FINANCIAL ACCOUNTING AND REPORTING ONLINE

A wide range of supporting resources is available at:

MyAccountingLab

Register to create your own personal account using the access code supplied with your copy of the book,* and access the following teaching and learning resources:

Resources for students

- **A dynamic eText** of the book that you can search, bookmark, annotate and highlight as you please
- **Self-assessment questions** that identify your strengths before recommending a personalised study plan that points you to the resources which can help you achieve a better grade

Resources for instructors

- **Instructor's manual**, with additional questions, complete and fully worked solutions, as well as case study debriefs
- **PowerPoint slides**, containing figures from the book

For more information, please contact your local Pearson Education sales representative or visit **www.myaccountinglab.com**.

* If you don't have an access code, you can still access the resources. Visit **www.myaccountinglab.com** for details.

PEARSON

At Pearson, we take learning personally. Our courses and resources are available as books, online and via multi-lingual packages, helping people learn whatever, wherever and however they choose.

We work with leading authors to develop the strongest learning experiences, bringing cutting-edge thinking and best learning practice to a global market. We craft our print and digital resources to do more to help learners not only understand their content, but to see it in action and apply what they learn, whether studying or at work.

Pearson is the world's leading learning company. Our portfolio includes Penguin, Dorling Kindersley, the Financial Times and our educational business, Pearson International. We are also a leading provider of electronic learning programmes and of test development, processing and scoring services to educational institutions, corporations and professional bodies around the world.

Every day our work helps learning flourish, and wherever learning flourishes, so do people.

To learn more please visit us at: www.pearson.com/uk

Financial Accounting and Reporting

SIXTEENTH EDITION

Barry Elliott and Jamie Elliott

PEARSON

Harlow, England • London • New York • Boston • San Francisco • Toronto • Sydney • Auckland • Singapore • Hong Kong
Tokyo • Seoul • Taipei • New Delhi • Cape Town • São Paulo • Mexico City • Madrid • Amsterdam • Munich • Paris • Milan

Pearson Education Limited
Edinburgh Gate
Harlow CM20 2JE
United Kingdom
Tel: +44 (0)1279 623623
Web: www.pearson.com/uk

First published 1993 (print)
Second edition 1996 (print)
Third edition 1999 (print)
Fourth edition 2000 (print)
Fifth edition 2001 (print)
Sixth edition 2002 (print)
Seventh edition 2003 (print)
Eighth edition 2004 (print)
Ninth edition 2005 (print)
Tenth edition 2006 (print)
Eleventh edition 2007 (print)
Twelfth edition 2008 (print)
Thirteenth edition 2009 (print)
Fourteenth edition 2011 (print)
Fifteenth edition 2012 (print and electronic)
Sixteenth edition 2013 (print and electronic)

© Pearson Education Limited 2000, 2011, 2012 (print)
© Pearson Education Limited 2013 (print and electronic)

The rights of Barry Elliott and Jamie Elliott to be identified as authors of this work have been asserted by them in accordance with the Copyright, Designs and Patents Act 1988.

The print publication is protected by copyright. Prior to any prohibited reproduction, storage in a retrieval system, distribution or transmission in any form or by any means, electronic, mechanical, recording or otherwise, permission should be obtained from the publisher or, where applicable, a licence permitting restricted copying in the United Kingdom should be obtained from the Copyright Licensing Agency Ltd, Saffron House, 6–10 Kirby Street, London EC1N 8TS.

The ePublication is protected by copyright and must not be copied, reproduced, transferred, distributed, leased, licensed or publicly performed or used in any way except as specifically permitted in writing by the publishers, as allowed under the terms and conditions under which it was purchased, or as strictly permitted by applicable copyright law. Any unauthorised distribution or use of this text may be a direct infringement of the author's and the publisher's rights and those responsible may be liable in law accordingly.

All trademarks used herein are the property of their respective owners. The use of any trademark in this text does not vest in the author or publisher any trademark ownership rights in such trademarks, nor does the use of such trademarks imply any affiliation with or endorsement of this book by such owners.

Contains public sector information licensed under the Open Government Licence (OGL) v1.0. http://www.nationalarchives.gov.uk/doc/open-government-licence.

Pearson Education is not responsible for the content of third-party Internet sites.

ISBN: 978-0-273-77817-2 (print)
978-0-273-77821-9 (PDF)
978-0-273-77818-9 (eText)

British Library Cataloguing-in-Publication Data
A catalogue record for the print edition is available from the British Library

Library of Congress Cataloging-in-Publication Data
Elliott, Barry.
  Financial accounting and reporting / Barry Elliott and Jamie Elliott. -- Sixteenth edition.
    pages cm
  ISBN 978-0-273-77817-2 (alk. paper)
  1. Accounting. 2. Financial statements. I. Elliott, Jamie. II. Title.
  HF5636.E47 2013
  657--dc23
                                                                    2013015510

10 9 8 7 6 5 4 3 2 1
17 16 15 14 13

Print edition typeset in 10/12pt Ehrhardt MT by 35
Printed by Ashford Colour Press Ltd., Gosport

NOTE THAT ANY PAGE CROSS REFERENCES REFER TO THE PRINT EDITION

Brief contents

Full contents

Preface and acknowledgements

Our objective is to provide a balanced and comprehensive framework to enable students to acquire the requisite knowledge and skills to appraise current practice critically and to evaluate proposed changes from a theoretical base. To this end, the text contains:

- extracts from current IASs and IFRSs;
- illustrations from published accounts;
- a range of review questions;
- exercises of varying difficulty;
- extensive references.

Solutions to selected exercises can be found on MyAccountingLab.

We have assumed that readers will have an understanding of financial accounting to a foundation or first-year level, although the text and exercises have been designed on the basis that a brief revision is still helpful. For the preparation of financial statements in Part 1 and Part 5 we have structured the chapters to assist readers who may have no accounting knowledge.

Lecturers are using the text selectively to support a range of teaching programmes for second-year and final-year undergraduate and postgraduate programmes. We have therefore attempted to provide subject coverage of sufficient breadth and depth to assist selective use.

The text has been adopted for financial accounting, reporting and analysis modules on:

- second-year undergraduate courses for Accounting, Business Studies and Combined Studies;
- final-year undergraduate courses for Accounting, Business Studies and Combined Studies;
- MBA courses;
- specialist MSc courses; and
- professional courses preparing students for professional accountancy examinations.

Changes to the sixteenth edition

Our emphasis has been on keeping the text current and responsive to constructive comments from reviewers and lecturers.

National accounting standards and the IASB

Since 2005 UK listed companies have followed international standards EU-IFRS for their consolidated accounts.

From 2013 large and medium-sized private companies in the UK will follow FRS 102 *The Financial Reporting Standard*. This standard is based (with UK modifications) on *IFRS for SMEs* which was issued by the IASB in 2009.

Smaller entities will continue to follow FRSSE.

Accounting standards – sixteenth edition updates

Chapters covering the following International Standards have been revised. They are as follows:

Chapter 3	Preparation of financial statements	IAS 1
Chapter 4	Preparation of additional financial statements	IAS 10, IAS 24, IFRS 5 and IFRS 8
Chapter 5	Statements of cash flows	IAS 7
Chapter 7	Accounting for price-level changes	IAS 29
Chapter 8	Revenue recognition	ED/2011/6
Chapter 13	Liabilities	IAS 37/ED/2010/1
Chapter 14	Financial instruments	IAS 32, IFRS 7 and IFRS 9
Chapter 15	Employee benefits	IAS 19 (revised 2011), IAS 26 and IFRS 2
Chapter 16	Taxation in company accounts	IAS 12
Chapter 17	Property, plant and equipment (PPE)	IAS 16, IAS 20, IAS 23, IAS 36, IAS 40 and IFRS 5
Chapter 18	Leasing	IAS 17 and ED/2010/9
Chapter 19	Intangible assets	IAS 38 and IFRS 3
Chapter 20	Inventories	IAS 2
Chapter 21	Construction contracts	IAS 11 and ED/2011/6
Chapters 22–26	Consolidation	IAS 21, IAS 28, IFRS 3, 10, 11 and 12
Chapter 27	Earnings per share	IAS 33

Part 1 Preparation of financial statements

Chapters 1 and 2 continue to cover accounting and reporting on a cash flow and accrual basis. Chapters 3 to 5 have been revised. They cover the preparation of statements of income, changes in equity, financial position and cash flows.

Part 2 Income and asset value measurement systems

Chapters 6 and 7 covering the economic income approach and accounting for price-level changes have been retained. Chapter 8 discusses the IASB exposure proposals for revenue recognition.

Part 3 Regulatory framework – an attempt to achieve uniformity

Chapters 9 and 10 have been revised.

Part 4 Statement of financial position

Chapters 12–21 are core chapters which have been retained and updated as appropriate.

Part 5 Consolidated accounts

Chapters 22–26 have been updated and revised to improve accessibility with explanations from first principles.

Part 6 Interpretation

Chapters 28 and 29 are two new replacement chapters aiming at encouraging good report writing based on the pyramid approach to ratios and an introduction to other tools and techniques for specific assignments.

Part 7 Accountability

Chapters 31 and 32 have been rewritten to focus more on the accountant's role in corporate governance and in the development of sustainability reporting.

Recent developments

In addition to the steps being taken towards the development of IFRSs that will receive broad consensus support, regulators have been active in developing further requirements concerning corporate governance. These have been prompted by the accounting scandals in the USA and, more recently, in Europe and by shareholder activism fuelled by the apparent lack of any relationship between increases in directors' remuneration and company performance.

The content of financial reports continues to be subjected to discussion with tension between preparers, stakeholders, auditors, academics and standard setters; this is mirrored in the tension that exists between theory and practice.

- Preparers favour reporting transactions on a historical cost basis, which is reliable but does not provide shareholders with relevant information to appraise past performance or to predict future earnings.
- Shareholders favour forward-looking reports relevant in estimating future dividend and capital growth and in understanding environmental and social impacts.
- Stakeholders favour quantified and narrative disclosure of environmental and social impacts and the steps taken to reduce negative impacts.
- Auditors favour reports that are verifiable so that the figures can be substantiated to avoid them being proved wrong at a later date.
- Academic accountants favour reports that reflect economic reality and are relevant in appraising management performance and in assessing the capacity of the company to adapt.
- Standard setters lean towards the academic view and favour reporting according to the commercial substance of a transaction.

In order to understand the tensions that exist, students need:

- the skill to prepare financial statements in accordance with the historical cost and current cost conventions, both of which appear in annual financial reports;
- an understanding of the main thrust of mandatory and voluntary standards;
- an understanding of the degree of flexibility available to the preparers and the impact of this on reported earnings and the figures in the statement of financial position;
- an understanding of the limitations of financial reports in portraying economic reality; and
- an exposure to source material and other published material in so far as time permits.

Instructor's Manual

A separate Instructor's Manual has been written to accompany this text. It contains fully worked solutions to all the exercises and is of a quality that allows them to be used as overhead transparencies. The Manual is available at no cost to lecturers on application to the publishers.

Website

An electronic version of the Instructor's Manual is also available for download at www.pearsoned.co.uk/elliott-elliott.

An electronic version of selected questions marked with an asterisk in the text is accessible by students in MyAccountingLab which may be available with this copy of the book, or otherwise can be purchased separately.

Acknowledgements

Financial reporting is a dynamic area and we see it as extremely important that the text should reflect this and be kept current. Assistance has been generously given by colleagues and many others in the preparation and review of the text and assessment material. This sixteenth edition continues to be very much a result of the authors, colleagues, reviewers and Pearson editorial and production staff working as a team and we are grateful to all concerned for their assistance in achieving this.

We owe particular thanks to Charles Batchelor, formerly of FTC Kaplan, for 'Financial instruments' (Chapter 14); Ozer Erman of Kingston University for 'Share capital, distributable profits and reduction of capital' (Chapter 12); Paul Robins of the Financial Training Company for Interpretation chapters; Professor Garry Tibbits of the University of Western Sydney for 'Revenue recognition' (Chapter 8); Hendrika Tibbits of the University of Western Sydney for 'An introduction to financial reporting on the Internet' (Chapter 30); and David Towers, formerly of Keele University, for Consolidation chapters.

The authors are grateful for the constructive comments received over various editions from the following reviewers who have assisted us in making improvements: Pik Liew of Essex University; Anitha Majeed of Coventry University; Allison Wylde of London Metropolitan University; Terry Morris of Queen Mary University of London; Ajjay Mandal of London South Bank University; and Michael Jeffrey of Manchester Metropolitan University. We would also like to thank the reviewers of this new edition of the book.

Thanks are owed to Keith Brown, formerly of De Montfort University; Kenneth N. Field of the University of Leeds; Sue McDermott of London Metropolitan Business School; David Murphy of Manchester Business School; Bahadur Najak of the University of Durham; Graham Sara of the University of Warwick; and Laura Spira of Oxford Brookes University.

Thanks are also due to the following organisations: the Accounting Standards Board, the International Accounting Standards Board, the Association of Chartered Certified Accountants, the Association of International Accountants, the Chartered Institute of Management Accountants, the Institute of Certified Public Accountants (CPA) in Ireland, the Institute of Chartered Accountants of England and Wales, the Institute of Chartered Accountants of Scotland and the Institute of Chartered Secretaries and Administrators.

We would also like to thank the authors of some of the end-of-chapter exercises. Some of these exercises have been inherited from a variety of institutions with which we have been associated, and we have unfortunately lost the identities of the originators of such material with the passage of time. We are sorry that we cannot acknowledge them by name and hope that they will excuse us for using their material.

We are indebted to Katie Rowland and Lucy Winder and the editorial team at Pearson Education for active support in keeping us largely to schedule and the attractively produced and presented text.

Finally we thank our wives, Di and Jacklin, for their continued good-humoured support during the period of writing and revisions, and Giles Elliott for his critical comment from the commencement of the project. We alone remain responsible for any errors and for the thoughts and views that are expressed.

Barry and Jamie Elliott

Publisher's acknowledgements

We are grateful to the following for permission to reproduce copyright material:

Figures

Figure page 755 from Marks and Spencer Group plc's 2012 Annual Report, http://annualreport.marksandspencer.com/_assets/downloads/Marks-and-Spencer-Annual-report-and-financial-statements-2012.pdf

Text

Questions and model answers from the Association of International Accountants and from the Institute of Certified Public Accountants in Ireland (CPA)

In some instances we have been unable to trace the owners of copyright material, and we would appreciate any information that would enable us to do so.

Guided tour of MyAccountingLab

MyAccountingLab is an online assessment and revision system that puts you in control of your learning through a suite of study and practice tools tied to the online eText.

Why should I use *MyAccountingLab?*

With more than 300,000 registered students in 2010 doing four million assignments, *MyAccountingLab* is the most effective and reliable learning solution for accounting available today.

We polled 10,000 student users of *MyAccountingLab* from around the globe in 2010:

- 92% of students said that *MyAccountingLab* learning aids helped them while completing homework and/or preparing or exams.
- 89% of students said that *MyAccountingLab* helped them earn a higher grade.
- 92% of students would recommend *MyAccountingLab* for future courses.

How do I use *MyAccountingLab?*

The **Course Home Page** is where you can view announcements from your instructor and see an erview of your progress.

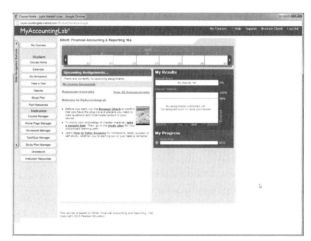

Course Home Page

View the **Calendar** to see dates for online homework, quizzes and tests.

Your lecturer may have chosen *MyAccountingLab* to provide online **Homework**, quizzes and ests. check here to access the homework hat has been set for you.

Practice tests or each chapter of the text enable you to check your understanding and identify areas in which you need to do further work. Your lecturers can customise and assign practice tests or you can complete them on your own.

Practice Test

Keep track of your **results** in your own gradebook.

Work through the questions in your personalised **Study Plan** at your own pace. Because the Study Plan is tailored to each student, you will be able to study more efficiently by only reviewing areas where you still need practice. The Study Plan also saves your results, helping you see at a glance exactly which topics you need to review.

Study Plan

Additional instruction is provided in the form of detailed, step-by-step **solutions** to worked exercises. The numbers in many of the exercises in *MyAccountingLab* are generated algorithmically, containing different values each time they are used. This means that you can practice individual concepts as often as you like.

There is also a link to the **eText** from every question in the Study Plan, so you can easily review and master the content.

View supporting multimedia resources such as links to the eText, Key Concept narratives and Glossary Flashcards.

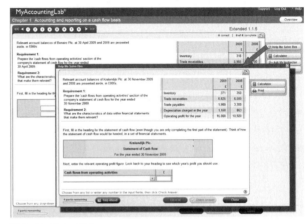

Help Me Solve This

Lecturer training and support

Our dedicated team of Technology Specialists offer personalised training and support for *MyAccountingLab*, ensuring that you can maximise the benefits of *MyAccountingLab*. To make contact with your Technology Specialist please email **feedback-cw@pearson.com**.

For a visual walkthrough of how to make the most of *MyAccountingLab*, visit

www.myaccountinglab.com

Lecturers can find details for local sales representatives at **www.pearsoned.co.uk/replocator**.

PART I

Preparation of financial statements

CHAPTER 1

Accounting and reporting on a cash flow basis

1.1 Introduction

Accountants are communicators. Accountancy is the art of communicating financial information about a business entity to users such as shareholders and managers. The communication is generally in the form of financial statements that show in money terms the economic resources under the control of the management. The art lies in selecting the information that is relevant to the user and is reliable.

Shareholders require periodic information that the managers are accounting properly for the resources under their control. This information helps the shareholders to evaluate the performance of the managers. The performance measured by the accountant shows the extent to which the economic resources of the business have grown or diminished during the year.

The shareholders also require information to **predict future performance**. At present companies are not required to publish forecast financial statements on a regular basis and the shareholders use the report of past performance when making their predictions.

Managers require information in order to control the business and make investment decisions.

Objectives

By the end of this chapter, you should be able to:

- explain the extent to which cash flow accounting satisfies the information needs of shareholders and managers;
- prepare a cash budget and operating statement of cash flows;
- explain the characteristics that make cash flow data a reliable and fair representation;
- critically discuss the use of cash flow accounting for predicting future dividends.

1.2 Shareholders

Shareholders are external users. As such, they are unable to obtain access to the same amount of detailed historical information as the managers, e.g. total administration costs are disclosed in the published profit and loss account, but not an analysis to show how the figure is made up. Shareholders are also unable to obtain associated information, e.g. budgeted sales and costs. Even though the shareholders own a company, their entitlement to information is restricted.

The information to which shareholders are entitled is restricted to that specified by statute, e.g. the Companies Acts, or by professional regulation, e.g. Financial Reporting Standards, or by market regulations, e.g. Listing requirements. This means that there may be a tension between the **amount** of information that a shareholder would like to receive and the amount that the directors are prepared to provide. For example, shareholders might consider that forecasts of future cash flows would be helpful in predicting future dividends, but the directors might be concerned that such forecasts could help competitors or make directors open to criticism if forecasts are not met. As a result, this information is not disclosed.

There may also be a tension between the **quality** of information that shareholders would like to receive and that which directors are prepared to provide. For example, the shareholders might consider that judgements made by the directors in the valuation of long-term contracts should be fully explained, whereas the directors might prefer not to reveal this information given the high risk of error that often attaches to such estimates. In practice, companies tend to compromise: they do not reveal the judgements to the shareholders, but maintain confidence by relying on the auditor to give a clean audit report.

The financial reports presented to the shareholders are also used by other parties such as lenders and trade creditors, and they have come to be regarded as general-purpose reports. However, it may be difficult or impossible to satisfy the needs of all users. For example, users may have different time-scales – shareholders may be interested in the long-term trend of earnings over three years, whereas creditors may be interested in the likelihood of receiving cash within the next three months.

The information needs of the shareholders are regarded as the primary concern. The government perceives shareholders to be important because they provide companies with their economic resources. It is shareholders' needs that take priority in deciding on the nature and detailed content of the general-purpose reports.[1]

1.3 What skills does an accountant require in respect of external reports?

For external reporting purposes the accountant has a two-fold obligation:

- an obligation to ensure that the financial statements comply with statutory, professional and Listing requirements; this requires the accountant to possess **technical expertise**;
- an obligation to ensure that the financial statements present the substance of the commercial transactions the company has entered into; this requires the accountant to have **commercial awareness**.

1.4 Managers

Managers are internal users. As such, they have access to detailed financial statements showing the current results, the extent to which these vary from the budgeted results and the future budgeted results. Examples of internal users are sole traders, partners and, in a company context, directors and managers.

There is no statutory restriction on the amount of information that an internal user may receive; the only restriction would be that imposed by the company's own policy. Frequently, companies operate a 'need to know' policy and only the directors see all the financial statements; employees, for example, would be most unlikely to receive information that would assist them in claiming a salary increase – unless, of course, it happened to be a time of recession, when information would be more freely provided by management as a means of containing claims for an increase.

1.5 What skills does an accountant require in respect of internal reports?

For the internal user, the accountant is able to tailor his or her reports. The accountant is required to produce financial statements that are specifically relevant to the user requesting them.

The accountant needs to be skilled in identifying the information that is needed and conveying its implication and meaning to the user. The user needs to be confident that the accountant understands the user's information needs and will satisfy them in a language that is understandable. The accountant must be a skilled communicator who is able to instil confidence in the user that the information is:

- relevant to the user's needs;
- measured objectively;
- presented within a time-scale that permits decisions to be made with appropriate information;
- verifiable, in that it can be confirmed that the report represents the transactions that have taken place;
- reliable, in that it is as free from bias as is possible;
- a complete picture of material items;
- a fair representation of the business transactions and events that have occurred or are being planned.

The accountant is a trained reporter of financial information. Just as for external reporting, the accountant needs commercial awareness. It is important, therefore, that he or she should not operate in isolation.

1.5.1 Accountant's reporting role

The accountant's role is to ensure that the information provided is useful for making decisions. For external users, the accountant achieves this by providing a general-purpose financial statement that complies with statute and is reliable. For internal users, this is done by interfacing with the user and establishing exactly what financial information is relevant to the decision that is to be made.

We now consider the steps required to provide relevant information for internal users.

1.6 Procedural steps when reporting to internal users

A number of user steps and accounting action steps can be identified within a financial decision model. These are shown in Figure 1.1.

Note that, although we refer to an accountant/user interface, this is not a single occurrence because the user and accountant interface at each of the user decision steps.

At **step 1**, the accountant attempts to ensure that the decision is based on the appropriate appraisal methodology. However, the accountant is providing a service to a user and, while the accountant may give guidance, the final decision about methodology rests with the user.

Figure 1.1 General financial decision model to illustrate the user/accountant interface

USER		ACCOUNTANT
User step 1		Identify the material information
Identify decision and		needed by the user
how it is to be made		Measure the relevant
User step 2		information
Establish with the	**USER/ACCOUNTANT**	Prepare report for user to
accountant the	**INTERFACE**	allow user to make decision
information necessary		Provide an understandable
for decision making		report to the user
User step 3		
Seek relevant data		
from the accountant		

At **step 2**, the accountant needs to establish the information necessary to support the decision that is to be made.

At **step 3**, the accountant needs to ensure that the user **understands** the full impact and financial implications of the accountant's report taking into account the user's level of understanding and prior knowledge. This may be overlooked by the accountant, who feels that the task has been completed when the written report has been typed.

It is important to remember in following the model that the accountant is attempting to satisfy the information needs of the individual user rather than those of a 'user group'. It is tempting to divide users into groups with apparently common information needs, without recognising that a group contains individual users with different information needs. We return to this later in the chapter, but for the moment we continue by studying a situation where the directors of a company are considering a proposed capital investment project.

Let us assume that there are three companies in the retail industry: Retail A Ltd, Retail B Ltd and Retail C Ltd. The directors of each company are considering the purchase of a warehouse. We could assume initially that, because the companies are operating in the same industry and are faced with the same investment decision, they have identical information needs. However, enquiry might establish that the directors of each company have a completely different attitude to, or perception of, the primary business objective.

For example, it might be established that Retail A Ltd is a large company and under the Fisher/Hirshleifer separation theory the directors seek to maximise profits for the benefit of the equity investors; Retail B Ltd is a medium-sized company in which the directors seek to obtain a satisfactory return for the equity shareholders; and Retail C Ltd is a smaller company in which the directors seek to achieve a satisfactory return for a wider range of stakeholders, including, perhaps, the employees as well as the equity shareholders.

The accountant needs to be aware that these differences may have a significant effect on the information required. Let us consider this diagrammatically in the situation where a capital investment decision is to be made, referring particularly to user step 2: 'Establish with the accountant the information necessary for decision making'.

Figure 1.2 Impact of different user attitudes on the information needed in relation to a capital investment proposal

	USER A Directors of Retail A Ltd	**USER B** Directors of Retail B Ltd	**USER C** Directors of Retail C Ltd
User attitude	PROFIT MAXIMISER for SHAREHOLDERS	PROFIT SATISFICER for SHAREHOLDERS	PROFIT SATISFICER for SHAREHOLDERS/ STAFF
Relevant data to measure	CASH FLOWS	CASH FLOWS	CASH FLOWS
Appraisal method (decided on by user)	IRR	NPV	NPV
Appraisal criterion (decided on by user)	HIGHEST IRR	NPV but only if positive	NPV possibly even if negative

We can see from Figure 1.2 that the accountant has identified that:

- the relevant financial data are the same for each of the users, i.e. cash flows; but
- the appraisal methods selected, i.e. internal rate of return (IRR) and net present value (NPV), are different; and
- the appraisal criteria employed by each user, i.e. higher IRR and NPV, are different.

In practice, the user is likely to use more than one appraisal method, as each has advantages and disadvantages. However, we can see that, even when dealing with a single group of apparently homogeneous users, the accountant has first to identify the information needs of the particular user. Only then is the accountant able to identify the relevant financial data and the appropriate report. It is the user's needs that are predominant.

If the accountant's view of the appropriate appraisal method or criterion differs from the user's view, the accountant might decide to report from both views. This approach affords the opportunity to improve the user's understanding and encourages good practice.

The diagrams can be combined (Figure 1.3) to illustrate the complete process. The user is assumed to be Retail A Ltd, a company that has directors who are profit maximisers.

The accountant is reactive when reporting to an internal user. We observe this characteristic in the Norman example set out in Section 1.8. Because the cash flows are identified as relevant to the user, it is these flows that the accountant will record, measure and appraise.

The accountant can also be proactive, by giving the user advice and guidance in areas where the accountant has specific expertise, such as the appraisal method that is most appropriate to the circumstances.

Figure 1.3 User/accountant interface where the user is a profit maximiser

General model	Specific application for Retail A Ltd A PROFIT MAXIMISER		General model	Specific application for Retail A Ltd
USER			**ACCOUNTANT**	**ACCOUNTANT**
Step 1				
Decision to be made	Appraise which project warrants capital investment		Identify information needed by the user	User decision criterion is IRR
Step 2		**USER/ ACCOUNTANT INTERFACE**	Measure	Measure the project cash flows
Information needed				
	Project with the highest IRR		Prepare report	Prepare report of highest IRR
Step 3				
Seek relevant data				
	Report of IRR project		Provide report	Submit report of project with highest IRR per £ invested

1.7 Agency costs[2]

The information in Figure 1.2 assumes that the directors have made their investment decision based on the assumed preferences of the shareholders. However, in real life, the directors might also be influenced by how the decision impinges on their own position. If, for example, their remuneration is a fixed salary, they might select not the investment with the highest IRR, but the one that maintains their security of employment. The result might be suboptimal investment and financing decisions based on risk aversion and over-retention. To the extent that the potential cash flows have been reduced, there will be an agency cost to the shareholders. This agency cost is an opportunity cost – the amount that was forgone because the decision making was suboptimal – and, as such, it will not be recorded in the books of account and will not appear in the financial statements.

1.8 Illustration of periodic financial statements prepared under the cash flow concept to disclose realised operating cash flows

In the above example of Retail A, B and C, the investment decision for the acquisition of a warehouse was based on an appraisal of cash flows. This raises the question: 'Why not continue with the cash flow concept and report the financial changes that occur after the investment has been undertaken using that same concept?'

To do this, the company will record the consequent cash flows through a number of subsequent accounting periods; report the cash flows that occur in each financial period; and produce a balance sheet at the end of each of the financial periods. For illustration we follow this procedure in Sections 1.8.1 and 1.8.2 for transactions entered into by Mr S. Norman.

1.8.1 Appraisal of the initial investment decision

Mr Norman is considering whether to start up a retail business by acquiring the lease of a shop for five years at a cost of £80,000.

Our first task has been set out in Figure 1.1 above. It is to establish the information that Mr Norman needs, so that we can decide what data need to be collected and measured. Let us assume that, as a result of a discussion with Mr Norman, it has been ascertained that he is a profit satisficer who is looking to achieve at least a 10% return, which represents the time value of money. This indicates that, as illustrated in Figure 1.2:

- the relevant data to be measured are **cash flows**, represented by the outflow of cash invested in the lease and the inflow of cash represented by the realised operating cash flows;
- the appropriate appraisal method is **NPV**; and
- the appraisal criterion is a **positive NPV** using the discount rate of 10%.

Let us further assume that the cash to be invested in the lease is £80,000 and that the realised operating cash flows over the life of the investment in the shop are as shown in Figure 1.4. This shows that there is a forecast of £30,000 annually for five years and a final receipt of £29,000 in 20X6 when he proposes to cease trading.

We already know that Mr Norman's investment criterion is a positive NPV using a discount factor of 10%. A calculation (Figure 1.5) shows that the investment easily satisfies that criterion.

Figure 1.4 Forecast of realised operating cash flows

	Annually years 20X1–20X5	Cash in year 20X6 after shop closure
	£	£
Receipts from		
Customers	400,000	55,000
Payments to		
Suppliers	(342,150)	(20,000)
Expense creditors	(21,600)	(3,000)
Rent	(6,250)	(3,000)
Total payments	(370,000)	(26,000)
Realised operating cash flows	30,000	29,000

Figure 1.5 NPV calculation using discount tables

	£	£
Cost of lease		(80,000)
£30,000 annually for 5 years (30,000 × 3.79)	113,700	
£29,000 received in year 6 (29,000 × 0.564)	16,356	
		130,056
Positive net present value		50,056

1.8.2 Preparation of periodic financial statements under the cash flow concept

Having **predicted** the realised operating cash flows for the purpose of making the investment decision, we can assume that the owner of the business will wish to obtain **feedback** to evaluate the correctness of the investment decision. He does this by reviewing the actual results on a regular **timely** basis and **comparing** these with the predicted forecast. Actual results should be reported quarterly, half-yearly or annually in the same format as used when making the decision in Figure 1.4. The actual results provide management with the feedback information required to audit the initial decision; it is a technique for achieving accountability. However, frequently, companies do not provide a report of actual cash flows to compare with the forecast cash flows, and fail to carry out an audit review.

In some cases, the transactions relating to the investment cannot be readily separated from other transactions, and the information necessary for the audit review of the investment cannot be made available. In other cases, the routine accounting procedures fail to collect such cash flow information because the reporting systems have not been designed to provide financial reports on a cash flow basis; rather, they have been designed to produce reports prepared on an accrual basis.

What would financial reports look like if they were prepared on a cash flow basis?

To illustrate cash flow period accounts, we will prepare half-yearly accounts for Mr Norman. To facilitate a comparison with the forecast that underpinned the investment decision, we will redraft the forecast annual statement on a half-yearly basis. The data for the first year given in Figure 1.4 have therefore been redrafted to provide a forecast for the half-year to 30 June, as shown in Figure 1.6.

We assume that, having applied the net present value appraisal technique to the cash flows and ascertained that the NPV was positive, Mr Norman proceeded to set up the business on 1 January 20X1. He introduced capital of £50,000, acquired a five-year lease for £80,000 and paid £6,250 in advance as rent to occupy the property to 31 December 20X1. He has decided to prepare financial statements at half-yearly intervals. The information given in Figure 1.7 concerns his trading for the half-year to 30 June 20X1.

Mr Norman was naturally eager to determine whether the business was achieving its forecast cash flows for the first six months of trading, so he produced the statement of realised

Figure 1.6 Forecast of realised operating cash flows

	Half-year to 30 June 20X1 £
Receipts from	
Customers	165,000
Payments to	
Suppliers	(124,000)
Expense creditors	(18,000)
Rent	(6,250)
Total payments	(148,250)
Realised operating cash flows	16,750

Figure 1.7 Monthly sales, purchases and expenses for six months ended 30 June 20X1

Month	Sales invoiced £	Cash received £	Purchases invoiced £	Cash paid £	Expenses invoiced £	Cash paid £
January	15,000	7,500	16,000		3,400	3,100
February	20,000	17,500	19,000	16,000	3,500	3,400
March	35,000	27,500	29,000	19,000	3,800	3,500
April	40,000	37,500	32,000	29,000	3,900	3,800
May	40,000	40,000	33,000	32,000	3,900	3,900
June	45,000	42,500	37,000	33,000	4,000	3,900
TOTAL	195,000	172,500	166,000	129,000	22,500	21,600

Note: The following items were included under the Expenses invoiced heading:

Expense creditors	– amount
Wages	– £3,100 per month paid in the month
Commission	– 2% of sales invoiced payable one month in arrears

Figure 1.8 Monthly realised operating cash flows

	Jan £	Feb £	Mar £	Apr £	May £	Jun £	Total £
Receipts							
Customers	7,500	17,500	27,500	37,500	40,000	42,500	172,500
Less payments							
Suppliers		16,000	19,000	29,000	32,000	33,000	129,000
Expense creditors	3,100	3,400	3,500	3,800	3,900	3,900	21,600
Rent	6,250						6,250
Realised	(1,850)	(1,900)	5,000	4,700	4,100	5,600	15,650

operating cash flows (Figure 1.8) from the information provided in Figure 1.7. From this statement we can see that the business generated positive cash flows after the end of February. These are, of course, only the cash flows relating to the trading transactions.

The information in the 'Total' row of Figure 1.7 can be extracted to provide the financial statement for the six months ended 30 June 20X1, as shown in Figure 1.9.

The figure of £15,650 needs to be compared with the forecast cash flows used in the investment appraisal. This is a form of auditing. It allows the assumptions made on the initial investment decision to be confirmed. The forecast/actual comparison (based on the information in Figures 1.6 and 1.9) is set out in Figure 1.10.

What are the characteristics of these data that make them relevant?

● The data are **objective**. There is no judgement involved in deciding the values to include in the financial statement, as each value or amount represents a verifiable cash transaction with a third party.

Figure 1.9 Realised operating cash flows for the six months ended 30 June 20X1

		£
Receipts from		
Customers		172,500
Payments to		
Suppliers	(129,000)	
Expense creditors	(21,600)	
Rent	(6,250)	
		156,850
Realised operating cash flow		15,650

Figure 1.10 Forecast/actual comparison

		Actual £	Forecast £
Receipts from			
Customers		172,500	165,000
Payment to			
Suppliers	(129,000)		(124,000)
Expense creditors	(21,600)		(18,000)
Rent	(6,250)		(6,250)
Total payments		(156,850)	(148,250)
Realised operating cash flow		15,650	16,750

- The data are **consistent**. The statement incorporates the same cash flows within the periodic financial report of trading as the cash flows that were incorporated within the initial capital investment report. This permits a logical comparison and confirmation that the decision was realistic.
- The results have a **confirmatory** value by helping users confirm or correct their past assessments.
- The results have a **predictive** value, in that they provide a basis for revising the initial forecasts if necessary.
- There is **no requirement for accounting standards** or disclosure of accounting policies that are necessary to regulate accrual accounting practices, e.g. depreciation methods.

1.9 Illustration of preparation of statement of financial position

Although the information set out in Figure 1.10 permits us to compare and evaluate the initial decision, it does not provide a sufficiently sound basis for the following:

- assessing the stewardship over the total cash funds that have been employed within the business;
- signalling to management whether its working capital policies are appropriate.

1.9.1 Stewardship

To assess the stewardship over the total cash funds we need to:

(a) evaluate the effectiveness of the accounting system to make certain that all transactions are recorded;

(b) extend the cash flow statement to take account of the capital cash flows; and

(c) prepare a statement of financial position or balance sheet as at 30 June 20X1.

The additional information for (b) and (c) above is set out in Figures 1.11 and 1.12 respectively.

The cash flow statement and statement of financial position, taken together, are a means of assessing stewardship. They identify the movement of **all** cash and derive a **net** balance figure. These statements are a normal feature of a sound system of internal control, but they have not been made available to external users.

1.9.2 Working capital policies

By 'working capital' we mean the current assets and current liabilities of the business. In addition to providing a means of making management accountable, cash flows are the raw data required by financial managers when making decisions on the management of working capital. One of the decisions would be to set the appropriate terms for credit policy. For example, Figure 1.11 shows that the business will have a £14,350 overdraft at 30 June 20X1. If this is not acceptable, management will review its working capital by reconsidering

Figure 1.11 Cash flow statement to calculate the net cash balance

	Jan £	Feb £	Mar £	Apr £	May £	Jun £	Total £
Operating cash	(1,850)	(1,900)	5,000	4,700	4,100	5,600	15,650
New capital	50,000						50,000
Lease payment	(80,000)						(80,000)
Cash balance	(31,850)	(33,750)	(28,750)	(24,050)	(19,950)	(14,350)	(14,350)

Figure 1.12 Statement of financial position

	Opening 1 Jan 20X1 £	Closing 30 Jun 20X1 £
Capital introduced	50,000	50,000
Net operating cash flow		15,650
	50,000	65,650
Lease		80,000
Net cash balance	50,000	−14,350
	50,000	65,650

the credit given to customers, the credit taken from suppliers, stock-holding levels and the timing of capital cash inflows and outflows.

If, in the example, it were possible to obtain 45 days' credit from suppliers, then the creditors at 30 June would rise from £37,000 to a new total of £53,500. This increase in trade credit of £16,500 means that half of the May purchases (£33,000/2) would not be paid for until July, which would convert the overdraft of £14,350 into a positive balance of £2,150. As a new business it might not be possible to obtain credit from all of the suppliers. In that case, other steps would be considered, such as phasing the payment for the lease of the warehouse or introducing more capital.

An interesting research report[3] identified that for small firms survival and stability were the main objectives rather than profit maximisation. This, in turn, meant that cash flow indicators and managing cash flow were seen as crucial to survival. In addition, cash flow information was perceived as important to external bodies such as banks in evaluating performance.

1.10 Treatment of non-current assets in the cash flow model

The statement of financial position in Figure 1.12 does not take into account any **unrealised** cash flows. Such flows are deemed to occur as a result of any rise or fall in the realisable value of the lease. This could rise if, for example, the annual rent payable under the lease were to be substantially lower than the rate payable under a new lease entered into on 30 June 20X1. It could also fall with the passing of time, with six months having expired by 30 June 20X1. We need to consider this further and examine the possible treatment of non-current assets in the cash flow model.

Using the cash flow approach, we require an independent verification of the realisable value of the lease at 30 June 20X1. If the lease has fallen in value, the difference between the original outlay and the net realisable figure could be treated as a negative unrealised operating cash flow.

For example, if the independent estimate was that the realisable value was £74,000, then the statement of financial position would be prepared as in Figure 1.13. The fall of £6,000 in realisable value is an unrealised cash flow and, while it does not affect the calculation of the net cash balance, it does affect the statement of financial position.

Figure 1.13 Statement of financial position as at 30 June 20X1 (assuming that there were unrealised operating cash flows)

	£
Capital introduced	50,000
Net operating flow: **realised**	15,650
: unrealised	(6,000)
	59,650
Lease: **net realisable value**	74,000
Net cash balance	−14,350
	59,650

The same approach would be taken to all non-current assets and could result in there being an unrealised cash flow where there is limited resale market for an asset, even though it might be productive and have value in use by the firm that owns it.

The additional benefit of the statement of financial position, as revised, is that the owner is able clearly to identify the following:

● the operating cash inflows of £15,650 that have been realised from the business operations;

● the operating cash outflow of £6,000 that has not been realised, but has arisen as a result of investing in the lease;

● the net cash balance of −£14,350;

● the statement provides a **stewardship-orientated** report: that is, it is a means of making the management accountable for the cash within its control.

1.11 What are the characteristics of these data that make them reliable?

We have already discussed some characteristics of cash flow reporting which indicate that the data in the financial statements are **relevant**, e.g. their predictive and confirmatory roles. We now introduce five more characteristics of cash flow statements which indicate that the information is also **reliable**, i.e. free from bias. These are prudence, neutrality, completeness, faithful representation and substance over form.

1.11.1 Prudence characteristic

Revenue and profits are included in the cash flow statement only when they are realised. Realisation is deemed to occur when cash is received. In our Norman example, the £172,500 cash received from debtors represents the revenue for the half-year ended 30 June 20X1. This policy is described as prudent because it **does not anticipate** cash flows: cash flows are recorded only when they actually occur and not when they are reasonably certain to occur. This is one of the factors that distinguishes cash flow from accrual accounting.

1.11.2 Neutrality characteristic

Financial statements are not neutral if, by their selection or presentation of information, they influence the making of a decision in order to achieve a predetermined result or outcome. With cash flow accounting, the information is not subject to management selection criteria.

Cash flow accounting avoids the tension that can arise between prudence and neutrality because, whilst neutrality involves freedom from deliberate or systematic bias, prudence is a potentially biased concept that seeks to ensure that, under conditions of uncertainty, gains and assets are not overstated and losses and liabilities are not understated.

1.11.3 Completeness characteristic

The cash flows can be verified for completeness provided there are adequate internal control procedures in operation. In small and medium-sized enterprises there can be a weakness if one person, typically the owner, has control over the accounting system and is able to under-record cash receipts.

1.11.4 Faithful representation characteristic

Cash flows can be depended upon by users to represent faithfully what they purport to represent provided, of course, that the completeness characteristic has been satisfied.

1.11.5 Substance over form

Cash flow accounting does not necessarily possess this characteristic which requires that transactions should be accounted for and presented in accordance with their substance and economic reality and not merely their legal form.

1.12 Reports to external users

1.12.1 Stewardship orientation

Cash flow accounting provides objective, consistent and prudent financial information about a business's transactions. It is stewardship-orientated and offers a means of achieving accountability over cash resources and investment decisions.

1.12.2 Prediction orientation

External users are also interested in the ability of a company to pay dividends. It might be thought that the past and current cash flows are the best indicators of future cash flows and dividends. However, the cash flow might be misleading, in that a declining company might sell non-current assets and have a better **net cash position** than a growing company that buys non-current assets for future use. There is also no matching of cash inflows and out-flows, in the sense that a benefit is matched with the sacrifice made to achieve it.

Consequently, it has been accepted accounting practice to view the income statement prepared on the accrual accounting concept as a better predictor of future cash flows to an investor than the cash flow statements that we have illustrated in this chapter.

However, the operating cash flows arising from trading and the cash flows arising from the introduction of capital and the acquisition of non-current assets can become significant to investors, e.g. they may threaten the company's ability to survive or may indicate growth.

In the next chapter, we revise the preparation of the same three statements using the **accrual accounting** model.

1.12.3 Going concern

The Financial Reporting Council suggests in its Consultation Paper *Going Concern and Financial Reporting*[4] that directors in assessing whether a company is a going concern may prepare monthly cash flow forecasts and monthly budgets covering, as a minimum, the period up to the next statement of financial position date. The forecasts would also be supported by a detailed list of assumptions which underlie them.

1.12.4 Tax authorities

In the UK accounts prepared on a cash flow basis will, from April 2013, be acceptable to the tax authorities for small unincorporated businesses. Companies are still required to deter-mine income on an accrual accounting basis. This reflects economic substance in that most incorporated businesses would have inventory or work in progress, or have creditors for the supply of materials.

Summary

To review our understanding of this chapter, we should ask ourselves the following questions.

How useful is cash flow accounting for internal decision making?

Forecast cash flows are relevant for the appraisal of proposals for capital investment. Actual cash flows are relevant for the confirmation of the decision for capital investment.

Cash flows are relevant for the management of working capital. Financial managers might have a variety of mathematical models for the efficient use of working capital, but cash flows are the raw data upon which they work.

How useful is cash flow accounting for making management accountable?

The cash flow statement is useful for confirming decisions and, together with the statement of financial position, provides a stewardship report. Lee states that 'Cash flow accounting appears to satisfy the need to supply owners and others with stewardship-orientated information as well as with decision-orientated information.'[5]

Lee further states that:

> By reducing judgements in this type of financial report, management can report factually on its stewardship function, whilst at the same time disclosing data of use in the decision-making process. In other words, cash flow reporting eliminates the somewhat artificial segregation of stewardship and decision-making information.

This is exactly what we saw in our Norman example – the same realised operating cash flow information was used for both the investment decision and financial reporting. However, for stewardship purposes it was necessary to extend the cash flow to include **all** cash movements and to extend the statement of financial position to include the **unrealised** cash flows.

How useful is cash flow accounting for reporting to external users?

Cash flow information is relevant:

● as a basis for making internal management decisions in relation to both non-current assets and working capital;
● for stewardship and accountability; and
● for assessing whether a business is a going concern.

Cash flow information is reliable and a fair representation, being:

● objective; consistent; prudent; and neutral.

However, professional accounting practice requires reports to external users to be on an accrual accounting basis. This is because the accrual accounting profit figure is a better predictor for investors of the future cash flows likely to arise from the dividends paid to them by the business, and of any capital gain on disposal of their investment. It could also be argued that cash flows may not be a fair representation of the commercial substance of transactions, e.g. if a business allowed a year's credit to all its customers there would be no income recorded.

REVIEW QUESTIONS

1 Explain why it is the user who should determine the information that the accountant collects, measures and reports, rather than the accountant who is the expert in financial information.

2 'Yuji Ijiri rejects decision usefulness as the main purpose of accounting and puts in its place account-ability. Ijiri sees the accounting relationship as a tripartite one, involving the accountor, the accountee, and the accountant . . . the decision useful approach is heavily biased in favour of the accountee . . . with little concern for the accountor . . . in the central position Ijiri would put fairness.'[6] Discuss Ijiri's view in the context of cash flow accounting.

3 Explain the effect on the statement of financial position in Figure 1.13 if the non-current asset consisted of expenditure on industry-specific machine tools rather than a lease.

4 'It is essential that the information in financial statements has a prudent characteristic if the financial statements are to be objective.' Discuss.

5 Explain why realised cash flow might not be appropriate for investors looking to predict future dividends.

6 Discuss why it might not be sufficient for a small businessperson who is carrying on business as a sole trader to prepare accounts on a cash flow basis.

7 'Unrealised operating cash flows are only of use for internal management purposes and are irrelevant to investors.' Discuss.

8 'While accountants may be free from bias in the measurement of economic information, they cannot be unbiased in identifying the economic information that they consider to be relevant.' Discuss.

EXERCISES

* Question 1

Jane Parker is going to set up a new business on 1 January 20X1. She estimates that her first six months in business will be as follows:

(i) She will put £150,000 into a bank account for the firm on 1 January 20X1.

(ii) On 1 January 20X1 she will buy machinery £30,000, motor vehicles £24,000 and premises £75,000, paying for them immediately.

(iii) All purchases will be effected on credit. She will buy £30,000 goods on 1 January and will pay for these in February. Other purchases will be: rest of January £48,000; February, March, April, May and June £60,000 each month. Other than the £30,000 worth bought in January, all other purchases will be paid for two months after purchase.

(iv) Sales (all on credit) will be £60,000 for January and £75,000 for each month after. Customers will pay for the goods in the fourth month after purchase, i.e. £60,000 is received in May.

(v) She will make drawings of £1,200 per month.

(vi) Wages and salaries will be £2,250 per month and will be paid on the last day of each month.

(vii) General expenses will be £750 per month, payable in the month following that in which they are incurred.

(viii) Rates will be paid as follows: for the three months to 31 March 20X1 by cheque on 28 February 20X1; for the 12 months ended 31 March 20X2 by cheque on 31 July 20X1. Rates are £4,800 per annum.

(ix) She will introduce new capital of £82,500 on 1 April 20X1.

(x) Insurance covering the 12 months of 20X1 of £2,100 will be paid for by cheque on 30 June 20X1.

(xi) All receipts and payments will be by cheque.

(xii) Inventory on 30 June 20X1 will be £30,000.

(xiii) The net realisable value of the vehicles is £19,200, machinery £27,000 and premises £75,000.

Required: Cash flow accounting
(i) Draft a cash budget (includes bank) month by month for the period January to June, showing clearly the amount of bank balance or overdraft at the end of each month.
(ii) Draft an operating cash flow statement for the six-month period.
(iii) Assuming that Jane Parker sought your advice as to whether she should actually set up in business, state what further information you would require.

* Question 2

Mr Norman set up a new business on 1 January 20X8. He invested €50,000 in the new business on that date. The following information is available.

1 Gross profit was 20% of sales. Monthly sales were as follows:

Month	Sales €
January	15,000
February	20,000
March	35,000
April	40,000
May	40,000
June	45,000
July	50,000

2 50% of sales were for cash. Credit customers (50% of sales) pay in month following sale.

3 The supplier allowed one month's credit.

4 Monthly payments were made for rent and rates €2,200 and wages €600.

5 On 1 January 20X8 the following payments were made: €80,000 for a five-year lease of business premises and €3,500 for insurances on the premises for the year. The realisable value of the lease was estimated to be €76,000 on 30 June 20X8 and €70,000 on 31 December 20X8.

6 Staff sales commission of 2% of sales was paid in the month following the sale.

Required:
(a) A purchases budget for each of the first six months.
(b) A cash flow statement for the first six months.
(c) A statement of operating cash flows and financial position as at 30 June 20X8.
(d) Write a brief letter to the bank supporting a request for an overdraft.

References

1 *Framework for the Preparation and Presentation of Financial Statements*, IASC, 1989, para. 10.
2 G. Whittred and I. Zimmer, *Financial Accounting: Incentive Effects and Economic Consequences*, Holt, Rinehart & Winston, 1992, p. 27.
3 R. Jarvis, J. Kitching, J. Curran and G. Lightfoot, *The Financial Management of Small Firms: An Alternative Perspective*, ACCA Research Report No. 49, 1996.
4 *Going Concern and Financial Reporting – Proposals V. Revise the Guidance for Directors of Listed Companies*, FRC, 2008, para. 29.
5 T.A. Lee, *Income and Value Measurement: Theory and Practice* (3rd edition), Van Nostrand Reinhold (UK), 1985, p. 173.
6 D. Solomons, *Making Accounting Policy*, Oxford University Press, 1986, p. 79.

CHAPTER 2

Accounting and reporting on an accrual accounting basis

2.1 Introduction

The main purpose of this chapter is to extend cash flow accounting by adjusting for the effect of transactions that have not been completed by the end of an accounting period.

Objectives

By the end of this chapter, you should be able to:

- explain the historical cost convention and accrual concept;
- adjust cash receipts and payments in accordance with IAS 18 *Revenue*;
- account for the amount of non-current assets used during the accounting period;
- prepare a statement of income and a statement of financial position;
- reconcile cash flow accounting and accrual accounting data.

2.1.1 Objective of financial statements

The *Framework for the Preparation and Presentation of Financial Statements*[1] issued by the International Accounting Standards Committee (IASC) has stated that the objective of financial statements is to provide information about the financial position, performance and capability of an enterprise that is useful to a wide range of users in making economic decisions.

Common information needs for decision making

The IASC recognises that all the information needs of all users cannot be met by financial statements, but it takes the view that some needs are common to all users: in particular, they have some interest in the financial position, performance and adaptability of the enterprise as a whole. This leaves open the question of which user is the primary target; the IASC states that, as investors are providers of risk capital, financial statements that meet their needs would also meet the needs of other users.

Stewardship role of financial statements

In addition to assisting in making economic decisions, financial statements also show the results of the stewardship of management: that is, the accountability of management for the resources entrusted to it. The IASC view is that users who assess the stewardship do so in order to make economic decisions, e.g. whether to hold or sell shares in a particular company or change the management.

Decision makers need to assess ability to generate cash

The IASC considers that economic decisions also require an evaluation of an enterprise's ability to generate cash, and of the timing and certainty of its generation. It believes that users are better able to make the evaluation if they are provided with information that focuses on the financial position, performance and cash flow of an enterprise.

2.1.2 Financial information to evaluate the ability to generate cash differs from financial information on actual cash flows

The IASC approach differs from the cash flow model used in Chapter 1, in that, in addition to the cash flows and statement of financial position, it includes within its definition of performance a reference to profit. It states that this information is required to assess changes in the economic resources that the enterprise is likely to control in the future. This is useful in predicting the capacity of the enterprise to generate cash flows from its existing resource base.

2.1.3 Statements making up the financial statements published for external users

In 2007 the IASB stated[2] that a complete set of financial statements should comprise:

- a statement of financial position as at the end of the period;
- a statement of comprehensive income for the period;
- a statement of changes in equity for the period;
- a statement of cash flows for the period;
- notes comprising a summary of significant accounting policies and other explanatory information.

In this chapter we consider two of the conventions under which the statement of comprehensive income and statement of financial position are prepared: the historical cost convention and the accrual accounting concept. In Chapters 3–5 we consider each of the above statements.

2.2 Historical cost convention

The historical cost convention results in an appropriate measure of the economic resource that has been withdrawn or replaced.

Under it, transactions are reported at the £ amount recorded at the date the transaction occurred. Financial statements produced under this convention provide a basis for determining the outcome of agency agreements with reasonable certainty and predictability because the data are relatively objective.[3]

By this we mean that various parties who deal with the enterprise, such as lenders, will know that the figures produced in any financial statement are objective and not manipulated by subjective judgements made by the directors. A typical example occurs when a lender attaches a covenant to a loan that the enterprise shall not exceed a specified level of gearing.

At an operational level, revenue and expense in the statement of comprehensive income are stated at the £ amount that appears on the invoices. This amount is objective and verifiable.

Because of this, the historical cost convention has strengths for stewardship purposes, but inflation-adjusted figures which we discuss in Chapter 7 may well be more appropriate for decision making.

2.3 Accrual basis of accounting

The accrual basis dictates when transactions with third parties should be recognised and, in particular, determines the accounting periods in which they should be incorporated into the financial statements. Under this concept the cash receipts from customers and payments to creditors are replaced by revenue and expenses respectively.

Revenue and expenses are derived by adjusting the realised operating cash flows to take account of business trading activity that has occurred during the accounting period, but has not been converted into cash receipts or payments by the end of the period.

2.3.1 Accrual accounting is a better indicator than cash flow accounting of ability to generate cash

The IASC supported the Financial Accounting Standards Board (FASB) view in 1989 when it stated that financial statements prepared on an accrual basis inform users not only of past transactions involving the payment and receipt of cash, but also of obligations to pay cash in the future and of resources that represent cash to be received in the future, and that they provide the type of information about past transactions and other events that is most useful in making economic decisions.[4]

Having briefly considered why accrual accounting may be more useful than cash flow accounting, we will briefly revise the preparation of financial statements under the accrual accounting convention.

2.4 Mechanics of accrual accounting – adjusting cash receipts and payments

We use the cash flows set out in Figure 1.7. The derivation of the revenue and expenses for this example is set out in Figures 2.1 and 2.2. We assume that the enterprise has incomplete records, so that the revenue is arrived at by keeping a record of unpaid invoices and adding these to the cash receipts. Clearly, if the invoices are not adequately controlled, there will be no assurance that the £22,500 figure is correct. This is a relatively straightforward process at a mechanistic level. The uncertainty is not how to adjust the cash flow figures, but when to adjust them. This decision requires managers to make subjective judgements. We now look briefly at the nature of such judgements.

Figure 2.1 Derivation of revenue

	£
Cash received	172,500
Invoices not paid (= Sales invoiced – Cash received)	22,500
Revenue = Total invoiced	195,000

Figure 2.2 Derivation of expense

	Materials £	Services £
Cash paid	129,000	21,600
Invoices not paid	37,000	900
Expense = Total invoiced	166,000	22,500

2.5 Subjective judgements required in accrual accounting – adjusting cash payments in accordance with the matching principle

We have seen that the enterprise needs to decide when to recognise the revenue. It then needs to decide when to include an item as an expense in the statement of comprehensive income. This decision is based on an application of the matching principle.

The matching principle means that financial statements must include costs related to the achievement of the reported revenue. These include the internal transfers required to ensure that reductions in the assets held by a business are recorded at the same time as the revenues.

The expense might be more or less than the cash paid. For example, in the Norman example, £37,000 was invoiced but not paid on materials, and £900 on services; £3,125 was prepaid on rent for the six months after June. The cash flow information therefore needs to be adjusted as in Figure 2.3.

2.6 Mechanics of accrual accounting – the statement of financial position

The statement of financial position, as set out in Figure 1.12, needs to be amended following the change from cash flow to accrual accounting. It needs to include the £ amounts that have arisen from trading but have not been converted to cash, and the £ amounts of cash that

Figure 2.3 Statement of income for the six months ended 30 June 20X1

	Operating cash flow £	ADJUST cash flow £	Business activity £
Revenue from business activity	172,500	22,500	195,000
Less: Matching expenses			
Transactions for materials	129,000	37,000	166,000
Transactions for services	21,600	900	22,500
Transaction with landlord	6,250	(3,125)	3,125
OPERATING CASH FLOW from business activity	15,650		
Transactions NOTconverted to cash or relating to a subsequent period		(12,275)	
PROFIT from business activity			3,375

Figure 2.4 Statement of financial position adjusted to an accrual basis

	£
Capital	50,000
Net operating cash flow: **realised**	15,650
Net operating cash flow: **to be realised next period**	(12,275)
	53,375
Lease	80,000
Net cash balance (refer to Figure 1.11)	(14,350)
Net amount of activities not converted to cash or relating to	
subsequent periods	(12,275)
	53,375

have been received or paid but relate to a subsequent period. The adjusted statement of financial position is set out in Figure 2.4.

2.7 Reformatting the statement of financial position

The item 'net amount of activities not converted to cash or relating to subsequent periods' is the net debtor/creditor balance. If we wished, the statement of financial position could be reframed into the customary statement of financial position format, where items are classified as assets or liabilities. The IASC defines assets and liabilities in its *Framework*:

● An asset is a resource:
  – controlled by the enterprise;
  – as a result of past events;
  – from which future economic benefits are expected to flow.
● A liability is a present obligation:
  – arising from past events;
  – the settlement of which is expected to result in an outflow of resources.

The reframed statement set out in Figure 2.5 is in accordance with these definitions. Note that the same amount of £3,375 results from calculating the difference in the opening and closing net assets in the statements of financial position as from calculating the residual amount in the statement of comprehensive income. When the amount derived from both approaches is the same, the statement of financial position and statement of comprehensive income are said to **articulate**. The statement of comprehensive income provides the detailed explanation for the difference in the net assets and the amount is the same because the same concepts have been applied to both statements.

2.8 Accounting for the sacrifice of non-current assets

The statement of comprehensive income and statement of financial position have both been prepared using verifiable data that have arisen from transactions with third parties outside the business. However, in order to determine the full sacrifice of economic resources that a

Figure 2.5 Reframed statement as at 30 June

	Reframed	
	£	£
CAPITAL	50,000	50,000
Net operating cash flow: **realised**	15,650	
Net operating cash flow: **to be realised**	(12,275)	
NET INCOME		3,375
	53,375	53,375
NON-CURRENT ASSETS	80,000	80,000
NET CURRENT ASSETS		
Net amount of activities not converted to cash	(12,275)	
CURRENT ASSETS		
Trade receivables		22,500
Other receivables: prepaid rent		3,125
CURRENT LIABILITIES		
Trade payables		(37,000)
Other payables: service suppliers		(900)
Net cash balance	(14,350)	(14,350)
	53,375	53,375

business has made to achieve its revenue, it is necessary also to take account of the use made of the non-current assets during the period in which the revenue arose.

In the Norman example, the non–current asset is the lease. The extent of the sacrifice is a matter of judgement by the management. This is influenced by the prudence principle, which regulates the matching principle. The prudence principle determines the extent to which transactions that have already been included in the accounting system should be recognised in the statement of comprehensive income.

2.8.1 Treatment of non-current assets in accrual accounting

Applying the matching principle, it is necessary to estimate how much of the initial outlay should be assumed to have been revenue expenditure, i.e. used in achieving the revenue of the accounting period. The provisions of IAS 16 on **depreciation** assist by defining depreciation and stating the duty of allocation, as follows:

Depreciation is the systematic allocation of the depreciable amount of an asset over its useful life.[5]

Depreciable amount is the cost of an asset, or other amount substituted for cost in the financial statements, less its residual value.

The depreciation method used should reflect the pattern in which the asset's economic benefits are consumed by the enterprise.

This sounds a rather complex requirement. It is therefore surprising, when one looks at the financial statements of a multinational company such as in the 2005 Annual Report of BP plc, to find that depreciation on tangible assets other than mineral production is simply provided on a straight-line basis of an equal amount each year, calculated so as to write off the cost by equal instalments. In the UK, this treatment was recognised in FRS 15 which stated that where the pattern of consumption of an asset's economic benefits was uncertain, a straight-line method of depreciation was usually adopted.[6] The reason is that, in accrual accounting, the depreciation charged to the statement of comprehensive income is a measure of the amount of the economic benefits that have been consumed, rather than a measure of the fall in realisable value. In estimating the amount of service potential expired, a business is following the **going concern assumption**.

2.8.2 Going concern assumption

The going concern assumption is that the business enterprise will continue in operational existence for the foreseeable future. This assumption introduces a constraint on the prudence concept by allowing the account balances to be reported on a depreciated cost basis rather than on a net realisable value basis.

It is more relevant to use the loss of service potential than the change in realisable value because there is no intention to cease trading and to sell the fixed assets at the end of the accounting period.

In our Norman example, the procedure would be to assume that, in the case of the lease, the economic resource that has been consumed can be measured by the amortisation that has occurred due to the effluxion of time. The time covered by the accounts is half a year: this means that one-tenth of the lease has expired during the half-year. As a result, £8,000 is treated as revenue expenditure in the half-year to 30 June.

This additional revenue expenditure reduces the income in the income account and the asset figure in the statement of financial position. The effects are incorporated into the two statements in Figures 2.6 and 2.7. The asset amounts and the income figure in the statement

Figure 2.6 Statement of income for the six months ending 30 June

	Operating cash flow CURRENT period £	Adjust cash flow £	Business activity CURRENT period £
Revenue from business activity	172,500	22,500	195,000
Less			
Expenditure to support this activity:			
Transactions with suppliers	129,000	37,000	166,000
Transactions with service providers	21,600	900	22,500
Transaction with landlord	6,250	(3,125)	3,125
OPERATING CASH FLOW from activity	15,650	———	
TRANSACTIONS NOT CONVERTED TO CASH		(12,275)	———
INCOME from business activity			3,375
Allocation of non-current asset cost to this period			8,000
INCOME			(4,625)

Figure 2.7 Statement of financial position as at 30 June

	Transaction cash flows £	Notional flows £	Reported £
CAPITAL	50,000		50,000
Net operating cash flow: **realised**	15,650		
Net operating cash flow: **to be realised**	(12,275)		
Net income before depreciation		3,375	
AMORTISATION		(8,000)	
Net income after amortisation			(4,625)
	53,375		45,375
NON-CURRENT ASSETS	80,000	80,000	
Less amortisation		(8,000)	
Net book value			72,000
NET CURRENT ASSETS			
Net amount not converted to cash	(12,275)		
CURRENT ASSETS			
Trade receivables			22,500
Other receivables – prepaid rent			3,125
CURRENT LIABILITIES			
Trade payables			(37,000)
Other payables: service suppliers			(900)
Net cash balance	(14,350)		(14,350)
	53,375		45,375

of financial position are also affected by the exhaustion of part of the non-current assets, as set out in Figure 2.7.

It is current accounting practice to apply the same concepts to determining the entries in both the statement of comprehensive income and the statement of financial position. The amortisation charged in the statement of comprehensive income at £8,000 is the same as the amount deducted from the non-current assets in the statement of financial position. As a result, the two statements articulate: the statement of comprehensive income explains the reason for the reduction of £4,625 in the net assets.

How decision-useful to the management is the income figure that has been derived after deducting a depreciation charge?

The loss of £4,625 indicates that the distribution of any amount would further deplete the financial capital of £50,000 which was invested in the company by Mr Norman on setting up the business. This is referred to as **capital maintenance**; the particular capital maintenance concept that has been applied is the **financial capital maintenance concept**.

2.8.3 Financial capital maintenance concept

The financial capital maintenance concept recognises a profit only after the original monetary investment has been maintained. This means that, as long as the cost of the assets representing the initial monetary investment is recovered against the profit, by way of a depreciation charge, the initial monetary investment is maintained.

The concept has been described in the IASC *Framework for the Preparation and Presentation of Financial Statements*:

> a profit is earned only if the financial or money amount of the net assets at the end of the period exceeds the financial or money amount of the net assets at the beginning of the period, after excluding any distributions to, and contributions from, owners during the period. Financial capital maintenance can be measured in either nominal monetary units [as we are doing in this chapter] or in units of constant purchasing power [as we will be doing in Chapter 7].

2.8.4 Summary of views on accrual accounting

Standard setters:

The profit (loss) is considered to be a guide when assessing the amount, timing and uncertainty of prospective cash flows as represented by future income amounts. The IASC, FASB in the USA and ASB in the UK clearly stated that the accrual accounting concept was more useful in predicting future cash flows than cash flow accounting.

Academic researchers:

Academic research provides conflicting views. In 1986, research carried out in the USA indicated that the FASB view was inconsistent with its findings and that cash flow information was a better predictor of future operating cash flows;[7] research carried out in the UK, however, indicated that accrual accounting using the historical cost convention was 'a more relevant basis for decision making than cash flow measures'.[8]

2.9 Reconciliation of cash flow and accrual accounting data

The accounting profession attempted to provide users of financial statements with the benefits of both types of data, by requiring a cash flow statement to be prepared as well as the statement of comprehensive income and statement of financial position prepared on an accrual basis.

From the statement of comprehensive income prepared on an accrual basis, an investor is able to obtain an indication of a business's present ability to generate favourable cash flows; from the statement of financial position prepared on an accrual basis (as in Figure 2.7) an investor is able to obtain an indication of a business's continuing ability to generate favourable cash flows; from the cash flow statement (as in Figure 2.9) an investor is able to reconcile the income figure with the change in net cash balance.

Figure 2.8 reconciles the information produced in Chapter 1 under the cash flow basis with the information produced under the accrual basis. It could be expanded to provide information more clearly, as in Figure 2.9. Here we are using the information from Figures 1.9 and 1.12, but within a third statement rather than the statement of comprehensive income and statement of financial position.

Figure 2.8 Reconciliation of income figure with net cash balance

	£
Income per income statement	(4,625)
Add: unrealisable cash outflow	8,000
	3,375
Add: unrealised operating cash flows	12,275
Operating cash flow	15,650
Other sources:	
Capital	50,000
Total cash available	65,650
Applications	
Lease	(80,000)
Net cash balance	(14,350)

Figure 2.9 Statement of cash flows netting amounts that have not been converted to cash

	£	£
Sales	195,000	
Trade receivables	(22,500)	172,500
Purchases	166,000	
Trade payables	(37,000)	(129,000)
Expenses	22,500	
Other payables	(900)	(21,600)
Rent	3,125	
Other receivables: Prepaid rent	3,125	(6,250)
Net cash inflow from operating activities		15,650
Cash flows from investing activities		
Lease		(80,000)
Cash flows from financing activities		
Issue of capital		50,000
Decrease in cash		(14,350)

2.9.1 Published cash flow statement

IAS 7 *Statement of Cash Flows*[9] specifies the standard headings under which cash flows should be classified. They are:

● cash flows from operating activities;
● cash flows from investing activities;

Figure 2.10 Cash flow statement in accordance with IAS 7 *Statement of Cash Flows*

	£
Net cash inflow from operating activities	15,650
Investing activities	
Payment to acquire lease	(80,000)
Net cash outflow before financing	(64,350)
Financing activities	
Issue of capital	50,000
Decrease in cash	(14,350)
Reconciliation of operating loss to net cash	
inflow from operating activities	£
Operating profit/loss	(4,625)
Amortisation charges	8,000
Increase in trade receivables	(22,500)
Increase in prepayments	(3,125)
Increase in trade payables	37,000
Increase in accruals	900
	15,650

● cash flows from financing activities;

● net increase in cash and cash equivalents.

To comply with IAS 7, the cash flows from Figure 2.9 would be set out as in Figure 2.10. IAS 7 is mentioned at this stage only to illustrate that cash flows can be reconciled to the accrual accounting data. There is further discussion of IAS 7 in Chapter 5.

Summary

Accrual accounting replaces cash receipts and payments with revenue and expenses by adjusting the cash figures to take account of trading activity which has not been converted into cash.

Accrual accounting is preferred to cash accounting by the standard setters on the assumption that accrual-based financial statements give investors a better means of predicting future cash flows.

The financial statements are transaction based, applying the historical cost accounting concept which attempts to minimise the need for personal judgements and estimates in arriving at the figures in the statements.

Under accrual-based accounting the expenses incurred are matched with the revenue earned. In the case of non-current assets, a further accounting concept has been adopted, the going concern concept, which allows an entity to allocate the cost of non-current assets over their estimated useful life.

REVIEW QUESTIONS

1   'Cash flow accounting and accrual accounting information are both required by a potential shareholder.' Discuss.

2   'The asset measurement basis applied in accrual accounting can lead to financial difficulties when assets are due for replacement.' Discuss.

3   'Accrual accounting is preferable to cash flow accounting because the information is more relevant to all users of financial statements.' Discuss.

4   'Information contained in a statement of income and a statement of financial position prepared under accrual accounting concepts is factual and objective.' Discuss.

5   The *Framework for the Preparation and Presentation of Financial Statements* identified seven user groups: investors, employees, lenders, suppliers and other trade creditors, customers, government and the public.

Discuss which of the financial statements illustrated in Chapters 1 and 2 would be most useful to each of these seven groups if they could only receive one statement.

6   The annual financial statements of companies are used by various parties for a wide variety of purposes. For each of the seven different 'user groups', explain their presumed interest with reference to the performance of the company and its financial position.

EXERCISES

* Question 1

Jane Parker is going to set up a new business in Bruges on 1 January 20X1. She estimates that her first six months in business will be as follows:

(i)   She will put €150,000 into the firm on 1 January 20X1.

(ii)   On 1 January 20X1 she will buy machinery €30,000, motor vehicles €24,000 and premises €75,000, paying for them immediately.

(iii)   All purchases will be effected on credit. She will buy €30,000 goods on 1 January and she will pay for these in February. Other purchases will be: rest of January €48,000; February, March, April, May and June €60,000 each month. Other than the €30,000 worth bought in January, all other purchases will be paid for two months after purchase, i.e. €48,000 in March.

(iv)   Sales (all on credit) will be €60,000 for January and €75,000 for each month after that. Customers will pay for goods in the third month after purchase, i.e. €60,000 in April.

(v)   Inventory on 30 June 20X1 will be €30,000.

(vi)   Wages and salaries will be €2,250 per month and will be paid on the last day of each month.

(vii)   General expenses will be €750 per month, payable in the month following that in which they are incurred.

(viii) She will introduce new capital of €75,000 on 1 June 20X1. This will be paid into the business bank account immediately.

(ix)   Insurance covering the 12 months of 20X1 of €26,400 will be paid for by cheque on 30 June 20X1.

(x)   Local taxes will be paid as follows: for the three months to 31 March 20X1 by cheque on 28 February 20X2, delay due to an oversight by Parker; for the 12 months ended 31 March 20X2 by cheque on 31 July 20X1. Local taxes are €8,000 per annum.

(xi)   She will make drawings of €1,500 per month by cheque.

(xii) All receipts and payments are by cheque.

(xiii) Depreciate motor vehicles by 20% per annum and machinery by 10% per annum, using the straight-line depreciation method.

(xiv) She has been informed by her bank manager that he is prepared to offer an overdraft facility of €30,000 for the first year.

Required:
(a) Draft a cash budget (for the firm) month by month for the period January to June, showing clearly the amount of bank balance at the end of each month.
(b) Draft the projected statement of comprehensive income for the first six months' trading, and a statement of financial position as at 30 June 20X1.
(c) Advise Jane on the alternative courses of action that could be taken to cover any cash deficiency that exceeds the agreed overdraft limit.

* Question 2

Mr Norman is going to set up a new business in Singapore on 1 January 20X8. He will invest $150,000 in the business on that date and has made the following estimates and policy decisions:

1 Forecast sales (in units) made at a selling price of $50 per unit are:

Month	Sales units
January	1,650
February	2,200
March	3,850
April	4,400
May	4,400
June	4,950
July	5,500

2 50% of sales are for cash. Credit terms are payment in the month following sale.

3 The units cost $40 each and the supplier is allowed one month's credit.

4 It is intended to hold inventory at the end of each month sufficient to cover 25% of the following month's sales.

5 Administration $8,000 and wages $17,000 are paid monthly as they arise.

6 On 1 January 20X8, the following payments will be made: $80,000 for a five-year lease of the business premises and $350 for insurance for the year.

7 Staff sales commission of 2% of sales will be paid in the month following sale.

Required:
(a) A purchases budget for each of the first six months.
(b) A cash flow forecast for the first six months.
(c) A budgeted statement of comprehensive income for the first six months' trading and a budgeted statement of financial position as at 30 June 20X8.
(d) Advise Mr Norman on the investment of any excess cash.

References

1 *Framework for the Preparation and Presentation of Financial Statements*, IASC, 1989, para. 12.
2 IAS 1 *Presentation of Financial Statements*, IASB, revised 2007, para. 10.
3 M. Page, *British Accounting Review*, vol. 24(1), 1992, p. 80.
4 *Framework for the Preparation and Presentation of Financial Statements*, IASC, 1989, para. 20.
5 IAS 16 *Property, Plant and Equipment*, IASC, revised 2004, para. 6.
6 FRS 15 *Tangible Fixed Assets*, ASB, 1999, para. 81.
7 R.M. Bowen, D. Burgstahller and L.A. Daley, 'Evidence on the relationship between earnings and various measures of cash flow', *Accounting Review*, October 1986, pp. 713–725.
8 J.I.G. Board and J.F.S. Day, 'The information content of cash flow figures', *Accounting and Business Research*, Winter 1989, pp. 3–11.
9 IAS 7 *Statement of Cash Flows*, IASB, revised 2007.

CHAPTER 3

Preparation of financial statements of comprehensive income, changes in equity and financial position

3.1 Introduction

Annual Reports consist of primary financial statements, additional disclosures and narrative.

The primary financial statements should be presented using standardised formats as prescribed by International Financial Reporting Standards and include [IAS 1.10]:

- a statement of income;
- a statement of other comprehensive income;
- a statement of changes in equity;
- a statement of financial position;
- a statement of cash flows (covered in Chapter 5);
- explanatory notes to the accounts.

Objectives

By the end of this chapter, you should be able to:

- understand the structure and content of published financial statements;
- prepare statements of comprehensive income, changes in equity and financial position;
- explain the nature of and reasons for notes to the accounts.

3.2 Preparing an internal statement of income from a trial balance

In this section we revise the steps taken to prepare an internal statement of income from a trial balance. These are to:

- identify year-end adjustments;
- calculate these adjustments;
- prepare an internal statement of income taking adjustments into account.

3.2.1 The trial balance of Wiggins SA

Accounts will be prepared for Wiggins SA from the trial balance set out in Figure 3.1.

Figure 3.1 The trial balance for Wiggins SA as at 31 December 20X3

	€000	€000
Issued share capital (€1)		16,500
Share premium		750
Retained earnings		57,500
10% long-term loan (20X9)		63,250
Bank overdraft		6,325
Trade payables		30,650
Depreciation – buildings		2,300
– equipment		3,450
– vehicles		9,200
Freehold land	57,500	
Freehold buildings	57,500	
Equipment	14,950	
Motor vehicles	20,700	
Inventory at 1 January 20X3	43,125	
Trade receivables	28,750	
Cash in hand	4,600	
Purchases	258,750	
Bank interest	1,150	
Dividends	1,725	
Interest on loan	6,325	
Insurance	5,290	
Salaries and wages	20,355	
Motor expenses	9,200	
Taxation that was under provided	750	
Light, power, miscellaneous	4,255	
Sales		345,000
	534,925	534,925

3.2.2 Identify the year-end adjustments

During the year cash and credit transactions are recorded by posting to the individual ledger accounts as cash is paid or received and invoices received or issued. It is only when financial statements are being prepared that adjustments are made to ensure that the statement of income includes only income and expenses related to the current financial period.

The following information relating to accruals and prepayments has not yet been taken into account in the amounts shown in the trial balance:

● Inventory valued at cost at 31 December 20X3 was €25,875,000.
● Depreciation is to be provided as follows:
  – 2% on freehold buildings using the straight-line method;
  – 10% on equipment using the reducing balance method;
  – 25% on motor vehicles using the reducing balance method.
● €2,300,000 was prepaid for light, power and miscellaneous expenses and €5,175,000 has accrued for wages.
● Freehold land was revalued on 31 December 20X3 at €77,500,000 resulting in a gain of €20,000,000.
● Assume income tax at 20% of pre-tax profit.
● 1,500 €1 shares had been issued on 1 January 20X3 at a premium of 50c each.

3.2.3 Calculate the year-end adjustments

In this example they relate to accrued and prepaid expenses and depreciation.

W1 Salaries and wages:

€20,355,000 + accrued €5,175,000 = €25,530,000

W2 Depreciation:

Buildings	2% of €57,500,000	€1,150,000
Equipment	10% of (€14,950,000 – €3,450,000)	€1,150,000
Vehicles	25% of (€20,700,000 – €9,200,000)	€2,875,000
Total		€5,175,000

W3 Light, power and miscellaneous

€4,255,000 – prepaid €2,300,000 = €1,955,000

3.2.4 Prepare an internal statement of income after making the year-end adjustments

By way of revision, we have set out a statement of income prepared for internal purposes in Figure 3.2. We have arranged the expenses in descending monetary value. The method for doing this is not prescribed and companies are free to organise the expenses in other ways, for example in alphabetical order.

Figure 3.2 Statement of income of Wiggins SA for the year ended 31 December 20X3

		€000	€000
Sales			345,000
Less:			
Opening inventory		43,125	
Purchases		258,750	
		301,875	
Closing inventory		25,875	
Cost of sales			276,000
Gross profit			69,000
Less expenses:			
Salaries and wages	WI	25,530	
Motor expenses		9,200	
Loan interest		6,325	
Depreciation	W2	5,175	
Insurance		5,290	
Bank interest		1,150	
Light, power and miscellaneous	W3	1,955	
			54,625
Profit before tax			14,375
Income taxation (includes under-provision)			3,625
Profit after tax			10,750
Dividends (are disclosed in Statement of Changes in Equity in published format)			1,725
Retained earnings			9,025

3.3 Reorganising the income and expenses into one of the formats required for publication

Public companies are required to present their statement of income in a prescribed format to assist users making inter-company comparisons. IAS 1 allows a company two choices in the way in which it analyses the expenses, and the formats[1] are as follows:

● Format 1: Vertical with costs analysed according to function, e.g. cost of sales, distribution costs and administration expenses, or

● Format 2: Vertical with costs analysed according to nature, e.g. raw materials, employee benefits expenses, operating expenses and depreciation.

Many companies use Format 1 (unless there is an industry preference or possible national requirement to use Format 2) with the costs analysed according to function. If this format is used the information regarding the nature of expenditure (e.g. raw materials, wages and depreciation) must be disclosed in a note to the accounts. The analysis of expenses classified either by the nature of the expenses or by their function within the entity is decided by whichever provides information that is reliable and more relevant.

3.4 Format 1: classification of operating expenses and other income by function

In order to arrive at its operating profit (a measure of profit often recognised by many companies), a company needs to classify all of the operating expenses of the business into one of four categories:

- cost of sales;
- distribution and selling costs;
- administrative expenses;
- other operating income or expense.

We comment briefly on each to explain how a company might classify its trading transactions.

3.4.1 Cost of sales

Expenditure classified under cost of sales will typically include direct costs, overheads, depreciation and amortisation expense and adjustments. The items that might appear under each heading are as follows:

- Direct costs: direct materials purchased; direct labour; other external charges that comprise production costs from external sources, e.g. hire charges and subcontracting costs.
- Overheads: variable and fixed production overheads.
- Depreciation and amortisation: depreciation of non-current assets used in production and impairment expense.
- Adjustments: capitalisation of own work as a non-current asset. Any amount of the costs listed above that have been incurred in the construction of non-current assets for retention by the company will not appear as an expense in the statement of comprehensive income: it will be capitalised. Any amount capitalised in this way would be treated for accounting purposes as a non-current asset and depreciated.

3.4.2 Distribution costs

These are costs incurred after the production of the finished article and up to and including transfer of the goods to the customer. Expenditure classified under this heading will typically include the following:

- warehousing costs associated with the operation of the premises, e.g. rent, rates, insurance, utilities, depreciation, repairs and maintenance; wage costs, e.g. gross wages and pension contributions of warehouse staff;
- promotion costs, e.g. advertising, trade shows;
- selling costs, e.g. salaries, commissions and pension contributions of sales staff; costs associated with the premises, e.g. rent, rates; cash discounts on sales; travelling and entertainment;
- transport costs, e.g. gross wages and pension contributions of transport staff, vehicle costs, e.g. running costs, maintenance and depreciation.

3.4.3 Administrative expenses

These are the costs of running the business that have not been classified as either cost of sales or distribution costs. Expenditure classified under this heading will typically include:

- administration, e.g. salaries, commissions, and pension contributions of administration staff;
- costs associated with the premises, e.g. rent, rates;

- amounts written off the receivables that appear in the statement of financial position under current assets;
- professional fees.

3.4.4 Other operating income or expense

Under this heading a company discloses material income or expenses derived from ordinary activities of the business that have not been included elsewhere. If the amounts are not material, they would not be separately disclosed but included within the other captions. Items classified under these headings may typically include the following:

- income derived from intangible assets, e.g. royalties, commissions;
- income derived from third-party use of property, plant and equipment that is surplus to the current productive needs of the company;
- income received from employees, e.g. canteen, recreation fees;
- payments for rights to use intangible assets not directly related to operations, e.g. licences.

3.4.5 Finance costs

In order to arrive at the profit for the period, interest received or paid on loans and bank over-draft and investment income is disclosed under the Finance cost heading.

3.4.6 An analysis of expenses by function

An analysis of expenses would be carried out in practice in order to classify these under their appropriate function heading. These are allocated or apportioned as appropriate. The assumptions for this exercise are shown in Figure 3.3.

3.4.7 Accounting for current tax

The profit reported in the statement of income is subject to taxation at a percentage rate set by government. The resulting amount is treated as an expense in the statement of income and a current liability in the statement of financial position. However, this is an estimated figure and the amount agreed with the tax authorities in the following accounting period might be higher or lower than the estimate.

Underprovisions

If the agreed amount should be higher, it means the company has underprovided and will be required to pay an amount higher than the liability reported in the statement of financial position – this results in a debit balance appearing in the trial balance prepared at the end of the following period. This underprovision will be added to the following year's estimated tax charged in the statement of income.

For example, if the company estimates €5,750,000 in Year 20X1 and pays €6,000,000 in 20X2 and estimates €5,220,000 in 20X2 on its 20X2 profits, then the charge in the statement of income for 20X2 will be €5,470,000 (€5,220,000 + €250,000).

Overprovisions

If overprovided the agreed tax payable will be lower, say €5,150,000 then the charge in 20X2 will be reduced by €600,000 (€5,750,000 − €5,150,000).

Figure 3.3 Assumptions made in analysing the costs

	Total €000	Cost of sales €000	Distribution costs €000	Administration expenses €000
Allocation of salaries and wages				
Factory staff	12,650	12,650		
Sales and warehouse	10,580		10,580	
Administration and accounts staff	2,300			2,300
Subtotal	25,530	12,650	10,580	2,300
An analysis of depreciation				
Freehold buildings	1,150	575	287.5	287.5
Equipment	1,150	575	287.5	287.5
Motor vehicles (allocated)	2,875		2,875	
Subtotal	5,175	1,150	3,450	575
Motor expenses (allocated)	9,200		9,200	
An apportionment of operating expenses on the basis of space occupied				
Insurance	5,290	2,645	1,322.5	1,322.5
Light, power and miscellaneous	1,955	977.5	488.75	488.75
Subtotal	16,445	3,622.5	11,011.25	1,811.25
TOTAL EXPENSES	47,150	17,422.5	25,041.25	4,686.25
Add material consumed	276,000	276,000		
TOTALS for statement of income	323,150	293,422.5	25,041.25	4,686.25

3.4.8 The statement of income using Format 1

Format 1 provides a multi-stage presentation reporting four profit measures for gross, operating, pre-tax and post-tax profit, as in Figure 3.4.

Figure 3.4 Statement of income of Wiggins SA for the year ended 31 December 20X3

	€000
Revenue	345,000.00
Cost of sales	293,422.50
Gross profit	51,577.50
Distribution costs	25,041.25
Administrative expenses	4,686.25
Operating profit	21,850.00
Finance costs	7,475.00
Profit on ordinary activities before tax	14,375.00
Income tax (2,875 + 750)	3,625.00
Profit for the year	10,750.00

Figure 3.5 Wiggins SA statement of income for the year ended 31 December 20X3

	€000	€000
Revenue		345,000
Decrease in inventory	(17,250)	
Raw materials	(258,750)	(276,000)
Employee benefit expense		
Salaries		(25,530)
Depreciation		(5,175)
Other operating expenses		
Motor expenses	(9,200)	
Insurance	(5,290)	
Light, power and miscellaneous	(1,955)	(16,445)
Operating profit		21,850

3.5 Format 2: classification of operating expenses according to their nature

Note that if Format 2 is used the expenses are classified as change in inventory, raw materials, employee benefits expense, other expenses and depreciation as in Figure 3.5. The operating profit is unchanged from that appearing in Figure 3.4 using Format 1. If this format is used, the cost of sales has to be disclosed.

3.6 Other comprehensive income

When IAS 1 was revised in 2008 the profit and loss account or 'income statement' was replaced by the statement of comprehensive income, and a new section of 'Other comprehensive income' was added to the previous statement of income. The statement was then retitled as 'Statement of Comprehensive Income'.

3.6.1 What is meant by comprehensive income?

Comprehensive income recognises the gains and losses, both realised and unrealised, that have increased or decreased the owners' equity in the business. Such gains and losses arise, for example, from the revaluation of non-current assets and from other items that are discussed later in Chapters 14 (Financial instruments) and 15 (Employee benefits). These are referred to as *Other comprehensive income*.

3.6.2 How to report other comprehensive income

IAS 1 allows a choice. It can be presented as a separate statement or as an extension of the statement of income. In our example we have presented it as an extension of the statement of income.

In this example, there is a revaluation gain on the freehold land which needs to be added to the profit on ordinary activities for the year in order to arrive at the comprehensive income. This is shown in Figure 3.6.

Figure 3.6 Statement of comprehensive income of Wiggins SA for the year ended 31.12.20X3

	€000
Revenue	345,000.00
Cost of sales	293,422.50
Gross profit	51,577.50
Distribution costs	25,041.25
Administrative expenses	4,686.25
Operating profit	21,850.00
Finance costs	7,475.00
Profit on ordinary activities before tax	14,375.00
Income tax	3,625.00
Profit for the year	10,750.00
Other comprehensive income:	
Gains on property revaluation	20,000.00
Comprehensive income for the year	30,750.00

3.7 How non-recurring or exceptional items can affect operating income

Operating income is one of the measures used by investors when attempting to predict future income. Management are, therefore, keen to highlight if the current year's operating income has been adversely affected by events that are unlikely to occur in future periods – these are referred to as 'exceptional items'. Such items are within the normal operating activities of the business but require to be separately disclosed because they are significant due to their non-recurring nature and materiality in both size and nature.

There could be a number of exceptional reasons that result in a lower profit, for example costs incurred in restructuring the business or unusually high allowances for bad debts or material write-downs of inventories to net realisable value or non-current assets to recoverable amounts.

Exceptional items are not, however, always adverse – there might, for example, have been significant gains arising from the disposal of non-current assets.

3.7.1 Notes to the accounts

It is important to refer to information in the Notes because these items can have a material impact as seen in the Carrefour 2011 Annual Report where an operating profit is turned into an operating loss:

	2011	2010	% change
Total revenue	82,764	81,840	1.1%
Cost of sales	(64,912)	(63,969)	1.5%
Gross margin from recurring operations	17,852	17,871	(0.1)%
Sales, general and administrative expenses	(13,969)	(13,494)	3.5%
Depreciation, amortisation and provisions	(1,701)	(1,675)	1.6%
Recurring operating income	2,182	2,701	(19.2)%
Non-recurring income and expenses, net	(2,662)	(999)	–
Operating profit/(loss)	(481)	1,703	(128.2)%

Non-recurring income and expenses consist mainly of gains and losses on disposal of property and equipment or intangible assets, impairment losses on property and equipment or intangible assets (including goodwill), restructuring costs and provisions for claims and litigation that are material at Group level. They are presented separately in the income statement to 'help users of the financial statements to better understand the Group's underlying operating performance and provide them with useful information to assess the earnings outlook'.

3.7.2 Columnar format

Whilst the information could be disclosed as a note, some companies emphasise the impact by preparing a three-column statement of income. For example, International Power plc state in their 2010 Annual Report:

> In order to allow a better understanding of the financial information presented, and specifically the Group's underlying business performance, the Group presents its income statement in three columns such that it identifies (i) results excluding exceptional items, (ii) the effect of exceptional items and (iii) results for the year . . . Those items that the Group separately presents as exceptional are items which, in the judgement of the Directors, need to be disclosed separately by virtue of their size or incidence in order to obtain a proper understanding of the financial information.

3.8 How decision-useful is the statement of comprehensive income?

A key question we should ask whenever there is a proposal to present additional financial information is 'How will this be useful to users of the accounts?' There is no definitive answer, because some commentators[2] argue that there is no decision-usefulness in providing the comprehensive net income figure for investors, whereas others[3] take the opposite view. Intuitively, one might take a view that investors are interested in the total movement in equity regardless of the cause, which would lead to support for the comprehensive income figure. However, given that there is this difference of opinion and research findings, this would seem to be an area open to further empirical research to further test the decision-usefulness of each measure to analysts.

Interesting research[4] has since been carried out which supports the view that net income and comprehensive income are both decision-useful. The findings suggested that comprehensive income was more decision-relevant for assessing share returns and traditional net income more decision-relevant for setting executive bonus incentives.

3.9 Statement of changes in equity

This statement is designed to show the following:

- *Prior period adjustments.* The effect of any prior period adjustments is shown by adjusting the retained earnings figure brought forward (we will cover this in Chapter 4).
- *Capital transactions with the owners.* This includes dividends and a reconciliation between the opening and closing equity capital, reporting any change such as increases from bonus, rights or new cash issues and decreases from any buyback of shares.

Figure 3.7 Statement of changes in equity for the year ended 31 December 20X3

	Share capital	Share premium	Retained earnings	Revaluation surplus	Total
Balance as at 1 January 20X3	15,000	—	57,500		74,750
Changes in equity for 20X3					
New shares issued	1,500	750			
Dividends			(1,725)		(1,725)
Total comprehensive income for the year			10,750	20,000	30,750
Balance as at 31 December 20X3	16,500	750	66,525	20,000	103,775

- *Transfers from revaluation reserves.* When a revalued asset is disposed of, any revaluation surplus may be transferred directly to retained earnings, or it may be left in equity under the heading revaluation surplus.
- *Comprehensive income.* The comprehensive income for the period is disclosed.

The statement for Wiggins SA is shown in Figure 3.7.

Note that the statement of changes in equity is a primary statement and is required to be presented with the same prominence as the other primary statements.

3.10 The statement of financial position

IAS 1 specifies which items are to be included on the face of the statement of financial position. These are referred to as alpha headings (a) to (r) – for example (a) Property, plant and equipment, (b) Investment property, . . . , (g) Inventories, . . . , (k) Trade and other payables.

It does not prescribe the order and presentation that are to be followed. It would be acceptable to present the statement as assets less liabilities equalling equity, or total assets equalling total equity and liabilities.

3.10.1 Current/non-current classification

- The standard does not absolutely prescribe that enterprises need to split assets and liabilities into current and non–current. However, it does state that this split would need to be done if the nature of the business indicates that it is appropriate.
- If it is more relevant, a presentation could be based on liquidity and if so, all assets and liabilities would be presented broadly in order of liquidity. However, in almost all cases it would be appropriate to split items into current and non–current and the statement in Figure 3.8 follows the headings prescribed in IAS 1.

Figure 3.8 Wiggins SA statement of financial position as at 31.12.20X3

	€000	€000
Non-current assets:		
Property, plant and equipment (see Figure 3.10)		150,525
Current assets:		
Inventory	25,875	
Receivables	28,750	
Cash at bank and in hand	4,600	
Prepayments	2,300	
		61,525
Total assets		212,050
Equity:		
Share capital		16,500
Share premium		750
Revaluation reserve		20,000
Retained earnings		66,525
		103,775
Non-current liabilities:		
10% loan (20X9)		63,250
Current liabilities:		
Payables	30,650	
Provisions for income tax	2,875	
Accruals	5,175	
Bank overdraft	6,325	45,025
Total equity and liabilities		212,050

3.11 The explanatory notes that are part of the financial statements

Published accounts are supported by a number of explanatory notes. These have been expanded over time to satisfy various user needs. We will comment briefly on (a) notes setting out accounting policies, (b) notes giving greater detail of the make-up of items that appear in the statement of financial position, (c) notes providing additional information to assist predicting future cash flows, and (d) notes giving information of interest to other stakeholders.

(a) Accounting policies

Accounting policies are chosen by a company as being the most appropriate to the company's circumstances and **best able to produce a fair view**. They typically disclose the accounting policies followed for the basis of accounting, for example that the accounts have been prepared on a historical cost basis and how revenue, assets and liabilities have been reported. The policies relating to assets and liabilities will cover non-current and current items, for example the depreciation method used for non-current assets (as in Figure 3.9) and the valuation method used for inventory such as FIFO or weighted average.

Figure 3.9 Extract from the financial statements of the Nestlé Group

Property, plant and equipment

Property, plant and equipment are shown in the statement of financial position at their historical cost. Depreciation is provided on components that have homogeneous useful lives by using the straight-line method so as to depreciate the initial cost down to the residual value over the estimated useful lives. The residual values are 30% on head office, 20% on distribution centres for products stored at ambient temperature and nil for all other asset types.

The useful lives are as follows:

Buildings	20–35 years
Machinery and equipment	10–20 years
Tools, furniture, information technology and sundry equipment	3–8 years
Vehicles	5 years

Land is not depreciated.

Useful lives, components and residual amounts are reviewed annually. Such a review takes into consideration the nature of the assets, their intended use and the evolution of technology.

Depreciation of property, plant and equipment is allocated to the appropriate headings of expenses by function in the statement of comprehensive income.

How do users know the effect of changes in accounting policy?

Accounting policies are required by IAS 1 to be applied consistently from one financial period to another. It is only permissible to change an accounting policy if required by a standard or if the directors consider that a change results in financial statements that are reliable and more relevant. When a change does occur IAS 8 requires:

● the comparative figures of the previous financial period to be amended if possible;

● the disclosure of the reason for the change;

● the effect of the adjustment in the statement of comprehensive income of the period and the effect on all other periods presented with the current period financial statements.

(b) Notes giving greater detail of the make-up of statement of financial position figures

Each of the alpha headings may have additional detail disclosed by way of a note to the accounts. For example, inventory of £25.875 million in the statement of financial position may have a note of its detailed make-up as follows:

	£m
Raw materials	11.225
Work in progress	1.500
Finished goods	13.150
	25.875

Property, plant and equipment normally have a schedule as shown in Figure 3.10. From this the net book value is read off the total column for inclusion in the statement of financial position.

Figure 3.10 Disclosure note: Property, plant and equipment movements

	Freehold land	Freehold buildings	Equipment	Motor vehicles	Total
	€000	€000	€000	€000	€000
Cost/valuation					
As at 1.1.20X3	57,500	57,500	14,950	20,700	150,650
Revaluation	20,000				20,000
Additions					
Disposals					
As at 31.12.20X3	77,500	57,500	14,950	20,700	170,650
Accumulated depreciation					
As at 1.1.20X3		2,300	3,450	9,200	14,950
Charge for the year		1,150	1,150	2,875	5,175
As at 31.12.20X3		3,450	4,600	12,075	20,125
Net book value					
As at 31.12.20X3	**77,500**	**54,050**	**10,350**	**8,625**	**150,525**
As at 31.12.20X2	57,500	55,200	11,500	11,500	135,700

(c) Notes giving additional information to assist prediction of future cash flows

These are notes intended to assist in predicting future cash flows. They give information on matters such as:

- capital commitments that have been contracted for but not provided in the accounts;
- capital commitments that have been authorised but not contracted for;
- future commitments, e.g. share options that have been granted; and
- contingent liabilities, e.g. guarantees given by the company in respect of overdraft facilities arranged by subsidiary companies or customers.

In deciding upon disclosures, management have an obligation to consider whether the omission of the information is material and could influence users who base their decisions on the financial statements. The management decision would be influenced by the size or nature of the item and the characteristics of the users. They are entitled to assume that the users have a reasonable knowledge of business and accounting and a willingness to study the information with reasonable diligence.

(d) Notes giving information that is of interest to other stakeholders

An example is information relating to staff. It is common for enterprises to provide a disclosure of the average number of employees in the period or the number of employees at the end of the period. IAS 1 does not require this information but it is likely that many businesses would provide and categorise the information, possibly following functions such as production, sales, and administration as in the following extract from the 2009 Annual Report of Wienerberger:

	Total (2009)	Total (2008)
Production	8,430	10,695
Administration	1,222	1,392
Sales	3,024	3,080
Total	12,676	15,167
Apprentices	70	152

This shows a significant reduction in staff numbers with reasons given within the Report. However, the annual report is not the only source of information – there might be separate employee reports and information obtained during labour negotiations such as the ratio of short-term and long-term assets to employee numbers, the capital–labour ratios and the average sales and net profits per employee in the company compared, if possible, to benchmarks from the same economic sector.

3.12 Has prescribing the formats meant that identical transactions are reported identically?

That is the intention, but there are various reasons why there may still be differences. For example, let us consider some of the reasons for differences in calculating the cost of sales: (a) how inventory is valued, (b) the choice of depreciation policy, (c) management attitudes, and (d) the capability of the accounting system.

(a) Differences arising from the choice of the inventory valuation method

Different companies may assume different physical flows when calculating the cost of direct materials used in production. This will affect the inventory valuation. One company may assume a first-in-first-out (FIFO) flow, where the cost of sales is charged for raw materials used in production as if the first items purchased were the first items used in production. Another company may use an average basis. This is illustrated in Figure 3.11 for a company that started trading on 1 January 20X1 without any opening inventory and sold 40,000 items on 31 March 20X1 for £4 per item.

Inventory valued on a FIFO basis is £60,000 with the 20,000 items in inventory valued at £3 per item, on the assumption that the purchases made on 1 January 20X1 and

Figure 3.11 Effect on sales of using FIFO and weighted average

Physical flow assumption	Items	£	FIFO £	Average £
Raw materials purchased				
On 1 Jan 20X1 at £1 per item	20,000	20,000		
On 1 Feb 20X1 at £2 item	20,000	40,000		
On 1 Mar 20X1 at £3 per item	20,000	60,000		
On 1 Mar 20X1 in inventory	60,000	120,000	120,000	120,000
On 31 Mar 20X1 in inventory	20,000		60,000	40,000
Cost of sales	40,000		60,000	80,000

Figure 3.12 Effect of physical inventory flow assumptions on the percentage gross profit

	Items	FIFO £	Average £	% difference in gross profit
Sales	40,000	160,000	160,000	
Cost of sales	40,000	60,000	80,000	
		100,000	80,000	
Gross profit %		62.5%	50%	25%

1 February 20X1 were sold first. Inventory valued on an average basis is £40,000 with the 20,000 items in inventory valued at £2 per item on the assumption that sales made in March cannot be matched with a specific item.

The effect on the gross profit percentage would be as shown in Figure 3.12. This demonstrates that, even from a single difference in accounting treatment, the gross profit for the same transaction could be materially different in both absolute and percentage terms.

How can an investor determine the effect of different assumptions?
Although companies are required to disclose their inventory valuation policy, the level of detail provided varies and we are not able to quantify the effect of different inventory valuation policies.

For example, a clear description of an accounting policy is provided by AstraZeneca. Even so, it does not allow the user to know how net realisable value was determined. Was it, for example, primarily based upon forecasted short-term demand for the product?

AstraZeneca inventory policy (2011) Annual Report

Inventories

Inventories are stated at the lower of cost or net realisable value.

The first in, first out or an average method of valuation is used.

For finished goods and work in progress, cost includes directly attributable costs and certain overhead expenses (including depreciation).

Selling expenses and certain other overhead expenses (principally central administration costs) are excluded.

Net realisable value is determined as estimated selling price less all estimated costs of completion and costs to be incurred in selling and distribution.

Write-downs of inventory occur in the general course of business and are included in cost of sales in the income statement. However, if the write-off is regarded as material it would be reported as an exceptional item.

The following illustration is an extract from the 2011 Annual Report of R & R Ice Cream plc:

	Before exceptional items (€000)	Exceptional items (€000)	After exceptional items (€000)
Revenue	501,028	—	501,028
Cost of sales (Note 2)	(394,932)	(1,150)	(396,082)
Gross profit	106,096	(1,150)	104,946

Note 2. Exceptional items:
Recognised in arriving at results from operating activities (€000):

	2011
Inventory write-off	(873)
Restructuring and redundancies	(277)
Total cost of sales exceptional items	(1,150)

Inventory write-off:

In the year, we incurred two exceptional inventory write-offs, one in respect of poor quality bought-in products which the third-party supplier refused to refund in full, and one in respect of flash-priced packaging which became redundant as a result of the price increases we were forced to implement to recover rising commodity prices.

(b) Differences arising from the choice of depreciation method and estimates

Companies may make different choices:

● the accounting base to use, e.g. historical cost or revaluation; and

● the method that is used to calculate the charge, e.g. straight-line or reducing balance.

Companies make estimates that might differ:

● assumptions as to an asset's productive use, e.g. different estimates made as to the economic life of an asset; and

● assumptions as to the total cost to be expensed, e.g. different estimates of the residual value.

(c) Differences arising from management attitudes

Losses might be anticipated and measured at a different rate. For example, when assessing the likelihood of the net realisable value of inventory falling below the cost figure, the management decision will be influenced by the optimism with which it views the future of the economy, the industry and the company. There could also be other influences. For example, if bonuses are based on net income, there is an incentive to overestimate the net realisable value; whereas, if management is preparing a company for a management buy-out, there is an incentive to underestimate the net realisable value in order to minimise the net profit for the period.

(d) Differences arising from the capability of the accounting system to provide data

Accounting systems within companies differ and costs that are collected by one company may well not be collected by another company. For example, the apportionment of costs might be more detailed with different proportions being allocated or apportioned.

3.13 Fair presentation

IAS 1 *Presentation of Financial Statements* requires financial statements to give a **fair presentation** of the financial position, financial performance and cash flows of an enterprise. In paragraph 17 it states that:

> In virtually all circumstances, a fair presentation is achieved by compliance with applicable IFRSs. A fair presentation also requires an entity to:
>
> (a) select and apply accounting policies in accordance with IAS 8 *Accounting Policies, Changes in Accounting Estimates and Errors* [this is dealt with in Chapter 4]

(b) present information, including accounting policies, in a manner that provides relevant, reliable, comparable and understandable information;

(c) provide additional disclosures when compliance with the specific requirements in IFRSs is insufficient to enable users to understand the impact of particular transactions, other events and conditions on the entity's financial position and financial performance.

3.13.1 Legal opinions

In the UK we require financial statements to give a **true and fair view**. True and fair is a legal concept and can be authoritatively decided only by a court. However, the courts have never attempted to define 'true and fair'. In the UK the Accounting Standards Committee (ASC) obtained a legal opinion which included the following statement:

> Accounts will not be true and fair unless the information they contain is sufficient in quantity and quality to satisfy the reasonable expectations of the readers to whom they are addressed.[5]

A further counsel's opinion was attained by the Accounting Standards Board (ASB) in 1991 and published in its foreword to Accounting Standards. It advised that accounting standards are an authoritative source of accounting practice and it is now the norm for financial statements to comply with them. In consequence the court may take accounting standards into consideration when forming an opinion on whether the financial statements give a true and fair view.

However, an Opinion obtained by the FRC in May 2008 advised that true and fair still has to be taken into consideration by preparers and auditors of financial statements whether prepared under UK company law or IFRSs. Directors have to consider whether the statements are appropriate and auditors have to exercise professional judgement when giving an audit opinion – it is not sufficient for either directors or auditors to reach a conclusion solely because the financial statements were prepared in accordance with applicable accounting standards.

3.13.2 Fair override

Standards are not intended to be a straitjacket and IAS 1 recognises that there may be occasions when application of an IAS/IFRS might be misleading and departure from the IAS/IFRS treatment is permitted. This is referred to as the **fair override** provision. If a company makes use of the override it is required to explain why compliance with IASs/IFRSs would be misleading and also give sufficient information to enable the user to calculate the adjustments required to comply with the standard.

Although IAS 1 does not refer to true and fair, the International Accounting Standards Regulation 1606/2002 (paragraph 9) states that: 'To adopt an international accounting standard for application in the Community, it is necessary . . . that its application results in a true and fair view of the financial position and performance of an enterprise'. However, overrides under IFRS are likely to be less common, as IAS 1 states that departures from IAS should be 'extremely rare' (paragraph 17) and should only happen where compliance with the standard together with additional disclosure would not result in a fair presentation. Examples of the use of the IAS 1 override among European companies are very rare.

When do companies use the fair override?

Fair override can occur for a number[6] of reasons with the most frequent being the situation where the Accounting Standards may prescribe one method, which contradicts company law and thus requires an override, for example, providing no depreciation on investment properties. Next would be where Accounting Standards may offer a choice between accounting procedures, at least one of which contradicts company law. If that particular choice is adopted, the override should be invoked, for example grants not being shown as deferred income.

Fair override can be challenged

If a company in the UK relies on the fair override provision, it may be challenged by the Financial Reporting Review Panel and the company's decision overturned. For example, although Eurovestech had adopted an accounting policy in its 2005 and 2006 accounts not to consolidate two of its subsidiaries because its directors considered that to do so would not give a true and fair view, the FRRP decision was that this was unacceptable because the company was unable to demonstrate special circumstances warranting this treatment.

3.14 What does an investor need in addition to the primary financial statements to make decisions?

Investors attempt to estimate future cash flows when making an investment decision. As regards future cash flows, these are normally perceived to be influenced by past profits as reported in the statements of income and the asset base as shown by the statement of financial position.

In order to assist shareholders to predict future cash flows with an understanding of the risks involved, more information has been required by the IASB. For example:

- More quantitative information (discussed in Chapter 4):
  - financial statements are required to take account of events and information becoming available after the period-end;
  - segment reports are required;
  - disclosure is required of the impact of changes on the operation, e.g. a breakdown of turnover, costs and profits for both new and discontinued operations.
- More qualitative narrative information, including:
  - mandatory disclosures;
  - IFRS practice statement – management commentary.
- UK requirements:
  - Chairman's Statement;
  - Directors' Report;
  - Best practice disclosures: Operating and Financial Review;
  - Business review in the Directors' Report;
  - Strategic Report.

We will comment briefly on the qualitative narrative disclosures.

3.14.1 IFRS mandatory disclosures

When making future predictions, investors need to be able to identify that part of the net income that is likely to be maintained in the future. IAS 1 provides assistance to users in this by requiring that certain items are separately disclosed. These are items within the ordinary activities of the enterprise which are of such size, nature or incidence that their separate disclosure is required in the financial statements in order for the financial statements to show a fair view.

These items are not extraordinary and must, therefore, be presented above the tax line. It is usual to disclose the nature and amount of these items in a note to the financial statements, with no separate mention on the face of the statement of comprehensive income; however, if sufficiently material, they can be disclosed on the face of the statement.

Examples of the type of item that may give rise to separate disclosures are:

- the write-down of assets to realisable value or recoverable amount;
- the restructuring of activities of the enterprise; discontinued operations;
- disposals of items of property, plant and equipment and long-term investments;
- litigation settlements.

3.14.2 IFRS management commentary

In December 2010 the IASB issued an IFRS Practice Statement *Management Commentary*. Management commentary is defined in the statement as:

> A narrative report that relates to financial statements that have been prepared in accordance with IFRSs. Management commentary provides users with historical explanations of the amounts presented in the financial statements, specifically the entity's financial position, financial performance and cash flows. It also provides commentary on an entity's prospects and other information not presented in the financial statements. Management commentary also serves as a basis for understanding management's objectives and its strategies for achieving those objectives.

The commentary should give management's view not only about what has happened, including both positive and negative circumstances, but also why it has happened and what the implications are for the entity's future.

Following the Practice Statement is not mandatory and the financial statements and annual report of a business can still be compliant with IFRS even if the requirements are not followed. However, it is the first document to be issued by the IASB that solely covers information that is provided by companies outside the financial statements.

The guidance does not attempt to dictate exactly how management commentary should be prepared so as to avoid the tick-box approach to compliance. Instead it indicates the information that should be included within the commentary:

(a) the nature of the business;

(b) management's objectives and its strategies for meeting those objectives;

(c) the entity's most significant resources, risks and relationships;

(d) the results of operations and prospects; and

(e) the critical performance measures and indicators that management uses to evaluate the entity's performance against stated objectives.

It will be interesting to observe the effect that this has on future annual reports.

Who presents and approves a management commentary may depend on jurisdictional requirements. For example, in the United Kingdom the Companies Act 2006 has required a Business Review as part of the Directors' Report, and for quoted companies the OFR Reporting Statement is approved by the directors.

3.14.3 Chairman's Statement

This often tends to be a brief upbeat comment on the current year. For example, the following is a brief extract from Findel plc's 2012 Annual Report to illustrate the type of information provided:

> Second-half group sales were ahead by 1.6%. This reflects the actions that we are taking and highlights the momentum building within the business. Profit before tax for the year increased by 53% to £10.7m (FY2011: £7.0m) as a result of substantially reduced finance costs following the refinancing. The group incurred exceptional restructuring and finance costs, primarily relating to various internal restructurings and management changes undertaken during the year, of £14.5m. . . . We continue to have sufficient headroom in our banking facilities and ample liquidity to execute our Full Potential plan.

3.14.4 Directors' Report

The paragraph headings from Findel's 2010 Annual Report illustrate the type of information that is published. The report headings were Activities; Review of the year and future prospects; Dividends; Capital structure; Suppliers' payment policy; Directors; Employees' Donations; Substantial holdings and Auditors.

There is a brief comment under each heading, for example:

Activities
The principal activities of the Group are home shopping and educational supplies through mail order catalogues and the provision of outsourced healthcare services.

Review of the Year and Future Prospects
The key performance indicators which management consider important are:

- operating margins
- average order value
- retention rates in Home Shopping
- on-time collections and deliveries within Healthcare.

3.14.5 OFR Reporting Standard RS 1

In the UK the Accounting Standards Board published RS 1 in 2005. This is not a statutory standard and is intended to inform best practice. The intention was that directors should focus on the information needs specific to their company and its shareholders rather than follow a rigid list of items to be disclosed. RS 1 assisted directors in this approach by setting down certain principles and providing illustrations of key performance indicators. Local standard setters have also published guidance on narrative disclosures.

The seven principles were that the OFR should:

1 reflect the directors' view of the business;

2 focus on matters that are relevant to investors in assessing the strategies adopted and the potential for those strategies to succeed. Whilst maintaining the primacy of meeting investors' needs, directors should take a 'broad view' in deciding what should be included in their OFR, on the grounds that the decisions and agendas of other stakeholders can influence the performance and value of a company;

3 have a forward-looking orientation with an analysis of the main trends and factors which are likely to affect the entity's future development, performance and position;

4 complement as well as supplement the financial statements with additional explanations of amounts included in the financial statements;

5 be comprehensive and understandable but avoid the inclusion of too much information that is not directly relevant;

6 be balanced and neutral – in this way the OFR can produce reliable information;

7 be comparable over time – the ability to compare with other entities in the same industry or sector is encouraged.

Key performance indicators (KPIs)

There has been a concern that OFR would lack quantifiable information. This was addressed with a list of potentially useful KPIs. These covered a wide range of interests, including:

- Economic measures of ability to create value (with the terms defined):
  - Return on capital employed
  - Economic profit-type measures, i.e. post-tax profit less cost of capital
- Market position
- Market share
- Development, performance and position:
  - traditional financial measures; cash conversion rate: industry-specific such as sales per square foot; products in the development pipeline; cost per unit produced
- Persons with whom the entity has relations and which could have a significant impact
- Customers, employees and suppliers: how do they view the company?
- Social, environmental and community issues.

3.14.6 Business Review in the Directors' Report

This has been a requirement in the UK. The intention is that the Review should provide a balanced and comprehensive analysis of the business including social and environmental aspects to allow shareholders to assess how directors have performed their statutory duty to promote the company's success.

3.14.7 Survey of meeting narrative reporting needs for the future

In 2010 the ACCA issued the results of an International Survey[5] of CFOs' views on narrative reporting, 'Hitting the notes, but what's the tune?', based on a joint survey with Deloitte of some 230 chief financial officers and other preparers in listed companies in nine countries (Australia, China, Kenya, Malaysia, Singapore, Switzerland, the UAE, the UK and the US). The major findings were that:

- the principal audiences for narrative information were shareholders and regulators;
- the most important disclosures for shareholders were the explanation of financial results and financial position, identifying the most important risks and how they were managed, an outline of future plans and prospects, a description of the business model and a description of key performance indicators (KPIs);
- the interviewees supported a reporting environment with more discretion and less regulation.

As with all approaches to standard setting, there is the need to balance discretion and regulation.

The following is an extract from an ACCA paper 'Writing the narrative: the triumphs and tribulations'[7] by Afra Sajjad:

> We believe that the future of narrative reporting lies in reconciliation of competing information needs and expectations of primary users of annual reports i.e. regulators and shareholders. This should be accompanied by nurturing of a culture of corporate reporting where integrity, probity and transparency are fundamental to reporting. Regulators also need to facilitate change in the culture of reporting by giving preparers the flexibility to use discretion and facilitate market led best practices. Shareholders . . . need also to be mature enough to encourage real transparency. If they respond with panic to disappointing news, it will inhibit the preparer's disclosure process.

3.14.8 Strategic Report

The Strategic Report[8] will be similar to the business review, but quoted companies will be required to report, to the extent necessary for an understanding of the business, on their strategy, their business model, and any human rights issues. Quoted companies will also be asked to report on the number of men and women on their board, in executive committees and in the organisation as a whole. Guidance on the preparation of the report is being drafted by the government in consultation with the FRC to be available for companies reporting in 2014.

Summary

In this chapter we have revised the preparation of internal financial statements making accrual adjustments to trial balance figures.

In order to assess stewardship and management performance, there have been mandatory requirements for standardised presentation, using the two formats prescribed by International Financial Reporting Standards. The required disclosures were explained for both formats.

The importance of referring to Notes to the accounts was illustrated with discussion of exceptional items and their impact on reported operating income.

The disclosure of accounting policies which allow shareholders to make comparisons between years by requiring companies to be consistent in the application of accounting policies or requiring disclosure if there has been a change was discussed.

The need for explanatory notes was explained and described.

The need for financial statements to give a true and fair view of the income and net assets was explained with recognition that this requires the exercise of professional judgement. Having recorded the transactions and made the normal adjustments for accruals, do the resulting financial statements give a fair presentation?

The evolving practices for narrative reporting under IASB and UK were discussed with the IFRS Practice Statement Management Commentary and the UK Strategic Report.

REVIEW QUESTIONS

1 Explain the effect on income and financial position if (a) the amount of accrued expense were to be underestimated and (b) the inventory at the year-end omitted inventory held in a customs warehouse awaiting clearance.

2 Explain why two companies carrying out identical trading transactions could produce different gross profit figures.

3 Classify the following items into cost of sales, distribution costs, administrative expenses, other operating income or item to be disclosed after trading profit:

(a) Personnel department costs

(b) Computer department costs

(c) Cost accounting department costs

(d) Financial accounting department costs

(e) Bad debts

(f) Provisions for warranty claims

(g) Interest on funds borrowed to finance an increase in working capital

(h) Interest on funds borrowed to finance an increase in property, plant and equipment.

4 'We analyze a sample of UK public companies that invoked a TFV override during 1998–2000 to assess whether overrides are used opportunistically. We find overrides increase income and equity significantly, and firms with weaker performance and higher levels of debt employ overrides that are more costly . . . financial statements are not less informative than control sample.'[9]

Discuss the enquiries and action that you think an auditor should take to ensure that the financial statements give a more true and fair view than from applying standards.

5 When preparing accounts under Format 1, how would a bad debt that was materially larger than normal be disclosed?

6 'Annual accounts have been put into such a straitjacket of overemphasis on uniform disclosure that there will be a growing pressure by national bodies to introduce changes unilaterally which will again lead to diversity in the quality of disclosure. This is both healthy and necessary.' Discuss.

7 Explain the relevance to the user of accounts if expenses are classified as 'administrative expenses' rather than as 'cost of sales'.

8 IAS 1 *Presentation of Financial Statements* requires 'other comprehensive income' items to be included in the statement of comprehensive income and it also requires a statement of changes in equity.

Explain the need for publishing this information, and identify the items you would include in them.

9 Discuss the major benefit to an investor from the UK Strategic Report if it purports to be similar to the Business Review.

10 The following are three KPIs for the retail sector:[10] capital expenditure, expected return on new stores, and customer satisfaction.

Discuss two further KPIs that might be significant.

* Question 1

The following trial balance was extracted from the books of Old NV on 31 December 20X1.

	€000	€000
Sales		12,050
Returns outwards		313
Provision for depreciation		
Plant		738
Vehicles		375
Rent receivable		100
Trade payables		738
Debentures		250
Issued share capital – ordinary €1 shares		3,125
Issued share capital – preference shares (treated as equity)		625
Share premium		350
Retained earnings		875
Inventory	825	
Purchases	6,263	
Returns inwards	350	
Carriage inwards	13	
Carriage outwards	125	
Salesmen's salaries	800	
Administrative wages and salaries	738	
Land	100	
Plant (includes €362,000 acquired in 20X1)	1,562	
Motor vehicles	1,125	
Goodwill	1,062	
Distribution costs	290	
Administrative expenses	286	
Directors' remuneration	375	
Trade receivables	3,875	
Cash at bank and in hand	1,750	
	19,539	19,539

Note of information not taken into the trial balance data:

(a) Provide for:

    (i)   An audit fee of €38,000.

    (ii) Depreciation of plant at 20% straight-line.

    (iii) Depreciation of vehicles at 25% reducing balance.

    (iv) The goodwill suffered an impairment in the year of €177,000.

    (v) Income tax of €562,000.

    (vi) Debenture interest of €25,000.

(b) Closing inventory was valued at €1,125,000 at the lower of cost and net realisable value.

(c) Administrative expenses were prepaid by €12,000.

(d) Land was to be revalued by €50,000.

Required:

(a) Prepare a statement of income for internal use for the year ended 31 December 20X1.

(b) Prepare a statement of comprehensive income for the year ended 31 December 20X1 and a statement of financial position as at that date in Format 1 style of presentation.

* Question 2

Formatone plc produced the following trial balance as at 30 June 20X6:

	£000	£000
Land at cost	2,160.0	—
Buildings at cost	1,080.0	—
Plant and Equipment at cost	1,728.0	—
Intangible assets	810.0	—
Accum. depreciation – 30.6.20X5		
Buildings	—	432.0
Plant and equipment	—	504.0
Interim dividend paid	108.0	
Receivables and payables	585.0	532.8
Cash and bank balance	41.4	—
Inventory as at 30.6.20X6	586.8	—
Taxation	—	14.4
Deferred tax	—	37.8
Distribution cost	529.2	—
Administrative expenses	946.8	—
Retained earnings b/f	—	891.0
Sales revenue	—	9,480.6
Cost of sales	5,909.4	—
Ordinary shares of 50p each	—	2,160.0
Share premium account	—	432.0
	14,484.6	14,484.6

The following information is available:

(i) A revaluation of the Land and Buildings on 1 July 20X5 resulted in an increase of £3,240,000 in the Land and £972,000 in the Buildings. This has not yet been recorded in the books.

(ii) Depreciation:
Plant and Equipment are depreciated at 10% using the reducing balance method.
Intangible assets are to be written down by £540,000.
Buildings have an estimated life of 30 years from date of the revaluation.

(iii) Taxation
The current tax is estimated at £169,200.
There had been an overprovision in the previous year.
Deferred tax is to be increased by £27,000.

(iv) Capital
150,000 shares were issued and recorded on 1 July 20X5 for 80p each.
A further dividend of 5p per share has been declared on 30 June 20X6.

Required:

Prepare for the year ended 30 June 20X6 the statement of comprehensive income, statement of changes in equity and statement of financial position.

* Question 3

Basalt plc is a wholesaler. The following is its trial balance as at 31 December 20X0.

	Dr £000	Cr £000
Ordinary share capital: £1 shares		300
Share premium		20
General reserve		16
Retained earnings as at 1 January 20X0		55
Inventory as at 1 January 20X0	66	
Sales		962
Purchases	500	
Administrative costs	10	
Distribution costs	6	
Plant and machinery – cost	220	
Plant and machinery – provision for depreciation		49
Returns outwards		25
Returns inwards	27	
Carriage inwards	9	
Warehouse wages	101	
Salesmen's salaries	64	
Administrative wages and salaries	60	
Hire of motor vehicles	19	
Directors' remuneration	30	
Rent receivable		7
Trade receivables	326	
Cash at bank	62	
Trade payables		66
	1,500	1,500

The following additional information is supplied:

(i)   Depreciate plant and machinery 20% on straight-line basis.

(ii)   Inventory at 31 December 20X0 is £90,000.

(iii)   Accrue auditors' remuneration £2,000.

(iv)   Income tax for the year will be £58,000 payable October 20X1.

(v)   It is estimated that 7/11 of the plant and machinery is used in connection with distribution, with the remainder for administration. The motor vehicle costs should be allocated to distribution.

Required:
Prepare a statement of income and statement of financial position in a form that complies with IAS 1. No notes to the accounts are required.

* Question 4

HK Ltd has prepared its draft trial balance to 30 June 20X1, which is shown below.

Trial balance at 30 June 20X1

	$000	$000
Freehold land	2,100	
Freehold buildings (cost $4,680,000)	4,126	
Plant and machinery (cost $3,096,000)	1,858	
Fixtures and fittings (cost $864,000)	691	
Goodwill	480	
Trade receivables	7,263	
Trade payables		2,591
Inventory	11,794	
Bank balance	11,561	
Development grant received		85
Profit on sale of freehold land		536
Sales		381,600
Cost of sales	318,979	
Administration expenses	9,000	
Distribution costs	35,100	
Directors' emoluments	562	
Bad debts	157	
Auditors' remuneration	112	
Hire of plant and machinery	2,400	
Loan interest	605	
Dividends paid during the year – preference	162	
Dividends paid during the year – ordinary	426	
9% loan		7,200
Share capital – preference shares (treated as equity)		3,600
Share capital – ordinary shares		5,400
Retained earnings		6,364
	407,376	407,376

The following information is available:

(a) The authorised share capital is 4,000,000 9% preference shares of $1 each and 18,000,000 ordinary shares of 50c each.

(b) Provide for depreciation at the following rates:

    (i)   Plant and machinery 20% on cost
    (ii) Fixtures and fittings 10% on cost
    (iii) Buildings 2% on cost

    Charge all depreciation to cost of sales.

(c) Provide $5,348,000 for income tax.

(d) The loan was raised during the year and there is no outstanding interest accrued at the year-end.

(e) Government grants of $85,000 have been received in respect of plant purchased during the year and are shown in the trial balance. One-fifth is to be taken into profit in the current year.

(f) During the year a fire took place at one of the company's depots, involving losses of $200,000. These losses have already been written off to cost of sales shown in the trial balance. Since the end of the financial year a settlement of $150,000 has been agreed with the company's insurers.

(g) $500,000 of the inventory is obsolete. This has a realisable value of $250,000.

(h) Acquisitions of property, plant and equipment during the year were:

Plant $173,000   Fixtures $144,000

(i) During the year freehold land which cost $720,000 was sold for $1,316,000.

(j) A final ordinary dividend of 3c per share is declared and was an obligation before the year-end, together with the balance of the preference dividend. Neither dividend was paid at the year-end.

(k) The goodwill has not been impaired.

(l) The land was revalued at the year-end at $2,500,000.

Required:
(a) **Prepare the company's statement of comprehensive income for the year to 30 June 20X1 and a statement of financial position as at that date, complying with the relevant accounting standards in so far as the information given permits.**
    (All calculations to nearest $000.)
(b) **Explain the usefulness of the schedule prepared in (a).**

* Question 5

Phoenix plc's trial balance at 30 June 20X7 was as follows:

	£000	£000
Freehold premises	2,400	
Plant and machinery	1,800	540
Furniture and fittings	620	360
Inventory at 30 June 20X7	1,468	
Sales		6,465
Administrative expenses	1,126	
Ordinary shares of £1 each		4,500
Trade investments	365	
Revaluation reserve		600
Development cost	415	
Share premium		500
Personal ledger balances	947	566
Cost of goods sold	4,165	
Distribution costs	669	
Overprovision for tax		26
Dividend received		80
Interim dividend paid	200	
Retained earnings		488
Disposal of warehouse		225
Cash and bank balances	175	
	14,350	14,350

The following information is available:

1 Freehold premises acquired for £1.8 million were revalued in 20X4, recognising a gain of £600,000. These include a warehouse, which cost £120,000, was revalued at £150,000 and was sold in June 20X7 for £225,000. Phoenix does not depreciate freehold premises.

2 Phoenix wishes to report plant and machinery at open market value which is estimated to be £1,960,000 on 1 July 20X6.

3 Company policy is to depreciate its assets on the straight-line method at annual rates as follows:

Plant and machinery   10%
Furniture and fittings   5%

4 Until this year the company's policy has been to capitalise development costs, to the extent permitted by relevant accounting standards. The company must now write off the development costs, including £124,000 incurred in the year, as the project no longer meets the capitalisation criteria.

5 During the year the company has issued one million shares of £1 at £1.20 each.

6 Included within administrative expenses are the following:

Staff salary (including £125,000 to directors)   £468,000
Directors' fees   £96,000
Audit fees and expenses   £86,000

7 Income tax for the year is estimated at £122,000.

8 Directors propose a final dividend of 4p per share declared and an obligation, but not paid at the year-end.

Required:
In respect of the year ended 30 June 20X7:
(a) The statement of comprehensive income.
(b) The statement of financial position as at 30 June 20X7.
(c) The statement of movement of property, plant and equipment.

Question 6

Olive A/S, incorporated with an authorised capital consisting of one million ordinary shares of €1 each, employs 64 persons, of whom 42 work at the factory and the rest at the head office. The trial balance extracted from its books as at 30 September 20X4 is as follows:

	€000	€000
Land and buildings (cost €600,000)	520	—
Plant and machinery (cost €840,000)	680	—
Proceeds on disposal of plant and machinery	—	180
Fixtures and equipment (cost €120,000)	94	—
Sales	—	3,460
Carriage inwards	162	—
Share premium account	—	150
Advertising	112	—
Inventory on 1 Oct 20X3	211	—
Heating and lighting	80	—
Prepayments	115	—
Salaries	820	—
Trade investments at cost	248	—
Dividend received (net) on 9 Sept 20X4	—	45
Directors' emoluments	180	—
Pension cost	100	—
Audit fees and expense	65	—
Retained earnings b/f	—	601
Sales commission	92	—
Stationery	28	—
Development cost	425	—
Formation expenses	120	—
Receivables and payables	584	296
Interim dividend paid on 4 Mar 20X4	60	—
12% debentures issued on 1 Apr 20X4	—	500
Debenture interest paid on 1 Jul 20X4	15	—
Purchases	925	—
Income tax on year to 30 Sept 20X3	—	128
Other administration expenses	128	—
Bad debts	158	—
Cash and bank balance	38	—
Ordinary shares of €1 fully called	—	600
	5,960	5,960

You are informed as follows:

(a) As at 1 October 20X3 land and buildings were revalued at €900,000. A third of the cost as well as all the valuation is regarded as attributable to the land. Directors have decided to report this asset at valuation.

(b) New fixtures were acquired on 1 January 20X4 for €40,000; a machine acquired on 1 October 20X1 for €240,000 was disposed of on 1 July 20X4 for €180,000, being replaced on the same date by another acquired for €320,000.

(c) Depreciation for the year is to be calculated on the straight-line basis as follows:

Buildings: 2% p.a.
Plant and machinery: 10% p.a.
Fixtures and equipment: 10% p.a.

(d) Inventory, including raw materials and work in progress on 30 September 20X4, has been valued at cost at €364,000.

(e) Prepayments are made up as follows:

	€000
Amount paid in advance for a machine	60
Amount paid in advance for purchasing raw materials	40
Prepaid rent	15
	€115

(f) In March 20X3 a customer had filed legal action claiming damages at €240,000. When accounts for the year ended 30 September 20X3 were finalised, a provision of €90,000 was made in respect of this claim. This claim was settled out of court in April 20X4 at €150,000 and the amount of the underprovision adjusted against the profit balance brought forward from previous years.

(g) The following allocations have been agreed upon:

	Factory	Administration
Depreciation of buildings	60%	40%
Salaries other than to directors	55%	45%
Heating and lighting	80%	20%

(h) Pension cost of the company is calculated at 10% of the emoluments and salaries.

(i) Income tax on 20X3 profit has been agreed at €140,000 and that for 20X4 estimated at €185,000.

(j) Directors wish to write off the formation expenses as far as possible without reducing the amount of profits available for distribution.

Required:
Prepare for publication:
(a) **The statement of comprehensive income of the company for the year ended 30 September 20X4,**
(b) **the statement of financial position as at that date along with as many notes (other than the one on accounting policy) as can be provided on the basis of the information made available, and**
(c) **the statement of changes in equity.**

Question 7

The following is an extract from the trial balance of Imecet at 31 October 2005:

	$000	$000
Property valuation	8,000	
Factory at cost	2,700	
Administration building at cost	1,200	
Delivery vehicles at cost	500	
Sales		10,300
Inventory at 1 November 2004	1,100	
Purchases	6,350	
Factory wages	575	
Administration expenses	140	
Distribution costs	370	
Interest paid (6 months to 30 April 2005)	100	
Accumulated profit at 1 November 2004		3,701
10% loan stock		2,000
$1 ordinary shares (incl. issue on 1 May 2005)		4,000
Share premium (after issue on 1 May 2005)		1,500
Dividends (paid 1 June 2005)	400	
Revaluation reserve		2,500
Deferred tax		650

Other relevant information:

(i) One million $1 ordinary shares were issued 1 May 2005 at the market price of $1.75 per ordinary share.

(ii) The inventory at 31 October 2005 has been valued at $1,150,000.

(iii) A current tax provision for $350,000 is required for the period ended 31 October 2005 and the deferred tax liability at that date has been calculated to be $725,000.

(iv) The property has been further revalued at 31 October 2005 at the market price of $9,200,000.

(v) No depreciation charges have yet been recognised for the year ended 31 October 2005.

The depreciation rates are:

> Factory – 5% straight-line.
> Administration building – 3% straight-line.
> Delivery vehicles – 25% reducing balance. The accumulated depreciation at 31 October 2004 was $10,000. No new vehicles were acquired in the year to 31 October 2005.

Required:
(a) Prepare the income statement for Imecet for the year ended 31 October 2005.
(b) Prepare the statement of changes in equity for Imecet for the year ended 31 October 2005.

(The Association of International Accountants)

Question 8

Graydon Ross, CFO of Diversified Industries PLC, is discussing the publication of the annual report with his managing director Phil Davison. Graydon says: 'The law requires us to comply with accounting standards and at the same time to provide a true and fair view of the results and financial position. As half of the business consists of the crockery and brickmaking business which your great-great-grandmother started, and the other half is the insurance company which your father started, I am not sure that the consolidated accounts are very meaningful. It is hard to make sense of any of the ratios as you don't know what industry to compare them with. What say we also give them the comprehensive income statements and balance sheets of the two subsidiary companies as additional information, and then no one can complain that they didn't get a true and fair view?'

Phil says: 'I don't think we should do that. The more information they have the more questions they will ask. Also they might realise we have been smoothing income by changing our level of pessimism in relation to the provisions for outstanding insurance claims. Anyway I don't want them to interfere with my business. Can't we just include a footnote, preferably a vague one, that stresses we are not comparable to either insurance companies or brickmakers or crockery manufacturers because of the unique mix of our businesses? Don't raise the matter with the auditors because it will put ideas into their heads. But if it does come up we may have to charge head office costs to the two subsidiaries. You need to think up some reason why most of the charges should be passed on to the crockery operations. We don't want to show everyone how profitable that area is. I trust you will give that some thought so you will have a good answer ready.'

Required:
Discuss the professional, legal and ethical implications for Ross.

References

1 IAS 1 *Presentation of Financial Statements*, IASB, December 2008.
2 D. Dhaliwal, K. Subramnayam and R. Trezevant, 'Is comprehensive income superior to net income as a measure of firm performance?', *Journal of Accounting and Economics*, vol. 26(1), 1999, pp. 43–67.
3 D. Hirst and P. Hopkins, 'Comprehensive income reporting and analysts' valuation judgments', *Journal of Accounting Research*, vol. 36 (Supplement), 1998, pp. 47–74.
4 G.C. Biddles and J.-H. Choi, 'Is comprehensive income irrelevant?', 12 June 2002. Available at SSRN: http://ssrn.com/abstract=316703.
5 http://www.accaglobal.com/pubs/af/narrative/new/hitting_the_notes.pdf
6 G. Livne and M. McNichols, *An Empirical Investigation of the True and Fair Override*, LBS Accounting Subject Area Working Paper No. 031 (http://www.bm.ust.hk/acct/acsymp2004/Papers/Livne.pdf).
7 http://www.accaglobal.com/content/dam/acca/global/PDF-technical/narrative-reporting/writing_the_narrative.pdf
8 http://www.bis.gov.uk/assets/BISCore/business-law/docs/F/12-979-future-of-narrative-reporting-new-structure.pdf
9 G. Livne and M.F. McNichols, 'An empirical investigation of the true and fair override', *Journal of Business, Finance and Accounting*, pp. 1–30, January/March 2009.
10 http://www.pwc.com/gx/en/corporate-reporting/assets/pdfs/UK_KPI_guide.pdf

CHAPTER **4**

Annual Report: additional financial disclosures

The main purpose of this chapter is to explain the additional content in an Annual Report that assists users to make informed assessments of stewardship and informed estimates of future financial performance. Investors need to be able to assess the effect on the published accounts of (a) transactions occurring after the year-end and (b) transactions occurring during the year that might not have been at arm's length. In looking at the future, investors need information on (a) the profitability of different product lines and markets and (b) the potential financial impact if any part of the business has been discontinued.

Objectives

By the end of this chapter, you should be able to:

● make appropriate entries in the financial statements and/or disclosure in the notes to the accounts in accordance with IAS 10 *Events after the Reporting Period*;
● make appropriate entries in the financial statements in accordance with IAS 8 *Accounting Policies, Changes in Accounting Estimates and Errors*;
● identify reportable segments in accordance with IFRS 8 *Operating Segments*;
● critically discuss the benefits and continuing concerns of segmental reporting;
● explain the meaning of the term and account for 'discontinued operations' in accordance with IFRS 5 *Non-current Assets Held for Sale and Discontinued Operations*;
● prepare financial statements applying IFRS 5;
● discuss the impact of such operations on the statement of comprehensive income;
● explain the criteria laid out in IFRS 5 that need to be satisfied before an asset (or disposal group) is classified as 'held for sale';
● explain how to identify key personnel for the purposes of IAS 24 *Related Party Disclosures* and why this is considered to be important.

We have seen that transactions listed in the trial balance need to be adjusted for accruals and prepayments. They may also need to be adjusted as a result of further information becoming available after the year-end. This is covered in IAS 10.

IAS 10 requires preparers of financial statements to review events that occur after the reporting date but before the financial statements have been authorised for issue by the directors to decide whether an **adjustment** is required to be made to the financial statements or explanatory information is required to be **disclosed** by way of a note.

4.2.1 Adjusting events

These are events after the reporting period that provide additional evidence of conditions that existed at the period-end. Examples of such events include, but are not limited to:

- *Inventory*: After-date sales of inventory that provide additional evidence that the net realisable value of the inventory at the reporting date was lower than cost.

- *Liabilities*: Evidence received after the year-end that provides additional evidence of the appropriate measurement of a liability that existed at the reporting date, such as the settlement of a contingent liability or the calculation of bonuses for which an obligation existed at the end of the reporting period.

- *Non-current assets*: The revaluation of an asset such as a property that indicates the likelihood of impairment at the reporting date.

- The discovery of fraud or errors that show that the financial statements are incorrect.

Under IAS 10 such information becoming available after the period-end means that the financial statements themselves have to be adjusted **provided** the information becomes available before the accounts have been approved. It is important to consider the date of the period-end, the date when the financial statements are approved and the date when transactions/events occurred.

For example, consider the following scenario. Financial statements are being prepared for the year ended 31 March 20X4 and are expected to be approved in the Annual General Meeting announced for 25 May 20X4. Reviewing the audit file on 15 May, it was noted that the audit staff had identified on 29 April that stores staff had misappropriated a material amount of stock and concealed it by reporting it as damaged. The police have been informed and are investigating. Should the financial statements be adjusted?

Solution: As the fraud involves a material amount occurring during the reporting period but which is only discovered after the period-end, it is classified as an adjusting event and the financial statements would require amendment.

Consideration would then be required of the accounting implications. For example, what is the impact on the cost of sales and the gross profit if closing inventory has been understated? Is it necessary to disclose the loss as an exceptional item? What is the likelihood of recovering recompense from the staff themselves or the company's insurers? Is any recovery an asset or contingent asset?

4.2.2 Non-adjusting events

These are events occurring after the reporting period that concern conditions that did not exist at the statement of financial position date. Examples would include:

- Dividends proposed. These must be disclosed in the notes [IAS 1.137]: 'the amount of dividends proposed or declared before the financial statements were authorised for issue but not recognised as a distribution to owners during the period'. The concept of a 'dividend liability' for equity shares has effectively disappeared.

- Interim dividends are not non-adjusting events, because they will have been paid during the reporting period, whereas final dividends are at the discretion of the reporting entity until approved by shareholders at a general meeting.

- An issue or redemption of shares after the reporting date, as in the following extract from the 2010 Annual Report of Wolters Kluwer:

  Events after the reporting period
  The company intends to execute a €100 million share buy-back plan in 2011.

- The acquisition of a new business after the reporting date, as in the following extract from the 2011 Annual Report of the Lanxess Group:

  On February 28, 2011, the LANXESS Group acquired the material protection business of Syngenta AG, Basle, Switzerland. . . . Based on figures from 2010, the acquisitions will contribute sales of around €400 million to the results of operations in 2011. It is also expected that the new activities will make a positive contribution to net income in the current fiscal year.

- An announcement after the reporting date of a plan to discontinue an operation or entering into binding agreements to sell.

- The loss or other decline in value of assets due to events occurring after the reporting date.

- Entering into significant contracts, as in the following extract from the Deutz 2011 Annual Report:

  On 12 January 2012, DEUTZ AG signed an agreement with the Chinese construction and agricultural equipment manufacturer Shandong Changlin Machinery Group to establish a company for the production of engines. . . . Over the medium term, the new plant will have a production capacity of around 65,000 engines. . . . At the moment, China represents the greatest area of potential growth for DEUTZ within the Asia region as a whole.

4.2.3 Going concern issues

Deterioration in the operating results or other major losses that occur after the period-end are basically non-adjusting events. However, if they are of such significance as to affect the going concern basis of preparation of the financial statements, then this impacts on the numbers in the financial statements, because the going concern assumption would no longer be appropriate. In this limited set of circumstances if the going concern assumption is no longer appropriate, IAS 10 requires the financial statements to be produced on a liquidation rather than going concern basis.

4.3 IAS 8 Accounting Policies, Changes in Accounting Estimates and Errors[2]

IAS 8 gives guidance when deciding whether to make a retrospective or prospective change to financial statements. A retrospective change means that the financial statements of the current and previous years will be affected. A prospective change means that accounting treatments in future years will be affected.

Let us now consider how to treat accounting policy changes, prior period adjustments and changes in accounting estimates in accordance with IAS 8.

4.3.1 Accounting policy changes

Accounting policies may be changed when required by a new IFRS or when management decide that it results in more relevant and reliable information being provided to users.

(a) When this occurs as a result of changes arising from the first application of a new IFRS

In this case there is normally a retrospective impact. For example, consider the effect on the financial statements if research costs had been capitalised by a company and a subsequent mandatory change then requires these costs to be expensed.

The research asset brought forward at the beginning of the year is treated as though it had already been expensed, which means it is eliminated and the retained earnings brought forward are reduced. The net result is that the opening assets and opening retained earnings are both reduced. Any research costs incurred in the current period will be charged to the current statement of income.

(b) When this occurs as a result of a change in circumstances

In this case, an entity might have applied one standard to an asset quite appropriately in one year and applied a different standard quite appropriately in the following year as its business circumstances change. For example, inventory reported under IAS 2 might be reported under IAS 16 if it is used in the construction of a capital asset. There would be no retrospective impact. The valuation would move from IAS 2 reporting at the lower of cost and net realisable value to reporting at cost/valuation less depreciation.

4.3.2 Prior period errors including both honest mistakes and fraud

Materiality

Changes are only required if the errors are material. Omissions or misstatements of items are material if they could, individually or collectively, influence the economic decisions that users make on the basis of the financial statements. Materiality depends on the size and nature of the omission or misstatement judged in the surrounding circumstances.

A decision as to their materiality depends on the entity-specific circumstances and questions would need to be asked. For example, does it change a loss to a profit? Does it avoid failing to comply with a loan covenant? Does it have the effect of increasing management's bonuses?

Criteria

We need to be familiar with the criteria set out in the standard for prior period errors. These are as follows:

- Omissions from, and misstatements in, the entity's financial statements for one or more prior periods arising from a failure to use, or misuse of, reliable information that:
  - was available when financial statements for those periods were authorised for issue, and
  - could reasonably be expected to have been obtained and taken into account when preparing the financial statements.
- Possible scenarios:
  - *Classification*: current accounts payable have been classified as long-term liabilities. This might have occurred due to error or a deliberate attempt to improve the liquidity ratio – either way, the accounts payable and long-term debt must be restated;
  - *Omission*: trade payable invoices might have been concealed;

– *Valuation*: inventory might have been overvalued by failing to record effect of obsolescence or trade receivables overstated by failing to make adequate provision for bad debts. Expenses might have been incorrectly capitalised.

Retained earnings restated

In each case we have to consider the effect on the retained earnings brought forward. For example, a material expense that was incorrectly capitalised would require both retained earnings and the asset to be reduced. In such a case, we would need to also consider other consequential changes such as the reversal of depreciation if that had been charged against the capital item.

4.3.3 Accounting estimates

Changes in methods, such as a change from straight-line depreciation to reducing balance, and changes in assumptions, such as a change in the expected economic life of an asset, do not result in any adjustment of retained earnings. These are changes being made at the end of the financial period which have a *current* and *prospective* impact in future periods.

Management should disclose, in a note to the financial statements, details of the nature of the change, and the related amounts if the change in accounting estimate has a material effect on the current period.

4.4 What do segment reports provide?

Segment reports provide a more detailed breakdown of key numbers from the financial statements. Such a breakdown potentially allows a user to:

● be more aware of the balance between the different operations and thus able to assess the quality of the entity's reported earnings, the specific risks to which the company is subject, and the areas where long-term growth may be expected;

● appreciate more thoroughly the results and financial position by permitting a better understanding of past performance and thus a better assessment of future prospects;

● be aware of the impact that changes in significant components of a business may have on the business as a whole.

The IASB requirements are set out in IFRS 8 *Operating Segments*.

4.5 IFRS 8 *Operating Segments*[1]

IFRS 8 applies to both separate and consolidated financial statements of entities

● whose debt or equity instruments are traded in a public market; or

● that file financial statements with a securities commission or other regulatory organisation for the purpose of issuing any class of instruments in the public market.

We will comment briefly on the following four key areas:

● identification of segments;

● identification of reportable segments;

● measurement of segment information; and

● disclosures.

4.5.1 Identification of segments

IFRS 8 requires the identification of operating segments on the basis of internal reports that are regularly reviewed by the entity's chief operating decision maker (CODM) in order to allocate resources to the segment and assess its performance. A segment that sells exclusively or mainly to other operating segments of the group meets the definition of an operating segment if the business is managed in that way.

Criteria for identifying a segment

An operating segment is a component of an entity:

(a) that engages in business activities from which it may earn revenues and incur expenses;

(b) whose operating results are regularly reviewed by the entity's chief operating decision maker, to make decisions about resources to be allocated to the segment and to assess its performance; and

(c) for which discrete financial information is available.

Not every part of the entity will necessarily be an operating segment. For example, a corporate headquarters may not earn revenues.

Criteria for identifying the chief operating decision maker

The chief operating decision maker (CODM) may be an individual or a group of directors or others. The key identifying factors will be those of performance assessment and resource allocation. Some organisations may have overlapping sets of components for which managers are responsible, e.g. some managers may be responsible for specific geographic areas and others for products worldwide. If the CODM reviews the operating results of both sets of components, the entity determines which constitutes the operating segments using the core principles (a)–(c) above.

4.5.2 Identifying reportable segments

Once an operating segment has been identified, a decision has to be made as to whether it has to be reported. The segment information is required to be reported for any operating segment that meets any of the following criteria:

(a) its reported revenue, from internal and external customers, is 10% or more of the combined revenue (internal and external) of all operating segments; or

(b) the absolute measure of its reported profit or loss is 10% or more of the greater in absolute amount of (i) the combined profit of all operating segments that did not report a loss and (ii) the combined reported loss of all operating segments that reported a loss; or

(c) its assets are 10% or more of the combined assets of all operating segments.

Failure to meet any of the criteria does not, however, preclude a company from reporting a segment's results. Operating segments that do not meet any of the criteria may be disclosed voluntarily, if management think the information would be useful to users of the financial statements.

The 75% test

If the total external revenue of the reportable operating segments is less than 75% of the entity's revenue, additional operating segments need to be identified as reportable segments (even if they don't meet the criteria in (a)–(c) above) until 75% of the entity's revenue is included.

Combining segments

IFRS 8 includes detailed guidance on which operating segments may be combined to create a reportable segment, e.g. if they have mainly similar products, processes, customers, distribution methods and regulatory environments.

Although IFRS 8 does not specify a maximum number of segments, it suggests that if the reportable segments exceed 10, the entity should consider whether a practical limit had been reached, as the disclosures may become too detailed.

EXAMPLE ● Varia plc is a large training and media entity with an important international component. It operates a state-of-the-art management information system which provides its directors with the information they require to plan and control the various businesses. The directors' reporting requirements are quite detailed and information is collected about the following divisions: Exam-based Training, E-Learning, Corporate Training, Print Media, Online Publishing and Cable Television. The following information is available for the year ended 31 December 2009:

Division	Total revenue	Profit	Assets
	£m	£m	£m
Exam-based Training	360	21	176
E-Learning	60	3	13
Corporate Training	125	5	84
Print Media	232	27	102
Online Publishing	124	2	31
Cable TV	73	5	39
	974	63	445

Question

Which of Varia plc's divisions are reportable segments in accordance with IFRS 8 *Operating segments*?

Solution

● The revenues of Exam-based Training, Corporate Training, Print Media and Online Publishing are clearly more than 10% of total revenues and so these segments are reportable.

● All three numbers for E-Learning and Cable TV are under 10% of entity totals for revenue, profit and assets and so, unless these segments can validly be combined with others for reporting purposes, they are not reportable separately, although Varia could choose to provide separate information.

As a final check we need to establish that the combined revenues of reportable segments we have identified (£360 million + £125 million + £232 million + £124 million = £841 million) is at least 75% of the total revenues of Varia of £974 million. £841 million is 86% of £974 million so this condition is satisfied. Therefore no other segments need to be added.

4.5.3 Measuring segment information

IFRS 8 specifies that the amount reported for each segment should be the measures reported to the chief operating decision maker for the purposes of allocating resources and assessing performance. It does not define segment revenue, segment expense, segment result, segment assets, and segment liabilities but rather requires an explanation of how segment profit or loss and segment assets and segment liabilities are measured for each reportable segment.

Allocations and adjustments to revenues and profit should only be included in segment disclosures if they are reviewed by the CODM.

4.5.4 Disclosure requirements for reportable segments

The principle in IFRS 8 is that an entity should disclose 'information to enable users to evaluate the nature and financial effect of the business activities in which it engages and the economic environment in which it operates'.

IFRS 8 requires disclosure of the following segment information:

(i)   Factors used to identify the entity's operating segments such as whether management organises the entity around products and services, geographical areas, regulatory environments, or a combination of factors and whether segments have been aggregated.

(ii) Types of products and services from which each reportable segment derives its revenues.

(iii) A measure of profit or loss for each reportable segment.

(iv) A measure of liabilities for each reportable segment if it is regularly provided to the chief operating decision maker.

(v)   The following items if they are disclosed in the performance statement reviewed by the chief operating decision maker:

- revenues from external customers and from transactions with other operating segments
- interest revenue and interest expense
- depreciation and amortisation
- 'exceptional' items
- income tax income or expense
- other material non-cash items.

(vi) Total assets; total amounts for additions to non-current assets if they are regularly provided to the chief operating decision maker.

(vii) Reconciliations of profit or loss to the group totals for the entity.

(viii) Reliance on major customers. If revenues from a single external customer are 10% or more of the entity's total revenue, it must disclose that fact and the segment reporting the revenue. It need not disclose the identity of the major customer or the amount of the revenue.

4.5.5 Sample disclosures under IFRS 8

We consider (1) the format for disclosure of segment profits or loss, assets and liabilities, (2) the reconciliations of reportable segment revenues and assets, and (3) information about major customers.

	Hotels	Software	Finance	Other	Entity totals
	£m	£m	£m	£m	£m
Revenue from external customers	**800**	**2,150**	**500**	**100**[(a)]	**3,550**
Intersegment revenue	—	450	—	—	450
Interest revenue	125	250	—	—	375
Interest expense	95	180	—	—	275
Net interest revenue[(b)]	—	—	100	—	100
Depreciation and amortisation	30	155	110	—	295
Reportable segment profit	*27*	*320*	*50*	*10*	*407*
Other material non-cash items – impairment of assets	20	—	—	—	20
Reportable segment assets	*700*	*1,500*	*5,700*	*200*	*8,100*
Expenditure for reportable segment non-current assets	100	130	60	—	290
Reportable segment liabilities	*405*	*980*	*3,000*	—	*4,385*

Reconciliations to group totals are in **bold italics**. Notes:

(a) Revenue from segments below the quantitative thresholds are attributed to four operating divisions. Those segments include a small electronics company, a warehouse leasing company, a retailer and an undertakers. None of these segments has ever met any of the quantitative thresholds for determining reportable segments.

(b) The finance segment derives most of its revenue from interest. Management primarily relies on net interest revenue, not the gross revenue and expense amounts, in managing that segment. Therefore, as permitted by paragraph 23, only net interest is disclosed.

Reconciliations are required for every material item disclosed. The following are just sample reconciliations.

Revenues	£m
Total revenues for reportable segments	3,900
Other revenues	100
Elimination of intersegment revenues	(450)
Entity's revenue	**3,550**

Profit or loss	£m
Total profit or loss for reportable segments	397
Other profit or loss	10
Entity profit	**407**

Assets	£m
Total assets for reportable segments	7,900
Other assets	200
Entity assets	**8,100**

(3) Information about major customers

A sample disclosure might be:

> Revenues from one customer of the software and hotels segments represent approximately £400 million of the entity's total revenue.

(Note that disclosure is not required of the customer's name or of the revenue for each operating segment.)

4.6 Benefits and continuing concerns following the issue of IFRS 8

4.6.1 The benefits of segment reporting

The majority of listed and other large entities derive their revenues and profits from a number of sources (or segments). This has implications for the investment strategy of the entity, as different segments require different amounts of investment to support their activities. Conventionally produced statements of financial position and statements of comprehensive income capture financial position and financial performance in a single column of figures.

The following is an extract from the Tesco 2011/12 Annual Report reporting on five segments within the group:

	Trading profit	Trading margin %	Growth %	Sales	Growth %
Group results	3,761m	5.8%	1.3%	72,035m	7.4%
UK	2,480m	5.8%	(1.0)%	47,355m	6.2%
Asia	737m	6.8%	21.5%	11,627m	10.4%
Europe	529m	5.3%	(0.4)%	11,371m	7.8%
US	(153m)	(24.2)%	17.7%	638m	31.5%
Tesco Bank	168m	16.1%	(36.4)%	1,044m	13.6%

We can see that the group is showing a trading profit growth of 1.3%. Within that, segments vary from negative growth of 36.4% to positive growth of 21.5%. Individual segments are also interesting, with sales in the US increasing by 31.5% whilst there is a trading loss.

To put the segment results into a group context we can see their relative importance to the group expressed as a percentage of the group totals as follows:

	Trading profit %	Sales %
UK	66	66
Asia	20	16
Europe	14	16
US	(4)	1
Tesco Bank	4	1

The losses are a red flag to investors and the problem is addressed in the Annual Report by the Chairman, who writes as follows:

> Elsewhere, we have continued the substantial reorientation of the US business to give it the best possible opportunity to secure its future with all the potential for longer-term growth that would bring. We have announced our intention to exit from Japan. We are willing to invest for the long term but where we cannot see a profitable, scalable business earning good returns within an acceptable timescale, we prefer to

pursue better opportunities. And we have slowed down the development of Tesco Bank to increase its focus on quality, service and risk management.

4.6.2 Concerns following the issue of IFRS 8

Despite the existence of IFRS 8, there are many concerns about the extent of segmental disclosure and its limitations must be recognised. A great deal of discretion is given to the directors concerning the **definition of each segment**. However, 'the factors which provide guidance in determining an industry segment are often the factors which lead a company's management to organise its enterprise into divisions, branches or subsidiaries'.

There is discretion concerning the **allocation of common costs** to segments on a reasonable basis. There is flexibility in the **definition of some of the items** to be disclosed (particularly net assets). These concerns have been recognised at government level and will be held under review by the European Parliament.

European Parliament reservations

In November 2007 the European Parliament accepted the Commission's proposal to endorse IFRS 8, incorporating US Statement of Financial Accounting Standard No. 131 into EU law, which will require EU companies listed in the European Union to disclose segmental information in accordance with the 'through-the-eyes-of-management' approach.

However, it regretted[4] that the impact assessment carried out by the Commission did not sufficiently take into account the interests of users as well as the needs of small and medium-sized companies located in more than one member state and companies operating only locally. Its view was that such impact assessments must incorporate quantitative information and reflect a balancing of interests among stakeholders.

It did not accept that the convergence of accounting rules was a one-sided process where one party (the IASB) simply copies the financial reporting standards of the other party (the FASB). In particular it expressed reservations that disclosure of geographical information on the basis of IFRS 8 would be comparable to that disclosed under IAS 14. A post-implementation review was carried out by EFRAG in 2012 (www.efrag.org).

The ESMA report

The European Securities and Markets Authority reported back[5] in 2011 that four topics emerged as a basis of their review:

- There might be some confusion over the definition of the CODM.

- The level of subjectivity in deciding how aggregation should be applied may lead to diversity in practice.

- In many instances, information about allocation policies of profit or loss, assets and liabilities to reporting segments, definition of non-GAAP measures and the reconciliation between segment information and the amounts reported in the financial statements were not disclosed properly.

- Analysis of entity-wide disclosures: although 58% of issuers in their sample provided information about revenues and non-current assets by geographical area in accordance with IFRS 8, ESMA noted that the notes to the financial statements rarely present information for individual foreign countries and that there is no common understanding on how the materiality concept should be applied in this context.

UK reservations

The FRRP reviewed a sample of 2009 interim accounts and 2008 annual accounts. On the basis of this review, the FRRP has highlighted situations where companies were asked to provide additional information:

- Only one operating segment is reported, but the group appears to be diverse with different businesses or with significant operations in different countries.
- The operating analysis set out in the narrative report differs from the operating segments in the financial report.
- The titles and responsibilities of the directors or executive management team imply an organisational structure which is not reflected in the operating segments.
- The commentary in the narrative report focuses on non-IFRS measures, whereas the segmental disclosures are based on IFRS amounts.

It also suggested a number of questions that directors should ask themselves when preparing segmental reports, such as:

- What are the key operating decisions made in running the business?
- Who makes the key operating decisions?
- Who are the segment managers and who do they report to?
- How are the group's activities reported in the information used by management?
- Have the reported segment amounts been reconciled to the IFRS aggregate amounts?
- Do the reported segments appear consistent with their internal reporting?

4.6.3 Constraints on comparison between entities

Segment reporting is intrinsically subjective. This means that there are likely to be major differences in the way segments are determined, and because costs, for instance, may be allocated differently by entities in the same industry, it is difficult to make inter-entity comparisons at the segment level and the user still has to take a great deal of responsibility for the interpretation of that information.

4.7 Discontinued operations – IFRS 5 Non-current Assets Held for Sale and Discontinued Operations[6]

IFRS 5 deals, as its name suggests, with two separate but related issues. We will first discuss the treatment of discontinued operations.

4.7.1 Criteria

We need to be familiar with the IFRS 5 definition of a discontinued operation. It is a component of an entity that, during the reporting period, either:

- has been disposed of (whether by sale or abandonment); or
- has been classified as held for sale, and *also*
  - represents a separate major line of business or geographical area of operations; or
  - is part of a single coordinated plan to dispose of a separate major line of business or geographical area of operations; or

– is a subsidiary acquired exclusively with a view to resale (possibly as part of the acquisition of an existing group with a subsidiary that does not fit into the long-term plans of the acquirer).

Defining a component

The IFRS defines a component as a part of an entity which comprises operations and cash flows that can be clearly distinguished, operationally and for financial reporting purposes, from the rest of the entity. This definition is somewhat subjective and the IASB is considering amending this definition to align it with that of an operating segment in IFRS 8 and has issued an exposure draft to this effect.

4.7.2 Disclosure in the statement of income

The results of discontinued operations should be separately disclosed from those of other, continuing, operations in the income statement. As a minimum, on the face of the statement, entities should show, as a single amount, the total of:

● the post-tax profit or loss of discontinued operations; and

● the post-tax gain or loss recognised on the measurement to fair value less cost to sell or on the disposal of the assets or disposal group(s) constituting the discontinued operation.

Further analysis of this amount required, either on the face of the statement of comprehensive income or in the notes:

● the revenue, expenses and pre-tax profit or loss of discontinued operations;

● the related income tax expense as required by IAS 12;

● the gain or loss recognised on the measurement to fair value less costs to sell or on the disposal of the assets or disposal group(s) constituting the discontinued operation; and

● the related income tax expense as required by IAS 12.

The following is an extract from Premier Foods' 2011 consolidated income statement:

	2011 £m	2010 £m
Continuing operations		
Gross profit	**563.4**	711.7
Operating (loss)/profit	**(176.3)**	219.9
Before impairment and loss on disposal of operations	116.9	219.9
Impairment of goodwill and intangible assets	(282.0)	—
Loss on disposal of operations	(11.2)	—
Finance expense	(126.9)	(160.1)
Finance income	7.2	12.0
Net movement on fair valuation of interest rate financial instruments	36.9	(43.3)
(Loss)/profit before taxation from continuing operations	**(259.1)**	28.5
Taxation credit/(charge)	29.1	(24.4)
(Loss)/profit after taxation from continuing operations	**(230.0)**	4.1
Loss from discontinued operations	**(109.0)**	(103.4)
Loss for the year attributable to equity shareholders of the Parent Company	**(339.0)**	(99.3)

Note 11 in the Annual Report giving details of make-up of the post-tax loss of £109m is as follows:

	£m
Revenue	218.6
Operating expenses	(325.1)
Operating loss before loss on disposal	(106.5)
Interest payable	(0.1)
Interest receivable	—
Loss before taxation	(106.6)
Taxation credit	12.2
Loss after taxation on discontinued operations for the year	(94.4)
Loss on disposal before taxation	(14.6)
Tax credit on loss on disposal	—
Loss on disposal after taxation	(14.6)
Total loss arising from discontinued operations	(109.0)

4.8 Held for sale – IFRS 5 *Non-current Assets Held for Sale and Discontinued Operations*

Let us now discuss the treatment of assets which have been classified as held for sale.

IFRS 5 deals with the appropriate reporting of an asset (or group of assets – referred to in IFRS 5 as a 'disposal group') that management has decided to dispose of. It states that an asset (or disposal group) is classified as 'held for sale' if its carrying amount will be recovered principally through a sale transaction rather than through continuing use.

It further provides that:

● the asset or disposal group must be **available for immediate sale** in its present condition; and

● its sale must be **highly probable**.

The criteria for the sale to be highly probable are:

● The appropriate level of management must be committed to a plan to sell the asset or disposal group.

● An active programme to locate a buyer and complete the plan must have been initiated.

● The asset or disposal group must be actively marketed for sale at a price that is reasonable in relation to its current fair value.

● The sale should be expected to qualify for recognition as a completed sale within one year from the date of classification.

● Actions required to complete the plan should indicate that it is unlikely that significant changes to the plan will be made or that the plan will be withdrawn.

There is a pragmatic recognition that there may be events outside the control of the enterprise which prevent completion within one year. In such a case the held for sale classification is retained, provided there is sufficient evidence that the entity remains committed to its plan to sell the asset or disposal group and has taken all reasonable steps to resolve the delay.

It is important to note that IFRS 5 specifies that this classification is appropriate for assets (or disposal groups) that are to be **sold** or distributed. The classification does not apply to assets or disposal groups that are to be **abandoned**.

4.8.1 IFRS 5 – implications of classification as held for sale

Assets, or disposal groups, that are classified as held for sale should be removed from their previous position in the statement of financial position and shown under a single 'held for sale' caption – usually as part of **current** assets. Any liabilities directly associated with disposal groups that are classified as held for sale should be separately presented within liabilities.

As far as disposal groups are concerned, it is acceptable to present totals on the face of the statement of financial position, with a more detailed breakdown in the notes. The following is a disclosure note from the published financial statements of Unilever for the year ended 31 December 2009:

Assets classified as held for sale

	2009 £m	2008 £m
Disposal groups held for sale		
Property, plant and equipment	7	7
Inventories	1	15
	8	22
Non-current assets held for sale		
Property, plant and equipment	9	14
	17	36

Depreciable assets that are classified as 'held for sale' should not be depreciated from classification date, as the classification implies that the intention of management is primarily to recover value from such assets through sale, rather than through continued use.

When assets (or disposal groups) are classified as held for sale, their carrying value(s) at the date of classification should be compared with the 'fair value less costs to sell' of the asset (or disposal group). If the carrying value exceeds fair value less costs to sell then the excess should be treated as an impairment loss. In the case of a disposal group, the impairment loss should be allocated to the specific assets in the order specified in IAS 36 *Impairment of Assets*. The treatment of impairment losses is discussed in detail in Chapter 17.

4.9 IAS 24 *Related Party Disclosures*[7]

In the previous chapter we saw that after the financial statements have been drafted it is necessary to form a judgement as to whether or not they give a fair presentation of the entity's activities.

One of the considerations is whether there are any indications that transactions have not been carried out at arm's length. This can occur when one of the parties to the transaction is able to influence the management to enter into transactions which are not primarily in the best interest of the company. Where such a possibility exists, the person (or business) able to exert this influence is referred to in accounting terms as a 'related party'.

The users of financial statements would normally assume that the transactions of an entity have been carried out at arm's length and under terms which are in the best interests of the entity. The existence of related party relationships may mean that this assumption is not appropriate and IAS 24 therefore requires disclosure of such existence.

4.9.1 How to determine what is 'arm's length'

The Board of a company should consider a number of surrounding factors when determining whether a transaction has been at arm's length. These include considering:

- how the terms of the overall transaction compare with those of any comparable transactions between parties dealing on an arm's length basis in similar circumstances;
- the level of risk – how the transaction impacts on the company's financial position and performance, its ability to follow its business plan and the expected rate of return on the assets given the level of risk;
- other options – what other options were available to the company and whether any expert advice was obtained by the company.

4.9.2 IAS 24 disclosures required

The purpose of IAS 24 is to define the meaning of the term 'related party' and prescribe the disclosures that are appropriate for transactions with related parties (and in some cases for their mere existence). From the outset it is worth remembering that the term 'party' could refer to an individual (referred to as a person) or to another entity. IAS 24 breaks the definition down into two main sections relating to (a) persons and (b) entities. We will consider both below.

4.9.3 Definition of 'related party' when the party is a person

A person, or a close member of that person's family, whom we will refer to as P, is a related party to the reporting entity (RE) if:

- P has control or joint control over RE;
- P has significant influence over RE; or
- P is a member of the key management personnel of RE.

Close members of the family of P are those family members who may be expected to influence, or be influenced by, P in their dealings with RE and include:

- P's children and spouse or domestic partner; and
- children of the spouse or domestic partner; and
- dependants of P or P's spouse or domestic partner.

Key management personnel of RE are those persons having authority and responsibility for planning, directing and controlling the activities of RE, directly or indirectly, including any director (whether executive or otherwise) of RE.

Example: Individual as investor

Let us assume that Arthur has 60% of the shares in and so controls Garden Supplies Ltd and:

(a) he also has a 45% significant interest in Plant Growers Ltd. This means that in Garden Supplies Ltd's financial statements Plant Growers Ltd are a related party, and in Plant Growers Ltd's financial statements Garden Supplies Ltd are a related party; or

(b) a close member of his family (in this case his domestic partner) owns a 45% interest in Plant Growers Ltd. This means that a similar treatment would be required and the two companies are related; or

(c) Arthur still has the 60% interest in Garden Supplies Ltd but instead of having an investment in Plant Growers Ltd he is a member of Plant Growers Ltd's key management personnel. This means that a similar treatment would be required and the two companies are related.

4.9.4 Definition of 'related party' when the party is another entity

We have discussed the position where the related party relationship arises from an individual's relationship with two businesses. It also arises when companies are involved.

For example, let us now assume that Arthur, Garden Supplies and Plant Growers are all limited companies. We classify each company as follows:

● Arthur Ltd holds 60% of the shares and so is a parent of Garden Supplies Ltd.

● Plant Growers Ltd is an associate of Arthur Ltd because Arthur Ltd can exercise significant influence over Plant Growers Ltd.

This means that when any of the companies prepares its financial statements:

● Arthur Ltd is related to both Garden Supplies Ltd and Plant Growers Ltd.

● Garden Supplies Ltd is related to Plant Growers Ltd.

● Plant Growers Ltd is related to Garden Supplies Ltd.

4.9.5 Identifying related parties is not always clear

In the above examples we have clear knowledge of the relationship. However, there could be an intention to conceal the relationship, which requires ingenuity from any auditor. Steps might need to be taken such as discussions with lawyers and searching company records, referring to daily newspapers, trade magazines and phone books and, of course, using the Internet and social network sites.

4.9.6 Parties deemed not to be related parties

IAS 24 emphasises that it is necessary to consider carefully the substance of each relationship to see whether or not a related party relationship exists. However, the standard highlights a number of relationships that would not normally lead to related party status:

● two entities simply because they have a director or other member of the key management personnel in common or because a member of the key management personnel of one entity has significant influence over the other entity;

● two venturers simply because they share control over a joint venture;

● providers of finance, trade unions, public utilities or government departments in the course of their normal dealings with the entity;

● a single customer, supplier, franchisor, distributor or general agent with whom an entity transacts a significant volume of business merely by virtue of the resulting economic dependence.

4.9.7 Disclosure of controlling relationships

IAS 24 requires that relationships between a parent and its subsidiaries be disclosed irrespective of whether there have been transactions between them. Where the entity is controlled, it should disclose:

- the name of its parent;
- the name of its ultimate controlling party (which could be an individual or another entity);
- if neither the parent nor the ultimate controlling party produces consolidated financial statements available for public use, the name of the next most senior parent that does produce such statements.

4.9.8 Exemption from disclosures re government-related entities

A reporting entity is exempt from the detailed disclosures referred to in Section 4.9.10 below in relation to related party transactions and outstanding balances with:

- a government that has control, joint control or significant influence over the reporting entity; and
- another entity that is a related party because the same government has control, joint control or significant influence over both parties.

If this exemption is applied, the reporting entity is nevertheless required to make the following disclosures about transactions with government-related entities:

- the name of the government and the nature of its relationship with the reporting entity;
- the following information in sufficient detail to enable users of the financial statements to understand the effect of related party transactions:
  - the nature and amount of each individually significant transaction; and
  - for other transactions that are collectively, but not individually, significant, a qualitative or quantitative indication of their extent.

The reason for the exemption is essentially pragmatic. In some jurisdictions where government control is pervasive it can be difficult to identify other government-related entities. In some circumstances the directors of the reporting entity may be genuinely unaware of the related party relationship. Therefore, the basis of conclusions to IAS 24 (BC 43) states that, in the context of the disclosures that are needed in these circumstances:

> The objective of IAS 24 is to provide disclosures necessary to draw attention to the possibility that the financial position and profit or loss may have been affected by the existence of related parties and by transactions and outstanding balances, including commitments, with such parties. To meet that objective, IAS 24 requires some disclosure when the exemption applies. Those disclosures are intended to put users on notice that related party transactions have occurred and to give an indication of their extent. The Board did not intend to require the reporting entity to identify **every** government-related entity, or to quantify in detail **every** transaction with such entities, because such a requirement would negate the exemption.

4.9.9 Disclosure of compensation of key management personnel

Compensation can be influenced by a person in this position. Consequently IAS 24 requires the disclosure of short-term employee benefits, post-employment benefits, other long-term benefits (e.g. accrued sabbatical leave), termination benefits, and share-based payment.

4.9.10 Disclosure of related party transactions

A related party transaction is a transfer of resources or obligations between a reporting entity and a related party, regardless of whether a price is charged. Where such transactions have occurred, the entity should disclose the nature of the related party relationship as well as information about those transactions and outstanding balances to enable a user to understand the potential effect of the relationship on the financial statements. As a minimum, the disclosures should include:

- the amount of the transactions;
- the amount of the outstanding balances and:
  - their terms and conditions, including whether they are secured, and the nature of the consideration to be provided in settlement; and
  - details of any guarantees given or received;
- provisions for doubtful debts related to the amount of outstanding balances; and
- the expense recognised during the period in respect of bad or doubtful debts due from related parties.

The following extract from the Unilever 2011 Annual Report is an example of the required disclosures:

30 Related party transactions
A related party is a person or entity that is related to the Group. These include both people and entities that have, or are subject to the influence or control of the Group. The following related party balances existed with associate or joint venture businesses at 31 December:

Related party balances

	2011 €million	2010 €million
Trading and other balances due from joint ventures	243	233

4.9.11 Possible impact of transactions with related parties

It is possible that there could be both beneficial and prejudicial impacts.

Beneficial transactions with related parties

It could be that the related party is actually offering support to the business. For example, the business might have received benefits in a variety of ways ranging from financial support on favourable terms such as guarantees or low or no interest loans to the provision of goods or services at less than market rates.

Prejudicial transactions with related parties

These can arise when the business enters into transactions on terms that would not be offered to an unrelated party. There are numerous ways that this could be arranged, such as:

- **Loans**:
  - borrowing at above market rates;
  - lending at below market rates;
  - lending with no agreement as to date for repayment;
  - lending with little prospect of being repaid;
  - lending with the intention of writing off;
  - guaranteeing debts where there is no commercial advantage to the business.
- **Assets**:
  - selling non-current assets at below market value;
  - selling goods at less than normal trade price;
  - providing services at less than normal rates;
  - transfer of know-how, or research and development transfers.
- **Trading**:
  - sales made where there is secret agreement to repurchase to inflate current period revenue;
  - sales to inflate revenue with funds advanced to the debtor to allow the debt to be paid;
  - paying for services which have not been provided.

Summary

The published accounts of a listed company are intended to provide a report to enable shareholders to assess current-year stewardship and management performance and to predict future cash flows. Financial statements prepared from a trial balance and adjusted for accruals might require further adjustments. These arise from:

1 events after the reporting period that provide additional evidence of conditions that existed at the period-end which might require the financial statements to be adjusted; or

2 prior period errors that may require retrospective changes to the opening balances in the statement of financial position that could affect assets, liabilities and retained earnings.

In addition to these adjustments, in order to assist shareholders to predict future cash flows with an understanding of the risks involved, more information has been required by the IASB. This has taken two forms:

1 more quantitative information in the accounts, e.g. segmental analysis, and the impact of changes on the operation, e.g. a breakdown of turnover, costs and profits for both new and discontinued operations; and

2 more qualitative information, e.g. related party disclosures and events occurring after the reporting period.

REVIEW QUESTIONS

1 Explain why non-adjusting items are not reported in the financial statements if they are of sufficient materiality to be disclosed.

2 Explain the criteria that have to be satisfied when identifying an operating segment.

3 Explain the criteria that have to be satisfied to identify a reportable segment.

4 Explain why it is necessary to identify a chief operating decision maker and describe the key identifying factors.

5 Discuss the review findings of the European Securities and Markets Authority (ESMA) in relation to the role of the chief operating decision maker.

6 A research report[8] found that users were worried about the lack of comparability among segmental disclosures of different companies following the issue of IFRS 8. Discuss:

(a) why it should have resulted in a lack of comparability;

(b) whether it is more relevant because its format and content are not closely defined;

(c) whether any of the other financial statements would be more relevant to users if they were free to format as they wished;

(d) whether inter-firm comparability is more important than inter-period comparability.

7 Explain the conditions set out in IFRS 5 for determining whether operations have been discontinued and the problems that might arise in applying them.

8 Explain the conditions that must be satisfied if a non-current asset is to be reported in the statement of financial position as held for sale.

9 Explain why it is important to an investor to be informed about assets held for sale.

10 Discuss how transactions with related parties can have

(a) a beneficial impact

(b) a prejudicial impact

on (i) the reported income and (ii) the financial position.

EXERCISES

Question 1

IAS 10 deals with events after the reporting period.

Required:
(a) Define the period covered by IAS 10.
(b) Explain when the financial statements should be adjusted.
(c) Why should non-adjusting events be disclosed?
(d) A customer made a claim for £50,000 for losses suffered by the late delivery of goods. The main part (£40,000) of the claim referred to goods due to be delivered before the year-end. Explain how this would be dealt with under IAS 10.
(e) After the year-end a substantial quantity of inventory was destroyed in a fire. The loss was not adequately covered by insurance. This event is likely to threaten the ability of the business to continue as a going concern. Discuss the matters you would consider in making a decision under IAS 10.
(f) The business entered into a favourable contract after the year-end that would see its profits increase by 15% over the next three years. Explain how this would be dealt with under IAS 10.

Question 2

Epsilon is a listed entity. You are the financial controller of the entity and its consolidated financial statements for the year ended 30 September 2008 are being prepared. Your assistant, who has prepared the first draft of the statements, is unsure about the correct treatment of a transaction and has asked for your advice. Details of the transaction are given below.

On 31 August 2008 the directors decided to close down a business segment which did not fit into its future strategy. The closure commenced on 5 October 2008 and was due to be completed on 31 December 2008. On 6 September 2008 letters were sent to relevant employees offering voluntary redundancy or redeployment in other sectors of the business. On 13 September 2008 negotiations commenced with relevant parties with a view to terminating existing contracts of the business segment and arranging sales of its assets. Latest estimates of the financial implications of the closure are as follows:

(i)   Redundancy costs will total $30 million, excluding the payment referred to in (ii) below.

(ii) The cost of redeploying and retraining staff who do not accept redundancy will total $6 million.

(iii) Plant having a net book value of $11 million at 30 September 2008 will be sold for $2 million.

(iv) The operating losses of the business segment for October, November and December 2008 are estimated at $10 million.

Your assistant is unsure of the extent to which the above transactions create liabilities that should be recognised as a closure provision in the financial statements. He is also unsure as to whether or not the results of the business segment that is being closed need to be shown separately.

Required:
Explain how the decision to close down the business segment should be reported in the financial statements of Epsilon for the year ended 30 September 2008.

* Question 3

Epsilon is a listed entity. You are the financial controller of the entity and its consolidated financial statements for the year ended 31 March 2009 are being prepared. The board of directors is responsible for all key financial and operating decisions, including the allocation of resources.

Your assistant is preparing the first draft of the statements. He has a reasonable general accounting knowledge but is not familiar with the detailed requirements of all relevant financial reporting standards. He requires your advice and he has sent you a note as shown below.

We intend to apply IFRS 8 *Operating segments* in this year's financial statements. I am aware that this standard has attracted a reasonable amount of critical comment since it was issued in November 2006.

The board of directors receives a monthly report on the activities of the five significant operational areas of our business. Relevant financial information relating to the five operations for the year to 31 March 2009, and in respect of our head office, is as follows:

Operational area	Revenue for year to 31 March 2009 $000	Profit/(loss) for year to 31 March 2009 $000	Assets at 31 March 2009 $000
A	23,000	3,000	8,000
B	18,000	2,000	6,000
C	4,000	(3,000)	5,000
D	1,000	150	500
E	3,000	450	400
Sub-total	49,000	2,600	19,900
Head office	Nil	Nil	6,000
Entity total	49,000	2,600	25,900

I am unsure of the following matters regarding the reporting of operating segments:

● How do we decide what our operating segments should be?

● Should we report segment information relating to head office?

● Which of our operational areas should report separate information? Operational areas A, B and C exhibit very distinct economic characteristics but the economic characteristics of operational areas D and E are very similar.

● Why has IFRS 8 attracted such critical comment?

Required:
Draft a reply to the questions raised by your assistant.

* Question 4

Filios Products plc owns a chain of hotels through which it provides three basic services: restaurant facilities, accommodation, and leisure facilities. The latest financial statements contain the following information:

Statement of financial position of Filios Products

	£m
ASSETS	
Non-current assets at book value	1,663
Current assets	
Inventories and receivables	381
Bank balance	128
	509
Total Assets	**2,172**
EQUITY AND LIABILITIES	
Equity	
Share capital	800
Retained earnings	1,039
	1,839
Non-current liabilities:	
Long-term borrowings	140
Current liabilities	193
Total Equity and liabilities	**2,172**

Statement of comprehensive income of Filios Products

	£m	£m
Revenue		1,028
Less: Cost of sales	684	
Administration expenses	110	
Distribution costs	101	
Interest charged	14	(909)
Net profit		119

The following breakdown is provided of the company's results into three divisions and head office:

	Restaurants £m	Hotels £m	Leisure £m	Head office £m
Revenue	508	152	368	—
Cost of sales	316	81	287	—
Administration expenses	43	14	38	15
Distribution costs	64	12	25	—
Interest charged	10	—	—	4
Non-current assets at book value	890	332	364	77
Inventories and receivables	230	84	67	—
Bank balance	73	15	28	12
Payables	66	40	56	31
Long-term borrowings	100	—	—	40

Required:

(a) Outline the nature of segmental reports and explain the reason for presenting such information in the published accounts.

(b) Prepare a segmental statement for Filios Products plc complying, so far as the information permits, with the provisions of IFRS 8 *Operating Segments* so as to show for each segment and the business as a whole:

(i)   revenue;

(ii) profit;

(iii) net assets.

(c) Examine the relative performance of the operating divisions of Filios Products. The examination should be based on the following accounting ratios:

(i)   operating profit percentage;

(ii) net asset turnover;

(iii) return on net assets.

Question 5

The following is the draft trading and income statement of Parnell Ltd for the year ending 31 December 2003:

	$m	$m
Revenue		563
Cost of sales		310
		253
Distribution costs	45	
Administrative expenses	78	
		123
Profit on ordinary activities before tax		130
Tax on profit on ordinary activities		45
Profit on ordinary activities after taxation – all retained		85
Profit brought forward at 1 January 2003		101
Profit carried forward at 31 December 2003		186

You are given the following additional information, which is reflected in the above statement of comprehensive income only to the extent stated:

1 Distribution costs include a bad debt of $15 million which arose on the insolvency of a major customer. There is no prospect of recovering any of this debt. Bad debts have never been material in the past.

2 The company has traditionally consisted of a manufacturing division and a distribution division. On 31 December 2003, the entire distribution division was sold for $50 million; its book value at the time of sale was $40 million. The profit on disposal was credited to administrative expenses. (Ignore any related income tax.)

3 During 2003, the distribution division made sales of $100 million and had a cost of sales of $30 million. There will be no reduction in stated distribution costs or administration expenses as a result of this disposal.

4 The company owns offices which it purchased on 1 January 2001 for $500 million, comprising $200 million for land and $300 million for buildings. No depreciation was charged in 2001 or 2002, but the company now considers that such a charge should be introduced. The buildings were

expected to have a life of 50 years at the date of purchase, and the company uses the straight-line basis for calculating depreciation, assuming a zero residual value. No taxation consequences result from this change.

5   During 2003, part of the manufacturing division was restructured at a cost of $20 million to take advantage of modern production techniques. The restructuring was not fundamental and will **not** have a material effect on the nature and focus of the company's operations. This cost is included under administration expenses in the statement of comprehensive income.

Required:

(a) State how each of the items 1–5 above must be accounted for in order to comply with the requirements of international accounting standards.

(b) Redraft the income statement of Parnell Ltd for 2003, taking into account the additional information so as to comply, as far as possible, with relevant standard accounting practice. Show clearly any adjustments you make. Notes to the accounts are not required. Where an IAS recommends information to be on the face of the income statement it could be recorded on the face of the statement.

* Question 6

Springtime Ltd is a UK trading company buying and selling as wholesalers fashionable summer clothes. The following balances have been extracted from the books as at 31 March 20X4:

	£000
Auditor's remuneration	30
Income tax based on the accounting profit:	
For the year to 31 March 20X4	3,200
Overprovision for the year to 31 March 20X3	200
Delivery expenses (including £300,000 overseas)	1,200
Dividends: final (proposed – to be paid 1 August 20X4)	200
interim (paid on 1 October 20X3)	100
Non-current assets at cost:	
Delivery vans	200
Office cars	40
Stores equipment	5,000
Dividend income (amount received from listed companies)	1,200
Office expenses	800
Overseas operations: closure costs of entire operations	350
Purchases	24,000
Sales (net of sales tax)	35,000
Inventory at cost:	
At 1 April 20X3	5,000
At 31 March 20X4	6,000
Storeroom costs	1,000
Wages and salaries:	
Delivery staff	700
Directors' emoluments	400
Office staff	100
Storeroom staff	400

Notes:

1   Depreciation is provided at the following annual rates on a straight-line basis: delivery vans 20%; office cars 25%; stores 1%.
2   The following taxation rates may be assumed: corporate income tax 35%; personal income tax 25%.
3   The dividend income arises from investments held in non-current investments.
4   It has been decided to transfer an amount of £150,000 to the deferred taxation account.
5   The overseas operations consisted of exports. In 20X3/X4 these amounted to £5,000,000 (sales) with purchases of £4,000,000. Related costs included £100,000 in storeroom staff and £15,000 for office staff.
6   Directors' emoluments include:

Chairperson	100,000	
Managing director	125,000	
Finance director	75,000	
Sales director	75,000	
Export director	25,000	(resigned 31 December 20X3)
	£400,000	

Required:
(a) Produce a statement of comprehensive income suitable for publication and complying as far as possible with generally accepted accounting practice.
(b) Comment on how IFRS 5 has improved the quality of information available to users of accounts.

Question 7

Omega prepares financial statements under International Financial Reporting Standards. In the year ended 31 March 2007 the following transaction occurred:

Omega follows the revaluation model when measuring its property, plant and equipment. One of its properties was carried in the balance sheet at 31 March 2006 at its market value at that date of $5 million. The depreciable amount of this property was estimated at $3.2 million at 31 March 2006 and the estimated future economic life of the property at 31 March 2006 was 20 years.

On 1 January 2007 Omega decided to dispose of the property as it was surplus to requirements and began to actively seek a buyer. On 1 January 2007 Omega estimated that the market value of the property was $5.1 million and that the costs of selling the property would be $80,000. These estimates remained appropriate at 31 March 2007.

The property was sold on 10 June 2007 for net proceeds of $5.15 million.

Required:
Explain, with relevant calculations, how the property would be treated in the financial statements of Omega for the year ended 31 March 2007 and the year ending 31 March 2008.

* Question 8

The following trial balance has been extracted from the books of Hoodurz as at 31 March 2006:

	$000	$000
Administration expenses	210	
Ordinary share capital, $1 per share		600
Trade receivables	470	
Bank overdraft		80
Provision for warranty claims		205
Distribution costs	420	
Non-current asset investments	560	
Investment income		75
Interest paid	10	
Property, at cost	200	
Plant and equipment, at cost	550	
Plant and equipment, accumulated depreciation (at 31.3.2006)		220
Accumulated profits (at 31.3.2005)		80
Loans (repayable 31.12.2010)		100
Purchases	960	
Inventories (at 31.3.2005)	150	
Trade payables		260
Sales		2,010
2004/2005 final dividend paid	65	
2005/2006 interim dividend paid	35	
	3,630	3,630

The following information is relevant:

(i)   The trial balance figures include the following amounts for a disposal group that has been classified as 'held for sale' under IFRS 5 *Non-current Assets Held for Sale and Discontinued Operations*:

	$000
Plant and equipment, at cost	150
Plant and equipment, accumulated depreciation	15
Trade receivables	70
Bank overdraft	10
Trade payables	60
Sales	370
Inventories (at 31.12.2005)	25
Purchases	200
Administration expenses	55
Distribution costs	60

The disposal group had no inventories at the date classified as 'held for sale'.

(ii)   Inventories (excluding the disposal group) at 31.3.2006 were valued at $160,000.

(iii)   The depreciation charges for the year have already been accrued.

(iv) The income tax for the year ended 31.3.2006 is estimated to be $74,000. This includes $14,000 in relation to the disposal group.

(v) The provision for warranty claims is to be increased by $16,000. This is classified as administration expense.

(vi) Staff bonuses totalling $20,000 for administration and $20,000 for distribution are to be accrued.

(vii) The property was acquired during February 2006, therefore, depreciation for the year ended 31.3.2006 is immaterial. The directors have chosen to use the fair value model for such an asset. The fair value of the property at 31.3.2006 is $280,000.

Required:

Prepare for Hoodurz:

(a) an income statement for the year ended 31 March 2006; and

(b) a balance sheet as at 31 March 2006.

Both statements should comply as far as possible with relevant International Financial Reporting Standards. No notes to the financial statements are required nor is a statement of changes in equity, but all workings should be clearly shown.

(The Association of International Accountants)

Question 9

Omega prepares financial statements under International Financial Reporting Standards. In the year ended 31 March 2007 the following transaction occurred. On 31 December 2006 the directors decided to dispose of a property that was surplus to requirements. They instructed selling agents to procure a suitable purchaser and advertised the property at a commercially realistic price.

The property was being measured under the revaluation model and had been revalued at $15 million on 31 March 2006. The depreciable element of the property was estimated as $8 million at 31 March 2006 and the useful economic life of the depreciable element was estimated as 25 years from that date. Omega depreciates its non-current assets on a monthly basis.

On 31 December 2006 the directors estimated that the market value of the property was $16 million, and that the costs incurred in selling the property would be $500,000. The property was sold on 30 April 2007 for $15.55 million, being the agreed selling price of $16.1 million less selling costs of $550,000. The actual selling price and costs to sell were consistent with estimated amounts as at 31 March 2007.

The financial statements for the year ended 31 March 2007 were authorised for issue on 15 May 2007.

Required:

Show the impact of the decision to sell the property on the income statement of Omega for the year ended 31 March 2007, and on its balance sheet as at 31 March 2007. You should state where in the income statement and the balance sheet relevant balances will be shown. You should make appropriate references to international financial reporting standards.

(IFRS)

Question 10

Bat, a public limited company, is currently preparing its financial statements for the year ended 31 October 2011. In order to spread risk, Bat has diversified its product base into five areas. Three of these areas, leisure goods, household products and fashion, are economically distinct, but two of the areas, finance and insurance, are quite similar. Bat's board of directors are responsible for all significant financial and operating decisions and for the allocation of resources to the five key operational activities. The board receives regular performance reports on each of these activities.

The directors fully appreciate the need to disclose segmental information to capital providers but do not fully understand the requirements of IFRS.

The following information relating to Bat's five operational activities has been extracted from the board's regular performance reports for the year ended 31 October 2011.

Operational activity	Revenue	Profit (loss)	Gross assets at year end
	$m	$m	$m
Leisure goods	12	(8)	14
Household products	63	9	22
Fashion	50	6	16
Finance	13	3	2
Insurance	8	1	1
	146	11	55
Unallocated assets (corporate head office)			15
			70

Three-quarters of the leisure goods sold are sold to the household products segment.

The directors are concerned about a number of issues relating to the implementation of IFRS 8 *Operating Segments*. These relate to two issues:

1 How the IFRS proposes Bat should:
  - identify operating segments;
  - identify those operating segments which should be reported as such in the financial statements;
  - deal with the unallocated assets; and
  - decide whether any of the operational activities should report separate information or could be combined.

2 The directors are concerned about the amount of negative comment concerning the implementation of IFRS 8 *Operating Segments*.

The finance and insurance activities are set up as operating subsidiaries and whilst the directors are planning a future strategy of growing the revenue and profits of the leisure, household and fashion activities, they plan to reduce those for the finance and insurance activities with a view to their eventual disposal. The directors believe the two activities are too dissimilar to the company's core business and wonder whether for this reason they could be presented as a separate set of operating segments or ignored for consolidation purposes.

Required:
(a) Prepare a report for the directors to address their concerns related to the implementation of IFRS 8.
(b) Advise the directors on whether or not the finance and insurance operating subsidiaries can be ignored for consolidation purposes.

(The Association of International Accountants)

Question 11

(a) In 20X3 Arthur is a large loan creditor of X Ltd and receives interest at 20% p.a. on this loan. He also has a 24% shareholding in X Ltd. Until 20X1 he was a director of the company and left after a disagreement. The remaining 76% of the shares are held by the remaining directors.

(b) Brenda joined Y Ltd, an insurance broking company, on 1 January 20X0 on a low salary but high commission basis. She brought clients with her that generated 30% of the company's 20X0 revenue.

(c) Carrie is a director and major shareholder of Z Ltd. Her husband, Donald, is employed in the company on administrative duties for which he is paid a salary of £25,000 p.a. Her daughter, Emma, is a business consultant running her own business. In 20X0 Emma carried out various consultancy exercises for the company for which she was paid £85,000.

(d) Fred is a director of V Ltd. V Ltd is a major customer of W Ltd. In 20X0 Fred also became a director of W Ltd.

Required:
Discuss whether parties are related in the above situations.

* Question 12

Maxpool plc, a listed company, owned 60% of the shares in Ching Ltd. Bay plc, a listed company, owned the remaining 40% of the £1 ordinary shares in Ching Ltd. The holdings of shares were acquired on 1 January 20X0.

On 30 November 20X0 Ching Ltd sold a factory outlet site to Bay plc at a price determined by an independent surveyor.

On 1 March 20X1 Maxpool plc purchased a further 30% of the £1 ordinary shares of Ching Ltd from Bay plc and purchased 25% of the ordinary shares of Bay plc.

On 30 June 20X1 Ching Ltd sold the whole of its fleet of vehicles to Bay plc at a price determined by a vehicle auctioneer.

Required:
Explain the implications of the above transactions for the determination of related party relationships and disclosure of such transactions in the financial statements of (a) Maxpool Group plc, (b) Ching Ltd and (c) Bay plc for the years ending 31 December 20X0 and 31 December 20X1.

(ACCA)

Question 13

Gamma is a company that manufactures power tools. Gamma was established by Mr Lee, who owns all of Gamma's shares. Mrs Lee, Mr Lee's wife, owns a controlling interest in Delta, a distributor of power tools. Delta is one of Gamma's biggest customers, accounting for 70% of Gamma's sales. Delta buys exclusively from Gamma.

Gamma's official price list is based on the policy of selling goods at cost plus 50%; however, sales to Delta are priced at normal selling price less a discount of 30% to reflect the scale of the business transacted.

Gamma's terms of sale require payment within one month, but Delta is permitted three months to pay.

Mrs Lee has decided to sell her shares in Delta and has provided a potential buyer with financial information including the following:

Sales revenue for the year ended 30 September 2011	$12.0m
Cost of sales	$8.0m
Gross profit %	33%
Current assets (including bank $0.3m)	$4.0m
Trade payables	$3.0m
Other current liabilities	$0.8m
Current ratio	1.1:1 (in line with the ratios reported in each of the past three years)

The buyer conducted a due diligence investigation and discovered the relationship between Gamma and Delta. She has decided to restate the figures provided in the table above to reflect a 'worst case' scenario before arriving at a final decision concerning the purchase.

Required:
(a) Discuss the manner in which IAS 24 *Related Party Disclosures* should have alerted the potential buyer in this case.
(b) Recalculate the table of figures provided by Mrs Lee on the basis that Delta will not receive favourable terms from Gamma if Mrs Lee sells her shares, and discuss the resulting changes.

(The Association of International Accountants)

* Question 14

IAS 8 *Accounting Policies, Changes in Accounting Estimates and Errors* lays down criteria for selection of accounting policies and prescribes circumstances in which an entity may change an accounting policy. The standard also deals with accounting treatment of changes in accounting policies, changes in accounting estimates and correction of prior errors.

You are the financial controller of Lifewest Ltd. The company began trading on 1 January 2007 and is currently involved in the preparation of financial statements for the year ended 31 December 2010. You have recently attended a one-day seminar on the application of International Financial Reporting Standards, organised by the Institute of Certified Public Accountants in Ireland (CPA). On 1 January 2010, the company had 50 million €1 ordinary shares in issue. On 30 June 2010, Lifewest Ltd issued 10 million 10% €1 irredeemable preference shares at par. There have been no other changes in share capital in the last five years. The appropriate dividend in respect of these shares was paid on 31 December 2010. A property revaluation at the year end gave a surplus of €250,000.

During the year ended 31 December 2010, Lifewest Ltd changed its accounting policy for depreciation in relation to the depreciation of property, plant and equipment. The depreciation charges calculated using the previous accounting policy and shown in the company's financial statements for three years ending 31 December 2009 were as follows:

	€000
Year to 31 December 2007	690
Year to 31 December 2008	810
Year to 31 December 2009	870

Assuming the new accounting policy had been applied in previous years, depreciation charges would have been:

	€000
Year to 31 December 2007	1,170
Year to 31 December 2008	930
Year to 31 December 2009	690

An extract from Lifewest Ltd's Statement of Comprehensive Income for the year to 31 December 2010 (before making any adjustments to reflect the change in accounting policy for the year 31 December 2009) shows the following:

	2010 €000	2009 €000
Profit before depreciation	7,530	7,350
Depreciation of property, plant and equipment	570	870
Profit before taxation	6,960	6,480
Taxation	2,088	1,944
Profit after taxation	4,872	4,536
Other Comprehensive Income:		
Gains on property revaluation	250	

Lifewest Ltd's retained earnings were reported as €8,829,000 at 31 December 2008. No dividends have been paid in any year. The company pays tax at 30% on the profit.

Required:

(a) Distinguish between accounting policies, accounting estimates and prior period errors.

(b) Present the extract from the Statement of Comprehensive Income so as to reflect the change in accounting policy, in accordance with IAS 8.

(c) Compute Lifewest Ltd's retained earnings at 31 December 2010 and the restated retained earnings as at 31 December 2008 and 2009.

(d) Prepare a statement of changes in equity for the year ended 31 December 2010.

(Institute of Certified Public Accountants (CPA), Professional Stage 1 Corporate Reporting Examination, August 2011)

References

1 IAS 10 *Events after the Reporting Period*, IASB, revised 2003.
2 IAS 8 *Accounting Policies, Changes in Accounting Estimates and Errors*.
3 IFRS 8 *Operating Segments*, IASB, 2006.
4 www.europarl.europa.eu/sides/getDoc.do?Type=TA&Reference=P6-TA-2007-0526&language=EN
5 http://www.esma.europa.eu/system/files/2011_372.pdf
6 IFRS 5 *Non-current Assets Held for Sale and Discontinued Operations*, IASB, revised 2009.
7 IAS 24 *Related Party Disclosures*, IASB, revised 2009.
8 L. Crawford, H. Extance and C. Helliar, *Operating Segments: The Usefulness of IFRS 8*, The Institute of Chartered Accountants of Scotland, 2012.

CHAPTER 5

Statements of cash flows

5.1 Introduction

The main purpose of this chapter is to explain the reasons for preparing a statement of cash flows and how to prepare a statement applying IAS 7.

Objectives

By the end of this chapter, you should be able to:

- prepare a statement of cash flows in accordance with IAS 7;
- analyse a statement of cash flows;
- critically discuss their strengths and weaknesses.

5.2 Development of statements of cash flows

We saw in Chapter 3 that, at the end of an accounting period, a statement of income is prepared which explains the change in the retained earnings at the beginning and end of an accounting period. In this chapter we prepare a statement of cash flows in accordance with IAS 7 *Statements of Cash Flows*.

IAS 7 explains the changes that have occurred in the amount of liquid assets easily accessible – these are defined as cash + cash equivalents.

5.2.1 Statements of cash flows – their benefits

As far back as 1991 Professor Arnold wrote in a report by the ICAEW Research Board and ICAS Research Advisory Committee *The Future Shape of Financial Reports*:[1]

> little attention is paid to the reporting entity's cash or liquidity position. Cash is the lifeblood of every business entity. The report . . . advocates that companies should provide a cash flow statement . . . preferably using the direct method.

Statements of cash flows are now primary financial statements and as important as statements of comprehensive income:

The emphasis on cash flows, and the emergence of the statement of cash flows as an important financial report, does not mean that operating cash flows are a substitute for, or are more important than, net income. In order to analyse financial statements correctly we need to consider **both** operating cash flows and net income.[2]

They are now primary financial statements because the financial viability and survival prospects of any organisation rest on the ability to generate positive operating cash flows. These are necessary in order to be able to pay the interest on loans and repay the loans, finance capital expenditure to maintain or expand operating capacity, and reward the investors with an acceptable dividend policy. If there is still a positive cash flow after this, it will help to reduce the need for additional external loan or equity funding.

The message is that, independent of reported profits, if an organisation is unable to generate sufficient cash, it will eventually become insolvent and fail.

The following extract from Heath and Rosenfield's article on solvency[3] is a useful conclusion to our analysis of the benefits of cash flow statements, emphasising that they also provide a basis for predicting future performance:

Solvency is a money or cash phenomenon. A solvent company is one with adequate cash to pay its debts; an insolvent company is one with inadequate cash . . . Any information that provides insight into the amounts, timings and certainty of a company's future cash receipts and payments is useful in evaluating solvency. Statements of past cash receipts and payments are useful for the same basic reason that statements of comprehensive income are useful in evaluating profitability: both provide a basis for predicting future performance.

5.3 Applying IAS 7 (revised) *Statements of Cash Flows*

5.3.1 IAS 7 format

The cash flows are analysed under three standard headings to explain the net increase/decrease in cash and cash equivalents and the effect on the opening amount of cash and cash equivalents. The headings are:

● Net cash generated by operating activities

● Cash flows from investing activities

● Cash flows from financing activities.

5.3.2 The two methods of presenting cash flows from operating activities

In the quote from *The Future Shape of Financial Reports* above, reference was made to the direct method. This preference was expressed because there are two methods, both of which are permitted by IAS 7. These are the direct method and the indirect method.

● The **direct** method reports cash inflows and outflows directly, starting with the major categories of gross cash receipts and payments. This means that cash flows such as receipts from customers and payments to suppliers are stated separately within the operating activities.

● The **indirect** method starts with the profit before tax and then adjusts this figure for non-cash items such as depreciation and changes in working capital.

5.3.3 Statement of cash flows illustrated using the direct method

The following shows the statement of cash flows for Tyro Bruce for the period ended 31.3.20X4.

	£000	£000
Cash flows from operating activities		
Cash received from customers (note (a))	11,740	
Cash paid to suppliers and employees (note (b))	(11,431)	
Cash generated from operations	309	
Interest paid (expense + (closing accrual – opening accrual))	(20)	
Income taxes paid (expense + (closing accrual – opening accrual))	(220)	
Net cash (used in) generated by operating activities		69
Cash flows from investing activities		
Purchase of property, plant and equipment	(560)	
Proceeds from sale of equipment	241	
Net cash used in investing activities		(319)
Cash flows from financing activities		
Proceeds from issue of shares at a premium	300	
Redemption of loan	(50)	
Dividends paid	(120)	
Net cash from financing activities		130
Net increase in cash and cash equivalents		(120)
Cash and cash equivalents at beginning of period		72
Cash and cash equivalents at end of period		(48)

Notes:

(a) Cash received from customers

	£000
Sales	12,000
Receivables increase	(260)
	11,740

(b) Cash paid to suppliers and employees

	£000
Cost of sales	10,000
Payables decreased	140
Inventory increased	900
Depreciation	(102)
Profit on sale	13
Distribution costs	300
Administration expenses	180
	11,431

5.3.4 Statement of cash flows illustrated using the indirect method

The two methods provide different types of information to the users. The indirect method applies changes in working capital to net income. In our illustration, for example, the cash generated from operations would be calculated as follows:

	£000
Cash flows from operating activities	
Profit before tax	1,500
Adjustments for non-cash items:	
Depreciation	102
Profit on sale of plant	(13)
Adjustments for changes in working capital:	
Increase in trade receivables	(260)
Increase in inventories	(900)
Decrease in trade payables	(140)
Interest expense (added back)	20
Cash generated from operations	309

5.3.5 Appraising the use of the direct method

The direct method demonstrates more of the qualities of a true cash flow statement because it provides more information about the sources and uses of cash. This information is not available elsewhere and helps in the estimation of future cash flows.

The principal advantage of the direct method is that it shows operating cash receipts and payments. Knowledge of the specific sources of cash receipts and the purposes for which cash payments were made in past periods may be useful in assessing future cash flows. Disclosure of *cash from customers* could provide additional information about an entity's ability to convert revenues to cash.

When is the direct method beneficial?

One such time is when the user is attempting to predict bankruptcy or future liquidation of the company. A research study looking at the cash flow differences between failed and non-failed companies[4] established that seven cash flow variables and suggested ratios captured statistically significant differences between failed and non-failed firms as much as five years prior to failure. The study further showed that the research findings supported the use of a direct cash flow statement, and the authors commented:

> An indirect cash flow statement will not provide a number of the cash flow variables for which we found significant differences between bankrupt and non-bankrupt companies. Thus, using an indirect cash flow statement could lead to ignoring important information about creditworthiness.

The direct method is the method preferred by the standard but preparers have a choice. In the UK the indirect method is often used; in other regions (e.g. Australia) the direct method is more common. It has been proposed in a review of IAS 7 that the direct method should be mandated and the alternative removed and this is the likely requirement in a new standard to eventually replace IAS 7.

5.3.6 Appraising the use of the indirect method

The principal advantage of the indirect method is that it highlights the differences between operating profit and net cash flow from operating activities to provide a measure of the quality of income. Many users of financial statements believe that such reconciliation is essential to give an indication of the quality of the reporting entity's earnings. Some investors and creditors assess future cash flows by estimating future income and then allowing for accruals adjustments; thus information about past accruals adjustments may be useful to help estimate future adjustments.

Preparer and user response

The IASB indicates that the responses to the discussion paper were mixed with the preparers tending to prefer the indirect method and the users having a mixed response. There was a view that the direct method would be improved if the movements on working capital were disclosed as supplementary information, and the indirect method would be improved if the cash from customers and payments to suppliers was disclosed as supplementary information; i.e., both are found useful.

5.3.7 Cash equivalents

IAS 7 recognised that companies' cash management practices vary in the amount of cash and range of short- to medium-term deposits that are held. The standard standardised the treatment of near-cash items by applying the following definition when determining whether items should be aggregated with cash in the statement of cash flows:

> Cash equivalents are short-term, highly liquid investments which are readily convertible into known amounts of cash and which are subject to an insignificant risk of changes in value.

Near-cash items are normally those that are within three months of maturity at the date of acquisition. Investments falling outside this definition are reported under the heading of 'investing activities'. In view of the variety of cash management practices and banking arrangements around the world and in order to comply with IAS 1 *Presentation of Financial Statements*, an entity discloses the policy which it adopts in determining the composition of cash and cash equivalents.

5.4 Step approach to preparation of a statement of cash flows – indirect method

We will now explain how to prepare a statement of cash flows for Tyro Bruce (Section 5.3.3) taking a step approach. We have shown our workings on the face of the statements of financial position and income.

Step 1: Calculate the differences in the statements of financial position and decide whether to report under operating, investing or financing activities or as a cash equivalent.

Statements of financial position of Tyro Bruce as at 31.3.20X3 and 31.3.20X4

	20X3		20X4		Calculate the differences	Decide which activities to report under
	£000	£000	£000	£000		
Non-current assets at cost	2,520		2,760		See PPE note	
Accumulated depreciation	452	2,068	462	2,298	for acquisitions or disposals	Investing/financing
Current assets						
Inventory	800		1,700		900	Operating
Trade receivables	640		900		260	Operating
Securities maturing less than 3 months at acquisition	—		20		20	Cash equivalent
Cash	80		10		70	Cash equivalent
	1,520		2,630			
Current liabilities						
Trade payables	540		400		140	Operating
Taxation	190		170		20	Operating
Overdraft	8		78		70	Cash equivalent
	738		648			
Net current assets		782		1,982		
		2,850		4,280		
Share capital	1,300		1,400		100	Financing
Share premium a/c	200		400		200	Financing
Retained earnings	1,150	2,650	1,150	2,950		
Profit for year		—		1,180		
10% loan 20×7		200		150	50	Financing
		2,850		4,280		

Step 2: Identify any items in the statement of income for the year ended 31.3.20X4 after profit before interest and tax (PBIT) to be entered under operating, investing or financing activities.

	£000	£000	
Sales		12,000	
Cost of sales		10,000	
Gross profit		2,000	
Distribution costs	300		
Administrative expenses	180	480	
PBIT		1,520	
Interest expense		(20)	Operating
Profit before tax		1,500	Operating
Income tax expense		(200)	Operating
Profit after tax		1,300	
Dividend paid		(120)	Financing
Retained earnings for year		1,180	

Step 3: Refer to the PPE schedule to identify any acquisitions, disposals and depreciation charges that affect the cash flows. The Tyro Bruce schedule showed:

	£000
Cost	
As at 31 March 20X3	2,520
(i) Additions	560
(iii) Disposal	(320)
As at 31.3.20X4	2,760
Accumulated depreciation	
As at 31.3.20X3	452
(ii) Charge for year	102
(iii) Disposal	(92)
As at 31.3.20X4	462
NBV as at 31.3.20X4	2,298
NBV as at 31.3.20X3	2,068

Note: Disposal proceeds were £241,000.

From Step 3 we can see that there are four impacts:

(i) Additions: The cash of £560,000 paid out on additions will appear under Investing.

(ii) The depreciation charge: This is a non-cash item and the £102,000 will be added back as a non-cash item to the profit before tax in the operating activities section.

(iii) Disposal proceeds: The cash received of £241,000 from the disposal was given in the Note and will appear under Investing activities. *If the note had provided you with the profit instead of the proceeds, then you would need to calculate the proceeds by taking the NBV and adjusting for any profit or loss. In this case it would be calculated as NBV of £228,000 (320,000 − 92,000) + the profit figure of £13,000 = £241,000.*

(iv) Profit on disposal: As the full proceeds of £241,000 are included under Investing activities there would be double counting to leave the profit of £13,000 within the profit before tax figure. It is therefore deducted as a non-cash item from PBT in the Operating activities section.

5.4.1 The statement of cash flows

The cash flow items can then be entered into the statement of cash flows in accordance with IAS 7.

		£000
Cash flows from operating activities		
Profit before tax		1,500
Adjustments for non-cash items:		
Depreciation	From Step 3 (ii)	102
Profit on sale of plant	From Step 3 (iv)	(13)
Adjustments for changes in working capital:		
Increase in trade receivables		(260)
Increase in inventories		(900)
Decrease in trade payables		(140)
Interest expense		20
Cash generated from operations		309
Interest paid (there are no closing or opening accruals)		(20)
Income taxes paid (expense + (opening accrual − closing accrual))	200 + (190 − 170)	(220)
Net cash (used in)/generated by operating activities		69
Cash flows from investing activities		
Purchase of property, plant and equipment	From Step 3 (i)	(560)
Proceeds from sale of equipment	From Step 3 (iii)	241
Net cash used in investing activities		(319)
Cash flows from financing activities		
Proceeds from issue of shares at a premium		300
Redemption of loan		(50)
Dividends paid		(120)
Net cash from financing activities		130
Net increase in cash and cash equivalents		(120)
Cash and cash equivalents at beginning of period	80 − 8	72
Cash and cash equivalents at end of period	(10 + 20) − 78	(48)

Note that interest paid and interest and dividends received could be classified either as operating cash flows or as financing (for interest paid) and investing cash flows (for receipts). Dividends paid could be presented either as financing cash flows or as operating cash flows. However, it is a requirement that whichever presentation is adopted by an enterprise should be consistently applied from year to year.

5.5 Additional notes required by IAS 7

As well as the presentation on the face of the cash flow statement, IAS 7 requires notes to the cash flow statement to help the user understand the information. The notes that are required are as follows.

Major non-cash transactions

If the entity has entered into major non-cash transactions that are therefore not represented on the face of the statement of cash flows, sufficient further information to understand the transactions should be provided in a note to the financial statements. Examples of major non-cash transactions might be:

- the acquisition of assets by way of finance leases;
- the conversion of debt to equity.

Components of cash and cash equivalents

An enterprise must disclose the components of cash and cash equivalents and reconcile these into the totals in the statement of financial position. An example of a suitable disclosure in the case of Tyro Bruce is:

	20X4	20X3
Cash	10	80
Securities	20	
Overdraft	(78)	(8)
Cash and cash equivalents	(48)	72

Disclosure must also be given on restrictions on the use by the group of any cash and cash equivalents held by the enterprise. These restrictions might apply if, for example, cash was held in foreign countries and could not be remitted back to the parent company.

Segmental information

IAS 7 encourages enterprises to disclose information about operating, investing and financing cash flows for each business and geographical segment. This disclosure may be relevant. IFRS 8 does not require a cash flow by segment.

5.6 Analysing statements of cash flows

Arranging cash flows into specific classes provides users with relevant and decision-useful information by classifying cash flows as cash generated from operations, net cash from operating activities, net cash flows from investing activities, and net cash flows from financing activities.

Lack of a clear definition

However, this does not mean that companies will necessarily report the same transaction in the same way. Although IAS 7 requires cash flows to be reported under these headings, it does not define operating activities except to say that it includes all transactions and other events that are not defined as investing or financing activities.

Alternative treatments

Alternative treatments for interest and dividends paid could be presented as either operating or financing cash flows. Whilst most companies choose to report the dividends as financing cash flows, when making inter-firm comparisons we need to see which alternative has been chosen. The choice can have a significant impact. If, for example, in the Tyro Bruce illustration the dividends of £120,000 were reported as an operating cash flow, then the net cash (used in)/generated by operating activities would change from an inflow of £69,000 to an outflow of £51,000.

The classifications assist users in making informed predictions about future cash flows or raising questions for further enquiry which would be difficult to make using traditional accrual-based techniques.[5]

We will briefly comment on the implication of each classification.

5.6.1 Cash generated from operations

In the Tyro Bruce example (Section 5.3.3) we can see that there has been a significant increase in working capital of £1,300,000 (£260,000 + £900,000 + £140,000).

The effect is to reduce the profit before tax from £1,500,000 to the £309,000 reported as cash flow from operations.

Lenders look to the cash generated from operations to pay interest and taxation, both of which are unavoidable – it is an indication of the safety margin, i.e. how long a business could continue to pay unavoidable costs.

Lenders in Tyro Bruce concerned with interest cover could see that there is sufficient cash available to meet their interest charges in the current year even though there has been a significant impact from the investment in working capital.

Interest cover

Interest cover is normally defined as the number of times the profit before interest and tax covers the interest charge: in the Tyro Bruce example this is 76 times (1,520/20). The position as disclosed in the statement of cash flows is a little weaker although, even so, the interest is still covered more than 15 times (309,000/20,000).

Cash debt coverage

In addition to interest cover, lenders want to be satisfied that their loan will be repaid. Failure to do so could lead to a going-concern problem for the company. One measure used is to calculate the ratio of cash flow generated by operating activities less dividend payments to total debt and, of more immediate interest, to loans that are about to mature.

The ratio can be adjusted to reflect the company's current position. For example, if there is a significant cash balance, it might be appropriate to add this on the basis that it would be available to meet the loan repayment.

In our example the cash coverage in the current year is low due to the heavy investment in working capital and payment of a dividend.

Cash dividend coverage

The ratio of cash flow from operating activities less interest paid to dividends paid indicates the ability to meet the current dividend. If the dividend rate shows a rising trend, dividends declared might be used rather than the cash flow dividend paid figure. This would give a better indication of the coverage ratio for future dividends. In our example coverage is again reduced by the working capital investment.

5.6.2 Future cash flows from operations

We need to consider trends, the discretionary costs and the investment in working capital.

Trends

We need to look at previous periods to identify the trend. Trends are important with investors naturally hoping to invest in a company with a rising trend. If there is a loss or a downward trend, this is a cause for concern and investors should make further enquiries to identify any proposed steps to improve the position.

This is where narrative may be helpful, such as that proposed in the IFRS Practice Statement *Management Commentary*, in the Strategic Review in the UK and in a Chairman's Statement. Reading these may give some indication as to how the company will be addressing the situation. For example, is the company planning a cost reduction programme or disposing of loss-making activities? If it is not possible to improve the trend or reverse the negative cash flow, then there could be future liquidity difficulties.

Discretionary costs

The implication for future cash flow is that such difficulties could have an impact on future discretionary costs, e.g. the curtailment of research, marketing or advertising expenditure; on investment decisions, e.g. postponing capital expenditure; and on financing decisions, e.g. the need to raise additional equity or loan capital.

Working capital

We can see the cash implication but would need to make further enquiries to establish the reasons for the change and the likelihood of similar cash outflow movements recurring in future years. If, for example, the increased investment in inventory resulted from an increase in turnover, then a similar increase could recur if the forecast turnover continued to increase. If, on the other hand, the increase was due to poor inventory control, then it is less likely that the increase will recur: in fact, quite the opposite as management addresses the problem.

The cash flow statement indicates the cash extent of the change; additional ratios (see Chapter 28) and enquiries are required to allow us to evaluate the change.

5.6.3 Evaluating the investing activities cash flows

These arise from the acquisition and disposal of non-current assets and investments.

It is useful to consider how much of the expenditure is to replace existing non-current assets and how much is to increase capacity. One way is to relate the cash expenditure to the depreciation charge; this indicates that the cash expenditure is more than five times greater than the depreciation charge, calculated as £540,000/£102,000. This seems to indicate a possible increase in productive capacity. However, the cash flow statement does not itemise the expenditure, as the extract from the non-current asset schedule does not reveal how much was spent on plant – this information would be available in practice.

How to inform investors how much of the capital expenditure relates to replacing existing non-current assets

There has been a criticism that it is not possible to assess how much of the investing activities cash outflow related to simply maintaining operations by replacing non-current assets that were worn out rather than to increasing existing capacity with a potential for an increase in turnover and profits. The solution proposed was that investment that is merely maintained should be shown as an operating cash flow and that the investing cash flow should be restricted to increasing capacity. The IASB doubted the reliability of such a distinction but there is a view that such an analysis provides additional information, provided the breakdown between the two types of expenditure can be reliably ascertained.

5.6.4 Evaluating the financing cash flows

Additional capital of £300,000 has been raised. After repaying a loan of £50,000 and payment of a dividend of £120,000, only £130,000 was left towards a net outflow of £250,000 (£319,000 − £69,000).

This does not allow us to assess the financing policy of the company, e.g. whether the capital was raised the optimum way. Nor does it allow us to assess whether the company would have done better to provide finance by improved control over its assets, e.g. working capital reduction.[6]

The indications are healthy in that the company is relying on earnings and equity capital to finance growth. It is lowly geared and further funds could be sought, possibly from the bank or private equity, particularly if it is required for capacity building purposes.

5.6.5 Reconciliation of net cash flows to net debt

Reconciling the movement in cash flows to the movement in net debt provides information that assists in the assessment of liquidity and solvency, e.g. investors review net debt levels for signs of financial distress. By way of illustration, the notes prepared for Tyro Bruce (see Section 5.4 above) would appear as follows:

		20X4		20X3
1 Borrowings		(150)		(200)
Overdraft	(78)		(8)	
Securities	20			
Cash	10		80	
		(48)		72
		(198)		(128)

2 Reconcile net cash flow to movement in net debt

Decrease in cash	(48 + 72)	(120)
Change in net debt resulting from cash	(200 − 150)	50
Movement in net debt	(198 − 128)	(70)
Net debt at beginning of period		(128)
Net debt at end of period		(198)

3 Analysis of net debt

	20X3	Cash flow	20X4
Cash at bank	80	(120)	10
Government securities			20
Overdraft	(8)		(78)
Debt outstanding	(200)	50	(150)
Net debt	(128)	(70)	(198)

5.6.6 Free cash flow (FCF)

This is a performance measure showing how much cash a company has for further investment after deducting from net cash generated by operating capital the amount spent on capital expenditure to maintain or expand its asset base. For example, Colt SA in its 2011 Annual Report states:

> Free cash flow is net cash generated from operating activities less net cash used to purchase non-current assets and net interest paid.

Free cash flow is reported by many companies and emphasised for different reasons. There is, however, no standardised definition. For example, the Kingfisher Group's 2010 Annual Report defines it after cash used for investment activities:

> The Group will maintain a high focus on free cash flow generation going forward to fund dividends to shareholders and increased investment in growth opportunities where returns are attractive.

However, Merck in its 2011 Annual Report states:

> Free cash flow and underlying free cash flow are indicators that we use internally to measure the contribution of our divisions to liquidity.

The amount of free cash flow will be normally positive for a mature company and negative for a younger company.

Capital expenditure ratio

This is a ratio where the numerator is *net cash flow generated by operating activities* and the denominator is *capital expenditures*. This ratio measures the capital available for internal reinvestment and for meeting existing debt. We look for a ratio that exceeds 1.0, showing that the company has funds to maintain its operational capability and has cash towards meeting its debt repayments and dividends. The ratio would be expected to be lower for companies in growth industries as opposed to those in mature industries and more variable in cyclical industries, such as housing.

It should be recognised, however, that there is a risk if a company has significant free cash flow that its managers may be too optimistic about future performance. When they are not reliant on satisfying external funders there could be less constraint on their investment decisions. If there is negative free cash flow then the opposite applies and the business would require external finance.

5.6.7 Voluntary disclosures

IAS 7 (paragraphs 50–52) lists additional information, supported by a management commentary that may be relevant to understanding:

- liquidity, e.g. the amount of undrawn borrowing facilities;
- future profitability, e.g. cash flow representing increases in operating capacity separate from cash flow maintaining operating capacity; and
- risk, e.g. cash flows for each reportable segment, to better understand the relationship between the entity's cash flows and each segment's cash flows.

5.7 Approach to answering questions with time constraints

We have explained the step approach with the explanatory detail on the statements of financial position and income. In an examination it is preferable to show the workings on the statement of cash flows itself as shown in the examination question for Riddle worked below.

The following are the statements of financial position and income for Riddle plc.

Statements of financial position as at 31 March

	20X8 $000	20X8 $000	20X9 $000	20X9 $000
Non-current assets:				
Property, plant and equipment, at cost	540		720	
Less accumulated depreciation	(145)		(190)	
		395		530
Investments		115		140
Current assets:				
Inventory	315		418	
Trade receivables	412		438	
Bank	48	775	51	907
Total assets		1,285		1,577
Capital and reserves:				
Ordinary shares	600		800	
Share premium	40		55	
Retained earnings	217	857	311	1,166
Non-current liabilities:				
12% debentures		250		200
Current liabilities:				
Trade payables	139		166	
Taxation	39	178	45	211
Total equity and liabilities		1,285		1,577

Statement of income for the year ended 31 March 20X9

	$000	$000
Revenue		2,460
Cost of sales		1,780
Gross profit		680
Distribution costs	(124)	
Administration expenses	(300)	(424)
Operating profit		256
Interest on debentures		(24)
Profit before tax		232
Tax		(48)
Profit after tax		184

Note: The statement of changes in equity disclosed a dividend of $90,000.

Teaching note: Take an initial look at the statement of financial position and notes to check whether or not there has been any disposal of non-current assets which would give rise to a profit or loss adjustment as a non-cash adjustment to the profit after tax figure in the statement of income. In the case of Riddle there have only been acquisitions.

Required
(a) Prepare the statement of cash flows for Riddle plc for the year ended 31 March 20X9 and show the operating cash flows using the 'indirect method'.
(b) Calculate the cash generated from operations using the 'direct method'.

Solution

(a) Using indirect method

Statement of cash flows for the year ended 31 March 20X9

		$000	$000
Cash from operating activities			
Profit before tax	Income statement		232
Adjustments for:			
Depreciation	190 – 145	45	
Interest expense		24	69
Operating profit before working capital changes			301
Increase in inventory	418 – 315	(103)	
Increase in trade receivables	438 – 412	(26)	
Increase in trade payables	166 – 139	27	(102)
Cash generated from operations			199
Interest paid		(24)	
Tax paid	39 + 48 – 45	(42)	(66)
Net cash used in operating activities			133
Cash flows from investing activities:			
Purchase of PPE	720 – 540	(180)	
Disposal proceeds of PPE	None in question		
Investments	140 – 115	(25)	(205)
Cash flows from financing activities:			
Share capital	800 – 600	200	
Share premium	55 – 40	15	
Debentures	200 – 250	(50)	
Dividends paid	Given in note	(90)	75
Net increase in cash and cash equivalents			3
Cash and cash equivalents at beginning of year			48
Cash and cash equivalents at end of year			51

(b) Cash generated from operations using the direct method

	$000	$000
(i) Received from customers		2,434
(ii) Paid to suppliers	1,856	
(iii) Paid expenses (124 + 300 – depreciation 45)	379	2,235
Cash generated from operations		199

(i) Received from customers

	$000
Trade receivables at beginning of year	412
Sales	2,460
	2,872
Less: Trade receivables at end of year	438
Cash received from customers	2,434

(ii) Paid to suppliers

	$000	$000
Trade payables at beginning of year		139
Cost of sales	1,780	
Closing inventory	418	
	2,198	
Less: Opening inventory	315	1,883
		2,022
Less: Trade payables at end of year		166
Cash paid to trade payables		1,856

Teaching note: Interest on the debentures is added back when preparing the statement using the indirect method. When using the direct method there is no need to include it within the payables calculation.

5.8 Critique of cash flow accounting

IAS 7 (revised) applies uniform requirements to the format and presentation of cash flow statements. It still, however, allows companies to choose between the direct and the indirect methods, and the presentation of interest and dividend cash flows. It can be argued, therefore, that it has failed to rectify the problem of a lack of comparability between statements.

An important point is that, in its search for improved comparability, IAS 7 (revised) reduced the scope for innovation. It might be argued that standard setters should not be reducing innovation, but that there should be concerted effort to increase innovation and improve the information available to user groups. The acceptability of innovation is a fundamental issue in a climate that is becoming increasingly prescriptive.

Summary

IAS 7 (revised) defines the format and treatment of individual items within the cash flow statement. This leads to uniformity and greater comparability between companies. However, there is still some criticism of the current IAS 7:

- There are options within IAS 7 for presentation, since either the direct or the indirect method can be used; and there are choices about the presentation of dividends and interest.
- The cash flow statement does not distinguish between discretionary and non-discretionary cash flows, which would be valuable information to users.
- There is no separate disclosure of cash flows for expansion from cash flows to maintain current capital levels. This distinction would be useful when assessing the position and performance of companies, and is not always easy to identify in the current presentation.
- The definition of cash and cash equivalents can cause problems in that companies may interpret which investments are cash equivalents differently, leading to a lack of comparability. Statements of cash flows could be improved by removing cash equivalents and concentrating solely on the movement in cash, which is the current UK practice.

REVIEW QUESTIONS

1 Explain the information that a user can obtain from a statement of cash flows that cannot be obtained from the current or comparative statements of financial position.

2 Discuss the limitations of a statement of cash flows when evaluating a company's control over its working capital.

3 Discuss the relationship between future discretionary costs and the statement of cash flows.

4 Many people preferred the direct method for cash flow preparation, but IAS 7 did not require it. Discuss possible circumstances when the direct method may be beneficial.

5 Discuss why the IASB preferred to reconcile to cash equivalents rather than reconciling to cash.

6 Explain why the financing section of a statement of cash flows does not allow a user to assess a company's financing policy.

7 A negative free cash flow is always a sign of a company in trouble. Discuss.

8 Explain the entries in the statement of cash flows when a non-current asset is sold (a) at a loss and (b) at a profit.

9 There is a view that if a company shows a healthy operating profit but low or negative operating cash flows then there might be a suspicion that there has been earnings manipulation. Discuss why there might be such suspicion.

EXERCISES

* Question 1

Direct plc provided the following information from its records for the year ended 30 September 20X9:

	€000	
Sales	316,000	
Cost of goods sold	110,400	
Other expenses	72,000	
Rent expense	14,400	
Dividends	10,000	
Amortisation expense – PPE	8,000	
Advertising expense	4,800	
Gain on sale of equipment	2,520	
Interest expense	320	

	20X9	20X8
Accounts receivable	13,200	15,200
Unearned revenue	8,000	9,600
Inventory	18,400	19,200
Prepaid advertising	0	400
Accounts payable	11,200	8,800
Rent payable	0	1,200
Interest payable	40	0

Required:

Using the direct method of presentation, prepare the cash flows from the operating activities section of the statement of cash flows for the year ended 30 September 20X9.

* Question 2

Marwell plc reported a profit after tax of €14.04m for 20X2 as follows:

	€m	€m
Revenue		118.82
Materials	29.70	
Wages	30.80	
Depreciation	22.68	
Loss on disposal of plant	3.78	
Profit on sale of buildings	(6.48)	
		80.48
Operating profit		38.34
Interest payable		16.20
Profit before tax		22.14
Income tax expense		8.10
Profit after tax		14.04

The statements of financial position and changes in equity showed:

(i)   Inventories at the year end were €5.94m higher than the previous year.

(ii)   Trade receivables were €10.26m higher.

(iii)   Trade payables were €4.86m lower.

(iv)   Tax payable had increased by €2.7m.

(v)   Dividends totalling €18.36m had been paid during the year.

Required:

(a) Calculate the net cash flow from operating activities.

(b) Explain why depreciation and a loss made on disposal of a non-current asset are both treated as a source of cash.

* Question 3

The statements of financial position of Flow Ltd for the years ended 31 December 20X5 and 20X6 were as follows:

	20X5		20X6	
	€	€	€	€
Non-current assets				
Tangible assets				
PPE at cost	1,743,750		1,983,750	
Accumulated depreciation	551,250	1,192,500	619,125	1,364,625
Current assets				
Inventory		101,250		85,500
Trade receivables		252,000		274,500
		1,545,750		1,724,625
Capital and reserves				
Common shares of €1 each		900,000		1,350,000
Share premium				30,000
Retained earnings		387,000		176,625
Current liabilities				
Trade payables		183,750		159,750
Bank overdraft		75,000		8,250
		1,545,750		1,724,625

Note that during the year ended 31 December 20X6:

1 Equipment that had cost €25,500 and with a net book value of €9,375 was sold for €6,225.
2 The company paid a dividend of €45,000.
3 A bonus issue was made at the beginning of the year of one bonus share for every three shares.
4 A new issue of 150,000 shares was made on 1 July 20X6 at a price of €1.20 for each share.
5 A dividend of €60,000 was declared but no entries had been made in the books of the company.

Required:
(a) Prepare a statement of cash flows for the year ended 31 December 20X6 that complies with IAS 7.
(b) Briefly explain ways in which statements of cash flows may be more useful than statements of income.

* Question 4

The statements of financial position of Radar plc at 30 September were as follows:

	20X8		20X9	
	$000	$000	$000	$000
Non-current assets:				
Property, plant and equipment, at cost	760		920	
Less accumulated depreciation	(288)		(318)	
		472		602
Investments		186		214
Current assets:				
Inventory	596		397	
Trade receivables	332		392	
Bank	5	933	—	789
Total assets		1,591		1,605
Capital and reserves:				
Ordinary shares	350		500	
Share premium	75		125	
Retained earnings	137	562	294	919
Non-current liabilities:				
12% debentures		400		100
Current liabilities:				
Trade payables	478		396	
Accrued expenses	64		72	
Taxation	87		96	
Overdraft	—		22	
		629		586
Total equity and liabilities		1,591		1,605

The following information is available:

(i) An impairment review of the investments disclosed that there had been an impairment of $20,000.

(ii) The depreciation charge made in the statement of comprehensive income was $64,000.

(iii) Equipment costing $72,000 was sold for $54,000 which gave a profit of $16,000.

(iv) The debentures redeemed in the year were redeemed at a premium of 25%.

(v) The premium paid on the debentures was written off to the share premium account.

(vi) The income tax expense was $92,000.

(vii) A dividend of $25,000 had been paid and dividends of $17,000 had been received.

Required:
Prepare a statement of cash flows for the year ended 30 September using the indirect method.

Question 5

Shown below are the summarised final accounts of Martel plc for the last two financial years:

Statements of financial position as at 31 December

	20X1		20X0	
	£000	£000	£000	£000
Non-current assets				
Tangible				
Land and buildings	1,464		1,098	
Plant and machinery	520		194	
Motor vehicles	140		62	
		2,124		1,354
Current assets				
Inventory	504		330	
Trade receivables	264		132	
Government securities	40		—	
Bank	—		22	
	808		484	
Current liabilities				
Trade payables	266		220	
Taxation	120		50	
Proposed dividend	72		40	
Bank overdraft	184		—	
	642		310	
Net current assets		166		174
Total assets less current liabilities		2,290		1,528
Non-current liabilities				
9% debentures		(432)		(350)
		1,858		1,178
Capital and reserves				
Ordinary shares of 50p each fully paid		900		800
Share premium account	120		70	
Revaluation reserve	360		—	
General reserve	100		50	
Retained earnings	378		258	
		958		378
		1,858		1,178

Summarised statement of comprehensive income for the year ending 31 December

	20X1	20X0
	£000	£000
Operating profit	479	215
Interest paid	52	30
Profit before taxation	427	185
Tax	149	65
Profit after taxation	278	120

Additional information:

1 The movement in non-current assets during the year ended 31 December 20X1 was as follows:

	Land and buildings	Plant, etc.	Motor vehicles
	£000	£000	£000
Cost at 1 January 20X1	3,309	470	231
Revaluation	360	—	—
Additions	81	470	163
Disposals	—	(60)	—
Cost at 31 December 20X1	3,750	880	394
Depreciation at 1 January 20X1	2,211	276	169
Disposals	—	(48)	—
Added for year	75	132	85
Depreciation at 31 December 20X1	2,286	360	254

The plant and machinery disposed of during the year was sold for £20,000.

2 During 20X1, a rights issue was made of one new ordinary share for every eight held at a price of £1.50.

3 A dividend of £36,000 (20X0 £30,000) was paid in 20X1. A dividend of £72,000 (20X0 £40,000) was proposed for 20X1. A transfer of £50,000 was made to the general reserve.

Required:

(a) Prepare a statement of cash flows for the year ended 31 December 20X1, in accordance with IAS 7.

(b) Prepare a report on the liquidity position of Martel plc for a shareholder who is concerned about the lack of liquid resources in the company.

The statements of financial position of Maytix as at 31 October 2005 and 31 October 2004 are as follows:

	2005		2004	
	$000	$000	$000	$000
Non-current assets:				
Property, at cost	4,000		3,000	
Plant and equipment, at cost	7,390		4,182	
Less accumulated depreciation	(1,450)		(1,452)	
		9,940		5,730
Current assets:				
Inventory	5,901		4,520	
Trade receivables	2,639		2,233	
Bank	—	8,540	1,007	7,760
		18,480		13,490
Capital and reserves:				
Ordinary shares	5,000		3,500	
Share premium	2,500		1,000	
Retained earnings	2,110	9,610	3,090	7,590
Non-current liabilities:				
10% loan stock		4,750		3,750
Current liabilities:				
Trade payables	1,237		1,700	
Taxation	550		450	
Bank overdraft	2,333	4,120	—	2,150
		18,480		13,490

The statement of comprehensive income of Maytix for the year ended 31 October 2005 is as follows:

	$000	$000
Credit sales		9,500
Cash sales		1,047
Cost of sales		(8,080)
Gross profit		2,467
Distribution costs	(501)	
Administration expenses	(369)	(870)
Operating profit		1,597
Interest on loan stock		(425)
Loss on disposal of non-current assets		(102)
Profit before tax		1,070
Tax		(550)
Profit after tax		520

Notes:
(i) The 'statement of changes in equity' disclosed a dividend paid figure of $1,500,000 during the year to 31 October 2005.

(ii) The non-current asset schedule revealed the following details:

Property: Additions cost $1,000,000.

Plant and equipment	Cost	Depreciation	NBV
	$000	$000	$000
Balance at 31.10.2004	4,182	(1,452)	2,730
Additions	6,278	—	6,278
Annual charge	—	(540)	(540)
	10,460	(1,992)	8,468
Disposal	(3,070)	542	(2,528)
Balance at 31.10.2005	7,390	(1,450)	5,940

Required:

(a) Prepare the cash flow statement of Maytix for the year ended 31 October 2005. Use the format required by IAS 7 *Cash Flow Statements* and show operating cash flows using the indirect method.

(b) Describe the additional information that would be included in a cash flow statement showing operating cash flows using the direct method and discuss the proposition that such disclosures be made compulsory under IAS 7.

(The Association of International Accountants)

Question 7

The financial statements of Saturn plc have been prepared as follows:

Statements of financial position as at 30 June	20X2 €000	20X2 €000	20X1 €000	20X1 €000
Non-current assets:				
Property, plant and equipment at cost	6,600		5,880	
Accumulated depreciation	(1,680)	4,920	(1,380)	4,500
Development costs		540		480
Investments		420		300
Current assets:				
Inventory	1,665		1,872	
Trade receivables	1,446		1,188	
Cash	9	3,120	42	3,102
		9,000		8,382
Equity and reserves				
Ordinary shares of €1 each	3,000		2,700	
Share premium account	600		270	
Retained earnings	3,084	6,684	2,622	5,592
Non-current liability:				
7% debentures	—			1,200
Current liabilities:				
Trade payables	1,632		1,104	
Taxation	507		396	
Dividend declared	60		90	
Bank overdraft	117	2,316	—	1,590
		9,000		8,382

Further information:

(a) Extract from statement of income

	€000
Operating profit	1,008
Dividend received	36
Premium on debentures	(120)
Interest paid	(144)
Profit before taxation	780
Income tax	(258)
Profit after tax	522

(b) Operating expenses written off in the year include the following:

	€000
Amortisation of development costs	102
Depreciation of property, plant and equipment	318

(c) Equipment which had cost €240,000 was sold in the year, incurring a loss of €156,000.

(d) The debentures were redeemed at a premium of 10%.

Required:
Prepare a statement of cash flows for the year ended 30 June 20X2.

References

1 J. Arnold *et al.*, *The Future Shape of Financial Reports*, ICAEW and ICAS, 1991.
2 G.H. Sorter, M.J. Ingberman and H.M. Maximon, *Financial Accounting: An Events and Cash Flow Approach*, McGraw-Hill, 1990.
3 L.J. Heath and P. Rosenfield, 'Solvency: the forgotten half of financial reporting', in R. Bloom and P.T. Elgers (eds), *Accounting Theory and Practice*, Harcourt Brace Jovanovich, 1987, p. 586.
4 J.M. Gahlon and R.L. Vigeland, 'Early warning signs of bankruptcy using cash flow analysis', *Journal of Commercial Lending*, December 1988, pp. 4–15.
5 J.W. Henderson and T.S. Maness, *The Financial Analyst's Deskbook*, Van Nostrand Reinhold, 1989, p. 72.
6 G. Holmes and A. Sugden, *Interpreting Company Reports and Accounts* (5th edition), Woodhead-Faulkner, 1995, p. 134.

PART 2

Income and asset value measurement systems

Income and asset value measurement: an economist's approach

6.1 Introduction

The main purpose of this chapter is to explain the need for income measurement, to compare the methods of measurement adopted by the accountant with those adopted by the economist, and to consider how both are being applied within the international financial reporting framework.

Objectives

By the end of this chapter, you should be able to:

- explain the role and objective of income measurement;
- explain the accountant's view of income, capital and value;
- critically comment on the accountant's measure;
- explain the economist's view of income, capital and value;
- critically comment on the economist's measure;
- define various capital maintenance systems.

6.2 Role and objective of income measurement

Although accountancy has played a part in business reporting for centuries, it is only since the Companies Act 1929 that financial reporting has become income orientated. Prior to that Act, a statement of income was of minor importance. It was the statement of financial position that mattered, providing a list of capital, assets and liabilities that revealed the financial soundness and solvency of the business.

According to some commentators,[1] this scenario may be attributed to the sources of capital funding. Until the late 1920s, as in present-day Germany, external capital finance in the UK was mainly in the hands of bankers, other lenders and trade creditors. As the main users of published financial statements, they focused on the company's ability to pay trade creditors and the interest on loans, and to meet the scheduled dates of loan repayment: they were interested in the short-term liquidity and longer-term solvency of the entity.

Thus the statement of financial position was the prime document of interest. Perhaps in recognition of this, the English statement of financial position, until recent times, tended to show liabilities on the left-hand side, thus making them the first part of the statement of financial position read.

The gradual evolution of a sophisticated investment market, embracing a range of financial institutions, together with the growth in the number of individual investors, caused a reorientation of priorities. Investor protection and investor decision-making needs started to dominate the financial reporting scene, and the revenue statement replaced the statement of financial position as the sovereign reporting document.

Consequently, attention became fixed on the statement of comprehensive income and on concepts of accounting for profit. Moreover, investor protection assumed a new meaning. It changed from simply protecting the **capital** that had **been invested** to protecting the **income information** used by investors when making an investment decision.

However, the sight of major companies experiencing severe liquidity problems over the past decade has revived interest in the statement of financial position; while its light is perhaps not of the same intensity as that of the profit and loss account, it cannot be said to be totally subordinate to its accompanying statement of income.

The main objectives of income measurement are to provide:

● a means of control in a micro- and macroeconomic sense;

● a means of prediction;

● a basis for taxation.

We consider each of these below.

6.2.1 Income as a means of control

Assessment of stewardship performance

Managers are the stewards appointed by shareholders. Income, in the sense of net income or net profit, is the crystallisation of their accountability. Maximisation of income is seen as a major aim of the entrepreneurial entity, but the capacity of the business to pursue this aim may be subject to political and social constraints in the case of large public monopolies, and private semi-monopolies such as British Telecommunications plc.

Maximisation of net income is reflected in the earnings per share (EPS) figure, which is shown on the face of the published statement of income. The importance of this figure to the shareholders is evidenced by contracts that tie directors' remuneration to growth in EPS. A rising EPS may result in an increased salary or bonus for directors and upward movement in the market price of the underlying security. The effect on the market price is indicated by another extremely important statistic, which is influenced by the statement of comprehensive income: namely, the price/earnings (PE) ratio. The PE ratio reveals the numerical relationship between the share's current market price and the last reported EPS. EPS and PE ratios are discussed in Chapters 27 and 29.

Actual performance versus predicted performance

This comparison enables the management and the investing public to use the lessons of the past to improve future performance. The public, as shareholders, may initiate a change in the company directorate if circumstances necessitate it. This may be one reason why management is generally loath to give a clear, quantified estimate of projected results – such an estimate is a potential measure of efficiency. The comparison of actual with projected results identifies apparent underachievement.

The macroeconomic concept

Good government is, of necessity, involved in managing the macroeconomic scene and as such is a user of the income measure. State policies need to be formulated concerning the allocation of economic resources and the regulation of firms and industries, as illustrated by the measures taken by Oftel and Ofwat to regulate the size of earnings by British Telecom and the water companies.

6.2.2 Income as a means of prediction

Dividend and retention policy

The profit generated for the year influences the payment of a dividend, its scale and the residual income after such dividend has been paid. Other influences are also active, including the availability of cash resources within the entity, the opportunities for further internal investment and the dividend policies of capital-competing entities with comparable shares.

However, some question the soundness of using the profit generated for the year when making a decision to invest in an enterprise. Their view is that such a practice misunderstands the nature of income data, and that the appropriate information is the prospective cash flows. They regard the use of income figures from past periods as defective because, even if the future accrual accounting income could be forecast accurately, 'it is no more than an imperfect surrogate for future cash flows'.[2]

The counter-argument is that there is considerable resistance by both managers and accountants to the publication of future operating cash flows and dividend payments.[3] This means that, in the absence of relevant information, an investor needs to rely on a surrogate. The question then arises: which is the best surrogate?

In the short term, the best surrogate is the information that is currently available, i.e. income measured according to the accrual concept. In the longer term, management will be pressed by the shareholders to provide the actual forecast data on operating cash flows and dividend distribution, or to improve the surrogate information, by for example reporting the cash earnings per share.

More fundamentally, Revsine has suggested that ideal information for investors would indicate the economic value of the business (and its assets) based on expected future cash flows. However, the Revsine suggestion itself requires information on future cash flows that it is not possible to obtain at this time.[4] Instead, he considered the use of replacement cost as a surrogate for the economic value of the business, and we return to this later in the chapter.

Future performance

While history is not a faultless indicator of future events and their financial results, it does have a role to play in assessing the level of future income. In this context, historic income is of assistance to existing investors, prospective investors and management.

6.2.3 Basis for taxation

The contemporary taxation philosophy, in spite of criticism from some economists, uses income measurement to measure the taxable capacity of a business entity.

However, the determination of income by HM Revenue and Customs is necessarily influenced by socioeconomic fiscal factors, among others, and thus accounting profit is subject to adjustment in order to achieve taxable profit. As a tax base, it has been continually eroded as the difference between accounting income and taxable income has grown.[2]

Her Majesty's Revenue and Customs in the UK has tended to disallow expenses that are particularly susceptible to management judgement. For example, a uniform capital allowance is substituted for the subjective depreciation charge that is made by management, and certain provisions that appear as a charge in the statement of income are not accepted as an expense for tax purposes until the loss crystallises, e.g. a charge to increase the doubtful debts provision may not be allowed until the debt is recognised as bad.

6.3 Accountant's view of income, capital and value

Variations between accountants and economists in measuring income, capital and value are caused by their different views of these measures. In this section, we introduce the accountant's view and, in Section 6.5, the economist's, in order to reconcile variations in methods of measurement.

6.3.1 The accountant's view

Income is an important part of accounting theory and practice, although until 1970, when a formal system of propagating standard accounting practice throughout the accountancy profession began, it received little attention in accountancy literature. The characteristics of measurement were basic and few, and tended to be of an intuitive, traditional nature, rather than being spelled out precisely and given mandatory status within the profession.

Accounting tradition of historical cost

The statement of income is based on the actual costs of business transactions, i.e. the costs incurred in the currency and at the price levels pertaining at the time of the transactions.

Accounting income is said to be historical income, i.e. it is an *ex post* measure because it takes place after the event. The traditional statement of income is historical in two senses: because it concerns a past period, and because it utilises historical cost, being the cost of the transactions on which it is based. It follows that the statement of financial position, being based on the residuals of transactions not yet dealt with in the statement of income, is also based on historical cost.

In practice, certain amendments may be made to historical cost in both the statement of comprehensive income and statement of financial position, but historical cost still predominates in both statements. It is justified on a number of counts which, in principle, guard against the manipulation of data.

The main characteristics of historical cost accounting are as follows:

- **Objectivity**. It is a predominantly objective system, although it does exhibit aspects of subjectivity. Its nature is generally understood and it is invariably supported by independent documentary evidence, e.g. an invoice, statement, cheque, cheque counterfoil, receipt or voucher.

- **Factual**. As a basis of fact (with exceptions such as when amended in furtherance of revaluation), it is verifiable and to that extent is beyond dispute.

- **Profit or income concept**. Profit as a concept is generally well understood in a capital market economy, even if its precise measurement may be problematic. It constitutes the difference between revenue and expenditure or, in the economic sense, between opening and closing net assets.

Unfortunately, historical cost is not without its weaknesses. It is not always objective, owing to alternative definitions of revenue and costs and the need for estimates.

For example, although inventories are valued at the lower of cost or net realisable value, the cost will differ depending upon the definition adopted, e.g. first-in-first-out, last-in-first-out or standard cost.

Estimation is needed in the case of inventory valuation, assessing possible bad debts, accruing expenses, providing for depreciation and determining the profit attributable to long-term contracts. So, although it is transaction based, there are aspects of historical cost reporting that do not result from an independently verifiable business transaction. This means that profit is not always a unique figure.

Assets are often subjected to revaluation. In an economy of changing price levels, the historical cost system has been compromised by a perceived need to restate the carrying value of those assets that comprise a large proportion of a company's capital employed, e.g. land and buildings. This practice is controversial, not least because it is said to imply that a statement of financial position is a list of assets at market valuation, rather than a statement of unamortised costs not yet charged against revenue.

However, despite conventional accountancy income being partly the result of subjectivity, it is largely the product of the historical cost concept. A typical accounting policy specified in the published accounts of companies now reads as follows:

> The financial statements are prepared under the historical cost conventions as modified by the revaluation of certain non-current assets.

Nature of accounting income as an ex post measure

Accounting income is defined in terms of the business entity. It is the excess of revenue from sales over direct and allocated indirect costs incurred in the achievement of such sales. Its measure results in a net figure. It is the numerical result of the matching and accruals concepts discussed in the preceding chapter.

Accounting income is transaction based and therefore can be said to be factual, in as much as the revenue and costs have been realised and will be reflected in cash inflow and outflow, although not necessarily within the financial year.

Under accrual accounting, the sales for a financial period are offset by the expenses incurred in generating such sales. Objectivity is a prime characteristic of accrual accounting, but the information cannot be entirely objective because of the need to break up the ongoing performance of the business entity into calendar periods or financial years for purposes of accountability reporting. The allocation of expenses between periods requires a prudent estimate of some costs, e.g. the provision for depreciation and bad debts attributable to each period.

Accounting income is presented in the form of the conventional statement of income. This statement of income, in being based on actual transactions, is concerned with a past-defined period of time. Thus accounting profit is said to be historical income, i.e. an *ex post* measure because it is after the event.

Nature of accounting capital

The business enterprise requires the use of non-monetary assets, e.g. buildings, plant and machinery, office equipment, motor vehicles, stock of raw materials and work in progress. Such assets are not consumed in any one accounting period, but give service over a number of periods; therefore, the unconsumed portions of each asset are carried forward from period to period and appear in the statement of financial position. This document itemises the unused asset balances at the date of the financial year-end. In addition to listing unexpired costs of non-monetary assets, the statement of financial position also displays monetary assets such as trade receivables and cash balances, together with monetary liabilities, i.e.

moneys owing to trade creditors, other creditors and lenders. Funds supplied by shareholders and retained income following the distribution of dividend are also shown. Retained profits are usually added to shareholders' capital, resulting in what is known as shareholders' funds. These represent the company's equity capital.

Statement of income as a linking statement

The net assets of the firm, i.e. that fund of unconsumed assets which exceeds moneys attributable to payables and lenders, constitutes the company's net capital, which is the same as its equity capital. Thus the statement of income of a financial period can be seen as a linking statement between that period's opening and closing statement of financial positions: in other words, income may be linked with opening and closing capital. This linking may be expressed by formula, as follows:

$$Y_{0-1} = NA_1 - NA_0 + D_{0-1}$$

where Y_{0-1} = income for the period of time t_0 to t_1; NA_0 = net assets of the entity at point of time t_0; NA_1 = net assets of the entity at point of time t_1; and D_{0-1} = dividends or distribution during period t_{0-1}.

Less formally: Y = income of financial year; NA_0 = net assets as shown in the statement of financial position at beginning of financial year; NA_1 = net assets as shown in the statement of financial position at end of financial year; and D_{0-1} = dividends paid and proposed for the financial year. We can illustrate this as follows:

Income Y_{0-1} for the financial year t_{0-1} as compiled by the accountant was £1,200

Dividend D_{0-1} for the financial year t_{0-1} was £450

Net assets NA_0 at the beginning of the financial year were £6,000

Net assets NA_1 at the end of the financial year were £6,750.

The income account can be linked with opening and closing statements of financial position, namely:

$$
\begin{aligned}
Y_{0-1} &= NA_1 - NA_0 + D_{0-1} \\
&= £6,750 - £6,000 + £450 \\
&= £1,200 = Y_{0-1}
\end{aligned}
$$

Thus Y has been computed by using the opening and closing capitals for the period where capital equals net assets.

In practice, however, the accountant would compute income Y by compiling a statement of income. So, of what use is this formula? For reasons to be discussed later, the economist finds use for the formula when it is amended to take account of what we call **present values**. Computed after the end of a financial year, it is the *ex post* measure of income.

Nature of traditional accounting value

As the values of assets still in service at the end of a financial period have been based on the unconsumed costs of such assets, they are the by-product of compiling the statement of income. These values have been fixed not by direct measurement, but simply by an assessment of costs consumed in the process of generating period turnover. We can say, then, that the statement of financial position figure of net assets is a residual valuation after measuring income.

However, it is not a value in the sense of worth or market value as a buying price or selling price; it is merely a **value of unconsumed costs of assets**. This is an important point that will be encountered again later.

6.4 Critical comment on the accountant's measure

6.4.1 Virtues of the accountant's measure

As with the economist's, the accountant's measure is not without its virtues. These are invariably aspects of the historical cost concept, such as objectivity, being transaction based and being generally understood.

6.4.2 Faults of the accountant's measure

Principles of historical cost and profit realisation

The historical cost and profit realisation concepts are firmly entrenched in the transaction basis of accountancy. However, in practice, the two concepts are not free of adjustments. Because of such adjustments, some commentators argue that the system produces a hetero-geneous mix of values and realised income items.[5]

For example, in the case of asset values, certain assets such as land and buildings may have a carrying figure in the statement of financial position based on a revaluation to market value, while other assets such as motor vehicles may still be based on a balance of unallocated cost. The statement of financial position thus pretends on the one hand to be a list of result-ant costs pending allocation over future periods, and on the other hand to be a statement of current values.

Prudence concept

This concept introduces caution into the recognition of assets and income for financial reporting purposes. The cardinal rule is that income should not be recorded or recognised within the system until it is realised, but unrealised losses should be recognised immediately.

However, not all unrealised profits are excluded. For example, practice is that attribut-able profit on long-term contracts still in progress at the financial year-end may be taken into account. As with non-current assets, rules are not applied uniformly.

Unrealised capital profits

Capital profits have been ignored as income until they are realised, when, in the accounting period of sale, they are acknowledged by the reporting system. This has meant that all the profit has been recognised in one financial period when, in truth, the surplus was generated over successive periods by gradual growth, albeit unrealised until disposal of the asset. Thus a portion of what are now realised profits applies to prior periods. Not all of this profit should be attributed to the period of sale. The introduction of the statement of comprehen-sive income has addressed this by including revaluation gains.

Going concern

The going concern concept is fundamental to accountancy and operates on the assumption that the business entity has an indefinite life. It is used to justify basing the periodic reports of asset values on carrying forward figures that represent unallocated costs, i.e. to justify the non-recognition of the realisable or disposal values of non-monetary assets and, in so doing, the associated unrealised profits/losses. Although the life of an entity is deemed indefinite, there is uncertainty, and accountants are reluctant to predict the future. When they are matching costs with revenue for the current accounting period, they follow the prudence concept of reasonable certainty.

In the long term, economic income and accountancy income are reconciled. The unreal-ised profits of the economic measure are eventually realised and, at that point, they will be recognised by the accountant's measure. In the short term, however, they give different results for each period.

What if we cannot assume that a business will continue as a going concern?

There may be circumstances, as in the case of HMV which in 2012 warned that, following falling sales, there was a material uncertainty on being able to continue as a going concern. The uncertainty may be reduced by showing that active steps are being taken such as introducing new sales initiatives, restructuring, cost reduction and raising additional share capital which will ensure the survival of the business. If survival is not possible, the business will prepare its accounts using net realisable values, which are discussed in the next chapter.

The key considerations for shareholders are whether there will be sufficient profits to support dividend distributions and whether they will be able to continue to dispose of their shares in the open market. The key consideration for the directors is whether there will be sufficient cash to allow the business to trade profitably. We can see all these considerations being addressed in the following extract from the 2011 Annual Report of Grontmij N.V.

> **Going concern**
> the Group faced declines in its operating results during 2011 and was unable to meet its original debt covenant ratios . . . the Company obtained a waiver . . . met the covenant levels set by the waiver . . . a deferral was granted . . . apparent that a redesign of the capital structure of the Company is required to sustain the operations of the Company in the long term . . . after a financial review by the management, it was concluded that the capital structure of the Company should consist of a committed credit facility agreement and additional equity ('the rights issue') . . . the Company reached, in principle, agreement with its major shareholders and the banks . . . as a consequence of the above, the 2011 financial statements are prepared on a going concern basis. The Company does, however, draw attention to the fact that the ability to continue as a going concern is dependent on the continuing support of its shareholders and banks . . .

6.5 Economist's view of income, capital and value

Let us now consider the economist's tradition of present value and the nature of economic income.

6.5.1 Economist's tradition of present value

Present value is a technique used in valuing a future money flow, or in measuring the money value of an existing capital stock in terms of a predicted cash flow *ad infinitum*.

Present value (PV) constitutes the nature of economic capital and, indirectly, economic income. Given the choice of receiving £100 now or £100 in one year's time, the rational person will opt to receive £100 now. This behaviour exhibits an intuitive appreciation of the fact that £100 today is worth more than £100 one year hence. Thus the mind has **discounted** the value of the future sum: £100 today is worth £100; but compared with today, i.e. **compared with present value**, a similar sum receivable in twelve months' time is worth less than £100. How much less is a matter of subjective evaluation, but compensation for the time element may be found by reference to interest: a person forgoing the spending of £1 today and spending it one year later may earn interest of, say, 10% per annum in compensation for the sacrifice undergone by deferring consumption.

So £1 today invested at 10% p.a. will be worth £1.10 one year later, £1.21 two years later, £1.331 three years later, and so on. This is the concept of compound interest. It may be calculated by the formula $(1 + r)^n$, where 1 = the sum invested; r = the rate of interest; and n = the number of periods of investment (in our case years). So for £1 invested at 10% p.a. for four years:

$$(1 + r)^n = (1 + 0.10)^4$$
$$= (1.1)^4$$
$$= £1.4641$$

and for five years:

$$= (1.1)^5$$
$$= £1.6105, \text{ and so on.}$$

Notice how the **future value** increases because of the compound interest element – it **varies** over time – whereas the investment of £1 remains constant. So, conversely, the sum of £1.10 received at the end of year 1 has a PV of £1, as does £1.21 received at the end of year 2 and £1.331 at the end of year 3.

It has been found convenient to construct tables to ease the task of calculating present values. These show the cash flow, i.e. the future values, at a constant figure of £1 and allow the investment to vary. So:

$$PV = \frac{CF}{(1 + r)^n}$$

where CF = anticipated cash flow; and r = the discount (i.e. interest) rate. So the PV of a cash flow of £1 receivable at the end of one year at 10% p.a. is:

$$\frac{£1}{(1 + r)^1} = £0.9091$$

and of £1 at the end of two years:

$$\frac{£1}{(1 + r)^2} = £0.8264$$

and so on over successive years. The appropriate present values for years 3, 4 and 5 would be £0.7513, £0.6830, £0.6209 respectively.

£0.9091 invested today at 10% p.a. will produce £1 at the end of one year. The PV of £1 receivable at the end of two years is £0.8264 and so on.

Tables presenting data in this way are called 'PV tables', while the earlier method compiles tables usually referred to as 'compound interest tables'. Both types of table are compound interest tables; only the presentation of the data has changed.

To illustrate the ease of computation using PV tables, we can compute the PV of £6,152 receivable at the end of year 5, given a discount rate of 10%, as being £6,152 × £0.6209 = £3,820. Thus £3,820 will total £6,152 in five years given an interest rate of 10% p.a. So the PV of that cash flow of £6,152 is £3,820, because £3,820 would generate interest of £2,332 (i.e. 6,152 – 3,820) as compensation for losing use of the principal sum for five years. Future flows must be discounted to take cognisance of the time element separating cash flows. Only then are we able to compare like with like by reducing all future flows to the comparable loss of present value.

This concept of PV has a variety of applications in accountancy and will be encountered in many different areas requiring financial measurement, comparison and decision. It originated as an economist's device within the context of economic income and economic capital models,

Figure 6.1 Dissimilar cash flows

Cash flows		
Machine A	Machine B	Receivable end of year
£	£	
1,000	5,000	1
2,000	4,000	2
7,000	1,000	3
10,000	10,000	

but in accountancy it assists in the making of valid comparisons and decisions. For example, two machines may each generate an income of £10,000 over three years. However, timing of the cash flows may vary between the machines. This is illustrated in Figure 6.1.

If we simply compare the profit-generating capacity of the machines over the three-year span, each produces a total profit of £10,000. But if we pay regard to the time element of the money flows, the machines are not so equal.

However, the technique has its faults. Future money flows are invariably the subject of **estimation** and thus the actual flow experienced may show variations from forecast. Also, the element of **interest**, which is crucial to the calculation of present values, is **subjective**. It may, for instance, be taken as the average prevailing rate operating within the economy or a rate peculiar to the firm and the element of risk involved in the particular decision. In this chapter we are concerned only with PV as a tool of the economist in evaluating economic income and economic capital.

6.5.2 Nature of economic income

Economics is concerned with the economy in general, raising questions such as: how does it function? how is wealth created? how is income generated? why is income generated? The economy as a whole is activated by income generation. The individual is motivated to generate income because of a need to satisfy personal wants by consuming goods and services. Thus the economist becomes concerned with the individual consumer's psychological state of personal **enjoyment and satisfaction**. This creates a need to treat the economy as a **behavioural entity**.

The behavioural aspect forms a substantial part of micro- and macroeconomic thought, emanating particularly from the microeconomic. We can say that the economist's version of income measurement is microeconomics orientated in contrast to the accountant's business entity orientation.

The origination of the economic measure of income commenced with Irving Fisher in 1930.[6] He saw income in terms of consumption, and consumption in terms of individual perception of personal enjoyment and satisfaction. His difficulty in formulating a standard measure of this personal psychological concept of income was overcome by equating this individual experience with the consumption of goods and services and assuming that the cost of such goods and services formed the measure.

Thus, he reasoned, consumption (C) equals income (Y); so $Y = C$. He excluded savings from income because savings were not consumed. There was no satisfaction derived from savings; enjoyment necessitated consumption, he argued. Money was worthless until spent; so growth of capital was ignored, but reductions in capital became part of income because such reductions had to be spent.

In Fisher's model, capital was a stock of wealth existing at a point in time, and as a stock it generated income. Eventually, he reconciled the value of capital with the value of income by employing the concept of present value. He assessed the PV of a future flow of income by **discounting** future flows using the discounted cash flow (DCF) technique. Fisher's model adopted the prevailing average market rate of interest as the discount factor.

Economists since Fisher have introduced savings as part of income. Sir John Hicks played a major role in this area.[7] He introduced the idea that income was the maximum consumption enjoyed by the individual without reducing the individual's capital stock, i.e. the amount a person could consume during a period of time that still left him or her with the same value of capital stock at the end of the period as at the beginning. Hicks also used the DCF technique in the valuation of capital.

If capital increases, the increase constitutes savings and grants the opportunity of consumption. The formula illustrating this was given in Section 6.3.1, i.e. $Y_{0-1} = NA_1 - NA_0 + D_{0-1}$.

However, in the Hicksian model, $NA_1 - NA_0$, given as £6,750 and £6,000 respectively in that section, would have been discounted to achieve present values.

The same formula may be expressed in different forms. The economist is likely to show it as $Y = C + (K_1 - K_0)$ where C = consumption, having been substituted for dividend, and K_1 and K_0 have been substituted for NA_1 and NA_0 respectively.

Hicks's income model

Hicks's income model is often spoken of as an *ex ante* model because it is usually used for the measurement of **expected** income in advance of the time period concerned. Of course, because it specifically introduces the present value concept, present values replace the statement of financial position values of net assets adopted by the accountant. Measuring income **before the event** enables the individual to estimate the level of consumption that may be achieved without depleting capital stock. Before-the-event computations of income necessitate predictions of future cash flows.

Suppose that an individual proprietor of a business anticipated that his investment in the enterprise would generate earnings over the next four years as specified in Figure 6.2. Furthermore, such earnings would be retained by the business for the financing of new equipment with a view to increasing potential output.

We will assume that the expected rate of interest on capital employed in the business is 8% p.a.

The economic value of the business at K_0 (i.e. at the beginning of year 1) will be based on the discounted cash flow of the future four years. Figure 6.3 shows that K_0 is £106,853, calculated as the present value of anticipated earnings of £131,000 spread over a four-year term.

The economic value of the business at K_1 (i.e. at the end of year 1, which is the same as saying the beginning of year 2) is calculated in Figure 6.4. This shows that K_1 is

Figure 6.2 Business cash flows for four years

Years	Cash inflows
	£
1	26,000
2	29,000
3	35,000
4	41,000

Figure 6.3 Economic value at K_0

	(a)	(b)	(c)
Year	Cash flow	$DCF = \dfrac{1}{(1+r)^n}$	$PV = (a) \times (b)$
	£		£
K_1	26,000	$\dfrac{1}{(1.08)^1} = 0.9259$	24,073
K_2	29,000	$\dfrac{1}{(1.08)^2} = 0.8573$	24,862
K_3	35,000	$\dfrac{1}{(1.08)^3} = 0.7938$	27,783
K_4	41,000	$\dfrac{1}{(1.08)^4} = 0.7350$	30,135
	131,000		106,853

Figure 6.4 Economic value at K_1

	(a)	(b)	(c)
Year	Cash flow	$DCF = \dfrac{1}{(1+r)^n}$	PV (a) × (b)
	£		£
K_1	26,000	1.0000	26,000
K_2	29,000	$\dfrac{1}{(1+r)^1} = 0.9259$	26,851
K_3	35,000	$\dfrac{1}{(1+r)^2} = 0.8573$	30,006
K_4	41,000	$\dfrac{1}{(1+r)^3} = 0.7938$	32,546
	131,000		115,403

£115,403 calculated as the present value of anticipated earnings of £131,000 spread over a four-year term.

From this information we are able to calculate Y for the period Y_1, as in Figure 6.5. Note that C (consumption) is nil because, in this exercise, dividends representing consumption

Figure 6.5 Calculation of Y for the period Y_1

$$Y = C + (K_1 - K_0)$$
$$Y = 0 + (115,403 - 106,853)$$
$$= 0 + 8,550$$
$$= £8,550$$

have not been payable for Y_1. In other words, income Y_1 is entirely in the form of projected capital growth, i.e. savings.

By year-end K_1, earnings of £26,000 will have been received; in projecting the capital at K_2 such earnings will have been reinvested and at the beginning of year K_2 will have a PV of £26,000. These earnings will no longer represent a **predicted** sum because they will have been **realised** and therefore will no longer be subjected to discounting.

The income of £8,550 represents an anticipated return of 8% p.a. on the economic capital at K_0 of £106,853 (8% of £106,853 is £8,548, the difference of £2 between this figure and the figure calculated above being caused by rounding).

As long as the expectations of future cash flows and the chosen interest rate do not change, then Y_1 will equal 8% of £106,853.

What will the anticipated income for the year Y_2 amount to?

Applying the principle explained above, the anticipated income for the year Y_2 will equal 8% of the capital at the end of K_1 amounting to £115,403 = £9,233. This is proved in Figure 6.6, which shows that K_2 is £124,636 calculated as the present value of anticipated earnings of £131,000 spread over a four-year term.

From this information we are able to calculate Y for the period Y_2 as in Figure 6.7. Note that capital value attributable to the end of year K_2 is being assessed at the beginning of K_2. This means that the £26,000 due at the end of year K_1 will have been received and re-invested, earning interest of 8% p.a. Thus by the end of year K_2 it will be worth £28,080. The sum of £29,000 will be realised at the end of year K_2 so its present value at that time will be £29,000.

If the anticipated future cash flows change, the expected capital value at the successive points in time will also change. Accordingly, the actual value of capital may vary from that forecast by the *ex ante* model.

Figure 6.6 Economic value at K_2

Year	(a) Cash flow	(b) $DCF = \dfrac{1}{(1+r)^n}$	(c) $PV = (a) \times (b)$
	£	£	£
K_1	26,000	1.08	28,080
K_2	29,000	1.0000	29,000
K_3	35,000	0.9259	32,407
K_4	41,000	0.8573	35,149
	131,000		124,636

Figure 6.7 Calculation of Y for the period Y_2

$$Y = C + (K_2 - K_1)$$
$$Y = 0 + (124,636 - 115,403)$$
$$= 0 + 9,233$$
$$= £9,233$$

6.6 Critical comment on the economist's measure

While the income measure enables us to formulate theories regarding the behaviour of the economy, it has inherent shortcomings not only in the economic field but particularly in the accountancy sphere.

- The calculation of economic capital, hence economic income, is subjective in terms of the present value factor, often referred to as the DCF element. The factor may be based on any one of a number of factors, such as opportunity cost, the current return on the firm's existing capital employed, the contemporary interest payable on a short-term loan such as a bank overdraft, the average going rate of interest payable in the economy at large, or a rate considered justified on the basis of the risk attached to a particular investment.
- Investors are not of one mind or one outlook. For example, they possess different risk and time preferences and will therefore employ different discount factors.
- The model constitutes a compound of unrealised and realised flows, i.e. profits. Because of the unrealised element, it has not been used as a base for computing tax or for declaring a dividend.
- The projected income is dependent upon the success of a planned financial strategy. Investment plans may change, or fail to attain target.
- Windfall gains cannot be foreseen, so they cannot be accommodated in the *ex ante* model. Our prognostic cash flows may therefore vary from the actual flows generated, e.g. an unexpected price movement.
- It is difficult to construct a satisfactory, meaningful statement of financial position detailing the unused stock of net assets by determining the present values of individual assets. Income is invariably the consequence of deploying a group of assets working in unison.

6.7 Income, capital and changing price levels

A primary concern of income measurement to both economist and accountant is the maintenance of the capital stock, i.e. the maintenance of capital values. The assumption is that income can only arise **after** the capital stock has been maintained at the same amount as at the beginning of the accounting period.

However, this raises the question of how we should define the capital that we are attempting to maintain. There are a number of possible definitions:

- **Money capital**. Should we concern ourselves with maintaining the fund of capital resources initially injected by the entrepreneur into the new enterprise? This is indeed one of the aims of traditional, transaction-based accountancy.
- **Potential consumption capital**. Is it this that should be maintained, i.e. the economist's present value philosophy expressed via the discounted cash flow technique?
- **Operating capacity capital**. Should maintenance of productive capacity be the rule, i.e. capital measured in terms of tangible or physical assets? This measure would utilise the current cost accounting system.

Revsine attempted to construct an analytical bridge between replacement cost accounting that maintains the operating capacity, and the economic concepts of **income** and **value**, by demonstrating that the distributable operating flow component of economic income is equal to the current operating component of replacement cost income, and that the unexpected income component of economic income is equal to the unrealisable cost savings of replacement cost income.[4] This will become clearer when the replacement cost model is dealt with in the next chapter.

- **Financial capital.** Should capital be maintained in terms of a fund of general purchasing power (sometimes called 'real' capital)? In essence, this is the consumer purchasing power (or general purchasing power) approach, but not in a strict sense as it can be measured in a variety of ways. The basic method uses a general price index. This concept is likely to satisfy the criteria of the proprietor/shareholders of the entity. The money capital and the financial capital concepts are variations of the same theme, the former being founded on the historical cost principle and the latter applying an adjustment mechanism to take account of changing price levels.

The money capital concept has remained the foundation stone of traditional accountancy reporting, but the operating and financial capital alternatives have played a controversial secondary role over the past 25 years.

Potential consumption capital is peculiar to economics in terms of measurement of the business entity's aggregate capital, although, as discussed in Section 6.5.2, it has a major role to play as a decision-making model in financial management.

6.7.1 Why are these varying methods of concern?

The problem tackled by these devices is that plague of the economy known as 'changing price levels', particularly the upward spiralling referred to as **inflation**. Throughout this chapter we have assumed that there is a stable monetary unit and that income, capital and value changes over time have been in response to operational activity and the interaction of supply and demand or changes in expectations.

Following the historical cost convention, capital maintenance has involved a comparison of opening and closing capital in each accounting period. It has been assumed that the purchasing power of money has remained constant over time.

If we take into account moving price levels, particularly the fall in the purchasing power of the monetary unit due to inflation, then our measure of **income** is affected if we insist upon **maintaining capital in real terms**.

6.7.2 Is it necessary to maintain capital in real terms?

Undoubtedly it is necessary if we wish to prevent an erosion of the operating capacity of the entity and thus its ability to maintain real levels of income. If we do not maintain the capacity of capital to generate the current level of profit, then the income measure, being the difference between opening and closing capitals, will be overstated or overvalued. This is because the capital measure is being understated or undervalued. In other words, there is a danger of dividends being paid out of real capital rather than out of real income. It follows that, if the need to retain profits is overlooked, the physical assets will be depleted.

In accountancy there is no theoretical difficulty in measuring the impact of changing price levels. There are, however, two practical difficulties:

- A number of methods, or mixes of methods, are available and it has proved impossible to obtain consensus support for one method or compound of methods.
- There is a high element of subjectivity, which detracts from the objectivity of the information.

In the next chapter we deal with inflation and analyse the methods formulated, together with the difficulties that they in turn introduce into the financial reporting system.

Summary

In measuring income, capital and value, the accountant's approach varies from the sister discipline of the economist, yet both are trying to achieve similar objectives.

The accountant uses a traditional transaction-based model of computing income, capital being the residual of this model.

The economist's viewpoint is anchored in a behavioural philosophy that measures capital and deduces income to be the difference between the capital at the beginning of a period and that at its end.

The objectives of income measurement are important because of the existence of a highly sophisticated capital market. These objectives involve the assessment of steward-ship performance, dividend and retention policies, comparison of actual results with those predicted, assessment of future prospects, payment of taxation and disclosure of matched costs against revenue from sales.

The natures of income, capital and value must be appreciated if we are to understand and achieve measurement. The apparent conflict between the two measures can be seen as a consequence of the accountant's need for periodic reporting to shareholders. In the longer term, both methods tend to agree.

Present value as a concept is the foundation stone of the economist, while historical cost, adjusted for prudence, is that of the accountant. Present value demands a subjec-tive discount rate and estimates that time may prove incorrect; historical cost ignores unrealised profits and in application is not always transaction based.

The economist's measure, of undoubted value in the world of micro- and macroeco-nomics, presents difficulty in the accountancy world of annual reports. The accountant's method, with its long track record of acceptance, ignores any generated profits, which caution and the concept of the going concern deem not to exist.

The economic trauma of changing price levels is a problem that both measures can embrace, but consensus support for a particular model of measurement has proved elusive.

REVIEW QUESTIONS

1 What is the purpose of measuring income?

2 Explain the nature of economic income.

3 The historical cost concept has withstood the test of time. Specify the reasons for this success, together with any aspects of historical cost that you consider are detrimental in the sphere of finan-cial reporting.

4 What is meant by present value? Does it take account of inflation?

5 Explain what you understand by an *ex ante* model.

6 Explain the principal criticisms of the economist's measure of income.

7 To an accountant, net income is essentially a historical record of the past. To an economist, net income is essentially a speculation about the future. Examine the relative merits of these two approaches for financial reporting purposes.

8 Examine and contrast the concepts of profit that you consider to be relevant to:

(a) an economist;

(b) a speculator;

(c) a business executive;

(d) the managing director of a company;

(e) a shareholder in a private company;

(f) a shareholder in a large public company.

EXERCISES

* Question 1

(a) 'Measurement in financial statements', Chapter 6 of the ASB's *Statement of Principles,* was published in 1999. Among the theoretical valuation systems considered is value in use, more commonly known as economic value.

Required:

Describe the Hicksian economic model of income and value, and assess its usefulness for financial reporting.

(b) Jim Bowater purchased a parcel of 30,000 ordinary shares in New Technologies plc for £36,000 on 1 January 20X5. Jim, an Australian on a four-year contract in the UK, has it in mind to sell the shares at the end of 20X7, just before he leaves for Australia. Based on the company's forecast growth and dividend policy, his broker has advised him that his shares are likely to fetch only £35,000 then.

In its annual report for the year ended 31 December 20X4 the company had forecast annual dividend payouts as follows:

Year ended: 31 December 20X5, 25p per share
31 December 20X6, 20p per share
31 December 20X7, 20p per share

Required:

Using the economic model of income:

(i) Compute Jim's economic income for each of the three years ending on the dates indicated above.

(ii) Show that Jim's economic capital will be preserved at 1 January 20X5 level. Jim's cost of capital is 20%.

* Question 2

(a) Describe briefly the theory underlying Hicks's economic model of income and capital. What are its practical limitations?

(b) Spock purchased a space invader entertainment machine at the beginning of year 1 for £1,000. He expects to receive at annual intervals the following receipts: at the end of year 1 £400; at end of year 2 £500; at end of year 3 £600. At the end of year 3 he expects to sell the machine for £400.

Spock could receive a return of 10% in the next best investment.

The present value of £1 receivable at the end of a period discounted at 10% is as follows:

End of year 1	£0.909
End of year 2	£0.826
End of year 3	£0.751

Required:

Calculate the ideal economic income, ignoring taxation and working to the nearest £.

Your answer should show that Spock's capital is maintained throughout the period and that his income is constant.

Question 3

Jason commenced with £135,000 cash. He acquired an established shop on 1 January 20X1. He agreed to pay £130,000 for the fixed and current assets and the goodwill. The replacement cost of the shop premises was £100,000, stock £10,000 and debtors £4,000; the balance of the purchase price was for the goodwill. He paid legal costs of £5,000. No liabilities were taken over. Jason could have resold the business immediately for £135,000. Legal costs are to be expensed in 20X1.

Jason expected to draw £25,000 per year from the business for three years and to sell the shop at the end of 20X3 for £150,000.

At 31 December 20X1 the books showed the following tangible assets and liabilities:

Cost to the business before any drawings by Jason:	£	He estimated that the net realisable values were:	£
Shop premises	100,000		85,000
Stock	15,500		20,000
Debtors	5,200		5,200
Cash	40,000		40,000
Creditors	5,000		5,000

Based on his experience of the first year's trading, he revised his estimates and expected to draw £35,000 per year for three years and sell the shop for £175,000 on 31 December 20X3.

Jason's opportunity cost of capital was 20%.

Required:

(a) Calculate the following income figures for 20X1:
    (i)   accounting income;
    (ii) income based on net realisable values;
    (iii) economic income *ex ante*;
    (iv) economic income *ex post*.
    State any assumptions made.
(b) Evaluate each of the four income figures as indicators of performance in 20X1 and as a guide to decisions about the future.

References

1 T.A. Lee, *Income and Value Measurement: Theory and Practice* (3rd edition), Van Nostrand Reinhold (UK), 1985, p. 20.
2 D. Solomons, *Making Accounting Policy*, Oxford University Press, 1986, p. 132.
3 R.W. Scapens, *Accounting in an Inflationary Environment* (2nd edition), Macmillan, 1981, p. 125.
4 *Ibid.*, p. 127.
5 T.A. Lee, *op. cit.*, pp. 52–54.
6 I. Fisher, *The Theory of Interest*, Macmillan, 1930, pp. 171–181.
7 J.R. Hicks, *Value and Capital* (2nd edition), Clarendon Press, 1946.

Bibliography

American Institute of Certified Public Accountants, *Objectives of Financial Statements*, Report of the Study Group, 1973.

The Corporate Report, ASC, 1975, pp. 28–31.

N. Kaldor, 'The concept of income in economic theory', in R.H. Parker and G.C. Harcourt (eds), *Readings in the Concept and Measurement of Income*, Cambridge University Press, 1969.

T.A. Lee, 'The accounting entity concept, accounting standards and inflation accounting', *Accounting and Business Research*, Spring 1980, pp. 1–11.

J.R. Little, 'Income measurement: an introduction', *Student Newsletter*, June 1988.

D. Solomons, 'Economic and accounting concepts of income', in R.H. Parker and G.C. Harcourt (eds), *Readings in the Concept and Measurement of Income*, Cambridge University Press, 1969.

R.R. Sterling, *Theory of the Measurement of Enterprise Income*, University of Kansas Press, 1970.

CHAPTER 7

Accounting for price-level changes

7.1 Introduction

The main purpose of this chapter is to explain the impact of inflation on profit and capital measurement and the concepts that have been proposed to incorporate the effect into financial reports by adjusting the historical cost data. These concepts are periodically discussed but there is no general support for any specific concept among practitioners in the field.

Objectives

By the end of the chapter, you should be able to:

● describe the problems of historical cost accounting (HCA);
● explain the approach taken in each of the price-level changing models;
● prepare financial statements applying each model (HCA, CPP, CCA, NRVA);
● critically comment on each model (HCA, CPP, CCA, NRVA);
● describe the approach being taken by standard setters and future developments.

7.2 Review of the problems of historical cost accounting (HCA)

The transaction-based historical cost concept was unchallenged in the UK until price levels started to hedge upwards at an ever-increasing pace during the 1950s and reached an annual rate of increase of 20% in the mid-1970s. The historical cost base for financial reporting witnessed growing criticism. The inherent faults of the system were discussed in Chapter 6, but inflation exacerbates the problem in the following ways:

● Profit is overstated when inflationary changes in the value of assets are ignored.

● Comparability of business entities, which is so necessary in the assessment of performance and growth, becomes distorted when assets are acquired at different times.

● The decision-making process, the formulation of plans and the setting of targets may be suboptimal if financial base data are out of date.

● Financial reports become confusing at best, misleading at worst, because revenue is mismatched with differing historical cost levels as the monetary unit becomes unstable.

● Unrealised profits arising in individual accounting periods are increased as a result of inflation.

In order to combat these serious defects, current value accounting became the subject of research and controversy as to the most appropriate method to use for financial reporting.

7.3 Inflation accounting

A number of versions of current value accounting (CVA) were eventually identified, but the current value postulate was said to suffer from the following disadvantages:

● It destroys the factual nature of HCA, which is transaction based: the factual characteristic is to all intents and purposes lost as transaction-based historic values are replaced by judgemental values.

● It is not as objective as HCA because it is less verifiable from auditable documentation.

● It entails recognition of unrealised profit, a practice that is anathema to the traditionalist.

● The claimed improvement in comparability between commercial entities is a myth because of the degree of subjectivity in measuring current value by each.

● The lack of a single accepted method of computing current values compounds the subjectivity aspect. One fault-laden system is being usurped by another that is also faulty.

In spite of these criticisms, the search for a system of financial reporting devoid of the defects of HCA and capable of coping with inflation has produced a number of CVA models.

7.4 The concepts in principle

Several current income and value models have been proposed to replace or operate in tandem with the historical cost convention. However, in terms of basic characteristics, they may be reduced to the following three models:

● current purchasing power (CPP) or general purchasing power (GPP);

● current entry cost or replacement cost (RC);

● current exit cost or net realisable value (NRV).

We discuss each of these models below.

7.4.1 Current purchasing power accounting (CPPA)

The CPP model measures income and value by adopting a price index system. Movements in price levels are gauged by reference to price changes in a group of goods and services in **general** use within the economy. The aggregate price value of this **basket** of commodities-cum-services is determined at a base point in time and indexed as 100. Subsequent changes in price are compared on a regular basis with this base period price and the change recorded. For example, the price level of our chosen range of goods and services may amount to £76 on 31 March 20X1, and show changes as follows:

£76	at 31 March 20X1
£79	at 30 April 20X1
£81	at 31 May 20X1
£84	at 30 June 20X1

and so on.

The change in price may be indexed with 31 March as the base:

20X1	Calculation	Index
31 March	i.e. £76	100
30 April	i.e. $\frac{79}{76} \times 100$	103.9
31 May	i.e. $\frac{81}{76} \times 100$	106.6
30 June	i.e. $\frac{84}{76} \times 100$	110.5

In the UK, index systems similar in construction to this are known as the Retail or Consumer Price Index (RPI). The index is a barometer of fluctuating price levels covering a miscellany of goods and services as used by the average household. Thus it is a **general** price index. It is amended from time to time to take account of new commodities entering the consumer's range of choice and needs. As a model, it is unique owing to the introduction of the concept of gains and losses in **purchasing power**.

7.4.2 Current entry or replacement cost accounting (RCA)

The replacement cost (RC) model assesses income and value by reference to entry costs or current replacement costs of materials and other assets utilised within the business entity. The valuation attempts to replace like with like and thus takes account of the quality and condition of the existing assets. A motor vehicle, for instance, may have been purchased brand new for £25,000 with an expected life of five years, an anticipated residual value of nil and a straight-line depreciation policy. Its HCA carrying value in the statement of financial position at the end of its first year would be £25,000 less £5,000 = £20,000. However, if a similar new replacement vehicle cost £30,000 at the end of year 1, then its gross RC would be £30,000; depreciation for one year based on this sum would be £6,000 and the net RC would be £24,000. The increase of £4,000 is a holding gain and the vehicle with a HCA carrying value of £20,000 would be revalued at £24,000.

7.4.3 Current exit cost or net realisable value accounting (NRVA)

The net realisable value (NRV) model is based on the economist's concept of opportunity cost. It is a model that has had strong academic support, most notably in Australia from Professor Ray Chambers who referred to this approach as Continuous Contemporary Accounting (CoCoA). If an asset cost £25,000 at the beginning of year 1 and at the end of that year it had a NRV of £21,000 after meeting selling expenses, it would be carried in the NRV statement of financial position at £21,000. This amount represents the cash forgone by holding the asset, i.e. the opportunity of possessing cash of £21,000 has been sacrificed in favour of the asset. There is effectively a holding loss for the year of £25,000 less £21,000 = £4,000.

7.5 The four models illustrated for a company with cash purchases and sales

We will illustrate the effect on the profit and net assets of Entrepreneur Ltd.

Entrepreneur Ltd commenced business on 1 January 20X1 with a capital of £3,000 to buy and sell second-hand computers. The company purchased six computers on 1 January 20X1 for £500 each and sold three of the computers on 15 January for £900 each.

The following data are available for January 20X1:

	Retail Price Index	Replacement cost per computer £	Net realisable value £
1 January	100		
15 January	112	610	
31 January	130	700	900

The statements of income and financial position are set out in Figure 7.1 with the detailed workings in Figure 7.2.

7.5.1 Financial capital maintenance concept

HCA and CPP are both transaction-based models that apply the financial capital maintenance concept. This means that profit is the difference between the opening and closing net

Figure 7.1 Trading account for the month ended 31 January 20X1

Statements of income for the month ended 31 January 20X1

	HCA £		CPP CPP£		RCA £		NRVA £	
Sales	2,700	W1	3,134	W5	2,700	W1	2,700	W1
Opening inventory	—		—		—		—	
Purchases	3,000	W2	3,900	W6	3,000	W2	3,000	W2
Closing inventory	(1,500)	W3	(1,950)	W7	(1,500)	W3	(1,500)	W3
COSA	na		na		330	W10	na	
Cost of sales	1,500		1,950		1,830		1,500	
Holding gain	na		na		na		1,200	W15
Profit	1,200		1,184		870		2,400	

Statement of financial position as at 31 January 20X1

	£		PCP£		£		£	
Current assets								
Inventory	1,500	W3	1,950	W7	2,100	W11	2,700	W14
Cash	2,700	W4	2,700		2,700		2,700	
Capital employed	4,200		4,650		4,800		5,400	
Capital	3,000		3,900	W8	3,000		3,000	
Holding gains								
On inventory consumed	na		na		330	W12		
On inventory in hand	na		na		600	W13		
Profit	1,200		1,184		870		2,400	
Loss on monetary items	na		(434)	W9	na		na	
	4,200		4,650		4,800		5,400	

na = not applicable

Figure 7.2 Workings (W)

HCA

W1 Sales	3 × £900 = £2,700	
W2 Purchases	6 × £500 = £3,000	
W3 Closing inventory	3 × £500 = £1,500	
W4 Cash	1 January 20X1 Capital	3,000
	1 January 20X1 Purchases	(3,000)
	1 January 20X1 Balance	nil
	15 January 20X1 Sales	
	3 × £900 =	£2,700
	31 January 20X1 Balance	£2,700

CPP

		CPP£
W5 Sales	£2,700 × 130/112 =	3,134
W6 Purchases	£3,000 × 130/100 =	3,900
W7 Closing inventory	£1,500 × 130/100 =	1,950
W8 Capital	£3,000 × 130/100 =	3,900

W9   Balance of cash was nil until 15 January when sales generated £2,700. This sum was held until 31 January during which period cash, a monetary item, lost purchasing power. The loss of purchasing power is measured by applying the general index to the cash held: £2,700 × 130/112 − £2,700 = CPP £434.

RCA

W10   Additional replacement cost of inventory consumed as at the date of sale is measured as a cost of sales adjustment (COSA). COSA is calculated as follows:

3 × £610 =	1,830
Less: 3 × £500 =	1,500
COSA	£330

W11   Closing inventory: 3 × £700 = £2,100

W12   Holding gains on inventory consumed: as for W10   = £330

W13 Inventory at replacement cost	= 3 × £700 = 2,100
Less: inventory at cost	= 3 × £500 = 1,500
Holding gains on closing inventory	£600

NRVA

W14   Closing inventory at net realisable value = 900 × 3 = £2,700

W15 3 × £900 =	2,700
3 × £500 =	1,500
Holding gain	£1,200

assets (expressed in HC £) or the opening and closing net assets (expressed in HC £ indexed for RPI changes) adjusted for any capital introduced or withdrawn during the month.

CPP adjustments

- All historical cost values are adjusted to a common index level for the month. In theory this can be the index applicable to any day of the financial period concerned. However, in practice it has been deemed preferable to use the last day of the period; thus the financial statements show the latest price level appertaining to the period.

- The application of a general price index as an adjusting factor results in the creation of an **alien** currency of **purchasing power**, which is used in place of sterling. Note, particularly, the impact on the entity's sales and capital compared with the other models. **Actual** sales shown on **invoices** will still read £2,700.

- Note the application of the concept of gain or loss on holding monetary items. In this example there is a monetary loss of CPP £434 as shown in Working 9 in Figure 7.2.

7.5.2 Operating capital maintenance concept

Under this concept capital is only maintained if sufficient income is retained to maintain the business entity's physical operating capacity, i.e. its ability to produce the existing level of goods or services. Profit is, therefore, the residual after increasing the cost of sales to the cost applicable at the date of sale.

- Basically, only two adjustments are involved: the additional replacement cost of inventory consumed and holding gains on closing inventories. However, in a comprehensive exercise an adjustment will be necessary regarding non-current assets and you will also encounter a gearing adjustment.

- Notice the concept of holding gains. This model introduces, in effect, unrealised profits in respect of closing inventories. The holding gain concerning inventory consumed at the time of sale has been realised and deducted from what would have been a profit of £1,200. The statement discloses profits of £870.

7.5.3 Capacity to adapt concept under the NRVA model

The HCA, CPP and RCA models have assumed that the business will continue as a going concern and only distribute realised profits after retaining sufficient profits to maintain either the financial or operating capital.

The NRVA concept is that a business has the capacity to realise its net assets at the end of each financial period and reinvest the proceeds and that the NRV accounts provide management with this information.

- This produces the same initial profit as HCA, namely £1,200, but a peculiarity of this system is that this realised profit is supplemented by **unrealised** profit generated by holding stocks. Under RCA accounting, such gains are shown in a separate account and are not treated as part of real income.

- This simple exercise has ignored the possibility of investment in non-current assets, thus depreciation is not involved. A reduction in the NRV of non-current assets at the end of a period compared with the beginning would be treated in a similar fashion to depreciation by being charged to the revenue account, and consequently profits would be reduced. An increase in the NRV of such assets would be included as part of the profit.

7.5.4 The four models compared

Dividend distribution

We can see from Figure 7.1 that if the business were to distribute the profit reported under HCA, CPP or NRVA the physical operating capacity of the business would be reduced and it would be paying dividends out of capital:

	HCA	CPP	RCA	NRVA
Realised profit	1,200	1,184	870	1,200
Unrealised profit	—	—	—	1,200
Profit for month	1,200	1,184	870	2,400

Shareholder orientation

The CPP model is shareholder orientated in that it shows whether shareholders' funds are keeping pace with inflation by maintaining their purchasing power. Only CPP changes the value of the share capital.

Management orientation

The RCA model is management orientated in that it identifies holding gains which represent the amounts required to be retained in order to simply maintain the operating capital.

RCA measures the impact of inflation on the individual firm, in terms of the change in price levels of its **raw materials and assets**, i.e. inflation peculiar to the company, whereas CPP measures general inflation in the economy as a whole. CPP may be meaningless in the case of an individual company. Consider a firm that carries a constant volume of stock valued at £100 in HCA terms. Now suppose that price levels double when measured by a general price index (GPI), so that its inventory is restated to £200 in a CPP system. If, however, the cost of that **particular** inventory has risen by 500%, then under the RCA model the value of the stock should be £500.

In the mid-1970s, when the accountancy profession was debating the problem of changing price-level measurement, the general price level had climbed by some 23% over a period during which petroleum-based products had risen by 500%.

7.6 Critique of each model

A critique of the various models may be formulated in terms of their characteristics and peculiarities as virtues and defects in application.

7.6.1 HCA

This model's virtues and defects have been discussed in Chapter 6 and earlier in this chapter.

7.6.2 CPP

Virtues

- It is an **objective measure** since it is still transaction based, as with HCA, and the possibility of subjectivity is constrained if a GPI is used that has been constructed by a central agency such as a government department. This applies in the UK, where the Retail Price Index is currently published by the Office for National Statistics.

- It is a **measure of shareholders' capital** and that capital's maintenance in terms of purchasing power units. Profit is the residual value after maintaining the money value of capital funds, taking account of changing price levels. Thus it is a measure readily understood by the shareholder/user of the accounts. It can prevent payment of a dividend out of real capital as measured by GPPA.

- It **introduces the concept of monetary items** as distinct from non-monetary items and the attendant concepts of gains and losses in holding net monetary liabilities compared with holding net monetary assets. Such gains and losses are experienced on a disturbing scale in times of inflation. They are **real** gains and losses. The **basic** RCA and NRV models do not recognise such 'surpluses' and 'deficits'.

Defects

- It is **HCA based but adjusted** to reflect general price movements. Thus it possesses the characteristics of HCA, good and bad, but with its values updated in the light of an arithmetic measure of general price changes. The major defect of becoming out of date is mitigated to a degree, but the impact of inflation on the entity's income and capital may be at variance with the rate of inflation affecting the economy in general.

- It may be **wrongly assumed that the CPP statement of financial position is a current value statement**. It is not a current value document because of the defects discussed above; in particular, asset values may be subject to a different rate of inflation than that reflected by the GPI.

- It **creates an alien unit of measurement** still labelled by the £ sign. Thus we have the HCA £ and the CPP £. They are different pounds: one is the *bona fide* pound, the other is a synthetic unit. This may not be fully appreciated or understood by the user when faced with the financial accounts for the recent accounting period.

- Its **concept of profit is dangerous**. It pretends to cater for changing prices, but at the same time it fails to provide for the additional costs of replacing stocks sold or additional depreciation due to the escalating replacement cost of assets. The inflation encountered by the business entity will not be the same as that encountered by the whole economy. Thus the maintenance of the CPP of shareholders' capital via this concept of profit is not the maintenance of the entity's operating capital in physical terms, i.e. its capacity to produce the same volume of goods and services. The use of CPP profit as a basis for decision making without regard to RCA profit can have disastrous consequences.

7.6.3 RCA

Virtues

- Its **unit of measurement** is the monetary unit and consequently it is understood and accepted by the user of accountancy reports. In contrast, the CPP system employs an artificial unit based on arithmetic relationships, which is different and thus unfamiliar.

- It **identifies and isolates holding gains** from operating income. Thus it can prevent the inadvertent distribution of dividends in excess of operating profit. It satisfies the prudence criterion of the traditional accountant and **maintains the physical operating capacity** of the entity.

- It introduces **realistic current values** of assets in the statement of financial position, thus making the statement of financial position a 'value' statement and consequently more meaningful to the user. This contrasts sharply with the statement of financial position as a list of unallocated carrying costs in the HCA system.

Defects

- It is a **subjective measure**, in that replacement costs are often necessarily based on estimates or assessments. It does not possess the factual characteristics of HCA. It is open to manipulation within constraints. Often it is based on index numbers which themselves may be based on a compound of prices of a mixture of similar commodities used as raw material or operating assets. This subjectivity is exacerbated in circumstances where rapid technological advance and innovation are involved in the potential new replacement asset, e.g. computers and printers.
- It **assumes replacement of assets** by being based on their replacement cost. Difficulties arise if such assets are not to be replaced by similar assets. Presumably, it will then be assumed that a replacement of equivalent value to the original will be deployed, however differently, as capital within the firm.

7.6.4 NRVA

Virtues

- It is a concept readily understood by the user. The value of any item invariably has two measures – a buying price and a selling price – and the twain do not usually meet. However, when considering the value of an **existing** possession, the owner instinctively considers its 'value' to be that in potential sale, i.e. NRV.
- It **avoids the need to estimate depreciation** and, in consequence, the attendant problems of assessing lifespan and residual values. Depreciation is treated as the arithmetic difference between the NRV at the end of a financial period and the NRV at its beginning.
- It is **based on opportunity cost** and so can be said to be more meaningful. It is the **sacrificial** cost of possessing an asset, which, it can be argued, is more authentic in terms of being a true or real cost. If the asset were not possessed, its cash equivalent would exist instead and that cash would be deployed in other opportunities. Therefore, NRV = cash = opportunity = cost.

Defects

- It is a **subjective measure** and in this respect it possesses the same major fault as RCA. It can be said to be less prudent than RCA because NRV will tend to be higher in some cases than RCA. For example, when valuing finished inventories, a profit content will be involved.
- It is **not a realistic measure** as most assets, except finished goods, are possessed in order to be utilised, not sold. Therefore, NRV is irrelevant.
- It is **not always determinable**. The assets concerned may be highly specialist and there may be no ready market by which a value can be easily assessed. Consequently, any particular value may be fictitious or erroneous, containing too high a holding gain or, indeed, too low a holding loss.
- It **violates the concept of the going concern**, which demands that the accounts are drafted on the basis that there is no intention to liquidate the entity. Admittedly, this concept was formulated with HCA in view, but the acceptance of NRV implies the possibility of a cessation of trading.
- It is less reliable and verifiable than HC.

- The statement of comprehensive income will report a more volatile profit if changes in NRV are taken to the statement of comprehensive income each year.
- The profit arising from the changes in NRV may not have been realised.

7.7 Operating capital maintenance – a comprehensive example

In Figure 7.1 we considered the effect of inflation on a cash business without fixed assets, credit customers or credit suppliers. In the following example, Economica plc, we now consider the effect where there are non-current assets and credit transactions.

The HCA statements of financial position as at 31 December 20X4 and 20X5 are set out in Figure 7.3 and index numbers required to restate the non-current assets, inventory and monetary items in Figure 7.4.

Figure 7.3 Economica plc HCA statement of financial position

Statements of financial position as at 31 December on the basis of HCA

	20X5		20X4	
	£000	£000	£000	£000
Non-current assets:				
Cost	85,000		85,000	
Depreciation	34,000		25,500	
		51,000		59,500
Current assets:				
Inventory	25,500		17,000	
Trade receivables	34,000		23,375	
Cash and bank	17,000		1,875	
	76,500		42,250	
Current liabilities:				
Trade payables	25,500		17,000	
Income tax	8,500		4,250	
Dividend declared	5,000		4,000	
	39,000		25,250	
Net current assets	37,500		17,000	
Less: 8% debentures	11,000		11,000	
		26,500		6,000
		77,500		65,500
Share capital and reserves:				
Authorised and issued £1 ordinary shares		50,000		50,000
Share premium		1,500		1,500
Retained earnings		26,000		14,000
		77,500		65,500

Figure 7.4 Index data relating to Economica plc

1 Index numbers as prepared by the Office for National Statistics for non-current assets:

1 January 20X2	100
1 January 20X5	165
1 January 20X6	185
Average for 20X4	147
Average for 20X5	167

2 All non-current assets were acquired on 1 January 20X2. There were no further acquisitions or disposals during the four years ended 31 December 20X5.

3 Indices as prepared by the Office for National Statistics for inventories and monetary working capital adjustments were:

1 October 20X4	115
31 December 20X4	125
15 November 20X4	120
1 October 20X5	140
31 December 20X5	150
15 November 20X5	145
Average for 20X5	137.5

4 Three months' inventory is carried.

5 Depreciation: historical cost based on 10% p.a. straight-line with residual value of nil:

	£ HCA
20X4	8,500,000
20X5	8,500,000

7.7.1 Restating the opening statement of financial position to current cost

The non-current assets and inventory are restated to their current cost as at the date of the opening statement as shown in W1 and W2 below. The increase from HC to CC represents an unrealised holding gain which is debited to the asset account and credited to a reserve account called a current cost reserve, as in W3 below.

The calculations are as follows. First we shall convert the HCA statement of financial position in Figure 7.3, as at 31 December 20X4, to the CCA basis, using the index data in Figure 7.4.

The **non-monetary items**, comprising the non-current assets and inventory, are converted and the converted amounts are taken to the CC statement and the increases taken to the current cost reserve, as follows.

(W1) Property, plant and equipment

	HCA £000	Index	CCA £000	Increase £000
Cost	85,000	$\times \dfrac{165}{100} =$	140,250	55,250
Depreciation	25,500	$\times \dfrac{165}{100} =$	42,075	16,575
	59,500		98,175	38,675

The CCA valuation at 31 December 20X4 shows a net increase in terms of numbers of pounds sterling of £38,675,000. The £59,500,000 in the HCA statement of financial position will be replaced in the CCA statement by £98,175,000.

(W2) Inventories

HCA £000		Index		CCA £000		Increase £000
17,000	×	$\dfrac{125}{120}$	=	17,708	=	708

Note that Figure 7.4 specifies that three months' inventories are held. Thus on average they will have been purchased on 15 November 20X4, on the assumption that they have been acquired and consumed evenly throughout the calendar period. Hence, the index at the time of purchase would have been 120. The £17,000,000 in the HCA statement of financial position will be replaced in the CCA statement of financial position by £17,708,000.

(W3) Current cost reserve

The total increase in CCA carrying values for non-monetary items is £39,383,000, which will be credited to CC reserves in the CC statement. It comprises £38,675,000 on the non-current assets and £708,000 on the inventory.

Note that monetary items do not change by virtue of inflation. Purchasing power will be lost or gained, but the carrying values in the CCA statement will be identical to those in its HCA counterpart. We can now compile the CCA statement as at 31 December 20X4 – this will show net assets of £104,883,000.

7.7.2 Adjustments that affect the profit for the year

The statement of comprehensive income for the year ended 31 December 20X5 set out in Figure 7.5 discloses a profit before interest and tax of £26,350,000. We need to deduct realised holding gains from this profit to avoid the distribution of dividends that would reduce the operating capital. These deductions are a cost of sales adjustment (COSA), a depreciation adjustment (DA) and a monetary working capital adjustment (MWCA). The accounting treatment is to debit the statement of comprehensive income and credit the current cost reserve.

The adjustments are calculated as follows.

(W4) Cost of sales adjustment (COSA) using the average method

We will compute the cost of sales adjustment by using the average method. The average purchase price index for 20X5 is 137.5. If price increases have moved at an even pace throughout the period, this implies that consumption occurred, on average, at 30 June, the mid-point of the financial year.

	HCA £000		Adjustment		CCA £000		Difference £000
Opening inventory	17,000	×	$\dfrac{137.5}{120}$	=	19,479	=	2,479
Purchases	——		—		——		—
	17,000				19,479		
Closing inventory	(25,500)	×	$\dfrac{137.5}{145}$	=	24,181	=	1,319
	(8,500)				(4,702)		3,798

Figure 7.5 Economica plc HCA statement of comprehensive income

Statement of income for the year ended 31 December 20X5, on the basis of HCA

		20X5		20X4
		£000		£000
Turnover		42,500		38,250
Less: Cost of sales		(12,070)		(23,025)
Gross profit		30,430		15,225
Less: Distribution costs	2,460		2,210	
Less: Administrative expenses	1,620		1,540	
		(4,080)		(3,750)
Profit before interest and tax		26,350		11,475
Interest		(880)		(880)
Profit before tax		25,470		10,595
Income tax expense		(8,470)		(4,250)
Profit after tax		17,000		6,345
Dividend		(5,000)		(4,000)
Retentions		12,000		2,345
Balance b/f		14,000		11,655
Balance c/f		26,000		14,000
EPS		34p		13p

The impact of price changes on the cost of sales would be an increase of £3,798,000, causing a profit decrease of like amount and a current cost reserve increase of like amount.

(W5) Depreciation adjustment: average method

As assets are consumed throughout the year, the CCA depreciation charge should be based on average current costs.

	HCA £000		Adjustment		CCA £000		Difference £000
Depreciation	8,500	×	$\dfrac{167}{100}$	=	14,195	=	5,695

(W6) Monetary working capital adjustment (MWCA)

The objective is to transfer from the statement of comprehensive income to CC reserve the amount by which the need for monetary working capital (MWC) has increased due to rising price levels. The change in MWC from one statement of financial position to the next will be the consequence of a combination of changes in volume and escalating price movements. Volume change may be segregated from the price change by using an average index.

	20X5	20X4		Change
	£000	£000		£000
Trade receivables	34,000	23,375		
Trade payables	25,500	17,000		
MWC =	8,500	6,375	Overall change =	2,125

The MWC is now adjusted by the average index for the year. This adjustment will reveal the change in volume.

$$\left(8,500 \times \frac{137.5}{150}\right) - \left(6,375 \times \frac{137.5}{125}\right)$$

$$= \quad 7,792 \quad - \quad 7,012 \qquad\qquad = \text{Volume change} \quad \underline{780}$$

So price change = $\underline{1,345}$

The profit before interest and tax will be reduced as follows:

	£000	£000
Profit before interest and tax		26,350
Less:		
COSA (from W4)	(3,798)	
DA (from W5)	(5,695)	
MWCA (from W6)	(1,345)	
Current cost operating adjustments		(10,838)
Current cost operating profit		15,512

The adjustments will be credited to the current cost reserve.

7.7.3 Unrealised holding gains on non-monetary assets as at 31 December 20X5

The holding gains as at 31 December 20X4 were calculated in Section 7.7.1 above for non-current assets and inventory. A similar calculation is required to restate these at 20X5 current costs for the closing statement of financial position. The calculations are as in Working 7 below.

(W7) Non-monetary assets

(i) Holding gain on non-current assets	£000
Revaluation at year-end	
Non-current assets at 1 January 20X5 (as W1) at CCA revaluation	140,250
CCA value at 31 December 20X5 = $140,250 \times \dfrac{185}{165} =$	157,250
Revaluation holding gain for 20X5 to CC reserve in W8	**17,000**

This holding gain of £17,000,000 is transferred to CC reserves.

(ii) Backlog depreciation on non-current assets

CCA aggregate depreciation at 31 December 20X5 for
CC statement of financial position

$£000$

$= \text{HCA } £34,000,000 \times \dfrac{185}{100} \text{ in CC statement of financial position}$ 62,900

Less: CCA aggregate depreciation at 1 January 20X5
  (as per W1 and statement of financial position at 1 January 20X5)   42,075

Being CCA depreciation as revealed between opening
  and closing statements of financial position   20,825

But CCA depreciation charged in revenue accounts
  (i.e. £8,500,000 in £HCA plus additional depreciation of
  £5,695,000 per W5) =   14,195

So total backlog depreciation to CC reserve in W8   **6,630**

The CCA value of non-current assets at 31 December 20X5: $£000$

Gross CCA value (above)   157,250

Depreciation (above)   62,900

Net CCA carrying value in the CC statement of
  financial position in W8   **94,350**

This £6,630,000 is backlog depreciation for 20X5. Total backlog depreciation is not expensed (i.e. charged to revenue account) as an adjustment of HCA profit, but is charged against CCA reserves. The net effect is that the CC reserve will increase by £10,370,000, i.e. £17,000,000 − £6,630,000.

(iii) Inventory valuation at year-end

CCA valuation at 31 December 20X5

HCA £000	*CCA £000*	*CCA £000*
= 25,500 × 150/145 = 26,379 = increase of		879
CCA valuation at 1 January 20X5 (per W2)		
= 17,000 × 125/120 = 17,708 = increase of		708
Inventory holding gain occurring during 20X5 to W8		**171**

7.7.4 Current cost statement of financial position as at 31 December 20X5

The current cost statement as at 31 December 20X5 now discloses non-current assets and inventory adjusted by index to their current cost and the retained profits reduced by the current cost operating adjustments. It appears as in Working 8 below.

(W8) Economica plc: CCA statement of financial position as at 31 December 20X5

Non-current assets	£000	20X5 £000	£000	20X4 £000
Cost	157,250 (W7(i))		140,250 (W1)	
Depreciation	62,900 (W7(ii))		42,075 (W1)	
		94,350 (W7(ii))		98,175
Current assets				
Inventory	26,379 (W7(iii))		17,708 (W2)	
Trade receivables	34,000		23,375	
Cash	17,000		1,875	
	77,379		42,958	
Current liabilities				
Trade payables	25,500		17,000	
Income tax	8,500		4,250	
Dividend declared	5,000		4,000	
	39,000		25,250	
Net current assets	38,379		17,708	
Less: 8% debentures	11,000		11,000	
		27,379		6,708
		121,729		104,883
Financed by				
Share capital: authorised and issued £1 shares		50,000		50,000
Share premium		1,500		1,500
CC reserve (Note 1)		55,067		39,383
Retained profit (Note 2)		15,162		14,000
Shareholders' funds		121,729		104,883

Note 1: **CC reserve**	£000	£000
Opening balance		39,383 (W3)
Holding gains		
Non-current assets	17,000 (W7(i))	
Inventory	171 (W7(iii))	
		17,171
COSA	3,798 (W4)	
MWCA	1,345 (W6)	
Less: backlog depreciation	(6,630) (W7(ii))	(1,487)
		55,067

Note 2: **Retained profit**

Opening balance		14,000 (Figure 7.5)
HCA profit for 20X5	12,000	
COSA	(3,798) (W4)	
Extra depreciation	(5,695) (W5)	
MWCA	(1,345) (W6)	
		1,162
CCA profit for 20X5		15,162

7.7.5 How to take the level of borrowings into account

We have assumed that the company will need to retain £10,838,000 from the current year's earnings in order to maintain the physical operating capacity of the company. However, if the business is part financed by borrowings then part of the amount required may be assumed to come from the lenders. One of the methods advocated is to make a gearing adjustment. The gearing adjustment that we illustrate here has the effect of reducing the impact of the adjustments on the profit after interest, i.e. it is based on the realised holding gains only.

The gearing adjustment will change the carrying figures of CC reserves and retained profit, but not the shareholders' funds, as the adjustment is compensating. The gearing adjustment cannot be computed before the determination of the shareholders' interest because that figure is necessary in order to complete the gearing calculation.

(W9) Gearing adjustment

The CC operating profit of the business is quantified after making such retentions from the historical profit as are required in order to maintain the physical operating capacity of the entity. However, from a shareholder standpoint, there is no need to maintain in real terms the portion of the entity financed by loans that are fixed in monetary values. Thus, in calculating profit attributable to shareholders, that part of the CC adjustments relating to the proportion of the business financed by loans can be deducted:

Gearing adjustment =

$$\frac{\text{Average net borrowings for year}}{\text{Average net borrowings for year} + \text{Average shareholders' funds for year}} \times \begin{array}{c} \text{Aggregate} \\ \text{adjustments} \end{array}$$

This formula is usually expressed as $\dfrac{L}{(L+S)} \times A$ where L = loans (i.e. net borrowings); S = shareholders' interest or funds; and A = adjustments (i.e. extra depreciation + COSA + MWCA). Note that $L/(L+S)$ is often expressed as a percentage of A (see example below where it is 6.31%).

Net borrowings

This is the sum of all liabilities less current assets, excluding items included in MWC or utilised in computing COSA. In this instance it is as follows.

Note: in some circumstances (e.g. new issue of debentures occurring during the year) a weighted average will be used.

	Closing balance £'000	Opening balance £'000
Debentures	11,000	11,000
Income tax	8,500	4,250
Cash	(17,000)	(1,875)
Total net borrowings, the average of which equals L	2,500	13,375

$$\text{Average net borrowings} = \frac{2,500,000 + 13,375,000}{2} = £7,937,500$$

Net borrowings plus shareholders' funds

Shareholders' funds in CC £ (inclusive of proposed dividends)	126,729	108,883
Add: net borrowings	2,500	13,375
	129,229	122,258

Or, alternatively:

	£'000	£'000
Non-current assets	94,350	98,175
Inventory	26,379	17,708
MWC	8,500	6,375
	129,229	122,258

$$\text{Average } L + S = \frac{129,229,000 + 122,258,000}{2}$$
$$= 125,743,500$$

$$\text{So gearing} = \frac{L}{L+S} \times A$$
$$= \frac{7,937,500}{125,743,500} \times \frac{(\text{COSA} + \text{MWCA} + \text{extra depreciation})}{(3,798,000 + 1,345,000 + 5,695,000)}$$
$$= 6.31\% \text{ of } £10,838,000 = £683,877, \text{ say } £684,000$$

Thus the CC adjustment of £10,838,000 charged against historical profit may be reduced by £684,000 due to a gain being derived from net borrowings during a period of inflation as shown in Figure 7.6. The £684,000 is shown as a deduction from interest payable.

Figure 7.6 Economica plc CCA statement of income

Economica plc CCA statement of comprehensive income for year ended 31 December 20X5
(i.e. under the operating capital maintenance concept)

		£000
Turnover		42,500
Cost of sales		(12,070)
Gross profit		30,430
Distribution costs		(2,460)
Administrative expenses		(1,620)
Historical cost operating profit		26,350
Current cost operating adjustments (from Section 7.7.2 above)		**(10,838)**
Current cost operating profit		15,512
Interest payable	(880)	
Gearing adjustment	**684**	(196)
Current profit on ordinary activities before taxation		15,316
Tax on profit on ordinary activities		(8,470)
Current cost profit for the financial year		6,846
Dividends declared		(5,000)
Current cost profit retained		1,846
EPS		13.7p

7.7.6 The closing current cost statement of financial position

The closing statement with the non-current assets and inventory restated at current cost and the retained profit adjusted for current cost operating adjustments as reduced by the gearing adjustment is set out in Figure 7.7.

7.7.7 Real terms system

The real terms system combines both CPP and current cost concepts. This requires a calculation of total unrealised holding gains and an inflation adjustment as calculated in Workings 10 and 11 below.

(W10) Total unrealised holding gains to be used in Figure 7.8

[Closing statement of financial position at CC – Closing statement of financial position at HC] – [Opening statement of financial position at CC – Opening statement of financial position at HC]

= (£121,729,000 – £77,500,000) – (£104,883,000 – £65,500,000) = £4,846,000

(Working 8)   (Figure 7.3)   (Working 8)   (Figure 7.3)

Figure 7.7 Economica plc CCA statement of financial position

Economica plc CCA statement of financial position as at 31 December 20X5

20X4			20X5	
£000	£000	Non-current assets	£000	£000
140,250		Property, plant and equipment	157,250	
42,075		Depreciation	62,900	
	98,175			94,350
		Current assets		
17,708		Inventory	26,379	
23,375		Trade receivables	34,000	
1,875		Cash	17,000	
42,958			77,379	
		Current liabilities		
17,000		Trade payables	25,500	
		Other payables		
4,250		— income tax	8,500	
4,000		— dividend declared	5,000	
25,250			39,000	
	17,708	Net current assets		38,379
		Non-current liabilities		
	(11,000)			(11,000)
	6,708			27,379
	104,883			121,729
	£000	Capital and reserves		£000
	50,000	Called-up share capital		50,000
	1,500	Share premium account		1,500
	53,383	Total of other reserves		70,229
	104,883			121,729

Analysis of 'Total of other reserves'

	£000			£000
	14,000	Statement of income		15,846
	39,383	Current cost reserve		54,383
	53,383			70,229

continued

Figure 7.7 (continued)

Movements on reserves

(a) Statement of income:

	£000
Balance at 1 January 20X5	14,000 (from Figure 7.5)
Current cost retained profit	1,846 (from Figure 7.6)
Balance at 31 December 20X5	15,846

(b) Current cost reserve:

	Total £000	Non-current assets £000	Inventory £000	MWCA £000	Gearing £000
Balance as at 1 January 20X5	39,383	38,675	708		
Movements during the year:					
Unrealised holding gains in year	10,541	10,370	171		
Gearing adjustment	(684)				(684)
MWCA	1,345			1,345	
COSA	3,798		3,798		
Balance as at 31 December 20X5	54,383	49,045	4,677	1,345	(684)

(W11) General price index numbers to be used to calculate the inflation adjustment in Figure 7.8

General price index at 1 January 20X5   = 317.2
General price index at 31 December 20X5 = 333.2
Opening shareholders' funds at CC × percentage change in GPI during the year =

$$104,883,000 \times \frac{333.2 - 317.2}{317.2} = £5,290,435 \text{ , say } £5,290,000$$

The GPP (or CPP) real terms financial capital

The real terms financial capital maintenance concept may be incorporated within the CCA system as in Figure 7.8 by calculating an inflation adjustment.

7.8 Critique of CCA statements

Considerable effort and expense are involved in compiling and publishing CCA statements. Does their usefulness justify the cost? CCA statements have the following uses:

1 The operating capital maintenance statement reveals CCA profit. Such profit has removed inflationary price increases in raw materials and other inventories, and thus is more realistic than the alternative HCA profit.

2 Significant increases in a company's buying and selling prices will give the HCA profit a holding gains content. That is, the reported HCA profit will include gains consequent upon holding inventories during a period when the cost of buying such inventories increases. Conversely, if specific inventory prices fall, HCA profit will be reduced as it takes account of losses sustained by holding inventory while its price drops. Holding gains and losses are quite different from operating gains and losses. HCA profit does not distinguish between the two, whereas CCA profit does.

Figure 7.8 Economica plc real terms statement of comprehensive income

Economica plc CCA statement of income under the real terms system
for the year ended 31 December 20X5

	£000	£000
Historical cost profit after tax for the financial year		17,000
Add: Total unrealised holding gains arising during the year (see W10)	4,846	
Less: Realised holding gains previously recognised as unrealised	none	
	4,846	
Less: Inflation adjustment to CCA shareholders' funds (W11)	(5,290)	
Real holding gains		(444)
Total real gains		16,556
Deduct: dividends declared		5,000
Amount retained		11,556

Real terms system: analysis of reserves

20X4 £000		20X5 £000
53,383	*Statement of income*	64,939
—	Financial capital maintenance reserve	5,290
53,383		70,229

Movements on reserves

	Income statement £000	Financial capital maintenance reserve £000
Balances at 1 January 20X5	53,383	—
Amount retained	11,556	—
Inflation adjustment for year		5,290
Balances as at 31 December 20X5	64,939	5,290

3 HCA profit might be adjusted to reflect the moving price-level syndrome:

   (a) by use of the operating capital maintenance approach, which regards only the CCA **operating** profit as the authentic result for the period and which treats any holding gain or loss as a movement on reserves;

   (b) by adoption of the real terms **financial** capital maintenance approach, which applies a general inflation measure via the RPI, combined with CCA information regarding holding gains.

Thus the statement can reveal information to satisfy the demands of the management of the entity itself – as distinct from the shareholder/proprietor, whose awareness of inflation may centre on the RPI. In this way the concern of operating management can be accommodated with the different interest of the shareholder. The HCA profit would fail on both these counts.

4 CC profit is important because:

(a) it quantifies cost of sales and depreciation after allowing for changing price levels; hence trading results, free of inflationary elements, grant a clear picture of entity activities and management performance;

(b) resources are maintained, as a result of having eliminated the possibility of paying dividend out of real capital;

(c) yardsticks for management performance are more comparable as a time series within the one entity and between entities, the distortion caused by moving prices having been alleviated.

7.9 The ASB approach

The ASB has been wary of this topic. It is only too aware that standard setters in the past have been unsuccessful in obtaining a consensus on the price-level adjusting model to be used in financial statements. The chronology in Figure 7.9 illustrates the previous attempts to deal with the topic. Consequently, the ASB has clearly decided to follow a gradualist approach and to require uniformity in the treatment of specific assets and liabilities where it is current practice to move away from historical costs.

The ASB view was set out in a Discussion Paper, *The Role of Valuation in Financial Reporting*, issued in 1993.[1] The ASB had three options when considering the existing system of modified historic costs:

- to remove the right to modify cost in the statement of financial position;
- to introduce a coherent current value system immediately;
- to make *ad hoc* improvements to the present modified historic cost system.

Figure 7.9 Standard setters' unsuccessful attempts to replace HCA

1974	Statement of Accounting Practice SSAP 7 *Accounting for Changes in the Purchasing Power of Money* advocating the CPP model.
1975	*Inflation Accounting*, Report of the Inflation Accounting Committee (The Sandilands Report) advocating current cost accounting (CCA) rather than the CPP, RCA or NRVA model. The CCA system recommended by Sandilands was based on the deprival value of an asset, i.e. the value based on the loss, direct or indirect, sustainable by an entity if it were to be deprived of the asset concerned.
1984	SSAP 16 *Current Cost Accounting* was issued by the ASC requiring listed companies to produce CCA accounts as their primary financial report. There was widespread non-compliance and a new exposure draft ED 35 was issued effectively retaining HCA accounts as the primary financial report with supplementary current cost information.
1985	SSAP 16 was withdrawn and the ASC issued *Accounting for the Effects of Changing Prices: A Handbook*. The Handbook was interesting in that it set out four valuation bases if the financial capital maintenance concept was applied and four valuation bases if the operating capital maintenance concept was applied. Its preferred options were CCA under the financial capital maintenance concept which it referred to as real terms accounting (RTA) and CCA under the operating capital maintenance concept.

7.9.1 Remove the right to modify cost in the statement of financial position

This would mean pruning the system back to one rigorously based on the principles of historical costs, with current values shown by way of note.

This option has strong support from the profession not only in the UK, e.g. 'in our view . . . the most significant advantage of historical cost over current value accounting . . . is that it is based on the actual transactions which the company has undertaken and the cash flows that it has generated . . . this is an advantage not just in terms of reliability, but also in terms of relevance',[2] but also in the USA, e.g. 'a study showed that users were opposed to replacing the current historic cost based accounting model . . . because it provides them with a stable and consistent benchmark that they can rely on to establish historical trends'.[3]

Although this would have brought UK practice into line with that of the USA and some of the EU countries, it has been rejected. This is no doubt on the basis that the ASB wishes to see current values established in the UK in the longer term.

7.9.2 Introduce a coherent current value system immediately

This would mean developing the system into one more clearly founded on principles embracing current values. One such system, advocated by the ASB in Chapter 6 of its *Statement of Accounting Principles*, is based on **value to the business**. The value to the business measurement model is eclectic in that it draws on various current value systems. The approach to establishing the value to the business of a specific asset is quite logical:

● If an asset is worth replacing, then use replacement cost (RC).

● If it is not worth replacing, then use:

   – value in use (economic value) if it is worth keeping; or

   – net realisable value (NRV) if it is not worth keeping.

The reasoning is that the value to the business is represented by the action that would be taken by a business if it were to be deprived of an asset – this is also referred to as the **deprival value**.

For example, assume the following:

	£
Historical cost	200,000
Accumulated depreciation (6 years straight line)	120,000
Net book value	80,000
Replacement cost (gross)	300,000
Aggregate depreciation	180,000
Depreciated replacement cost	120,000
Net realisable value (NRV)	50,000
Value in use (discounted future income)	70,565

If the asset were destroyed then it would be irrational to replace it at its depreciated replacement cost of £120,000 considering that the asset has a value in use of only £70,565.

However, the ASB did not see it as feasible to implement this system at that time because 'there is much work to be done to determine whether or not it is possible to devise a system that would be of economic relevance and acceptable to users and preparers of financial statements in terms of sufficient reliability without prohibitive cost'.[4]

7.9.3 Make *ad hoc* improvements to the present modified historical cost system

In the UK the *Statement of Accounting Principles* envisages that a mixed measurement system will be used and it focuses on the mix of historical cost and current value to be adopted.[5]

It is influenced in choosing this option by the recognition that there are anxieties about the costs and benefits of moving to a full current value system, and by the belief that a considerable period of experimentation and learning would be needed before such a major change could be successfully introduced.[6]

The historical cost based system and the current value based system have far more to commend them than the *ad hoc* option chosen by the ASB. However, as a short-term measure, it leaves the way open for the implementation in the longer term of its preferred value to the business model.

7.10 The IASC/IASB approach

The IASB has struggled in the same way as the ASB in the UK in deciding how to respond to inflation rates that have varied so widely over time. Theoretically there is a case for inflation-adjusting financial statements whatever the rate of inflation, but standard setters need to carry the preparers and users of accounts with them – this means that there has to be a consensus that the traditional HCA financial statements are failing to give a true and fair view. Such a consensus is influenced by the current rate of inflation.

When the rates around the world were in double figures, there was pressure for a **mandatory** standard so that financial statements were comparable. This led to the issue in 1983 of IAS 15 *Information Reflecting the Effects of Changing Prices* which required companies to restate the HCA accounts using either a general price index or replacement costs with adjustments for depreciation, cost of sales and monetary items.

As the inflation rates fell below double figures, there was less willingness by companies to prepare inflation-adjusted accounts and so, in 1989, the mandatory requirement was relaxed and the application of IAS 15 became **optional**.

In recent years the inflation rates in developed countries have ranged between 1% and 4% and so in 2003, 20 years after it was first issued, IAS 15 was **withdrawn** as part of the ASB Improvement Project.

These low rates have not been universal outside the developed world and there has remained a need to prepare inflation-adjusted financial statements where there is hyper-inflation and the rates are so high that HCA would be misleading.

7.10.1 The IASB position where there is hyperinflation

What do we mean by hyperinflation?

IAS 29 *Financial Reporting in Hyperinflationary Economies* states that hyperinflation occurs when money loses purchasing power at such a rate that comparison of amounts from transactions that have occurred at different times, even within the same accounting period, is misleading.

What rate indicates that hyperinflation exists?

IAS 29 does not specify an absolute rate – this is a matter of qualitative judgement – but it sets out certain pointers, such as people preferring to keep their wealth in non-monetary assets, people preferring prices to be stated in terms of an alternative stable currency rather than the domestic currency, wages and prices being linked to a price index, or the cumulative inflation rate over three years approaching 100%.

Countries where hyperinflation has occurred recently include Angola, Burma and Turkey.

How are financial statements adjusted?

The current year financial statements, whether HCA or CCA, must be restated using the domestic measuring unit current at the statement of financial position date; if the current year should be the first year that restatement takes place then the opening statement of financial position also has to be restated.

Illustration of accounting policy in IAS 29 adjusted accounts

The following is an extract from the 2011 Annual Report of Coca-Cola Hellenic Bottling Company S.A.

Basis of preparation and accounting policies (continued)
Entities operating in hyperinflationary economies prepare financial statements that are recorded in accordance with IAS 29 *Financial Reporting in Hyperinflationary Economies.* The gain or loss on net monetary position is recorded in finance costs. The application of hyperinflation accounting includes:

- Adjustment of the historical cost of non-monetary assets and liabilities and the various items of equity from their date of acquisition or inclusion in the balance sheet to the end of the year for the changes in purchasing power of the currency caused by inflation.

- The various components in the income statement and statement of cash flows have been adjusted for the inflation index since their generation.

- The subsidiary's financial statements are translated at the closing exchange rate.

7.11 Future developments

A mixed picture emerges when we try to foresee the future of changing price levels and financial reporting. The accounting profession has been reluctant to abandon the HC concept in favour of a 'valuation accounting' approach. In the UK and Australia many companies have stopped revaluing their non-current assets, with a large proportion opting instead to revert to the historical cost basis, with the two main factors influencing management's decision being cost-effectiveness and future reporting flexibility.[7]

The pragmatic approach is prevailing with each class of asset and liability being considered on an individual basis. For example, non-current assets are reported at depreciated replacement cost unless this is higher than the economic value we discussed in Chapter 6; financial assets are reported at market value (exit value in the NRV model); and current assets reported at the lower of HC and NRV. In each case the resulting changes, both realised and unrealised, in value will find their way into the financial performance statement(s).

Fair values

A number of IFRSs now require or allow the use of fair values, e.g. IFRS 3 *Business Combinations* in which fair value is defined as 'the amount for which an asset could be exchanged or a liability settled between knowledgeable, willing parties in an arm's length transaction'. This is equivalent to the NRVA model discussed above. It is defined as an exit value rather than a cost value but like NRVA it does not imply a forced sale, i.e. it is the best value that could be obtained.

It is interesting to note that in the US there is a view that financial statements should be primarily decision-useful. This is a move away from the position adopted by the IASB in its conceptual framework in which it states that financial statements have two functions – one to provide investors with the means to assess stewardship and the other to provide them with the means to make sound economic decisions.

How will financial statements be affected if fair values are adopted?

The financial statements will have the same virtues and defects as the NRVA model (section 7.6.4 above). Some concerns have been raised that reported annual income will become more volatile and the profit that is reported may contain a mix of realised and unrealised profits. Supporters of the use of fair values see the statements of income and financial position as more relevant for decision making whilst accepting that the figures might be less reliable and not as effective as a means of assessing the stewardship by the directors.

Stewardship

Before the growth of capital markets, stewardship was the primary objective of financial reporting. This is reflected in company law, which viewed management as agents of the shareholders who should periodically provide an account of their performance to explain the use they have made of the resources that the owners put under their control, i.e. it is a means of governance by providing *retrospective* accountability.

With the growth of capital markets, the ability to generate cash flows became important when making decisions as to whether to buy, sell or hold shares, i.e. it is concerned with *prospective* performance.

This has given rise to an ongoing debate over the relative importance of stewardship reporting and there is a fundamental difference between the US and Europe. In the US, stewardship is seen as secondary to decision-usefulness, whereas in Europe reporting the past use of resources is seen as just as important as reporting the future wealth-generating potential of those resources.

In their efforts to agree on a common approach, the IASB and FASB issued a Discussion Paper entitled *Preliminary Views on an Improved Conceptual Framework for Financial Reporting* which proposed that the converged framework should specify only one objective of financial reporting, namely the provision of information useful in making future resource allocation decisions. However, there is a strong argument to support the explicit recognition of two equal objectives.

The first is retrospective and stewardship based, and helps investors to assess the management: Have their strategies been effective? Have the assets been protected? Have the resources produced an adequate return? The second is prospective, helping investors to make a judgement as to future performance – a judgement that might well be influenced by their assessment of the past.

It is interesting to note that the IASB *Framework*[8] currently supports the importance of financial statements as a means of assessing stewardship, stating:

> Financial statements also show the results of the stewardship of management, or the accountability of management for the resources entrusted to it. Those users who wish to assess the stewardship or accountability of management do so in order that they make economic decisions; these decisions may include, for example, whether to hold or sell their investment in the enterprise or whether to reappoint or replace the management.

Any revision to the conceptual framework should hold firm to equal weight being given to retrospective and prospective objectives.

The gradualist approach

It is very possible that the number of international standards requiring or allowing fair values will increase over time and reflect the adoption on a piecemeal basis. In the meantime, efforts[9] are in hand for the FASB and IASB to arrive at a common definition of fair value which can be applied to value assets and liabilities where there is no market value available. Agreeing a definition, however, is only a part of the exercise. If analysts are to be able to compare corporate performance across borders, then it is essential that both the FASB and the IASB agree that all companies should adopt fair value accounting – it has been proving difficult to gain acceptance for this in the US.

This means that in the future historical cost and realisation will be regarded as less relevant[10] and investors, analysts and management will need to come to terms with increased volatility in reported annual performance.

Summary

The traditional HCA system reveals disturbing inadequacies in times of changing price levels, calling into question the value of financial reports using this system. Considerable resources and energy have been expended in searching for a substitute model able to counter the distortion and confusion caused by an unstable monetary unit.

Three basic models have been developed: RCA, NRVA and CPP. Each has its merits and defects; each produces a different income value and a different capital value. However, it is important that inflation-adjusted values be computed in order to avoid a possible loss of entity resources and the collapse of the going concern.

In assessing future prospects, it would seem that more useful financial information is needed. This need will be met by changes in the reporting system, which are beginning to include some form of 'value accounting' as distinct from HC accounting. Such value accounting will probably embrace inflationary adjustments to enable comparability to be maintained, as far as possible, in an economic environment of changing prices.

The contemporary financial reporting scene continues to be dynamic, including addressing measurement problems such as identifying impairment of tangible and intangible assets based on deprival values (discussed in Chapter 17) and measuring financial assets using discounted future cash flows and various valuation models (discussed in Chapter 14).

REVIEW QUESTIONS

1 Explain why financial reports prepared under the historical cost convention are subject to the following major limitations:

- inventory is undervalued;
- the depreciation charge to the statement of comprehensive income is understated;
- gains and losses on net monetary assets are undisclosed;
- statement of financial position values are understated;
- periodic comparisons are invalidated.

2 Explain how each of the limitations in Question 1 could be overcome.

3 Compare the operating and financial capital maintenance concepts.

4 Explain the features of the CPP model in contrast with those of the CCA model.

5 '... the IASB's failure to decide on a capital maintenance concept is regrettable as users have no idea as to whether total gains represent income or capital and are therefore unable to identify a meaningful "bottom line".'[11] Discuss.

6 'To be relevant to investors, the profit for the year should include both realised and unrealised gains/losses.' Discuss.

7 Discuss why there are objections to financial statements being prepared using the NRVA model.

8 Explain the criteria for determining whether hyperinflation exists.

EXERCISES

* Question 1

Raiders plc prepares accounts annually to 31 March. The following figures, prepared on a conventional historical cost basis, are included in the company's accounts to 31 March 20X5.

1 In the income statement:

	£000	£000
(i) Cost of goods sold:		
Inventory at 1 April 20X4	9,600	
Purchases	39,200	
	48,800	
Inventory at 31 March 20X5	11,300	37,500
(ii) Depreciation of equipment		8,640

2 In the statement of financial position:

	£000	£000
(iii) Equipment at cost	57,600	
Less: Accumulated depreciation	16,440	41,160
(iv) Inventory		11,300

The inventory held on 31 March 20X4 and 31 March 20X5 was in each case purchased evenly during the last six months of the company's accounting year.

Equipment is depreciated at a rate of 15% per annum, using the straight-line method. Equipment owned on 31 March 20X5 was purchased as follows: on 1 April 20X2 at a cost of £16 million; on 1 April 20X3 at a cost of £20 million; and on 1 April 20X4 at a cost of £21.6 million.

	Current cost of inventory	Current cost of equipment	Retail Price Index
1 April 20X2	109	145	313
1 April 20X3	120	162	328
30 September 20X3	128	170	339
31 December 20X3	133	175	343
31 March/1 April 20X4	138	180	345
30 September 20X4	150	191	355
31 December 20X4	156	196	360
31 March 20X5	162	200	364

Required:
(a) Calculate the following current cost accounting figures:
   (i)   The cost of goods sold of Raiders plc for the year ended 31 March 20X5.
   (ii) The statement of financial position value of inventory at 31 March 20X5.
   (iii) The equipment depreciation charge for the year ended 31 March 20X5.
   (iv) The net statement of financial position value of equipment at 31 March 20X5.
(b) Discuss the extent to which the figures you have calculated in (a) above (together with figures calculated on a similar basis for earlier years) provide information over and above that provided by the conventional historical cost statement of comprehensive income and statement of financial position figures.
(c) Outline the main reasons why the standard setters have experienced so much difficulty in their attempts to develop an accounting standard on accounting for changing prices.

Question 2

The finance director of Toy plc has been asked by a shareholder to explain items that appear in the current cost statement of comprehensive income for the year ended 31.8.20X9 and the statement of financial position as at that date:

		£	£
Historical cost profit			143,000
Cost of sales adjustment	(1)	10,000	
Additional depreciation	(2)	6,000	
Monetary working capital adjustment	(3)	2,500	18,500
Current cost operating profit before tax			124,500
Gearing adjustment	(4)		2,600
CCA operating profit			127,100
Non-current assets at gross replacement cost		428,250	
Accumulated current cost depreciation	(5)	(95,650)	332,600
Net current assets			121,400
12% debentures			(58,000)
			396,000
Issued share capital			250,000
Current cost reserve	(6)		75,000
Retained earnings			71,000
			396,000

Required:
(a) Explain what each of the items numbered 1–6 represents and the purpose of each.
(b) What do you consider to be the benefits to users of providing current cost information?

* Question 3

The statements of financial position of Parkway plc for 20X7 and 20X8 are given below, together with the income statement for the year ended 30 June 20X8.

	Statement of financial position					
	20X8			20X7		
	£000	£000	£000	£000	£000	£000
Non-current assets	Cost	Depn	NBV	Cost	Depn	NBV
Freehold land	60,000	—	60,000	60,000	—	60,000
Buildings	40,000	8,000	32,000	40,000	7,200	32,800
Plant and machinery	30,000	16,000	14,000	30,000	10,000	20,000
Vehicles	40,000	20,000	20,000	40,000	12,000	28,000
	170,000	44,000	126,000	170,000	29,200	140,800
Current assets						
Inventory		80,000			70,000	
Trade receivables		60,000			40,000	
Short-term investments		50,000			—	
Cash at bank and in hand		5,000			5,000	
		195,000			115,000	
Current liabilities						
Trade payables		90,000			60,000	
Bank overdraft		50,000			45,000	
Taxation		28,000			15,000	
Dividends declared		15,000			10,000	
		183,000			130,000	
Net current assets			12,000			(15,000)
			138,000			125,800
Financed by						
Ordinary share capital			80,000			80,000
Share premium			10,000			10,000
Retained profits			28,000			15,800
			118,000			105,800
Long-term loans			20,000			20,000
			138,000			125,800

Statement of income of Parkway plc
for the year ended 30 June 20X8

	£000
Sales	738,000
Cost of sales	620,000
Gross profit	118,000

Notes

1 The freehold land and buildings were purchased on 1 July 20X0. The company policy is to depreciate buildings over 50 years and to provide no depreciation on land.
2 Depreciation on plant and machinery and motor vehicles is provided at the rate of 20% per annum on a straight-line basis.
3 Depreciation on buildings and plant and equipment has been included in administration expenses, while that on motor vehicles is included in distribution expenses.
4 The directors of Parkway plc have provided you with the following information relating to price rises:

	RPI	Inventory	Land	Buildings	Plant	Vehicles
1 July 20X0	100	60	70	50	90	120
1 July 20X7	170	140	290	145	135	180
30 June 20X8	190	180	310	175	165	175
Average for year ending 30 June 20X8	180	160	300	163	145	177

Required:
(a) Making and stating any assumptions that are necessary, and giving reasons for those assumptions, calculate the monetary working capital adjustment for Parkway plc.
(b) Critically evaluate the usefulness of the monetary working capital adjustment.

* Question 4

The historical cost accounts of Smith plc are as follows:

Smith plc Statement of income for the year ended 31 December 20X8

	£000	£000
Sales		2,000
Cost of sales:		
Opening inventory 1 January 20X8	320	
Purchases	1,680	
	2,000	
Closing inventory at 31 December 20X8	280	
		1,720
Gross profit		280
Depreciation	20	
Administration expenses	100	
		120
Net profit		160

Statement of financial position of Smith plc as at 31 December 20X8

		20X7		20X8
		£000		£000
Non-current assets				
Land and buildings at cost		1,360		1,360
Less aggregate depreciation		(160)		(180)
		1,200		1,180
Current assets				
Inventory	320		280	
Trade receivables	80		160	
Cash at bank	40		120	
	440		560	
Trade payables	200		140	
		240		420
		1,440		1,600
Ordinary share capital		800		800
Retained profit		640		800
		1,440		1,600

Notes

1 Land and buildings were acquired in 20X0 with the buildings component costing £800,000 and depreciated over 40 years.
2 Share capital was issued in 20X0.
3 Closing inventories were acquired in the last quarter of the year.
4 RPI numbers were:

Average for 20X0	120
20X7 last quarter	216
At 31 December 20X7	220
20X8 last quarter	232
Average for 20X8	228
At 31 December 20X8	236

Required:

(i) Explain the basic concept of the CPP accounting system.

(ii) Prepare CPP accounts for Smith plc for the year ended 20X8.

The following steps will assist in preparing the CPP accounts:

(a) Restate the statement of comprehensive income for the current year in terms of £CPP at the year-end.

(b) Restate the closing statement of financial position in £CPP at year-end, but excluding monetary items, i.e. trade receivables, trade payables, cash at bank.

(c) Restate the opening statement of financial position in £CPP at year-end, but including monetary items, i.e. trade receivables, trade payables and cash at bank, and showing equity as the balancing figure.

(d) Compare the opening and closing equity figures derived in (b) and (c) above to arrive at the total profit/loss for the year in CPP terms. Compare this figure with the CPP profit calculated in (a) above to determine the monetary gain or monetary loss.

(e) Reconcile monetary gains/loss in (d) with the increase/decrease in net monetary items during the year expressed in £CPP compared with the increase/decrease expressed in £HC.

* Question 5

Shower Ltd was incorporated towards the end of 20X2, but it did not start trading until 20X3. Its historical cost statement of financial position at 1 January 20X3 was as follows:

	£
Share capital, £1 shares	2,000
Loan (interest free)	8,000
	£10,000
Non-current assets, at cost	6,000
Inventory, at cost (4,000 units)	4,000
	£10,000

A summary of Shower Limited's bank account for 20X3 is given below:

		£	£
1 Jan 20X3	Opening balance		nil
30 Jun 20X3	Sales (8,000 units)		20,000
Less			
29 Jun 20X3	Purchase (6,000 units)	9,000	
	Sundry expenses	5,000	14,000
31 Dec 20X3	Closing balance		£6,000

All the company's transactions are on a cash basis.

The non-current assets are expected to last for five years and the company intends to depreciate its non-current assets on a straight-line basis. The non-current assets had a resale value of £2,000 at 31 December 20X3.

Notes
1. The closing inventory is 2,000 units and the inventory is sold on a first-in-first-out basis.
2. All prices remained constant from the date of incorporation to 1 January 20X3, but thereafter, various relevant price indices moved as follows:

		Specific indices	
	General price level	Inventory	Non-current assets
1 January 20X3	100	100	100
30 June 20X3	120	150	140
31 December 20X3	240	255	200

Required:
Produce statements of financial position as at December 20X3 and statements of comprehensive income for the year ended on that date on the basis of:
(i) historical cost;
(ii) current purchasing power (general price level);
(iii) replacement cost;
(iv) continuous contemporary accounting (NRVA).

Question 6

Aspirations Ltd commenced trading as wholesale suppliers of office equipment on 1 January 20X1, issuing ordinary shares of £1 each at par in exchange for cash. The shares were fully paid on issue, the number issued being 1,500,000.

The following financial statements, based on the historical cost concept, were compiled for 20X1.

Aspirations Ltd

Statement of income for the year ended 31 December 20X1

	£	£
Sales		868,425
Purchases	520,125	
Less: Inventory 31 December 20X1	24,250	
Cost of sales		495,875
Gross profit		372,550
Expenses	95,750	
Depreciation	25,250	
		121,000
Net profit		251,550

Statement of financial position as at 31 December 20X1

Non-current assets	Cost £	Depreciation £	£
Freehold property	650,000	6,500	643,500
Office equipment	375,000	18,750	356,250
	1,025,000	25,250	999,750
Current assets			
Inventories		24,250	
Trade receivables		253,500	
Cash		1,090,300	
		1,368,050	
Current liabilities		116,250	
		1,251,800	
Non-current liabilities		500,000	751,800
			1,751,550
Issued share capital			
1,500,000 £1 ordinary shares			1,500,000
Retained earnings			251,550
			1,751,550

The year 20X1 witnessed a surge of inflation and in consequence the directors became concerned about the validity of the revenue account and statement of financial position as income and capital statements. Index numbers reflecting price changes were:

Specific index numbers reflecting replacement costs

	1 January 20X1	31 December 20X1	Average for 20X1
Inventory	115	150	130
Freehold property	110	165	127
Office equipment	125	155	145
General price index numbers	135	170	155

Regarding current exit costs

Inventory is anticipated to sell at a profit of 75% of cost.

Value of assets at 31 December 20X1

	£
Freehold property	640,000
Office equipment	350,000

Initial purchases of inventory were effected on 1 January 20X1 amounting to £34,375; the balance of purchases was evenly spread over the 12-month period. The non-current assets were acquired on 1 January 20X1 and, together with the initial inventory, were paid for in cash on that day.

Required:
Prepare the accounts adjusted for current values using each of the three proposed models of current value accounting: namely, the accounting methods known as replacement cost, general (or current) purchasing power and net realisable value.

Question 7

Antonio Rossi set up a part-time business on 1 November 2004 buying and selling second-hand sports cars. On 1 November 2004 he commenced business with $66,000 which he immediately used to purchase 10 identical sports cars costing $6,600 each, paying in cash. On 1 May 2005 he sold seven of the sports cars for $8,800 each, receiving the cash immediately. Antonio estimates that the net realisable value of each sports car remaining unsold was $8,640 as at 31 October 2005.

The replacement cost of similar sports cars was $6,800 as at 1 May 2005 and $7,000 as at 31 October 2005, and the value of a relevant general price index was 150 as at 1 November 2004, 155 as at 1 May 2005 and 159 as at 31 October 2005.

Antonio paid the proceeds from the sales on 1 May 2005 into a special bank account for the business and made no drawings and incurred no expenses over the year ending 31 October 2005.

Antonio's accountant has told him that there are different ways of calculating profit and financial position and has produced the following figures:

Current purchasing power accounting Profit and Loss Account for the year ended 31 October 2005

	$
Sales	63,190
less Cost of sales	48,972
	14,218
Loss on monetary item	(1,590)
CPP net income	12,628

Balance sheet as at 31 October 2005

	$
Assets	
Inventory	20,988
Cash	61,600
	82,588
Financed by:	
Opening capital	69,960
Profit for the year	12,628
	82,588

Current cost accounting Profit and Loss Account for the year ended 31 October 2005

	$
Historical cost profit	15,400
less Cost of sales adjustment	1,400
Current cost income	14,000

Balance sheet as at 31 October 2005

	$
Assets	
Inventory	21,000
Cash	61,600
	82,600
Financed by:	
Opening capital	66,000
Current cost reserve	2,600
Profit for the year	14,000
	82,600

Required:
(a) Prepare Antonio's historical cost profit and loss account for the year ended 31 October 2005 and his balance sheet as at 31 October 2005.
(b) (i) Explain how the figures for Sales and Cost of sales were calculated for the current purchasing power profit and loss account. You need not provide detailed calculations.
   (ii) Explain what the 'loss on monetary item' means. In what circumstances would there be a profit on monetary items?
(c) (i) Explain how the 'cost of sales adjustment' was calculated and what it means. You need not provide detailed calculations.
   (ii) Identify and explain the purpose of any three other adjustments which you might expect to see in a current cost profit and loss account prepared in this way.
(d) State, giving your reasons, which of the three bases gives the best measure of Antonio's financial performance and financial position.

(The Association of International Accountants)

References

1 *The Role of Valuation in Financial Reporting*, ASB, 1993.
2 Ernst & Young, *UK GAAP* (4th edition), 1994, p. 91.
3 *The Information Needs of Investors and Creditors*, AICPA Special Committee on Financial Reporting.
4 *The Role of Valuation in Financial Reporting*, ASB, 1993, para. 31(ii).
5 *Statement of Accounting Principles*, ASB, December 1999, para. 6.4.
6 *The Role of Valuation in Financial Reporting*, ASB, 1993, para. 33.
7 Ernst & Young, 'Revaluation of non-current assets', Accounting Standard, Ernst & Young, January 2002, www.ey.com/Global/gcr.nsf/Australia.
8 *Framework for the Preparation and Presentation of Financial Statements*, IASC, 1989, adopted by IASB 2001, para. 14.
9 SFAS 157 *Fair Value Measurement*, FASB, 2006.
10 A. Wilson, 'IAS: the challenge for measurement', *Accountancy*, December 2001, p. 90.
11 N. Fry and D. Bence, 'Capital or income?', *Accountancy*, April 2007, p. 81.

Bibliography

W.T. Baxter, *Depreciation*, Sweet and Maxwell, 1971.
W.T. Baxter, *Inflation Accounting*, Philip Alan, 1984.
W.T. Baxter, *The Case for Deprival Accounting*, ICAS, 2003.
E.O. Edwards and P.W. Bell, *The Theory and Measurement of Business Income*, University of California Press, 1961.
J.R. Hicks, *Value and Capital* (2nd edition), OUP, 1975.
T.A. Lee, *Income and Value Measurement: Theory and Practice* (3rd edition), Van Nostrand Reinhold (UK), 1985, Chapter 5.
D.R. Myddleton, *On a Cloth Untrue – Inflation Accounting: The Way Forward*, Woodhead-Faulkner, 1984.
R.H. Parker and G.C. Harcourt (eds), *Readings in the Concept and Measurement of Income*, Cambridge University Press, 1969.
D. Tweedie and G. Whittington, *Capital Maintenance Concepts*, ASC, 1985.
D. Tweedie and G. Whittington, *The Debate on Inflation in Accounting*, Cambridge University Press, 1985.

CHAPTER 8

Revenue recognition

8.1 Introduction

Revenue recognition is at the core of the accounting process. A critical part of this process is to accurately identify those earnings outcomes which have been achieved during the period. The trend of earnings is important to investors as it affects the share price and to management as it is often the basis for determining their bonuses.

It is in seeking to maintain an upward trend that scandals involving the manipulation of earnings have arisen on a regular basis, frequently caused by the overstatement by some companies of their revenue. The extent of such manipulation and its adverse impacts is evidenced by the considerable research undertaken in the US which has provided us with reliable statistics.

Adverse effect on capital markets

The US Government Accountability Office reports[1] that in 2005 6.8% of listed companies had to restate earnings, and during the period July 2002 to September 2005, the restatements affected market values by $36 billion. Of those restatements, 20.1% of the restatements were in relation to revenue recognition. Thus correct revenue recognition is important for the effective operation of the capital markets.

Adverse effect on staff prospects

It is not only investors who suffer. Collins *et al.* (2009)[2] suggest that chief financial officers of restating companies have an enhanced likelihood of losing their job and find it harder to get comparable jobs subsequently.

This chapter will discuss the principles underlying revenue recognition and measurement, and the ethical issues arising out of attempts to circumvent the rules. The discussion will primarily be based on the exposure draft *Revenue from Contracts with Customers*, ED/2011/6, issued jointly by the Financial Accounting Standards Board in the USA and the International Accounting Standards Board in November 2011.

Objectives

By the end of this chapter, you should be able to:

- apply the principles of revenue recognition and measurement to typical accounting situations;
- understand the complexities of developing universally applicable revenue recognition standards;
- understand the importance of complying with the spirit as well as the detail of the revenue accounting standard;
- identify the situations in which there are industry-specific revenue recognition rules covered by separate standards.

8.2 The issues

Revenue broadly defined is the gross benefit arising from provision of goods and services to external parties for which remuneration is receivable. If the provision of goods or services is immediately followed by the receipt of remuneration in cash or cash equivalents (e.g. entitlement to cash from a credit card provider) then there is little controversy.

The accounting difficulties arise when

- there is a significant probability that the full amount invoiced will not be received in full;
- gains arise from unusual or infrequent transactions with a decision required as to whether they are to be treated in revenue or kept separate;
- transactions are spread over several accounting periods so that it is not clear when the services have been provided;
- a single contract involves the supply of multiple goods and services which may not have similar patterns of delivery;
- the value of the transaction is difficult to determine because it involves payment in kind, volume discounts or the possibility of contract variations during the course of the contract;
- the application is so difficult in a particular industry that there has to be guidance to clarify the application of the general principles in that industry. This includes the construction industry where contracts may take several years, for example road, ship and aircraft building. (Construction contracts are discussed in Chapter 21);
- in addition, all other standards which are impacted have to be modified to bring them into agreement with the revised revenue standard or vice versa. For example, the leasing standard involves revenue recognition, so the two standards have to be made consistent. Similarly the timing of revenue recognition affects the timing of transfers from inventory into cost of goods sold and the assessment of the recoverable amount of the asset in the inventory standard. In comparable ways the revenue standard impinges on many other standards which also have to be modified.

Note that separate standards are required as for leases (see Chapter 18), the recognition of changes in market values of financial instruments (see Chapter 14), and biological assets (see Chapter 20).

The changes from the previous exposure draft in 2010 highlight some of the issues in arriving at a revenue standard. In particular the 2011 exposure draft has simplified the earlier exposure draft by allowing revenue to be recorded at the gross amount and not net of expected bad debts as was previously suggested; the treatment of warranties has been simplified rather than a distinction being made between those required under the law and those additional warranties offered by the company; allowed implied interest is to be ignored in contracts which are of less than one year; as a practical expedient allowed costs of acquiring new contracts are to be written off as an expense if the contract is for less than one year; and revenue recognition in construction contracts is to be made more explicit. These modifications highlight that the standard setters are under continued pressure from financial statement preparers to sacrifice some of the conceptual niceties in order to make the application of the standards easier.

The other complication in developing a new standard is that it is intended to be applied in the USA which is used to having much more detailed guidance in general, and many more industry guidelines. In the USA, a very litigious society, there is a philosophy that they need detailed and precise rules which they can follow. Further, there is a widespread perception that if it is not covered by rules the company is free to choose what suits it rather than trying to gauge the intent of the standard and attempting to implement that intent.

8.3 The challenge

A fair view

Accountants, in addition to checking that each transaction has been recorded in accordance with the accounting standards, still need to ask whether the resulting accounting statements give a fair view of the situation. In the final analysis it will be the courts who decide whether clever ploys to get around standards, or the taking advantage of technical accounting rules, is legitimate. In New York v Ernst & Young (Part II)[3] 451586/2010 New York State Supreme Court (Manhattan) the complaint said it was still necessary to ensure the accounts were fair. If considered unfair, they need to disclose sufficient information to rectify the situation.

Example of complexity

In the case of revenue recognition standard setters have been faced with the problem as to how to define revenue in such a way that it precludes transactions being artificially structured. Such a problem arose when Lehman Brothers in its last year entered into agreements to sell securities to a third party who agreed to sell them back after the reporting date, allowing Lehman Brothers to treat the transfer of securities as sales, thus increasing its revenue and reducing its leverage. So the major issue was whether the sale and the repurchase agreements should be treated as two separate transactions or as a single transaction.

This gave rise to the grey area as to whether to report according to the substance or according to the technical form. One could argue that reporting according to the technical form (i.e. applying an existing technical guidance) was legal; another could argue that it was misleading and could be construed as fraudulent manipulation. Of course it is desirable that accounting standards reduce the likelihood that such situations will arise, and following this case the SEC and FASB have issued new rules hoping to achieve reporting that reflects the economic substance.

8.4 Proposed IFRS *Revenue from Contracts with Customers*

There is no modification in the definition of revenues, which are still:

> Increases in economic benefits during the accounting period in the form of inflows or enhancements of assets or decreases in liabilities that result in increases in equity, other than those relating to contributions from equity participants, and that arise in the course of an entity's ordinary activities. (paragraph 1)

The proposal is restricted to coverage of contracts with customers and excludes changes in values such as when some biological and agricultural assets are revalued annually to recognise changes in values due to growth, and natural increases and decreases.

The core principle is that

> . . . an entity shall recognise revenue to depict the transfer of promised goods or services to customers in an amount that reflects the consideration to which the entity expects to be entitled in exchange for goods or services. (paragraph 3)

Note that the new proposal looks at revenue in terms of the provision of service obligations and in that way tries to incorporate both goods and services in one set of rules. Also the emphasis is on the amount which the entity is entitled to under the contract. No reduction is required in recording revenue for estimated bad debts. (In the earlier exposure draft in 2010 the estimated bad debts were deducted from revenue on the basis that such transfers in hindsight represented gifts to the recipient rather than a sale.) However, items such as VAT or equivalent are excluded because they do not increase equity but rather generate a liability to the government.

A sale of goods on credit for €1,000 plus €100 VAT would be recorded as:

Dr	Accounts receivable	1,100	
Cr	Revenue		1,000
Cr	VAT liability		100

recording the revenue plus the money being collected on behalf of the government.

In order to identify the amount and timing of the recognition of revenue, the entity has to go through five steps (paragraph 4):

(a) identify the contract with a customer;

(b) identify the separate performance obligations in the contract;

(c) determine the transaction price;

(d) allocate the transaction price to the separate performance obligations in the contract; and

(e) recognise revenue when (or as) the entity satisfies a performance obligation.

8.4.1 Identify the contract with a customer (Step 1)

The first step is to ensure there is an enforceable agreement so the terms and conditions are specified. Different countries will have different legal systems and may include in the contract additional terms and conditions. Further, there may be industry practices which are recognised by the courts.

The terms and conditions may be explicit, such as where the price is specified or the terms may specify how the price is to be ascertained. The price could be dependent on the quantity supplied under the contract or could be ascertainable by reference to a specific market. In regard to the quantity the contract may say that up to 10,000 units in the year the price shall be €10 and above that quantity the price shall be €9. An example of a reference to a market is where the price of petrol is specified as 3% below the listed market price for petrol in the Singapore market, for example, on the date of delivery.

Only when the full terms and conditions of the contract are ascertainable can it be accounted for.

Then Step 2 (see below) focuses on clarifying the nature of the different obligations involved in the contract and accounting for them separately if they do not have the same pattern of delivery. Steps 3 to 5 involve arriving at the revenue value as at the date reported.

What is a service obligation?

A service obligation would include the supply of goods, the provision of services such as consulting or dry cleaning, and compensation for making available assets such as capital (interest), intellectual property (royalties), property, plant and equipment (lease payments) and software.

8.4.2 Separate service obligations within the same contract (Step 2)

A decision has to be made as to whether the contract involves the supply of one or multiple service obligations. If you normally sell the items subject to the contract separately then there is a presumption that there is probably a supply for separate service obligations. On the other hand, if the items are highly dependent on each other or are closely interrelated then they could represent one service obligation. The other issue that would be taken into consideration is whether the pattern or timing of the delivery is the same or different. As a practical matter, if items are delivered at the same time they will be treated as a single obligation.

A contract to supply equipment and to service it for a period of years in the future would be split into two components, namely, the supply of equipment and the supply of maintenance services. The justification for treating them as separate service obligations could be that if the equipment and service contracts could be purchased separately from your company this would suggest distinct service obligations, or that the time of delivery differs, with the equipment being supplied first and the servicing occurring in subsequent periods. There is no definitive answer and each case has to be decided on its merits.

Let us illustrate the above with the following Consensus example.

Consensus Supplies plc – information on contract

Let us assume that Consensus Supplies plc sells 10 printers on credit at a price of €4,000 each when the manufactured cost was €2,000 each. Let us further assume that Consensus offers its customers a combined contract for €4,800 for each printer which includes the provision of maintenance cover for two years. The cost of manufacture remains the same at €2,000 each and the cost of supplying maintenance is €250 per machine per year.

Let us also assume that customers could purchase separate maintenance cover from other suppliers for two years at a cost of €1,000 per printer.

Consensus Supplies plc – accounting for contract

To keep this introductory example simple, we ignore the financing elements.*

The contract is for two separate service obligations with different timing of the services and so the revenue has to be apportioned between the contracts and then recognised as the individual services are provided. The normal selling prices are:

Supply of printers	€40,000
Supply of maintenance in Year 1	€5,000
Supply of maintenance in Year 2	€5,000
Total services provided	€50,000
Combined price	€48,000

This shows that Consensus is selling at 48,000/50,000 or 96% of the normal price i.e. 4% below normal selling price. Each component part of the contract is reduced by 4% as follows:

Supply of printers	40,000 × .96	€38,400
Supply of maintenance in Year 1	5,000 × .96	€4,800
Supply of maintenance in Year 2	5,000 × .96	€4,800
Combined price		€48,000

* It could be argued that the customer is prepaying the service contract particularly for the second year and hence we should recognise the payment of interest to the customer, and then offset that by recognising a higher service fee to cover the contract amount and to recover the imputed interest (see paragraphs 58 to 62). There is a clause which allows items of one year or less to be ignored. Thus if the relevant interest rate was 6% and the financing was deemed applicable to prepayment of the maintenance for the second year to be $1\frac{1}{2}$ years to the middle of the second year, then the interest deemed payable would be 6% of €500 or €30 in year 1 and €15.9 in year 2, being 6% of €530 for half a year. Then the revenue for the maintenance in year 2 would be 500 + 30 + 15.9 = €545.9.

(This process represents Step 4 of the requirements, which is to allocate the transaction price to the separate performance obligations in the contract.)

The entries for a contract under the proposed system would be:

Dr	Trade receivables	€48,000	
Cr	Sales revenue (equipment sales)		€38,400
Cr	Sales revenue (maintenance)		€4,800
Cr	Revenue in advance liability		€4,800

being the recording of a sale and maintenance package

Dr	Cost of goods sold (equipment)	€20,000	
Dr	Cost of goods sold (maintenance)	€2,500	
Cr	Inventory		€20,000
Cr	Bank		€2,500

Recording costs of providing services and the outlays for wages and materials used for maintenance

Note: Under the proposed standard the company would have to disclose in its annual report the amount and timing of the future revenue secured by existing contracts. A possible way of disclosing this could be as follows:

Contracts for the supply of maintenance

	Period 2	Period 3
Prepaid amounts	£4,800	XXX
Executory contracts	XXX	XXX

The entries for period 2 would be:

Dr	Revenue in advance	€4,800	
Cr	Sales revenue (maintenance)		€4,800

Transferring revenue in advance to current

Dr	Cost of goods sold (maintenance)	€2,500	
Cr	Bank		€2,500

Payment for materials and wages

Note that in the above example not all the disclosure requirements are covered. Paragraph 109 of the proposed standard says:

> The objective of the disclosure requirements is to enable users of financial statements to understand the nature, amount, timing and uncertainty of revenue and cash flows arising from contracts with customers. To achieve that objective, an entity shall disclose qualitative and quantitative information about all of the following:
>
> **(a)** its contracts with customers . . .;
>
> **(b)** the significant judgements, and changes in judgements, made. . . . ;
>
> **(c)** Any assets recognised from the costs to obtain or fulfil a contract. . . .

8.4.3 Pricing the transaction (Step 3)

The third step involves the pricing of the performance obligations in the contract. In many contracts that process is relatively simple. The contract is for one item and the price is unambiguously specified in the contract. However, it is possible that the contract is more complicated. Next, some common pricing arrangements will be examined.

Annual refund

Dee Pharmaceutical sells to pharmacies whereby it charges the standard price and at the close of the year pays a 5% discount based on the total purchases for the year. During January Dee Pharmaceutical invoices customers €5,000,000 for goods supplied. The entry would be:

Dr	Accounts receivable	5,000,000	
Cr	Sales revenue		4,750,000
Cr	Sales rebate liability		250,000

being gross sales of €5,000,000 less the obligation to refund 5% at the end of the financial year.

Quantity discounts

Suppose Gee Pharmaceuticals has a system of only giving annual refunds to customers who buy more than €400,000-worth in the calendar year, in which case they get a 6% discount on all purchases during the year.

Suppose Gee Pharmaceuticals sells goods worth €20,000 to Neu Chemists in January. Gee Pharmaceuticals does not anticipate that Neu Chemists will buy €400,000-worth or more in the year, so records the sale as:

Dr	Accounts receivable	20,000	
Cr	Sales revenue		20,000

being sale of goods not subject to discounts.

However, the new customer is much more successful than anticipated and purchases in February and March are €65,000 and €75,000 respectively. During March Gee Pharmaceuticals reconsiders its earlier forecasts and now expects Neu Chemists to exceed the discount threshold. So in the month of February the recording would still have been as before:

Dr	Accounts receivable	65,000	
Cr	Sales revenue		65,000

being February sales to Neu Chemists.

During March sales revenue needs to be decreased to reflect discounts for January, February and March:

Dr	Accounts receivable	75,000	
Cr	Sales discount liability		9,600
Cr	Sales revenue		65,400

being sales for March and discounts for January 1,200, February 3,900 and March 4,500.

Variable prices

It is possible that the contract price has a variable component such as when the contract price for the purchase of a million tons of commodity X is based on the average price during the following three months on a specified spot market such as the US commodity market. The reference to the spot market is a reference to current purchases which are not part of a longer-term contract. In such cases the revenue is recorded at the expected value (that is, the weighted average of the likely outcomes for the next three months) or the most likely average price. The entity should choose between those two possibilities based on which is expected to most accurately predict the final price.

So the general principle is that where the contract price is not a fixed amount but is variable, the aim is to record the transfer of the goods at the amount at which the entity expects to become entitled. There are two possible ways to estimate the entitlement. The first is to predict each of the possible prices which may be applicable. Then the probability of each outcome is estimated. The weighted average is then calculated by multiplying each predicted price by its associated estimated probability of occurring and adding all the answers. Thus if the expected outcomes are 10, 15 and 20 and the associated probabilities are 0.35, 0.40 and 0.25, the weighted average would be $0.35 \times 10 + 0.40 \times 15 + 0.25 \times 20 = 14.5$.

The alternative approach is to ask 'What is the most probable outcome?', meaning the outcome with the highest estimated probability. In this case it would be 15 as it has the highest probability.

The choice between the two should be based on what experience has shown to be the most accurate in predicting the actual outcomes.

8.4.4 Timing of revenue recognition (Steps 4 and 5)

Major principles

Revenue recognition occurs under the new criteria when a service (asset) or good is transferred to a customer. When an asset is transferred the customer obtains control (paragraph 31) and the performance obligation has been performed. Thus gaining control of the asset is the primary criterion for revenue recognition.

Traditionally we have recognised revenue when the service has been performed and that is compatible with the new criteria as the customer then 'controls' the service which was provided. With goods traditionally we have primarily, but not exclusively, recognised revenue when title passes. When title passes a customer is deemed to control the asset because at that time they can control the asset through sale, exchange, or pledging the asset as security for loans. Hence control has passed.

If the company is delivering to customers whose creditworthiness is doubtful, there may be a fear that in the event of a bankruptcy or liquidation the company will have lost control of the goods. In that event they must then compete with other creditors for a fraction of the inadequate resources available after paying liquidation costs and priority payments such as wages and discharging any secured charges.

To avoid this risk, some companies deliver goods on the basis that the customer is free to use the goods in manufacturing or to sell the goods on in the normal course of business, *but* until the customer does so the property rights in the goods remain with the supplying company. In the past revenue has in such circumstance often been recognised based on the actual quantity of goods used or sold by the customer. Under the new criteria the revenue would be recognised before the title passes, because the customer has control over the goods from the time of receipt of the goods.

The above discussion revolves around easy identification of when control passes and the price. The next major issue concerns multiple performance obligations.

Multiple performance objectives

In the event of multiple performance objectives there is a need to first identify the various performance objectives and to relate the revenue in the contract to the objectives. If the objectives are independent and priced separately in the contract, the process is easy. If the contract provides an overall price then the total amount has to be split up between the performance objectives. The exception is where the performance objectives are delivered at the same time and rate, when the step of splitting is not necessary. If the timing of the delivery differs for the various performance objectives then the total price has to be allocated to the specific performance obligations.

There are two possible ways of allocating the contract proceeds:

(a) allocate based on the basis of the amounts which would normally be paid by customers for the component obligations; or

(b) allocate the revenue between performance objectives on the basis of the relative costs of providing the various performance objectives.

The first case of allocation of the total contract price is on the basis of the normal selling price for one performance objective as a proportion of the amount that would be paid to buy all the service obligations individually.* You have already done this for Consensus Supplies plc in Section 8.4.2. Returning to that example, there is a single contract for €4,800 per printer covering the cost of the printer and maintenance for two years. The printer could be purchased for €4,000 and the maintenance contract for €1,000. The revenue could be recognised as follows:

Revenue allocated to the printer =

$$\text{combination contract price per printer} \times \frac{\text{normal selling price for a printer}}{\text{total selling price of printer and maintenance}}$$

$= 4,800 \times 4,000/(4,000 + 1,000) = 3,840$ per printer or 38,400 for 10 printers

Revenue allocated to the maintenance contract $= 4,800 \times 1,000/(4,000 + 1,000) = 960$, or 480 each year

If separate selling prices are not available then the expected costs of satisfying the performance obligations can be used to allocate the revenue between the various service obligations.

Another interesting application is where a contract extends over multiple periods and the performance obligations have to be allocated to each period. In other words, if it is reasonable to divide the contract into distinct service obligations for each period and it is possible to allocate costs to periods then profits can be identified with periods. (This will be discussed further under longer-term contracts.)

Suppose we have a service contract for maintaining equipment on a remote island which is subject to extreme weather conditions. The total contract is for €300,000 and involves annual payments of €100,000 at the start of each year. Given the unique conditions there is no market price for the individual annual maintenance contracts. This justifies allocation based on expected costs. The engineers estimate that the costs of satisfying the requirements of the contract will rise as the equipment gets older, so the estimated costs are:

Year 1	€30,000
Year 2	€80,000
Year 3	€160,000
Total	€270,000

The revenue of €300,000 could be allocated as follows:

$$\text{Total revenue} \times \frac{\text{expected costs for the year}}{\text{total expected costs over the total contract}}$$

Revenue for year 1 $= 300,000 \times 30,000/270,000 = 33,333$
Revenue for year 2 $= 300,000 \times 80,000/270,000 = 88,889$
Revenue for year 3 $= 300,000 \times 160,000/270,000 = 177,778$
Total revenue   300,000

* There is one possible complication. If two performance obligations are often sold as a combination, then those two items can be treated as a single performance obligation.

The accounting entries would be:

Year 1
Dr   Bank   100,000
Cr   Sales revenue   33,333
Cr   Revenue in advance   66,667

being recording of the bank receipt, acknowledging that given the higher amount of work in later periods only 33,000 is recognised as earned and the remainder is not earned until later.

Year 2
Dr   Bank   100,000
Cr   Sales revenue   88,889
Cr   Revenue in advance   11,111

allocating the receipt between periods.

Year 3
Dr   Bank   100,000
Cr   Sales revenue   177,778
Dr   Revenue in advance   77,778

reversing the previous prepayments of 66,667 and 11,111.

Longer-term contracts

Another interesting application is where a contract extends over multiple periods, such as when the entity is either:

(a) building an asset over which the customer has control, or

(b) creating an asset for which the entity has no use other than satisfying the customer because of the nature of the asset or because its alternative use is restricted by the agreement with the customer.

Under the former scenario, revenue is recognised as the work is performed, since the output is under the control of the customer. In the second case at least one of the following criteria must be met under the requirements of the 2011 exposure draft if the supplier entity is to recognise revenue over time (paragraph 35):

(i) the customer consumes the benefits as work proceeds; or

(ii) another entity could complete the obligation without access to the work in progress or re-doing the work already done; or

(iii) there is a right to be paid for the work done and the company expects to complete the contract.*

If one or more of the conditions specified in the second case is satisfied then revenue can be recognised as the project progresses according to the proportion of the obligation completed.

The above set of requirements is designed to broaden the revenue regulations so that they are comprehensive and to create consistency across standards. Those clauses will be particularly relevant when construction contracts are examined.

If the control of the asset has not passed and revenue cannot yet be recognised then the costs incurred to date would possibly be treated as an asset. They must satisfy the normal

* It is likely that these requirements will be modified by combining some of the criteria to make the tests clearer, but the intent will be the same.

rules for recognition of such assets. There are four possible categories of assets which may be satisfied. They are inventories which would be dealt with under IAS 2 including satisfying the net realisable value rule; property, plant and equipment under IAS 16 and intangible assets under IAS 38 including the impairment testing associated with such; and costs to fulfil a contract which is also subject to a cost recovery test.

To qualify as a cost to fulfil a contract, the costs must relate to a specific contract or an anticipated contract, and must contribute to satisfying the performance obligation, and there must be an expectation that those costs will be recovered (see paragraph 91).

8.4.5 Time value of money

The transaction price should reflect the time value of money and wherever the effect is material use a discount rate that reflects a financing transaction between the entity and its customer, taking into account the customer's credit characteristics to determine the discount rate used.

Treatment where payment is made in arrears

Let us assume that Alfa plc sells a mechanical digger for €100,000 allowing a credit period of two years from date of delivery and that a discount rate of 10% is appropriate.

As Alfa plc has an unconditional right to consideration on delivery it will recognise sales revenue of €82,645 (€100,000/(1.1 × 1.1)) rather than the contract price. Subsequently the interest revenue component will be recognised as earned.

The entries would be:

Year 1

Dr	Accounts receivable	100,000	
Cr	Sales revenue		82,645
Cr	Revenue in advance		17,355

recording the initial transaction.

Dr	Revenue in advance	8,264	
Cr	Interest revenue		8,264

(10% interest on 82,645 for the first year).

Year 2

Dr	Revenue in advance	9,091	
Cr	Interest revenue		9,091

being interest on the new balance of 82,645 + 8,264.

Treatment where payment is made in advance

Let us assume that Alfa plc sells a crane for €40,000 provided the customer pays one year and one day before delivery. When payment is made Alfa recognises a contract liability of €40,000 and estimating that a 5% interest rate is appropriate recognises interest expense of €2,000 ((€40,000 × 1.05) – €40,000) and increases the performance obligation by that amount during the year before its delivery.

The carrying amount of the contract liability is €42,000 (€40,000 + €2,000) immediately before the performance obligation is satisfied and Alfa reports revenue of €42,000 when the product is delivered.

Note that by accounting for the time value of money under the proposed treatment the amount of revenue to be recognised could be greater than the amount of the consideration that is ultimately received.

The entries would be:

Year 1

Dr	Bank	40,000
Cr	Revenue in advance liability		40,000

being payment by customer one year in advance.

Dr	Interest expense	2,000
Cr	Revenue in advance liability		2,000

(imputed interest at 5%).

Year 2

Dr	Revenue in advance liability	42,000
Cr	Sales revenue		42,000

recording implied revenue.

As a practical expedient the 2011 exposure draft allows us to ignore interest if the interest is not significant and if the period is one year or less.

8.5 Harmonisation

The objective of the proposed standard is to harmonise the US standard and the international standards, together with the harmonisation of all standards dealing with the recognition of gains and losses on transfers of assets. To this end, IAS 11 *Construction Contracts* will be altered to adopt all the revenue recognition and measurement criteria. Also IAS 16 *Property, Plant and Equipment* and IAS 40 *Investment Property* will be amended to be consistent with *Revenue from Contracts with Customers*.

Summary

This chapter has stressed the importance of matching service revenue with periods and then correctly assigning values to those services as provided. The first critical process is to dissect the contract into the various distinct service obligations if they have different patterns of delivery. Obviously if they have the same patterns of delivery separation is not necessary.

Then we need to identify when the goods or services are supplied to the customer. In the case of goods the point at which the goods have traditionally been treated as passing to the customer has normally been the time of shipment because at that point or shortly thereafter title passes. However, with more companies trying to protect themselves against insolvency of customers, retention of title clauses is becoming more common. In this environment it becomes appropriate to reconsider the recognition criteria, and the point of transfer of control of the goods is being proposed.

In the case of services these are often provided over several periods and the services provided in each period have to be separated out to allow revenue to be matched with periods.

Then the value of the service obligations has to be assigned to the various components of the overall service package. The selling prices of the stand-alone components of the goods and services provided by the company or its competitors may assist in this allocation.

Whatever rules are promulgated, a small number of practitioners will doubtless attempt to circumvent those rules. Such activities undermine the long-term credibility of the profession if the examples which come to light are frequent enough or of significant magnitude.

REVIEW QUESTIONS

1 Explain why the idea of recognising revenue on exchange of ownership title rights is no longer considered adequate.

2 A continuing problem in accounting is where companies use multiple contracts to circumvent the intentions of rules. Sometimes this is called the need for accounting to reflect substance over form. Lehman Brothers in the USA entered into a contract for sale of some securities which it agreed to buy back after balance date. What are the advantages and disadvantages of the substance over form approach?

3 One of the problems faced by the standard setters was the untangling of contracts which delivered multiple service obligations. Identify a business which supplies multiple services in one contract and identify the individual service components. Then discuss the following:

  (a) whether the two service components have similar or dissimilar patterns of delivery;

  (b) whether the components are sold by that business or other businesses as separate contracts or as stand-alone services;

  (c) the significance of the presence of other companies selling the services as individual services;

  (d) the likely impact on the business if the two service components have to be recognised individually.

4 The bloggers Anthony H. Catanach Jr and J. Edward Ketz discussed in their blog Grumpy Old Accountants on 27 August 2012 the accounting for Internet companies. The article is titled 'What is Zynga's "real" growth rate?'. They quote from the accounting policies of Zynga as follows: 'We recognise revenue from the sale of durable virtual goods ratably over the estimate average playing period of paying players for the applicable game . . .'. Discuss whether the preceding policy would be an appropriate policy under the proposed standard and whether Internet companies need their own revenue standard.

5 The ASB made a submission on the 2010 proposed revenue standard in which they indicated that the revenue allocation in relation to a contract which involved multiple service obligations should reflect the normal margins of the various service obligations. This is in contrast to the standard which allocated revenue in relation to the stand-alone prices of the various service obligations. Discuss the merits of the two alternatives.

6 In the technology sector there has been a high proportion of problems centred on what accountants call improper 'revenue recognition' – the recording of revenue that does not exist. Discuss why the technology sector might be more likely to do this and how it would have been justified to the auditors.

7 Do the proposed/new recognition rules give primary importance to calculating income or fairly presenting the statement of financial position (balance sheet)? How do you support that conclusion?

8 Executory contracts are contracts where both sides have not yet performed their obligations. If your company has a long-term contract for the supply of raw materials to XYZ Ltd for 50,000 tons per year for five years at a selling price of €10,000 per ton and the market price has fallen to €8,000 per ton, should this be recorded as a €2,000 a ton revenue in the current period? Justify your answer.

9 During the 'dot com' boom two major companies with excess data transmission lines in different areas arranged a sale whereby company X transferred lines in city A to company Y who in return transferred their excess lines in city B to company X. No cash changed hands. The contract specified the agreed value of the assets transferred. Identify and explain the potential problems in accounting for such a transaction. Would it make any difference if cash had changed hands?

10 There is a company which facilitates barter exchanges. Thus the barter company may ask a restaurant to make available a number of free meals which are then effectively exchanged for other services such as a painter repainting the building in which the restaurant is located. The painter can use only some of the free meals, so with the help of the barter company he exchanges the balance of the meals with a manufacturer/paint supplier for his paint needs on several projects. The paint manufacturer uses the meals in their staff training activities. The barter company which facilitates these exchanges also gets remunerated by the companies involved for its brokering activities so may also get a small quantity of meals. Discuss the recording issues for the restaurant and the barter company.

11 As soon as the authorities identify new rules accountants for hire will attempt to find ways around the rules. Identify as many ways as you can in which the new rules can be circumvented.

12 The Australian Securities and Investment Commission (ASIC) required a company called Flight Centre to amend the way in which it recorded revenue. It had previously recorded revenue based on the gross value of the flights it had booked for customers, whereas the ASIC wanted it to record revenue based on the commissions it received. The change would have no impact on the reported profit of the company. Given that the company disclosed its accounting policies and was consistent from year to year, it appears no one was misled. Explain why the company would prefer the gross approach, and the regulator the net revenue approach, and whether the issue is worthy of such a debate. Provide justification for your conclusions.

13 Access the IASB website and critically review the various decisions made to arrive at the final IFRS on revenue recognition.

14 The traditional method for recognising revenue made no allowance for possible bad debts. The first (2010) exposure draft reduced the amount of revenue by the estimated amount of bad debts. In the second exposure draft the standard setters reverted to the traditional method of revenue recognition. Given the contribution of possible bad debts to the great financial crisis, was the reversion to the traditional method wise? Discuss.

EXERCISES

* Question 1

Senford PLC entered into a contract to sell 3,000 telephones each with a two-year provider contract. The total cost of the contract was €120 per month payable at the end of the month. The phones were bought for cash from a supplier for €480 each and the cost of providing the telephone service is estimated at €30 per month for each phone. Senford PLC sells two-year service contracts (without supplying a phone) for €90 a month. The balance date for the company is three months after the date of the sales.

Required:
(a) Prepare all the journal entries for the current financial year that are possible from the data given.
(b) Show the disclosures which will be necessary in the annual report in relation to these phone contracts.
Show your calculations.

* Question 2

Strayway PLC sells two planes to Elliott & Elliott Budget Airlines PLC for five million euros each payable in two years' time on presentation of an accepted bill of exchange to be presented through Lloyd's Bank. The face value of the bill is €10,000,000. Further enquiry ascertains that government bonds with two years to maturity yield 4% pa and Strayway borrow from their bank at 9%, and the average yield on commercial bills of exchange payable in two years time is 8%.

Required:
Record the sale and associated transactions in the books of Strayway PLC.

* Question 3

Penrith European Car Sales plc sells a new car with 'free' 5,000 kilometre and 20,000 kilometre services for a combined price of €41,500. The cost of the car from the manufacturer is €30,000. The two services normally cost €400 and €600 to do and are charged to casual customers at the rate of €800 and €1,200 respectively.

Required:
Record all the transactions associated with the sale.

* Question 4

Henry Falk subscribes to an online monthly gardening magazine and selects the option of a three-year subscription from the following options:

One issue	€12
Twelve issues	€120
Twenty-four issues	€200
Thirty-six issues	€300

The publisher, English Magazine Specialties plc, estimates that it will cost €60, €62 and €64 per annum respectively to supply the magazines for the respective years.

Henry duly pays by credit card as part of the subscribing process.

Required:
(a) Show the entries in the books of English Magazine Specialties plc to record the transactions associated with the sale and supply for years 1, 2 and 3.
(b) Assuming a 10% borrowing rate and a constant revenue stream, show the accounting entries. Use 2% for credit card fees.
(c) Provide the disclosures which would need to be made in the annual report at the end of the first year of the contract under your answer to (a).
(d) What other patterns of revenue recognition could be used?

* Question 5

Assume the same facts as in Question 4 but add the presence of a 7.5% value added tax on the sales and a 1% transaction cost paid to the supplier of credit card transactions.

Required:
(a) Show the entries to record the transactions associated with the sale and supply for years 1, 2 and 3. (Ignore imputed interest costs.)
(b) Provide the disclosures which would need to be made in the annual report at the end of the first year of the contract.

* Question 6

Five G Telephones enters into telephone contracts on the following terms and options:

Xyz mobile phones	€1,000
Basic Y phones	€200

Basic connection service options:

A	€40 per month
B	€15 plus 50 cents per call

Combined services:

Supply of Xyz and connection service €79 per month with a minimum contract period of 24 months.

Required:
Record the entries for the first month for each of the possible transactions, assuming the following information:
(a) Xyz phones are purchased from a supplier for €500.
(b) Basic phones are purchased from a supplier for €120.
(c) The average user makes 100 calls a month at a variable cost of five cents per call.
(d) Ignore imputed interest.

Question 7

Assume the same facts as in Question 6 with the following additional costs:

There is a €5 cost to add a customer to the phone system, and those who buy the phone outright do not default on payments for the phone or the service contract, but those who have a combined service contract default in 10% of the cases.

Required:
(a) Show the entries to record the transactions associated with the sale and supply for years 1, 2 and 3.
(b) Provide the disclosures which would need to be made in the annual report at the end of the first year of the contract.

Question 8

Assume that in Question 3 you had also been told that cars without the inclusion of free services are typically sold by other sales outlets for €40,000.

Required:
(a) Redo the entries for the sale and the servicing. (Ignore interest, as the timing of the servicing is not given and the amounts are modest.)
(b) If you were then told that past experience for the timing of the 20,000 km service was 15% after two months, 30% after four months, 45% after six months and 10% after eight months and you wanted to take the prepayment/interest component into account, when would you assume the service took place? Justify your answer.

Question 9

Complete Computer Services (CCS) sells computer packages which include supply of a computer which carries the normal warranty against faulty parts plus a two-year assistance package covering problems encountered using any software sold or supplied with the computer. This package is designed for the person who lacks confidence in the use of the computer and likes to feel they have help available if they want it. The costs which CCS incurs are €600 for the purchase of the computer, €20 for normal warranty costs and €30 a year to service the assistance service component. The sales revenue is €950, being assigned as €100 for the service assistance and €850 for the computer.

Required:
Show all relevant journal entries.

Question 10

Henry plc has established a reputation as a company which generates growth in sales from year to year and those growth prospects have been incorporated into share prices. However, the current year has been more difficult and the managing director does not want to disappoint the market. He has approached a friend with an idea he got from one of the auditors for pulling a rabbit out of the hat. The friend spends €3,000 to establish a company called Dreams Come True Pty Ltd and contributes a further €2m as the new company's paid-up capital. Henry plc then enters into a contract to lend €3m to Dreams Come True Pty Ltd. Next, Henry plc sells a building to Dreams Come True Pty Ltd for €3m for cash. A week after the end of the financial year Henry plc enters into a contract to repurchase the building from Dreams Come True for €3.5m with an effective date six months into the new financial year. The managing director wants the accountant to record the building as sales revenue.

Required:
(a) Discuss the technical issues of the proposals.
(b) Discuss the ethical issues of the proposals.

Question 11

Exess Steel plc specialises in steel making and is located in the north-west of the country. Due to an unexpected downturn in demand for its steel products it has excess coking coal. South East Steel Products plc has also been caught by the unexpected economic downturn and has an excess of steel pellets. At the steel producers' annual conference the two managing directors discuss how their different auditors want them to write down the value of the excess stock because of the economic circumstances. They agree to do an exchange of the two commodities with the contracts including selling prices at the cost values in their books and a small cash payment to cover the difference between the two valuations. The two items are recorded in the books at the agreed purchase and selling prices respectively.

Required:
Comment critically on this proposal.

Question 12

New Management plc is a pharmaceutical company selling to wholesalers and retail pharmacies. The new CEO was appointed at the start of the financial year and was full of enthusiasm. For the first six months her new ideas created a 10% increase in sales and then the economy crashed as the government cut spending and monetary policy was tightened. Sales dropped 20% as customers had slower sales and were required by their banks to reduce their overdrafts. A new strategy was adopted in the last two months of the year. Sales representatives were told to sell on the basis that customers would not have to pay for three months by which time they would have sold the stock. They were also told that if sales for the month to that customer were not 5% higher than the sales for the corresponding month for the previous year they could say to the customer, off the record of course, that they could return any unsold stock after four months. In the last two months of the financial year sales were up 10% and 11% on the respective previous corresponding periods. The first month of the new financial year recorded a 10% drop in sales.

Required:
Critically discuss from the point of view of (a) an investor, (b) the auditor and (c) the CEO.

References

1 US Government Accountability Office, *Financial Restatements Update of Public Company Trends, Market Impacts and Regulatory Enforcement Activities*, GAO, 2007.
2 D. Collins, A. Masli, A.L. Reitenga and J.M. Sanchez, 'Earnings restatements, the Sarbanes–Oxley Act and the disciplining of chief financial officers', *Journal of Accounting, Auditing and Finance*, vol. 24(1), 2009, pp. 1–34.
3 New York v Ernst & Young (Part II), http://accounting.smartpros.com/X71245.xml and www.ag.ny.gov/media_center/2010/dec/ErnstYoungComplaint.pdf

PART 3

Regulatory framework – an attempt to achieve uniformity

CHAPTER 9

Financial reporting – evolution of global standards

9.1 Introduction

The main purpose of this chapter is to describe the movement towards global standards for publicly and non-publicly accountable entities.

Objectives

By the end of the chapter, you should be able to:

● critically discuss the arguments for and against standards;
● describe standard setting and enforcement in the UK, EU and US;
● critically evaluate the UK approach to financial reporting by smaller entities (FRSSE);
● describe and comment on the IASB approach to financial reporting by small and medium-sized entities (IFRS for SMEs);
● critically discuss the advantages and disadvantages of global standards;
● describe the reasons for differences in financial reporting.

9.2 Why do we need financial reporting standards?

Standards are needed because accounting numbers are important when defining contractual entitlements. Contracting parties frequently define the rights between themselves in terms of accounting numbers.[1] For example, the remuneration of directors and managers might be expressed in terms of a salary plus a bonus based on an agreed performance measure, e.g. Johnson Matthey's 2010 Annual Report states:

> Annual Bonus – which is paid as a percentage of basic salary . . . based on consolidated underlying profit before tax (PBT) compared with the annual budget. The board of directors rigorously reviews the annual budget to ensure that the budgeted PBT is sufficiently stretching.

However, there is a risk of irresponsible behaviour by directors and managers if it appears that earnings will not meet performance targets. They might be tempted to adopt measures that increase the PBT but which are not in the best interest of the shareholders.

This risk is specifically addressed in the Johnson Matthey Annual Report as shown in the following extract:

> The Committee has discretion in awarding annual bonuses and . . . ensures that the incentive structure for senior management does not raise environmental, social and governance risks by inadvertently motivating irresponsible behaviour.

This would not, however, preclude companies from taking typical steps such as **deferring discretionary expenditure**, e.g. research, advertising or training expenditure; **deferring amortisation**, e.g. making optimistic sales projections in order to classify research as development expenditure which can be capitalised; and **reclassifying** deteriorating current assets as non-current assets to avoid the need to recognise a loss under the lower of cost and net realisable value rule applicable to current assets.

The introduction of a mandatory standard that changes management's ability to adopt such measures **affects wealth distribution** within the firm. For example, if managers are able to delay the amortisation of development expenditure, then bonuses related to profit will be higher and there will effectively have been a transfer of wealth to managers from shareholders.

9.3 Why do we need standards to be mandatory?

Mandatory standards are needed, therefore, to define the way in which accounting numbers are presented in financial statements, so that their measurement and presentation are less subjective. It had been thought that the accountancy profession could obtain uniformity of disclosure by persuasion but, in reality, the profession found it difficult to resist management pressures.

During the 1960s the financial sector of the UK economy lost confidence in the accountancy profession when internationally known UK-based companies were seen to have published financial data that were materially incorrect. Shareholders are normally unaware that this occurs and it tends to become public knowledge only in restricted circumstances, e.g. when a third party has a **vested interest** in revealing adverse facts following a takeover, or when a company falls into the hands of an administrator, inspector or liquidator, **whose duty it is to enquire and report** on shortcomings in the management of a company.

Two scandals which disturbed the public at the time, GEC/AEI and Pergamon Press,[2] were both made public in the restricted circumstances referred to above, when financial reports prepared from the same basic information disclosed a materially different picture.

9.3.1 GEC takeover of AEI in 1967

The first calamity for the profession involved GEC Ltd in its takeover bid for AEI Ltd when the pre-takeover accounts prepared by the old AEI directors differed materially from the post-takeover accounts prepared by the new AEI directors.

Under the control of the directors of GEC the accounts of AEI were produced for 1967 showing **a loss of £4.5 million**. Unfortunately, this was from basic information that was largely the same as that used by AEI when producing its profit forecast of £10 million.

There can be two reasons for the difference between the figures produced. Either the facts have changed or the judgements made by the directors have changed. In this case, it seems there was a change in the facts to the extent of a post-acquisition closure of an AEI factory; this explained £5 million of the £14.5 million difference between the forecast profit and the actual loss. The remaining £9.5 million arose because of differences in judgement. For example, the new directors took a different view of the value of stock and work in progress.

9.3.2 Pergamon Press

Audited accounts were produced by Pergamon Press Ltd for 1968 showing a profit of approximately £2 million.

An independent investigation by Price Waterhouse suggested that this profit should be reduced by 75% because of a number of unacceptable valuations, e.g. there had been a failure to reduce certain stock to the lower of cost and net realisable value, and there had been a change in policy on the capitalisation of printing costs of back issues of scientific journals – they were treated as a cost of closing stock in 1968, but not as a cost of opening stock in 1968.

9.3.3 Public view of the accounting profession following such cases

It had long been recognised that accountancy is not an exact science, but it had not been appreciated just how much latitude there was for companies to produce vastly different results based on the same transactions. Given that the auditors were perfectly happy to sign that those accounts showing either a £10 million profit or a £4.5 million loss were true and fair, the public felt the need for action if investors were to have any trust in the figures that were being published.

The difficulty was that each firm of accountants tended to rely on precedents within its own firm in deciding what was true and fair. In fairness, there could be consistency within an audit firm's approach but not across all firms in the profession. The auditors were also under pressure to agree to practices that the directors wanted because there were no pro- fessional mandatory standards.

This was the scenario that galvanised the City press and the investing public. An embarrassed, disturbed profession announced in 1969, via the ICAEW, that there was a majority view supporting the introduction of Statements of Standard Accounting Practice to supplement the legislation.

9.3.4 Does the need for standards and effective enforcement still exist in the twenty-first century?

The scandals involving GEC and Pergamon Press occurred more than 30 years ago. However, the need for the ongoing enforcement of standards for financial reporting and auditing continues unabated. We only need to look at the unfortunate events with Enron and Ahold to arrive at an answer.

Enron

Enron was formed in the mid-1980s and became by the end of the 1990s the seventh-largest company in revenue terms in the USA. However, this concealed the fact that it had off-balance-sheet debts and that it had overstated its profits by more than $500 million – falling into bankruptcy (the largest in US corporate history) in 2001.

Ahold

In 2003 Ahold, the world's third-largest grocer, reported that its earnings for the past two years were overstated by more than $500 million as a result of local managers recording promotional allowances provided by suppliers to promote their goods at a figure greater than the cash received. This may reflect on the pressure to inflate profits when there are option schemes for managers.

9.4 Arguments in support of standards

The setting of standards has both supporters and opponents. Those who support standards have a view that they are important in giving investors confidence and encouraging informed investment. In this section we discuss credibility, discipline and comparability.

Credibility

The accountancy profession would lose all credibility if it permitted companies experiencing similar events to produce financial reports that disclosed markedly different results simply because they could select different accounting policies. Uniformity was seen as essential if financial reports were to disclose a true and fair view. However, it has been a continuing view in the UK and IASB that standards should be based on principles and not be seen as rigid rules – they were not to replace the exercise of informed judgement in determining what constituted a true and fair view in each circumstance. The US approach has been different – its approach has been to prescribe detailed rules.

Discipline

Directors are under pressure to maintain and improve the market valuation of their company's securities. There is a temptation, therefore, to influence any financial statistic that has an impact on the market valuation, such as the trend in the earnings per share (EPS) figure, the net asset backing for the shares or the gearing ratios which show the level of borrowing relative to the amount of equity capital put in by the shareholders.

This is an ever-present risk and the Financial Reporting Council showed awareness of the need to impose discipline when it stated in its Annual Review as far back as 1991 that the high level of company failures in the then recession, some of which were associated with **obscure financial reporting**, damaged confidence in the high standard of reporting by the majority of companies.

Comparability

In addition to financial statements allowing investors to evaluate the management's performance i.e. their stewardship, they should also allow investors to make predictions of future cash flows and make comparisons with other companies.

In order to be able to make valid inter-company comparisons of performance and trends, investors need relevant and reliable data that have been standardised. If companies were to continue to apply different accounting policies to identical commercial activities, innocently or with the deliberate intention of disguising bad news, then investors could be misled in making their investment decisions.

9.5 Arguments against standards

We have so far discussed the arguments in support of standard setting. However, there are also arguments that have been made against, such as consensus-seeking and information overload with IFRSs themselves exceeding 3,000 pages.

Consensus-seeking

Consensus-seeking can lead to the issuing of standards that are over-influenced by those who fear that a new standard will adversely affect their statements of financial position. For example, we see retail companies, who lease many of their stores, oppose the proposal to put operating leases onto the statement of financial position rather than reporting simply the future commitment as a note to the accounts.

Overload

Standard overload is not a new charge. It has been put forward by those who consider that:

- There are too many standard setters with differing requirements, e.g. the FRC in the UK with FRSs; the FASB in the US with the Accounting Standards Codification; the IASB with IFRSs and IFRICs; the EU with separate endorsement of IFRS giving us EU-IFRS; and the EU with its Directives and national Stock Exchange listing requirements.

- There are too many Notes to the accounts to satisfy regulatory requirements. Standards are too detailed if rule based and not sufficiently detailed if principle based, leading to the need for yet further guidance – for example, further guidance has to be issued by the International Financial Reporting Interpretations Committee (IFRIC) when existing IFRSs do not provide the answer.

- There are too many Notes to the accounts put in by companies themselves. Various surveys by professional accounting firms including one by Baker Tilly in 2012[3] showed that the majority of financial directors were keen to cut 'clutter' from financial disclosures, believing that the financial statements are too long, and that key messages are being lost as a result. It was felt that existing standards lead to a checklist mentality and boiler-plate disclosures that are not material and can obscure relevant information.

- There has been no definition of a Note by the standard setters. This is being addressed by EFRAG with the issue of a Discussion Paper in 2012, *Towards a Disclosure Framework for the Notes*,[4] which proposes how notes should be defined. For example, it is proposed that relevance, for instance, should only apply to disclosures that fulfil some *specific* users' needs.

- International standards have, until 2009 with the issue of *IFRS for SMEs*, focused on the large multinational companies and failed to recognise the different users and information needs between large and smaller entities.

9.6 Standard setting and enforcement by the Financial Reporting Council (FRC) in the UK

The Financial Reporting Council (FRC) was set up in 1990 as an independent regulator. Under the FRC the Accounting Standards Board (ASB) issued standards and the Financial Reporting Review Panel (FRRP) reviewed compliance to encourage high-quality financial reporting.

Due to its success in doing this, the government decided, following corporate disasters such as that of Enron in the USA, to give it a more **proactive** role from 2004 onwards in the areas of corporate governance, compliance with statutes and accounting and auditing standards.

Countries experience alternating periods of favourable and unfavourable economic conditions – often described as boom and bust. The FRC directs its reviews towards those sectors most likely to experience difficulties at the time. For example, it announced that its review activity in 2011/12 would focus on companies operating in niche markets, companies outside the FTSE 350, and companies providing support services with significant exposure to public spending cuts. It identified Commercial property, Insurance, Support services and Travel as priority sectors for review. It also pays particular attention to the reports and accounts of companies whose shareholders have raised concerns about governance or where there have been specific complaints.

9.6.1 The FRC structure

The FRC structure has evolved to meet changing needs. It was restructured in 2012 to operate as a unified regulatory body with enhanced independence. The new structure is shown in Figure 9.1.

9.6.2 The FRC Board

The FRC Board is supported by three Committees: the Codes and Standards Committee, the Conduct Committee and the Executive Committee.

The Codes and Standards Committee
This will advise the FRC Board on matters relating to codes, standard setting and policy questions, through its Accounting, Actuarial and Audit & Assurance Councils. The *Accounting Council* replaces the Accounting Standards Board. It reports to the Codes and Standards Committee and is responsible for providing strategic input into the work-plan of the FRC as a whole and advising on draft national and international standards to ensure that high-quality, effective standards are produced.

The Conduct Committee
This will advise the FRC Board in matters relating to conduct to promote high-quality corporate reporting, including monitoring, oversight, investigative and disciplinary functions,

Figure 9.1 FRC structure from 2012

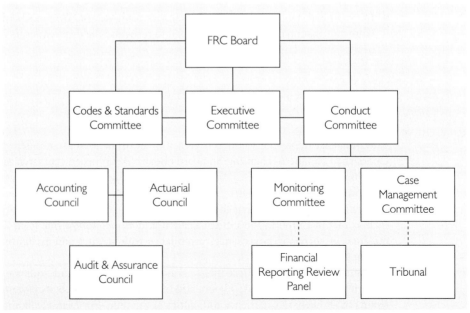

through its Monitoring Committee and Case Management Committee. The *Monitoring Committee* will be concerned with the assessment and reviews of audit quality and decisions as to possible resulting sanctions and investigation leading to possible disciplinary action being taken.

The Executive Committee

This will support the Board by advising on strategic issues and providing day-to-day oversight of the work of the FRC.

9.6.3 The Financial Reporting Review Panel (FRRP)

The FRRP has a policing role with responsibility for overseeing some 2,500 companies. Its role is to review material departures from accounting standards and, where financial statements are defective, to require the company to take appropriate remedial action. It has the right to apply to the court to make companies comply, but it prefers to deal with defects by agreement and there has never been recourse to the court.

Creative accounting

A research study[5] into companies that have been the subject of a public statement suggests that when a firm's performance comes under severe strain, even apparently well-governed firms can succumb to the pressure for creative accounting, and that good governance alone is not a sufficient condition for ensuring high-quality financial reporting.

Risk-based proactive approach

The Committee of European Securities Regulators (CESR), at the request of the European Commission, developed proposals which required enforcement bodies to take a proactive approach. In its *Proposed Statement of Principles of Enforcement of Accounting Standards in Europe* issued in 2002, it proposed that there should be a selection of companies and documents to be examined using a risk-based approach or a mixed model where a risk-based approach is combined with a rotation and/or a sampling approach – a pure rotation approach or a pure reactive approach would not be acceptable.[6] The FRRP follows this approach.

Cooperative approach to enforcement

The FRC published a report in 2012 showing that the FRRP had reviewed 326 sets of accounts selected from FTSE 100, FTSE 250, AIM and other listed and unlisted companies.[7] The Panel found the general quality of reporting by companies whose accounts it reviewed to be 'Good' with further improvement in all aspects of reporting of principal risks and uncertainties.

There was some evidence of boards focusing on key messages by eliminating unnecessary and obscuring detail, giving greater prominence to material disclosures and changing the order of content to assist shareholders' understanding of their company's business, policies, performance and position.

There were, however, reservations expressed about the quality of reporting by some smaller listed and AIM quoted companies that lacked the accounting expertise of their larger listed counterparts.

The Panel welcomed the fact that boards of directors continued to cooperate well with it during the year, often voluntarily giving undertakings to improve the quality of their future reporting.

9.7 The International Accounting Standards Board

The International Accounting Standards Board (IASB) has responsibility for all technical matters including the preparation and implementation of standards. The IASB website (www.iasb.org.uk) explains that:

> The IASB is committed to developing, in the public interest, a single set of high quality, understandable and enforceable global accounting standards that require transparent and comparable information in general purpose financial statements. In addition, the IASB co-operates with national accounting standard–setters to achieve convergence in accounting standards around the world.

The IASB adopted all current IASs and began issuing its own standards, International Financial Reporting Standards (IFRSs). The body of IASs and IFRSs are referred to collectively as 'IFRS'.

The process of producing a new IFRS is similar to the processes of some national account-ing standard setters. Once a need for a new (or revised) standard has been identified, a steering committee is set up to identify the relevant issues and draft the standard. Drafts are produced at varying stages and are exposed to public scrutiny. Subsequent drafts take account of comments obtained during the exposure period. The final standard is approved by the Board and an effective date agreed. IFRS currently in effect are referred to through-out the rest of this book.

The IASC also issued a *Framework for the Preparation and Presentation of Financial Statements*[8] in 2001. This continues to assist in the development of accounting standards and improve harmonisation by providing a basis for reducing the number of accounting treatments permitted by IFRS. It is currently being revised.

It is interesting to see how by 2012 more than 100 jurisdictions have permitted or mandated the use of IFRS and the process is continuing throughout the world. There is a natural tendency for countries to adopt the same standards if they are trading or geographical partners.

Extant IASs and IFRSs are listed in Figure 9.2.

Figure 9.2 Extant international standards

IAS 1	Presentation of Financial Statements
IAS 2	Inventories
IAS 7	Statement of Cash Flows
IAS 8	Accounting Policies, Changes in Accounting Estimates and Errors
IAS 10	Events after the Reporting Period
IAS 11	Construction Contracts
IAS 12	Income Taxes
IAS 16	Property, Plant and Equipment
IAS 17	Leases
IAS 18	Revenue
IAS 19	Employee Benefits
IAS 20	Accounting for Government Grants and Disclosure of Government Assistance
IAS 21	The Effects of Changes in Foreign Exchange Rates
IAS 23	Borrowing Costs
IAS 24	Related Party Disclosures
IAS 26	Accounting and Reporting by Retirement Benefit Plans
IAS 27	Separate Financial Statements

Figure 9.2 (*continued*)

IAS 28	Investments in Associates and Joint Ventures
IAS 29	Financial Reporting in Hyperinflationary Economies
IAS 32	Financial Instruments: Presentation
IAS 33	Earnings per Share
IAS 34	Interim Financial Reporting
IAS 36	Impairment of Assets
IAS 37	Provisions, Contingent Liabilities and Contingent Assets
IAS 38	Intangible Assets
IAS 39	Financial Instruments: Recognition and Measurement
IAS 40	Investment Properties
IAS 41	Agriculture
IFRS 1	First-time Adoption of International Financial Reporting Standards
IFRS 2	Share-based Payment
IFRS 3	(Revised) Business Combinations
IFRS 4	Insurance Contracts
IFRS 5	Non-current Assets Held for Sale and Discontinued Operations
IFRS 6	Exploration for and Evaluation of Mineral Resources
IFRS 7	Financial Instruments Disclosures
IFRS 8	Operating Segments
IFRS 9	Financial Instruments
IFRS 10	Consolidated Financial Statements
IFRS 11	Joint Arrangements
IFRS 12	Disclosure of Interests in Other Entities
IFRS 13	Fair Value Measurement

9.8 Standard setting and enforcement in the European Union[9]

The European Economic Community was established by the Treaty of Rome in 1957 to promote the free movement of goods, services, people and capital. In 1993 it was renamed the European Union (the EU). A major aim has been to create a single financial market that requires access by investors to financial reports which have been prepared using common financial reporting standards. The initial steps were the issue of accounting directives – these were the Fourth Directive, the Seventh Directive and the Eighth Directive which are required to be adopted by each EU country into their national laws.

The **Fourth Directive**[10] prescribed the information to be published by individual companies:

- annual accounts comprising a profit and loss account and statement of financial position with supporting notes to the accounts;
- a choice of formats, e.g. vertical or horizontal presentation;
- the assets and liabilities to be disclosed;
- the valuation rules to be followed, e.g. historical cost accounting;
- the general principles underlying the valuations, e.g. prudence to avoid overstating asset values and understating liabilities, and consistency to allow for inter-period comparisons;
- various additional information such as research and development activity and any material events that have occurred after the end of the financial year.

The directive is routinely updated to reflect increasing stakeholder pressure for greater transparency such as additional provisions relating to the reporting of off-balance-sheet commitments. There is also pressure to reduce the regulatory burden on small and medium-sized enterprises. An interesting survey[11] was undertaken into possible changes to the Directive which reports on matters such as time to implement changes, cost/benefit and potential help or otherwise to stakeholders.

The **Seventh Directive** requires:

- the consolidation of subsidiary undertakings across national borders, i.e. worldwide;
- uniform accounting policies to be followed by all members of the group;
- the elimination of the effect of inter-group transactions, e.g. eliminating inter-company profit and cancelling inter-company debt;
- the use of the formats prescribed in the Fourth Directive adjusted for the treatment of non-controlling interests.

We look in more detail at consolidation in Chapters 22–26.

The **Eighth Directive** issued in 1984 defined the qualifications of persons responsible for carrying out the statutory audits of the accounting documents required by the Fourth and Seventh Directives.

Just as the Fourth and Seventh Directives have been updated to reflect changing commercial practices, so the Eighth Directive has required updating. In the case of the Eighth Directive the need has been to restore investor confidence in the financial reporting system following the financial scandals in the US with Enron in 2001 and in the EU with Parmalat in 2004 where aspects of the auditing were heavily criticised.

The amended directive requires:

- independent audit committees to have one financial expert as a member;
- audit committees to recommend an auditor for shareholder approval;
- audit partners to be rotated every seven years;
- public oversight to ensure quality audits;
- the group auditor to bear full responsibility for the audit report even where other audit firms may have audited subsidiaries around the world.

It clarifies the duties and ethics of statutory auditors but has not prohibited auditors from carrying out consultancy work, which some strongly criticise on the grounds that it compromises the independence of auditors. Recently the emphasis has been on checking that each member state has a legally established operational public oversight system with adequate and independent financial and human resources.

9.8.1 EU adoption of IFRSs

Both the European Union (EU) and the International Accounting Standards Board have been active in seeking to standardise financial reports. The EU recognised that the Accounting Directives which provided accounting rules for limited liability companies were not, in themselves, sufficient to meet the needs of companies raising capital on the international securities markets. There was a need for more detailed standards so that investors could have adequate and transparent disclosures that would allow them to assess risks and opportunities and make inter-company comparisons – standards that would result in annual reports giving a fair view.

The IASB is the body that produces such standards and from 2005 the EU required[12] the consolidated accounts of all listed companies to comply with International Financial Reporting Standards. However, to give the IFRS legal force within the EU, each IFRS has to be endorsed by the EU. This is not a rubber-stamping process.

9.8.2 Enforcement of standards in Europe

The European Enforcers Co-ordination Sessions (EECS) is a forum containing 37 European enforcers from 29 countries in the EEA which aims to promote a high level of consistency amongst enforcers in the decisions they take in respect of their reviews of financial statements.

It has as its main objective the coordination of the enforcement activities of member states in order to foster investor confidence.

A report[13] issued in 2012 provided an overview of the monitoring of compliance in 2011 with International Financial Reporting Standards (IFRS). It was not a rubber-stamping exercise and it was reported that:

- In 2011, European enforcers performed full reviews of around 850 companies' accounts (annual and interim), covering some 12% of listed entities in Europe.

- Action was taken in almost 70% of companies with 18 revised financial statements issued, around 150 public corrective notes and around 420 corrections required to be made in future financial statements.

9.8.3 The importance of enforcement

There is research evidence[14] that the cost of capital falls following the mandatory adoption of IFRS and that there is an increase in foreign equity investment. However, in addition to the standards, effective enforcement has to be in place.[15]

Even following the mandatory adoption of IFRS and enforcement of reporting standards, investors continue to take into account national considerations such as the existence of good corporate governance, the degree of shareholder protection and the level of corruption.

9.9 Standard setting and enforcement in the US

Reporting standards are set by the Financial Accounting Standards Board (FASB) and enforced by the Securities Exchange Commission. Since 2002 it has also been necessary to satisfy the requirements of the Sarbanes–Oxley Act (normally referred to as SOX) which was passed following the Enron disaster.

9.9.1 Standard setting by the FASB and other bodies

The Financial Accounting Standards Board (FASB) is responsible for setting accounting standards in the USA. The FASB is financed by a compulsory levy on public companies, which should ensure its independence. (The previous system of voluntary contributions ran the risk of major donors trying to exert undue influence on the Board.) In 2009 the FASB launched the FASB *Accounting Standards Codification* as the single source of authoritative non-governmental US GAAP, combining and replacing the jumbled mix of accounting standards that have evolved over the last half-century.

9.9.2 Enforcement by the SEC

The Securities and Exchange Commission (SEC) is responsible for requiring the publication of financial information for the benefit of shareholders. It has the power to dictate the form and content of these reports. The largest companies whose shares are listed must register with the SEC and comply with its regulations. The SEC monitors financial reports filed in great detail and makes useful information available to the public via its website.[16] However, it is important to note that the majority of companies fall outside the SEC's jurisdiction.

9.9.3 SOX (the Sarbanes–Oxley Act 2002)

SOX came as a response to the failures in Enron. It is different from the UK's Code of Corporate Governance in that, rather than the comply-or-explain approach, compliance is mandatory with significant potential sanctions for individual directors where there is non-compliance.

Prevention of fraud

The SOX objectives are to reduce the risk of fraud. It provides that

> Whoever knowingly alters, destroys, mutilates, conceals, covers up, falsifies, or makes a false entry in any record, document, or tangible object with the intent to impede, obstruct, or influence the investigation or proper administration of any matter within the jurisdiction of any department or agency of the United States . . . shall be fined under this title, imprisoned not more than 20 years, or both. (Section 802(a))

Following the Enron and other scandals, a number of weaknesses were identified which allowed the frauds to go undetected. Weaknesses included (a) the accounting profession where there was inadequate oversight and conflicts of interest, (b) company management who had poor internal controls and had been subject to weak corporate governance procedures, and (c) investors under-protected with stock analysts giving biased investment advice, the FASB which was responsible for inadequate disclosure rules, and an under-funded enforcement agency in the Securities and Exchange Commission (SEC).

The accounting profession

The Public Company Accounting Oversight Board (PCAOB)[17] is a non-profit corporation which was established by Congress to oversee the audits of public companies in order to protect the interests of investors and further the public interest in the preparation of informative, accurate and independent audit reports.

Management

CEOs of publicly traded companies are now directly responsible for ensuring that financial reports are accurate.

Internal controls

To protect themselves CEOs rely on a sound system of internal control and management is accountable for the quality of those controls. Under SOX, management is required to certify the company's financial reports and both management and an independent accountant are required to certify the organisation's internal controls.

Companies use a report, *Internal Control – Integrated Framework*, issued in 1992 by the Committee of Sponsoring Organizations of the Treadway Commission (COSO) as a basis for establishing internal control systems and determining their effectiveness. For further information refer to www.coso.org for further detailed information on its exposure draft issued in 2012, *Internal Control over External Financial Reporting* (ICEFR).

Investors

SOX aimed to reduce fraud and improve investor confidence in financial reports and the capital market by seeking improvements in corporate accounting controls. In doing so it has created mandatory requirements that might have disadvantaged US companies operating in a global market where there is a comply-or-explain approach to compliance as in the UK and OECD countries.

9.9.4 Progress towards adoption by the USA of international standards

Global standards will only be achieved when the US fully adopts IFRSs to replace existing US GAAP. This process started in October 2002 when the IASB and the SEC jointly published details of what is known as the Norwalk Agreement. This included an undertaking to make their financial reporting standards fully compatible as soon as possible and to coordinate future work programmes to maintain that compatibility and to eventually mandate the use of IFRS by US listed companies. The process started with the Norwalk Agreement, followed by the IASB carrying out a Convergence Programme and finally joint standards being issued. The detailed progress was as follows.

9.9.5 The Norwalk Agreement

At their joint meeting in Norwalk in 2002, the Financial Accounting Standards Board (FASB) and the International Accounting Standards Board (IASB) committed to the development of high-quality, compatible accounting standards that could be used for both domestic and cross-border financial reporting aiming to:

- make their existing financial reporting standards fully compatible by undertaking a short-term project aimed at removing a variety of individual differences between US GAAP and International Financial Reporting Standards; and
- remove other differences between IFRSs and US GAAP remaining at 1 January 2005 (when IFRS became compulsory for consolidated accounts in Europe) through coordination of their future work programmes by undertaking discrete, substantial projects on which both Boards would work concurrently.

9.9.6 The short-term project

The aim was for the IASB and FASB to remove minor differences by changing their standards, which would remove the need for the reconciliation requirement for non-US companies that use IFRSs and are registered in the United States of America.

It is a two-way traffic. For example, by 2008 a number of projects were completed. For example, the FASB issued new or amended standards to bring standards in line with IFRS, e.g. it adopted the IFRS approach to accounting for R&D assets acquired in a business combination (SFAS 141R); in others the IASB converged IFRS with US GAAP, e.g. the new standard on segment reporting (IFRS 8).

The SEC was sufficiently persuaded by the progress made by the Boards that in 2007 it removed the reconciliation requirement for non-US companies that are registered in the USA and accepts the use of IFRSs as issued by the IASB.

9.9.7 Possible way forward

There is little support in the US for the adoption of IFRS as authoritative guidance. There is more support, however, for exploring other methods of incorporating IFRS such as the endorsement method that is applied in the EU. This is tied in with the US reservation that IFRSs are not being applied with consistency across all national adopters. The endorsement method means that the FASB would remain the US standard setter overseeing the incorporation of IFRS into the US financial reporting system over an extended period of time.

9.10 Advantages and disadvantages of global standards for publicly accountable entities

Publicly accountable entities are those whose debt or equity is publicly traded. Many are multinational and listed on a stock exchange in more than one country.

9.10.1 Advantages

The main advantages arising from the development of international standards are that it reduces the cost of reporting under different standards, makes it easier to raise cross-border finance, leads to a decrease in firms' costs of capital with a corresponding increase in share prices, and enables investors to compare performance. For developing countries there is also the incentive to improve accountants' technical training and expertise.

9.10.2 Disadvantages

Complexity

However, one survey[18] carried out in the UK indicated that finance directors and auditors surveyed felt that IFRSs undermined UK reporting integrity. In particular, there was little support for the further use of fair values as a basis for financial reporting, which was regarded as making the accounts less reliable with comments such as 'I think the use of fair values increases the subjective nature of the accounts and confuses unqualified users.'

There was further reference to this problem of understanding with a further comment: 'IFRS/US GAAP have generally gone too far – now nobody other than the Big 4 technical departments and the SEC know what they mean. The analyst community doesn't even bother trying to understand them – so who exactly do the IASB think they are satisfying?'

Net income change

In some instances the changes have a dramatic effect on headline figures, e.g. the Dutch company, Wessanen, reported an increase of over 400% in its net income figure when the Dutch GAAP accounts were restated under IFRS. In other cases, there may be some large adjustments to individual balances, but the net effect may be less obvious.

Asset and liability changes

In certain countries there will be major changes in specific components of equity in the year of transition as particular assets or liabilities fall to be recognised differently from in the past. For example, the European hotel group Accor reported a reduction in total assets of only 1% when its 2004 statement of financial position was restated from French GAAP to IFRS, but within this, 'other receivables and accruals' had fallen by €294 million, a reduction of over 30% of the previously reported balance.

In the UK many companies made increased provisions for deferred tax liabilities on revalued properties and Australian companies made large adjustments to their statements of financial position through the derecognition of intangible assets.

In the short term, these changes in reported figures can have important consequences for companies' contractual obligations (e.g. they may not be able to maintain the level of liquidity required by their loan agreements) and their ability to pay dividends. There may be motivational issues to consider where staff bonuses have traditionally been based on reported accounting profit. As a result, companies may find that they need to adjust their management accounting system to align it more closely with IFRS.

Volatility in the accounts

In most countries the use of IFRS will mean that earnings and statement of financial position values will be more volatile than in the past. This could be quite a culture shock for analysts and others used to examining trends that follow a fairly predictable straight line.

Lack of familiarity

While the change to IFRS was covered in the professional and the more general press, it was not clear whether users of financial statements fully appreciated the effect of the change in accounting regulations, although surveys by KPMG[19] and PricewaterhouseCoopers[20] indicated that most analysts and investors were confident that they understood the implications of the change. A survey following the issue of *IFRS for SMEs* in 2009 indicated that, as a new standard, there was naturally a fairly widespread lack of understanding of its provisions. This has been well addressed[21] by the IASB with supporting workshops and educational material.

9.11 How do reporting requirements differ for non-publicly accountable entities?

Governments and standard setters have realised that there are numerous small and medium-sized businesses that do not raise funds on the stock exchange and do not prepare general-purpose financial statements for external users.

9.11.1 Role of small firms in the UK economy

Small firms play a major role in the UK economy (as they do throughout the world) and are seen to be the main job creators. Interesting statistics on SMEs from a report[22] carried out by the Warwick Business School showed for the UK:

By size:

2,200,000 businesses have no employees (about 61% of SMEs).

1,450,000 businesses have an annual turnover of less than £50,000 (about 40% of SMEs).

350,000 businesses have less than £10,000 worth of assets.

By legal form:

Almost two in three businesses are sole traders (2,400,000 businesses).

Less than one in four businesses are limited liability companies (870,000 businesses).

About one in 10 businesses are partnerships (including limited liability partnerships).

By age:

The majority of businesses (51%) are aged more than 15 years (1,900,000 businesses).

About 7% of SMEs are start-ups (aged less than two years) (250,000 businesses).

By growth rate:

About 11% of businesses (320,000 businesses) are high growth businesses, having an average turnover growth of 30% or more per annum over a period going back up to three years.

· Certain companies are relieved of statutory and mandatory reporting and audit requirements on account of their size.

9.11.2 Statutory requirements

Every year the directors of companies are required to submit accounts to the shareholders
and file a copy with the Registrar of Companies. In recognition of the cost implications and
need for different levels of privacy, there is provision for small and medium-sized companies
to file abbreviated accounts.

A small company satisfies two or more of the following conditions:

● Turnover does not exceed £6.5 million.
● Assets do not exceed £3.26 million.
● Average number of employees does not exceed 50.

The company is excused from filing a profit and loss account, and the directors' report
and statement of financial position need only be an abbreviated version disclosing major
asset and liability headings. Its privacy is protected by excusing disclosure of directors'
emoluments.

From 2012 the companies need not have their accounts audited unless requested by more
than 10% of the shareholders.

A medium-sized company satisfies two or more of the following conditions:

● Turnover does not exceed £25.9 million.
● Assets do not exceed £12.9 million.
● Average number of employees does not exceed 250.

It is excused far less than a small company: the major concession is that it need not disclose
sales turnover and cost of sales, and the profit and loss account starts with the gross profit
figure. This is to protect its competitive position.

9.11.3 National standards

Countries are permitted to adopt IFRS for publicly accountable entities and adopt their own
national standards for non-publicly accountable entities. In the UK it is proposed to allow
smaller entities to adopt the national Financial Reporting Standard for Smaller Entities
(FRSSE). Larger and medium-sized private companies can adopt FRS 102. This replaces
UK GAAP and is based on the IFRS for SMEs issued by the IASB in 2009 with amendments
to suit UK conditions.

First FRSSE issued[23]

In 1997 the ASB issued the first FRSSE. There was a concern as to the legality of setting
different measurement and disclosure requirements; the ASB took legal advice which confirmed that smaller entities can properly be allowed exemptions or differing treatments in
standards and UITFs provided such differences were justified **on rational grounds**.

How can rational grounds be established?

The test as to whether a decision is rational is based on obtaining answers to nine questions.
If there are more negative responses than positive, there are rational grounds for a different
treatment. The nine questions can be classified as follows:

Generic relevance

1 Is the standard essential practice for all entities?

2 Is the standard likely to be widely relevant to small entities?

Proprietary relevance

3 Would the treatment required by the standard be readily recognised by the proprietor or manager as corresponding to their understanding of the transaction?

Relevant measurement requirements

4 Is the treatment compatible with that used by HM Revenue and Customs in computing tax?

5 Are the measurement methods in a standard reasonably practical for small entities?

6 Is the accounting treatment the least cumbersome?

User relevance

7 Is the standard likely to meet information needs and legitimate expectations of the users?

8 Is the disclosure likely to be meaningful and comprehensible to users?

Expanding statutory provision

9 Do the requirements of the standard significantly augment the treatment required by statute?

How are individual standards dealt with in the FRSSE?

Standards have been dealt with in six ways as explained in (a) to (f) below:

(a) Adopted without change. FRSSE adopted certain standards and UITFs without change.

(b) Not addressed. Certain standards were not addressed in the FRSSE, e.g. FRS 22 *Earnings per Share*.

(c) Disclosure requirements removed. Certain standards apply but the disclosure requirement is removed, e.g. FRS 10 *Goodwill and Intangible Assets*.

(d) Disclosure requirements reduced. Certain standards apply but there is a reduced disclosure requirement, e.g. SSAP 9 *Stocks and Long-term Contracts* applies but there is no requirement to sub-classify stock nor to disclose the accounting policy.

(e) Exempt but provisions within FRSSE. Certain standards are exempt e.g. under FRS 8 *Related Party Disclosures* but separate provisions in FRSSE itself.

(f) Main requirements included. Certain standards have their main requirements included, e.g. FRS 5 *Reporting the Substance of Transactions*, FRS 16 *Current Tax*, FRS 18 *Accounting Policies* and FRS 19 *Deferred Tax*.

The revised FRSSE

A revised FRSSE was issued in 2008 to incorporate changes in company law arising from the Companies Act 2006, which defines small companies as having an annual turnover of up to £6.5 million. No changes were made to the requirements that are based upon Generally Accepted Accounting Practice.

Entities adopting the FRSSE continue to be exempt from applying all other accounting standards, which reduces the volume of standards that a small entity needs to apply. They may of course still choose not to adopt the FRSSE and to comply with the other UK accounting standards and UITF Abstracts instead or, if they are companies, international accounting standards.

9.12 IFRS for SMEs

The IASB issued *IFRS for SMEs* in July 2009. The approach follows that adopted by the ASB with:

- some topics omitted, e.g. IAS 33 *Earnings per Share*, IFRS 8 *Operating Segments*, IAS 34 *Interim Financial Reporting*, IFRS 5 *Assets Held for Sale*, and IFRS 4 *Insurance Contracts*;
- some additional requirements as companies adopting the IFRS will have to comply with its mandatory requirement to produce a statement of cash flows and more information as to related party transactions;
- simpler options allowed, e.g. expensing rather than capitalising borrowing cost;
- simpler recognition, e.g. following an amortisation (with a maximum life of 10 years) rather than an annual impairment review for goodwill;
- simpler measurement, e.g. using the historical cost–depreciation model for property, plant and equipment;
- SMEs are not prevented from adopting other options available under full IFRS and may elect to do this if they so decide.

However, in defining an SME it has moved away from the size tests towards a definition based on qualitative factors such as public accountability whereby an SME would be a business that does not have public accountability. Public accountability is implied if outside stakeholders have a high degree of either investment, commercial or social interest and if the majority of stakeholders have no alternative to the external financial report for financial information.

Adoption

Adoption has been encouraged for companies outside the EU with more than 80 countries adopting. Within the EU it is a very different story because a significant number of member states have compulsory filing and publication requirements for SMEs with some member states strongly opposing.

However, whereas with publicly accountable companies there is a clear understanding that the primary user is the equity investor, the question remains for SMEs as to (a) the primary user, e.g. whether it is the non-managing owner, the long-term lender, the trade creditor or the tax authorities, and (b) the primary user's needs, e.g. whether maximising long-term growth, medium-term viability or short-term liquidity.

Questions remain such as whether the financial statements need to be a stewardship report or decision-useful and, then, how the characteristics such as relevance, reliability and comparability are to be ranked and prioritised.

It is intended to have a three-yearly review of the implementation of the standard and it is reasonable to expect that the IFRS will evolve based on review findings.

9.13 Why have there been differences in financial reporting?

Although there have been national standard-setting bodies, this has not resulted in uniform standards. A number of attempts have been made to identify reasons for differences in financial reporting.[24] The issue is far from clear but most writers agree that the following are among the main factors influencing the development of financial reporting:

- the character of the national legal system;
- the way in which industry is financed;
- the relationship of the tax and reporting systems;
- the influence and status of the accounting profession;
- the extent to which accounting theory is developed;
- accidents of history;
- language.

We will consider the effect of each of these.

9.13.1 The character of the national legal system

There are two major legal systems, that based on common law and that based on Roman law. It is important to recognise this because the legal systems influence the way in which behaviour in a country, including accounting and financial reporting, is regulated.

Countries with a legal system based on common law include England and Wales, Ireland, the USA, Australia, Canada and New Zealand. These countries rely on the application of equity to specific cases rather than a set of detailed rules to be applied in all cases. The effect in the UK, as far as financial reporting was concerned, was that there was limited legislation regulating the form and content of financial statements until the government was required to implement the EC Fourth Directive. The directive was implemented in the UK by the passing of the Companies Act 1981 and this can be seen as a watershed because it was the first time that the layout of company accounts had been prescribed by statute in England and Wales.

English common law heritage was accommodated within the legislation by the provision that the detailed regulations of the Act should not be applied if, in the judgement of the directors, strict adherence to the Act would result in financial statements that did not present a true and fair view.

Countries with a legal system based on Roman law include France, Germany and Japan. These countries rely on the codification of detailed rules, which are often included within their companies legislation. The result is that there is less flexibility in the preparation of financial reports in those countries. They are less inclined to look to fine distinctions to justify different reporting treatments, which is inherent in the common law approach. The existence of detailed rules or existing effective publication requirements also determines their approach to reporting standards as, for example, the reluctance in Germany to support the adoption of IFRS for SMEs.

However, it is not just that common law countries have fewer codified laws than Roman law countries. There is a fundamental difference in the way in which the reporting of commercial transactions is approached. In the common law countries there is an established practice of creative compliance. By this we mean that the spirit of the law is elusive[25] and management is more inclined to act with creative compliance in order to escape effective legal control. By creative compliance we mean that management complies with the form of the regulation but in a way that might be against its spirit, e.g. structuring leasing agreements in the most acceptable way for financial reporting purposes.

9.13.2 The way in which industry is financed

Accountancy is the art of communicating relevant financial information about a business entity to users. One of the considerations to take into account when deciding what is relevant

Figure 9.3 Domestic equity market capitalisation/gross domestic product

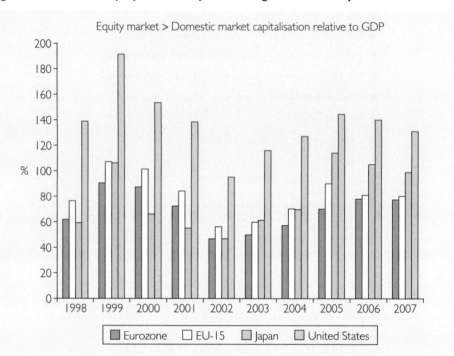

is the way in which the business has been financed, e.g. the information needs of equity investors will be different from those of loan creditors. This is one factor responsible for international financial reporting differences because the predominant provider of capital is different in different countries.[26] Figure 9.3 makes a simple comparison between domestic equity market capitalisation and Gross Domestic Product (GDP).[27] The higher the ratio, the greater the importance of the equity market compared with loan finance.

We see that in the USA companies have relied more heavily on individual investors to provide finance than in Europe or Japan. An active stock exchange has developed to allow shareholders to liquidate their investments. A system of financial reporting has evolved to satisfy a stewardship need where prudence and conservatism predominate, and to meet the capital market need for fair information[28] which allows interested parties to deal on an equal footing where the accruals concept and the doctrine of substance over form predominate. It is important to note that European statistics are *averages* that do not fully reflect the variation in sources of finance used between, say, the UK (where equity investment is very important) and Germany (where lending is more important). These could be important factors in the development of accounting.

We can see that the European countries have made continuing use of equity finance since 1998 rather than loan finance and this has led to a greater interest in the issue of International Financial Reporting Standards. Whereas lenders had access to management to obtain the information they sought, equity investors rely more on published information.

Since the 1990s there has been a growth globally of institutional investors, such as banks, insurance companies, retirement or pension funds, hedge funds and sovereign wealth funds. These form an ever-increasing proportion of shareholders. In theory, the information needs of these institutional investors should be the same as those of individual investors. However, in practice, they might be in a position to obtain information by direct access to management and the directors. One effect of this might be that they will become less interested in seeking disclosures in the financial statements – they will have already picked up the significant information at an informal level.

9.13.3 The relationship of the tax and reporting systems

In the UK separate rules have evolved for computing profit for tax and computing profit for financial reporting purposes in a number of areas. The legislation for tax purposes tends to be more prescriptive, e.g. there is a defined rate for capital allowances on fixed assets, which means that the reduction in value of fixed assets for tax purposes is decided by the government. The financial reporting environment is less prescriptive but this is compensated for by requiring greater disclosure. For example, there is no defined rate for depreciating non-current assets but there is a requirement for companies to state their depreciation accounting policy. Similar systems have evolved in the USA and the Netherlands.

However, certain countries give primacy to taxation rules and will only allow expenditure for tax purposes if it is given the same treatment in the financial accounts. In France and Germany, the tax rules effectively become the accounting rules for the accounts of individual companies, although the tax influence might be less apparent in consolidated financial statements.

This can lead to difficulties of interpretation, particularly when capital allowances, i.e. depreciation for tax purposes, are changed to secure public policy objectives such as encouraging investment in fixed assets by permitting accelerated write-off when assessing taxable profits. In fact, the depreciation charge against profit would be said by a UK accountant not to be fair, even though it could certainly be legal or correct.[29]

Depreciation has been discussed to illustrate the possibility of misinterpretation because of the different status and effect of tax rules on annual accounts. Other items that require careful consideration include inventory valuations, bad debt provisions, development expenditure and revaluation of non-current assets. There might also be public policy arrangements that are unique to a single country, e.g. the existence of special reserves to reduce taxable profits was common in Scandinavia. It has recently been suggested that level of connection between tax and financial reporting follows a predictable pattern.[30]

9.13.4 The influence and status of the accounting profession

The development of a capital market for dealing in shares created a need for reliable, relevant and timely financial information. Legislation was introduced in many countries requiring companies to prepare annual accounts and have them audited. This resulted in the growth of an established and respected accounting profession able to produce relevant reports and attest to their reliability by performing an audit.

In turn, the existence of a strong profession had an impact on the development of accounting regulations. It is the profession that has been responsible for the promulgation of accounting standards and recommendations in a number of countries, such as the UK, the USA, Australia, Canada and the Netherlands.

In countries where there was not the same need to provide market-sensitive information, e.g. in Eastern Europe in the 1980s, accountants were seen purely as bookkeepers and were accorded a low status. However, the position has changed rapidly and there has been a growth in the training, professionalism and contribution for both financial and management accountants as these economies have become market economies.

9.13.5 The extent to which accounting theory is developed

Accounting theory can influence accounting practice. Theory can be developed at both an academic and a professional level, but for it to take root it must be accepted by the profession.

For example, in the UK, theories such as current purchasing power and current cost accounting first surfaced in the academic world and there were many practising accountants who regarded them then, and still regard them now, as academic.

In the Netherlands, professional accountants receive academic accountancy training as well as the vocational accountancy training that is typical in the UK. Perhaps as a result of that, there is less reluctance on the part of the profession to view academics as isolated from the real world. This might go some way to explaining why it was in the Netherlands that we saw general acceptance by the profession for the idea that for information to be relevant it needed to be based on current value accounting. Largely as a result of pressure from the Netherlands, the Fourth Directive contained provisions that allowed member states to introduce inflation accounting systems.[31]

Attempts have been made to formulate a conceptual framework for financial reporting in countries such as the UK, the USA, Canada and Australia,[32] and the International Standards Committee has also contributed to this field. One of the results has been the closer collaboration between the regulatory bodies, which might assist in reducing differences in underlying principles in the longer term.

9.13.6 Accidents of history

The development of accounting systems is often allied to the political history of a country. Scandals surrounding company failures, notably in the USA in the 1920s and 1930s and in the UK in the 1960s and 1980s, had a marked impact on financial reporting in those countries. In the USA the Securities and Exchange Commission was established to control listed companies, with responsibility to ensure adequate disclosure in annual accounts. Ever-increasing control over the form and content of financial statements through improvements in the accounting standard-setting process has evolved from the difficulties that arose in the UK.

International boundaries have also been crossed in the evolution of accounting. In some instances it has been a question of pooling of resources to avoid repeating work already carried out elsewhere, e.g. the Norwegians studied the report of the Dearing Committee in the UK before setting up their new accounting standard-setting system in the 1980s.[33] Other changes in nations' accounting practices have been a result of external pressure, e.g. Spain's membership of the European Community led to radical changes in accounting.[34]

9.13.7 Language

Language has often played an important role in the development of different methods of accounting for similar items. Certain nationalities are renowned for speaking only their own language, which has prevented them from benefiting from the wisdom of other nations. There is also the difficulty of translating concepts as well as phrases, where one country has influenced another.

9.14 Move towards a conceptual framework

The process of formulating standards has encouraged a constructive appraisal of the policies being proposed for individual reporting problems and has stimulated the development of a conceptual framework. For example, the standard on leasing introduced the idea in UK standards of considering the commercial substance of a transaction rather than simply the legal position.

When the ASC was set up in the 1970s there was no clear statement of accounting principles other than that accounts should be prudent, be consistent, follow accrual accounting procedures and be based on the initial assumption that the business would remain a going concern.

The immediate task was to bring some order into accounting practice. The challenge of this task is illustrated by the ASC report *A Conceptual Framework for Financial Accounting and Reporting: The Possibilities for an Agreed Structure* by R. Macve, published in 1981, which considered that the possibility of an agreed body of accounting principles was remote at that time.

However, the process of setting standards has stimulated accounting thought and literature to the point where, by 1989, the IASC had issued the *Framework for the Presentation and Preparation of Financial Statements*. In 1994, the ASB produced its exposure drafts of *Statement of Accounting Principles*, which appeared in its final form in December 1999.

The development of conceptual frameworks is discussed further in Chapter 10.

Summary

It is evident from cases such as AEI/GEC, Enron and Parmalat that management cannot be permitted to have total discretion in the way in which it presents financial information in its accounts and rules are needed to ensure uniformity in the reporting of similar commercial transactions. Decisions must then be made as to the nature of the rules and how they are to be enforced.

In the UK the standard-setting bodies have tended to lean towards rules being framed as general principles and accepting the culture of voluntary compliance with explanation for any non-compliance.

Although there is a preference on the part of the standard setters to concentrate on general principles, there is growing pressure from the preparers of the accounts for more detailed illustrations and explanations as to how the standards are to be applied.

Standard setters have recognised that small and medium-sized businesses are not publicly accountable to external users and are given the opportunity to prepare financial statements under standards specifically designed to be useful and cost-effective.

The expansion in the number of multinational enterprises and transnational investments has led to a demand for a greater understanding of financial statements prepared in a range of countries. This has led to pressure for a single set of high-quality international accounting standards. IFRS are being used increasingly for reporting to capital markets. At the same time, national standards are evolving to come into line with IFRS.

REVIEW QUESTIONS

1 Why is it necessary for financial reporting to be subject to (a) mandatory control and (b) statutory control?

2 'The effective working of the financial aspects of a market economy rests on the validity of the underlying premises of integrity in the conduct of business and reliability in the provision of information. Even though in the great majority of cases that presumption is wholly justified, there needs to be strong institutional underpinning.

'That institutional framework has been shown to be inadequate. The last two to three years have accordingly seen a series of measures by the financial and business community to strengthen it. Amongst these has been the creation of the Financial Reporting Council and the bodies which it in turn established.'[35]

Discuss the above statement with particular reference to the Financial Reporting Review Panel. Illustrate with reference to its publications or decisions.

3 The increasing perception is that IFRS is overly complex and is complicating the search for appropriate forms of financial reporting for entities not covered by the EU Regulation.[36] Discuss:

(a) whether the current criteria for defining small and medium-sized companies are appropriate; and

(b) whether adopting

- FRSSE for small-sized entities;
- FRS 102 (based on *IFRS for SMEs*) for medium-sized entities; and
- IFRS for large private companies

might alleviate the problem.

4 'The most favoured way to reduce information overload was to have the company filter the available information set based on users' specifications of their needs.'[37] Discuss how this can be achieved given that users have differing needs.

5 Research[38] has indicated that narrative reporting in annual reports is not neutral, with good news being highlighted more than is supported by the statutory accounts and more than bad news. Discuss whether mandatory or statutory regulation could enforce objectivity in narrative disclosures and who should be responsible for such enforcement.

6 'The current differences between IASs and US GAAP are extensive and the recent pairing of the US Financial Accounting Standards Board and IASB to align IAS and US GAAP will probably result in IASB moving further from current UK GAAP.'[39] Discuss the implication of this on any choice that non-listed UK companies might make regarding complying with IFRS rather than a UK (adapted IFRS) GAAP.

7 How is it possible to make shareholders aware of the significance of the exercise of judgement by directors which can turn profits of £6 million into losses of £2 million?

8 Discuss the effect on reporting standards of the way in which industry is financed.

9 Foreign equity investment increases when countries have mandatory adoption of IFRS and effective enforcement. Discuss why this may not be required by investors in bonds.

10 The existence of a strong accounting profession is more important than uniform accounting standards in providing relevant information. Discuss.

EXERCISES

Question 1

Constructive review of the regulators.

Required:
(a) Obtain a copy of the Financial Reporting Review Panel's Annual Report.
(b) Critically discuss the major areas of criticism raised by the Panel in relation to Statements of Cash Flows and the improvements that could be expected in future years.

Question 2

IFRS for SMEs has been adopted by many countries internationally. Critically discuss reasons why it has not yet been adopted by the EU.

Question 3

Consider the interest of the tax authorities in financial reporting regulations. Explain why national tax authorities might be concerned about the transition from domestic accounting standards to IFRS in companies' annual reports.

Question 4

Access the Financial Reporting Council website and

(i)   Identify the industries that the FRRP will be currently reviewing and discuss the pros and cons of their choice and of giving prior notice of their intention.

(ii) Identify the results of the previous year's investigations and the implication for future enforcement.

(iii) Critically assess the result of your enquiries on the audit expectation gap.

Question 5

(i)   Critically discuss the rationale for allowing businesses in the UK a choice as to which accounting standards to apply, such as IFRS for the Group accounts and FRS 102 for UK subsidiaries.

(ii) Critically evaluate the IASB decision to move from a size criterion to a qualitative criterion in issuing *IFRS for SMEs*.

Question 6

The FRC in its 2010 publication *Cutting Clutter in Annual Reports* observed that much immaterial information is included in an Annual Report.

Required:
Obtain an Annual Report of a company that interests you and (a) as a potential investor critically comment on information you consider immaterial and (b) as the preparer justify its inclusion.

References

1 G. Whittred and I. Zimmer, *Financial Accounting Incentive Effects and Economic Consequences*, Holt, Rinehart & Winston, 1992, p. 8.
2 E.R. Farmer, *Making Sense of Company Reports*, Van Nostrand Reinhold, 1986, p. 16.
3 Baker Tilly, http://www.bakertilly.co.uk
4 EFRAG, *Towards a Disclosure Framework for the Notes*, Discussion Paper, 2012.
5 K. Peasnell, P. Pope and S. Young, 'Breaking the rules', *Accountancy International*, February 2000, p. 76.
6 CESR, *Proposed Statement of Principles of Enforcement of Accounting Standards in Europe*, CESR02–188b Principle 13, October 2002.
7 http://www.frc.org.uk/getattachment/f46d075e-7d0b-439c-aaf6-d557de55f93f/Financial-Reporting-Review-Panel-Annual-Report-2012.aspx
8 IASC, *Framework for the Preparation and Presentation of Financial Statements*, 1989, adopted by IASB 2001.
9 http://ec.europa.eu/internal_market/accounting/ias_en.htm#regulation
10 http://europa.eu/legislation_summaries/internal_market/business/company_law/126009_en.htm
11 http://ec.europa.eu
12 EU, *Regulation of the European Parliament and of the Council on the Application of International Accounting Standards*, Brussels, 2002.
13 http://www.esma.europa.eu/system/files/2012-412.pdf
14 S. Li, 'Does mandatory adoption of International Financial Reporting Standards in the European Union reduce the cost of equity capital?', *The Accounting Review*, vol. 85(2), 2009, pp. 607–636.
15 K.M. Shima and E.A. Gordon, 'ITFRS and the regulatory environment: The case of U.S. investor allocation choice', *Journal of Accounting and Public Policy*, vol. 30(5), 2011, pp. 481–500.
16 www.sec.gov
17 www.pcaobus.org
18 V. Beattie, S. Fearnley and T. Hines, 'Does IFRS undermine UK reporting integrity?', *Accountancy*, December 2008, pp. 56–57.
19 www.kpmg.co.uk/pubs/215748.pdf
20 download.pwc.com/ie/pubs/ifrs_survey.pdf
21 http://www.ifrs.org/IFRS-for-SMEs/Pages/SME-Workshops.aspx
22 S. Fraser, *Finance for Small and Medium-Sized Enterprises: A Report on the 2004 UK Survey of SME Finances*, Centre for Small and Medium-Sized Enterprises, Warwick Business School, University of Warwick, http://www.wbs.ac.uk/downloads/research/wbs-sme-main.pdf
23 ASB, *Financial Reporting Standard for Smaller Entities*, 1997.
24 C. Nobes and R. Parker, *Comparative International Accounting* (7th edition), Pearson Education, 2002, pp. 17–33.
25 J. Freedman and M. Power, *Law and Accountancy: Conflict and Cooperation in the 1990s*, Paul Chapman Publishing, 1992, p. 105.
26 For more detailed discussion see C. Nobes, 'Towards a general model of the reasons for international differences in financial reporting', *Abacus*, vol. 3(2), 1998, pp. 162–187.
27 Source: www.eurocapitalmarkets.org/files/images/equity_capGDP_col.jpg
28 C. Nobes, *Towards 1992*, Butterworths, 1989, p. 15.
29 Nobes, *op. cit.*, p. 8.
30 C. Nobes and H.R. Schwencke, 'Modelling the links between tax and financial reporting: a longitudinal examination of Norway over 30 years up to IFRS adoption', *European Accounting Review*, vol. 15(1), 2006, pp. 63–87.
31 Nobes and Parker, *op. cit.*, pp. 73–75.
32 See S.P. Agrawal, P.H. Jensen, A.L. Meader and K. Sellers, 'An international comparison of conceptual frameworks of accounting', *International Journal of Accounting*, vol. 24, 1989, pp. 237–249.
33 *Accountancy*, June 1989, p. 10.
34 See, e.g., B. Chauveau, 'The Spanish *Plan General de Contabilidad*: Agent of development and innovation?', *European Accounting Review*, vol. 4(1), 1995, pp. 125–138.

35 *The State of Financial Reporting*, Financial Reporting Council Second Annual Review, November 1992.

36 S. Fearnley and T. Hines, 'How IFRS has destabilised financial reporting for UK non-listed entities', *Journal of Financial Regulation and Compliance*, vol. 15(4), 2007, pp. 394–408.

37 V. Beattie, *Business Reporting: The Inevitable Change?*, ICAS, 1999, p. 53.

38 V. Tauringana and C. Chong, 'Neutrality of narrative discussion in annual reports of UK listed companies', *Journal of Applied Accounting Research*, vol. 7(1), 2004, pp. 74–107.

39 Y. Dinwoodie and P. Holgate, 'Singing from the same songsheet?', *Accountancy*, May 2003, pp. 94–95.

CHAPTER 10

Concepts – evolution of an international conceptual framework

The main purpose of this chapter is to discuss the rationale underlying financial reporting standards and concepts to apply when there are transactions for which there are no relevant standards.

Objectives

By the end of this chapter, you should be able to:

- discuss how financial accounting theory has evolved;
- discuss the accounting principles set out in:
  - the IASC *Framework for the Preparation and Presentation of Financial Statements*;
  - the IASB *Conceptual Framework for Financial Reporting 2010*;
  - the ASB *Statement of Principles*;
- comment critically on rule-based and principles-based approaches.

In the previous chapter we discussed the evolution of national and international accounting standards. The need for standards arose initially as a means by which the accounting profession protected itself against litigation for negligence by relying on the fact that financial statements complied with the published professional standards. The standards were based on existing best practice and little thought was given to a theoretical basis.

Standards were developed by individual countries and it was a reactive process. For example, in the US the Securities and Exchange Commission (SEC) was set up in 1933 to restore investor confidence in financial reporting following the Great Depression. The SEC is an enforcement agency that enforces compliance with US GAAP, which comprises often rule-based standards issued by the FASB.

There has been a similar reactive response in other countries often reacting to major financial crises and fraud, which has undermined investor confidence in financial statements. As a result, there has been a variety of national standards with national enforcement, e.g. in the UK principles-based standards are issued by the FRC Board.

With the growth of the global economy there has been a corresponding growth in the need for global standards, so that investors around the world receive the same fair view of a company's results regardless of the legal jurisdiction in which the company is registered. National standards varied in their quality and in the level of enforcement. This is illustrated by the following comment by the International Forum on Accountancy Development (IFAD):

> **Lessons from the crisis**
> . . . the Asian crisis showed that under the forces of financial globalisation it is essential for countries to improve . . . the supervision, regulation and transparency of financial systems . . . Efficiency of markets requires reliable financial information from issuers. With hindsight, it was clear that local accounting standards used to prepare financial statements did not meet international standards. Investors, both domestic and foreign, did not fully understand the weak financial position of the companies in which they were investing.

We will see in this chapter that, in addition to the realisation that global accounting standards were required, there was also growing interest in basing the standards on a conceptual framework rather than fire-fighting with pragmatic standards often dealing with an immediate problem. However, just as there have been different national standards, so there have been different conceptual frameworks.

Rationale for accounting standards

It is interesting to take a historical overview of the evolution of the financial accounting theory underpinning standards and guiding standard setters to see how it has moved through three phases from the empirical inductive to the deductive and then to a formalised conceptual framework.

10.3 Historical overview of the evolution of financial accounting theory

Financial accounting practices have not evolved in a vacuum. They are dynamic responses to changing macro- and micro-conditions which may involve political, fiscal, economic and commercial changes. For example, possible approaches to the accounting treatment of changing prices could be to:

- ignore if they do not represent a material change with a low rate of inflation as seen in many European countries;
- ignore and apply historical cost accounting;
- adopt a modified historical cost system where tangible non-current assets are revalued, which has been the norm in the UK; or
- adopt a physical capital maintenance concept and report using current costs.

It is clear from considering just the treatment of changing prices that there could be a variety of accounting treatments for similar transactions. If annual financial reports are to be useful in making economic decisions, there is a need for uniformity and consistency in reporting.

Attempts to achieve consistency have varied over time.

10.3.1 An empirical inductive approach

This was the approach followed by the accounting profession prior to 1970. It looked at the practices that existed and attempted to generalise from them.

This tended to be how the technical departments of accounting firms operated. By rationalising what they did, they ensured that the firm avoided accepting different financial reporting practices for similar transactions. The technical department's role was to advise partners and staff, i.e. it was a defensive role to avoid any potential charge from a user of the accounts that they had been misled.

Initially a technical circular was regarded as a private good and distribution was restricted to the firm's own staff. However, it then became recognised that it could benefit the firm if its practices were accepted as the industry benchmark, so that in the event of litigation it could rely on this fact.

When the technical advice ceased to be a private good, there was a perceived additional benefit to the firm if the nature of the practice could be changed from being a positive statement, i.e. this is how we report profits on uncompleted contracts, to a normative statement, i.e. this is how we report and this is how all other financial reporters ought to report.

Consequently, there has been a growing trend since the 1980s for firms to publish rationalisations for their financial reporting practices. It has been commercially prudent for them to do so. It has also been extremely helpful to academic accountants and their students.

Typical illustrations of the result of such empirical induction are the wide acceptance of the historical cost model and various concepts such as matching and realisation that we discussed in Chapter 2. The early standards were produced under this regime, e.g. IAS 2, the standard on inventory valuation.

This approach has played an important role in the evolution of financial reporting practices and will continue to do so. After all, it is the preparers of the financial statements and their auditors who are first exposed to change, whether economic, political or commercial. They are the ones who have to think their way through each new problem that surfaces, for example how to measure and report financial instruments. This means that a financial reporting practice already exists by the time the problem comes to the attention of theoreticians.

This resulted in standards or reporting practices that were based on rationalising what happened in practice, i.e. it established best current practice as the norm. Under this approach there was a general disclosure standard, e.g. IAS 1 *Disclosure of Accounting Policies*, and standards for major specific items, e.g. IAS 2 *Inventories*.

It was thought that the limitations implicit in the empirical inductive approach could be overcome by the deductive approach.

10.3.2 A deductive approach

The deductive approach is not dependent on existing practice, which is often perceived as having been tainted because it has been determined by finance directors and auditors. However, the problem remains: from whose viewpoint is the deduction to be made?

Possible alternatives to the preparers and auditors of the accounts are economists and users. However, economists are widely perceived as promoting unrealistic models and users as having needs so diverse that they cannot be realistically satisfied in a single set of accounts. Consider the attempts made to define income. Economists have supported the concept of a true income, while users have indicated the need for a range of relevant incomes.

10.3.3 A conceptual framework approach

This was promoted in the late 1980s. It was recognised that standards needed to be decision-useful, that they should satisfy cost/benefit criteria and that their implementation could only be achieved by consensus. Consensus was generally only achievable where there was a clearly perceived rationale underpinning a standard and, even so, alternative treatments were initially required in order to gain support.

The outcome of the wish for a conceptual framework was the publication by the IASC in 1989 of its *Framework for the Preparation and Presentation of Financial Statements.*

10.4 IASC *Framework for the Preparation and Presentation of Financial Statements*

The *Framework* is not a reporting standard. Its purpose is to describe the basic concepts by which financial statements are prepared. It acts as a guide to the Board when developing accounting standards and as a guide to management when deciding how to report on transactions for which there is no relevant international standard.

It is concerned with general-purpose financial statements that a business enterprise prepares and presents to meet the common information needs of a wide range of users to help them make decisions.

The user groups include current and potential investors, employees, lenders, suppliers and other trade creditors, customers, governments and their agencies and the general public. The approach taken by the *Framework* is that it accepts that not all of the information needs of each of the user groups can be met by a single set of financial statements.

It assumes, however, that as all users are making economic decisions, there is information in which all users have a common interest and that general-purpose financial statements should satisfy this. It further assumes that because investors are providers of risk capital to the enterprise, financial statements that meet their needs will also meet most of the general financial information needs of other users.

Typical economic decisions that are being made include:

- Assessing:
  - when to buy, hold or sell an equity investment;
  - the stewardship or accountability of management;
  - how much of the distributable profits to pay out as dividends;
  - the ability of the entity to pay and provide other benefits to its employees;
  - the security for amounts lent to the entity.
- Determining:
  - taxation policies;
  - how to regulate the activities of entities.

10.4.1 The *Framework* content

The *Framework* deals with:

(a) the objective of financial statements;

(b) underlying assumptions;

(c) the qualitative characteristics that determine the usefulness of information provided in financial statements;

(d) definition, recognition and measurement of the elements from which financial statements are constructed; and

(e) concepts of capital and capital maintenance.

As the *Conceptual Framework for Financial Reporting* issued in 2010 has replaced (a) and (c) with the issue of its Chapter 1 *The objective of general purpose financial reporting* and Chapter 3 *Qualitative characteristics of useful financial information*, we will discuss these in Section 10.5. We now comment briefly on (b), (d) and (e), which have not yet been replaced.

10.4.2 Underlying assumptions

The underlying assumptions of financial statements are that they are prepared on the basis of the following:

- **Accruals.** The effects of transactions and other events are recognised when they occur, rather than when cash or its equivalent is received or paid, and they are reported in the financial statements of the periods to which they relate. We have seen in Chapter 2 that, in addition to cash receipts and payments, obligations to pay cash in the future and resources that represent cash to be received in the future are also reported.

- **Going concern.** The financial statements presume that an enterprise will continue in operation indefinitely or, if that presumption is not valid, disclosure and a different basis of reporting are required, such as preparing the statements using the net realisable value accounting model described in Chapter 7.

- **Consistency.** In order to achieve comparability of the financial statements of an enterprise through time, the accounting policies are followed consistently from one period to another; a change in an accounting policy is made only in certain exceptional circumstances.

10.4.3 Definition, recognition and measurement of elements

Financial statements portray the financial effects of transactions and other events by grouping them into broad classes according to their economic characteristics. These broad classes are termed the elements of financial statements.

(i) The elements relating to financial position

The elements that appear in the balance sheet are Assets, Liabilities and Equity.

Definitions of the elements relating to financial position

- **Asset.** An asset is a resource *controlled* by the enterprise as a result of *past* events and from which *future* economic benefits are expected to flow to the enterprise.

- **Liability.** A liability is a *present* obligation of the enterprise arising from *past* events, the settlement of which is expected to result in an *outflow* from the enterprise of resources embodying economic benefits.

- **Equity.** Equity is the *residual* interest in the assets of the enterprise after deducting all its liabilities.

Recognition in the balance sheet

An **asset** is recognised in the balance sheet when it is **probable** that the **future economic benefits** will flow to the enterprise and the asset has a cost or value that can be **measured reliably**.

A **liability** is recognised in the balance sheet when it is **probable** that **an outflow of resources** embodying economic benefits will result from the settlement of a **present obligation** and the amount at which the settlement will take place can be **measured reliably**.

(ii) The elements relating to financial performance

The elements that appear in the income statement are income and expenses.

Definitions of the elements relating to financial performance

- **Income**. Income is increases in economic benefits from revenue or gains during the accounting period in the form of inflows or enhancements of assets or decreases of liabilities that result in increases in equity, other than contributions from equity shareholders.

- **Expenses**. Expenses are decreases in economic benefits from expenses incurred in the ordinary business and losses arising during the accounting period in the form of outflows or depletions of assets or incurrences of liabilities that result in decreases in equity, other than those relating to distributions to equity shareholders.

Recognition in the income statement

Income is recognised in the income statement when an increase in future economic benefits related to an increase in an asset or a decrease of a liability has arisen that can be measured reliably. This means, in effect, that recognition of income occurs simultaneously with the recognition of increases in assets or decreases in liabilities.

Expenses are recognised when a decrease in future economic benefits related to a decrease in an asset or an increase of a liability has arisen that can be measured reliably. This means, in effect, that recognition of expenses occurs simultaneously with the recognition of an increase in liabilities or a decrease in assets.

(iii) Measurement of all the elements of financial statements

Measurement involves assigning monetary amounts at which the elements of the financial statements are to be recognised and reported. The *Framework* acknowledges that a variety of bases were used, including historical cost, current cost, net realisable value and present value. It does not give any guidance for selecting which measurement basis should be used for particular elements of financial statements or in particular circumstances.

10.4.4 Concepts of capital and capital maintenance

We saw in Chapter 7 that the choice of capital maintenance concept impacts on the amount of profit that is reported.

Financial capital maintenance

Under this concept, a profit is earned only if the financial (or money) amount of the net assets at the end of the period exceeds the financial (or money) amount of net assets at the beginning of the period, after excluding any distributions to, and contributions from, owners during the period. Financial capital maintenance can be measured in either nominal monetary units or units of constant purchasing power.

Physical capital maintenance

Under this concept, a profit is earned only if the physical productive capacity (or operating capability) of the enterprise at the end of the period exceeds the physical productive capacity at the beginning of the period, after excluding any distributions to, and contributions from, owners during the period. The physical capital maintenance concept requires the adoption of the current cost basis of measurement.

10.5 *Conceptual Framework for Financial Reporting 2010*

The purpose of the *Conceptual Framework* is to assist:

- the Board
  - in the development of future IFRSs and in its review of existing IFRSs;
  - in promoting harmonisation of regulations, accounting standards and procedures relating to the presentation of financial statements by providing a basis for reducing the number of alternative accounting treatments permitted by IFRSs;
- national standard-setting bodies in developing national standards;
- preparers of financial statements in applying IFRSs and in dealing with topics that have yet to form the subject of an IFRS;
- auditors in forming an opinion on whether financial statements comply with IFRSs;
- users of financial statements in interpreting the information contained in financial statements prepared in compliance with IFRSs.

10.5.1 Piecemeal development

The IASB and FASB started a convergence project in 2004 to prepare an agreed *Framework* over eight phases. These are:

Phase A: Objective and qualitative characteristics (final chapter published)

Phase B: Elements and recognition

Phase C: Measurement

Phase D: Reporting entity (ED/2010/2)

Phase E: Presentation and disclosure

Phase F: Purpose and status of framework

Phase G: Applicability to not-for-profit entities

Phase H: Other issues, if necessary.

The *Conceptual Framework* (2010) is produced in chapters as follows:

Chapter 1 The objective of general purpose financial reporting

Chapter 2 The reporting entity

Chapter 3 Qualitative characteristics of useful financial information

Chapter 4 The *Framework* (1989): the remaining text.

10.6 Phase A of the *Conceptual Framework*

The main points of Phase A which includes Chapter 1 (The objective of general purpose financial reporting) and Chapter 3 (Qualitative characteristics of useful financial information) are described below.

10.6.1 The objective of financial reporting

The fundamental objective of general-purpose financial reporting is to provide financial information about the reporting entity that is useful to present and potential equity investors, lenders and other creditors when making investment and loan decisions. Information is needed to help them assess the prospects for future cash flows which, based to an extent on the review of past performance, will assist in assessing stewardship.

However, general-purpose financial reports do not and cannot provide all of the information that existing and potential investors, lenders and other creditors need. Those users need to consider pertinent information from other sources, for example general economic conditions and expectations, political events and political climate, and industry and company outlooks.

10.6.2 Qualitative characteristics of useful financial information

There are two fundamental qualitative characteristics if information is to be decision-useful and not misleading. These are **relevance** and **faithful representation**.

Relevance

Relevant financial information is capable of making a difference to the decisions made by users. Financial information is capable of making a difference to decisions if it has **predictive value**, **confirmatory value** or both.

Predictive value
Financial information has predictive value if it can be used as an input to processes employed by users to predict future outcomes. It is used by users in making their own predictions.

Confirmatory value
Financial information has confirmatory value if it provides feedback about (confirms or changes) previous evaluations.

Predictive and confirmatory values
Predictive and confirmatory values are interrelated. For example, revenue information for the current year, which can be used as the basis for predicting revenues in future years, can also be compared with revenue predictions for the current year that were made in past years.

Faithful representation

Financial reports represent the effect of economic activities in words and numbers. A faithful representation would need to be complete, neutral and free from error.

Neutral
This means that the information has not been slanted, weighted, emphasised, de-emphasised or otherwise manipulated to increase the probability that financial information will be received favourably or unfavourably by users.

Freedom from error
Faithful representation does not mean the information is 100% accurate. 'Free from error' means there are no errors or omissions in the description of the event or transaction and no errors in the process used to produce the reported information. Taking the reporting of an estimate as an example, a representation of that estimate can be faithful if the amount is described clearly and accurately as being an estimate, the nature and limitations of the estimating process are explained, and no errors have been made in selecting and applying an appropriate process for developing the estimate.

Enhancing qualities

There are other characteristics that may make the information more useful. These are comparability, consistency, verifiability, timeliness and understandability.

Characteristics considered but not included

Some characteristics were considered but not included on the grounds that they were covered by the above characteristics. For instance, 'true and fair view' and 'fair presentation' were not included because they were considered to be equivalent to faithful representation.

Constraints

As with other frameworks, there are constraints on the information to be disclosed. These are materiality, defined in the usual way as being information whose omission or misstatement could influence decisions, and cost, if this exceeds the benefit of providing the information.

10.6.3 Review of progress

We can see that the project by the IASB to develop an agreed *Conceptual Framework* is progressing in a piecemeal fashion with only Chapters 1 and 3 finalised and the date for the finalisation of some of the other chapters still to be announced. This might be seen as a strength in that time and thought are being given to the project.

Downside to piecemeal progress

However, there is also a downside as seen in the ASB response to the IASB which expressed the following concerns:

● The current *Framework* applies to financial *statements* rather than financial *reporting*. If it is to be extended to financial reporting, this could include other areas such as prospectuses, news releases and management forecasts, but this has not been defined.
● There is a risk that the piecemeal approach could lead to internal inconsistencies, and decisions being made in the earlier chapters could have as yet unforeseen adverse consequences.
● The consequences of adopting the entity approach on the remainder of the *Framework* may be extensive. For example, there is a link between the stewardship objective and the proprietary view, and dismissing that view from the *Framework* entirely may lead to difficulties for entities in providing information in the financial reports that fulfils that objective.

The last point concerning the implication for stewardship reporting reflects the US influence on the *Framework* with less emphasis being given to it.

The piecemeal approach perhaps reflects the differences that need to be resolved between the IASB and the FASB, from differences in terminology, for example substituting *faithful representation* for *reliability*, to more fundamental differences relating to the scope of the *Framework*, for example its very objective and its boundaries as to whether it relates to financial *statements* or financial *reports*.

Principles versus rules

The FASB in the USA and the IASB have been collaborating on revising the IASB *Framework* and the FASB *Concepts Statements*. The intention is to adopt a principles-based approach. This is also supported by a report[1] from the Institute of Chartered Accountants of Scotland which concludes that the global convergence of accounting standards cannot be achieved by a 'tick-box' rules-driven approach but should rely on judgement-based principles.

A principles-based approach allows companies the flexibility to deal with new situations. A rules-based approach provides the auditor with protection against litigious claims because it can be shown that other auditors would have adopted the same accounting treatment. However, following the Enron disaster, the rules-based approach was heavily criticised in America and it was felt that a principles-based approach would have been more effective in preventing it.

A rules-based approach means that financial statements are more comparable. Recognising that a principles-based approach could lead to different professional judgements for the same commercial activity, it is important that there should be full disclosure and transparency.

The *Framework*'s influence on other frameworks

The *Framework* has initiated the development of conceptual frameworks by other national standard setters for both private sector and public sector financial statements. Since then and up to the present day other jurisdictions have been influenced when drafting their own national conceptual frameworks; for example Australia, Canada, New Zealand, South Africa and the UK have similar conceptual frameworks.

One of the earliest conceptual frameworks developed subsequently was that developed by the ASB in the UK as the *Statement of Principles* – this expanded on the ideas underlying the *Framework* and the ASB deserves praise for this.

10.7 ASB *Statement of Principles* 1999[2]

In the UK the *Statement* fleshed out the ideas contained in the *Framework*.

As Sir David Tweedie, Chairman of the ASB, commented, 'The Board has developed its *Statement of Principles* in parallel with its development of accounting standards . . . It is in effect the Board's compass for when we navigate uncharted waters in the years ahead. This is essential reading for those who want to know where the Board is coming from, and where it is aiming to go.'

The *Statement* contains eight chapters dealing with key issues. Each of the chapters is commented on below.

10.7.1 Chapter 1: 'The objective of financial statements'

The *Statement of Principles* follows the IASC *Framework* in the identification of user groups. It identifies the investor group as the primary group for whom the financial statements are being prepared. It then states the information needs of each group as follows:

● **Investors**. These need information to:
  – assess the stewardship of management, e.g. in safeguarding the entity's resources and using them properly, efficiently and profitably;
  – take decisions about management, e.g. assessing need for new management;
  – take decisions about their investment or potential investment, e.g. deciding whether to hold, buy or sell shares and assessing the ability to pay dividends.

● **Lenders**. These need information to:
  – determine whether their loans and interest will be paid on time;
  – decide whether to lend and on what terms.

- **Suppliers**. These need information to:
  - decide whether to sell to the entity;
  - determine whether they will be paid on time;
  - determine longer-term stability if the company is a major customer.
- **Employees**. These need information to:
  - assess the stability and profitability of the company;
  - assess the ability to provide remuneration, retirement benefits and employment opportunities.
- **Customers**. These need information to:
  - assess the probability of the continued existence of the company taking account of their own degree of dependence on the company, e.g. for future provision of specialised replacement parts and servicing product warranties.
- **Government and other agencies**. These need information to:
  - be aware of the commercial activities of the company;
  - regulate these activities;
  - raise revenue;
  - produce national statistics.
- **Public**. Members of the public need information to:
  - determine the effect on the local economy of the company's activities, e.g. employment opportunities, use of local suppliers;
  - assess recent developments in the company's prosperity and changes in its activities.

The information needs of which group are to be dominant?

Seven groups are identified, but there is only one set of financial statements. Although they are described as general-purpose statements, a decision has to be made about which group's needs take precedence.

The *Statement of Principles* identifies the **investor** group as the defining class of user, i.e. the primary group for whom the financial statements are being prepared.

It takes the view that financial statements 'are able to focus on the common interest of users'. The common interest is described thus: 'all potential users are interested, to a varying degree, in the financial performance and financial position of the entity as a whole'.

This means that it is a prerequisite that the information must be relevant to the investor group. This suggests that any need of the other groups that is not also a need of the investors will not be met by the financial statements. However, the 1995 Exposure Draft stated: 'Awarding primacy to investors does not imply that other users are to be ignored. The information prepared for investors is useful as a frame of reference for other users, against which they can evaluate more specific information that they may obtain in their dealings with the enterprise.'

What information should be provided to satisfy the information needs?

The *Statement* proposes that information is required in four areas: financial performance, financial position, generation and use of cash, and financial adaptability.

Financial performance

Financial performance is defined as the return an entity obtains from the resources it controls. This return is available from the profit and loss account and provides a means to assess past management performance, how effectively resources have been utilised and the capacity to generate cash flows.

Financial position

Financial position is available from an examination of the statement of financial position and includes:

- the economic resources controlled by an entity, i.e. assets and liabilities;
- financial structure, i.e. capital gearing indicating how profits will be divided between the different sources of finance and the capacity for raising additional finance in the future;
- liquidity and solvency, i.e. current and liquid ratios;
- capacity to adapt to changes – see below under Financial adaptability.

Generation and use of cash

Information is available from the cash flow statement which shows cash flows from operating, investment and financing activities providing a perspective that is largely free from allocation and valuation issues. This information is useful in assessing and reviewing previous assessments of cash flows.

Financial adaptability

This is an entity's ability to alter the amount and timing of its cash flows. It is desirable in order to be able to cope with difficult periods, e.g. when losses are incurred and to take advantage of unexpected investment opportunities. It is dependent on factors such as the ability, at short notice, to:

- raise new capital;
- repay capital or debt;
- obtain cash from disposal of assets without disrupting continuing business, i.e. realise readily marketable securities that might have been built up as a liquid reserve;
- achieve a rapid improvement in net cash flows from operations.

10.7.2 Chapter 2: 'The reporting entity'

This chapter focuses on identifying when an entity should report and which activities to include in the report.

When an entity should report

The principle is that an entity should prepare and publish financial statements if:

- there is a legitimate demand for the information, i.e. it is the case both that it is decision-useful and that benefits exceed the cost of producing the information; and
- it is a cohesive economic unit, i.e. a unit under a central control that can be held accountable for its activities.

Which activities to include

The principle is that those activities should be included that are within the direct control of the entity, e.g. assets and liabilities which are reported in its own statement of financial position, or indirect control, e.g. assets and liabilities of a subsidiary of the entity which are reported in the consolidated statement of financial position.

Control is defined as (a) the ability to deploy the resources and (b) the ability to benefit (or to suffer) from their deployment. Indirect control by an investor can be difficult to determine. The test is not to apply a theoretical level of influence such as holding x% of shares but to review the relationship that exists between the investor and investee in practice, such as the investor having the power to veto the investee's financial and operating policies and benefit from its net assets.

10.7.3 Chapter 3: 'The qualitative characteristics of financial information'

The *Statement of Principles* is based on the IASC *Framework* and contains the same four principal qualitative characteristics relating to the content of information and how the information is presented. The two primary characteristics relating to content are the need to be relevant and reliable; the two relating to presentation are the need to be understandable and comparable. The characteristics appear diagrammatically in Figure 10.1.

From the diagram we can see that for information content to be **relevant** it must have:

- the ability to influence the economic decisions of users;
- predictive value, i.e. help users to evaluate or assess past, present or future events; or
- confirmatory value, i.e. help users to confirm their past evaluations.

For information to be **reliable** it must be:

- free from material error, i.e. transactions have been accurately recorded and reported;
- a faithful representation, i.e. reflecting the commercial substance of transactions;
- neutral, i.e. not presented in a way to achieve a predetermined result;
- prudent, i.e. not creating hidden reserves or excessive provisions, deliberately understating assets or gains, or deliberately overstating liabilities or losses; and
- complete, i.e. the information is complete subject to a materiality test.

Figure 10.1 What makes financial information useful?

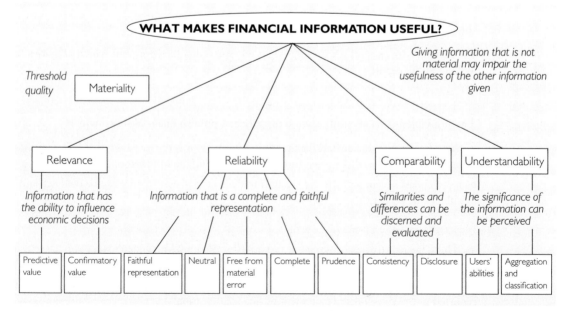

To be useful, the financial information also needs to be **understandable** and **comparable** over time and between companies.

Understandability

The financial information satisfies the criteria for understandability if it is capable of being understood by a user with a reasonable knowledge of business activities and accounting, and a willingness to study the information with reasonable diligence.

Materiality

Materiality is a threshold quality which is described as follows: 'An item of information is material to the financial statements if its misstatement or omission might reasonably be expected to influence the economic decisions of users of those financial statements, including their assessment of management's stewardship.'[3]

The important consideration is not user expectation (e.g. that users might expect turnover to be accurate to within 1%) but the effect on decision making (e.g. that there might be an effect only if turnover were over- or understated by more than 10%, in which case only errors exceeding 10% are material).

Materiality benchmarks

Materiality depends on the size of the item or error judged in the particular circumstances of its omission or misstatement. The need to exercise judgement means that the preparer needs to have a benchmark.

A discussion paper issued in January 1995 by the Financial Reporting and Auditing Group of the ICAEW entitled *Materiality in Financial Reporting FRAG 1/95* identified that there were few instances where an actual figure was given by statute or by standard setters, e.g. FRS 6,[4] paragraph 76 referred to a material minority and indicates that this was defined as 10%.

The paper also referred to a rule of thumb used in the USA:

> The staff of the US Securities and Exchange Commission have an informal rule of thumb that errors of more than 10% are material, those between 5% and 10% may be material and those under 5% are usually not material. These percentages are applied to gross profit, net income, equity and any specific line in the financial statements that is potentially misstated.

However, the ASB has moved away from setting percentage benchmarks and there is now a need for more explicit guidance on the application of the materiality threshold.

10.7.4 Chapter 4: 'The elements of financial statements'

This chapter gives guidance on the items that *could* appear in financial statements. These are described as **elements** and have the following essential features:

- **Assets**. These are rights to future economic benefits controlled by an entity as a result of past transactions or events.
- **Liabilities**. These are obligations of an entity to transfer future economic benefits as a result of past transactions or events, i.e. ownership is not essential.
- **Ownership interest**. This is the residual amount found by deducting all liabilities from assets which belong to the owners of the entity.
- **Gains**. These are increases in ownership interest not resulting from contributions by the owners.

- **Losses**. These are decreases in ownership interest not resulting from distributions to the owners.
- **Contributions by the owners**. These are increases in ownership interest resulting from transfers from owners in their capacity as owners.
- **Distributions to owners**. These are decreases in ownership interest resulting from transfers to owners in their capacity as owners.

These definitions have been used as the basis for developing standards, e.g. assessing the substance of a transaction means identifying whether the transaction has given rise to new assets or liabilities.

10.7.5 Chapter 5: 'Recognition in financial statements'

The *Statement of Principles* approach is different from that which focuses on matching costs to revenue in that it identifies the amount of the expenditure to be recognised as an asset and the balance is transferred to the statement of income, i.e. the question is 'Should this expenditure be recognised as an asset (capitalised) and, if so, should any part of it be derecognised (written off as a loss element)?'

This means that the allocation process now requires an assessment as to whether an asset exists at the statement of financial position date by applying the following test:

1 If the future economic benefits are eliminated at a single point in time, it is at that point that the loss is recognised and the expenditure derecognised, i.e. the debit balance is transferred to the profit and loss account.

2 If the future economic benefits are eliminated over several accounting periods – typically because they are being consumed over a period of time – the cost of the asset that comprises the future economic benefits will be recognised as a loss in the performance statement over those accounting periods, i.e. written off as a loss element as their future economic benefit reduces.

The result of this approach should not lead to changes in the accounts as currently prepared but it does emphasise that matching cost and revenue is not the main driver of recognition, i.e. the question is not 'How much expenditure should we match with the revenue reported in the profit and loss account?' but rather 'Are there future economic benefits arising from the expenditure to justify inclusion in the statement of financial position?' and, if not, derecognise it, i.e. write it off.

Dealing with uncertainty

There is almost always some uncertainty as to when to recognise an event or transaction, e.g. when is the asset element of raw material inventory to be disclosed as the asset element work in progress? Is it when an inventory requisition is issued, when the storekeeper isolates it in the bay for inventory to be issued, when it is issued onto the workshop floor, or when it begins to be worked on?

The *Statement of Principles* states that the principle to be applied if a transaction has created or added to an existing asset or liability is to recognise it if:

1 sufficient evidence exists that the new asset or liability has been created or that there has been an addition to an existing asset or liability; and

2 the new asset or liability or the addition to the existing asset or liability can be measured at a monetary amount with sufficient reliability.

The use of the word sufficient reflects the uncertainty that surrounds the decision when to recognise, and the *Statement* states: 'In the business environment, uncertainty usually exists in a continuum, so the recognition process involves selecting the point on the continuum at which uncertainty becomes acceptable.'[5]

Before that point it may, for example, be appropriate to disclose by way of a note to the accounts a contingent liability that is possible (less than 50% chance of crystallising into a liability) but not probable (more than 50% chance of crystallising).

10.7.6 Chapter 6: 'Measurement in financial statements'

The majority of listed companies in the UK use the mixed measurement system whereby some assets and liabilities are measured using historical cost and some are measured using a current value basis. The *Statement of Principles* envisages that this will continue to be the practice and states that the aim is to select the basis that:

- provides information about financial performance and financial position that is useful in evaluating the reporting entity's cash-generation abilities and in assessing its financial adaptability;

- carries values which are sufficiently reliable: if the historical cost and current value are equally reliable, the better measure is the one that is the most relevant; current values may frequently be no less reliable than historical cost figures given the level of estimation that is required in historical cost figures, e.g. determining provisions for bad debts, stock provisions, product warranties;

- reflects what the asset or liability represents: e.g. the relevance of short-term investments to an entity will be the specific future cash flows and these are best represented by current values.

ASB gradualist approach

The underlying support of the ASB for a gradualist move towards the use of current values is reflected in its statement that 'Although the objective of financial statements and the qualitative characteristics of financial information, in particular relevance and reliability may not change . . . as markets develop, measurement bases that were once thought unreliable may become reliable. Similarly, as access to markets develops, so a measurement basis that was once thought insufficiently relevant may become the most relevant measure available.'

Determining current value

Current value systems could be defined as replacement cost (entry value), net realisable value (exit value) or value in use (discounted present value of future cash flows). The approach of the *Statement* is to identify the value to the business by selecting from these three alternatives the measure that is most relevant in the circumstances. This measure is referred to as deprival value and represents the loss that the entity would suffer if it were deprived of the asset.

The value to the business is determined by considering whether the company would replace the asset. If the answer is *yes*, then use replacement cost; if the answer is *no* but the asset is worth keeping, then use value in use; and if *no* and the asset is not worth keeping, then use net realisable value.

This can be shown diagrammatically as in Figure 10.2.

Figure 10.2 Value to the business

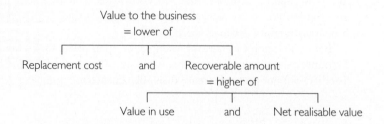

10.7.7 Chapter 7: 'Presentation of financial information'

Chapter 7 states that the objective of the presentation adopted is to communicate clearly and effectively and in as simple and straightforward a manner as is possible without loss of relevance or reliability and without significantly increasing the length of the financial statements.

The point about length is well made given the length of current annual reports and accounts. Recent examples include the Stagecoach Group (over 100 pages) and Jenoptik AG (extending to over 190 pages).

The *Statement* analyses the way in which information should be presented in financial statements to meet the objectives set out in Chapter 1. It covers the requirement for items to be aggregated and classified and outlines good presentation practices in the statement of income, statement of financial position, statement of cash flows and accompanying information.

For example, as regards the statement of income, good presentation involves:

- recognising only gains and losses;
- classifying items by function, e.g. production, selling, administrative, and nature, e.g. interest payable;
- showing separately amounts that are affected in different ways by economic or commercial conditions, e.g. continuing, acquired and discontinued operations, segmental geographical information;
- showing separately:
  - items unusual in amount or incidence;
  - expenses that are not operating expenses, e.g. financing costs and taxation;
  - expenses that relate primarily to future periods, e.g. research expenditure.

10.7.8 Chapter 8: 'Accounting for interests in other entities'

Interests in other entities can have a material effect on the company's own financial perform-ance and financial position and need to be fully reflected in the financial statements. As an example, an extract from the 2012 Annual Report and Accounts of Stagecoach plc shows:

	Company statement of financial position	Consolidated statement of financial position
Tangible assets	£0.8m	£961.6m
Investments	£1,025.3m	—

In deciding whether to include the assets in the consolidated statement of financial position, a key factor is the degree of influence exerted over the activities and resources of the investee:

- If the degree of influence allows control of the operating and financial policies, the financial statements are aggregated.

- If the investor has joint control or significant influence, the investor's shares of the gains and losses are recognised in the consolidated statement of comprehensive income and reflected in the carrying value of the investment.

However, there is no clear agreement on the treatment of interests in other entities, and further developments can be expected.

Summary

Directors and accountants are constrained by a mass of rules and regulations which govern the measurement, presentation and disclosure of financial information. Regulations are derived from three major sources: the legislature in the form of statutes, the accountancy profession in the form of standards, and the Financial Services Authority in the form of Listing Rules.

There have been a number of reports relating to financial reporting. The preparation and presentation of financial statements continue to evolve. Steps are being taken to provide a conceptual framework and there is growing international agreement on the setting of global standards.

User needs have been accepted as paramount; qualitative characteristics of information have been specified; the elements of financial statements have been defined precisely; the presentation of financial information has been prescribed; and comparability between companies is seen as desirable.

However, the intention remains to produce financial statements that present a fair view. This is not achieved by detailed rules and regulations; the exercise of judgement will continue to be needed. This opens the way for creative accounting practices that bring financial reporting and the accounting profession into disrepute. Strenuous efforts will continue to be needed from the auditors and regulators to contain the use of unacceptable practices. The regulatory bodies show that they have every intention of accepting the challenge.

The question of the measurement base that should be used has yet to be settled. The measurement question still remains a major area of financial reporting that needs to be addressed.

The *Framework* sees the objective of financial statements as providing information about the financial position, performance and financial adaptability of an enterprise that is useful to a wide range of users in making economic decisions. It recognises that they are limited because they largely show the financial effects of past events and do not necessarily show non-financial information.

On the question of measurement the view has been expressed that:

historical cost has the merit of familiarity and (to some extent) objectivity; current values have the advantage of greater relevance to users of the accounts who wish to assess the current state or recent performance of the business, but they may sometimes be unreliable or too expensive to provide. It concludes that practice should develop by evolving in the direction of greater use of current values to the extent that this is consistent with the constraints of reliability, cost and acceptability to the financial community.[6]

There are critics[7] who argue that the concern with recording current asset values rather than historical costs means that:

> the essential division between the IASC and its critics is one between those who are more concerned about where they want to be and those who want to be very clear about where they are now. It is a division between those who see the purpose of financial statements as taking economic decisions about the future, and those who see it as a basis for making management accountable and for distributing the rewards among the stakeholders.

Finally, it is interesting to give some thought to extracts from two publications which indicate that there is still a long way to go in the evolution of financial reporting, and that there is little room for complacency. The first is from *The Future Shape of Financial Reports:*[8]

> As Solomons[9] and *Making Corporate Reports Valuable* discussed in detail, the then system of financial reporting in the UK fails to satisfy the purpose of providing information to shareholders, lenders and others to appraise past performance in order to form expectations about an organisation's future performance in five main respects:
>
> 1 . . . measures of performance . . . are based on original or historical costs . . .
> 2 Much emphasis is placed on a single measure of earnings per share . . .
> 3 . . . insufficient attention is paid to changes in an enterprise's cash or liquidity position.
> 4 The present system is essentially backward looking . . .
> 5 Emphasis is often placed on the legal form rather than on the economic substance of transactions . . .

We have seen that some of these five limitations are being addressed, but not all, e.g. the provision of projected figures.

The second extract is from *Making Corporate Reports Valuable:*[10]

> The present statement of financial position almost defies comprehension. Assets are shown at depreciated historical cost, at amounts representing current valuations and at the results of revaluations of earlier periods (probably also depreciated); that is there is no consistency whatsoever in valuation practice. The sum total of the assets, therefore, is meaningless and combining it with the liabilities to show the entity's financial position does not in practice achieve anything worthwhile.

The IASC has taken steps to deal with the frequency of revaluations, but the criticism still holds in that financial statements will continue to be produced incorporating mixed measurement bases.

The point made by some critics remains unresolved:

> Accountability and the IASC's decision usefulness are not compatible. Forward-looking decisions require forecasts of future cash flows, which in the economic model are what determines the values of assets. These values are too subjective to form the basis of accountability. The definition of assets and the recognition rules restrict assets to economic benefits the enterprise controls as a result of past events and that are measurable with sufficient reliability. But economic decision making requires examination of all sources of future cash flows, not just a restricted sub-set of them.

In the USA, Australia, Canada, the UK and the IASB, the approach has been the same, i.e. commencing with a consideration of the objectives of financial statements, qualitative characteristics of financial information, definition of the elements, and when these are to be recognised in the financial statements. There is a general agreement on these areas. Agreement on measurement has yet to be reached. A global framework is being developed between the IASB and the FASB and it is interesting to see that the same tensions exist, for example, between accountability and decision-usefulness.

REVIEW QUESTIONS

1 Name the user groups and information needs of the user groups identified in the *Statement of Principles*.

2 R. Macve in *A Conceptual Framework for Financial Accounting and Reporting: The Possibilities for an Agreed Structure* suggested that the search for a conceptual framework was a political process. Discuss the effect that this thinking has had and will have on standard setting.

3 'The replacement of accrual accounting with cash flow accounting would avoid the need for a conceptual framework.'[11] Discuss.

4 Financial accounting theory has accumulated a vast literature. A cynic might be inclined to say that the vastness of the literature is in sharp contrast to its impact on practice.

 (a) Describe the different approaches that have evolved in the development of accounting theory.

 (b) Assess its impact on standard setting.

 (c) Discuss the contribution of accounting theory to the understanding of accounting practice, and suggest contributions that it might make in the future.

5 Rules-based accounting adds unnecessary complexity, encourages financial engineering and does not necessarily lead to a 'true and fair view' or a 'fair presentation'. Discuss.

6 Explain what you understand by a balance sheet approach to income determination.

7 Explain how a company assesses materiality when attempting to report a true and fair view of its income and financial position.

8 The key qualitative characteristics in the *Framework* are relevance and reliability. Preparers of financial statements may face a dilemma in satisfying both criteria at once. Discuss.

9 An asset is defined in the *Framework* as a resource which an entity controls as a result of past events and from which future economic benefits are expected to flow to the entity. Discuss whether property, plant and equipment automatically qualify as assets.

EXERCISES

Question 1

The following extract is from *Conceptual Framework for Financial Accounting and Reporting: Elements of Financial Statements and Their Measurement*, FASB 3, December 1976.

The benefits of achieving agreement on a conceptual framework for financial accounting and reporting manifest themselves in several ways. Among other things, a conceptual framework can (1) guide the body responsible for establishing accounting standards, (2) provide a frame of reference for resolving accounting questions in the absence of a specific promulgated standard, (3) determine bounds for judgement in preparing financial statements, (4) increase financial statement users' understanding of and confidence in financial statements, and (5) enhance comparability.

Required:

(a) Define a conceptual framework.

(b) Critically examine why the benefits provided in the above statements are likely to flow from the development of a conceptual framework for accounting.

Question 2

The following extract is from 'Comments of Leonard Spacek', in R.T. Sprouse and M. Moonitz, *A Tentative Set of Broad Accounting Principles for Business Enterprises*, Accounting Research Study No. 3, AICPA, New York, 1962, reproduced in A. Belkaoui, *Accounting Theory*, Harcourt Brace Jovanovich.

A discussion of assets, liabilities, revenue and costs is premature and meaningless until the basic principles that will result in a fair presentation of the facts in the form of financial accounting and financial reporting are determined. This fairness of accounting and reporting must be for and to people, and these people represent the various segments of our society.

Required:

Discuss the extent to which the IASB conceptual framework satisfies the above definition of fairness.

Question 3

The following is an extract from *Accountancy Age*, 25 January 2001.

A powerful and 'shadowy' group of senior partners from the seven largest firms has emerged to move closer to edging control of accounting standards from the world's accountancy regulators . . . they form the Global Steering Committee . . . The GSC has worked on plans to improve standards for the last two years after scathing criticism from investors that firms produced varying standards of audit in different countries.

Discuss the effect on standard setting if control were to be edged from the world's accountancy regulators and back in the hands of the profession.

Question 4

The FRC in its 2009 publication *Louder than Words – Principles and Actions for Making Corporate Reports Less Complex and More Relevant* included a call for action to 'Ensure disclosure requirements are relevant and proportionate to the risks', stating that 'We would like to see a project on disclosure which investigates the characteristics of useful disclosures and the main objectives of financial reporting disclosure. . . . Ideally, we believe another organisation could constructively kick off this work with a view to providing recommendations to the relevant regulators, including the International Accounting Standards Board (IASB).'

Required:

Critically discuss how a company could determine whether any disclosure is proportionate to the risks and whether this implies that there should be less mandatory disclosures which lead to ever more complexity.

References

1 ICAS, 'Principles not rules – a question of judgement', www.icas.org.uk/site/cms/contentView Article.asp?article=4597

2 ASB, *Statement of Principles for Financial Reporting*, 1999.

3 *Ibid.*, para. 3.27.

4 ASB, FRS 6 *Acquisition and Mergers*, 1994.

5 ASB, *Statement of Principles for Financial Reporting*, 1999, para. 5.10.

6 A. Lennard, 'The peg on which standards hang', *Accountancy*, January 1996, p. 80.

7 S. Fearnley and M. Page, 'Why the ASB has lost its bearings', *Accountancy*, April 1996, p. 94.

8 J. Arnold *et al.*, *The Future Shape of Financial Reports*, ICAEW/ICAS, 1991.

9 D. Solomons, *Guidelines for Financial Reporting Standards*, ICAEW, 1989, p. 32.

10 ICAS, *Making Corporate Reports Valuable*, 1988, p. 35.

11 R. Skinner, *Accountancy*, January 1990, p. 25.

CHAPTER 11

Ethical behaviour and implications for accountants

11.1 Introduction

The main purpose of this chapter is for you to have an awareness of the need for ethical behaviour by accountants to complement the various accounting and audit standards issued by the International Accounting Standards Board (IASB), the International Auditing and Assurance Standards Board (IAASB) and professional accounting bodies.

Objectives

By the end of this chapter, you should be able to discuss:

● the meaning of ethical behaviour;
● the relationship of ethics to standard setting;
● the main provisions of the IFAC *Code of Ethics for Professional Accountants*;
● the implications of ethical values for the principles- versus rules-based approaches to accounting standards;
● the problem of defining principles and standards where there are cultural differences;
● the implications of unethical behaviour for stakeholders using the financial reports;
● the type of ethical issues raised for accountants in business;
● the role of whistle-blowing.

11.2 The meaning of ethical behaviour

Individuals in an organisation have their own ethical guidelines which may vary from person to person. These may perhaps be seen as social norms which can vary over time. For example, the relative importance of individual and societal responsibility varies over time.

11.2.1 Individual ethical guidelines

Individual ethical guidelines or personal ethics are the result of a varied set of influences or pressures. As an individual each of us 'enjoys' a series of ethical pressures or influences including the following:

● Parents – the first and, according to many authors, the most crucial influence on our ethical guidelines.

- Family – the *extended* family which is common in Eastern societies (aunts, uncles, grand-parents and so on) can have a significant impact on personal ethics; the *nuclear* family which is more common in Western societies (just parent(s) and siblings) can be equally as important but more narrowly focused.

- Social group – the ethics of our 'class' (either actual or aspirational) can be a major influence.

- Peer group – the ethics of our 'equals' (again either actual or aspirational) can be another major influence.

- Religion – ethics based in religion are more important in some cultures, e.g. Islamic societies have some detailed ethics demanded of believers as well as major guidelines for business ethics. However, even in supposedly secular cultures, individuals are influenced by religious ethics.

- Culture – this is also a very effective formulator of an individual's ethics.

- Professional – when an individual becomes part of a professional body then they are subject to the ethics of the professional body.

Given the variety of influences it is natural that there will be a variety of views on what is acceptable ethical behaviour. For example, as an accounting student, how would you handle ethical issues? Would you personally condone cheating? Would you refrain from reporting cheating in exams and assignments by friends? Would you resent other students being selfish such as hiding library books which are very helpful for an essay? Would you resent cheating in exams by others because you do not cheat and therefore are at a disadvantage? Would that resentment be strong enough to get you to report the fact that there is cheating to the authorities even if you did not name the individuals involved?

11.2.2 Professional ethical guidelines

A managing director of a well-known bank described his job as deciding contentious matters for which, after extensive investigation by senior staff, there was no obvious solution. The decision was referred to him because all proposed solutions presented significant down-side risks for the bank. Ethical behaviour can be similarly classified. There are matters where there are clearly morally correct answers and there are dilemmas where there are conflicting moral issues.

Professional codes of conduct tend to provide solutions to common issues which the profession has addressed many times. However, the professional code of ethics is only the starting point in the sense that it can never cover all the ethical issues an accountant will face and does not absolve accountants from dealing with other ethical dilemmas.

11.3 The accounting standard-setting process and ethics

Standard setters seem to view the process as similar to physics in the sense of trying to set standards with a view to achieving an objective measure of reality. However, some academics suggest that such an approach is inappropriate because the concepts of profit and value are not physical attributes but 'man made' dimensions. For instance, for profit we measure the progress of the business but the concept of progress is a very subjective attribute which has traditionally omitted public costs such as environmental and social costs. The criterion of fairness has been seen as satisfied by preparing profit statements on principles such as going concern and accrual when measuring profit and neutrality when presenting the profit statement.

What if fairness is defined differently? For example, the idea of basing accounting on the criterion of fairness to all stakeholders (financiers, workers, suppliers, customers and the community) was made by Leonard Spacek[1] before the formation of the FASB. However, this view was not appreciated by the profession at that time. We now see current developments in terms of environmental and social accounting which are moves in that direction but, even so, CSR is not incorporated into the financial statements prepared under IFRSs and constitutes supplementary information that is not integrated into the accounting measures themselves.

The accounting profession sees ethical behaviour in standard setting as ensuring that accounting is neutral. Their opponents think that neutrality is impossible and that accounting has a wide impact on society and thus to be ethical the impact on all parties affected should be taken into consideration. The ASB and EFRAG addressed this with the issue of a Discussion Paper: *Considering the Effects of Accounting Standards* in January 2011.

The accounting profession does not address ethics at the macro level other than pursuing neutrality, but rather focuses its attention on actions after the standards and laws are in place. The profession seeks to provide ethical standards which will increase the probability of those standards being applied in an ethical fashion at the micro level where accountants apply their individual skills.

The accounting profession through its body the International Federation of Accountants (IFAC) has developed a *Code of Ethics for Professional Accountants.*[2] That code looks at fundamental principles as well as specific issues which are frequently encountered by accountants in public practice, followed by those commonly faced by accountants in business. The intention is that the professional bodies and accounting firms '. . . shall not apply less stringent standards than those stated in this code' (p. 4).

11.4 The IFAC Code of Ethics for Professional Accountants

The IFAC Fundamental Principles are:

(i) 'A distinguishing mark of the accountancy profession is its acceptance of the responsibility to act in the public interest . . .' (100.1).

(ii) 'A professional accountant shall comply with the following fundamental principles:

(a) *Integrity* – to be straightforward and honest in all professional and business relationships.

(b) *Objectivity* – to not allow bias, conflict of interest or undue influence of others to override professional or business judgements.

(c) *Professional Competence and Due Care* – to maintain professional knowledge and skill at the level required to ensure that a client or employer receives competent professional services and act diligently in accordance with applicable technical and professional standards.

(d) *Confidentiality* – to respect the confidentiality of information acquired as a result of professional and business relationships and, therefore, not disclose any such information to third parties without proper and specific authority, unless there is a legal or professional right or duty to disclose, nor use the information for the personal advantage of the professional accountant or third parties.

(e) *Professional Behaviour* – to comply with relevant laws and regulations and avoid any action that discredits the profession' (100.5).

11.4.1 Acting in the public interest

The first underlying statement that accountants should act in the public interest is probably more difficult to achieve than is imagined. This requires accounting professionals to stand firm against accounting standards which are not in the public interest, even when the politicians and company executives may be pressing for their acceptance. Owing to the fact that, in the conduct of an audit, the auditors have mainly dealings with the management it is easy to lose sight of who the clients actually are. For example, the expression 'audit clients' is commonly used in professional papers and academic books when they are referring to the management of the companies being audited. It immediately suggests a relationship which is biased towards management when, legally, the client may be either the shareholders as a group or specific stakeholders. Whilst it is a small but subtle distinction it could be the start of a misplaced orientation towards seeing the management as the client.

11.4.2 Fundamental principles

The five fundamental principles are probably uncontentious guides to professional conduct. It is the application of those guides in specific circumstances which provides the greatest challenges. The IFAC paper provides guidance in relation to public accountants covering appointments, conflicts of interest, second opinions, remuneration, marketing, acceptance of gratuities, custody of client assets, objectivity and independence. In regard to accountants in business they provide guidance in the areas of potential conflicts, preparation and reporting of information, acting with sufficient expertise, financial interests and inducements.

It is not intended to provide here all the guidance which the IFAC *Code of Ethics* provides, and if students want that detail they should consult the original document. This chapter will provide a flavour of the coverage relating to accountants in public practice and accountants in business.

11.4.3 Problems arising for accountants in practice

Appointments

Before accepting appointments public accountants should consider the desirability of accepting the client given the business activities involved, particularly if there are questions of their legality. They also need to consider (a) whether the current accountant of the potential client has advised of any professional reasons for not becoming involved and (b) whether they have the competency required considering the industry and their own expertise. Nor should they become involved if they already provide other services which are incompatible with being the auditor or if the size of the fees would threaten their independence. (Whilst it is not stated in the code the implication is that it is better to avoid situations which are likely to lead to difficult ethical issues.)

Second opinions

When an accountant is asked to supply a second opinion on an accounting treatment it is likely that the opinion will be used to undermine an accountant who is trying to do the right thing. It is therefore important to ascertain that all relevant information has been provided before issuing a second opinion, and if in doubt decline the work.

Remuneration

Remuneration must be adequate to allow the work to be done in a professional manner.

Commissions received from other parties must not be such as to make it difficult to be objective when advising your client and in any event must at least be disclosed to clients.

Some accountants have addressed that by passing the commissions on to their client and charging a flat fee for the consulting.

Marketing

Marketing should be professional and should not exaggerate or make negative comments about the work of other professionals.

Independence

The accountant and their close relatives should not accept gifts, other than insubstantial ones, from clients. IFAC para 280.2 provides that:

> A professional accountant in public practice who provides an assurance service shall be independent of the assurance client. Independence of mind and in appearance is necessary to enable the professional accountant in public practice to express a conclusion.

Professional firms have their own criterion level as to the value of gifts that can be accepted. For example, the following is an extract from the KPMG Code of Conduct:

> Qn: I manage a reproduction center at a large KPMG office. We subcontract a significant amount of work to a local business. The owner is very friendly and recently offered to give me two free movie passes. Can I accept the passes?

> Ans: Probably. Here, the movie passes are considered a gift because the vendor is not attending the movie with you. In circumstances where it would not create the appearance of impropriety, you may accept reasonable gifts from third parties such as our vendors, provided that the value of the gift is not more than $100 and that you do not accept gifts from the same vendor more than twice in the same year.

11.4.4 Problems arising for accountants in business

In relation to accountants in business the major problem identified by the code seems to be the financial pressures which arise from substantial financial interests in the form of shares, options, pension plans and dependence on employment income to support themselves and their dependants. When these depend on reporting favourable performance it is difficult to withstand the pressure.

Every company naturally wants to present its results in the most favourable way possible and investors expect this and it is part of an accountant's expertise to do this. However, the ethical standards require compliance with the law and accounting standards subject to the overriding requirement for financial statements to present a fair view. Misreporting and the omission of additional significant material which would change the assessment of the financial position of the company are unacceptable.

Accountants need to avail themselves of any internal steps to report pressure to act unethically and if that fails to produce results they need to be willing to resign.

11.4.5 Threats to compliance with the fundamental principles

The IFAC document has identified five types of threats to compliance with their fundamental principles and they will be outlined below. The objective of outlining these potential threats is to make you sensitive to the types of situations where your ethical judgements may be clouded and where you need to take extra steps to ensure you act ethically. The statements are deliberately broad to help you handle situations not covered specifically by the guidelines. IFAC para 100.12 provides the following classification:

Threats fall into one or more of the following categories:

(a) Self-interest threat – the threat that a financial or other interest will inappropriately influence the accountant's judgment or behavior;

(b) Self-review threat – the threat that a professional accountant will not appropriately evaluate the results of a previous judgment made or service performed by another individual within the professional accountant's firm or employing organization;

(c) Advocacy threat – the threat that a professional accountant will promote a client's or employer's position to the point that the professional accountant's objectivity is compromised;

(d) Familiarity threat – the threat that due to a long or close relationship with a client or employer, a professional accountant will be too sympathetic to their interests or too accepting of their work; and

(e) Intimidation threat – the threat that a professional accountant will be deterred from acting objectively because of actual or perceived pressures.

11.5 Implications of ethical values for the principles- versus rules-based approaches to accounting standards

It is common in the literature for authors to quote Milton Friedman as indicating that the role of business is to focus on maximising profits, and also to cite Adam Smith as justification for not interfering in business affairs. In many cases those arguments are misinterpreting the authors.

Milton Friedman recognised that what business people should do was maximise profits *within the norms of society*. He knew that without laws to give greater certainty in regard to business activities, and the creation of trust, it was not possible to have a highly efficient economy. Thus he accepted laws which facilitated business transactions and norms in society which also helped to create a cooperative environment. Thus the norms in society set the minimum standards of ethical and social activity which businesses must engage in to be acceptable to those with whom they interact.

Adam Smith (in *The Wealth of Nations*) did not say do not interfere with business; rather, he assumed the existence of the **conditions necessary to facilitate fair and equitable exchanges**. He also suggested that government should interfere to prevent monopolies but should not interfere as a result of lobbying of business groups because their normal behaviour is designed to create monopolies. He also assumed that those who did not meet ethical standards might make initial gains but would be found out and shunned. His other major book (*The Theory of Moral Sentiments*) was on morality so there is no doubt that he thought ethics were a normal and essential part of society and business.

How does this relate to accounting standards?

The production of accounting standards is only the starting point in the application of accounting standards. We have seen that accountants can apply the standards to the letter of the law and still not achieve reporting that conveys the substance of the performance and financial state of the business. This is because businesses can structure transactions so as to avoid the application of a standard. For example, by taking liabilities off the balance sheet, such as when a company does not want to capitalise a lease, it arranges for a change in the lease terms so that it is reported as a note and not shown as a liability on the face of the accounts.

It is that type of gamesmanship which has worried accounting standard setters. The issue is whether such games are appropriate, and if they aren't, why haven't they been prevented by the ethical standards of the accountants?

How does the accounting profession attempt to ensure that financial reports reflect the substance of a transaction?

We have seen that standards have been set in many national jurisdictions and now internationally by the IASB, in order to make financial statements fair and comparable. The number of standards varies between countries and is described as rules based or principles based according to the number of standardised accounting treatments.

Rules based

Where there are many detailed standards as in the US, the system is described as rules based in that it attempts to specify the uniform treatment for many types of transactions. This is both a strength and also a weakness in that the very use of precise standards as the only criterion leads to the types of games to get around the criteria that were mentioned earlier for lease accounting. One solution to combat this behaviour is to resort to override criteria such as the 'true and fair' override to support (or replace) the rules.

Principles based

Where there are fewer standards as in the UK, the system is referred to as principles based. In the principles-based system there is greater reliance on the application of the 'true and fair' override to (a) report unusual situations and (b) address the issue of whether the accounts prepared in accordance with existing standards provide a fair picture for the decisions to be made by the various users and provide additional information where necessary.

Whilst these are positive applications the override criteria can also be misused. For example, many companies during the 'dot com' boom around the year 2000 produced statements of **normalised** earnings. The argument was that they were in the set-up phase and many of the costs they were incurring were one-offs. To get a better understanding of the business readers were said to need to know what an ongoing result was likely to be. So they removed set-up costs and produced **normalised** or **sustainable** earnings which suggested the company was inherently profitable. Unfortunately, many of these companies failed because those one-off costs were not one-off and had to be maintained to keep a customer base.

Does a principles-based approach achieve true and fair reports?

The US regulators and the IASB have agreed that the principles-based approach should be adopted. However, this still leaves unanswered the question as to whether this approach can give a true and fair view to every stakeholder. Shareholders are recognised in all jurisdictions but the rights of other parties may vary according to the legal system. When, for example, do the rights of lenders become paramount? Should the accounts be tailored to suit employees when the legal system in some jurisdictions recognises that companies are not just there to support owners but have major responsibilities to recognise the preservation of employment wherever possible?

Can general-purpose accounts (whether rules based or principles based) ever be appropriate for the many purposes for which they are routinely used?

11.5.1 The problem of linking principles to accounting standards

The current conceptual framework assumes that we need to produce general-purpose financial accounts using understandability, relevance, reliability and comparability as guiding criteria. However, the individual standards do not demonstrate how those principles lead to the standards which have been produced.

11.5.2 The principles-based approach and ethics

The preceding discussion looked at the principle of true and fair or its equivalent from an accountant's perspective, but ultimately what it means will be determined by the courts. They might take a different perspective again, which is one of the problems of having a criterion which is subjective and liable to be defined more precisely after the event.

If accounting is to be primarily or partially principles based then those principles need to be clearly spelt out in such a manner that those applying them, and those who are reviewing their application, clearly understand what they mean. Furthermore, those who will adjudicate in disputes over whether the criteria have been properly applied, which normally only occurs when substantial sums have been lost or unfairly gained, must at least have basically the same perspective. This is not to suggest that law courts have to follow accountants. In application it is probable that the accountants will have to adopt the stance of the courts irrespective of whether they have correctly understood the subtleties of accounting. This means the principles must be expressed in everyday language. 'True and fair' could perhaps be applied but it would have to have an everyday interpretation, such as Rawls[3] expressed when he spoke of justice as fairness or what Baumol called superfairness. Baumol, a celebrated economist, provides an interesting concept of superfairness[4] which would help with this type of ethical decision. He says if you didn't know what side of the transaction you were going to be on, what would you consider to be fair? If you didn't know whether you were going to be a company executive, or an auditor, or a buyer of shares, or a seller of shares, what do you think would be a fair representation of the company's performance and financial position?

It would, in order to avoid ambiguity, have to spell out 'fair to whom and for what purpose'. This is because at the present time society is in a process of reassessing the role of business relative to the demands by society to achieve high employment rates, to overcome environmental problems and to achieve fair treatment of all countries. Essentially this is suggesting that, given the changing orientation, consideration may have to be given to ethical criteria even if there is only a partial shift from a shareholder orientation to a balancing of competing claims in society. Daniel Friedman (2008, p. 179)[5] says: 'The greatest challenge is to realign morals and markets so that they work together, rather than at cross purposes.' This will need a balancing act specific to the problem faced. In other words it would have to be principle driven.

11.5.3 The problem of defining principles and standards where there are cultural differences

Cultural differences may lead to different principles being formulated and applied. For example, the IASB has defined assets to be reported in the financial statements in such a way that human assets and social costs are not included. As regards application, an accountant in preparing accounts will always have a potential clash between what his or her employer and superior wants, what his or her profession requires and what is best from an ethical or community perspective.

This raises questions such as:

- 'What grounds are there for different accounting being applicable to different countries?'
- 'Should there be different principles if the purpose of accounting is not the same in all countries, with some countries placing, say, greater emphasis on the impact on employees or the community?'
- 'How do cultural norms and religion affect ethics in both the formulation and the interpretation of individual guidelines?
- 'Is it correct to assume that shareholders in every country have identical information needs and apply identical ethical criteria in assessing a company's operations?

11.5.4 Research into the impact of different cultural characteristics on behaviour

An interesting piece of research compared the attitudes of students in the USA and the UK to cheating and found the US students more likely to cheat.[6] The theoretical basis of the research was that different cultural characteristics, such as uncertainty avoidance or conversely the tolerance for ambiguity, lead to different attitudes to ethics.

Implication for multinationals

This means uniform ethical guidelines will not lead to uniform applications in multinational companies unless the corporate culture is much stronger than the country culture. This has implications for multinational businesses that want the accounts prepared in the different countries to be uniform in quality. It is significant for audit firms that want their sister firms in other countries to apply the same standards to audit judgements. It is important to investment firms that are making investments throughout the world on the understanding that accounting and ethical standards mean the same things in all major security markets.

Where there are differences in legal and cultural settings then potentially the correct accounting will also differ if a principles-based approach is adopted. Currently Western concepts dominate accounting but if the world power base shifts, either to several world centres of influence or to a new dominant world power, then principles of accounting may have to reflect that.

11.6 Ethics in the accountants' work environment – a research report

The Institute of Chartered Accountants in Scotland issued a discussion paper report[7] titled 'Taking ethics to heart' based on research into the application of ethics in practice. This section will discuss some of the findings of that report.

From a student's perspective one of the interesting findings was that many accountants could not remember the work on ethics which they did as students and therefore had little to draw upon to guide them when problems arose. There was agreement that students need to get more experience in dealing with case studies so as to enhance their ethical-decision-making skills. This should be reinforced throughout their careers by continuing professional development. The training should sensitise accountants so that they can easily recognise ethical situations and develop skills in resolving the dilemmas.

Exposure to ethical issues is usually low for junior positions, although even then there can be clear and grey issues. For example, padding an expense claim and overstating overtime are clear issues, whereas how to deal with information that has been heard in a private conversation between client staff is less clear. What if a conversation is overheard where one of the factory staff says that products which are known to be defective have been dispatched at the year-end? Would your response be different if you had been party to the conversation? Would your response be different if it had been suggested that there was a risk of injury due to the defect? Is it ethical to inform your manager or is it unethical not to inform?

Normally exposure to ethical issues increases substantially at the manager level and continues in senior management positions. However, the significance of ethical decision making has increased with the expansion of the size of both companies and accounting practices. The impact of decisions can be more widespread and profound. Further, there has been an increase in litigation, potentially exposing the accountant to more external review. Greater numbers of accounting and auditing standards can lead to a narrower focus, making it harder for individual accountants to envisage the wider ethical dimensions and to get people to consider more than the detailed rules.

Given the likelihood of internal or external review, the emphasis that many participants in the study placed on asking 'How would this decision look to others?' seems a sensible criterion. In light of that emphasis by participants in the research it is interesting to consider the 'Resolving conflicts' section of BT PLC's document called *The Way We Work*[8] which among other things says:

> How would you explain your decision to your colleagues in different countries?
>
> How would you explain your decision to your family or in public?
>
> Does it conflict with your own or BT's commitment to integrity?

This emphasis on asking how well ethical decisions would stand public scrutiny, including scrutiny in different countries, would be particularly relevant to accountants in businesses operating across national borders.

The role of the organisational setting in improving or worsening ethical decision making was given considerable attention in the ICAS report. A key starting point is having a set of ethical policies which are practical and are reinforced by the behaviour of senior management. Another support is the presence of a clearly defined process for referring difficult ethical decisions upward in the organisation.

For those in small organisations there needs to be an opportunity for those in difficult situations to seek advice about the ethical choice or the way to handle the outcomes of making an ethical stand. Most professional bodies either have senior mentors available or have organised referrals to bodies specialising in ethical issues.

The reality is that some who have taken ethical stands have lost their jobs, but some of those who haven't stood their ground have lost their reputations or their liberty.

11.7 Implications of unethical behaviour for stakeholders using the financial reports

One of the essential aspects of providing complete and reliable information which are taken seriously by the financial community is to have a set of rigorous internal controls. However, ultimately those controls are normally dependent on checks and balances within the system and the integrity of those with the greatest power within the system. In other words the checks and balances, such as requiring two authorisations to issue a cheque or transfer money, presume that at least one of those with authority will act diligently and will be alert to the possibility of dishonest or misguided behaviour by the other. Further, if necessary or desirable, they will take firm action to prevent any behaviour that appears suspicious. The internal control system depends on the integrity and diligence, in other words the ethical behaviour, of the majority of the staff in the organisation.

11.7.1 Increased cost of capital

The presence of unethical behaviour in an organisation will raise questions about the reliability of the accounts. If unethical behaviour is suspected by investors, they will probably raise the cost of capital for the individual business. If there are sufficient cases of unethical behaviour across all companies, the integrity of the whole market will be brought into question and the liquidity of the whole market is reduced. That would affect the cost of funds across the board and increase the volatility of share prices.

11.7.2 Hidden liabilities

A liability, particularly an environmental one, might not crystallise for a number of years, as with the James Hardie Group in Australia. The James Hardie Group was a producer of asbestos sheeting whose fibres can in the long term damage the lungs and lead to death. The challenge the company faced was the long gestation period between the exposure to the dust from the asbestos and the appearance of the symptoms of the disease. It can be up to 40 years before the victim finds out that they have a death sentence.

Liability transferred to a separate entity

The company reorganised so that there was a separate entity which was responsible for the liabilities and that entity was supposed to have sufficient funds to cover future liabilities as they came to light. When it was apparent that the funds set aside were grossly inadequate and that the assessment of adequacy had been based on old data rather than using the more recent data which showed an increasing rate of claims, there was widespread community outrage. As a result the James Hardie Group felt that irrespective of their legal position they had to negotiate with the state government and the unions to set aside a share of their cash flows from operations each year to help the victims. Thus the unfair arrangements set in place came back to create the equivalent of liabilities and did considerable damage to the public image of the company. This also made some people reluctant to be associated with the company as customers or as employees. The current assessment of liability (as at 2009) is set out in a KPMG Actuarial Report.[9]

11.7.3 Effect of ethical collapse in an organisation

There is an increasing need to be wary of unethical behaviour by management leading to fraud.

Jennings (2006)[10] points out that while most of the major frauds that make the headlines tend to be attributed to a small number of individuals, there have to be many other participants who allow them to happen. For every CEO who bleeds the company through payment for major personal expenses, or through gross manipulation of accounts, or backdating of options, there have to be a considerable number of people who know what is happening but who choose not to bring it to the attention of the appropriate authorities. The appropriate authority could be the board of directors, or the auditors or regulatory authorities. Jennings attributes this to the culture of the organisation and suggests there are seven signs of ethical collapse in an organisation. They include pressure to maintain the numbers, suppression of dissent and bad news, iconic CEOs surrounding themselves with young executives whose careers are dependent on them, a weak board of directors, numerous conflicts of interest, innovation excess, and goodness in some areas being thought to atone for evil in others.

Others have suggested that companies with high levels of takeover activity and high leverage are often prime candidates for fraud because of the pressures to achieve the numbers. Also, if the attitude is that the sole purpose of the firm is to make money subject to compliance with the letter of the law, that is also a warning sign.

The ICAS report[7] 'Taking ethics to heart' noted that it appeared that the current business and commercial environment placed an enormous pressure on accountants, wherever they work, which may result in decisions and judgements that compromise ethical standards. It noted also that increased commercial pressures on accountants may be viewed by many within the profession as heralding a disquieting new era.

The accountant working within business has a different set of problems due to his or her dual position as an employee and a professional accountant. There is a potential clash of issues where the interests of the business could be at odds with professional standards.

11.7.4 Auditor reaction to risk of unethical behaviour

In addition to the above items, unethical behaviour should make auditors and investors scrutinise accounts more closely. Following the experiences with companies such as Enron the auditing standards have placed greater emphasis on auditors being sceptical. This means that if they identify instances of unethical behaviour they should ask more searching questions. Depending on the responses they get, they may need to undertake more testing to satisfy themselves of the reliability of the accounts.

11.7.5 Action by professional accounting bodies to assist members

The various professional bodies approach things in different ways. For example, the ICAEW established the Industrial Members Advisory Committee on Ethics (IMACE) in the late 1970s to give specific advice to members with ethical problems in business. This is supported by a strong local support network as well as a national helpline for the guidance of accountants. At the moment IMACE is dealing with 200 to 300 problems per year but this is more a reflection of the numbers of chartered accountants in business than a reflection on the lack of ethical problems.

The type of problem raised is a good indication of the ethical issues raised for accountants in business. They include:

● requests by employers to manipulate tax returns;
● requests to produce figures to mislead shareholders;
● requests to conceal information;
● requests to manipulate overhead absorption rates to extort more income from customers (an occurrence in the defence industries);
● requests to authorise and conceal bribes to buyers and agents, a common request in some exporting businesses;
● requests to produce misleading projected figures to obtain additional finance;
● requests to conceal improper expense claims put in by senior managers;
● requests to over- or undervalue assets;
● requests to misreport figures in respect of government grants;
● requests for information which could lead to charges of 'insider dealing';
● requests to redefine bad debts as 'good' or vice versa.

For accountants in industry the message is that if your employer has a culture which is not conducive to high ethical values then a good career move would be to look for employment elsewhere. For auditors the message is that the presence of symptoms suggested above is grounds for employing greater levels of scepticism in the audit.

11.7.6 Action taken by governments

The Sarbanes–Oxley Act (SOX) has had a major impact on company management and auditors to address what had been seen as an inadequate oversight of the accounting profession and conflicts of interest involving the auditors.

Management

Following the collapse of the auditors Arthur Andersen, the introduction of SOX placed personal responsibility on the CEO and the CFO for the accounts, with serious penalties for publishing misleading accounts. This led to these officers seeking reassurance that there were adequate systems and internal controls in place. This has in turn led to complaints that management effort is being directed away from growing the business and earnings.

Accountants and auditors

Management and audit committees since SOX are more focused on financial reporting. SOX gave rise to a major demand by business for internal auditors to undertake this work with the focus moving to assessing financial controls, as opposed to operational processes.

As for auditors, they have to confirm that companies have adequate systems and internal controls and are required to report to the audit committee rather than management.

11.7.7 Negative pressures on standard setters

Standard setters have been under pressure, which could result in lower quality or expedient accounting as reflected in FASB and SEC rulings. This pressure comes from industry and commerce, both directly, and indirectly through threats from the legislators who are beholden to industry. For example, there were proposals to replace the SEC's role in standard setting by transferring the role to a new regulator. The proposal was unsuccessful but illustrates the pressures that can be brought to bear on the standard setters in the US.

The SEC has statutory authority to establish financial accounting and reporting standards for publicly held companies under the Securities Exchange Act of 1934. Historically, however, the SEC has supported FASB's independence and relied on FASB and its predecessors in the private sector to set accounting standards.

The original amendment, which was introduced by Rep. Ed Perlmutter, D-Colo., would have transferred the SEC's accounting standards oversight authority to a proposed new regulator with a mandate to take an active role in accounting standards that it deemed could pose systemic risks.

11.7.8 Action by companies – company codes of ethics

Most companies now adopt codes of ethics. They may have alternative titles such as 'our values', codes of conduct, or codes of ethics. For example, BP has a code of conduct whose coverage, which is listed below, is what one would expect of a company involved in its industry and its activities covering a large number of countries. Its Code of Conduct includes the following major categories:

● Our commitment to integrity

● Health, safety, security and the environment

● Employees

● Business partners

● Governments and communities

● Company assets and financial integrity.

However, the challenge is to make the code an integral part of the day-to-day behaviour of the company and to be perceived as doing so by outsiders. Obviously top management have to act in ways so as to reinforce the values of the code and to eliminate existing activities which are incompatible with the new values.

BP has been criticised for behaviour inconsistent with its values but such behaviour may relate to actions taken before the adoption of the code (see Beder[11]).

Thus it is important to ensure that the corporate behaviour is consistent with the code of conduct, and that staff are rewarded for ethical behaviour and suffer penalties for non-compliance. Breaches, irrespective of whether they are in the past, are difficult to erase from the memories of society.

Stohl *et al.* (2009)[12] suggest that the content of codes of conduct can be divided into three levels:

- Level 1 is where there is an attempt to ensure that the company is in compliance with all the laws which impact on it in the various countries in which it operates.

- Level 2 focuses on ensuring fair and equitable relations with all parties with which the company has direct relations. In this category would be the well-publicised adverse publicity which Nike received when it was alleged that their subcontractors were exploiting child labour in countries where such treatment is legal. The adverse publicity and boycotts meant that many companies reviewed their operations and expanded their codes to cover such situations and thus moved into the second level of ethical awareness.

- Level 3 is where companies take a global perspective and recognise their responsibility to contribute to the likelihood of peace and favourable global environmental conditions. In most companies the level 1 concerns are more dominant than the level 2, and the level 2 more than the level 3. European firms are more likely than US firms to have a level 3 orientation.

11.7.9 Conflict between codes and targets

On the one hand we see companies developing codes of ethical conduct, whilst on the other hand we see some of these same companies developing management by objectives which set staff unachievable targets and create pressures that lead to unethical behaviour. Where this occurs there is the risk that an unhealthy corporate climate may develop, resulting in the manipulation of accounting figures and unethical behaviour.

There is a view[13] that there is a need to create an ethical climate that transcends a compliance approach to ethics and focuses instead on fostering socially harmonious relationships. An interesting article[14] proceeds to make the argument that the recent accounting scandals may be as much a reflection of a deficient corporate climate, with its concentration on setting unrealistic targets and promoting competition between the staff, as of individual moral failures of managers.

11.7.10 Multinationals face special problems

Modern multinational companies experience special problems in relation to ethics.

Firstly, the transactions are often extremely large, so that there are greater pressures to bend the rules so as to get the business.

Secondly, the ethical values as reflected in some of the countries may be quite different from those in the head office of the group. One company did business in a developing country where the wages paid to public officials were so low as to be insufficient to support a family even at the very modest living standards of that country. Many public officials had a second job so as to cope. Others saw it as appropriate to demand kick-backs in order for them to process any government approvals, as for them there was a strong ethical obligation to ensure their family was properly looked after, which in their opinion outweighs their obligation to the community.

Is it ethical for other nations to condemn such behaviour in the extreme cases? Should a different standard apply? What is the business to do if that is the norm in a country? Some may decline to do business in those countries, others may employ intermediaries. In the latter case, a company sells the goods to an intermediary company which then resells the goods in the problem country. The intermediary obviously has to pay fees and bribes to make the sale but that is not the concern of the multinational company! They deliberately do not ask the intermediary what they do. However, it could become a concern if a protest group identifies the questionable behaviour of the agent and decides to hold the multinational responsible. A third option is just to pay the fees and bribes. The problem with the second and third positions is that the company may be held responsible by one of the countries in which they operate which has laws making it illegal to corrupt public officials in their country or any other country. Also there is the problem that if companies pay bribes, that behaviour reinforces the corrupt forces in the target country which, in turn, makes it difficult for the government of that country to eliminate corruption.

Thirdly, governments are taking a closer look at company activities. The Serious Fraud Office in the UK[15] and the Department of Justice in the US are actively investigating corrupt practices. For example, in 2010 BAE Systems had to pay substantial fines for being involved in bribery. In the US it had to pay $400 million to settle allegations of bribery in relation to arms deals with Saudi Arabia. The Serious Fraud Office in the UK made BAE Systems pay £30 million in relation to overpriced military radar sold to Tanzania whilst taking into account the implementation by the company of substantial ethical and compliance reforms. Part of the fines is being passed on to the people of Tanzania to compensate for the damage done.

11.7.11 The support given by professional bodies in the designing of ethical codes

There are excellent support facilities available. For example, the Association of Chartered Certified Accountants' website (www.accaglobal.com) makes a toolkit available for accountants who might be involved with designing a code of ethics. The site also provides an overview which considers matters such as why ethics are important, links to other related sites, e.g. the Center for Ethics and Business at Loyola Marymount University in Los Angeles[16] with a quiz to establish one's ethical style as an ethic of justice or an ethic of care, and a toolkit from the Ethics Resource Center[17] to assist in the design of a code of ethics.

11.8 The increasing role of whistle-blowing

It is recognised that normally when the law or the ethical code is being broken by the company, a range of people inside and outside the company are aware of the illegal activities or have sufficient information to raise suspicions. To reduce the likelihood of illegal activity or to help identify its occurrence, a number of regulatory organisations have set up mechanisms for whistle-blowing to occur. Also a number of companies have set up their own units, often through a consulting firm, whereby employees can report illegal activities and breaches of the firm's code of ethics or any other activities which are likely to bring the company into disrepute.

11.8.1 Immunity to the first party to report

For example, in many countries the regulatory authority responsible for pursuing price fixing has authority to give immunity or favourable treatment to the first party to report the occurrence of price fixing. It may be possible for the person's lawyer to ascertain whether the item has already been reported without disclosing the identity of their client. This arrangement is in place because of the difficulty of collecting information on such activities of sufficient quality and detail to prosecute successfully. For example, British Airways was fined about £270m after it admitted collusion in fixing the prices of fuel surcharges. The US Department of Justice fined it $300m (£148m) for colluding on how much extra to charge on passenger and cargo flights to cover fuel costs, and the UK's Office of Fair Trading fined it £121.5m after it held illegal talks with rival Virgin Atlantic. Virgin was given immunity after it reported the collusion and was not fined.

11.8.2 Anonymous whistle-blowing

In the case of large companies it is difficult for top management to be fully informed as to whether subordinates throughout the organisation are acting responsibly. One solution has been to arrange for an accounting firm to have a contact number where people can anonymously report details of breaches of the law or breaches of ethics or other activities impacting on the good name of the company. It has to be anonymous for several reasons. Firstly, people will often be reporting on activities which they have been 'forced' to do or on activities of their superior or colleagues. Given that those colleagues will not take kindly to being reported on, and are capable of making life very difficult for the informant, it is important that reports can be made anonymously. Also, even those who are not directly affected will often view whistle-blowing as letting the side down. The whistle-blower, if identified, could well be ostracised. Whilst firms who have anonymous hotlines may well support the individual if they ask for it, whistle-blowers need to realise from the beginning that ultimately they may have to seek alternative employment. This is not to suggest they shouldn't blow the whistle. Rather it is to reflect the history of whistle-blowers. However, this should be contrasted with the alternative. If the behaviour you are being required to take exposes you to criminal actions, it is better to do the hard work now than suffer the con-sequences of lost reputation, possibly lost liberty, severe financial penalties, and the stress of drawn-out law cases. If you are not involved but are just trying to prevent the company from getting further into negative territory, you may be doing many people a favour. You may prevent the company from getting into a position from which there may be no recovery. You will avoid other people suffering the same stress which you are under.

Take Enron as an example. The collapse of the company meant many people lost their jobs and a substantial portion of their superannuation. Others served time in prison. This included executives, and external parties who benefited from or supported the illegal or unethical behaviour. Also the events surrounding the failure contributed to the series of events which destroyed their auditors Arthur Andersen. If someone had blown the whistle much earlier then perhaps a number of those serious consequences would never have occurred. As it was, the staff member who raised the issue of dubious accounting with the CEO Kenneth Lay shortly before the collapse made it harder for him to deny responsibility when he was tried for fraud.

11.8.3 Proportionate response

In spite of the above comments it is important to keep in mind that the steps taken should reflect the seriousness of the event and that the whistle-blowing should be the final strategy rather than the first. In other words the normal actions should be to use the internal forums such as debating issues in staff meetings or raising the issue with an immediate superior or their boss when the superior is not approachable for some reason. Nor are disagreements over business issues a reason for reporting. The motivation should be to report breaches which represent legal, moral or public interest concerns and not matters purely relating to differences of opinion on operational issues, personality differences or jealousy.

11.8.4 Government support

There are legal protections against victimisation but it would be more useful if the government provided positive support such as assistance with finding other employment or, perhaps, some form of financial reward to compensate for public-spirited actions that actually lead to professional or financial hardship for the whistle-blower.

11.9 The role of financial reporting authorities

The financial markets are very dependent on the presence of trust in the integrity of the system and all major players in its operation. It is noticeable that in periods when there have been lower levels of trust, participation rates have fallen, prices are lower and prices are more volatile. To maintain trust in the system, financial regulatory authorities monitor inappropriate behaviour and take action against offenders. We comment briefly on FINRA in the US and on the Accounting and Actuarial Disciplinary Board in the UK.

11.9.1 FINRA (Financial Industry Regulatory Authority)

In announcing its creation of the 'Office of the Whistleblower' on 5 March 2009 FINRA said:[18]

> Some of FINRA's most significant enforcement actions have resulted from investor complaints or anonymous insider tips. They include FINRA's 2007 action against Citigroup Global Markets, ordering the firm to pay a $3 million fine and $12.2 million in restitution to customers to settle charges of misleading Bell South employees in North and South Carolina at early retirement seminars; FINRA's 2006 fine of $5 million against Merrill Lynch to resolve charges related to supervisory violations at its customer Call Center; FINRA's 2005 landmark action against the Kansas firm Waddell & Reed, Inc., in which the firm was fined $5 million and ordered to pay $11 million in restitution to customers to resolve charges related to variable annuity switching; and FINRA's 2002 action against Credit Suisse First Boston to resolve charges of siphoning tens of millions of dollars of customers' profits in exchange for 'hot' IPO shares, which resulted in a $50 million fine imposed by FINRA and an additional $50 million fine imposed by the Securities and Exchange Commission.

11.9.2 The Accounting and Actuarial Disciplinary Board

In the UK the Accounting and Actuarial Disciplinary Board investigates and hears complaints. It has on its web pages details of pending cases and reports on completed cases. People with complaints are referred to the relevant accounting professional bodies (ICAEW, ACCA, CIMA, CIFPA) who will try to resolve the issues and if appropriate will refer them to the tribunal.

11.9.3 Whistle-blowing – protection in the UK

In the UK the Public Interest Disclosure Act came into force in 1999 protecting whistle-blowers who raised genuine concerns about malpractice from dismissal and victimisation in order to promote the public interest. The scope of malpractice is wide-ranging, including, e.g., the covering up of a suspected crime, a civil offence such as negligence, a miscarriage of justice, and health and safety or environmental risks.

11.9.4 Whistle-blowing – policies

Companies should have in place a policy which gives clear guidance to employees on the appropriate internal procedures to follow if there is a suspected malpractice. Employees, including accountants and internal auditors, are expected to follow these procedures as well as acting professionally and in accordance with their own professional code.

The following is an extract from the Vodafone 2009 Annual Report:

Ethics

Vodafone's success is underpinned by our commitment to ethical conduct in the way we do business and interact with key stakeholders.

Business principles

Our *Business Principles* define how we intend to conduct our business and our relationships with key stakeholders. They require employees to act with honesty, integrity and fairness.

The principles cover ethical issues including:

- Bribery and corruption
- Conflicts of interest
- Human rights

The Business Principles set a policy of zero tolerance on bribery and corruption. Our *Anti-corruption Compliance Guidelines* help ensure employees comply with all applicable anti-corruption laws and regulations. We have also introduced an anti-bribery online training course.

11.9.5 Reporting violations

The following is also from the Vodafone Annual Report:

Employees can report any potential violations of the Business Principles to their line manager or local human resources manager in the first instance. Alternatively, they can raise concerns anonymously to our Group Audit Director or our Group Human Resources Director via an online whistle-blowing system.

Our Duty to Report policy applies to suppliers and contractors as well as employees. Concerns can be reported either by contacting Vodafone's Group Fraud Risk and Security Department directly, or via a third party confidential telephone hotline service. The line is available 24 hours a day. All calls are taken by an independent organisation with staff trained to handle calls of this nature.

However, although the whistle-blowing policies might have been followed and the accountants protected by the provisions of the Public Interest Disclosure Act, whistle-blowing could result in a breakdown of trust making the whistle-blower's position untenable; this means that a whistle-blower might be well advised to have an alternative position in mind.

11.9.6 Breach of confidentiality

Auditors are protected from the risk of liability for breach of confidence provided that:

- disclosure is made in the public interest;
- disclosure is made to a proper authority;
- there is no malice motivating the disclosure.

11.9.7 Legal requirement to report – national and international regulation

It is likely that there will be an increase in formal regulation as the search for greater transparency and ethical business behaviour continues. We comment briefly on national and international regulation relating to money laundering and bribery.

Money laundering – overview

There are various estimates of the scale of money laundering ranging up to over 2% of global gross domestic product. Certain businesses are identified as being more prone to money laundering, e.g. import/export companies and cash businesses such as antiques and art dealers, auction houses, casinos and garages. However, the avenues are becoming more and more sophisticated with methods varying between countries, e.g. in the UK there is the increasing use of smaller non-bank institutions whereas in Spain it includes cross-border carrying of cash, money-changing at bureaux de change and investment in real estate.

Money laundering – implications for accountants

In 2006 the Auditing Practices Board (APB) in the UK issued a revised Practice Note 12 *Money Laundering* which required auditors to take the possibility of money laundering into account when carrying out their audit and to report to the appropriate authority if they become aware of suspected laundering.

Money laundering – the Financial Action Task Force (FATF)

The Financial Action Task Force (FATF) is an independent inter-governmental body that develops and promotes policies to protect the global financial system against money laundering and terrorist financing. Recommendations issued by the FATF define criminal justice and regulatory measures that should be implemented to counter this problem. These recommendations also include international cooperation and preventive measures to be taken by financial institutions and others such as casinos, real-estate dealers, lawyers and accountants. The recommendations are recognised as the global anti-money-laundering (AML) and counter-terrorist-financing (CTF) standard.

FATF issued a report[19] in 2009 titled *Money Laundering through the Football Sector.* This report identified the vulnerabilities of the sector arising from transactions relating to the ownership of football clubs, the transfer market and ownership of players, betting activities and image rights, sponsorship and advertising arrangements. The report is an excellent introduction to the complex web that attracts money launderers.

11.10 Why should students learn ethics?

Survival of the profession

There is debate over whether the attempts to teach ethics are worthwhile. However, this chapter is designed to raise awareness of how important ethics are to the survival of the accounting profession. Accounting is part of the system to create trust in the financial information provided. The financial markets will not operate efficiently and effectively if there is not a substantial level of trust in the system. Such trust is a delicate matter and if the accounting profession is no longer trusted then there is no role for them to play in the system. In that event the accounting profession will vanish. It may be thought that the loss of trust is so unlikely that it need not be contemplated. But who imagined that Arthur Andersen, one of the 'Big Five' as we knew it, would vanish from the scene so quickly? As soon as the public correctly or incorrectly decided they could no longer trust Arthur Andersen, the business crashed.

A future role for accountants in ethical assurance

The accountant within business could also be seeing a growth in the ethical policing role as internal auditors take on the role of assessing the performance of managers as to their adherence to the ethical code of the organisation. This is already partly happening as conflicts of interest are often highlighted by internal audits and comments raised on managerial practices. This is after all a traditional role for accountants, ensuring that the various codes of practice of the organisation are followed. The level of adherence to an ethical code is but another assessment for the accountant to undertake.

Implications for training

If, as is likely, the accountant has a role in the future as 'ethical guardian', additional training will be necessary. This should be done at a very early stage, as in the US, where accountants wishing to be Certified Public Accountants (CPAs) are required to pass formal exams on ethical practices and procedures before they are allowed the privilege of working in practice. Failure in these exams prevents the prospective accountant from practising in the business environment.

In the UK, for example, ethics is central to the ACCA qualification in recognition that values, ethics and governance are themes which organisations are now embedding into company business plans, and expertise in these areas is highly sought after in today's employment market. ACCA has adopted a holistic approach to a student's ethical development through the use of 'real-life' case studies and embedding ethical issues within the exam syllabi. For example, ACCA's Paper P1, *Professional Accountant*, covers personal and professional ethics, ethical frameworks and professional values, as applied in the context of the accountant's duties and as a guide to appropriate professional behaviour and conduct in a variety of situations. In addition, as part of their ethical development, students will be required to complete a two-hour online training module, developed by ACCA. This will give students exposure to a range of real-life ethical case studies and will require them to reflect on their own ethical behaviour and values. Students will be expected to complete the ethics module before commencing their professional-level studies. Similar initiatives are being taken by the other professional accounting bodies.

How will decisions be viewed?

Another aspect of ethical behaviour is that others will often be judging the morality of action using hindsight or whilst coming from another perspective. This is the 'how would it appear on the front page of the newspaper?' aspect. So being aware of what could happen is often part of ethical sensitivity. In other words, being able to anticipate possible outcomes or how other parties will view what you have done is a necessary part of identifying that ethical issues have to be addressed.

What if there are competing solutions?

Ethical behaviour involves making decisions which are as morally correct and fair as possible, recognising that sometimes there will have to be decisions in relation to two or more competing aspects of what is morally correct which are in unresolvable conflict. One has to be sure that any trade-offs are made for the good of society and that decisions are not blatantly or subtly influenced by self-interest. They must appear fair and reasonable when reviewed subsequently by an uninvolved outsider who is not an accountant. This is because the community places their trust in professionals because they have expertise that others do not, but at the same time it is necessary to retain that trust.

Summary

At the macro level the existence of the profession and the careers of all of us are dependent on the community's perception of the profession as being ethical. Students need to be very conscious of that as they will make up the profession of the future.

At a more micro level all accountants will face ethical issues during their careers, whether they recognise them or not. This chapter attempts to increase awareness of the existence of ethical questions. The simplest way to increase awareness is to ask the question:

- Who is directly or indirectly affected by this accounting decision?

Then the follow-up question is:

- If I was in their position how would I feel about the accounting decision in terms of its fairness? (This is Rawls' (1971, revised 1999)[3] and Baumol's (1982)[4] superfairness proposal.)

By increasing awareness of the impact of decisions, including accounting decisions, on other parties, hopefully the dangers of decisions which are unfair will be recognised. By facing the implications head-on, the accountant is less likely to make wrong decisions. Also keep in mind those accountants who never set out to be unethical but by a series of small incremental decisions found themselves at the point of no return. The personal consequences of being found to be unethical can cover financial disasters, a long period of stress as civil or criminal cases wind their way through the courts, and at the extreme suicide or prison.

Another aspect of this chapter has been the attempt to highlight the vulnerability of companies to accusations of both direct and indirect unethical impacts and hence the need to be aware of trends to increasing levels of accountability.

Finally you need to be aware of the avenues for getting assistance if you find yourself under pressure to ignore ethics or to turn a blind eye to the inappropriate behaviour of others. You should be aware of built-in avenues for addressing such concerns within your own organisation. Further, you should make yourself familiar with the assistance which your professional body can provide, such as providing experienced practitioners to discuss your options and the likely advantages and disadvantages of those alternatives.

REVIEW QUESTIONS

1 Identify two ethical issues which university students experience and where they look for guidance. How useful is that guidance?

2 The following is an extract from a *European Accounting Review*[20] article:

> On the teaching front, there is a pressing need to challenge more robustly the tenets of modern day business, and specifically accounting, education which have elevated the principles of property rights and narrow self-interest above broader values of community and ethics.

Discuss how such a challenge might impact on accounting education.

3 The International Association for Accounting Education and Research states that: 'Professional ethics should pervade the teaching of accounting' (www.iaaer.org). Discuss how this can be achieved on an undergraduate accounting degree.

4 As a trainee auditor, what ethical issues are you most likely to encounter?

5 Explain what you think are four common types of ethical issues associated with (a) auditing, (b) public practice and (c) accounting in a corporate environment.

6 Lord Borrie QC has said[21] of the Public Interest Disclosure Bill that came into force in July 1999 that the new law would encourage people to recognise and identify with the wider public interest, not just their own private position, and it will reassure them that if they act reasonably to protect the legitimate interest of others, the law will not stand idly by should they be vilified or victimised. Confidentiality should only be breached, however, if there is a statutory obligation to do so. Discuss.

7 Confidentiality means that an accountant in business has a loyalty to the business which employs him or her which is greater than any commitment to a professional code of ethics. Discuss.

8 An interesting ethical case arose when an employee of a Swiss bank stole records of the accounts of international investors. The records were then offered for sale to the German government on the basis that many of them would represent unreported income and thus provide evidence of tax evasion. Should the government buy the records? Provide arguments for and against.

9 Refer to the Ernst & Young Code of Conduct and discuss the questions they suggest when putting their Global Code of Conduct into action.[22]

10 Should ethics be applicable at the standard-setting level? Express and justify your own views on this as distinct from repeating the material in the chapter.

11 Discuss the role of the accounting profession in the issue of ethics.

12 The management of a listed company has a fiduciary duty to act in the best interest of the current shareholders and it would be unethical for them to act in the interest of other parties if this did not maximise the existing earnings per share. Discuss.

13 How might a company develop a code of ethics for its own use?

14 Outline the advantages and disadvantages of a written code of ethics.

15 In relation to the following scenarios explain why it is a breach of ethics and what steps could have been taken to avoid the issue:

(a) The son of the accountant of a company is employed during the university holiday period to undertake work associated with preparation for a visit of the auditors.

(b) A senior executive is given a first-class seat to travel to Chicago to attend an industry fair where the company is launching a new product. The executive decides to cash in the ticket and to get two economy-class tickets so her boyfriend can go with her. The company picks up the hotel bill and she reimburses the difference between what it would have cost if she went alone and the final bill. The frequent flier points were credited to her personal frequent flier account. Would it make any difference if the company was not launching a new product at the fair?

(c) You pay a sizeable account for freight on the internal shipping of product deliveries in an underdeveloped country. At morning tea the gossip is that the company is paying bribes to a general in the underdeveloped country as protection money.

(d) The credit card statement for the managing director includes payments to a casino. The managing director says it is for the entertainment of important customers.

(e) You are processing a payment for materials which have been approved for repairs and maintenance when you realise the delivery is not to one of the business addresses of the company.

16 In each of the following scenarios, outline the ethical problem and suggest ways in which the organisation may solve the problem and prevent its recurrence:

(a) A director's wife uses his company car for shopping.

(b) Groceries bought for personal use are included on a director's company credit card.

(c) A director negotiates a contract for management consultancy services but it is later revealed that her husband is a director of the management consultancy company.

(d) The director of a company hires her son for some holiday work within the company but does not mention the fact to her fellow directors.

(e) You are the accountant to a small engineering company and you have been approached by the Chairman to authorise the payment of a fee to an overseas government employee in the hope that a large contract will be awarded.

(f) Your company has had some production problems which have resulted in some electrical goods being faulty (possibly dangerous) but all production is being dispatched to customers regardless of condition.

17 In each of the following scenarios, outline the ethical or potential ethical problem and suggest ways in which it could be resolved or avoided:

(a) Your company is about to sign a contract with a repressive regime in South America for equipment which **could** have a military use. Your own government has given you no advice on this matter.

(b) Your company is in financial difficulties and a large contract has just been gained in partnership with an overseas supplier who employs children as young as seven years old on their production line. The children are the only wage earners for their families and there is no welfare available in the country where they live.

(c) You are the accountant in a large manufacturing company and you have been approached by the manufacturing director to prepare a capital investment proposal for a new production line. After your calculations the project meets **none** of the criteria necessary to allow the project to proceed but the director instructs you to change the financial forecast figures to ensure the proposal is approved.

(d) Review the last week's newspapers and select **three** examples of failures of business ethics and justify your choice of examples.

(e) The company deducts from the monthly payroll employees' compulsory contribution to their superannuation accounts. The payment to the superannuation fund, which also includes the company's matching contribution, is being made only six-monthly because the cash flow of the company is tight following rapid expansion.

18 It has been said that football clubs are seen by criminals as the perfect vehicles for money laundering. Discuss the reason for this view.

EXERCISES

Question 1

You have recently qualified and set up in public practice under the name Patris Zadan. You have been approached to provide accounting services for Joe Hardiman. Joe explains that he has had a lawyer set up six businesses and he asks you to do the books and to handle tax matters. The first thing you notice is that he is running a number of laundromats which are largely financed by relatives from overseas. As the year progresses you realise those businesses are extremely profitable, given industry averages.

Required:
Discuss: What do you do?

Question 2

Joe Withers is the chief financial officer for Withco plc responsible for negotiating bank loans. It has been the practice to obtain loans from a number of merchant banks. He has recently met Ben Billings who had been on the same undergraduate course some years earlier. They agree to meet for a game of squash and during the course of the evening Joe learns that Ben is the chief loans officer at The Swift Merchant Bank.

During the next five years Joe negotiates all of the company's loan requirements through Swift, and Ben arranges for Joe to receive substantial allocations in initial public offerings. Over that period Joe has done quite well out of taking up allocations and selling them within a few days on the market.

Required:
Discuss the ethical issues.

Question 3

Kim Lee is a branch accountant in a multinational company Green Cocoa plc responsible for purchasing supplies from a developing country. Kim Lee is authorised to enter into contracts up to $100,000 for any single transaction. Demand in the home market is growing and Head Office are pressing for an increase in supplies. A new government official in the developing country says that Kim needs an export permit from his department and that he needs a payment to be made to his brother-in-law for consulting services if the permit is to be granted. Kim quickly checks alternative sources and finds that the normal price combined with the extra 'facilitation fee' is still much cheaper than the alternative sources of supply. Kim faces two problems, namely, whether to pay the bribe and, if so, how to record it in the accounts so it is not obvious what it is.

Required:
Discuss the ethical issues.

Question 4

Jemma Burrett is a public practitioner. Four years earlier she had set up a family trust for a major client by the name of Simon Trent. The trust is for the benefit of Simon and his wife Marie. Marie is also a client of the practice and the practice prepares her tax returns. Subsequently Marie files for divorce. In her claim for a share of the assets she claims a third share of the business and half the other assets of the family which are listed. The assets of the family trust are not included in the list.

Required:
Discuss the ethical issues raised by the case and what action the accountant should take (if any).

Question 5

George Longfellow is a financial controller with a listed industrial firm which has a long period of sustained growth. This has necessitated substantial use of external borrowing.

During the great financial crisis it has become harder to roll over the loans as they mature. To make matters worse sales revenues have fallen 5% for the financial year, debtors have taken longer to pay, and margins have fallen. The managing director has said that he doesn't want to report a loss for the first time in the company's history as it might scare financiers.

The finance director (FD) has told George to make every effort to get the result to come out positively. He suggests that a number of expenses should be shifted to prepayments, provisions for doubtful debts should be lowered, and new assets should not be depreciated in the year of purchase but rather should only commence depreciation in the next financial year on the argument that new assets take a while to become fully operational.

In the previous year the company had moved into a new line of business where a small number of customers paid in advance. Because these were exceptional the auditors were persuaded to allow you to avoid the need to make the systems more sophisticated to decrease revenue and to recognise a liability. After all, it was immaterial in the overall group. Fortunately, that new line of business has grown substantially in the current financial year and it was suggested that the auditors be told that the revenue in advance should not be taken out of sales because a precedent had been set the year before.

George saw this as a little bit of creative accounting and was reluctant to do what he was instructed. When he tentatively made this comment to the FD he was assured that this was only temporary to ensure the company could refinance and that next year, when the economy recovered, all the discretionary adjustments would be reversed and everyone would be happy. After all, the employment of the 20,000 people who work for the group depends upon the refinancing and it was not as if the company was not going to be prosperous in the future. The FD emphasised that the few adjustments were, after all, a win–win situation for everyone and George was threatening the livelihood of all of his colleagues – many with children and with mortgage payments to meet.

Required:
Discuss who would or could benefit or lose from the Finance Director's proposals.

References

1 L. Spacek, 'The need for an accounting court', *The Accounting Review*, 1958, pp. 368–379.
2 IFAC, *Code of Ethics for Professional Accountants*.
3 J. Rawls, *A Theory of Justice*, Oxford University Press, 1971, 1999.
4 W.J. Baumol, *Superfairness: Applications and Theory*, MIT Press, 1982.
5 D. Friedman, *Morals and Markets*, Palgrave Macmillan, 2008.
6 S.B. Salter, D.M. Guffey and J.J. McMillan, 'Truth, consequences and culture: a comparative examination of cheating and attitudes about cheating among U.S. and U.K. students', *Journal of Business Ethics*, vol. 31(1), May 2001, pp. 37–50, Springer.
7 C. Helliar and J. Bebbington, 'Taking ethics to heart', ICAS, 2004, http://www.icas.org.uk
8 See http://www.btplc.com/TheWayWeWork/Businesspractice/twww_english.pdf
9 See http://www.ir.jameshardie.com.au/jh/asbestos_compensation.jsp
10 M.M. Jennings, *Seven Signs of Ethical Collapse: Understanding What Causes Moral Meltdowns in Organizations*, St Martin's Press, 2006.
11 S. Beder, *Beyond Petroleum*, http://www.uow.edu.au/~sharonb/bp.html
12 C. Stohl, M. Stohl and L. Popova, 'A new generation of codes of ethics', *Journal of Business Ethics*, vol. 90, 2009, pp. 607–622.
13 T. Morris, *If Aristotle Ran General Motors*, New York: Henry Holt and Company, 1997, pp. 118–145.
14 J.F. Castellano, K. Rosenweig and H.P. Roehm, 'How corporate culture impacts unethical distortion of financial numbers', *Management Accounting Quarterly*, vol. 5(4), Summer 2004.
15 See http://www.sfo.gov.uk

16 See http://www.lmu.edu/Page23070.aspx
17 See Ethics Resource Center, www.ethics.org
18 FINRA announces creation of 'Office of the Whistleblower', http://www.finra.org
19 See http://www.oecd.org
20 D. Owen, 'CSR after Enron: a role for the academic accounting profession?', *European Accounting Review*, vol. 14(2), 2005.
21 W. Raven, 'Social auditing', *Internal Auditor*, February 2000, p. 8.
22 See http://www.ey.com/Publication/vwLUAssets/Ernst-Young_Global_Code_of_Conduct/$FILE/EY_Code_of_Conduct.pdf

Statement of financial position – equity, liability and asset measurement and disclosure

CHAPTER 12

Share capital, distributable profits and reduction of capital

12.1 Introduction

The main purpose of this chapter is to explain the issue and reduction of capital and distributions to shareholders in the context of creditor protection.

Objectives

By the end of this chapter, you should be able to:

- describe the reasons for the issue of shares;
- describe the rights of different classes of shares;
- prepare accounting entries for issue of shares;
- explain the rules relating to distributable profits;
- explain when capital may be reduced;
- prepare accounting entries for reduction of capital;
- discuss the rights of different parties on a capital reduction.

12.2 Common themes

Companies may be financed by equity investors, loan creditors and trade creditors. Governments have recognised that for an efficient capital market to exist the rights of each of these stakeholders need to be protected. This means that equity investors require a clear statement of their powers to appoint and remunerate directors and of their entitlement to share in residual income and net assets; loan creditors and trade creditors require assurance that the directors will not distribute funds to the equity investors before settling outstanding debts in full.

Statutory rules have, therefore, evolved which attempt a balancing act by protecting the creditors on the one hand, e.g. by restricting dividend distributions to realised profits, whilst, on the other hand, not unduly restricting the ability of companies to organise their financial affairs, e.g. by reviewing a company's right to purchase and hold treasury shares. Such rules may not be totally consistent between countries but there appear to be some common themes in much of the legislation. These are:

- Share capital can be broadly of two types, equity or preference.
- Equity shares are entitled to the residual income in the statement of comprehensive income after paying expenses, loan interest and tax.

- Equity itself is a residual figure in that the standard setters have taken the approach of defining assets and liabilities and leaving equity as the residual difference in the statement of financial position.
- Equity may consist of ordinary shares or equity elements of **participating** preference shares and compound instruments which include debt and equity, i.e. where there are conversion rights when there must be a split into their debt and equity elements, with each element being accounted for separately.
- Preference shareholders are not entitled (unless participating) to share in the residual income but may be entitled to a fixed or floating rate of interest on their investment.
- Distributable reserves equate to retained earnings when these have arisen from realised gains.
- Trade payables require protection to prevent an entity distributing assets to shareholders if creditors are not paid in full.
- Capital restructuring may be necessary when there are sound commercial reasons.

However, the rules are not static and there are periodic reviews in most jurisdictions, e.g. the proposal that an entity should make dividend decisions based on its ability to pay rather than on the fact that profits have been realised.

- The distributable reserves of entities are those that have arisen due to realised gains and losses (retained profits), as opposed to unrealised gains (such as revaluation reserves).
- There must be protection for trade payables to prevent an entity distributing assets to shareholders to the extent that the trade payables are not paid in full. An entity must retain net assets at least equal to its share capital and non-distributable reserves (a capital maintenance concept).
- The capital maintenance concept also applies with regard to reducing share capital, with most countries generally requiring a replacement of share capital with a non-distributable reserve if it is redeemed.

Because all countries have company legislation and these themes are common, the authors felt that, as the UK has relatively well-developed company legislation, it would be helpful to consider such legislation as illustrating a typical range of statutory provisions. We therefore now consider the constituents of total shareholders' funds (also known as total owners' equity) and the nature of distributable and non-distributable reserves. We then analyse the role of the capital maintenance concept in the protection of creditors, before discussing the effectiveness of the protection offered by the Companies Act 2006 in respect of both private and public companies.

12.3 Total owners' equity: an overview

Total owners' equity consists of the issued share capital stated at nominal (or par) value, non-distributable and distributable reserves. Here we comment briefly on the main constituents of total shareholders' funds. We go on to deal with them in greater detail in subsequent sections.

12.3.1 Right to issue shares

Companies incorporated[1] under the Companies Act 2006 are able to raise capital by the issue of shares and debentures. There are two main categories of company: private limited companies and public limited companies. Public limited companies are designated by the letters plc and have the right to issue shares and debentures to the public. Private limited companies are often family companies; they are not allowed to seek share capital by invitations to the public. The shareholders of both categories have the benefit of limited personal indemnity, i.e. their liability to creditors is limited to the amount they agreed to pay the company for the shares they bought.

12.3.2 Types of share

Broadly, there are two types of share: ordinary and preference.

Ordinary shares

Ordinary shares, often referred to as equity shares, carry the main risk and their bearers are entitled to the residual profit after the payment of any fixed interest or fixed dividend to investors who have invested on the basis of a fixed return. Distributions from the residual profit are made in the form of dividends, which are normally expressed as pence per share.

Preference shares

Preference shares usually have a fixed rate of dividend, which is expressed as a percentage of the nominal value of the share. The dividend is paid before any distribution to the ordinary shareholders. The specific rights attaching to a preference share can vary widely.

12.3.3 Non-distributable reserves

There are a number of types of **statutory** non-distributable reserve, e.g. when the paid-in capital exceeds the par value as a share premium. In addition to the statutory non-distributable reserves, a company might have restrictions on distribution within its memorandum and articles, stipulating that capital profits are non-distributable as dividends.

12.3.4 Distributable reserves

Distributable reserves are normally represented by the retained earnings that appear in the statement of financial position and belong to the ordinary shareholders. However, as we shall see, there may be circumstances where credits that have been made to the statement of comprehensive income are not actually distributable, usually because they do not satisfy the **realisation** concept.

Although the retained earnings in the statement of financial position contain the cumulative residual distributable profits, it is the earnings per share (EPS), based on the post-tax earnings for the year as disclosed in the profit and loss account, that influences the market valuation of the shares, applying the price/earnings ratio.

When deciding whether to issue or buy back shares, the directors will therefore probably consider the impact on the EPS figure. If the EPS increases, the share price can normally be expected also to increase.

12.4 Total shareholders' funds: more detailed explanation

12.4.1 Ordinary shares – risks and rewards

Ordinary shares (often referred to as equity shares) confer the right to:

● share proportionately in the rewards, i.e.:
  – the residual profit remaining after paying any loan interest or fixed dividends to investors who have invested on the basis of a fixed return;
  – any dividends distributed from these residual profits;

- any net assets remaining after settling all creditors' claims in the event of the company ceasing to trade;
- share proportionately in the risks, i.e.:
  - lose a proportionate share of invested share capital if the company ceases to trade and there are insufficient funds to pay all the creditors and the shareholders in full.

12.4.2 Ordinary shares – powers

The owners of ordinary shares generally have one vote per share which can be exercised on a routine basis, e.g. at the Annual General Meeting to vote on the appointment of directors, and on an *ad hoc* basis, e.g. at an Extraordinary General Meeting to vote on a proposed capital reduction scheme.

However, there are some companies that have issued non-voting ordinary shares which may confer the right to a proportional share of the residual profits but not to vote.

Non-voting shareholders can attend and speak at the Annual General Meeting but, as they have no vote, are unable to have an influence on management if there are problems or poor performance – apart from selling their shares.

The practice varies around the world and is more common in continental Europe. In the UK, institutional investors have made it clear since the early 1990s that they regard it as poor corporate governance and companies have taken steps to enfranchise the non-voting shareholders. The following is an extract from a letter from John Laing plc to shareholders setting out its enfranchisement proposals:

LAING SETS OUT ENFRANCHISEMENT PROPOSALS *23 March 2000*
John Laing plc today issues enfranchisement proposals to change the Group voting structure.

The key points are as follows:

- Convert the Ordinary A (non-voting) Shares into Ordinary Shares
- All redesignated shares to have full voting rights ranking pari passu in all respects with the existing Ordinary Shares
- Compensatory Scrip Issue for holders of existing Ordinary Shares of one New Ordinary Share for every 20 Ordinary Shares held [authors' note: this is in recognition of the fact that the proportion of votes of the existing ordinary shareholders has been reduced – an alternative approach would be to ask the non-voting shareholders to pay a premium in exchange for being given voting rights]
- EGM to be held on 18th May 2000

Reasons for enfranchisement

- To increase the range of potential investors in the company which the directors believe should enhance the marketability and liquidity of the company's shares.
- To enable all classes of equity shareholders, who share the same risks and rewards, to share the same voting rights.
- To ensure the company has maximum flexibility to manage its capital structure in order to reduce its cost of capital and to enhance shareholder value.

In other countries, however, there may be sound commercial reasons why non-voting shares are issued. In Japan, for example, the Japanese Commercial Code was amended in 2002 to allow companies to issue shares with special rights, e.g. power to veto certain company decisions, and to increase the proportion of non-voting shares in issue. The intention was to promote successful restructuring of ailing companies and stimulate demand for Japanese equity investments.

12.4.3 Methods and reasons for issuing shares

Methods of issuing shares

Some of the common methods of issuing shares are *offer for subscription*, where the shares are offered directly to the public; *placings*, where the shares are arranged (placed) to be bought by financial institutions; and *rights issues*, whereby the new shares are offered to the existing shareholders at a price below the market price of those shares. The rights issue might be priced significantly below the current market price but this may not mean that the shareholder is benefiting from cheap shares as the price of existing shares will be reduced, e.g. the British Telecommunications plc £5.9 billion rights issue announced in 2001 made UK corporate history in that no British company had attempted to raise so much cash from its shareholders. The offer was three BT shares for every 10 held and, to encourage take-up, the new shares were offered at a deeply discounted rate of £3 which was at a 47% discount to the share price on the day prior to the launch.

Reasons for issuing shares

- **For future investment**, e.g. Watford Leisure plc (Watford Football Club) offered and placed 540,000,000 ordinary shares and expected to raise cash proceeds of about £4.7 million. The company has since been floated on the AIM.

- **As consideration on an acquisition**, e.g. Microsoft Corporation acquired Great Plains Software Incorporated, a leading supplier of mid-market business applications. The acquisition was structured as a stock purchase and was valued at approximately $1.1 billion. Each share of Great Plains common stock was exchanged for 1.1 shares of Microsoft common stock.

- **To shareholders to avoid paying out cash from the company's funds**, e.g. the Prudential plc Annual Report 2009 has a scrip dividend scheme which enables shareholders to receive new ordinary shares instead of the cash dividends they would normally receive. This means they can build up their shareholding in Prudential without going to the market to buy new shares and so will not incur any dealing costs or stamp duty.

- **To directors and employees to avoid paying out cash in the form of salary from company funds**, e.g. the Anglo Pacific Group plc:

  Shares Issued in lieu of Remuneration to Executive Directors (9 December 2010)
  Anglo Pacific Group plc announces that, as of 8 December 2010 and following the recommendation of the Remuneration Committee, it has issued 36,640 Ordinary Shares of 2p each in the Company at a price of 327.5p per share to the Executive Directors as part of their remuneration.

- **To shareholders to encourage reinvestment**, e.g. some companies operate a Dividend Reinvestment Plan whereby the dividends of shareholders wishing to reinvest are pooled and reinvested on the Stock Exchange. A typical plan is operated by Santander:

  Santander Shareholder Account and Dividend Re-investment Plan
  An easy way to increase your holding of Santander shares whilst earning a fantastic rate of 5% gross p.a./AER (variable) on your Santander share dividends
  The Santander Shareholder Account and Dividend Re-investment Plan is a great savings option – exclusive to people based in the UK who own Santander shares and hold them through the Santander Nominee Service. It offers a variable rate of interest of 5% gross p.a./AER (variable) on deposited Santander share dividends between re-investments.

- **To shareholders by way of a rights issue** to shore up statements of financial position weakened in the credit crisis by reducing debt and to avoid breaching debt covenants, e.g. in February 2009 the Cookson Group plc announced a 12 for 1 rights issue to raise net proceeds of approximately £240 million in order to provide a more suitable capital structure for the current environment and enhance covenant and longer-term liquidity headroom under current debt facilities.

- **To loan creditors in exchange for debt**, e.g. Sirius XM, a satellite radio station, with about $1 billion debt due to mature in February 2009, exchanged shares for $2\frac{1}{2}\%$ convertible debt in January 2009.

- **To obtain funds for future acquisitions**, e.g. SSL International, a successful company that had outperformed the FTSE All-Share Index 2008, raised £87 million to fund its medium-term growth plans. Other companies were raising funds to acquire assets that were being sold by companies needing to obtain cash to reduce their debt burden.

- **To reduce levels of debt** to avoid credit-rating agencies downgrading the company, which would make it difficult or more expensive to borrow.

- **To overcome liquidity problems**, e.g. Brio experienced liquidity problems and refinanced with the isue of 300 million shares to raise over £25 million.

12.4.4 Types of preference shares

The following illustrate some of the ways in which specific rights can vary.

Cumulative preference shares
Dividends not paid in respect of any one year because of a lack of profits are accumulated for payment in some future year when distributable profits are sufficient.

Non-cumulative preference shares
Dividends not paid in any one year because of a lack of distributable profits are permanently forgone.

Participating preference shares
These shares carry the right to participate in a distribution of additional profits over and above the fixed rate of dividend after the ordinary shareholders have received an agreed percentage. The participation rights are based on a precise formula.

Redeemable preference shares
These shares may be redeemed by the company at an agreed future date and at an agreed price.

Convertible preference shares
These shares may be converted into ordinary shares at a future date on agreed terms. The conversion is usually at the preference shareholder's discretion.

There can be a mix of rights, e.g. Getronics entered into an agreement in 2005 with its cumulative preference shareholders whereby Getronics had the right in 2009 to repurchase (redeem) the shares and, if it did not redeem the shares, the cumulative preference shareholders had the right to convert into ordinary shares.

12.5 Accounting entries on issue of shares

12.5.1 Shares issued at nominal (par) value

If shares are issued at nominal value, the company simply debits the cash account with the amount received and credits the ordinary share capital or preference share capital, as appropriate, with the **nominal value** of the shares.

12.5.2 Shares issued at a premium

The market price of the shares of a company, which is based on the prospects of that company, is usually different from the par (nominal) value of those shares.

On receipt of consideration for the shares, the company again debits the cash account with the amount received and credits the ordinary share capital or preference share capital, as appropriate, with the **nominal value** of the shares.

Assuming that the market price exceeds the nominal value, a premium element will be credited to a share premium account. The share premium is classified as a **non-distributable reserve** to indicate that it is not repayable to the shareholders who have subscribed for their shares: it remains a part of the company's permanent capital.

The accounting treatment for recording the issue of shares is straightforward. For example, the journal entries to record the issue of 1,000 £1 ordinary shares at a market price of £2.50 per share payable in instalments of:

on application	on 1 January 20X1	25p
on issue	on 31 January 20X1	£1.75 including the premium
on first call	on 31 January 20X2	25p
on final call	on 31 January 20X4	25p

would be as follows:

1 Jan 20X1	Dr £	Cr £
Cash account	250	
Application account		250

31 Jan 20X1	Dr £	Cr £
Cash account	1,750	
Issue account		1,750

31 Jan 20X1	Dr £	Cr £
Application account	250	
Issue account	1,750	
Share capital account		500
Share premium in excess of par value		1,500

The first and final call would be debited to the cash account and credited to the share capital account on receipt of the date of the calls.

12.6 Creditor protection: capital maintenance concept

To protect creditors, there are often rules relating to the use of the total shareholders' funds which determine how much is distributable.

As a general rule, the paid-in share capital is not repayable to the shareholders and the reserves are classified into two categories: distributable and non-distributable. The directors have discretion as to the amount of the distributable profits that they recommend for distribution as a dividend to shareholders. However, they have no discretion as to the treatment of the non-distributable funds. There may be a statutory requirement for the company to retain within the company net assets equal to the non-distributable reserves. This requirement is to safeguard the interests of creditors and is known as **capital maintenance**.

12.7 Creditor protection: why capital maintenance rules are necessary

It is helpful at this point to review the position of unincorporated businesses in relation to capital maintenance.

12.7.1 Unincorporated businesses

An unincorporated business such as a sole trader or partnership is not required to maintain any specified amount of capital within the business to safeguard the interests of its creditors. The owners are free to decide whether to introduce or withdraw capital. However, they remain personally liable for the liabilities incurred by the business, and the creditors can have recourse to the personal assets of the owners if the business assets are inadequate to meet their claims in full.

When granting credit to an unincorporated business, the creditors may well be influenced by the personal wealth and apparent standing of the owners and not merely by the assets of the business as disclosed in its financial statements. This is why in an unincorporated business there is no external reason for the capital and the profits to be kept separate.

In partnerships, there are frequently internal agreements that require each partner to maintain his or her capital at an agreed level. Such agreements are strictly a matter of contract between the owners and do not prejudice the rights of the business creditors.

Sometimes owners attempt to influence creditors unfairly, by maintaining a lifestyle in excess of what they can afford, or try to frustrate the legal rights of creditors by putting their private assets beyond their reach, e.g. by transferring their property to relatives or trusts. These subterfuges become apparent only when the creditors seek to enforce their claim against the private assets. Banks are able to protect themselves by seeking adequate security, e.g. a charge on the owners' property.

12.7.2 Incorporated limited liability company

Because of limited liability, the rights of creditors against the private assets of the owners, i.e. the shareholders of the company, are restricted to any amount unpaid on their shares. Once the shareholders have paid the company for their shares, they are not personally liable for the company's debts. Creditors are restricted to making claims against the assets of the company.

Hence, the legislature considered it necessary to ensure that the shareholders did not make distributions to themselves such that the assets needed to meet creditors' claims were put beyond creditors' reach. This may be achieved by setting out statutory rules.

12.8 Creditor protection: how to quantify the amounts available to meet creditors' claims

Creditors are exposed to two types of risk: the business risk that a company will operate unsuccessfully and will be unable to pay them; and the risk that a company will operate successfully, but will pay its shareholders rather than its creditors.

The legislature has never intended trade creditors to be protected against ordinary business risks, e.g. the risk of the debtor company incurring either trading losses or losses that might arise from a fall in the value of the assets following changes in market conditions.

In the UK, the Companies Act 2006 requires the amount available to meet creditors' claims to be calculated by reference to the company's annual financial statements. There are two possible approaches:

- The **direct** approach which requires the **asset** side of the statement of financial position to contain assets with a realisable value sufficient to cover all outstanding liabilities.

- The **indirect** approach which requires the **liability** side of the statement of financial position to classify reserves into distributable and non-distributable reserves (i.e. respectively, available and not available to the shareholders by way of dividend distributions).

The Act follows the indirect approach by specifying capital maintenance in terms of the total shareholders' funds. However, this has not stopped certain creditors taking steps to protect themselves by following the direct approach, e.g. it is bank practice to obtain a mortgage debenture over the assets of the company. The effect of this is to disadvantage the trade creditors. The statutory restrictions preventing shareholders from reducing capital accounts on the liability side are weakened when management grants certain parties priority rights against some or all of the company's assets.

We will now consider total shareholders' funds and capital maintenance in more detail, starting with share capital. Two aspects of share capital are relevant to creditor protection: minimum capital requirements and reduction of capital.

12.9 Issued share capital: minimum share capital

The creditors of public companies may be protected by the requirements that there should be a minimum share capital and that capital should be reduced only under controlled conditions.

In the UK, the minimum share capital requirement for a public company is currently set at £50,000 or its euro equivalent, although this can be increased by the Secretary of State for the Department for Business, Innovation and Skills.[2] A company is not permitted to commence trading unless it has issued this amount. However, given the size of many public companies, it is questionable whether this figure is adequate.

The minimum share capital requirement refers to the nominal value of the share capital. In the UK, the law requires each class of share to have a stated nominal value. This value is used for identification and also for capital maintenance. The law ensures that a company receives an amount that is at least equal to the nominal value of the shares issued, less a controlled level of commission, by prohibiting the issue of shares at a discount and by limiting any underwriting commissions on an issue. This is intended to avoid a material discount being granted in the guise of commission. However, the requirement is concerned more with safeguarding the relative rights of existing shareholders than with protecting creditors.

There is effectively no minimum capital requirement for private companies. We can see many instances of such companies having an issued and paid-up capital of only a few £1 shares, which cannot conceivably be regarded as adequate creditor protection. The lack of adequate protection for the creditors of private companies is considered again later in the chapter.

12.10 Distributable profits: general considerations

We have considered capital maintenance and non-distributable reserves. However, it is not sufficient to attempt to maintain the permanent capital accounts of companies unless there are clear rules on the amount that they can distribute to their shareholders as profit. Without such rules, they may make distributions to their shareholders out of capital. The question of what can legitimately be distributed as profit is an integral part of the concept of capital maintenance in company accounts. In the UK, there are currently statutory definitions of the amount that can be distributed by private, public and investment companies.

12.10.1 Distributable profits: general rule for private companies

The definition of distributable profits under the Companies Act 2006 is:

> Accumulated, realised profits, so far as not previously utilised by distribution or capitalisation, less its accumulated, realised losses, as far as not previously written off in a reduction or reorganisation of capital.

This means the following:

● Unrealised profits cannot be distributed.
● There is no difference between realised revenue and realised capital profits.
● All accumulated net realised profits (i.e. realised profits less realised losses) on the statement of financial position date must be considered.

On the key question of whether a profit is realised or not, the Companies Act (paragraph 853) simply says that realised profits or realised losses are

> such profits or losses of the company as fall to be treated as realised in accordance with principles generally accepted, at the time when the accounts are prepared, with respect to the determination for accounting purposes of realised profits or losses.

Hence, the Act does not lay down detailed rules on what is and what is not a realised profit; indeed, it does not even refer specifically to 'accounting principles'. Nevertheless, it would seem reasonable for decisions on realisation to be based on generally **accepted accounting principles** at the time, subject to the court's decision in cases of dispute.

12.10.2 Distributable profits: general rule for public companies

According to the Companies Act, the undistributable reserves of a public company are its share capital, share premium, capital redemption reserve and also 'the excess of accumulated unrealised profits over accumulated unrealised losses at the time of the intended distribution and . . . any reserves not allowed to be distributed under the Act or by the company's own Memorandum or Articles of Association'.

This means that, when dealing with a public company, the distributable profits have to be reduced by any net unrealised loss.

12.10.3 Investment companies

The Companies Act 2006 allows for the special nature of some businesses in the calculation of distributable profits. There are additional rules for investment companies in calculating their distributable profits. For a company to be classified as an investment company, it must invest its funds mainly in securities with the aim of spreading investment risk and giving its members the benefit of the results of managing its funds.

Such a company has the option of applying one of two rules in calculating its distributable profits. These are either:

● the rules that apply to public companies in general, but excluding any realised capital profits, e.g. from the disposal of investments; or
● the company's accumulated realised revenue less its accumulated realised and unrealised revenue losses, provided that its assets are at least one and a half times its liabilities both before and after such a distribution.

The reasoning behind these special rules seems to be to allow investment companies to pass the dividends they receive to their shareholders, irrespective of any changes in the values of their investments, which are subject to market fluctuations. However, the asset cover ratio of liabilities can easily be manipulated by the company simply paying creditors, whereby the ratio is improved, or borrowing, whereby it is reduced.

12.11 Distributable profits: how to arrive at the amount using relevant accounts

In the UK, the Companies Act 2006 stipulates that the distributable profits of a company must be based on **relevant accounts**. Relevant accounts may be prepared under either UK GAAP or EU adopted IFRS. On occasions a new IFRS might have the effect of making a previously realised item reclassified as unrealised, which would then become undistributable. For a more detailed description on the determination of realised profits for distribution refer to the ICAEW Technical Release 01/09 (www.icas.org.uk). These would normally be the audited annual accounts, which have been prepared according to the requirements of the Act to give a true and fair view of the company's financial affairs. In the case of a qualified audit report, the auditor is required to prepare a written statement stating whether such a qualification is material in determining a company's distributable profit. Interim dividends are allowed to be paid provided they can be justified on the basis of the latest annual accounts, otherwise interim accounts will have to be prepared that would justify such a distribution.

12.11.1 Effect of fair value accounting on decision to distribute

In the context of fair value accounting, volatility is an aspect where directors will need to consider their fiduciary duties. The fair value of financial instruments may be volatile even though such fair value is properly determined in accordance with IAS 39 *Financial Instruments: Recognition and Measurement*. Directors should consider, as a result of their fiduciary duties, whether it is prudent to distribute profits arising from changes in the fair values of financial instruments considered to be volatile, even though they may otherwise be realised profits in accordance with the technical guidance.

12.12 When may capital be reduced?

Once the shares have been issued and paid up, the contributed capital together with any payments in excess of par value are normally regarded as permanent. However, there might be commercially sound reasons for a company to reduce its capital and we will consider three such reasons. These are:

● writing off part of capital which has already been lost and is not represented by assets;

● repayment of part of paid-up capital to shareholders or cancellation of unpaid share capital;

● purchase of own shares.

In the UK it has been necessary for both private and public companies to obtain a court order approving a reduction of capital. In line with the wish to reduce the regulatory burden on private companies, the government legislated[3] in 2008 for private companies to be able to reduce their capital by special resolution subject to the directors signing a solvency statement to the effect that the company would remain able to meet all of its liabilities for at least a year. At the same time a reserve arising from the reduction is treated as realised and may be distributed, although it need not be and could be used for other purposes, e.g. writing off accumulated trading losses.

12.13 Writing off part of capital which has already been lost and is not represented by assets

This situation normally occurs when a company has accumulated trading losses which prevent it from making dividend payments under the rules relating to distributable profits. The general approach is to eliminate the debit balance on retained earnings by setting it off against the share capital and non-distributable reserves.

12.13.1 Accounting treatment for a capital reduction to eliminate accumulated trading losses

The accounting treatment is straightforward. A capital reduction account is opened. It is debited with the accumulated losses and credited with the amount written off the share capital and reserves.

For example, assume that the capital and reserves of Hopeful Ltd were as follows at 31 December 20X1:

	£
200,000 ordinary shares of £1 each	200,000
Retained earnings	(180,000)

The directors estimate that the company will return to profitability in 20X2, achieving profits of £4,000 per annum thereafter. Without a capital reduction, the profits from 20X2 must be used to reduce the accumulated losses. This means that the company would be unable to pay a dividend for 45 years if it continued at that level of profitability and ignoring tax. Perhaps even more importantly, it would not be attractive for shareholders to put additional capital into the company because they would not be able to obtain any dividend for some years.

There might be statutory procedures such as the requirement for the directors to obtain a special resolution and court approval to reduce the £1 ordinary shares to ordinary shares of 10p each. Subject to satisfying such requirements, the accounting entries would be:

	Dr	Cr
	£	£
Capital reduction account	180,000	
Retained earnings:		180,000
Transfer of debit balance		
Share capital	180,000	
Capital reduction account:		180,000
Reduction of share capital		

Accounting treatment for a capital reduction to eliminate accumulated trading losses and loss of value on non-current assets – losses borne by equity shareholders

Companies often take the opportunity to revalue all of their assets at the same time as they eliminate the accumulated trading losses. Any loss on revaluation is then treated in the same way as the accumulated losses and transferred to the capital reduction account.

For example, assume that the capital and reserves and assets of Hopeful Ltd were as follows at 31 December 20X1:

	£	£
200,000 ordinary shares of £1 each		200,000
Retained earnings		(180,000)
		20,000
Non-current assets		
Plant and equipment		15,000
Current assets		
Cash	17,000	
Current liabilities		
Trade payables	12,000	
Net current assets		5,000
		20,000

The plant and equipment is revalued at £5,000 and it is resolved to reduce the share capital to ordinary shares of 5p each. The accounting entries would be:

	Dr	Cr
	£	£
Capital reduction account	190,000	
Statement of income		180,000
Plant and machinery:		10,000
Transfer of accumulated losses and loss on revaluation		
Share capital	190,000	
Capital reduction account:		190,000
Reduction of share capital to 200,000 shares of 5p each		

The statement of financial position after the capital reduction shows that the share capital fairly reflects the underlying asset values:

	£	£
200,000 ordinary shares of 5p each		10,000
		10,000
Non-current assets		
Plant and equipment		5,000
Current assets		
Cash	17,000	
Current liabilities		
Trade payables	12,000	5,000
		10,000

The pro forma statement of financial position shown in Figure 12.1 is from the Pilkington's Tiles Group plc's 2002 Annual Report. It shows the position when the company proposed the creation of distributable reserves after a substantial deficit in the reserves had been caused by the writing down of an investment – this was to be achieved by transferring to the profit and loss account the sums currently standing to the credit of the capital redemption reserve and share premium account.

The proposal was the subject of a special resolution to be confirmed by the High Court – the court would consider the proposal taking creditor protection into account. The company recognised this with the following statement:

the Company will need to demonstrate to the satisfaction of the High Court that no creditor of the Company who has consented to the cancellations will be prejudiced by them. At present, it is anticipated that the creditor protection will take the form of an undertaking . . . not to treat as distributable any sum realised . . . which represents the realisation of hidden value in the statement of financial position.

Figure 12.1 Pilkington's Tiles Group pro forma balance sheet assuming the competition of the restructuring plan

	31 March 2002 £000	Adjustment £000	Adjusted balance £000
Capital and reserves			
Share capital	9,247		9,247
Share premium	25,429	(25,429)	—
Capital redemption reserve	645	(645)	—
Merger reserve	(1,001)	1,001	—
Revaluation reserve	1,581	—	1,581
Profit and loss account	(21,738)	25,073	3,335
Equity shareholders' funds	14,163	—	14,163

Accounting treatment for a capital reduction to eliminate accumulated trading losses and loss of value on non-current assets – losses borne by equity and other stakeholders

In the Hopeful Ltd example above, the ordinary shareholders alone bore the losses. It might well be, however, that a reconstruction involves a compromise between shareholders and creditors, with an amendment of the rights of the latter. Such a reconstruction would be subject to any statutory requirements within the jurisdiction, e.g. the support, say, of 75% of each class of creditor whose rights are being compromised, 75% of each class of share-holder and the permission of the court. For such a reconstruction to succeed there needs to be reasonable evidence of commercial viability and that anticipated profits are sufficient to service the proposed new capital structure.

Assuming in the Hopeful Ltd example that the creditors agree to bear £5,000 of the losses, the accounting entries would be as follows:

	£	£
Share capital	185,000	
Creditors	5,000	
Capital reduction account:		190,000
Reduction of share capital to 200,000 shares of 7.5p each		

Reconstruction schemes can be complex, but the underlying evaluation by each party will be the same. Each will assess the scheme to see how it affects their individual position.

Trade payables

In their decision to accept £5,000 less than the book value of their debt, the trade payables of Hopeful Ltd would be influenced by their prospects of receiving payment if Hopeful were to cease trading immediately, the effect on their results without Hopeful as a continuing customer and the likelihood that they would continue to receive orders from Hopeful following reconstruction.

Loan creditors

Loan creditors would take into account the expected value of any security they possess and a comparison of the opportunities for investing any loan capital returned in the event of liquidation with the value of their capital and interest entitlement in the reconstructed company.

Preference shareholders

Preference shareholders would likewise compare prospects for capital and income following a liquidation of the company with prospects for income and capital from the company as a going concern following a reconstruction.

Relative effects of the scheme

In practice, the formulation of a scheme will involve more than just the accountant, except in the case of very small companies. A merchant bank, major shareholders and major debenture holders will undoubtedly be concerned. Each vested interest will be asked for its opinion on specific proposals: unfavourable reactions will necessitate a rethink by the accountant. The process will continue until a consensus begins to emerge.

Each stakeholder's position needs to be considered separately. For example, any attempt to reduce the nominal value of all classes of shares and debentures on a proportionate basis would be unfair and unacceptable. This is because a reduction in the nominal values of preference shares or debentures has a different effect from a reduction in the nominal value of ordinary shares. In the former cases, the dividends and interest receivable will be reduced; in the latter case, the reduction in nominal value of the ordinary shares will have no effect on dividends as holders of ordinary shares are entitled to the residue of profit, whatever the nominal value of their shares.

Total support may well be unachievable. The objective is to maintain the company as a going concern. In attempting to achieve this, each party will continually be comparing its advantages under the scheme with its prospects in a liquidation.

Illustration of a capital reconstruction

XYZ plc has been making trading losses, which have resulted in a substantial debit balance on the profit and loss account. The statement of financial position of XYZ plc as at 31 December 20X3 was as follows:

		£000
Ordinary share capital (£1 shares)		1,000
Less: Accumulated losses on retained earnings	Note 1	(800)
		200
10% debentures (£1)		600
Net assets at book value	Note 2	800

Notes:

1 The company is changing its product and markets and expects to make £150,000 profit before interest and tax every year from 1 January 20X4.

2 (a) The estimated break-up or liquidation value of the assets at 31 December 20X3 was £650,000.

  (b) The going concern value of assets at 31 December 20X3 was £700,000.

The directors are faced with a decision to liquidate or reconstruct. Having satisfied themselves that the company is returning to profitability, they propose the following reconstruction scheme:

- Write off losses and reduce asset values to £700,000.
- Cancel all existing ordinary shares and debentures.
- Issue 1,200,000 new ordinary shares of 25p each and 400,000 12.5% debentures of £1 each as follows:
  - the existing shareholders are to be issued with 800,000 ordinary 25p shares;
  - the existing debenture holders are to be issued with 400,000 ordinary 25p shares and the new debentures.

The stakeholders, i.e. the ordinary shareholders and debenture holders, have first to decide whether the company has a reasonable chance of achieving the estimated profit for 20X4. The company might carry out a sensitivity analysis to show the effect on dividends and interest over a range of profit levels.

Next, stakeholders must consider whether allowing the company to continue provides a better return than that available from the liquidation of the company. Assuming that it does, they assess the effect of allowing the company to continue without any reconstruction of capital and with a reconstruction of capital.

The accountant writes up the reconstruction accounts and produces a statement of financial position after the reconstruction has been effected.

The accountant will produce the following information:

Effect of liquidating

	£	Debenture holders £	Ordinary shareholders £
Assets realised	650,000		
Less: Prior claim	(600,000)	600,000	
Less: Ordinary shareholders	(50,000)		50,000
	—	600,000	50,000

This shows that the ordinary shareholders would lose almost all of their capital, whereas the debenture holders would be in a much stronger position. This is important because it might influence the amount of inducement that the debenture holders require to accept any variation of their rights.

Company continues without reconstruction

	£	Debenture holders £	Ordinary shareholders £
Expected annual income:			
Expected operating profit	150,000		
Debenture interest	(60,000)	60,000	
Less: Ordinary dividend	(90,000)		90,000
Annual income	—	60,000	90,000

However, as far as the ordinary shareholders are concerned, no dividend will be allowed to be paid until the debit balance of £800,000 has been eliminated, i.e. there will be no dividend for more than nine years (for simplicity the illustration ignores tax effects).

Company continues with a reconstruction

	£	Debenture holders £	Ordinary shareholders £
Expected annual income:			
Expected operating profit	150,000		
Less: Debenture interest	(50,000)	50,000	
(12.5% on £400,000)			
Less: Dividend on shares	(33,000)	33,000	
Less: Ordinary dividend	(67,000)		67,000
Annual income	—	83,000	67,000

How will debenture holders react to the scheme?

At first glance, debenture holders appear to be doing reasonably well: the £83,000 provides a return of almost 14% on the amount that they would have received in a liquidation (83,000/600,000 × 100), which exceeds the 10% currently available, and it is £23,000 more than the £60,000 currently received. However, their exposure to risk has increased because £33,000 is dependent upon the level of profits. They will consider their position in relation to the ordinary shareholders.

For the ordinary shareholders the return should be calculated on the amount that they would have received on liquidation, i.e. 134% (67,000/50,000 × 100). In addition to receiving a return of 134%, they would hold two-thirds of the share capital, which would give them control of the company.

A final consideration for the debenture holders would be their position if the company were to fail after a reconstruction. In such a case, the old debenture holders would be materially disadvantaged as their prior claim will have been reduced from £600,000 to £400,000.

Accounting for the reconstruction

The reconstruction account will record the changes in the book values as follows:

Reconstruction account

	£000		£000
Retained earnings	800	Share capital	1,000
Assets (losses written off)	100	Debentures	600
		(old debentures cancelled)	
Ordinary share capital (25p)	300		
12.5% debentures (new issue)	400		
	1,600		1,600

The post-reconstruction statement of financial position will be as follows:

Ordinary share capital (25p)	300,000
12.5% debentures of £1	400,000
	700,000

12.14 Repayment of part of paid-in capital to shareholders or cancellation of unpaid share capital

This can occur when a company wishes to reduce its unwanted liquid resources. It takes the form of a *pro rata* payment to each shareholder and may require the consent of the creditors.

At the same time, the Directors need to retain sufficient to satisfy the company's capital investment requirements. The following is an extract from the AstraZeneca 2005 Annual Report:

Dividend and share re-purchases

In line with the policy stated last year, the Board intends to continue its practice of growing dividends in line with earnings (maintaining dividend cover in the two to three times range) whilst substantially distributing the balance of cash flow via share re-purchases. During 2005, we returned $4,718 million out of free cash of $6,052 million to shareholders through a mix of share buy-backs and dividends. The Board firmly believes that the first call on free cash flow is business need and, having fulfilled that, will return surplus cash flow to shareholders.

The primary business need is to build the product pipeline by supporting internal and external opportunities. Accordingly, in 2006, the Board intends to re-purchase shares at around the same level as 2005, with any balance of free cash flow available firstly for investment in the product pipeline or subsequent return to shareholders.

12.15 Purchase of own shares

This might take the form of the redemption of redeemable preference shares, the purchase of ordinary shares which are then cancelled and the purchase of ordinary shares which are not cancelled but held in treasury.

12.15.1 Redemption of preference shares

In the UK, when redeemable preference shares are redeemed, the company is required either to replace them with other shares or to make a transfer from distributable reserves to non-distributable reserves in order to maintain permanent capital. The accounting entries on redemption are to credit cash and debit the redeemable preference share account.

12.15.2 Buyback of own shares – intention to cancel

There are a number of reasons for companies buying back shares. These provide a benefit when taken as:

- a strategic measure, e.g. recognising that there is a lack of viable investment projects, i.e. expected returns being less than the company's weighted average cost of capital and so returning excess cash to shareholders to allow them to search out better growth investments;
- a defensive measure, e.g. an attempt to frustrate a hostile takeover or to reduce the power of dissident shareholders;
- a reactive measure, e.g. taking advantage of the fact that the share price is at a discount to its underlying intrinsic value or stabilising a falling share price;
- a proactive measure, e.g. creating shareholder value by reducing the number of shares in issue which increases the earnings per share, or making a distribution more tax efficient than the payment of a cash dividend;
- a tax efficient measure, e.g. Rolls-Royce made a final payment to shareholders in 2004 of 5.00p, making a total of 8.18p per ordinary share (2003 8.18p), stating that: 'The Company will continue to issue B Shares in place of dividends in order to accelerate the recovery of its advance corporation tax.'

There is also a potential risk if the company has to borrow funds in order to make the buyback, leaving itself liable to service the debt. Where it uses free cash rather than loans it is attractive to analysts and shareholders. For example, in the BP share buyback scheme (one of the UK's largest), the chief executive, Lord Browne, said that any free cash generated from BP's assets when the oil price was above $20 a barrel would be returned to investors over the following three years.

12.15.3 Buyback of own shares – treasury shares

The benefits to a company holding treasury shares are that it has greater flexibility to respond to investors' attitude to gearing, e.g. reissuing the shares if the gearing is perceived to be too high. It also has the capacity to satisfy loan conversions and employee share options without the need to issue new shares which would dilute the existing shareholdings.

National regimes where buyback is already permitted

In Europe and the USA it has been permissible to buy back shares, known as treasury shares, and hold them for reissue. In the UK this has been permissible since 2003. There are two common accounting treatments – the cost method and the par value method. The most common method is the cost method, which provides the following:

On purchase
The treasury shares are debited at gross cost to a Treasury Stock account – this is deducted as a one-line entry from equity, e.g. a statement of financial position might appear as follows:

Owners' equity section of statement of financial position

	£
Common stock, £1 par, 100,000 shares authorised, 30,000 shares issued	30,000
Paid-in capital in excess of par	60,000
Retained earnings	165,000
Treasury Stock (15,000 shares at cost)	(15,000)
Total owners' equity	240,000

In some countries, e.g. Switzerland, the treasury shares have been reported in the statement of financial position as a financial asset. When a company moves to IFRS this is not permitted and it is required that the shares are disclosed as negative equity.

On resale

- If on resale the sale price is higher than the cost price, the Treasury Stock account is credited at cost price and the excess is credited to Paid-in Capital (Treasury Stock).

- If on resale the sale price is lower than the cost price, the Treasury Stock account is credited with the proceeds and the balance is debited to Paid-in Capital (Treasury Stock). If the debit is greater than the credit balance on Paid-in Capital (Treasury Stock), the difference is deducted from retained earnings.

The UK experience

Treasury shares have been permitted in the UK since 2003. The regulations relating to Treasury shares are now contained in the Companies Act 2006.[4] These regulations permit companies with listed shares that purchase their own shares out of distributable profits to hold them 'in treasury' for sale at a later date or for transfer to an employees' share scheme.

There are certain restrictions whilst shares are held in treasury, namely:

- Their aggregate nominal value must not exceed 10% of the nominal value of issued share capital (if it exceeds 10% then the excess must be disposed of or cancelled).
- Rights attaching to the class of share – e.g. receiving dividends, and the right to vote – cannot be exercised by the company.

Treasury shares – cancellation

- Where shares are held as treasury shares, the company may at any time cancel some or all of the shares.
- If shares held as treasury shares cease to be qualifying shares, then the company must cancel the shares.
- On cancellation the amount of the company's share capital is reduced by the nominal amount of the shares cancelled.

The Singapore experience

It is interesting to note that until 1998 companies in Singapore were not permitted to purchase their own shares and had to rely on obtaining a court order to reduce capital. It was realised, however, that regimes such as those in the UK allowed a quicker and less expensive way to return capital to shareholders. UK experience meant that public companies were able to return capital if there were insufficient investment opportunities, and private companies were able to repurchase shares to resolve disputes between family members or minority and majority shareholders.

The following criteria apply:

- the company should have authority under its Articles of Association;
- the repayment should be from distributable profits that are realised;
- the creditors should be protected by requiring the company to be solvent before and after the repayment (assets and liabilities to be restated to current values for this exercise);
- on-market acquisitions require an ordinary resolution;
- selective off-market acquisitions require a special resolution because of the risk that directors may manipulate the transaction.

The amount paid by the company will be set against the carrying amount of the contributed capital, i.e. the nominal value plus share premium attaching to the shares acquired and the retained earnings. In order to maintain capital, there will be a transfer from retained earnings to a capital redemption reserve. For example, a payment of $100,000 to acquire shares with a nominal value of $20,000 would be recorded as:

	Dr	Cr
Share capital	$20,000	
Retained earnings	$80,000	
Cash		$100,000

being purchase of 20,000 $1 shares for $100,000 and their cancellation

	Dr	Cr
Retained earnings	$20,000	
Capital redemption reserve		$20,000

being the creation of capital redemption reserve to maintain capital.

Summary

Creditors of companies are not expected to be protected against ordinary business risks as these are taken care of by financial markets, e.g. through the rates of interest charged on different capital instruments of different companies. However, the creditors are entitled to depend on the non-erosion of the permanent capital unless their interests are considered and protected.

The chapter also discusses the question of capital reconstructions and the need to consider the effect of any proposed reconstruction on the rights of different parties.

REVIEW QUESTIONS

1 Discuss how the Companies Act 2006 defines distributable profits in the UK.

2 Why do companies reorganise their capital structure when they have accumulated losses?

3 What factors would a loan creditor take into account if asked to bear some of the accumulated loss?

4 Explain a debt/equity swap and the reasons for debt/equity swaps, and discuss the effect on existing shareholders and loan creditors.

5 The following relates to RWE AG:

> On April 22, 2009, the Annual General Meeting authorized us again to buy back shares. Hence, the Executive Board is entitled to acquire shares in the amount of up to 10% of the share capital until October 21, 2010.[5]

Explain why companies hold treasury shares.

EXERCISES

* Question 1

The draft statement of financial position of Telin plc at 30 September 20X5 was as follows:

	£000		£000
Ordinary shares of £1 each, fully paid	12,000	Product development costs	1,400
12% preference shares of £1 each, fully paid	8,000	Sundry assets	32,170
Share premium	4,000	Cash and bank	5,450
Retained (distributable) profits	4,600		
Payables	10,420		
	39,020		39,020

Preference shares of the company were originally issued at a premium of 2p per share. The directors of the company decided to redeem these shares at the end of October 20X5 at a premium of 5p per share. They also decided to write off the balances on development costs and discount on debentures (see below).

All write-offs and other transactions are to be entered into the accounts according to the provisions of the Companies Acts and in a manner financially advantageous to the company and to its shareholders.

The following transactions took place during October 20X5:

(a) On 4 October the company issued for cash 2,400,000 10% debentures of £1 each at a discount of $2\frac{1}{2}\%$.

(b) On 6 October the balances on development costs and discount of debentures were written off.

(c) On 12 October the company issued for cash 6,000,000 ordinary shares at a premium of 10p per share. This was a specific issue to help redeem preference shares.

(d) On 29 October the company redeemed the 12% preference shares at a premium of 5p per share and included in the payments to shareholders one month's dividend for October.

(e) On 30 October the company made a bonus issue, to all ordinary shareholders, of one fully paid ordinary share for every 20 shares held.

(f) During October the company made a net profit of £275,000 from its normal trading operations. This was reflected in the cash balance at the end of the month.

Required:
(a) Write up the ledger accounts of Telin plc to record the transactions for October 20X5.
(b) Prepare the company's statement of financial position as at 31 October 20X5.
(c) Briefly explain accounting entries which arise as a result of redemption of preference shares.

* Question 2

The following is the statement of financial position of Alpha Ltd as on 30 June 20X8:

	£000	£000	£000
	Cost	Accumulated depreciation	
Non-current assets			
Freehold property	46	5	41
Plant	85	6	79
	131	11	120
Investments			
Shares in subsidiary company		90	
Loans		40	130
Current assets			
Inventory		132	
Trade receivables		106	
		238	
Current liabilities			
Trade payables		282	
Bank overdraft		58	
		340	
Net current liabilities			(102)
Total assets less liabilities			148
Capital and reserves			
250,000 $8\frac{1}{2}\%$ cumulative redeemable preference shares of £1 each fully paid			250
100,000 ordinary shares of £1 each 75p paid			75
			325
Retained earnings			(177)
			148

The following information is relevant:

1 There are contingent liabilities in respect of (i) a guarantee given to bankers to cover a loan of £30,000 made to the subsidiary and (ii) uncalled capital of 10p per share on the holding of 100,000 shares of £1 each in the subsidiary.

2 The arrears of preference dividend amount to £106,250.

3 The following capital reconstruction scheme, to take effect as from 1 July 20X8, has been duly approved and authorised:

   (i)   the unpaid capital on the ordinary shares to be called up;

   (ii) the ordinary shares thereupon to be reduced to shares of 25p each fully paid up by cancelling 75p per share and then each fully paid share of 25p to be subdivided into five shares of 5p each fully paid;

   (iii) the holders to surrender three of such 5p shares out of every five held for reissue as set out below;

   (iv) the $8\frac{1}{2}$% cumulative preference shares together with all arrears of dividend to be surrendered and cancelled on the basis that the holder of every 50 preference shares will pay to Alpha a sum of £30 in cash, and will be issued with:

         (a) one £40 convertible $7\frac{3}{4}$% note of £40 each, and

         (b) 60 fully paid ordinary shares of 5p each (being a redistribution of shares surrendered by the ordinary shareholders and referred to in (iii) above);

   (v)   the unpaid capital on the shares in the subsidiary to be called up and paid by the parent company whose guarantee to the bank should be cancelled;

   (vi) the freehold property to be revalued at £55,000;

   (vii) the adverse balance on retained earnings to be written off, £55,000 to be written off the shares in the subsidiary and the sums made available by the scheme to be used to write down the plant.

Required:
(a) Prepare a capital reduction and reorganisation account.
(b) Prepare the statement of financial position of the company as it would appear immediately after completion of the scheme.

Question 3

A summary of the statement of financial position of Doxin plc, as at 31 December 20X0, is given below:

	£		£
800,000 ordinary shares of		Assets other than bank	
£1 each	800,000	(at book values)	1,500,000
300,000 6% preference			
shares of £1 each	300,000	Bank	200,000
General reserves	200,000		
Payables	400,000		
	1,700,000		1,700,000

During 20X1, the company:

(i) issued 200,000 ordinary shares of £1 each at a premium of 10p per share (a specific issue to redeem preference shares);

(ii) redeemed all preference shares at a premium of 5%. These were originally issued at 25% premium;

(iii) issued 4,000 7% debentures of £100 each at £90;

(iv) used share premium, if any, to issue fully paid bonus shares to members; and

(v) made a net loss of £500,000 by end of year which affected the bank account.

Required:

(a) Show the effect of each of the above items in the form of a moving statement of financial position (i.e. additions/deductions from original figures) and draft the statement of financial position of 31 December 20XI.

(b) Consider to what extent the interests of the creditors of the company are being protected.

Question 4

Discuss the advantages to a company of:

(a) purchasing and cancelling its own shares;

(b) purchasing and holding its own shares in treasury.

* Question 5

Speedster Ltd commenced trading in 1986 as a wholesaler of lightweight travel accessories. The company was efficient and traded successfully until 2000 when new competitors entered the market selling at lower prices which Speedster could not match. The company has gradually slipped into losses and the bank is no longer prepared to offer overdraft facilities. The directors are considering liquidating the company and have prepared the following statement of financial position and supporting information:

Statement of financial position	£000	£000
Non-current assets		
Freehold land at cost		1,500
Plant and equipment (NBV)		1,800
Current assets		
Inventories	600	
Trade receivables	1,200	
	1,800	
Current liabilities		
Payables	1,140	
Bank overdraft (secured on the plant and equipment)	1,320	
	2,460	
Net current assets		(660)
Non-current liabilities		
Secured loan (secured on the land)		(1,200)
		1,440
Financed by		
Ordinary shares of £1 each		3,000
Statement of comprehensive income		(1,560)
		1,440

Supporting information:

(i) The freehold land has a market value of £960,000 if it continues in use as a warehouse. There is a possibility that planning permission could be obtained for a change of use allowing the warehouse to be converted into apartments. If planning permission were to be obtained, the company has been advised that the land would have a market value of £2,500,000.

(ii) The net realisable values on liquidation of the other assets are:

Plant and equipment	£1,200,000
Inventory	£450,000
Trade receivables	£1,050,000

(iii) An analysis of the payables indicated that there would be £300,000 owing to preferential creditors for wages, salaries and taxes.

(iv) Liquidation costs were estimated at £200,000.

Required:
Prepare a statement showing the distribution on the basis that:
(a) planning permission was not obtained; and
(b) planning permission was obtained.

Question 6

Delta Ltd has been developing a lightweight automated wheelchair. The research costs written off have been far greater than originally estimated and the equity and preference capital has been eroded as seen on the statement of financial position.

The following is the statement of financial position of Delta Ltd as at 31.12.20X9:

	£000	£000
Intangible assets		
Development costs		300
Non-current assets		
Freehold property	800	
Plant, vehicles and equipment	650	1,450
		1,750
Current assets		
Inventory	480	
Trade receivables	590	
Investments	200	
	1,270	
Current liabilities		
Trade payables	(1,330)	
Bank overdraft	(490)	(550)
		1,200
10% debentures (secured on freehold premises)		(1,000)
Total assets less liabilities		200
Capital and reserves		
Ordinary shares of 50p each		800
7% cumulative preference shares of £1 each		500
Retained earnings (debit)		(1,100)
		200

The finance director has prepared the following information for consideration by the board.

1 Estimated current and liquidation values were estimated as follows:

	Current values £000	Liquidation values £000
Capitalised development costs	300	—
Freehold property	1,200	1,200
Plant and equipment	600	100
Inventory	480	300
Trade receivables	590	590
Investments	200	200
		2,390

2 If the company were to be liquidated there would be disposal costs of £100,000.

3 The preference dividend had not been paid for five years.

4 It is estimated that the company would make profits before interest over the next five years of £150,000 rising to £400,000 by the fifth year.

5 The directors have indicated that they would consider introducing further equity capital.

6 It was the finance director's opinion that for any scheme to succeed, it should satisfy the following conditions:

(a) The shareholders and creditors should have a better benefit in capital and income terms by reconstructing rather than liquidating the company.

(b) The scheme should have a reasonable possibility of ensuring the long-term survival of the company.

(c) There should be a reasonable assurance that there will be adequate working capital.

(d) Gearing should not be permitted to become excessive.

(e) If possible, the ordinary shareholders should retain control.

Required:
(a) **Advise the unsecured creditors of the minimum that they should accept if they were to agree to a reconstruction rather than proceed to press for the company to be liquidated.**
(b) **Propose a possible scheme for reconstruction.**
(c) **Prepare the statement of financial position of the company as it would appear immediately after completion of the scheme.**

References

1 The Companies Act 2006.
2 Ibid., para. 764.
3 Companies (Reduction of Share Capital) Order 2008.
4 The Companies Act 2006, paras 724–732.
5 http://www.rwe.com

CHAPTER 13

Liabilities

13.1 Introduction

In order for financial statements to show a true and fair view it is essential that reporting entities recognise all the liabilities that satisfy the *Framework* criteria, but **only** those liabilities that satisfy the criteria. Given that the recognition of a liability often involves a charge against profits, and the derecognition of a liability sometimes involves a credit to profits, there is the possibility that, unless this area of financial reporting is appropriately regulated, there is scope for manipulation of reporting profits when liabilities are recognised or derecognised inappropriately.

There are a number of financial reporting standards dealing with the recognition and measurement of specific liabilities that are dealt with elsewhere in this book:

- Financial liabilities (including, *inter alia*, trade payables and loans) are dealt with in IAS 39 *Financial Instruments: Recognition and Measurement* and, in the future, in IFRS 9 *Financial Instruments* (see Chapter 14).
- Pension liabilities are dealt with in IAS 19 *Employee Benefits* (see Chapter 15).
- Income tax liabilities are dealt with in IAS 12 *Income Taxes* (see Chapter 16).
- Lease liabilities are dealt with in IAS 17 *Leases* (see Chapter 18).

The above financial reporting standards deal with many types of liability but not with all liabilities. Examples of liabilities, or potential liabilities, not dealt with by the above financial reporting standards include:

- liabilities arising from legal disputes;
- liabilities arising due to corporate restructurings;
- environmental and decommissioning obligations;
- liabilities arising under contracts that have become onerous.

IAS 37 *Provisions, Contingent Liabilities and Contingent Assets* deals with the recognition, measurement and disclosure of these liabilities or potential liabilities.

Objectives

By the end of this chapter, you should be able to:

- account for provisions, contingent liabilities and contingent assets under IAS 37;
- explain the potential change the IASB is considering in relation to provisions.

13.2 Provisions – a decision tree approach to their impact on the statement of financial position

The IASC (now the IASB) approved IAS 37 *Provisions, Contingent Liabilities and Contingent Assets*[1] in July 1998. The key objective of IAS 37 is to ensure that appropriate recognition criteria and measurement bases are applied and that sufficient information is disclosed in the notes to enable users to understand their nature, timing and amount.

The IAS sets out a useful **decision tree**, shown in Figure 13.1, for determining whether an event requires the creation of a provision, the disclosure of a contingent liability or no action.

Figure 13.1 Decision tree

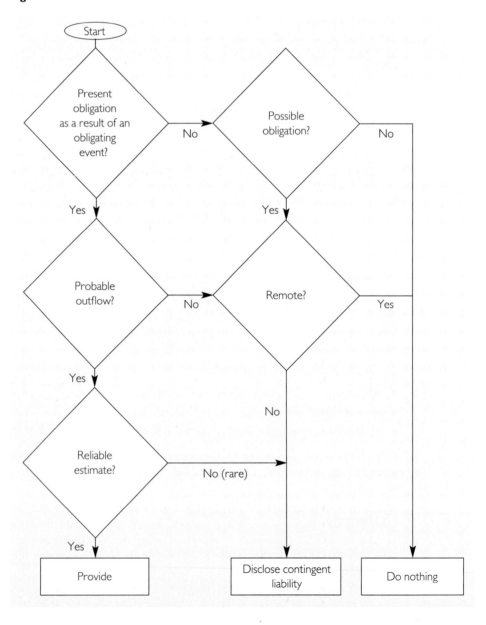

In June 2005 the IASB issued an exposure draft, IAS 37 *Non-Financial Liabilities*, to revise IAS 37. A further exposure draft clarifying the proposed amendments was issued in January 2010. However, the current IASB timetable does not envisage a new accounting standard on liabilities very soon. We will now consider the current IAS 37 treatment of provisions, contingent liabilities and contingent assets.

13.3 Treatment of provisions

IAS 37 is mainly concerned with provisions and the distorting effect they can have on profit trends, income and capital gearing. It defines a provision as 'a liability of uncertain timing or amount'.

In particular it targets 'big-bath' provisions that companies historically have been able to make. This is a type of creative accounting that it has been tempting for directors to make in order to smooth profits without any reasonable certainty that the provision would actually be required in subsequent periods. Sir David Tweedie, the chairman of the IASB, has said:

> A main focus [of IAS 37] is 'big-bath' provisions. Those who use them sometimes pray in aid of the concept of prudence. All too often however the provision is wildly excessive and conveniently finds its way back to the statement of comprehensive income in a later period. The misleading practice needed to be stopped and [IAS 37] proposed that in future provisions should only be allowed when the company has an unavoidable obligation – an **intention** which may or may not be fulfilled will **not be enough**. Users of accounts can't be expected to be mind readers.

13.4 The general principles that IAS 37 applies to the recognition of a provision

The general principles are that a provision should be recognised when:[2]

(a) an entity has a present obligation (legal or constructive) as a result of past events;

(b) it is probable that a transfer of economic benefits will be required to settle the obligation;

(c) a reliable estimate can be made of the amount of the obligation.

Provisions by their nature relate to the future. This means that there is a need for estimation, and IAS 37 comments[3] that the use of estimates is an essential part of the preparation of financial statements and does not undermine their reliability. The IAS addresses the uncertainties arising in respect of present obligation, past event, probable transfer of economic benefits and reliable estimates when deciding whether to recognise a provision.

Present obligation

Provisions can arise under law or because the entity has created an expectation due to its past actions that it cannot realistically avoid.

The test to be applied is whether it is more likely than not, i.e. has more than a 50% chance of occurring. For example, if involved in a disputed lawsuit, the company is required to take account of all available evidence including that of experts and of events after the reporting period to decide if there is a greater than 50% chance that the lawsuit will be decided against the company.

Where it is more likely that no present obligation exists at the period-end date, the company discloses a contingent liability, unless the possibility of a transfer of economic resources is remote.

Past event[4]

A past event that leads to a present obligation is called an **obligating event**. This is a new term with which to become familiar. This means that the company has no realistic alternative to settling the obligation. The IAS defines no alternative as being only where the settlement of the obligation can be enforced by law or, in the case of a constructive obligation, where the event creates valid expectations in other parties that the company will discharge the obligation.

The IAS stresses that it is only those obligations arising from past events existing independently of a company's future actions that are recognised as provisions, e.g. clean-up costs for unlawful environmental damage that has occurred require a provision; environmental damage that is not unlawful but is likely to become so and involve clean-up costs will not be provided for until legislation is virtually certain to be enacted as drafted.

Probable transfer of economic benefits[5]

The IAS defines probable as meaning that the event is more likely than not to occur. Where it is not probable, the company discloses a contingent liability unless the possibility is remote.

13.5 Management approach to measuring the amount of a provision

IAS 37 states[6] that the amount recognised as a provision should be the *best estimate* of the expenditure required to settle the present obligation at the period-end date.

Best estimate is defined as the amount that a company would rationally pay to settle the obligation or to transfer it to a third party. The estimates of outcome and financial effect are determined by the judgement of management supplemented by experience of similar transactions and reports from independent experts. Management deal with the uncertainties as to the amount to be provided in a number of ways:

- A class obligation exists:
  - where the provision involves a large population of items as with a warranty provision, statistical analysis of expected values should be used to determine the amount of the provision.
- A single obligation exists but a number of outcomes may be possible:
  - where a single obligation is measured, the individual most likely outcome may be the best estimate;
  - more than one outcome exists or the outcome is anywhere within a range; or
  - expected values may be most appropriate.

For example, a company had been using unlicensed parts in the manufacture of its products and, at the year-end, no decision had been reached by the court. The plaintiff was seeking damages of $10 million.

In the draft accounts a provision had been made of $5.85 million using expected values. This had been based on the estimate by the entity's lawyers that there was a 20% chance that the plaintiff would be unsuccessful and a 25% chance that the entity would be required to pay $10 million and a 55% chance of $7 million becoming payable to the plaintiff. The provision had been calculated as 25% of $0 + 55% of $7 million + 20% of $10 million.

The finance director, however, disagreed with this on the grounds that it was a single obligation and more likely than not there would be an outflow of funds of $7 million, and required an additional $1.15 million to be provided.

Avoiding once of excessive provisions

Avoiding once of excessive provisions

Management must avoid creating excessive provisions based on a prudent view. Uncertainty does not justify the creation of excessive provisions.[7] If the projected costs of a particular adverse outcome are estimated on a prudent basis, that outcome should not then be deliberately treated as more probable than is realistically the case.

The measurement requirements of the current IAS 37 are somewhat imprecise and can be interpreted in more than one way. One of the objectives of the proposed amendment to IAS 37 is to remove the imprecision in the current standard. We will discuss the amendments proposed in this exposure draft in Section 13.10.

Approach when time value of money is material

The IAS states[8] that 'where the effect of the time value of money is material, the amount of a provision should be the present value of the expenditures expected to be required to settle the obligation'.

Present value is arrived at by discounting the future obligation at 'a pre-tax rate (or rates) that reflect(s) current market assessments of the time value of money and the risks specific to the liability. The discount rate(s) should not reflect risks for which future cash flow estimates have been adjusted.'

If provisions are recognised at present value, a company will have to account for the unwinding of the discounting. As a simple example, assume a company is making a provision at 31 December 2010 for an expected cash outflow of €1 million on 31 December 2012. The relevant discount factor is estimated at 10%. Assume the estimated cash flows do not change and the provision is still required at 31 December 2011.

	€000
Provision recognised at 31 December 2010 (€1m × 1/1.121)	826
Provision recognised at 31 December 2011 (€1m × 1/1.1)	909
Increase in the provision	83

This increase in the provision is purely due to discounting for one year in 2011 as opposed to two years in 2010. This increase in the provision must be recognised as an expense in profit or loss, usually as a finance cost, although IAS 37 does not make this mandatory.

The following is an extract from the Minefinders Corporation Ltd 2011 Annual Report:

> A provision for site closure and reclamation is recorded when the Company incurs liability for costs associated with the eventual retirement of tangible long-lived assets (for example, reclamation costs). The liability for such costs exists from the time the legal or constructive obligation first arises, not when the actual expenditures are made.
>
> Such obligations are based on estimated future cash flows discounted at a rate specific to the liability. . . . The amount added to the asset is amortized in the same manner as the asset.
>
> The liability is increased in each accounting period by the amount of the implied interest inherent in the use of discounted present value methodology. . . .

13.6 Application of criteria illustrated

Scenario 1

An offshore oil exploration company is required by its licence to remove the rig and restore the seabed. Management have estimated that 85% of the eventual cost will be incurred in removing the rig and 15% through the extraction of oil. The company's practice on similar projects has been to account for the decommissioning costs using the 'unit of production' method whereby the amount required for decommissioning was built up year by year, in line with production levels, to reach the amount of the expected costs by the time production ceased.

Decision process

1 **Is there a present obligation as a result of a past event?**
   The construction of the rig has created a legal obligation under the licence to remove the rig and restore the seabed.

2 **Is there a probable transfer of economic benefits?**
   This is probable.

3 **Can the amount of the outflow be reasonably estimated?**
   A best estimate can be made by management based on past experience and expert advice.

4 **Conclusion**
   A provision should be created of 85% of the eventual future costs of removal and restoration. This provision should be discounted if the effect of the time value of money is material.
   A provision for the 15% relating to restoration should be created when oil production commences.

The unit of production method is not acceptable in that the decommissioning costs relate to damage already done.

Scenario 2

A company has a private jet costing £24 million. Air regulations required it to be overhauled every four years. An overhaul costs £1.6 million. The company policy has been to create a provision for depreciation of £2 million on a straight-line basis over 12 years and an annual provision of £400,000 to meet the cost of the required overhaul every four years.

Decision process

1 **Is there a present obligation as a result of a past obligating event?**
   There is no present obligation. The company could avoid the cost of the overhaul by, for example, selling the aircraft.

2 **Conclusion**
   No provision for cost of overhaul can be recognised. Instead of a provision being recognised, the depreciation of the aircraft takes account of the future incidence of maintenance costs, i.e. an amount equivalent to the expected maintenance costs is depreciated over four years.

13.7 Provisions for specific purposes

Specific purposes could include considering the treatment of future operating losses, onerous contracts, restructuring and environmental liabilities. Let us consider each of these.

13.7.1 A provision for future operating losses

Such losses should not be recognised if there is no obligation at the reporting date on the basis that the entity could decide to discontinue that particular business activity. However, if it is contractually unable to discontinue then it classifies the contract as an onerous contract and makes provision.

13.7.2 Onerous contracts

A provision should be recognised if there is an onerous contract. An onerous contract is one entered into with another party under which the unavoidable costs of fulfilling the contract exceed the revenues to be received and where the entity would have to pay compensation to the other party if the contract was not fulfilled. A typical example in times of recession is the requirement to make a payment to secure the early termination of a lease where it has been impossible to sub-let the premises. This situation could arise where there has been a downturn in business and an entity seeks to reduce its annual lease payments on premises that are no longer required.

The following is an extract from the 2011 Preliminary Results of the Spirit Pub Company plc:

Onerous lease provisions

The Group provides for its onerous obligations under operating leases where the property is closed or vacant and for properties where rental expense is in excess of income. The estimated timings and amounts of cash flows are determined using the experience of internal and external property experts; however, any changes to the estimated method of exiting from the property could lead to changes to the level of the provision recorded.

13.7.3 Restructuring provisions

- **A provision for restructuring** should only be recognised when there is a commitment supported by:

  (a) a detailed formal plan for the restructuring identifying at least:

    (i) the business or part of the business concerned;

    (ii) the principal locations affected;

    (iii) details of the approximate number of employees who will receive compensation payments;

    (iv) the expenditure that will be undertaken; and

    (v) when the plan will be implemented; and

  (b) a valid expectation in those affected that the business will carry out the restructuring by implementing its restructuring plans or announcing its main features to those affected by it.

- **A provision for restructuring should not be created merely on the intention to restructure**. For example, a management or board decision to restructure taken before the reporting date does not give rise to a constructive obligation at the reporting date unless the company has, before the reporting date:

  – started to implement the restructuring plan, e.g. by dismantling plant or selling assets; or

  – announced the main features of the plan with sufficient detail to raise the valid expectation of those affected that the restructuring will actually take place.

- **A provision for restructuring** should only include the direct expenditures arising from the restructuring which are necessarily entailed and not associated with the ongoing activities of the company. For example, redundancy costs would be included, but note that the following costs which relate to the future conduct of the business are not included: retraining costs, relocation costs, marketing costs, and investment in new systems and distribution networks.

13.7.4 Environmental liabilities and decommissioning costs

- **A provision for environmental liabilities** should be recognised at the time and to the extent that the entity becomes obliged, legally or constructively, to rectify environmental damage or to perform restorative work on the environment. This means that a provision should be set up only for the entity's costs to meet its *legal* or *constructive* obligations. It could be argued that any provision for any additional expenditure on environmental issues is a public relations decision and should be written off.

- **A provision for decommissioning costs** should be recognised to the extent that decommissioning costs relate to damage already done or goods and services already received.

Provisions for decommissioning costs often relate to non-current assets, e.g. power stations. Where a liability for decommissioning exists at the date of construction, it is recognised, normally at the present value of the expected future outflow of cash, and added to the cost of the non-current asset.

EXAMPLE ● An entity constructs a nuclear power station at a cost of €20 million. The estimated useful life of the power station is 25 years. The entity has a legal obligation to decommission the power station at the end of its useful life and the estimated costs of this are €15 million in 25 years' time. A relevant annual discount factor is 5% and the present value of a payment of €15 million in 25 years' time is approximately €4.43 million.

In these circumstances a liability of €4.43 million is recognised at the completion of the construction of the facility. The debit side of this accounting entry is to property, plant and equipment, giving a total carrying amount for the power station of €24.43 million. This amount is then depreciated over 25 years which gives an annual charge (assuming straight-line depreciation with no residual value) of approximately €977,200.

The discounting of the liability is 'unwound' over the 25-year life of the power station, the annual unwinding being shown as a finance cost. The unwinding in the first year of operation is approximately €221,500 (€4.43 million × 5%).

13.7.5 Disclosures required by IAS 37 for provisions

Specific disclosures,[9] for each material class of provision, should be given as to the amount recognised at the year-end and about any movements in the year, e.g.:

- **Increases in provisions** – any new provisions; any increases to existing provisions; and, where provisions are carried at present value, any change in value arising from the passage of time or from any movement in the discount rate.

- **Reductions in provisions** – any amounts utilised during the period. Management are required to review provisions at each reporting date and adjust to reflect the current best estimates. If it is no longer probable that a transfer of economic benefits will be required to settle the obligation, the provision should be reversed. Note, however, that only expenditure that relates to the original provision may be set against that provision.

Disclosures need not be given in cases where to do so would be seriously prejudicial to the company's interests. For example, an extract from the Technotrans 2002 Annual Report states:

> A competitor filed patent proceedings in 2000, . . . the court found in favour of the plaintiff . . . paves the way for a claim for compensation which may have to be determined in further legal proceedings . . . the particulars pursuant to IAS 37.85 are not disclosed, in accordance with IAS 37.92, in order not to undermine the company's situation substantially in the ongoing legal dispute.

13.8 Contingent liabilities

IAS 37 deals with provisions and contingent liabilities within the same IAS because the IASB regarded all provisions as contingent as they are uncertain in timing and amount. For the purposes of the accounts, it distinguishes between provisions and contingent liabilities in that:

- Provisions are a present obligation requiring a probable transfer of economic benefits that can be reliably estimated – a provision can therefore be recognised as a liability.
- Contingent liabilities fail to satisfy these criteria, e.g. lack of a reliable estimate of the amount; not probable that there will be a transfer of economic benefits; yet to be confirmed that there is actually an obligation. A contingent liability cannot therefore be recognised in the accounts but may be disclosed by way of note to the accounts or not disclosed if an outflow of economic benefits is remote.

Where the occurrence of a contingent liability becomes sufficiently probable, it falls within the criteria for recognition as a provision as detailed above and should be accounted for accordingly and recognised as a liability in the accounts.

Where the likelihood of a contingent liability is possible but not probable and not remote, disclosure should be made, for each class of contingent liability, where practicable, of:

(a) an estimate of its financial effect, taking into account the inherent risks and uncertainties and, where material, the time value of money;

(b) an indication of the uncertainties relating to the amount or timing of any outflow; and

(c) the possibility of any reimbursement.

For example, an extract from the 2011 Annual Report of the Nottingham Forest Football Club Ltd informs us that:

> Additional transfer fees amounting to £1,075,000 (2010: £1,470,000) in total will become payable to their previous clubs if certain players make an agreed number of international appearances, first team appearances or the club achieves defined feats. Signing on fees of £306,000 (2010: £451,000) will become due to certain players if they are still in the service of Nottingham Forest Football Club Limited on specific future dates.

13.9 Contingent assets

A contingent asset is a possible asset that arises from past events whose existence will be confirmed only by the occurrence of one or more uncertain future events not wholly within the entity's control.

Recognition as an asset is only allowed if the asset is *virtually certain*, and therefore by definition no longer contingent.

Disclosure by way of note is required if an inflow of economic benefits is *probable*. The disclosure would include a brief description of the nature of the contingent assets at the reporting date and, where practicable, an estimate of their financial effect taking into account the inherent risks and uncertainties and, where material, the time value of money.

No disclosure is required where the chance of occurrence is anything less than probable. For the purposes of IAS 37, probable is defined as more likely than not, i.e. with more than a 50% chance.

13.10 ED IAS 37 *Non-financial Liabilities*

In June 2005, the International Accounting Standards Board (IASB) proposed amendments to IAS 37 *Provisions, Contingent Liabilities and Contingent Assets*. These strip IAS 37 of the words 'Provisions', 'Contingent' and 'Assets' and add the term 'Non-financial' to create the new title IAS 37 *Non-financial Liabilities*.[10] It is interesting to see that the new standard has been developed around the *Framework*'s definitions of an asset and a liability.

It appears that the word 'non-financial' has been added to distinguish the subject from 'financial liabilities' which are covered by IAS 32 and IAS 39. It should be noted that whilst the exposure draft remains in issue a new standard based on these proposals is not in the current IASB workplan.

13.10.1 The 'old' IAS 37 *Provisions, Contingent Liabilities and Contingent Assets*

To understand the 'new' approach in ED IAS 37 *Non-financial Liabilities*, it is necessary first to look at the 'old' IAS 37. The old treatment can be represented by the following table:

Probability	*Contingent liabilities*	*Contingent assets*
Virtually certain	Liability	Asset
Probable ($p > 50\%$)	Provide	Disclose
Possible ($p < 50\%$)	Disclose	No disclosure
Remote	No disclosure	No disclosure

Note that contingent liabilities are those items where the probability is less than 50% ($p < 50\%$). Where, however, the liability is probable, i.e. the probability is $p > 50\%$, the item is classified as a provision and not a contingent liability. Normally, such a provision will be reported as the product of the value of the potential liability and its probability.

Note that the approach to contingent assets is different in that the 'prudence' concept is used which means that only virtually certain assets are reported as assets. If the probability is probable, i.e. $p > 50\%$, then contingent assets are disclosed by way of a note to the accounts, and if the probability is $p < 50\%$ then there is no disclosure.

Criticisms of the 'old' IAS 37

The criticisms included the following:

- The 'old' IAS 37 was not even-handed in its treatment of contingent assets and liabilities. In ED IAS 37 the treatment of contingent assets is similar to that of contingent liabilities, and provisions are merged into the treatment of contingent liabilities.

- The division between 'probable' and 'possible' was too strict or crude (at the $p = 50\%$ level) rather than being proportional. For instance, if a television manufacturer was considering the need to provide for guarantee claims (e.g. on televisions sold with a three-year warranty), then it is probable that each television sold would have a less than 50% chance of being subject to a warranty claim and so no provision would need to be made. However, if the company sold 10,000 televisions, it is almost certain that there would be some claims which would indicate that a provison should be made. A company could validly take either treatment, but the effect on the financial statements would be different.

- If there was a single possible legal claim, then the company could decide it was 'possible' and just disclose it in the financial statements. However, a more reasonable treatment would be to assess the claim as the product of the amount likely to be paid and its probability. This latter treatment is used in the new ED IAS 37.

13.10.2 Approach taken by ED IAS 37 Non-financial Liabilities

The new proposed standard uses the term 'non-financial liabilities' which it defines as 'a liability other than a financial liability as defined in IAS32 *Financial Instruments: Presentation*'. In considering ED IAS 37, we will look at the proposed treatment of contingent liabilities/ provisions and contingent assets, starting from the *Framework*'s definitions of a liability and an asset.

The *Framework*'s definition

The *Framework*, paragraph 91, requires a liability to be recognised as follows:

> A liability is recognised in the statement of financial position when it is probable that an outflow of resources embodying economic benefits will result from the settlement of a present obligation and the amount at which the settlement will take place can be measured reliably.

The ED IAS 37 approach to provisions

Considering a provision first, the old IAS 37 (paragraph 10) defines it as follows:

> A provision is distinguished from other liabilities because there is uncertainty about the timing or amount of the future expenditure required in settlement.

ED IAS 37 argues that a provision should be reported as a liability, as it satisfies the *Framework*'s definition of a liability. It makes the point that there is no reference in the *Framework* to 'uncertainty about the timing or amount of the future expenditure required in settlement'. It considers a provision to be just one form of liability which should be treated as a liability in the financial statements.

Will the item 'provision' no longer appear in financial statements?

One would expect that to be the result of the ED classification. However, the proposed standard does not take the step of prohibiting the use of the term, as seen in the following extract (paragraph 9):

> In some jurisdictions, some classes of liabilities are described as provisions, for example those liabilities that can be measured only by using a substantial degree of estimation. Although this [draft] Standard does not use the term 'provision', it does not prescribe how entities should describe their non-financial liabilities. Therefore, entities may describe some classes of non-financial liabilities as provisions in their financial statements.

The ED IAS 37 approach to contingent liabilities

Now considering contingent liabilities, the old IAS 37 (paragraph 10) defines these as:

(a) a possible obligation that arises from past events and whose existence will be confirmed only by the occurrence or non-occurrence of one or more uncertain future events not wholly within the control of the entity; or

(b) a present obligation that arises from past events, but is not recognised because:

  (i) it is not probable that an outflow of resources embodying economic benefits will be required to settle the obligation; or

  (ii) the amount of the obligation cannot be measured with sufficient reliability.

This definition means that the old IAS 37 has taken the strict approach of using the term 'possible' ($p < 50\%$) when it required no liability to be recognised.

ED IAS 37 is different in that it takes a two-stage approach in considering whether 'contingent liabilities' are 'liabilities'. To illustrate this, we will take the example of a restaurant where some customers have suffered food poisoning.

First determine whether there is a present obligation

The restaurant's year-end is 30 June 20X6. If the food poisoning took place after 30 June 20X6, then this is not a 'present obligation' at the year-end, so it is not a liability. If the food poisoning occurred up to 30 June, then it is a 'present obligation' at the year-end, as there are possible future costs arising from the food poisoning. This is the first stage in considering whether the liability exists.

Then determine whether a liability exists

The second stage is to consider whether a 'liability' exists. The *Framework*'s definition of a liability says it is a liability if 'it is probable that an outflow of resources will result from the settlement of the present obligation'. So, there is a need to consider whether any payments (or other expenses) will be incurred as a result of the food poisoning. This may involve settling legal claims, other compensation or giving 'free' meals. The estimated cost of these items will be the liability (and expense) included in the financial statements.

The rationale

ED IAS 37 explains this process as:

- the unconditional obligation (stage 1) establishes the liability; and
- the conditional obligation (stage 2) affects the amount that will be required to settle the liability.

The liability is the amount that the entity would rationally pay to settle the present obligation or to transfer it to a third party on the statement of financial position date. Often, the liability will be estimated as the product of the maximum liability and the probability of it occurring, or a decision tree will be used with a number of possible outcomes (costs) and their probability.

In many cases, the new ED IAS 37 will cover the 'possible' category for contingent liabilities and include the item as a liability (rather than as a note to the financial statements). This gives a more 'proportional' result than the previously strict line between 'probable' ($p > 50\%$) (when a liability is included in the financial statements) and 'possible' ($p < 50\%$) (when only a note is included in the financial statements and no charge is included for the liability).

What if they cannot be measured reliably?

For other 'possible' contingent liabilities, which have not been recognised because they cannot be measured reliably, the following disclosure should be made:

- a description of the nature of the obligation;
- an explanation of why it cannot be measured reliably;
- an indication of the uncertainties relating to the amount or timing of any outflow of economic benefits; and
- the existence of any rights to reimbursement.

What disclosure is required for maximum potential liability?

ED IAS 37 does not require disclosure of the maximum potential liability, e.g. the maximum damages if the entity loses the legal case.

13.10.3 Measured reliably

The *Framework*'s definition of a liability includes the condition 'and the amount at which the settlement will take place can be measured reliably'. This posed a problem when drafting ED IAS 37 because of the concern that an entity could argue that the amount of a contingent liability could not be measured reliably and that there was therefore no need to include it as a liability in the financial statements – i.e. to use this as a 'cop out' to give a 'rosier' picture in the financial statements. Whilst acknowledging that in many cases a non-financial liability cannot be measured exactly, it considered that it could (and should) be estimated. It then says that cases where the liability cannot be measured reliably are 'extremely rare'. We can see from this that the ED approach is that 'measured reliably' does not mean 'measured exactly' and that cases where the liability 'cannot be measured reliably' will be 'extremely rare'.

13.10.4 Contingent asset

The *Framework*, paragraph 89, requires recognition of an asset as follows:

> An Asset is recognised in the statement of financial position when it is probable that the future economic benefits will flow to the entity and the asset has a cost or value that can be measured reliably.

Note that under the old IAS 37, contingent assets included items where they were 'probable' (unlike liabilities, when this was called a 'provision'). However, probable contingent assets are not included as assets but only included in the notes to the financial statements.

The ED IAS 37 approach

ED IAS 37 takes a similar approach to 'contingent assets' as it does to 'provisions/contingent liabilities'. It abolishes the term 'contingent asset' and replaces it with the term 'contingency'. The term contingency refers to uncertainty about the amount of the future economic benefits embodied in an asset, rather than uncertainty about whether an asset exists.

Essentially, the treatment of contingent assets is the same as that of contingent liabilities. The first stage is to consider whether an asset exists and the second stage is concerned with valuing the asset (i.e. the product of the value of the asset and its probability). A major change is to move contingent assets to IAS 38 *Intangible Assets* (and not include them in IAS 37).

The treatment of 'contingent assets' under IAS 38 is now similar to that for 'contingent liabilities/provisions'. This seems more appropriate than the former 'prudent approach' used by the old IAS 37.

13.10.5 Reimbursements

Under the old IAS 37 an asset could be damaged or destroyed, when the expense would be included in profit or loss (and any future costs included as a provision). If the insurance claim relating to this loss was made after the year-end, it is likely that no asset could be included in the financial statements as compensation for the loss, as the insurance claim was 'not virtually certain'. In reality, this did not reflect the true situation when the insurance claim would compensate for the loss, and there would be little or no net cost.

With the new rules under ED IAS 37, the treatment of contingent assets and contingent liabilities is the same, so an asset would be included in the statement of financial position as the insurance claim, which would offset the loss on damage or destruction of the asset. The ED position is that an asset exists because there is an unconditional right to reimbursement – the only uncertainty is to the amount that will be received. But ED IAS 37 says the liability relating to the loss (e.g. the costs of repair) must be stated separately from the asset for the reimbursement (i.e. the insurance claim) – they cannot be netted off (although they will be in profit or loss).

13.10.6 Constructive and legal obligations

The term 'constructive obligation' is important in determining whether a liability exists. ED IAS 37 (paragraph 10) defines it as follows:

> A constructive obligation is a present obligation that arises from an entity's past actions when:
>
> (a) by an established pattern of past practice, published policies or a sufficiently specific current statement, the entity has indicated to other parties that it will accept particular responsibilities, and
>
> (b) as a result, the entity has created a valid expectation in those parties, that they can **reasonably rely on it** to discharge those responsibilities.

It also defines a legal obligation as follows:

> A legal obligation is a present obligation that arises from the following:
>
> (a) a contract (through its explicit or implicit terms)
>
> (b) legislation, or
>
> (c) other operating law.

A contingent liability/provision is a liability only if it is either a constructive and/or a legal obligation. Thus, an entity would not normally make a provision (recognise a liability) for the potential costs of rectifying faulty products outside their guarantee period.

13.10.7 Present value

ED IAS 37 says that future cash flows relating to the liability should be discounted at the pre-tax discount rate. Unwinding of the discount would still need to be recognised as an interest cost.

13.10.8 Subsequent measurement and derecognition

On subsequent measurement, ED IAS 37 says the carrying value of the non-financial liability should be reviewed at each reporting date. The non-financial liability should be derecognised when the obligation is settled, cancelled or expires.

13.10.9 Onerous contracts

If a contract becomes onerous, the entity is required to recognise a liability as the present obligation under the contract. However, if the contract becomes onerous as a result of the entity's own actions, the liability should not be recognised until it has taken the action. For example, let us assume that an entity has a non-cancellable 10-year lease on a warehouse and decides during year 7 to vacate the property. Under the old IAS 37 the present obligation arises when the entity communicates this to the lessor, whereas under ED IAS 37 the present obligation does not arise until the property is actually vacated. The contract is still onerous but there may be a later recognition.

13.10.10 Restructurings

ED IAS 37 says:

An entity shall recognise a non-financial liability for a cost associated with a restructuring only when the definition of a liability has been satisfied.

There are situations where management has made a decision to restructure and the ED provides that in these cases a decision by the management of an entity to undertake a restructuring is not the requisite past event for recognition of a liability. The ED position is that an announcement is insufficient, even if there is a detailed plan, if the entity continues to be able to modify the plan. A cost associated with a restructuring is recognised as a liability on the same basis as if that cost arose independently of the restructuring. This change would, if implemented, align IAS 37 with the equivalent US standard in this area.

13.10.11 Other items

These include the treatment of termination costs and future operating losses where the approach is still to assess whether a liability exists. The changes to termination costs will require an amendment to IAS 19 *Employee Benefits*. In the case of termination costs, these are only recognised when a liability is incurred: e.g. the costs of closure of a factory become a liability only when the expense is incurred, and redundancy costs become a liability only when employees are informed of their redundancy. In the case of future operating losses, these are not recognised as they do not relate to a past event.

Under the new ED IAS 37, the liability arises no earlier than under the old IAS 37 and sometimes later.

13.10.12 Disclosure

ED IAS 37 requires the following disclosure of non-financial liabilities:

For each class of non-financial liability, the carrying amount of the liability at the period-end together with a description of the nature of the obligation.

For any class of non-financial liability with uncertainty about its estimation:

(a) a reconciliation of the carrying amounts at the beginning and end of the period showing:

  (i) liabilities incurred;

  (ii) liabilities derecognised;

  (iii) changes in the discounted amount resulting from the passage of time and the effect of any change in the discount rate; and

  (iv) other adjustments to the amount of the liability (e.g. revisions in the estimated cash flows that will be required to settle it);

(b) the expected timing of any resulting outflows of economic benefits;

(c) an indication of the uncertainties about the amount or timing of those outflows. If necessary, to provide adequate information on the major assumptions made about future events;

(d) the amount of any right to reimbursement, stating the amount of any asset that has been recognised.

If a non-financial liability is not recognised because it cannot be measured reliably, that fact should be disclosed together with:

(a) a description of the nature of the obligation;

(b) an explanation of why it cannot be measured reliably;

(c) an indication of the uncertainties relating to the amount or timing of any outflow of economic benefits; and

(d) the existence of any right to reimbursement.

13.10.13 Conclusion on ED IAS 37 *Non-financial Liabilities*

This proposed standard makes significant changes to the subject of 'Provisions, Contingent Liabilities and Contingent Assets', which are derived from the general principles of accounting. Its good features include:

(a) It is conceptually sound by basing changes on the *Framework*'s definitions of an asset and a liability.

(b) It is more appropriate that the treatment of provisions/contingent liabilities and contingent assets should be more 'even-handed'.

(c) It avoids the 'strict' breaks at 50% probability between 'probable' and 'possible'. It uses probability in estimating the liability down (effectively) to 0%.

(d) The definition of a constructive obligation has been more clearly defined.

(e) It overcomes the previous anomaly of not allowing reimbursements after the year-end (e.g. where there is an unsettled insurance claim at the year-end).

However, in some ways it could be argued that the proposed standard goes too far, particularly in its new terminology:

(a) The abolition of the term 'contingent liability' and not defining 'provision'. The new term 'non-financial liability' does not seem as meaningful as 'contingent liability'. It would seem better (more meaningful) to continue to use the term 'contingent liability' and make this encompass provisions (as it does for contingent assets).

(b) It would seem more appropriate to continue to include 'contingent assets' in this standard, rather than move them to 'intangible assets', as the treatment of these items is similar to that of 'contingent liabilities'.

ED IAS 37 has proved to be a controversial exposure draft where there have been significant discussions surrounding the potential changes. In addition this project could be influenced by other projects that the IASB has in development, such as on leasing and revenue recognition.

13.11 ED/2010/1 *Measurement of Liabilities in IAS 37*[11]

This ED is a limited re-exposure of a proposed amendment to IAS 37. It deals with only one of the measurement requirements for liabilities. The ED proposes that the non-financial liability should be measured at the amount that the entity would rationally pay to be relieved of the liability.

If the liability cannot be cancelled or transferred, the liability is measured as the present value of the resources required to fulfil the obligation. It may be that the resources required are uncertain. If so, the expected value is estimated based on the probability-weighted average of the outflows. The expected value is then increased to take into account the risk that the actual outcome might be higher, estimating the amount a third party would require to take over this risk. Where there is an obligation to undertake a service at a future date such as decommissioning plant and there is no market for such a service, it is proposed that the amount of any provision should be the cost that the entity would itself charge another party to carry out the work, including a profit margin.

If the liability can be cancelled or transferred, there is a choice available – to fulfil the obligation, to cancel the obligation or to transfer the liability. The logical choice is to choose the lower of the present value of fulfilling the obligation and the amount that would have to be paid to either cancel or transfer.

Potential impact on ratios and transparency

A new standard that applies this measurement approach will not have an identical impact on all entities – some will have to include higher non-financial liabilities on their statement of financial position, others will have to reduce the non-financial liabilities. This means that there will be different impacts on returns on equity, gearing and debt covenants.

Given the process of establishing expected values and risk adjustments, it might be that additional narrative explanation will be required in the annual report, particularly if the non-financial liabilities are material.

Summary

The *Framework* defines a liability as a present obligation arising from a past event, the settlement of which is expected to result in an outflow from the entity of economic resources. The treatment of provisions has been the subject of an ED IAS 37 which considers that a provision should be reported as a liability.

The chapter considers the approach to be taken when accounting for a variety of scenarios including the treatment of onerous contracts, future operating losses, restructuring and environmental liabilities and decommissioning costs.

REVIEW QUESTIONS

1 The Notes in the BG Group 2011 Annual Report included the following extract:

Provisions for liabilities

Decommissioning

	2011	2010
	£m	£m
As at 1 January	1,424	1,154
Unwinding of discount	57	49

Decommissioning costs

The estimated cost of decommissioning at the end of the producing lives of fields is reviewed at least annually and engineering estimates and reports are updated periodically. Provision is made for the estimated cost of decommissioning at the statement of financial position date, to the extent that current circumstances indicate BG Group will ultimately bear this cost.

Explain why the provision has been increased in 2010 and 2011 by the unwinding of discount and why these increases are for different amounts.

2 Mining, nuclear and oil companies historically provided an amount each year over the life of an enterprise to provide for decommissioning costs. Explain why the IASB considered this to be an inappropriate treatment and how these companies would be affected by IAS 37 *Provisions, Contingent Liabilities and Contingent Assets* and ED IAS 37 *Non-financial Liabilities*.

3 The following note appeared in the Amey plc 2011 Annual Report:

> The onerous lease provision is in respect of property leases and is expected to be utilised over the remaining lease terms.

Discuss the criteria for assessing whether a provision may be created in these circumstances under both IAS 37 and ED IAS 37 and explain what is meant by 'utilised'. Discuss the criteria for assessing whether a contract is onerous.

4 One of the reasons why the IASB considered in their EDs an amendment to IAS 37 is that the criteria within that standard for the recognition of provisions are allegedly inconsistent with those in other international financial reporting standards. Discuss the extent to which you believe this statement to be true, and the improvements proposed in the 2005 and 2010 exposure drafts.

5 Given the uncertainty inherent in the recognition of provisions or contingent liabilities, financial statements would be much more reliable if the existence of potential liabilities were disclosed, rather than being recognised under conditions of potential uncertainty. Discuss this statement.

6 The current version of IAS 37 requires the recognition of a restructuring provision at the earlier of the commencement of the restructuring and its public announcement. This requirement has led some critics to suggest that the IAS 37 approach countenances 'big-bath' provisioning – the very practice the standard was produced to avoid. Assess the validity of the arguments of such critics.

The exposure draft proposing changes to IAS 37 was originally issued in 2005 and then added to in 2010. Explain the clarifications that were made in the 2010 draft and outline why the 2005 draft was deficient in these areas.

EXERCISES

Question 1

(a) Provisions are particular kinds of liabilities. It therefore follows that provisions should be recognised when the definition of a liability has been met. The key requirement of a liability is a present obligation and thus this requirement is critical also in the context of the recognition of a provision. IAS 37 *Provisions, Contingent Liabilities and Contingent Assets* deals with this area.

Required:
(i) Explain why there was a need for detailed guidance on accounting for provisions.
(ii) Explain the circumstances under which a provision should be recognised in the financial statements according to IAS 37 *Provisions, Contingent Liabilities and Contingent Assets*.

(b) World Wide Nuclear Fuels, a public limited company, disclosed the following information in its financial statements for the year ending 30 November 20X9:

> The company purchased an oil company during the year. As part of the sale agreement, oil has to be supplied to the company's former holding company at an uneconomic rate for a period of five years. As a result, a provision for future operating losses has been set up of $135m, which relates solely to the uneconomic supply of oil. Additionally the oil company is exposed to environmental liabilities arising out of its past obligations, principally in respect of soil and ground

water restoration costs, although currently there is no legal obligation to carry out the work. Liabilities for environmental costs are provided for when the group determines a formal plan of action on the closure of an inactive site. It has been decided to provide for $120m in respect of the environmental liability on the acquisition of the oil company. World Wide Nuclear Fuels has a reputation for ensuring the preservation of the environment in its business activities. The company is also facing a legal claim for $200 million from a competitor who claims they have breached a patent in one of their processes. World Wide Nuclear Fuels has obtained legal advice that the claim has little chance of success and the insurance advisers have indicated that to insure against losing the case would cost $20 million as a premium.

Required:
Discuss whether the provision has been accounted for correctly under IAS 37 *Provisions, Contingent Liabilities and Contingent Assets*, and whether any changes are likely to be needed under ED IAS 37.

* Question 2

On 20 December 20X6 one of Incident plc's lorries was involved in an accident with a car. The lorry driver was responsible for the accident and the company agreed to pay for the repair to the car. The company put in a claim to its insurers on 17 January 20X7 for the cost of the claim. The company expected the claim to be settled by the insurance company except for a £250 excess on the insurance policy. The insurance company may dispute the claim and not pay out; however, the company believes that the chance of this occurring is low. The cost of repairing the car was estimated as £5,000, all of which was incurred after the year-end.

Required:
Explain how this item should be treated in the financial statements for the year ended 31 December 20X6 according to both IAS 37 and ED IAS 37 *Non-financial Liabilities*.

Question 3

Plasma Ltd, a manufacturer of electrical goods, guarantees them for 12 months from the date of purchase by the customer. If a fault occurs after the guarantee period but is due to faulty manufacture or design of the product, the company repairs or replaces the product. However, the company does not make this practice widely known.

Required:
Explain how repairs after the guarantee period should be treated in the financial statements.

Question 4

In 20X6 Alpha AS made the decision to close a loss-making department in 20X7. The company proposed to make a provision for the future costs of termination in the 20X6 profit or loss. Its argument was that a liability existed in 20X6 which should be recognised in 20X6. The auditor objected to recognising a liability, but agreed to recognition if it could be shown that the management decision was irrevocable.

Required:
Discuss whether a liability exists and should be recognised in the 20X6 statement of financial position.

* Question 5

Easy View Ltd had started business publishing training resource material in ring binder format for use in primary schools. Later it diversified into the hiring out of videos and had opened a chain of video hire shops. With the growing popularity of a mail order video/DVD supplier the video hire shops had become loss-making.

The company's year-end was 31 March and in February the financial director (FD) was asked to prepare a report for the board on the implications of closing this segment of the business.

The position at the board meeting on 10 March was as follows:

1 It was agreed that the closure should take place from 1 April 2010 to be completed by 31 May 2010.

2 The premises were freehold except for one that was on a lease with six years to run. It was in an inner-city shopping complex where many properties were empty and there was little chance of sub-letting. The annual rent was £20,000 per annum. Early termination of the lease could be negotiated for a figure of £100,000. An appropriate discount rate is 8%.

3 The office equipment and vans had a book value of £125,000 and were expected to realise £90,000, a figure tentatively suggested by a dealer who indicated that he might be able to complete by the end of April.

4 The staff had been mainly part-time and casual employees. There were 45 managers, however, who had been with the company for a number of years. These were happy to retrain to work with the training resources operation. The cost of retraining to use publishing software was estimated at £225,000.

5 Losses of £300,000 were estimated for the current year and £75,000 for the period until the closure was complete.

A week before the meeting the managing director made it clear to the FD that he wanted the segment to be treated as a discontinued operation so that the continuing operations could reflect the profitable training segment's performance.

Required:
Draft the finance director's report to present to the MD before the meeting to clarify the financial reporting implications.

Question 6

Suktor is an entity that prepares financial statements to 30 June each year.

On 30 April 20X1 the directors decided to discontinue the business of one of Suktor's operating divisions. They decided to cease production on 31 July 20X1, with a view to disposing of the property, plant and equipment soon after 31 August 20X1.

On 15 May 20X1 the directors made a public announcement of their intentions and offered the employees affected by the closure termination payments or alternative employment opportunities elsewhere in the group. Relevant financial details are as follows:

(a) On 30 April 20X1 the directors estimated that termination payments to employees would total $12 million and the costs of retraining employees who would remain employed by other group companies would total $1.2 million. Actual termination costs paid out on 31 May 20X1 were $12.6 million and the latest estimate of total retraining costs is $960,000.

(b) Suktor was leasing a property under an operating lease that expires on 30 September 20Y0. On 30 June 20X1 the present value of the future lease rentals (using an appropriate discount rate) was $4.56 million. On 31 August 20X1 Suktor made a payment to the lessor of $4.56 million in return for early termination of the lease. There were no rental payments made in July or August 20X1.

(c) The loss after tax of Suktor for the year ended 30 June 20X1 was $14.4 million. Suktor made further operating losses totalling $6 million for the two-month period 1 July 20X1 to 31 August 20X1.

Required:
Compute the provision that is required in the financial statements of Suktor at 30 June 20X1 in respect of the decision to close.

* Question 7

On 1 April 20W9 Kroner began to lease an office block on a 20-year lease. The useful economic life of the office buildings was estimated at 40 years on 1 April 20W9. The supply of leasehold properties exceeded the demand on 1 April 2009 so as an incentive the lessor paid Kroner $1 million on 1 April 20W9 and allowed Kroner a rent-free period for the first two years of the lease, followed by 36 payments of $250,000, the first being due on 1 April 20X1.

Between 1 April 20W9 and 30 September 20W9 Kroner carried out alterations to the office block at a total cost of $3 million. The terms of the lease require Kroner to vacate the office block on 31 March 20Y9 and leave it in exactly the same condition as it was at the start of the lease. The directors of Kroner have consistently estimated that the cost of restoring the office block to its original condition on 31 March 20Y9 will be $2.5 million at 31 March 20Y9 prices.

An appropriately risk-adjusted discount rate for use in any discounting calculations is 6% per annum. The present value of $1 payable in $19\frac{1}{2}$ years at an annual discount rate of 6% is 32 cents.

Required:
Prepare extracts from the financial statements of Kroner that show the depreciation of leasehold improvements and unwinding of discount on the restoration liability in the statement of comprehensive income for *both* of the years ended 31 March 20X0 and 20X1.

Question 8

Epsilon is a listed entity. You are the financial controller of the entity and its consolidated financial statements for the year ended 31 March 2009 are being prepared. The board of directors is responsible for all key financial and operating decisions, including the allocation of resources.

Your assistant is preparing the first draft of the statements. He has a reasonable general accounting knowledge but is not familiar with the detailed requirements of all relevant financial reporting standards. There is one issue on which he requires your advice and he has sent you a note as shown below:

I note that on 31 January 2009 the board of directors decided to discontinue the activities of a number of our subsidiaries. This decision was made, I believe, because these subsidiaries did not fit into the long-term plans of the group and the board did not consider it likely that the subsidiaries could be sold. This decision was communicated to the employees on 28 February 2009 and the activities of the subsidiaries affected were gradually curtailed starting on 1 May 2009, with an expected completion date of 30 September 2009. I have the following information regarding the closure programme:

(a) All the employees in affected subsidiaries were offered redundancy packages and some of the employees were offered employment in other parts of the group. These offers had to be accepted or rejected by 30 April 2009. On 31 March 2009 the directors estimated that the cost of redundancies would be $20 million and the cost of relocation of employees who accepted alternative employment would be $10 million. Following 30 April 2009 these estimates were revised to $22 million and $9 million respectively.

(b) Latest estimates are that the operating losses of the affected subsidiaries for the six months to 30 September 2009 will total $15 million.

(c) A number of the subsidiaries are leasing properties under non-cancellable operating leases. I believe that at 31 March 2009 the present value of the future lease payments relating to these properties totalled $6 million. The cost of immediate termination of these lease obligations would be $5 million.

(d) The carrying values of the freehold properties owned by the affected subsidiaries at 31 March 2008 totalled $25 million. The estimated net disposal proceeds of the properties are $29 million and all properties should realise a profit.

(e) The carrying value of the plant and equipment owned by the affected subsidiaries at 31 March 2008 was $18 million. The estimated current disposal proceeds of this plant and equipment is $2 million and its estimated value in use (including the proceeds from ultimate disposal) is $8 million.

I am unsure regarding a number of aspects of accounting for this decision by the board. Please tell me how the decision to curtail the activities of the three subsidiaries affects the financial statements.

Required:
Draft a reply to the questions raised by your assistant.

* Question 9

Epsilon is a listed entity. You are the financial controller of the entity and its consolidated financial statements for the year ended 30 September 2008 are being prepared. Your assistant, who has prepared the first draft of the statements, is unsure about the correct treatment of a transaction and has asked for your advice. Details of the transaction are given below.

On 31 August 2008 the directors decided to close down a business segment which did not fit into its future strategy. The closure commenced on 5 October 2008 and was due to be completed on 31 December 2008. On 6 September 2008 letters were sent to relevant employees offering voluntary redundancy or redeployment in other sectors of the business. On 13 September 2008 negotiations commenced with relevant parties with a view to terminating existing contracts of the business segment and arranging sales of its assets. Latest estimates of the financial implications of the closure are as follows:

(i) Redundancy costs will total $30 million, excluding the payment referred to in (ii) below.

(ii) The pension plan (a defined benefit plan) will make a lump sum payment totalling $8 million to the employees who accept voluntary redundancy in termination of their rights under the plan. Epsilon will pay this amount into the plan on 31 January 2009. The actuaries have advised that the accumulated pension rights that this payment will extinguish have a present value of $7 million and this sum is unlikely to alter significantly before 31 January 2009.

(iii) The cost of redeploying and retraining staff who do not accept redundancy will total $6 million.

(iv) The business segment operates out of a leasehold property that has an unexpired lease term of 10 years from 30 September 2008. The annual lease rentals on this property are $1 million, payable on 30 September in arrears. Negotiations with the owner of the freehold indicate that the owner would accept a single payment of $5.5 million in return for early termination of the lease. There are no realistic opportunities for Epsilon to sub-let this property. An appropriate rate to use in any discounting calculations is 10% per annum. The present value of an annuity of $1 receivable annually at the end of years 1 to 10 inclusive using a discount rate of 10% is $6.14.

(v) Plant having a net book value of $11 million at 30 September 2008 will be sold for $2 million.

(vi) The operating losses of the business segment for October, November and December 2008 are estimated at $10 million.

Your assistant is unsure of the extent to which the above transactions create liabilities that should be recognised as a closure provision in the financial statements. He is also unsure as to whether or not the results of the business segment that is being closed need to be shown separately.

Required:

Explain how the decision to close down the business segment should be reported in the financial statements of Epsilon for the year ended 30 September 2008.

Question 10

Thetic, a public limited company, is a worldwide distributor of chemicals. The company was founded in the eighteenth century and until the current year manufactured one of its products, ink for the Ritestyle pen, from the company's original factory. However, the profitability of the product had declined and during the current year the factory was closed. The company's finance department has prepared the following draft statement of comprehensive income for the year ended 31 October 2010:

Statement of comprehensive income for the year ended 31 October 2010

		$m
Turnover	i	260
Cost of sales	ii	150
Gross profit		110
Operating expenses	iii	80
Operating profit		30
Other operating income	iv	60
Profit for the year		90
Dividends paid on ordinary shares		10
Profit for the year retained		80

The following information is relevant to Thetic's financial statements:

(i) Turnover includes $40 million in respect of the ink factory.

(ii) Cost of sales includes the following in respect of the ink factory:

	$m
● Labour	2
● Materials	18
● Redundancy costs	6
● Restructuring of remaining business after closure of ink factory	10
● Depreciation of plant	1

Thetic has a detailed formal plan for the restructuring and has announced its intentions to the workforce. The provision of $10 million includes $3 million related to retraining the existing workforce and $1 million to market the new business.

(iii) Operating expenses include the following in respect of the ink factory:

	$m
● Salaries	3
● Running costs (rent, maintenance, etc.)	8
● Closure costs	4

(iv) Operating income includes the following:

	$m
● Gain on revaluation of property (not ink factory). Assessment made by an independent expert	20
● Gain on sale of ink factory	45
● Loss on disposal of ink factory property, plant and equipment	(5)

(v) Owing to the closure of the ink factory, the Ritestyle pen had reduced market potential. At 31 October 2010 the carrying value of inventory was $1.5 million at which date Thetic believed the pens had a net realisable value of $0.5 million. This event has not yet been recorded in the financial statements.

(vi) Thetic wishes to show the results of discontinued operations as a one-line entry in the income statement.

Required:

(a) Produce a new version of Thetic's statement of comprehensive income for the year ended 31 October 2010 taking into consideration the above information. Explain your workings. Ignore taxation.

(b) Assume the financial statements were authorised for issuance on 7 November 2010 and that Thetic entered into an agreement to sell the Ritestyle pens to a competitor for $0.8 million after that date. Discuss the impact this event would have, if any, on the above financial statements.

(c) Discuss how the *Framework for the Preparation and Presentation of Financial Statements* (the *'Framework'*) would support your treatment of the gain on revaluation of property.

(The Association of International Accountants)

References

1 IAS 37 *Provisions, Contingent Liabilities and Contingent Assets*, IASC, 1998.
2 *Ibid.*, para. 2.
3 *Ibid.*, para. 25.
4 *Ibid.*, para. 17.
5 *Ibid.*, para. 23.
6 *Ibid.*, para. 36.
7 *Ibid.*, para. 43.
8 *Ibid.*, para. 45.
9 *Ibid.*, para. 84.
10 ED IAS 37 *Non-financial Liabilities*, IASB, 2005.
11 ED/2010/1 *Measurement of Liabilities in IAS 37*, IASB, 2010.

CHAPTER 14

Financial instruments

14.1 Introduction

Accounting for financial instruments has proven to be one of the most difficult areas for the IASB to provide guidance on, and the current standards are far from perfect. In 2009 the IASB began a process to amend the existing financial instrument accounting with the issue of revised guidance on the recognition and measurement of financial instruments. It is expected over 2013 or later that new guidance on impairment, hedging and derecognition of assets and liabilities will also be issued. The new guidance is unlikely to be mandatory before 2015. In this chapter we will consider the main requirements of IAS 32 *Financial Instruments: Presentation*, IAS 39 *Financial Instruments: Recognition and Measurement* and IFRS 7 *Financial Instruments: Disclosure* as well as the main changes introduced by the revised standard IFRS 9 *Financial Instruments* and the potential future changes in other areas of financial instruments.

Objectives

By the end of this chapter, you should be able to:

- define what financial instruments are and be able to outline the main accounting requirements under IFRS;
- comment critically on the international accounting requirements for financial instruments and understand why they continue to prove both difficult and controversial topics in accounting;
- account for different types of common financial instrument that companies may use.

14.2 Financial instruments – the IASB's problem child

International accounting has had standards on financial instruments since the late 1990s and, ever since they were introduced, they have proved the most controversial requirements of IFRS. In the late 1990s, in order to make international accounting standards generally acceptable to stock exchanges, the International Accounting Standards Committee (forerunner of the International Accounting Standards Board) introduced IAS 32 and 39. These standards drew heavily on US GAAP as that was the only comprehensive regime that had guidance in this area. Even now some national accounting standards, such as the UK regime, do not have compulsory comprehensive accounting standards on financial instruments for all companies.

Ever since their issue the guidance on financial instruments has been criticised by users, preparers, auditors and others and has also been the only area of accounting that has caused real political problems. In the financial crisis of 2008 and 2009 IAS 39 was the only international accounting standard that was extensively discussed and debated within the G20 and other political forums. It was suggested that the rules, particularly on fair value measurement and impairment, could have contributed to the financial crisis and this led to the rules being examined and calls for changes.

14.2.1 Rules versus principles

IAS 32 and 39 are sourced from US GAAP (although not fully consistent with US GAAP) and this has led to one of the first major criticisms of the guidance, that it is too 'rules' based. The international accounting standards aim is to be a principles-based accounting regime where the accounting standards establish good principles that underpin the accounting treatments, but not every possible situation or transaction is covered in guidance. Generally US GAAP, whilst still having underpinning principles, tends to have a significantly greater number of 'rules'. As a result IAS 32 and 39 have significant and detailed rules within them.

The difficulty with the rules-based approach is that some companies claim that they cannot produce financial statements that reflect the intent behind their transactions. For example, an area we will be considering in this chapter is hedge accounting. Some companies have claimed that the very strict hedge accounting requirements in IAS 39 are so difficult to comply with that they cannot reflect what they consider are genuine hedge transactions appropriately in their financial statements. The extract below is from the 2011 Annual Report of Rolls-Royce and shows the importance of the 'underlying' performance of the business:

> Underlying figures are considered more representative of the trading performance by excluding the impact of year end mark-to-market adjustments of outstanding financial instruments on the reported performance, principally relating to the GBP/USD hedge book. In addition the net post-retirement financing is excluded and, in 2011, adjustments have been made to exclude one-off past-service credits on post-retirement schemes and the effect of acquisition accounting. The adjustments between the underlying income statement and the reported income statement are set out in more detail in note 2 of the financial statements. This basis of presentation has been applied consistently since the transition to IFRS in 2005.

14.2.2 The 2008 financial crisis

The financial crisis that began in 2008 highlighted problems with IAS 39 and caused more political intervention in accounting standard setting than had previously been seen. Also the IASB was forced into a position where it had to change an accounting standard without any due process, an action which the IASB felt was necessary but that has drawn widespread criticism.

As you read this chapter you will appreciate that IAS 39 requires different measurement bases for different types of financial assets and liabilities. How a company determines which measurement to use, broadly the choice being fair value or amortised cost, depends on how instruments are classified, there being four different asset classifications allowed by IAS 39. Many banks in the financial crisis were caught in a position where they had loan assets measured at fair value, and the fair value of those loans was reducing significantly, with the potential for major losses.

The impact on profits of moving from fair value to amortised cost

Banks will keep their loan assets generally in two books, a 'trading' book where the loans are measured at fair value through profit or loss, and a 'banking' book where the loans are measured at amortised cost. Up to October 2008, under IAS 39, if a company chose to measure its financial assets or liabilities at fair value through profit or loss, it was not allowed to subsequently reclassify those loans and measure them at amortised cost. Many banks had included loans in the 'trading' book which, because of illiquidity in financial markets, they could not sell. As a result, market values were significantly reduced. The losses on revaluation were all going to be charged against their profit and this was causing some concern.

The issue came to a head when the European Union identified that under US GAAP reclassification was allowed and, therefore, European banks were potentially in a worse competitive position than their American counterparts. The European Union concluded that this was unacceptable and that if IAS 39 was not altered they would 'carve out' the section of IAS 39 restricting the transfer, and, as a result, not make that part of the standard relevant to EU businesses. This was perceived as a major threat by the IASB (in particular to its convergence work with US GAAP) and therefore the IASB amended IAS 39 to allow reclassification. For the first time ever an amendment was made that had not been issued as a discussion paper or exposure draft but was simply a change to the standard. This has led to significant criticism of the IASB and calls for its due process to be revisited to ensure this does not happen again.

Political pressure on the IASB

The political interest in accounting has continued with global politicians putting pressure on the IASB to speed up its work on certain areas. In addition it has led to calls for the IASB to examine the way it operates and its governance: a number of governments are concerned that a board, on which they have no representation, can set accounting standards which have to be followed by companies in their country. To highlight how high these issues have been on the agenda of politicians, the following are extracts from the G20 communiqué issued after the meeting on 15 November 2008:

Strengthening Transparency and Accountability
Immediate Actions by March 31, 2009.
The key global accounting standards bodies should work to enhance guidance for valuation of securities, also taking into account the valuation of complex, illiquid products, especially during times of stress.

Accounting standard setters should significantly advance their work to address weaknesses in accounting and disclosure standards for off balance sheet vehicles.

Regulators and accounting standard setters should enhance the required disclosure of complex financial instruments by firms to market participants.

With a view toward promoting financial stability, the governance of the international accounting standard setting body should be further enhanced, including by undertaking a review of its membership, in particular in order to ensure transparency, accountability, and an appropriate relationship between this independent body and the relevant authorities.

Promoting Integrity in Financial Markets Immediate Actions by March 31, 2009.
Medium-term actions
The key global accounting standards bodies should work intensively toward the objective of creating a single high-quality global standard.

Regulators, supervisors, and accounting standard setters, as appropriate, should work with each other and the private sector on an ongoing basis to ensure consistent application and enforcement of high-quality accounting standards.

14.3 IAS 32 *Financial Instruments: Disclosure and Presentation*[1]

The dynamic nature of the international financial markets has resulted in a great variety of financial instruments from traditional equity and debt instruments to derivative instruments such as futures or swaps. These instruments are a mixture of on- and off-balance-sheet instruments, and they can significantly contribute to the risks that an enterprise faces. IAS 32 was introduced to highlight to users of financial statements the range of financial instruments used by an enterprise and how they affect the financial position, performance and cash flows of the enterprise.

IAS 32 only considers the areas of presentation of financial instruments; recognition and measurement are considered in a subsequent standard, IAS 39.

14.3.1 Scope of the standard

IAS 32 should be applied by all enterprises and should consider all financial instruments with the exceptions of:

(a) share-based payments as defined in IFRS 2;

(b) interests in subsidiaries as defined in IAS 27;

(c) interests in associates as defined in IAS 28;

(d) interests in joint ventures as defined in IAS 31;

(e) employers' rights and ligations under employee benefit plans;

(f) rights and obligations arising under insurance contracts (except embedded derivatives requiring separate accounting under IAS 39).

14.3.2 Definition of terms[2]

The following definitions are used in IAS 32 and also in IAS 39, which is to be considered later.

A **financial instrument** is any contract that gives rise to both a financial asset of one enterprise and a financial liability or equity instrument of another enterprise.

A **financial asset** is any asset that is:

(a) cash;

(b) a contractual right to receive cash or another financial asset from another entity;

(c) a contractual right to exchange financial instruments with another entity under conditions that are potentially favourable; or

(d) an equity instrument of another entity.

A **financial liability** is any liability that is a contractual obligation:

(a) to deliver cash or another financial asset to another entity; or

(b) to exchange financial instruments with another entity under conditions that are potentially unfavourable.

An **equity instrument** is any contract that evidences a residual interest in the assets of an entity after deducting all of its liabilities.

Following the introduction of IAS 39 extra clarification was introduced into IAS 32 in the application of the definitions. First, a commodity-based contract (such as a commodity future) is a financial instrument if either party can settle in cash or some other financial instrument. Commodity contracts would not be financial instruments if they were expected to be settled by delivery, and this was always intended.

The second clarification is for the situation where an enterprise has a financial liability that can be settled with either financial assets or the enterprise's own equity shares. If the number of equity shares to be issued is variable, typically so that the enterprise always has an obligation to give shares equal to the fair value of the obligation, they are treated as a financial liability.

14.3.3 Presentation of instruments in the financial statements

Two main issues are addressed in the standard regarding the presentation of financial instruments. These issues are whether instruments should be classified as liabilities or equity instruments, and how compound instruments should be presented.

Liabilities versus equity

IAS 32 follows a substance approach[3] to the classification of instruments as liabilities or equity. If an instrument has terms such that there is an obligation on the enterprise to transfer financial assets to redeem the obligation then it is a liability instrument regardless of its legal nature. Preference shares are the main instrument where in substance they could be liabilities but legally are equity. The common conditions on the preference share that would indicate it is to be treated as a liability instrument are as follows:

● annual dividends are compulsory and not at the discretion of directors; or

● the share provides for mandatory redemption by the issuer at a fixed or determinable amount at a future fixed or determinable date; or

● the share gives the holder the option to redeem upon the occurrence of a future event that is highly likely to occur (e.g. after the passing of a future date).

If a preference share is treated as a liability instrument, it is presented as such in the statement of financial position. Any dividends paid or payable on that share are calculated in the same way as interest and presented as a finance cost in the statement of comprehensive income. The presentation on the statement of comprehensive income could be as a separate item from other interest costs, but this is not mandatory. Any gains or losses on the redemption of financial instruments classified as liabilities are also presented in profit or loss.

Impact on companies

The presentation of preference shares as liabilities does not alter the cash flows or risks that the instruments give, but there is a danger that the perception of a company may change. This presentational change has the impact of reducing net assets and increasing gearing. This could be very important, for example, if a company had debt covenants on other borrowings that required the maintenance of certain ratios such as gearing or interest cover. Moving preference shares to debt and dividends to interest costs could mean the covenants are breached and other loans become repayable.

In addition, the higher gearing and reduced net assets could mean the company is perceived as more risky, and therefore could result in the company being perceived to have a higher credit risk. This in turn might lead to a reduction in the company's credit rating, making obtaining future credit more difficult and expensive.

These very practical issues need to be managed by companies converting to IFRS from a local accounting regime that treats preference shares as equity or non-equity funds. Good communication with users is key to smoothing the transition.

Compound instruments[4]

Compound instruments are financial instruments that have the characteristics of both debt and equity. A convertible loan, which gives the holder the option to convert into equity shares at some future date, is the most common example of a compound instrument. The view of the IASB is that the proceeds received by a company for these instruments are made up of two parts: (i) a debt obligation and (ii) an equity option. Following the substance of the instruments, IAS 32 requires that the two parts be presented separately, a 'split accounting' approach.

The split is made by measuring the debt part and making the equity the residual of the proceeds. This approach is in line with the definitions of liabilities and equity, where equity is treated as a residual. The debt is calculated by discounting the cash flows on the debt at a market rate of interest for similar debt without the conversion option.

The following is an extract from the 2011 Balfour Beatty Annual Report relating to convertible preference shares:

> The Company's cumulative convertible redeemable preference shares are regarded as a compound instrument, comprising a liability component and an equity component. The fair value of the liability component at the date of issue was estimated using the prevailing market interest rate for a similar non-convertible instrument. The difference between the proceeds of issue of the preference shares and the fair value assigned to the liability component, representing the embedded option to convert the liability into the Company's ordinary shares, is included in equity.
>
> The interest expense on the liability component is calculated by applying the market interest rate for similar non-convertible debt prevailing at the date of issue to the liability component of the instrument. The difference between this amount and the dividend paid is added to the carrying amount of the liability component and is included in finance charges, together with the dividend payable.

Illustration for compound instruments

Rohan plc issues 1,000 £100 5% convertible debentures at par on 1 January 2000. The debentures can be either converted into 50 ordinary shares per £100 of debentures, or redeemed at par at any date from 1 January 2005. Interest is paid annually in arrears on 31 December. The interest rate on similar debentures without the conversion option is 6%.

To split the proceeds the debt value must be calculated by discounting the future cash flows on the debt instrument. The value of debt is therefore:

Present value of redemption payment (discounted @ 6%)	£74,726
Present value of interest (5 years) (discounted @ 6%)	£21,062
Value of debt	£95,788
Value of the equity proceeds: (£100,000 – £95,788)	
(presented as part of equity)	£4,212

The following is an extract from the 2011 Annual Report of Aspen Pharmacare Holdings Ltd:

> For accounting purposes the preference shares have been split into an equity and a liability component. Refer to the accounting policy for detail.

		R million
Preference shares – equity component		**162.0**
(per statement of changes in equity)		
Deferred tax effect		(8.7)
Net equity component		153.3
Preference shares – liability component		381.3
(per the statement of financial position)		
Amount expensed in 2011		(183.2)
Cumulative notional interest on liability component		
Opening balance	20.1	
For the year	5.3	25.4
		376.8

Perpetual debt

Following a substance approach, perpetual or irredeemable debt could be argued to be an equity instrument as opposed to a debt instrument. IAS 32, however, takes the view that it is a debt instrument because the interest must be paid (as compared to dividends which are only paid if profits are available for distribution and if directors declare a dividend approved by the shareholders). The present value of all the future obligations to pay interest will equal the proceeds of the debt if discounted at a market rate. The proceeds on issue of a perpetual debt instrument are therefore a liability obligation.

14.3.4 Calculation of finance costs on liability instruments

The finance costs will be charged to profit or loss. The finance cost of debt is the total payments to be incurred over the lifespan of that debt less the initial carrying value. Such costs should be allocated to profit or loss over the lifetime of the debt at a constant rate of interest based on the outstanding carrying value per period. If a debt is settled before maturity, any profit or loss should be reflected immediately in profit or loss – unless the substance of the settlement transaction fails to generate any change in liabilities and assets.

Illustration of the allocation of finance costs and the determination of carrying value

On 1 January 20X6 a company issued a debt instrument of £1,000,000 spanning a four-year term. It received from the lender £890,000, being the face value of the debt less a discount of £110,000. Interest was payable yearly in arrears at 8% per annum on the principal sum of £1,000,000. The principal sum was to be repaid on 31 December 20X9.

To determine the yearly finance costs and year-end carrying value it is necessary to compute:

- the aggregate finance cost;
- the implicit rate of interest carried by the instrument (referred to in IAS 39 as the effective yield);
- the finance charge per annum; and
- the carrying value at successive year-ends.

Aggregate finance cost

This is the difference between the total future payments of interest plus principal, less the net proceeds received less costs of the issue, i.e. £430,000 in column (i) of Figure 14.1.

Figure 14.1 Allocation of finance costs and determination of carrying value

	(i)		(ii) Finance charge to statement of comprehensive income £000		(iii) Carrying value in statement of financial position £000
	Cash flows £000				
At I Jan 20X6	(890)	(1,000 – 110)	—		890
At 31 Dec 20X6	80	(8% × 1,000)	103.2	(11.59% × 890)	913.2
At 31 Dec 20X7	80	(8% × 1,000)	105.8	(11.59% × 913.2)	939.2
At 31 Dec 20X8	80	(8% × 1,000)	108.8	(11.59% × 939)	967.8
At 31 Dec 20X9	1,080	(1,000 + (8% × 1,000))	112.2	(11.59% × 967.8)	—
Net cash flow	430	= Cost	430		

Implicit rate of interest carried by the instrument
This can be computed by using the net present value (NPV) formula:

$$\sum_{t=1}^{t=n} \frac{A_t}{(1+r)^t} - I = 0$$

where A is forecast net cash flow in year A, t time (in years), n the lifespan of the debt in years, r the company's annual rate of discount and I the initial net proceeds. Note that the application of this formula can be quite time-consuming. A reasonable method of assessment is by interpolation of the interest rate.

The aggregate formula given above may be disaggregated for calculation purposes:

$$\frac{A_1}{(1+r)} + \frac{A_2}{(1+r)^2} + \frac{A_3}{(1+r)^3} + \frac{A_4}{(1+r)^4} - I = 0$$

Using the data concerning the debt and assuming (allowing for discount and costs) an implicit constant rate of, say, 11%:

$$\sum = \frac{80,000}{(1.11)^1} + \frac{80,000}{(1.11)^2} + \frac{80,000}{(1.11)^3} + \frac{1,080,000}{(1.11)^4} - 890,000 = 0$$

$$= 72,072 + 64,930 + 58,495 + 711,429 - 890,000 = +16,926$$

The chosen implicit rate of 11% is too low. We now choose a higher rate, say 12%:

$$\sum = \frac{80,000}{(1.12)^1} + \frac{80,000}{(1.12)^2} + \frac{80,000}{(1.12)^3} + \frac{1,080,000}{(1.12)^4} - 890,000 = 0$$

$$= 71,429 + 63,776 + 56,942 + 686,360 - 890,000 = -11,493$$

This rate is too high, resulting in a negative net present value. Interpolation will enable us to arrive at an implicit rate:

$$11\% + \left[\frac{16,926}{16,926 + 11,493} \times (12\% - 11\%) \right]$$

$$= 11\% + 0.59\% = 11.59\%$$

This is a trial and error method of determining the implicit interest rate. In this example the choice of rates, 11% and 12%, constituted a change of only 1%. It would be possible to choose, say, 11% and then 14%, generating a 3% gap within which to interpolate. This wider margin would result in a less accurate implicit rate and an aggregate interest charge at variance with the desired £430,000 of column (ii). The aim is to choose interest rates as close as possible to either side of the monetary zero, so that the exact implicit rate may be computed.

The object is to determine an NPV of zero monetary units, i.e. to identify the discount rate that will enable the aggregate future discounted net flows to equate to the initial net proceeds from the debt instrument. In the above illustration, a discount (interest) rate of 11.59% enables £430,000 to be charged to profit or loss after allowing for payment of all interest, costs and repayment of the face value of the instrument.

The finance charge per annum and the successive year-end carrying amounts
The charge to the statement of comprehensive income and the carrying values in the statement of financial position are shown in Figure 14.1.

14.3.5 Offsetting financial instruments[5]

Financial assets and liabilities can only be offset and presented net if the following conditions are met:

(a) the enterprise has a legally enforceable right to set off the recognised amounts; and

(b) the enterprise intends either to settle on a net basis, or to realise the asset and settle the liability simultaneously.

IAS 32 emphasises the importance of the intention to settle on a net basis as well as the legal right to do so. Offsetting should only occur when the cash flows and therefore the risks associated with the financial asset and liability are offset and therefore to present them net in the statement of financial position shows a true and fair view. An example of a situation where offsetting may be appropriate would be if a company has a receivable and a payable to the same counterparty, has a legal right to offset the two, and does offset the amounts in practice when settling the cash flows.

Situations where offsetting might be considered but which would not normally be appropriate are where:

● several different financial instruments are used to emulate the features of a single financial instrument;

● financial assets and financial liabilities arise from financial instruments having the same primary risk exposure but involve different counterparties;

● financial or other assets are pledged as collateral for non-recourse financial liabilities;

● financial assets are set aside in trust by a debtor for the purpose of discharging an obligation without those assets having been accepted by the creditor in settlement of the obligation;

● obligations incurred as a result of events giving rise to losses are expected to be recovered from a third party by virtue of a claim made under an insurance policy.

14.4 IAS 39 *Financial Instruments: Recognition and Measurement*

IAS 39 is the first comprehensive standard on the recognition and measurement of financial instruments and completes the guidance that was started with the introduction of IAS 32.

14.4.1 Scope of the standard

IAS 39 should be applied by all enterprises to all financial instruments except those excluded from the scope of IAS 32 (see Section 14.3.1) and the following additional instruments:

- rights and obligations under leases to which IAS 17 applies (except for embedded derivatives);
- equity instruments of the reporting entity including options, warrants and other financial instruments that are classified as shareholders' equity;
- contracts between an acquirer and a vendor in a business combination to buy or sell or acquire at a future date;
- rights to payments to reimburse the entity for expenditure it is required to make to settle a liability under IAS 37.

14.4.2 Definitions of the categories of financial instruments

The four categories of financial assets are (a) financial assets at fair value through profit or loss, (b) held-to-maturity investments, (c) loans and receivables, and (d) available-for-sale financial assets. The definition of each is as stated below.

Financial liabilities are less complicated to classify than financial assets. There are only two categories of financial liability, fair value through profit or loss, and other financial liabilities. Financial liabilities at fair value through profit or loss are defined consistently with those below. Other financial liabilities are measured at amortised cost.

(a) Financial assets or liabilities at fair value through profit or loss

Assets and liabilities under this category are reported in the financial statements at fair value. Changes in the fair value from period to period are reported as a component of net income. There are two types of investments that are accounted for under this heading, namely, *held-for-trading investments* and those *designated on initial recognition* under the fair value option.

Held-for-trading investments
These are financial instruments where (i) the investor's principal intention is to sell or repurchase a security in the near future and where there is normally active trading for profit-taking in the securities, or (ii) they are part of a portfolio of identified financial instruments that are managed together and for which there is evidence of a recent pattern of short-term profit-taking, or (iii) they are derivatives. This category includes commercial papers, certain government bonds and treasury bills.

A **derivative** is a financial instrument:

- whose value changes in response to the change in a specified interest rate, security price, commodity price, foreign exchange rate, index of prices or rates, a credit rating or credit index or similar variable (sometimes called the 'underlying');
- that requires no initial net investment or an initial net investment that is smaller than would be required for other types of contract that would be expected to have a similar response to changes in market factors; and
- that is settled at a future date.

Designated on initial recognition – the 'fair value option'

A company has the choice of designating as fair value through profit or loss on the initial recognition of an investment in the following situations:

- it eliminates or significantly reduces a measurement or recognition inconsistency (sometimes referred to as an 'accounting mismatch') that would otherwise arise from measuring assets or liabilities or recognising the gains and losses on them on different bases; or

- a group of financial assets, financial liabilities or both is managed and performance is evaluated on a fair value basis, in accordance with a documented risk management or investment strategy; or

- the financial asset or liability contains an embedded derivative that would otherwise require separation from the host.

The following is an extract from the Annual Consolidated Financial Statements of BNP Paribas Bank Polska SA Group for 2011:

Financial assets measured to fair value through profit or loss

Financial assets measured to fair value through profit or loss are the assets:

(a) classified at initial recognition as held for trading if they were acquired mainly to be sold in the near term, i.e. within six months of the acquisition date;

(b) that are part of a portfolio of identified financial instruments that are managed together and for short-term profit taking;

(c) that are derivative instruments (excluding derivative instruments that constitute effective hedging instruments); or

(d) classified at the initial recognition as measured to fair value through profit or loss.

The Group did not classify assets at their initial recognition as measured to fair value through profit and loss account.

The Bank classifies held-for-trading financial assets into the category of financial assets, in particular:

(a) held-for-trading securities,

(b) derivative instruments (excluding derivative instruments that constitute effective hedging instruments).

Prior to October 2008 it was prohibited to transfer instruments either into or out of the fair value through profit or loss category after initial recognition of the instrument. Following significant pressure from the European Union that the international standards were more restrictive than US GAAP in this area, the IASB amended the standard to allow reclassification of financial instruments in rare circumstances. The financial crisis of 2008 was deemed to be a rare situation that would justify reclassification.

The reclassification requirements allow instruments to be transferred from the fair value through profit and loss to the loans and receivables category. They also allow reclassifications from the available-for-sale category (discussed below) to the loans and receivables category. The IASB allowed a short-term exemption from the general requirement that the transfer is at fair value, and permitted the transfers to be undertaken at the fair values of instruments on 1 July 2008, a date before significant reductions in fair value on debt instruments arose.

(b) Held-to-maturity investments

Held-to-maturity investments consist of instruments with fixed or determinable payments and fixed maturity for which the entity positively intends and has the ability to hold to maturity. For items to be classified as held-to-maturity an entity must justify that it will hold them to maturity. The tests that a company must pass to justify this classification are summarised in Figure 14.2.

The investments are initially measured at fair value (including transaction costs) and subsequently measured at amortised cost using the effective interest method, with the periodic amortisation recorded in the statement of comprehensive income. As they are reported at amortised cost, temporary fluctuations in fair value are not reflected in the entity's financial statements.

Such investments include corporate and government bonds and redeemable preference shares which can be held to maturity. They do not include investments designated as at fair value through profit or loss on initial recognition, those designated as available for sale and those defined as loans and receivables. They also do not include ordinary shares in other entities because these do not have a maturity date.

(c) Loans and receivables

Loans and receivables include financial assets with fixed or determinable payments that are not quoted in an active market. They are initially measured at fair value (including transaction costs) and subsequently measured at amortised cost using the effective interest method, with the periodic amortisation in the statement of comprehensive income.

Amortised cost is normally the amount at which a financial asset or liability is measured at initial recognition minus principal repayments, minus the cumulative amortisation of any premium and minus any write-down for impairment.

Figure 14.2 Tests for classification as held-to-maturity investment

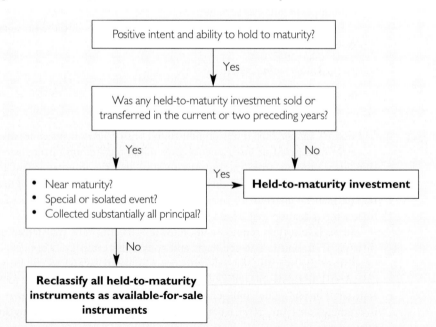

This category includes trade receivables, accrued revenues for services and goods, loan receivables, bank deposits and cash at hand. It does not include financial assets held for trading, those designated on initial recognition as at fair value through profit or loss, those designated as available-for-sale and those for which the holder may not recover substantially all of its initial investment, other than because of credit deterioration.

(d) Available-for-sale financial assets

The available-for-sale category is a 'catch-all' that includes all financial assets that have not been classified as fair value through profit or loss, held-to-maturity or loans and receivables. Because of its nature as a catch-all it effectively gives entities a choice of classification for some instruments. For example, if an entity did not include an investment in a non-trading bond within loans and receivables or held-to-maturity it would, by default, be classified as available-for-sale.

A common financial asset that would be classified as available-for-sale is equity investments in another entity.

On initial recognition an asset is reported at fair value (including transaction costs) and at period-ends it is restated to fair value with changes in fair value reported under other comprehensive income. If the fair value falls below amortised cost and the fall is not determined to be temporary, it is reported in the investor's statement of comprehensive income.

Any revaluations to fair value of available-for-sale assets are recognised in other comprehensive income until the asset is derecognised. On derecognition any cumulative gain or loss recognised in other comprehensive income is transferred to profit or loss as part of the gain or loss on derecognition. Consider the example of Kathryn plc below.

Illustration of available-for-sale accounting

On 1 January 2010 Kathryn plc acquires an equity investment for €100,000 which is classified as available-for-sale. On 31 December 2010 the investment is valued at €110,000, and on 31 March 2011 it is sold for €115,000. The accounting entries that would be reflected in the year ended 31 December 2010 and 2011 are as follows:

2010

		€	€
On acquisition of the investment:			
Dr	Available-for-sale asset	100,000	
Cr	Cash		100,000

		€	€
On revaluation at the year-end:			
Dr	Available-for-sale asset	10,000	
Cr	Available-for-sale revaluation reserve		10,000
	(presented as a gain in other comprehensive income (OCI))		

2011

		€	€
On disposal of the investment:			
Dr	Cash	115,000	
Cr	Available-for-sale asset		110,000
Cr	Profit on sale		5,000

		€	€
On disposal recycle the gain in OCI:			
Dr	Available-for-sale revaluation reserve	10,000	
Cr	Profit on sale		10,000

The impact of the above is that when in 2011 the investment is sold, the profit recognised (€15,000) is the difference between the sale proceeds (€115,000) and cost (€100,000).

The fair value of publicly traded securities is normally based on quoted market prices at the year-end date. The fair value of securities that are not publicly traded is assessed using a variety of methods and assumptions based on market conditions existing at each year-end date referring to quoted market prices for similar or identical securities if available or employing other techniques such as option pricing models and estimated discounted values of future cash flows.

Available-for-sale does not include debt and equity securities classified as held for trading or held-to-maturity.

Example of accounting for an available-for-sale financial asset: the acquisition by Brighton plc of shares in Hove plc

On 1 September 20X9 Brighton purchased 15 million of the 100 million shares in Hove for £1.50 per share. This purchase was made with a view to further purchases in future. The Brighton directors are not able to exercise any influence over the operating and financial policies of Hove. The shares are currently in the statement of financial position as at 31 December 20X9 at cost and the fair value of a share was £1.70.

Accounting treatment at the year-end

Brighton owns 15% of the Hove issued shares. As the directors are not able to exercise any influence, the investment is dealt with under IAS 39 *Financial Instruments: Recognition and Measurement* and under its provisions the investment is an available-for-sale financial asset. This means that it is to be valued at fair value, with gains or losses taken to equity.

In this case the investment is valued at £25.5 million (15 million × £1.70) and the gain of £3 million (15 million × (£1.70 – £1.50)) is taken to equity through other comprehensive income.

Headings under which reported

Assets are reported as appropriate in the statement of financial position under Other non-current assets, Trade and other receivables, Interest-bearing receivables, or Cash and cash equivalents. For example, financial liabilities measured at amortised cost comprise financial liabilities such as borrowings, trade payables, accrued expenses for services and goods, and certain provisions settled in cash. These are reported in the statement of financial position under Long-term and short-term borrowings, Other provisions, Other long-term liabilities, Trade payables and Other current liabilities.

Impact of classification on the financial statements

The impact of the classification of financial instruments on the financial statements is important as it affects the value of assets and liabilities and also the income recognised. For example, assume that Henry plc had the following financial assets and liabilities at its year-end. All the instruments had been taken out at the start of the current year:

1 A forward exchange contract. At the period-end date the contract was an asset with a fair value of £100,000.

2 An investment of £1,000,000 in a 6% corporate bond. At the period-end date the market rate of interest increased and the bond fair value fell to £960,000.

3 An equity investment of £500,000. This investment was worth £550,000 at the period-end.

The classification of these instruments is important and choices are available as to how they are accounted for. For example, the investment in the corporate bond above could be accounted for as a held-to-maturity investment (if Henry plc had the intent and ability to hold it to maturity), or it could be an available-for-sale investment if so chosen by Henry. The bond and the equity investment could even be recognised as fair value through profit or loss if they met the criteria to be designated as such on initial recognition.

To highlight the impact on the financial statements, the tables below show the accounting positions for the investments on different assumptions. Not all possible classifications are shown in the tables.

Option 1

Instrument	Classification	Statement of financial position	Profit or loss	Other comprehensive income
Forward contract	FV-P&L	£100,000	£100,000	—
Corporate bond	Held-to-maturity	£1,000,000	*(£60,000)	—
Equity investment	Available-for-sale	£550,000	—	£50,000

* Interest on the bond of £1,000,000 × 6%

The bond is not revalued because held-to-maturity investments are recognised at amortised cost.

Option 2

Instrument	Classification	Statement of financial position	Profit or loss	Other comprehensive income
Forward contract	FV-P&L	£100,000	£100,000	—
Corporate bond	Available-for-sale	£960,000	(£60,000)	(£40,000)
Equity investment	Available-for-sale	£550,000	—	£50,000

Interest is still recognised on the bond but at the year-end it is revalued through equity to its fair value of £960,000.

Option 3

Instrument	Classification	Statement of financial position	Profit or loss	Other comprehensive income
Forward contract	FV-P&L	£100,000	£100,000)	—
Corporate bond	Held-to-maturity	£1,000,000	(£60,000)	—
Equity investment	FV-P&L	£550,000	£50,000	—

The equity investment is revalued through profit and loss as opposed to through other comprehensive income as it would be if classified as available-for-sale.

14.4.3 Recognition of financial instruments

Initial recognition

A financial asset or liability should be recognised when an entity becomes party to the contractual provisions of the instrument. This means that derivative instruments must be recognised if a contractual right or obligation exists.

Derecognition

Derecognition of financial assets is a complex area which has extensive rules in IAS 39. These rules have also been included within IFRS 9 *Financial Instruments*. The main principle is that financial assets should only be derecognised when the entity transfers the risks and rewards that comprise the asset. This could be because the benefits are realised, the rights expire or the enterprise surrenders the benefits.

If it is not clear whether the risks and rewards have been transferred, the entity considers whether control has passed. If control has passed, the entity should derecognise the asset; whereas if control is retained, the asset is recognised to the extent of the entity's continuing involvement in the asset.

On derecognition any gain or loss should be recorded in profit or loss. Also any gains or losses previously recognised in reserves relating to the asset should be transferred to the profit or loss on sale.

Financial liabilities should only be derecognised when the obligation specified in the contract is discharged, is cancelled or expires.

The rule on the derecognition of liabilities means that it is not possible to write off liabilities unless they are discharged, cancelled or expired. In some industries this will lead to a change in business practice. For example, banks are not allowed to remove dormant accounts from their statements of financial position unless the liability has been legally extinguished.

14.4.4 Embedded derivatives

Sometimes an entity will enter into a contract that includes both a derivative and a host contract, with the effect that some of the cash flows of the combined contract vary in a similar way to a stand-alone derivative. Examples of such embedded derivatives could be a put option on an equity instrument held by an enterprise, or an equity conversion feature embedded in a debt instrument.

An embedded instrument should be separated from the host contract and accounted for as a derivative under IAS 39 if all of the following conditions are met:

(a) the economic characteristics and risks of the embedded derivative are not closely related to the economic characteristics and risks of the host contract;

(b) a separate instrument with the same terms as the embedded derivative would meet the definition of a derivative; and

(c) the hybrid instrument is not measured at fair value with changes in fair value reported in profit or loss.

If an entity is required to separate the embedded derivative from its host contract but is unable to measure the embedded derivative separately, the entire hybrid instrument should be treated as a financial instrument held at fair value through profit or loss and as a result changes in fair value should be reported through profit or loss.

14.4.5 Measurement of financial instruments

Initial measurement

Financial assets and liabilities (other than those at fair value through profit or loss) should be initially measured at fair value plus transaction costs. In almost all cases this would be at cost. For instruments at fair value through profit and loss, transaction costs are not included and instead are expensed as incurred.

Subsequent measurement

Figure 14.3 summarises the way that financial assets and liabilities are to be subsequently measured after initial recognition.

Figure 14.3 Subsequent measurement

Category	Measurement
Financial assets at fair value through profit or loss*	Fair value without any deduction for transaction costs on sale or disposal
Held-to-maturity investments	Amortised cost using the effective interest method
Loans and receivables	Amortised cost using the effective interest method
Available-for-sale financial assets*	Fair value without any deduction for transaction costs on sale or disposal
Financial liabilities at fair value through profit or loss	Fair value
Other financial liabilities	Amortised cost using the effective interest method

* If these categories include unquoted equity instruments (or derivative liabilities that are settled in unquoted equity instruments) where fair value cannot be measured reliably then they are measured at cost. This, however, should be very rare.

The measurement after initial recognition is at either fair value or amortised cost. The only financial instruments that can be recognised at cost (not amortised) are unquoted equity investments for which there is no measurable fair value. These should be very rare.

The fair value is the amount for which an asset could be exchanged, or a liability settled, between knowledgeable, willing parties in an arm's-length transaction.

The methods for fair value measurement allow a number of different bases to be used for the assessment of fair value. These include:

- published market prices; transactions in similar instruments; discounted future cash flows; valuation models.

From January 2013 fair value will be assessed under IFRS 13 *Fair Value Measurement*. The method used will be the one which is most reliable for the particular instrument.

In the 2008 financial crisis there were calls on the IASB to either abolish or suspend the fair value measurement basis in IAS 39 as it has been perceived as requiring companies to recognise losses greater than their true value. The reason for this is that some claim the market value was being distorted by a lack of liquidity and that markets are not functioning efficiently with willing buyers and sellers. The IASB has resisted the calls but has issued guidance on valuation in illiquid markets that emphasises the different ways that fair value can be determined. For instruments that operate in illiquid markets there is sometimes a need to value the instruments based on valuation models and discounted cash flows; however, these models take into account factors that a market participant would consider in the current circumstances.

Amortised cost is calculated using the effective interest method on assets and liabilities. For the definition of effective interest it is necessary to look at IAS 39, paragraph 9. The effective rate is defined as:

> the rate that exactly discounts estimated future cash receipts or payments through the expected life of the financial instrument.

The definition then goes on to require that the entity shall:

- estimate cash flows considering all contractual terms of the financial instrument (for example, prepayment, call and similar options), but not future credit losses;
- include all necessary fees and points paid or received that are an integral part of the effective yield calculation (IAS 18);
- make a presumption that the cash flows and expected life of a group of similar financial instruments can be estimated reliably.

Illustration of the effective yield method

George plc lends £10,000 to a customer for fixed interest based on the customer paying 5% interest per annum (annually in arrears) for two years, and then 6% fixed for the remaining three years with the full £10,000 repayable at the end of the five-year term.

The tables below show the interest income over the loan period assuming:

(a) it is not expected that the customer will repay early (effective rate is 5.55% per annum derived from an internal rate of return calculation); and

(b) it is expected the customer will repay at the end of year 3 but there are no repayment penalties (effective rate is 5.3% per annum derived from an internal rate of return calculation).

The loan balance will alter as follows:

No early repayment

Period	B/F	Interest income (5.55%)	Cash received	C/F
Year 1	10,000	555	(500)	10,055
Year 2	10,055	558	(500)	10,113
Year 3	10,113	561	(600)	10,074
Year 4	10,074	559	(600)	10,033
Year 5	10,033	557	(10,600)	(10)*

* Difference due to rounding

Early repayment

Period	B/F	Interest income (5.3%)	Cash received	C/F
Year 1	10,000	530	(500)	10,030
Year 2	10,030	532	(500)	10,062
Year 3	10,062	533	(10,600)	(5)*

* Difference due to rounding

Gains or losses on subsequent measurement

When financial instruments are remeasured to fair value the rules for the treatment of the subsequent gain or loss are as shown in Figure 14.4. Gains or losses arising on financial instruments that have not been remeasured to fair value will arise when either the assets are impaired or the instruments are derecognised. These gains and losses are recognised in profit or loss for the period.

14.4.6 Hedging

If a financial instrument has been taken out to act as a hedge, and this position is clearly identified and expected to be effective, hedge accounting rules can be followed.

There are three types of hedging relationship: fair value hedge, cash flow hedge and net investment hedge.

Figure 14.4 Gains or losses on subsequent measurements

Instrument	Gain or loss
Instruments at fair value through profit or loss	Profit or loss
Available-for-sale	Other comprehensive income (except for impairments and foreign exchange gains and losses) until derecognition, at which time the cumulative gain/loss in equity is recognised in profit or loss. Dividend income is recognised in profit or loss when the right to receive payment is established.

1 Fair value hedge

A hedge of the exposure to changes in fair value of a recognised asset or liability or an unrecognised firm commitment that will affect reported net income. Any gain or loss arising on remeasuring the hedging instrument and the hedged item should be recognised in profit or loss in the period.

2 Cash flow hedge

A hedge of the exposure to variability in cash flows that is attributable to a particular risk associated with the recognised asset or liability and that will affect reported net income. A hedge of foreign exchange risk on a firm commitment may be a cash flow or a fair value hedge. The gain or loss on the hedging instrument should be recognised directly in other comprehensive income. Any gains or losses recognised in other comprehensive income should be included in profit or loss in the period that the hedged item affects profit or loss. If the instrument being hedged results in the recognition of a non-financial asset or liability, the gain or loss on the hedging instrument can be recognised as part of the cost of the hedged item.

Cash flow hedge illustrated

Harvey plc directors agreed at their July 2006 meeting to acquire additional specialist computer equipment in September 2007 at an estimated cost of $500,000.

The company entered into a forward contract in July 2006 to purchase $500,000 in September 2007 and pay £260,000. At the year-end in December 2006 the $500,000 has appreciated and has a sterling value of £276,000.

At the year-end the increase of £16,000 will be debited to Forward Contract and credited to a hedge reserve.

In September 2007 when the equipment is purchased the £16,000 will be deducted in its entirety from the Equipment carrying amount or transferred annually as a reduction of the annual depreciation charge.

3 Net investment hedge

A hedge of an investment in a foreign entity. The gain or loss on the hedging instrument should be recognised directly in other comprehensive income to match against the gain or loss on the hedged investment.

Conditions for hedge accounting

In order to be able to apply the hedge accounting techniques detailed above, an entity must meet a number of conditions. These conditions are designed to ensure that only genuine hedging instruments can be hedge accounted, and that the hedged positions are clearly identified and documented.

The conditions are:

- at the inception of the hedge there is formal documentation of the hedge relationship and the enterprise's risk management objective and strategy for undertaking the hedge;
- the hedge is expected to be highly effective at inception and on an ongoing basis in achieving offsetting changes in fair values or cash flows;
- the effectiveness of the hedge can be reliably measured, that is the fair value of the hedged item and the hedging instrument can be measured reliably;
- for cash flow hedges, a forecasted transaction that is the subject of the hedge must be highly probable; and
- the hedge was assessed on an ongoing basis and determined actually to have been effective throughout the accounting period (effective between 80% and 125%).

14.5 IFRS 7 *Financial Instruments: Disclosure*[6]

14.5.1 Introduction

This standard came out of the ongoing project of improvements to the accounting and disclosure requirements relating to financial instruments.

For periods before those starting on or after 1 January 2007 disclosures in respect of financial instruments were governed by two standards:

1 IAS 30 *Disclosures in the Financial Statements of Banks and Similar Financial Institutions*; and

2 IAS 32 *Financial Instruments: Disclosure and Presentation*.

In drafting IFRS 7, the IASB:

- reviewed existing disclosures in the two standards, and removed duplicative disclosures;
- simplified the disclosure about concentrations of risk, credit risk, liquidity risk and market risk under IAS 32; and
- transferred disclosure requirements from IAS 32.

14.5.2 Main requirements

The standard applies to all entities, regardless of the quantity of financial instruments held. However, the extent of the disclosures required will depend on the extent of the entity's use of financial instruments and of its exposure to risk.

The standard requires disclosure of:

- the significance of financial instruments for the entity's financial position and performance (many of these disclosures were previously in IAS 32); and
- the nature and extent of risks arising from financial instruments to which the entity is exposed during the period and at the end of the reporting period, and how the entity manages those risks.

The qualitative disclosures describe management's objectives, policies and processes for managing those risks.

The quantitative disclosures provide information about the extent to which the entity is exposed to risk, based on the information provided internally to the entity's key management personnel.

For the disclosure of the significance of financial instruments for the entity's financial position and performance, a key aspect will be to clearly link the statement of financial position and the statement of comprehensive income to the classifications in IAS 39. The requirements from IFRS 7 in this respect are as follows:

8   The carrying amounts of each of the following categories, as defined in IAS 39, shall be disclosed either on the face of the statement of financial position or in the notes:

(a) financial assets at fair value through profit or loss, showing separately (i) those designated as such upon initial recognition and (ii) those classified as held for trading in accordance with IAS 39;

(b) held-to-maturity investments;

(c) loans and receivables;

(d) available-for-sale financial assets;

(e) financial liabilities at fair value through profit or loss, showing separately (i) those designated as such upon initial recognition and (ii) those classified as held for trading in accordance with IAS 39; and

(f) financial liabilities measured at amortised cost.

20 An entity shall disclose the following items of income, expense, gains or losses either on the face of the financial statements or in the notes:

(a) net gains or net losses on:

(i) financial assets or financial liabilities at fair value through profit or loss, showing separately those on financial assets or financial liabilities designated as such upon initial recognition, and those on financial assets or financial liabilities that are classified as held for trading in accordance with IAS 39;

(ii) available-for-sale financial assets, showing separately the amount of gain or loss recognised directly in equity during the period and the amount removed from equity and recognised in profit or loss for the period;

(iii) held-to-maturity investments;

(iv) loans and receivables; and

(v) financial liabilities measured at amortised cost;

(b) total interest income and total interest expense (calculated using the effective interest method) for financial assets or financial liabilities that are not at fair value through profit or loss;

(c) fee income and expense (other than amounts included in determining the effective interest rate) arising from:

(i) financial assets or financial liabilities that are not at fair value through profit or loss; and

(ii) trust and other fiduciary activities that result in the holding or investing of assets on behalf of individuals, trusts, retirement benefit plans, and other institutions;

(d) interest income on impaired financial assets accrued in accordance with paragraph AG93 of IAS 39; and

(e) the amount of any impairment loss for each class of financial asset.

EXAMPLE ● Extract from the disclosures given by Findel plc in 2010 compliant with IFRS 7:

FINANCIAL INSTRUMENTS

Capital risk management

The group manages its capital to ensure that the group will be able to continue as a going concern while maximising the return to stakeholders through the optimisation of the net debt and equity balance. The board of directors reviews the capital structure of the group regularly considering both the costs and risks associated with each class of capital. The capital structure of the group consists of:

	2010 £000	2009 £000 (Restated)
Net debt		
Obligations under finance leases (note 24)	1,011	2,247
Borrowings (note 25)	352,918	383,762
Cash at bank and in hand (note 22)	(44,331)	(9,924)
	309,598	376,085
Equity		
Share capital (note 30)	24,472	4,257
Capital reserves (note 31)	111,493	54,290
Translation reserve (note 32)	702	1,292
Accumulated losses (note 33)	(103,094)	(27,531)
	33,573	32,308
Gearing (being net debt divided by equity above)	9.2	11.6

Significant accounting policies

Details of the significant accounting policies and methods adopted, including the criteria for recognition, the basis of measurement and the basis on which income and expenses are recognised, in respect of each class of financial asset, financial liability and equity instrument are disclosed in note 1 to the financial statements.

Categories of financial instruments

	Carrying value	
	2010 £000	2009 £000 (Restated)
Financial assets		
Held for trading	—	—
Loans and receivables (including cash and cash equivalents)	254,686	273,158
Financial liabilities		
Held for trading	6	3,219
Amortised cost	435,198	484,299

Financial risk management objectives

The group's financial risks include market risk (including currency risk and interest risk), credit risk, liquidity risk and cash flow interest rate risk. The group seeks to minimise the effects of these risks by using derivative financial instruments to manage its exposure. The use of financial derivatives is governed by the group's policies approved by the board of directors. The group does not enter into or trade financial instruments, including derivative financial instruments, for speculative purposes.

Market risk

The group's activities expose it primarily to the financial risks of changes in foreign currency exchange rates and interest rates. The group enters into a variety of derivative financial instruments to manage its exposure to interest rate and foreign currency risk, including:

- forward foreign exchange contracts to hedge the exchange rate risk arising on the purchase of inventory in US dollars; and
- interest rate swaps to mitigate the risk of rising interest rates.

Foreign currency risk management

The group undertakes certain transactions denominated in foreign currencies. Hence, exposures to exchange rate fluctuations arise. Exchange rate exposures are managed utilising forward foreign exchange contracts.

Foreign currency sensitivity analysis

A significant proportion of products sold through the group's Home Shopping and Educational Supplies divisions are procured through the group's Far East buying office. The currency of purchase for these goods is principally the US dollar, with a proportion being in Hong Kong dollars . . . details the group's sensitivity to a 10% increase and decrease in the Sterling against the relevant foreign currencies. 10% represents management's assessment of the reasonably possible change in foreign exchange rates.

Interest rate risk management

The group is exposed to interest rate risk as the group borrows funds at both fixed and floating interest rates. The risk is managed by the group by maintaining a mix between fixed and floating rate borrowings, and the use of interest rate swap contracts and forward interest rate contracts when considered necessary.

Credit risk management

Credit risk refers to the risk that a counterparty will default on its contractual obligations resulting in financial loss to the group. The group's credit risk is primarily attributable to its trade receivables. The amounts presented in the balance sheet are net of allowances for doubtful receivables. An allowance for impairment is made when there is an identified loss event which, based on previous experience, is evidence of a reduction in the recoverability of the cash flows.

Liquidity risk management

Ultimate responsibility for liquidity risk management rests with the board of directors, which has built an appropriate liquidity risk management framework for the management of the group's short-, medium- and long-term funding and liquidity management requirements. The group manages liquidity risk by maintaining adequate reserves, banking facilities and reserve borrowing facilities by continuously monitoring forecast and actual cash flows and matching the maturity profiles of financial assets and liabilities. Included in note 25 is a description of additional undrawn facilities that the group has at its disposal to further reduce liquidity risk.

The group has access to financing and securitisation facilities, the total unused amount of which is £10,840,000 (2009: £76,162,000) at the balance sheet date. The group expects to meet its other obligations from operating cash flows and proceeds of maturing financial assets.

Fair value of financial instruments

The directors consider that the carrying amounts of financial assets and financial liabilities recorded at amortised cost in the financial statements approximate their fair value. The group is required to analyse financial instruments that are measured subsequent to initial recognition at fair value, grouped into levels 1 to 3 based on the degree to which the fair value is observable.

- Level 1 fair value measurements are those derived from quoted prices (unadjusted) in active markets for identical assets or liabilities;
- Level 2 fair value measurements are those derived from inputs other than quoted prices included within level 1 that are observable for the asset or liability, either directly (i.e. as prices) or indirectly (i.e. derived from prices); and
- Level 3 fair value measurements are those derived from valuation techniques that include inputs for the asset or liability that are not based on observable market data (unobservable inputs).

The above financial assets and liabilities were measured at fair value on level 2 fair value measurement bases.

[These are extracts from the disclosures; full disclosures can be seen in Findel plc 2010 Annual Report.]

14.5.3 Effective date

The standard must be applied for annual accounting periods commencing on or after 1 January 2007, although early adoption is encouraged. Certain amendments have been made to IFRS 7 since 2007 which are effective at later dates.

IAS 32 was renamed[7] in 2005 as *Financial Instruments: Presentation*, following the transfer of the disclosure requirements to IFRS 7.

14.6 Financial instruments developments

As a result of the 2008 financial crisis and the subsequent criticism of the accounting standards on financial instruments, the IASB committed to revising IAS 39 and replacing it with a simpler standard that was easier to apply. In order to be able to progress this project quickly, the IASB split the project into a number of areas and IFRS 9 *Financial Instruments* is the outcome of the first part of the project. The areas to be considered are:

(i)   recognition and measurement (IFRS 9);

(ii) impairment and the effective yield model;

(iii) hedge accounting;

(iv) derecognition of financial assets and liabilities (no longer an active project)

(v) financial liability measurement.

By early 2011 the IASB had issued IFRS 9 and had also issued exposure drafts on the impairment model, derecognition and hedge accounting. IFRS 9 is mandatory from accounting periods beginning on or after 1 January 2015, but earlier adoption is permitted. As yet (May 2013) the European Union has not endorsed the standard and therefore it cannot be used in Europe.

14.6.1 IFRS 9 – recognition and measurement

As discussed earlier in this chapter, the existing IAS 39 is complex, involving four different potential classifications of financial assets (held-to-maturity, loans and receivables, available-for-sale and fair value through profit or loss), each with its own measurement requirements. These classifications can be difficult to apply and also can give inconsistencies between entities and between the accounting and the commercial intentions of some instruments (highlighted in the changes made to IAS 39 to allow reclassification in 2008). The primary focus of the IASB was to simplify these categories and also to be clearer in how to determine which instruments are recognised in each category.

Classification

IFRS 9 has only two measurement bases for financial assets, fair value or amortised cost. It also only allows gains and losses on equity instruments to be presented in other comprehensive income; fair value gains and losses on other instruments are recognised in profit or loss. The diagram in Figure 14.5 summarises the classification approach.

The two key factors in determining the accounting treatment are the business model adopted by an entity for the instrument and the nature of the cash flows. The alternative business models could be to collect principal and interest or to trade the instruments by selling them on, for example. The contractual cash flows requirement ensures that an instrument held at amortised cost only exhibits the basic loan features of repayment of interest and capital. IFRS 9 does, however, retain the fair value option in IAS 39 although it is not expected to be as significant a choice, as the first two criteria will generally determine the treatment. Reclassification between the categories is acceptable only if an entity changes its business model, and only applies prospectively.

Figure 14.5 The classification approach of IFRS 9

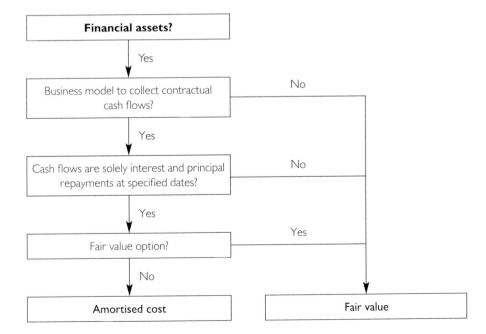

Presentation of gains and losses

Once the measurement at fair value or amortised cost is determined, the standard gives a choice of the presentation of fair value gains and losses only for equity instruments. Any debt instruments or derivatives are measured at fair value with gains and losses in profit or loss. However, for equity instruments which are not trading instruments there is a choice for entities to present the gains and losses from movements in fair value in other comprehensive income. This choice is irrevocable and therefore subsequent reclassification is not appropriate.

14.6.2 Impairment of financial assets

The issues surrounding impairment have proved difficult for the IASB and they have faced significant pressure to change the current impairment models in IAS 39, in particular for instruments measured at amortised cost. To the date of writing this text the IASB has issued two exposure drafts on amortised cost and impairment but final guidance has not been issued. Below we discuss the major concern that the IASB has been asked to address. A revised exposure draft, ED/2013/3 *Financial Instruments: Expected Credit Losses* was issued in early 2013.

Incurred versus expected losses

The debate on impairment largely revolves around whether financial asset impairment should be calculated following an incurred or expected loss model. IAS 39 uses an incurred loss model; however, in the 2008 financial crisis many commentators have suggested that this model delayed the recognition of losses on loans, resulting in misleading results for financial institutions. The key difference between the two approaches is that an incurred loss model provides for impairments only when an event has occurred which causes that impairment. An expected loss model provides for impairment if there is reason to expect that it will arise at some point over the life of the loan (even if it has not arisen at the balance sheet date). For example, if a bank makes a loan to a customer and the customer becomes unemployed and therefore defaults on the loan, under the incurred loss model an impairment would only be recognised when the customer loses their job. Under the expected loss model, the bank would have made an estimate of the likelihood of the customer losing his job from the inception of the loan and provide based on that probability. The provision on the expected loss model is therefore recognised earlier but it does depend much more on the estimation and judgement of management of a company.

ED/2009/12 was issued to address impairment and the way that the amortised cost method of accounting is applied. The ED proposes an expected loss model but does this by proposing changes in the way that the amortised cost model is applied. The amortised cost model determines an effective interest rate by determining the rate at which the initial loan and the cash flows over its life are discounted to zero, effectively the internal rate of return on the loan. IAS 39 requires the rate to be determined on cash flows before future credit losses, whereas the exposure draft requires the calculation on cash flows including expected future credit losses. In every period the expected cash flows would need to be adjusted and discounted back at the original effective rate; any difference in the loan value is then adjusted against profit or loss. The impact of this new approach is that losses would tend to be recognised earlier and no separate impairment model is required; if impairment is expected, the cash flow estimates will automatically adjust for that. It is still to be seen how straightforward the approach will be in practice and whether financial institutions can adapt their systems and processes easily to the revised approach. A further ED was issued in 2013 as many financial institutions had expressed concerns about the proposed model.

14.6.3 Hedge accounting

The final phase of the IASB project to replace IAS 39 concerns proposals on hedge accounting. The hedge accounting models in IAS 39 have come under criticism for a number of reasons:

(i) entities claim that the requirements are complex and difficult to apply. For example, it can be difficult to distinguish a cash flow hedge from a fair value hedge;

(ii) investors regularly resort to pro forma or underlying information produced by entities outside the financial statements to understand risk management (for example, in the case of Rolls-Royce discussed in Section 14.2.1); and

(iii) the hedge accounting requirements can be incompatible with the commercial practices adopted. For example, IAS 39 does not allow hedge accounting of a net position.

These criticisms have led the IASB to look at hedging as part of the review of IAS 39. In December 2010 an exposure draft was issued that proposes amendments to the requirements. Assuming new guidance is issued, it will be added to IFRS 9.

The new guidance attempts to address some of the key criticisms of IAS 39. In particular it proposes to follow an approach that attempts to align accounting with risk management activities. The aim is that if risk management activities are to hedge this should be reflected in the financial statements, thereby making the financial statements more meaningful to investors. In addition the IASB is proposing to address specific criticisms, for example by allowing net positions to be designated as hedged items.

The changes in recognition of hedging will also be accompanied by new disclosures that focus on the risks being hedged, the risk management practices and the impact on the primary financial statements.

Summary

This chapter has given some insight into the difficulties and complexities of accounting for financial instruments and the ongoing debate on this topic, highlighted by the financial crisis that began in 2008. The approach of the IASB is to adhere to the principles contained in the *Framework* but to also issue guidance that is robust enough to prevent manipulation and abuse. Whether the IASB has achieved this is open to debate. Some might view the detailed requirements of the standards, particularly IAS 39, to be so onerous that companies will not be able to show their real intentions in the financial statements. This would be particularly true, for instance, with the detailed criteria on hedging. These criteria have led to many businesses not hedge accounting even though they are hedging commercially to manage their risks. The hedge accounting criteria do not fit with the way they run or manage their risk profiles. This may change with future developments currently under discussion by the IASB.

The principles in IAS 39 are still developing. Since December 2003 there have already been many amendments to the standards.

As can be seen, there is much to criticise in these requirements, but it should be borne in mind that the IASB has grasped this issue better than many other standard setters. Financial instruments may be complex and subject to debate but guidance is required in this area, and the IASB has given guidance where many others have not.

In addition to giving an insight into the development of standards, our aim has been that you should be able to calculate the debt/equity split on compound instruments and the finance cost on liability instruments and classify and account for the four categories of financial instrument.

REVIEW QUESTIONS

1 Explain what is meant by the term split accounting when applied to convertible debt or convertible preference shares and the rationale for splitting.

2 Discuss the implications for a business if a substance approach is used for the reporting of convertible loans.

3 Explain how a gain or loss on a forward contract is dealt with in the accounts if the contract is not completed until after the period-end.

4 Explain how redeemable preference shares, perpetual debt, loans and equity investments are reported in the financial statements.

5 The authors[8] contend that the use of current valuations can present an inaccurate view of a firm's true financial status. When assets are illiquid, current value represents only a guess. When assets participate in an economic 'bubble', current value is invariably unsustainable. Accounting standards, the authors conclude, should be flexible enough to fairly assess value in these circumstances. Discuss the alternatives that standard setters could permit in order to fairly assess values in an illiquid market.

6 Disclosure of the estimated fair values of financial instruments is better than adjusting the values in the financial statements with the resulting volatility that affects earnings and gearing ratios. Discuss.

7 Companies were permitted in 2008 to reclassify financial instruments that were initially designated as at fair value through profit. Critically discuss the reasons for the standard setters changing the existing standard.

8 Explain the difference between the incurred loss model and the expected loss model in determining impairment and suggest limitations of both approaches.

9 The only true way to simplify IAS 39 would be for all financial assets and liabilities to be measured at fair value with gains and losses recognised in profit or loss. Discuss.

EXERCISES

* Question 1

On 1 April year 1, a deep discount bond was issued by DDB AG. It had a face value of £2.5 million covering a five-year term. The lenders were granted a discount of 5%. The coupon rate was 10% on the principal sum of £2.5 million, payable annually in arrears. The principal sum was repayable in cash on 31 March year 5. Issuing costs amounted to £150,000.

Required:
Compute the finance charge per annum and the carrying value of the loan to be reported in each year's profit or loss and statement of financial position respectively.

* Question 2

Fairclough plc borrowed €10 million from a bank on 1 January 2011. Fees of €100,000 were charged by the bank which were paid by Fairclough plc at inception of the loan. The terms of the loan are:

Interest

- Interest of 6% until 31 December 2013
- Interest dropping to 5% from 31 December 2013 to 31 December 2015

Repayment schedule

- Repayment of €5 million on 31 December 2013
- Repayment of €5 million on 31 December 2015

Interest is paid annually in arrears.

The effective yield on the loan is 6.07%.

Required:
(i)   What is the total finance cost on the loan over the five-year period?
(ii) What will be reflected as a liability in the financial statements for each 31 December year-end and what interest costs will be recognised in the statement of comprehensive income?

* Question 3

Isabelle Limited borrows £100,000 from a bank on the following terms:

(i)   arrangement fees of £2,000 are charged by the bank and deducted from the initial proceeds on the loan;

(ii) interest is payable at 5% for the first three years of the loan and then increases to 7% for the remaining two years of the loan;

(iii) the full balance of £100,000 is repaid at the end of year 5.

Required:
(a) What interest should be recognised in the statement of comprehensive income for each year of the loan?
(b) If Isabelle Limited repaid the loan after three years for £100,000, what gain or loss would be recognised in the statement of comprehensive income?

* Question 4

On 1 January 2009 Henry Ltd issued a convertible debenture for €200 million carrying a coupon interest rate of 5%. The debenture is convertible at the option of the holders into 10 ordinary shares for each €100 of debenture stock on 31 December 2013. Henry Ltd considered borrowing the €200 million through a conventional debenture that repaid in cash; however, the interest rate that could be obtained was estimated at 7%, therefore Henry Ltd decided on the issue of the convertible.

Required:
Show how the convertible bond issue will be recognised on 1 January 2009 and determine the interest charges that are expected in the statement of comprehensive income over the life of the convertible bond.

Question 5

On 1 October year 1, RPS plc issued one million £1 5% redeemable preference shares. The shares were issued at a discount of £50,000 and are due to be redeemed on 30 September Year 5. Dividends are paid on 30 September each year.

Required:
Show the accounting treatment of the preference shares throughout the lifespan of the instrument calculating the finance cost to be charged to profit or loss in each period.

* Question 6

Milner Ltd issues a 6% cumulative preference share for €1 million that is repayable in cash at par 10 years after issue. The only condition on the dividends is that if the directors declare an ordinary dividend the preference dividend (and any arrears of preference dividend) must be paid first. Arrears of dividend do not need to be paid on redemption of the instrument.

Required:

Explain how this preference share should be accounted for over its life.

Question 7

Creasy plc needs to raise €20 million and is considering two different instruments that could be issued:

(i) A 7% debenture with a par value of €20 million, repayable at par in five years. Interest is paid annually in arrears.

(ii) A 5% convertible debenture with a par value of €20 million, repayable at par in five years or convertible into 5 million €1 shares. Interest is paid annually in arrears.

Required:

Comment on the effect on the statement of comprehensive income and the statement of financial position of issuing these different instruments.

* Question 8

On 1 October 20X1, Little Raven plc issued 50,000 debentures, with a par value of £100 each, to investors at £80 each. The debentures are redeemable at par on 30 September 20X6 and have a coupon rate of 6%, which was significantly below the market rate of interest for such debentures issued at par. In accounting for these debentures to date, Little Raven plc has simply accounted for the cash flows involved, namely:

● On issue: debenture 'liability' included in the statement of financial position at £4,000,000.

● Statements of comprehensive income: interest charged in years ended 30 September 20X2, 20X3 and 20X4 (published accounts) and 30 September 20X5 (draft accounts) – £300,000 each year (being 6% of £5,000,000).

The new finance director, who sees the likelihood that further similar debenture issues will be made, considers that the accounting policy adopted to date is not appropriate. He has asked you to suggest a more appropriate treatment.

Little Raven plc intends to acquire subsidiaries in 20X6.

Statements of comprehensive income for the years ended 30 September 20X4 and 20X5 are as follows:

	Y/e 30 Sept 20X5 (Draft) £000	Y/e 30 Sept 20X4 (Actual) £000
Turnover	6,700	6,300
Cost of sales	(3,025)	(2,900)
Gross profit	3,675	3,400
Overheads	(600)	(550)
Interest payable – debenture	(300)	(300)
– others	(75)	(50)
Profit for the financial year	2,700	2,500
Retained earnings brought forward	4,300	1,800
Retained earnings carried forward	7,000	4,300

Extracts from the statement of financial position are:

	At 30 Sept 20X5 (Draft) £000	At 30 Sept 20X4 (Actual) £000
Share capital	2,250	2,250
Share premium	550	550
Retained earnings	7,000	4,300
	9,800	7,100
6% debentures	4,000	4,000
	13,800	11,100

Required:

(a) Outline the considerations involved in deciding how to account for the issue, the interest cost and the carrying value in respect of debenture issues such as that made by Little Raven plc. Consider the alternative treatments in respect of the statement of comprehensive income and refer briefly to the appropriate statement of financial position disclosures for the debentures. Conclude in terms of the requirements of IAS 32 (on accounting for financial instruments) in this regard.

(b) Detail an alternative set of entries in the books of Little Raven plc for the issue of the debentures and subsequently; under this alternative the discount on the issue should be dealt with under the requirements of IAS 32. The constant rate of interest for the allocation of interest cost is given to you as 11.476%. Draw up a revised statement of comprehensive income for the year ended 30 September 20X5, together with comparatives, taking account of the alternative accounting treatment.

* Question 9

George plc adopted IFRS for the first time on 1 January 2008 and has three different instruments whose accounting George is concerned will change as a result of the adoption of the standard. The three instruments are:

1   An investment in 15% of the ordinary shares of Joshua Ltd, a private company. This investment cost €50,000, but had a fair value of €60,000 on 1 January 2008, €70,000 on 31 December 2008 and €65,000 on 31 December 2009.

2   An investment of €40,000 in 6% debentures. The debentures were acquired at their face value of €40,000 on 1 July 2007 and pay interest half-yearly in arrears on 31 December and 30 June each year. The bonds had a fair value of €41,000 at 1 January 2008, €43,000 at 31 December 2008 and €38,000 at 31 December 2009.

3   An interest rate swap taken out to swap floating-rate interest on an outstanding loan to fixed-rate interest. Since taking out the swap the loan has been repaid; however, George plc decided to retain the swap as it was 'in the money' at 1 January 2008. The fair value of the swap was a €10,000 asset on 1 January 2008; however, it became a liability of €5,000 by 31 December 2008 and the liability increased to €20,000 by 31 December 2009. In 2008 George paid €1,000 to the counterparty to the swap and in 2009 paid €5,000 to the counterparty.

Required:

Show the amount that would be recognised for all three instruments in the statement of financial position, in profit and loss and in other comprehensive income on the following assumptions:

(i)   Equity and debt investments are available for sale.
(ii) Where possible, investments are treated as held to maturity.
(iii) Where equity investments are treated as fair value through profit and loss, and debt investments are treated as loans and receivables.

Question 10

On 1 January 2009 Hazell plc borrows €5 million on terms with interest of 3% for the period to 31 December 2009, going to variable rate thereafter (at inception the variable rate is 6%). The loan is repayable at Hazell plc's option between 31 December 2011 and 31 December 2013.

Initially Hazell plc estimates that the loan will be repaid on 31 December 2011; however, at 31 December 2010 Hazell plc revises this estimate and assumes the loan will only be repaid on 31 December 2013.

Assume that the variable rate remains at 6% throughout the period and that interest is paid annually in arrears.

Required:
(i) Determine the total expected finance costs and effective yield on the loan at 1 January 2009.
(ii) Show the impact of the loan on the statement of comprehensive income and statement of financial position for periods ended 31 December 2009 and 31 December 2010.

Question 11

Baudvin Ltd has an equity investment that cost €1 million on 1 January 2008. The investment is classified as an available-for-sale investment. The value of the investment at each period-end is:

31 December 2008	€950,000
31 December 2009	€1,030,000
31 December 2010	€1,080,000

Baudvin Ltd sold the investment for €1,100,000 on 31 March 2011.

Required:
Show what should be reflected for the investment in Baudvin Ltd's financial statements for each period from 31 December 2008 to 2011.

* Question 12

A company borrows on a floating-rate loan, but wishes to hedge against interest variations so swaps the interest for fixed rate. The swap should be perfectly effective and has zero fair value at inception. Interest rates increase and therefore the swap becomes a financial asset to the company at fair value of £5 million.

Required:
Describe the impact on the financial statements for the following situations:
(a) The swap is accounted for under IAS 39, but is not designated as a hedge.
(b) The swap is accounted for under IAS 39, and is designated as a hedge.

Question 13

Charles plc is applying IAS 32 and IAS 39 for the first time this year and is uncertain about the application of the standard. Charles plc's balance sheet is as follows:

	£000	Financial asset/liability	IAS 32/39?	Category	Measurement
Non-current assets					
Goodwill	2,000				
Intangible	3,000				
Tangible	6,000				
Investments					
Corporate bond	1,500				
Equity trade					
investments	900				
	13,400				
Current assets					
Inventory	800				
Receivables	700				
Prepayments	300				
Forward contracts					
(note 1)	250				
Equity investments					
held for future sale	1,200				
	3,250				
Current liabilities					
Trade creditors	(3,500)				
Lease creditor	(800)				
Income tax	(1,000)				
Forward contracts					
(note 1)	(500)				
	(5,800)				
Non-current liabilities					
Bank loan	(5,000)				
Convertible debt	(1,800)				
Deferred tax	(500)				
Pension liability	(900)				
	(8,200)				
Net assets	**2,650**				

Note

1 The forward contracts have been revalued to fair value in the balance sheet. They do not qualify as hedging instruments.

Required:

Complete the above balance sheet and consider under IAS 39:

(i)   Which items on the balance sheet are financial assets/liabilities?

(ii) Are the balances within the scope of IAS 39?

(iii) How they should be classified under IAS 39:

    HTM   Held-to-maturity

    LR   Loans and receivables

    FVPL Fair value through profit and loss

    AFS   Available-for-sale

    FL   Financial liabilities

(iv) How they should be measured under IAS 39:

FV   Fair value

C   Amortised cost

Assume that the company includes items in 'fair value through profit and loss' only when required to do so, and also chooses where possible to include items in 'loans and receivables'.

* Question 14

Tan plc owns an available-for-sale equity investment that cost £2 million. At 31 December 2008 the investment was recognised on the balance sheet at £2.1 million.

At 31 December 2009 the investment had declined in value to £1.5 million; however, Tan plc did not assume that the investment had impaired. By 31 December 2010 the investment had not recovered in value (it was still worth £1.5 million) and Tan plc concluded that its decline in value was permanent and it had impaired.

In June 2011 (after the 2010 financial statements had been issued) circumstances changed and the investment recovered in value to £2.2 million.

Required:

Show the accounting entries you would expect Tan plc to make for each December year-end from 2009 to 2011.

Question 15

At the start of the year Cornish plc entered into a number of financial instruments and is considering how to classify these instruments under IAS 39. The instruments are as follows:

(a) Investment in listed 3% government bonds for €2 million. Cornish acquired the bonds when they were issued at their nominal value of €2 million. By the year-end, 31 December 2010, interest rates had fallen and the bonds had a market value of €2,025,000.

(b) Investment in shares in Schaenzler plc, a listed company, for €1,300,000. At 31 December 2010 the investment had fallen in value and was estimated to be worth only €1,200,000.

(c) Cornish plc borrowed €5 million at floating rate in the year and to hedge the interest rate took out an interest rate swap (floating to fixed) on the loan. The swap cost nothing to enter into but by 31 December 2010 because interest rates had fallen it had a fair value (liability) of €50,000. Cornish plc does not use hedge accounting.

Required:

Discuss how the investments could be classified and measured under IAS 39 and the implications of the choices for the financial statements of Cornish plc.

References

1 IAS 32 *Financial Instruments: Disclosure and Presentation*, IASC, revised 1998.
2 *Ibid.*, para. 5.
3 *Ibid.*, para. 18.
4 *Ibid.*, para. 23.
5 *Ibid.*, para. 33.
6 IFRS 7 *Financial Instruments: Disclosure*, IASB, 2005.
7 IAS 32 *Financial Instruments: Presentation*, IASB, revised 2005.
8 S. Fearnley and S. Sunder, 'Bring back prudent', *Accountancy*, vol. 140(1370), 2007, pp. 76–77.

CHAPTER 15

Employee benefits

15.1 Introduction

In this chapter we consider the application of IAS 19 *Employee Benefits*.[1] IAS 19 is concerned with the determination of the cost of retirement benefits in the financial statements of **employers** having retirement benefit plans (sometimes referred to as 'pension schemes', 'superannuation schemes' or 'retirement benefit schemes'). The requirements of IFRS 2 *Share-based Payment* will also be considered here. Even though IFRS 2 covers share-based payments for almost any good or service a company can receive, in practice it is employee service that is most commonly rewarded with share-based payments. We also consider the disclosure requirements of IAS 26 *Accounting and Reporting by Retirement Benefit Plans*.[2]

Objectives

By the end of this chapter, you should be able to:

- critically comment on the approaches to pension accounting that have been used under international accounting standards;
- understand the nature of different types of pension plan and account for the different types of pension plan that companies may have;
- explain the accounting treatment for other long-term and short-term employee benefit costs;
- understand and account for share-based payments that are made by companies to their employees;
- outline the required approach of pension schemes to presenting their financial position and performance.

15.2 Greater employee interest in pensions

The percentages of pensioners and public pension expenditure are increasing.

| | % of population over 60 | | Public pensions as % of GDP |
| | 2000 | 2040 | 2040 |
	%	% (projected)	% (projected)
Germany	24	33	18
Italy	24	37	21
Japan	23	34	15
UK	21	30	5
US	17	29	7

This has led to gloomy projections that countries could even be bankrupted by the increasing demand for state pensions. In an attempt to avert what governments see as a national disaster, there have been increasing efforts to encourage private funding of pensions.

As people become more and more aware of the possible failure of governments to provide adequate basic state pensions, they recognise the advisability of making their own provision for their old age. This has raised their expectation that their employers should offer a pension scheme and other post-retirement benefits. These have increased, particularly in Ireland, the UK and the USA, and what used to be a 'fringe benefit' for only certain categories of staff has been broadened across the workforce. This has been encouraged by various governments with favourable tax treatment of both employers' and employees' contributions to pension schemes, and requirements for companies to contribute to pension funds of employees.

15.3 Financial reporting implications

The provision of pensions for employees as part of an overall remuneration package has led to the related costs being a material part of the accounts. The very nature of such arrangements means that the commitment is a long-term one that may well involve estimates. The way the related costs are allocated between accounting periods and are reported in the financial statements needs careful consideration to ensure that a fair view of the position is shown.

In recent years there has been a shift of view on the way that pension costs should be accounted for. The older view was that pension costs (as recommended by IAS 19 prior to its revision in 1998) should be matched against the period of the employee's service so as to create an even charge for pensions in the statement of comprehensive income. However, this approach could result in the statement of financial position being misleading. The more recent approach is to make the statement of financial position more sensible, but perhaps accept greater variation in the pension cost in the statement of comprehensive income. The new view is the one endorsed by IAS 19 (revised) and is the one now in use by companies preparing accounts to international accounting standards.

Before examining the detail of how IAS 19 (revised) requires pensions and other long-term benefits to be accounted for, we need to consider the types of pension scheme that are commonly used.

15.4 Types of scheme

15.4.1 *Ex gratia* arrangements

These are not schemes at all but are circumstances where an employer agrees to grant a pension to be paid for out of the resources of the firm. Consequently these are arrangements where pensions have not been funded but decisions are made on an *ad hoc* or case-by-case basis, sometimes arising out of custom or practice. No contractual obligation to grant or pay a pension exists, although a constructive obligation may exist which would need to be provided for in accordance with IAS 37 *Provisions, Contingent Liabilities and Contingent Assets*.

15.4.2 Defined contribution schemes

These are schemes in which the employer undertakes to make certain contributions each year, usually a stated percentage of salary. These contributions are usually supplemented by contributions from the employee. The money is then invested and, on retirement, the employee gains the pension benefits that can be purchased from the resulting funds.

Such schemes have uncertain future benefits but fixed, predetermined costs. Schemes of this sort were very common among smaller employers but fell out of fashion for a time. In recent years, due to the fixed cost to the company and the resulting low risk to the employer for providing a pension, these schemes have become increasingly popular. They are also popular with employees who regularly change employers, since the funds accrued within the schemes are relatively easy to transfer.

The contributions may be paid into a wide variety of plans, e.g. government plans to ensure state pensions are supplemented (these may be optional or compulsory), or schemes operated by insurance companies.

The following is an extract from the 2011 Annual Report of Nokia:

Pensions
The Group's contributions to defined contribution plans, multi-employer and insured plans are recognised in the income statement in a period which the contributions relate to.

15.4.3 Defined benefit schemes

Under these schemes the employees will, on retirement, receive a pension based on the length of service and salary, usually final salary or an average of the last few (usually three) years' salary.

These schemes have become less popular when new schemes are formed because the cost to employers is uncertain and there are greater regulatory requirements being introduced. Three key factors contributing to the increased costs to employers are:

● the increased life expectancy for retired employees in many countries – meaning that benefits are payable for a longer period;

● the trend towards lower interest rates in many countries. This is relevant because lower interest rates lead to lower discount rates, so liabilities that are discounted are measured at higher amounts in financial statements; and

● the generally disappointing return on equity and property investments in many countries – meaning that the return on investments made by pension schemes is adversely affected.

Whilst the benefits to the employee are not certain, they are more predictable than under a defined contribution scheme. The cost to the employer, however, is uncertain as the employer will need to vary the contributions to the scheme to ensure it is adequately funded to meet the pension liabilities when employees eventually retire.

The following is an extract from the accounting policies in the 2011 Annual Report of the Nestlé Group:

Employee benefits
The liabilities of the Group arising from defined benefit obligations, and the related current service cost, are determined using the projected unit credit method. Actuarial advice is provided both by external consultants and by actuaries employed by the Group. The actuarial assumptions used to calculate the defined benefit obligations vary according to the economic conditions of the country in which the plan is located. Such plans are either externally funded (in the form of independently administered funds) or unfunded.

For the funded defined benefit plans, the deficit or excess of the fair value of plan assets over the present value of the defined benefit obligation is recognised as a liability or an asset in the balance sheet, taking into account any unrecognised past service cost.

However, an excess of assets is recognised only to the extent that it represents a future economic benefit which is available in the form of refunds from the plan or reductions in future contributions to the plan. When these criteria are not met, it is not recognised but is disclosed in the notes. Impacts of minimum funding requirements in relation to past service are considered when determining pension obligations.

Actuarial gains and losses arise mainly from changes in actuarial assumptions and differences between actuarial assumptions and what has actually occurred. They are recognised in the period in which they occur in other comprehensive income.

For defined benefit plans, the pension cost charged to the income statement consists of current service cost, interest cost, expected return on plan assets, effects of early retirements, curtailments or settlements, and past service cost. The past service cost for the enhancement of pension benefits is accounted for when such benefits vest or become a constructive obligation.

Some benefits are also provided by defined contribution plans. Contributions to such plans are charged to the income statement as incurred.

The accounting policy is quite complex to apply and we will illustrate the detailed calculations involved below.

15.4.4 Equity compensation plans

IAS 19 does not specify recognition or measurement requirements for equity compensation plans such as shares or share options issued to employees at less than fair value. The valuation of share options has proved an extremely contentious topic and we will consider the issues that have arisen. IFRS 2 *Share-based Payment* covers these plans.[3]

The following is an extract from the accounting policies in the 2011 Annual Report of the Nestlé Group:

> **Equity compensation plans**
> The Group has equity-settled and cash-settled share-based payment transactions.
>
> Equity-settled share-based payment transactions are recognised in the income statement with a corresponding increase in equity over the vesting period. They are fair valued at grant date and measured using generally accepted pricing models. The cost of equity-settled share-based payment transactions is adjusted annually by the expectations of vesting, for the forfeitures of the participants' rights that no longer satisfy the plan conditions, as well as for early vesting.
>
> Liabilities arising from cash-settled share-based payment transactions are recognised in the income statement over the vesting period. They are fair valued at each reporting date and measured using generally accepted pricing models. The cost of cash-settled share-based payment transactions is adjusted for the forfeitures of the participants' rights that no longer satisfy the plan conditions, as well as for early vesting.

15.5 Defined contribution pension schemes

Defined contribution schemes (otherwise known as money purchase schemes) have not presented any major accounting problems. The cost of providing the pension, usually a percentage of salary, is recorded as a remuneration expense in the statement of comprehensive income in the period in which it is due. Assets or liabilities may exist for the pension contributions if the company has not paid the amount due for the period. If a contribution was payable more than 12 months after the reporting date for services rendered in the current period, the liability should be recorded at its discounted amount (using a discount rate based on the market rate for high-quality corporate bonds).

Disclosure is required of the pension contribution charged to the statement of comprehensive income for the period.

Illustration of Andrew plc defined contribution pension scheme costs

Andrew plc has payroll costs of £2.7 million for the year ended 30 June 2011. Andrew plc pays pension contributions of 5% of salary, but for convenience paid £10,000 per month standard contribution with any shortfall to be made up in the July 2011 contribution.

Statement of comprehensive income charge
The pension cost is £2,700,000 × 5% = £135,000.

Statement of financial position
The amount paid over the period is £120,000 and therefore an accrual of £15,000 will be made in the statement of financial position at 30 June 2011.

15.6 Defined benefit pension schemes

15.6.1 The fundamental accounting issue

A problem that arises in accounting for defined benefit schemes that does not arise when accounting for defined contribution schemes is the much greater uncertainty of the actual benefit payable. There is no guarantee, even after the contributing company has contributed the contractually required amount, that the assets of the scheme will be sufficient to settle the likely future liabilities. Therefore the contributing company may have to provide additional contributions to finance a shortfall and these need to be provided for.

15.6.2 Efforts to arrive at a solution

In order to assess the likely level of exposure for contributing companies, it is necessary to look at the work of the actuaries – specialists who advise on the funding of the scheme and its overall financial position. The actuaries will assess the financial position of the scheme on a regular basis and identify whether the liabilities of the scheme (to pay future benefits already earned out of past service) are covered by the market value of the assets into which contributions are invested until required to pay benefits. These actuarial assessments resulted in the identification of deficits or (occasionally) surpluses for such schemes.

Previous accounting standards in this area tended to focus on the charge to profit and loss for retirement benefits. The charge was typically split into two elements:

● The regular cost – a long-term estimate largely consistent with the contributions made.

● Variations from the regular cost – recognising the actuarial deficit or surplus over the period to the next actuarial assessment.

Differences between the charge to profit and loss and the contributions paid in the period were recognised as liabilities or assets on the statement of financial position. This approach led to a number of problems. Two key problems were:

● The figure in the statement of financial position was difficult to explain.

● The charge to profit and loss depended, *inter alia*, on the frequency of the actuarial assessments.

It was in order to address these issues that a fundamentally different approach was advocated in IAS 19 (revised), published in 1998.

15.7 IAS 19 (revised 1998) *Employee Benefits*

After a relatively long discussion and exposure period IAS 19 (revised 1998) was issued in 1998 and redefined how all employee benefits were to be accounted for.

IAS 19 has chosen to follow an 'asset or liability' approach to accounting for the pension scheme contributions by the employer and, therefore, it defines how the statement of financial position asset or liability should be built up. The statement of comprehensive income charge is effectively the movement in the asset or liability. The pension fund must be valued sufficiently regularly so that the statement of financial position asset or liability is kept up-to-date. The valuation would normally be done by a qualified actuary and is based on actuarial assumptions.

In June 2011 the IASB issued an amended IAS 19 which makes changes to the recognition, measurement and presentation of pension liabilities for periods beginning on or after 1 January 2013. The changes made by IAS 19 (2011) are included in Section 15.17.

15.8 The liability for pension and other post-retirement costs

The liability for pension costs is made up from the following amounts:

(a) the present value of the defined benefit obligation at the period-end date;

(b) plus any actuarial gains (less actuarial losses) not yet recognised;

(c) minus any past service cost not yet recognised;

(d) minus the fair value at the period-end date of plan assets (if any) out of which the obligations are to be settled directly.

If this calculation comes out with a negative amount, the company should recognise a pension asset in the statement of financial position. There is a limit on the amount of the asset, if the asset calculated above is greater than the total of:

(i) any unrecognised actuarial losses and past service cost; plus

(ii) the present value of any future refunds from the scheme or reductions in future contributions.

Within IAS 19 there are rules regarding the maximum pension asset that can be created. Effective from 1 January 2009, IFRIC 14 *Limit on a Defined Benefit Asset, Minimum Funding Requirements and their Interaction* was issued. It provides further guidance in respect of the maximum pension asset that can be recognised. It gives guidance that where a pension has minimum funding obligations to cover future pension service, these reduce the amount of the asset that can be recognised.

Each of the elements making up the asset or liability position (a) to (d) above can now be considered.

15.8.1 Obligations of the fund

The pension fund obligation must be calculated using the 'projected unit credit method'. This method of allocating pension costs builds up the pension liability each year for an extra year of service and a reversal of discounting. Discounting of the liability is done using the market yields on high-quality corporate bonds with similar currency and duration.

The Grado illustration below shows how the obligation to pay pension accumulates over the working life of an employee.

Grado illustration

A lump sum benefit is payable on termination of service and equal to 1% of final salary for each year of service. The salary in year 1 is £10,000 and is assumed to increase at 7% (compound) each year. The discount rate used is 10%. The following table shows how an obligation (in £) builds up for an employee who is expected to leave at the end of year 5. For simplicity, this example ignores the additional adjustment needed to reflect the probability that the employee may leave service at an earlier or a later date.

Year	1	2	3	4	5
Benefit attributed to prior years	0	131	262	393	524
Benefit attributed to current year (1% of final salary)*	131	131	131	131	131
Benefit attributed to current and prior years	131	262	393	524	655
Opening obligation (present value of benefit attributed to prior years)	—	89	196	324	476
Interest at 10%	—	9	20	33	48
Current service cost (present value of benefit attributed to current year)	89	98	108	119	131
Closing obligation (present value of benefit attributed to current and prior years)**	89	196	324	476	655

* Final salary is £10,000 × (1.07)^4 = £13,100.
** Discounting the benefit attributable to current and prior years at 10%.

15.8.2 Actuarial gains and losses

Actuarial gains or losses result from either changes in the present value of the defined benefit obligation or changes in the market value of the plan assets. They arise from experience adjustments – that is, differences between actuarial assumptions and actual experience. Typical reasons for the gains or losses would be:

● unexpectedly low or high rates of employee turnover;

● the effect of changes in the discount rate;

● differences between the **actual** return and the **expected** return on plan assets.

Accounting treatment

Since a revision of IAS 19 in 2004 there has been a choice of accounting treatment for actuarial gains and losses. One approach follows a '10% corridor' and requires recognition of gains and losses in the profit or loss, whereas other alternatives make no use of the corridor and require gains and losses to be recognised immediately, either in profit and loss or in other comprehensive income.

10% corridor approach

- If actual gains and losses are greater than the higher of 10% of the present value of the defined benefit obligation or 10% of the market value of the plan assets, the excess gains and losses should be charged or credited to the profit or loss over the average remaining service lives of current employees. Any shorter period of recognition of gains or losses is acceptable, provided it is systematic.

- If beneath the 10% thresholds, they can be part of the defined benefit liability for the year; however, the standard also allows them to be recognised in the profit or loss.

Any actuarial gains and losses that are recognised in the profit or loss are recognised in the periods following the one in which they arise. For example, if an actuarial loss arose in the year ended 31 December 2010 that exceeded the 10% corridor and therefore required recognition in the statement of comprehensive income, that recognition would begin in the 2011 year. This means that to calculate the income statement charge or credit for the current year, the cumulative unrecognised gains or losses at the end of the previous year are compared to the corridor at the end of the previous year (or the beginning of the current year).

The comprehensive illustration in Section 15.10 below illustrates this treatment.

Immediate recognition approach

It is acceptable to recognise actuarial gains and losses immediately, either in profit and loss or in other comprehensive income.

This approach has the benefit over the corridor approach in that it does not require any actuarial gains and losses to be recognised in profit or loss; however, its drawback comes in volatility on the statement of financial position. Under this approach all actuarial gains and losses are recognised and therefore no unrecognised ones are available for offset against the statement of financial position asset or liability. As the actuarial valuations are based on fair values the volatility could be significant.

15.8.3 Past service costs

Past service costs are costs that arise for a pension scheme as a result of improving the scheme or when a business introduces a plan. They are the extra liability in respect of previous years' service by employees. Note, however, that past service costs can only arise if actuarial assumptions did not take into account the reason why they occurred. Typically they would include:

- estimates of benefit improvements as a result of actuarial gains (if the company proposes to give the gains to the employees);
- the effect of plan amendments that increase or reduce benefits for past service.

Accounting treatment

The past service cost should be recognised on a straight-line basis over the period to which the benefits vest. If already vested, the cost should be recognised immediately in profit or loss in the statement of comprehensive income. A benefit vests when an employee satisfies preconditions. For example, if a company offered a scheme where employees would only be entitled to a pension if they worked for at least five years, the benefits would vest as soon as they started their sixth year of employment. The company will still have to make provision for pensions for the first five years of employment (and past service costs could arise in this period), as these will be pensionable service years provided the employees work for more than five years.

15.8.4 Fair value of plan assets

This is usually the market value of the assets of the plan (or the estimated value if no immediate market value exists). The plan assets exclude unpaid contributions due from the reporting enterprise to the fund.

15.9 The statement of comprehensive income

The statement of comprehensive income charge for a period should be made up of the following parts:

(a) current service cost;

(b) interest cost;

(c) the expected return on any plan assets;

(d) actuarial gains and losses to the extent that they are recognised under the 10% corridor;

(e) past service cost to the extent that it is recognised;

(f) the effect of any curtailments or settlements.

If a company takes the option of recognising all actuarial gains and losses outside profit or loss then they are recognised in full in the 'other comprehensive income' section of the statement of comprehensive income.

The items above are all the things that cause the statement of financial position liability for pensions to alter, and the statement of comprehensive income is consequently based on the movement in the liability. Because of the potential inclusion of actuarial gains and losses and past service costs in comprehensive income, the total comprehensive income is liable to fluctuate much more than the charge made under the original IAS 19.

15.10 Comprehensive illustration

The following comprehensive illustration is based on an example in IAS 19 (revised)[4] and demonstrates how a pension liability and profit or loss charge is calculated. The example does not include the effect of curtailments or settlements. This illustration demonstrates the 10% corridor approach for actuarial gains and losses.

Illustration

The following information is given about a funded defined benefit plan. To keep the computations simple, all transactions are assumed to occur at the year-end. The present value of the obligation and the market value of the plan assets were both 1,000 at 1 January 20X1. The average remaining service lives of the current employees is 10 years.

	20X1	20X2	20X3
Discount rate at start of year	10%	9%	8%
Expected rate of return on plan assets at start of year	12%	11%	10%
Current service cost	160	140	150
Benefits paid	150	180	190
Contributions paid	90	100	110
Present value of obligations at 31 December	1,100	1,380	1,455
Market value of plan assets at 31 December	1,190	1,372	1,188

In 20X2 the plan was amended to provide additional benefits with effect from 1 January 20X2. The present value as at 1 January 20X2 of additional benefits for employee service before 1 January 20X2 was 50, all for vested benefits.

Required:
Show how the pension scheme would be shown in the accounts for 20X1, 20X2 and 20X3.

Solution

Step 1 Change in the obligation

The changes in the present value of the obligation must be calculated and used to determine what, if any, actuarial gains and losses have arisen. This calculation can be done by comparing the expected obligations at the end of each period with the actual obligations as follows:

	20X1	20X2	20X3
Present value of obligation, 1 January	1,000	1,100	1,380
Interest cost	100	99	110
Current service cost	160	140	150
Past service cost – vested benefits	—	50	—
Benefits paid	(150)	(180)	(190)
Actuarial (gain) loss on obligation			
(balancing figure)	(10)	171	5
Present value of obligation, 31 December	1,100	1,380	1,455

Step 2 Change in the assets

The changes in the fair value of the assets of the fund must be calculated and used to determine what, if any, actuarial gains and losses have arisen. This calculation can be done by comparing the asset values at the end of each period with the actual asset values as follows:

	20X1	20X2	20X3
Fair value of plan assets, 1 January	1,000	1,190	1,372
Expected return on plan assets	120	131	137
Contributions	90	100	110
Benefits paid	(150)	(180)	(190)
Actuarial gain (loss) on plan assets			
(balancing figure)	130	131	(241)
Fair value of plan assets, 31 December	1,190	1,372	1,188

Step 3 The 10% corridor calculation

The limits of the '10% corridor' need to be calculated in order to establish whether actuarial gains or losses exceed the corridor limit and therefore need recognising in profit or loss. Actuarial gains and losses are recognised in profit or loss if they exceed the 10% corridor, and they are recognised by being amortised over the remaining service lives of employees.

The limits of the 10% corridor (at 1 January) are set at the greater of:

(a) 10% of the present value of the obligation before deducting plan assets (100, 110 and 138); and

(b) 10% of the fair value of plan assets (100, 119 and 137).

	20X1	20X2	20X3
Limit of '10% corridor' at 1 January	100	119	138
Cumulative unrecognised gains (losses), 1 January	—	140	98
Gains (losses) on the obligation	10	(171)	(5)
Gains (losses) on the assets	130	131	(241)
Cumulative gains (losses) before amortisation	140	100	(148)
Amortisation of excess over 10 years (see working)	—	(2)	—
Cumulative unrecognised gains (losses), 31 December	140	98	(148)

Working: $\dfrac{(140-119)}{10 \text{ years}} = 2$ = amortisation charge in 20X2.

Step 4 Calculate the profit or loss entry

	20X1	20X2	20X3
Current service cost	160	140	150
Interest cost	100	99	110
Expected return on plan assets	(120)	(131)	(137)
Recognised actuarial (gains) losses		(2)	
Recognised past service cost		50	
Profit or loss charge	140	156	123

Step 5 Calculate the statement of financial position entry

	20X1	20X2	20X3
Present value of obligation, 31 December	1,100	1,380	1,455
Fair value of assets, 31 December	(1,190)	(1,372)	(1,188)
Unrecognised actuarial gains (losses) from Step 3	140	98	(148)
Liability in statement of financial position	50	106	119

15.11 Plan curtailments and settlements

A curtailment of a pension scheme occurs when a company is committed to making a material reduction in the number of employees in a scheme or when the employees will receive no benefit for a substantial part of their future service. A settlement occurs when an enterprise enters into a transaction that eliminates any further liability from arising under the fund.

The accounting for a settlement or curtailment is that a gain or loss is recognised in profit or loss when the settlement or curtailment occurs. The gain or loss on a curtailment or settlement should comprise:

(a) any resulting change in the present value of the defined benefit obligation;

(b) any resulting change in the fair value of the plan assets;

(c) any related actuarial gain/loss and past service cost that had not previously been recognised.

Before determining the effect of the curtailment the enterprise must remeasure the obligation and the liability to get it to the up-to-date value.

15.12 Multi-employer plans

The definition of a multi-employer plan according to IAS 19[5] is that it is a defined contribution or defined benefit plan that:

(a) pools the assets contributed by various enterprises that are not under common control; and

(b) uses those assets to provide benefits to employees of more than one enterprise, on the basis that contribution and benefit levels are determined without regard to the identity of the enterprise that employs the employees concerned.

An enterprise should account for a multi-employer defined benefit plan as follows:

- it should account for its share of the defined benefit obligation, plan assets and costs associated with the plan in the same way as for any defined benefit plan; or
- if insufficient information is available to use defined benefit accounting, it should:
  - account for the plan as if it were a defined contribution plan; and
  - give extra disclosures.

In 2004 the IASB revised IAS 19 and changed the position for group pension plans in the financial statements of the individual companies in the group. Prior to the revision a group pension scheme could not be treated as a multi-employer plan and therefore any group schemes would have had to be split across all the individual contributing companies. The amendment to IAS 19, however, made it acceptable to treat group schemes as multi-employer schemes. This means that the defined benefit accounting is only necessary in the consolidated accounts and not in the individual company accounts of all companies in the group. It is necessary, however, to recognise the full group defined benefit accounting in at least one entity in the group. The requirements for full defined benefit accounting are included in the individual sponsor company financial statements.

This amendment to IAS 19 was not effective until accounting periods commencing in 2006; however, earlier adoption was allowed.

15.13 Disclosures

The major disclosure requirements[6] of the standard are:

- the enterprise's accounting policy for recognising actuarial gains and losses;
- a general description of the type of plan;
- a reconciliation of the assets and liabilities including the present value of the obligations, the market value of the assets, the actuarial gains/losses and the past service cost;
- a reconciliation of the movement during the period in the net liability;
- the total expense in the statement of comprehensive income broken down into different parts;
- the actual return on plan assets; and
- the principal actuarial assumptions used as at the period-end date.

15.14 Other long-service benefits

So far in this chapter we have considered the accounting for post-retirement costs for both defined contribution and defined benefit pension schemes. As well as pensions, IAS 19 (revised) considers other forms of long-service benefit paid to employees.[7] These other forms of long-service benefit include:

(a) long-term compensated absences such as long-service or sabbatical leave;

(b) jubilee or other long-service benefits;

(c) long-term disability benefits;

(d) profit-sharing and bonuses payable 12 months or more after the end of the period in which the employees render the related service; and

(e) deferred compensation paid 12 months or more after the end of the period in which it is earned.

The measurement of these other long-service benefits is not usually as complex or uncertain as it is for post-retirement benefits and therefore a more simplified method of accounting is used for them. For other long-service benefits any actuarial gains and losses and past service costs (if they arise) are recognised immediately in profit or loss and no '10% corridor' is applied.

This means that the statement of financial position liability for other long-service benefits is just the present value of the future benefit obligation less the fair value of any assets that the benefit will be settled from directly.

The profit or loss charge for these benefits is therefore the total of:

(a) current service cost;

(b) interest cost;

(c) expected return on plan assets (if any);

(d) actuarial gains and losses;

(e) past service cost; and

(f) the effect of curtailments or settlements.

15.15 Short-term benefits

In addition to pension and other long-term benefits considered earlier, IAS 19 gives accounting rules for short-term employee benefits.

Short-term employee benefits include items such as:

- wages, salaries and social security contributions;

- short-term compensated absences (such as paid annual leave and paid sick leave) where the absences are expected to occur within 12 months after the end of the period in which the employees render the related employee service;

- profit-sharing and bonuses payable within 12 months after the end of the period in which the employees render the related service; and

- non-monetary benefits (such as medical care, housing or cars) for current employees.

All short-term employee benefits should be recognised at an undiscounted amount:

- as a liability (after deducting any payments already made); and

- as an expense (unless another international standard allows capitalisation as an asset).

If the payments already made exceed the undiscounted amount of the benefits, an asset should be recognised only if it will lead to a future reduction in payments or a cash refund.

Compensated absences

The expected cost of short-term compensated absences should be recognised:

(a) in the case of accumulating absences, when the employees render service that increases their entitlement to future compensated absences; and

(b) in the case of non-accumulating compensated absences, when the absences occur.

Accumulating absences occur when the employees can carry forward unused absence from one period to the next. They are recognised when the employee renders services regardless of whether the benefit is vesting (the employee would get a cash alternative if they left employment) or non-vesting. The measurement of the obligation reflects the likelihood of employees leaving in a non-vesting scheme.

It is common practice for leave entitlement to be an accumulating absence (perhaps restricted to a certain number of days) but for sick pay entitlement to be non-accumulating.

Profit-sharing and bonus plans

The expected cost of a profit-sharing or bonus plan should be recognised only when:

(a) the enterprise has a present legal or constructive obligation to make such payments as a result of past events; and

(b) a reliable estimate of the obligation can be made.

15.16 Termination benefits[8]

These benefits are treated separately from other employee benefits in IAS 19 (revised) because the event that gives rise to the obligation to pay is the termination of employment as opposed to the service of the employee.

The accounting treatment for termination benefits is consistent with the requirements of IAS 37 and the rules concern when the obligation should be provided for and the measurement of the obligation.

Recognition

Termination benefits can be recognised as a liability only when the enterprise is demonstrably committed to either:

(a) terminating the employment of an employee or group of employees before the normal retirement date; or

(b) providing termination benefits as a result of an offer made in order to encourage voluntary redundancy.

The enterprise would be considered to be demonstrably committed to a termination only when a detailed plan for the termination is made and there is no realistic possibility of withdrawal from that plan. The plan should include as a minimum:

● the location, function and approximate number of employees whose services are to be terminated;

● the termination benefits for each job classification or function; and

● the time at which the plan will be implemented.

In June 2005 the IASB issued an exposure draft of IAS 37 *Provisions, Contingent Liabilities and Contingent Assets*. When they issued this exposure draft they also proposed an amendment to IAS 19 regarding provisions for termination benefits. The proposal is that for voluntary redundancy payments provision can only be made once the employees have accepted the offer as opposed to when the detailed plan has been announced. The IASB view is that this is the date the payment becomes an obligation.

Measurement

If the termination benefits are to be paid more than 12 months after the period-end date, they should be discounted, at a discount rate using the market yield on good quality corporate bonds. Prudence should also be exercised in the case of an offer made to encourage voluntary redundancy, as provision should only be based on the number of employees expected to accept the offer.

15.17 IAS 19 *Employee Benefits* (revised 2011)

In June 2011 the International Accounting Standards Board published a revised version of IAS 19 making limited changes, largely to the accounting for defined benefit post-employment benefit plans. The revised standard is effective from accounting periods beginning on or after 1 January 2013, although early adoption is permitted provided that entities disclose that fact.

The changes proposed in the exposure draft remove certain choices from companies and also should lead to more consistency in the presentation of the financial statements. The main changes are in the areas of (i) recognition of actuarial gains and losses, (ii) the discount rate to be applied to pension assets or liabilities, and (iii) the presentation of elements of the post-employment benefit cost. The effect of each of these changes is considered below.

15.17.1 Recognition of actuarial gains and losses

The previous version of IAS 19 has a number of different approaches to the recognition of actuarial gains and losses, being:

(a) to recognise in full within other comprehensive income (OCI);

(b) to recognise in full in the income statement; or

(c) to use the corridor approach and recognise actuarial gains and losses in excess of the '10% corridor' over the average remaining working lives of employees, or any systematic shorter period.

The revised standard requires that actuarial gains and losses are recognised in full in OCI. Actuarial gains and losses are categorised as 'remeasurements' and the IASB has specified that they must be presented within OCI. The impact of this will be significant on both the balance sheet asset or liability and potentially the income statement charge for pensions for those entities that use the corridor approach.

15.17.2 Discount rate to apply

The revised standard specifies that the discount rate to be applied to post-employment benefit obligations is determined by reference to market yields at the end of the reporting period on high-quality corporate bonds. In countries where there is no deep market in such bonds, the market yields on government bonds should be used.

This requirement removes the distinction that previously existed in IAS 19 between applying one discount rate to liabilities and a different expected rate on scheme assets. The discount rate in the revised standard is consistent with the rate applied in the old standard on pension liabilities. The impact of this change on the reported profits of entities will depend on the difference between the expected rate of return on assets previously used and the new discount rate to be applied. One potential benefit of the change is that it should remove a situation where a post-employment benefit scheme could have a net liability recognised on the balance sheet but with net interest income recognised in profit or loss (and vice versa).

15.17.3 Presentation of the elements of post-employment benefit cost

The revised standard requires that the service cost and net interest on the defined benefit liability or asset should be presented in profit or loss. Gains and losses on remeasurement (actuarial gains and losses) are presented within other comprehensive income. The standard does not specify how an entity should present service cost and net interest on the defined benefit liability (asset). However, it does require that those components are presented in accordance with IAS 1.

IAS 1 presentation requires that finance costs are separately presented on the face of the statement of comprehensive income. It is likely, as a result of this, that it will be more difficult for entities to justify including net interest within operating costs than it was under the previous version of IAS 19.

15.17.4 Comprehensive illustration (revisited)

Using the illustration in Section 15.10, the following shows how the pension scheme would be recognised under the revised IAS 19.

Step 1 Change in the net pension obligation

	20X1	20X2	20X3
Present value of obligation, 1 January	—	(90)	8
Net interest cost at 10%, 9%, 8%	—	(8)	1
Current service cost	160	140	150
Past service cost	—	50	—
Contributions paid	(90)	(100)	(110)
Actuarial (gain) loss on obligation (balancing figure)	(160)	16	218
Present value of the obligation (asset), 31 December	(90)	8	267

Step 2 Calculate the impact on the statement of comprehensive income

	20X1	20X2	20X3
Operating costs:			
Current service cost	160	140	150
Past service cost		50	
Net interest cost	—	(8)	1
Profit and loss charge	160	182	151
Other comprehensive income:			
Actuarial gains (losses)	160	(16)	(218)

Step 3 Calculate the statement of financial position

	20X1	*20X2*	*20X3*
Present value of pension obligation, 31 December	1,100	1,380	1,455
Fair value of plan assets, 31 December	(1,190)	(1,372)	(1,188)
Liability (asset) recognised	*(90)*	8	267

15.18 IFRS 2 *Share-based Payment*

Share awards, either directly through shares or through options, are very common ways of rewarding employee performance. These awards align the interests of the directors with those of the shareholders and, as such, are aimed at motivating the directors to perform in the way that benefits the shareholders. In particular, there is a belief that they will motivate the directors towards looking at the long-term success of the business as opposed to focusing solely on short-term profits. They have additional benefits also to the company and employees, for example in relation to cash and tax. If employees are rewarded in shares or options, the company will not need to pay out cash to reward the employees, and in a start-up situation where cash flow is very limited this can be very beneficial. Many 'dot com' companies initially rewarded their staff in shares for this reason. There are also tax benefits to employees with shares in some tax regimes which give an incentive to employees to accept share awards.

Whilst commercially share-based payments have many benefits, the accounting world has struggled in finding a suitable way to account for them. IAS 19 only covered disclosure requirements for share-based payments and had no requirements for the recognition and measurement of the payments when it was issued. The result of this was that many companies that gave very valuable rewards to their employees in the form of shares or options did not recognise any charge associated with this. The IASB addressed this by issuing, in February 2004, IFRS 2 *Share-based Payment*, which is designed to cover all aspects of accounting for share-based payments.

15.18.1 Should an expense be recognised?

Historically there has been some debate about whether a charge should be recognised in the statement of comprehensive income for share-based payments. One view is that the reward is given to employees in their capacity as shareholders and, as a result, it is not an employee benefit cost. Also supporters of the 'no-charge' view claimed that to make a charge would be a double hit to earnings per share in that it would reduce profits and increase the number of shares, which they felt was unreasonable.

Supporters of a charge pointed to opposite arguments that claimed having no charge underestimated the reward given to employees and therefore overstated profit. The impact of this was to give a misleading view of the profitability of the company. Also, making a charge gave comparability between companies that rewarded their staff in different ways. Comparability is one of the key principles of financial reporting.

For many years these arguments were not resolved and no standard was in issue, but the IASB eventually decided that a charge is appropriate and issued IFRS 2. In drawing up IFRS 2 a number of obstacles had to be overcome and decisions had to be made, for example:

- What should the value of the charge be – fair value or intrinsic value?
- At what point should the charge be measured – grant date, vesting date or exercise date?

- How should the charge be spread over a number of periods?
- If the charge is made to the statement of comprehensive income, where is the opposite entry to be made?
- What exemptions should be given from the standard?

IFRS 2 has answered these questions, and when introduced it made substantial changes to the profit recognised by many companies. In the UK, for example, the share-based payments charge for many businesses was one of their largest changes to profit on adopting IFRS.

15.19 Scope of IFRS 2

IFRS 2 is a comprehensive standard that covers all aspects of share-based payments. Specifically IFRS 2 covers:

- equity-settled share-based payment transactions, in which the entity receives goods or services as consideration for equity instruments issued;
- cash-settled share-based payment transactions, in which the entity receives goods or services by incurring liabilities to the supplier of those goods or services for amounts that are based on the price of the entity's shares or other equity instruments; and
- transactions in which the entity receives goods or services and either the entity or the supplier of those goods or services may choose whether the transaction is settled in cash (based on the price of the entity's shares or other equity instruments) or by issuing equity instruments.

There are no exemptions from the provisions of the IFRS except for:

(a) acquisitions of goods or other non-financial assets as part of a business combination; and

(b) acquisitions of goods or services under derivative contracts where the contract is expected to be settled by delivery as opposed to being settled net in cash.

15.20 Recognition and measurement

The general principles of recognition and measurement of share-based payment charges are as follows:

- Entities should recognise the goods or services acquired in a share-based payment transaction over the period the goods or services are received.
- The entity should recognise an increase in equity if the share-based payment is equity-settled and a liability if the payment is a cash-settled payment transaction.
- The share-based payment should be measured at fair value.

15.21 Equity-settled share-based payments

For equity-settled share-based payment transactions, the entity shall measure the goods and services received, and the corresponding increase in equity:

- **directly** at the fair value of the goods and services received, unless that fair value cannot be estimated reliably;

- **indirectly**, by reference to the fair value of the equity instruments granted, if the entity cannot estimate reliably the fair value of the goods and services received.

For transactions with employees, the entity shall measure the fair value of services received by reference to the fair value of the equity instruments granted, because typically it is not possible to estimate reliably the fair value of the services received.

In transactions with employees the IASB has decided that it is appropriate to value the benefit at the fair value of the instruments granted at their *grant date*. The IASB could have picked a number of different dates at which the options could have been valued:

- grant date – the date on which the options are given to the employees;
- vesting date – the date on which the options become unconditional to the employees; or
- exercise date – the date on which the employees exercise their options.

The IASB went for the grant date as it felt that the grant of options was the reward to the employees and not the exercise of the options. This means that after the grant date any movements in the share price, whether upwards or downwards, do not influence the charge to the financial statements.

Employee options

In order to establish the fair value of an option at grant date the market price could be used (if the option is traded on a market), but it is much more likely that an option pricing model will need to be used. Examples of option pricing models that are possible include:

- *Black–Scholes*. An option pricing model used for options with a fixed exercise date that does not require adjustment for the inability of employees to exercise options during the vesting period.
- *Binomial model*. An option pricing model used for options with a variable exercise date that will need adjustment for the inability of employees to exercise options during the vesting period.

Disclosures are required of the principal assumptions used in applying the option pricing model.

IFRS 2 does not recommend any one pricing model but insists that whichever model is chosen a number of factors affecting the fair value of the option such as exercise price, market price, time to maturity and volatility of the share price must be taken into account. In practice the Black–Scholes model is probably most commonly used; however, many companies vary the model to some extent to ensure it fits with the precise terms of their options.

Once the fair value of the option has been established at the grant date it is charged to profit or loss over the vesting period. The vesting period is the period in which the employees are required to satisfy conditions, for example service conditions, that allow them to exercise their options. The vesting period might be within the current financial accounting period and all options exercised.

EXAMPLE ● Employees were granted options to acquire 100,000 shares at $20 per share if still in employment at the end of the financial year. The market value of an option was $1.50 per share. All employees exercised their option at the year-end and the company received $2,000,000. There will be a charge in the income statement of $150,000. Although the company has not transferred cash, it has transferred value to the employees. IFRS 2 requires the charge to be measured as the market value of the option, i.e. $1.50 per share.

However, it is more usual for options to be exercised over longer periods. In this case, the charge is spread over the vesting period by calculating a revised cumulative charge each year, and then apportioning that over the vesting period with catch-up adjustments made to amend previous under- or over-charges to profit or loss. The illustration below shows how this approach works.

When calculating the charge in profit or loss the likelihood of options being forfeited due to non-market price conditions (e.g., because the employees leave in the conditional period) should be adjusted for. For non-market conditions the charge is amended each year to reflect any changes in estimates of the numbers expected to vest.

The charge cannot be adjusted, however, for market price conditions. If, for example, the share price falls and therefore the options will not be exercised due to the exercise price being higher than the market price, no adjustment can be made. This means that if options are 'under water' the statement of comprehensive income will still be recognising a charge for those options.

The charge is made to the statement of comprehensive income but there was some debate about how the credit entry should be made. The credit entry must be made either as a liability or as an entry to equity, and the IASB has decided that it should be an entry to equity. The logic for not including a liability is that the future issue of shares is not an 'obligation to transfer economic benefits' and therefore does not meet the definition of a liability. When the shares are issued it will increase the equity of the company and be effectively a contribution from an owner.

Even though the standard specifies that the credit entry is to equity, it does not specify which item in equity is to be used. In practice it seems acceptable either to use a separate reserve or to make the entry to retained earnings. If a separate reserve is used and the options are not ultimately exercised, this reserve can be transferred to retained earnings.

Illustration of option accounting

A Ltd issued share options to staff on 1 January 20X0, details of which are as follows:

Number of staff	1,000
Number of options to each staff member	500
Vesting period	3 years
Fair value at grant date (per option)	£3
Expected employee turnover (per annum)	5%

In the 31 December 20X1 financial statements, the company revised its estimate of employee turnover to 8% per annum for the three-year vesting period.

In the 31 December 20X2 financial statements, the actual employee turnover had averaged 6% per annum for the three-year vesting period.

Options vest as long as the staff remain with the company for the three-year period.

The charge for share-based payments under IFRS 2 would be as follows:

Year ended 31 December 20X0

In this period the charge would be based on the original terms of the share option issue. The total value of the option award at fair value at the grant date is:

	£000
1,000 staff × 500 options × £3 × (0.95 × 0.95 × 0.95)	1,286

The charge to the statement of comprehensive income for the period is therefore:

£1,286 ÷ 3	429

Year ended 31 December 20X1

In this year the expected employee turnover has risen to 8% per annum. The estimate of the effect of the increase is taken into account. Amended total expected share option award at grant date:

	£000	£000
1,000 staff × 500 options × £3 × (0.92 × 0.92 × 0.92)		1,168

The charge to the statement of comprehensive income is therefore

£1,168 × $^2/_3$	779	
Less: recognised to date	(429)	
		350

Year ended 31 December 20X2

The actual number of options that vest is now known. The actual value of the option award that vests at the grant date is:

	£000	£000
1,000 staff × 500 options × £3 × (0.94 × 0.94 × 0.94)		1,246

The charge to the statement of comprehensive income is therefore:

Total value over the vesting period	1,246	
Less: recognised to date	(779)	
		467

Re-priced options

If an entity re-prices its options, for instance in the event of a falling share price, the incremental fair value should be spread over the remaining vesting period. The incremental fair value per option is the difference between the fair value of the option immediately before re-pricing and the fair value of the re-priced option.

Market-related vesting conditions

We have already seen that most vesting conditions (e.g. the requirement for employees to remain employed over the vesting period) are allowed for in estimating the number of options that are likely to vest. Where the vesting condition is a market-related condition, e.g. the share price must exceed a target amount or perform to a specified standard relative to other listed securities, then the condition is allowed for in computing the fair value of the option at grant date using an appropriate model. Given that the condition is taken into account in this way, it is ignored when considering the likely vesting of the option to avoid double-counting. This means that, where such conditions exist, it is at least theoretically possible for there to be a charge to profit and loss for an equity-settled share-based payment where the options do not actually vest!

15.22 Cash-settled share-based payments

Cash-settled share-based payments result in the recognition of a liability. The entity measures the goods or services acquired and the liability incurred at fair value. Until the liability is settled, the entity remeasures the fair value of the liability at each reporting date, with any changes in fair value recognised in profit or loss.

For example, an entity might grant share appreciation rights to employees as part of their pay package, whereby the employees will become entitled to a future cash payment (rather than an equity instrument), based on the increase in the entity's share price from a specified level over a specified period.

The entity recognises the services received, and a liability to pay for those services, as the employees render service. For example, some share appreciation rights vest immediately, and the employees are therefore not required to complete a specified period of service to become entitled to the cash payment. In the absence of evidence to the contrary, the entity presumes that the services rendered by the employees in exchange for the share appreciation rights have been received. Thus, the entity recognises immediately the services received and a liability to pay for them. If the share appreciation rights do not vest until the employees have completed a specified period of service, the entity recognises the services received, and a liability to pay for them, as the employees render service during that period.

The liability is measured, initially and at each reporting date until settled, at the fair value of the share appreciation rights, by applying an option pricing model, taking into account the terms and conditions on which the share appreciation rights were granted, and the extent to which the employees have rendered service to date. The entity remeasures the fair value of the liability at each reporting date until settled.

Disclosure is required of the difference between the amount that would be charged to the statement of comprehensive income if the share appreciation rights are paid out in cash as opposed to being paid out with shares.

15.23 Transactions which may be settled in cash or shares

Some share-based payment transactions can be settled in either cash or shares with the settlement option being with the supplier of the goods or services and/or with the entity.

The accounting treatment is dependent upon which counterparty has the choice of settlement.

Supplier choice

If the supplier of the goods or services has the choice over settlement method, the entity has issued a compound instrument. The entity has an obligation to pay out cash (as the supplier can take this choice), but also has issued an equity option, as the supplier may decide to take equity to settle the transaction. The entity therefore recognises both a liability and an equity component.

The fair value of the equity option is the difference between the fair value of the offer of the cash alternative and the fair value of the offer of the equity payment. In many cases these are the same value, in which case the equity option has no value.

Once the split has been determined, each part is accounted for in the same way as other cash-settled or equity-settled transactions.

If cash is paid in settlement, any equity option recognised may be transferred to a different category in equity. If equity is issued, the liability is transferred to equity as the consideration for the equity instruments issued.

Entity choice

For a share-based payment transaction in which an entity may choose whether to settle in cash or by issuing equity instruments, the entity determines whether it has a present obligation to settle in cash and account for the share-based payment transaction accordingly. The entity has a present obligation to settle in cash if the choice of settlement in equity instruments is not substantive, or if the entity has a past practice or a stated policy of settling in cash.

If such an obligation exists, the entity accounts for the transaction in accordance with the requirements applying to cash-settled share-based payment transactions.

If no such obligation exists, the entity accounts for the transaction in accordance with the requirements applying to equity-settled transactions.

15.24 IAS 26 *Accounting and Reporting by Retirement Benefit Plans*

This standard provides complementary guidance in addition to IAS 19 regarding the way that the pension fund should account and report on the contributions it receives and the obligations it has to pay pensions. The standard mainly contains the presentation and disclosure requirements of the schemes as opposed to the accounting methods that they should adopt.

15.24.1 Defined contribution plans

The report prepared by a defined contribution plan should contain a statement of net assets available for benefits and a description of the funding policy.

With a defined contribution plan it is not normally necessary to involve an actuary, since the pension paid at the end is purely dependent on the amount of fund built up for the employee. The obligation of the employer is usually discharged by the employer paying the agreed contributions into the plan. The main purpose of the report of the plan is to provide information on the performance of the investments, and this is normally achieved by including the following statements:

(a) a description of the significant activities for the period and the effect of any changes relating to the plan, its membership and its terms and conditions;

(b) statements reporting on the transactions and investment performance for the period and the financial position of the plan at the end of the period; and

(c) a description of the investment policies.

15.24.2 Defined benefit plans

Under a defined benefit plan (as opposed to a defined contribution plan) there is a need to provide more information, as the plan must be sufficiently funded to provide the agreed pension benefits at the retirement of the employees. The objective of reporting by the defined benefit plan is to periodically present information about the accumulation of resources and plan benefits over time that will highlight an excess or shortfall in assets.

The report that is required should contain[9] either:

(a) a statement that shows:

   (i) the net assets available for benefits;

   (ii) the actuarial present value of promised retirement benefits, distinguishing between vested benefits and non-vested benefits; and

   (iii) the resulting excess or deficit; or

(b) a statement of net assets available for benefits, including either:

   (i) a note disclosing the actuarial present value of promised retirement benefits, distinguishing between vested benefits and non-vested benefits; or

   (ii) a reference to this information in an accompanying report.

The most recent actuarial valuation report should be used as a basis for the above disclosures and the date of the valuation should be disclosed. IAS 26 does not specify how often actuarial valuations should be done but suggests that most countries require a triennial valuation.

When the fund is preparing the report and using the actuarial present value of the future obligations, the present value could be based on either projected salary levels or current salary levels. Whichever basis has been used should be disclosed. The effect of any significant changes in actuarial assumptions should also be disclosed.

Report format

IAS 26 proposes three different report formats that will fulfil the content requirements detailed above. These formats are:

(a) A report that includes a statement that shows the net assets available for benefits, the actuarial present value of promised retirement benefits, and the resulting excess or deficit. The report of the plan also contains statements of changes in net assets available for benefits and changes in the actuarial present value of promised retirement benefits. The report may include a separate actuary's report supporting the actuarial present value of promised retirement benefits.

(b) A report that includes a statement of net assets available for benefits and a statement of changes in net assets available for benefits. The actuarial present value of the promised retirement benefits is disclosed in a note to the statements. The report may also include a report from an actuary supporting the actuarial value of the promised retirement benefits.

(c) A report that includes a statement of net assets available for benefits and a statement of changes in net assets available for benefits with the actuarial present value of promised retirement benefits contained in a separate actuarial report.

In each format a trustees' report in the nature of a management or directors' report and an investment report may also accompany the statements.

15.24.3 All plans – disclosure requirements[10]

For all plans, whether defined contribution or defined benefit, some common valuation and disclosure requirements exist.

Valuation

The investments held by retirement benefit plans should be carried at fair value. In most cases the investments will be marketable securities and the fair value is the market value. If it is impossible to determine the fair value of an investment, disclosure should be made of the reason why fair value is not used.

Market values are used for the investments because the market value is felt to be the most appropriate value at the report date and the best indication of the performance of the investments over the period.

Disclosure

In addition to the specific reports detailed above for defined contribution and defined benefit plans, the report should also contain:

(a) a statement of net assets available for benefits disclosing:

- assets at the end of the period suitably classified;
- the basis of valuation of assets;

- details of any single investment exceeding either 5% of the net assets available for benefits or 5% of any class or type of security;
- details of any investment in the employer;
- liabilities other than the actuarial present value of promised retirement benefits;

(b) a statement of changes in net assets for benefits showing the following:

- employer contributions;
- employee contributions;
- investment income such as interest or dividends;
- other income;
- benefits paid or payable;
- administrative expenses;
- other expenses;
- taxes on income;
- profits or losses on disposal of investment and changes in value of investments;
- transfers from and to other plans;

(c) a summary of significant accounting policies; and

(d) a description of the plan and the effect of any changes in the plan during the period.

Summary

Accounting for employee benefits has always been a difficult problem with different views as to the appropriate methods.

The different types of pension scheme and the associated risks add to the difficulties in terms of accounting. The accounting treatment for these benefits has recently changed, the current view being that the asset or liability position takes priority over the profit or loss charge. However, one consequence of giving the statement of financial position priority is that this change to the statement of comprehensive income can be much more volatile and this is considered by some to be undesirable.

Within the international community agreement does not exist on how these benefits should be accounted for. An interesting recent development is the option to use 'other comprehensive income' to record variations from the normal pension costs, i.e. for actuarial gains and losses, rather than taking them to profit or loss. There is significant choice to companies in how they account for their pension schemes, which could be a criticism of the standard. Pension accounting is a very difficult area to gain global agreement on, and therefore IAS 19 (revised) could be construed as an early step towards more global convergence.

IFRS 2 is the first serious attempt of the IASB to deal with accounting for share-based payments. It requires companies to recognise that a charge should be made for share-based payments and, in line with other recent standards such as financial instruments, it requires that charge to be recognised at fair value. There has been criticism of the standard in that it brings significant estimation into assessing the amount of charges to profit; however, overall the standard has been relatively well received with companies coping well with its requirements so far. What is unclear at present is whether the requirements will change the way that companies reward their staff; for this we will have to wait and see.

REVIEW QUESTIONS

1 Outline the differences between a defined benefit and a defined contribution pension scheme.

2 If a defined contribution pension scheme provided a pension that was 6% of salary each year, the company had a payroll cost of €5 million, and the company paid €200,000 in the year, what would be the statement of comprehensive income charge and the statement of financial position liability at the year-end?

3 'The approach taken in IAS 19 before its 1998 revision was to match an even pension cost against the period the employees provided service. This follows the accruals principle and is therefore fundamentally correct.' Discuss.

4 Under the revised IAS 19 (post-1998) what amount of actuarial gains and losses should be recognised in profit or loss? Following the revision to IAS 19 in 2011, is this expected to change?

5 Past service costs are recognised under IAS 19 (revised) immediately if the benefit is 'vested'. In what circumstances would the benefits not be vested?

6 What is the required accounting treatment for a curtailment of a defined benefit pension scheme?

7 What distinguishes a termination benefit from the other benefits considered in IAS 19 (revised)?

8 The issue of shares by companies, even to employees, should not result in a charge against profits. The contribution in terms of service that employees give to earn their rewards are contributions as owners and not as employees and when owners buy shares for cash there is no charge to profit. Discuss.

9 The use of option pricing models to determine the charges to profit or loss brings undesired estimation and subjectivity into the financial statements. Discuss.

10 Briefly summarise the required accounting if a company gives its staff a cash bonus directly linked to the share price.

11 Explain what distinguishes the different types of share-based payment: equity-settled, cash-settled and equity with a cash alternative.

EXERCISES

* Question 1

Donna, Inc. operates a defined benefit pension scheme for staff. The pension scheme has been operating for a number of years but not following IAS 19. The finance director is unsure of which accounting policy to adopt under IAS 19 because he has heard very conflicting stories. He went to one presentation in 2003 that referred to a '10% corridor' approach to actuarial gains and losses, recognising them in profit or loss, but went to another presentation in 2004 that said actuarial gains and losses could be recognised in other comprehensive income.

The pension scheme had market value of assets of £3.2 million and a present value of obligations of £3.5 million on 1 January 2002. There were no actuarial gains and losses brought forward into 2002.

The details relevant to the pension are as follows (in £000):

	2002	2003	2004
Discount rate at start of year	6%	5%	4%
Expected rate of return on plan assets at start of year	10%	9%	8%
Current service cost	150	160	170
Benefits paid	140	150	130
Contributions paid	120	120	130
Present value of obligations at 31 December	3,600	3,500	3,200
Market value of plan assets at 31 December	3,400	3,600	3,600

In all years the average remaining service life of the employees was 10 years. Under the 10% corridor approach any gains or losses above the corridor would be recognised over the average remaining service lives of the employees.

Required:
(a) Advise the finance director of the differences in the approach to actuarial gains and losses following the '10% corridor' and the recognition in equity. Illustrate your answer by showing the impact on the pension for 2002 to 2004 under both bases.
(b) Comment on how you answer to (a) would change if the requirements of IAS 19 (2011) are applied.

* Question 2

The following information (in £m) relates to the defined benefit scheme of Basil plc for the year ended 31 December 20X7:

Fair value of plan assets at 1 January 20X7 £3,150 and at 31 December 20X7 £3,386; contributions £26; current service cost £80; benefits paid £85; past service cost £150; present value of the obligation at 1 January 20X7 £3,750 and at 31 December 20X7 £4,192.

The discount rate was 7% at 31 December 20X6 and 8% at 31 December 20X7. The expected rate of return on plan assets was 9% at 31 December 20X6 and 10% at 31 December 20X7.

Required:
(a) Show the amounts that will be recognised in the statement of comprehensive income and statement of financial position for Basil plc for the year ended 31 December 20X7 under IAS 19 Employee Benefits and the movement in the net liability.
(b) Show how the answer to (a) would change if the requirements of IAS 19 (2011) are applied.

* Question 3

The following information is available for the year ended 31 March 20X6 (values in $m):

Present value of scheme liabilities at 1 April 20X5 $1,007; fair value of plan assets at 1 April 20X5 $844; benefits paid $44; expected return on plan assets $67; contributions paid by employers $16; current service costs $28; past service costs $1; actuarial gains on assets $31; actuarial losses on liabilities $10; interest costs $58.

Required:
(a) Calculate the net liability to be recognised in the statement of financial position.
(b) Show the amounts recognised in the statement of comprehensive income.
Prepare your answers based on IAS 19 before its revision in 2011.

Question 4

(a) IAS 19 *Employee Benefits* was amended in December 2004 to allow a choice of methods for the recognition of actuarial gains and losses.

Required:

Explain the treatments of actuarial gains and losses currently permitted by IAS 19, and how these will change for periods beginning on or after 1 January 2013.

(b) The following information relates to the defined benefit employee compensation scheme of an entity:

Present value of obligation at start of 2008 ($000)	20,000
Market value of plan assets at start of 2008 ($000)	20,000
Expected annual return on plan assets	10%
Discount rate per year	8%

	2008	2009
	$000	$000
Current service cost	1,250	1,430
Benefits paid out	987	1,100
Contributions paid by entity	1,000	1,100
Present value of obligation at end of the year	23,000	25,500
Market value of plan assets at end of the year	21,500	22,300

Actuarial gains and losses outside the 10% corridor are to be recognised in full in the income statement. Assume that all transactions occur at the end of the year.

Required:

(i) Calculate the present value of the defined benefit plan obligation as at the start and end of 2008 and 2009 showing clearly any actuarial gain or loss on the plan obligation for each year.

(ii) Calculate the market value of the defined benefit plan assets as at the start and end of 2008 and 2009 showing clearly any actuarial gain or loss on the plan assets for each year.

(iii) Applying the 10% corridor show the total charge in respect of this plan in the income statement for 2008 and the statement of comprehensive income for 2009.

(The Association of International Accountants)

(c) Show the impact of applying IAS 19 (revised 2011) on the statement of comprehensive income and the statement of financial position.

* Question 5

On 1 October 2005 Omega granted 50 employees options to purchase 500 shares in the entity. The options vest on 1 October 2007 for those employees who remain employed by the entity until that date. The options allow the employees to purchase the shares for $10 per share. The market price of the shares was $10 on 1 October 2005 and $10.50 on 1 October 2006. The market value of the options was $2 on 1 October 2005 and $2.60 on 1 October 2006. On 1 October 2005 the directors estimated that 5% of the relevant employees would leave in each of the years ended 30 September 2006 and 2007 respectively. It turned out that 4% of the relevant employees left in the year ended 30 September 2006 and the directors now believe that a further 4% will leave in the year ended 30 September 2007.

Required:

Show the amounts that will appear in the balance sheet of Omega as at 30 September 2006 in respect of the share options, and the amounts that will appear in the income statement for the year ended 30 September 2006.

You should state where in the balance sheet and where in the income statement the relevant amounts will be presented. Where necessary you should justify your treatment with reference to appropriate international financial reporting standards.

(Dip IFR December 2006)

* Question 6

On 1 January 20X1 a company obtained a contract in order to keep its factory in work but had obtained it on a very tight profit margin. Liquidity was a problem and there was no prospect of offering staff a cash bonus. Instead, the company granted its 80 production employees share options for 1,000 shares each at £10 per share. There was a condition that they would only vest if they still remained in employment at 31 December 20X2. The options were then exercisable during the year ended 31 December 20X3. Each option had an estimated fair value of £6.50 at the grant date.

At 31 December 20X1:

● The fair value of each option was £7.50.

● Four employees had left.

● It was estimated that 16 of the staff would have left by 31 December 20X2.

● The share price had increased from £9 on 1 January 20X1 to £9.90.

Required:
Calculate the charge to the income statement for the year ended 31 December 20X1.

* Question 7

C plc wants to reward its directors for their service to the company and has designed a bonus package with two different elements as follows. The directors are informed of the scheme and granted any options on 1 January 20X7.

1   Share options over 300,000 shares that can be exercised on 31 December 20Y0. These options are granted at an exercise price of €4 each, the share price of C plc on 1 January 20X7. Conditions of the options are that the directors remain with the company, and the company must achieve an average increase in profit of at least 10% per year, for the years ending 31 December 20X7 to 31 December 20X9. C plc obtained a valuation on 1 January 20X7 of the options which gave them a fair value of €3.

   No directors were expected to leave the company but, surprisingly, on 30 November 20X9 a director with 30,000 options did leave the company and therefore forfeited his options. At the 31 December 20X7 and 20X8 year-ends C plc estimated that they would achieve the profit targets (they said 80% sure) and by 31 December 20X9 the profit target had been achieved.

   By 31 December 20Y0 the share price had risen to €12, giving the directors who exercised their options an €8 profit per share on exercise.

2   The directors were offered a cash bonus payable on 31 December 20X8 based on the share price of the company. Each of the five directors was granted a €5,000 bonus for each €1 rise in the share price or proportion thereof by 31 December 20X8.

   On 1 January 20X7 the estimated fair value of the bonus was €75,000; this had increased to €85,000 by 31 December 20X7, and the share price on 31 December 20X8 was €8 per share.

Required:
Show the accounting entries required in the years ending 31 December 20X7, 20X8 and 20X9 for the directors' options and bonus above.

Question 8

Kathryn plc, a listed company, provides a defined benefit pension for its staff, the details of which are given below.

As at 30 April 2004, actuaries valued the company's pension scheme and estimated that the scheme had assets of £10.5 million and obligations of £10.2 million (using the valuation methods prescribed in IAS 19).

The actuaries made assumptions in their valuation that the assets would grow by 11% over the coming year to 30 April 2005, and that the obligations were discounted using an appropriate corporate bond rate of 10%. The actuaries estimated the current service cost at £600,000. The actuaries informed the company that pensions to retired directors would be £800,000 during the year, and the company should contribute £700,000 to the scheme.

At 30 April 2005 the actuaries again valued the pension fund and estimated the assets to be worth £10.7 million, and the obligations of the fund to be £10.9 million.

Assume that contributions and benefits are paid on the last day of each year.

Required:

(a) Explain the reasons why IAS 19 was revised in 1998, moving from an actuarial income-driven approach to a market-based asset- and liability-driven approach. Support your answer by referring to the *Framework* principles.

(b) Show the extracts from the statement of comprehensive income and statement of financial position of Kathryn plc in respect of the information above for the year ended 30 April 2005. You do not need to show notes to the accounts.

(The accounting policy adopted by Kathryn plc is to recognise actuarial gains and losses immediately in other comprehensive income.)

(c) Discuss how the above accounting will change in 2013 when IAS 19 (revised 2011) becomes effective.

* Question 9

Oberon prepares financial statements to 31 March each year. Oberon makes contributions to a defined benefit post-employment benefit plan for its employees. Oberon accounts for actuarial gains and losses arising on these arrangements using the corridor method. Relevant data are as follows:

(a) At 1 April 20X0 the plan obligation was €35 million and the fair value of the plan assets was €30 million. Unrecognised actuarial losses at that date totalled €6.5 million.

(b) The actuary advised that the current service cost for the year ended 31 March 20X1 was €4 million. Oberon paid contributions of €3.6 million to the plan on 31 March 20X1. These were the only contributions paid in the year.

(c) The expected annual rate of return on plan assets at 1 April 20X0 was 5%. The actuary revised this estimate to 4% at 31 March 20X1.

(d) The appropriate annual rate at which to discount the plan liabilities was 6% on 1 April 20X0 and 5.5% on 31 March 20X1.

(e) The plan paid out benefits totalling €2 million to retired members on 31 March 20X1.

(f) At 31 March 20X1 the plan obligation was €41.5 million and the fair value of the plan assets was €32.5 million.

(g) The average remaining service life of plan members still in employment was estimated to be 20 years.

Required:

(a) Compute the amounts that will appear in the statement of comprehensive income of Oberon for the year ended 31 March 20X1 and the statement of financial position at 31 March 20X1 in respect of the post-employment benefit plan. You should indicate where in each statement the relevant amounts will be presented.

(b) Show how the above will change in 2013 with the introduction of IAS 19 (revised 2011).

* Question 10

On 1 April 20W9 Oliver granted share options to 20 senior executives. The options are due to vest on 31 March 20X2 provided the senior executives remain with the company for the period between 1 April 20W9 and 31 March 20X2. The number of options vesting to each director depends on the cumulative profits over the three-year period from 1 April 20W9 to 31 March 20X2:

● 10,000 options per director if the cumulative profits are between €5 million and €10 million;

● 15,000 options per director if the cumulative profits are more than €10 million.

On 1 April 20W9 and 31 March 20X0 the best estimate of the cumulative profits for the three-year period ending on 31 March 20X2 was €8 million. However, following very successful results in the year ended 31 March 20X1 the latest estimate of the cumulative profits in the relevant three-year period is €14 million.

On 1 April 20W9 it was estimated that all 20 senior executives would remain with Oliver for the three-year period but on 31 December 20W9 one senior executive left unexpectedly. None of the other executives have since left and none are expected to leave before 31 March 20X2.

A further condition for vesting of the options is that the share price of Oliver should be at least €12 on 31 March 20X2. The share price of Oliver over the last two years has changed as follows:

● €10 on 1 April 20W9;

● €11.75 on 31 March 20X0;

● €11.25 on 31 March 20X1.

On 1 April 20W9 the fair value of the share options granted by Oliver was €4.80 per option. This had increased to €5.50 by 31 March 20X0 and €6.50 by 31 March 20X1.

Required:

Produce extracts, with supporting explanations, from the statements of financial position at 31 March 20X0 and 20X1 and from the statements of comprehensive income for the years ended 31 March 20X0 and 20X1 that show how the granting of the share options will be reflected in the financial statements of Oliver. Ignore deferred tax.

Question 11

A plc issues 50,000 share options to its employees on 1 January 2008 which the employees can only exercise if they remain with the company until 31 December 2010. The options have a fair value of £5 each on 1 January 2008.

It is expected that the holders of options over 8,000 shares will leave A plc before 31 December 2010.

In March 2008 adverse press comments regarding A plc's environmental policies and a downturn in the stock market cause the share price to fall significantly to below the exercise price on the options. The share price is not expected to recover in the foreseeable future.

Required:

What charge should A plc recognise for share options in the financial statements for the year ended 31 December 2008?

References

1 IAS 19 *Employee Benefits*, IASB, amended 2002.
2 IAS 26 *Accounting and Reporting by Retirement Benefit Plans*, IASC, reformatted 1994.
3 IFRS 2 *Share-based Payment*, IASB, 2004.
4 IAS 19 *Employee Benefits*, IASB, amended 2002, Appendix 1.
5 *Ibid.*, para. 7.
6 *Ibid.*, para. 120.
7 *Ibid.*, para. 126.
8 *Ibid.*, para. 132.
9 IAS 26 *Accounting and Reporting by Retirement Benefit Plans*, IASC, reformatted 1994, para. 28.
10 *Ibid.*, para. 32.

CHAPTER 16

Taxation in company accounts

16.1 Introduction

The main purpose of this chapter is to explain the corporation tax system and the accounting treatment of deferred tax.

Objectives

By the end of this chapter, you should be able to:

- discuss the theoretical background to corporation tax systems;
- critically discuss tax avoidance and tax evasion;
- prepare deferred tax calculations;
- critically discuss deferred tax provisions.

16.2 Corporation tax

Limited companies, and indeed all corporate bodies, are treated for tax purposes as being legally separate from their proprietors. Thus, a limited company is itself liable to pay tax on its profits. This tax is known as **corporation tax**. The shareholders are accountable for tax only on the income they receive by way of any dividends distributed by the company. If the shareholder is an individual, then **income tax** becomes due on their dividend income received.

This is in contrast to the position in a partnership, where each partner is individually liable for the tax on their share of the pre-tax profit that has been allocated. A partner is taxed on the profit and not simply on drawings. Note that this is different from the treatment of an employee who is charged tax on the amount of salary that is paid.

In this chapter we consider the different types of company taxation and their accounting treatment. The International Accounting Standard that applies specifically to taxation is IAS 12 *Income Taxes*. The standard was last revised by the IASB in 2010. Those UK unquoted companies that choose not to follow international standards will follow FRSs 100–102 from 2015 (with earlier adoption allowed).

Corporation tax is calculated under rules set by Parliament each year in the Finance Act. The Finance Act may alter the existing rules; it also sets the rate of tax payable. Because of this annual review of the rules, circumstances may change year by year, which makes comparability difficult and forecasting uncertain.

The reason for the need to adjust accounting profits for tax purposes is that although the tax payable is based on the accounting profits as disclosed in the profit and loss account, the tax rules may differ from the accounting rules which apply prudence to income recognition. For example, the tax rules may not accept that all the expenses which are recognised by the accountant under the IASB's *Framework for the Preparation and Presentation of Financial Statements* and the IAS 1 *Presentation of Financial Statements* accrual concept are deductible when arriving at the taxable profit. An example of this might be a bonus, payable to an employee (based on profits), which is payable in arrears but which is deducted from account-ing profit as an accrual under IAS 1. This expense is allowed in calculating taxable profit on a cash basis only when it is paid in order to ensure that one taxpayer does not reduce his potential tax liability before another becomes liable to tax on the income received.

The accounting profit may therefore be lower or higher than the taxable profit. For example, the Companies Acts require that the formation expenses of a company, which are the costs of establishing it on incorporation, must be written off in its first accounting period; the rules of corporation tax, however, state that these are a capital expense and cannot be deducted from the profit for tax purposes. This means that more tax will be assessed as payable than one would assume from an inspection of the published statement of income.

Similarly, although most businesses would consider that entertaining customers and other business associates was a normal commercial trading expense, it is not allowed as a deduction for tax purposes.

A more complicated situation arises in the case of depreciation. Because the directors have the choice of method of depreciation to use, the legislators have decided to require all companies to use the same method when calculating taxable profits. If one thinks about this, then it would seem to be the equitable practice. Each company is allowed to deduct a uni-form percentage from its profits in respect of the depreciation that has arisen from the wear and tear and diminution in value of non-current assets.

The substituted depreciation that the tax rules allow is known as a **capital allowance**. The capital allowance is calculated in the same way as depreciation; the only difference is that the rates are those set out in the Finance Acts.

16.3 Corporation tax systems – the theoretical background

It might be useful to explain that there are three possible systems of company taxation: classical, imputation and partial imputation.[1] These systems differ solely in their tax treat-ment of the relationship between the limited company and those shareholders who have invested in it.

16.3.1 The classical system

In the classical system, a company pays tax on its profits, and then the shareholders suffer a second and separate tax liability when their share of the profits is distributed to them. In effect, the dividend income of the shareholder is regarded as a second and separate source of income from that of the profits of the company. The payment of a dividend creates an additional tax liability which falls directly on the shareholders. It could be argued that this double taxation is inequitable when compared to the taxation system on unincorporated bodies where the rate of taxation suffered overall remains the same whether or not profits are withdrawn from the business. It is suggested that this classical system discourages the distribution of profits to shareholders, since the second tranche of taxation (the tax on dividend income of the shareholders) only becomes payable on payment of the dividend, although some argue that the effect of the burden of double taxation on the economy is less serious than it might seem.[2]

16.3.2 The imputation system

In an imputation system, the dividend is regarded merely as a flow of the profits on each sale to the individual shareholders, as there is considered to be merely one source of income which could be either retained in the company or distributed to the shareholders. It is certainly correct that the payment of a dividend results from the flow of monies into the company from trading profits, and that the choice between retaining profits to fund future growth and the payment of a dividend to investing shareholders is merely a strategic choice unrelated to a view as to the nature of taxable profits. In an imputation system the total of the tax paid by the company and by the shareholder is unaffected by the payment of dividends, and the tax paid by the company is treated as if it were also a payment of the individual shareholders' liabilities on dividends received. It is this principle of the flow of net profits from particular sales to individual shareholders that has justified the repayment of tax to shareholders with low incomes or to non-taxable shareholders of tax paid by the limited company, even though that tax credit has represented a reduction in the overall tax revenue of the state because the tax credit repaid also represented a payment of the company's own corporation tax liability. If the dividend had not been distributed to such a low-income or non-taxable shareholder who was entitled to repayment, the tax revenue collected would have been higher overall. France and Germany have such an imputation system. The UK modified its imputation system in 1999, so that a low-income or non-taxable shareholder (such as a charity) could no longer recover any tax credit.

16.3.3 The partial imputation system

In a partial imputation system only part of the underlying corporation tax paid is treated as a tax credit.

16.3.4 Common basis

All three systems are based on the taxation of profits earned as shown under the same basic principles used in the preparation of financial statements.

16.4 Corporation tax systems – avoidance and evasion

Governments have to follow the same basic principles of management as individuals. To spend money, there has to be a source of funds. The sources of funds are borrowing and income. With governments, the source of income is taxation. As with individuals, there is a practical limit as to how much they can borrow; to spend for the benefit of the populace, taxation has to be collected. In a democracy, the tax system is set up to ensure that the more prosperous tend to pay a greater proportion of their income in order to fund the needs of the poorer; this is called a progressive system. As Franklin Roosevelt, the American politician, stated, 'taxes, after all, are the dues that we pay for the privileges of membership in an organised society'.[3] Corporation tax on company profits represents 10% of the taxation collected by HM Revenue and Customs in the UK from taxes on income and wages.

It appears to be a general rule that taxpayers do not enjoy paying taxation (despite the fact that they may well understand the theory underpinning the collection of taxation).

This fact of human nature applies just as much to company directors handling company resources as it does to individuals. Every extra pound paid in taxation by a company reduces the resources available for retention for funding future growth.

16.4.1 Tax evasion

Politicians often complain about tax evasion. Evasion is the illegal (and immoral) manipulation of business affairs to escape taxation. An example could be the directors of a family-owned company taking cash sales for their own expenditure. Another example might be the payment of a low salary (below the threshold of income tax) to a family member not working in the company, thus reducing profits in an attempt to reduce corporation tax. It is easy to understand the illegality and immorality of such practices. Increasingly the distinction between tax avoidance and tax evasion has been blurred.[4] When politicians complain of tax evasion, they tend not to distinguish between evasion and avoidance.

16.4.2 Tax avoidance

Tax avoidance could initially be defined as a manipulation of one's affairs, within the law, so as to reduce liability; indeed, as it is legal, it can be argued that it is not immoral. There is a well-established tradition within the UK that 'every man is entitled if he can to order his affairs so that the tax attaching under the appropriate Acts is less than it otherwise would be'.[5]

Indeed the government deliberately sets up special provisions to reduce taxes in order to encourage certain behaviours. The more that employers and employees save for employee retirement, the less social security benefits will be paid out in the future. Thus both companies and individuals obtain full relief against taxation for pension contributions. Another example might be increased tax depreciation (capital allowances) on capital investment, in order to increase industrial investment and improve productivity within the UK economy.

The use of such provisions, as intended by the legislators, is not criticised by anyone, and might better be termed 'tax planning'. The problem area lies between the proper use of such tax planning, and illegal activities. This 'grey area' could best be called 'tax avoidance'.

The Institute for Fiscal Studies has stated:

> We think it is impossible to define the expression 'tax avoidance' in any truly satisfactory manner. People routinely alter their behaviour to reduce or defer their taxation liabilities. In doing so, commentators regard some actions as legitimate tax planning and others as tax avoidance. We have regarded tax avoidance (in contra-indication to legitimate . . . tax planning) as action taken to reduce or defer tax liabilities in a way Parliament plainly did not intend. . . .[6]

The law tends to define tax avoidance as an artificial element in the manipulation of one's affairs, within the law, so as to reduce liability.[7]

16.4.3 The problem of distinguishing between avoidance and evasion

The problem lies in distinguishing clearly between legal avoidance and illegal evasion. It can be difficult for accountants to walk the careful line between helping clients (in tax avoidance) and colluding with them against HM Revenue and Customs.[8]

When clients seek advice, accountants have to be careful to ensure that they have integrity in all professional and business relationships. Integrity implies not merely honesty but fair dealing and truthfulness. 'In all dealings relating to the tax authorities, a member must act honestly and do nothing that might mislead the authorities.'[9]

As an example to illustrate the problems that could arise, a client company has carried out a transaction to avoid taxation, but failed to minute the details as discussed at a directors' meeting. If the accountant were to correct this act of omission in arrears, this would be a move from tax avoidance towards tax evasion. Another example of such a move from tax avoidance to tax evasion might be where an accountant in informing HM Revenue and Customs of a tax-avoiding transaction fails to detail aspects of the transaction which might show it in a disadvantageous light.

Companies can move profit centres from high-taxation countries to low-taxation countries by setting up subsidiaries therein. These areas, known in extreme cases as tax havens, are disliked by governments.

Tax havens are countries with very low or zero tax rates on some or all forms of income. They could be classified into two groups:

1 the zero rate and low-tax havens;

2 the tax havens that impose tax at normal rates but grant preferential treatment to certain activities.

The use of zero rate and low-tax havens could be considered a form of tax avoidance, although sometimes they are used by tax evaders for their lack of regulation.

A similar problem has arisen in the use of charitable donations where tax relief is allowed to the donor and is a legitimate avoidance to encourage donations, except that the system has been manipulated as a form of tax evasion. This is an international problem and an OECD *Report on Abuse of Charities for Money-laundering and Tax Evasion* issued in 2009 stated that 'Tax evasion and tax fraud through the abuse of charities is a serious and increasing risk in many countries although its impact is variable. Some countries estimate that the abuse of charities costs their treasury many hundreds of millions of dollars and is becoming more prevalent'.[10]

16.4.4 Countering tax avoidance

An interesting discussion paper, *Countering Tax Avoidance in the UK: Which Way Forward?*, was published by the IFS in 2009.[11] It recognises that there is a difficulty in defining what constitutes avoidance.

It is a grey area and possibly not capable of a precise definition. Revenue authorities may often appear to consider tax avoidance to occur where it is sought to reduce the tax burden of individuals, businesses and other entities below the level envisaged by the government; the problem is, however, that the envisaged level is usually unclear.

In the public eye there is a view that certain types of avoidance are unacceptable. This leaves open the question, however, as to what is acceptable. What is acceptable to a taxpayer might be unacceptable to the tax collector. In principle, what is acceptable should be clear from the government as the body responsible for the raising of taxes. In practice it is incredibly difficult to cover all schemes through legislation. Detailed legislation, for instance, to indicate what is acceptable risks becoming more and more complex. This leads to the possibility for schemes to be designed which reflect the legal position but not the commercial substance. It is a similar problem to that faced by standard setters who have adopted the substance over form approach in areas such as accounting for leases.

Adopting a fuzzy approach rather than detailed legislation might appear to give the tax collector greater ability to counteract avoidance, but there is a downside – multinational companies might decide that there is too much uncertainty and base themselves in another jurisdiction.

16.4.5 International approaches

The discussion paper considers the approaches taken to counteracting avoidance in countries such as the UK and the Netherlands. It sets out that the Netherlands, for example, has both a case-based and a practical approach to avoidance.

The **case-based** concept is known as 'fraus legis'. Fraus legis means that the person has acted contrary to the intention of the law even though they have complied with the letter of the law. In order for it to apply, the avoidance of tax must be the only or paramount motive for the transaction and there must be a conflict with the intention and purpose of the law. Once applied, the judges may decide to ignore the tax avoidance transaction or replace it with other transactions if that would better fit with the purpose of the law.

The **practical approach** is to manage the taxpayer relationship. Since 2005, the Dutch tax authorities have entered into 'enforcement covenants' with certain multinationals. Currently, more than 40 have concluded these agreements. The Dutch tax authorities agree to reduce their supervision of the taxpayer's affairs and in return the taxpayer agrees to report tax risks. The taxpayer must be recognised as compliant for this option to be offered to them. The taxpayer effectively agrees to abide by not only the letter of the law but also its spirit and has to be seen to be paying a fair share of tax. A multinational with its tax burden reduced to nil would not be viewed as suitable for this approach.

16.5 Corporation tax and dividends

A company pays corporation tax on its income. When that company pays a dividend to its shareholders it is distributing some of its taxed income among the proprietors. In an imputation system the tax paid by the company is 'imputed' to the shareholders who therefore receive a dividend which has already been taxed.

This means that, from the paying company's point of view, the concept of gross dividends does not exist. From the paying company's point of view, the amount of dividend paid shown in the profit and loss account will equal the cash that the company will have paid.

However, from the shareholder's point of view, the cash received from the company is treated as a net payment after deduction of tax. The shareholders will have received, with the cash dividend, a note of a tax credit, which is regarded as equal to basic rate income tax on the total of the dividend plus the tax credit. For example:

	£
Dividend being the cash paid by the company and disclosed in the company's profit and loss account	400.00
Imputed tax credit of 1/9 of dividend paid (being the rate from 6 April 1999)	44.44
Gross dividend	444.44

The imputed tax credit calculation (as shown above) has been based on a basic tax rate of 10% for dividends paid, being the basic rate of income tax on dividend income from 6 April 1999. This means that an individual shareholder who only pays basic rate income tax has no further liability in that the assumption is that the basic rate tax has been paid by the company. A non-taxpayer cannot obtain a repayment of tax.

Although a company pays corporation tax on its income, when that company pays a dividend to its shareholders it is still considered to be distributing some of its taxed income among the proprietors. In this system the tax payable by the company is 'imputed' to the shareholders who therefore receive a dividend which has already been taxed. This means that, from the paying company's point of view, the concept of 'gross' dividends does not exist. From the paying company's point of view, the amount of dividends paid shown in the profit and loss account will equal the cash that the company will have paid to the shareholders.

The essential point is that the dividend-paying company makes absolutely no deduction from the dividend, **nor is any payment made by the company to HM Revenue and Customs**. The addition of 1/9 of the dividend paid as an imputed tax credit is purely nominal. A tax credit of 1/9 of the dividend will be deemed to be attached to that dividend (in effect an income tax rate of 10%). That credit is notional in that no payment of the 10% will be made to HM Revenue and Customs.[12] The payment of taxation is not associated with dividends.

Large companies (those with taxable profits of over £1,500,000) pay their corporation tax liability in quarterly instalments starting within the year of account, rather than paying their corporation tax liability nine months thereafter. The payment of taxation is not associated with the payment of dividends. Smaller companies pay their corporation tax nine months after the year-end.

16.6 IAS 12 – accounting for current taxation

The essence of IAS 12 is that it requires an enterprise to account for the tax consequences of transactions and other events in the same way that it accounts for the transactions and other events themselves. Thus, for transactions and other events recognised in the statement of comprehensive income, any related tax effects are also recognised in the statement of comprehensive income.

The details of how IAS 12 requires an enterprise to account for the tax consequences of transactions and other events follow below.

Statement of comprehensive income disclosure

The standard (paragraph 77) states that the tax expense related to profit or loss from ordinary activities should be presented on the face of the statement of comprehensive income. It also provides that the major components of the tax expense should be disclosed separately. These separate components of the tax expense may include (paragraph 80):

(a) current tax expense for the period of account;

(b) any adjustments recognised in the current period of account for prior periods (such as where the charge in a past year was underprovided);

(c) the amount of any benefit arising from a previously unrecognised tax loss, tax credit or temporary difference of a prior period that is used to reduce the current tax expense; and

(d) the amount of tax expense (income) relating to those changes in accounting policies and fundamental errors which are included in the determination of net profit or loss for the period in accordance with the allowed alternative treatment in IAS 8 *Net Profit or Loss for the Period, Fundamental Errors and Changes in Accounting Policies.*

Statement of financial position disclosure

The standard states that current tax for current and prior periods should, to the extent unpaid, be recognised as a liability. If the amount already paid in respect of current and prior periods exceeds the amount due for those periods, the excess should be recognised as an asset.

The treatment of tax losses

As regards losses for tax purposes, the standard states that the benefit relating to a tax loss that can be carried back to recover current tax of a previous period should be recognised as an asset. Tax assets and tax liabilities should be presented separately from other assets and liabilities in the statement of financial position. An enterprise should offset (paragraph 71) current tax assets and current tax liabilities if, and only if, the enterprise:

(a) has a legally enforceable right to set off the recognised amounts; and

(b) intends either to settle on a net basis, or to realise the asset and settle the liability simultaneously.

The standard provides (paragraph 81) that the following should also be disclosed separately:

(a) tax expense (income) relating to extraordinary items recognised during the period;

(b) an explanation of the relationship between tax expense (income) and accounting profit in either or both of the following forms:

(i) a numerical reconciliation between tax expense (income) and the product of accounting profit multiplied by the applicable tax rate(s), disclosing also the basis on which the applicable tax rate(s) is/are computed; or

(ii) a numerical reconciliation between the average effective tax rate and the applicable tax rate, disclosing also the basis on which the applicable tax rate is computed; and

(c) an explanation of changes in the applicable tax rate(s) compared to the previous accounting period.

The relationship between tax expense and accounting profit

The standard set out the following example in Appendix B of an explanation of the relationship between tax expense (income) and accounting profit:

Current Tax Expense

	X5	X6
Accounting profit	8,775	8,740
Add		
Depreciation for accounting purposes	4,800	8,250
Charitable donations	500	350
Fine for environmental pollution	700	—
Product development costs	250	250
Health care benefits	2,000	1,000
	17,025	18,590
Deduct		
Depreciation for tax purposes	(8,100)	(11,850)
Taxable profit	8,925	6,740
Current tax expense at 40%	3,570	
Current tax expense at 35%		2,359

16.7 Deferred tax

16.7.1 IAS 12 – background to deferred taxation

The profit on which tax is paid may differ from that shown in the published profit and loss account. This is caused by two separate factors.

Permanent differences

One factor that we looked at above is that certain items of expenditure may not be legitimate deductions from profit for tax purposes under the tax legislation. These differences are referred to as **permanent** differences because they will not be allowed at a different time and will be permanently disallowed, even in future accounting periods.

Timing differences

Another factor is that there are some other expenses that are legitimate deductions in arriving at the taxable profit which are allowed as a deduction for tax purposes at a later date. These might be simply **timing** differences in that tax relief and charges to the profit and loss account occur in different accounting periods. The accounting profit is prepared on an accruals basis but the taxable profit might require certain of the items to be dealt with on a cash basis. Examples of this might include bonuses payable to senior management, properly included in the financial statements under the accruals concept but not eligible for tax relief until actually paid some considerable time later, thus giving tax relief in a later period.

Temporary differences

The original IAS 12 allowed an enterprise to account for deferred tax using the statement of comprehensive income liability method which focused on timing differences. IAS 12 (revised) requires the statement of financial position liability method, which focuses on temporary differences, to be used. Timing differences are differences between taxable profit and accounting profit that originate in one period and reverse in one or more subsequent periods. Temporary differences are differences between the tax base of an asset or liability and its carrying amount in the statement of financial position. The tax base of an asset or liability is the amount attributed to that asset or liability for tax purposes. All timing differences are temporary differences.

The most significant temporary difference is depreciation. The depreciation charge made in the financial statements must be added back in the tax calculations and replaced by the official tax allowance for such an expense. The substituted expense calculated in accordance with the tax rules is rarely the same amount as the depreciation charge computed in accordance with IAS 16 *Property, Plant and Equipment*.

Capital investment incentive effect

It is common for legislation to provide for higher rates of tax depreciation than are used for accounting purposes, for it is believed that the consequent deferral of taxation liabilities serves as an incentive to capital investment (this incentive is not forbidden by European Union law or the OECD rules). The classic effect of this is for tax to be payable on a lower figure than the accounting profit in the earlier years of an asset's life because the tax allowances usually exceed depreciation in those years. In later accounting periods, the tax allowances will be lower than the depreciation charges and the taxable profit will then be higher than the accounting profit that appears in the published profit and loss account.

Deferred tax provisions

The process whereby the company pays tax on a profit that is lower than the reported profit in the early years and on a profit that is higher than reported profit in later years is known as **reversal**. Given the knowledge that, ultimately, these timing differences will reverse, the accruals concept requires that consideration be given to making provision for the future liability in those early years in which the tax payable is calculated on a lower figure. The provision that is made is known as a **deferred tax provision**.

Alternative methods for calculating deferred tax provisions

As you might expect, there has been a history of disagreement within the accounting profession over the method to use to calculate the provision. There have been, historically, two methods of calculating the provision for this future liability – the **deferral** method and the **liability** method.

The deferral method

The deferral method, which used to be favoured in the USA, involves the calculation each year of the tax effects of the timing differences that have arisen in that year. The tax effect is then debited or credited to the profit and loss account as part of the tax charge; the double entry is effected by making an entry to the deferred tax account. This deferral method of calculating the tax effect ignores the effect of changing tax rates on the timing differences that arose in earlier periods. This means that the total provision may consist of differences calculated at the rate of tax in force in the year when the entry was made to the provision.

The liability method

The liability method requires the calculation of the total amount of potential liability each year at current rates of tax, increasing or reducing the provision accordingly. This means that the company keeps a record of the timing differences and then recalculates at the end of each new accounting period using the rate of corporation tax in force as at the date of the current statement of financial position.

To illustrate the two methods we will take the example of a single asset, costing £10,000, depreciated at 10% using the straight-line method, but subject to a tax allowance of 25% on the reducing balance method. The workings are shown in Figure 16.1. This shows that, if there were no other adjustments, for the first four years the profits subject to tax would be lower than those shown in the accounts, but afterwards the situation would reverse.

Charge to statement of comprehensive income under the deferral method

The deferral method would charge to the profit and loss account each year the variation multiplied by the current tax rate, e.g. 20X5 at 25% on £1,500 giving £375.00, and 20X8 at 24%

Figure 16.1 Deferred tax provision using deferral method

		Accounts (depreciation) £	Tax (allowances) £	Difference (temporary) £	Tax (rate)
01.01.20X5	Cost of asset	10,000	10,000		
31.12.20X5	Depn/tax allowance	1,000	2,500	1,500	25%
		9,000	7,500	1,500	
31.12.20X6	Depn/tax allowance	1,000	1,875	875	25%
		8,000	5,625	2,375	
31.12.20X7	Depn/tax allowance	1,000	1,406	406	25%
		7,000	4,219	2,781	
31.12.20X8	Depn/tax allowance	1,000	1,055	55	24%
		6,000	3,164	2,836	
31.12.20X9	Depn/tax allowance	1,000	791	(209)	24%
		5,000	2,373	2,627	

Figure 16.2 Summary of deferred tax provision using the deferral method

Year ended	Timing difference £	Basic rate %	Deferred tax charge in year £	Deferred tax provision (deferral method) £
31.12.20X5	1,500	25%	375.00	375.00
31.12.20X6	875	25%	218.75	593.75
31.12.20X7	406	25%	101.50	695.25
31.12.20X8	55	24%	13.20	708.45
31.12.20X9	(209)	24%	(50.16)	658.29

on £55 giving £13.20. This is in accordance with the accruals concept which matches the tax expense against the income that gave rise to it. Under this method the deferred tax provision will be credited with £375 in 20X6 and this amount will not be altered in 20X8 when the tax rate changes to 24%. In the example, the calculation for the five years would be as in Figure 16.2.

Charge to statement of comprehensive income under the liability method
The liability method would make a charge so that the total balance on deferred tax equalled the cumulative variation multiplied by the current tax rate. The intention is that the statement of financial position liability should be stated at a figure which represents the tax effect as at the end of each new accounting period. This means that there would be an adjustment made in 20X8 to recalculate the tax effect of the timing difference that was provided for in earlier years. For example, the provision for 20X6 would be recalculated at 24%, giving a figure of £360 instead of the £375 that was calculated and charged in 20X6. The decrease in the expected liability will be reflected in the amount charged against the profit and loss account in 20X6. The £15 will in effect be credited to the 20X6 profit statement.

The effect on the charge to the 20X9 profit statement (Figures 16.2 and 16.3) is that there will be a charge of £13.20 using the deferral method and a **credit** of £14.61 using the liability method. The £14.61 is the reduction in the amount provided from £695.25 at the end of 20X8 to the £680.64 that is required at the end of 20X9.

World trend towards the liability method

There has been a move in national standards away from the deferral method towards the liability method, which is a change of emphasis from the statement of comprehensive

Figure 16.3 Deferral tax provision using the liability method

Year ended	Temporary difference £	Basic rate	Deferred tax charge in year £	Deferred tax provision (deferral method) £	Rate in 20X9	Deferred tax provision (liability method) £
31.12.20X6	1,500	25%	375.00	375.00	24%	360.00
31.12.20X7	875	25%	218.75	593.75	24%	210.00
31.12.20X8	406	25%	101.50	695.25	24%	97.44
31.12.20X9	55	24%	13.20	708.45	24%	13.20
				708.45		680.64

income to the statement of financial position because the deferred tax liability is shown at current rates of tax in the liability method. This is in accordance with the IASB's conceptual framework which requires that all items in the statement of financial position, other than shareholders' equity, must be either assets or liabilities as defined in the framework. Deferred tax as it is calculated under the traditional deferral method is not in fact a calculation of a liability, but is better characterised as deferred income or expenditure. This is illustrated by the fact that the sum calculated under the deferral method is not recalculated to take account of changes in the rate of tax charged, whereas it is recalculated under the liability method.

The world trend towards using the liability method also results in a change from accounting only for timing differences to accounting for temporary differences.

Temporary versus timing: conceptual difference

These temporary differences are defined in the IASB standard as 'differences between the carrying amount of an asset or liability in the statement of financial position and its tax base'.[13] The conceptual difference between these two views is that under the liability method provision is made for only the future reversal of these timing differences, whereas the temporary difference approach provides for the tax that would be payable if the company were to be liquidated at statement of financial position values (i.e. if the company were to sell all assets at statement of financial position values).

The US standard SFAS 109 argues the theoretical basis for these temporary differences to be accounted for on the following grounds:

> A government levies taxes on net taxable income. Temporary differences will become taxable amounts in future years, thereby increasing taxable income and taxes payable, upon recovery or settlement of the recognised and reported amounts of an enterprise's assets or liabilities . . . A contention that those temporary differences will never result in taxable amounts . . . would contradict the accounting assumption inherent in the statement of financial position that the reported amounts of assets and liabilities will be recovered and settled, respectively; thereby making that statement internally inconsistent.[14]

A consequence of accepting this conceptual argument in IAS 12 is that provision must also be made for the potential taxation effects of asset revaluations.

16.7.2 IAS 12 – deferred taxation

The standard requires that the financial statements are prepared using the liability method described above (which is sometimes known as the statement of financial position liability method).

An example of how deferred taxation operates follows.

EXAMPLE ● An asset which cost £150 has a carrying amount of £100. Cumulative depreciation for tax purposes is £90 and the tax rate is 25% as shown in Figure 16.4.

Figure 16.4 Cumulative depreciation

	In accounts	For tax
Cost	150	150
Depreciation	50	90
Carrying amount	100	60

Figure 16.5 Deferred tax liability

Income to recover	
Carrying amount	£100
Carrying amount for tax	£60
Temporary difference	£40
Tax rate	25%
Deferred tax	£10

The tax base of the asset is £60 (cost of £150 less cumulative tax depreciation of £90). To recover the carrying amount of £100, the enterprise must earn taxable income of £100, but will only be able to deduct tax depreciation of £60. Consequently, the enterprise will pay taxes of £10 (£40 at 25%) when it recovers the carrying amount of the asset. The difference between the carrying amount of £100 and the tax base of £60 is a taxable temporary difference of £40. Therefore, the enterprise recognises a deferred tax liability of £10 (£40 at 25%) representing the income taxes that it will pay when it recovers the carrying amount of the asset as shown in Figure 16.5.

The accounting treatment over the life of an asset

The following example, taken from IAS 12,[15] illustrates the accounting treatment over the life of an asset.

EXAMPLE ● An enterprise buys equipment for £10,000 and depreciates it on a straight-line basis over its expected useful life of five years. For tax purposes, the equipment is depreciated at 25% per annum on a straight-line basis. Tax losses may be carried back against taxable profit of the previous five years. In year 0, the enterprise's taxable profit was £5,000. The tax rate is 40%. The enterprise will recover the carrying amount of the equipment by using it to manufacture goods for resale. Therefore, the enterprise's current tax computation is as follows:

Year	1	2	3	4	5
Taxable income (£)	2,000	2,000	2,000	2,000	2,000
Depreciation for tax purposes	2,500	2,500	2,500	2,500	0
Tax profit (loss)	(500)	(500)	(500)	(500)	2,000
Current tax expense (income) at 40%	(200)	(200)	(200)	(200)	800

The enterprise recognises a current tax asset at the end of years 1 to 4 because it recovers the benefit of the tax loss against the taxable profit of year 0.

The temporary differences associated with the equipment and the resulting deferred tax asset and liability and deferred tax expense and income are as follows:

Year	1	2	3	4	5
Carrying amount (£)	8,000	6,000	4,000	2,000	0
Tax base	7,500	5,000	2,500	0	0
Taxable temporary difference	500	1,000	1,500	2,000	0
Opening deferred tax liability	0	200	400	600	800
Deferred tax expense (income)	200	200	200	200	(800)
Closing deferred tax liability	200	400	600	800	0

The enterprise recognises the deferred tax liability in years 1 to 4 because the reversal of the taxable temporary difference will create taxable income in subsequent years. The enterprise's statement of comprehensive income is as follows:

Year	1	2	3	4	5
Income (£)	2,000	2,000	2,000	2,000	2,000
Depreciation	2,000	2,000	2,000	2,000	2,000
Profit before tax	0	0	0	0	0
Current tax expense (income)	(200)	(200)	(200)	(200)	800
Deferred tax expense (income)	200	200	200	200	(800)
Total tax expense (income)	0	0	0	0	0
Net profit for the period	0	0	0	0	0

Further examples of items that could give rise to temporary differences are:

● Retirement benefit costs may be deducted in determining accounting profit as service is provided by the employee, but deducted in determining taxable profit either when contributions are paid to a fund by the enterprise or when retirement benefits are paid by the enterprise. A temporary difference exists between the carrying amount of the liability (in the financial statements) and its tax base (the carrying amount of the liability for tax purposes); the tax base of the liability is usually nil.

● Research costs are recognised as an expense in determining accounting profit in the period in which they are incurred but may not be permitted as a deduction in determining taxable profit (tax loss) until a later period. The difference between the tax base (the carrying amount of the liability for tax purposes) of the research costs, being the amount the taxation authorities will permit as a deduction in future periods, and the carrying amount of nil is a deductible temporary difference that results in a deferred tax asset.

Treatment of asset revaluations

The original IAS 12 permitted, but did not require, an enterprise to recognise a deferred tax liability in respect of asset revaluations. If such assets were sold at the revalued sum then a profit would arise that could be subject to tax. IAS 12 as currently written requires an enterprise to recognise a deferred tax liability in respect of asset revaluations.

Such a deferred tax liability on a revalued asset might not arise for many years, for there might be no intention to sell the asset. Many would argue that IAS 12 should allow for such timing differences by discounting the deferred liability (for a sum due many years in advance is certainly recognised in the business community as a lesser liability than the sum due immediately, for the sum could be invested and produce income until the liability would become due; this is termed the time value of money). The standard does not allow such discounting.[16] Indeed, it could be argued that in reality most businesses tend to have a policy of continuous asset replacement, with the effect that any deferred liability will be further deferred by these future acquisitions, so that the deferred tax liability would only become payable on a future cessation of trade. Not only does the standard preclude discounting, it also does not permit any account being made for future acquisitions by making a partial provision for the deferred tax.

Accounting treatment of deferred tax following a business combination

In a business combination that is an acquisition, the cost of the acquisition is allocated to the identifiable assets and liabilities acquired by reference to their fair values at the date of the exchange transaction. Temporary differences arise when the tax bases of the identifiable assets and liabilities acquired are not affected by the business combination or are affected differently. For example, when the carrying amount of an asset is increased to fair value but the tax base of the asset remains at cost to the previous owner, a taxable temporary difference arises which results in a deferred tax liability. Paragraph B16(i) of IFRS 3 *Business Combinations* prohibits discounting of deferred tax assets acquired and deferred tax liabilities assumed in a business combination, as does IAS 12 (revised). IAS 12 states that deferred tax should not be provided on goodwill if amortisation of it is not allowable for tax purposes (as is the case in many states). Deferred tax arising on a business combination that is an acquisition is an exception to the rule that changes in deferred tax should be recognised in the statement of comprehensive income (rather than as an adjustment by way of a note to the financial statements).

Another exception to this rule relates to items charged (or credited) directly to equity. Examples of such items are:

● a change in the carrying amount arising from the revaluation of property, plant and equipment (IAS 16 *Property, Plant and Equipment*);

● an adjustment to the opening balance of retained earnings resulting from either a change in accounting policy that is applied retrospectively or the correction of an error (IAS 8 *Accounting Policies, Changes in Accounting Estimates and Errors*);

● exchange differences arising on the translation of the financial statements of a foreign entity (IAS 21 *The Effects of Changes in Foreign Exchange Rates*); and

● amounts arising on initial recognition of the equity component of a compound financial instrument.

Deferred tax asset

A deferred tax asset should be recognised for the carry-forward of unused tax losses and unused tax credits to the extent that it is probable that future taxable profit will be available against which the unused tax losses and unused tax credits can be utilised.

At each statement of financial position date, an enterprise should reassess unrecognised deferred tax assets. The enterprise recognises a previously unrecognised deferred tax asset to the extent that it has become probable that future taxable profit will allow the deferred tax asset to be recovered. For example, an improvement in trading conditions may make it more probable that the enterprise will be able to generate sufficient taxable profit in the future for the deferred tax asset.

The Financial Reporting Review Panel in its 2012 Annual Report stated that 'As reported last year, the Panel continued to have to remind a number of companies with a record of losses of the need to recognise a deferred tax asset for the carry forward of unused tax losses and credits only to the extent that it is probable that future taxable profit will be available against which the temporary differences can be utilised. When a company has a history of losses, in the absence of sufficient taxable temporary differences "convincing other evidence" is required to support the company's judgement that it is probable that future taxable profits will be available against which the tax losses can be utilised. The Panel sought undertakings that, in future, as required by the standard the deferred tax asset should be quantified and the nature of the evidence supporting its recognition disclosed.'

The carrying amount of a deferred tax asset has to be reviewed at the end of each reporting period and reduced to the extent that it is no longer probable that sufficient taxable profit will be available to allow the benefit of the asset to be utilised. However, any such reduction can be reversed later if it becomes probable that sufficient taxable profit will be available.

At the October 2009 joint meeting of the IASB and the FASB, both boards indicated that they would consider undertaking a fundamental review of accounting for income taxes at some time in the future. In the meantime, the IASB is considering which issues it should address in a limited-scope project to amend IAS 12.

16.8 A critique of deferred taxation

It could be argued that deferred tax is not a legal liability until it accrues. The consequence of this argument would be that deferred tax should not appear in the financial statements, and financial statements should:

- present the tax expense for the year equal to the amount of income taxes that has been levied based on the income tax return for the year;
- accrue as a receivable any income refunds that are due from taxing authorities or as a payable any unpaid current or past income taxes;
- disclose in the notes to the financial statements differences between the income tax bases of assets and liabilities and the amounts at which they appear in the statement of financial position.

The argument is that the process of accounting for deferred tax is confusing what **did** happen to a company, i.e. the agreed tax payable for the year, and what **did not** happen to the company, which is the tax that would have been payable if the adjustments required by the tax law for timing differences had not occurred. It is felt that the investor should be provided with details of the tax charge levied on the profits for the year and an explanation of factors that might lead to a different rate of tax charge appearing in future financial statements. The argument against adjusting the tax charge for deferred tax and the creation of a deferred tax provision holds that shareholders are accustomed to giving consideration to many other imponderables concerning the amount, timing and uncertainty of future cash receipts and payments, and the treatment of tax should be considered in the same way. This view has received support from others,[17] who have held that tax attaches to taxable income and not to the reported accounting income and that there is no legal requirement for the tax to bear any relationship to the reported accounting income. Indeed it has been argued that 'deferred tax means income smoothing'.[18]

The creation of a charge in the statement of income for a deferred tax liability has an impact on the EPS in the year in which it arises and when it reverses. However, it is suggested that the arguments for and against deferred taxation accounting must be based solely on the theory underpinning accounting, and be unaffected by commercial considerations.

Accrual accounting assumption

It is also suggested that the above arguments against the use of deferred tax accounting are unconvincing if one considers the IASB's underlying assumption about accrual accounting, as stated in the *Framework*:

In order to meet their objectives, financial statements are prepared on the accrual basis of accounting . . . Financial statements prepared on the accrual basis inform users not only of past transactions involving the payment and receipt of cash but also of obligations to pay cash in the future and of resources that represent cash to be received in the future.[19]

This underlying assumption confirms that deferred tax accounting makes the fullest possible use of accrual accounting.

Pursuing this argument further, the *Framework* states:

The future economic benefit embodied in an asset is the potential to contribute, directly or indirectly, to the flow of cash and cash equivalents to the enterprise. The potential may be a productive one that is part of the operating activities of the enterprise.[20]

If a statement of financial position includes current market valuations based on this view of an asset, it is difficult to argue logically that the implicit taxation arising on this future economic benefit should not be provided for at the same time. The previous argument for excluding the deferred tax liability cannot therefore be considered persuasive on this basis.

On the other hand, it is stated in the *Framework* that 'An essential characteristic of a liability is that the enterprise has a present obligation.'[21] One could argue solely from these words that deferred tax is not a liability, but this conflicts with the argument based on the definition of an asset; consequently when considered in context this does not provide a sustainable argument against a deferred tax provision. The fact is that accounting practice has moved definitively towards making such a provision for deferred taxation.

Substance over form assumption

The legal argument that deferred tax is not a legal liability until it accrues runs counter to the criterion of substance over form which gives weight to the economic aspects of the event rather than the strict legal aspects. The *Framework* states:

Substance Over Form
If information is to represent faithfully the transactions and other events that it purports to represent, it is necessary that they are accounted for and presented in accordance with their substance and economic reality and not merely their legal form. The substance of transactions or other events is not always consistent with that which is apparent from their legal or contrived form.[22]

It is an interesting fact that substance over form has achieved a growing importance since the 1980s and the legal arguments are receiving less recognition. Investments are made on economic criteria, investors make their choices on the basis of anticipated cash flows, and such flows would be subject to the effects of deferred taxation.

16.9 Examples of companies following IAS 12

Figure 16.6 is from the Roche Group 2012 Annual Report. Figure 16.7 is from the Bayer Group 2011 Annual Report. It should be noted that these published examples do not always comply in full with all aspects of IAS 12 (revised).

Figure 16.6 Extract from Roche Group 2012 Annual Report

6. Income taxes

Income tax expenses | in millions of CHF

	2012	2011
Current income taxes	(3,402)	(2,693)
Adjustments recognised for current tax of prior periods	70	(5)
Deferred income taxes	782	357
Total income (expense)	**(2,550)**	**(2,341)**

The Group's effective tax rate can be reconciled to the Group's average expected tax rate as follows:

Reconciliation of the Group's effective tax rate

	2012	2011
Average expected tax rate	20.3%	19.6%

Tax effect of

	2012	2011
— Equity compensation plans	−0.3%	−0.1%
— Non-taxable income/non-deductible expenses	+1.8%	+1.1%
— Research, development and other manufacturing tax credits	−2.1%	−2.1%
— US state tax impacts	+0.8%	+0.9%
— Other differences	+0.2%	+0.3%
Group's effective tax rate before exceptional items	**20.7%**	**19.7%**

Figure 16.7 Extract from Bayer Group 2011 Annual Report

14. Income taxes

The breakdown of income taxes by origin was as follows:

Income tax expense by origin

	2010	2011
	€ million	€ million
Income taxes paid or accrued		
Germany	(118)	(313)
other countries	(779)	(754)
	(897)	**(1,067)**
Deferred taxes		
from temporary differences	534	223
from tax loss carryforwards	(33)	(28)
from tax credits	(15)	(19)
	486	**176**
Total	**(411)**	**(891)**

16.10 Value added tax (VAT)

VAT is one other tax that affects most companies and for which there is an accounting standard (SSAP 5 *Accounting for Value Added Tax*), which was established on its introduction. This standard was issued in 1974 when the introduction of value added tax was imminent and there was considerable worry within the business community on its accounting treatment. We can now look back, having lived with VAT for well over three decades, and wonder, perhaps, why an SSAP was needed. VAT is essentially a tax on consumers collected by traders and is accounted for in a similar way to PAYE income tax, which is a tax on employees collected by employers.

IAS 18 (paragraph 8) makes clear that the same principles are followed:

> Revenue includes only the gross inflows of economic benefits received and receivable by the enterprise on its own account. Amounts collected on behalf of third parties such as sales taxes, goods and services taxes and value added taxes are not economic benefits which flow to the enterprise and do not result in increases in equity. Therefore, they are excluded from revenue.[23]

16.10.1 The effects of the standard

The effects of the standard vary depending on the status of the accounting entity under the VAT legislation. The term 'trader' appears in the legislation and is the terminology for a business entity. The 'traders' or companies, as we would normally refer to them, are classified under the following headings:

(a) Registered trader

For a registered trader, accounts should only include figures net of VAT. This means that the VAT on the sales will be deducted from the invoice amount. The VAT will be payable to the government and the net amount of the sales invoice will appear in the profit and loss account in arriving at the sales turnover figure. The VAT on purchases will be deducted from the purchase invoice. The VAT will then be reclaimed from the government and the net amount of the purchases invoice will appear in the profit and loss account in arriving at the purchases figure.

The only exception to the use of amounts net of VAT is when the input tax is not recoverable, e.g. on entertaining and on 'private' motor cars.

(b) Non-registered or exempt trader

For a company that is classified as non-registered or exempt, the VAT that it has to pay on its purchases and expenses is not reclaimable from the government. Because the company cannot recover the VAT, it means that the expense that appears in the profit and loss account must be inclusive of VAT. It is treated as part of each item of expenditure and the costs treated accordingly. It will be included, where relevant, with each item of expense (including capital expenditure) rather than being shown as a separate item.

(c) Partially exempt trader

An entity which is partially exempt can only recover a proportion of input VAT, and the proportion of non-recoverable VAT should be treated as part of the costs on the same lines as with an exempt trader. The VAT rules are complex but, for the purpose of understanding the figures that appear in published accounts of public companies, treatment as a registered trader would normally apply.

Summary

Corporation tax is charged on the taxable profit of a company after adjusting the accounting profit for non-allowable deductions and temporary differences.

The imputation system means that dividends are reported at the amount of cash paid out by the company and a credit is allowed on the dividend received by the shareholder.

Deferred tax is provided for under IAS 12 reflecting the amount that is expected to be settled as a liability. The requirement to make such a provision is supported by the *Framework for the Preparation and Presentation of Financial Statements*.

Tax avoidance and tax evasion have been perceived by the public as being unfair and governments have internationally attempted to combat the problem through legislation, case law and encouraging positive consumer reaction to put pressure on companies not appearing to pay a fair amount of tax nationally.

REVIEW QUESTIONS

1 Why does the charge to taxation in a company's accounts not equal the profit multiplied by the current rate of corporation tax?

2 Deferred tax accounting may be seen as an income-smoothing device which distorts the true and fair view. Explain the impact of deferred tax on reported income and justify its continued use.

3 Distinguish between (a) the deferral and (b) the liability methods of company deferred tax.

4 If a deferred liability or asset is not expected to crystallise they should at least be discounted. Discuss.

5 The effective tax rate of all companies should be published and any with a rate below the average for the sector should be subjected to consumer or government commercial pressure to make additional payments. Discuss.

6 Discuss the problems in distinguishing tax evasion from tax avoidance.

7 Discuss whether there is a socially responsible right amount of tax for a company to pay and who is to determine what is socially responsible.

8 A tax adviser has a duty of care to a client to legally minimise a company's tax bill and would be professionally negligent not to do so. Discuss.

9 A company justified paying little tax on the grounds that it invested funds more effectively than government by creating employment. It further argued that this view was supported when it appears that governments lack the technical skills to control expenditure effectively. Discuss.

10 The Financial Reporting Review Panel (FRRP) in its 2012 Annual Report stated that: 'Several companies had to be reminded that current and deferred tax liabilities and assets are to be measured using the tax rates that have been enacted or substantively enacted by the end of the reporting period'. Discuss why this is necessary.

EXERCISES

Question 1

In your capacity as chief assistant to the financial controller, your managing director has asked you to explain to him the differences between tax planning, tax avoidance and tax evasion.

He has also asked you to explain to him your feelings as a professional accountant about these topics.

Write some notes to assist you in answering these questions.

* Question 2

A non-current asset (a machine) was purchased by Adjourn plc on 1 July 20X2 at a cost of £25,000.

The company prepares its annual accounts to 31 March in each year. The policy of the company is to depreciate such assets at the rate of 15% straight line (with depreciation being charged *pro rata* on a time-apportionment basis in the year of purchase). The company was granted capital allowances at 25% per annum on the reducing balance method (such capital allowances are apportioned *pro rata* on a time-apportionment basis in the year of purchase).

The rate of corporation tax has been as follows:

Year ended   31 Mar 20X3 20%
            31 Mar 20X4 30%
            31 Mar 20X5 20%
            31 Mar 20X6 19%
            31 Mar 20X7 19%

Required:
(a) Calculate the deferred tax provision using both the deferred method and the liability method.
(b) Explain why the liability method is considered by commentators to place the emphasis on the statement of financial position, whereas the deferred method is considered to place the emphasis on the profit and loss account.

* Question 3

The following information is given in respect of Unambitious plc:

(a) Non-current assets consist entirely of plant and machinery. The net book value of these assets as at 30 June 2010 is £100,000 in excess of their tax written-down value.

(b) The provision for deferred tax (all of which relates to fixed asset timing differences) as at 30 June 2010 was £21,000.

(c) The company's capital expenditure forecasts indicate that capital allowances and depreciation in future years will be:

Year ended 30 June	Depreciation charge for year	Capital allowances for year
£	£	£
2011	12,000	53,000
2012	14,000	49,000
2013	20,000	36,000
2014	40,000	32,000
2015	44,000	32,000
2016	46,000	36,000

For the following years, capital allowances are likely to continue to be in excess of depreciation for the foreseeable future.

(d) Corporation tax is to be taken at 21%.

Required:
Calculate the deferred tax charges or credits for the next six years, commencing with the year ended 30 June 2011, in accordance with the provisions of IAS 12.

Question 4

The move from the preparation of accounts under UK GAAP to the users of IFRS by United Kingdom quoted companies for years beginning 1 January 2005 had an effect on the level of profits reported. How will those profits arising from the change in accounting standards be treated for taxation purposes?

Question 5

Discuss the arguments for and against discounting the deferred tax charge.

Question 6

Austin Mitchell MP proposed an Early Day Motion in the House of Commons on 17 May 2005 as follows:

That this House urges the Government to clamp down on artificial tax avoidance schemes and end the . . . tax avoidance loop-holes that enable millionaires and numerous companies trading in the UK to avoid UK taxes; and further urges the Government to . . . so that transactions lacking normal commercial substance and solely entered into for the purpose of tax avoidance are ignored for tax purposes, thereby providing certainty, fairness and clarity, which the UK's taxation system requires to prevent abusive tax avoidance, to protect the interests of ordinary citizens who are committed to making their contribution to society, to avoid an unnecessary burden of tax on individual tax-payers and to ensure that companies pay fair taxes on profits generated in this country.

Required:
(a) The Motion refers to tax avoidance. In your opinion, does the Early Day Motion tend to confuse the boundaries between tax avoidance and tax evasion?
(b) The Motion refers to nullifying the effects of tax avoidance to protect the interests of ordinary citizens who are making their contribution to society, to avoid an unnecessary burden of tax on individual taxpayers. If ordinary citizens require such protection, would it be possible to argue that even if tax avoidance were legal, it might well be immoral?

* Question 7

Dee For has recently qualified as a pilot and is now intending to set up a private company in the near future to run small charter passenger flights from her home town. Most of her business plan has been written but she has recently learned that the company's forecast statement of comprehensive income and statement of financial position may be incorrect as she has not taken into account the likely impact of deferred tax on those financial statements. She has therefore asked you for help and, following a meeting, the following facts come to light:

(i)   The aircraft would cost $1m. It would have a life of five years after which it would have no residual value and will then be scrapped. Depreciation will be on a straight-line basis.

(ii) The government of the country in which she lives has recently introduced a scheme for new entrepreneurs which provides a tax allowance on capital expenditure of this type of 25% per annum using the reducing balance method. In this country, depreciation is not a deductible expense for tax purposes. Also in this country, a balancing adjustment is allowed whenever the asset is sold or scrapped.

(iii) Corporate income tax is currently set at 30%. It has remained unchanged for many years now and the government has indicated there are no plans to change it.

(iv) The company's forecast annual accounting profit before tax is $2m per annum over the next five years.

Required:

(a) Demonstrate the impact of the above on the company's forecast profit and loss accounts and balance sheets for each of the next five years by comparing the 'nil provision' method with the 'full provision method'.

(b) Explain how your answer to (a) would be affected by a government announcement that it intends to increase the corporate income tax rate in the near future.

(The Association of International Accountants)

Question 8

Hanson Products Ltd is a newly formed company. The company commenced trading on 1 January 20X1 when it purchased an item of plant and equipment for $240,000. The plant and equipment has an expected life of five years with zero residual value, and will be depreciated on a straight-line basis on cost over that period. The company's profits before depreciation (of the plant) are expected to be $1 million each year.

Tax allowances for plant are a 40% initial allowance with an annual 25% writing-down allowance on tax written-down value in subsequent years. The company will have a life of five years and, on closure, any unused tax allowances will be allowed as a deduction from the final year's taxable profit.

The rate of corporation tax is 20%. The company does not provide for deferred taxation.

Required:

(a) For each of the years from 20X1 to 20X5, calculate:
   (i)   the capital allowances,
   (ii) the taxable profit,
   (iii) the tax payable on the year's profit.
(b) Discuss the advantages and disadvantages of not providing for deferred taxation.

Question 9

The accountant of Hanson Products Ltd has asked you how your answer to Question 8 above would be affected using the following two methods of calculating deferred taxation.

Required:
(a) For each of the years from 20X1 to 20X5, calculate the deferred tax balance if:
   (i) full provision is made for deferred tax in accordance with IAS 12 *Income Taxes*,
   (ii) the company decided to calculate the deferred tax balance using a discount rate of 5%.
(b) Discuss the advantages and disadvantages of discounting deferred tax balances. Use the following table of discount factors:

Year	Discount factor
1	0.9524
2	0.9070
3	0.8638
4	0.8227
5	0.7835

Question 10

The following information relates to Deferred plc:

- EBITDA (earnings before interest, tax, depreciation and amortisation) for year ended 31.12.20X1 is £300,000
- No interest payable in 20X1
- No amortisation
- Equipment cost £100,000 at 1.1.20X1
   - Depreciation rate is 10% straight line
   - Nil scrap value
- Tax rate is 20%
- Capital allowance is 25% on reducing balance basis.

Required:
Calculate:
(a) deferred tax;
(b) statement of income entries;
(c) statement of financial position entries.

References

1 OECD, *Theoretical and Empirical Aspects of Corporate Taxation*, Paris, 1974; van den Temple, *Corporation Tax and Individual Income Tax in the EEC*, EEC Commission, Brussels, 1974.
2 G.H. Partington and R.H. Chenhall, *Dividends, Distortion and Double Taxation*, Abacus, June 1983.
3 Franklin D. Roosevelt, 1936 Speech at Worcester, Mass., 1936. Roosevelt Museum.
4 *Countering Tax Avoidance in the UK: Which Way Forward?*, A Report for the Tax Law Review Committee, The Institute for Fiscal Studies, 2009, para. 4.2.
5 Tomlin, L.J. in *Duke of Westminster v CIR*, HL 1935, 19 TC 490.

6 *Tax Avoidance*, A Report for the Tax Law Review Committee, The Institute for Fiscal Studies, 1997, para. 7.

7 *WT Ramsay Ltd v CIR*, HL 1981, 54 TC 101; [1981] STC 174; [1981] 2 WLR 449; [1981] 1 All ER 865.

8 Robert Maas, *Beware Tax Avoidance Drifting into Evasion*, Taxline, Tax Planning 2003–2004, Institute of Chartered Accountants in England & Wales.

9 *Professional Conduct in Relation to Taxation*, Ethical Statement 1.308, Institute of Chartered Accountants in England & Wales, para. 2.13 (this is similar to the statements issued by the other accounting bodies).

10 http://www.oecd.org/tax/exchangeofinformation/42232037.pdf

11 http://www.ifs.org.uk/comms/dp7.pdf

12 R. Altshul, 'Act now', *Accountancy Age*, 5 February 1998, p. 19.

13 IAS 12 *Income Taxes*, IASB, revised 2000, para. 5.

14 SFAS 109, *Accounting for Income Taxes*, FASB, 1992, extracts therefrom.

15 IAS 12 *Income Taxes*, IASB, revised 2000, Example 1 to Appendix B.

16 *Ibid.*, para. 54.

17 R.J. Chambers, *Tax Allocation and Financial Reporting*, Abacus, 1968.

18 Prof. D.R. Middleton, letters to the Editor, *The Financial Times*, 29 September 1994.

19 *Framework for the Preparation and Presentation of Financial Statements*, IASB, 2001, para. 22.

20 *Ibid.*, para. 53.

21 *Ibid.*, para. 60.

22 *Ibid.*, para. 35.

23 IAS 18 *Revenue*, IASB, 2001, para. 8.

CHAPTER 17

Property, plant and equipment (PPE)

17.1 Introduction

The main purpose of this chapter is to explain how to determine the initial carrying value of PPE and to explain and account for the normal movements in PPE that occur during an accounting period.

Objectives

By the end of this chapter, you should be able to:

- explain the meaning of PPE and determine its initial carrying value;
- account for subsequent expenditure on PPE that has already been recognised;
- explain the meaning of depreciation and compute the depreciation charge for a period;
- account for PPE measured under the revaluation model;
- explain the meaning of impairment;
- compute and account for an impairment loss;
- explain the criteria that must be satisfied before an asset is classified as held for sale and account for such assets;
- explain the accounting treatment of government grants for the purchase of PPE;
- identify an investment property and explain the alternative accounting treatment of such properties;
- explain the impact of alternative methods of accounting for PPE on key accounting ratios.

17.2 PPE – concepts and the relevant IASs and IFRSs

For PPE the accounting treatment is based on the accruals or matching concepts, under which expenditure is capitalised until it is charged as depreciation against revenue in the periods in which benefit is gained from its use. Thus, if an item is purchased that has an economic life of two years, so that it will be used over two accounting periods to help earn profit for the entity, then the cost of that asset should be apportioned in some way between the two accounting periods.

However, this does not take into account the problems surrounding PPE accounting and depreciation, which have so far given rise to six relevant international accounting standards. We will consider these problems in this chapter and cover the following questions.

IAS 16 and IAS 23

- What is PPE (IAS 16)?

- How is the cost of PPE determined (IAS 16 and IAS 23)?

- How is depreciation of PPE computed (IAS 16)?

- What are the regulations regarding carrying PPE at revalued amounts (IAS 16)?

Other relevant international accounting standards and pronouncements

- How should grants receivable towards the purchase of PPE be dealt with (IAS 20)?

- Are there ever circumstances in which PPE should not be depreciated (IAS 40)?

- What is impairment and how does this affect the carrying value of PPE (IAS 36)?

- What are the key changes made by the IASB concerning the disposal of non-current assets (IFRS 5)?

17.3 What is PPE?

IAS 16 *Property, Plant and Equipment*[1] defines PPE as tangible assets that are:

(a) held by an entity for use in the production or supply of goods and services, for rental to others, or for administrative purposes; and

(b) expected to be used during more than one period.

It is clear from the definition that PPE will normally be included in the non-current assets section of the statement of financial position.

17.3.1 Problems that may arise

Problems may arise in relation to the interpretation of the definition and in relation to the application of the materiality concept.

The definitions give rise to some areas of practical difficulty. For example, an asset that has previously been held for use in the production or supply of goods or services but is now going to be sold should, under the provisions of IFRS 5, be classified separately on the statement of financial position as an asset 'held for sale'.

Differing accounting treatments arise if there are different assessments of materiality. This may result in the same expenditure being reported as an asset in the statement of financial position of one company and as an expense in the statement of comprehensive income of another company. In the accounts of a self-employed carpenter, a kit of hand tools that, with careful maintenance, will last many years will, quite rightly, be shown as PPE. Similar assets used by the maintenance department in a large factory will, in all probability, be treated as 'loose tools' and written off as acquired.

Many entities have *de minimis* policies, whereby only items exceeding a certain value are treated as PPE; items below the cut-off amount will be expensed through the statement of comprehensive income.

For example, the MAN 2003 Annual Report stated in its accounting policies:

Tangible assets are depreciated according to the straight-line method over their estimated useful lives. Low-value items (defined as assets at cost of €410 or less) are fully written off in the year of purchase.

17.4 How is the cost of PPE determined?

17.4.1 Components of cost[2]

According to IAS 16, the cost of an item of PPE comprises its purchase price, including import duties and non-refundable purchase taxes, plus any directly attributable costs of bringing the asset to working condition for its intended use. Examples of such directly attributable costs include:

(a) the costs of site preparation;

(b) initial delivery and handling costs;

(c) installation costs;

(d) professional fees such as for architects and engineers;

(e) the estimated cost of dismantling and removing the asset and restoring the site, to the extent that it is recognised as a provision under IAS 37 *Provisions, Contingent Liabilities and Contingent Assets*.

Administration and other general overhead costs are not a component of the cost of PPE unless they can be directly attributed to the acquisition of the asset or bringing it to its working condition. Similarly, start-up and similar pre-production costs do not form part of the cost of an asset unless they are necessary to bring the asset to its working condition.

17.4.2 Self-constructed assets[3]

The cost of a self-constructed asset is determined using the same principles as for an acquired asset. If the asset is made available for sale by the entity in the normal course of business then the cost of the asset is usually the same as the cost of producing the asset for sale. This cost would usually be determined under the principles set out in IAS 2 *Inventories*.

The normal profit that an enterprise would make if selling the self-constructed asset would not be recognised in 'cost' if the asset were retained within the entity. Following similar principles, where one group company constructs an asset that is used as PPE by another group company, any profit on sale is eliminated in determining the initial carrying value of the asset in the consolidated accounts (this will also clearly affect the calculation of depreciation).

If an item of PPE is exchanged in whole or in part for a dissimilar item of PPE then the cost of such an item is the fair value of the asset received. This is equivalent to the fair value of the asset given up, adjusted for any cash or cash equivalents transferred or received.

17.4.3 Capitalisation of borrowing costs

Where an asset takes a substantial period of time to get ready for its intended use or sale then the entity may incur significant borrowing costs in the preparation period. Under the accruals basis of accounting there is an argument that such costs should be included as a directly attributable cost of construction. IAS 23 *Borrowing Costs* was issued to deal with this issue.

IAS 23 states that borrowing costs that are directly attributable to the acquisition, construction or production of a 'qualifying asset' should be included in the cost of that asset.[4] A 'qualifying asset' is one that necessarily takes a substantial period of time to get ready for its intended use or sale.

Borrowing costs that would have been avoided if the expenditure on the qualifying asset had not been undertaken are eligible for capitalisation under IAS 23. Where the funds are borrowed specifically for the purpose of obtaining a qualifying asset, the borrowing costs that are eligible for capitalisation are those incurred on the borrowing during the period less any investment income on the temporary investment of those borrowings. Where the funds are borrowed generally and used for the purpose of obtaining a qualifying asset, the entity should use a capitalisation rate to determine the borrowing costs that may be capitalised. This rate should be the weighted average of the borrowing costs applicable to the entity, other than borrowings made specifically for the purpose of obtaining a qualifying asset. Capitalisation should commence when:

● expenditures for the asset are being incurred;
● borrowing costs are being incurred;
● activities that are necessary to prepare the asset for its intended use or sale are in progress.

When substantially all the activities necessary to prepare the qualifying asset for its intended use or sale are complete, capitalisation should cease.

Borrowing costs treatment in the UK

The UK standard that deals with this issue is FRS 15 *Tangible Fixed Assets*. FRS 15 makes the capitalisation of borrowing costs optional, rather than compulsory. FRS 15 requires that the policy be applied consistently, however. This used to be the treatment under IAS 23 before that standard was revised in 2007.

Borrowing costs for SMEs

IAS 23 *Borrowing Costs* requires borrowing costs directly attributable to the acquisition, construction or production of a qualifying asset (including some inventories) to be capitalised as part of the cost of the asset. For cost-benefit reasons, the IFRS for SMEs requires such costs to be charged to expense.

IFRS for SMEs

All borrowing costs are charged to expense when incurred. Borrowing costs are not capitalised.

17.4.4 Subsequent expenditure

Subsequent expenditure relating to an item of PPE that has already been recognised should normally be recognised as an expense in the period in which it is incurred. The exception to this general rule is where it is probable that future economic benefits in excess of the originally assessed standard of performance of the existing asset will, as a result of the expenditure, flow to the entity. In these circumstances, the expenditure should be added to the carrying value of the existing asset. Examples of expenditure that might fall to be treated in this way include:

● modification of an item of plant to extend its useful life, including an increase in its capacity;
● upgrading machine parts to achieve a substantial improvement in the quality of output;
● adoption of new production processes enabling a substantial reduction in previously assessed operating costs.

Conversely, expenditure that restores, rather than increases, the originally assessed standard of performance of an asset is written off as an expense in the period incurred.

Some assets have components that require replacement at regular intervals. Two examples of such components would be the lining of a furnace and the roof of a building. IAS 16 states[5] that, provided such components have readily ascertainable costs, they should be accounted for as separate assets because they have useful lives different from the items of PPE to which they relate. This means that when such components are replaced they are accounted for as an asset disposal and acquisition of a new asset.

17.5 What is depreciation?

IAS 16 defines depreciation[1] as the systematic allocation of the depreciable amount of an asset over its life. The depreciable amount is the cost of an asset or other amount substituted for cost in the financial statements, less its residual value.

Note that this definition places an emphasis on the consumption in a particular accounting period rather than an average over the asset's life. We will consider two aspects of the definition: the measure of wearing out; and the useful economic life.

17.5.1 Allocation of depreciable amount

Depreciation is a measure of wearing out that is calculated annually and charged as an expense against profits. Under the 'matching concept', the depreciable amount of the asset is allocated over its productive life.

It is important to make clear what depreciation is *not*:

- It is not 'saving up for a new one'; it is not setting funds aside for the replacement of the existing asset at the end of its life; it is the matching of cost to revenue. The effect is to reduce the profit available for distribution, but this is not accompanied by the setting aside of cash of an equal amount to ensure that liquid funds are available at the end of the asset's life.

- It is not 'a way of showing the real value of assets on the statement of financial position' by reducing the cost figure to a realisable value.

We emphasise what depreciation is *not* because both of these ideas are commonly held by non-accountant users of accounts; it is as well to realise these possible misconceptions when interpreting accounts for non-accountants.

Depreciation is currently conceived as a charge for funds **already expended**, and thus it cannot be considered as the setting aside of funds to meet future expenditure. If we consider it in terms of capital maintenance, then we can see that it results in the maintenance of the initial invested monetary capital of the company. It is concerned with the allocation of that expenditure over a period of time, without having regard for the **value** of the asset at any intermediate period of its life.

Where an asset has been revalued the depreciation is based on the revalued amount. This is because the revalued amount has replaced cost (less residual value) as the depreciable amount.

17.5.2 Useful life

IAS 16 defines this as:

(a) the period of time over which an asset is expected to be used by an entity; or

(b) the number of production or similar units expected to be obtained from the asset by an entity.[1]

The IAS 16 definition is based on the premise that almost all assets have a finite useful economic life. This may be true in principle, but it is incredibly difficult in real life to arrive at an average economic life that can be applied to even a single class of assets, e.g. plant. This is evidenced by the accounting policy in the AkzoNobel 2010 Annual Report which states:

> Depreciation is calculated using the straight-line method based on the estimated useful life. In the majority of cases the useful life of plant, equipment and machinery is ten years, and for buildings ranges from 20 to 30 years. Land is not depreciated. In the majority of cases residual value is assumed to be insignificant. Depreciation methods, lives and residual values are reassessed annually.

In addition to the practical difficulty of estimating economic lives, there are also exceptions where nil depreciation is charged. Two common exceptions found in the accounts of UK companies relate to freehold land and certain types of property.

17.5.3 Freehold land

Freehold land (but not the buildings thereon) is considered to have an infinite life unless it is held simply for the extraction of minerals, etc. Thus land held for the purpose of, say, mining coal or quarrying gravel will be dealt with for accounting purposes as a coal or gravel deposit. Consequently, although the land may have an infinite life, the deposits will have an economic life only as long as they can be profitably extracted. If the cost of extraction exceeds the potential profit from extraction and sale, the economic life of the quarry has ended. When assessing depreciation for a commercial company, we are concerned only with these private costs and benefits, and not with public costs and benefits which might lead to the quarry being kept open.

The following extract from the Goldfields 2010 Annual Report illustrates accounting policies for land and mining assets.

Land
Land is shown at cost and is not depreciated.

Amortisation and depreciation of mining assets
Amortisation is determined to give a fair and systematic charge in the statement of comprehensive income taking into account the nature of a particular ore body and the method of mining that ore body. To achieve this the following calculation methods are used:

- Mining assets, including mine development and infrastructure costs, mine plant facilities and evaluation costs, are amortised over the lives of the mines using the units-of-production method, based on estimated proved and probable ore reserves above infrastructure.

- Where it is anticipated that the mine life will significantly exceed the proved and probable reserves, the mine life is estimated using a methodology that takes account of current exploration information to assess the likely recoverable gold from a particular area. Such estimates are used only for the level of confidence in the assessment and the probability of conversion to reserves.

- At certain of the group's operations, the calculation of amortisation takes into account future costs which will be incurred to develop all the proved and probable ore reserves.

- Proved and probable ore reserves reflect estimated quantities of economically recoverable reserves, which can be recovered in future from known mineral deposits. Certain mining plant and equipment included in mine development and infrastructure are depreciated on a straight-line basis over their estimated useful lives.

Mineral and surface rights
Mineral and surface rights are recorded at cost of acquisition. When there is little likelihood of a mineral right being exploited, or the value of mineral rights have diminished below cost, a write-down is effected against income in the period that such determination is made.

Few jurisdictions have comprehensive accounting standards for extractive activities. IFRS 6 *Exploration for and Evaluation of Mineral Resources* is an interim measure pending a more comprehensive view by the ASB in future. IFRS 6 allows an entity to develop an accounting policy for exploration and evaluation assets without considering the consistency of the policy with the IASB framework. This may mean that for an interim period accounting policies might permit the recognition of both current and non-current assets that do not meet the criteria laid down in the IASB *Framework*. This is considered by some commentators to be unduly permissive. Indeed, about the only firm requirement IFRS 6 can be said to contain is the requirement to test exploration and evaluation assets for impairment whenever a change in facts and circumstances suggests that impairment exists.

17.6 What are the constituents in the depreciation formula?

In order to calculate depreciation it is necessary to determine three factors:

1 Cost (or revalued amount if the company is following a revaluation policy)
2 Economic life
3 Residual value.

A simple example is the calculation of the depreciation charge for a company that has acquired an asset on 1 January 20X1 for £1,000 with an estimated economic life of four years and an estimated residual value of £200. Applying a straight-line depreciation policy, the charge would be £200 per year using the formula of:

$$\frac{\text{Cost} - \text{estimated residual value}}{\text{Estimated economic life}} = \frac{£1,000 - £200}{4} = £200 \text{ per annum}$$

We can see that the charge of £200 is influenced in all cases by the definition of cost, the estimate of the residual value, the estimate of the economic life, and the management decision on depreciation policy.

In addition, if the asset were to be revalued at the end of the second year to £900, then the depreciation for 20X3 and 20X4 would be recalculated using the revised valuation figure. Assuming that the residual value remained unchanged, the depreciation for 20X3 would be:

$$\frac{\text{Revalued asset} - \text{estimated residual value}}{\text{Estimated economic life}} = \frac{£900 - £200}{2} = £350 \text{ per annum}$$

17.6.1 How is the useful life of an asset determined?

The IAS 16 definition of useful life is given in Section 17.5.2 above. This is not necessarily the total life expectancy of the asset. Most assets become less economically and technologically efficient as they grow older. For this reason, assets may well cease to have an economic life long before their working life is over. It is the responsibility of the preparers of accounts to estimate the economic life of all assets.

It is conventional for entities to consider the economic lives of assets by class or category, e.g. buildings, plant, office equipment, or motor vehicles. However, this is not necessarily appropriate, since the level of activity demanded by different users may differ. For example, compare two motor cars owned by a business: one is used by the national sales manager, covering 100,000 miles per annum visiting clients; the other is used by the accountant to drive from home to work and occasionally the bank, covering perhaps one-tenth of the mileage.

In practice, the useful economic life would be determined by reference to factors such as repair costs, the cost and availability of replacements, and the comparative cash flows of existing and alternative assets. The problem of optimal replacement lives is a normal financial management problem; its significance in financial reporting is that the assumptions used within the financial management decision may provide evidence of the expected economic life.

17.6.2 Other factors affecting the useful life figure

We can see that there are technical factors affecting the estimated economic life figure. In addition, other factors have prompted companies to set estimated lives that have no relationship to the active productive life of the asset. One such factor is the wish of management to take into account the effect of inflation. This led some companies to reduce the estimated economic life, so that a higher charge was made against profits during the early period of the asset's life to compensate for the inflationary effect on the cost of replacement. The total charge will be the same, but the timing is advanced. This does not result in the retention of funds necessary to replace; but it does reflect the fact that there is at present no coherent policy for dealing with inflation in the published accounts – consequently, companies resort to *ad hoc* measures that frustrate efforts to make accounts uniform and comparable. *Ad hoc* measures such as these have prompted changes in the standards.

17.6.3 Residual value

IAS 16 defines residual value as the net amount which an entity expects to obtain for an asset at the end of its useful life after deducting the expected costs of disposal. Where PPE is carried at cost, the residual value is initially estimated at the date of acquisition. In subsequent periods the estimate of residual value is revised, the revision being based on conditions prevailing at each statement of financial position date. Such revisions have an effect on future depreciation charges.

Besides inflation, residual values can be affected by changes in technology and market conditions. For example, during the period 1980–90 the cost of small business computers fell dramatically in both real and monetary terms, with a considerable impact on the residual (or second-hand) value of existing equipment.

17.7 Calculation of depreciation

Having determined the key factors in the computation, we are left with the problem of how to allocate that cost between accounting periods. For example, with an asset having an economic life of five years:

	£
Asset cost	11,000
Estimated residual value	1,000
(no significant change anticipated over useful economic life)	
Depreciable amount	10,000

How should the depreciable amount be charged to the statement of comprehensive income over the five years? IAS 16 tells us that it should be allocated on a systematic basis and the depreciation method used should reflect as fairly as possible the pattern in which the asset's economic benefits are consumed. The two most popular methods are **straight-line**, in which the depreciation is charged evenly over the useful life, and **diminishing balance**, where depreciation is calculated annually on the net written-down amount. In the case above, the calculations would be as in Figure 17.1.

Note that, although the diminishing balance is generally expressed in terms of a percentage, this percentage is arrived at by inserting the economic life into the formula as n; the 38% reflects the expected economic life of five years. As we change the life, so we change the percentage that is applied. The normal rate applied to vehicles is 25% diminishing balance; if we apply that to the cost and residual value in our example, we can see that we would be assuming an economic life of eight years. It is a useful test when using reducing balance percentages to refer back to the underlying assumptions.

We can see that the end result is the same. Thus, £10,000 has been charged against income, but with a dramatically different pattern of statement of comprehensive income charges. The charge for straight-line depreciation in the first year is less than half that for reducing balance.

Figure 17.1 Effect of different depreciation methods

	Straight-line (£2,000) £	Diminishing balance (38%) £	Difference £
Cost	11,000	11,000	
Depreciation for year 1	2,000	4,180	2,180
Net book value (NBV)	9,000	6,820	
Depreciation for year 2	2,000	2,592	592
NBV	7,000	4,228	
Depreciation for year 3	2,000	1,606	(394)
NBV	5,000	2,622	
Depreciation for year 4	2,000	996	(1,004)
NBV	3,000	1,626	
Depreciation for year 5	2,000	618	(1,382)
Residual value	1,000	1,008	

The diminishing balance formula was $1 - \sqrt[n]{(\text{Residual value/Cost})}$

17.7.1 Arguments in favour of the straight-line method

The method is simple to calculate. However, in these days of calculators and computers this seems a particularly facile argument, particularly when one considers the materiality of the figures.

17.7.2 Arguments in favour of the diminishing balance method

First, the charge reflects the efficiency and maintenance costs of the asset. When new, an asset is operating at its maximum efficiency, which falls as it nears the end of its life. This may be countered by the comment that in year 1 there may be 'teething troubles' with new equipment, which, while probably covered by a supplier's guarantee, will hamper efficiency.

Secondly, the pattern of diminishing balance depreciation gives a net book amount that approximates to second-hand values. For example, with motor cars the initial fall in value is very high.

17.7.3 Other methods of depreciating

Besides straight-line and diminishing balance, there are a number of other methods of depreciating, such as the sum of the units method, the machine-hour method and the annuity method. We will consider these briefly.

Sum of the units method

A compromise between straight-line and reducing balance that is popular in the USA is the sum of the units method. The calculation based on the information in Figure 17.1 is now shown in Figure 17.2. This has the advantage that, unlike diminishing balance, it is simple to obtain the exact residual amount (zero if appropriate), while giving the pattern of high initial charge shown by the diminishing balance approach.

Machine-hour method

The machine-hour system is based on an estimate of the asset's service potential. The economic life is measured not in accounting periods but in working hours, and the depreciation

Figure 17.2 Sum of the units method

		£
Cost		11,000
Depreciation for year 1	£10,000 × 5/15	3,333
Net book value (NBV)		7,667
Depreciation for year 2	£10,000 × 4/15	2,667
NBV		5,000
Depreciation for year 3	£10,000 × 3/15	2,000
NBV		3,000
Depreciation for year 4	£10,000 × 2/15	1,333
NBV		1,667
Depreciation for year 5	£10,000 × 1/15	667
Residual value		1,000

is allocated in the proportion of the actual hours worked to the potential total hours available. This method is commonly employed in aviation, where aircraft are depreciated on the basis of flying hours.

Annuity method

With the annuity method, the asset, or rather the amount of capital representing the asset, is regarded as being capable of earning a fixed rate of interest. The sacrifice incurred in using the asset within the business is therefore two-fold: the loss arising from the exhaustion of the service potential of the asset; and the interest forgone by using the funds invested in the business to purchase the non-current asset. With the help of annuity tables, a calculation shows what equal amounts of depreciation, written off over the estimated life of the asset, will reduce the book value to nil, after debiting interest to the asset account on the diminishing amount of funds that are assumed to be invested in the business at that time, as represented by the value of the asset.

Figure 17.3 contains an illustration based on the treatment of a five-year lease which cost the company a premium of £10,000 on 1 January year 1. It shows how the total depreciation charge is computed. Each year the charge for depreciation in the statement of comprehensive income is the equivalent annual amount that is required to repay the investment over the five-year period at a rate of interest of 10% less the notional interest available on the remainder of the invested funds.

An extract from the annuity tables to obtain the annual equivalent factor for year 5 and assuming a rate of interest of 10% would show:

Year	Annuity $A_{\overline{n}\rceil}^{-1}$
1	1.1000
2	0.5762
3	0.4021
4	0.3155
5	0.2638

Therefore, at a rate of interest of 10% five annual payments to repay an investor of £10,000 would each be £2,638.

A variation of this system involves the investment of a sum equal to the net charge in fixed interest securities or an endowment policy, so as to build up a fund that will generate cash to replace the asset at the end of its life.

Figure 17.3 Annuity method

Year	Opening written-down value £	Notional interest (10%) £	Annual payment £	Net movement £	Closing written-down value £
1	10,000	1,000	(2,638)	(1,638)	8,362
2	8,362	836	(2,638)	(1,802)	6,560
3	6,560	656	(2,638)	(1,982)	4,578
4	4,578	458	(2,638)	(2,180)	2,398
5	2,398	240	(2,638)	(2,398)	Nil

This last system has significant weaknesses. It is based on the misconception that depreciation is 'saving up for a new one', whereas in reality depreciation is charging against profits funds already expended. It is also dangerous in a time of inflation, since it may lead management not to maintain the capital of the entity adequately, in which case they may not be able to replace the assets at their new (inflated) prices.

The annuity method, with its increasing net charge to income, does tend to take inflationary factors into account, but it must be noted that the *total* net profit and loss charge only adds up to the cost of the asset.

17.7.4 Which method should be used?

The answer to this seemingly simple question is 'it depends'. On the matter of depreciation IAS 16 is designed primarily to force a fair charge for the use of assets into the statement of comprehensive income each year, so that the earnings reflect a true and fair view.

Straight-line is most suitable for assets such as leases which have a definite fixed life. It is also considered most appropriate for assets with a short working life, although with motor cars the diminishing balance method is sometimes employed to match second-hand values. Extraction industries (mining, oil wells, quarries, etc.) sometimes employ a variation on the machine-hour system, where depreciation is based on the amount extracted as a proportion of the estimated reserves.

Despite the theoretical attractiveness of other methods the straight-line method is, by a long way, the one in most common use by entities that prepare financial statements in accordance with IFRSs. Reasons for this are essentially pragmatic:

● It is the most straightforward to compute.

● In the light of the three additional subjective factors – cost (or revalued amount), residual value and useful life – that need to be estimated, any imperfections in the charge for depreciation caused by the choice of the straight-line method are not likely to be significant.

● It conforms to the accounting treatment adopted by peers. For example, one group reported that it currently used the reducing balance method but, as peer companies used the straight-line method, it decided to change and adopt that policy.

17.8 Measurement subsequent to initial recognition

17.8.1 Choice of models

An entity needs to choose either the cost or the revaluation model as its accounting policy for an entire class of PPE. The cost model (definitely the most common) results in an asset being carried at cost less accumulated depreciation and any accumulated impairment losses.

17.8.2 The revaluation model

Under the revaluation model the asset is carried at revalued amount, being its fair value at the date of the revaluation less any subsequent accumulated depreciation and subsequent accumulated impairment losses. The fair value of an asset is defined in IAS 16 as 'the amount for which an asset could be exchanged between knowledgeable and willing parties in an arm's length transaction'. Thus fair value is basically market value. If a market value is not available, perhaps in the case of partly used specialised plant and equipment that is rarely bought and sold other than as new, then IAS 16 requires that revaluation be based on depreciated replacement cost.

EXAMPLE ● An entity purchased an item of plant for £12,000 on 1 January 20X1. The plant was depreciated on a straight-line basis over its useful economic life, which was estimated at six years. On 1 January 20X3 the entity decided to revalue its plant. No fair value was available for the item of plant that had been purchased for £12,000 on 1 January 20X1 but the replacement cost of the plant at 1 January 20X3 was £21,000.

The carrying value of the plant immediately before the revaluation would have been:

- Cost £12,000
- Accumulated deprecation £4,000 [(£12,000/6) × 2]
- Written-down value £8,000.

Under the principles of IAS 16 the revalued amount would be £14,000 (£21,000 × 4/6). This amount would be reflected in the financial statements by either:

- showing a revised gross figure of £14,000 and reversing out all the accumulated depreciation charged to date so as to give a carrying value of £14,000; or
- restating both the gross figure and the accumulated depreciation by the proportionate change in replacement cost. This would give a gross figure of £21,000, with accumulated depreciation restated at £7,000 to once again give a net carrying value of £14,000.

17.8.3 Detailed requirements regarding revaluations

The frequency of revaluations depends upon the movements in the fair values of those items of PPE being revalued. In jurisdictions where the rate of price changes is very significant revaluations may be necessary on an annual basis. In other jurisdictions revaluations every three or five years may well be sufficient.

Where an item of PPE is revalued, the entire class of PPE to which that asset belongs should be revalued.[6] A class of PPE is a grouping of assets of a similar nature and use in an entity's operations. Examples would include:

- land;
- land and buildings;
- machinery.

This is an important provision because without it entities would be able to select which assets they revalued on the basis of best advantage to the financial statements. Revaluations will usually increase the carrying values of assets and equity and leave borrowings unchanged. Therefore gearing (or leverage) ratios will be reduced. It is important that, if the revaluation route is chosen, assets are revalued on a rational basis.

The following is an extract from the financial statements of Coil SA, a company incorporated in Belgium that prepares financial statements in euros in accordance with international accounting standards: 'Items of PPE are stated at historical cost modified by revaluation and are depreciated using the straight-line method over their estimated useful lives.'

17.8.4 Accounting for revaluations

When the carrying amount of an asset is increased as a result of a revaluation, the increase should be credited directly to other comprehensive income, being shown in equity under the heading of revaluation surplus. The only exception is where the gain reverses a revaluation decrease previously recognised as an expense **relating to the same asset**.

This means that, in the example we considered under Section 17.8.2 above, the revaluation would lead to a credit of £6,000 (£14,000 – £8,000) to other comprehensive income.

If, however, the carrying amount of an asset is decreased as a result of a revaluation, the decrease should be recognised as an expense. The only exception is where that asset had previously been revalued. In those circumstances the loss on revaluation is charged against the revaluation surplus to the extent that the revaluation surplus contains an amount **relating to the same asset**.

EXAMPLE 1 ● REVALUED BUT NOT SOLD   An entity buys freehold land for £100,000 in year 1. The land is revalued to £150,000 in year 3 and £90,000 in year 5. The land is not depreciated.

● In year 3 a surplus of £50,000 (£150,000 – £100,000) is reported as other comprehensive income and included in equity under the heading 'revaluation surplus'.

● In year 5 a deficit of £60,000 (£90,000 – £150,000) arises on the second revaluation. £50,000 of this deficit is deducted from the revaluation surplus and £10,000 is charged as an expense.

● It is worth noting that £10,000 is the amount by which the year 5 carrying amount is lower than the original cost of the land.

EXAMPLE 2 ● REVALUED AND THEN SOLD WITH THE REVALUATION SURPLUS REALISED AT TIME OF SALE Where an asset that has been revalued is sold, the revaluation surplus becomes realised.[7] It may be transferred to retained earnings when this happens but this transfer is not made through the statement of comprehensive income.

Continuing with our example in Section 17.8.2, let us assume that:

● the plant was sold on 1 January 20X5 for £5,000; and

● the carrying amount of the asset in the financial statements immediately before the sale was £7,000 [£14,000 – (2 × £3,500)].

This means that a loss on sale of £2,000 would be taken to the statement of comprehensive income, and the revaluation surplus of £6,000 would be transferred to retained earnings.

EXAMPLE 3 ● REVALUED AND THEN SOLD WITH THE EXCESS DEPRECIATION RECOGNISED EACH YEAR IAS 16 allows for the possibility that the revaluation surplus is transferred to retained earnings as the asset is depreciated. To turn once again to our example, we see that:

● the revaluation on 1 January 20X3 increased the annual depreciation charge from £2,000 (£12,000/6) to £3,500 (£21,000/6);

● following revaluation an amount equivalent to the 'excess depreciation' may be transferred from the revaluation surplus to retained earnings as the asset is depreciated. This would lead in our example to a transfer of £1,500 each year; and

● if this occurs then the revaluation surplus that is transferred to retained earnings on sale is £3,000 [£6,000 – (2 × £1,500)].

17.8.5 IFRS for SMEs

The IFRS for SMEs does not permit the use of the revaluation model and only requires a review if there is an indication that there has been a significant change since the last annual reporting date.

17.9 IAS 36 *Impairment of Assets*

17.9.1 IAS 36 approach

IAS 36 sets out the principles and methodology for accounting for impairments of non-current assets and goodwill. Where possible, individual non-current assets should be individually tested for impairment. However, where cash flows do not arise from the use of a single non-current asset, impairment is measured for the smallest group of assets which generates income that is largely independent of the company's other income streams. This smallest group is referred to as a cash-generating unit (CGU).

Impairment of an asset, or CGU (if assets are grouped), occurs when the carrying amount of an asset or CGU is greater than its recoverable amount, where

- the carrying amount is the depreciated historical cost (or depreciated revalued amount);
- the recoverable amount is the higher of the net selling price and the value in use, where
  - the net selling price is the amount at which an asset could be disposed of, less any direct selling costs; and
  - the value in use is the present value of the future cash flows obtainable as a result of an asset's continued use, including those resulting from its ultimate disposal.

When impairment occurs, a **revised carrying amount** is calculated for the statement of financial position as follows:

It is not always necessary to go through the potentially time-consuming process of computing the value in use of an asset. If the net selling price can be shown to be higher than the existing carrying value then the asset cannot possibly be impaired and no further action is necessary. However, this is not always the case for non-current assets and a number of assets (e.g. goodwill) cannot be sold, so several value in use computations are inevitable.

The revised carrying amount is then depreciated over the remaining useful economic life.

17.9.2 Dividing activities into CGUs

In order to carry out an impairment review it is necessary to decide how to divide activities into CGUs. There is no single answer to this – it is extremely judgemental, e.g. if the company has multi-retail sites, the cost of preparing detailed cash flow forecasts for each site could favour grouping.

The risk of grouping is that poorly performing operations might be concealed within a CGU and it would be necessary to consider whether there were any commercial reasons for breaking a CGU into smaller constituents, e.g. if a location was experiencing its own unique difficulties such as local competition or inability to obtain planning permission to expand to a more profitable size.

17.9.3 Indications of impairment

A review for impairment is required when there is an indication that an impairment has actually occurred. The following are indicators of impairment:

- External indicators:
  - a fall in the market value of the asset;
  - material adverse changes in regulatory environment;
  - material adverse changes in markets;
  - material long-term increases in market rates of return used for discounting.
- Internal indicators:
  - material changes in operations;
  - major reorganisation;
  - loss of key personnel;
  - loss or net cash outflow from operating activities if this is expected to continue or is a continuation of a loss-making situation.

If there is such an indication, it is necessary to determine the depreciated historical cost of a single asset, or the net assets employed if a CGU, and compare this with the net realisable value and value in use.

Akzonobel stated in its 2010 Annual Report:

> We assess the carrying value of intangible assets and property, plant and equipment whenever events or changes in circumstances indicate that the carrying amount of an asset may not be recoverable. In addition, for goodwill and other intangible assets with an indefinite useful life, we review the carrying value annually in the fourth quarter.
>
> The recoverable amount of an asset or its cash-generating unit is the greater of its value in use and its fair value less costs to sell, whereby estimated future cash flows are discounted to their present value. The discount rate used reflects current market assessments of the time value of money and, if appropriate, the risks specific to the assets. If the carrying value of an asset or its cash-generating unit exceeds its estimated recoverable amount, an impairment loss is recognized in the statement of income. The assessment for impairment is performed at the lowest level of assets generating largely independent cash inflows, which we have determined to be at business unit level (one level below segment). We allocate impairment losses in respect of cash-generating units first to goodwill and then to the carrying amount of the other assets on a pro rata basis.

17.9.4 Value in use calculation

Value in use is arrived at by estimating and discounting the income stream. The **income streams**:

- are likely to follow the way in which management monitors and makes decisions about continuing or closing the different lines of business;
- may often be identified by reference to major products or services;
- should be based on reasonable and supportable assumptions;
- should be consistent with the most up-to-date budgets and plans that have been formally approved by management, or if they are for a period beyond that covered by formal budgets and plans should, unless there are exceptional circumstances, assume a steady or declining growth rate;[8]
- should be projected cash flows unadjusted for risk, discounted at a rate of return expected from a similarly risky investment, or should be projected risk-adjusted pre-tax cash flows discounted at a risk-free rate.

The **discount rate** should be:

- calculated on a pre-tax basis;
- an estimate of the rate that the market would expect on an equally risky investment excluding the effects of any risk for which the cash flows have been adjusted:[9]
  - increased to reflect the way the market would assess the specific risks associated with the projected cash flows;
  - reduced to a risk-free rate if the cash flows have been adjusted for risk.

The following illustration is from the Roche Holdings, Inc. 2011 Annual Report:

> When the recoverable amount of an asset, being the higher of its net selling price and its value in use, is less than the carrying amount, then the carrying amount is reduced to its recoverable amount. This reduction is reported in the income statement as an impairment loss. Value in use is calculated using estimated cash flows, generally over a five-year period, with extrapolating projections for subsequent years. These are discounted using an appropriate long-term pre-tax interest rate. When an impairment arises, the useful life of the asset in question is reviewed and, if necessary, the future depreciation/amortisation charge is amended.

17.9.5 Treatment of impairment losses

If the carrying value exceeds the higher of net selling price and value in use, then an impairment loss has occurred. The accounting treatment of such a loss is as follows.

Asset not previously revalued

An impairment loss should be recognised in the statement of comprehensive income in the year in which the impairment arises.

Asset previously revalued

An impairment loss on a revalued asset is effectively treated as a revaluation deficit. As we have already seen, this means that the decrease should be recognised as an expense. The only exception is where that asset had previously been revalued. In those circumstances the loss on revaluation is charged against the revaluation surplus to the extent that the revaluation surplus contains an amount **relating to the same asset**.

Allocation of impairment losses

Where an impairment loss arises, the loss should ideally be set against the specific asset to which it relates. Where the loss cannot be identified as relating to a specific asset, it should be apportioned within the CGU to reduce the most subjective values first, as follows:

- first, to reduce any goodwill within the CGU;
- then to the unit's other assets, allocated on a *pro rata* basis;
- with the proviso that no individual asset should be reduced below the higher of:
  - its net selling price (if determinable);
  - its value in use (if determinable);
  - zero.

The following is an example showing the allocation of an impairment loss.

EXAMPLE ● A cash–generating unit contains the following assets:

	£
Goodwill	70,000
Intangible assets	10,000
PPE	100,000
Inventory	40,000
Receivables	30,000
	250,000

The unit is reviewed for impairment due to the existence of indicators and the recoverable amount is estimated at £150,000. The PPE includes a property with a carrying amount of £60,000 and a market value of £75,000. The net realisable value of the inventory is greater than its carrying values and none of the receivables is considered doubtful.

The table below shows the allocation of the impairment loss:

	Pre-impairment £	Impairment £	Post-impairment £
Goodwill	70,000	(70,000)	Nil
Intangible assets	10,000	(6,000)	4,000
PPE	100,000	(24,000)	76,000
Inventory	40,000	Nil	40,000
Receivables	30,000	Nil	30,000
	250,000	(100,000)	150,000

Notes to table:

1 The impairment loss is first allocated against goodwill. After this has been done £30,000 (£100,000 − £70,000) remains to be allocated.

2 No impairment loss can be allocated to the property, inventory or receivables because these assets have a recoverable amount that is higher than their carrying value.

3 The remaining impairment loss is allocated *pro rata* to the intangible assets (carrying amount £10,000) and the plant (carrying amount £40,000 (£100,000 − £60,000)).

Restoration of past impairment losses

Past impairment losses in respect of an asset other than goodwill may be restored where the recoverable amount increases due to an improvement in economic conditions or a change in use of the asset. Such a restoration should be reflected in the statement of comprehensive income to the extent of the original impairment previously charged to the statement of comprehensive income, adjusting for depreciation which would have been charged otherwise in the intervening period.

17.9.6 Illustration of data required for an impairment review

Pronto SA has a product line producing wooden models of athletes for export. The carrying amount of the net assets employed on the line as at 31 December 20X3 was £114,500. The scrap value of the net assets at 31 December 20X6 is estimated to be £5,000.

There is an indication that the export market will be adversely affected in 20X6 by competition from plastic toy manufacturers. This means that the net assets employed to produce this product might have been impaired.

The finance director estimated the net realisable value of the net assets at 31 December 20X3 to be £70,000. The value in use is now calculated to check if it is higher or lower than

£70,000. If it is higher it will be compared with the carrying amount to see if impairment has occurred; if it is lower the net realisable value will be compared with the carrying amount.

Pronto SA has prepared budgets for the years ended 31 December 20X4, 20X5 and 20X6. The assumptions underlying the budgets are as follows:

Unit costs and revenue:

	£
Selling price	10.00
Buying-in cost	(4.00)
Production cost: material, labour, overhead	(0.75)
Head office overheads apportioned	(0.25)
Cash inflow per model	5.00

Estimated sales volumes:

	20X3	20X4	20X5	20X6
Estimated at 31 December 20X2	6,000	8,000	11,000	14,000
Revised estimate at 31 December 20X3	—	8,000	11,000	4,000

Determining the discount rate to be used:

	20X4	20X5	20X6
Rate obtainable elsewhere at same level of risk	10%	10%	10%

The discount factors to be applied to each year are then calculated using cost of capital discount rates as follows:

20X4	1/1.1	= 0.909
20X5	1/(1.1)²	= 0.826
20X6	1/(1.1)³	= 0.751

17.9.7 Illustrating calculation of value in use

Before calculating value in use, it is necessary to ensure that the assumptions underlying the budgets are reasonable, e.g. is the selling price likely to be affected by competition in 20X6 in addition to loss of market? Is the selling price in 20X5 likely to be affected? Is the estimate of scrap value reasonably accurate? How sensitive is value in use to the scrap value? Is it valid to assume that the cash flows will occur at year-ends? How accurate is the cost of capital? Will components making up the income stream, e.g. sales, materials, labour, be subject to different rates of inflation?

Assuming that no adjustment is required to the budgeted figures provided above, the estimated income streams are discounted using the normal DCF approach as follows:

	20X4	20X5	20X6
Sales (models)	8,000	11,000	4,000
Income per model	£5	£5	£5
Income stream (£)	40,000	55,000	20,000
Estimated scrap proceeds			5,000
Cash flows to be discounted	40,000	55,000	25,000
Discounted (using cost of capital factors)	0.909	0.826	0.751
Present value	36,360	45,430	18,775

Value in use = £100,565

If the carrying amount at the statement of financial position date exceeds net realisable value and value in use, it is revised to an amount which is the higher of net realisable value and value in use. For Pronto SA:

	£
Carrying amount as at 31 December 20X3	114,500
Net realisable value	70,000
Value in use	100,565
Revised carrying amount	**100,565**

17.10 IFRS 5 Non-current Assets Held for Sale and Discontinued Operations

IFRS 5 sets out requirements for the classification, measurement and presentation of non-current assets held for sale. The requirements which replaced IAS 35 *Discontinuing Operations* were discussed in Chapter 4. The IFRS is the result of the joint short-term project to resolve differences between IFRSs and US GAAP.

Classification as 'held for sale'

The IFRS (paragraph 6) classifies a non-current asset as 'held for sale' if its carrying amount will be recovered principally through a sale transaction rather than through continuing use. The criteria for classification as 'held for sale' are:

● the asset must be available for immediate sale in its present condition; and
● its sale must be *highly probable*.

The criteria for a sale to be highly probable are:

● the appropriate level of management must be committed to a plan to sell the asset;
● an active programme to locate a buyer and complete the plan must have been initiated;
● the asset must be actively marketed for sale at a price that is reasonable in relation to its current fair value;
● the sale should be expected to qualify for recognition as a completed sale within one year from the date of classification unless the delay is caused by events or circumstances beyond the entity's control and there is sufficient evidence that the entity remains committed to its plan to sell the asset; and
● actions required to complete the plan should indicate that it is unlikely that significant changes to the plan will be made or that the plan will be withdrawn.

Measurement and presentation of assets held for sale

The IFRS requires that assets 'held for sale' should:

● be measured at the lower of carrying amount and *fair value* less costs to sell;
● not continue to be depreciated; and
● be presented separately on the face of the statement of financial position.

The following additional disclosures are required in the notes in the period in which a non-current asset has been either classified as held for sale or sold:

● a description of the non-current asset;
● a description of the facts and circumstances of the sale;

- the expected manner and timing of that disposal;
- the gain or loss if not separately presented on the face of the statement of comprehensive income; and
- the caption in the statement of comprehensive income that includes that gain or loss.

17.10.1 IFRS for SMEs

The IFRS does not require separate presentation in the statement of financial position of 'non-current assets held for sale'. However, if an entity has plans to discontinue or restructure the operation to which an asset belongs and has plans to dispose of an asset before the previously expected date, then this is to be treated as an indication that an asset may be impaired and in such a case an impairment test is required.

17.11 Disclosure requirements

For each class of PPE the financial statements need to disclose:

- the measurement bases used for determining the gross carrying amount;
- the depreciation methods used;
- the useful lives or the depreciation rates used;
- the gross carrying amount and the accumulated depreciation (aggregated with accumulated impairment losses) at the beginning and end of the period;
- a reconciliation of the carrying amount at the beginning and end of the period.

The style employed by British Sky Broadcasting Group plc in its 2010 accounts is almost universally employed for this:

Tangible fixed assets (or PPE)
The movements in the year were as follows:

	Land and freehold buildings	Leasehold improvements	Equipment, furniture and fixtures	Assets not yet available for use	Total
	£m	£m	£m	£m	£m
Cost					
At 1 July 2009	128	77	931	191	1,327
Foreign exchange movements	—	—	(4)	—	(4)
Additions	58	2	152	64	276
Disposals	—	(6)	(69)	(3)	(78)
Transfers	—	—	30	(31)	(1)
At 30 June 2010	186	73	1,040	221	1,520
Depreciation					
At 1 July 2009	22	29	477	—	528
Foreign exchange movements			(4)		(4)
Depreciation	4	4	160	—	168
Impairments	—	—	2	3	5
Disposals	—	(6)	(67)	(3)	(76)
At 30 June 2010	26	27	568	—	621
Carrying amounts					
At 30 June 2009	106	48	454	191	799
At 30 June 2010	160	46	472	221	899

Additionally the financial statements should disclose:

● the existence and amounts of restrictions on title, and PPE pledged as security for liabilities;

● the accounting policy for the estimated costs of restoring the site of items of PPE;

● the amount of expenditures on account of PPE in the course of construction; and

● the amount of commitments for the acquisition of PPE.

17.12 Government grants towards the cost of PPE

The accounting treatment of government grants is covered by IAS 20. The basis of the standard is the accruals concept, which requires the matching of cost and revenue so as to recognise both in the statements of comprehensive income of the periods to which they relate. This should, of course, be tempered with the prudence concept, which requires that revenue is not anticipated. Therefore, in the light of the complex conditions usually attached to grants, credit should not be taken until receipt is assured.

Similarly, there may be a right to recover the grant wholly or partially in the event of a breach of conditions, and on that basis these conditions should be regularly reviewed and, if necessary, provision made.

Should the tax treatment of a grant differ from the accounting treatment, the effect of this would be accounted for in accordance with IAS 12 *Income Taxes*.

IAS 20

Government grants should be recognised in the statement of comprehensive income so as to match the expenditure towards which they are intended to contribute. If this is retrospective, they should be recognised in the period in which they became receivable.

Grants in respect of PPE should be recognised over the useful economic lives of those assets, thus matching the depreciation or amortisation.

IAS 20 outlines two acceptable methods of presenting grants relating to assets in the statement of financial position:

(a) The first method sets up the grant as deferred income, which is recognised as income on a systematic and rational basis over the useful life of the asset.

> EXAMPLE ● An entity purchased a machine for £60,000 and received a grant of £20,000 towards its purchase. The machine is depreciated over four years.
>
> The 'deferred income method' would result in an initial carrying amount for the machine of £60,000 and a deferred income credit of £20,000. In the first year of use of the plant the depreciation charge would be £15,000. £5,000 of the deferred income would be recognised as a credit in the statement of comprehensive income, making the net charge £10,000. At the end of the first year the carrying amount of the plant would be £45,000 and the deferred income included in the statement of financial position would be £15,000.
>
> The following is an extract from the 2010 Go-Ahead Annual Report:
>
> **Government grants**
> Government grants are recognised at their fair value where there is reasonable assurance that the grant will be received and all attaching conditions will be complied with. When the grant relates to an expense item, it is recognised in the income statement over the period necessary to match on a systematic basis to the costs that it is intended to compensate. *Where the grant relates to a non-current asset,*

value is credited to a deferred income account and is released to the income statement over the expected useful life of the relevant asset.

(b) The second method deducts the grant in arriving at the carrying amount of the relevant asset. If we were to apply this method to the above example then the initial carrying amount of the asset would be £40,000. The depreciation charged in the first year would be £10,000. This is the same as the net charge to income under the 'deferred credit' method. The closing carrying amount of the plant would be £30,000. This is of course the carrying amount under the 'deferred income method' (£45,000) less the closing deferred income under the 'deferred income method' (£15,000).

The following extract is from the 2010 Annual Report of A & J Muklow plc:

Capital grants
Capital grants received relating to the building or refurbishing of investment properties are deducted from the cost of the relevant property. Revenue grants are deducted from the related expenditure.

17.12.1 Arguments in favour of each approach

The capital approach

Supporters of the capital approach argue that (a) government grants are a means of financing and should therefore be reported as such in the statement of financial position rather than be recognised in profit or loss to offset the items of expense which they finance, and (b) it is inappropriate to recognise government grants in profit or loss, because they are not earned but represent an incentive provided by government without related costs.

The income approach

Supporters of this approach argue that (a) government grants are receipts from a source other than shareholders which should not, therefore, be recognised directly in equity but should be recognised in profit or loss in appropriate periods, and (b) they are not without cost in that the entity earns them through its compliance with their conditions. Their preferred treatment is, therefore, to recognise in profit or loss over the periods in which the entity recognises as expenses the related costs for which the grant was intended to compensate.

17.12.2 IASB future action

The IASB is currently considering drafting an amended standard on government grants. Among the reasons for the Board amending IAS 20 were the following:

● The recognition requirements of IAS 20 often result in accounting that is inconsistent with the *Framework*, in particular the recognition of a deferred credit when the entity has no liability, e.g. the following is an extract from the Annual Report of SSL International plc (now part of Reckitt Benckiser):

Grant income
Capital grants are shown in other creditors within the statement of financial position and released to match the depreciation charge on associated assets.

● IAS 20 contains numerous options. Apart from reducing the comparability of financial statements, the options in IAS 20 can result in understatement of the assets controlled by the entity and do not provide the most relevant information to users of financial statements.

In due course there is the prospect of the IASB issuing a revised standard which requires entities to recognise grants as income as soon as their receipt becomes unconditional. This is consistent with the specific requirements for the recognition of grants relating to agricultural activity laid down in IAS 41 *Agriculture*. This matter is discussed in more detail in Chapter 20.

IFRS for SMEs

Government grants are measured at the fair value of the asset received or receivable and treated as income when the proceeds are receivable if there are no future performance conditions attached. If there are performance conditions, the grant is recognised in profit or loss when the conditions are satisfied.

17.13 Investment properties

While IAS 16 requires all PPE to be subjected to a systematic depreciation charge, this may be considered inappropriate for properties held as assets but not employed in the normal activities of the entity, rather being held as investments. For such properties a more relevant treatment is to take account of the current market value of the property. The accounting treatment is set out in IAS 40 *Investment Property*.

Such properties may be held either as a main activity (e.g. by a property investment company) or by a company whose main activity is not the holding of such properties. In each case the accounting treatment is similar.

Definition of an investment property[10]

For the purposes of the statement, an investment property is property held (by the owner or by the lessee under a finance lease) to earn rentals or capital appreciation or both.

Investment property does **not** include:

(a) property held for use in the production or supply of goods or services or for administrative purposes (dealt with in IAS 16);

(b) property held for sale in the ordinary course of business (dealt with in IAS 2);

(c) an interest held by a lessee under an operating lease, even if the interest was a long-term interest acquired in exchange for a large upfront payment (dealt with in IAS 17);

(d) forests and similar regenerative natural resources (dealt with in IAS 41 *Agriculture*); and

(e) mineral rights, the exploration for and development of minerals, oil, natural gas and similar non-regenerative natural resources (dealt with in project on Extractive Industries).

Accounting models

Under IAS 40, an entity must choose either:

● a fair value model: investment property should be measured at fair value and changes in fair value should be recognised in the statement of comprehensive income; or

● a cost model (the same as the benchmark treatment in IAS 16 *Property, Plant and Equipment*): investment property should be measured at depreciated cost (less any accumulated impairment losses). An entity that chooses the cost model should disclose the fair value of its investment property.

An entity should apply the model chosen to all its investment property. A change from one model to the other model should be made only if the change will result in a more appropriate presentation. The standard states that this is highly unlikely to be the case for a change from the fair value model to the cost model.

In exceptional cases, there is clear evidence when an entity that has chosen the fair value model first acquires an investment property (or when an existing property first becomes investment property following the completion of construction or development, or after a change in use) that the entity will not be able to determine the fair value of the investment property reliably on a continuing basis. In such cases, the entity measures that investment property using the benchmark treatment in IAS 16 until the disposal of the investment property. The residual value of the investment property should be assumed to be zero. The entity measures all its other investment property at fair value.

IFRS for SME treatment

Under this IFRS the accounting for investment property is driven by circumstances. If an entity knows or can measure the fair value without undue cost or effort on an ongoing basis, it must use the fair value through profit or loss model for that investment property. If not, it must use the cost–depreciation–impairment model but, in that case, it is not required to disclose the fair values.

17.14 Effect of accounting policy for PPE on the interpretation of the financial statements

A number of difficulties exist when attempting to carry out inter-firm comparisons using the external information that is available to a shareholder.

17.14.1 Effect of inflation on the carrying value of the asset

The most serious difficulty is the effect of inflation, which makes the charges based on historical cost inadequate. Companies have followed various practices to take account of inflation. None of these is as effective as an acceptable surrogate for index adjustment using specific asset indices on a systematic annual basis: this is the only way to ensure uniformity and comparability of the cost/valuation figure upon which the depreciation charge is based.

The method that is currently allowable under IAS 16 is to revalue the assets. This is a partial answer, but it results in lack of comparability of ratios such as gearing or leverage.

17.14.2 Effect of revaluation on ratios

The rules of double entry require that when an asset is revalued the 'profit' (or, exceptionally, 'loss') must be credited somewhere. As it is not a 'realised' profit, it would not be appropriate to credit the statement of comprehensive income, so a 'revaluation reserve' must be created. As the asset is depreciated, this reserve may be realised to income; similarly, when an asset is ultimately disposed of, any residue relevant to that asset may be taken into income.

One significant by-product of revaluing assets is the effect on gearing. The revaluation reserve, while not distributable, forms part of the shareholders' funds and thus improves the debt/equity ratio. Care must therefore be taken in looking at the revaluation policies and reserves when comparing the gearing or leverage of companies.

The problem is compounded because the carrying value may be amended at random periods and on a selective category of asset.

17.14.3 Choice of depreciation method

There are a number of acceptable depreciation methods that may give rise to very different patterns of debits against the profits of individual years.

17.14.4 Inherent imprecision in estimating economic life

One of the greatest difficulties with depreciation is that it is inherently imprecise. The amount of depreciation depends on the estimate of the economic life of assets, which is affected not only by the durability and workload of the asset, but also by external factors beyond the control of management. Such factors may be technological, commercial or economic. Here are some examples:

● the production by a competitor of a new product rendering yours obsolete, e.g. watches with battery-powered movements replacing those with mechanical movements;

● the production by a competitor of a product at a price lower than your production costs, e.g. imported goods from countries where costs are lower;

● changes in the economic climate which reduce demand for your product.

This means that the interpreter of accounts must pay particular attention to depreciation policies, looking closely at the market where the entity's business operates. However, this understanding is not helped by the lack of requirement to disclose specific rates of depreciation and the basis of computation of residual values. Without such information, the potential effects of differences between policies adopted by competing entities cannot be accurately assessed.

17.14.5 Mixed values in the statement of financial position

The effect of depreciation on the statement of financial position is also some cause for concern. The net book amount shown for non-current assets is the result of deducting accumulated depreciation from cost (or valuation); it is not intended to be (although many non-accountants assume it is) an estimate of the value of the underlying assets. The valuation of a business based on the statement of financial position is extremely difficult.

17.14.6 IFRS for SMEs

This IFRS differs from IAS 16 in that:

● PPE is reported at historical cost less depreciation and less any impairment of the carrying amount. The revaluation model is not permitted.

● A review of the useful life, residual value or depreciation rate is only carried out if there is a significant change in the asset or how it is used. Any adjustment is a change in estimate.

● Assets held for sale are not reported separately, although the fact that an asset is held for sale might be an indication that there has been an impairment.

● Most investment property is treated in the same way as PPE. However, if the fair value of investment property can be measured reliably without excessive cost then the fair value model applies with changes being through profit or loss.

● Separate significant components should be depreciated separately if there are significantly different patterns of consumption of economic benefits.

17.14.7 Different policies may be applied within the same sector

Inter-company comparisons are even more difficult. Two entities following the historical cost convention may own identical assets, which, as they were purchased at different times, may well appear as dramatically different figures in the accounts. This is particularly true of interests in land and buildings.

17.14.8 Effect on the return on capital employed

There is an effect not only on the net asset value, but also on the return on capital employed. To make a fair assessment of return on capital it is necessary to know the current replacement cost of the underlying assets, but, under present conventions, up-to-date valuations are required only for investment properties.

17.14.9 Effect on EPS

IAS 16 is concerned to ensure that the earnings of an entity reflect a fair charge for the use of the assets by the enterprise. This should ensure an accurate calculation of earnings per share. But there is a weakness here. If assets have increased in value without revaluations, then depreciation will be based on the historical cost.

Summary

Before IAS 16 there were significant problems in relation to the accounting treatment of PPE such as the determination of a cost figure and the adjustment for inflation; companies providing nil depreciation on certain types of asset; and revaluations being made selectively and not kept current.

With IAS 16 the IASB has made the accounts more consistent and comparable. This standard has resolved some of these problems, principally requiring companies to provide for depreciation and if they have a policy of revaluation to keep such valuations reasonably current and applied to all assets within a class, i.e. removing the ability to cherry-pick which assets to revalue.

However, certain difficulties remain for the user of the accounts in that there are different management policies on the method of depreciation, which can have a major impact on the profit for the year; subjective assessments of economic life that may be reviewed each year with an impact on profits; and inconsistencies such as the presence of modified historical costs and historical costs in the same statement of financial position. In addition, with pure historical cost accounting, where non-current asset carrying values are based on original cost, no pretence is made that non-current asset net book amounts have any relevance to current values. The investor is expected to know that the depreciation charge is arithmetical in character and will not wholly provide the finance for tomorrow's assets or ensure maintenance of the business's operational base. To give recognition to these factors requires the investor to grapple with the effects of lost purchasing power through inflation; the effect of changes in supply and demand on replacement prices; technological change and its implication for the company's competitiveness; and external factors such as exchange rates. To calculate the effect of these variables necessitates not only considerable mental agility, but also far more information than is contained in a set of accounts. This is an area that needs to be revisited by the standard setters.

REVIEW QUESTIONS

1 Define PPE and explain how materiality affects the concept of PPE.

2 Define depreciation. Explain what assets need not be depreciated and list the main methods of calculating depreciation.

3 What is meant by the phrases 'useful life' and 'residual value'?

4 Define 'cost' in connection with PPE.

5 What effect does revaluing assets have on gearing (or leverage)?

6 How should grants received towards expenditure on PPE be treated?

7 Define an investment property and explain its treatment in financial statements.

8 'Depreciation should mean that a company has sufficient resources to replace assets at the end of their economic lives.' Discuss.

EXERCISES

* Question 1

Simple SA has just purchased a roasting/salting machine to produce roasted walnuts. The finance director asks for your advice on how the company should calculate the depreciation on this machine. Details are as follows:

Cost of machine	SF800,000
Residual value	SF104,000
Estimated life	4 years
Annual profits	SF2,000,000
Annual turnover from machine	SF850,000

Required:
(a) Calculate the annual depreciation charge using the straight-line method and the reducing balance method. Assume that an annual rate of 40% is applicable for the reducing balance method.
(b) Comment upon the validity of each method, taking into account the type of business and the effect each method has on annual profits. Are there any other methods which would be more applicable?

* Question 2

(a) Discuss why IAS 40 *Investment Property* was produced.
(b) Universal Entrepreneurs plc has the following items on its PPE list:
   (i) £1,000,000 – the right to extract sandstone from a particular quarry. Geologists predict that extraction at the present rate may be continued for 10 years.
   (ii) £5,000,000 – a freehold property, let to a subsidiary on a full repairing lease negotiated on arm's-length terms for 15 years. The building is a new one, erected on a greenfield site at a cost of £4,000,000.
   (iii) A fleet of motor cars used by company employees. These have been purchased under a contract which provides a guaranteed part exchange value of 60% of cost after two years' use.

(iv) A company helicopter with an estimated life of 150,000 flying hours.

(v) A 19-year lease on a property let out at arm's-length rent to another company.

Required:

Advise the company on the depreciation policy it ought to adopt for each of the above assets.

(c) The company is considering revaluing its interests in land and buildings, which comprise freehold and leasehold properties, all used by the company or its subsidiaries.

Required:

Discuss the consequences of this on the depreciation policy of the company and any special instructions that need to be given to the valuer.

* Question 3

You have been given the task, by one of the partners of the firm of accountants for which you work, of assisting in the preparation of a trend statement for a client, Mercury.

Mercury has been in existence for four years. Figures for the three preceding years are known but those for the fourth year need to be calculated. Unfortunately, the supporting workings for the preceding years' figures cannot be found and the client's own ledger accounts and workings are not available.

One item in particular, plant, is causing difficulty and the following figures have been given to you:

12 months ended 31 March	20X6	20X7	20X8	20X9
	£	£	£	£
(A) Plant at cost	80,000	80,000	90,000	?
(B) Accumulated depreciation	(16,000)	(28,800)	(28,080)	?
(C) Net (written down) value	64,000	51,200	61,920	?

The only other information available is that disposals have taken place at the beginning of the financial years concerned:

	Date of Disposal 12 months ended 31 March	Original acquisition 12 months ended 31 March	Original cost £	Sales proceeds £
First disposal	20X8	20X6	15,000	8,000
Second disposal	20X8	20X6	30,000	21,000

Plant sold was replaced on the same day by new plant. The cost of the plant which replaced the first disposal is not known but the replacement for the second disposal is known to have cost £50,000.

Required:

(a) Identify the method of providing for depreciation on plant employed by the client, stating how you have arrived at your conclusion.

(b) Show how the figures shown at line (B) for each of the years ended 31 March 20X6, 20X7 and 20X8 were calculated. Extend your workings to cover the year ended 31 March 20X9.

(c) Produce the figures that should be included in the blank spaces on the trend statement at lines (A), (B) and (C) for the year ended 31 March 20X9.

(d) Calculate the profit or loss arising on each of the two disposals.

Question 4

In the year to 31 December 20X9, Amy bought a new machine and made the following payments in relation to it:

	£	£
Cost as per supplier's list	12,000	
Less: Agreed discount	1,000	11,000
Delivery charge		100
Erection charge		200
Maintenance charge		300
Additional component to increase capacity		400
Replacement parts		250

Required:
(a) State and justify the cost figure which should be used as the basis for depreciation.
(b) What does depreciation do, and why is it necessary?
(c) Briefly explain, without numerical illustration, how the straight-line and diminishing balance methods of depreciation work. What different assumptions does each method make?
(d) Explain the term 'objectivity' as used by accountants. To what extent is depreciation objective?
(e) It is common practice in published accounts in Germany to use the diminishing balance method for PPE in the early years of an asset's life, and then to change to the straight-line method as soon as this would give a higher annual charge. What do you think of this practice? Refer to relevant accounting conventions in your answer.

(ACCA)

* Question 5

The finance director of Small Machine Parts Ltd is considering the acquisition of a lease of a small workshop in a warehouse complex that is being redeveloped by City Redevelopers Ltd at a steady rate over a number of years. City Redevelopers are granting such leases for five years on payment of a premium of £20,000.

The accountant has obtained estimates of the likely maintenance costs and disposal value of the lease during its five-year life. He has produced the following table and suggested to the finance director that the annual average cost should be used in the financial accounts to represent the depreciation charge in the profit and loss account.

Table prepared to calculate the annual average cost

Years of life	1	2	3	4	5
	£	£	£	£	£
Purchase price	20,000	20,000	20,000	20,000	20,000
Maintenance/repairs					
Year 2		1,000	1,000	1,000	1,000
3			1,500	1,500	1,500
4				1,850	1,850
5					2,000
	20,000	21,000	22,500	24,350	26,350
Resale value	11,500	10,000	8,010	5,350	350
Net cost	8,500	11,000	14,490	19,000	26,000
Annual average cost	8,500	5,500	4,830	4,750	5,200

The finance director, however, was considering whether to calculate the depreciation chargeable using the annuity method with interest at 15%.

Required:
(a) Calculate the entries that would appear in the statement of comprehensive income of Small Machine Parts Ltd for each of the five years of the life of the lease for the amortisation charge, the interest element in the depreciation charge and the income from secondary assets using the *annuity method*. Calculate the net profit for each of the five years assuming that the operating cash flow is estimated to be £25,000 per year.
(b) Discuss briefly which of the two methods you would recommend.
   The present value at 15% of £1 per annum for five years is £3.35214.
   The present value at 15% of £1 received at the end of year 5 is £0.49717.
   Ignore taxation.

(ACCA)

Question 6

(a) IAS 16 *Property, Plant and Equipment* requires that where there has been a permanent diminution in the value of property, plant and equipment, the carrying amount should be written down to the recoverable amount. The phrase 'recoverable amount' is defined in IAS 16 as 'the amount which the entity expects to recover from the future use of an asset, including its residual value on disposal'. The issues of how one identifies an impaired asset, the measurement of an asset when impairment has occurred and the recognition of impairment losses were not adequately dealt with by the standard. As a result the International Accounting Standards Committee issued IAS 36 *Impairment of Assets* in order to address the above issues.

Required:
(i)   Describe the circumstances which indicate that an impairment loss relating to an asset may have occurred.
(ii) Explain how IAS 36 deals with the recognition and measurement of the *impairment of assets*.

(b) AB, a public limited company, has decided to comply with IAS 36 *Impairment of Assets*. The following information is relevant to the impairment review:

(i)   Certain items of machinery appeared to have suffered a permanent diminution in value. The inventory produced by the machines was being sold below its cost and this occurrence had affected the value of the productive machinery. The carrying value at historical cost of these machines is $290,000 and their net selling price is estimated at $120,000. The anticipated net cash inflows from the machines are now $100,000 per annum for the next three years. A market discount rate of 10% per annum is to be used in any present value computations.

(ii) AB acquired a car taxi business on 1 January 20X1 for $230,000. The values of the assets of the business at that date based on net selling prices were as follows:

	$000
Vehicles (12 vehicles)	120
Intangible assets (taxi licence)	30
Trade receivables	10
Cash	50
Trade payables	(20)
	190

On 1 February 20X1, the taxi company had three of its vehicles stolen. The net selling value of these vehicles was $30,000 and because of non-disclosure of certain risks to the insurance company, the vehicles were uninsured. As a result of this event, AB wishes to recognise an impairment loss of $45,000 (inclusive of the loss of the stolen vehicles) due to the decline in the value in use of the

cash generating unit, that is the taxi business. On 1 March 20X1 a rival taxi company commenced business in the same area. It is anticipated that the business revenue of AB will be reduced by 25%, leading to a decline in the present value in use of the business, which is calculated at $150,000. The net selling value of the taxi licence has fallen to $25,000 as a result of the rival taxi operator. The net selling values of the other assets have remained the same as at 1 January 20X1 throughout the period.

Required:

Describe how AB should treat the above impairments of assets in its financial statements.

(In part (b) (ii) you should show the treatment of the impairment loss at 1 February 20X1 and 1 March 20X1.)

(ACCA)

* Question 7

Infinite Leisure Group owns and operates a number of pubs and clubs across Europe and South East Asia. Since inception the group has made exclusive use of the cost model for the purpose of its annual financial reporting. This has led to a number of shareholders expressing concern about what they see as a consequent lack of clarity and quality in the group's financial statements.

The CEO does not support use of the alternative to the cost model (the revaluation model), believing it produces volatile information. However, she is open to persuasion and so, as an example of the impact of a revaluation policy, has asked you to carry out an analysis (using data concerning 'Soo^z' – one of the group's nightclubs sold during the year to 31 October 2006) to show the impact the revaluation model would have had on the group's financial statements had the model been adopted from the day the club was acquired.

The following extract has been taken from the company's asset register:

Outlet: 'Soo^z'

Acquisition data

Date acquired	1 November 2001
Total cost	€10.24m
Cost components:	
Plant and equipment	
Cost	€0.24m
Economic life	6 years
Residual value	nil
Property	
Buildings	
Cost	€7.0m
Economic life	50 years
Land	
Cost	€3.0m

Updates

1 November 2003   Replacement cost of plant and equipment €0.42m. No fair value available (mainly specialised audio visual equipment). No change to economic life. Property revaluation €13m (land €4m, buildings €9m). Future economic life as at 1 November 2003 50 years.

Disposal

Date committed to a plan to sell	January 2006
Date sold	June 2006
Net sale price	€9.1m
Sale price components	
Plant and equipment	€0.1m
Property	€9.0m

Note: the Group accounts for property and for plant and equipment as separate non-current assets in its statement of financial position using straight-line depreciation.

Required:

Prepare an analysis to show the impact on Infinite Leisure's financial statements for each year the *'Soo"* nightclub was owned had the revaluation model been in place from the day the nightclub was acquired.

(The Association of International Accountants)

Question 8

The Blissopia Leisure Group consists of three divisions: Blissopia 1, which operates mainstream bars; Blissopia 2, which operates large restaurants; and Blissopia 3, which operates one hotel – the Eden.

Divisions 1 and 2 have been trading very successfully and there are no indications of any potential impairment. It is a different matter with the Eden, however. The Eden is a 'boutique' hotel and was acquired on 1 November 2006 for $6.90m. The fair value (using net selling price) of the hotel's net assets at that date and their carrying value at the year-end were as follows:

	Fair value 1.11.06 $m	Carrying value 31.10.07 $m
Land and buildings	3.61	3.18
Plant and equipment	0.90	0.81
Cash	1.40	1.12
Vehicles	0.10	0.09
Trade receivables	0.34	0.37
Trade payables	(0.60)	(0.74)
	5.75	4.83

The following facts were discovered following an impairment review as at 31 October 2007:

(i) During August 2007, a rival hotel commenced trading in the same location as the Eden. The Blissopia Leisure Group expects hotel revenues to be significantly affected and has calculated the value-in-use of the Eden to be $3.52m.

(ii) The company owning the rival hotel has offered to buy the Eden (including all of the above net assets) for $4m. Selling costs would be approximately $50,000.

(iii) One of the hotel vehicles was severely damaged in an accident whilst being used by an employee to carry shopping home from a supermarket. The vehicle's carrying value at 31 October 2007 was $30,000 and insurers have indicated that as it was being used for an uninsured purpose the loss is not covered by insurance. The vehicle was subsequently scrapped.

(iv) A corporate client, owing $40,000, has recently gone into liquidation. Lawyers have estimated that the company will receive only 25% of the amount outstanding.

Required:

Prepare a memo for the directors of the Blissopia Leisure Group explaining how the group should account for the impairment to the Eden Hotel's assets as at 31 October 2007.

(The Association of International Accountants)

Question 9

Cryptic plc extracted its trial balance on 30 June 20X5 as follows:

	£000	£000
Land and buildings at cost	750	—
Plant and machinery at cost	480	—
Accumulated depreciation on plant and machinery at 30 June 20X5	—	400
Depreciation on plant and machinery	80	—
Furniture, tools and equipment at cost	380	—
Accumulated depreciation on furniture, etc. at 30 June 20X4	—	95
Receivables and payables	475	360
Inventory of raw materials at 30 June 20X4	112	—
Work in progress at factory cost at 30 June 20X4	76	—
Finished goods at cost at 30 June 20X4	264	—
Sales including selling taxes	—	2,875
Purchases of raw materials including selling taxes	1,380	—
Share premium account	—	150
Advertising	65	—
Deferred taxation	—	185
Salaries	360	—
Rent	120	—
Retained earnings at 30 June 20X4	—	226
Factory power	48	—
Trade investments at cost	240	—
Overprovision for tax for the year ended 30 June 20X4	—	21
Electricity	36	—
Stationery	12	—
Dividend received (net)	—	24
Dividend paid on 15 April 20X5	60	—
Other administration expenses	468	—
Disposal of furniture	—	64
Selling tax control account	165	—
Ordinary shares of 50p each	—	1,000
12% preference shares of £1 each (IAS 32 liability)	—	200
Cash and bank balance	29	—
	5,600	5,600

The following information is relevant:

(i) The company discontinued a major activity during the year and replaced it with another. All non-current assets involved in the discontinued activity were redeployed for the new one. The following expenses incurred in this respect, however, are included in 'Other administration expenses':

	£000
Cancellation of contracts re terminated activity	165
Fundamental reorganisation arising as a result	145

Cryptic has decided to present its results from discontinued operations as a single line on the face of the statement of comprehensive income with analysis in the notes to the accounts as allowed by IFRS 5.

(ii) On 1 January 20X5 the company acquired new land and buildings for £150,000. The remainder of land and buildings, acquired nine years earlier, have *not* been depreciated until this year. The company has decided to depreciate the buildings, on the straight-line method, assuming that one-third of the cost relates to land and that the buildings have an estimated economic life of 50 years. The company policy is to charge a full year of depreciation in the year of purchase and none in the year of sale.

(iii) Plant and machinery was all acquired on 1 July 20X0 and has been depreciated at 10% per annum on the straight-line method. The estimate of useful economic life had to be revised this year when it was realised that if the market share is to be maintained at current levels, the company has to replace all its machinery by 1 July 20X6. The balance in the 'Accumulated provision for depreciation' account on 1 July 20X4 was amended to reflect the revised estimate of useful economic life and the impact of the revision adjusted against the retained earnings brought forward from prior years.

(iv) Furniture acquired for £80,000 on 1 January 20X3 was disposed of for £64,000 on 1 April 20X5. Furniture, tools and equipment are depreciated at 5% p.a. on cost. Depreciation for the current year has not been provided.

(v) Results of the inventory counting at year-end are as follows:

Inventory of raw materials at cost including selling tax	£197,800
Work in progress at factory cost	£54,000
Finished goods at cost	£364,000

(vi) The company allocates its expenditure as follows:

	Production cost	Factory overhead	Distribution cost	Administrative expenses
Salaries and wages	65%	15%	5%	15%
Rent	—	60%	15%	25%
Electricity	—	10%	20%	70%
Depreciation of building	—	40%	10%	50%

(vii) The directors wish to make an accrual for audit fees of £18,000 and estimate the income tax for the year at £65,000. £11,000 should be transferred from the deferred tax account. The directors have to pay the preference dividend.

(viii) The following analysis has been made:

	New activity	Discontinued activity
Sales excluding selling taxes	£165,000	£215,000
Cost of sales	£98,000	£155,000
Distribution cost	£16,500	£48,500
Administrative expenses	£22,500	£38,500

(ix) Assume that the rate of selling taxes applicable to all purchases and sales is 15%, the basic rate of personal income tax is 25% and the corporate income tax rate is 35%.

Required:
(a) Advise the company on the accounting treatment in respect of information stated in (ii) above.
(b) In respect of the information stated in (iii) above, state whether a company is permitted to revise its estimate of the useful economic life of a non-current asset and comment on the appropriateness of the accounting treatment adopted.
(c) Set out a statement of movement of property, plant and equipment in the year to 30 June 20X5.
(d) Set out for publication the statement of income for the year ended 30 June 20X5, the statement of financial position as at that date and any notes other than that on accounting policy, in accordance with relevant standards.

* Question 10

Omega prepares financial statements under International Financial Reporting Standards. In the year ended 31 March 2007 the following transaction occurred.

On 1 April 2006 Omega began the construction of a new production line. Costs relating to the line are as follows:

Details	Amount $000
Costs of the basic materials (list price $12.5 million less a 20% trade discount)	10,000
Recoverable sales taxes incurred, not included in the purchase cost	1,000
Employment costs of the construction staff for the three months to 30 June 2006 (Note 1)	1,200
Other overheads directly related to the construction (Note 2)	900
Payments to external advisors relating to the construction	500
Expected dismantling and restoration costs (Note 3)	2,000

Note 1

The production line took two months to make ready for use and was brought into use on 30 June 2006.

Note 2

The other overheads were incurred in the two months ended 31 May 2006. They included an abnormal cost of $300,000 caused by a major electrical fault.

Note 3

The production line is expected to have a useful economic life of eight years. At the end of that time Omega is legally required to dismantle the plant in a specified manner and restore its location to an acceptable standard. The figure of $2 million included in the cost estimates is the amount that is expected to be incurred at the end of the useful life of the production plant. The appropriate rate to use in any discounting calculations is 5%. The present value of $1 payable in eight years at a discount rate of 5% is approximately $0.68.

Note 4

Four years after being brought into use, the production line will require a major overhaul to ensure that it generates economic benefits for the second half of its useful life. The estimated cost of the overhaul, at current prices, is $3 million.

Note 5

Omega computes its depreciation charge on a monthly basis.

Note 6

No impairment of the plant had occurred by 31 March 2007.

The financial statements for the year ended 31 March 2007 were authorised for issue on 15 May 2007.

Required:
Show the impact of the construction of the production line on the income statement of Omega for the year ended 31 March 2007, and on its balance sheet as at 31 March 2007. You should state where in the income statement and the balance sheet relevant balances will be shown. You should make appropriate references to international financial reporting standards.

(IFRS)

References

1 IAS 16 *Property, Plant and Equipment*, IASB, revised 2004, para. 6.
2 *Ibid.*, para. 16.
3 *Ibid.*, para. 22.
4 IAS 23 *Borrowing Costs*, IASB, revised 2007, para. 8.
5 IAS 16 *Property, Plant and Equipment*, IASB, revised 2004, para. 18.
6 *Ibid.*, para. 29.
7 *Ibid.*, para. 41.
8 IAS 36 *Impairment of Assets*, IASB, 2004, para. 33.
9 *Ibid.*, paras 55–56.
10 IAS 40 *Investment Property*, IASB, 2004.

CHAPTER 18

Leasing

18.1 Introduction

The main purpose of this chapter is to introduce the accounting principles and policies that apply to lease agreements.

Objectives

By the end of this chapter, you should be able to:

- critically discuss the reasons for IAS 17;
- account for leases by the lessee;
- account for leases by the lessor;
- critically discuss the reasons for the proposed revision of IAS 17;
- critically discuss the reasons for revising IAS 17.

18.2 Background to leasing

In this section we consider the nature of a lease; why leasing has become popular; and why it was necessary to introduce IAS 17.

18.2.1 What is a lease?

IAS 17 *Leases* provides the following definition:

> A *lease* is an agreement whereby the lessor conveys to the lessee in return for a payment or series of payments the right to use an asset for an agreed period of time.

In practice, there might well be more than two parties involved in a lease. For example, on leasing a car the parties involved are the motor dealer, the finance company and the company using the car.

18.2.2 Why did leasing initially become popular?

Prior to the issue of IAS 17, three of the main reasons for the popularity of leasing were the tax advantage to the lessor able to make use of depreciation allowances (now called capital allowances), the commercial advantages to the lessee and the potential for off-balance-sheet financing.

Commercial advantages for the lessee

There are a number of advantages associated with leases. These are attributable in part to the ability to spread cash payments over the lease period instead of making a one-off lump sum payment. They include the following:

- **Cash flow management**. If cash is used to purchase non-current assets, it is not available for the normal operating activities of a company.
- **Conservation of capital**. Lines of credit may be kept open and may be used for purposes where finance might not be available easily (e.g. financing working capital).
- **Continuity**. The lease agreement is itself a line of credit that cannot easily be withdrawn or terminated due to external factors, in contrast to an overdraft that can be called in by the lender.
- **Flexibility of the asset base**. The asset base can be more easily expanded and contracted. In addition, the lease payments can be structured to match the income pattern of the lessee.

18.2.3 Off-balance-sheet financing

Leasing previously provided the lessee with the possibility of off-balance-sheet financing,[1] whereby a company had the use of an economic resource that did not appear in the statement of financial position, with the corresponding omission of the liability.

An attraction of off-balance-sheet financing was that the gearing ratio is not increased by the inclusion of the liability.

18.2.4 Why was IAS 17 necessary?

As with many of the standards, action was required because there was no uniformity in the treatment and disclosure of leasing transactions. The need became urgent following the massive growth in the leasing industry and the growth in off-balance-sheet financing which by 2007 had grown to US$760 billion worldwide.

Leasing has become a material economic resource but the accounting treatment of the lease transaction was seen to distort the financial reports of a company so that they did not represent a true and fair view of its commercial activities.

IAS 17, therefore, required lease agreements that transferred substantially all the risks and rewards to the lessee to be reported in the financial statements. The asset and liability were both brought onto the statement of financial position.

There was some concern that this might have undesirable economic consequences[2] by reducing the volume of leasing, and that the inclusion of the lease obligation might affect the lessee company's gearing adversely, possibly causing it to exceed its legal borrowing powers. However, in the event, the commercial reasons for leasing and the capacity of the leasing industry to structure lease agreements to circumvent the standard prevented a reduction in lease activity. Evidence of lessors varying the term of the lease agreements to ensure that they remained off balance sheet is supported by Cranfield[3] and by Abdel-Khalik et al.[4]

A standard was necessary to ensure uniform reporting and to prevent the accounting message being manipulated.

18.2.5 The approach taken by IAS 17

The approach taken by the standard was to distinguish between two types of lease – finance and operating – and to recommend a different accounting treatment for each. In brief, the definitions were as follows:

- **Finance lease**: a lease that transfers substantially all the risks and rewards of ownership of an asset. Title may or may not eventually be transferred.
- **Operating lease**: a lease other than a finance lease.

Finance leases were required to be capitalised in the lessee's accounts. This means that the leased item should be recorded as an asset in the statement of financial position, and the obligation for future payments should be recorded as a liability in that statement. It was not permissible for the leased asset and lease obligation to be left out of the statement.

In the case of operating leases, the lessee is required only to expense the annual payments as a rental through the statement of comprehensive income.

18.3 Why was the IAS 17 approach so controversial?

The proposal to classify leases into finance and operating leases, and to capitalise those which are classified as finance leases, appears to be a feasible solution to the accounting problems that surround leasing agreements. So, why did the standard setters encounter so much controversy in their attempt to stop the practice of charging all lease payments to the statement of comprehensive income?

The whole debate centres on one accounting policy: **substance over form**. Although this is not cited as an accounting concept in the IASC *Framework*, paragraph 35 states:

> If information is to represent faithfully the transactions and other events that it purports to represent, it is necessary that they are accounted for and presented in accordance with their substance and economic reality and not merely their legal form.

The real sticking point was that IAS 17 invoked a substance-over-form approach to accounting treatment that was completely different from the traditional approach, which has strict regard to legal ownership. The IASC argued that in reality there were two separate transactions taking place. In one transaction, the company was borrowing funds to be repaid over a period. In the other, it was making a payment to the supplier for the use of an asset.

The correct accounting treatment for the borrowing transaction, based on its substance, was to include in the lessee's statement of financial position a liability representing the obligation to meet the lease payments, and the correct accounting treatment for the asset acquisition transaction, based on its substance, was to include an asset representing the asset supplied under the lease.

IAS 17, paragraph 10, states categorically that 'whether a lease is a finance lease or an operating lease depends on the substance of the transaction rather than the form of the contract'.

18.3.1 How do the accounting and legal professions differ in their approach to the reporting of lease transactions?

The accounting profession sees itself as a service industry that prepares financial reports in a dynamic environment, in which the user is looking for reports that reflect commercial reality. Consequently, the profession needs to be sensitive and responsive to changes in commercial practice.

There was still some opposition within the accounting profession to the inclusion of a finance lease in the statement of financial position as an 'asset'. The opposition rested on the fact that the item that was the subject of the lease agreement did not satisfy the existing criterion for classification as an asset because it was not 'owned' by the lessee. To accommodate this, the definition of an asset has been modified from 'ownership' to 'control' and 'the ability to contribute to the cash flows of the enterprise'.

EXAMPLE ● OPERATING LEASE Clifford plc is a manufacturing company. It negotiates a lease to begin on 1 January 20X1 with the following terms:

Term of lease	4 years
Estimated useful life of machine	9 years
Purchase price of new machine	£75,000
Annual payments	£8,000

This is an *operating lease* as it does not apply only to a major part of the asset's useful life, and the present value of the lease payments does not constitute substantially all of the fair value.

The amount of the annual rental paid – £8,000 p.a. – will be charged to the statement of comprehensive income and disclosed. There will also be a disclosure of the ongoing commitment with a note that £8,000 is payable within one year and £24,000 within two to five years.

18.6 Accounting requirements for finance leases

We follow a step approach to illustrate the accounting entries in both the statement of financial position and the statement of comprehensive income.

When a lessee enters into a finance lease, both the leased asset and the related lease obligations need to be shown in the statement of financial position.

18.6.1 Statement of financial position step approach to accounting for a finance lease

Step 1 The leased asset should be capitalised in property, plant and equipment (and recorded separately) at the lower of the present value of lease payments and its fair value.

Step 2 The annual depreciation charge for the leased asset should be calculated by depreciating the asset over the shorter of its estimated useful life or the lease period.

Step 3 The net book value of the leased asset should be reduced by the annual depreciation charge.

Step 4 The finance lease obligation is a liability which should be recorded. At the inception of a lease **agreement**, the value of the leased asset and the leased liability will be the same.

Step 5 (a) The finance charge for the finance lease should be calculated as the difference between the total of the minimum lease payments and the fair value of the asset (or the present value of the minimum lease payments if lower), i.e. it represents the charge made by the lessor for the credit that is being extended to the lessee.

  (b) The finance charge should be allocated to the accounting periods over the term of the lease. Three methods for allocating finance charges are used in practice:

   ● **Actuarial method**. This applies a constant periodic rate of charge to the balance of the leasing obligation. The rate of return applicable can be calculated by applying present value tables to annual lease payments.

- **Sum of digits method**. This method ('Rule of 78') is much easier to apply than the actuarial method. The finance charge is apportioned to accounting periods on a reducing scale.
- **Straight-line method**. This spreads the finance charge equally over the period of the lease (it is only acceptable for immaterial leases).

Step 6 The finance lease obligation should be reduced by the difference between the lease payment and the finance charge. This means that first the lease payment is used to repay the finance charge, and then the balance of the lease payment is used to reduce the book value of the obligation.

18.6.2 Statement of comprehensive income step approach to accounting for a finance lease

Step 1 The annual depreciation charge should be recorded.

Step 2 The finance charge allocated to the current period should be recorded.

18.7 Example allocating the finance charge using the sum of the digits method

EXAMPLE ● FINANCE LEASE Clifford plc negotiates another lease to commence on 1 January 20X1 with the following terms:

Term of lease	3 years
Purchase price of new machine	£16,500
Annual payments (payable in advance)	£6,000
Clifford plc's borrowing rate	10%

Finance charges are allocated using the sum of the digits method.

18.7.1 Categorise the transaction

First we need to decide whether the lease is an operating or a finance lease. We do this by applying the present value criterion.

- Calculate the fair value:
  Fair value of asset = £16,500
- Calculate the present value of minimum lease payments:

$$£6,000 + \frac{£6,000}{1.1} + \frac{£6,000}{(1.1)^2} = £16,413$$

- Compare the fair value and the present value. It is a finance lease because the present value of the lease payments is substantially all of the fair value of the asset.

18.7.2 Statement of financial position step approach to accounting for a finance lease

Step 1 Capitalise the lease at fair value (the present value is immaterially different):
  Asset value = £16,500

Step 2 Calculate the depreciation (using the straight-line method):
  £16,500/3 = £5,500

Step 3 Reduce the asset in the statement of financial position:

Extract as at		31 Dec 20X1	31 Dec 20X2	31 Dec 20X3
Asset	Opening value	16,500	11,000	5,500
(right to	Depreciation	5,500	5,500	5,500
use asset)	Closing value	11,000	5,500	—

Or if we keep the asset at cost as in published accounts:

Asset	Cost	16,500	16,500	16,500
(right to	Depreciation	5,500	11,000	16,500
use asset)	Closing value	11,000	5,500	—

Step 4 Obligation on inception of finance lease:
Liability = £16,500

Step 5 Finance charge:

Total payments, $3 \times £6,000$	£18,000
Asset value	£16,500
Finance charge, being the difference	£1,500

Finance charge allocated using sum of digits:

Year 1 = $2/(1 + 2) \times £1,500 = £1,000$
Year 2 = $1/(1 + 2) \times £1,500 = £500$

Note that the allocation is over only two periods because the instalments are being made in advance. If the instalments were being made in arrears, the liability would continue over three years and the allocation would be over three years.

Step 6 Reduce the obligation in the statement of financial position:

Extract as at		31 Dec 20X1	31 Dec 20X2	31 Dec 20X3
Liability	Opening value	16,500	11,500	6,000
(obligation	Lease payment	6,000	6,000	6,000
under finance		10,500	5,500	—
lease)	Finance charge	1,000	500	—
	Closing value	11,500	6,000	—

Note that the closing balance on the asset represents unexpired service potential and the closing balance on the liability represents the capital amount outstanding at the period-end date.

18.7.3 Statement of comprehensive income step approach to accounting for a finance lease

Step 1 A depreciation charge is made on the basis of use. The charge would be calculated in accordance with existing company policy relating to the depreciation of that type of asset.

Step 2 A finance charge is levied on the basis of the amount of financing outstanding.

Both then appear in the statement of comprehensive income as expenses of the period:

Extract for year ending	31 Dec 20X1	31 Dec 20X2	31 Dec 20X3
Depreciation	5,500	5,500	5,500
Finance charge	1,000	500	—
Total	6,500	6,000	5,500

18.8 Example allocating the finance charge using the actuarial method

In the Clifford example, we used the sum of the digits method to allocate the finance charge over the period of the repayment. In the following example, we will illustrate the actuarial method of allocating the finance charge.

EXAMPLE ● FINANCE LEASE Witts plc negotiates a four-year lease for an item of plant with a cost price of £35,000. The annual lease payments are £10,000 payable in advance. The cost of borrowing for Witts plc is 15%.

First we need to determine whether this is a finance lease. Then we need to calculate the implicit interest rate and allocate the total finance charge over the period of the repayments using the actuarial method.

● Categorise the transaction to determine whether it is a finance lease.

Fair value of asset $= £35,000$
Present value of future lease payments:
$£10,000 + (10,000 \times a_{\overline{3}|15})$
$£10,000 + (10,000 \times 2.283)$ $= £32,830$

The present value of the minimum lease payments is substantially the fair value of the asset. The lease is therefore categorised as a finance lease.

● Calculate the 'interest rate implicit in the lease'.

Fair value = lease payments discounted at the implicit interest rate
$£35,000 \quad = £10,000 + (10,000 \times a_{\overline{3}|i})$
$a_{\overline{3}|i} \quad = £25,000/10,000 = 2.5$
$i \quad = 9.7\%$

● Allocate the finance charge using the actuarial method.

Figure 18.2 shows that the finance charge is levied on the obligation during the period at 9.7%, which is the implicit rate calculated above.

18.9 Disclosure requirements for finance leases

IAS 17 requires that assets subject to finance leases should be identified separately and the net carrying amount disclosed. This can be achieved either by separate entries in the property, plant and equipment schedule or by integrating owned and leased assets in this schedule and disclosing the breakdown in the notes to the accounts.

The obligations relating to finance leases can also be treated in two different ways. The leasing obligation should be either shown separately from other liabilities in the statement of financial position or integrated into 'current liabilities' and 'non-current liabilities' and disclosed separately in the notes to the accounts.

Figure 18.2 Finance charge allocation using actuarial method

Period	Obligation (start) £	Rentals paid £	Obligation (during) £	Finance 9.7% £	Obligation (end) £
Year 1	35,000	10,000	25,000	2,425	27,425
Year 2	27,425	10,000	17,425	1,690	19,115
Year 3	19,115	10,000	9,115	885	10,000
Year 4	10,000	10,000	—	—	—

The notes to the accounts should also analyse the leasing obligations in terms of the timing of the payments. The analysis of the amounts payable should be broken down into those obligations falling due within one year, two to five years, and more than five years.

Note that Figure 18.2 also provides the information required for the period-end date. For example, at the end of year 1 the table shows, in the final column, a total obligation of £27,425. This can be further subdivided into its non-current and current components by using the next item in the final column, which represents the amount outstanding at the end of year 2. This amount of £19,115 represents the non-current element, and the difference of £8,310 represents the current liability element at the end of year 1.

This method of calculating the current liability from the table produces a different current figure each year. For example, the current liability at the end of year 2 is £9,115, being £19,115 – £10,000. This has been discussed in *External Financial Reporting*, where the point was made that the current liability should be the present value of the payment that is to be made at the end of the next period, i.e. £10,000 discounted at 9.7%, which gives a present value for the current liability of £9,115 for inclusion at each period-end until the liability is discharged.[5] We use the conventional approach in working illustrations and exercises, but you should bear this point in mind.

EXAMPLE ● DISCLOSURE REQUIREMENTS IN THE LESSEE'S ACCOUNTS It is interesting to refer to the disclosures found in published accounts as illustrated by the Nestlé Group accounts.

Extract from the Nestlé Group – Annual Report and Accounts 2011

Accounting policies

Leased assets
Assets acquired under finance leases are capitalised and depreciated in accordance with the Group's policy on property, plant and equipment unless the lease term is shorter. Land and building leases are recognised separately provided an allocation of the lease payments between these categories is reliable. The associated obligations are included under financial liabilities.

Rentals payable under operating leases are expensed.

The costs of the agreements that do not take the legal form of a lease but convey the right to use an asset are separated into lease payments and other payments if the entity has the control of the use or of the access to the asset or takes essentially all the output of the asset. Then the entity determines whether the lease component of the agreement is a finance or an operating lease.

Other notes

Lease commitments
The following charges arise from these commitments:

Operating leases

Lease commitments refer mainly to buildings, industrial equipment, vehicles and IT equipment.

In millions of CHF	2011	2010
	Minimum lease payments future value	
Within one year	595	600
In the second year	442	467
In the third to fifth year inclusive	866	939
After the fifth year	516	569
	2,419	2,575

Operating lease charge for the year 2011 amounts to CHF 657 million (2010: CHF 701 million)

Finance leases

In millions of CHF	2011		2010	
	Minimum lease payments			
	Present value	*Future value*	*Present value*	*Future value*
Within one year	57	63	68	74
In the second year	50	61	57	68
In the third to fifth year inclusive	90	136	106	155
After the fifth year	51	101	69	145
	248	361	300	442

The difference between the future value of the minimum lease payments and their present value represents the discount on the lease obligations.

18.10 Accounting for the lease of land and buildings

Land and buildings are dealt with separately. Each has to be reviewed to determine whether to classify the lease as an operating or a finance lease. This is illustrated in the following Warehouse Company example. Let us assume that:

● The Warehouse Company Ltd, whose borrowing rate was 10% per annum, entered into a 10-year lease under which it made payments of $106,886 annually in advance.

● The present value of the land was $500,000 and that of the buildings was $500,000.

● The value of the land at the end of 10 years was $670,000 and the value of the buildings was $50,000.

Classifying the land segment of the lease

We first need to classify the land lease. As there is no contract to pass title at the end of the contract and the land is expected to increase in value, it is clear that the land segment of the contract does not involve the lessor transferring the risk and benefits to the lessee. This means that the lessee has to account for the lease of the land as an operating lease.

Classifying the building segment of the lease

The building segment of the lease is different. The residual value has fallen to $50,000 which has a present value of $19,275 (50,000 × 0.3855). This means that 96% of the benefit has been transferred (500,000 – 19,275) and the building segment is, therefore, a finance lease with a present value of $480,725.

How to apportion the lease payment in the statement of comprehensive income

The payment should be split at the commencement of the lease according to the fair value of the components covered by the lease. In the case of the land, the present value of the land is $500,000 of which $258,285 (670,000 × 0.3855) represents the present value of the land at the end of the contract, so the balance of $241,715 represents the present value of the operating lease.

As the present value of the finance lease for the building segment is $480,725, the lease payment of $106,886 is split in those proportions (241,715:480,725) giving $35,763 for the land component and $71,123 for the finance lease representing the buildings leased.

How to report in the statement of financial position

For the finance lease covering the building the lessee will have to show a $480,725 asset initially which will be depreciated over the 10 years of the lease according to the normal policy of depreciating buildings which are going to last 10 years. At the same time a liability representing an obligation to the legal owner of the buildings (the lessor) for the same amount will be created. As lease payments are made the interest component will be treated as an expense and the balance will be used to reduce the liability.

In this example the risk and rewards relating to the building segment were clearly transferred to the lessee. If the residual value had been, say, $350,000 rather than $50,000 then the present value at the end of the lease would have been $134,925, which represents 27% of the value. This does not indicate that substantially all the benefits of ownership have been transferred and hence it would be classified as an operating lease. The lessee would not, therefore, capitalise the lease but would charge each period with the same leasing expense.

18.11 Leasing – a form of off-balance-sheet financing

Prior to IAS 17, one of the major attractions of leasing agreements for the lessee was the off-balance-sheet nature of the transaction. However, the introduction of IAS 17 required the capitalisation of finance leases and removed part of the benefit of off-balance-sheet financing.

The capitalisation of finance leases effectively means that all such transactions will affect the lessee's gearing, return on assets and return on investment. Consequently, IAS 17 substantially alters some of the key accounting ratios which are used to analyse a set of financial statements.

Operating leases, on the other hand, are not required to be capitalised. This means that operating leases still act as a form of financing that is off the statement of financial position.[6] Hence, they are extremely attractive to many lessees. Indeed, leasing agreements are increasingly being structured specifically to be classified as operating leases, even though they appear to be more financial in nature.[7]

An important conclusion is that some of the key ratios used in financial analysis become distorted and unreliable in instances where operating leases form a major part of a company's financing.[8]

To illustrate the effect of leasing on the financial structure of a company, we present a buy versus leasing example.

EXAMPLE ● RATIO ANALYSIS OF BUY VERSUS LEASE DECISION Kallend Tiepins plc requires one extra machine for the production of tiepins. The MD of Kallend Tiepins plc is aware that the gearing ratio and the return on capital employed ratio will change depending on whether the company buys or leases (on an operating lease) this machinery. The relevant information is as follows.

The machinery costs £100,000, but it will improve the operating profit by 10% p.a. The current position, the position if the machinery is bought and the position if the machinery is leased are as follows, assuming that lease costs match depreciation charges:

	Current £	Buy £	Lease £
Operating profit	40,000	44,000	44,000
Equity capital	200,000	200,000	200,000
Long-term debt	100,000	200,000	100,000
Total capital employed	300,000	400,000	300,000
Gearing ratio	0.5:1	1:1	0.5:1
ROCE	13.33%	11%	14.66%

It is clear that the impact of a leasing decision on the financial ratios of a company can be substantial.[9] Although this is a very simple illustration, it does show that the buy versus lease decision has far-reaching consequences in the financial analysis of a company.

18.12 Accounting for leases – a new approach

The total annual leasing volume was estimated in 2011 as being in excess of US$1 trillion. Whilst finance leases are reported on the statement of financial position, many of the lease contracts have been classified as operating leases and do not appear on the statement.

There has been criticism on theoretical grounds that this effectively ignores assets and liabilities that fall within the definition of assets and liabilities in the Conceptual Framework and on practical grounds that the difference in the accounting treatment of finance leases and operating leases provides opportunities to structure transactions so as to achieve a particular lease classification. This means that the same transaction could be reported differently by companies and comparability reduced.

Some users have attempted to overcome this by adjusting the statement of financial position to capitalise the operating leases. For example, credit rating agencies capitalise operating lease obligations on the basis that all leasing is a form of financing that creates a claim on future cash flows and the distinction between finance and operating leases is artificial. The approach taken by the credit agency Standard & Poor is to capitalise operating leases by discounting the minimum lease commitments using the entity's borrowing rate to calculate the present value of the commitments.

The data in the financial statements are then adjusted, for example EBITDA is recalculated with the interest element of the lease payments deducted from the rental figure that had been deducted in arriving at the EBITDA. Other adjustments are made as discussed below in considering the impact on financial statements.

However, the staff of the IASB have noted that there can be considerable differences in the estimates of different analysts when they adjust the financial statements.[10] The standard setters (the IASB and FASB) have therefore proposed that operating leases give rise to an asset which is the right-of-use and a liability, and both should be reported on the statement of financial position.

Following initial exposure of the proposals in August 2010 by both the FASB and the IASB, there was considerable feedback. The proposals were claimed to be impractical, and gave inappropriate patterns of expense allocations. At the time of writing the standard setters are preparing another exposure draft which is expected to retain the capitalisation of leases except those of insignificant amounts, being leases for less than one year. Leases for less than a year would be treated on a flow-through basis. In other words, they would be treated as expenses as incurred and would not be capitalised. All other leases would be capitalised; however, the accounting would differ depending on the significance of the proportion of the asset expected to be consumed during the course of the lease period.

18.13 Classification of leases

The new approach relies on the right-of-use approach rather than assuming a hypothetical purchase by the lessee and a hypothetical use of loan finance. The proposed accounting is to recognise the rights and obligations created by the lease contract combined with the legal consequences of delivery of the leased asset or the taking of possession of a property.

Thus the lease provides the lessee with the intangible right to use the asset and in return an acceptance of the obligation to pay for the use of the asset. The asset and liability are both recorded at the present value of the 'payments' under the lease.

The leases are then divided into two separate categories, namely:

(a) those where the lessee does not consume more than an insignificant portion of the leased asset; and

(b) those where the lessee consumes more than an insignificant portion of the leased asset.

There are two important issues to note: (i) the significant/insignificant divide is not defined by a set percentage as was previously the case for the financial/operating classification, which is likely to create concerns on the part of some users and preparers; and (ii) the accounting for expenses in the statement of income depends on the classification.

Whether the usage is more than an insignificant portion of the asset could be assessed by looking at the term of the lease compared to the estimated life of the asset or by comparing the present value of the lease payments compared to the fair value of the asset at the commencement of the lease.

18.13.1 Lessee accounting

The lessee has to record a right-of-use asset and a lease liability at the commencement of the lease and these have to be adjusted each period to reflect the reduction in the remaining term of the lease. This requirement holds irrespective of the classification.

Where an insignificant portion is consumed

Where the lessee uses an insignificant portion of the asset, the lease payments are essentially a payment for the use of the asset. Once this is identified, the use expense is normally recognised on a straight-line basis, but another pattern may be used if its use more adequately reflects the ensuing flow of benefits. This approach was viewed by many commentators on the first exposure draft as being more consistent with the economic reality as viewed by business people. This category was designed primarily to suit the majority of property leases where typically the lease is short relative to the life of the building and the land component is not consumed at all. However, not all property (land and/or buildings) has to fall into this category.

Example of accounting by lessee with an insignificant portion consumed

Magnificant Retailor enters into a two-year lease agreement with Mega Shopping Centres plc to lease a small shop at £50,000 per annum payable at the start of each year. Given the period of the lease and the nature of the item being leased, it is deemed to be a lease for an insignificant portion of the leased asset. Assume the relevant interest rate is 10% per annum.

The accounting would be as follows:

Dr	Leased asset	95,455	
Cr	Lease liability		95,455

(being the recognition of the lease based on its present value)

Dr	Lease rental expense	50,000	
Cr	Bank		50,000

(being payment of the first instalment)

Dr	Lease liability	45,455	
Cr	Leased asset		45,455

(to bring the lease asset and liability back to the present value of future payments at the end of the first year)

Dr	Lease expense	50,000	
Cr	Bank		50,000

(to record the payment of the second lease payment at the commencement of the second year)

Dr	Leased asset	50,000	
Cr	Lease liability		50,000

(to eliminate the asset and liability now that all payments under the lease have been made).

Where more than an insignificant portion is consumed

Where the lessee consumes more than an insignificant portion of the leased asset, the lessee is paying for both the consumption of the asset and the financing of the asset in the form of interest. This is then essentially the same as the treatment under the old financial leases.

The lessee establishes a right-of-use asset at the commencement of the lease equal to the present value of the expected payments under the lease. There is a corresponding lease liability. The right-of-use asset is amortised over the life of the lease. The lease payment first goes to pay the implied interest on the liability and then to reduce the principle.

Where the lease payment is a constant amount and the right-of-use asset is amortised on a straight-line basis, there will be a charge for (a) interest expense, which is higher in earlier periods and lower each subsequent year, and (b) amortisation expense in respect of the right-of-use asset, which is normally constant.

Example of lessee accounting when more than an insignificant portion of the asset is consumed

Market Specialists plc leases a motor vehicle for its managing director from K G Financiers plc for a five-year period at £27,618 per annum payable in advance. The expected life of the vehicle is eight years, so the lease is for more than an insignificant portion of its life. The relevant interest rate is 10% per annum. This requires that Market Specialists plc establish a right-of-use asset (leased motor vehicle) and a corresponding liability at the commencement of the lease. The amount of the right-of-use asset is £115,164, determined by taking the present value of the lease payments of £27,618 for years 0, 1, 2, 3 and 4 using a 10% discount rate.

The initial entries are:

Dr	Leased vehicle	115,164	
Cr	Lease liability		115,164
(establishment of lease contract)			

Dr	Lease liability	27,618	
Cr	Bank		27,618
(upfront payment of lease).			

Then at the end of the first year the entries for interest and amortisation would need to be made:

Dr	Interest expense	8,755	
Cr	Lease liability		8,755

(being 10% interest on the balance of the liability account immediately after the upfront payment, i.e. 10% of (115,164 − 27,618))

Dr	Amortisation of leased vehicle	23,032	
Cr	Provision for amortisation of leased vehicle		23,032

(write-off for the first year, being one-fifth of the leased asset).

At the beginning of the second year there would be another lease payment:

Dr	Lease liability	27,618	
Cr	Bank		27,618

(a payment reducing the lease liability to £68,683).

At the end of the second year there would be entries to identify the expenses for the year:

Dr	Interest expense	6,868	
Cr	Lease liability		6,868

Dr	Amortisation of leased vehicle	23,033	
Cr	Provision for amortisation of leased vehicle		23,033
(amortisation for one year).			

18.13.2 Lessor accounting

The lessor accounting is also determined by the previous classification, distinguishing between the cases where the lessee does or does not consume more than an insignificant portion of the leased asset.

Where an insignificant portion is consumed

Where the lessee does not consume more than an insignificant portion, the lessee is paying for the right of use. In this case:

(a) the leased asset is recorded by the lessor in the normal way at cost or fair value;

(b) capital allowance/amortisation (if any) is recorded on the asset which is being leased;

(c) if the leased asset is an asset recorded at fair value then the change in fair value for the period is recognised as an expense or gain as the case may be; and

(d) lease payments are recognised by the lessor as revenue.

Where more than an insignificant portion of the asset is consumed

Where the lessee consumes more than an insignificant proportion of the leased asset, the lessor initially records the asset at the cost of acquisition plus any additional expenses incurred in getting the asset ready for leasing.

Then when the lease becomes operational by allowing the lessee access to the asset in question, the lessor needs to establish an accounts receivable equal to the present value of the lease 'payments'.

This essentially reduces the value of the leased asset as it is now encumbered and the remaining balance should represent the present value of the expected residual of the leased asset at the end of the lease. Another way of expressing this is to say that the original carrying amount of the asset is apportioned between the amount that is currently owed under the lease contract and the residual asset.

Note how in each period interest revenue is recognised both on the lease receivable and on the residual asset.

Example of accounting by the lessor where more than an insignificant portion of the asset is consumed

The following information is available:

- K G Financiers plc purchased a vehicle for £137,000 at the request of Market Specialists plc who agreed to lease the vehicle. Further costs of £3,000 were incurred by K G Financiers plc in order to customise the vehicle ready for use by the lessee.
- The lease was for five years.
- Annual payments were £27,618 payable in advance.
- The estimated residual value was £40,000.
- The appropriate discount rate was 10%.
- The present value of the five lease payments (£115,164) and the residual value (£24,836), both using an interest rate of 10%, was £140,000.
- The leased asset realised £43,500 at the conclusion of the lease.

The asset was initially recorded by the lessor (K G Financiers plc) at £140,000. Then when the lease became operational by delivery of the vehicle to Market Specialists plc, the cost of the vehicle was allocated between the lease receivable and the residual interest in the asset retained by K G Financiers plc.

The entries to record this are as follows:

Dr	Motor vehicle	137,000	
Cr	Bank		137,000
(purchase of vehicle)			

Dr	Motor vehicle	3,000	
Cr	Bank		3,000
(further costs to customise the vehicle in readiness for use by the lessee)			

Dr	Lease receivable	115,164	
Dr	Residual interest in asset	24,836	
Cr	Motor vehicle		140,000

(to allocate the cost of the vehicle between the amount receivable from the lessee, that is the present value of the series of lease payments under the contract, and the balance of the cost, being the residual claim in the asset whose possession will revert to the lessor at the end of the contract).

At the end of the first year the interest on the financing arrangements will be recorded in the books as follows:

Dr	Lease receivable	8,755	
Dr	Residual interest in asset	2,484	
Cr	Interest income		11,239

(The lessor is expecting to get a 10% return on the financing. It has effectively financed £112,382, being the cost of the vehicle of £140,000 less the immediate lease payment of £27,618. Ten per cent of that amount is £11,238 and the £1 difference is due to rounding differences. Thus interest is associated both with the amount owing under the lease and also with the residual interest in the vehicle which the lessor has to finance until the asset is sold at the end of the lease.)

In year 2 the entries will be:

Dr	Bank	27,618	
Cr	Lease receivable		27,618

(being the payment at the commencement of the second year which will reduce the balance of the lease receivable to £68,683)

Dr	Lease receivable	6,868	
Dr	Residual interest in asset	2,732	
Cr	Interest income		9,600

(being interest accruing in relation to year 2 financing).

By the end of the five years the residual interest in the lease asset will have a balance of £40,000 made up as follows:

Initial amount	24,836
Interest in year 1	2,484
Interest in year 2	2,732
Interest in year 3	3,005
Interest in year 4	3,306
Interest in year 5	3,637
Total	40,000

At the end of the lease the asset is sold for £43,500. The entry to record this would be as follows:

Dr	Bank	43,500	
Cr	Residual interest in lease		40,000
Cr	Profit on sale of asset		3,500

(recording sale of asset on conclusion of the lease).

18.14 The significance of options to extend the lease

A contentious area in leasing is how to recognise options to extend a lease. It is not unusual for leases to include an option to extend a lease, particularly where the lease is a lease of premises or where a specialised asset is involved. If you establish a shop then it may be that the customers associate the shop with that location, so the goodwill of the business is partially dependent on maintaining the location. If the asset is specialised then the lessor may find it difficult to realise much money on the sale of the asset and would be very open to the lessee extending the period of the lease.

How do we account for such options?

If the option is solely at the discretion of the lessee the value of the lessor's residual asset may be diminished. From the perspective of the lessee the right-of-use asset is increased, but as we are only recording it at cost it is normally difficult to ascertain how much, if anything, was paid for the option.

If the option requires the consent of both parties it has no special value because in the absence of the option the parties could have negotiated a new lease agreement. Further, when we are recording the lease liability in the books of the lessee the option would not create a legal obligation, as the lessee is by definition not compelled to exercise the option and hence does not have a binding obligation.

Remember that companies often have long-term agreements with suppliers which are not reflected in the statement of financial position. The justification for the different treatment is that under the lease the asset has been made available to the lessee whereas the future goods have not been delivered. So until the option is exercised not all elements of the second lease contract have been finalised and thus it is not recorded.

In a like manner, if the lease arrangement includes both a fixed payment and a variable or contingent element such as a fixed percentage of the sales of the shopping centre as a whole or the individual shop's sales, there is uncertainty as to the future amount of the contingent/variable component and hence the appropriate amount of the lease liability.

The main question that arises in relation to options is the extent to which companies will try to use options to diminish the extent of capitalisation of leased (right-to-use) assets and the associated lease liabilities. Perhaps the authorities should include disclosures by lessees of the average term remaining on leases (excluding option possibilities) so that gamesmanship can be identified.

18.15 Implications of the revenue recognition standard

The discussion in the earlier sections of the chapter has assumed the transaction is a financing transaction. However, in some instances the lessor is both the manufacturer and the retailer of the goods, such that the transaction is a combination of a sale of whole or part of the asset together with an associated financing transaction. The new lease standard will focus on ensuring that the sale recognition, under a leasing transaction, conforms to the revenue standard requirements.

An example might be a manufacturer of trucks who provides lease contracts to enable drivers to 'acquire' a vehicle. If the lease contract essentially passes the risk of ownership to the truck driver and all other conditions of revenue recognition are satisfied, then the transaction can be recognised in two stages. Firstly the sales transaction is recognised and then the financing is considered. If the lease term is only for part of the life of the asset then reference would have to be made to the revenue recognition standard to decide whether some or none of the truck asset can be deemed to have been sold to the truck driver.

Summary

Off-balance-sheet financing was considered a particular advantage of lease financing. IAS 17 recognised this and attempted to introduce stricter accounting policies and requirements. However, although IAS 17 introduced the concept of 'substance over form', the hazy distinction between finance and operating leases still allows companies to structure lease agreements to achieve either type of lease. This is important because, while stricter accounting requirements apply to finance leases, operating leases can still be used as a form of accounting off the statement of financial position.

We do not know the real extent to which IAS 17 is either observed or ignored. However, it is true to say that creative accountants and finance companies are able to circumvent IAS 17 by using 'structured' leases. Future developments are attempting to reduce the opportunities for such off-balance-sheet financing. It is likely that companies will next focus on minimising the amount of the leasing assets and liabilities which they have to include in the statement of financial position.

REVIEW QUESTIONS

1 Can the legal position on leases be ignored now that substance over form is used for financial reporting? Discuss.

2 (a) Consider the importance of decisions over the categorisation of lease transactions into operating leases or finance leases when carrying out financial ratio analysis. What ratios might be affected if a finance lease is structured to fit the operating lease classification?

(b) Discuss the effects of renegotiating/reclassifying all operating leases into finance leases. For which industries might this classification have a significant impact on the financial ratios?

3 State the factors that indicate that a lease is a finance lease under IAS 17.

4 The favourite off-balance-sheet financing trick used to be leasing. Use any illustrative numerical examples you may wish to:

(a) Define the term 'off-balance-sheet financing' and state why it is popular with companies.

(b) Illustrate what is meant by the above term in the context of leases and discuss the accounting treatments and disclosures required by IAS 17 which have limited the usefulness of leasing as an off-balance-sheet financing technique.

(c) Suggest two other off-balance-sheet financing techniques and discuss the effect that each technique has on statement of financial position assets and liabilities, and on the income statement.

5 The Tesco 2011 Annual Report included the following accounting policy:

Assets held under finance leases are recognised as assets of the Group at their fair value or, if lower, at the present value of the minimum lease payments, each determined at the inception of the lease. The corresponding liability is included in the Group Balance Sheet as a finance lease obligation. Lease payments are apportioned between finance charges and a reduction of the lease obligations so as to achieve a constant rate of interest on the remaining balance of the liability. Finance charges are charged to the Group Income Statement. Rentals payable under operating leases are charged to the Group Income Statement on a straight-line basis over the term of the lease.

Rental income from operating leases is recognised on a straight-line basis over the term of the lease.

(a) Explain the meaning of 'minimum lease payments and fair value'.

(b) Explain why fair value might be higher than the discounted minimum lease payments.

(c) Explain why the aim is to arrive at a constant rate of interest.

6 The accountant in a small entity, Balloon Daredevils Ltd, was looking at a number of leases and attempting to decide whether each was definitely a finance lease. The lease conditions were as follows:

Lease 1 The company could cancel the lease but would be required to compensate the lessor for any resulting losses.

Lease 2 The lease transfers ownership of the asset to Balloon Daredevils.

Lease 3 Balloon Daredevils could continue the lease for a secondary period at a rent that was substantially lower than market rent.

Lease 4 Balloon Daredevils had the option to purchase balloons at the end of the lease at a bargain price. It had been company policy in the past to exercise this option.

Lease 5 The lease was for a specialist balloon designed to operate at high altitudes.

Lease 6 This was for a three-year rental to cover a contract to provide balloons for a client's staff motivational courses. It was a new venture for the company and was unlikely to be repeated as the client was attempting to negotiate a price that would leave the company making losses.

7 Given that the details of operating leases are disclosed in the notes to the accounts, why is it necessary to propose a new standard which incorporates these into the statement of financial position when sophisticated investors already do such adjustments themselves?

8 Under the first exposure draft in 2010 lessees had to account for all leases in terms of their amortisation of the right-of-use asset and the interest expense implied in the contract. There was considerable lobbying against that approach in relation to property leases. Discuss whether the distinction between whether the lessee does, or does not, consume more than an insignificant portion of the leased asset is a valid distinction.

9 Companies sometimes get special prices from suppliers if they undertake to purchase specified commodities from the supplier over a designated future period. These supply arrangements do not have to be recorded as assets and liabilities. However, in future leases will give rise to recording of assets and liabilities. Discuss why the transactions are to be treated differently.

10 Under the proposed system of lease accounting the lessor recognises interest on the residual asset as well as the lease receivable item.

(a) Why is interest charged on the lease receivable asset?

(b) Why is interest accrued on the residual asset?

EXERCISES

* Question 1

On 1 January 20X8, Grabbit plc entered into an agreement to lease a widgeting machine for general use in the business. The agreement, which may not be terminated by either party to it, runs for six years and provides for Grabbit to make an annual rental payment of €92,500 on 31 December each year. The cost of the machine to the lessor was €350,000, and it has no residual value. The machine has a useful economic life of eight years and Grabbit depreciates its property, plant and equipment using the straight-line method.

Required:

(a) Show how Grabbit plc will account for the above transaction in its statement of financial position at 31 December 20X8, and in its statement of comprehensive income for the year then ended, if it capitalises the leased asset in accordance with the principles laid down in IAS 17.
(Hint: the rate which equates the lease payments with the cost is 15%.)

(b) Explain why the standard setters considered accounting for leases to be an area in need of standardisation and discuss the rationale behind the approach adopted in the standard.

(c) The lessor has suggested that the lease could be drawn up with a minimum payment period of one year and an option to renew. Discuss why this might be attractive to the lessee.

* Question 2

(a) When accounting for finance leases, accountants prefer to overlook legal form in favour of commercial substance.

Required:
Discuss the above statement in the light of the requirements of IAS 17 *Leases*.

(b) State briefly how you would distinguish between a finance lease and an operating lease.

(c) Smarty plc finalises its accounts annually on 31 March. It reduces its machinery at 20% per annum on cost and adopts the 'Rule of 78' for allocating finance charges among different accounting periods. On 1 August 20X7 it acquired machinery on a finance lease on the following agreement:

   (i)   a lease rent of £500 per month is payable for 36 months commencing from the date of acquisition;
   (ii) cost of repairs and insurance are to be met by the lessee;
   (iii) on completion of the primary period the lease may be extended for a further period of three years, at the lessee's option, for a peppercorn rent.

   The cash price of the machine is £15,000.

Required:

(1) Set out how all ledger accounts reflecting these transactions will appear in each of the four accounting periods 20X7/8, 20X8/9, 20X9/Y0 and 20Y0/1.

(2) Show the statement of comprehensive income entries for the year ended 31 March 20X8 and statement of financial position extracts as at that date.

* Question 3

The Mission Company Ltd, whose year-end is 31 December, has acquired two items of machinery on leases, the conditions of which are as follows:

Item Y: Ten annual instalments of £20,000 each, the first payable on 1 January 20X0. The machine was completely installed and first operated on 1 January 20X0 and its purchase price on that date was £160,000. The machine has an estimated useful life of 10 years, at the end of which it will be of no value.

Item Z: Ten annual instalments of £30,000 each, the first payable on 1 January 20X2. The machine was completely installed and first operated on 1 January 20X2 and its purchase price on that date was £234,000. The machine has an estimated useful life and is used for 12 years, at the end of which it will be of no value.

The Mission Company Ltd accounts for finance charges on finance leases by allocating them over the period of the lease on the sum of the digits method.

Depreciation is charged on a straight-line basis. Ignore taxation.

Required:
(a) Calculate and state the charges to the statement of comprehensive income for 20X6 and 20X7 if the leases were treated as operating leases.
(b) Calculate and state the charges to the statement of comprehensive income for 20X6 and 20X7 if the leases were treated as finance leases and capitalised using the sum of the digits method for the finance charges.
(c) Show how items Y and Z should be incorporated in the statement of financial position, and notes thereto, at 31 December 20X7, if capitalised.

Question 4

X Ltd entered into a lease agreement on the following terms:

Cost of leased asset	€100,000
Lease term	5 years
Rentals six-monthly in advance	€12,000
Anticipated residual on disposal of the assets at end of lease term	€0
Economic life	5 years
Inception date	1 January 20X4
Lessee's financial year-end	31 December
Implicit rate of interest is applied half-yearly	4.3535%

Required:
Show the statement of comprehensive income entries for the years ended 31 December 20X4 and 20X7 and statement of financial position extracts at those dates.

Question 5

At 1 January 20X5 Bridge Finance plc agreed to finance the lease of machinery costing $37,200 to Rapid Growth plc at a lease cost of $10,000 per annum payable at the end of the year, namely 31 December. The period of the lease is five years. Bridge Finance plc incurred direct costs of $708 in setting up the contract.

Required:
Show for Bridge Finance plc the amount that would appear in the statement of comprehensive income for the year ending 31 December 20X7 and the amount of the leased asset that would appear in the statement of financial position at that date. (Apply a rate of 10%.)

Question 6

Alpha entered into an operating lease under which it was committed to five annual payments of £50,000 per year. It was subsequently decided to treat the lease as a right-of-use asset reported on the statement of financial position. Alpha's borrowing rate was 10%.

Required:
Calculate the amounts to be reported in the statement of financial position and the statement of comprehensive income.

Question 7

Construction First provides finance and financial solutions to companies in the construction industry. On 1 January 2007 the company agreed to finance the lease of equipment costing $145,080 to Bodge Brothers over its useful life of five years at an annual rental of $39,000 payable annually in arrears. The interest rate associated with this transaction is 10% and Construction First incurred direct costs of $2,761 in setting up the lease.

Construction First agreed with the manufacturer of the equipment to pay the amount owing in three equal six-monthly instalments beginning on 31 January 2007.

Required:
Show the entries that would appear in Construction First's statement of income and statement of financial position (balance sheet) for the year ended 31 December 2008 together with comparative figures and an appropriate disclosure note.

(Association of International Accountants)

References

1 G. Allum *et al.*, 'Fleet focus: to lease or not to lease', *Australian Accountant*, September 1989, pp. 31–58; R.L. Benke and C.P. Baril, 'The lease vs. purchase decision', *Management Accounting*, March 1990, pp. 42–46.
2 B. Underdown and P. Taylor, *Accounting Theory and Policy Making*, Heinemann, 1985, p. 273.
3 Cranfield School of Management, *Financial Leasing Report*, Bedford, 1979.
4 A.R. Abdel-Khalik *et al.*, 'The economic effects on lessees of FASB Statement No. 13', *Accounting for Leases*, FASB, 1981.
5 R. Main, in *External Financial Reporting*, ed. B. Carsberg and S. Dev, Prentice Hall, 1984.
6 R.H. Gamble, 'Off-balance-sheet diet: greens on the side', *Corporate Cashflow*, August 1990, pp. 28–32.
7 R.L. Benke and C.P. Baril, 'The lease vs. purchase decision', *Management Accounting*, March 1990, pp. 42–46; N. Woodhams and P. Fletcher, 'Operating leases to take bigger market share with changing standards', *Rydge's (Australia)*, September 1985, pp. 100–110.
8 C.H. Volk, 'The risks of operating leases', *Journal of Commercial Bank Lending*, May 1988, pp. 47–52.
9 Chee-Seong Tah, 'Lease or buy?', *Accountancy*, December 1992, pp. 58–59.
10 Staff presentation entitled 'Leases: Project update July 2012' (being the views of the staff making the presentation and not representing the official views of the FASB and IASB).

CHAPTER 19

Intangible assets

19.1 Introduction

The statement of financial position or balance sheet has traditionally reported tangible non-current assets and working capital. In order to protect future economic benefits, i.e. profits, companies have paid for legal or contractual intangible assets such as patents and copyright. As these were evidenced by a payment, they satisfied the accounting definition of an asset with a measurable cost and probable future economic benefit.

As business has become more complex, future economic benefits have become more reliant on internally generated intellectual capital that does not satisfy all the criteria for inclusion as an asset in the statement of financial position. For example, expenditure on a skilled workforce, training, research, and the development of a loyal customer base are all charged as an expense in the statement of income.

There are two adverse results that may arise from this: (a) the current year's profits are reduced by the charge and the company may be at risk in the short term from a predatory takeover; and (b) there is a mismatch between the market value of a company and the book value of its net assets.

The main purpose of this chapter is to consider the approach taken by IAS 38 *Intangible Assets*[1] and IFRS 3 *Business Combinations*[2] to the accounting treatment of intangible assets.

Objectives

By the end of this chapter, you should be able to:

- define and explain how to account for:
  - legally enforceable intangibles and internally generated intangibles;
  - research and development (R&D);
  - goodwill;
  - brands; and
  - emissions trading certificates;
- account for development costs;
- comment critically on the IASB requirements in IAS 38 and IFRS 3.

19.2 Intangible assets defined

Intangible assets are identifiable non-monetary assets that cannot be seen, touched or physically measured but are identifiable as a separate asset.

19.2.1 Criteria for recognition as an asset in the statement of financial position

IAS 38 *Intangible Assets* states that an asset is recognised in respect of an intangible item if the asset is characterised by the following properties:

- **The asset is identifiable.**
  The standard states that for an intangible asset to exist (or be identifiable) it must either be separable or arise from contractual or other legal rights (such as a patent), whether or not the asset can be separately disposed of (such as goodwill).

- **The asset is controlled by the entity.**
  Control is one of the central features of the *Framework* definition of an asset. Control is said to exist if the entity has the power to obtain the future economic benefits flowing from the underlying resource and to restrict the access of others to those benefits. *It is failing to satisfy the control criterion that prevents the skills of the workforce being recognised as an asset in the statement of financial position.*

- **The asset gives future economic benefits.**
  Again, it is inherent in the *Framework* definition of an asset that the potential future economic benefits can be identified with reasonable certainty.

If the identifiability and control tests are satisfied then IAS 38 allows recognition of an intangible asset if:

- it is **probable** that the expected future economic benefits that are attributable to the asset will flow to the entity; and

- the cost of the asset can be **measured reliably**.

Application of these criteria means that the costs associated with most internally generated intangible assets are expensed to the statement of income. An exception is development costs, **provided** these meet additional recognition criteria required by the standard.

19.2.2 Recognition criteria illustrated

Devon Cheeses Ltd decided to diversify into the production of vegetarian organic sausages. The project team produced a list of cost headings for the acquisition of:

(a) recipes from an international chef;

(b) a licence to use a specialised computer-controlled oven;

(c) registration of a trade name 'The Organo One'; and

(d) training courses for management in sausage making.

Their auditors were asked for advice on the possibility of capitalising all costs arising in respect of the above. The advice received was that the cost of recipes, the licence and the trade name registration could be capitalised, since:

- they were identifiable arising from contractual rights;
- Devon Cheeses Ltd controlled the future economic benefits;
- the costs could be measured reliably;
- it was probable that there would be future economic benefits; and
- the trade name was a defensive intangible that protected the receipt of the future economic benefits.

The training courses would improve management expertise but failed the control criterion and should be expensed.

19.2.3 Accounting treatment of recognised intangible assets at year-ends

The accounting treatment depends on whether the asset has a finite or an indefinite life.

Intangible assets with a finite life

IAS 38 states that recognised intangible non-current assets should be reported at cost less accumulated amortisation or, as when a parent acquires a subsidiary with intangible assets, fair value less accumulated amortisation.

The asset should be amortised over its estimated useful economic life, in a manner that is very similar to the treatment of property, plant and equipment under IAS 16. Amortisation must be on a systematic basis. This is frequently on a straight-line basis as with patents which have a legal life. The following extract is from the Bayer Group 2010 Annual Report:

> The Bayer Group currently owns some 78,000 patents or patent applications. . . .
> Patents are valid for varying periods, depending on the laws of the jurisdiction
> granting the patent. . . . Intangible assets are recognised at the cost of acquisition
> or generation. . . . Those with a determinable useful life are amortised accordingly
> on a straight-line basis over a period of up to 30 years, except where their actual
> depletion demands a different amortisation pattern.

Intangible assets are also tested for impairment where there is a triggering event. The following Accounting Policy extract from the SABMiller 2012 Annual Report explains the amortisation and impairment policy for intangibles with finite lives:

> Intangible assets are stated at cost less accumulated amortisation on a straight-line basis
> (if applicable) and impairment losses . . . Amortisation is included within net operating
> expenses in the income statement . . . Intangible assets with finite lives are amortised
> over their estimated useful economic lives, and only tested for impairment where there
> is a triggering event.

Intangible assets with an indefinite life

Where the estimated useful economic life is indefinite, such as with goodwill, there is no amortisation but the asset is subject to annual impairment reviews under IAS 36. Other intangible assets such as trademarks might be less definite and be subject to an amortisation charge and an impairment charge. This treatment is illustrated in the following extract from the Bayer Group 2010 Annual Report:

	Trademarks
	€
Cost of acquisition or generation	4.028m
Amortisation in 2010	163m
Impairment in 2010	429m

Expenditure on intangibles that does not satisfy recognition criteria is expensed through the statement of income.

19.2.4 Disclosure of intangible assets under IAS 38

IAS 38 requires the disclosure of the following for each type of intangible asset:[3]

- whether useful lives are indefinite or finite;
- the amortisation methods used for intangible assets with finite useful lives;
- the gross carrying amount and accumulated amortisation at the beginning and end of the period;
- increases or decreases resulting from revaluations and from impairment losses recognised or reversed directly in equity (IAS 36 *Impairment of Assets*); and
- for R&D, disclosure in the financial statements of the charge for research and development in the period.[4]

Where an intangible asset is assessed as having an indefinite useful life, the carrying value of the asset must be stated[5] along with the reasons for supporting the assessment of an indefinite life.

19.3 Accounting treatment for research and development

Under IAS 38 *Intangible Assets*, research expenditure **must be expensed** whereas development expenditure **must be capitalised** provided a strict set of criteria is met. In this section we will consider R&D activities, why research expenditure is written off and the tests for capitalising development expenditure.

19.3.1 Research activities

IAS 38 states[6] 'expenditure on research shall be recognised as an expense when it is incurred'. This means that it cannot be included as an intangible asset in the statement of financial position. The standard gives examples of research activities[7] as:

- activities aimed at obtaining new knowledge;
- the search for, evaluation and final selection of, applications of research findings or other knowledge;
- the search for alternatives for materials, devices, products, processes, systems and services; and
- the formulation, design, evaluation and final selection of possible alternatives for new or improved materials, devices, products, processes, systems or services.

Normally, research expenditure is not related directly to any of the company's products or processes. For instance, development of a high-temperature material which could be used in any aero engine would be 'research', but development of a honeycomb for a particular engine would be 'development'. Whilst it is in the research phase, the IAS position[8] is that an entity cannot demonstrate that an intangible asset exists that will generate probable future economic benefits. It is this inability that justifies the IAS requirement for research expenditure not to be capitalised but to be charged as an expense when it is incurred.

19.3.2 Development activities

Expenditure is recognised[9] as development if the entity can identify an intangible asset and demonstrate that the asset will generate probable future economic benefits. The standard gives examples of development activities:[10]

(a) the design, construction and testing of pre-production and pre-use prototypes and models;

(b) the design of tools, jigs, moulds and dies involving new technology;

(c) the design, construction and operation of a pilot plant that is not of a scale economically feasible for commercial production; and

(d) the design, construction and testing of a chosen alternative for new or improved materials, devices, products, processes, systems or services.

19.4 Why is research expenditure not capitalised?

Many readers will think of research not as a cost but as a strategic investment which is essential to remain competitive in world markets. Indeed, this was the view[11] taken by the House of Lords Select Committee on Science and Technology, stating that 'R&D has to be regarded as an investment which leads to growth, not a cost'.

It is reported[12] that Global R&D spending is expected to grow by about 5.2% to more than $1.4 trillion in 2012, according to an analysis performed by Battelle and *R&D Magazine*. Most of the global funding growth is being driven by Asian economies, which are expected to increase nearly 9% in 2012, while European R&D will grow by about 3.5% and North American R&D by 2.8%. US R&D is forecast to grow 2.1% in 2012 to $436 billion.

Globally, such expenditure is in excess of 3% of sales, taking place particularly in the advanced technical industries such as pharmaceuticals, where a sustained high level of R&D investment is required – almost 80% occurring in five countries: the USA, Japan, Germany, France and the UK. The regulators, however, do not consider that the expenditure can be classified as an asset for financial reporting purposes.

Why do the regulators not regard research expenditure as an asset?

The IASC in its *Framework for the Preparation and Presentation of Financial Statements*[13] defines an asset as a resource that is controlled by the enterprise, as a result of past events and from which future economic benefits are expected to flow.

Research is controlled by the enterprise and results from past events but there is no reasonable certainty that the intended economic benefits will be achieved. Because of this uncertainty, the accounting profession has traditionally considered it more prudent to write off the investment in research as a cost rather than report it as an asset in the statement of financial position.

It might be thought that this is concealing an asset from investors, but in research on the reactions of both analysts[14] and accountants[15] to R&D expenditure Nixon found that: 'Two important dimensions of the corporate reporting accountants' perspective emerge: first, disclosure is seen as more important than the accounting treatment of R&D expenditure and, second, the financial statements are not viewed as the primary channel of communication for information on R&D.'

This highlights the importance of reading carefully the narrative in financial reports. An interesting study in Singapore[16] examined the impact of annual report disclosures on analysts' forecasts for a sample of firms listed on the Stock Exchange of Singapore (SES) and showed that the level of disclosure affected the accuracy of earnings forecasts among analysts and also led to greater analyst interest in the firm.

Management might prefer in general to be able to capitalise research expenditure but there could be circumstances where writing off might be preferred. For example, directors might be pleased to take the expense in a year when they know its impact rather than carry it forward. They are aware of profit levels in the year in which the expenditure arises and could, perhaps, find it embarrassing to take the charge in a subsequent year when profits were lower or the company even reported a trading loss.

Development expenditure, on the other hand, has more probability of achieving future economic benefits and the regulators, therefore, require such expenditure to be capitalised.

19.5 Capitalising development costs

19.5.1 Conditions to be satisfied

The relevant paragraph of IAS 38[17] says an intangible asset for development expenditure must be recognised if and only if an entity can demonstrate **all** of the following:

(a) the technical feasibility of completing the intangible asset so that it will be available for use or sale;

(b) the intention to complete the intangible asset and use or sell it;

(c) its ability to use or sell the intangible asset;

(d) how the intangible asset will generate probable future economic benefits;

(e) the availability of adequate technical, financial and other resources to complete the development and to use or sell the intangible asset;

(f) its ability to measure reliably the expenditure attributable to the intangible asset during its development.

It is important to note that if the answers to all the conditions (a) to (f) above are 'Yes' then the entity *must* capitalise the development expenditure subject to reviewing for impairment.

19.5.2 What costs can be included?

The costs that can be included in development expenditure are similar to those used in determining the cost of inventory (IAS 2 *Inventories*).

It is important to note that only expenditure incurred after the project satisfies the IAS 38 criteria can be capitalised – all expenditure incurred prior to this date must be written off as an expense in the statement of income. Experience tends to indicate that people who develop products are notoriously optimistic. In practice, they encounter many more problems than they imagined and the cost is much greater than estimates. This means that the development project may well be approaching completion before future development costs can be estimated reliably.

At the year-ends development costs are usually amortised over the sales of the product (i.e. the charge in 20X5 would be: 20X5 sales/total estimated sales × capitalised development expenditure) with straight-line as the default.

19.6 Disclosure of R&D

R&D is important to many manufacturing companies, such as pharmaceutical companies, car and defence manufacturers. Disclosure is required of the aggregate amount of research and development expenditure recognised as an expense during the period.[4] Normally, this total expenditure will be:

(a) research expenditure;

(b) development expenditure amortised;

(c) development expenditure not capitalised; and

(d) impairment of capitalised development expenditure.

Under IAS 38 more companies may capitalise development expenditure. Management view of the probability of making future profits from the sale of the product is a critical element in making a decision. The following is the R&D policy extract from the Rolls-Royce Annual Report for the year ended 31 December 2010:

> In accordance with IAS 38 'Intangible Assets', expenditure incurred on research and development . . . is distinguished as relating either to a research phase or to a development phase. All research phase expenditure is charged to the income statement. For development expenditure, this is capitalised as an internally generated intangible asset, only if it meets strict criteria, relating in particular to technical feasibility and generation of future economic benefits.
>
> Expenditure that cannot be classified into these two categories is treated as being incurred in the research phase. The Group considers that, due to the complex nature of new equipment programmes, it is not possible to distinguish reliably between research and development activities until relatively late in the programme.
>
> Expenditure capitalised is amortised over its useful economic life, up to a maximum of 15 years from the entry-into-service of the product.

The financial statements of Rolls-Royce for the year ended 31 December 2010 show capitalised development expenditure of £630 million at the year-end, £121 million additions and £29 million amortisation in the year.

19.7 IFRS for SMEs treatment of intangible assets

Internally generated intangible assets

The IFRS provides that internally generated intangible assets are not recognised. This means that both research and development costs are expensed.

Separately purchased intangible assets

The IFRS provides the following:

● Such assets should be amortised over the asset's useful life; and

● if the useful life cannot be estimated, then a 10-year useful life is presumed.

● If there is a significant change in the asset or how it is used, then the useful life, residual value and depreciation rate are reviewed.

● Impairment testing is carried out where there are impairment indications.

● The revaluation of intangible assets is prohibited.

19.8 Internally generated and purchased goodwill

IFRS 3 *Business Combinations* defines goodwill[18] as: 'future economic benefits arising from assets that are not capable of being individually identified and separately recognised'. The definition effectively affirms that the value of a business as a whole is more than the sum of the accountable and identifiable net assets. Goodwill can be internally generated through the normal operations of an existing business or purchased as a result of a business combination.

19.8.1 Internally generated goodwill

Internally generated goodwill falls within the scope of IAS 38 *Intangible Assets* which states that 'Internally Generated Goodwill (or "self generated goodwill") shall not be recognised as an asset'. If companies were allowed to include internally generated goodwill as an asset in the statement of financial position, it would boost total assets and produce a more favourable view of the statement of financial position, for example by reducing the gearing ratio.

19.8.2 Purchased goodwill

How goodwill is calculated

The key distinction between internally generated goodwill and purchased goodwill is that purchased goodwill has an identifiable 'cost', being the difference between the fair value of the total consideration that was paid to acquire a business and the fair value of the identifiable net assets acquired. This is the initial cost reported in the statement of financial position.

What was received in return for the payment for goodwill?

Companies reporting under IFRS are required to disclose the nature of the intangible assets comprising goodwill and explain why they cannot be valued separately.

For example, the pharmaceutical group Bayer acquired a majority interest in Schering in June 2006 for a net total of €16.2 billion. Of this, €12.0 billion was allocated to intangible assets in five separate classes including marketing and technology-related assets. Goodwill of €5.8 billion is described as relating to synergies and cost savings across various business functions, as well as the strengthening of Bayer's global market position.[19]

19.9 The accounting treatment of goodwill

Now that we have a definition of goodwill, we need to consider how to account for it in subsequent years. One might have reasonably thought that a simple requirement to amortise the cost over its estimated useful life would have been sufficient. This has been far from the case. Over the past 40 years, there have been a number of approaches to accounting for purchased goodwill, including:

(a) writing off the cost of the goodwill directly to reserves in the year of acquisition;
(b) reporting goodwill at cost in the statement of financial position (this was attractive to management as there was no charge against profits in any year);
(c) reporting goodwill at cost, amortising over its expected life; and
(d) reporting goodwill at cost, but checking it annually for impairment.

The last (d) is now the treatment required by IFRS 3.

19.9.1 The current IFRS 3 treatment

IFRS 3 prohibits the amortisation of goodwill. It treats goodwill as if it has an indefinite life with the amount reviewed annually for impairment. If the carrying value is greater than the recoverable value of the goodwill, the difference is written off.

Whereas goodwill amortisation gave rise to an annual charge, impairment losses will arise at irregular intervals. This means that the profit for the year will become more volatile. This is why companies and analysts rely more on the EBITDA (earnings before interest, tax, depreciation and amortisation) when assessing a company's performance, assuming that this is a better indication of maintainable profits.

This is illustrated by the following extract from the 2012 Vodafone Annual Report which shows the volatile effect of impairment charges on maintainable profits:

	2012 £m	2011 £m	2010 £m
Revenue	46,417	45,884	44,472
Gross profit	14,871	15,070	15,033
Impairment losses	(4,050)	(6,150)	(2,100)
Operating profit	11,187	5,596	9,480

This illustrates the volatility when impairment charges are included when calculating operating profit or loss with a pre-impairment profit reporting a profit increase in 2012 of 100% instead of 30% and a fall in 2011 instead of an increase.

19.9.2 Identifying intangible assets to reduce the amount of goodwill

Because goodwill is reviewed annually for impairment under IFRS 3 and other intangible assets are amortised annually under IAS 38, standard setters wanted companies to identify any intangible assets that were acquired on an acquisition of another company and not to include them within a global figure of goodwill.

This has two effects: (a) there is greater transparency and control over assets by identifying the asset that the parent acquired; and (b) intangible assets are amortised rather than being reviewed annually for impairment, so reducing the volatility in the reported operating profits.

Examples of intangible assets that should be recognised and reported in the statement of financial position are set out in IAS 38.[20] They include:

● **Marketing-related** intangible assets which are used primarily in the marketing or promotion of products or services such as trademarks, newspaper mastheads, Internet domain names and non-compete agreements.

● **Technology-related** intangible assets which arise from contractual rights to use technology (patented and unpatented), databases, formulae, designs, software, processes and recipes.

● **Customer or supplier-related** intangible assets which arise from relationships with or knowledge of customers or suppliers such as licensing, royalty and standstill agreements, servicing contracts, use rights such as airport landing slots and customer lists.

● **Artistic-related** intangible assets which arise from the right to benefits such as royalties from artistic works such as plays, books, films and music, and from non-contractual copyright protection.

Greater transparency should be achieved following the amendment in July 2009 to IFRS 3 which provides that if an intangible asset can be separately identified then it can be measured reliably, as the two conditions are interdependent. This will place further pressure on companies to properly consider the nature and value of any intangible assets they acquire.

19.10 Critical comment on the various methods that have been used to account for goodwill

Let us consider briefly the alternative accounting treatments.

(a) Reporting goodwill unchanged at cost

It is (probably) wrong to keep goodwill unchanged in the statement of financial position, as its value will decline with time. Its value may be *maintained* by further expenditure, e.g. continued advertising, but this expenditure is essentially creating 'internally generated goodwill' which is not allowed to be capitalised. Sales of most manufactured products often decline during their life and their selling price falls. Eventually, the products are replaced by a technically superior product. An example is computer microprocessors, which initially command a high price and high sales. The selling price and sales quantities decline as faster microprocessors are produced. Much of the goodwill of businesses is represented by the products they sell. Hence, it is wrong to not amortise the goodwill.

(b) Writing off the cost of the goodwill directly to reserves in the year of acquisition

A buyer pays for goodwill on the basis that future profits will be improved. It is wrong, therefore, to write it off in the year of acquisition against previous years in the reserves. The loss in value of the goodwill does not occur at the time of acquisition but occurs over a longer period. The goodwill is losing value over its life, and this loss in value should be charged to the statement of comprehensive income each year. Making the charge direct to reserves stops this charge from appearing in the future income statements.

(c) Amortising the goodwill over its expected useful life

Amortising goodwill over its life could achieve a matching under the accrual concept with a charge in the statement of comprehensive income. However, there are problems (i) in determining the life of the goodwill and (ii) in choosing an appropriate method for amortising.

(i) What is the life of the goodwill?

Companies wishing to minimise the amortisation charge could make a high estimate of the economic life of the goodwill and auditors have to be vigilant in checking the company's justification. The range of lives can vary widely. For example, goodwill paid to acquire a business in the fashion industry could be quite short compared to that paid to acquire an established business with a loyal customer base.

(ii) The method for amortising

Straight-line amortisation is the simplest method. However, as the benefits are likely to be greater in earlier years than in later ones, amortisation could use 'actual sales'/'expected total sales' or the reducing balance method.

It could be argued that amortising goodwill is equivalent to depreciating tangible fixed assets as prescribed by IAS 16 *Property, Plant and Equipment* and that the amortisation approach appears to be the best way of treating goodwill in the statement of financial position and statement of comprehensive income. This is effectively following a 'statement of comprehensive income' approach to 'expense' (e.g. depreciation) with the expense charged over the life of the asset or in relation to the profits obtained from the acquisition.

There are difficulties but these should not prevent us from using this method. After all, accountants have to make many judgements when valuing items in the statement of financial position, such as assessing the life of property, plant and equipment, the value of inventory and bad debt provisions.

(d) An annual impairment check

IFRS 3 introduced a new treatment for purchased goodwill when it arises from a business combination (i.e. the purchase of a company which becomes a subsidiary). It assumes that goodwill has an indefinite economic life, which means that it is not possible to make a realistic estimate of its economic life and a charge should be made to the statement of income only when it becomes impaired.

This is called a 'statement of financial position' approach to accounting, as the charge is made only when the value (in the statement of financial position) falls below its original cost.

The IFRS 3 treatment is consistent with the *Framework*,[21] which says: 'Expenses are recognised in the statement of comprehensive income when a decrease in future economic benefits related to a decrease in an asset or an increase of a liability has arisen that can be measured reliably.'

Criticism of the 'statement of financial position' approach

However, there has been much criticism of the 'statement of financial position' approach of the *Framework*.

For example, if a company purchased specialised plant which had a resale value of 5% of its cost, then it could be argued that the depreciation charge should be 95% of its cost immediately after it comes into use. This is not sensible, as the purpose of buying the plant is to produce a product, so the depreciation charge should be over the life of the product.

Alternatively, if the 'future economic benefit' approach was used to value the plant, there would be no depreciation until the future economic benefit was less than its original cost. So, initial sales would incur no depreciation charge, but later sales would have an increased charge.

This example shows the weakness of using impairment and the 'statement of financial position' approach for charging goodwill to the statement of comprehensive income – the charge occurs at the wrong time. The charge should be made earlier when sales, selling prices and profits are high, not when the product becomes out of date and sales and profits are falling.

Why the impairment charge occurs at the wrong time

Although the IFRS 3 treatment of impairment appears to be correct according to the *Framework*, it could be argued that the impairment approach is not correct, as the charge occurs at the wrong time (i.e. when there is a loss in value, rather than when profits are being made), it is very difficult to estimate the future economic benefit of the goodwill and those estimates are likely to be over-optimistic.

In addition, it means that the treatment of goodwill for IFRS 3 transactions is different from the treatment in IAS 38 *Intangible Assets*. This shows the inconsistency of the standards – they should use a single treatment, either IAS 38 amortisation or IFRS 3 impairment.

19.10.1 Why does the IFRS 3 treatment of goodwill differ from the treatment of intangible assets in IAS 38?

The answer is probably related to the convergence of International Accounting Standards to US accounting standards, and pressure from listed companies.

Convergence pressure

In issuing recent International Standards, the IASB has not only aimed to produce 'worldwide' standards but also standards which are acceptable to US standard setters. The IASB wanted their standards to be acceptable for listing on the New York Stock Exchange (NYSE), so there was strong pressure on the IASB to make their standards similar to US standards. The equivalent US standard to IFRS 3 uses impairment of goodwill as the charge against profits (rather than amortisation). Thus, IFRS 3 uses the same method and it prohibits amortisation.

Commercial pressure

A further pressure for impairment rather than amortisation comes from listed companies. Essentially, listed companies want to maximise their reported profit, and amortisation reduces profit. For most of the time, companies can argue that the future economic benefit of the goodwill is greater than its original cost (or carrying value if it has been previously impaired), and thus avoid a charge to the statement of comprehensive income. Also, companies could argue that the 'impairment charge' is an unexpected event and charge it as an exceptional item.

In the UK, many companies publicise their profit before exceptional items and impairment to highlight maintainable profits.

19.11 Negative goodwill

Negative goodwill arises when the amount paid is less than the fair value of the net assets acquired. IFRS 3 says the acquirer should:

(a) reassess the identification and measurement of the acquiree's identifiable assets, liabilities and contingent liabilities and the measurement of the cost of the combination in case the assets have been undervalued or the liabilities overstated; and

(b) recognise immediately in the statement of comprehensive income any excess remaining after that reassessment.

The immediate crediting of negative goodwill to the statement of comprehensive income seems difficult to justify when, as in many situations, the reason why the consideration is less than the value of the net identifiable assets is that there are expected to be future losses or redundancy payments. Whilst the redundancy payments could be included in the 'contingent liabilities' at the date of acquisition, standard setters are very reluctant to allow a provision to be made for future losses (this has been prohibited in recent accounting standards). This means that the only option is to say the negative goodwill should be credited to the statement of comprehensive income at the date of acquisition. This results in the group profit being inflated when a subsidiary with negative goodwill is acquired.

In some ways, it would be better to credit the negative goodwill to the statement of comprehensive income over the years the losses are expected. However, the 'provision for future losses' (i.e. the negative goodwill) does not fit in very well with the *Framework*'s definition of a liability as being recognised 'when it is probable that an outflow of resources embodying economic benefits will result from the settlement of a present obligation and the amount at which the settlement will take place can be measured reliably'. It is questionable whether future losses are a 'present obligation' and whether they can be 'measured reliably', so it is very unlikely that future losses can be included as a liability in the statement of financial position.

19.12 Brands

We have discussed intangible assets and goodwill above but brands deserve a separate consideration because of their major significance in some companies. For example, the following information appears in the 2011 Diageo annual report:

	£m	£m
Total equity (i.e. net assets)		5,985
Intangible assets:		
Brands	4,805	
Goodwill	418	
Other intangible assets	1,138	
Computer software	184	
Total intangible assets		6,545

We can see that brands alone are 80% of total equity. It is interesting to take a look at the global importance of brands within sectors.

19.12.1 The importance of brands to particular sectors

It is interesting to note that certain sectors have high global brand valuations. For example, the Best Global Brands Report 2011[22] showed beverages (Coca-Cola $71,861m), computer services (IBM $69,905m), computer software (Microsoft $59,087m), Internet services (Google $55,317m), diversified (GE $42,808m), restaurants (McDonald's $35,593m) and electronics (Apple $33,492m). Even the hundredth exceeded $3,000 million (Harley Davidson $3,512m).

This indicates the importance of investors having as much information as possible to assess management's stewardship of brands. If this cannot be reported on the face of the statement of financial position then there is an argument for having an additional statement to assist shareholders, including the information that the directors consider when managing brands.

19.12.2 Justifications for reporting all brands as assets

We now consider some other justifications that have been put forward for the inclusion of brands as a separate asset in the statement of financial position.

Reduce equity depletion

For acquisitive companies it could be attributed to the accounting treatment required for measuring and reporting goodwill. The London Business School carried out research into the 'brands phenomenon' and found that 'a major aim of brand valuation has been to repair or pre-empt equity depletion caused by UK goodwill accounting rules'.[23]

Strengthen the statement of financial position

Non-acquisitive companies do not incur costs for acquiring goodwill, so their reserves are not eroded by writing off purchased goodwill. However, these companies may have incurred promotional costs in creating home-grown brands and it would strengthen the statement of financial position if they were permitted to include a valuation of these brands.

Effect on equity shareholders' funds

Immediate goodwill write-off results in a fall in net tangible assets as disclosed by the statement of financial position, even though the market capitalisation of the company increases. One way to maintain the asset base and avoid such a depletion of companies' reserves is to divide the purchased goodwill into two parts: the amount attributable to brands and the remaining amount attributable to pure goodwill. For instance, WPP capitalised two corporate brand names in 1988; without that capitalisation, the share owners' funds of £187.7 million in the 1998 accounts would have been reduced by £350 million to a *negative* figure of £162.3 million. The 2010 Annual Report shows that total equity now exceeds the brand value but would be reduced to a negative figure if goodwill were not included as an asset.

Effect on borrowing powers

The borrowing powers of public companies may be expressed in terms of multiples of net assets. In Articles of Association there may be strict rules regarding the multiple that a company must not exceed. In addition, borrowing agreements and Stock Exchange listing agreements are generally dependent on net assets.

Effect on ratios

Immediate goodwill write-off distorts the gearing ratios, but the inclusion of brands as intangible assets minimises this distortion by providing a more realistic value for shareholders' funds.

Effect on management decisions

Including brands on the statement of financial position should lead to more informed and improved management decision making. As brands represent one of the most important assets of a company, management should be aware of the success or failure of each individual brand. Knowledge about the performance of brands ensures that management reacts accordingly to maintain or improve competitive advantage.

Effect on management decisions where brands are not capitalised

Whether or not a brand is capitalised, management do take its existence into account when making decisions affecting a company's gearing ratios. For example, in 2007 the Hugo Boss management in explaining its thinking about the advisability of making a Special Dividend payment[24] recognised that one effect was to reduce the book value of equity and increase the gearing ratio but commented:

> The book value of the equity capital of the HUGO BOSS Group will be reduced by the special dividend. However this perception does not take into consideration that the originally created market value 'HUGO BOSS' is not reflected in the book value of the equity capital. This does not therefore mirror the strong economic position of HUGO BOSS fully.

The implication is that the existence of brand value is recognised by the market and leads to a more sustainable market valuation.

There is also evidence[25] that companies with valuable brand names are not including these in their statements of financial position and are not, therefore, taking account of the assets for insurance purposes.

The above are the justifications for recognising internally generated brands as assets. However, IAS 38 prohibits[26] this by saying: 'Internally generated brands, mastheads, publishing titles, customer lists and items similar in substance shall not be recognised as intangible assets.'

19.13 Accounting for acquired brands

Acquired brands require to be valued. In 2009, the International Valuation Standards Council issued an Exposure Draft, *Valuation of Intangible Assets for IFRS Reporting Purposes*,[27] which considers the need to define more clearly terms used within IFRSs such as 'active' and 'inactive' markets.

A decision is then made in respect of each brand as to whether it should be treated in the financial statements as having a definite or an indefinite life. The following is an extract from the accounting policies of WPP in their 2011 Annual Report:

> Corporate brand names, customer relationships and proprietary tools acquired as part of acquisitions of business are capitalised separately from goodwill as intangible assets if their value can be measured reliably on initial recognition and it is probable that the expected economic benefits that are attributable to the asset will flow to the Group.
>
> Certain corporate brands of the Group are considered to have an indefinite economic life because of the institutional nature of the corporate brand names, their proven ability to maintain market leadership and profitable operations over long periods of time and the Group's commitment to develop and enhance their value. The carrying value of these intangible assets is reviewed at least annually for impairment and adjusted to the recoverable amount if required.

19.13.1 How effective have IFRS 3 and IAS 38 been?

There is still a temptation for companies to treat the excess paid on acquiring a subsidiary as goodwill. If it is treated as goodwill, then there is no requirement to make an annual amortisation charge. If any part of the excess is attributed to an intangible, then this has to be amortised. For example, in the UK the FRRP required Brewin Dolphin Holdings plc to implement a change of accounting policy in the forthcoming financial statements of the company for the period ended 27 September 2009. The company agreed that intangible assets representing client relationships would now be recognised separately from goodwill.

The Panel's principal concern related to the company's practice of not separately recognising customer-related intangible assets in the purchase of investment management businesses. IFRS 3 (2004) *Business Combinations* requires an acquirer to recognise intangible assets separately if they meet the definition of an intangible asset in IAS 38 *Intangible Assets* and their fair value can be measured reliably.

This is a clear indication in the UK that the FRRP will be policing the allocation of any excess on acquisitions to ensure that there is appropriate effort to attribute to intangible asset categories if that is the economic reality.

However, even so, the information is limited in that only acquired brands can be reported on the statement of financial position, which gives an incomplete picture of an entity's value. Even with acquired brands, their value can only remain the same or be revised downward following an impairment review. This means that there is no record of any added value that might have been achieved by the new owners to allow shareholders to assess the current stewardship.

19.14 Emissions trading

Under the European Union Emissions Trading Scheme (EU ETS) governments issue companies with free certificates allowing them to emit a stated amount of CO_2. If a company is not going to emit that quantity of CO_2, it can sell the excess in the market, which companies

502 • Statement of financial position − equity, liability and asset measurement and disclosure

exceeding the limit can buy. Standard setters have yet to decide (a) how these certificates should be valued in companies' financial statements, and (b) where they should be included in the statement of financial position.

Three possible approaches to valuation could be:

1 If the company receives the certificates free from the government, their value in the financial statements should be zero. It would be unreasonable to put a value on them in the company's financial statement (e.g. number of tonnes of CO_2 × CO_2 emissions value per tonne). This would be 'boosting the statement of financial position'. Presumably their treatment will eventually be addressed by a revision to IAS 20 *Accounting for Government Grants.*

2 If the company is trading in the certificates, they are financial instruments under IAS 39 *Financial Instruments: Recognition and Measurement*. They can be valued at cost, with impairment if their value becomes less than cost. However, it is probably more appropriate to treat them as 'fair value through profit or loss', value them at market value, and include profits or losses in the statement of comprehensive income.

3 If a company buys the certificates to use in its business, they could be accounted for like inventory and valued at the lower of original cost and net realisable value. When the CO_2 emission takes place, their cost will be included in cost of sales.

Four possible solutions to the question of where to report could be to include them as:

● an intangible asset subject to the conditions studied in this chapter;
● a financial instrument;
● a prepayment; or
● inventory.

Considering approaches 1 to 3 above in turn:

1 If the certificates have no value, they do not appear in the statement of financial position.

2 If they are classified as a financial instrument, they will be included in current assets if their life is less than one year.

3 This is a problem which will be considered below.

CO_2 emissions certificates have many characteristics of inventory, and the most appropriate accounting treatment is to treat them like inventory. Normally, they will be valued at cost, and they will be charged as cost of sales when the CO_2 emissions take place. Net realisable value (NRV) will apply when the process which produces the CO_2 makes a loss. NRV will be the value which gives a zero profit from the process, but NRV will not be less than zero (negative). The problem with including them as inventory is that inventory is a physical asset, and these emission certificates are not a physical asset; they are an intangible asset.

The certificates could be a financial instrument and valued at either cost, market value or net realisable value. As they are held for use in a production process (which produces CO_2), market value does not seem appropriate. As the CO_2 is emitted, their value will be reduced and the amount charged to cost of sales. It will be like selling part of a holding of shares, but the 'sale' will be a consumption in a production process. Overall, it does not seem appropriate to include the certificates as a financial instrument, as there are more negative factors than when including them as inventory.

The certificates could be included as an intangible asset, like the items considered in this chapter. However, most intangible assets last a number of years, and these certificates will probably be used within a year. The accounting standards prohibit amortisation of certain types of goodwill. This should not apply to emission certificates, as they are being consumed in the production process (i.e. as the CO_2 is being emitted, the units of the emission certificates left diminish).

It is apparent that emission certificates are a current asset, as their life is probably less than a year, and they are consumed in the production process. They come into the category of 'receivables', although they are not an amount owed by a customer. They are more like a prepayment. The company buys the certificates (like buying insurance for the future) and consumes them in the future. Most prepayments relate to payments in advance for a future period (e.g. a year for insurance). Emission certificates are different, as they are consumed in proportion to the amount of CO_2 emitted in the future. However, they are probably more like a prepayment than the other items considered.

This discussion is a view based on various arguments. It is not a definitive answer. You could consider these and other arguments and come to a different conclusion. In November 2010, the IASB and FASB agreed to defer this project to be considered as part of the agenda consultation process in 2012.

19.14.1 Accounting policy illustrated

There is no standard treatment. An example of one company's accounting policy is seen in the following Accounting Policy from the British Energy (now part of EDF) 2008 Annual Report:

> Under the EU Emissions Trading Scheme (EU ETS), granted carbon allowances received in a period are initially recognised at nil value within intangible assets. Purchased carbon allowances are initially recognised at cost within intangible assets. Allowances granted are apportioned over the year in line with actual and forecast emissions for the relevant emissions year.
>
> A liability is recognised when actual emissions are greater than the granted allowances apportioned for the year. The liability is measured at the cost of purchased allowances up to the level of purchased allowances held, and then at the market price of allowances ruling at the statement of financial position date, with movements in the liability recognised in operating profit.
>
> Forward contracts for the purchase or sale of carbon allowances are measured at fair value with gains and losses arising from changes in fair value recognised in the consolidated statement of comprehensive income in the unrealised net gains or losses on derivative financial instruments and commodity contracts line. On delivery of forward contracts, carbon allowances are capitalised in intangible assets at cost, with any permanent reduction to bring the carrying value in line with market prices being presented within fuel costs. Carbon allowances have a sustainable value and can be used in settlement of the Group's EU ETS obligation at any time within the corresponding EU ETS Phase. As a result, carbon allowances are not amortised.

19.15 Intellectual capital disclosures (ICDs) in the annual report

The problem of valuing for financial reporting purposes has meant that investors need to look outside the annual report for information which tends to be predominately narrative. This is highlighted in an ICAEW Research Report[28] which comments:

> A wide range of media were used to report ICDs, with the annual report accounting for less than a third of total ICDs across all reporting media. Furthermore, the pattern of

ICDs in the annual report did not reflect the pattern of ICDs in other reports, so examination of ICDs in annual reports was not a good proxy for overall ICD practices in the sample studied . . . disclosures are overwhelmingly narrative. Previous studies have tended to indicate that monetary expression of IC elements in corporate reports is a relatively rare practice (see, for example, Beattie *et al.*, 2004).[29] This current study of UK ICR practices reinforces this observation.

The report also referred to the fact that preparers of reports did not see that the annual report was the appropriate place to be providing stakeholders with new information on intellectual capital – the annual report being seen as having a confirmatory role in relation to information that was already in the public domain.

It would seem that companies do not consider that their market value is undervalued by the omission of an 'intellectual property' asset provided they keep investors and analysts up-to-date with developments. A contrary approach could be taken by companies that see an economic value in valuing and reporting in acquisition situations, e.g. payment to acquire customer lists.

19.16 Review of implementation of IFRS 3

IFRS 3 *Business Combinations* was designed to give greater transparency to how companies account for acquisitions. However, studies in 2006 and 2008 indicated that IFRS 3 was not always being correctly applied by leading companies in the UK, the US and the 'Rest of the World' (ROW).

A report was issued in 2008, *An Analysis of the International Application of IFRS 3 Business Combinations*,[30] based on the study of annual reports of FT Global 500 companies which report under IFRS and are outside the UK. The study included companies in all European countries, Australia, Hong Kong, China, South Africa and Switzerland.

A previous study in 2006 had looked at the UK and US and found that the standards (IFRS 3 and SFAS 141) were not being adhered to fully, allocating too much to inadequately explained goodwill and not enough to identifiable intangible assets.

The following is an extract from the report:

	UK	US	ROW
Source of data	FTSE 100, 2006	S&P 100, 2001–2007, under SFAS 141	FT Global 500 that report under IFRS outside the UK
Amount spent on acquisitions	£40bn	£516bn	£226bn
Total allocation to tangible assets	17%	24%	21%
	£6bn	£126bn	£48bn
Total allocation to goodwill	53%	48%	47%
	£21bn	£245bn	£105bn
Total allocation to identifiable intangible assets	37%	35%	32%
Proportion of intangible value attributed to goodwill	63%	65%	68%

Companies reporting under IFRS are required to disclose the nature of the intangible assets comprising goodwill and explain why they cannot be valued separately. 53% of companies in the ROW (Rest of the World) failed to describe the acquired goodwill (totalling

£57 billion) at all, and a further 16% made only a limited attempt (for goodwill of £13 billion). Less than one-third made what we would consider to be a reasonable attempt to explain the nature of goodwill (worth £34 billion) to their shareholders.

The study commented that it was believed that the level of identifiable intangible assets as a proportion of the total, including goodwill, and taking account of the sector in which each company operates, was a good indicator of the adequacy of the valuation process. However, it was felt that while there were companies for whom this proportion seemed reasonable, the overall position in the ROW was too low with an average of only 32% of intangibles identified, leaving 68% in goodwill.

Findings by country were interesting as the spread was wide, ranging from 20% in Australia to 37% in the UK, with the average percentage described as goodwill ranging from 63% in the UK to 80% in Australia. While the average for Chinese companies is 35%, a quarter of them reported no identifiable intangibles at all, while the top quartile reported at least 61%.

For further interesting analysis see www.intangiblebusiness.com.

A certain amount of goodwill is, of course, inevitable. A premium will generally have to be paid to convince shareholders to sell their investment. While this premium by definition is more than the sum of the company's assets, it can still be identified. And one would hope that it already had been identified prior to the takeover approach or else how would the acquiring company know that it can make a return on its investment, thereby justifying the acquisition?

Prior to an acquisition, companies would generally identify likely benefits. This would generate a range within which the acquiring company must remain for the deal to make commercial sense. This could include a premium for value the buyer can bring. The premium could be justified by economies of scale, possible synergies such as reducing overheads like head office costs, or the portfolio effect.

Summary

Intangible assets have grown in importance with the rise of the new economy. This has been principally driven by information and knowledge. It has been identified by the Organisation for Economic Co-operation and Development (OECD) as explaining the increased prominence of intellectual capital as a business and research topic.[31]

Since the industrial revolution, the following chain of events is observable:[32]

(a) Capital and labour were brought together and the factors of production became localised and accessible.

(b) Firms pushed to increase volumes of production to meet the demands of growing markets.

(c) Firms began to build intangibles like brand equity and reputation (goodwill) in order to create a competitive advantage in markets where new entrants limited the profit-making potential of a strategy of mass production.

(d) Firms invested heavily in information technology to increase the quality of products and improve the speed with which those products could be brought to market.

(e) Firms invested heavily in human capital with staff development and customer loyalty creation.

At each stage of this corporate evolution non–current tangible assets became less important, in relative terms, compared with intangible assets in determining a company's success. Accounting and financial reporting practices, however, have remained largely unchanged. Expenditure on intellectual capital (except for development costs) is expensed, net assets are understated and book values of the assets bear little relationship to market values.

This makes it more important for stakeholders to refer to non–financial disclosures in the annual reports and elsewhere. As with all information, more detailed explanations about intellectual capital investment should see a fall in the cost of capital and encourage management to provide more as found in a research study.[33]

IAS 38 requires development costs to be recognised if they satisfy strict criteria. IFRS 3 requires purchased goodwill to be reviewed annually for impairment and not amortised.

REVIEW QUESTIONS

1 Why do standard setters consider it necessary to distinguish between research and development expenditure, and how does this distinction affect the accounting treatment?

2 Discuss the suggestion that the requirement for companies to write off research investment rather than showing it as an asset exposes companies to short-term pressure from acquisitive companies that are damaging to the country's interest.

3 Discuss why the market value of a business may increase to reflect the analysts' assessment of future growth but the asset(s) responsible for the growth may not appear in the statement of financial position.

4 The following is an extract from the 2010 WPP Annual Report:

Corporate brand names, customer relationships and proprietary tools acquired as part of acquisitions of businesses are capitalised separately from goodwill as intangible assets if their value can be measured reliably on initial recognition and it is probable that the expected future economic benefits that are attributable to the asset will flow to the Group.

Certain corporate brands of the Group are considered to have an indefinite economic life because of the institutional nature of the corporate brand names, their proven ability to maintain market leadership and profitable operations over long periods of time and the Group's commitment to develop and enhance their value. The carrying value of these intangible assets is reviewed at least annually for impairment and adjusted to the recoverable amount if required.

Amortisation is provided at rates calculated to write off the cost less estimated residual value of each asset on a straight-line basis over its estimated useful life as follows:

Acquired intangibles

- Brand names (with finite lives) – 10–20 years.
- Customer-related intangibles – 3–10 years.
- Other proprietary tools – 3–10 years.
- Other (including capitalised computer software) – 3–5 years.

Discuss why maintenance of a brand is treated differently in the statement of income from maintenance of a non-current tangible asset.

5 Discuss the advantages and disadvantages of the proposal that there should be a separate category of asset in the statement of financial position clearly identified as 'research investment – outcome uncertain'.

6 IFRS 3 has introduced a new concept into accounting for purchased goodwill – annual impairment testing, rather than amortisation. Consider the effect of a change from amortisation of goodwill (in IAS 22) to impairment testing and no amortisation in IFRS 3, and in particular:

- the effect on the financial statements;

- the effect on financial performance ratios;

- the effect on the annual impairment or amortisation charge and its timing;

- which method gives the fairest charge over time for the value of the goodwill when a business is acquired;

- whether impairment testing with no amortisation complies with the IASC's *Framework for the Preparation and Presentation of Financial Statements*;

- why there has been a change from amortisation to impairment testing – is this pandering to pressure from the US FASB and/or listed companies?

7 Discuss reasons for the undervaluing of intangibles and subsuming within goodwill.

8 One goodwill impairment indicator is the loss of key personnel. Discuss two further possible indicators.

9 There has been a requirement for companies to disaggregate the amount paid for goodwill into other intangible assets. This has led to the valuation of certain of the relational intellectual capital items such as customer lists. Recent research[34] indicates that there is a variety of structural, human and relational capital components which are considered by a representative cross-section of pre-parers to be significantly more important than others and these key components should be a focus for future research. The researchers raise the need to investigate whether a set of industry-specific standardised metrics can be developed and their disclosure regulated and recommend that IASB include the intangibles project on its active agenda.

Discuss the argument that potentially the future of the accounting profession and its role as the key reporting function could depend on addressing this issue effectively.

10 Critically evaluate the basis of the following assertion: 'I am sceptical that the impairment test will work reliably in practice, given the complexity and subjectivity that lie within the calculations'.[34]

EXERCISES

Question 1

IAS 38 *Intangible Assets* was issued primarily in order to identify the criteria that need to be present before expenditure on intangible items can be recognised as an asset. The standard also prescribes the subsequent accounting treatment of intangible assets that satisfy the recognition criteria and are recognised in the statement of financial position.

Required:
(a) Explain the criteria that need to be satisfied before expenditure on intangible items can be recognised in the statement of financial position as intangible assets.
(b) Explain how the criteria outlined in (a) are applied to the recognition of separately purchased intangible assets, intangible assets acquired in a business combination, and internally generated intangible assets. You should give an example of each category discussed.

(c) Explain the subsequent accounting treatment of intangible assets that satisfy the recognition criteria of IAS 38.

Iota prepares financial statements to 30 September each year. During the year ended 30 September 20X6 Iota (which has a number of subsidiaries) engaged in the following transactions:

1 On 1 April 20X6 Iota purchased all the equity capital of Kappa, and Kappa became a subsidiary from that date. Kappa sells a branded product that has a well-known name and the directors of Iota have obtained evidence that the fair value of this name is $20 million and that it has a useful economic life that is expected to be indefinite. The value of the brand name is not included in the statement of financial position of Kappa, as the directors of Kappa do not consider that it satisfies the recognition criteria of IAS 38 for internally developed intangible assets. However, the directors of Kappa have taken legal steps to ensure that no other entities can use the brand name.

2 On 1 October 20X4 Iota began a project that sought to develop a more efficient method of organising its production. Costs of $10 million were incurred in the year to 30 September 20X5 and debited to the statement of comprehensive income in that year. In the current year the results of the project were extremely encouraging and on 1 April 20X6 the directors of Iota were able to demonstrate that the project would generate substantial economic benefits for the group from 31 March 20X7 onwards as its technical feasibility and commercial viability were clearly evident. Throughout the year to 30 September 20X6 Iota spent $500,000 per month on the project.

Required:
(d) Explain how both of the above transactions should be recognised in the financial statements of Iota for the year ending 30 September 20X6. You should quantify the amounts recognised and make reference to relevant provisions of IAS 38 wherever possible.

Question 2

Environmental Engineering plc is engaged in the development of an environmentally friendly personal transport vehicle. This will run on an electric motor powered by solar cells, supplemented by passenger effort in the form of pedal assistance.

At the end of the current accounting period, the following costs have been attributed to the project:

(a) A grant of £500,000 to the Polytechnic of the South Coast Faculty of Solar Engineering to encourage research.

(b) Costs of £1,200,000 expended on the development of the necessary solar cells prior to the decision to incorporate them in a vehicle.

(c) Costs of £5,000,000 expended on designing the vehicle and its motors, and the planned promotional and advertising campaign for its launch on the market in 12 months' time.

Required:
(i)   Explain, with reasons, which of the above items could be considered for treatment as deferred development expenditure, quoting any relevant International Accounting Standard.
(ii) Set out the criteria under which any items can be so treated.
(iii) Advise on the accounting treatment that will be afforded to any such items after the product has been launched.

* Question 3

As chief accountant at Italin NV, you have been given the following information by the director of research:

Project Luca

	€000
Costs to date (pure research 25%, applied research 75%)	200
Costs to develop product (to be incurred in the year to 30 September 20X1)	300
Expected future sales per annum for 20X2–20X7	1,000

Fixed assets purchased in 20X1 for the project:

Cost	2,500
Estimated useful life	7 years
Residual value	400

(These assets will be disposed of at their residual value at the end of their estimated useful lives.)

The board of directors considers that this project is similar to the other projects that the company undertakes, and is confident of a successful outcome. The company has enough finances to complete the development and enough capacity to produce the new product.

Required:
(a) Prepare a report for the board outlining the principles involved in accounting for research and development and showing what accounting entries will be made in the company's accounts for each of the years ending 30 September 20X1–20X7 inclusive.
(b) Indicate what factors need to be taken into account when assessing each research and development project for accounting purposes, and what disclosure is needed for research and development in the company's published accounts.

* Question 4

Oxlag plc, a manufacturer of pharmaceutical products, has the following research and development projects on hand at 31 January 20X2:

(A) A general survey into the long-term effects of its sleeping pill Chalcedon upon human resistance to infections. At the year-end the research is still at a basic stage and no worthwhile results with any particular applications have been obtained.

(B) A development for Meebach NV in which the company will produce market research data relating to Meebach's range of drugs.

(C) An enhancement of an existing drug, Euboia, which will enable additional uses to be made of the drug and which will consequently boost sales. This project was completed successfully on 30 April 20X2, with the expectation that all future sales of the enhanced drug would greatly exceed the costs of the new development.

(D) A scientific enquiry with the aim of identifying new strains of antibiotics for future use. Several possible substances have been identified, but research is not sufficiently advanced to permit patents and copyrights to be obtained at the present time.

The following costs have been brought forward at 1 February 20X1:

Project	A £000	B £000	C £000	D £000
Specialised laboratory				
Cost	—	—	500	—
Depreciation	—	—	25	—
Specialised equipment				
Cost	—	—	75	50
Depreciation	—	—	15	10
Capitalised development costs	—	—	200	—
Market research costs	—	250	—	—

The following costs were incurred during the year:

Project	A £000	B £000	C £000	D £000
Research costs	25	—	265	78
Market research costs	—	75	—	—
Specialised equipment cost	50	—	—	50

Depreciation on specialised laboratories and special equipment is provided by the straight-line method and the assets have an estimated useful life of 25 and five years respectively. A full year's depreciation is provided on assets purchased during the year.

Required:

(a) Write up the research and development, fixed asset and market research accounts to reflect the above transactions in the year ended 31 January 20X2.

(b) Calculate the amount to be charged as research costs in the statement of comprehensive income of Oxlag plc for the year ended 31 January 20X2.

(c) State on what basis the company should amortise any capitalised development costs and what disclosures the company should make in respect of amounts written off in the year to 31 January 20X3.

(d) Calculate the amounts to be disclosed in the statement of financial position in respect of fixed assets, deferred development costs and work in progress.

(e) State what disclosures you would make in the accounts for the year ended 31 January 20X2 in respect of the new improved drug developed under project C, assuming sales begin on 1 May 20X2, and show strong growth to the date of signing the accounts, 14 July 20X2, with the expectation that the new drug will provide 25% of the company's pre-tax profits in the year to 31 January 20X3.

Question 5

Ross Neale is the divisional accountant for the Research and Development division of Critical Pharmaceuticals PLC. He is discussing the third-quarter results with Tina Snedden who is the manager of the division. The conversation focuses on the fact that whilst they have already fully committed the development capital expenditure budget for the year, the annual expense budget for research is well under-spent because of the staff shortages which occurred in the last quarter. Tina mentions that she is under pressure to meet or exceed her expense budgets this year as the industry is renegotiating prescription costs this year and doesn't want to be seen to be too profitable.

Ross suggests that there are several strategies they could employ, namely:

(a) Several of the subcontractors have us as their largest customer and so we could ask them to describe the services in the fourth quarter, which are essentially development cost, as research costs.

(b) We could ask them to charge us in advance for research work that will be required in the first quarter of next year without mentioning that it is an advance in documentation. That would be good for them as it would improve their cash flow and it would guarantee that they would get the work next year.

(c) We could ask some of the subcontractors on development projects to charge us in the first quarter of next year and we could hold out to them that we would give them some better-priced projects next year to compensate them for the interest incurred as a result of the delayed payment.

Required:
Discuss the advantages and disadvantages of adopting these strategies.

Question 6

The brands debate

Under IAS 22, the depletion of equity reserves caused by the accounting treatment for purchased goodwill resulted in some companies capitalising brands on their statements of financial position. This practice was started by Rank Hovis McDougall (RHM) – a company which has since been taken over. Martin Moorhouse, the group chief accountant at RHM, claimed that putting brands on the statement of financial position forced a company to look to their value as well as to profits. It served as a reminder to management of the value of the assets for which they were responsible and that at the end of the day those companies which were prepared to recognise brands on the statement of financial position could be better and stronger for it.[35]

There were many opponents to the capitalisation of brands. A London Business School research study found that brand accounting involves too many risks and uncertainties and too much subjective judgement. In short, the conclusion was that 'the present flexible position, far from being neutral, is potentially corrosive to the whole basis of financial reporting and that to allow brands – whether acquired or homegrown – to continue to be included in the statement of financial position would be highly unwise'.[23]

Required:
Consider the arguments for and against brand accounting. In particular, consider the issues of brand valuation; the separability of brands; purchased versus home-grown brands; and the maintenance/ substitution argument.

Question 7

Brands plc is preparing its accounts for the year ended 31 October 20X8 and the following information is available relating to various intangible assets acquired on the acquisition of Countrywide plc:

(a) A milk quota of 2,000,000 litres at 30p per litre. There is an active market trading in milk and other quotas.

(b) A government licence to experiment with the use of hormones to increase the cream content of milk had been granted to Countrywide shortly before the acquisition by Brands plc. No fee had been required. This is the first licence to be granted by the government and was one of the reasons why Brands acquired Countrywide. The licence is not transferable but the directors estimate that it has a value to the company based on discounted cash flows for a five-year period of £1 million.

(c) A full-cream yoghurt sold under the brand name 'Naughty but Nice' was valued by the directors at £2 million. Further enquiry established that a similar brand name had been recently sold for £1.5 million.

Required:

Explain how each of the above items would be treated in the consolidated financial statements using IAS 38.

Question 8

The following is the summarised balance sheet of Grimsel, a limited liability company, as at 31 October 2007.

ASSETS		$000
Non-current assets:		
Property, plant and equipment		7,540
Current assets:		
Inventory	2,230	
Receivables	4,120	
Cash	430	
		6,780
		14,320
LIABILITIES AND EQUITY		
Current liabilities		3,775
Non-current liabilities		12,500
Equity:		
Issued share capital	5,000	
Accumulated losses	6,955	
		(1,955)
		14,320

Grimsel has been a very successful company in its time. However, a series of losses due to a declining share in the market and demands from its bankers for repayment of significant bank debt included in current and non-current liabilities have left its shareholders keen to sell.

Brenner, another limited liability company, operates in the same line of business as Grimsel. Brenner has been very successful and sees an opportunity to acquire Grimsel at a bargain price.

Brenner has successfully concluded negotiations with Grimsel and has agreed a price of $2,000,000 for all the issued share capital of Grimsel.

The following additional information is available:

(i) The value of all the assets and liabilities identified in Grimsel's balance sheet were agreed as fair values for the purposes of the purchase with the exception of the following assets:

Fair values	$000
Property, plant and equipment	8,000
Inventory	2,000
Receivables	3,710

(ii) Grimsel has a deferred income tax asset of $2,200,000. This is not shown in Grimsel's balance sheet because it was unlikely that Grimsel would be able to recover this amount because of its continuing losses. Brenner is trading profitably in the same type of business and will be able to realise this benefit.

(iii) Grimsel has significant patents which were internally developed. These patents are still useful and an independent valuer has given them a fair value of $1,000,000.

(iv) Brenner will also take over Grimsel's customer list. This is a sensitive area. While the customer list was not of much value to Grimsel, the directors of Brenner feel that it could be of significant value but wish to continue keeping it off the balance sheet. An independent valuer has estimated the fair value of the customer list to Brenner as $1,500,000.

Required:
(a) Applying the rules in IFRS 3, calculate the amount of goodwill arising on the acquisition of Grimsel by Brenner.
(b) Summarise the guidance in IFRS 3 when goodwill turns out to be a negative.

(The Association of International Accountants)

Question 9

James Bright has just taken up the position of managing director following the unsatisfactory achievements of the previous incumbent. James arrives as the accounts for the previous year are being finalised. James wants the previous performance to look poor so that whatever he achieves will look good in comparison. He knows that if he can write off more expenses in the previous year, he will have lower expenses in his first year and possibly a lower asset base. He gives directions to the accountants to write off as many bad debts as possible and to make sure accruals can be as high as they can get past the auditors. Further, he wants all brand name assets reviewed using assumptions that the sales levels achieved during the economic downturn are only going to improve slightly over the foreseeable future. Also he mentions that the cost of capital has risen over the period of the financial crisis so the projected benefits are to be discounted at a higher rate, preferably at a much higher rate than that used in the previous reviews!

Required:
Discuss the accountant's professional responsibility and any ethical questions arising in this case.

* Question 10

International Accounting Standards IFRS 3 and IAS 38 address the accounting for goodwill and intangible assets.

Required:
(a) Describe the requirements of IFRS 3 regarding the initial recognition and measurement of goodwill and intangible assets.
(b) Explain the proposed approach set out by IFRS 3 for the treatment of positive goodwill in subsequent years.

(c) Territory plc acquired 80% of the ordinary share capital of Yukon Ltd on 31 May 20X6. The statement of financial position of Yukon Ltd at 31 May 20X6 was as follows:

	£000
Non-current assets	
Intangible assets	6,020
Tangible assets	38,300
	44,320
Current assets	
Inventory	21,600
Receivables	23,200
Cash	8,800
	53,600
Current liabilities	24,000
Net current assets	29,600
Total assets less current liabilities	73,920
Non-current liabilities	12,100
Provision for liabilities and charges	3,586
	58,234
Capital reserves	
Called-up share capital	10,000
(ordinary shares of £1)	
Share premium account	5,570
Retained earnings	42,664
	58,234

Additional information relating to the above statement of financial position:

(i) The intangible assets of Yukon Ltd were brand names currently utilised by the company. The directors felt that they were worth £7 million but there was no readily ascertainable market value at the statement of financial position date, nor any information to verify the directors' estimated value.

(ii) The provisional market value of the land and buildings was £20 million at 31 May 20X6. This valuation had again been determined by the directors. A valuers' report received on 30 November 20X6 stated the market value of land and buildings to be £23 million as at 31 May 20X6. The depreciated replacement cost of the remainder of the tangible fixed assets was £18 million at 31 May 20X6.

(iii) The replacement cost of inventories was estimated at £25 million and its net realisable value was deemed to be £20 million. Trade receivables and trade payables due within one year are stated at the amounts expected to be received and paid.

(iv) The non-current liability was a long-term loan with a bank. The initial loan on 1 June 20X5 was for £11 million at a fixed interest rate of 10% per annum. The total amount of the interest is to be paid at the end of the loan period on 31 May 20X9. The current bank lending rate is 7% per annum.

(v) The provision for liabilities and charges relates to costs of reorganisation of Yukon Ltd. This provision had been set up by the directors of Yukon Ltd prior to the offer by Territory plc and the reorganisation would have taken place even if Territory plc had not purchased the shares of Yukon Ltd. Additionally Territory plc wishes to set up a provision for future losses of £10 million which it feels will be incurred by rationalising the group.

(vi) The offer made to all of the shareholders of Yukon Ltd was 2.5 £1 ordinary shares of Territory plc at the market price of £2.25 per share plus £1 cash, per Yukon Ltd ordinary share.

(vii) The directors of Yukon Ltd informed Territory plc that as at 31 May 20X7, the brand names were worthless as the products to which they related had recently been withdrawn from sale because they were deemed to be a health hazard.

(viii) In view of the adverse events since acquisition, the directors of Territory plc have impairment-tested the goodwill relating to Yukon Ltd, and they estimate its current value is £1 million.

Calculate the charge for impairment of goodwill in the Group Statement of Comprehensive Income of Territory plc for the accounting period ending on 31 May 20X7.

References

1 IAS 38 *Intangible Assets*, IASC, revised March 2004.
2 IFRS 3 *Business Combinations*, IASB, revised 2008.
3 IAS 38 *Intangible Assets*, IASC, revised March 2004, para. 118.
4 *Ibid.*, para. 126.
5 *Ibid.*, para. 122.
6 *Ibid.*, para. 54.
7 *Ibid.*, para. 56.
8 *Ibid.*, para. 55.
9 *Ibid.*, para. 58.
10 *Ibid.*, para. 59.
11 B. Nixon and A. Lonie, 'Accounting for R&D: the need for change', *Accountancy*, February 1990, p. 91; B. Nixon, 'R&D disclosure: SSAP 13 and after', *Accountancy*, February 1991, pp. 72–73.
12 http://www.rdmag.com/Featured-Articles/2011/12/2012-Global-RD-Funding-Forecast-RD-Spending-Growth-Continues-While-Globalization-Accelerates/
13 IASC, *Framework for the Preparation and Presentation of Financial Statements*, IASB, April 2001, para. 49.
14 A. Goodacre and J. McGrath, 'An experimental study of analysts' reactions to corporate R&D expenditure', *British Accounting Review*, vol. 29, 1997, pp. 155–179.
15 B. Nixon, 'The accounting treatment of research and development expenditure: views of UK company accountants', *European Accounting Review*, vol. 6(2), 1997, pp. 265–277.
16 Li Li Eng, Hong Kiat Teo, 'The relation between annual report disclosures, analysts' earnings forecast and analysts following: evidence from Singapore', *Pacific Accounting Review*, vol. 121(1/2), 1999, pp. 21–239.
17 IAS 38 *Intangible Assets*, IASC, revised March 2004, para. 57.
18 IFRS 3 *Business Combinations*, IASB, 2004, para. 51.
19 http://www.intangiblebusiness.com/Reports/International-IFRS-3~1175.html
20 IAS 38 *Intangible Assets*, IASC, revised March 2004, para. 119.
21 IASC, *Framework for the Preparation and Presentation of Financial Statements*, IASB, April 2001, para. 94.
22 www.interbrand.com/best_global_brands.aspx
23 P. Barwise, C. Higson, A. Likierman and P. Marsh, *Accounting for Brands*, ICAEW, June 1989; M. Cooper and A. Carey, 'Brand valuation in the balance', *Accountancy*, June 1989.
24 http://group.hugoboss.com/en/faq_special_dividend.htm
25 M. Gerry, 'Companies ignore value of brands', *Accountancy Age*, March 2000, p. 4.
26 IAS 38 *Intangible Assets*, IASC, revised March 2004, para. 63.
27 www.ivsc.org
28 J. Unerman, J. Guthrie and M. Striukova, *UK Reporting of Intellectual Capital*, ICAEW, 2007, www.icaew.co.uk

29 V. Beattie and S.J. Thompson, *Intellectual Capital Reporting: Academic Utopia or Corporate Reality in a Brave New World?*, 2010, www.icas.org.uk

30 http://www.intangiblebusiness.com/store/data/files/437-International_IFRS_3.pdf

31 OECD, *Final Report: Measuring and Reporting Intellectual Capital: Experience, Issues and Prospects*, Paris: OECD, 2000.

32 J. Guthrie and R. Petty, 'Knowledge management: the information revolution has created the need for a codified system of gathering and controlling knowledge', *Company Secretary*, vol. 9(1), January 1999, pp. 38–41; R. Tissen *et al.*, *Value-Based Knowledge Management*, Longman Nederland BV, 1998, pp. 25–44.

33 M. Mangena, R. Pike and J. Li, *Intellectual Capital Disclosure Practices and Effects on the Cost of Equity Capital: UK Evidence*, ICAS, 2010.

34 V. Beattie and S.J. Thomson, *Intellectual Capital Reporting: Academic Utopia or Corporate Reality in a Brave New World?*, ICAS, 2010, http://www.icas.org.uk/site/cms/contentviewarticle.asp?article=6837

35 M. Moorhouse, 'Brands debate: wake up to the real world', *Accountancy*, July 1990, p. 30.

CHAPTER 20

Inventories

The main purpose of this chapter is to explain the accounting principles involved in the valuation of inventory and biological assets.

Objectives

By the end of this chapter, you should be able to:

- define inventory in accordance with IAS 2;
- explain why valuation has been controversial;
- describe acceptable valuation methods;
- describe procedure for ascertaining cost;
- calculate inventory value;
- explain how inventory could be used for creative accounting;
- explain IAS 41 provisions relating to agricultural activity;
- calculate biological value.

IAS 2 *Inventories* defines inventories as assets:

(a) held for sale in the ordinary course of business;

(b) in the process of production for such sale;

(c) in the form of materials or supplies to be consumed in the production process or in the rendering of services.[1]

The valuation of inventory involves:

(a) the establishment of physical existence and ownership;

(b) the determination of unit costs;

(c) the calculation of provisions to reduce cost to net realisable value, if necessary.[2]

The resulting evaluation is then disclosed in the financial statements.

These definitions appear to be very precise. We shall see, however, that although IAS 2 was introduced to bring some uniformity into financial statements, there are many areas where professional judgement must be exercised. Sometimes this may distort the financial statements to such an extent that we must question whether they do represent a 'true and fair' view.

20.3 The controversy

The valuation of inventory has been a controversial issue in accounting for many years. The inventory value is a crucial element not only in the computation of profit, but also in the valuation of assets for statement of financial position purposes.

Figure 20.1 presents information relating to Nissan Motor Co. Ltd. It shows that the inventory is material in relation to pre-tax profits. In relation to the profits we can see that an error of 5% in the 2010 inventory values would potentially cause the pre-tax profit to fall by 28%. As inventory is usually a multiple rather than a fraction of profit, inventory errors may have a disproportionate effect on the accounts. Valuation of inventory is therefore crucial in determining earnings per share, net asset backing for shares and the current ratio. Consequently, the basis of valuation should be consistent, so as to avoid manipulation of profits between accounting periods, and comply with generally accepted accounting principles, so that profits are comparable between different companies.

Unfortunately, there are many examples of manipulation of inventory values in order to create a more favourable impression. By increasing the value of inventory at the year-end, profit and current assets are automatically increased (and vice versa). Of course, closing inventory of one year becomes opening inventory of the next, so profit is thereby reduced. Such manipulation provides opportunities for profit-smoothing.

Figure 20.2 illustrates the point. Simply by increasing the value of inventory in year 1 by £10,000, profit (and current assets) is increased by a similar amount. Even if the two values are identical in year 2, such manipulation allows profit to be 'smoothed' and £10,000 profit switched from year 2 to year 1.

According to normal accrual accounting principles, profit is determined by matching costs with related revenues. If it is unlikely that the revenue will in fact be received, prudence dictates that the irrecoverable amount should be written off immediately against current revenue.

It follows that inventory should be valued at cost less any irrecoverable amount. But what is cost? Entities have used a variety of methods of determining costs, and these are explored later in the chapter. There have been a number of disputes relating to the valuation of inventory which affected profits (e.g. the AEI/GEC merger of 1967).[3] Such circumstances tend to come to light with a change of management, but it was considered important that a definitive statement of accounting practice be issued in an attempt to standardise treatment.

Figure 20.1 Nissan Motor Co. Ltd

	2010	Inventory reduced by 5%	% change
Pre-tax profits (million yen)	141,680	101,566	28%
Inventories	802,278	762,164	5%

Figure 20.2 Inventory values manipulated to smooth income

	Year 1		Year 1 With inventory inflated
Sales		100,000	100,000
Opening inventory	—		—
Purchases	65,000		65,000
Less: Closing inventory	5,000		15,000
COST OF SALES		60,000	50,000
PROFIT		40,000	50,000

	Year 2		Year 2 With inventory inflated
Sales		150,000	150,000
Opening inventory	5,000		15,000
Purchases	100,000		100,000
	105,000		115,000
Less: Closing inventory	15,000		15,000
COST OF SALES		90,000	100,000
PROFIT		60,000	50,000

20.4 IAS 2 *Inventories*

No area of accounting has produced wider differences in practice than the computation of the amount at which inventory is stated in financial accounts. An accounting standard on the subject needs to define the practices, to narrow the differences and variations in those practices and to ensure adequate disclosure in the accounts.

IAS 2 requires that the amount at which inventory is stated in periodic financial statements should be the total of the lower of cost and net realisable value of the separate items of inventory or of groups of similar items. The standard also emphasises the need to match costs against revenue, and it aims, like other standards, to achieve greater uniformity in the measurement of income as well as improving the disclosure of inventory valuation methods. To an extent, IAS 2 relies on management to choose the most appropriate method of inventory valuation for the production processes used and the company's environment. Various methods of valuation are theoretically available, including FIFO, LIFO and weighted average or any similar method (see below). In selecting the most suitable method, management must exercise judgement to ensure that the methods chosen provide the fairest practical approximation to cost. IAS 2 does not allow the use of LIFO because it often results in inventory being stated in the statement of financial position at amounts that bear little relation to recent cost levels.

At the end of the day, even though there is an International Accounting Standard in existence, the valuation of inventory can provide areas of subjectivity and choice to management. We will return to this theme many times in the following sections of this chapter.

20.5 Inventory valuation

The valuation rule outlined in IAS 2 is difficult to apply because of uncertainties about what is meant by cost (with some methods approved by IAS 2 and others not) and what is meant by net realisable value.

20.5.1 Methods acceptable under IAS 2

The acceptable methods of inventory valuation include FIFO, AVCO and standard cost.

First-in-first-out (FIFO)

Inventory is valued at the most recent 'cost', since the cost of oldest inventory is charged out first, whether or not this accords with the actual physical flow. FIFO is illustrated in Figure 20.3.

Average cost (AVCO)

Inventory is valued at a 'weighted average cost', i.e. the unit cost is weighted by the number of items carried at each 'cost', as shown in Figure 20.4. This is popular in organisations holding a large volume of inventory at fluctuating 'costs'. The practical problem of actually

Figure 20.3 First-in-first-out method (FIFO)

Date	Receipts Quantity	Rate	£	Issues Quantity	Rate	£	Balance Quantity	Rate	£
January	10	15	150				10		150
February				8	15	120	2		30
March	10	17	170				12		200
April	20	20	400				32		600
May				2	15	30			
				10	17	170			
				12	20	240			
				Cost of goods sold		560			
				Inventory			8	20	160

Figure 20.4 Average cost method (AVCO)

Date	Receipts Quantity	Rate	£	Issues Quantity	Rate	£	Balance Quantity	Rate	£
January	10	15	150				10		150
February				8	15	120	2		30
March	10	17	170				12		200
April	20	20	400				32		600
May				24	18.75	450			600
				Cost of goods sold		570			
				Inventory			8	18.75	150

recording and calculating the weighted average cost has been overcome by the use of sophisticated computer software.

The following is an extract from the J Sainsbury plc 2011 Annual Report:

Inventories
Inventories are valued on a weighted average cost basis and carried at the lower of cost and net realisable value. Cost includes all direct expenditure and other appropriate attributable costs incurred in bringing inventories to their present location and condition.

Standard cost

In many cases this is the only way to value manufactured goods in a high-volume/high-turnover environment. However, the standard is acceptable only if it approximates to actual cost. This means that variances need to be reviewed to see if they affect the standard cost and for inventory evaluation.

Retail method

IAS 2 recognises that an acceptable method of arriving at cost is the use of selling price, less an estimated profit margin. This method is only acceptable if it can be demonstrated that it gives a reasonable approximation of the actual cost.

IAS 2 does not recommend any specific method. This is a decision for each organisation based upon sound professional advice and the organisation's unique operating conditions.

20.5.2 Methods rejected by IAS 2

Methods rejected by IAS 2 include LIFO and (by implication) replacement cost.

Last-in-first-out (LIFO)

The cost of the inventory most recently received is charged out first at the most recent 'cost'. The practical upshot is that the inventory value is based upon an 'old cost', which may bear little relationship to the current 'cost'. LIFO is illustrated in Figure 20.5.

Figure 20.5 Last-in-first-out method (LIFO)

Date	Receipts Quantity	Rate	£	Issues Quantity	Rate	£	Balance Quantity	Rate	£
January	10	15	150				10		150
February				8	15	120	2		30
March	10	17	170				12		200
April	20	20	400				32		600
May				20	20	400			
				4	17	68			
				Cost of goods sold		588			
				Inventory			8		132

May closing balance = $[(2 \times 15) + (6 \times 17)]$

US companies commonly use the LIFO method as illustrated by this extract from the Wal-Mart Stores, Inc. 2012 Annual Report:

Inventories

The Company values inventories at the lower of cost or market as determined primarily by the retail method of accounting, using the last-in, first-out ('LIFO') method for substantially all of the Wal-Mart Stores segment's merchandise inventories. . . . Inventories of foreign operations are primarily valued by the retail method of accounting, using the first-in, first-out ('FIFO') method. At January 31, 2012 and 2011, our inventories valued at LIFO approximate those inventories as if they were valued at FIFO.

Replacement cost

The inventory is valued at the current cost of the individual item (i.e. the cost to the organisation of replacing the item) rather than the actual cost at the time of manufacture or purchase. This is an attractive idea since the 'value' of inventory could be seen as the cost at which a similar item could be currently acquired. The problem again is in arriving at a 'reliable' profit figure for the purposes of performance evaluation. Wild fluctuation of profit could occur simply because of such factors as the time of the year, the vagaries of the world weather system, the manipulation of market forces and political unrest as evidenced by the movements in oil prices.

The use of replacement cost is not specifically prohibited by IAS 2 but is out of line with the basic principle underpinning the standard, which is to value inventory at the actual costs incurred in its purchase or production. The IASC *Framework for the Preparation and Presentation of Financial Statements* describes historical cost and current cost as two distinct measurement bases, and where a historical cost measurement base is used for assets and liabilities the use of replacement cost is inconsistent.

Although LIFO does not have IAS 2 approval, it is still used in practice. For example, LIFO is commonly used by UK companies with US subsidiaries, since LIFO is the main method of inventory valuation in the USA.

20.5.3 Procedure to ascertain cost

Having decided upon the accounting policy of the company, there remains the problem of ascertaining the cost. In a retail environment, the 'cost' is the price the organisation had to pay to acquire the goods, and it is readily established by reference to the purchase invoice from the supplier. However, in a manufacturing organisation the concept of cost is not as simple. Should we use prime cost, or production cost, or total cost? IAS 2 attempts to help by defining cost as 'all costs of purchase, costs of conversion and other costs incurred in bringing the inventories to their present location and condition'.

In a manufacturing organisation each expenditure is taken to include three constituents: direct materials, direct labour and appropriate overhead.

Direct materials

These include not only the costs of raw materials and component parts, but also the costs of insurance, handling (special packaging) and any import duties. An additional problem is waste and scrap. For instance, if a process inputs 100 tonnes at £45 per tonne, yet outputs only 90 tonnes, the output's inventory value **must** be £4,500 (£45 × 100) and not £4,050 (90 × £45). (This assumes the 10 tonnes loss is a normal, regular part of the process.) An adjustment may be made for the residual value of the scrap/waste material, if any.

The treatment of component parts will be the same, provided they form part of the finished product.

Direct labour

This is the cost of the actual production in the form of gross pay and those incidental costs of employing the direct workers (employer's national insurance contributions, additional pension contributions, etc.). The labour costs will be spread over the goods' production.

Appropriate overhead

It is here that the major difficulties arise in calculating the true cost of the product for inventory valuation purposes. Normal practice is to classify overheads into five types and decide whether to include them in inventory. The five types are as follows:

- Direct overheads – subcontract work, royalties.
- Indirect overheads – the cost of running the factory and supporting the direct workers, and the depreciation of capital items used in production.
- Administration overheads – the office costs and salaries of senior management.
- Selling and distribution overheads – advertising, delivery costs, packaging, salaries of sales personnel, and depreciation of capital items used in the sales function.
- Finance overheads – the cost of borrowing and servicing debt.

We will look at each of these in turn, to demonstrate the difficulties that the accountant experiences.

Regular, routine direct overhead will be included in the inventory valuation, but a non-routine cost could present difficulties, especially in a high-volume/high-turnover organ-isation. Special subcontract work would form part of the inventory value where it is readily identifiable to individual units of inventory such as in a customised car manufacturer making 20 cars a month.

Indirect overheads. These always form part of the inventory valuation, as such expenses are incurred in support of production. They include factory rent and rates, factory power and depreciation of plant and machinery; in fact, any indirect factory-related cost, including the warehouse costs of storing completed goods, will be included in the value of inventory.

Administration overheads. This overhead is in respect of the whole business, so only that portion easily identifiable to production should form part of the inventory valuation. For instance, the costs of the personnel or wages department could be apportioned to produc-tion on a head-count basis and that element would be included in the inventory valuation. Any production-specific administration costs (welfare costs, canteen costs, etc.) would also be included in the inventory valuation. If the expense cannot be identified as forming part of the production function, it will not form part of the inventory valuation.

Selling and distribution overheads. These costs will not normally be included in the inventory valuation as they are incurred after production has taken place. However, if the goods are on a 'sale or return' basis and are on the premises of the customer but remain the supplier's property, the delivery and packing costs will be included in the inventory value of goods held on a customer's premises.

An additional difficulty concerns the modern inventory technique of 'just-in-time' (JIT). Here, the customer does not keep large inventories, but simply 'calls off' inventory from the supplier and is invoiced for the items delivered. There is an argument for the inventory still in the hands of the supplier to bear more of this overhead within its valuation, since the only selling and distribution overhead to be charged/incurred is delivery. The goods have in fact been sold, but ownership has not yet changed hands. As JIT becomes more popular, this problem may give accountants and auditors much scope for debate.

Finance overheads. Normally these overheads would never be included within the inventory valuation because they are not normally identifiable with production. In a job-costing context, however, it might be possible to use some of this overhead in inventory valuation. Let us take the case of an engineering firm being requested to produce a turbine engine, which requires parts/components to be imported. It is logical for the financial charges for these imports (e.g. exchange fees or fees for letters of credit) to be included in the inventory valuation.

Thus it can be seen that the identification of the overheads to be included in inventory valuation is far from straightforward. In many cases it depends upon the judgement of the accountant and the unique operating conditions of the organisation.

In addition to the problem of deciding **whether** the five types of overhead should be included, there is the problem of deciding **how much** of the total overhead to include in the inventory valuation at the year-end. IAS 2 stipulates the use of 'normal activity' when making this decision on overheads. The vast majority of overheads are 'fixed', i.e. do not vary with activity, and it is customary to share these out over a normal or expected output.

The following is an extract from the Agrana Group 2011/12 Annual Report:

Inventories

Inventories are measured at the lower of cost of purchase and/or conversion and net selling price. The weighted average formula is used. In accordance with IAS 2, the conversion costs of unfinished and finished products include – in addition to directly attributable unit costs – reasonable proportions of the necessary material costs and production overheads inclusive of depreciation of manufacturing plant (*based on the assumption of normal capacity utilisation*) *as well as production-related administrative costs* [our italics]. Financing costs are not taken into account. To the extent that inventories are at risk because of prolonged storage or reduced saleability, a write-down is recognised. If this expected output [based on normal capacity utilisation] is not reached, it is not acceptable to allow the actual production to bear the full overhead for inventory purposes.

A numerical example will illustrate this:

Overhead for the year	£200,000	
Planned activity	10,000 units	
Closing inventory	3,000 units	
Direct costs	£2 per unit	
Actual activity	6,000 units	

Inventory value based on actual activity

Direct costs	$3,000 \times £2$	£6,000
Overhead	$\dfrac{3,000 \times £200,000}{6,000}$	£100,000
Closing inventory value		£106,000

Inventory value based on planned or normal activity

Direct cost	$3,000 \times £2$	£6,000
Overhead	$\dfrac{3,000 \times £200,000}{10,000}$	£60,000
Closing inventory value		£66,000

Comparing the value of inventory based upon actual activity with the value based upon planned or normal activity, we have a £40,000 difference. This could be regarded as increasing the current year's profit by carrying forward expenditure of £40,000 to set against the following year's profit.

The problem occurs because of the organisation's failure to meet expected output level (6,000 actual versus 10,000 planned). By adopting the **actual activity basis**, the organisation makes a profit out of failure. This cannot be an acceptable position when evaluating performance. Therefore, IAS 2 stipulates **the planned or normal activity model** for inventory valuation. The failure to meet planned output could be due to a variety of sources (e.g. strikes, poor weather, industrial conditions); the cause, however, is classed as abnormal or non-routine, and all such costs should be excluded from the valuation of inventory.

20.5.4 What is meant by net realisable value?

We have attempted to identify the problems of arriving at the true meaning of cost for the purpose of inventory valuation. Net realisable value is an alternative method of inventory valuation if 'cost' does not reflect the true value of the inventory. Prudence dictates that net realisable value will be used if it is lower than the 'cost' of the inventory (however that may be calculated). These occasions will vary among organisations, but can be summarised as follows:

- There is a permanent fall in the market price of inventory. Short-term fluctuations should not cause net realisable value to be implemented.
- The organisation is attempting to dispose of high inventory levels or excessively priced inventory to improve its liquidity position (quick ratio/acid test ratio) or reduce its inventory holding costs. Such high inventory volumes or values are primarily a result of poor management decision making.
- The inventory is physically deteriorating or is of an age where the market is reluctant to accept it. This is a common feature of the food industry, especially with the use of 'sell by' dates in the retail environment.
- Inventory suffers obsolescence through some unplanned development. (Good management should never be surprised by obsolescence.) This development could be technical in nature, or due to the development of different marketing concepts within the organisation or a change in market needs.
- The management could decide to sell the goods at 'below cost' for sound marketing reasons. The concept of a 'loss leader' is well known in supermarkets, but organisations also sell below cost when trying to penetrate a new market or as a defence mechanism when attacked.

Such decisions are important and the change to net realisable value should not be undertaken without considerable forethought and planning. Obsolescence should be a decision based upon sound market intelligence and not a managerial 'whim'. The auditors of companies always examine such decisions to ensure they were made for sound business reasons. The opportunities for fraud in such 'price-cutting' operations validate this level of external control.

Realisable value is, of course, the price the organisation receives for its inventory from the market. However, getting this inventory to market may involve additional expense and effort in repackaging, advertising, delivery and even repairing of damaged inventory. This additional cost must be deducted from the realisable value to arrive at the net realisable value.

For example, goods costing £1,000 had been flood damaged and were not covered by insurance. It was estimated that if £200 were spent on cleaning the goods could be sold for £550 giving a NRV for inventory of £350.

A numerical example will demonstrate this concept:

Item	Cost (£)	Net realisable value (£)	Inventory value (£)
1 No. 876	7,000	9,000	7,000
2 No. 997	12,000	12,500	12,000
3 No. 1822	8,000	4,000	4,000
4 No. 2076	14,000	8,000	8,000
5 No. 4732	27,000	33,000	27,000
	(a) 68,000	(b) 66,500	(c) 58,000

The inventory value chosen for the accounts is (c) £58,000, although each item is assessed individually.

20.6 Work in progress

Inventory classified as work in progress (WIP) is mainly found in manufacturing organisations and is simply the production that has not been completed by the end of the accounting period.

The valuation of WIP must follow the same IAS 2 rules and be the lower of cost or net realisable value. We again face the difficulty of deciding what to include in cost. The three basic classes of cost – direct materials, direct labour and appropriate overhead – will still form the basis of ascertaining cost.

20.6.1 Direct materials

It is necessary to decide what proportion of the total materials have been used in WIP. The proportion will vary with different types of organisation, as the following two examples illustrate:

● If the item is complex or materially significant (e.g. a custom-made car or a piece of specialised machinery), the WIP calculation will be based on actual recorded materials and components used to date.

● If, however, we are dealing with mass production, it may not be possible to identify each individual item within WIP. In such cases, the accountant will make a judgement and define the WIP as being $x\%$ complete in regard to raw materials and components. For example, a drill manufacturer with 1 million tools per week in WIP may decide that in respect of raw materials they are 100% complete; WIP then gets the full materials cost of one million tools.

In both cases **consistency** is vital so that, however WIP is valued, the same method will always be used.

20.6.2 Direct labour

Again, it is necessary to decide how much direct labour the items in WIP have actually used. As with direct materials, there are two broad approaches:

● Where the item of WIP is complex or materially significant, the actual time 'booked' or recorded will form part of the WIP valuation.

- In a mass production situation, such precision may not be possible and an accounting judgement may have to be made as to the average percentage completion in respect of direct labour. In the example of the drill manufacturer, it could be that, on average, WIP is 80% complete in respect of direct labour.

20.6.3 Appropriate overhead

The same two approaches as for direct labour can be adopted:

- With a complex or materially significant item, it should be possible to allocate the overhead actually incurred. This could be an actual charge (e.g. subcontract work) or an application of the appropriate overhead recovery rate (ORR). For example, if we use a direct labour hour recovery rate and we have an ORR of £10 per direct labour hour and the recorded labour time on the WIP item is 12 hours, then the overhead charge for WIP purposes is £120.

EXAMPLE ● A custom-car company making sports cars has the following costs in respect of No. 821/C, an unfinished car, at the end of the month:

Materials charged to job 821/C	£2,100
Labour 120 hours @ £4	£480
Overhead £22/DLH × 120 hours	£2,640
WIP value of 821/C	£5,220

This is an accurate WIP value provided *all* the costs have been accurately recorded and charged. The amount of accounting work involved is not great as the information is required by a normal job cost system. An added advantage is that the figure can be formally audited and proven.

- With mass production items, the accountant must either use a budgeted overhead recovery rate approach or simply decide that, in respect of overheads, WIP is y% complete.

EXAMPLE ● A company produces drills. The costs of a completed drill are:

	£	
Direct materials	2.00	
Direct labour	6.00	
Appropriate overhead	10.00	
Total cost	18.00	(for finished goods inventory value purposes)

Assuming that the company accountant takes the view that for WIP purposes the following applies:

Direct material	100% complete
Direct labour	80% complete
Appropriate overhead	30% complete

then, for one WIP drill:

Direct material	£2.00 × 100% = £2.00
Direct labour	£6.00 × 80% = £4.80
Appropriate overhead	£10.00 × 30% = £3.00
WIP value	£9.80

If the company has 100,000 drills in WIP, the value is:

100,000 × £9.80 = £980,000

This is a very simplistic view, but the principle can be adapted to cover more complex issues. For instance, there could be 200 different types of drill, but the same calculation can be done on each. Of course, sophisticated software makes the accountant's job mechanically easier.

This technique is particularly useful in processing industries, such as petroleum, brewing, dairy products or paint manufacture, where it might be impossible to identify WIP items precisely. The approach must be consistent and the role of the auditor in validating such practices is paramount.

20.7 Inventory control

The way in which inventory is physically controlled should not be overlooked. Discrepancies are generally of two types: disappearance through theft and improper accounting.[4,5] Management will, of course, be responsible for adequate systems of internal control, but losses may still occur through theft or lack of proper controls and recording. Inadequate systems of accounting may also cause discrepancies between the physical and book inventories, with consequent correcting adjustments at the year-end.

Many companies are developing in-house computer systems or using bought-in packages to account for their inventories. Such systems are generally adequate for normal recording purposes, but they are still vulnerable to year-end discrepancies arising from errors in establishing the physical inventory on hand at the year-end, and problems connected with the paperwork and the physical movement of inventories.

A major cause of discrepancy between physical and book inventory is the 'cut-off' date. In matching sales with cost of sales, it may be difficult to identify exactly into which period of account certain inventory movements should be placed, especially when the annual inventory count lasts many days or occurs at a date other than the last day of the financial year. It is customary to make an adjustment to the inventory figure, as shown in Figure 20.6. This depends on an accurate record of movements between the inventory count date and the financial year-end.

Auditors have a special responsibility in relation to inventory control. They should look carefully at the inventory counting procedures and satisfy themselves that the accounting arrangements are satisfactory. For example, in September 1987 Harris Queensway announced an inventory reduction of some £15 million in projected profit caused by write-downs in its furniture division. It blamed this on the inadequacy of control systems to 'identify ranges that were selling and ensure their replacement'. Interestingly, at the preceding AGM, no hint of the overvaluation was given and the auditors insisted that 'the company had no problem from the accounting point of view'.[6]

In many cases the auditor will be present at the inventory count. Even with this apparent safeguard, however, it is widely accepted that sometimes an accurate physical inventory take

Figure 20.6 Adjusted inventory figure

	£
Inventory on 7 January 20X1	XXX
Less: Purchases	(XXX)
Add: Cost of sales	XXX
Inventory at 31 December 20X0	XXX

is almost impossible. The value of inventory should nevertheless be based on the best information available; and the resulting disclosed figure should be acceptable and provide a true and fair view on a going concern basis.

In practice, errors may continue unidentified for a number of years,[7] particularly if there is a paper-based system in operation. This was evident when T.J. Hughes reduced its profit for the year ended 31 January 2001 by £2.5–3 million from a forecast £8 million when stock discrepancies came to light following the implementation of a new stock management system.

20.8 Creative accounting

No area of accounting provides more opportunities for subjectivity and creative accounting than the valuation of inventory. This is illustrated by the report *Fraudulent Financial Reporting: 1987–1997 – An Analysis of U.S. Public Companies* prepared by the Committee of Sponsoring Organizations of the Treadway Commission.[8] This report, which was based on the detailed analysis of approximately 200 cases of fraudulent financial reporting, identified that the fraud often involved the overstatement of revenues and assets with inventory fraud featuring frequently – assets were overstated by understating allowances for receivables, overstating the value of inventory and other tangible assets, and recording assets that did not exist.

This section summarises some of the major methods employed.

20.8.1 Year-end manipulations

There are a number of stratagems companies have followed to reduce the cost of goods sold by inflating the inventory figure. These include the following.

Manipulating cut-off procedures

Goods are taken into inventory but the purchase invoices are not recorded.

The authors of *Fraudulent Financial Reporting: 1987–1997 – An Analysis of U.S. Public Companies* found that over half the frauds involved overstating revenues by recording revenues prematurely or fictitiously and that such overstatement tended to occur right at the end of the year – hence the need for adequate cut-off procedures. This was illustrated by Ahold's experience in the USA where subsidiary companies took credit for bulk discounts allowed by suppliers before inventory was actually received.

Fictitious transfers to overseas locations

Year-end inventory is inflated by recording fictitious transfers of non-existent inventory, e.g. it was alleged by the SEC that certain officers of the Miniscribe Corporation had increased the company's inventory by recording fictitious transfers of non-existent inventory from a Colorado location to overseas locations where physical inventory counting would be more difficult for the auditors to verify or the goods are described as being 'in transit'.[9]

Inaccurate inventory records

Where inventory records are poorly maintained it has been possible for senior management to fail to record material shrinkage due to loss and theft as in the matter of Rite Aid Corporation.[10]

Journal adjustments

In addition to suppressing purchase invoices, making fictitious transfers and failing to write off obsolete inventory or recognise inventory losses, the senior management may simply reduce the cost of goods sold by adjusting journal entries. Auditors pay particular attention to journal adjustments, questioning whether there have been significant adjusting entries that have increased the inventory balance and whether there have been material reversing entries made to the inventory account after the close of an accounting period.

20.8.2 Net realisable value (NRV)

Although the determination of net realisable value is dealt with extensively in the appendix to IAS 2, the extent to which provisions can be made to reduce cost to NRV is highly subjective and open to manipulation. A provision is an effective smoothing device and allows overcautious write-downs to be made in profitable years and consequent write-backs in unprofitable ones.

20.8.3 Overheads

The treatment of overheads has been dealt with extensively above and is probably the area that gives the greatest scope for manipulation. Including overhead in the inventory valuation has the effect of deferring the overhead's impact and so boosting profits. IAS 2 allows expenses incidental to the acquisition or production cost of an asset to be included in its cost. We have seen that this includes not only directly attributable production overheads, but also those which are indirectly attributable to production and interest on borrowed capital. IAS 2 provides guidelines on the classification of overheads to achieve an appropriate allocation, but in practice it is difficult to make these distinctions and auditors may find it difficult to challenge management on such matters.

The statement suggests that the allocation of overheads included in the valuation needs to be based on the company's normal level of activity. The cost of unused capacity should be written off in the current year. The auditor will insist that allocation should be based on normal activity levels, because if the company underproduces, the overhead per unit increases and can therefore lead to higher year-end values. The creative accountant will be looking for ways to manipulate these year-end values, so that in bad times costs are carried forward to more profitable accounting periods.

20.8.4 Other methods of creative accounting

Over- or understated quantities

A simple manipulation is to show more or less inventory than actually exists. If the commodity is messy and indistinguishable, the auditor may not have either the expertise or the will to verify measurements taken by the client's own employees. This lack of auditor measuring knowledge and involvement allowed one of the biggest frauds ever to take place, which became known as 'the great salad oil swindle'.[11]

Understated obsolete inventory

Another obvious ploy is to include, in the inventory valuation, obsolete or 'dead' inventory. Of course, such inventory should be written off. However, management may be 'optimistic' that it can be sold, particularly in times of economic recession. In high-tech industries, unrealistic values may be placed on inventory that in times of rapid development becomes obsolete quickly.

This can be highly significant, as in the case of Cal Micro.[12] On 6 February 1995, Cal Micro restated its financial results for fiscal year 1994. The bulk of the adjustments to Cal Micro's financial statements – all highly material – occurred in the areas of accounts inventory, accounts receivable and property and, from an originally reported net income of approximately $5.1 million for the year ended 30 June 1994, the restated allowance for additional inventory obsolescence decreased net income by approximately $9.3 million.

Lack of marketability

This is a problem that investors need to be constantly aware of, particularly when a company experiences a downturn in demand but a pressure to maintain the semblance of growth. An example is provided by Lexmark[13] which was alleged to have made highly positive statements regarding strong sales and growth for its printers although there was intense competition in the industry – the company reporting quarter after quarter of strong financial growth, whereas the actual position appeared to be very different with unmarketable inventory in excess of $25 million to be written down in the fourth quarter of fiscal year 2001. The share price of a company that conceals this type of information is maintained and allows insiders to offload their shareholding on an unsuspecting investing public.

20.9 Audit of the year-end physical inventory count

The problems of accounting for inventory are highlighted at the company's year-end. This is when the closing inventory figure to be shown in both the statement of comprehensive income and the statement of financial position is calculated. In practice, the company will assess the final inventory figure by physically counting all inventory held by the company for trade. The year-end inventory count is therefore an important accounting procedure, one in which the auditors are especially interested.

The auditor generally attends the inventory count to verify both the physical quantities and the procedure of collating those quantities. At the inventory count, values are rarely assigned to inventory items, so the problems facing the auditor relate to the identification of inventory items, their ownership, and their physical condition.

20.9.1 Identification of inventory items

The auditor will visit many companies in the course of a year and will spend a considerable time looking at accounting records. However, it is important for the auditor also to become familiar with each company's products by visiting the shop floor or production facilities during the audit. This makes identification of individual inventory items easier at the year-end. Distinguishing between two similar items can be crucial where there are large differences in value. For example, steel-coated brass rods look identical to steel rods, but their value to the company will be very different. It is important that they are not confused at inventory count because, once recorded on the inventory sheets, values are assigned, production carries on, and the error cannot be traced.

20.9.2 Physical condition of inventory items

Inventory in premium condition has a higher value than damaged inventory. The auditor must ensure that the condition of inventory is recorded at inventory count, so that the correct value is assigned to it. Items that are damaged or have been in inventory for a long period will be written down to their net realisable value (which may be nil) as long as adequate details are given by the inventory counter. Once again, this is a problem of identification, so the auditor must be able to distinguish between, for instance, rolls of first quality and faulty fabric. Similarly, items that have been in inventory for several inventory counts may have little value, and further enquiries about their status should be made at the time of inventory count.

20.9.3 Adjustment if inventory is taken after the year-end date

If inventory is counted after the year-end then an adjustment will need to be made to add back the cost of items sold and deduct the cost of purchases made after the year-end that have been taken into stock.

For example, assume that after the year-end sales of £100,000 at cost plus 25% were made and dispatched and purchases of £45,000 were made and received. Inventory would be increased by £100,000 × 20/100 = £80,000 and reduced by £45,000.

20.9.4 Adjustment if errors are discovered

Typical errors could include:

● Sales invoices raised and posted but goods are awaiting dispatch – these should be excluded from the year-end inventory.

● Purchase invoices received and posted without waiting for the goods received note – the purchases figure should be reduced.

● Errors on pricing items or casting inventory sheets – these should be corrected when identified.

● Consumable stock might have been included – this should be taken out of inventory. The cost of sales will be higher, gross profit lower and the consumables expense reduced with no effect on the net profit.

● Omitting stock held by third parties on approval or consignment – these would need to be taken into closing inventory at cost.

20.10 Published accounts

Disclosure requirements in IAS 2 have already been indicated. The standard requires the accounting policies that have been applied to be stated and applied consistently from year to year. Inventory should be sub-classified in the statement of financial position or in the notes to the financial statements so as to indicate the amounts held in each of the main categories in the standard statement of financial position formats. But will the ultimate user of those financial statements be confident that the information disclosed is reliable, relevant and useful? We have already indicated many areas of subjectivity and creative accounting, but are such possibilities material?

In 1982 Westwick and Shaw examined the accounts of 125 companies with respect to inventory valuation and its likely impact on reported profit.[14] The results showed that the effect on profit before tax of a 1% error in closing inventory valuation ranged from a low of 0.18% to a high of 25.9% (in one case) with a median of 2.26%. The industries most vulnerable to such errors were household goods, textiles, mechanical engineering, contracting and construction.

Clearly, the existence of such variations has repercussions for such measures as ROCE, EPS and the current ratio. The research also showed that, in a sample of audit managers,

Figure 20.7 Impact of a 5% change in closing inventory

Company:	1	2	3	4	5	6	7	8
	£m	£m	£m	£m	£m	£m	£m	£m
Actual inventory	390.0	428.0	1,154.0	509.0	509.0	280.0	360.0	232.0
Actual pre-tax profit	80.1	105.6	479.0	252.5	358.4	186.3	518.2	436.2
Change in pre-tax profit	19.5	21.4	57.7	25.2	25.5	14.0	18.0	11.6
	Impact of a 5% change in closing inventory (%)							
(i) Pre-tax profit	24.3	20.3	12.0	10.0	7.1	7.5	3.5	2.7
(ii) Earnings per share	27.0	25.0	12.0	9.3	8.4	6.9	3.4	3.4

Key to companies:

1 Electrical retailer
2 Textile, etc., manufacturer
3 Brewing, public houses, etc.
4 Retailer – diversified

5 Pharmaceutical and retail chemist
6 Industrial paints and fibres
7 Food retailer
8 Food retailer

85% were of the opinion that the difference between a pessimistic and an optimistic valuation of the same inventory could be more than 6%.

IAS 2 has since been strengthened and these results may not be so indicative of the present situation. However, using the same principle, let us take a random selection of eight companies' recent annual accounts, apply a 5% increase in the closing inventory valuation and calculate the effect on EPS (taxation is simply taken at 35% on the change in inventory).

Figure 20.7 shows that, in absolute terms, the difference in pre-tax profits could be as much as £57.7 million and the percentage change ranges from 2.7% to 24.3%. Of particular note is the change in EPS, which tends to be the major market indicator of performance. In the case of the electrical retailer (company 1), a 5% error in inventory valuation could affect EPS by as much as 27%. The inventory of such a company could well be vulnerable to such factors as changes in fashion, technology and economic recession.

20.11 Agricultural activity

20.11.1 The overall problem

Agricultural activity is subject to special considerations and so is governed by a separate IFRS, namely IAS 41. IAS 41 defines agricultural activity as 'the management by an entity of the biological transformation of biological assets for sale, into agricultural produce or into additional biological assets'. A biological asset is a living animal or plant.

The basic problem is that biological assets, and the produce derived from them (referred to in IAS 41 as 'agricultural produce'), cannot be measured using the cost-based concepts that form the bedrock of IAS 2 and IAS 16. This is because biological assets, such as cattle, for example, are not usually purchased; they are born and develop into their current state. Therefore different accounting methods are necessary.

20.11.2 The recognition and measurement of biological assets and agricultural produce

IAS 41 states that an entity should recognise a biological asset or agricultural produce when:

- the entity controls the asset as a result of a past event;
- it is probable that future economic benefits associated with the asset will flow to the entity;
- the fair value or cost of the asset can be measured reliably.

Rather than the usual cost-based concepts of measurement that are used for assets, IAS 41 states that assets of this type should be measured at their fair value less estimated costs of sale. The only (fairly rare) exception to this general measurement principle is if the asset's fair value cannot be estimated reliably. In such circumstances a biological asset is measured at cost (if available). Research[15] indicates that the adoption of fair value is avoided in countries such as France where there is a culture of conservatism, which means that they rebut the presumption that fair values can be determined with reliability to justify the use of historical cost. It also means that they are able to avoid the onerous valuation requirements of the standard.

The following is an extract from the 2011 Holmen AB annual report:

Biological assets
The Group divides all its forest assets for accounting purposes into growing forests, which are recognised as biological assets at fair value, and land, which is stated at acquisition cost. Any changes in the fair value of the growing forests are recognised in the income statement. Holmen's assessment is that there are no relevant market prices available that can be used to value forest holdings as extensive as Holmen's. They are therefore valued by estimating the present value of expected future cash flows (after deduction of selling costs) from the growing forests.

20.11.3 An illustrative example

A farmer owned a dairy herd. At the start of the period the herd contained 100 animals that were two years old and 50 newly born calves. At the end of the period a further 30 calves were born. None of the herd died during the period. Relevant fair value details were as follows:

	Start of period $	End of period $
Newly born calves	50	55
One-year-old animals	60	65
Two-year-old animals	70	75
Three-year-old animals	75	80

The change in the fair value of the herd is $3,400, made up as follows:

Fair value at end of the year = $(100 \times \$80) + (50 \times \$65) + (30 \times \$55)$	= $12,900
Fair value at start of the year = $(100 \times \$70) + (50 \times \$50)$	= $9,500

IAS 41 requires that the change in the fair value of the herd be reconciled as follows:

	$
Price change – opening newly born calves: 50($55 − $50)	250
Physical change of opening newly born calves: 50($65 − $55)	500
Price change of opening two-year-old animals: 100($75 − $70)	500
Physical change of opening two-year-old animals: 100($80 − $75)	500
Due to birth of new calves: 30 × $55	1,650
Total change	**3,400**

The costs incurred in maintaining the herd would all be charged in the statement of comprehensive income in the relevant period.

20.11.4 Agricultural produce

Examples of agricultural produce would be milk from a dairy herd or crops from a cornfield. Such produce is sold by a farmer in the ordinary course of business and is inventory. The initial carrying value of the inventory at the point of 'harvest' is its fair value less costs to sell at that date. Agricultural entities then apply IAS 2 to the inventory using the initial carrying value as 'cost'.

20.11.5 Land

Despite its importance in agricultural activity, IAS 41 does not apply to agricultural land, which is accounted for in accordance with IAS 16. Where biological assets are physically attached to land (e.g. crops in a field) then it is often possible to compute the fair value of the biological assets by computing the fair value of the combined asset and deducting the fair value of the land alone.

20.11.6 Minerals

The standard does not apply to the measurement of inventories of producers of agricultural and forest products, agricultural produce after harvest, and minerals and mineral products, to the extent that they are measured at net realisable value in accordance with well-established industry practices.

20.11.7 Government grants relating to biological assets

As mentioned in Chapter 17 such grants are not subject to IAS 20 – the general standard on this subject. Under IAS 41 the IASB view is more consistent with the principles of the *Framework* than the provisions of IAS 20. Under IAS 41 grants are recognised as income when the entity becomes entitled to receive it. This removes the fairly dubious credit balance 'Deferred income' that arises under the IAS 20 approach and does not appear to satisfy the *Framework* definition of a liability.

20.11.8 Fair value or historic cost option?

An interesting research project[15] carrying out an empirical investigation of the implications of IAS 41 for the harmonisation of farm accounting practices in Australia, France and the UK found that agricultural entities in all three countries are using a variety of valuation methods under IAS 41 and that there is a lack of comparability of disclosure practices. It was their view that IAS 41 has failed to enhance the international comparability of accounting practices in the agricultural sector. The following problems have been identified.

Valuation method

The researchers found that although historical cost is the most common valuation basis for biological assets, a variety of proxies for fair value are used, such as net present value, independent/external valuation, net realisable value and market price, both within and across countries.

National characteristics impact on choice of method

Some countries may be more conservative and private than others. These characteristics and attitudes existed pre-IFRS[16] and do not change merely because the IASB has produced IFRSs.

Fair national or fair global value?

In the European Union IAS 41 requires biological assets to be valued by reference to artificial and highly subsidised or politically mediated market prices. This allows European farmers to export to developing countries at prices which are substantially below production costs.

Cost/benefit considerations

Small and medium-sized companies consider that the cost of compliance is too high and this has been recognised by the IASB who provide that, for biological assets, the fair value through profit or loss model is required only when fair value is readily determinable without undue cost or effort. If fair value is not used SMEs follow the cost–depreciation–impairment model.

Summary

Examples of differences in inventory valuation are not uncommon.[11,17] For example, in 1984, Fidelity, the electronic equipment manufacturer, was purchased for £13.4 million.[18] This price was largely based on the 1983/84 profit figure of £400,000. Subsequently, it was maintained that this 'profit' should actually be a loss of £1.3 million – a difference of £1.7 million. Much of this difference was attributable to inventory discrepancies. The claim was contested, but it does illustrate that a disparity can occur when important figures are left to 'professional judgement'.

Another case involved the selling of British Wheelset by British Steel, just before privatisation in 1988, at a price of £16.9 million.[19] It was claimed that the accounts 'were not drawn up on a consistent basis in accordance with generally accepted accounting practice'. If certain inventory provisions had been made, these would have resulted in a £5 million (30%) difference in the purchase price.

Other areas that cause difficulties to the user of published information are the capitalisation of interest and the reporting of write-downs on acquisition. Post-acquisition profits can be influenced by excessive write-downs of inventory on acquisition, which has the effect of increasing goodwill. The written-down inventory can eventually be sold at higher prices, thus improving post-acquisition profits.

Although legal requirements and IAS 2 have improved the reporting requirements, many areas of subjective judgement can have substantial effects on the reporting of financial information.

REVIEW QUESTIONS

1 Discuss the extent to which individual judgements might affect inventory valuation, e.g. changing the basis of overhead absorption.

2 Discuss the acceptability of the LIFO and replacement cost methods of inventory valuation and why the IASB has not permitted all methods to be used.

3 Explain the criteria to be applied when selecting the method to be used for allocating administrative costs.

4 Discuss the effect on work in progress and finished goods valuation if the net realisable value of the raw material is lower than cost at the statement of financial position date.

5 Discuss why the accurate valuation of inventory is so crucial if the financial statements are to show a true and fair view.

6 The following is an extract from the Interbrew 2010 Annual Report:

Inventories

Inventories are valued at the lower of cost and net realizable value. Cost includes expenditure incurred in acquiring the inventories and bringing them to their existing location and condition. The weighted average method is used in assigning the cost of inventories.

The cost of finished products and work in progress comprises raw materials, other production materials, direct labor, other direct cost and an allocation of fixed and variable overhead based on normal operating capacity. Net realizable value is the estimated selling price in the ordinary course of business, less the estimated completion and selling costs.

Discuss the possible effects on profits if the company did not use normal operating activity. Explain an alternative definition for net realisable value and discuss the criterion to be applied when making a policy choice.

7 It has been suggested that

'Given national characteristics it will be impossible to ensure that financial statements that comply with IFRSs will ever be comparable.'

Discuss whether auditors can make this change.

8 The following is an extract from the 2011 Annual Report of SIPEF NV:

Auditor's Report

The statutory auditor has confirmed that his audit procedures, which have been substantially completed, have revealed no material adjustments that would have to be made to the accounting information included in this press release.

With regard to the valuation of the biological assets, the statutory auditor draws the reader's attention to the fact that, because of the inherent uncertainty associated with the valuation of the biological assets due to the volatility of the prices of the agricultural produce and the absence of a liquid market, their carrying value may differ from their realisable value.

Given the inherent uncertainty in applying IAS 41, discuss (a) whether the pre-IAS 41 practice of value at historical cost would be preferable for the statement of financial position, and (b) whether the new requirement to pass unrealised gains and losses through the statement of comprehensive income is more relevant to an investor.

Question 1

Sunhats Ltd manufactures patent hats. It carries inventory of these and sells to wholesalers and retailers via a number of salespeople. The following expenses are charged in the profit and loss account:

Wages of: Storemen and factory foremen

Salaries of: Production manager, personnel officer, buyer, salespeople, sales manager, accountant, company secretary

Other: Directors' fees, rent and rates, electric power, repairs, depreciation, carriage outwards, advertising, bad debts, interest on bank overdraft, development expenditure for new types of hat.

Required:
Which of these expenses can reasonably be included in the valuation of inventory?

* Question 2

Purchases of a certain product during July were: Units sold during the month were:

July	1	100 units @ £10.00	July	10	80 units
	12	100 units @ £9.80		14	100 units
	15	50 units @ £9.60		30	90 units
	20	100 units @ £9.40			

Required:
Assuming no opening inventories:
(a) Determine the cost of goods sold for July under three different valuation methods.
(b) Discuss the advantages and/or disadvantages of each of these methods.
(c) A physical inventory count revealed a shortage of five units. Show how you would bring this into account.

* Question 3

Alpha Ltd makes one standard article. You have been given the following information:

1 The inventory sheets at the year-end show the following items:

Raw materials:
100 tons of steel:
Cost £140 per ton
Present price £130 per ton

Finished goods:
100 finished units:
Cost of materials £50 per unit
Labour cost £150 per unit
Selling price £500 per unit

40 semi-finished units
Cost of materials £50 per unit
Labour cost to date £100 per unit
Selling price £500 per unit (completed)

10 damaged finished units:
Cost to rectify the damage £200 per unit
Selling price £500 per unit (when rectified)

2 Manufacturing overheads are 100% of labour cost.
Selling and distribution expenses are £60 per unit (mainly salespeople's commission and freight charges).

Required:
From the information in notes 1 and 2, state the amounts to be included in the statement of financial position of Alpha Ltd in respect of inventory. State also the principles you have applied.

* Question 4

Beta Ltd commenced business on 1 January and is making up its first year's accounts. The company uses standard costs. The company owns a variety of raw materials and components for use in its manufacturing business. The accounting records show the following:

	Standard cost of purchases	Adverse (favourable) variances Price variance	Usage variance
	£	£	£
July	10,000	800	(400)
August	12,000	1,100	100
September	9,000	700	(300)
October	8,000	900	200
November	12,000	1,000	300
December	10,000	800	(200)
Cumulative figures for whole year	110,000	8,700	(600)

Raw materials control account balance at year-end is £30,000 (at standard cost).

Required:
The company's draft statement of financial position includes 'Inventories, at the lower of cost and net realisable value £80,000'. This includes raw materials £30,000: do you consider this to be acceptable? If so, why? If not, state what you consider to be an acceptable figure.

(Note: for the purpose of this exercise, you may assume that the raw materials will realise more than cost.)

* Question 5

Uptodate plc's financial year ended on 31 March 20X8. Inventory taken on 7 April 20X8 amounted to £200,000. The following information needs to be taken into account:

(i) Purchases made during the seven days to 7 April amounted to £40,000. Invoices had not been received and only 20% had been delivered by 7 April. These had been taken into inventory.

(ii) Purchases of £10,000, which had been ordered but not paid for before the year-end, had been received before 31 March. However, as the invoices had not been received by 31 March they have not been included in the inventory.

(iii) Purchases of £5,000, which had been ordered and paid for before the year-end, had not been received by 31 March.

(iv) Purchases of £12,000, ordered and paid for by the year-end, were in a bonded warehouse awaiting customs clearance at 31 March. These were eventually delivered to the company on 9 April.

Required:
Calculate the revised year-end inventory as at 31 March 20X8.

Question 6

Hasty plc's financial year ended on 31 March 20X8. Inventory taken on 7 April 20X8 amounted to £100,000. The following information needs to be taken into account:

(i) Sales invoices totalling £9,000 were raised during the seven days after the year-end. £1,500 of this had not been dispatched by 7 April. The company policy was to add 20% to cost.

(ii) Sales returns received on 6 April totalled £600.

(iii) Goods with an invoice value of £6,000 had been sent to customers on approval in February 20X8. £3,600 had been returned in March 20X8. The company policy was to add 20% to cost and not to process the invoice until customers gave notice of purchasing.

(iv) Goods bought in to satisfy a one-off customer order at £575 had been sent on approval in November 20X7 on a pro forma invoice for £850. These had been taken into inventory at the pro forma price.

Required:
Calculate revised inventory as at 31 March 20X8.

Question 7

The statement of income of Bottom, a manufacturing company, for the year ending 31 January 20X2 is as follows:

	$000
Revenue	75,000
Cost of sales	(38,000)
Gross profit	37,000
Other operating expenses	(9,000)
Profit from operations	28,000
Investment income	
Finance cost	(4,000)
Profit before tax	24,000
Income tax expense	(7,000)
Net profit for the period	17,000

Note – accounting policies
Bottom has used the LIFO method of inventory valuation but the directors wish to assess the implications of using the FIFO method. Relevant details of the inventories of Bottom are as follows:

Date	Inventory valuation under:	
	FIFO	LIFO
	$000	$000
1 February 20X1	9,500	9,000
31 January 20X2	10,200	9,300

Required:
Redraft the statement of income of Bottom using the FIFO method of inventory valuation and explain how the change would need to be recognised in the published financial statements, if implemented.

* Question 8

Agriculture is a key business activity in many parts of the world, particularly in developing countries. Following extensive discussions with, and funding from, the World Bank, the International Accounting Standards Committee (IASC) developed an accounting standard relating to agricultural activity. IAS 41 *Agriculture* was published in 2001 to apply to accounting periods beginning on or after 1 January 2003.

Sigma prepares financial statements to 30 September each year. On 1 October 2003 Sigma carried out the following transactions:

● Purchased a large piece of land for $20 million.

● Purchased 10,000 dairy cows (average age at 1 October 2003, two years) for $1 million.

● Received a grant of $400,000 towards the acquisition of the cows. This grant was non-returnable.

During the year ending 30 September 2004 Sigma incurred the following costs:

● $500,000 to maintain the condition of the animals (food and protection).

● $300,000 in breeding fees to a local farmer.

On 1 April 2004, 5,000 calves were born. There were no other changes in the number of animals during the year ended 30 September 2004. At 30 September 2004, Sigma had 10,000 litres of unsold milk in inventory. The milk was sold shortly after the year-end at market prices.

Information regarding fair values is as follows:

Item	*Fair value less point-of-sale costs*		
	1 October 2003	*1 April 2004*	*30 September 2004*
	$	$	$
Land	20 m	22 m	24 m
New-born calves (per calf)	20	21	22
Six-month-old calves (per calf)	23	24	25
Two-year-old cows (per cow)	90	92	94
Three-year-old cows (per cow)	93	95	97
Milk (per litre)	0.6	0.55	0.55

Required:
(a) Discuss how the IAS 41 requirements regarding the recognition and measurement of biological assets and agricultural produce are consistent with the IASC *Framework for the Preparation and Presentation of Financial Statements*.
(b) Prepare extracts from the statement of comprehensive income and the statement of financial position that show how the transactions entered into by Sigma in respect of the purchase and maintenance of the dairy herd would be reflected in the financial statements of the entity for the year ended 30 September 2004. You do not need to prepare a reconciliation of changes in the carrying amount of biological assets.

(ACCA DipIFR 2004)

References

1 IAS 2 *Inventories*, IASB, revised 2004.
2 'A guide to accounting standards – valuation of inventory and work-in-progress', *Accountants Digest*, Summer 1984.
3 M. Jones, 'Cooking the accounts', *Certified Accountant*, July 1988, p. 39.
4 www.agrana.com/fileadmin/inhalte/agrana_group/annual_reports/AGRANA_JFB_201112_E_WEB.pdf
5 T.S. Dudick, 'How to avoid the common pitfalls in accounting for inventory', *The Practical Accountant*, January/February 1975, p. 65.
6 *Certified Accountant*, October 1987, p. 7.
7 M. Perry, 'Valuation problems force FD to quit', *Accountancy Age*, 15 March 2001, p. 2.
8 The report appears on www.coso.org/index.htm
9 See www.sec.gov/litigation/admin/34-41729.htm
10 See www.sec.gov/litigation/admin/34-46099.htm
11 E. Woolf, 'Auditing the stocks – part II', *Accountancy*, May 1976, pp. 108–110.
12 See www.sec.gov/litigation/admin/34-41720.htm
13 See http://securities.stanford.edu/1022/LXK01-01/
14 C. Westwick and D. Shaw, 'Subjectivity and reported profit', *Accountancy*, June 1982, pp. 129–131.
15 C. Elad and K. Herbohn, *Implementing Fair Value Accounting in the Agricultural Sector*, ICAS Research Report, 2011, http://www.icas.org.uk/site/cms/download/res/elad_Exec_Summary_Feb_2011.pdf
16 C. Nobes, 'Different versions of IFRS practice', in C. Nobes and R. Parker (eds), *Comparative International Accounting* (10th edition), FT Prentice Hall, 2008, pp. 145–156.
17 E. Woolf, 'Auditing the stocks – part I', *Accountancy*, April 1976, p. 106.
18 K. Bhattacharya, 'More or less true, quite fair', *Accountancy*, December 1988, p. 126.
19 R. Northedge, 'Steel attacked over Wheelset valuation', *Daily Telegraph*, 2 January 1991, p. 19.

CHAPTER 21

Construction contracts

21.1 Introduction

Construction contracts have been given special attention because of the size, duration and special challenges which arise in accounting for them. In this chapter we will be addressing the issues involved in supplying services which are of long duration and thus raise issues of whether revenue should be recognised continuously or whether the completion of the total contract is the delivery of the contracted service. In addition to the accounting for the revenue recognition there are a number of issues relating to the valuation of the work in progress.

The basic principles which apply to revenue recognition in general, and as outlined in Chapter 8, are applied in construction contracts. So in essence this chapter can be seen as illustrating the application of the revenue standard in a complex business situation together with the application of impairment accounting (see Chapter 17) in arriving at the valuation of the resulting assets. Both these issues will be addressed in this chapter.

We also explain the basic accounting for contracts of public–private partnerships, which have become increasingly popular for undertaking major infrastructure construction and operations.

Objectives

By the end of this chapter, you should be:

- aware of some of the historical developments in the accounting for construction contracts such that you understand how to read and prepare accounts involving construction activities following IAS 11;
- able to prepare construction accounts in accordance with the proposed revenue recognition rules and to record assets arising from construction contracts; and
- able to account for public–private partnerships (PPP).

21.2 The need to replace IAS 11 *Construction Contracts*[1]

Before 2011 it had been considered that construction contracts were of such complexity that they warranted a separate standard (IAS 11 *Construction Contracts*) and the general rules for revenue recognition set out in IAS 18 *Revenue*[2] were specially excluded. In their place IAS 11 established a separate set of rules under which revenue is recognised progressively as the item is built, matching expenses, writing off unrecoverable costs and identifying those costs to be carried forward as assets which are expected to be recovered in the future.

However, the presence of two different sets of rules in relation to revenue recognition has not sat comfortably with the idea of having a coherent set of standards. Accordingly the IASB and the FASB have been reviewing IAS 11 with a view to construction contracts being covered by the one Revenue Recognition standard.

21.2.1 IAS 11 Construction Contracts

IAS 11 *Construction Contracts* defines a construction contract as:

> A contract specifically negotiated for the construction of an asset or a combination of assets that are closely inter-related or inter-dependent in terms of their design, technology and function or their ultimate purpose or use.

Some construction contracts are **fixed-price contracts,** where the contractor agrees to a fixed contract price. However, where the contract extends over a longer period it is quite normal for such fixed-price contracts to include escalation clauses. An escalation clause essentially means that when specified events beyond the control of the contractor (such as new union wage rates or prices of specified material, such as iron reinforcement used in the construction) increase then the price of the contract is amended according to a previously agreed formula to allow the contractor to recover all or part of the cost increases. Thus escalation clauses are a device for sharing or transferring specified risks associated with the contract.

Other construction contracts are **cost-plus contracts,** where the contractor is reimbursed for allowable costs, plus a percentage of these costs or alternatively a fixed fee added to the allowable costs. This type of contract would be appropriate where the amount of materials or labour needed is unclear as may be the case in an innovative project.

Some examples of construction contracts would involve building ships, aeroplanes, buildings, dams and bridges.

Construction contracts are normally assessed and accounted for individually. However, in certain circumstances construction contracts may be combined or segmented. Combination or segmentation is appropriate when:

● a group of contracts is negotiated as a single package and the contracts are performed together in a continuous sequence (combination); and

● separate proposals have been submitted for each asset and the costs and revenues of each asset can be identified (segmentation).

A key accounting issue is when the revenues and costs (and therefore net income) under a construction contract should be recognised. There are two major possibilities:

● Only recognise net income when the contract is complete – the *completed contracts method.*

● Recognise a proportion of net income over the period of the contract – this is currently achieved using the *percentage of completion method.*

IAS 11 requires the latter approach, provided the overall contract result can be predicted with reasonable certainty. If that is not the case then the completed contract method is used.

21.3 Identification of contract revenue

Contract revenue should comprise:

(a) the initial amount of revenue agreed in the contract; and

(b) variations in contract work, claims and incentives payments, to the extent that

– it is probable that they will result in revenue; and

– they are capable of being reliably measured.

Variations to the initially agreed contract price occur due to events such as:

● cost escalation clauses;

● claims for additional revenue by the contractor due to customer-caused delays or changes in the specification or design;

● incentive payments when specified performance standards are met or exceeded;

● penalty clauses representing agreed damages caused by failure to complete by the contracted date.

Incentive payments might apply to a toll road where early completion would allow additional revenue to be collected by the owner of the road. Penalty clauses might apply to a construction contract because the client would incur additional costs as a result of delays such as temporary storage expenses if they cannot move into the new factory at the agreed handover date. Penalties are a way of ensuring the client can plan ahead for the transfer of their business to the new premises at an agreed date, confident that the contractor will do everything in their power to complete on time.

The same recognition rules apply to variations as apply to the original recognition, namely the probability of occurrence is high and the amount can be predicted with reasonable certainty.

21.4 Identification of contract costs

IAS 11 classifies costs that can be identified with contracts under three headings:

● Costs that directly relate to the specific contract, such as:

– site labour;

– cost of materials;

– depreciation of plant and equipment used on the contract;

– costs of moving plant and materials to and from the contract site;

– costs of hiring plant and equipment;

– costs of design and technical assistance that are directly related to the contract;

– the estimated costs of rectification and guarantee work;[3]

– claims from third parties.

● Costs that are attributable to contract activity in general and can be allocated to specific contracts, such as:

– insurance;

– costs of design and technical assistance that are not directly related to a specific contract;

– construction overheads.

Costs of this nature need to be allocated on a systematic and rational basis, based on the normal level of construction activity.

● The construction contract itself may specify costs which can be recovered under the contract and those of course can be charged to the contract.

An interesting area is the cost of tendering. This may seem an insignificant cost but in relation to major complex contracts these costs may amount to many millions of dollars. For example, in 2012 the UK government cancelled the current competition for the West Coast Main Line railway franchise and will pay back all costs incurred by bidding parties, which, when combined with the costs of retendering the franchise, could cost the taxpayer as much as £40 million.

The proposed standard says incremental costs of obtaining the contract may be treated as an asset provided there is an expectation that it will be recovered. That cost can then be allocated systematically to the construction cost over the life of the project. Each period the net balance in the asset account would have to be checked in terms of its continued likelihood of recovery and its write-down where applicable.

Johnson Matthey plc in their 2012 accounts, which follow IAS 11, state that their accounting policy is:

> Where the outcome of a long term contract can be estimated reliably, revenue and costs are recognised by reference to the stage of completion. This is measured by the proportion that contract costs incurred to date bear to the estimated total contract costs.
>
> Where the outcome of a long term contract cannot be estimated reliably, contract revenue is recognised to the extent of contract costs incurred that it is probable will be recoverable. Contract costs are recognised as expenses in the period in which they are incurred.
>
> When it is probable that the total contract costs will exceed total contract revenue, the expected loss is recognised as an expense immediately.

Note the following interesting issues:

(a) Revenue and expenses are recognised on the basis of stage of completion.

(b) When there is uncertainty regarding the ability of the contract to make a profit overall, the costs incurred that probably would not be recovered are immediately written off as an expense.

Balfour Beatty in their 2011 annual accounts report their accounting policies including the following two extracts:

Construction and service contracts
When the outcome of individual contracts can be estimated reliably, contract revenue and contract costs are recognised as revenue and expenses respectively by reference to the stage of completion at the reporting date. The stage of completion is measured by the proportion of the value of work done to the total value of work under the contract. Full provision is made for known or expected losses on individual contracts once such losses are foreseen. Revenue in respect of variations to contracts, claims and incentive payments is recognised when it is probable it will be agreed by the client. Profit for the year includes the benefit of claims settled on contracts completed in previous years.

Pre-contract bid costs and recoveries
Pre-contract costs are expensed as incurred until it is virtually certain that a contract will be awarded, from which time further pre-contract costs are recognised as an asset and charged as an expense over the period of the contract. Amounts recovered in

respect of pre-contract costs that have been written-off are deferred and amortised over the life of the contract.

For construction and services projects, the relevant contract is the construction or services contract respectively. With respect to PPP projects, there are potentially three contracts over which the recovered costs could be amortised, the concession itself, the construction contract or the services contract. An assessment is made as to which contractual element the pre-contract costs relate to, in order to determine the relevant period for amortization. . . .

These policies are also in accordance with IAS 11 but notice the emphasis placed on the difficulties in finalising the contract revenue given the variations for escalation allowances and modifications to contracts and rectification of claimed deficiencies. The treatment of pre-contract costs is also emphasised. (The proposed new standard will treat the pre-contract costs differently in that the incremental costs of acquiring a contract can be capitalised if there is an expectation that they will be recovered.)

The statement of financial position presentation for construction contracts should show as an asset – Gross amounts due from customers – the following net amount:

- total costs incurred to date;
- plus attributable profits (or less foreseeable losses);
- less any progress billings to the customer.

Where for any contract the above amount is negative, it should be shown as a liability – Gross amounts due to customers.

Advances – amounts received by the contractor before the related work is performed – should be shown as a liability, effectively a payment on account by the customer.

21.5 Proposed new accounting rules

Some of the important provisions of the proposed new revenue rules include the requirements to:

- recognise revenue when control passes;
- account for onerous performance obligations as soon as they become apparent so as to be consistent with rules relating to asset recognition and impairment; and
- disclose sufficient information to allow report readers to assess the risks and rewards likely to be associated with ongoing contracts.

Recognise revenue when control passes

We discussed in Chapter 8 on revenue recognition the fact that recognition is dependent on the transfer of control rather than the transfer of legal title. This will also apply to construction contracts. However, the fact that construction contracts often extend over several years and are often not easily subdivided into parts makes the issue of importance to companies involved in substantial contracts.

To assist with identifying when revenue is to be recognised, the proposed revenue standard provides guidance for performance obligations satisfied over time.

The first situation which is relevant is where the performance obligation creates or enhances an asset under the control of the customer. The situation is then fairly straightforward. An example might be a contract to build a large shopping centre. The customer might require that it be built in stages so that he can get tenants into each section whilst the next and sub-sequent sections are being built. In that way cash can start flowing earlier. When each section is completed the builder would be justified in recognising the revenue relating to that section even though there are not several independent contracts for construction but one overall contract. Similarly a contract to refurbish a multi-storey building could be done floor by floor.

The second situation involves the production of an asset for which the construction firm would not have an alternative use, expects to complete the contract, and has a right to payment for the work completed to date. The right to payment may be because of the terms of the contract or rights conferred by relevant laws. An example might be a 24-month contract to produce a substantial machine to the unique specifications of the customer where the contract provides for four-weekly progress payments.

The third situation would be a longer-term service contract where the customer consumes the service as it is developed and if the contract were terminated the new contractor would not have to duplicate the work already done. An example might be a contract to make an online accounting course more effective and interesting, module by module.

In each period it is necessary to recognise the revenue which has been earned and the expenses associated with generating that revenue. The expenses incurred in relation to a contract which relate to the incomplete components of the contract are carried forward as an asset provided they are expected to be recoverable.

Given the complexity of some long-term contracts it is not surprising that some of them do not proceed according to plan. As soon as it becomes apparent that expenses have been, or will be, incurred that are not recoverable the losses need to be recognised.

Accounting for onerous performance obligations

According to paragraph 87 of the proposed revenue standard:

A performance obligation is onerous if the lowest cost of settling the performance obligation exceeds the amount of the transaction price allocated to that performance obligation.

The above definition mirrors the definition in IAS 37 *Provisions, Contingent Liabilities and Contingent Assets* leading to greater consistency in standards. Its inclusion in the revenue standard is to that extent redundant.

There are two ways of ending a contract to provide performance obligations. The first is to complete the contract with the associated costs. The other way is to negotiate with someone else to complete the contract for a fee or to default on the contract and pay damages. Whichever of these alternatives is cheaper becomes the amount to be accounted for.

The accounting requirements in the standard relating to onerous performance do not appear to substantially alter normal accounting requirements. In other words, when it becomes apparent that the contract will *not* be profitable the first step will be to recognise that some, or all, of the previously recognised contract work in progress has been impaired and needs to be written off. The impairment is recorded as an expense. When that asset has been extinguished, it is necessary to create a liability to reflect the present value of obligations which are still to be incurred but that will not be recovered through the contract price. This is not a new provision.

Disclosure

The disclosure requirement is explained in the proposed guidance:

109 . . . to enable users of financial statements to understand the nature, amount, timing, and uncertainty of revenue and cash flows arising from contracts with

customers . . . , an entity shall disclose qualitative and quantitative information about all of the following:

(a) its contracts with customers . . . ;

(b) the significant judgments, and changes in judgments, made in applying the [draft] IFRS to those contacts . . . and

(c) any assets recognized from the costs to obtain or fulfil a contract with a customer . . .

To satisfy these requirements it would be necessary to divide revenue into meaningful categories to disclose revenues with different levels of uncertainty, all movements in contract assets and liabilities during the period, normal terms and conditions of contracts, significant judgements made in applying the IFRS and any changes in those judgements between periods.

21.6 Approach when a contract can be separated into components

To keep track of the construction contracts the accounting has many similarities with job costing where costs are accumulated by job and, if there are distinct components of the job, then separate records may be required for each component as a basis for invoicing and assessing profitability.

For example, if you are constructing a shopping centre and you want to complete it in stages so that the landlord can have the first stage operational whilst the second stage is still under construction, you may need two 'jobs' in the books. Care will need to be taken to ensure the expenses are charged to the right stage with subjective decisions such as how to allocate the costs for preparing the land and installing the services. Then when the first stage is complete it may be possible under the terms of the contract to invoice the landlord for progress to date. You will have to keep track of the revenue earned to that stage. That will enable you to calculate the profit to that stage and to assess whether the construction contract is on track or whether it is in trouble.

If the contract is not going according to plan you will have to recognise the losses you expect to make on the total contract by forecasting further costs to complete the overall contract and comparing it with the expected revenue. The total revenue would be the contract price plus allowances which can be invoiced under the escalation clauses plus any revenue arising from agreed variations to the original contract.

So from the above we have to keep track of:

(a) total costs incurred on the contract to date;

(b) the amount of revenue recognised in the accounts to date;

(c) the costs incurred in relation to the revenue which has been recognised;

(d) the amount of the profit or loss recorded on the contract so far;

(e) the amount invoiced to the customer so far; and

(f) the amount unpaid by the customer.

21.7 Accounting for a contract

As costs are incurred they are charged to construction work in progress ((a) above) and there would be a subsidiary ledger showing those costs assigned to stages one and two in the example given.

Assuming stage one is completed before the period-end, the customer would be invoiced and an account called 'Billings on construction contracts' would be credited. At the end of the period the revenue earned during the period is estimated.

The costs relating to that revenue are debited to cost of goods sold for construction contracts, the revenue account is credited and the difference, which is the profit, is debited or credited to work in progress. Why the entry to work in progress? The work in progress is being revalued to market value so that we can measure our profit or loss so far on the contract.

The profit/loss on construction contract ((d) above) is debited/credited to construction work in progress.

If the accounts were prepared at that point the profit calculation would include:

Revenue from construction contracts	XXXX
Less: Cost of goods sold for construction	XXX
Gross profit on construction contracts	XXXX

The statement of financial position would include:

Work in progress for construction (at cost)	XXXX
Plus: Profit recognised in the accounts so far (both current and past)	XXX
Total work in progress for construction	XXXX

If the customer is then invoiced for part of the work done, the entry would be to debit the debtor for the invoiced amount and to credit an account called 'Billings for construction work'. The profit calculations would be as shown above and now the statement of financial position would include the following:

Receivables for construction work		XXXX
(at amounts invoiced less cash received)		
Work in progress:		
Costs incurred to date (at cost)	XXXX	
Plus (*Minus*): Profits (losses) recognised to date	XXX	
Less: Billings to date (now appearing in receivables)	XXXX	
Net work in progress		XXXX

An extract from the Lend Lease Group 2011 accounts illustrates the above:

b. Construction Work in Progress	2010	2011
Construction work in progress comprises:	*A$m*	*A$m*
Contract costs incurred to date	59,315.7	56,438.6
Profit recognised to date	2,651.3	6,722.0
	61,967.0	63,160.6
Less: Progress billings received and receivable on contracts	(62,952.9)	(63,928.6)
Net construction work in progress	(985.9)	(768.0)
Costs in excess of billings – inventories	218.1	319.5
Billings in excess of costs – trade payables	(1,204.0)	(1,087.5)
	(985.9)	(768.0)

21.8 Illustration – profitable contract using step approach

First year of contract

ABC has two construction contracts (Contract A and Contract B) outstanding at the end of its financial year, 30 June 20X3. Details for Contract A are as follows:

	Contract A
	£000
Total contract price	25,000
Cost incurred to date	5,500
Anticipated future costs	14,500
Progress billing	—

Step one: Review the anticipated overall position for the contract

	Contract A
	£000
Total expected cost to complete the contract:	
Costs to date	5,500
Anticipated future costs	14,500
Expected total cost	20,000
Contract price	25,000
Forecast profit on the contract	5,000

Since the contract is expected to be profitable overall, the profit on the component completed to date can be fully realised. If, on the other hand, the forecast total cost for the total contract was greater than the revenue, then the anticipated cost overrun would need to be recorded as an expense/loss in the current period.

Step two: The statement of comprehensive income
Based on the proportion of the contract completed using costs as the guide, 5,500/20,000 or 0.275 of the revenue has been earned. Revenue = 25,000 × 0.275 = 6,875.

		Contract A
		£000
Revenue		6,875
Less:		
Cost incurred to date	5,500	
Allowance for future losses	—	
Total expenses		5,500
Net income		1,375

Step three: The statement of financial position entries
As the statement of financial position is a cumulative statement, all figures have to be prepared on that basis.

	Contract A
	£000
Costs incurred to date	5,500
Add: Profits to date	1,375
Less: Recognised losses to date	—
Gross work done for customer	6,875
Less: Amount billed to customer	—
Gross amount due from customer	6,875

Note that it is assumed that a direct estimate of the revenue earned was not available. A more common situation is that an independent architect's estimate of the proportion of the contract that has been completed is obtained. For example, assuming that the architect said the contract was 28% complete, then the revenue to be recognised would be that proportion of the total contract price of £25,000,000, i.e. £7,000,000.

Whether the percentage of revenue is based on a direct estimate of revenue or the percentage of costs is a practical consideration in terms of what information is readily available.

Second year of contract

Details of the transactions for Contract A for the year ended 30 June 20X4 are outlined below.

	Contract A £000
Total contract price	25,000
Costs incurred to date	16,000
Anticipated future costs to complete the contract	8,000
Progress billings	12,000
Payments received	4,000

Step one: Review the anticipated overall result for the contract

	Contract A £000
Costs incurred to date	16,000
Anticipated future costs to complete	8,000
Total expected costs	24,000
Contract price	25,000
Anticipated profit	1,000

Since the project is expected to be profitable there is no requirement to make accruals for losses.

Step two: Prepare the relevant part of the comprehensive income statement

Calculate the stage of completion as the ratio of expenses to date divided by the total forecast expenses to complete the project. That is, $16,000/24,000 = 0.667$. Revenue earned $= 0.667 \times 25,000 = 16,675$.

	Contract A £000	£000
Total revenue for years one and two		16,675
Less: Revenue already recognised		6,875
Revenue for the period		9,800
Less: Expenses:		
Additional expenses incurred in the period (16,000 – 5,500)	10,500	
Additional anticipated loss accrual	—	
Total expenses		10,500
Loss for the year		(700)

Step three: Prepare the statement of financial position entries

	Contract A £000
Work in progress	
Costs incurred to date	16,000
Add: Recognised profits	1,375
Less: Recognised losses	(700)
Work performed for customer	16,675
Less: Progress billings	12,000
Gross amount due from customer	4,675
Construction receivables	8,000

21.9 Illustration – loss-making contract using step approach

First year of contract

The terms of Contract B specify that 50% of the contract price is due on completion of stage one and 50% on completion of stage two. The details as at 30 June 20X3 are as follows:

	Contract B £000
Total contract price	20,000
Costs incurred to date	13,000
Anticipated future costs	11,000
Progress billings	10,000
Advance payments	nil

Assuming that stage one of Contract B is complete

Step one: Review the expected overall position of the contract as at 30 June 20X3

	Contract B £000
Costs incurred to date	13,000
Anticipated future costs	11,000
Forecast contract cost	24,000
Contract price (revenue)	20,000
Anticipated loss on contract	(4,000)

This loss has to be recognised at 30 June 20X3.

Step two: Prepare the relevant part of the comprehensive income statement

	Contract B £000	£000
Revenue earned to date (13,000/24,000) × 20,000		10,833
Less: Revenue previously recognised		nil
Revenue earned in the period		10,833
Costs incurred to date	13,000	
Less: Costs previously recorded as an expense	nil	
	(13,000)	
Anticipated future losses (9,167 – 11,000)	(1,833)	
Total expenses for the period		(14,833)
Loss on Contract B for the period		(4,000)

Step three: Prepare the statement of financial position entries

The entries in the statement of financial position represent the cumulative position.

	Contract B £000
Costs incurred to date	13,000
Add: Profits recognised to date	nil
Less: Losses recognised to date	(4,000)
Work performed to date at cost or net realisable value	9,000
Less: Billings to date	(10,000)
Net balance	(1,000)
Representing:	
Work in progress for work not yet invoiced (revenue 10,833 – 10,000 billed)	833
Liability for anticipated future loss in period 20X3–20X4	(1,833)
Net	(1,000)

Journal entries to record the above in the books of account are as follows:

Dr	Work in progress	13,000	
Cr	Bank/creditors		13,000

(expenditure in relation to the contract)

Dr	Cost of goods sold	14,833	
Cr	Revenue		10,833
Cr	Work in progress		4,000

(to recognise revenue and cost of goods sold, and to write off part of the work in progress as it will not be recovered in revenue)

Dr	Work in progress	1,833	
Cr	Liability for further contract commitments		1,833

(accruing expenses not expected to be covered by future revenue)

Dr	Debtors	10,000	
Cr	Billings on construction contracts		10,000

(invoicing the customer for progress payment on the contract)

Note that the balance in the billings on construction contracts account is offset against the work in progress to arrive at the balance for the statement of financial position.

21.10 Public–private partnerships (PPPs)

PPPs have become a common government policy whereby public bodies enter into contracts with private companies which have included contracts for the building and management of transport infrastructure, prisons, schools and hospitals. There are inherent risks in any project and the intention is that the government, through a PPP arrangement, should transfer some or all of such risks to private contractors. For this to work equitably there needs to be an incentive for the private contractors to be able to make a reasonable profit provided they are efficient whilst ensuring that the providers, users of the service, taxpayers and employees also receive a fair share of the benefits of the PPP.

Improved public services

It has been recognised that where such contracts satisfy a value for money test it makes economic sense to transfer some or all of the risks to a private contractor. In this way it has been possible to deliver significantly improved public services with:

- increases in the quality and quantity of investment, e.g. by the private contractor raising equity and loan capital in the market rather than relying simply on government funding;

- tighter control of contracts during the construction stage to avoid cost and time overruns, e.g. completing construction contracts within budget and within the agreed time – this is evidenced in a report from the National Audit Office[4] which indicates that the majority are completed on time and within budget; and

- more efficient management of the facilities after construction, e.g. maintaining the buildings, security, catering and cleaning of an approved standard for a specified number of years.

PPP defined

There is no clear definition of a PPP. It can take a number of forms, e.g. in the form of the improved use of existing public assets under the Wider Markets Initiative (WMI) or contracts for the construction of new infrastructure projects and services provided under a Private Finance Initiative (PFI).

The Wider Markets Initiative (WMI)[5]

The WMI encourages public sector bodies to become more entrepreneurial and to undertake commercial services based on the physical assets and knowledge assets (e.g. patents, databases) they own in order to make the most effective use of public assets. WMI does not relate to the use of surplus assets – the intention would be to dispose of these. However, wanting to become more entrepreneurial leads to the need to collaborate with private enterprises which have the necessary expertise.

The Private Finance Initiative (PFI)

The PFI has been described[6] as a form of public–private partnership (PPP) that 'differs from privatisation in that the public sector retains a substantial role in PFI projects, either as the main purchaser of services or as an essential enabler of the project . . . differs from contracting out in that the private sector provides the capital asset as well as the services . . . differs from other PPPs in that the private sector contractor also arranges finance for the project'.

In its 2004 Government Review, HM Treasury stated[7] that:

> The Private Finance Initiative is a small but important part of the Government's strategy for delivering high quality public services. In assessing where PFI is appropriate, the Government's approach is based on its commitment to efficiency, equity and accountability and on the Prime Minister's principles of public sector reform. PFI is only used where it can meet these requirements and deliver clear value for money without sacrificing the terms and conditions of staff. Where these conditions are met, PFI delivers a number of important benefits. By requiring the private sector to put its own capital at risk and to deliver clear levels of service to the public over the long term, PFI helps to deliver high quality public services and ensure that public assets are delivered on time and to budget.

At the time of the 2010 Budget, the following figures in relation to PFIs were published:[8]

Departmental estimates of capital spending by the private sector (signed deals) in £million:

	2010–11	2011–12
Communities and Local Government	230	92
Culture, Media and Sport	51	8
Education	574	143
Environment, Food and Rural Affairs	325	166
Transport	749	838
Health	584	356
Work and Pensions	56	55
Home Office	40	0
Defence	702	542
Northern Ireland Executive	242	109
Scotland	156	44
Wales	0	0
Other Departments	8	3
Total	3,722	2,363

(Similar statistics for 2012–13 are available at www.hm-treasury.gov.uk/d/summary_document_pfi_data_march_2012.pdf which contains statistics for some of the departments shown above.)

The PFI has meant that more capital projects have been or will be undertaken for a given level of public expenditure, and public service capital projects have been brought on stream earlier. However, it has to be recognised that this increased level of activity must be paid for by higher public expenditure in the future or by additional fees for services paid by the public. The aim is to offset some of those costs by additional income or better efficiency.

Thus the stream of contracted revenue payments to the private sector restricts the options which the current and future governments will have. PFI projects have committed governments to payments to private sector contractors between 2000/01 and 2025/26 of more than £100 billion.

Briefly, then, PFI allows the public sector to enter into a contract (known as a concession) with the private sector to provide quality services on a long-term basis, typically 25 to 30 years, so as to take advantage of private sector management skills working under contracts where private sector finance is at risk. The private sector has the incentive to operate efficiently and effectively if the service requirements are comprehensive and reflect public needs appropriately, and the future risks associated with the project are fairly shared by the two parties.

Refining the model in the UK

In 2012 the UK government sought feedback from industry participants with an active role in the delivery and operation of public facilities; from those with an interest in investing in these projects; and from across the public sector, academics, think tanks, employees and wider stakeholders. It is seeking to develop new delivery models to obtain long-term value for money for the taxpayer and more effective use of private sector innovation and skills, reducing costs, improving flexibility and increasing transparency. The Treasury observed that it would be looking to retain the benefits that a successful PFI can deliver – in getting projects built to time and to budget and increasing the correct disciplines and incentives on the private sector to manage risk effectively.

21.10.1 How does PFI operate?

In principle, private sector companies accept the responsibility for the design, raise the finance, and undertake the construction, maintenance and possibly the operation of assets for the delivery of public services. In return for this the public sector pays for the project by making annual payments that cover all the costs plus a return on the investment through performance payments which include incentives for being efficient.

In practice the construction company and other parties such as the maintenance companies become shareholders in a **project company** set up specifically to tender for a concession.

● The project company enters into the contract (the 'concession') with the public sector, then enters into two principal subcontracts with

– a construction company to build the project assets; and

– a facilities management company to maintain the asset – this is normally for a period of five or so years after which time it is renegotiated.

Note that the project company will pass down to the constructor and maintenance subcontractors any penalties or income deductions that arise as a result of their mismanagement.

● The project company raises a mixture of

– equity and subordinated debt from the principal private promoters, i.e. the construction company and the maintenance company; and

– long-term debt.

Note that the long-term debt may be up to 90% of the finance required on the basis that it is cheaper to use debt rather than equity. The loan would typically be obtained from banks and would be without recourse to the shareholders of the project company. As there is no recourse to the shareholders, lenders need to be satisfied that there is a reliable income stream coming to the project company from the public sector, i.e. the lender needs to be confident that the project company can satisfy the contractual terms agreed with the public sector. The subordinated debt made available to the project company by the promoters will be subordinated to the claims of the long-term lenders in that they will only be repaid after the long-term lenders.

● The project company receives regular payments, usually over a 25- to 30-year period, from the public sector once the construction has been completed to cover the interest, construction, operating and maintenance costs.

Note that such payments may be conditional on a specified level of performance and the private sector partners need to have carried out a detailed investigation of past practice for accommodation-type projects and/or detailed economic forecasting for throughput projects. If, for example, it is an accommodation-type project (e.g. prisons, hospitals and schools) then payment is subject to the buildings being available in an appropriate clean and decorated condition; if not, income deductions can result. If it is a throughput project (e.g. roads, water) with payment made on the basis of throughput such as number of vehicles and litres of water, then payment would be at a fixed rate per unit of throughput and the accuracy of the forecast usage has a significant impact on future income.

● The project company makes interest and dividend payments to the principal promoters.

● Finally, the project company returns the infrastructure assets in agreed condition to the public sector at the end of the 25- to 30-year contractual period.

This can be shown graphically as in Figure 21.1.

Figure 21.1 The operation of PFI

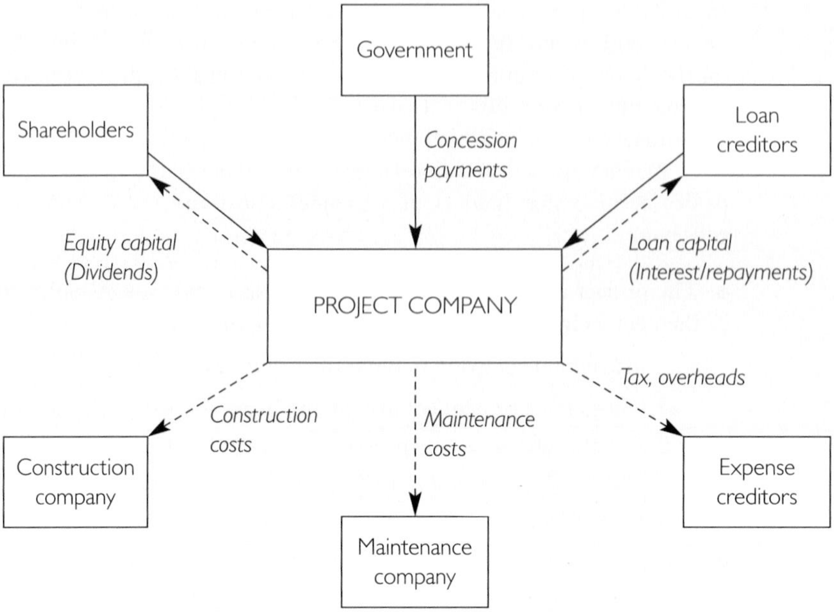

21.10.2 Profit and cash flow profile for the shareholders

Over a typical 30-year contract the profit and cash flow profiles would follow different growth patterns.

Profit profile

No profits are received as dividends during construction. Before completion the depreciation and loan interest charges can result in losses in the early years. As the loans are reduced the interest charge falls and profits then grow steadily to the end of the concession.

Cash flow

As far as the shareholders are concerned, cash flow is negative in the early years with the introduction of equity finance and subordinated loans. Cash begins to flow in when receipts commence from the public sector and interest payments commence on the subordinated loans, say from year 5, and dividend payments start to be made to the equity shareholders, say from year 15.

21.10.3 How is a concession dealt with in the annual accounts of a construction company?

Statement of comprehensive income entries

The accounting treatment will depend on the nature of the construction company's shareholding in the project company. If it has control, then it would consolidate. Frequently, however, it has significant influence without control and therefore accounts for its investment in concessions by taking to the statement of comprehensive income its share of the net income or expense of each concession, in line with IAS 28 *Investments in Associates*.

21.10.4 How is a concession dealt with in the annual accounts of a concession or project company?

The accounting for service concessions has been a difficult problem for accounting standard setters around the world and different models exist. The main difficulties are in determining the nature of the asset that should be recognised, whether that is a tangible fixed asset, a financial asset or an intangible asset, or even some combination of these different options.

Accounting for concessions in the UK is governed by Financial Reporting Standard 5 *Reporting the Substance of Transactions*, Application Note F, which is primarily concerned with how to account for the costs of constructing new assets.

Assets constructed by the concession may be considered either as a fixed asset of the concession or as a long-term financial asset ('contract receivable'), depending on the specific allocation of risks between the concession company and the public sector authority. In practice the main risk is normally the demand risk associated with the usage of the asset, e.g. number of vehicles using a road where the risk remains with the concession company.

Treated as a non-current asset

Where the concession company takes the greater share of the risks associated with the asset, the cost of constructing the asset is considered to be a fixed asset of the concession. The cost of construction is capitalised and depreciation is charged to the statement of comprehensive income over the life of the concession. Income is recognised as turnover in the statement of comprehensive income as it is earned.

Treated as a financial instrument

Where the public sector takes the greater share of the risks associated with the asset, the concession company accounts for the cost of constructing the asset as a long-term contract receivable, being a receivable from the public sector. Finance income on this contract receivable is recorded using a notional rate of return which is specific to the underlying asset, and included as part of non-operating financial income in the statement of comprehensive income.

Under the contract receivable treatment, the revenue received from the public sector is split. The element relating to the provision of services that are considered a separate transaction from the provision of the asset is recognised as turnover in the statement of comprehensive income. The element relating to the contract debtor is split between finance income and repayment of the outstanding principal.

The following are extracts from the Balfour Beatty 2011 Annual Report:

1.20(d) PPP concession companies

Assets constructed by PPP concession companies are classified principally as available-for-sale financial assets.

In the construction phase, income is recognized by applying an attributable profit margin on the construction costs representing the fair value of construction services. In the operational phase, income is recognized by allocating a proportion of total cash received over the life of the project to service costs by means of a deemed constant rate of return on those costs. The residual element of projected cash is allocated to the financial asset using the effective interest rate method, giving rise to interest income. Due to the nature of the contractual arrangements the projected cash flows can be estimated with a high degree of certainty.

In the construction phase the fair value of the Group's PPP financial assets is determined by applying an attributable profit margin on the construction costs representing the fair value of construction services performed. In the operational phase fair value is determined by discounting the future cashflows allocated to the financial assets using assumptions in respect of the of the discount rates which are based on long-term gilt rates adjusted for the risk levels associated with the assets. The subsequent movements in the fair value are taken to equity. Amounts accumulated in equity are transferred to the income statement upon disposal of the asset.

1.27(d) Available-for-sale financial assets

Assets constructed by the Group's PPP subsidiary, joint venture and associate companies are classified as 'available-for-sale financial assets' and at 31 December 2011 had a value of £1,897m. The fair value of these financial assets is measured at each reporting date by discounting the future value of the cash flows allocated to the financial asset. A range of discount rates, varying from 4.83% to 7.83%, is used which reflects the prevailing risk-free interest rates and the different risk profiles of the various concessions. A £204m gain was taken to equity in 2011 and a cumulative fair value gain of £342m had arisen on these financial assets as a result of movements in the fair value of these financial assets at 31 December 2011.

1.27(e) PPP derivative financial instruments

The Group's PPP subsidiary, joint venture and associate companies use derivative financial instruments, principally swaps, to manage the interest rate and inflation rate risks to which the concessions are exposed by their long-term contractual agreements. These derivatives are initially recognised as assets and liabilities at their fair value and subsequently remeasured at each reporting date at their fair value. The fair value of derivatives constantly changes in response to prevailing market conditions. A loss of £239m was taken to equity in 2011 and a cumulative fair value loss of £449m had arisen on these financial instruments at 31 December 2011.

The total profit earned from a concession will be the same whether it is treated as a fixed asset or a finance asset. There will, however, be a difference in the timing of the profit recognition, and a difference in the presentation of income and expenses in the statement of comprehensive income. When treated as a fixed asset, profits increase over time largely due to the reducing financing costs of the transaction as the outstanding loans are repaid; when treated as a finance asset, the finance income is calculated on the full value of the contract debtor and this finance income falls in line with the principal repayments over the life of the project.

IFRIC 12 service concession agreements

For enterprises preparing financial statements in accordance with IFRS, IFRIC 12 was issued in November 2006 and became effective for periods beginning on or after 31 January 2008. As we will see, this interpretation will result in accounting that has some similarities to that laid down for PFI contracts in UK FRS 5; however, the presentation of the assets recognised might differ.

Service concession agreements are arrangements where a government or other body grants contracts for the supply of public services to private operators. IFRIC 12 draws a distinction between two types of service concession arrangement.

In one case the operator receives a **financial asset**, specifically an unconditional contractual right to receive cash or another financial asset in return for constructing or upgrading the public sector asset. In the other case the operator receives an **intangible asset** – a right to charge for use of the public sector asset that it constructs or upgrades. IFRIC 12 allows for the possibility that both types of arrangement may exist within a single contract. Therefore, IFRIC 12 recognises two accounting models:

- Under the **financial asset model** the operator receives a financial asset. This arises where the operator has an unconditional contractual right to receive cash or another financial asset from the public sector body for relevant services. This is where the public sector body contractually guarantees to pay the operator:

  – specified or determinable amounts; or

  – the shortfall, if any, between amounts received from users of the public service and specified or determinable amounts.

  The operator measures the intangible asset initially at fair value. Subsequent to initial measurement the financial assets will be accounted for under IAS 39 and will be classified according to that standard. As a result the financial asset could be measured as follows:

  – if classified as a 'loan and receivable' it will be measured at amortised cost;

  – if classified as 'available for sale' it will be measured at fair value with gains and losses recognised in the other gains and losses section of the statement of comprehensive income; or

  – if classified as 'fair value through profit or loss' it will be measured at fair value with gains and losses reflected with net profit or loss in the statement of comprehensive income.

- Under the **intangible asset model** the operator recognises an intangible asset to the extent to which it receives a right to charge users of the public service. A right to charge users is not an unconditional right to receive cash because it depends on the extent to which the public uses the service. The operator measures the financial asset initially at fair value. Subsequent to initial recognition the intangible asset will be recognised in accordance with IAS 38 *Intangible Assets*. Subsequent to initial recognition the assets amortisation or impairment charges will need to be recognised as required by IAS 38.

Revenue is recognised by the operator in accordance with the general recognition principles.

Summary

Long-term contracts are those that cannot be completed within the current financial year. This means that a decision has to be made as to whether or not to include any profit before the contract is actually completed. The view taken by the standard setters pre-2011 is that contract revenue and costs should be recognised under IAS 11 using the percentage of completion method. There is a proviso that revenue and costs can only be recognised when the amounts are capable of independent verification and the contract has reached a reasonable stage of completion. Although profits are primarily attributed to the financial periods in which the work is carried out, there is a requirement that any foreseeable losses should be recognised immediately in the statement of comprehensive income of the current financial period and not apportioned over the life of the contract.

IAS 11 is intended to be amended when the proposed new standard on revenue is finalised. Under the proposed revenue approach revenue is recognised when the service has been rendered, control has passed and the results are measurable.

REVIEW QUESTIONS

1 Discuss the relative merits of recognising revenue under the percentage of completion method and the passing of control as major thresholds are met or the contract is finished.

2 'Profit on a contract is not realised until completion of the contract.' Discuss.

3 Discuss whether fixed price construction contracts should be accounted for differently from cost-plus contracts.

4 'Profit on a contract that is not complete should be treated as an unrealised holding gain.' Discuss.

5 What should the percentage of completion be before revenue recognition occurs in the accounts? Discuss.

6 Discuss what information should be disclosed in the annual report in relation to construction costs in order for it to be useful to report users.

7 The Treasury states that 'Talk of PFI liabilities with a present value of £110 million is wrong. Adding up PFI unitary payments and pretending they present a threat to the public finances is like adding up electricity, gas, cleaning and food bills for the next 30 years.' Discuss.

8 'The operator of an asset in a PFI contract should recognise the tangible assets on its balance sheet.' Discuss.

9 Discuss whether having different revenue recognition criteria for goods and services results in inconsistent approaches and misleading financial statements.

10 A submission on the revenue standard raised an issue of when revenue for variations to contracts should be recognised. One possibility is only after each variation has been approved by the customer should it be recognised, whereas the other argument is that as variations are a normal part of contract work they should be recognised immediately. Discuss.

11 Accounting for partly completed construction faces two risks. The first risk is a mismatch of revenue and expenses due to inaccurate estimates of the percentage of completion with actual expenses. The alternative risk is to account for contract progress as clearly defined milestones are reached, with the risk that expenses which have been incurred relate to the achievement of future stages of development. Which risk is more serious? Discuss.

MACTAR have a series of contracts to resurface sections of motorways. The scale of the contract means several years' work and each motorway section is regarded as a separate contract.

M1	€m
Contract sum	3.0
Costs to date	2.1
Estimated cost to complete	0.3
Progress billings applied for to date	1.75
Payment received to date	1.5

M6	€m
Contract sum	2.0
Costs to date	0.3
Estimated cost to complete	1.1
Progress billings applied for to date	0.1
Payment received to date	—

M62	€m
Contract sum	2.5
Costs to date	2.3
Estimated cost to complete	0.8
Progress billings applied for to date	1.0
Payment received to date	0.75

The M62 contract has had major difficulties due to difficult terrain, and the contract only allows for a 10% increase in contract sum for such events.

Required:

From the information above, calculate for each contract the amount of profit (or loss) you would show for the year and show how these contracts would appear in the statement of financial position with all appropriate notes. Assume that control passed at the time costs were certified.

Question 2

At 31 October 20X2, Lytax Ltd was engaged in the following five long-term contracts. In each contract Lytax were building cold storage warehouses on five sites where the land was owned by the customer. Details are given below:

	1	2	3	4	5
Site:	£000	£000	£000	£000	£000
Contract price	1,100	950	1,400	1,300	1,200
At 31 October					
Cumulative costs incurred	664	535	810	640	1,070
Estimated further costs to completion	106	75	680	800	165
Estimated cost of post-completion guarantee rectification work	30	10	45	20	5
Progress billings:					
Cumulative receipts	615	680	615	385	722
Invoiced					
– awaiting receipt	60	40	25	200	34
– retained by customer	75	80	60	65	84

There are retention clauses in the contracts which allow the customer not to pay an agreed amount until all problems have been rectified.

It is not expected that any customers will default on their payments.

Up to 31 October 20X1, the following amounts have been included in the revenue and cost of sales figures:

Site:	1	2	3	4	5
	£000	£000	£000	£000	£000
Cumulative revenue	560	340	517	400	610
Cumulative costs incurred transferred to cost of sales	460	245	517	470	610

It is the accounting policy of Lytax Ltd to arrive at contract revenue by adjusting contract cost of sales (including foreseeable losses) by the amount of contract profit or loss to be regarded as recognised, separately for each contract.

Required:

(a) Show how these items will appear in the statement of financial position of Lytax Ltd with all appropriate notes. Show all workings in tabular form.

(b) How much profit will be recognised in relation to these contracts in the 20X2 year?

* Question 3

During its financial year ended 30 June 20X7 Beavers, an engineering company, has worked on several contracts. Information relating to one for Dam Ltd which is being constructed to a specific customer design is given below:

Contract X201

Date commenced	1 July 20X6
Original estimate of completion date	30 September 20X7
Contract price	£240,000
Proportion of work certified as satisfactorily completed (and invoiced) up to 30 June 20X7	£180,000
Progress payments from Dam Ltd	£150,000
Costs up to 30 June 20X7	
Wages	£91,000
Materials sent to site	£36,000
Other contract costs	£18,000
Proportion of Head Office costs	£6,000
Plant and equipment transferred to the site (at book value on 1 July 20X6)	£9,000

The plant and equipment is expected to have a book value of about £1,000 when the contract is completed.

Inventory of materials at site 30 June 20X7	£3,000
Expected additional costs to complete the contract:	
Wages	£10,000
Materials (including stock at 30 June 20X7)	£12,000
Other (including Head Office costs)	£8,000

At 30 June 20X7 it is estimated that work to a cost value of £19,000 has been completed but not included in the certifications.

If the contract is completed one month earlier than originally scheduled, an extra £10,000 will be paid to the contractors. At the end of June 20X7 there seemed to be a 'good chance' that this would happen.

Required:
(a) Show the account for the contract in the books of Beavers up to 30 June 20X7 (including any transfer to the statement of comprehensive income which you think is appropriate).
(b) Show the statement of financial position entries.
(c) Calculate the profit (or loss) to be recognised in the 20X6–20X7 accounts.

Question 4

Newbild SA commenced work on the construction of a block of flats on 1 July 20X0.

During the period ended 31 March 20X1 contract expenditure was as follows:

	€
Materials issued from stores	13,407
Materials delivered direct to site	73,078
Wages	39,498
Administration expenses	3,742
Site expenses	4,693

On 31 March 20X1 there were outstanding amounts for wages €396 and site expenses €122, and the stock of materials on site amounted to €5,467.

The following information is also relevant:

1   On 1 July 20X0 plant was purchased for exclusive use on site at a cost of €15,320. It was estimated that it would be used for two years after which it would have a residual value of €5,000.

2   By 31 March 20X1 Newbild SA had received €114,580, being the amount of work certified by the architects up to 31 March 20X1 on completion and handover of the show flat, less a 15% retention.

3   The total contract price is €780,000. The company estimates that additional costs to complete the project will be €490,000. From costing records it is estimated that the costs of rectification and guarantee work will be 2.5% of the contract price.

Required:
(a) Prepare the contract account for the period, together with a statement showing your calculation of the net income to be taken to the company's statement of comprehensive income on 31 March 20X1. Assume for the purpose of the question that the contract is sufficiently advanced to allow for the taking of profit.
(b) Give the values which you think should be included in the figures of revenue and cost of sales, in the statement of comprehensive income, and those to be included in net amounts due to or from the customer in the statement of financial position in respect of this contract.

Question 5

(a) A concession company, WaterAway, has completed the construction of a wastewater plant. The plant will be transferred to the public sector unconditionally after 25 years. The public sector (the grantor) makes payments related to the volume of wastewater processed.

Required:
Discuss how this will be dealt with in the statement of comprehensive income and statement of financial position of the concession company.

(b) A concession company, LearnAhead, has built a school and receives income from the public sector (the grantor) based on the availability of the school for teaching.

Required:
Discuss how this will be dealt with in the statement of comprehensive income and statement of financial position of the concession company, under IFRIC 12.

Question 6

Quickbuild Ltd entered into a two-year contract on 1 January 20X7 at a contract price of £250,000. The estimated cost of the contract was £150,000. At the end of the first year the following information was available:

● contract costs incurred totalled £70,000;

● inventories still unused at the contract site totalled £10,000;

● progress payments received totalled £60,000;

● other non-contract inventories totalled £185,000.

The accounting is to be performed under the percentage of completion method as required under IAS 11.

Required:
Calculate the statement of comprehensive income entries for the contract revenue and the contract costs and the items in the statement of financial position.

* Question 7

(a) During 2006, Jack Matelot set up a company, JTM, to construct and refurbish marinas in various ports around Europe. The company's first accounting period ended on 31 October 2006 and during that period JTM won a contract to refurbish a small marina in St Malo, France. During the year ended 31 October 2007, the company won a further two contracts in Barcelona, Spain and Faro, Portugal. The following extract has been taken from the company's contract notes as at 31 October 2007:

Contract:	Barcelona	Faro	St Malo
	€m	€m	€m
Contract value	12.24	10.00	15.00
Payments received:			
To 31 October 2006	—	—	5.75
Year to 31 October 2007	3.76	—	1.75
To date	3.76	—	7.50
Invoices sent to client:			
To 31 October 2006	—	—	6.00
Year to 31 October 2007	5.00	0.50	2.76
To date	5.00	0.50	8.76
Costs incurred:			
To 31 October 2006	—	—	6.56
Year to 31 October 2007	11.50	1.50	3.94
To date	11.50	1.50	10.50
Estimated costs to complete:			
As at 31 October 2006			5.44
As at 31 October 2007	4.00	5.50	1.50

Notes
Barcelona: Experiencing difficulties. Although JTM does not anticipate any cost increases, the client has offered to increase the contract value by €0.76m as compensation.
Faro: No problems.
St Malo: Work slowed down during 2007, though the company feels it can continue profitably.

The company uses the value of work certified to estimate the percentage completion of each contract.

Required:
For each contract, calculate the profit or loss attributable to the year ended 31 October 2007 and show how it would be recognised in the company's balance sheet at that date. (Show your workings clearly.)

(b) As JTM's 2007 accounts were being prepared, it became evident that the St Malo contract had slowed down due to a dispute with a neighbouring marina which claimed that the JTM refurbishment had damaged part of its quayside. The company has been told that the cost of repairing the damage would be €150,000. Jack Matelot believes it is a fair estimate and, in the interests of completing the contract on time, has decided to settle the claim. He is not unduly concerned about the amount involved as such eventualities are adequately covered by insurance.

Required:
How should this event be dealt with in the 2007 accounts?

(c) During 2007, Jack Matelot had two major worries: (i) the operating performance of JTM had not been as good as expected; and (ii) the planned disposal of surplus property (to finance the agreed acquisition of a competitor, MoriceMarinas, and the payment of a dividend) had not been successful. As a result of these circumstances, Jack had been warning shareholders not to expect a dividend for 2007. However, during November 2007, the property was unexpectedly disposed of for €5m, which enabled the payment of a 2007 dividend of €1m and the acquisition of MoriceMarinas for €4m.

Required:
How should the above events be dealt with in the 2007 accounts?

(The Association of International Accountants)

Question 8

Backwater Construction Company is reviewing a major contract which is in serious difficulty. The contract price is €10,000,000. The project involves the construction of four buildings of equal size and complexity. The first building has been completed and costs to date are €3,000,000. The second building is expected to be completed after one more year, the third building after two years and the final building after three years. The relevant discount rate is 10% p.a.

Required:
Prepare the entries to record the revenue for the year just completed, to record the expenses incurred, and adjust assets (if any) and liabilities (if any) at the balance date.

Question 9

Norwik Construction plc is a large construction company involved in multiple large contracts around the world. One contract to build three stadiums is being undertaken by the Australasian division. Jim Norwik, who is the great-grandson of the founder, is in charge of that division. He is concerned that the first stadium is costing more than is included in the tender estimates. Rather than recognise an immediate loss on the contract, he orders his subordinates to charge some of the materials for stadium one to stadium two which seems to be on target.

Discuss the consequences of Jim Norwik's actions for Norwik Construction plc and the likely impact on the behaviour of Jim Norwik's subordinates.

References

1 IAS 11 *Construction Contracts*, IASB, 1995.
2 IAS 18 *Revenue*, IASB, revised 2005.
3 It is common in construction work for architects to certify the amount which the contractor is entitled to as various milestones are reached. The amount payable is often the amount earned less a percentage withheld until the contract is completed and all problems resolved. If resolution does not occur the customer can use the money withheld to get a third party to rectify the remaining mistakes.
4 National Audit Office, PFI: Construction Performance, February 2003, www.nao.org.uk/publications/nao_reports/02-03/0203371.pdf
5 *Selling Government Services into Wider Markets, Policy and Guidance Notes*, Enterprise and Growth Unit, HM Treasury, July 1998, www.hm-treasury.gov.uk/mediastore/otherfiles/agswm.pdf
6 Research Paper 01/0117 *Private Finance Initiative*, G. Allen, Economic Policy and Statistics Section, House of Commons, December 2001.
7 See www.hm-treasury.gov.uk/documents/public_private_partnerships/ppp_index.cfm?ptr=29
8 The economy and public finances – supplementary material, http://www.hm-treasury.gov.uk/d/junebudget_supplementary_material.pdf (Note the small discrepancies in the totals appear in the original document.)

PART **5**

Consolidated accounts

CHAPTER 22

Accounting for groups at the date of acquisition

The main purpose of this chapter is to explain how to prepare consolidated financial statements at the date of acquisition and the IFRS 10 and 13 requirements.

Objectives

By the end of this chapter, you should be able to:

- prepare consolidated accounts at the date of acquisition:
  - for a wholly owned subsidiary;
  - for a partly owned subsidiary with non-controlling interests, calculating goodwill under the two options available in IFRS 3;
  - where the fair value of a subsidiary's net assets are more or less than their book values;
- explain IFRS 10, IFRS 3 and IFRS 13 provisions;
- discuss the usefulness of group accounts to stakeholders.

The **fair value** of the parent company's investment in a subsidiary is set against the **fair value** of the identifiable net assets in the subsidiary at the date of acquisition. If the investment is greater than the share of net assets then the difference is regarded as the purchase of goodwill – see the Rose Group example below.

EXAMPLE ● THE ROSE GROUP On 1 January 20X0 Rose plc acquired 100% of the 10,000 £1 ordinary voting shares in Tulip plc for £1.50 per share in cash and so gained control. We are assuming for this example that the fair value of Tulip's net assets at that date was the same as their book value. The individual and group statements of financial position immediately after the acquisition were as in the following schedule:

	Rose plc £	Tulip plc £	Adjustments Dr	Cr	Group £	
Non-current assets	20,000	11,000			31,000	Step 2
Investment in Tulip	15,000	—		10,000 (a)	—	
				4,000 (b)	1,000	Step 1
Net current assets	8,000	3,000			11,000	
Net assets	43,000	14,000			43,000	
Share capital	16,000	10,000	10,000 (a)		16,000	Step 3
Retained earnings	27,000	4,000	4,000 (b)		27,000	Step 3
	43,000	14,000	14,000	14,000	43,000	

(a) and (b) identify the entries in the calculations below.

Step 1. First we calculate the goodwill

Goodwill arises if Rose has to pay the Tulip shareholders more than the book value of the net assets in order to acquire control over those net assets.

	£	£
The parent company's investment		15,000
Less: The parent's share of		
(a) the subsidiary's share capital (100% × 10,000)	10,000	
(b) the subsidiary's retained earnings (100% × 4,000)	4,000	14,000
Goodwill reported in statement of financial position		1,000

Step 2. Aggregate the assets and liabilities

Having cancelled the investment in Tulip against the share capital and reserves acquired, we then add together the assets and liabilities of the two companies including any goodwill:

	£
Non-current assets other than goodwill (20,000 + 11,000)	31,000
Goodwill (as calculated in Step 1)	1,000
Net current assets (8,000 + 3,000)	11,000
	43,000

Note that the total of the net assets in the consolidated account is the same as the net assets in the individual statement of financial position except that Rose's investment in Tulip has been replaced by Tulip's net assets of £14,000 **plus** the previously unrecorded £1,000 goodwill.

Step 3. Calculate the consolidated share capital and reserves

This is the final step.

	£
Share capital (parent company only)	16,000
Retained earnings (parent company only)	27,000
	43,000

Note that in a consolidated statement of financial position we only **ever** include the parent's share capital because, as we have seen above, the subsidiary's share capital has been cancelled as in Step 1 above.

22.3 Preparing consolidated accounts when there is a partly owned subsidiary

A parent company does not need to purchase all the shares of another company to gain control. The holders of any shares not acquired by the parent are collectively referred to as a **non-controlling interest**. They are part-owners of the subsidiary. However, although the parent does not **own** all the net assets of the acquired company, it does **control** them and the parent company directors are accountable for their use.

Indeed, one of the main purposes of preparing group accounts is to show how effectively the directors have used this power to control. Therefore, all of the net assets of the subsidiary will be included in the group statement of financial position and the non-controlling interest will be shown as partly financing those net assets.

How is a non-controlling interest measured?

IFRS 3 allows for two different methods of measuring the non-controlling interest in the statement of financial position:

● **Method 1** requires the non-controlling interest to be measured as the *proportionate share of the net assets* of the subsidiary at the date of acquisition. At each subsequent reporting date the non-controlling interest is measured as its percentage share of the subsidiary's net assets.

● **Method 2** requires the non-controlling interest to be measured at *fair value* at the date of acquisition. Using fair value rather than a percentage of book value means that there could be a difference for goodwill. At each subsequent reporting date the non-controlling interest is measured as the share of the net assets of the subsidiary, plus any goodwill.

22.3.1 Prepare consolidated accounts with non-controlling interest calculated using Method 1

We will continue with our Rose Group example on the basis that it acquired less than 100% of Tulip's shares.

On 1 January 20X0 Rose plc acquired 80% of the 10,000 £1 ordinary shares in Tulip plc for £1.50 per share in cash and so gained control. The fair value of Tulip's net assets at that date was the same as their book value.

The consolidation schedule is as follows:

	Rose	Tulip	Adjustment Dr	Cr	Group	
	£	£	£	£	£	
Non-current assets	20,000	11,000			31,000	Step 3
Investment in Tulip	12,000	—		8,000 (a)	—	
				3,200 (b)		
Goodwill	—	—			800	Step 1
Net current assets	11,000	3,000			14,000	Step 3
Net assets	43,000	14,000			45,800	
Share capital	16,000	10,000	8,000 (a)			Step 4
			2,000 (c)		16,000	
Retained earnings	27,000	4,000	3,200 (b)			Step 4
			800 (d)		27,000	
	43,000	14,000			43,000	
Non-controlling interest				2,000 (c)		Step 2
		—		800 (d)	2,800	
	43,000	14,000	14,000	14,000	45,800	

(a), (b), (c) and (d) identify the entries in the calculations below.

Step 1. Calculate goodwill

	£	£
The parent company's investment in Tulip		12,000
Less: (a) parent's share of Tulip's share capital (80% × 10,000)	8,000	
(b) parent's share of the retained earnings (80% × 4,000)	3,200	
Goodwill		11,200
		800

Step 2. Calculate the non-controlling interest in Tulip

		£
(c) Non-controlling interest in the share capital	(20% × 10,000)	2,000
(d) Non-controlling interest in the retained earnings (20% × 4,000)		800
Representing the non–controlling interest in Tulip's net assets		2,800

In the published consolidated accounts the non-controlling interest will be shown as a separate item in the equity of the group as follows:

	£
Share capital	16,000
Retained earnings	27,000
Rose shareholders' share of equity	43,000
Non-controlling interest	2,800
Total equity	45,800

This recognises that the non-controlling shareholders are part of the ownership of the group rather than a liability.

Step 3. Aggregate the assets and liabilities of the parent and subsidiary

		£
Non–current assets other than goodwill (20,000 + 11,000)		31,000
Goodwill (as calculated in Step 1)		800
Net current assets	(11,000 + 3,000)	14,000
		45,800

Step 4. Calculate the consolidated share capital and reserves

	£
Share capital *(parent company only)*	16,000
Retained earnings *(parent company only)*	27,000
	43,000

Note it is only the parent's share capital that is **ever** reported in the group accounts. As for the retained earnings, it is only the earnings that arise **after** the date when the parent obtains control that are reported as part of the group retained earnings – this is dealt with further in the next chapter.

22.3.2 Prepare consolidated accounts with non-controlling interest calculated using Method 2

Let us now consider the impact on the previous example of using Method 2 to measure the non-controlling interest. In order to use this method, we need to know the fair value of the non-controlling interest in the subsidiary at the date of acquisition. Let us assume in this case that this fair value is £2,900.

Two figures are different in the consolidated accounts if this method is used. The use of Method 2 affects two figures – goodwill and the non-controlling interest. Whereas under

Method 1 the goodwill represented the cost of Rose obtaining control, under Method 2 we also credit the non-controlling interest with its own goodwill. It is computed as follows:

	£
Fair value of non-controlling interest at date of acquisition	2,900
20% of the net assets at the date of acquisition (£14,000)	(2,800)
Attributable goodwill	100

The consolidated statement of financial position would now be as follows:

		£
Non-current assets other than goodwill		31,000
Goodwill	(£800 + £100)	900
Net current assets		14,000
		45,900
Share capital		16,000
Retained earnings		27,000
Non-controlling interest (£2,800 + £100)		2,900
		45,900

How to determine the value of a share not acquired by the parent

Note that we assumed that the fair value of the non-controlling interest at the date of acquisition was £2,900. If Tulip's shares are quoted then the fair value estimate would be based on the share price prior to a bid. This price could be different from that paid by Rose on the assumption that in seeking to obtain control it would probably have paid more than the current share price. In exercises or exam questions the total figure might be given (as in this example) or a price per share might be given.

In the Rose example the goodwill relating to the parent (Rose's) shareholding of 80% is £800, i.e. 10p per share. The goodwill relating to the non-controlling interest in 2,000 shares, however, based on a £2,900 valuation is £100, i.e. 5p per share.

22.3.3 Possible impact of Method 2

There could be a reduction in earnings if there is a need to recognise impairment losses under the Method 2 full goodwill method. This is because any recognition of goodwill on non-controlling interests will be reflected in an increase in any impairment charges arising in subsequent years.

22.4 The treatment of differences between a subsidiary's fair value and book value

In our examples so far we have assumed that the book value of the net assets in the subsidiary is equal to their fair value. In practice, book value rarely equals fair value and it is necessary to revalue the group's share of the assets and liabilities of the subsidiary prior to consolidation.

The following is an extract from the 2011 EnBW Annual Report:

Basis of consolidation
Subsidiaries are consolidated in accordance with the acquisition method. The cost of a business combination is measured based on the fair value of the assets acquired and

liabilities assumed or entered into at the acquisition date. Non-controlling interests are measured at the proportionate share of fair value of assets identified and liabilities assumed.

Note that, when consolidating, the **parent** company's assets and liabilities remain unchanged at book value – it is only the subsidiary's that are adjusted for the purpose of the consolidated accounts.

For example, let us assume that Tulip's non–current assets had a fair value of £11,600. This means that the non–current assets would be increased by £600 and a pre-acquisition revaluation reserve created of £600. If Rose owned 100% of Tulip, then the Rose share-holders would have the benefit of the £600 and the goodwill would be reduced from £800 to £200. However, as Tulip is part-financed by non-controlling shareholders, they are entitled to their 20% share of the £600 as seen in the following schedule:

	Rose	Tulip	Group	Dr	Cr	Group fair value	
	£	£	£			£	
Non-current assets	20,000	11,000	31,000	**600**		31,600	Step 3
Goodwill	—	—	800		**480**	320	Step 1
Investment in Tulip	12,000	—	—			—	
Net current assets	11,000	3,000	14,000			14,000	
Net assets	43,000	14,000	45,800			45,920	
Share capital	16,000	10,000	16,000			16,000	
Retained earnings	27,000	4,000	27,000			27,000	
	43,000	14,000	43,000			43,000	
Non-controlling interest	—	—	2,800		**120**	2,920	Step 2
	43,000	14,000	45,800			45,920	

Step 1. Goodwill is adjusted when fair value exceeds book value

			£
The parent company's investment in Tulip			12,000
Less: The parent's share of the subsidiary's share capital	(80% × 10,000)	8,000	
The parent's share of retained earnings	(80% × 4,000)	3,200	
The parent's share of the revaluation	(80% × 600)	480	11,680
Goodwill			320

* This is equivalent to the share of net assets, 80% × (11,000 + 3,000 + 600).

Step 2. Non-controlling interest adjusted for fair value in excess of book value

Non-controlling interest in share capital of Tulip	(20% × 10,000)	2,000
Non-controlling interest in retained earnings of Tulip	(20% × 4,000)	800
Revaluation to fair value of the subsidiary's assets	(20% × 600)	120
		2,920

Step 3. Aggregate the parent's non-current assets which remain at book value and the subsidiary's which have been restated to fair value

The non-current assets would be reported as £31,600 (20,000 + 11,000 + 600). Remember that the revaluation of the subsidiary's assets is only necessary for the consolidated accounts. No entries need be made in the individual accounts of the subsidiary or its books of account. The preparation of consolidated accounts is *a separate exercise* that in no way affects the records of the individual companies.

22.5 The parent issues shares to acquire shares in a subsidiary

Shares in another company can be purchased with cash or through an exchange of shares. In the former case, the cash will be reduced and exchanged for another asset called 'investment in the subsidiary company'. If there is an exchange of shares, there will be an increase in the parents' share capital and often in the share premium.

Let us assume that Rose issued its own shares to 80% of the Tulip shareholders who wanted £1.50 for each share, totalling £12,000. Rose would in this case have to set a value of its own shares that was acceptable to the Tulip shareholders.

For illustration purposes, let us assume that the Rose shares were valued at £2.50 each and 4,800 were issued (£12,000/£2.50). The consolidation schedule would show that Rose's cash had not been reduced but the share capital and share premium had increased as follows:

		Rose £	Tulip £	Group £
Non-current assets		20,000	11,600	31,600
Investment in Tulip		12,000	—	—
Goodwill		—	—	320
Net current assets	11,000 + 12,000*	23,000	3,000	26,000
Net assets		55,000	14,000	57,920
Share capital	16,000 + 4,800 at par	20,800	10,000	20,800
Share premium	4,800 × £1.50	7,200		7,200
Retained earnings		27,000	4,000	27,000
Parent company's equity		55,000	14,000	55,000
Non-controlling interest		—	—	2,920
		55,000	14,000	57,920

* This is showing cash at £23,000 which was the position before we assumed that the shares in Tulip had been acquired for cash.

Note that there is no effect on the accounts of the acquired company as the payment of cash or exchange of shares is with the subsidiary company's individual shareholders, not the company itself.

22.6 IFRS 10 provisions

IFRS 10 has provisions relating to how to define a group, how to identify whether there is control and the need to use fair values.

22.6.1 IFRS 10 definition of a group

One of IASB's main objectives had been to develop a consistent basis for determining when a company consolidates the financial statements of another company to prepare group accounts. For this, it has stated that **control** should be the determining factor.

Under IFRS 10 *Consolidated Financial Statements*, a group exists where one enterprise (the parent) *controls*, either directly or *indirectly*, another enterprise (the subsidiary). A group consists of a parent and its subsidiaries.[1]

22.6.2 IFRS 10 definition of control

Under IFRS 10 an investor is a parent[2] when it is exposed, or has rights, to *variable returns* from its involvement with the investee and has the *ability* to affect those returns through its *power* over the investee.

An investor *controls* an investee (IFRS 10:7) if and only if the investor satisfies all of the following requirements:

● exposure, or rights, to variable returns whether positive or negative from its involvement with the investee;

● power over the investee whereby the investor has existing rights that give it the ability to direct those activities that significantly affect the investee's returns;

● the ability to use its power over the investee to affect the amount of the investor's returns.

The following is an extract from the 2011 Linde AG annual report:

Scope of consolidation
The Group financial statements comprise Linde AG and all the companies over which Linde AG exercises direct or indirect control by virtue of its power to govern their financial and operating policies.

What if the shares acquired are less than 50%?

Even in this situation, it may still be possible to identify an acquirer when one of the combining enterprises, as a result of the business combination, acquires:

(a) power over more than one-half of the voting rights of the other enterprise by virtue of an agreement with other investors;

(b) power to govern the financial and operating policies of the other enterprise under a statute or an agreement;

(c) power to appoint or remove the majority of the members of the board of directors; or

(d) power to cast the majority of votes at a meeting of the board of directors.

What if the parent holds options?

IFRS 10 provides that if those options give the entity control then this could result in an entity being consolidated. For example, if the investee's management always followed the wishes of the option holder, this may be viewed as having control.

What if a company has significant voting rights in comparison to other shareholders?

If an investor is so powerful through their voting rights compared to others, for example one investor has 40% while the other 60% is widely dispersed between unconnected investors, this can also give control and result in the investee being consolidated. Both of these areas will require directors to exercise judgement in determining whether control exists.

22.6.3 Requirement to use fair values

When one company acquires a controlling interest in another and the combination is treated as an acquisition, the assets and liabilities of the subsidiary are recorded in the acquirer's consolidated statement of financial position at their fair value.

On consolidation, if the acquirer has acquired less than 100% of the ordinary shares, any differences (positive or negative) between the fair values of the net assets and their book value are recognised in full and the parent and non-controlling interests are credited or debited with their respective percentage interests.

22.7 IFRS 3 *Business Combinations* treatment of goodwill

Any differences between the fair values of the net assets and the consideration paid to acquire them is treated as positive or 'negative' goodwill and dealt with in accordance with IFRS 3 *Business Combinations*.

The treatment of positive goodwill

Positive purchased goodwill, where the investment exceeds the total of the net assets acquired, should be recognised as an asset with no amortisation. Goodwill must be subject to impairment tests in accordance with IAS 36 *Impairment of Assets*. These tests will be annual, or more frequently if circumstances indicate that the goodwill might be impaired.[3] Once recognised, an impairment loss for goodwill may not be reversed in a subsequent period,[4] which helps in preventing the manipulation of period profits.

The treatment of negative goodwill

The acquiring company does not always pay more than the fair value of the identifiable net assets. Paying less (sometimes referred to as negative goodwill) can arise[5] when

(a) there have been errors measuring the fair value of either the cost of the combination or the acquiree's identifiable assets, liabilities or contingent liabilities; or

(b) future costs such as losses have been taken into account; or

(c) there has been a bargain purchase.

Where negative goodwill apparently arises, IFRS 3 requires parent companies to review the fair value exercise to ensure that no assets are overstated or liabilities understated. Assuming this review reveals no errors, then the resulting negative goodwill is recognised immediately in the statement of income.

The following is an extract from the 2011 EnBW Annual Report:

> **Basis of consolidation**
> Goodwill is measured as the excess of the aggregate of the consideration transferred and the amount of any non-controlling interest in the acquiree over the group's net identified assets acquired and liabilities assumed. If this consideration is lower than the fair value of the net assets acquired, the difference is recognized immediately in profit or loss following further review.

22.8 When may a parent company not be required to prepare consolidated accounts?

It may not be necessary for a parent company to prepare consolidated accounts if the parent is itself a wholly owned subsidiary and the ultimate parent produces consolidated financial statements available for public use that comply with International Financial Reporting Standards (IFRSs).[6]

If the parent company is a partially owned subsidiary of another entity, then, if its other owners have been informed and do not object, the parent company need not present consolidated financial statements.

22.9 When may a parent company exclude or not exclude a subsidiary from a consolidation?

22.9.1 Exclusion permitted

Subsidiaries may be excluded if they are immaterial or there are substantial rights exercisable by non-controlling interests.

Materiality

Exclusion is permissible on grounds of non-materiality[7] as the International Accounting Standards are not intended to apply to immaterial items. For example, the Nissan group states in its 2009 Annual Report:

> **Unconsolidated subsidiaries**
> These unconsolidated subsidiaries are small in terms of their total assets, sales, net income or loss, retained earnings and others, and do not have a significant effect on the consolidated financial statements. As a result, they have been excluded from consolidation.

Substantial rights exercisable by the non-controlling interest

Exclusion might also be appropriate where there are substantial rights exercisable by a non-controlling interest as seen in the following extract from the 2011 Linde AG annual report:

> **Scope of consolidation**
> Companies in which Linde AG holds the majority of the voting rights, either directly or indirectly, but where it is unable to control the company due to substantial rights of non-controlling shareholders (significant influence), are also accounted for using the equity method.

22.9.2 Exclusion not permitted

Exclusion on the grounds that a subsidiary's activities are dissimilar from those of the others within a group is not permitted.[8] This is because information is required under IFRS 8 *Operating Segments* on the different activities of subsidiaries, and users of accounts can, therefore, make appropriate adjustments for their own purposes if required. IFRS 10 also does not allow subsidiaries to be excluded from consolidation on the grounds of severe long-term restrictions on control.

A subsidiary would be accounted for under IFRS 5 *Non-current Assets Held for Sale and Discontinued Operations* if it was acquired exclusively with a view to sale and it meets the criteria in IFRS 5. This is illustrated by an extract from the 2010 GKN annual report:

> **Basis of consolidation**
> The statements incorporate the financial statements of the Company and its subsidiaries . . . Subsidiaries are entities over which, either directly or indirectly, the Company has control through the power to govern financial operating policies so as to obtain benefit from their activities. Except as noted below, this power is accompanied by a shareholding of more than 50% of the voting rights. . . .

In a single case the Company indirectly owns 100% of the voting share capital of an entity but was precluded from exercising either control or joint control by a contractual agreement with the United States Department of Defense. In accordance with IAS 27 this entity has been excluded from the consolidation and treated as an investment.

22.10 IFRS 13 *Fair Value Measurement*

IFRS 13 *Fair Value Measurement*[9] defines fair value as the price that would be received to sell an asset or paid to transfer a liability in an orderly transaction between market participants at the measurement date. The detailed guidance for determining fair value is also set out in IFRS 3.

The main provisions are that as from the date of acquisition, an acquirer should:

(a) incorporate into the statement of income the results of operations of the acquiree; and

(b) recognise in the statement of financial position the identifiable assets, liabilities and contingent liabilities of the acquiree and any goodwill or negative goodwill arising on the acquisition.

The identifiable assets, liabilities and contingent liabilities acquired that are recognised should be those of the acquiree that existed at the date of acquisition.

Treatment of future liabilities

Liabilities should not be recognised at the date of acquisition if they result from the acquirer's intentions or actions. Therefore liabilities for terminating or reducing the activities of the acquiree should **only** be recognised where the acquiree has, at the acquisition date, an existing liability for restructuring recognised in accordance with IAS 37 *Provisions, Contingent Liabilities and Contingent Assets*.

Treatment of future losses

Liabilities should also not be recognised for future losses[10] or other costs expected to be incurred as a result of the acquisition, whether they relate to the acquirer or the acquiree.

Treatment of intangible assets

There is a requirement to identify both tangible and intangible assets that are acquired. For example, fair values would be attached to intangibles such as brands and customer lists if these can be measured reliably. If it is not possible to measure them reliably, then the goodwill would be reported at a higher figure as in the following extract from the 2011 AstraZeneca Annual Report:

Business Combinations and Goodwill
On the acquisition of a business, fair values are attributed to the identifiable assets and liabilities and contingent liabilities unless the fair value cannot be measured reliably in which case the value is subsumed into goodwill.

Why revalue net assets?

The reason why all the net assets of the subsidiary must be identified and fair-valued at the date of acquisition is to prevent distortion of EPS in periods following the acquisition. For example, we have seen in Chapter 19 that intangible assets are required to be amortised with an annual charge against profits, whereas goodwill is not subject to an annual amortisation charge but is reviewed for impairment. Subsuming intangible assets into the goodwill figure means that a regular amortisation charge is avoided.

22.11 What advantages are there for stakeholders from requiring groups to prepare consolidated accounts?

Advantages include investor protection, help in predicting future earnings per share and means to assess management performance.

(a) **Investor protection**: Consolidation prevents the publication of misleading accounts by such means as inflating the sales through selling to another member of a group.

(b) **Prediction**: Consolidation provides a more meaningful EPS figure. Consolidated accounts show the full earnings on a parent company's investment while the parent's individual accounts only show the dividend received from the subsidiaries.

(c) **Accountability**: Consolidation provides a better measurement of the performance of a parent company's directors as the total earnings of a group can be compared with its total assets in arriving at a group's return on capital employed (ROCE).

It is important to remember that the ROCE prepared from the consolidated financial statements is regarded by management as a ratio that is an important measure of performance and one to be maximised. For example, Northgate plc reported in its 2012 Annual Report:

> Return on capital employed (ROCE) – In a capital intensive business, ROCE is a more important measure of performance than profitability alone, as low margin business returns low value to shareholders . . . ROCE is maximised through a combination of managing utilisation, hire rates, vehicle holding costs and improvements in operational efficiency.

Summary

When one company acquires a controlling interest in another and the combination is treated as an acquisition, the investment in the subsidiary is recorded in the acquirer's statement of financial position at the fair value of the investment.

On consolidation, if the acquirer has acquired less than 100% of the common shares, any differences between the fair values of the assets or liabilities and their face value are recognised in full and the parent and non-controlling interests credited or debited with their respective percentage interests.

Also, on consolidation, any differences between the fair values of the net assets and the consideration paid to acquire them is treated as positive or negative goodwill and dealt with in accordance with IFRS 3 *Business Combinations*.

REVIEW QUESTIONS

1 Explain how negative goodwill may arise and its accounting treatment.

2 Explain how the fair value is calculated for:
- tangible non-current assets
- inventories
- monetary assets.

3 Explain why only the net assets of the subsidiary and not those of the parent are adjusted to fair value at the date of acquisition for the purpose of consolidated accounts.

4 Coil SA/NV is a company incorporated under the laws of Belgium. Its accounts are IAS compliant. It states in its 2003 accounts (in accordance with IAS 27, para. 13):

> Principles of consolidation
> The consolidated Financial statements include all subsidiaries which are controlled by the Parent Company, unless such control is assumed to be temporary or due to long-term restrictions significantly impairing a subsidiary's ability to transfer funds to the Parent Company.

Discuss whether these would be acceptable reasons for excluding a subsidiary from the consolidated financial statements under IFRS 10.

5 The 2008 Annual Report of Bayer AG states:

> Subsidiaries that do not have a material impact on the Group's net worth, financial position or earnings, either individually or in aggregate, are not consolidated.

Discuss what criteria might have applied in determining that a subsidiary does not have a material impact.

6 Parent plc acquired Son plc at the beginning of the year. At the end of the year there were intangible assets reported in the consolidated accounts for the value of a domain name and customer lists. These assets did not appear in either Parent or Son's statements of financial position.

Discuss why these assets only appeared in the consolidated accounts.

7 In each of the following cases you are required to give your opinion, with reasons, on whether or not there is a parent/subsidiary under IFRS 3. Suggest any other information, if any, that might be helpful in making a decision.

(a) Tin acquired 15% of the equity voting shares and 90% of the non-voting preferred shares of Copper. Copper has no other category of shares. The directors of Tin are also the directors of Copper, there is a common head office with shared administration departments and the functions of Copper are mainly the provision of marketing and transport facilities for Tin. Another company, Iron, holds 55% of the equity voting shares of Copper but has never used its voting power to interfere with the decisions of the directors.

(b) Hat plc owns 60% of the voting equity shares in Glove plc and 25% of the voting equity shares in Shoe plc. Glove owns 30% of the voting equity shares in Shoe plc and has the right to appoint a majority of the directors.

(c) Morton plc has 30% of the voting equity shares of Berry plc and also has a verbal agreement with other shareholders, who own 40% of the shares, that those shareholders will vote according to the wishes of Morton.

(d) Bean plc acquired 30% of the shares of Pea plc several years ago with the intention of acquiring influence over the operating and financial policies of that company. Pea sells 80% of its output to Bean. While Bean has a veto over the operating and financial decisions of Pea's board of directors it has only used this veto on one occasion, four years ago, to prevent that company from supplying one of Bean's competitors.

EXERCISES

Questions 1–5

Required in each case:
Prepare the statements of financial position of Parent Ltd and the consolidated statement of financial position as at 1 January 20X7 after each transaction, using for each question the statements of financial position of Parent Ltd and Daughter Ltd as at 1 January 20X7 which were as follows:

	Parent Ltd	Daughter Ltd
	£	£
Ordinary shares of £1 each	40,500	9,000
Retained earnings	4,500	1,800
	45,000	10,800
Cash	20,000	2,000
Other net assets	25,000	8,800
	45,000	10,800

* Question 1

(a) Assume that on 1 January 20X7 Parent Ltd acquired all the ordinary shares in Daughter Ltd for £10,800 cash. The fair value of the net assets in Daughter Ltd was their book value.

(b) The purchase consideration was satisfied by the issue of 5,400 new ordinary shares in Parent Ltd. The fair value of a £1 ordinary share in Parent Ltd was £2. The fair value of the net assets in Daughter Ltd was their book value.

Required: see above.

* Question 2

(a) On 1 January 20X7 Parent Ltd acquired all the ordinary shares in Daughter Ltd for £16,200 cash. The fair value of the net assets in Daughter Ltd was their book value.

(b) The purchase consideration was satisfied by the issue of 5,400 new ordinary shares in Parent Ltd. The fair value of a £1 ordinary share in Parent Ltd was £3. The fair value of the net assets in Daughter Ltd was their book value.

Required: see above.

* Question 3

(a) On 1 January 20X7 Parent Ltd acquired all the ordinary shares in Daughter Ltd for £16,200 cash. The fair value of the net assets in Daughter Ltd was £12,000.

(b) The purchase consideration was satisfied by the issue of 5,400 new ordinary shares in Parent Ltd. The fair value of a £1 ordinary share in Parent Ltd was £3. The fair value of the net assets in Daughter Ltd was £12,000.

Required: see above.

* Question 4

On 1 January 20X7 Parent Ltd acquired all the ordinary shares in Daughter Ltd for £6,000 cash. The fair value of the net assets in Daughter Ltd was their book value.

Required: see above.

Question 5

On 1 January 20X7 Parent Ltd acquired 75% of the ordinary shares in Daughter Ltd for £9,000 cash. The fair value of the net assets in Daughter Ltd was their book value. Assume in each case that the non-controlling interest is measured using Method 1.

Required: see above.

* Question 6

Rouge plc acquired 100% of the common shares of Noir plc on 1 January 20X0 and gained control. At that date the statements of financial position of the two companies were as follows:

	Rouge € million	Noir € million
ASSETS		
Non-current assets		
Property, plant and equipment	100	60
Investment in Noir	132	
Current assets	80	70
Total assets	312	130
EQUITY AND LIABILITIES		
Ordinary €1 shares	200	60
Retained earnings	52	40
	252	100
Current liabilities	60	30
Total equity and liabilities	312	130

Note: The fair values are the same as the book values.

Required:
Prepare a consolidated statement of financial position for Rouge plc as at 1 January 20X0.

Question 7

Ham plc acquired 100% of the common shares of Burg plc on 1 January 20X0 and gained control. At that date the statements of financial position of the two companies were as follows:

	Ham €000	Burg €000
ASSETS		
Non-current assets		
Property, plant and equipment	250	100
Investment in Burg	90	
Current assets	100	70
Total assets	440	170
EQUITY AND LIABILITIES		
Capital and reserves		
€1 shares	200	100
Retained earnings	160	10
	360	110
Current liabilities	80	60
Total equity and liabilities	440	170

Notes:

1 The fair value is the same as the book value.

2 €15,000 of the negative goodwill arises because the net assets have been acquired at below their fair value and the remainder covers expected losses of €3,000 in the year ended 31/12/20X0 and €2,000 in the following year.

Required:

(a) Prepare a consolidated statement of financial position for Ham plc as at 1 January 20X0.

(b) Explain how the negative goodwill will be treated.

Question 8

Set out below is the summarised statement of financial position of Berlin plc at 1 January 20X0.

	£000
ASSETS	
Non-current assets	
Property, plant and equipment	250
Current assets	150
Total assets	400
EQUITY AND LIABILITIES	
Capital and reserves	
Share capital (£5 shares)	200
Retained earnings	80
	280
Current liabilities	120
Total equity and liabilities	400

On 1/1/20X0 Berlin acquired 100% of the shares of Hanover for £100,000 and gained control.

Required:

Prepare the statement of financial position of Berlin immediately after the acquisition if:

(a) Berlin acquired the shares for cash.

(b) Berlin issued 10,000 shares of £5 (market value £10).

Question 9

Bleu plc acquired 80% of the shares of Verte plc on 1 January 20X0 and gained control. At that date the statements of financial position of the two companies were as follows:

	Bleu £m	Verte £m
ASSETS		
Non-current assets		
Property, plant and equipment	150	120
Investment in Verte	210	
Current assets	108	105
Total assets	468	225
EQUITY AND LIABILITIES		
Capital and reserves		
Share capital (£1 shares)	300	120
Retained earnings	78	60
	378	180
Current liabilities	90	45
Total equity and liabilities	468	225

Note: The fair values are the same as the book values.

Required:

Prepare a consolidated statement of financial position for Bleu plc as at 1 January 20X0. Non-controlling interests are measured using Method 1.

Question 10

Base plc acquired 60% of the common shares of Ball plc on 1 January 20X0 and gained control. At that date the statements of financial position of the two companies were as follows:

	Base £000	Ball £000
ASSETS		
Non-current assets		
Property, plant and equipment	250	100
Investment in Ball	90	
Current assets	100	70
Total assets	440	170
EQUITY AND LIABILITIES		
Capital and reserves		
Share capital	200	80
Share premium		20
Retained earnings	160	10
	360	110
Current liabilities	80	60
Total equity and liabilities	440	170

Note: The fair value of the property, plant and equipment in Ball at 1/1/20X0 was £120,000. The fair value of the non-controlling interest in Ball at 1/1/20X0 was £55,000. The 'fair value method' should be used to measure the non-controlling interest.

Required:
Prepare a consolidated statement of financial position for Base as at 1 January 20X0.

Question 11

On 1 January 20X0 Hill plc purchased 70% of the ordinary shares of Valley plc for £1.3 million. The fair value of the non-controlling interest at that date was £0.5 million. At the date of acquisition, Valley's retained earnings were £0.4 million.

The statements of financial position of Hill and Valley at 31 December 20X0 were:

	Hill £000	Valley £000
Capital and reserves		
Share capital	5,000	1,000
Retained earnings	3,500	200
	8,500	1,200
Net assets	8,500	1,200

Because of Valley's loss in 20X0, the directors of Hill decided to write down the value of goodwill by £0.3 million. The directors of Hill propose to use Method 2 to calculate goodwill in the consolidated statement of financial position. The goodwill is to be written down in proportion to the respective holdings of Valley's shares by Hill and the non-controlling interest.

Required:
(a) Calculate the goodwill of Valley relating to Hill plc and the non-controlling interest.
(b) Show how the goodwill will be written down at 31 December 20X0, for both Hill plc and the non-controlling interest.
(c) Comment on your answer to part (b).

* Question 12

The following accounts are the consolidated statement of financial position and parent company statement of financial position for Alpha Ltd as at 30 June 20X2.

	Consolidated statement of financial position		Parent company statement of financial position	
	£	£	£	£
Ordinary shares		140,000		140,000
Capital reserve		92,400		92,400
Retained earnings		79,884		35,280
Non-controlling interest		12,329		—
		324,613		267,680
Non-current assets				
Property		127,400		84,000
Plant and equipment		62,720		50,400
Goodwill		85,680		
Investment in subsidiary (50,400 shares)				151,200
Current assets				
Inventory	121,604		71,120	
Trade receivables	70,429		51,800	
Cash at bank	24,360		—	
	216,393		122,920	
Current liabilities				
Trade payables	140,420		80,920	
Income tax	27,160		20,720	
Bank overdraft	—		39,200	
	167,580		140,840	
Working capital		48,813		(17,920)
		324,613		267,680

Notes:
1 There was only one subsidiary, called Beta Ltd.
2 There were no capital reserves in the subsidiary.
3 Alpha produced inventory for sale to the subsidiary at a cost of £3,360 in May 20X2. The inventory was invoiced to the subsidiary at £4,200 and was still on hand at the subsidiary's warehouse on 30 June 20X2. The invoice had not been settled at 30 June 20X2.
4 The retained earnings of the subsidiary had a credit balance of £16,800 at the date of acquisition. No fair value adjustments were necessary.
5 There was a right of set-off between overdrafts and bank balances.
6 The parent owns 90% of the subsidiary.

Required:
Prepare the statement of financial position as at 30 June 20X2 of the subsidiary company from the information given above. The non-controlling interest is measured using Method 1.

Question 13

Applying the principles of control in IFRS 10 *Consolidated Financial Statements*, as described in Section 22.6.2 of this chapter, you are required to consider whether certain investments of Austin plc are subsidiaries.

Austin plc has investments in a number of companies, and the company's accountant has asked your advice on whether certain of these companies should be treated as subsidiaries under IFRS 10 *Consolidated Financial Statements*.

(a) Austin plc owns 45% of the voting shares of Bond Ltd.

(b) Austin plc owns 60% of the voting shares of Bradford Ltd and Bradford Ltd owns 30% of the voting shares of Derby Ltd. Recently, Austin plc purchased 70% of the voting shares of Coventry Ltd. Coventry Ltd owns 30% of the voting shares of Derby Ltd. The accountant believes Derby Ltd is not a subsidiary of Austin, as Austin effectively owns only 39% of the shares of Derby – 60% × 30% = 18% through Bradford and 70% × 30% = 21% through Coventry.

(c) Recently, Austin plc purchased 60% of the ordinary shares of Norwich plc.

Prior to the purchase, Norwich plc had in issue 6,000,000 'A' shares of £1 each. Each 'A' share carries a single vote. These shares were owned equally by each of the directors of Norwich plc. For the purchase, the directors of Norwich plc sold 2,000,000 'A' shares to Austin plc, and Norwich plc issued 4,000,000 'B' shares of £1 each to Austin plc. 'B' shares do not carry a vote.

Required:
Consider and, where appropriate, discuss whether the following companies are subsidiaries of Austin plc:
(a) Bond Ltd
(b) Derby Ltd
(c) Norwich plc.

References

1 IFRS 10 Consolidated Financial Settlements, IASB, 2011, para. 4a.
2 IAS 36 *Impairment of Assets*, 2004, BC 131A.
3 IAS 36 *Impairment of Assets*, IASB, revised 2004, para. 34.
4 IFRS 3 *Business Combinations*, 2008, para. 57.
5 IFRS 10 *Consolidated Financial Statements*, IASB, 2011, para. 1.
6 IAS 1 *Presentation of Financial Statements*, IASB, 2007, para. 31.
7 IFRS 10 *Consolidated Financial Statements*, IASB, 2011.
8 *Ibid.*, paras 5, 6 and 8.
9 IFRS 13 *Fair Value Measurement*, IASB, 2011, Appendix A.
10 IFRS 3 *Business Combinations*, 2008, para. 41.

CHAPTER 23

Preparation of consolidated statements of financial position after the date of acquisition

23.1 Introduction

The main purpose of this chapter is to prepare consolidated financial statements after a period of trading.

Objectives

By the end of this chapter, you should be able to:

- explain uniform accounting policies;
- account for the pre- and post-acquisition profits of a subsidiary;
- eliminate inter-company balances and deal with reconciling items;
- account for unrealised profits on inter-company transactions;
- calculate group retained earnings;
- prepare consolidated statements of financial position.

23.2 Uniform accounting policies and reporting dates

Consolidated financial statements are required to adopt uniform accounting policies on a consistent basis in accordance with IAS 27 *Consolidated and Separate Financial Statements*. The following is an extract from the 2011 Annual Report of Munksjo AB:

> Accounting policies for subsidiaries are changed where necessary to ensure consistent application of the Group's policies.

If this is not practicable then disclosure must be made of that together with details of the items involved.[1]

The financial statements of the parent and subsidiaries used in the consolidated accounts are usually drawn up to the same date but IFRS 10 continues to allow up to three months' difference providing that appropriate adjustments are made for significant transactions outside the common period.[2]

23.3 Pre- and post-acquisition profits/losses

Pre-acquisition profits

Any profits or losses of a subsidiary made **before** the date of acquisition are referred to as **pre-acquisition profits/losses** in the consolidated financial statements. These are represented by the retained earnings that existed in the subsidiary as at the date of acquisition and, as we have seen in Chapter 22, they are taken into account when calculating the goodwill.

It is important to remember that the calculation of the initial goodwill as at the date of acquisition is unchanged in subsequent accounting periods. The goodwill only changes in subsequent accounting periods if there should be an impairment charge.

Post-acquisition profits

Any profits or losses made **after** the date of acquisition are referred to as **post-acquisition profits**. Because these will have arisen whilst the subsidiary was under the control of the parent company, they will be included in the group consolidated statement of income and so will be included in the retained earnings figure in the statement of financial position. The following example for the Bend Group illustrates the approach for dealing with pre- and post-acquisition profits.

23.4 The Bend Group – assuming there have been no inter-group transactions

On 1 January 20X1 Bend plc acquired 80% of the 10,000 £1 ordinary shares in Stretch plc for £1.50 per share in cash which gave it control.

- Investment in the subsidiary cost £12,000.
- The retained earnings of Stretch plc were £4,000.
- The fair value of the non-current assets in Stretch plc was £600 above book value.
- The fair value of the non-controlling interest at the date of acquisition was £2,950 and Method 2 has been adopted.

Remember that in the subsidiary's own accounts the assets may be either left at book values or restated at their fair values. If restated at fair values, they will then become subject to the requirements of IAS 16 *Property, Plant and Equipment*[3] which states that revaluations should be made with sufficient regularity that the statement of financial position figure is not materially different from the fair value at that date. This is one reason why the fair value adjustment is usually treated simply as a consolidation adjustment each year.

At 31 December 20X1 the closing statements of financial position of Bend plc and Stretch plc together with the group accounts were as follows:

	Bend £	Stretch £	Group £	
ASSETS				
Non-current assets	26,000	12,000	38,600	Step 3
Goodwill	—	—	350	Step 1
Investment in Stretch	12,000	—	—	
Net current assets	13,000	4,000	17,000	Step 3
Net assets	51,000	16,000	55,950	
EQUITY				
Share capital	16,000	10,000	16,000	Step 4
Retained earnings	35,000	6,000	36,600	Step 4
	51,000	16,000	52,600	
Non-controlling interest	—	—	3,350	Step 2
	51,000	16,000	55,950	

Step 1. Goodwill calculated as at 1 January 20X1

	£	£
Goodwill on Bend's 80% shareholding in Stretch		
The cost of the parent company's investment in Stretch		12,000
Less:		
(a) Bend's share of Stretch share capital:		
80% × share capital of Stretch (80% × 10,000)	8,000	
(b) Pre-acquisition profit		
Bend's share of Stretch's retained earnings:		
80% × retained earnings as at 1 January 20X1 (80% × 4,000)	3,200	
(c) Fair value adjustment		
Bend's share of any change in the book values:		
80% × revaluation of fixed assets at 1 January 20X1 (80% × 600)	480	
		11,680
Goodwill attributable to the parent company shareholders		320
Goodwill on non-controlling interest's 20% shareholding in Stretch		
Fair value of non-controlling interest at date of acquisition		2,950
20% of net assets at date of acquisition (10,000 + 4,000 + 600)		(2,920)
Goodwill attributable to the non-controlling interest		30
Total goodwill of parent and non-controlling interest (£320 + £30)		£350

Step 2. Non-controlling interest in the net assets of subsidiary calculated as at 31.12.20X1

	£
(a) Subsidiary share capital	
Non-controlling interest in the share capital of Stretch (20% × 10,000)	2,000
(b) Total retained earnings as at 31.12.20X1	
Non-controlling interest in retained earnings of Stretch (20% × 6,000)	1,200
(c) Fair value adjustment of subsidiary's non-current assets	
Non-controlling interest in fair value increase (20% × 600)	120
Non-controlling interest in the net assets of Stretch as at 31.12.20X1	3,320
Non-controlling interest in goodwill	30
Reported in the statement of financial position as at 31 December 20X1	3,350

Step 3. Add together the assets and liabilities of the parent and subsidiary for the group

	Parent		Subsidiary	Group
	£		£	£
Non-current tangible assets	26,000	+	(12,000 + revaluation 600)	38,600
Goodwill as calculated in Step 1				350
Net current assets	13,000	+	4,000	17,000
Total				55,950

Step 4. Calculate the consolidated share capital and reserves for the group accounts

			£	£
Share capital	Parent only			16,000
Retained earnings	Parent		35,000	
	Bend's share of post-acquisition retained earnings	(80% of (6,000 − 4,000))	1,600	36,600
Total				52,600

Notes:

1 The separation of the retained earnings into pre- and post-acquisition is only of relevance to the parent with the pre-acquisition (£4,000) used when calculating the goodwill and the post-acquisition (£2,000) reported as part of the group earnings.

2 The non-controlling shareholders are entitled to their percentage share of the closing net assets. The pre-acquisition and post-acquisition division is irrelevant to the non-controlling interests – they are entitled to their percentage share of the **total** retained earnings at the date the consolidated statement of financial position is prepared.

23.5 Inter-company transactions

In the Bend example we assumed that there had been no inter-company transactions. Inter-company transactions that occur in practice include the transfer of property such as the sale of goods and depreciable assets; the provision of services such as renting property and management fees from head office; financial transactions such as making or receiving loans and interest; and dividend receipts from the subsidiary.

All inter-company transactions are to be eliminated. For example, if sales of £10,000 have been made by one group member to another, then the sales revenue and cost of sales will both be reduced by the amount invoiced. This is accomplished by a consolidation journal entry:

	Dr	Cr
Sales	10,000	
Cost of sales		10,000

Eliminating intra-group sales

Similar reversing entries would be made for services that have been provided and loans, loan interest and dividends. As well as these reversing entries there may be a need for further consolidation adjustments, for example if transfers have been made at cost plus a profit loading as when goods are sold within the group at cost plus a percentage markup.

These eliminations and adjustments are made in order that the group accounts do not double-count revenue, expenses, assets and/or liabilities. All such eliminations and adjustments should be authorised as consolidation journal entries by a responsible officer such as the finance director.

23.5.1 Inter-company balances arising from sales or other transactions

IFRS 10 requires inter-company balances to be eliminated in full.[4]

Eliminating inter-company balances

If entries in the parent's records and the subsidiary's records are up-to-date, the same figure will appear as a balance in the current assets of one company and in the current liabilities of the other. For example, if the parent company has supplied goods invoiced at £1,500 to its subsidiary, there will be a receivable for £1,500 in the parent statement of financial position and a payable for £1,500 in the subsidiary's statement of financial position. These need to be cancelled, i.e. eliminated, before preparing the consolidated accounts. In accounting terminology, this is also referred to as offsetting.

Reconciling inter-company balances

In practice, temporary differences may arise for such items as inventory or cash in transit that are recorded in one company's books but of which the other company is not yet aware, e.g. goods or cash in transit. In such a case the records will require reconciling and updating before proceeding.

Differences due to items in transit will need adjustment in the books of the recipient to the cash or goods. In a multinational company, this can be an extremely time-consuming exercise.

23.5.2 Inter-company dividends payable/receivable

If the subsidiary company has declared a dividend before the year-end, it will appear in the current liabilities of the subsidiary company and in the current assets of the parent company. It needs to be cancelled by set-off.

If the subsidiary is wholly owned by the parent the whole amount will be cancelled. If, however, there is a non-controlling interest in the subsidiary, the non-cancelled amount of the dividend payable in the subsidiary's statement of financial position will be the amount payable to the non-controlling interest and will be reported as part of the non-controlling interest in the consolidated statement of financial position.

Where a final dividend has not been declared by the year-end date there is no liability under IAS 10 *Events after the Reporting Period Date* and no liability will be reported.

23.5.3 Unrealised profit on inter-company sales

Where sales have been made between two companies within the group, it is only necessary to provide for an unrealised profit from intra-group sales to the extent that the goods are still in the inventories of the group at the date of the statement of financial position.

We will illustrate the accounting treatment where there is unrealised profit with the Many Group example. The Group consists of the parent, Many plc, and a subsidiary, Few plc.

Let us assume that Many plc buys £1,000 worth of goods for resale and sells them to Few plc for £1,500, making a profit of £500 in Many's own accounts.

We have already seen that one of the consolidated journal entries would be to debit sales £1,500 and credit cost of sales £1,500 whether or not the goods had been sold on to a third party.

If at the year-end Few plc still has these goods in inventory, the group has not yet made a sale to a third party and the £500 profit is therefore 'unrealised'. It must be removed from the consolidated statement of financial position by:

● reducing the retained earnings of Many by £500; and
● reducing the inventories of Few by £500.

The £500 is called a provision for unrealised profit.

If the sale is made by a subsidiary to the parent and there are non-controlling interests, these will be debited with their proportion of the unrealised profit.

Companies include a reference to these adjustments in their accounting policies as seen in the following extract from the 2011 Annual Report of Munksjo AB:

> Intra-Group transactions, balances and unrealised gains and losses on transactions between Group companies are eliminated.

The Prose Group example that follows incorporates the main points dealt with so far on the preparation of a consolidated statement of financial position.

23.6 The Prose Group – assuming there have been inter-group transactions

On 1 January 20X1 Prose plc acquired 80% of the equity shares in Verse plc for £21,100 to gain control and 10% of the 5% loans for £900. The retained earnings as at 1 January 20X1 were £4,000. The fair value of the land in Verse was £1,000 above book value.

During the year Prose sold some of its inventory to Verse for £3,000, which represented cost plus a markup of 25%. Half of these goods are still in the inventory of Verse at 31/12/20X1.

The consolidated statement of financial position as at 31 December 20X1 is shown below with supporting notes. Note that depreciation is not charged on land and Method 1 is used to compute the non-controlling interest.

	Prose £	Verse £	Adjustments Dr	Adjustments Cr	Group £	
ASSETS						
Non-current assets	25,920	33,400	1,000		60,320	
Investment in Verse/goodwill	22,000	—		21,500	500	Step 1
Current assets						
Inventories	9,600	4,000		300	13,300	Step 3
Verse current account	8,000			8,000	—	Step 2
Loan interest receivable	35			35	—	Step 2
Other current assets	3,965	13,350			17,315	
Total assets	69,520	50,750			91,435	
EQUITY and LIABILITIES						
Equity share capital	24,000	21,000	21,000		24,000	
Retained earnings	30,000	8,500	5,200		33,300	Step 5
Non-controlling interest	—	—		6,100	6,100	Step 4
Non-current liabilities						
5% loan 2017/18	5,000	7,000	700		11,300	Step 2
Current liabilities						
Prose current account		8,000	8,000		—	
Loan interest payable		350	35		315	
Other current liabilities	10,520	5,900			16,420	
	69,520	50,750	35,935	35,935	91,435	

Step 1. Calculation of goodwill (note that this calculation will be the same as when calculated at the date of acquisition)

	£	£
Cost of investment in shares and loan		22,000
Less:		
1 80% × equity shares of Verse (80% × 21,000)	16,800	
2 80% × retained earnings balance at 1.1.20X1 (80% × 4,000)	3,200	
3 80% × fair value increase at 1.1.20X1 (80% × 1,000)	800	
4 10% × loans of Verse (10% × 7,000)	700	21,500
5 Goodwill in statement of financial position		500

Step 2. Inter-company elimination by set-off of inter-company balances

1 The current accounts of £8,000 between the two companies are cancelled. Note that the accounts are equal, which indicates that there are no items such as goods in transit or cash in transit which would have required a reconciliation.

2 The loan interest receivable by Prose is cancelled with £35 (10% of £350) of the loan interest payable by Verse, leaving £315 (90% of £350) payable to outsiders. This is not part of the non-controlling interest as loan holders have no ownership rights in the company.

3 The loan of £700 in Prose's accounts is set off against the £7,000 in Verse's accounts, leaving 6,300 owing to non-group members.

Step 3. Unrealised profit in inventory

Markup on the inter-company sales (£3,000 × 20%)	£600
Half the goods are still in inventories at the year-end.	
Unrealised profit	£300

Step 4. Calculation of non-controlling interest as at 31/12/20X1

Note that the non-controlling interest is calculated as at the year-end while goodwill is calculated at the date of acquisition.

		£
Non-controlling interest in the equity shares of Verse	(20% × 21,000)	4,200
Non-controlling interest in the retained earnings of Verse	(20% × 8,500)	1,700
Non-controlling interest in the fair value increase	(20% × 1,000)	200
Statement of financial position figure		6,100

Step 5. Calculation of consolidated share capital and reserves for the group accounts

	£	£
Share capital:		
Equity share capital (parent company's only)		24,000
Retained earnings (parent company's)	30,000	
Less: Provision for unrealised profit	(300)	29,700
Parent's share of the post-acquisition profit of the subsidiary (80% × 8,500)	6,800	
Less: 80% of pre-acquisition profits (80% × 4,000)	(3,200)	3,600
Retained earnings in the consolidated statement of financial position		33,300

Note: Under the Adjustments (DR) column, the 21,000 comprises 4,200 in the Goodwill calculation and 4,200 in the Non-controlling interest column. The 8,500 comprises 3,200 under Goodwill, 1,700 under Non-controlling interest and 300 under retained earnings.

23.7 How is the investment in subsidiaries reported in the parent's own statement of financial position?

IAS 27 gives the parent a choice as to how to report the investment.[5] It can either report the investment at cost, or report it in accordance with the provisions of IAS 39 *Financial Instruments: Recognition and Measurement*. Cost in this context means the fair value of the consideration at the date of acquisition.

Summary

When consolidated accounts are prepared after the subsidiary has traded with other members of the group, the goodwill calculation remains as at the date of the acquisition but all inter-company transactions and unrealised profits arising from inter-company transactions must be eliminated.

1 The following is an extract from the UPM-Kymmene Corporation 2011 financial statements:

All intercompany transactions, receivables, liabilities and unrealised profits, as well as intragroup profit distributions, are eliminated.

(a) Discuss three examples of inter-company (also referred to as intra-group) transactions.

(b) Explain what is meant by 'are eliminated'.

(c) Explain what effect there could be on the reported group profit if inter-company transactions were not eliminated.

2 Explain why the non-controlling interest is not affected by the pre- and post-acquisition division.

3 Explain why pre-acquisition profits of a subsidiary are treated differently from post-acquisition profits when consolidating.

4 Explain the effect of a provision for unrealised profit on a non-controlling interest:

(a) where the sale was made by the parent to the subsidiary; and

(b) where the sale was made by the subsidiary to the parent.

5 A consolidated journal adjustment set off the dividend receivable reported in the parent's statement of financial position against the dividend declared by the subsidiary. Explain why this may not fully eliminate the dividend that is reported in the group statement of financial position.

6 Explain reasons why the current accounts in the parent and subsidiary may not agree. If not, how could the two accounts be set off?

* Question 1

Sweden acquired 100% of the equity shares of Oslo on 1 March 20X1 and gained control. At that date the balances on the reserves of Oslo were as follows:

Revaluation reserve   Kr10 million
Retained earnings   Kr70 million

The statements of financial position of the two companies at 31/12/20X1 were as follows:

	Sweden Krm	Oslo Krm
ASSETS		
Non-current assets		
Property, plant and equipment	264	120
Investment in Oslo	200	
Current assets	160	140
Total assets	624	260
EQUITY AND LIABILITIES		
Kr10 shares	400	110
Retained earnings	104	80
Revaluation reserve	20	10
	524	200
Current liabilities	100	60
Total equity and liabilities	624	260

Notes:

1 The fair values were the same as the book values on 1/3/20X1.
2 There have been no movements on share capital since 1/3/20X1.
3 20% of the goodwill is to be written off as an impairment loss.
4 Method 1 is to be used to compute the non-controlling interest.

Required:
Prepare a consolidated statement of financial position for Sweden as at 31 December 20X1.

* Question 2

Summer plc acquired 60% of the equity shares of Winter Ltd on 30 September 20X1 and gained control. At the date of acquisition, the balance of retained earnings of Winter was €35,000.

At 31 December 20X1 the statements of financial position of the two companies were as follows:

	Summer €000	Winter €000
ASSETS		
Non-current assets		
Property, plant and equipment	200	200
Investment in Winter	141	
Current assets	100	140
Total assets	441	340
EQUITY AND LIABILITIES		
Equity shares	200	180
Retained earnings	161	40
	361	220
Current liabilities	80	120
Total equity and liabilities	441	340

Notes:

1 The fair value of the non-controlling interest at the date of acquisition was £92,000. The non-controlling interest is to be measured using Method 2. The fair values of the identifiable net assets of Winter at the date of acquisition were the same as their book values.
2 There have been no movements on share capital since 30/9/20X1.
3 16.67% of the goodwill is to be written off as an impairment loss.

Required:
Prepare a consolidated statement of financial position for Summer plc as at 31 December 20X1.

Question 3

On 30 September 20X0 Gold plc acquired 75% of the equity shares, 30% of the preferred shares and 20% of the bonds in Silver plc and gained control. The balance of retained earnings on 30 September 20X0 was £16,000. The fair value of the land owned by Silver was £3,000 above book value. No adjustment has so far been made for this revaluation.

The statements of financial position of Gold and Silver at 31 December 20X1 were as follows:

	Gold £	Silver £
ASSETS		
Property, plant and equipment (including land)	82,300	108,550
Investment in Silver	46,000	—
Current assets:		
Inventory	23,200	10,000
Silver current account	20,000	
Bond interest receivable	175	
Other current assets	5,000	7,500
Total assets	176,675	126,050
EQUITY AND LIABILITIES		
Equity share capital	60,000	27,600
Preferred shares	10,000	20,000
Retained earnings	75,000	21,200
	145,000	68,800
Non-current liabilities – bonds	12,500	17,500
Current liabilities		
Gold current account		20,000
Bond interest payable	625	875
Other current liabilities	18,550	18,875
Total equity and liabilities	176,675	126,050

Notes:

1 20% of the goodwill is to be written off as an impairment loss.
2 During the year Gold sold some of its inventory to Silver for £3,000, which represented cost plus a markup of 25%. Half of these goods are still in the inventory of Silver at 31.12.20X1.
3 There is no depreciation of land.
4 There has been no movement on share capital since the acquisition.
5 Method 1 is to be used to compute the non-controlling interest.

Required:
Prepare a consolidated statement of financial position as at 31 December 20X1.

Prop and Flap have produced the following statements of financial position as at 31 October 2008:

	Prop		Flap	
	$m	$m	$m	$m
ASSETS				
Non-current assets				
Plant and equipment		2,100		480
Investments		800		
Current assets				
Inventories	880		280	
Receivables	580		420	
Cash and cash equivalents	400		8	
		1,860		708
Total assets		4,760		1,188
EQUITY and LIABILITIES				
Equity share capital		2,400		680
Retained earnings		860		200
		3,260		880
Non-current liabilities				
Long-term borrowing		400		
Current liabilities				
Payables	1,100		228	
Bank overdraft	—		80	
		1,100		308
Total equity and liabilities		4,760		1,188

The following information is relevant to the preparation of the financial statements of the Prop Group:

1 Prop acquired 80% of the issued ordinary share capital of Flap many years ago when the retained earnings of Flap were $72 million. Consideration transferred was $800 million. Flap has performed well since acqusition and so far there has been no impairment to goodwill.

2 At the date of acquisition the plant and equipment of Flap was revalued upwards by $40 million, although this revaluation was not recorded in the accounts of Flap. Depreciation would have been $32 million greater had it been based on the revalued figure.

3 Flap buys goods from Prop upon which Prop earns a margin of 20%. At 31 October 2008 Flap's inventories include $180 million goods purchased from Prop.

4 At 31 October 2008 Prop has receivables of $140 million owed by Flap and payables of $60 million owed to Flap.

5 The market price of the non-controlling interest shares just before Flap's acquisition by Prop was $1.30. It is the group's policy to value the non-controlling interest at fair value.

Required:
Prepare the Prop Group consolidated statement of financial position as at 31 October 2008.

(Association of International Accountants)

References

1 IFRS 10 *Consolidated Financial Statements*, IASB, 2011, para. 19.
2 *Ibid.*, B 92–93.
3 IAS 16 *Property, Plant and Equipment*, IASB, revised 2003, para. 31.
4 IFRS 10 *Consolidated Financial Statements*, IASB, 2011, B 86.
5 IAS 27 *Separate Financial Statements*, IASB, revised 2011.

CHAPTER 24

Preparation of consolidated statements of income, changes in equity and cash flows

24.1 Introduction

The main purpose of this chapter is to explain how to prepare a consolidated statement of income.

Objectives

By the end of this chapter, you should be able to:

- eliminate inter-company transactions;
- prepare a consolidated statement of income;
- attribute income to the non-controlling shareholders;
- prepare a consolidated statement of changes in equity;
- prepare a consolidated statement of income when a subsidiary is acquired part-way through a year;
- prepare a consolidated statement of cash flows.

24.2 Eliminate inter-company transactions

Many business combinations occur because the acquirer seeks closer links with the acquired company. There are many examples of this, such as a clothing manufacturer in Europe acquiring a denim supplier in Hong Kong with inter-company purchases and sales following the acquisition.

Inter-company sales

When the consolidated statement of income is prepared the inter-company sales are eliminated. This avoids the possibility that the group could inflate its revenue merely by group companies selling to each other. The sales and purchases both need to be reduced by the invoiced amount of the inter-company sales. This is achieved in the consolidation process by reducing the aggregate sales and aggregate cost of sales figures.

Unrealised profit

In the previous chapter we treated any unrealised profit by reducing the inventory figure and reducing the retained earnings figure. The retained earnings figure would have incorporated the retained earnings balance from the statement of income, i.e. the adjustment for the unrealised profit would have already been reported in the statement of income.

In the consolidation process the unrealised profit is added to the cost of sales to achieve the reduction in group gross profit.

Dividends and interest

Having set off the sales and cost of sales and adjusted for any unrealised profit, further adjustments may be required[1] to establish the profit before tax earned by the group as a whole. This requires us to eliminate any dividends (and interest if any) that have been credited in the parent's statement of income for amounts paid or payable to the parent by the subsidiaries.

If this were not done, there would be double-counting because we would be including in the consolidated statement of income the subsidiary's profit from operations and again as dividends and interest received/receivable by the parent.

Group profits before tax

We can see, therefore, that group profit before tax is arrived at after setting-off inter-company sales against the cost of sales, adding the unrealised profit to the cost of sales figure, and eliminating any dividends or interest received or receivable from a subsidiary.

We will illustrate this in the following Ante Group example.

24.3 Preparation of a consolidated statement of income – the Ante Group

The following information is available:

At the date of acquisition on 1 January 20X3
Ante plc acquired 75% of the ordinary shares in Post plc. (*This shows that Ante had control.*) At that date the retained earnings of Post were £30,000. (*These are pre-acquisition profits and should not be included in the group profit for the year.*)

At the end of 20X3
The retained earnings of Ante were £69,336 and the retained earnings of Post were £54,000.

During the year ended 31 December 20X4
Ante had sold Post goods at their cost price of £9,000 plus a markup of one-third. These were the only inter-company sales. (*This indicates that the group sales and cost of sales require reducing.*)

At the end of the financial year on 31 December 20X4
Half of these goods were still in the inventory at the end of the year. (*There is unrealised profit to be removed from the group gross profit by adding the unrealised amount to the cost of sales figure.*)

Dividends paid in 20X4 by group companies were as follows:

	Ante	Post
On ordinary shares	£40,000	£5,000

Set out below are the individual statements of income of Ante and Post together with the consolidated statement of income for the year ended 31 December 20X4 with explanatory notes.

Statements of comprehensive income for the year ended 31 December 20X4

	Ante £	Post £	Consolidated £	
Sales	200,000	120,000	308,000	Note 1
Cost of sales	60,000	60,000	109,500	Notes 1 and 2
Gross profit	140,000	60,000	198,500	
Expenses	59,082	40,000	99,082	Note 3
Profit from operations	80,918	20,000	99,418	
Dividends received – ordinary shares	3,750	—	—	
Profit before tax	84,668	20,000	99,418	Note 4
Income tax expense	14,004	6,000	20,004	Note 5
Profit for the period	70,664	14,000	79,414	
Attributable to:				
Ordinary shareholders of Ante (balance)			75,914	
Non-controlling shareholders in Post			3,500	Note 6
			79,414	

Notes:

1 Eliminate inter-company sales on consolidation

Cancel the inter-company sales of £12,000 (£9,000 × $1^1/_3$) by

(i) reducing the sales of Ante from £200,000 to £188,000; and

(ii) reducing the cost of sales of Post by the same amount from £60,000 to £48,000.

> (Remember that the same amount is deducted from both sales and cost of sales – a sale to one party is the amount of the purchase by the other party.)

(iii) Group sales are £188,000 + £120,000 = £308,000.

(iv) Group cost of sales (before any adjustment for unrealised profit) is £60,000 + £48,000 = £108,000.

2 Eliminate unrealised profit on inter-company goods still in closing inventory

(i) Ante had sold the goods to Post at a markup of £3,000.

(ii) Half of the goods remain in the inventory of Post at the year-end.

(iii) From the group's view there is an unrealised profit of half of the markup, i.e. £1,500. Therefore:

- deduct £1,500 from the gross profit of Ante by adding this amount to the cost of sales;

- reduce the inventories in the consolidated statement of financial position by the amount of the provision (as explained in the previous chapter).

(iv) Cost of sales has been increased from £108,000 to £109,500.

3 Aggregate expenses

In this example we do not have any inter-company transactions such as Head Office management fees that need to be set off. No adjustment is, therefore, required to the parent or subsidiary total figures.

4 Profit before tax, accounting for the inter-company dividends

The ordinary dividend of £3,750 received by Ante is an inter-company item that does not appear in the group profit before tax.

5 **Aggregate the taxation figures**
No adjustment is required to the parent or subsidiary total figures.

6 **Allocation of profit to equity holders and non-controlling interest**
Adjustment is required[2] to establish how much of the profit after tax is attributable to equity holders of the parent. The amount is that remaining after deducting the non-controlling interest's percentage of the subsidiary's after-tax figure, i.e. 25% of £14,000 = £3,500.

24.4 The statement of changes in equity (SOCE)[3]

In practice the opening figures for the SOCE would be available from the 20X3 group accounts. It is not uncommon in an examination context to require you to calculate the opening figure for the group SOCE. The calculation is as follows:

Opening balance for the Ante group

	£
Ante's retained earnings at the start of the year	69,336
Group share of Post's post-acquisition earnings (75% × (54,000 − 30,000))	18,000
	87,336

Opening balance for the non-controlling interest
Total retained earnings as at 31.12.20X3 of £54,000 × 25% = £13,500.

We can then complete the group SOCE as follows:

	Ante	Non-controlling interest	Total
	£	£	£
Opening balance	87,336	13,500	100,836
Income for the period	75,914	3,500	79,414
Dividends paid	(40,000)	(1,250)	(41,250)
Closing balance	123,250	15,750	139,000

Dividends paid

In the Ante column the dividends paid are those of the parent only. The parent company's share of Post's dividend cancels out with the parent company's investment income. The non-controlling share is £5,000 minus the £3,750 paid to the parent. This is the amount dealt with in their column.

24.5 Other consolidation adjustments

In the above example we dealt with adjustments for intra-group sale of goods, unrealised profit on inventories and dividends received from a subsidiary. There are other adjustments that often appear in examinations relating to depreciation and dividends paid by a subsidiary out of pre-acquisition profits.

24.5.1 Depreciation adjustment when fair value is higher than book value

If the fair value of depreciable non-current assets is different from their book value, it is necessary to adjust the depreciation that has been charged.

For example, assume that the parent acquired a non-current asset from a subsidiary which had a book value of £100,000 that was being depreciated by the subsidiary on a straight-line basis over five years and the scrap value was nil. The annual charge in the subsidiary's statement of income would be £20,000.

If the fair value on acquisition was £150,000, the charge in the consolidated statement of income should be based on the £150,000, i.e. £30,000 (£150,000/5) with the depreciation increased by £10,000. If there is no information as to the type of non-current asset, the £10,000 would be added to the cost of sales figure. If the type of asset is identified, for example as delivery vehicles, then the adjustment would be made to the appropriate expense, e.g. distribution costs.

24.5.2 Depreciation adjustment when transfer has been at cost plus a profit loading

Let us consider Digdeep plc, a civil engineering company that has a subsidiary, Heavylift plc, that manufactures digging equipment. Assume that at the beginning of the financial year Heavylift sold equipment costing £80,000 to Digdeep for £100,000. It is Digdeep's depreciation policy to depreciate at 5% using the straight-line method with nil scrap value.

On consolidation, the following adjustments are required:

(i) Revenue is reduced by £20,000 and the asset is reduced by £20,000 to bring the asset back to its cost of £80,000.

Dr: Revenue	£20,000	
Cr: Asset		£20,000

(ii) Revenue is then reduced by £80,000 and cost of sales reduced by £80,000 to eliminate the inter-company sale.

Dr: Revenue	£80,000	
Cr: Cost of sales		£80,000

(iii) Depreciation needs to be based on the cost of £80,000. The depreciation charge was £5,000 (5% of £100,000); it should be £4,000 (5% of £80,000) so the adjustment is:

Dr: Accumulated depreciation	£1,000	
Cr: Depreciation in the statement of income		£1,000

24.5.3 Dividends or interest paid by the subsidiary out of pre-acquisition profits

When a parent acquires the net assets of a subsidiary it is paying for all of the assets including the cash. If the subsidiary then pays part of this to the parent as a dividend it is in effect transferring an asset that the parent had already paid for. The dividend received by the parent is not, therefore, income but a return of part of the purchase price. It is credited by the parent to the investment in subsidiary account. This is illustrated in the Bow plc example below.

Illustration of a dividend paid out of pre-acquisition profits

Bow plc acquired 75% of the shares in Tie plc on 1 January 20X4 for £80,000 when the balance of the retained earnings of Tie was £40,000. On 10 January 20X4 Bow received a dividend of £3,000 from Tie out of the profits for the year ended 31/12/20X3. The draft summarised statements of income for the year ended 31/12/20X4 were as follows:

	Bow £	Tie £	Consolidated £
Gross profit	130,000	70,000	200,000
Expenses	50,000	40,000	90,000
Profit from operations	80,000	30,000	110,000
Dividends received from Tie (see note)	3,000	—	—
Profit before tax	83,000	30,000	110,000
Income tax expense	24,000	6,000	30,000
Profit for the period	59,000	24,000	80,000

Note:
The treatment is incorrect. The £3,000 dividend received from Tie is not income and must not therefore appear in Bow's statement of income. The correct treatment is to deduct it from the investment in Tie, which will then become £77,000 (80,000 − 3,000) with a debit to dividends received and a credit to the Investment in Tie.

24.5.4 Goodwill

We know that there is no amortisation charge for goodwill. However, if there has been any impairment then this would appear as an expense in the group column of the consolidated statement of income.

For example, if in our Ante example above you were informed that the goodwill on acquisition was £10,000 and that it had been impaired by £2,000, the consolidated statement of income would have an entry in the group column and appear as follows:

	Ante £	Post £	Consolidated £	
Sales	200,000	120,000	308,000	Note 1
Cost of sales	60,000	60,000	109,500	Notes 1/2
Gross profit	140,000	60,000	198,500	
Expenses	59,082	40,000	99,082	Note 3
Goodwill amortisation			2,000	
Profit from operations	80,918	20,000	97,418	

24.6 A subsidiary acquired part-way through the year

It would be attractive for a company whose results had not been as good as expected to acquire a profitable subsidiary at the end of the year and take its current year's profit into the group accounts. However, this is window dressing and it is not permitted. The group can only bring in a subsidiary's profits from the date of the acquisition when it assumed control. The Tight plc example below illustrates the approach.

24.6.1 Illustration of a subsidiary acquired part-way through the year – Tight plc

The following information is available:

At the date of acquisition on 30 September 20X1
Tight acquired 75% of the shares and 20% of the 5% long-term loans in Loose. The book value and fair value were the same amount.

During the year
There have been no inter-company sales. If there had been then normal set-off would apply. All income and expenses are deemed to accrue evenly through the year and the dividend receivable may be apportioned to pre- and post-acquisition on a time basis.

At the end of the financial year
The Tight Group prepares its accounts as at 31 December each year.

Set out below are the individual statements of income of Tight and Loose together with the consolidated statement of income for the year ended 31 December 20X1.

	Tight	Loose	Time-apportion		Consolidated
	£	£		£	£
Revenue	200,000	120,000	3/12	30,000	230,000
Cost of sales	60,000	60,000	3/12	15,000	75,000
Gross profit	140,000	60,000	3/12	15,000	155,000
Expenses	59,082	30,000	3/12	7,500	66,582
Interest paid on 5% loans		10,000		2,500	2,000
Interest received on Loose loans	2,000		Set off		NIL
	82,918	20,000			86,418
Dividends received	3,600	NIL	Set off		NIL
Profit before tax	86,518	20,000			86,418
Income tax expense	14,004	6,000	3/12	1,500	15,504
Profit for the period after tax	72,514	14,000		3,500	70,914
Attributable to:					
Ordinary shareholders of Tight (balance)					70,039
Non-controlling shareholders in Loose					875
					70,914

Notes:

1 **Time-apportion and aggregate the revenue, cost of sales, expenses and income tax**
Group items include a full year for the parent company and three months for the subsidiary (1 October to 31 December).

2 **Account for inter-company interest**
Inter-company expense items need to be eliminated or cancelled by set-off against the interest paid by Loose. Interest is an expense which is normally deemed to accrue evenly over the year and is to be apportioned on a time basis.

(i) It has been assumed that interest is paid annually in arrears. This means that the interest received by Tight has to be apportioned on a time basis: $\frac{9}{12} \times £2,000 = £1,500$ is treated as being pre-acquisition. It is therefore deducted from the cost of the investment in Loose.

(ii) The remainder (£500) is cancelled with £500 of the post-acquisition element of the interest paid by Loose. The interest paid figure in the consolidated financial statements will be the post-acquisition interest less the inter-company elimination, which represents the amount payable to the holders of 80% of the loan capital.

(iii) The interest of £10,000 paid by Loose to its loan creditors is time-apportioned with £7,500 being pre-acquisition. The post-acquisition amount of £2,500 includes £500 that was included in the £2,000 reported by Tight in its statement of income. This is cancelled, leaving £2,000 which was paid to the 80% non-group loan creditors.

3 Account for inter-company dividends

Amount received by Tight =	£3,600
The dividend received by Tight is apportioned on a time basis, and the pre-acquisition element is credited to the cost of investment in Tight, i.e. $^9/_{12} \times £3,600 =$	(£2,700)
The post-acquisition element is cancelled	(£900)
Amount credited to consolidated statement of income	NIL

4 Calculate the share of post-acquisition consolidated profits belonging to the non-controlling interest

As only the post-acquisition proportion of the subsidiary's profit after tax has been included in the consolidated statement of income, the amount deducted as the non-controlling interest in the profit after tax is also time-apportioned, i.e. 25% of £3,500 = £875.

24.7 Published format statement of income

The statement of comprehensive income follows the classification of expenses by function as illustrated in IAS 1:

	£
Revenue	230,000
Cost of sales	75,000
Gross profit	155,000
Distribution costs	xxxxxx
Administrative expense	xxxxxx
	66,582
	88,418
Finance cost	2,000
	86,418
Income tax expense	15,504
Profit for the period	70,914
Attributable to:	
Equity holders of the parent	70,039
Non-controlling interest	875
	70,914

24.8 Consolidated statements of cash flows

Statements of cash flows are explained in Chapter 5 for a single company. A consolidated statement of cash flows differs from that for a single company in two respects:

(a) there are additional items such as dividends paid to non-controlling interests; and

(b) adjustments may be required to the actual amounts to reflect the assets and liabilities brought in by the subsidiary which did not arise from cash movements.

24.8.1 Adjustments to changes between opening and closing statements of financial position

Adjustments are required if the closing statement of financial position items have been increased or reduced as a result of **non-cash movements**. Such movements occur if there has been a purchase of a subsidiary to reflect the fact that the assets and liabilities from the new subsidiary have not necessarily resulted from cash flows. The following illustrates such adjustments in relation to a subsidiary acquired at the end of the financial year where the net assets of the subsidiary were as follows:

Net assets acquired	£000	Effect in consolidated statement of cash flows
Working capital:		
Inventory	10	Reduce inventory increase
Trade payables	(12)	Reduce trade payables increase
Non-current assets:		
Vehicles	20	Reduce capital expenditure
Cash/bank:		
Cash	5	Reduce amount paid to acquire subsidiary in investing section
Net assets acquired	23	

Let us assume that the consideration for the acquisition was as follows:

Shares	10	Reduce share cash inflow
Share premium	10	Reduce share cash inflow
Cash	3	Payment to acquire subsidiary in investing section
	23	

The consolidated statement of cash flows can then be prepared using the indirect method.

Statement of cash flows using the indirect method

	£000	£000
Cash flows from operating activities		
Net profit before tax	500	
Adjustments for:		
Depreciation	102	
Operating profit before working capital changes	602	
Increase in inventories	(400)	
Less: **Inventory brought in on acquisition**	10	(390)
Decrease in trade payables	(40)	
Add: **Trade payables brought in on acquisition**	(12)	(52)
Cash generated from operations		160
Income taxes paid (200 + 190 − 170)		(220)
Net cash from operating activities		(60)
Cash flows from investing activities		
Purchase of property, plant and equipment	(563)	
Less: **Vehicles brought in on acquisition**	20	(543)
Payment to acquire subsidiary		(3)
Cash acquired with subsidiary		5
Net cash used in investing activities		(541)
Cash flows from financing activities		
Proceeds from issuance of share capital	300	
Less: **Shares issued on acquisition not for cash**	(20)	280
Dividends paid (from statement of income)		(120)
Net cash from financing activities		160
Net decrease in cash and cash equivalents		(441)
Cash and cash equivalents at the beginning of the period		72
Cash and cash equivalents at the end of the period		(369)

Supplemental disclosure of acquisition

	£
Total purchase consideration	23,000
Portion of purchase consideration discharged by means of cash or cash equivalents	3,000
Amount of cash and cash equivalents in the subsidiary acquired	5,000

Summary

The retained earnings of the subsidiary brought forward are divided into pre-acquisition profits and post-acquisition profits – the group share of the former are used in the goodwill calculation, and the share of the latter are brought into the consolidated shareholders' equity.

Revenue and cost of sales are adjusted in order to eliminate intra-group sales and unrealised profits.

Finance expenses and income are adjusted to eliminate inter-company payments of interest and dividends.

The non-controlling interest in the profit after tax of the subsidiary is deducted to arrive at the profit for the year attributable to the equity holders of the parent.

If a subsidiary is acquired during a financial year, the items in its statement of income require apportioning. In the illustration in the text we assumed that trading was evenly spread throughout the year – in practice you would need to consider any seasonal patterns that would make this assumption unrealistic, remembering that the important consideration is that the group accounts should only be credited with profits arising whilst the subsidiary was under the parent's control.

REVIEW QUESTIONS

1 Explain why the dividends deducted from the group in the statement of changes in equity are only those of the parent company.

2 Explain two ways in which unrealised profits might arise from transactions between companies in a group and why it is important to remove them.

3 Explain why it is necessary to apportion a subsidiary's profit or loss if acquired part-way through a financial year.

4 Explain why dividends paid by a subsidiary to a parent company are eliminated on consolidation.

5 Give four examples of inter-company income and expense transactions that will need to be eliminated on consolidation and explain why each is necessary.

6 A shareholder was concerned that following an acquisition the profit from operations of the parent and subsidiary were less than the aggregate of the individual profit from operations figures. She was concerned that the acquisition, which the directors had supported as improving earnings per share, appeared to have reduced the combined profits. She wanted to know where the profits had gone. Give an explanation to the shareholder.

7 Explain how a management charge made by a parent company would be dealt with on consolidation.

8 Explain how the impairment of goodwill is dealt with on consolidation.

9 Explain why unrealised profits on inventory purchased from another member of the group is added to the cost of sales when it is not a cost.

10 Explain why differences between the opening and closing statements of financial position are adjusted when preparing a consolidated statement of cash flows when a subsidiary is acquired.

EXERCISES

* Question 1

Hyson plc acquired 75% of the shares in Green plc on 1 January 20X0 for £6 million when Green plc's accumulated profits were £4.5 million. At acquisition, the fair value of Green's non-current assets were £1.2 million in excess of their carrying value. The remaining life of these non-current assets is six years.

The summarised statements of comprehensive income for the year ended 31.12.20X0 were as follows:

	Hyson £000	Green £000
Revenue	23,500	6,400
Cost of sales	16,400	4,700
Gross profit	7,100	1,700
Expenses	4,650	1,240
Profit before tax	2,450	460
Income tax expense	740	140
Profit for the period	1,710	320

There were no inter-company transactions. Depreciation of non-current assets is charged to cost of sales.

Required:
Prepare a consolidated statement of comprehensive income for the year ended 31 December 20X0.

* Question 2

Forest plc acquired 80% of the ordinary shares of Bulwell plc some years ago. At acquisition, the fair values of the assets of Bulwell plc were the same as their carrying value. Bulwell plc manufacture plant and equipment.

On 1 January 20X3, Bulwell sold an item of plant and equipment to Forest plc for $2 million. Forest plc depreciate plant and equipment at 10% per annum on cost, and charge this expense to cost of sales. Bulwell plc made a gross profit of 30% on the sale of the plant and equipment to Forest plc.

The income statements of Forest and Bulwell for the year ended 31 December 20X3 are:

	Forest $000	Bulwell $000
Revenue	21,300	8,600
Cost of sales	14,900	6,020
Gross profit	6,400	2,580
Other operating expenses	3,700	1,750
Profit before tax	2,700	830
Taxation	820	250
Profit after tax	1,880	580

Required:
Prepare an income statement for the Forest plc group for the year ended 31 December 20X3.

* Question 3

Bill plc acquired 80% of the common shares and 10% of the preferred shares in Ben plc on 31 December three years ago when Ben's accumulated retained profits were €45,000. During the year Bill sold Ben goods for €8,000 plus a markup of 50%. Half of these goods were still in stock at the end of the year. There was goodwill impairment loss of €3,000. Non-controlling interests are measured using Method 1.

The statements of comprehensive income of the two companies for the year ended 31 December 20X1 were as follows:

	Bill	Ben
	€	€
Revenue	300,000	180,000
Cost of sales	90,000	90,000
Gross profit	210,000	90,000
Expenses	88,623	60,000
	121,377	30,000
Dividends received – common shares	6,000	—
Dividends received – preferred shares	450	—
Profit before tax	127,827	30,000
Income tax expense	21,006	9,000
Profit for the period	106,821	21,000

Required:
Prepare a consolidated statement of comprehensive income for the year ended 31 December 20X1.

* Question 4

Morn Ltd acquired 90% of the shares in Eve Ltd on 1 January 20X1 for £90,000 when Eve Ltd's accumulated profits were £50,000. On 10 January 20X1 Morn Ltd received a dividend of £10,800 from Eve Ltd out of the profits for the year ended 31/12/20X0. On 31/12/20X1 Morn increased its non-current assets by £30,000 on revaluation. The summarised statements of comprehensive income for the year ended 31/12/20X1 were as follows:

	Morn	Eve
	£	£
Gross profit	360,000	180,000
Expenses	120,000	110,000
	240,000	70,000
Dividends received from Eve Ltd	10,800	—
Profit before tax	250,800	70,000
Income tax expense	69,000	18,000
Profit for the period	181,800	52,000

There were no inter-company transactions, other than the dividend. There was no goodwill.

Required:
Prepare a consolidated statement of comprehensive income for the year ended 31 December 20X1.

* Question 5

River plc acquired 90% of the common shares and 10% of the 5% bonds in Pool Ltd on 31 March 20X1. All income and expenses are deemed to accrue evenly through the year. On 31 January 20X1 River sold Pool goods for £6,000 plus a markup of one-third. 75% of these goods were still in stock at the end of the year. There was a goodwill impairment loss of £4,000. On 31/12/20X1 River increased its non-current assets by £15,000 on revaluation. Non-controlling interests are measured using Method 1. Set out below are the individual statements of comprehensive income of River and Pool:

Statements of comprehensive income for the year ended 31 December 20X1

	River £	Pool £
Net turnover	100,000	60,000
Cost of sales	30,000	30,000
Gross profit	70,000	30,000
Expenses	20,541	15,000
Interest payable on 5% bonds		5,000
Interest receivable on Pool Ltd bonds	500	
	49,959	10,000
Dividends received	2,160	NIL
Profit before tax	52,119	10,000
Income tax expense	7,002	3,000
Profit for the period	45,117	7,000

Required:
Prepare a consolidated statement of comprehensive income for the year ended 31 December 20X1.

Question 6

The statements of financial position of Mars plc and Jupiter plc at 31 December 20X2 are as follows:

	Mars £	Jupiter £
ASSETS		
Non-current assets at cost	550,000	225,000
Depreciation	220,000	67,500
	330,000	157,500
Investment in Jupiter	187,500	
Current assets		
Inventories	225,000	67,500
Trade receivables	180,000	90,000
Current account – Jupiter	22,500	
Bank	36,000	18,000
	463,500	175,500
Total assets	**981,000**	**333,000**
EQUITY AND LIABILITIES		
Capital and reserves		
£1 common shares	196,000	90,000
General reserve	245,000	31,500
Retained earnings	225,000	135,000
	666,000	256,500
Current liabilities		
Trade payables	283,500	40,500
Taxation	31,500	13,500
Current account – Mars		22,500
	315,000	76,500
Total equity and liabilities	**981,000**	**333,000**

Statements of comprehensive income for the year ended 31 December 20X2

	£	£
Sales	1,440,000	270,000
Cost of sales	1,045,000	135,000
Gross profit	395,000	135,000
Expenses	123,500	90,000
Dividends received from Jupiter	9,000	NIL
Profit before tax	280,500	45,000
Income tax expense	31,500	13,500
Profit for the period	249,000	31,500
Dividends paid	180,000	11,250
	69,000	20,250
Retained earnings brought forward from previous years	156,000	114,750
	225,000	135,000

Mars acquired 80% of the shares in Jupiter on 1 January 20X0 when Jupiter's retained earnings were £80,000 and the balance on Jupiter's general reserve was £18,000. Non-controlling interests are measured using Method 1. During the year Mars sold Jupiter goods for £18,000 which represented cost plus 50%. Half of these goods were still in stock at the end of the year.

During the year Mars and Jupiter paid dividends of £180,000 and £11,250 respectively. The opening balances of retained earnings for the two companies were £156,000 and £114,750 respectively.

Required:
Prepare a consolidated statement of income for the year ended 31/12/20X2, a statement of financial position as at that date, and a consolidated statement of changes in equity. Also prepare the retained earnings columns of the consolidated statement of changes in equity for the year.

Question 7

The statements of financial position of Red Ltd and Pink Ltd at 31 December 20X2 are as follows:

	Red $	Pink $
ASSETS		
Non-current assets	225,000	100,000
Depreciation	80,000	30,000
	145,000	70,000
Investment in Pink Ltd	110,000	
Current assets		
Inventories	100,000	30,000
Trade receivables	80,000	40,000
Current account – Pink Ltd	10,000	
Bank	16,000	8,000
	206,000	78,000
Total assets	**461,000**	**148,000**
EQUITY AND LIABILITIES		
Capital and reserves		
$1 common shares	176,000	40,000
General reserve	20,000	14,000
Revaluation reserve	25,000	
Retained earnings	100,000	60,000
	321,000	114,000
Current liabilities		
Trade payables	125,996	18,000
Taxation payable	14,004	6,000
Current account – Red Ltd		10,000
	140,000	34,000
Total equity and liabilities	**461,000**	**148,000**

Statements of comprehensive income for the year ended 31 December 20X2

	$	$
Sales	200,000	120,000
Cost of sales	60,000	60,000
Gross profit	140,000	60,000
Expenses	59,082	40,000
Dividends received	3,750	NIL
Profit before tax	84,668	20,000
Income tax expense	14,004	6,000
	70,664	14,000
Surplus on revaluation	25,000	—
Total comprehensive income	**95,664**	**14,000**

Red Ltd acquired 75% of the shares in Pink Ltd on 1 January 20X0 when Pink Ltd's retained earnings were $30,000 and the balance on Pink's general reserve was $8,000. The fair value of the non-controlling interest at the date was £32,000. Non-controlling interests are to be measured using Method 2.

On 31 December 20X2 Red revalued its non-current assets. The revaluation surplus of £25,000 was credited to the revaluation reserve.

During the year Pink sold Red goods for $9,000 plus a markup of one-third. Half of these goods were still in inventory at the end of the year. Goodwill suffered an impairment loss of 20%.

Required:
Prepare a consolidated statement of comprehensive income for the year ended 31/12/20X2 and a statement of financial position as at that date.

Question 8

H Ltd has one subsidiary, S Ltd. The company has held a controlling interest for several years. The latest financial statements for the two companies and the consolidated financial statements for the H Group are as shown below:

Statements of comprehensive income for the year ended 30 September 20X4

	H Ltd	S Ltd	H Group
	€000	€000	€000
Turnover	4,000	2,200	5,700
Cost of sales	(1,100)	(960)	(1,605)
	2,900	1,240	4,095
Administration	(420)	(130)	(550)
Distribution	(170)	(95)	(265)
Dividends received	180	—	—
Profit before tax	2,490	1,015	3,280
Income tax	(620)	(335)	(955)
Profit after tax	1,870	680	2,325
Attributable to:			
Equity shareholders of H Ltd			2,155
Non-controlling shareholders in S Ltd			170
			2,325

Statements of financial position at 30 September 20X4

	H Ltd €000	€000	S Ltd €000	€000	H Group €000	€000
Non-current assets:						
Tangible	7,053		2,196		9,249	
Investment in S Ltd	1,700	8,753	—	2,196	—	9,249
Current assets:						
Inventory	410		420		785	
Receivables	535		220		595	
Bank	27	972	19	659	46	1,426
Current liabilities:						
Payables	(300)		(260)		(355)	
Dividend to non-controlling interest	—		—		(45)	
Taxation	(605)	(905)	(375)	(635)	(980)	(1,380)
		8,820		2,220		9,295

	H Ltd £000	S Ltd £000	H Group £000
Share capital	4,500	760	4,500
Retained earnings	4,320	1,460	4,240
	8,820	2,220	8,740
Non-controlling interest	—	—	555
	8,820	2,220	9,295

Goodwill of €410,000 was written off at the date of acquisition following an impairment review.

Required:
(a) Calculate the percentage of S Ltd which is owned by H Ltd.
(b) Calculate the value of sales made between the two companies during the year.
(c) Calculate the amount of unrealised profit which had been included in the inventory figure as a result of inter-company trading and which had to be cancelled on consolidation.
(d) Calculate the value of inter-company receivables and payables cancelled on consolidation.
(e) Calculate the balance on S Ltd's retained earnings when H Ltd acquired its stake in the company. Non-controlling interests are measured using Method 1.

(CIMA)

Question 9

The following are the financial statements of White and its subsidiary Brown as at 30 September 20X9:

Statement of income for the year ended 30 September 20X9			Statements of financial position as at 30 September 20X9		
	White	Brown		White	Brown
	£000	£000		£000	£000
Sales revenue	245,000	95,000	Non-current assets:		
Cost of sales	(140,000)	(52,000)	Property, plant & equipment	110,000	40,000
Gross profit	105,000	43,000	Investments – 21 million	24,000	—
Distribution costs	(12,000)	(10,000)	shares in Brown		
Admin expenses	(55,000)	(13,000)	Current assets:		
Profit from operations	38,000	20,000	Inventory	13,360	3,890
Dividend from Brown	7,000	—	Trade receivables &	14,640	6,280
Profit before tax	45,000	20,000	dividend receivable		
Tax	(13,250)	(5,000)	Bank	3,500	2,570
Net profit for the year	31,750	15,000		165,500	52,740
			Equity and reserves:		
			Ordinary shares of £1 each	100,000	30,000
			Reserves	9,200	1,000
			Retained earnings	27,300	9,280
				136,500	40,280
			Current liabilities:		
			Trade payables	9,000	2,460
			Dividend declared	20,000	10,000
				165,500	52,740

The following information is also available:

(i)   White purchased its ordinary shares in Brown on 1 September 20X4 when Brown had credit balances on reserves of £0.5 million and on retained earnings of £1.5 million.

(ii) At 1 September 20X8 goodwill on the acquisition of Brown was £960,000. The impairment review at 30 September 20X9 reduced this to £800,000.

(iii) During the year ended 30 September 20X9 White sold goods which originally cost £12 million to Brown and were invoiced to Brown at cost plus 40%. Brown still had 30% of these goods in inventory as at 30 September 20X9.

(iv) Brown owed White £1.5 million at 30 September 20X9 for goods supplied during the year.

Required:
(a) Calculate the goodwill arising at the date of acquisition.
(b) Prepare the consolidated statement of income for the year ended 30 September 20X9.
(c) Prepare the consolidated statement of financial position at 30 September 20X9.

* Question 10

Alpha has owned 80% of the equity shares of Beta since the incorporation of Beta. On 1 July 20X6 Alpha purchased 60% of the equity shares of Gamma. The statements of comprehensive income and summarised statements of changes in equity of the three entities for the year ended 31 March 20X7 are given below:

Statement of comprehensive income

	Alpha	Beta	Gamma
	$000	$000	$000
Revenue (Note 1)	180,000	120,000	106,000
Cost of sales	(90,000)	(60,000)	(54,000)
Gross profit	90,000	60,000	52,000
Distribution costs	(9,000)	(8,000)	(8,000)
Administrative expenses	(10,000)	(9,000)	(8,000)
Investment income (Note 2)	26,450	NIL	NIL
Finance cost	(10,000)	(8,000)	(5,000)
Profit before tax	87,450	35,000	31,000
Income tax expense	(21,800)	(8,800)	(7,800)
Net profit for the period	65,650	26,200	23,200

Summarised statements of changes in equity

	Alpha	Beta	Gamma
Balance at 1 April 20X6	152,000	111,000	102,000
Net profit for the period	65,650	26,200	23,200
Dividends paid on 31 January 20X7	(30,000)	(13,000)	(15,000)
Revaluation of non-current assets	—	20,000	—
Balance at 31 March 20X7	187,650	144,200	110,200

Notes to the financial statements

Note 1 – Inter-company sales
Alpha sells products to Beta and Gamma, making a profit of 30% on the cost of the products sold. All the sales to Gamma took place in the post-acquisition period. Details of the purchases of the products by Beta and Gamma, together with the amounts included in opening and closing inventories in respect of the products, are given below:

	Purchased in year	Included in opening inventory	Included in closing inventory
	$000	$000	$000
Beta	20,000	2,600	3,640
Gamma	10,000	Nil	1,950

Note 2 – Investment income

Alpha's investment income includes dividends received from Beta and Gamma and interest receivable from Beta. The dividend received from Gamma has been credited to the statement of comprehensive income of Alpha without time-apportionment. The interest receivable is in respect of a loan of $60 million to Beta at a fixed rate of interest of 6% per annum. The loan has been outstanding for the whole of the year ended 31 March 20X7.

Note 3 – Details of acquisition of shares in Gamma

On 1 July 20X6 Alpha purchased 15 million of Gamma's issued equity shares by a share exchange. Alpha issued four new equity shares for every three shares acquired in Gamma. The market value of the shares in Alpha and Gamma at 1 July 20X6 was $5 and $5.50 respectively. The non-controlling interest in Gamma is measured using Method 1.

The fair values of the net assets of Gamma closely approximated to their carrying values in Gamma's financial statements with the exception of the following items:

(i) A property that had a carrying value of $20 million at the date of acquisition had a market value of $30 million. $16 million of this amount was attributable to the building, which had an estimated useful future economic life of 40 years at 1 July 20X6. In the year ended 31 March 20X7 Gamma had charged depreciation of $200,000 in its own financial statements in respect of this property.

(ii) Plant and equipment that had a carrying value of $6 million at the date of acquisition had a market value of $8 million. The estimated useful future economic life of the plant at 1 July 20X6 was four years. None of this plant and equipment had been sold or scrapped prior to 31 March 20X7.

(iii) Inventory that had a carrying value of $3 million at the date of acquisition had a fair value of $3.5 million. This entire inventory had been sold by Gamma prior to 31 March 20X7.

Note 4 – Other information

(i) Gamma charges depreciation and impairment of assets to cost of sales.

(ii) On 31 March 20X7 the directors of Alpha computed the recoverable amount of Gamma as a single cash-generating unit. They concluded that the recoverable amount was $150 million.

(iii) When the directors of Beta and Gamma prepared the individual financial statements of these companies no impairment of any assets of either company was found to be necessary.

(iv) On 31 March 20X7 Beta revalued its non-current assets. This resulted in a surplus of £20,000 which was credited to Beta's revaluation reserve.

Required:

Prepare the consolidated statement of comprehensive income and consolidated statement of changes in equity of Alpha for the year ended 31 March 20X7. Notes to the consolidated statement of comprehensive income are not required. Ignore deferred tax.

Splash plc has a number of subsidiaries, one of which, Muck Ltd, was acquired during the year ended 31 December 2009.

The draft consolidated financial statements for the year ended 31 December 2009 are as follows:

Consolidated statement of comprehensive income of Splash plc for the year ended 31 December 2009

	€000
Profit from operations	1,210
Interest	(100)
	1,110
Share of profits of associates	240
Profit before taxation	1,350
Taxation	(482)
	868
Non-controlling interest	(104)
Group profit	764

Statements of financial position

	Splash plc consolidated at 31/12/2009 €000	Splash plc consolidated at 31/12/2008 €000	Muck Ltd at acquisition €000
Assets			
Non-current assets			
Property, plant and equipment	4,730	2,610	610
Intangibles	350	310	—
Investment in associates	520	500	—
	5,600	3,420	610
Current assets			
Inventories	740	610	150
Trade and other receivables	390	350	85
Cash and cash equivalents	40	85	20
Total assets	6,770	4,465	865
Equity and liabilities			
€1 ordinary shares	1,400	1,000	500
Share premium	300	200	100
Retained earnings	1,615	865	80
	3,315	2,065	680
Non-controlling interest	580	610	—
	3,895	2,675	680
Non-current liabilities			
Long-term loans	1,900	1,100	—
Current liabilities			
Trade payables	520	480	75
Taxation	455	210	110
Total equity and liabilities	6,770	4,465	865

Additional information:

1   Splash plc issued 400,000 €1 ordinary shares at a premium of 25 cents and paid a cash consideration of €197,500 to acquire 75% of Muck Ltd. At the date of acquisition, Muck Ltd's assets and liabilities were recorded at their fair value with the exception of some plant which had a fair value of €90,000 in excess of its carrying value. Goodwill on acquisition was €120,000.

2   The property, plant and equipment during the year to 31 December 2009 shows plant with a carrying value of €800,000 which was sold for €680,000. Total depreciation for the year was €782,000.

Required:

(a) Prepare a consolidated statement of cash flows in accordance with IAS 7 *Statement of Cash Flows* for the year ended 31 December 2009.

(b) The Managing Director of Splash plc has asked you to draft a memorandum, briefly explaining the following:

   (i)   Why is it important to remove unrealised profits arising from transactions between companies in a group?
   (ii) Is it possible for a business to make losses year after year but still increase its bank balance?
   (iii) Explain the difference between the direct method and indirect methods of calculating the net cash flow from operating activities.

(Institute of Certified Public Accountants (ICPA), Professional I Stage I Corporate Reporting Examination, August 2010)

References

1 IFRS 10 *Consolidated Financial Statements*, IASB, 2011, B 86.
2 *Ibid.*, B 94, B 89.
3 IAS 1 *Presentation of Financial Statements*, IASB, revised 2007, Implementation Guidance.

CHAPTER 25

Accounting for associates and joint arrangements

25.1 Introduction

The previous three chapters have focused on the need for consolidated financial statements where an investor has control over an entity. In those circumstances line-by-line consolidation is appropriate. Where the size of an investment is not sufficient to give sole control, but where the investment gives the investor significant influence or joint control, then a modified form of accounting is appropriate. We will consider this issue further in this chapter.

Objectives

By the end of this chapter, you should be able to:

- define an associate;
- incorporate a profit-making associate into the consolidated financial statements using the equity method;
- incorporate a loss-making associate into the consolidated financial statements using the equity method;
- define and describe a joint operation and a joint venture and prepare financial statements incorporating interests in joint ventures;
- explain disclosure requirements.

25.2 Definitions of associates and of significant influence

An associate is an entity over which the investor has significant influence and which is neither a subsidiary nor a joint venture of the investor.[1] **Significant influence** is the power to participate in the financial and operating policy decisions of the investee but is not control over these policies.[1]

Significant influence will be assumed in situations where one company has 20% or more of the voting power in another company, unless it can be shown that there is no such influence. Unless it can be shown to the contrary, a holding of less than 20% will be assumed insufficient for associate status. The circumstances of each case must be considered.[2]

IAS 28 *Investments in Associates and Joint Ventures* suggests that one or more of the following might be evidence of an associate:

(a) representation on the board of directors or equivalent governing body of the investee;

(b) participation in policy-making processes;

(c) material transactions between the investor and the investee;

(d) interchange of managerial personnel; or

(e) provision of essential technical information.[3]

25.3 The treatment of associated companies in consolidated accounts

Associated companies will be shown in consolidated accounts under the equity method, unless the investment meets the criteria of a disposal group held for sale under IFRS 5 *Non-current Assets Held for Sale and Discontinued Operations*. If this is the case it will be accounted for under IFRS 5 at the lower of carrying value and fair value less costs to sell.

The equity method is a method of accounting whereby:

● The investment is reported in the consolidated statement of financial position in the non-current asset section.[4] It is reported initially at cost adjusted, at the end of each financial year, for the post-acquisition change in the investor's share of the net assets of the investee.[5]

● In the consolidated statement of comprehensive income, income from associates is reported after profit from operations together with finance costs and finance expenses.[6] The income reflects the investor's share of the post-tax results of operations of the investee.[5]

25.4 The Brill Group – group accounts with a profit-making associate

Brill plc was the parent of the Brill Group which consisted of Brill and a single subsidiary, Bream plc. On 1 January 20X0 Brill acquired 20% of the ordinary shares in Cod Ltd for £20,000. At that date the retained earnings of Cod were £22,500 and the general reserve was £6,000.

Set out below are the consolidated accounts of Brill and its subsidiary Bream and the individual accounts of the associated company, Cod, together with the consolidated group accounts.

25.4.1 Consolidated statement of financial position

Statements of financial position of the Brill Group (parent plus subsidiary already consolidated) and Cod (an associate company) as at 31 December 20X2 are as follows:

	Brill and subsidiary £	Cod £	Group £	
Non-current assets				
Property, plant and equipment	172,500	59,250	172,500	
Goodwill on consolidation	13,400		13,400	
Investment in Cod	20,000		23,600	Note 1
Current assets				
Inventories	132,440	27,000	132,440	
Trade receivables	151,050	27,000	151,050	
Current account – Cod	2,250		2,250	Note 2
Bank	36,200	4,500	36,200	
Total assets	527,840	117,750	531,440	
Current liabilities				
Trade payables	110,250	25,500	110,250	
Taxation	27,750	6,000	27,750	
Current account – Brill		2,250		
	138,000	33,750	138,000	
Total net assets	389,840	84,000	393,440	
EQUITY				
£1 ordinary shares	187,500	37,500	187,500	
General reserve	24,900	9,000	25,500	Note 3
Retained earnings	145,940	37,500	148,940	Note 4
	358,340	84,000	361,940	
Non-controlling interest	31,500	—	31,500	Note 5
	389,840	84,000	393,440	

Notes:

1 Investment in associate

	£	£
Initial cost of the 20% holding		20,000
Share of post-acquisition reserves of Cod:		
Retained earnings 20% × (37,500 − 22,500)	3,000	
General reserve 20% × (9,000 − 6,000)	600	3,600
		23,600

Note that (a) unlike subsidiaries the assets and liabilities are not joined line-by-line with those of the companies in the group; (b) where necessary the investment in the associate is tested for impairment under IAS 28;[7] and (c) goodwill is not reported separately and is only calculated initially to establish a figure when considering possible impairment.

2 The Cod current account is received from outside the group and must therefore continue to be shown as receivable by the group. *It is not cancelled.*

3 **General reserve consists of:**

	£
Parent's general reserve	24,900
General reserve of Cod:	
The group share of the post-acquisition general reserve,	
i.e. 20% × (9,000 − 6,000)	600
Consolidated general reserve	**25,500**

4 **Retained earnings consist of:**

Brill group's retained earnings	145,940
Retained earnings of Cod:	
The group share of the post-acquisition retained profits,	3,000
i.e. 20% × (37,500 − 22,500)	
Consolidated retained earnings	**148,940**

5 **Non-controlling interest**

Note that there is no non-controlling interest in Cod. Only the group share of Cod's net assets has been brought into the total net assets above (see Note 1). This is unlike the consolidation of a subsidiary when all of the subsidiary's assets and liabilities are aggregated into the consolidation.

25.4.2 Consolidated statement of income

Statements of income for the year ended 31 December 20X2 are as follows:

	Brill and subsidiary £	Cod £	Group £	
Sales	329,000	75,000	329,000	
Cost of sales	114,060	30,000	114,060	
Gross profit	214,940	45,000	214,940	
Expenses	107,700	22,500	107,700	
Profit from operations	107,240	22,500	107,240	
Dividends received	1,200	—	NIL	Note 1
Share of associate's **post-tax** profit	—	—	3,300	Note 2
Profit before tax	108,440	22,500	110,540	
Income tax expense	27,750	6,000	27,750	
Profit for the period	80,690	16,500	82,790	

Notes:

1 **Dividend received from Cod** is not shown because the share of Cod's profits (before dividend) has been included in the group account (see Note 2). To include the dividend as well would be double-counting.

2 **Share of Cod's profit after tax** = 20% × £16,500 = **£3,300**

As in the statement of financial position, there is no need to account for a non-controlling interest in Cod. This is because the consolidated statement of income only included the group share of Cod's profits.

There are no additional complications in the statement of changes in equity. The group retained earnings column will include the group share of Cod's post-acquisition retained earnings. There will be no additional column for a non-controlling interest in Cod.

25.4.3 The treatment of unrealised profits

It is never appropriate in the case of associated companies to remove 100% of any unrealised profit on inter-company transactions because only the group's share of the associate's profit and net assets are shown in the group accounts. For example, let us assume that Brill had purchased goods from Cod during the year at an agreed markup of £10,000, and a quarter of the goods were held by Brill in inventory at the year-end.

The Brill Group will provide for 20% of £2,500 (i.e. £500) by reducing the group share of the associate's profit in the statement of income and reducing the investment in the associate reported in the statement of financial position.

If the sale had been made by Brill, the cost of sales would be increased by £500 and the investment in the associate would be reduced by £500.

25.5 The Brill Group – group accounts with a loss-making associate

The treatment of losses in and impairment of an associate are described below.

Losses

Losses in an associate are normally treated the same way as profits. The group statement of income will show a loss after tax of the associate, and the statement of financial position will continue to show the associate at cost plus its share of post-acquisition profits or less its share of post-acquisition losses.

If the losses were such that they exceeded the carrying amount of the investment in the associate, the investment would be reduced to zero. After that point, additional losses are recognised by a provision (liability) only to the extent that the investor has incurred legal or constructive obligations or made payments on behalf of the associate.

If the associate subsequently reports profits, the investor resumes recognising its share of those profits only after its share of the profits equals the share of losses not recognised.[8]

Impairment

IAS 36 *Impairment of Assets* says (paragraph 9): 'An entity shall assess at the end of each reporting period whether there is any indication that an asset may be impaired. If any such indication exists [*such as making losses or small profits*], the entity shall estimate the recoverable amount of the asset.'

Brill and its subsidiary have a loss-making associate, Herring, which is 20% owned by Brill. On 1 January 20X0 Brill acquired 20% of the ordinary shares in Herring for £20,000. At that date the retained earnings of Herring were £22,500 and the general reserve was £6,000.

Because of the losses incurred by Herring, Brill has carried out an impairment test on the value of the investment in the associate. The recoverable amount of a 20% shareholding in Herring at 31 December 20X2 is £10,000.

**Statements of financial position of the Brill Group and Herring as at
31 December 20X2**

	Brill group £	Herring £	Group £	
Non-current assets				
Property, plant and equipment	172,500	59,250	172,500	
Goodwill on consolidation	13,400		13,400	
Investment in Herring	20,000		10,000	Note 1
Current assets				
Inventories	132,440	10,500	132,440	
Trade receivables	151,050	12,000	151,050	
Current account – Herring	2,250		2,250	Note 2
Bank	36,200	500	36,200	
	527,840	82,250	517,840	
Current liabilities				
Trade payables	110,250	25,500	110,250	
Taxation	27,750	—	27,750	
Current account – Herring		2,250		
	138,000	27,750	138,000	
Total net assets	389,840	54,500	379,840	
EQUITY				
£1 ordinary shares	187,500	37,500	187,500	
General reserve	24,900	7,000	25,100	Note 3
Retained earnings	145,940	10,000	135,740	Note 4
	358,340	54,500	348,340	
Non-controlling interest	31,500	—	31,500	
	389,840	54,500	379,840	

Notes:

1 **Investment in associate**

	£	£
Initial cost of 20% holding		20,000
Share of post-acquisition reserves of Herring		
20% × (10,000 − 22,500) (retained earnings)	(2,500)	
20% × (7,000 − 6,000) (general reserves)	200	(2,300)
Carrying value (before impairment)		17,700
Impairment (write down to recoverable amount)		(7,700)
Value in statement of financial position		10,000

The post-acquisition loss of £12,500 gives a loss of £2,500 in the group financial statements. As the carrying value (before impairment) is higher than the recoverable amount of £10,000, the value of the associate in Brill's statement of financial position is reduced to £10,000.

2 **The Herring current account** remains at £2,250.

3 **General reserve consists of:**

	£
Parent's general reserve	24,900
General reserve of Herring:	
The group share of the post-acquisition general reserve, i.e. 20% × (7,000 − 6,000)	200
Consolidated general reserve	25,100

4 **Retained earnings consist of:**

	£
Parent's retained earnings	145,940
Retained earnings of Herring:	
The group share of the post-acquisition retained earnings,	
i.e. 20% × (10,000 − 22,500)	(2,500)
Impairment of investment in associate (see Note 1)	(7,700)
Consolidated general reserve	135,740

Statements of income for the year ended 31 December 20X2

	Brill group £	Herring £	Group £	
Sales	329,000	75,000	329,000	
Cost of sales	114,060	66,000	114,060	
Gross profit	214,940	9,000	214,940	
Expenses	107,700	27,500	107,700	
Profit/(loss) from operations	107,240	(18,500)	107,240	
Share of associate's after-tax loss			(3,700)	Note 1
Impairment of investment in associate			(7,700)	Note 2
Profit before tax	107,240	(18,500)	95,840	
Income tax expense	27,750	—	27,750	
Profit/(loss) for the period	79,490	(18,500)	68,090	

Notes:

1 Share of associate's loss after tax = 20% × (18,500) = (3,700).

2 Impairment of investment in associate: this figure comes from the investment in associate in the statement of financial position. It reduces the carrying value of £17,700 to its recoverable amount of £10,000.

25.6 The acquisition of an associate part-way through the year

In order to match the cost (the investment) with the benefit (share of the associate's net assets), the associate's profit will only be taken into account from the date of acquiring the holding in the associate. The associate's profit at the date of acquisition represents part of the net assets that are being acquired at that date. The Puff example below is an illustration of the accounting treatment. The adjustment for unrealised profit is made against the group's share of the associate's profit and investment in the associate.

25.6.1 The Puff Group

At date of acquisition on 31 March 20X4 of shares in the associate:

● Puff plc acquired 30% of the shares in Blow plc.

● At that date the retained earnings of Blow were £61,500.

During the year:

● On 1/10/20X4 Blow sold Puff goods for £15,000 which was cost plus 25%.

● All income and expenditure for the year in Blow's statement of comprehensive income accrued evenly throughout the year.

At end of financial year on 31 December 20X4:

● 75% of the goods sold to Puff by Blow were still in inventory.

Set out below are the consolidated statement of income of Puff and its subsidiaries and the individual statement of income of an associated company, Blow, together with the consolidated group statement of income.

	Puff and subsidiaries	Blow	Group accounts	
	£	£	£	
Revenue	225,000	112,500	225,000	Note 1
Cost of sales	75,000	56,250	75,000	Note 2
Gross profit	150,000	56,250	150,000	
Expenses	89,850	30,000	89,850	
	60,150	26,250	60,150	
Dividends received from associate	1,350	NIL	NIL	Note 3
Share of associate's profit	—	—	3,713	Note 4
Profit before taxation	61,500	26,250	63,863	
Income tax for the period	15,000	6,750	15,000	
Profit for the period	46,500	19,500	48,863	

Notes:

1 The revenue, cost of sales and all other income and expenses of the associated company are not added on a line-by-line basis with those of the parent company and its subsidiaries. The group's share of the profit after taxation of the associate is shown as one figure (see Note 4) and added to the remainder of the group's profit before taxation.

2 The group accounts 'cost of sales' figure has not been adjusted for unrealised profit, as this has been deducted from the share of the associate's profit.

3 The dividend received of £1,350 is eliminated, being replaced by the group share of its underlying profits.

4 Share of profits after tax of the associate:

	£
Profit after tax	19,500
Apportion for 9 months ($\frac{9}{12} \times 19,500$)	14,625
Less: Unrealised profit ($\frac{25}{125} \times 15,000$) × 75%	2,250
	12,375
Group share (30% × 12,375)	3,713

5 There is no share of the associated company's retained earnings brought forward because the shares in the associate were purchased during the year.

25.7 Joint arrangements

IFRS 11 *Joint Arrangements* was issued by the IASB in 2011. Under this standard, joint arrangements are classified as either *joint operations* or *joint ventures* depending upon the parties' rights and obligations.

Joint control[9]

Notice that both joint operations and joint ventures require that there should be joint control. Joint control exists where there is a contractually agreed sharing of control of an arrangement under which decisions require the *unanimous* consent of the parties sharing control.

This may be by implicit agreement such as when two parties establish an arrangement in which each has 50% of the voting rights and the contractual arrangement between them specifies that at least 51% of the voting rights are required to make decisions, which results in joint control.

This does not mean the unanimous consent of *all* parties but of those who *collectively control* an arrangement, as illustrated in the following example.[10]

EXAMPLE ● Assume that three parties establish an arrangement: A has 50% of the voting rights in the arrangement, B has 30% and C has 20%. The contractual arrangement between A, B and C specifies that at least 75% of the voting rights are required to make decisions. Even though A can block any decision, it does not control the arrangement because it needs the agreement of B. The terms of their contractual arrangement requiring at least 75% of the voting rights to make decisions about the relevant activities imply that A and B have joint control of the arrangement, because decisions about the relevant activities of the arrangement cannot be made without both A and B agreeing.

Joint operations[11]

This is where the parties, called joint operators, have joint control of the arrangement which gives rights to the assets and obligations for the liabilities. It is the existence of rights and obligations that is critical to determining whether a joint operation exists as opposed to the legal structure of the joint venture. In the predecessor standard, IAS 31, a joint operation could only exist where no new entity was formed.

There may be situations where the ownership rights have been varied by contract. For example, the contractual arrangement might provide for the allocation of revenues and expenses on the basis of the relative performance of each party to the joint arrangement, such as when companies control and finance an oil pipeline equally but pay according to the amount of their throughput. In other instances, the parties might have agreed to share the profit or loss on the basis of a specified proportion such as the parties' ownership interest in the arrangement. These contractual arrangements would not prevent the arrangement from being a joint operation so long as the parties have rights to the assets and obligations for the liabilities.

Joint ventures[12]

This is where the parties, called joint venturers, have joint control of the arrangement which gives rights to the *net* assets of the arrangement. Typically in a joint venture the venturers take a share of the overall profit or loss earned by the joint venture as opposed to taking a share of the output of the venture.

25.7.1 Consolidated financial statements

Joint operations

IFRS 11 says:[13]
A joint operator shall recognise in relation to its interest in a joint operation:

(a) its assets, including its share of any assets held jointly;

(b) its liabilities, including its share of any liabilities incurred jointly;

(c) its revenue from the sale of its share of the output arising from the joint operation;

(d) its share of the revenue from the sale of the output by the joint operation; and

(e) its expenses, including its share of any expenses incurred jointly.

As there are no numerical examples in the standard, it is not clear how the assets, liabilities, revenue and expenses of the joint operation will be shown in the financial statements of each contributor to the joint venture.

The following example suggests how the joint operation would be shown in the financial statements of Sherwood plc:

EXAMPLE ● The joint operators are Sherwood plc and Arnold plc. Sherwood provides the land and buildings for the joint operation, and Sherwood and Arnold have provided equal cash sums to set up the joint venture. The profit is allocated equally between Sherwood and Arnold, after a payment to Sherwood of 5% of the carrying value of the land and buildings. On liquidation of the joint operation, the land and buildings will be returned to Sherwood, and the remaining assets and liabilities split equally between Sherwood and Arnold.

Sherwood's statement of financial position will include all the value of the land and buildings, and half the value of all the other assets and liabilities. It appears that these figures will be combined with the other assets and liabilities of Sherwood and not shown separately.

On the income statement, the joint operation's revenue will be included with other revenue. It would be helpful to the users of the financial statements if the revenue of the joint operation was shown separately.

On expenses, the standard is not clear whether they will be shown separately (in total) or combined with the other individual expense items of Sherwood. It may be shown as a separate figure (in total) as this would be helpful to the users of the financial statements. The rent on the land and buildings (of 5% of their carrying value) is likely to be shown separately in the income statement.

Joint operations can be very complex and require detailed analysis to identify the specific rights and obligations. Already audit firms are considering the practical implication of applying the standard and the possible restatement of prior years' financial statements if accounting policy and treatment changes.

Joint ventures

A joint venturer recognises[14] its interest in a joint venture as an investment which is accounted for using the equity method in accordance with IAS 28 *Investments in Associates and Joint Ventures.*

What if a party participates but does not have joint control?

If it is a joint operation the party would include its interest in the assets and liabilities. If a joint venture, the treatment then depends on the extent of influence that can be exerted. If it is significant then it is accounted for as an associate in accordance with IAS 28. If it is not significant then it is accounted for accordance with IFRS 9 *Financial Instruments.*

25.7.2 Determining whether a joint operation or a joint venture

The following is a helpful extract from www.kpmg.com:

An entity determines the type of joint arrangement by considering the structure, the legal form, the contractual arrangement and other facts and circumstances.

Structure	Is the arrangement structured through a vehicle that is separate from the parties?	No	Joint operation
	Yes		
Legal form	Does the legal form of the separate vehicle give the parties rights to the assets and obligations for the liabilities of the arrangement?	Yes	Joint operation
	No		
Contractual arrangement	Do the contractual arrangements give the parties rights to the assets and obligations for the liabilities of the arrangement?	Yes	Joint operation
	No		
Other facts and circumstances	Do the parties have rights to substantially all of the economic benefits of the assets relating to the arrangement; and does this arrangement depend on the parties on a continuous basis for settling its liabilities?	Yes	Joint operation
	No		
	Joint venture		

25.7.3 The accounting treatment required where the investment is a subsidiary, associate or joint operation

To illustrate the accounting treatments, we will take a parent company, Pete, which has an investment in another company, Sid.

Subsidiary – IFRS 10 Consolidated Financial Statements applies

If Pete owns more than 50% of the shares of Sid then Pete is presumed to have control of Sid. Sid is, therefore, classified as a subsidiary and the Pete group accounts will include all Sid's assets and liabilities as Pete has *control* over *all* of Sid's assets and liabilities.

Associate – IAS 28 Investments in Associates and Joint Ventures applies

If Pete owns between 20% and 50% of Sid's shares, then it is presumed that Pete is able to exercise significant influence and Sid will be classified as an associated company. In the Pete group accounts the investment in Sid is shown as a single figure in non-current assets. It will be reported at Pete's share of Sid's net assets at the date of acquisition plus goodwill plus post-acquisition profits.

Joint venture

If Sid is a joint venture, then Sid is treated like an associated company of Pete. Even if Pete owns more than 50% of the shares in Sid, it would be treated like an associated company (using equity accounting) rather than a subsidiary. The reason for this is that one of the requirements of a joint venture is that decisions must be with the agreement of all the parties to the joint venture so that Pete does not have control of Sid. Thus Sid cannot be a subsidiary.

Joint operation – IFRS 11 *Joint Arrangements* applies

At the time of writing it is not clear how a joint operation would be presented in the group financial statements. For instance, are all assets of the operation aggregated or are they shown as separate items? If Pete has provided the building as part of its contribution to the joint operation, and retained ownership of the building, then the building will be included in the group financial statements. A proportion of the other assets and liabilities of the joint operation will be shown in the group financial statements, according to the proportion of those assets and liabilities owned by way of the joint arrangement agreement.

25.7.4 Separate financial statements

The accounting for joint arrangements in an entity's separate financial statements depends on the involvement of the entity in that joint arrangement and the type of the joint arrangement.[15] For example, if the entity is a joint operator or joint venturer, it accounts for its interest in

- a joint operation in accordance with Section 25.7.1 above;
- a joint venture in accordance with paragraph 10 of IAS 27 *Separate Financial Statements.*

25.8 Disclosure in the financial statements

IFRS 12 *Disclosure of Interests in Other Entities* was issued by the IASB in 2011 to bring 'off-balance-sheet finance' onto the financial statements and to enable[16] users of financial statements to evaluate:

(a) the nature of, and risks associated with, its interests in other entities; and

(b) the effects of those interests on its financial position, financial performance and cash flows.

In terms of this chapter, there is a general requirement to disclose information about significant judgements and assumptions made when determining control, joint control, significant influence and classification of joint arrangements. In relation to interest in subsidiaries and joint arrangements, there are specific disclosure requirements.

Interests in subsidiaries disclosures

An entity shall disclose information that enables[17] users of its consolidated financial statements to:

(a) understand the composition of the group and the interest that non-controlling interests have in the group's activities and cash flows; and

(b) evaluate the nature and extent of significant restrictions on its ability to access or use assets, and settle liabilities, of the group; the nature of, and changes in, the risks associated with its interests in consolidated structured entities; the consequences of changes in its ownership interest in a subsidiary that do not result in a loss of control; and the consequences of losing control of a subsidiary during the reporting period.

Interests in joint arrangements and associates disclosures

An entity shall disclose information that enables[18] users of its financial statements to evaluate:

(a) the nature, extent and financial effects of its interests in joint arrangements and associates; and

(b) the nature of, and changes in, the risks associated with its interests in joint ventures and associates.

Summary

Associates and joint ventures are accounted for under IAS 28 (revised 2011) using the equity method whereby there is a single-line entry in the statement of financial position carried initially at cost and the balance adjusted annually for the investor's share of the associate's current year's profit or loss. For joint venture entities, IAS 31 (now superseded by IFRS 11) permitted alternative treatments with investors able to adopt the equity accounting method or proportionate consolidation. Proportionate consolidation is no longer permitted. Joint operations are accounted for in accordance with IFRS 11.

REVIEW QUESTIONS

1 Why are associated companies accounted for under the equity method rather than consolidated?

2 IAS 28, paragraph 17, states:

> The recognition of income on the basis of distributions received may not be an adequate measure of the income earned by an investor on an investment in an associate.

Explain why this may be so.

3 How does the treatment of inter-company unrealised profit differ between subsidiaries and associated companies?

4 The result of including goodwill by valuing the non-controlling shares at their market price using Method 2 is to value the non-controlling shares on a different basis to valuing an equity investment in an associate. Discuss whether there should be a uniform approach to both.

5 Where an associate has made losses, IAS 28, paragraph 30, states:

> After the investor's interest is reduced to zero, additional losses are provided for, and a liability is recognised, only to the extent that the investor has incurred legal or constructive obligations or made payments on behalf of the associate. If the associate subsequently reports profits, the investor resumes recognising its share of those profits only after its share of the profits equals the share of losses not recognised.

Explain why profits are recognised only after its share of the profits equals the share of losses not recognised.

6 The following is an extract from the notes to the 1999 consolidated financial statements of the Chugoku Electric Power Company, Incorporated:

Equity method
Investments in four (three in 1998) affiliated companies (20% to 50% owned) are accounted for by the equity method and, accordingly, are stated at cost adjusted for equity in undistributed earnings and losses from the date of acquisition.

(a) What is another name for most companies which are 20% to 50% owned?

(b) What is meant by the word 'equity' in the above statement?

(c) What are the entries in the statement of income under the equity method of accounting?

(d) What are the differences between the equity method and consolidation?

7 Explain the difference between a joint operation and a joint venture.

8 Explain the approach to determining whether an arrangement is a joint operation or a joint venture.

* Question 1

The statements of income for Continent plc, Island Ltd and River Ltd for the year ended 31 December 20X9 were as follows:

	Continent plc	Island Ltd	River Ltd
	€	€	€
Revenue	825,000	220,000	82,500
Cost of sales	(616,000)	(55,000)	(8,250)
Gross profit	209,000	165,000	74,250
Administration costs	(33,495)	(18,700)	(3,850)
Distribution costs	(11,000)	(14,300)	(2,750)
Dividends receivable from Island and River	4,620		
Profit before tax	169,125	132,000)	67,650
Income tax	(55,000)	(33,000)	(11,000)
Profit after tax	114,125	99,000	56,650

Continent plc acquired 80% of Island Ltd for €27,500 on 1 January 20X3, when Island Ltd's retained earnings were €22,000 and share capital was €5,500. During the year, Island Ltd sold goods costing €2,750 to Continent plc for €3,850. At the year end, 10% of these goods were still in Continent plc's inventory.

Continent plc acquired 40% of River Ltd for €100,000 on 1 January 20X5, when River Ltd's share capital and reserves totalled €41,250 (share capital consisted of 11,000 50c shares). During the year River Ltd sold goods costing €1,650 to Continent plc for €2,200. At the year-end, 50% of these goods were still in Continent plc's inventory.

Goodwill in Island Ltd had suffered impairment charges in previous years totalling €2,200 and goodwill in River Ltd impairment charges totalling €7,700. Impairment has continued during 2009, reducing the goodwill in Island by €550 and the goodwill in River by €3,850.

Continent plc includes in its revenue management fees of €5,500 charged to Island Ltd and €2,750 charged to River Ltd. Both companies treat the charge as an administration cost.

Non-controlling interests are measured using Method 1.

Required:
Prepare Continent plc's consolidated statement of income for the year ended 31 December 20X9.

Question 2

The statements of comprehensive income for Highway plc, Road Ltd and Lane Ltd for the year ended 31 December 20X9 were as follows:

	Highway plc $	Road Ltd $	Lane Ltd $
Revenue	184,000	152,000	80,000
Cost of sales	(48,000)	(24,000)	(16,000)
Gross profit	136,000	128,000	64,000
Administration costs	(13,680)	(11,200)	(20,800)
Distribution costs	(11,200)	(17,600)	(8,000)
Dividends receivable from Road	2,480		
Profit before tax	113,600	99,200	35,200
Income tax	(32,000)	(8,000)	(4,800)
Profit for the period	81,600	91,200	30,400

Highway plc acquired 80% of Road Ltd for $160,000 on 1.1.20X6 when Road Ltd's share capital was $64,000 and reserves were $16,000.

Highway plc acquired 30% of Lane Ltd for $40,000 on 1.1.20X7 when Lane Ltd's share capital was $8,000 and reserves were $8,000.

Goodwill of Road Ltd had suffered impairment charges of $14,400 in previous years and $4,800 was to be charged in the current year. Goodwill of Lane Ltd had suffered impairment charges of $3,520 in previous years and $1,760 was to be charged in the current year.

During the year Road Ltd sold goods to Highway plc for $8,000. These goods had cost Road Ltd $1,600. 50% were still in Highway's inventory at the year-end.

During the year Lane Ltd sold goods to Highway plc for $6,400. These goods had cost Lane Ltd $3,200. 50% were still in Highway's inventory at the year-end.

Highway's revenue included management fees of 5% of Road and Lane's turnover. Both of those companies have treated the charge as an administration cost.

Non-controlling interests are measured using Method 1.

Required:
Prepare Highway's consolidated statement of comprehensive income for the year ended 31.12.20X9.

The following are the statements of comprehensive income of four companies for the year ended 31 October 2006, the end of their most recent financial year.

Income statements for the year ended 31 October 2006

	Afjar $000	Jikki $000	Hupin $000	Sofrin $000
Revenue	8,890	4,580	4,470	2,760
Cost of sales	(3,000)	(2,200)	(1,800)	(1,700)
Gross profit	5,890	2,380	2,670	1,060
Distribution costs	(900)	(540)	(1,010)	(230)
Administrative expenses	(1,060)	(990)	(1,100)	(250)
Operating profit	3,930	850	560	580
Dividends receivable	410	130		
Interest receivable	230	321	150	
Interest payable	(1,188)	(455)	(380)	
Net profit before taxation	3,382	846	330	580
Income tax expense	(1,000)	(200)	(80)	(100)
Net profit after taxation	2,382	646	250	480
Earnings per share (in cents)	11.9	4.0	2.5	2.4

The following additional information is available:

(a) All shares issued by the companies have a face value of $1.

(b) The companies made the following dividend payments to shareholders during the year ended 31 October 2006:

	Afjar $000	Jikki $000	Hupin $000	Sofrin $000
Preference dividend				
– final for 2005, paid March 2006	400	120		
– interim for 2006, paid September 2006	400	120		
Ordinary dividend				
– final for 2005, paid March 2006	800	180	54	76
– interim for 2006, paid September 2006	800	180	54	76

Under IAS 32 *Financial Instruments: Disclosure and Presentation* dividends on preference shares have been included in interest payable.

(c) Afjar owns 60% of the ordinary shares in Jikki, 40% of the shares in Hupin and 25% of the shares in Sofrin. Jikki is a subsidiary of Afjar, Hupin is an associate of Afjar, and Sofrin is a joint venture.

(d) During the year ended 31 October 2006 Afjar sold inventory which had cost $640,000 to Jikki at a mark up of 25%. Jikki had resold 65% of these items by 31 October 2006.

(e) On 1 July 2006 Jikki made a long-term loan of $500,000 to Afjar. The loan bears interest at 12% a year payable every six months in arrears.

Required:
Prepare, in so far as the information given permits, the consolidated statement of comprehensive income of Afjar for the year ended 31 October 2006. Your statement of comprehensive income should include a figure for earnings per share with a supportive disclosure note.

(The Association of International Accountants)

Question 4

Alpha has owned 75% of the equity shares of Beta since the incorporation of Beta. Therefore, Alpha has prepared consolidated financial statements for some years. On 1 July 20X6 Alpha purchased 40% of the equity shares of Gamma. The statements of comprehensive income and summarised statements of changes in equity of the three entities for the year ended 30 September 20X6 are given below:

Statements of income

	Alpha	Beta	Gamma
	$000	$000	$000
Revenue (Note 1)	150,000	100,000	96,000
Cost of sales	(110,000)	(78,000)	(66,000)
Gross profit	40,000	22,000	30,000
Distribution costs	(7,000)	(6,000)	(6,000)
Administrative expenses	(8,000)	(7,000)	(7,200)
Profit from operations	25,000	9,000	16,800
Investment income (Note 2)	6,450	NIL	NIL
Finance cost	(5,000)	(3,000)	(4,200)
Profit before tax	26,450	6,000	12,600
Income tax expense	(7,000)	(1,800)	(3,600)
Net profit for the period	19,450	4,200	9,000
Summarised statements of changes in equity			
Balance at 1 October 20X5	122,000	91,000	82,000
Net profit for the period	19,450	4,200	9,000
Dividends paid on 31 July 20X6	(6,500)	(3,000)	(5,000)
Balance at 30 September 20X6	134,950	92,200	86,000

Notes to the financial statements

Note 1 – Inter-company sales

Alpha sells products to Beta and Gamma, making a profit of 25% on the cost of the products sold. All the sales to Gamma took place in the post-acquisition period. Details of the purchases of the products by Beta and Gamma, together with the amounts included in opening and closing inventories in respect of the products, are given below:

	Purchased in year	Included in opening inventory	Included in closing inventory
	$000	$000	$000
Beta	20,000	2,000	3,000
Gamma	10,000	NIL	1,500

There were no other inter-company sales between Alpha, Beta or Gamma during the period.

Note 2 – Investment income

Alpha's investment income includes dividends received from Beta and Gamma and interest receivable from Beta. The dividend received from Gamma has been credited to the statement of comprehensive income of Alpha without time-apportionment. The interest receivable is in respect of a loan of $20 million to Beta at a fixed rate of interest of 6% per annum. The loan has been outstanding for the whole of the year ended 30 September 20X6.

Note 3 – Details of acquisitions by Alpha

Entity	Date of acquisition	Fair value adjustment at date of acquisition $000
Beta	1 July 20X5	NIL
Gamma	1 June 20X6	6,400

There has been no impairment of the goodwill arising on the acquisition of Beta or of the investment in Gamma since the dates of acquisition of either entity.

The fair value adjustment has the effect of increasing the fair value of property, plant and equipment above the carrying value in the individual financial statements of Gamma. Group policy is to depreciate property, plant and equipment on a monthly basis over its estimated useful economic life. The estimated life of the property, plant and equipment of Gamma that was subject to the fair value adjustment is five years, with depreciation charged against cost of sales.

Note 4 – Other information

● The purchase of shares in Gamma entitled Alpha to appoint a representative to the board of directors of Gamma. This meant that Alpha was potentially able to participate in, and significantly influence, the policy decisions of Gamma.

● No other investor is able to control the operating and financial policies of Gamma, but on one occasion since 1 July 20X6 Gamma made a policy decision with which Alpha did not fully agree.

● Alpha has not entered into a contractual relationship with any other investor to exercise joint control over the operating and financial policies of Gamma.

● All equity shares in Beta carry one vote at general meetings.

● The policy of Alpha regarding the treatment of equity investments in its consolidated financial statements is as follows:
  - subsidiaries are fully consolidated;
  - joint ventures are proportionally consolidated;
  - associates are equity accounted; and
  - other investments are treated as available for sale financial assets.

Your assistant has been reading the working papers for the consolidated financial statements of Alpha for previous years. He has noticed that Beta has been consolidated as a subsidiary and has expressed the view that this must be because Alpha owns more than 50% of its shares. He has further stated that Gamma should be treated as an available-for-sale financial asset since Alpha is unable to control its operating and financial policies.

Required:
(a) Prepare the consolidated statement of income and consolidated statement of changes in equity of Alpha for the year ended 30 September 20X6. Notes to the consolidated statement of comprehensive income are not required. Ignore deferred tax.
(b) Assess the observations of your assistant regarding the appropriate method of consolidating Beta and Gamma. Your assessment need *not* include an explanation of the detailed mechanics of consolidation. You should refer to the provisions of international financial reporting standards where you consider they will assist your explanation.

The following are the financial statements of the parent company Alpha plc, a subsidiary company Beta and an associate company Gamma.

Statements of financial position as at 31 December 20X9

	Alpha £	Beta £	Gamma £
ASSETS			
Non-current assets			
Land at cost	540,000	256,500	202,500
Investment in Beta	216,000		
Investment in Gamma	156,600		
Current assets			
Inventories	162,000	54,000	135,000
Trade receivables	108,000	72,900	91,800
Dividend receivable from Beta	12,420		
Current account – Beta	10,800		
Current account – Gamma	13,500		
Cash	237,600	62,100	67,500
Total current assets	544,320	189,000	294,300
Total assets	1,456,920	445,500	496,800
EQUITY AND LIABILITIES			
£1 shares	540,000	67,500	27,000
Retained earnings	769,500	329,400	391,500
	1,309,500	396,900	418,500
Current liabilities			
Trade payables	93,420	24,300	59,400
Dividends payable	54,000	13,500	5,400
Current account – Alpha	—	10,800	13,500
Total equity and liabilities	1,456,920	445,500	496,800

On 1 January 20X5 Alpha plc acquired 80% of Beta plc for £216,000 when Beta plc's share capital and reserves were £81,000, and 30% of Gamma Ltd for £156,600 when Gamma Ltd's share capital and reserves were £40,500. The fair value of the land at the date of acquisition was £337,500 in Beta plc and £270,000 in Gamma Ltd. Both companies have kept land at cost in their statement of financial position. All other assets are recorded at fair value. There have been no further share issues or purchases of land since the date of acquisition.

At the year-end, Alpha plc has inventory acquired from Beta plc and Gamma Ltd. Beta plc had invoiced the inventory to Alpha plc for £54,000 – the cost to Beta plc had been £40,500. Gamma Ltd had invoiced Alpha plc for £13,500 – the cost to Gamma Ltd had been £8,100. Goodwill has been impaired by £52,650. The whole of the impairment relates to Beta.

Non-controlling interests are measured using Method 1.

Required:
Prepare Alpha plc's consolidated statement of financial position as at 31.12.20X9.

Question 6

The following are the statements of financial position of Garden plc, its subsidiary Rose Ltd and its associate Petal Ltd:

Statements of financial position as at 31 December 20X9

	Garden £	Rose £	Petal £
ASSETS			
Non-current assets			
Land at cost	240,000		84,000
Land at valuation		180,000	
Investment in Rose	300,000		
Investment in Petal	72,000		
Investments	18,000		
Current assets			
Inventories	15,000	99,000	5,400
Trade receivables	33,000	98,400	1,200
Current account – Rose	18,000		
Current account – Petal	2,400		
Cash	6,600	67,200	300
Total current assets	75,000	264,600	6,900
Total assets	705,000	444,600	90,900
EQUITY AND LIABILITIES			
£1 shares	300,000	120,000	30,000
Revaluation reserve		90,000	
Retained earnings	270,000	216,000	57,600
	570,000	426,000	87,600
Current liabilities			
Trade payables	135,000	3,600	900
Current account – Garden	—	15,000	2,400
Total equity and liabilities	705,000	444,600	90,900

On 1 January 20X3 Garden plc acquired 75% of Rose Ltd for £300,000 when Rose's share capital and reserves were £252,000. Prior to the acquisition, the net book value of Rose's non-current assets was £90,000. Rose revalued its non-current assets immediately prior to the acquisition to fair value and included the revaluation in its statement of financial position.

On 1 January 20X5 Garden acquired 20% of Petal Ltd for £72,000 when the fair value of Petal's net assets were £42,000.

Goodwill has been impaired in Rose by £77,700 and in Petal by £31,800.

At the year-end, Garden plc has inventory acquired from Rose and Petal. Rose had invoiced the inventory to Garden for £6,000 – the cost to Rose had been £1,200. Petal had invoiced Garden for £3,000 – the cost to Petal had been £1,800.

Non-controlling interests are measured using Method 1.

Required:
Prepare Garden plc's consolidated statement of financial position as at 31.12.20X9.

* Question 7

The following are the financial statements of the parent company Swish plc, a subsidiary company Broom and an associate company Handle.

Statements of financial position as at 31 December 20X3

	Swish £	Broom £	Handle £
ASSETS			
Non-current assets			
Property, plant and equipment at cost	320,000	180,000	100,000
Depreciation	200,000	70,000	21,000
	120,000	110,000	79,000
Investment in Broom	140,000		
Investment in Handle	40,000		
Current assets			
Inventories	120,000	60,000	36,000
Trade receivables	130,000	70,000	36,000
Current account – Broom	15,000		
Current account – Handle	3,000		
Bank	24,000	7,000	6,000
Total current assets	292,000	137,000	78,000
Total assets	592,000	247,000	157,000
EQUITY AND LIABILITIES			
£1 ordinary shares	250,000	60,000	50,000
General reserve	30,000	20,000	12,000
Retained earnings	150,000	120,000	50,000
	430,000	200,000	112,000
Current liabilities			
Trade payables	132,000	25,000	34,000
Taxation payable	30,000	7,000	8,000
Current account – Swish		15,000	3,000
Total equity and liabilities	592,000	247,000	157,000

Statement of income for the year ended 31 December 20X3

	£	£	£
Sales	300,000	160,000	100,000
Cost of sales	90,000	80,000	40,000
Gross profit	210,000	80,000	60,000
Expenses	95,000	50,000	30,000
Dividends received from Broom and Handle	11,000	NIL	NIL
Profit before tax	126,000	30,000	30,000
Income tax expense	30,000	7,000	8,000
Profit for the period	96,000	23,000	22,000
Dividend paid (shown in equity)	40,000	10,000	8,000

Swish acquired 90% of the shares in Broom on 1 January 20X1 when the balance on the retained earnings of Broom was £60,000 and the balance on the general reserve of Broom was £16,000. Swish also acquired 25% of the shares in Handle on 1 January 20X2 when the balance on Handle's accumulated retained profits was £30,000 and the general reserve £8,000.

During the year Swish sold Broom goods for £16,000, which included a markup of one-third. 80% of these goods were still in inventory at the end of the year.

Required:
(a) Prepare a consolidated statement of income, including the associated company Handle's results, for the year ended 31 December 20X3.
(b) Prepare a consolidated statement of financial position as at 31 December 20X3. The group policy is to measure non-controlling interests using Method 1.

Question 8

Set out below are the financial statements of Ant Co., its subsidiary Bug Co. and an associated company Nit Co. for the accounting year-end 31 December 20X9.

Statements of financial position as at 31 December 20X9

	Ant $	Bug $	Nit $
ASSETS			
Non-current assets			
Property, plant and equipment at cost	240,000	135,000	75,000
Depreciation	150,000	52,500	15,750
	90,000	82,500	59,250
Investment in Bug	90,000		
Investment in Nit	30,000		
Current assets			
Inventories	105,000	45,000	27,000
Trade receivables	98,250	52,500	27,000
Current account – Bug	11,250		
Current account – Nit	2,250		
Bank	17,250	5,250	4,500
Total current assets	234,000	102,750	58,500
Total assets	444,000	185,250	117,750
EQUITY AND LIABILITIES			
$1 ordinary shares	187,500	45,000	37,500
General reserve	22,500	15,000	9,000
Retained earnings	112,500	90,000	37,500
	322,500	150,000	84,000
Current liabilities			
Trade payables	99,000	18,750	25,500
Taxation payable	22,500	5,250	6,000
Current account – Ant		11,250	2,250
Total equity and liabilities	444,000	185,250	117,750

Statements of comprehensive income for the year ended 31 December 20X9

	Ant	Bug	Nit
	$	$	$
Sales	225,000	120,000	75,000
Cost of sales	67,500	60,000	30,000
Gross profit	157,500	60,000	45,000
Expenses	70,500	37,500	30,000
Dividends received	7,500	NIL	7,500
Profit before tax	94,500	22,500	22,500
Taxation	22,500	5,250	6,000
Profit for the year	72,000	17,250	16,500
Dividends paid in year	30,000	7,500	6,000

Ant Co. acquired 80% of the shares in Bug Co. on 1 January 20X7 when the balance on the retained earnings of Bug Co. was $45,000 and the balance on the general reserve of Bug Co. was $12,000. The fair value of the non-controlling interest in Bug on 1 January 20X7 was $21,000. Group policy is to measure non-controlling interests using Method 2. Ant Co. also acquired 25% of the shares in Nit Co. on 1 January 20X8 when the balance on Nit's retained earnings was $22,500 and the general reserve $6,000.

During the year Ant Co. sold Bug Co. goods for $12,000, which included a markup of one-third. 90% of these goods were still in inventory at the end of the year.

Required:
(a) Prepare a consolidated statement of income for the year ending 31/12/20X9, including the associated company Nit's results.
(b) Prepare a consolidated statement of financial position at 31/12/20X9, including the associated company.

* Question 9

Epsilon acquired 40% of Zeta when Zeta's retained earnings were $50,000, 25% of Kappa when Kappa's retained earnings were $40,000, and 25% of Lambda when Lambda's retained earnings were $50,000.

The four companies' statements of financial position as at 31 October 2011 were as follows:

	Epsilon $000	Zeta $000	Kappa $000	Lambda $000
ASSETS				
Non-current assets	1,900	170	140	160
Investment in Zeta	100			
Investment in Kappa	55			
Investment in Lambda	60			
	2,115	170	140	160
Current assets:				
Inventory	8	6	12	11
Trade receivables	12	5	4	7
Bank	5	4	3	2
	25	15	19	20
Total assets	2,140	185	159	180
LIABILITIES				
Equity:				
Share capital	500	50	60	70
Reserves	1,563	124	91	98
	2,063	174	151	168
Non-current liabilities	50			
Current liabilities:				
Trade payables	27	11	8	12
	2,140	185	159	180

Epsilon is entitled to appoint three members of Zeta's board. Zeta's articles state that the board of directors is restricted to five members and that board decisions are binding whenever a simple majority of the directors agree.

Epsilon used its voting rights to secure a place on Kappa's board for one of its own directors. This director has access to internal management reports and can exert some influence on decision making within the company.

Epsilon does not have a representative on the board of Lambda. The directors of Epsilon attempted to secure a place on the board, but were rebuffed by Ms Strong, who owns 75% of the shares. Ms Strong takes a very direct role in the management of Lambda.

Required:
(a) Discuss how each of Epsilon shareholdings should be accounted for in the Epsilon group's consolidated financial statements.
(b) Prepare a consolidated statement of financial position for the Epsilon Group as at 31 October 2011.

(The Association of International Accountants)

Question 10

This question concerns an associated company making a loss and possible impairment of goodwill.

Hyson plc acquired a 30% interest in the ordinary shares of Green plc on 1 January 20X3 when Green's general reserve was £25,000 and its retained earnings were £40,000.

In the year ended 31 December 20X8 Green made a loss after tax of £65,000 because of a recession in its principal sales market.

The statements of financial position of Hyson plc and Green plc at 31 December 20X8 are as follows:

	Hyson £	Green £
ASSETS		
Non-current assets:		
Property, plant and equipment	650,000	230,000
Depreciation	(310,000)	(105,000)
	340,000	125,000
Investment in Green	90,000	
Current assets:		
Inventories	145,000	64,000
Trade receivables	180,000	85,000
Current account – Green	5,000	
Bank	25,000	3,000
Total current assets	355,000	152,000
Total assets	785,000	277,000
EQUITY AND LIABILITIES		
£1 ordinary shares	300,000	200,000
General reserve	60,000	30,000
Retained earnings	225,000	(57,000)
	585,000	173,000
Current liabilities:		
Trade payables	163,000	99,000
Taxation payable	37,000	—
Current account – Hyson	—	5,000
Total equity and liabilities	785,000	277,000

The statements of income of Hyson and Green for the year ended 31 December 20X8 are:

	£	£
Sales	1,045,000	350,000
Cost of sales	683,000	320,000
Gross profit	362,000	30,000
Distribution expenses	42,000	20,000
Administration expenses	152,000	75,000
Profit/(loss) before tax	168,000	(65,000)
Income tax expense	33,000	—
Profit for the period	135,000	(65,000)
Dividend paid (shown in equity)	40,000	—

Because of the losses of Green in 20X8, the recoverable amount of a 30% interest in Green is £40,000 at 31 December 20X8.

Required:

(a) Prepare a consolidated statement of financial position of Hyson plc as at 31 December 20X8.

(b) Prepare a consolidated statement of income of Hyson plc, including the associated company Green, for the year ended 31 December 20X8.

(c) State the changes to your answers in (a) and (b) above if the recoverable amount of a 30% interest in Green was £65,000.

References

1 IAS 28 *Investments in Associates and Joint Ventures*, IASB, revised 2011, para. 3.
 2 *Ibid.*, para. 5.
 3 *Ibid.*, para. 8.
 4 *Ibid.*, para. 15.
 5 *Ibid.*, para. 10.
 6 IAS 1 *Presentation of Financial Statements*, IASB, revised 2003, Implementation Guidance.
 7 IAS 28 *Investments in Associates and Joint Ventures*, IASB, revised 2011, para. 40.
 8 *Ibid.*, para. 30.
 9 *Ibid.*, para. 7.
10 IFRS 11 *Joint Arrangements*, IASB, 2011, B8.
11 *Ibid.*, para. 15.
12 *Ibid.*, para. 16.
13 *Ibid.*, para. 20.
14 *Ibid.*, paras 24–25.
15 *Ibid.*, para. 26.
16 IFRS 12 *Disclosure of Interests in Other Entities*, IASB, 2011, para. 1.
17 *Ibid.*, para. 10.
18 *Ibid.*, para. 20.

CHAPTER 26

Introduction to accounting for exchange differences

26.1 Introduction

The increasing globalisation of business means that it is becoming more and more common for companies to enter into transactions that have to be paid for in a foreign currency.

When currency fluctuations occur the exchange rate will have changed between the date the goods or services have been invoiced and the date that payment is made. The difference impacts on cash flows and will be reported as a realised exchange gain or loss in the statement of income.

In this chapter we also consider how to prepare consolidated accounts when there is a foreign subsidiary that maintains its own accounts in the local currency which is different from that of its parent. IAS 21 refers to the local currency as the **functional** currency and the parent's currency as the **presentation** currency. The restatement of the functional currency into the presentation is referred to as translation. Any difference on exchange arising on translation has not been realised and is reported as other comprehensive income.

Objectives

By the end of this chapter, you should be able to:

- account for foreign transactions where differences arise on actual cash inflows and outflows resulting in realised gains or losses;
- translate the financial statements of foreign subsidiaries into the parent company's currency and report any exchange differences under other comprehensive income;
- explain the criteria when determining 'functional' and 'presentation' currency;
- prepare consolidated financial statements to include subsidiaries whose financial statements prepared using the local functional currency have to be translated into a different presentation currency on consolidation; and
- explain the characteristics of a hyperinflationary economy and restatement of the functional currency financial statements.

26.2 How to record foreign currency transactions in a company's own books

We will comment briefly on the IAS 21 provisions relating to (i) how a foreign currency transaction is defined, (ii) the amount entered into the company's accounting records on entering into a transaction, (iii) the accounting treatment of exchange differences when the transaction is settled within the current accounting period, (iv) the accounting treatment when settlement occurs in the next accounting period, (v) the accounting treatment when settlement occurs in an accounting period beyond the next, and (vi) hedging the amount payable.

26.2.1 Defining foreign transactions

IAS 21 *The Effects of Changes in Foreign Exchange Rates* defines foreign transactions as follows:[1]

> A foreign transaction is a transaction which is denominated in or requires settlement in a foreign currency, including transactions arising when an entity:
>
> (a) buys or sells goods or services whose price is denominated in a foreign currency;
>
> (b) borrows or lends funds when the amounts payable or receivable are denominated in a foreign currency;
>
> (c) otherwise acquires or disposes of assets, or incurs or settles liabilities, denominated in a foreign currency.

26.2.2 The amount recorded on entering into a transaction

On initial recognition,[2] transactions are entered in the books at the spot currency exchange rate at the transaction date.

For example, let us assume that Brie SA buys vintage cheese from a UK company, Cheddar Ltd, on 1 October 20X1 for £100,000 when the exchange rate was £1 = €1.20. This will be recorded by Brie as Purchases €120,000 and Trade payable (Cheddar) at €120,000.

Where it is more practical an average rate may be used for a period to translate the month's purchases (it will be inappropriate where exchange rates fluctuate significantly).

26.2.3 The accounting treatment of exchange differences when the transaction is settled within the current accounting period

Amounts paid or received in settlement of foreign currency monetary items during an accounting period are translated at the date of settlement, and any exchange difference is taken to the statement of income as a realised gain or loss.

For example, if the rate at the date of payment on 31 October 20X1 was £1 = €1.22, then Brie would pay €122,000 to obtain the sterling amount of £100,000. The exchange difference of €2,000 (€122,000 − €120,000) is debited to the statement of income as an operating expense. If the rate had changed to £1 = €1.18 then there would have been an operating income of €2,000.

The following is an extract from the accounting policies in Nemetschek's 2011 report:

Currency translation
Exchange rate differences arising on the settlement of monetary items at rates different from those at which they were initially recorded during the period, are recognized as other operating income or other operating expenses in the period in which they arise.

26.2.4 The accounting treatment of exchange differences at the year-end when settlement is to occur in the next accounting period

The treatment depends on the ledger balances outstanding. For instance:

- Monetary balances are retranslated at the closing rate as at the date of the statement of financial position.
- Non-monetary items such as property, plant, equipment and inventory reported at historical cost remain translated at their original transaction rate.
- Non-monetary items at fair value are translated at the rate on the date the fair value was determined.[3]

Continuing with our Brie example on accounting for inventory, there are the following possibilities.

Inventory has been sold but the account payable is still outstanding

Assuming that all of the cheese had been sold but Cheddar had still not been paid, then there is no inventory to consider, only the amount payable to Cheddar. This balance is required to be translated at the closing rate. If the closing rate is £1 = €1.24 then the liability to Cheddar would be restated at €124,000 and there would be a resulting exchange loss of €4,000 which is reported in the statement of income.

Inventory has still not been sold and the account payable is still outstanding

If the cheese had not been sold and was still held as inventory, it is required to be reported at the rate as at the date of the initial transaction and not the closing rate, i.e. reported in the statement of financial position as €120,000 – the cost as at 1 October 20X1, the date of purchase. The account payable would still be reported at €124,000.

Inventory has still not been sold but net realisable value is lower than cost

If enquiry established that the cheese had deteriorated and the net realisable value was 50% of cost, then this would be translated at the closing rate as €62,000 (£50,000 × 1.24) and a loss reported of €58,000.

26.2.5 The accounting treatment of exchange differences when settlement occurs in a yet later accounting period

If a monetary item remains unpaid beyond the next accounting period then it will need to be retranslated at the closing rate as at the end of that period.

Let us assume the following:

- Brie has translated the €120,000 due to Cheddar as €124,000 and recognised an operating loss of €4,000 in the year ended 31 December 20X1.
- Brie has reached an agreement with Cheddar that the cheese needs a further period to mature and settlement in full is to be on 1 January 20X3.
- The exchange rate is £1 = €1.23 on 31 December 20X2.

At 31 December 20X2 Brie would report that there was €123,000 owing and there would be an operating gain reported in the 20X2 statement of income of €1,000 (€124,000 – €123,000). If the exchange rate had weakened to a rate higher than £1 = €1.24 there would have been a further operating loss reported in 20X2.

26.2.6 Hedging a foreign currency transaction to crystallise the amount of any exchange difference

A company might enter into a hedging transaction under IAS 39 or IFRS 9 *Financial Instruments*. The intention is to neutralise the exchange risk so that the company knows exactly how much a transaction will cost when settlement is required at a later date. This can be achieved in a number of ways such as entering into a forward contract or an options contract.

For example, let us continue with our Brie example and assume that the euro is weakening and Brie's finance director wants to fix the exact amount it is required to pay in euros on 31 October 20X1 to settle the debt currently recorded as €120,000. His worry is that the end-of-month rate might be £1 = €1.30 which would result in an operating loss of €10,000. In order to take away the uncertainty, Brie enters into a forward contract to buy £100,000 at the end of the month at a rate of say €1.25. This means that there is a known loss of €5,000 as opposed to the risk of a potential loss of up to €10,000.

26.3 Boil plc – a more detailed illustration

Let us assume the following transactions were entered into by Boil plc, a UK company that buys and sells catering equipment in New Zealand during the year ended 31 December 20X4:

1/11	Buys goods for $30,000 on credit from Napier Ltd
15/11	Sells goods for $40,000 on credit to Wellington Ltd
15/11	Pays Napier Ltd $20,000 on account for the goods purchased
10/12	Receives $25,000 on account from Wellington Ltd in payment for the goods sold
10/12	Buys machinery for $80,000 from Auckland Ltd on credit
22/12	Pays Auckland Ltd $80,000 for the machinery

Boil's functional currency is sterling and the New Zealand companies' functional currency is NZ$.

The exchange rates at the relevant dates were:

1/11	£1 = $2.00	15/11	£1 = $2.20	10/12	£1 = $2.40
22/12	£1 = $2.50	31/12	£1 = $2.60		

(Assume that Boil plc buys foreign currency to pay for goods and non-current assets on the day of settlement and immediately converts into sterling any currency received from sales.)

Translating monetary accounts

We need to calculate any exchange differences on monetary accounts that are to be reported in the statement of income which arise on changes between the date of the initial transaction and the rate on the date of its settlement or the statement of financial position date, whichever is the earlier. Profits or losses on exchange differences will arise on the following monetary accounts:

Napier Ltd	Trade payables
Wellington Ltd	Trade receivable
Auckland Ltd	Payable for machinery

The profit or loss on foreign exchange in these cases will be as follows:

	Napier			Wellington			Auckland		
	Payable			Receivable			Payable		
	NZ$	Rate	£	NZ$	Rate	£	NZ$	Rate	£

(i) Record using the exchange rate on the date of transaction:
  30,000 @ 2.00 = 15,000   40,000 @ 2.20 = (18,182)   80,000 @ 2.40 = 33,333

(ii) Record using the exchange rate at the settlement date:
  20,000 @ 2.20 = (9,091)   25,000 @ 2.40 = 10,417   80,000 @ 2.50 = (32,000)

(iii) Retranslate and record using the closing exchange rate as at the year-end:
  10,000 @ 2.60 = (3,846)   15,000 @ 2.60 = 5,769

(iv) Calculate any gain (loss) on exchange:
  2,063   (1,996)   1,333

The exchange gains of £2,063 and £1,333 and exchange loss of £1,996 have been realised and are reported in the statement of income as operating income and operating expense.

Accounting treatment of other balances

All other balances, i.e. purchases and sales in the statement of income and machinery (non-monetary), will be translated on the day of the initial transaction and no profit or loss on foreign exchange will arise. These balances will therefore appear in the financial statements as follows:

Purchases	$30,000/2.00 = £15,000
Sales	$40,000/2.20 = £18,182
Machinery	$80,000/2.40 = £33,333

26.4 IAS 21 concept of functional and presentation currencies

All companies have a functional and a presentation currency. In a group with foreign subsidiaries these currencies often differ.

Many groups consist of a parent with a number of foreign subsidiaries that prepare their accounts in the local currency, their functional currency. At the year-end each set of foreign subsidiary accounts is translated into the currency of the parent, the presentation currency or presentational currency.

26.4.1 The functional currency

The functional currency is the currency of the primary economic environment in which the entity operates. For example, the following extract is from the Rio Tinto 2011 financial statements:

> The functional currency for each entity in the Group ... is the currency of the primary economic environment in which that entity operates. For many entities, this is the currency of the country in which they are located.

Factors to consider when determining the functional currency for an individual company

IAS 21 sets out the factors which a reporting entity (a company preparing financial statements) will consider in determining its functional currency.[1] These are:

- the currency that mainly influences sales prices for goods and services;

- the currency that mainly influences labour, materials and other costs of providing goods and services; and

- the currency in which funds from financing activities are generated and the currency in which the receipts from operating activities are usually retained, which also provide evidence of an entity's functional currency.[4]

If the functional currency is not obvious from the above, then managers have to make a judgement as to which currency most represents the economic effects of its transactions.

Factors a parent considers when deciding with a subsidiary on the subsidiary's functional currency

In making its decision the following factors will be considered:[5]

(a) Whether the activities of the foreign operation are carried out as an extension of the reporting entity (the parent), rather than being carried out with a significant degree of autonomy. An example of the former is when the foreign operation only sells goods imported from the parent and remits the proceeds to it. An example of the latter is when the operation accumulates cash and other monetary items, incurs expenses, generates income and arranges borrowings, all substantially in its local currency.

(b) Whether transactions with the parent are a high or low proportion of the foreign operation's activities.

(c) Whether cash flows from the activities of the foreign operation directly affect the cash flows of the parent and are readily available for remittance to it.

(d) Whether cash flows from the activities of the foreign operation are sufficient to service existing and normally expected debt obligations without funds being made available by the parent.

If the functional currency of the foreign operation is the same as that of the parent, there will of course be no need for translation and the consolidation will be just as for any other subsidiary.

26.4.2 The presentation currency[6]

The **presentation currency** is the currency a parent chooses for its financial statements. The parent is entitled to present its group accounts in any currency, so that in some cases the parent's presentation currency may differ from its own functional currency. There are various reasons for this, such as the principal or potential investors tending to function in a country with a different currency. For example, a parent whose functional currency is the euro might decide to raise finance in the US and so translates its euro financial statements into US$.

The following is an extract from a Press Announcement in 2010 by Tullow Oil plc:

Change in presentation currency
Tullow Oil plc ('the Company', together with its subsidiaries, 'the Group') will present its results in US dollars with effect from 1 January 2010. The Group has decided it is appropriate to change the presentational currency from Sterling as the majority of the Group's activities are in Africa where oil revenues and costs are dollar denominated.

26.5 Translating the functional currency into the presentation currency

Whenever the presentational currency is different from the functional currency, it is necessary to translate the financial statements into the presentational currency. In this situation there is no impact on cash flows and so there is no realised exchange gain or loss to be reported in the statement of income.

Any gain or loss will, therefore, be reported as other comprehensive income. The translation rules used in this situation are set out in paragraph 39 of IAS 21 as follows:

(a) assets and liabilities . . . shall be translated at the closing rate at the date of the statement of financial position;

(b) income and expenses . . . shall be translated at exchange rates at the dates of the transactions [or average rate if this is a reasonable approximation]; and

(c) all resulting exchange differences shall be recognised as a separate component of equity.

The following is an extract from Nemetschek AG's 2011 annual report:

Currency translation

The group's consolidated financial statements are presented in Euros, which is the group's presentation currency.

Functional currency policy

Each entity in the group determines its own functional currency. That is the currency of the primarily economic environment in which the company operates. Items included in the financial statements of each entity are measured using the functional currency. Transactions in foreign currencies are initially recorded at the functional currency rate ruling on the date of the transaction.

Monetary assets and liabilities denominated in foreign currencies are retranslated at the functional currency spot rate of exchange ruling at the balance sheet date. Foreign exchange differences are recorded in profit or loss . . .

Non-monetary items that are measured in terms of historical cost in a foreign currency are translated using the exchange rate as of the date of the initial transaction. Non-monetary items measured at fair value in a foreign currency are translated using the exchange rates at the date when the fair value is determined.

Group policy re subsidiaries

Assets and liabilities of foreign companies are translated to the Euro at the closing rate (incl. goodwill). Income and expenses are translated at the average exchange rate. Any resulting exchange differences are recognized separately in equity.

26.6 Preparation of consolidated accounts

The consolidated accounts are prepared for the Pau Group from the following data.

On 1 January 20X1 Pau Inc. acquired 80% of the ordinary shares of a Brazilian company Briona for $18m when Briona's retained earnings were R$2m and the share premium was R$7m. Briona's financial statements have been audited in their functional currency of Brazilian Reals and comply with IAS 21. The summarised statements of income and financial position as at 31 December 20X1 were as follows:

Statements of income for the year ended 31 December 20X1

	US$000	Pau US$000	R$000	Briona R$000
Sales		200,000		80,000
Opening inventories	20,000		10,000	
Purchases	130,000		60,000	
Closing inventories	(40,000)		(30,000)	
Cost of sales		110,000		40,000
Gross profit		90,000		40,000
Other expenses		(15,000)		(14,000)
Interest paid				(1,000)
Total expenses		(15,000)		(15,000)
Profit before taxation		75,000		25,000
Taxation		(15,000)		(5,000)
Profit after taxation		60,000		20,000

Statement of financial position as at 31 December 20X1

	US$000	R$000
Non-current assets	70,000	30,000
Investment in Briona	18,000	
Current assets		
Inventories	40,000	30,000
Trade receivables	27,000	25,000
Cash	2,000	1,000
Total current assets	69,000	56,000
Current liabilities		
Trade payables	35,000	12,000
Taxation	15,000	5,000
Total current liabilities	50,000	17,000
Debentures		6,000
Total assets less liabilities	107,000	63,000
Share capital	20,000	34,000
Share premium		7,000
Retained earnings	87,000	22,000
	107,000	63,000

The following information is also available:

(i) The opening inventory was acquired when the exchange rate was US$1 = R$2.0 and the closing inventory when the rate was US$1 = R$2.4.

(ii) Exchange rates were as follows:

At 1 January 20X1	US$1 = R$2.0
Average for the year ending 31 December 20X4	US$1 = R$2.25
At 31 December 20X1	US$1 = R$2.5

Required:

(a) Prepare a consolidated statement of income.

(b) Prepare a consolidated statement of financial position:

    (i) Show the goodwill calculation.

    (ii) Show the non-controlling interest calculation.

    (iii) Complete with retained earnings as a balancing figure.

(c) Reconcile the retained earnings figure showing exchange gains and losses.

26.6.1 Pau Group draft consolidated accounts

(a) Statement of income

	Pau US$000	Briona R$000	Rate	Briona US$000	Pau Group US$000
Sales	200,000	80,000	2.25	35,555.6	235,555.6
Opening inventories	20,000	10,000	2.0	5,000.0	25,000.0
Purchases	130,000	60,000	2.25	26,666.7	156,666.7
Closing inventories	−40,000	−30,000	2.4	−12,500.0	−52,500.0
Cost of sales	110,000	40,000		19,166.7	129,166.7
Gross profit	90,000	40,000		16,388.9	106,388.9
Other expenses	−15,000	−14,000	2.25	−6,222.2	−21,222.2
Interest paid		−1,000	2.25	−444.4	−444.4
Total expenses	15,000	15,000		6,666.7	21,666.7
Profit before tax	75,000	25,000		9,722.2	84,722.2
Income tax	−15,000	−5,000	2.5	−2,000.0	−17,000.0
Profit after tax	60,000	20,000		7,722.2	67,722.2

(b) Statement of financial position

	Pau US$000	Briona R$000	Rate	Briona US$000	Pau Group US$000
Non-current assets	70,000	30,000	2.5	12,000	82,000
Investment in Briona	18,000				Goodwill (b1) 640
Current assets					
Inventories	40,000	30,000	2.5	12,000	52,000
Trade receivables	27,000	25,000	2.5	10,000	37,000
Cash	2,000	1,000	2.5	400	2,400
	69,000	56,000		22,400	91,400
Current liabilities					
Trade payables	35,000	12,000	2.5	4,800	39,800
Taxation	15,000	5,000	2.5	2,000	17,000
Total current liabilities	50,000	17,000		6,800	56,800
Debentures		6,000	2.5	2,400	2,400
Total assets less liabilities	107,000	63,000		25,200	114,840
Share capital	20,000	34,000	2.5	13,600	20,000
Share premium		7,000	2.5	2,800	
Retained earnings	87,000	22,000	2.5	8,800	(b3) 89,800
	107,000	63,000		25,200	109,800
Non-controlling interest					(b2) 5,040
	107,000	63,000		25,200	114,840

(b1) Goodwill

	R$000	R$000	Rate at 1.1.20X1	US$000
Cost		36,000		
Share capital	34,000			
Share premium	7,000			
Retained earnings	2,000			
	43,000 × 80%	34,400		
Goodwill		1,600	2.0	800
Required to restate at year-end:				
Goodwill		1,600	2.5	640

(b2) Non-controlling interest (NCI) at 31.12.20X1

	R$000	Rate	US$000	US$000
Share capital	34,000	2.5	13,600	
Share premium	7,000	2.5	2,800	
Retained earnings	22,000	2.5	8,800	
			25,200 × 20%	5,040

(b3) The consolidated statement of financial position could be completed by inserting a balancing figure of US$89,800 for the retained earnings made up of Pau's retained earnings of £87,000 and Briona's post-acquisition profit of £2,800. This can be proved as follows:

(c) Subsidiary post-acquisition profit included in the $89,800 group retained earnings

	R$000	Rate	US$000	US$000 Parent	US$000 NCI
Retained profit per Income Statement			7,722.2	6,177.8	1,544.4
At closing rate	20,000	2.5	8,000		
Gain on exchange			277.8	222.2	55.6
Loss on opening shareholders' funds					
Share capital	34,000				
Share premium	7,000				
Retained earnings	2,000				
		Opening rate			
	43,000	2.0	21,500		
		Closing rate			
		2.5	17,200		
Loss			−4,300	(3,440)	(860)
Loss on goodwill		Opening rate			
Goodwill	1,600	2.0	800		
		Closing rate			
		2.5	640		
Loss			−160	(160)	
Post-acquisition profit of Briona attributable to Pau				2,800	

Post-acquisition profit attributable to NCI	740
Opening NCI (43,000 × 20% / 2.0)	4,300
Closing NCI (63,000 × 20% / 2.5)	5,040

	US$000
Group retained profit at 31.12.20X1	
Pau	87,000
Briona post–acquisition (above)	2,800
Group retained profit	89,800

Note that there is no post-acquisition share premium, as the subsidiary's balance at acquisition and at 31.12.20X1 is the same at R$7m.

26.7 How to reduce the risk of translation differences

We have seen that when a parent invests in a foreign subsidiary it is required at each year-end to translate the assets and liabilities from the subsidiary's functional currency into that of the parent.

For example, let us assume that a UK parent has spent $10m on acquiring a US trading subsidiary and at the year-end the net assets of the US subsidiary are also $10m.

On consolidation by the UK parent, the $10m net assets of the US subsidiary are translated into sterling for inclusion in the consolidated statement of financial position. At each year-end the sterling value of any foreign exchange differences are taken to reserves. This means that the group's consolidated shareholders' funds will fluctuate up and down as exchange rates move.

The parent is able to reduce the extent of such fluctuations by hedging the translation risk. It normally does so by acquiring a matching foreign exchange liability. One way is to take on a debt such as a $10m loan.

Assuming that the opening exchange rate is £1 = $2 and the closing rate is £1 = $2.5, without hedging there would be an exchange loss on holding the net assets of £1,000. If the same amount is borrowed there would be an exchange gain on holding the debt of £1,000 ($10m at 2.0 less $10m at 2.5).

In practice, it may be difficult for the parent to borrow as much as $10m unless it gave a guarantee to the lender. By borrowing all its investment in its subsidiary in dollars, the parent would minimise its exchange gains and losses in its subsidiary. In this example, the dollar depreciates against the pound and there is a loss (without hedging). If the dollar appreciated against the pound, there would be a gain (without hedging).

26.8 Critique of use of presentational currency

Multinational companies may have subsidiaries in many different countries, each of which may report by choice or legal requirement internally in their local currency. With globalisation, reporting the group in a presentation currency assists the efficiency of international capital markets, particularly where a group raises funds in more than one market. Although each subsidiary might be controlled through financial statements prepared in the local currency, realism requires the use of a single presentation currency.

26.9 IAS 29 *Financial Reporting in Hyperinflationary Economies*[7]

IAS 29 applies where an entity's functional currency is that of a hyperinflationary economy. Its objective is to give guidance on (a) determining when an economy is hyperinflationary, and (b) restating financial statements to make them meaningful.

26.9.1 Determining when an economy is hyperinflationary

There is no precise criterion, although there is a view that there is hyperinflation when the cumulative inflation rate over three years exceeds 100%. The IAS 29 approach is to leave it as a matter of judgement, based on indicators (IAS 29.3) such as:

- the general population preferring to keep its wealth in non-monetary assets or in a relatively stable foreign currency, with amounts of local currency held being immediately invested to maintain purchasing power;

- the general population regarding monetary amounts not in terms of the local currency but in terms of a relatively stable foreign currency in which prices may be quoted;

- sales and purchases on credit taking place at prices that compensate for the expected loss of purchasing power during the credit period, even if the period is short;

- interest rates, wages and prices being linked to a price index; and

- the cumulative inflation rate over three years approaching, or exceeding, 100%.

26.9.2 How to restate financial statements

Having decided that hyperinflation has occurred, the standard requires the financial statements (and corresponding figures for previous periods) of an entity with a functional currency that is hyperinflationary to be restated for the changes in the general pricing power of the functional currency using the measuring unit current at the year-end date.

26.9.3 Restatement treatment of statements of income and financial position

The statement of comprehensive income

All items in the statement of comprehensive income are expressed in terms of the measuring unit current at the end of the reporting period. All amounts need to be restated by applying the change in the general price index from the dates when the items of income and expenses were initially recorded in the financial statements.

The statement of financial position

Amounts not already expressed in terms of the measuring unit current at the end of the reporting period are restated by applying a general price index.

Monetary items

- **Monetary items are not restated because they are already expressed in terms of the monetary unit.**
- Inventory also as it has been written down to net realisable value under IAS 2.

Non-monetary items

Non-monetary items are restated from the date of acquisition if they are historical cost financial statements or from date of valuation if any asset has been reported at valuation.

If they are current cost financial statements then there is no restatement because they are already expressed in the unit of measurement current at the end of the reporting period.

26.9.4 Disclosures

The following disclosures are required:

(a) the fact that the financial statements and the corresponding figures for previous periods have been restated in terms of the measuring unit current at the end of the reporting period;

(b) whether the financial statements are based on a historical cost approach or a current cost approach; and

(c) the price index that has been used and the level of the price index at the end of the reporting period and the movement in the index during the current and the previous reporting periods.

Summary

When accounts are prepared in the functional currency, exchange differences arising on the settlement of monetary items or on translating monetary items at rates that are different from those which applied on initial recognition (i.e. settled in a later accounting period) are recognised in profit or loss in the period in which they arise.

When functional currency financial statements are translated into a different presentation currency, assets and liabilities are translated at closing rate, income and expenses are translated at the rate as at the date of the transactions (an average may be practical if appropriate), and resulting exchange gains are recognised in other comprehensive income.

REVIEW QUESTIONS

1 Discuss the desirability or otherwise of isolating profits or losses caused by exchange differences from other profit or losses in financial statements.

2 Explain the term functional currency and describe the factors an entity should take into account when determining which is the functional currency.

3 Explain why exchange differences are treated differently in financial statements prepared in a functional currency and those prepared in a presentation currency.

4 Discuss why a company that is not part of a group might decide to translate its financial statements into a presentation currency.

5 Explain why exchange differences might appear in other comprehensive income.

6 How does the treatment of changes in foreign exchange rates relate to the prudence and accruals concepts?

7 It was reported[8] that 'Belarus' cumulative inflation index will exceed 100%, which means that IAS 29 is likely to be applicable to Belarus up to 2014 . . . does not expect any significant microeconomic consequences of Belarus' qualifying as a country with hyperinflationary economy, except for the significant deterioration in financial performance indicators of banks and enterprises applying IFRS.'

Discuss what financial performance indicators might be adversely affected by applying IAS 29.

EXERCISES

Question 1

Fry Ltd has the following foreign currency transactions in the year to 31/12/20X0:

15/11	Buys goods for $40,000 on credit from Texas Inc
15/11	Sells goods for $60,000 on credit to Alamos Inc
20/11	Pays Texas Inc $40,000 for the goods purchased
20/11	Receives $30,000 on account from Alamos Inc in payment for the goods sold
20/11	Buys machinery for $100,000 from Chicago Inc on credit
20/11	Borrows $90,000 from an American bank
21/12	Pays Chicago Inc $80,000 for the machinery

The exchange rates at the relevant dates were:

15/11	£1 = $2.60
20/11	£1 = $2.40
21/12	£1 = $2.30
31/12	£1 = $2.10

Required:
Calculate the profit or loss to be reported in the financial statements of Fry Ltd at 31/12/20X0.

*Question 2

On 1 January 20X1 Fibre plc acquired 80% of the ordinary shares of a Singaporean company, Fastlink Ltd, for £6m when Fastlink's retained earnings were $15.5m and the share premium was $0.8m. Fastlink's financial statements have been prepared in their functional currency of Singapore dollars and comply with IAS 21. The summarised statements of income and financial position as at 31 December 20X1 were as follows:

Statements of income for the year ended 31 December 20X1

	Fibre	Fastlink
	£000	$000
Sales	200,000	50,000
Opening inventories	20,000	8,000
Purchases	130,000	30,000
Closing inventories	(40,000)	(6,000)
Cost of sales	110,000	32,000
Gross profit	90,000	18,000
Expenses	(15,000)	(6,500)
Profit before taxation	75,000	11,500
Taxation	(15,000)	(3,000)
Profit after taxation	60,000	8,500

Statement of financial position as at 31 December 20X1

	£000	$000
Non-current assets	90,000	25,000
Investment in Fastlink	6,000	
Current assets:		
Inventories	40,000	6,000
Trade receivables	27,000	5,000
Cash	2,000	4,000
Total current assets	69,000	15,000
Current liabilities:		
Trade payables	35,000	11,000
Taxation	15,000	3,000
Total current liabilities	50,000	14,000
Total assets less liabilities	115,000	26,000
Share capital	20,000	1,200
Share premium		800
Retained earnings	95,000	24,000
	115,000	26,000

The following information is also available:

(i) The opening inventory was acquired when the exchange rate was £1 = $2.6 and the closing inventory when the rate was £1 = $2.2.

(ii) Exchange rates were as follows:

At 1 January 20X1	£1 = $2.5
Average for the year ending 31 December 20X4	£1 = $2.25
At 31 December 20X1	£1 = $2.0

Required:
(a) Prepare a consolidated statement of income.
(b) Prepare a consolidated statement of financial position:
    (i) Show the goodwill calculation.
    (ii) Show the non-controlling interest calculation.
    (iii) Complete with retained earnings as a balancing figure.
(c) Reconcile the retained earnings figure showing exchange gains and losses.

Question 3

On 1 January 20X0 Walpole Ltd acquired 90% of the ordinary shares of a French subsidiary Paris SA. At that date the balance on the retained earnings of Paris SA was €10,000. The non-controlling interest in Paris was measured as a percentage of identifiable net assets. No shares have been issued by Paris since acquisition. Paris SA's dividend was paid on 31 December 20X2. The summarised statements of comprehensive income and statements of financial position of Walpole Ltd and Paris SA at 31 December 20X2 were as follows:

Statements of comprehensive income for the year ended 31 December 20X2

	Walpole Ltd £000	Paris SA £000
Sales	317,200	200,000
Opening inventories	50,000	22,000
Purchases	180,000	90,000
Closing inventories	60,000	12,000
Cost of sales	170,000	100,000
Gross profit	147,200	100,000
Dividend received from Paris SA	1,800	NIL
Depreciation	30,000	30,000
Other expenses	15,000	7,000
Interest paid	6,000	3,000
Total expenses	51,000	40,000
Profit before taxation	98,000	60,000
Taxation	21,000	15,000
Profit after taxation	77,000	45,000
Dividend paid	20,000	10,000

Statement of financial position as at 31 December 20X2

	Walpole Ltd £000	Paris SA £000
Non-current assets	94,950	150,000
Investment in Paris SA	41,050	
Current assets:		
Inventories	60,000	12,000
Trade receivables	59,600	40,000
Paris SA	2,400	
Cash	11,000	11,000
Total current assets	133,000	63,000
Current liabilities:		
Trade payables	45,000	18,000
Walpole Ltd		12,000
Taxation	21,000	15,000
Total current liabilities	66,000	45,000
Debentures	40,000	10,000
Total assets less liabilities	163,000	158,000
Share capital	80,000	60,000
Share premium	6,000	20,000
Revaluation reserve	10,000	12,000
Retained earnings	67,000	66,000
	163,000	158,000

The following information is also available:

(i)   The revaluation reserve in Paris SA arose from the revaluation of non-current assets on 1/1/20X2.

(ii) No impairment of goodwill has occurred since acquisition.

(iii) Exchange rates were as follows:

At 1 January 20X0	£1 = €2
Average for the year ending 31 December 20X2	£1 = €4
At 31 December 20X1/1 January 20X2	£1 = €3
At 31 December 20X2	£1 = €5

Required:
Assuming that the functional currency of Paris SA is the euro, prepare the consolidated accounts for the Walpole group at 31 December 20X2.

* Question 4

(a) According to IAS 21 *The Effects of Changes in Foreign Exchange Rates*, how should a company decide what its functional currency is?

(b) Until recently Eufonion, a UK limited liability company, reported using the euro (€) as its functional currency. However, on 1 November 2007 the company decided that its functional currency should now be the dollar ($).

The summarised balance sheet of Eufonion as at 31 October 2008 in € million was as follows:

ASSETS		€m
Non-current assets		420
Current assets		
Inventories	26	
Trade and other receivables	42	
Cash and cash equivalents	8	
		76
Total assets		496
EQUITY AND LIABILITIES		
Equity		
Share capital		200
Retained earnings		107
		307
Non-current liabilities	85	
Current liabilities		
Trade and other payables	63	
Current taxation	41	
	104	
Total liabilities		189
Total equity and liabilities		496

Non-current liabilities includes a loan of $70 million which was raised in dollars ($) and translated at the closing rate of $1 = €0.72425.

Trade receivables include an amount of $20 million invoiced in dollars ($) to an American customer which has been translated at the closing rate of $1 = €0.72425.

All items of property, plant and equipment were purchased in euros (€) except for plant which was purchased in British pounds (£) in 2007 and which cost £150 million. This was translated at the exchange rate of £1 = €1.46015 as at the date of purchase. The carrying value of the equipment was £90 million as at 31 October 2008.

Required:
Translate the balance sheet of Eufonion as at 31 October 2008 into dollars ($m), the company's new functional currency.

(c) The directors of Eufonion (as in (b) above) are now considering using the British pound (£) as the company's presentation currency for the financial statements for the year ended 31 October 2009.

Required:
Advise the directors how they should translate the company's income statement for the year ended 31 October 2009 and its balance sheet as at 31 October 2009 into the new presentation currency.

(d) Discuss whether or not a reporting entity should be allowed to present its financial statements in a currency which is different from its functional currency.

(The Association of International Accountants)

Question 5

Helvatia GmbH is a Swiss company which is a wholly owned subsidiary of Corolli, a UK company. Helvatia GmbH was formed on 1 November 2005 to purchase and manage a property in Zürich in Switzerland. The reporting and functional currency of Helvatia GmbH is the Swiss franc (CHF).

As a financial accountant in Corolli you are converting the financial statements of Helvatia GmbH into £ sterling in order to be consolidated with the results of Corolli which reports in £s.

The following are the summarised income statements and balance sheet (in thousands of Swiss francs) of Helvatia GmbH:

Helvatia GmbH income statement and retained earnings for the year ended 31 October 2007

	CHF (000)
Revenue	8,800
Depreciation	(1,370)
Other operating expenses	(1,900)
Net income	5,530
Retained earnings at 1 November 2006	3,760
	9,290
Dividends paid	(1,000)
Retained earnings at 31 October 2007	8,290

Helvatia GmbH balance sheet as at 31 October

		2007		2006
ASSETS		CHF (000)		CHF (000)
Non-current assets				
Land		6,300		3,300
Buildings		12,330		13,700
		18,630		17,000
Current assets				
Receivables	550		1,550	
Cash	5,610		610	
		6,160		2,160
		24,790		19,160
LIABILITIES AND EQUITY				
Non-current liabilities				
Mortgage loan		10,800		10,000
Current liabilities				
Payables		700		400
Equity				
Issued share capital	5,000		5,000	
Retained earnings	8,290	13,290	3,760	8,760
		24,790		19,160

The following exchange rates are available:

	1 Swiss franc = £
At 1 November 2005	0.40
At 1 November 2006	0.55
At 30 November 2006	0.53
At 31 January 2007	0.53
At 31 October 2007	0.45
Weighted average for the year ended 31 October 2007	0.50

The non-current assets and mortgage loan of Helvatia GmbH as at 31 October 2006 all date from 1 November 2005. Helvatia GmbH purchased additional land and increased the mortgage loan on 31 January 2007. There were no other purchases of non-current assets. Land is not depreciated but the building is depreciated at 10% a year using the reducing balance method. Helvatia GmbH's dividends were paid on 31 January 2007.

The sterling equivalent of Helvatia GmbH's retained earnings as at 31 October 2006 was £1,222,000.

Required:

Prepare the following statements for Helvatia GmbH *in £000 sterling*:

(a) A summarised income statement for the year ended 31 October 2007.

(b) A summarised balance sheet as at 31 October 2007.

(c) A statement of cash flows for the year ended 31 October 2007 using the indirect method. Additional notes are not required.

(The Association of International Accountants)

References

1 IAS 21 *The Effects of Changes in Foreign Exchange Rates*, IASB, revised 2003, para. 20.
2 *Ibid.*, para. 21.
3 *Ibid.*, para. 23.
4 *Ibid.*, para. 10.
5 *Ibid.*, para. 11.
6 *Ibid.*, para. 38.
7 IAS 29 *Financial Reporting in Hyperinflationary Economies*, IASB, 1989.
8 http://www.prime-tass.by/english/News/show.asp?id=96939

PART 6

Interpretation

CHAPTER 27

Earnings per share

27.1 Introduction

The main purpose of this chapter is to undertand the importance of earnings per share (EPS) and the PE ratio as a measure of the financial performance of a company (or 'an enterprise'). This chapter will enable you to calculate the EPS according to IAS 33 for both the current year and prior years, when there is an issue of shares in the year. Also, it will enable you to understand and calculate the diluted earnings per share, for future changes in share capital arising from exercising of share options and conversion of other financial instruments into shares.

Objectives

By the end of this chapter, you should be able to:

- define earnings per share and the PE ratio;
- comment critically on alternative EPS figures;
- calculate the basic earnings per share;
- calculate the diluted earnings per share.

27.2 Why is the earnings per share figure important?

One of the most widely publicised ratios for a public company is the price/earnings or PE ratio. The PE ratio is significant because, by combining it with a forecast of company earnings, analysts can decide whether the shares are currently over- or undervalued.[1]

The ratio is published daily in the financial press and is widely employed by those making investment decisions. The following is a typical extract:

Breweries, Pubs and Restaurants

Company	Price 31/10/12	PE ratio
Company A	283	8.9
Company B	471	11.0
Company C	705	17.0

The PE ratio is calculated by dividing the market price of a share by the earnings that the company generated for that share. Alternatively, the PE figure may be seen as a multiple of the earnings per share, where the multiple represents the number of years' earnings required to recoup the price paid for the share. For example, it would take a shareholder in Company B 11 years to recoup her outlay if all earnings were to be distributed, whereas it would take a shareholder in Company A almost nine years to recoup his outlay, and one in Company C 17 years.

27.2.1 What factors affect the PE ratio?

The PE ratio for a company will reflect investors' confidence and hopes about the international scene, the national economy and the industry sector, as well as about the current year's performance of the company as disclosed in its financial report. It is difficult to interpret a PE ratio in isolation without a certain amount of information about the company, its competitors and the industry within which it operates.

For example, a **high PE ratio** might reflect investor confidence in the existing management team: people are willing to pay a high multiple for expected earnings because of the underlying strength of the company. Conversely, it might also reflect lack of investor confidence in the existing management, but an anticipation of a takeover bid which will result in transfer of the company assets to another company with better prospects of achieving growth in earnings than has the existing team.

A **low PE ratio** might indicate a lack of confidence in the current management or a feeling that even a new management might find problems that are not easily surmounted. For example, there might be extremely high gearing, with little prospect of organic growth in earnings or new capital inputs from rights issues to reduce it.

These reasons for a difference in the PE ratios of companies, even though they are in the same industry, are market-based and not simply a function of earnings. However, both the current earnings per share figure and the individual shareholder's expectation of future growth relative to that of other companies also have an impact on the share price.

27.3 How is the EPS figure calculated?

Because of the importance attached to the PE ratio, it is essential that there be a consistent approach to the calculation of the EPS figure. IAS 33 *Earnings per Share*[2] was issued in 1998 for this purpose. A revised version of the standard was issued in 2003.

The EPS figure is of major interest to shareholders not only because of its use in the PE ratio calculation, but also because it is used in the earnings yield percentage calculation. It is a more acceptable basis for comparing performance than figures such as dividend yield percentage because it is not affected by the distribution policy of the directors. The formula is:

$$\text{EPS} = \frac{\text{Earnings}}{\text{Weighted number of ordinary shares}}$$

The standard defines two EPS figures for disclosure, namely,

- **basic** EPS based on ordinary shares currently in issue; and
- **diluted** EPS based on ordinary shares currently in issue *plus* potential ordinary shares.

27.3.1 Basic EPS

Basic EPS is defined in IAS 33 as follows:[3]

- Basic earnings per share is calculated by dividing the net profit or loss for the period attributable to ordinary shareholders by the weighted average number of ordinary shares outstanding during the period.

For the purpose of the BEPS definition:

- **Net profit** is the profit for the period attributable to the parent entity after deduction of preference dividends (assuming preference shares are equity instruments).[4]
- The **weighted average number of ordinary shares** should be adjusted for events, other than the conversion of potential ordinary shares, that have changed the number of ordinary shares outstanding, without a corresponding change in resources.[5]
- An **ordinary share** is an equity instrument that is subordinate to all other classes of equity instruments.[6]

Earnings per share is calculated on the overall profit attributable to ordinary shareholders but also on the profit from continuing operations if this is different from the overall profit for the period.

27.3.2 Diluted EPS

Diluted EPS is defined as follows:

- For the purpose of calculating diluted earnings per share, the net profit attributable to ordinary shareholders and the weighted average number of shares outstanding should be *adjusted for the effects of all dilutive potential ordinary shares.*[7]

This means that *both* the earnings *and* the number of shares used *may* need to be adjusted from the amounts that appear in the profit and loss account and statement of financial position.

- **Dilutive** means that earnings in the future may be spread over a larger number of ordinary shares.
- **Potential ordinary shares** are financial instruments that may entitle the holders to ordinary shares.

27.4 The use to shareholders of the EPS

Shareholders use the reported EPS to estimate future growth which will affect the future share price. It is an important measure of growth over time. There are, however, limitations in its use as a performance measure and for inter-company comparison.

27.4.1 How does a shareholder estimate future growth in the EPS?

The current EPS figure allows a shareholder to assess the wealth-creating abilities of a company. It recognises that the effect of earnings is to add to the individual wealth of shareholders in two ways: first, by the payment of a dividend which transfers cash from the company's control to the shareholder; and, secondly, by retaining earnings in the company for reinvestment, so that there may be increased earnings in the future.

The important thing when attempting to arrive at an estimate is to review the statement of comprehensive income of the current period and identify the earnings that can reasonably be expected to continue. In accounting terminology, you should identify the **maintainable post-tax earnings** that arise in the **ordinary course of business**.

Companies are required to make this easy for the shareholder by disclosing separately, by way of note, any unusual items and by analysing the profit and loss on trading between discontinuing and continuing activities.

Shareholders can use this information to estimate for themselves the maintainable post-tax earnings, assuming that there is no change in the company's trading activities.

Clearly, in a dynamic business environment it is extremely unlikely that there will be no change in the current business activities. The shareholder needs to refer to any information on capital commitments which appear as a note to the accounts and also to the chairman's statement and any coverage in the financial press. This additional information is used to adjust the existing maintainable earnings figure.

27.4.2 Limitations of EPS as a performance measure

EPS is thought to have a significant impact on the market share price. However, there are limitations to its use as a performance measure.

The limitations affecting the use of EPS as an inter-period performance measure include the following:

- It is based on historical earnings. Management might have made decisions in the past to encourage current earnings growth at the expense of future growth, e.g. by reducing the amount spent on capital investment and research and development. Growth in the EPS cannot be relied on as a predictor of the rate of growth in the future.
- EPS does not take inflation into account. Real growth might be materially different from the apparent growth.

The limitations affecting inter-company comparisons include the following:

- The earnings are affected by management's choice of accounting policies, e.g. whether non-current assets have been revalued or interest has been capitalised.
- EPS is affected by the capital structure, e.g. changes in number of shares by making bonus issues.

However, the **rate of growth** of EPS is important and this may be compared between different companies and over time within the same company.

27.5 Illustration of the basic EPS calculation

Assume that Watts plc had post-tax profits for 20X1 of £1,250,000 and an issued share capital of £1,500,000 comprising 1,000,000 ordinary shares of 50p each and 1,000,000 £1 10% preference shares that are classified as equity. The basic EPS (BEPS) for 20X1 is calculated at £1.15 as follows:

	£000
Profit on ordinary activities after tax	1,250
Less preference dividend	(100)
Profit for the period attributable to ordinary shareholders	1,150

BEPS = £1,150,000/1,000,000 shares = **£1.15**

Note that it is the *number* of issued shares that is used in the calculation and *not the nominal value* of the shares. The market value of a share is not required for the BEPS calculation.

27.6 Adjusting the number of shares used in the basic EPS calculation

The earnings per share is frequently used by shareholders and directors to demonstrate the growth in a company's performance over time. Care is required to ensure that the number of shares is stated consistently to avoid distortions arising from changes in the capital structure that have changed the number of shares outstanding without a corresponding change in resources during the whole or part of a year. Such changes occur with (a) bonus issues and share splits; (b) new issues and buybacks at full market price during the year; and (c) the bonus element of a rights issue.

We will consider the appropriate treatment for each of these capital structure changes in order to ensure that EPS is comparable between accounting periods.

27.6.1 Bonus issues

A bonus issue, or capitalisation issue as it is also called, arises when a company capitalises reserves to give existing shareholders more shares. In effect, a simple transfer is made from reserves to issued share capital. In real terms, neither the shareholder nor the company is giving or receiving any immediate financial benefit. The process indicates that the reserves will not be available for distribution, but will remain invested in the physical assets of the company. There are, however, more shares.

Treatment in current year

In the Watts plc example, assume that the company increased its shares in issue in 20X1 by the issue of another 1 million shares and achieved identical earnings in 20X1 as in 20X0. The EPS reported for 20X1 would be immediately halved from £1.15 to £0.575. Clearly, this does not provide a useful comparison of performance between the two years.

Restatement of previous year's BEPS

The solution is to restate the EPS for 20X0 that appears in the 20X1 accounts, using the number of shares in issue at 31.12.20X1, i.e. £1,150,000/2,000,000 shares = BEPS of **£0.575**.

27.6.2 Share splits

When the market value of a share becomes high some companies decide to increase the number of shares held by each shareholder by changing the nominal value of each share. The effect is to reduce the market price per share but for each shareholder to hold the same total value. A share split would be treated in the same way as a bonus issue.

For example, if Watts plc split the 1,000,000 shares of 50p each into 2,000,000 shares of 25p each, the 20X1 BEPS would be calculated using 2,000,000 shares. It would seem that the BEPS had halved in 20X1. This is misleading and the 20X0 BEPS is therefore restated using 2,000,000 shares. The total market capitalisation of Watts plc would remain unchanged. For example, if, prior to the split, each share had a market value of £4 and the company had a total market capitalisation of £4,000,000, after the split each share would have a market price of £2 and the company market capitalisation would remain unchanged at £4,000,000.

A split is frequently taken as a sign that the board is confident of improved future performance, plus the fact that the fall in the share price makes the shares become more attractive to smaller investors means that the share price might rise above £4 due to the increased demand.

Effect on ratios of a share split

Those ratios that are expressed as 'per share' are restated in proportion to the split as with the earnings, dividends and asset per share ratios. For example, if the earnings per share are

50c before a two-for-one split, this will be restated as 25c per share. Note that the PE ratio also needs to be restated – if before the split it was 8:50, after the split it will be 4:25.

Reverse share split

The board might decide to recommend a reverse if the share price is considered too low. Just as with a share split, the market capitalisation is unchanged. For example, if there were 5 million shares with a market value of €8 and there was a reverse split of one share for two currently held, the share price would double to €16 and the market capitalisation would remain at €40m.

The following is an extract relating to The Coca-Cola Company:

> **April 25, 2012** – The Board of Directors of The Coca-Cola Company today voted to recommend a two-for-one stock split to shareowners. The split would be the 11th in the stock's 92-year history and the first in 16 years.
>
> 'Our recommended two-for-one stock split reflects the Board of Directors' continued confidence in the long-term growth and financial performance of our Company,' said Muhtar Kent, Chairman and CEO of The Coca-Cola Company. 'Our system's 2020 Vision to double our revenues over this decade provides a clear roadmap for creating value for our consumers, customers, bottling partners and shareowners. A stock split reflects our desire to share value with an ever-growing number of people and organizations around the world.'

27.6.3 New issue at full market value

Selling more shares to raise additional capital should generate additional earnings. In this situation we have a real change in the company's capital and there is no need to adjust any comparative figures. However, a problem arises in the year in which the issue took place. Unless the issue occurred on the first day of the financial year, the new funds would have been *available to generate profits* for only a part of the year. It would therefore be misleading to calculate the EPS figure by dividing the earnings generated during the year by the number of shares in issue at the end of the year. The method adopted to counter this is to use a time-weighted average for the number of shares.

For example, let us assume in the Watts example that the following information is available:

	No. of shares
Shares (nominal value 50p) in issue at 1 January 20X1	1,000,000
Shares issued for cash at market price on 30 September 20X1	500,000

The time-weighted number of shares for EPS calculation at 31 December 20X1 will be:

	No. of shares
Shares in issue for 9 months to date of issue $(1,000,000 \times 9/12)$	750,000
Shares in issue for 3 months from date of issue $(1,500,000 \times 3/12)$	375,000
Time-weighted shares for use in BEPS calculation	1,125,000

EPS for 20X1 will be £1,150,000/1,125,000 shares = **£1.02**

27.6.4 Buybacks at market value

Companies are prompted to buy back their own shares when there is a fall in the stock market. The main arguments that companies advance for purchasing their own shares are:

- to reduce the cost of capital when equity costs more than debt;
- the shares are undervalued;
- to return surplus cash to shareholders; and
- to increase the apparent rate of growth in BEPS.

The following is an extract from the 2012 Vodafone Group plc Annual Report:

> Our business is highly cash generative and in the last four years we have returned over 30% of our market capitalisation to shareholders in the form of dividends and share buybacks, while still investing around £6 billion a year in our networks and infrastructure.
>
> **Earnings per share**
> Adjusted earnings per share was 14.91 pence, a decline of 11.0% year-on-year, reflecting the loss of our 44% interest in SFR and Polkomtel's profits, the loss of interest income from investment disposals and mark-to-market items charged through finance costs, *partially offset by a reduction in shares arising from the Group's share buyback programme*.

Shares bought back by the company are included in the basic EPS calculation time-apportioned from the beginning of the year to the date of buyback.

For example, let us assume in the Watts example that the following information is available:

	No. of shares
Shares (50p nominal value) in issue at 1 January 20X1	1,000,000
Shares bought back on 31 May 20X1	240,000
Profit attributable to ordinary shares	£1,150,000

The time-weighted number of shares for EPS calculation at 31 December 20X1 will be:

1.1.20X1 Shares in issue for 5 months to date of buyback (1,000,000 × 5/12)		416,667
31.5.20X1 Number of shares bought back by company	(240,000)	
31.12.20X1 Opening capital less shares bought back	(760,000 × 7/12)	443,333
Time-weighted shares for use in BEPS calculation		860,000

BEPS for 20X1 will be £1,150,000/860,000 shares = **£1.34**

Note that the effect of this buyback has been to increase the BEPS for 20X1 from £1.15 as calculated in Section 27.5 above. This is a mechanism for management to lift the BEPS and achieve EPS growth.

27.7 Rights issues

A rights issue involves giving existing shareholders 'the right' to buy a set number of additional shares at a price below the fair value which is normally the current market price. A rights issue has two characteristics, being both an issue for cash and, because the price is below fair value, a bonus issue. Consequently the rules for *both* a cash issue *and* a bonus issue need to be applied in calculating the weighted average number of shares for the basic EPS calculation.

This is an area where students frequently find difficulty with Step 1 and we will illustrate the rationale without accounting terminology.

The following four steps are required:

Step 1: Calculate the average price of shares before and after a rights issue to identify the amount of the bonus the company has granted.

Step 2: Calculate the weighted average number of shares for the current year.

Step 3: Calculate the BEPS for the current year.

Step 4: Adjust the previous year's BEPS for the bonus element of the rights issue.

Step 1: Calculate the average price of shares before and after a rights issue to identify the amount of the bonus the company has granted

Assume that Mr Radmand purchased two 50p shares at a market price of £4 each in Watts plc on 1 January 20X1 and that on 2 January 20X1 the company offered a 1:2 rights issue (i.e. one new share for every two shares held) at £3.25 per share.

If Mr Radmand had bought at the market price, the position would simply have been:

		£
Two shares at market price of £4 each on 1 January 20X1	=	8.00
One share at market price of £4 on 2 January 20X1	=	4.00
Total cost of three shares as at 2 January 20X1		12.00
Average cost per share unchanged at		4.00

However, this did not happen. Mr Radmand paid only £3.25 for the new share. This meant that the total cost of three shares to him was:

		£
Two shares at market price of £4 each on 1 January 20X1	=	8.00
One share at discounted price of £3.25 on 2 January 20X1	=	3.25
Total cost of three shares	=	11.25
Average cost per share (£11.25/3 shares)	=	3.75

The rights issue has had the effect of reducing the cost per share of each of the three shares held by Mr Radmand on 2 January 20X1 by £0.25 per share.

The accounting terms applied are:

- The average cost per share after the rights issue (£3.75) is *the theoretical ex-rights value*.
- The amount by which the average cost of each share is reduced (£0.25) is *the bonus element*.

In accounting terminology, Step 1 is described as follows:

> **Step 1:** *Theoretical ex-rights calculation.* The bonus element is ascertained by calculating the theoretical ex-rights value, i.e. the £0.25 is ascertained by calculating the £3.75 and deducting it from £4 pre-rights market price.

In accounting terminology, this means that existing shareholders get an element of bonus per share (£0.25) at the same time as the company receives additional capital (£3.25 per new share). The bonus element may be quantified by the calculation of a **theoretical ex-rights price (£3.75)**, which is compared with the last market price (£4.00) prior to the issue; the difference is a bonus. The theoretical ex-rights price is calculated as follows:

		£
Two shares at fair value of £4 each prior to rights issue	=	8.00
One share at discounted rights issue price of £3.25 each	=	3.25
Three shares at fair value after issue (i.e. ex-rights)	=	11.25
Theoretical ex-rights price (£11.25/3 shares)	=	3.75
Bonus element (fair value £4 less £3.75)	=	0.25

Note that for the calculation of the number of shares and the time-weighted number of shares for a bonus issue, share split and issue at full market price per share, the market price per share is not relevant. The position for a rights issue is different and the market price becomes a relevant factor in calculating the number of bonus shares.

Assume that Watts plc made a rights issue of one share for every two shares held on 1 January 20X1. There would be no need to calculate a weighted average number of shares. The total used in the BEPS calculation would be as follows:

		No. of shares
Shares to date of rights issue:		
1,000,000 shares held for a full year	=	1,000,000
Shares from date of rights issue:		
500,000 shares held for a full year	=	500,000
Total shares for BEPS calculation		1,500,000

However, if a rights issue is made part-way through the year, a time-apportionment is required. For example, if we assume that a rights issue is made on 30 September 20X1, the time-weighted number of shares is calculated as follows:

		No. of shares
Shares to date of rights issue:		
1,000,000 shares held for a full year	=	1,000,000
Shares from date of rights issue:		
500,000 shares held for 3 months $(500,000 \times 3/12)$	=	125,000
Weighted average number of shares		1,125,000

Note, however, that the 1,125,000 has not taken account of the fact that the new shares had been issued at less than market price and that the company had effectively granted the existing shareholders a bonus. We saw above that when there has been a bonus issue the number of shares used in the BEPS is increased. We need, therefore, to calculate the number of bonus shares that would have been issued to achieve the reduction in market price from £4.00 to £3.75 per share. This is calculated as follows:

Total market capitalisation 1,000,000 shares @ £4.00 per share	= £4,000,000
Number of shares that would reduce the market price to £3.75	= £4,000,000/£3.75
	= 1,066,667 shares
Number of shares prior to issue	= 1,000,000
Bonus shares deemed to be issued to existing shareholders	= 66,667
Bonus shares for period of 9 months to date of issue $(66,667 \times 9/12) =$	**50,000**

The bonus shares for the nine months are added to the existing shares and the time-apportioned new shares as follows:

Figure 27.1 Formula approach to calculating weighted average number of shares

No. of shares

Shares to date of rights issue:

No. of shares	×	Increase by bonus fraction	× Time adjustment		
1,000,000			× 9/12	=	750,000
Bonus:		((1,000,000 × 4/3.75) − 1,000,000)	× 9/12	=	50,000

Shares from date of issue:

1,500,000	×		× 3/12	= 375,000
Weighted average number of shares				1,175,000

No. of shares

Shares to date of rights issue:
1,000,000 shares held for a full year = 1,000,000
Shares from date of rights issue:
500,000 shares held for 3 months (500,000 × 3/12) = 125,000
Weighted average number of shares 1,125,000
Bonus shares:
66,667 shares held for 9 months (66,667 × 9/12) = 50,000
1,175,000

The same figure of 1,175,000 can be derived from the following approach using the relationship between the market price of £4.00 and the theoretical ex-rights price of £3.75 to calculate the number of bonus shares.

The relationship between the actual cum-rights price and theoretical ex-rights price is shown by the bonus fraction:

$$\frac{\text{Actual cum-rights share price}}{\text{Theoretical ex-rights share price}}$$

This fraction is applied to the number of shares before the rights issue to adjust them for the impact of the bonus element of the rights issue. This is shown in Figure 27.1.

Step 3: Calculate the BEPS for the current year
The BEPS for 20X1 is then calculated as £1,150,000/1,175,000 shares = **£0.979**.

Step 4: Adjust the previous year's BEPS for the bonus element of the rights issue
The 20X0 BEPS of £1.15 needs to be restated, i.e. reduced to ensure comparability with 20X1.

In Step 2 above we calculated that the company had made a bonus issue of 66,667 shares to existing shareholders. In recalculating the BEPS for 20X0 the shares should be increased by 66,667 to 1,066,667. The restated BEPS for 20X0 is as follows:

Earnings/restated number of shares
£1,150,000/1,066,667 = £1.078125

Assuming that the earnings for 20X0 and 20X1 were £1,150,000 in each year, the 20X0 BEPS figures will be reported as follows:

As reported in the 20X0 accounts as at 31.12.20X0 = £1,150,000/1,000,000 = **£1.15**

As restated in the 20X1 accounts as at 31.12.20X1 = £1,150,000/1,066,667 = **£1.08**

The same result is obtained using the bonus element approach by reducing the 20X0 BEPS as follows by multiplying it by the reciprocal of the bonus fraction:

$$\frac{\text{Theoretical ex-rights fair value per share}}{\text{Fair value per share immediately before the exercise of rights}} = \frac{£3.75}{£4.00}$$

As restated in the 20X1 accounts as at 31.12.20X1 = £1.15 × (3.75/4.00) = **£1.08**.

27.7.1 Would the BEPS for the current and previous years be the same if the company had made a separate full market price issue and a separate bonus issue?

This section is included to demonstrate that the BEPS is the same, i.e. £1.08, if we approach the calculation on the assumption that there was a full price issue followed by a bonus issue. This will demonstrate that the BEPS is the same as that calculated using theoretical ex-rights. There are five steps, as follows.

Step 1: Calculate the number of full value and bonus shares in the company's share capital

	No. of shares
Shares in issue *before* bonus	1,000,000
Rights issue at full market price	
(500,000 shares × £3.25 issue price/£4 full market price)	406,250
	1,406,250
Total number of bonus shares	93,750
Total shares	1,500,000

Step 2: Allocate the total bonus shares to the 1,000,000 original shares

(Note that the previous year will be restated using the proportion of original shares: original shares + bonus shares allocated to these original 1,000,000 shares.)

		No. of shares
Shares in issue before bonus		1,000,000
Bonus issue applicable to pre-rights:		
93,750 bonus shares × (1,000,000/1,406,250) = 66,667 × 9/12	= 50,000	
Bonus issue applicable to post-rights:		
93,750 bonus shares × (1,000,000/1,406,250) = 66,667 × 3/12	= 16,667	
Total bonus shares allocated to existing 1,000,000 shares		66,667
Total original holding plus bonus shares allocated to that holding		1,066,667

Step 3: Time-weight the rights issue and allocate bonus shares to rights shares

Rights issue at full market price:

500,000 shares × (£3.25 issue price/£4 full market price) = 406,250 × 3/12 =   101,563

Bonus issue applicable to rights issue:

93,750 bonus shares × (406,250/1,406,250) = 27,083 × 3/12   =   6,770

Weighted average ordinary shares (includes shares from Steps 2 and 3)   1,175,000

Calculate the BEPS using the post-tax profit and weighted average ordinary shares, as follows:

$$20\text{X}1 \text{ BEPS} = \frac{£1,150,000}{1,175,000} = £0.979$$

There were 93,750 bonus shares issued in 20X1. The 20X0 BEPS needs to be reduced, therefore, by the same proportion as applied to the 1,000,000 ordinary shares in 20X1, i.e. 1,000,000:1,066,667:

20X0 BEPS × bonus adjustment = restated 20X0 BEPS

$$= £1.15 \times (1,000,000/1,066,667) = £1.08.$$

This approach illustrates the rationale for the time-weighted average and the restatement of the previous year's BEPS. The adjustment using the theoretical ex-rights approach produces the same result and is simpler to apply but the rationale is not obvious.

27.8 Adjusting the earnings and number of shares used in the diluted EPS calculation

We will consider briefly what dilution means and the circumstances which require the weighted average number of shares and the net profit attributable to ordinary shareholders used to calculate BEPS to be adjusted.

27.8.1 What is dilution?

In a modern corporate structure, a number of classes of person such as the holders of convertible bonds, the holders of convertible preference shares, members of share option schemes and share warrant holders may be entitled as at the date of the statement of financial position to become equity shareholders at a future date.

If these people exercise their entitlements at a future date, the EPS would be reduced. In accounting terminology, the EPS will have been *diluted*. The effect on future share price could be significant. Assuming that the share price is a multiple of the EPS figure, any reduction in the figure could have serious implications for the existing shareholders; they need to be aware of the potential effect on the EPS figure of any changes in the way the capital of the company is or will be constituted. This is shown by calculating and disclosing both the basic and 'diluted EPS' figures.

IAS 33 therefore requires a diluted EPS figure to be reported using as the denominator potential ordinary shares that are dilutive, i.e. would decrease net profit per share or increase net loss from continuing operations.[7]

27.8.2 Circumstances in which the number of shares used for BEPS is increased

The holders of convertible bonds, the holders of convertible preference shares, members of share option schemes and the holders of share warrants will each be entitled to receive ordinary shares from the company at some future date. Such additional shares, referred to as potential ordinary shares, *may* need to be added to the basic weighted average number *if they are dilutive*. It is important to note that if a company has potential ordinary shares they are not automatically included in the fully diluted EPS calculation. There is a test to apply to see if such shares actually are dilutive – this is discussed further in Section 27.9 below.

27.8.3 Circumstances in which the earnings used for BEPS are increased

The earnings are increased to take account of the post-tax effects of amounts recognised in the period relating to dilutive potential ordinary shares that will no longer be incurred on their conversion to ordinary shares, e.g. the loan interest payable on convertible loans will no longer be a charge after conversion and earnings will be increased by the post-tax amount of such interest.

27.8.4 Procedure where there are share warrants and options

Where options, warrants or other arrangements exist which involve the issue of shares below their fair value (i.e. at a price lower than the average for the period) then the impact is calculated by notionally splitting the potential issue into shares issued at fair value and shares issued at no value for no consideration.[8] Since shares issued at fair value are not dilutive, that number is ignored, but the number of shares at no value is employed to calculate the dilution. The calculation is illustrated here for Watts plc.

Assume that Watts plc had at 31 December 20X1:

● an issued capital of 1,000,000 ordinary shares of 50p each nominal value;

● profit attributable to shareholders of £1,150,000;

● an average market price per share of £4; and

● share options in existence 500,000 shares issuable in 20X2 at £3.25 per share.

The computation of basic and diluted EPS is as follows:

	Per share	*Earnings*	*Shares*
Profit attributable to shareholders		£1,150,000	
Weighted average shares during 20X1			1,000,000
Basic EPS (£1,150,000/1,000,000)	1.15		
Number of shares under option			500,000
Number that would have been issued at fair value (500,000 × £3.25/£4)			(406,250)
Adjusted earnings and number of shares		£1,150,000	1,093,750
Diluted EPS (£1,150,000/1,093,750)	1.05		

27.8.5 Procedure where there are convertible bonds or convertible preference shares

The post-tax profit should be adjusted[9] for:

● any dividends on dilutive potential ordinary shares that have been deducted in arriving at the net profit attributable to ordinary shareholders;

● interest recognised in the period for the dilutive potential ordinary shares; and

● any other changes in income or expense that would result from the conversion of the dilutive potential ordinary shares, e.g. the reduction of interest expense related to convertible bonds results in a higher post-tax profit but this could lead to a consequential increase in expense if there were a non-discretionary employee profit-sharing plan.

27.8.6 Convertible preference shares calculation

Assume that Watts plc had at 31 December 20X1:

- an issued capital of 1,000,000 ordinary shares of 50p each nominal value;
- profit attributable to ordinary shareholders of £1,150,000;
- convertible 8% preference shares of £1 each totalling £1,000,000, convertible at one ordinary share for every five convertible preference shares.

The computation of basic and diluted EPS for convertible bonds is as follows:

	Per share	Earnings	Shares
Post-tax net profit for 20X1 (after interest)		£1,150,000	
Weighted average shares during 20X1			1,000,000
Basic EPS (£1,150,000/1,000,000)	£1.15		
Number of shares resulting from conversion			200,000
Add back the preference dividend paid in 20X1		80,000	
Adjusted earnings and number of shares		1,230,000	1,200,000
Diluted EPS (£1,230,000/1,200,000)	£1.025		

27.8.7 Convertible bonds calculation

Assume that Watts plc had at 31 December 20X1:

- an issued capital of 1,000,000 ordinary shares of 50p each nominal value;
- profit attributable to ordinary shareholders of £1,150,000;
- convertible 10% loan of £1,000,000;
- an average market price per share of £4;

and the convertible loan is convertible into 250,000 ordinary shares of 50p each.
The computation of basic and diluted EPS for convertible bonds is as follows:

	Per share	Earnings	Shares
Post-tax net profit for 20X1 (after interest)		£1,150,000	
Weighted average shares during 20X1			1,000,000
Basic EPS (£1,150,000/1,000,000)	£1.15		
Number of shares resulting from conversion			250,000
Interest expense on convertible loan		100,000	
Tax liability relating to interest expense, assuming the firm's marginal tax rate is 40%		(20,000)	
Adjusted earnings and number of shares		1,230,000	1,250,000
Diluted EPS (£1,230,000/1,250,000)	£0.98		

27.9 Procedure where there are several potential dilutions

Where there are several potential dilutions the calculation must be done in progressive stages starting with the most dilutive and ending with the least.[10] Any potential 'antidilutive' issues (i.e. potential issues that would increase earnings per share) are ignored.
Assume that Watts plc had at 31 December 20X1:

- an issued capital of 1,000,000 ordinary shares of 50p each nominal value;
- profit attributable to ordinary shareholders of £1,150,000;

- an average market price per share of £4;
- share options in existence of 500,000 shares exercisable in year 20X2 at £3.25 per share;
- a convertible 10% loan of £1,000,000 convertible in year 20X2 into 250,000 ordinary shares of 50p each; and
- convertible 8% preference shares of £1 each totalling £1,000,000 convertible in year 20X4 at one ordinary share for every 40 preference shares.

There are two steps in arriving at the diluted EPS, namely:

Step 1: Determine the increase in earnings attributable to ordinary shareholders on conversion of potential ordinary shares;

Step 2: Determine the potential ordinary shares to include in the computation of diluted earnings per share.

Step 1: Determine the increase in earnings attributable to ordinary shareholders on conversion of potential ordinary shares

	Increase in earnings	Increase in number of ordinary shares	Earnings per incremental share
Options			
Increase in earnings			
Incremental shares issued for no consideration			
500,000 × (£4 − 3.25)/£4	NIL	93,750	NIL
Convertible preference shares			
Increase in net profit 8% of £1,000,000	80,000		
Incremental shares 1,000,000/40		25,000	3.20
10% convertible bond			
Increase in net profit £1,000,000 × 0.10 × (60%)	60,000		
(assuming a marginal tax rate of 40%)			
Incremental shares 1,000,000/4		250,000	0.24

Step 2: Determine the potential ordinary shares to include in the computation of diluted earnings per share

	Net profit attributable to continuing operations	Ordinary shares	Per share
As reported for BEPS	1,150,000	1,000,000	1.15
Options	—	93,750	
	1,150,000	1,093,750	1.05 dilutive
10% convertible bonds	60,000	250,000	
	1,210,000	1,343,750	0.90 dilutive
Convertible preference shares	80,000	25,000	
	1,290,000	1,368,750	0.94 antidilutive

Since the diluted earnings per share is increased when taking the convertible preference shares into account (from 90p to 94p), the convertible preference shares are antidilutive and are ignored in the calculation of diluted earnings per share. The lowest figure is selected and the diluted EPS will, therefore, be disclosed as 90p.

27.10 Exercise of conversion rights during the financial year

Shares actually issued will be in accordance with the terms of conversion and will be included in the BEPS calculation on a time-apportioned basis from the date of conversion to the end of the financial year.

27.10.1 Calculation of BEPS assuming that convertible loan has been converted and options exercised during the financial year

This is illustrated for the calculation for the year 20X2 accounts of Watts plc as follows. Assume that Watts plc had at 31 December 20X2:

- an issued capital of 1,000,000 ordinary shares of 50p each as at 1 January 20X2;
- a convertible 10% loan of £1,000,000 **converted** on 1 January 20X2 into 250,000 ordinary shares of 50p each; and
- share options for 500,000 ordinary shares of 50p each **exercised** on 1 January 20X2.

The weighted average number of shares for BEPS is calculated as follows:

	Net profit attributable to continuing operations	Ordinary shares	Per share
As reported for BEPS	1,150,000	1,000,000	1.15
Options	—	93,750	
	1,150,000	1,093,750	1.05
10% convertible bonds	60,000	250,000	
	1,210,000	1,343,750	0.90
Convertible preference shares	80,000	25,000	
	1,290,000	1,368,750	0.94

27.11 Disclosure requirements of IAS 33

The standard[11] requires the following disclosures. For the current year:

- Companies should disclose the basic and diluted EPS figures for profit or loss from continuing operations and for profit or loss with equal prominence, whether positive or negative, on the face of the statement of comprehensive income for each class of ordinary share that has a different right to share in the profit for the period.
- The amounts used as the numerators in calculating basic and diluted earnings per share, and a reconciliation of those amounts to the net profit or loss for the period.
- The weighted average number of shares used as the denominator in calculating the basic and diluted earnings per share and a reconciliation of these denominators to each other.

For the previous year (if there has been a bonus issue, rights issue or share split):

- BEPS and diluted EPS should be adjusted retrospectively.

27.11.1 Alternative EPS figures

In the UK the Institute of Investment Management and Research (IIMR) published State-ment of Investment Practice No. 1, entitled *The Definition of Headline Earnings*,[12] in which it identified two purposes for producing an EPS figure:

- as a measure of the company's **maintainable earnings** capacity, suitable in particular for forecasts and for inter-year comparisons, and for use on a per-share basis in the calculation of the price/earnings ratio;

- as a factual headline figure for historical earnings, which can be a benchmark figure for the **trading outcome for the year**.

The Institute recognised that the maintainable earnings figure required exceptional or non-continuing items to be eliminated, which meant that, in view of the judgement involved in adjusting the historical figures, the calculation of maintainable earnings figures could not be put on a standardised basis. It took the view that there was a need for an earnings figure, calculated on a standard basis, which could be used as an unambiguous reference point among users. The Institute accordingly defined a **headline earnings** figure for that purpose.

An interesting recent research study[13] supports the finding that the additional EPS figures provide a better indication of future operating earnings one year ahead.

27.11.2 Definition of IIMR headline figure

The Institute criteria for the headline figure are that it should be:

1 **A measure of the trading performance**, which means that it will:

  (a) *exclude* capital items such as profits/losses arising on the sale or revaluation of non-current assets, profits/losses arising on the sale or termination of a discontinued operation and amortisation charges for goodwill, because these are likely to have a different volatility from trading outcomes;

  (b) *exclude* provisions created for capital items such as profits/losses arising on the sale of non-current assets or on the sale or termination of a discontinued operation; and

  (c) *include* abnormal items with a clear note and profits/losses arising on operations discontinued during the year.

2 **Robust**, in that the result could be arrived at by anyone using the financial report produced in accordance with IAS 1 and IFRS 5.

3 **Factual**, in that it will not have been adjusted on the basis of subjective opinions as to whether a cost is likely to continue in the future.

The strength of the Institute's approach is that, by defining a headline figure, it is producing a core definition. Additional earnings, earnings per share and price/earnings ratio figures can be produced by individual analysts, refining the headline figure in the light of their own evaluation of the quality of earnings.

27.11.3 IAS 33 disclosure requirements

If an enterprise discloses an additional EPS figure using a reported component of net profit other than net profit for the period attributable to ordinary shareholders, IAS 33 requires that:

- it must still use the weighted average number of shares determined in accordance with IAS 33;

- if the net profit figure used is not a line item in the statement of comprehensive income, then a reconciliation should be provided between the figure and a line item which is reported in the statement of comprehensive income; and

- the additional EPS figures cannot be disclosed on the face of the statement of comprehensive income.

The following is an extract from the 2012 Annual Report of Vodacom (Pty) Ltd:

	2012 Cents per share	2011 Cents per share
As calculated from IAS 33	694	561
Impairment losses	(15)	(95)
Headline earnings per share as defined by IIMR	709	656

27.12 The Improvement Project

IAS 33 was one of the IASs revised by the IASB as part of its Improvement Project. The objective of the revised standard was to continue to prescribe the principles for the determination and presentation of earnings per share so as to improve comparisons between different entities and different reporting periods. The Board's main objective when revising was to provide additional guidance on selected complex issues such as the effects of contingently issuable shares and purchased put and call options. However, the Board did not reconsider the fundamental approach to the determination and presentation of earnings per share contained in the original IAS 33.

27.13 The Convergence Project

The earnings used as the numerator and the number of shares used as the denominator are both calculated differently under IAS 33 and the US SFAS 128 *Earnings per Share* and so produce different EPS figures.

In 2008, as part of the Convergence Project, the IASB and FASB issued an Exposure Draft which aimed to achieve some convergence in the calculation of the denominator of earnings per share. They are, in the meanwhile, conducting a joint project on financial statement presentation. When they have completed that project and their joint project on liabilities and equity, they may consider whether to conduct a more fundamental review of the method for determining EPS which would look at an agreed approach to determining earnings and number of shares to be used in both the basic and diluted EPS calculation.

Summary

The increased globalisation of stock market transactions places an increasing level of importance on international comparisons. The EPS figure is regarded as a key figure with a widely held belief that management performance could be assessed by the comparative growth rate in this figure. This has meant that the earnings available for distribution, which was the base for calculating EPS, became significant. Management action has been directed towards increasing this figure: sometimes by healthy organic growth; sometimes by buying-in earnings by acquisition; sometimes by cosmetic manipulation, e.g. structuring transactions so that all or part of the cost bypassed the statement of comprehensive income; and at other times by the selective exercise of judgement, e.g. underestimating provisions. Regulation by the IASB has been necessary.

IAS 33 permits the inclusion of an EPS figure calculated in a different way, provided that there is a reconciliation of the two figures. Analysts have expressed the view that EPS should be calculated to show the future maintainable earnings and in the UK have arrived at a formula designed to exclude the effects of unusual events and of activities discontinued during the period.

REVIEW QUESTIONS

1 Explain: (i) basic earnings per share; (ii) diluted earnings per share; (iii) potential ordinary shares; and (iv) limitation of EPS as a performance measure.

2 In connection with IAS 33 *Earnings per Share*:

(a) Define the profit used to calculate basic and diluted EPS.

(b) Explain the relationship between EPS and the price/earnings (PE) ratio. Why may the PE ratio be considered important as a stock market indicator?

3 Would the following items justify the calculation of a separate EPS figure under IAS 33?

(a) A charge of £1,500 million that appeared in the accounts, described as additional provisions relating to exposure to countries experiencing payment difficulties.

(b) Costs of £14 million that appeared in the accounts, described as redundancy and other non-recurring costs.

(c) Costs of £62.1 million that appeared in the accounts, described as cost of rationalisation and withdrawal from business activities.

(d) The following items that appeared in the accounts:

(i) Profit on sale of property £80m

(ii) Reorganisation costs £35m

(iii) Disposal and discontinuance of hotels £659m.

4 In the 1999 Annual Report and Accounts of Associated British Ports Holdings plc, the directors report earnings per share – basic, and earnings per share – underlying, as follows:

	Goodwill £m	Exceptional amortisation £m	Total items £m	1999 £m	1998 £m
Earnings per share – basic	24.6	(1.1)	(21.9)	**1.6p**	22.4p
Earnings per share – underlying				**24.6p**	22.4p

Discuss the relevance of the basic figure of 1.6p reported for 1999.

5 The following note appeared in the 2011 Annual Report of Mercer International Inc.:

Net income (loss) per share attributable to common shareholders:

	2011	2010	2009
Basic	€1.00	€2.24	€(1.71)
Diluted	€0.89	€1.56	€(1.71)

Stock options and awards excluded from the calculation of diluted income (loss) per share attributable to common shareholders because they are anti-dilutive.

Explain:

what is meant by antidilutive.

6 Why are issues at full market value treated differently from rights issues?

7 Explain why companies buy back shares and the effect that this has on the earnings per share figure.

8 Explain reverse share splits and the effect that this has on a company's market capitalisation.

9 Discuss the limitations of an IAS 33 calculated EPS figure for performance reporting.

10 Discuss the limitations of EPS as a criterion for setting executive remuneration targets.

EXERCISES

Question 1

Alpha plc had an issued share capital of 2,000,000 ordinary shares at 1 January 20X1. The nominal value was 25p and the market value £1 per share. On 30 September 20X1 the company made a rights issue of 1 for 4 at a price of 80p per share. The post-tax earnings were £4.5m and £5m for 20X0 and 20X1 respectively.

Required:
(a) Calculate the basic earnings per share.
(b) Restate the basic earnings per share for 20X0.

* Question 2

Beta Ltd had the following changes during 20X1:

1 January	1,000,000 shares of 50c each
31 March	500,000 shares of 50c each issued at full market price of $5 per share
30 April	Bonus issue made of 1 for 2
31 August	1,000,000 shares of 50c each issued at full market price of $5.50 per share
31 October	Rights issue of 1 for 3. Rights price was $2.40 and market value was $5.60 per share.

Required:
Calculate the time-weighted average number of shares for the basic earnings per share denominator. Note that adjustments will be required for time, the bonus issue and the bonus element of the rights issue.

The computation and publication of earnings per share (EPS) figures by listed companies are governed by IAS 33 *Earnings per Share*.

Nottingham Industries plc
Statement of comprehensive income for the year ended 31 March 20X6
(extract from draft unaudited accounts)

		£000
Profit on ordinary activities before taxation	(Note 2)	(1,000)
Tax on profit on ordinary activities	(Note 3)	(420)
Profit on ordinary activities after taxation		580

Notes:

1   Called-up share capital of Nottingham Industries plc:
    In issue at 1 April 20X5:
    16,000,000 ordinary shares of 25p each
    1,000,000 10% cumulative preference shares of £1 each classified as equity
    1 July 20X5: Bonus issue of ordinary shares, 1 for 5.
    1 October 20X5: Market purchase of 500,000 of own ordinary shares at a price of £1.00 per share.

2   In the draft accounts for the year ended 31 March 20X6, 'profit on ordinary activities before taxation' is arrived at after charging or crediting the following items:

    (i)   accelerated depreciation on fixed assets, £80,000;

    (ii) book gain on disposal of a major operation, £120,000.

3   Profit after tax included a write-back of deferred taxation (accounted for by the liability method) in consequence of a reduction in the rate of corporation tax from 45% in the financial year 20X4 to 40% in the financial year 20X5.

4   The following were charged:

    (i)   Provision for bad debts arising on the failure of a major customer, £150,000. Other bad debts have been written off or provided for in the ordinary way.

    (ii) Provision for loss through expropriation of the business of an overseas subsidiary by a foreign government, £400,000.

5   In the published accounts for the year ended 31 March 20X5, basic EPS was shown as 2.2p; fully diluted EPS was the same figure.

6   Dividends paid totalled £479,000.

Required:

(a) On the basis of the facts given, compute the basic EPS figures for 20X6 and restate the basic EPS figure for 20X5, stating your reasons for your treatment of items that may affect the amount of EPS in the current year.

(b) Compute the diluted earnings per share for 20X6 assuming that on 1 January 20X6 executives of Nottingham plc were granted options to take up a total of 200,000 unissued ordinary shares at a price of £1.00 per share: no options had been exercised at 31 March 20X6. The average fair value of the shares during the year was £1.10.

(c) Give your opinion as to the usefulness (to the user of financial statements) of the EPS figures that you have computed.

The following information relates to Simrin plc for the year ended 31 December 20X0:

	£
Turnover	700,000
Operating costs	476,000
Trading profit	224,000
Net interest payable	2,000
	222,000
Exceptional charges	77,000
	145,000
Tax on ordinary activities	66,000
Profit after tax	79,000

Simrin plc had 100,000 ordinary shares of £1 each in issue throughout the year. Simrin plc has in issue warrants entitling the holders to subscribe for a total of 50,000 shares in the company. The warrants may be exercised after 31 December 20X5 at a price of £1.10 per share. The average fair value of shares was £1.28. The company had paid an ordinary dividend of £15,000 and a preference dividend of £9,000 on preference shares classified as equity.

Required:

(a) Calculate the basic EPS for Simrin plc for the year ended 31 December 20X0, in accordance with best accounting practice.

(b) Calculate the diluted EPS figure, to be disclosed in the statutory accounts of Simrin plc in respect of the year ended 31 December 20X0.

(c) Briefly comment on the need to disclose a diluted EPS figure and on the relevance of this figure to the shareholders.

(d) In the past, the single most important indicator of financial performance has been earnings per share. In what way has the profession attempted to destroy any reliance on a single figure to measure and predict a company's earnings, and how successful has this attempt been?

Gamma plc had an issued share capital at 1 April 20X0 of:

● £200,000 made up of 20p shares; and

● 50,000 £1 convertible preference shares classified as equity receiving a dividend of £2.50 per share. These shares were convertible in 20X6 on the basis of one ordinary share for one preference share.

There was also loan capital of:

● £250,000 10% convertible loans. The loan was convertible in 20X9 on the basis of 500 shares for each £1,000 of loan, and the tax rate was 40%.

Earnings for the year ended 31 March 20X1 were £5,000,000 after tax.

Required:

(a) Calculate the diluted EPS for 20X1.

(b) Calculate the diluted EPS assuming that the convertible preference shares were receiving a dividend of £6 per share instead of £2.50.

Question 6

Delta NV has share capital of €1m in shares of €0.25 each. At 31 May 20X9 shares had a market value of €1.1 each. On 1 June 20X9 the company makes a rights issue of one share for every four held at €0.6 per share. Its profits were €500,000 in 20X9 and €440,000 in 20X8. The year-end is 30 November.

Required:
Calculate
(a) the theoretical ex-rights price;
(b) the bonus issue factor;
(c) the basic earnings per share for 20X8;
(d) the basic earnings per share for 20X9.

Question 7

The following information is available for X Ltd for the year ended 31 May 20X1:

Net profit after tax and minority interest	£18,160,000
Ordinary shares of £1 (fully paid)	£40,000,000
Average fair value for year of ordinary shares	£1.50

Notes:

1 Share options have been granted to directors giving them the right to subscribe for ordinary shares between 20X1 and 20X3 at £1.20 per share. The options outstanding at 31 May 20X1 were 2,000,000 in number.

2 The company has £20 million of 6% convertible loan stock in issue. The terms of conversion of the loan stock per £200 nominal value of loan stock at the date of issue were:

Conversion date	No. of shares
31 May 20X0	24
31 May 20X1	23
31 May 20X2	22

No loan stock has as yet been converted. The loan stock had been issued at a discount of 1%.

3 There are 1,600,000 convertible preference shares in issue classified as equity. The cumulative dividend is 10p per share and each preference share can convert into two ordinary shares. The preference shares can be converted in 20X2.

4 Assume a corporation tax rate of 33% when calculating the effect on income of converting the convertible loan stock.

Required:
(a) Calculate the diluted EPS according to IAS 33.
(b) Discuss why there is a need to disclose diluted earnings per share.

Question 8

(a) The issued share capital of Manfred, a quoted company, on 1 November 2004 consisted of 36,000,000 ordinary shares of 75 cents each. On 1 May 2005 the company made a rights issue of 1 for 6 at $1.46 per share. The market value of Manfred's ordinary shares was $1.66 before announcing the rights issue. Tax is charged at 30% of profits.

Manfred reported a profit after taxation of $4.2 million for the year ended 31 October 2005 and $3.6 million for the year ended 31 October 2004. The published figure for earnings per share for the year ended 31 October 2004 was 10 cents per share.

Required:
Calculate Manfred's earnings per share for the year ended 31 October 2005 and the comparative figure for the year ended 31 October 2004.

(b) Brachly, a publicly quoted company, has 15,000,000 ordinary shares of 40 cents each in issue throughout its financial year ended 31 October 2005. There are also:

- 1,000,000 8.5% convertible preference shares of $1 each in issue classified as equity. Each preference share is convertible into 1.5 ordinary shares.

- $2,000,000 12.5% convertible loan notes. Each $1 loan note is convertible into two ordinary shares.

- Options granted to the company's senior management giving them the right to subscribe for 600,000 ordinary shares at a cost of 75 cents each.

The statement of comprehensive income of Brachly for the year ended 31 October 2005 reports a net profit after tax of $9,285,000 and preference dividends paid of $85,000. Tax on profits is 30%. The average market price of Brachly's ordinary shares was 84 cents for the year ended 31 October 2005.

Required:
Calculate Brachly's basic and diluted earnings per share figures for the year ended 31 October 2005.

(The Association of International Accountants)

Question 9

The capital structure of Chavboro, a quoted company, during the years ended 31 October 2005 and 2006 was as follows:

	$
6,000,000 ordinary shares of 50 cents	3,000,000
10% preferred shares of $1	200,000
300,000 deferred ordinary shares of $1	300,000
12% convertible loan stock	250,000

The company has an executive share option scheme which gives the company's directors the option to purchase a total of 100,000 ordinary shares for $2.10 each. During the year ended 31 October 2006 no shares were issued in accordance with the share incentive scheme and the company's obligations under the scheme remained unchanged.

On 31 August 2006 Chavboro plc made a 1 for 6 rights issue at $2.50 per share. The cum-rights price on the last day of quotation cum rights was $2.85 per share. The shares issued in the rights issue are not included in the figure for ordinary shares given above.

The deferred ordinary shares will not rank for dividends until 1 November 2010 when they will each be divided into two 50 cents ordinary shares ranking *pari passu* with the other ordinary shares then in issue.

The 12% loan stock is convertible into 50 cents ordinary shares on the following terms:

(i) if the option is exercised on 1 November 2007 each $100 of loan stock can be converted into 40 ordinary shares;

(ii) if the option is exercised on 1 November 2008 each $100 of loan stock can be converted into 35 ordinary shares.

The following information comes from the statement of comprehensive income of the company for the year ended 31 October 2006:

	$
Profit before interest and tax	1,253,000
Less: Interest	30,000
	1,223,000
Less: Income tax, at 30%	366,900
Profit attributable to shareholders	856,100

You may assume that the yield on 2.5% government consolidated stock was 7.5% on 1 November 2005 and 6% on 1 November 2006, and that the rate of income tax is 30% throughout. Chavboro plc's reported earnings per share for the year ended 31 October 2005 were 10 cents.

Required:
(a) Calculate Chavboro plc's basic earnings per share in cents for the year ended 31 October 2006.
(b) Calculate Chavboro plc's restated earnings per share in cents for the year ended 31 October 2005.
(c) Calculate Chavboro plc's fully diluted earnings per share in cents for the year ended 31 October 2006.
(d) Calculate Chavboro plc's fully diluted earnings per share in cents for the year ended 31 October 2005.
(e) How can an investor evaluate the quality of the earnings per share figure published in a company's financial statements?

(The Association of International Accountants)

* Question 10

(a) The Dent group earned profits from continuing operations attributable to the parent company for the year ended 31 October 2011 of $13.6 million. Losses from discontinued operations attributable to the parent company were $4 million. The group has a complex capital structure. The following transactions and events relate to changes in Dent's capital structure during the year ended 31 October 2011:

● *Ordinary shares.* The number of ordinary shares outstanding at 1 November 2010 was 6 million. On 1 February 2011 1 million ordinary shares were issued for cash.

● *Convertible bonds.* In 2009 10,000 $1,000 4% convertible bonds were issued for cash at par value. Each $1,000 bond is convertible into 35 ordinary shares. The entire issue was converted on 1 April 2011.

- *Preference shares.* On 1 November 2010, 100,000 non-convertible, non-redeemable cumulative preference shares classified as equity each with a par value of $100 were issued at $89 each. The shares are entitled to a cumulative annual dividend starting in two years' time and equivalent to the market rate dividend yield at the time of issue of 6%. In 2008 Dent had issued 1 million 5% convertible preference shares. Each share is convertible into one ordinary share. 75% of these were converted into ordinary shares on 1 May 2011. Preference dividends are paid half-yearly in arrears.

- *Warrants.* On 1 November 2010 Dent issued warrants to purchase 2 million ordinary shares at $6 per share for an exercise period of three years. All warrants were exercised on 1 October 2011. The average market price of each warrant during the period to 1 October 2011 was $7.50.

Required:

Calculate the basic earnings per share figures for Dent for the year ended 31 October 2011 and show how the information would be presented in Dent's financial statements.

(b) On 1 January 2011 Ram issued 100,000 ordinary shares for cash at $10 each. On 18 July 2011, Ram reacquired 10% of these shares for cash at a cost of $15 each. One month later the reacquired shares were all reissued for cash of $17 each. This type of transaction is new to the directors of Ram and they are unsure how they should be accounted for in the company's financial statements.

Required:

Advise Ram on the appropriate accounting treatment of these transactions in the company's financial statements.

(The Association of International Accountants)

References

1 J. Day, 'The use of annual reports by UK investment analysts', *Accounting Business Research*, Autumn 1986, pp. 295–307.
2 IAS 33 *Earnings per Share*, IASB, 2003.
3 *Ibid.*, para. 10.
4 *Ibid.*, para. 12.
5 *Ibid.*, para. 26.
6 *Ibid.*, para. 5.
7 *Ibid.*, para. 31.
8 *Ibid.*, para. 45.
9 *Ibid.*, para. 33.
10 *Ibid.*, para. 44.
11 *Ibid.*, paras 66 and 70.
12 Statement of Investment Practice No. 1, *The Definition of Headline Earnings*, IIMR, 1993.
13 Young-soo Choi, M. Walker and S. Young, 'Bridging the earnings GAAP', *Accountancy*, February 2005, pp. 77–78.

CHAPTER **28**

Review of financial statements for management purposes

28.1 Introduction

The key objective of financial statements is to provide useful financial information to the stakeholders, or 'users' – those with legitimate rights to such information. Different users have different information needs, for example:

- Existing and potential equity investors will be primarily interested in the profitability of an entity but will also require reassurance that the entity's liquidity (ability to generate cash) is such that it can continue in operational existence for the foreseeable future as a going concern.

- Lenders (both short and long term) will be primarily interested in the ability of the entity to generate the cash that is required to repay them and will focus on liquidity issues.

- Management will be concerned with both profitability (to satisfy the legitimate needs of the investors to whom they are accountable) and liquidity (to satisfy the legitimate needs of the lenders and suppliers to receive repayment of the amounts owed to them).

A financial analyst needs to be able to extract useful information from financial data, whether this is produced internally as detailed statements for the benefit of management or published externally for the benefit of external stakeholders, primarily the equity investors. The purpose of this chapter is to provide a framework for the analysis of financial data in order to write a report.

Objectives

By the end of this chapter, you should be able to:

- appreciate the potential of ratio analysis as an analytical tool;
- carry out an initial overview of financial statements;
- discuss the relationship between the return on capital employed and supporting accounting ratios through the 'pyramid of ratios';
- analyse the financial statements of a single entity;
- draft a report based on an inter-period and inter-firm comparison;
- explain the limitations of comparisons based on ratios.

28.2 Overview of techniques for the analysis of financial data

28.2.1 The 'golden rule of analysis'

This might be described as 'identify your yardstick of comparison'. Analysis without comparison is meaningless. For example, if you were simply told that an entity generated revenue of £10 million and made a profit of £900,000 it would be difficult or impossible to assess whether that was 'good' or 'bad' without reference to factors such as:

- the previous year's revenues and profits;
- the budgeted revenues and profits;
- the revenues and profits of competitors in the same industry; and
- the underlying expectations of the analyst based on their knowledge of relevant internal and external factors.

If we are making an inter-firm comparison for management purposes care has to be taken to select a company that is in the same industry.

Whilst it is possible to compare the return on investment that is obtainable in different industries when deciding whether to invest, it would be extremely difficult to compare management ratios in different industries looking at, say, how well managers are controlling the cash cycle. For example, the cash cycle of a retail company where customers generally pay on receipt of goods is completely different from that of a construction company. We need to be sure, as far as possible, that we are making a valid comparison.

28.2.2 The benefits of ratio analysis

The use of accounting ratios for analysis purposes has a number of important benefits for analysts:

- Ratios allow comparison with peers through inter-firm comparison schemes and comparison with industry averages so that possible strengths and weaknesses can be identified.
- Through the pyramid approach it is possible to carry out a structured analysis of financial performance and financial position by drilling down to identify ratios in ever greater detail, building up to the return on capital employed.
- It enables, for certain ratios, the comparison of entities of different sizes. For example, it is very difficult to compare the absolute profits of two entities without an appreciation of how 'large' one entity is relative to another. However, it might be perfectly legitimate to compare the ratio of profit to revenue of two entities of very different sizes in the same industry.

28.2.3 Ratio analysis – some notes of caution

In order to evaluate a ratio, it is customary to make a comparison with that of the previous year or with the industry average. However, remember to check if:

- The same accounting policies have been applied; for example, have non-current assets been reported using the same measurement bases (i.e. at depreciated cost or revalued amounts in both cases)?
  Inter-firm comparison schemes overcome this problem by requiring all member companies to report using uniform defined ratios.

- Note has been taken of different commercial practices. For example, some retail entities lease their properties on operating leases whilst others purchase them.
  Accounting ratios that use assets as their denominator will be affected.

- The ratios have been defined in the same way. This is important when comparing ratios from different companies' Annual Reports – check to see if the company has defined its ratios.

28.3 Ratio analysis – a case study

Vertigo plc is a family company which deals in building materials and garden supplies. It has been managed by non-family members since the principal shareholder/managing director retired from active management at the end of 20X6 on health grounds. Let us assume that you are a trainee in an accounting firm that has been approached by a client who is a family member for a report on the company's financial position and financial performance following a fall in profit available for dividend and a request by the management for an injection of more capital.

We will use the financial statements of Vertigo (see below) to illustrate the technique.

28.3.1 Financial statements for the case study

Vertigo plc: statement of income for year ended 31 December

	20X9 £000	20X9 £000	20X8 £000	20X8 £000
Revenues		3,461		3,296
Opening inventory	398		253	
Purchases	2,623		2,385	
Closing inventory	(563)		(398)	
Cost of goods sold		(2,458)		(2,240)
Gross profit		1,003		1,056
Distribution costs:				
Depreciation	187		239	
Irrecoverable debts	17		32	
Advertising	24		94	
		(228)		(365)
Administrative expenses:				
Rent	60		60	
Salaries and wages	362		316	
Miscellaneous expenses	177		159	
		(599)		(535)
Operating profit		176		156
Dividend received		—		51
Finance costs		(60)		(53)
Profit before tax		116		154
Income tax expense		(25)		(39)
Profit after taxation		91		115

Vertigo plc: statement of financial position at 31 December

	20X9 £000	20X8 £000
ASSETS		
Non-current assets:		
Machinery	2,100	2,240
Motor vehicles	394	441
Investments	340	340
	2,834	3,021
Current assets:		
Inventory	563	398
Trade receivables	1,181	912
Cash and cash equivalents	9	11
	1,753	1,321
	4,587	4,342
EQUITY AND LIABILITIES		
Equity:		
Ordinary shares of 50p each	3,000	3,000
Retained earnings	353	262
	3,353	3,262
Non-current liabilities:		
Long-term borrowings (repayable in 8 years)	600	600
Current liabilities:		
Trade payables	498	398
Accrued expenses	15	12
Taxation	24	29
Short-term borrowings	97	41
	634	480
	4,587	4,342

28.4 Introductory review

Before embarking on detailed ratio analysis, an analyst (whether an internal or an external user of the financial statements) would carry out a review to gain an overall impression of:

(a) the external trading conditions for the building materials sector, for example, refer to subscription sources such as the Markit/CIPS Purchasing Managers' Index (PMI) indices; and

(b) the financial statements as a whole.

We will illustrate one approach using common-sized statements for Vertigo before proceeding to consider more detailed ratios and the preparation of a report.

Overall impressions from initial review

Common-sized statements are a useful aid when making an initial review of a company's financial structure, such as seeing the percentage of cash to current assets, and cost structures such as the percentage of sales revenue that goes on administration.

28.4.1 The company's financial structure

Our first thought might be to gain an impression of the financial structure of a company.

Vertical analysis – common-sized statement

The vertical analysis approach highlights the structure of the statement of financial position by presenting non-current assets, working capital, debt and equity as a percentage of debt plus equity. It allows us to form a view on the financing of the business, in particular the extent to which a business is reliant on debt to finance its non-current assets. In times of recession this is of particular interest and is described as indicating the strength of the financial position.

	20X8 £000	20X8 %	20X9 £000	20X9 %
Non-current assets	3,021	69.6	2,834	61.8
Current assets	1,321	30.4	1,753	38.2
Total	4,342	100	4,587	100
Equity	3,262	75.1	3,353	73.1
Debt	600	13.8	600	13.1
Current liabilities	480	11.1	634	13.8
Total	4,342	100	4,587	100

This indicates that the financial strength is maintained in terms of the amount of debt compared to the amount of capital put in by the shareholders.

However, the non-current assets have fallen and the fall appears to be due to the depreciation charge. We need to assess whether this lack of investment in non-current assets is likely to be a concern for the future and to check if the management has identified and quantified future capital expenditure commitments.

Horizontal analysis – common-sized statement

A horizontal analysis looks at the percentage change that has occurred. We could calculate the percentage change for every asset and liability, but it is more helpful in Vertigo to concentrate on the area that seems to require closer investigation, i.e. current assets and liabilities. The analysis is as follows:

	20X8 £000	20X9 £000	Percentage change
Current assets:			
Inventory	398	563	+41.5
Trade receivables	912	1,181	+29.5
Cash and cash equivalents	11	9	−18.2
Trade payables	398	498	+25.1
Accrued expenses	12	15	+25.0
Taxation	29	24	−17.2
Bank overdraft	41	97	+136.6

Inventories and (to a lesser extent) trade receivables have risen significantly when we consider that sales have increased by only 5%.

This raises questions in our mind. For example, is it possibly because greater quantities of inventory are expected to be required in anticipation of growth in future sales? Alternatively, is the inventory slow moving with the possibility that net realisable value is lower than cost?

Trade payables have increased significantly. This could be due to poor cash flow putting pressure on liquidity (short-term borrowings have increased by around £50,000 and there has been no additional long-term equity or loan finance).

The common-sized analysis of the financial position has given us questions to have in our minds when carrying out a more detailed analysis. The next step would be to extract detailed turnover ratios for inventory, trade receivables and payables and ascertain the terms and limit of the overdraft. Before doing that we carry out a similar common-sized exercise to form a view of a company's cost structure.

28.4.2 The company's cost structure

Again, both a vertical and horizontal analysis is helpful.

Vertical analysis – common-sized statement

An overview is obtained by restating by function into a vertical common-sized statement format as follows:

	20X8 £000	20X8 %	20X9 £000	20X9 %
Sales	3,296	100.0	3,461	100.0
Cost of sales	2,240	68.0	2,458	71.0
Total gross profit	1,056	32.0	1,003	29.0
Distribution costs	365	11.1	228	6.6
Administration expenses	588	17.8	659	19.0
Net profit before tax	103	3.1	116	3.4

We can see that there has been a change in the cost structure with a fall in the gross profit from 32% to 29% compensated for by a significant fall in the distribution costs.

Horizontal analysis – common-sized statement

An overview is obtained by calculating the percentage change as follows:

	20X8 £000	20X9 £000	Percentage change
Sales	3,296	3,461	+5.0
Cost of sales	2,240	2,458	+9.7
Total gross profit	1,056	1,003	−5.0
Distribution costs	365	228	−37.5
Administration expenses	588	659	+12.1
Net profit before tax and dividend income	103	116	+12.6

Our initial observations are as follows:

- Revenues have risen slightly but gross profits have fallen. We need to establish the reasons for this.

- Other operating expenses (distribution costs and administrative expenses) have fallen significantly. This appears in the main to be caused by the reduction in depreciation charges and advertising expenditure.

- No income has been received from the financial asset in the period. This may be due to timing issues (given that dividend income is basically recognised only when received). However, we would need to carry out further investigations here.

We can now go on to a more detailed analysis.

28.5 Financial statement analysis, part 1 – financial performance

Return on investment

If the analysis is being performed exclusively for the shareholders then an appropriate ROI measure might be 'Return on Equity (ROE)'. This ratio would be calculated as:

$$\frac{\text{Profit attributable to the shareholders}}{\text{Equity}}$$

For Vertigo, ROE would be

	20X9	20X8
Profit after tax	91	115
Equity	3,353	3,262
So ROE equals	2.7%	3.5%

This shows a fall of more than 20%.

Return on capital employed

If the analysis is of the overall performance of the entity (however it is financed) then the appropriate ratio is 'Return on Capital Employed (ROCE)'. Management would be likely to consider this to be the best measure of ROI, as it shows the return on the assets under their control without any effect from the rates of tax and interest which operational management might regard as outside their control.

This ratio would be calculated as:

$$\frac{\text{Profit before interest and tax (PBIT)}}{\text{Capital employed (CE) (equity + borrowings)}}$$

Definitions of ratios vary

It should be remembered that there is no 'accounting standard' that governs the exact composition of this ratio and care needs to be taken when making inter-firm comparisons. For example, capital employed might be defined as:

(a) total assets, also expressed as equity plus long-term loans plus current liabilities; or

(b) net assets, also expressed as equity plus long-term loans. Even here, though, care is needed – if a company maintains a high level of relatively permanent overdraft it might be added to the long-term loans.

For the purposes of this analysis, we will take 'borrowings' to be long-term borrowings only. Therefore our ROCE would be as follows:

	20X9	20X8
Profit before interest and tax	116 + 60	154 + 53
Capital employed	3,353 + 600	3,262 + 600
So ROCE equals	4.4%	5.4%

Our initial conclusion would be that Vertigo is less profitable in 20X9 than it was in 20X8. We would need to investigate further to establish the reasons for this. In looking for a reason for the fall from 5.4% to 4.4% we propose to follow the pyramid approach.

28.5.1 The pyramid approach

In this approach we start at the top of the pyramid with the return on capital employed and systematically analyse those ratios that impact on the profit and those that impact on the

Figure 28.1 Pyramid for return on capital employed

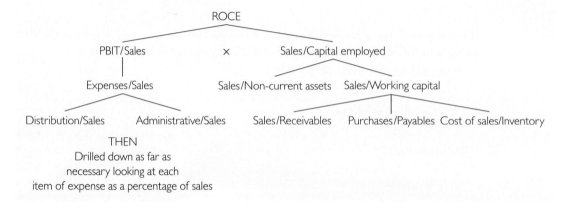

assets employed in the business. This approach is also the basis for a number of inter-firm comparison schemes.

Diagrammatically the pyramid is shown in Figure 28.1. We can see the pyramid starts with the following relationship:

$$\frac{\text{Profit before interest and tax}}{\text{Capital employed}} = \frac{\text{Profit before interest and tax}}{\text{Revenue}} \times \frac{\text{Revenue}}{\text{Capital employed}}$$

This is often expressed as:

ROCE = Profit margin × Asset turnover

This shows us that the two key components of the return on capital employed are **'margin'** (PBIT/Revenue) and **'volume'** (Revenue/Capital employed). It is to these two aspects that we now turn.

28.5.2 Margin and expense analysis

The first 'margin ratio' we compute is the 'net profit margin'. This is simply:

$$\frac{\text{'Profit' (PBIT as used in the ROCE ratio)}}{\text{Revenue}}$$

For Vertigo, the profit margins for 20X9 and 20X8 are:

	20X9	20X8
Profit	176	207
Revenue	3,461	3,296
So profit margin equals	5.1%	6.3%

This shows us that one of the reasons for the decline in ROCE is a decline in the profit margin. For our report we 'drill down' into the detail and investigate further why the margin has reduced. Is it because the gross profit has fallen or is it due to expenses?

Gross profit

One possibility is that the relationship between our revenues and our cost of sales has altered, so it is instructive to compute the gross profit margin. This ratio is computed as:

$$\frac{\text{Gross profit}}{\text{Revenue}}$$

For Vertigo, the gross profit margins for 20X9 and 20X8 are:

	20X9	20X8
Gross profit	1,003	1,056
Revenue	3,461	3,296
So profit margin equals	29.0%	32.0%

Clearly the reduction in gross margin is not a good thing and internal analysts would almost certainly call for further investigation. We do not have the data here to perform more detailed checks.

Remember, however, that in answering any interpretation question it is always important to identify the further questions you would ask and the further information you would request, giving your reasons. For example, questions would be asked as to whether there has been:

● a change in the sales mix, with a greater proportion of lower-margin items being sold this year than last year;

● a change to maintain sales volume at the expense of the profit margin;

● discounting or longer-running sales;

● a rise in raw material costs that could not be passed on to customers in the form of increased sales prices; or

● a rise in the employment costs of production workers that could not be passed on to customers in the form of increased sales prices. This is unlikely to be the reason for the change in the gross margin here, given that cost of sales appears to include purchases, rather than production costs. Apparently Vertigo is a retail organisation rather than a manufacturing organisation – unless, perhaps, it is involved in also constructing any of the building products such as conservatories and garden studios.

Operating expenses – administrative expenses

We could also compute:

	20X9	20X8
Administrative expenses	599	535
Revenues	3,461	3,296
Ratio	17.3%	16.2%

This ratio reveals a slightly less satisfactory position in 20X9 compared with 20X8. The information we have shows us that a key factor behind the increase is the rise in salary costs of approximately 15%. This seems excessive given that revenues have grown by only 5%.

Operating expenses – distribution costs

A further part of the analysis of the profit margin is to investigate the relationship between other operating expenses and revenues. For Vertigo, this would involve computing:

	20X9	20X8
Distribution costs	228	365
Revenues	3,461	3,296
Ratio	6.6%	11.1%

Clearly, for Vertigo, the adverse movement in the gross profit margin is at least partly mitigated by a reduction of the percentage of distribution costs to revenues. Given the information we have for Vertigo (not necessarily available to an external analyst), we can see that there has been a significant reduction in depreciation (all of which has been charged to this expense heading) and advertising costs.

We would at this stage drill down further, in the same way as when designing audit tests, to target areas of significant change.

	20X8 £000	20X9 £000	Percentage change
Sales revenue	3,296	3,461	+5.0
Inventory – opening	253	398	
Purchases	2,385	2,623	+10.0
Inventory – closing	(398)	(563)	+41.5
Cost of goods sold	(2,240)	(2,458)	+9.7
Gross profit	1,056	1,003	−5.0
Distribution costs:			
Depreciation	239	187	−21.8
Bad debts	32	17	−46.9
Advertising	94	24	−74.5
Administrative expenses:			
Rent	60	60	—
Salaries and wages	316	362	+14.6
Miscellaneous expenses	159	177	+11.3
Operating profit	156	176	+12.8

It is interesting to see that discretionary costs in the form of advertising have been reduced by 74.5%. However, if the advertising had been maintained at 20X8 levels the operating profit would be reduced by £70,000 to £106,000, which would have shown a fall from the previous year of 32% rather than an increase of 12.8%.

This is where it is important to look at trends, in particular from 1 January 20X6 which was the last year when the previous Managing Director had been in control. There should be further enquiry to establish (a) the normal level over the previous three years – whether there was heavier advertising in 20X8 to achieve the 5% increase in sales in the light of the company's intention to attempt to obtain further investment in 20X9; (b) whether the reduction is likely to have an adverse effect on future sales; (c) what the company's reason was for reduced spending; and (d) the necessity or otherwise to return to a higher level in future years. This is more of commercial relevance to the client who is already concerned about the fall in profits than audit relevance.

28.5.3 Volume analysis – asset turnover

The basic 'volume ratio' is:

$$\frac{\text{Revenue}}{\text{Capital employed}}$$

This ratio is commonly referred to as the *asset turnover ratio*. For Vertigo, this ratio is:

	20X9	20X8
Revenue	3,461	3,296
Capital employed	3,953	3,862
Asset turnover	87.6%	85.3%
Turnover expressed as a multiple	0.876 ×	0.853 ×

This shows us that the asset turnover has in fact slightly improved in 20X9 compared with 20X8. Therefore an overall conclusion we can make is that the decline in ROCE is due to a declining margin rather than a decline in the utilisation of assets. Using our formula we can now see that:

ROCE (4.4%) = profit margin (5.1%) × asset turnover (0.876)

Although the asset turnover rate has improved, we still need to analyse the reasons for the change, because the change can have resulted from changes in sales or any of the non-current and current assets.

Non-current asset turnover

The non-current asset turnover is:

$$\frac{\text{Revenue}}{\text{Non-current assets}}$$

For Vertigo, this ratio is:

	20X9	20X8
Revenue	3,461	3,296
Non-current assets	2,834	3,021
Non-current asset turnover	122.1%	109.1%
Turnover expressed as a multiple	1.22 ×	1.09 ×

From a profitability point of view, this is an improvement. However, we should remember that there has been no investment in non-current assets this year and, after depreciation, the asset turnover would appear to have improved simply because the written-down value of the non-current assets is lower.

An increasing ratio is not always an improving ratio and might not always be good for the long-term health of the business. For example, if we had made an investment in non-current assets this year we would have quite possibly replaced older, fully depreciated, assets with newer assets that have higher net book values. This might be good for the long term but in the short term the fall in the rate of turnover of non-current assets would have a negative impact on the ROCE.

New, growth companies are likely to have a fall in the rate of non-current asset turnover as they expand. We must take care that our use of ratios does not take us into 'short-term thinking'.

Asset turnover – working capital

When we analyse net current assets (or 'working capital') we generally do this by an individual focus on the three key components of inventory, trade receivables and trade payables.

Inventory turnover

The ratio we use to assess the effectiveness of our inventory management is the 'inventory days ratio'. This would normally be computed as:

$$\frac{\text{Closing inventory} \times 365}{\text{Cost of sales}}$$

The rationale behind the ratio is that we are effectively dividing closing inventory by 'one day's usage' to give us a hypothetical period for how long it will take us to sell the inventory. Whilst this analysis can be useful, we need to sound two notes of caution:

- We are relating the closing inventory to the average 'usage' in the previous year. The closing inventory will of course be used next year and so a more 'realistic' figure would be to base it on next year's projected usage, but of course this often is not available to the analyst.
- With this (and other) ratios we are comparing a 'point of time' figure (closing inventory) with a 'period' figure (cost of sales).

To a certain extent, both of the above factors are at least partly mitigated by the fact that, when using ratio analysis, we are comparing one ratio with another, and if the above factors apply to both the ratio and its comparative, to a certain extent the above 'defects' can cancel each other out.

That said, our inventory days ratio will be:

	20X9	20X8
Closing inventory × 365	$\dfrac{563 \times 365}{2,458}$	$\dfrac{398 \times 365}{2,240}$
Cost of sales		
Inventory days	84 days	65 days
Turnover expressed as a multiple	4.4 ×	5.6 ×

Inventory is not being turned over as quickly in 20X9. This is not a positive sign. Not only does it affect the profitability of Vertigo but it also affects its liquidity, as we will see in the next section.

Trade receivables

The second key component of working capital is trade receivables. The equivalent ratio for trade receivables is:

$$\frac{\text{Trade receivables} \times 365}{\text{Revenue}}$$

For Vertigo, this ratio would be

	20X9	20X8
Trade receivables × 365	$\dfrac{1,181 \times 365}{3,461}$	$\dfrac{912 \times 365}{3,296}$
Sales		
Trade receivables days	125 days	101 days
Turnover expressed as a multiple	2.9 ×	3.6 ×

It appears that Vertigo is collecting its cash from its customers less quickly in 20X9 than was the case in 20X8. This has a negative impact on profitability as the working capital cycle is lengthened when customers take longer to pay. This in turn has a negative impact on liquidity.

Late payment is a serious problem and a study in 2012 by the Clydesdale Bank and Yorkshire Bank in the UK reported that 10% of businesses say closing or seriously scaling back operations would have to be looked at if customers took more than 90 days to pay invoices. This poses a problem for management who need to tighten up their systems and controls and introduce procedures such as agreeing payment terms and conditions upfront or using incentives for early payment. Vertigo's management need to review their current procedures.

Trade payables

The third key component of working capital is trade payables. The equivalent ratio for trade payables is:

$$\frac{\text{Trade payables} \times 365}{\text{Credit purchases}}$$

For Vertigo, this ratio would be

	20X9	20X8
Trade payables × 365	498 × 365	398 × 365
Credit purchases	2,623	2,385
Trade payables days	69 days	61 days
Turnover expressed as a multiple	5.3 ×	6.0 ×

It appears that Vertigo is taking slightly longer to pay its suppliers in 20X9 than in 20X8. Given the way we have computed the profitability ratios (capital employed is total assets less current liabilities) this will actually improve the asset turnover and hence the ROCE. Given that our suppliers effectively provide us with interest-free finance there is, in a sense, a liquidity benefit in extending the credit we take from our suppliers.

However, this can also be indicative of liquidity problems that make it difficult for us to settle our debts as they fall due and, if we allow the level of our trade payables to get too high, it could lead to problems with future supplies and ultimately could lead to the entity being wound up. Overall the 'real' level of trade payables of Vertigo is probably not a major concern but management will need to monitor this going forward.

It should be noted that, whilst the trade payables ratio can be calculated from the accounts of Vertigo, those accounts are more detailed than the information available in the published financial statements. Credit purchases would not normally be available from the published financial statements. In practice external analysts would use cost of sales as a 'proxy' for credit purchases. As stated before, whilst this practice clearly isn't strictly correct, the fact that interpretation involves a comparison of ratios means that, if used consistently, this slightly contrived ratio can be used as a means of comparing the payment policies of a single entity over time or two comparable entities over a corresponding period.

The cash cycle

The cash cycle, also referred to as the cash conversion cycle, measures the number of days it takes to acquire and sell inventory and convert sales into cash. It measures how effective managers are in managing this process.

For Vertigo the cash cycle is:

$$\text{Accounts Receivable days} + \text{Inventory days} - \text{Accounts Payable days} = \text{Cash Cycle}$$
$$125 \quad + \quad 84 \quad - \quad 69 \quad = 140 \text{ days}$$

This means it takes Vertigo 140 days from the time the company acquires inventory from its suppliers, completes the sale of the inventory to its customers and collects the cash from accounts receivable.

The 140 days can be regarded as the length of time the company needs to have cash to cover the cash cycle or, thinking defensively, to cover its operating expenses. The means that the management of the cash cycle is critical to the cash flow and profitability of the company.

High working capital turnover rate

As with all ratios, a high rate does not always indicate that it is acceptable. For example, a high turnover rate can indicate overtrading, i.e. the sales volume is excessive in relation to the equity investment in the business. A high turnover might be an indication that the business relies too much on credit granted by suppliers or the bank instead of providing an adequate margin of operating funds.

28.6 Financial statement analysis, part 2 – liquidity

Liquidity is the lifeblood of any business. The ultimate price for poor liquidity is insolvency and therefore internal managers cannot ignore it. External users who have lent or who are thinking about lending money to the entity, whether on a short-term or a long-term basis, will almost certainly be more concerned with liquidity than with profitability.

Analysts can consider the liquidity of an entity in two ways. The first is through ratio analysis. We discussed in the previous section the fact that investment in working capital, as revealed when calculating changes in inventory days, trade receivables days and trade payables days, had an impact on liquidity.

However, there are also other ratios that are commonly used to assess liquidity. These include the current ratio, the quick ratio and cash flow ratios.

28.6.1 The current ratio

This ratio is simply the ratio of current assets to current liabilities. In the case of Vertigo, this ratio would be:

	20X9	20X8
Current assets	1,753	1,321
Current liabilities	634	480
So current ratio equals	2.76	2.75

The rationale behind the ratio is that the current assets are a short-term source of cash for the entity, whilst the current liabilities are the amounts that need settling reasonably quickly.

It is very difficult to give a general level for this ratio which analysts would regard as 'satisfactory' because different entities vary so much in their working capital cycles. In most cases you would expect this ratio to be well in excess of 1 for analysts to feel comfortable. However, entities that can generate cash easily are often able to operate with current ratios well below 1.

Consider a food retailer: food retailers have little if any trade receivables, since they sell to their customers for cash. Their inventory levels necessarily have to be quite low, since their products are often perishable. However, their trade payables days would be just as large as for any manufacturing entity and, if they reinvest the cash they generate quickly, their current ratios are often less than $\frac{1}{2}$:1. This does not mean they have liquidity problems, however!

Rather, therefore, than identifying an absolute level at which the current ratio should be, it is probably better to monitor whether or not there has been a significant change from one period to another and compare with the industry average or peer group. Comparing it with the previous year we can see that it is virtually unchanged – this does not mean, however, that it is acceptable. We would need to look further at the trend over the past four years and also at competitors' current ratios.

An increase in the current ratio beyond the company's own normal range may arise for a number of reasons, some beneficial, others unwelcome.

Beneficial reasons

These include:

● A build-up of inventory in order to support increased sales following an advertising campaign or increasing popular demand as for, say, a PlayStation. Management action will be to establish from a cash budget that the company will not experience liquidity problems from holding such inventory, e.g. there may be sufficient cash in hand or from operations, short-term loans, extended credit or bank overdraft facilities.

● A permanent expansion of the business which will require continuing higher levels of inventory. Management action will be to consider existing cash resources or future cash flows from operations or arrange additional long-term finance, e.g. equity or long-term borrowings to finance the increased working capital.

Unwelcome reasons

These include:

● Operating losses may have eroded the working capital base. Management action will vary according to the underlying problem, e.g. disposing of underperforming segments, arranging a sale of non-current assets or inviting a takeover.

● Inefficient control over working capital, e.g. poor inventory or accounts receivable control allowing a build-up of slow-moving inventories or doubtful trade receivables.

● Adverse trading conditions, e.g. inventory becoming obsolete or introduction of new models by competitors.

28.6.2 The quick ratio

Another ratio that is used for liquidity assessment purposes is the quick ratio (also known as the acid test ratio). This ratio is:

$$\frac{\text{Current assets} - \text{inventory}}{\text{Current liabilities}}$$

The rationale for using the quick ratio is that entities cannot regard their inventory as a short-term source of cash because of the time it takes to realise cash through its sale. Whether this is true depends on the nature of the entity. This would certainly be true for entities in the construction sector, but for many entities in the retail sector, particularly those entities who sell their goods directly to the general public for cash, the current ratio would be a better measure of liquidity.

For Vertigo, the quick ratio would be:

	20X9	20X8
Current assets − inventory	1,753 − 563	1,321 − 398
Current liabilities	634	480
So quick ratio equals	1.88	1.92

There has been a small decline in this ratio given the higher trade payables levels but the decline is not significant.

28.6.3 Cash flow ratios

Even if a statement of cash flows is not provided in a question it is worth preparing and analysing one. If we prepared such a statement for Vertigo for the year ended 31 December 20X9 we would get the following:

	£000	£000
Profit before tax	116	
Finance costs	60	
Depreciation	187	
Increase in inventory	(165)	
Increase in trade receivables	(269)	
Increase in trade payables	100	
Increase in accrued expenses	3	
Cash generated from operations		32
Interest paid		(60)
Tax paid		(30)
Reduction in cash and cash equivalents		(58)
Cash and cash equivalents, 1 January 20X9 (11 – 41)		(30)
Cash and cash equivalents, 31 December 20X9 (9 – 97)		(88)

This statement shows that the entity is struggling to generate cash from its operations. This is mainly due to the increased levels of working capital; all three components have increased in real terms as we have already seen.

This increase has absorbed significant amounts of cash such that cash from operating activities is negative. There has been no investment in non-current assets or additional equity or loan capital raised, and cash flow fails to cover the current year's interest and any dividend payments.

Interest cover

The lenders would be interested in their interest cover, i.e. the number of times that their interest could be paid out of cash generated by the operations. In this case, the interest cover is $32/60 = 0.53$ times. Notice that this is far worse than the interest cover based on the statement of income which indicates that there is adequate cover at 2.93 times (176/60).

Servicing future debt

As we have already seen, the entity has not purchased any non-current assets this year but sooner or later they may have to. Their borrowing levels are not currently excessive (see Section 28.7 below) but their ability to service additional debt is questionable. Based on this, it would appear that consideration may need to be given to raising further long-term finance if future expansion of the business is envisaged.

28.6.4 The cash ratio

This is a more conservative ratio than the quick ratio as it shows the ratio of cash and cash equivalents to current liabilities. Suppliers are able to see whether these are enough to settle the amount owed to them. In this case, of course, it is a negative figure.

It is certainly not a problem that faces Vertigo but there are companies sitting on hoards of cash either to meet cyclical demands or because they are nervous about investing in the uncertain economic climate or they are unable to find investment opportunities. We see major companies like Apple, therefore, setting aside US$10 billion for stock buybacks.

28.7 Financial statement analysis, part 3 – financing

One of the key issues for analysts is the way a business is financed. Of particular concern is the relationship between borrowings (debt finance) and equity finance. Because most equity investors are risk averse, the return required by the providers of debt finance is lower than that required by equity investors as they would normally have fixed or floating security. However, management must balance the benefit of 'cheaper' debt finance against the fact that the greater the proportion of finance provided through borrowings the greater the risk for both as measured by the gearing ratio.

28.7.1 The gearing ratio

There are a number of ways in which the gearing ratio can be computed but the two most common are:

$$\frac{\text{Debt finance}}{\text{Debt finance} + \text{equity finance}}$$

and

$$\frac{\text{Debt finance}}{\text{Equity finance}}$$

Both these ratios will increase as the proportion of debt finance gets greater. We will use the former ratio to illustrate the gearing of Vertigo:

	20X9	20X8
Debt finance (long-term only)	600	600
Debt finance + equity finance	600 + 3,353	600 + 3,262
So gearing ratio equals	15.2%	15.5%

Gearing is relatively stable, the only fluctuation being caused by the retention of 20X9 profits increasing equity whilst long-term borrowings stay static. It is difficult to generalise, but this is a relatively low gearing ratio – ratios of less than $\frac{1}{3}$ would normally be regarded as 'low' and gearing would normally only be regarded as 'high' when it exceeded 50%. There would appear to be plenty of scope for Vertigo to obtain more debt finance subject to being able to produce forecasts showing its ability to service the debt.

28.7.2 How should a potential investor decide on an acceptable level of gearing?

This is initially influenced by the political and economic climate of the time. We have seen that prior to the credit crisis arising in 2007 high gearing was not seen by many as risky and there was a general feeling that borrowing was good, leverage was respectable, and capital gains were inevitable. This might have reduced the importance of questions that would normally have been asked, such as the following.

Asset values

- Are the values in the statement of financial position reasonably current? If much lower than current then the gearing ratio may be significantly overstated.

Gearing ratios

- Is the gearing ratio constant or has it increased over time with heavier borrowing? If higher:
  - further borrowing might be difficult;
  - it might indicate that there has been investment that will lead to higher profits, so details are needed as to how the funds borrowed have been used.

- What covenants are in place and what is the risk that they might be breached? A breach could lead to a company having to renegotiate finance at a higher interest rate or even go into administration or liquidation.
- How does the gearing compare to other companies in the same sector?

Use of funds

- If gearing has increased, what were the funds used for? Was it to:
  - restructure debt following inability to meet current repayment terms?
  - finance new maintenance/expansion capital expenditure?
  - improve liquid ratios?

Interest commitment

- How variable is the rate of interest that is being charged on the borrowings? If rates are falling then equity shareholders benefit, but if rates rise then expenses are higher.
- How many times does the earnings before tax cover the interest? A highly geared company is more at risk if the business cycle moves into recession because the company has to continue to service the debts even if sales fall substantially.
- How many times does the cash flow from operations currently cover the interest? This is a useful ratio if profits are not converted into cash, e.g. they might be reinvested in working capital.

Cash flows

- How variable is the company's cash flow from operations? A company with a stable cash flow is less at risk, so the trend is important.
- What is the likely effect of contingent liabilities if they crystallise on the cash flows and debt ratio? Could it have a significant adverse impact?

A company's attitude to leverage may vary over time

This is often dependent on the availability of finance and the possibility of profitable capital investment. If there is uncertainty about either then there will an unwillingness to lend and an unwillingness to borrow.

28.8 Peer comparison

We have so far prepared internal ratios for two years making our comparison with 20X8. We have now selected comparative ratios from a competitor and set out some comparative ratios where Vertigo's ratios seem too high or too low:

	20X9	20X8	20X7	20X6	20X5
Asset turnover ratio:					
Vertigo	0.88	0.85			
Competitor*	2.77	2.10	1.96	1.59	1.43
Inventory turnover:					
Vertigo	84 days	65 days			
Competitor	58 days	70 days	62 days	80 days	87 days

* For illustration, the competitor comparisons were ratios reported in the Everest Industries 2012 Annual Report.

	20X9	20X8	20X7	20X6	20X5
Profit before interest and tax margin:					
Vertigo	5.1%	6.3%			
Competitor	7.9%	6.41%	7.2%	6.9%	4.38%
Debt/equity ratio:					
Vertigo	0.15	0.15			
Competitor	0.28	0.53	0.69	1.13	0.94
Current ratio:					
Vertigo	2.76	2.75			
Competitor	0.86	1.33	1.07	0.90	0.89
Quick ratio:					
Vertigo	1.88	1.92			
Competitor	0.66	0.63	0.70	0.67	0.70

Looking at the profit before interest and tax, it is interesting to see that the competitor has had a rising trend over the five years with alternating positive and negative changes but the overall trend is up. An examination of the past five years' figures for Vertigo would be helpful in identifying its trend.

The inventory turnover has risen in 20X9 for Vertigo but it is interesting to see that again the trend with the competitor is falling with uneven positive and negative changes over the five years. The competitor has clearly addressed the level of inventory held in the last year. This could well indicate that a target of 70 days for Vertigo should be achievable.

The debt/equity ratio is steady at 0.15 in Vertigo. This is almost half of the gearing in the competitor where the gearing has fallen year on year to less threatening levels.

The asset turnover, however, paints a different picture with the competitor turning over its assets three times faster than Vertigo. This would seem to indicate that Vertigo needs to work its assets more effectively and aim at increasing its sales. A 5% increase in sales compares with a 22% increase in the competitor's sales.

The current ratio and quick ratio are more than double those of the competitor whose trend figures show that it is operating on levels of less than 1:1 for both ratios.

Note that it is important to obtain a comparator from the same industry and size, as far as possible.

28.9 Report based on the analysis

A report based on the above analysis might read as follows:

Report:
From:
To:
Date:

Subject: Financial Performance of Vertigo Ltd

Profitability
Vertigo's profitability has declined compared with 20X8, with the ROCE declining from 5.4% in 20X8 to 4.4% in 20X9. This decline is mainly due to a reduction in the profit margin (see appendix). The reduction is a combination of three factors:

- A reduction in the gross margin. Reasons for this need to be investigated further.

- An increase in administrative expenses. This is mainly caused by a 15% rise in salary costs which is a little surprising given the rise in revenue is only 5%.

- The reduction in the profit margin is slightly mitigated by a fall in distribution costs. The key reason for this is a significant reduction (almost 75%) in advertising expenditure. This reduction might be beneficial for profitability in the short term, but as a long-term measure this may be unwise.

Liquidity

Liquidity ratios are conservative but seem excessive when compared to the current and quick ratios of the competitor (see appendix).

The cash generated from operations is very low given the level of profits and this amount does not cover the interest and tax payments made in the year. During 20X9 the cash balances declined by £88,000. A key reason for the disappointing cash flow is the significant increase in working capital, particularly inventory and trade receivables.

The reason for the increase in the inventory turnover needs to be discussed further with management. As far as the impact on cash is concerned, if inventory is brought back to the 65 days turnover level, the increase of £165,000 would be reduced by more than £120,000 – more than enough to pay off the existing short-term borrowings. An improvement to 70 days would be sufficient to clear all short-term borrowings.

Further investigation of the management of receivables is required, particularly in the present credit climate.

The overall rise in working capital is mitigated to a certain extent by a rise in trade payables. This needs to be carefully monitored to ensure that the credit status of Vertigo is not compromised.

Financial position

As stated above, overall liquidity ratios are unchanged in both years but the management of the working capital needs to be addressed. There has been no investment in non-current assets during 20X9 and the shareholders have not received a dividend. Both these factors may be due to a cash shortage and Vertigo would appear to require additional long-term finance. Compared to the competitor the gearing is low which, on the basis of the current level of borrowing, would allow Vertigo to seek additional debt finance.

Conclusion

Profits are under pressure. Although revenues are continuing to rise there appears to be a decline in the gross margin which needs investigating further.

As far as the possibility of an improvement in profitability is concerned, there is concern that the asset turnover is low and sales are increasing but at a slower rate than the competitor's. There has at the same time been a significant reduction in advertising spend, which seems strange in a competitive environment and with the slow rate of sales growth.

It is noted that there has been no investment in non-current assets in 20X9. It is not clear without further enquiry whether the current level of non-current assets can sustain an increase in sales. If not, the need for further capital expenditure could not be provided by the current level of operating cash-flow.

Further attention urgently needs to be paid to working capital management.

As far as obtaining additional loan or equity capital, profitability needs to be addressed. The ROE is low at 2.7% and operating cash is insufficient to fully cover interest payments. The more positive aspect is that, given an improvement in profitability, it would appear possible to obtain this through issuing more debt as gearing levels are fairly low.

To support a request for additional funding a feasible three-year forecast would be required and we would be pleased to assist with this if so instructed.

Appendix – detailed ratios (not reproduced here as computed earlier)

Subscription sources are available for inter-firm ratios such as *RMA Annual Statement Studies* (Risk Management Association) and *Financial Studies of the Small Business* by Karen Goodman (Financial Research Associates).

28.10 Caution when using ratios for prediction

At the beginning of the chapter we mentioned the importance of taking an overview which influenced your expectations as to, say, the level of sales or profits that could be expected.

The same approach has to be taken when interpreting the ratios. This involves considering external and internal factors that could help explain current ratios and what might be predicted from them.

28.10.1 External factors

There are a number of external factors that need to be considered when interpreting ratios bearing in mind the economic context within which a business has been and will be operating. Consider, for example, assuming that Vertigo is a retail company:

- Have the retail sales been adversely or positively affected by growth of Internet sales?
- Has there been a change in fashion or downturn in the market?
- Will this mean inventory write-downs? Discounted sales?
- Have wage costs gone up (or will they be going up) following legislation for equal pay for women/part-time staff/maternity/paternity leave?
- Have credit sales been affected by less being spent on non-essential items?
- Has the company had to respond to pressure to pay small suppliers on time?
- Has there been a change in the sales mix that has impacted (or will impact) on sales or profits?
- Is property leased and, if so, are any rent reviews due? Are there any onerous covenants on the leases?

28.10.2 Internal factors

There are internal factors to consider:

- Ratios need to be interpreted in conjunction with reading the narrative and notes in the annual reports. The narrative could be helpful in explaining changes in the ratios, e.g. whether an inventory build-up is in anticipation of sales or a fall in demand. The notes could be helpful in corroborating the narrative, e.g. if the narrative explains that the increase in inventory is due to anticipated further production and sales, check whether the non-current assets have increased or whether there is a note about future capital expenditure.
- Ratios might be distorted because they are based on period-end figures. The end-of-year figures are static and might not be a fair reflection of normal relationships such as when

a business is seasonal, e.g. an arable farm might have no inventory until the harvest and a toy manufacturer might have little inventory after supplying wholesalers in the lead-up to Christmas. Any ratios based on the inventory figure such as inventory turnover could be misleading if calculated at, say, a 31 December year-end.

- The use of norms can be misleading, e.g. the current ratio of 2:1 might be totally inappropriate for an entity like Asda which does not have long inventory turnover periods and, as its sales are for cash, it would not produce trade receivable collection period ratios.

- Factors that could invalidate inter-firm comparisons, such as:
  - use of different measurement bases with non-current assets reported at historical cost or revaluation and revaluations carried out at different dates;
  - use of different commercial practices, e.g. factoring trade receivables so that cash is increased – a perfectly normal transaction but one that could cause the comparative ratio of days' credit allowed to be significantly reduced;
  - applying different accounting practice, e.g. adopting different depreciation methods such as straight-line and reducing balance; adopting different inventory valuation methods such as FIFO and weighted average; or assuming different degrees of optimism or pessimism when making judgement-based adjustments to non-current and current assets;
  - having different definitions for ratios, e.g. the numerator for ROCE could be operating profit, profit before interest, profit before interest and tax (PBIT), earnings before interest, tax, depreciation and amortisation (EBITDA), profit after tax, etc.; the denominator for ROCE could be total assets, total assets less intangibles, net assets, average total assets, etc.

28.10.3 Degree of scepticism

This depends on the role of the person using the ratios. For example, a financial controller/ FD preparing a report to the Board would have local knowledge of the company's business activities. In the Vertigo circumstances a reporting accountant, and to a lesser extent an external auditor, might not have this local knowledge and their starting point would be to form an overall impression followed by a more detailed analysis.

In expressing an opinion they might need to be more investigative and consider:

- Whether there is a risk of window dressing to improve sales, e.g. dispatching goods at the end of the period knowing them to be defective so that they appear in the current year's sales and accepting that they will be returned later in the next period.

- Whether liabilities have been omitted to improve the quick ratio, e.g. simply by suppressing purchase invoices at the year-end.

- Whether liabilities have been omitted to improve gearing, e.g. by the use of off-balance-sheet finance such as structuring the terms of a lease to ensure that it is treated as an operating lease and not a finance lease and special-purpose enterprises to keep debts off the statement of financial position.

- Whether there has been full disclosure in the notes of, say, contingent liabilities, which could result in ratios not being accurate predictors of future earnings and solvency.

Summary

Ratios are an aid in interpreting financial performance and liquidity. Comparison with prior periods and competitor/industry averages can provide a business with an indication of its relative performance – has it improved and how does it compare to its competitors? In this chapter we have followed a common-sized approach to the initial overview and the pyramid approach to calculating the ratios for two years to provide a basis for a report.

A comparison was made with a competitor's ratios for those areas that required further investigation. In practice it would be helpful to have data for 3–5 years in order to review trends. Reference was then made to the need to be cautious when using the ratios for prediction – remembering that at all times there needs to be a degree of scepticism when interpreting the ratios.

REVIEW QUESTIONS

1 State and express two ratios that can be used to analyse each of the following:

(i)   profitability;

(ii) liquidity;

(iii) management control.

2 Discuss the importance of the disclosure of exceptional items to the users of the annual report in addition to the operating profit.

3 Explain how a reader of the accounts might be able to assess whether the non-current asset base is being maintained.

4 Explain in what circumstances an increase in the revenue to current assets might be an indication of a possible problem.

5 Explain in what circumstances a decrease in the rate of non-current asset turnover might be a positive indicator.

6 Discuss why an increasing current ratio might not be an indicator of better working capital management.

7 The management of Alpha Ltd calculates ROCE using profit before interest and tax as a percentage of net closing assets. Discuss how this definition might be improved.

8 The asset turnover rate has increased by 50% over the previous year. Explain the questions you would have in mind and what other ratios you would review.

9 The current ratio has doubled since the previous year. Explain the questions that you would have in mind when reviewing the accounts.

10 Explain the problems a creditor might have when assessing the creditworthiness of a subsidiary entity.

11 You ascertain that inventories and (to a lesser extent) trade receivables have risen significantly when you consider that sales have increased by only 5%. Discuss the questions that you ask and the possible impact of each answer on the ratios.

12 Access the annual reports of two companies in the same industry and identify (a) the ratios that they report in common, (b) how these have been defined, and (c) why some ratios are not common to both.

13 A company has a very high rate of inventory turnover. Discuss circumstances when this might be of concern to management.

14 The ratio of current liabilities to net worth (equity + retained earnings) was 75%. Discuss how this would be viewed by suppliers and management.

15 The ratio of non-current assets to net worth was 75%. Discuss the risk that this poses for a company.

EXERCISES

Question 1

Flash Fashions plc has had a difficult nine months and the management team is discussing strategy for the final quarter.

In the last nine months the company has survived by cutting production, reducing staff and reducing overheads wherever possible. However, the share market, whilst recognising that sales across the industry have been poor, has worried about the financial strength of the business and as a result the share price has fallen 40%.

The company is desperate to increase sales. It has been recognised that the high fixed costs of the factory are not being fully absorbed by the lower volumes which are costed at standard cost. If sales and production can be increased then more factory costs will be absorbed and increased sales volume will raise staff morale and make analysts think the firm is entering a turnaround phase.

The company decides to drop prices by 15% for the next two months and to change the terms of sale so that property does not pass until the clothes are paid for. This is purely a reflection of the tough economic conditions and the need to protect the firm against customer insolvency. Further, it is decided that if sales have not increased enough by the end of the two months, the company representatives will be advised to ship goods to customers on the understanding that they will be invoiced but if they don't sell the goods in two months they can return them. Volume discounts will be stressed to keep the stock moving.

These actions are intended to increase sales, increase profitability, justify higher stocks, and ensure that more overheads are transferred out of the profit statement into stocks.

For the purposes of annual reporting it was decided not to spell out sales growth in financial figure terms in the managing director's report but rather to focus on units shipped in graphs using scales (possibly log scales) designed to make the fall look less dramatic. Also comparisons will be made against industry volumes as the fashion industry has been more affected by economic conditions than the economy as a whole.

To make the ratios look better, the company will enter into an agreement on the last week of the year with a two-dollar company called Upstart Ltd owned by Colleen Livingston, friend of the managing director of Flash Fashions, Sue Cotton. Upstart Ltd will sign a contract to buy a property for £30 million from Flash Fashions and will also sign promissory notes payable over the next three quarters for £10 million each. The auditors will not be told, but Flash Fashions will enter into an agreement to buy back the property for £31 million any time after the start of the third month in the new financial year.

Required:
Critically discuss each of the proposed strategies.

* Question 2

Relationships plc

You are informed that the non-current assets totalled €350,000, current liabilities €156,000, the opening retained earnings totalled €103,000, the administration expenses totalled €92,680 and that the available ratios were the current ratio 1.5, the acid test ratio 0.75, the trade receivables collection period was six weeks, the gross profit was 20% and the net assets turned over 1.4 times.

Required:
Prepare the Relationships plc statement of financial position from the above information.

* Question 3

The major shareholder/director of Esrever Ltd has obtained average data for the industry as a whole. He wishes to see what the forecast results and position of Esrever Ltd would be if in the ensuing year its performance were to match the industry averages.

At 1 July 20X0, actual figures for Esrever Ltd included:

	£
Land and buildings (at written-down value)	132,000
Fixtures, fittings and equipment (at written-down value)	96,750
Inventory	22,040
12% loan (repayable in 20X5)	50,000
Ordinary share capital (50p shares)	100,000

For the year ended 30 June 20X1 the following forecast information is available:

1 Depreciation of non-current assets (on reducing balance)

Land and buildings	2%
Fixtures, fittings and equipment	20%

2 Net current assets will be financed by a bank overdraft to the extent necessary.

3 At 30 June 20X0 total assets minus current liabilities will be £231,808.

4 Profit after tax for the year will be 23.32% of gross profit and 11.16% of total assets minus all external liabilities, both long-term and short-term.

5 Tax will be at an effective rate of 20% of profit before tax.

6 Cost of sales will be 68% of turnover (excluding VAT).

7 Closing inventory will represent 61.9 days' average cost of sales (excluding VAT).

8 Any difference between total expenses and the aggregate of expenses ascertained from this given information will represent credit purchases and other credit expenses, in each case excluding VAT input tax.

9 A dividend of 2.5p per share will be proposed.

10 The collection period for the VAT-exclusive amount of trade receivables will be an average of 42.6 days of the annual turnover. All the company's supplies are subject to VAT output tax at 15%.

11 The payment period for the VAT-exclusive amount of trade payables (purchases and other credit expenses) will be an average of 29.7 days. All these items are subject to (reclaimable) VAT input tax at 15%. This VAT rate has been increased to 17.5% and may be subject to future changes, but for the purpose of this question the theory and workings remain the same irrespective of the rate.

12 Payables, other than trade payables, will comprise tax due, proposed dividends and VAT payable equal to one-quarter of the net amount due for the year.

13 Calculations are based on a year of 365 days.

Required:
Construct a forecast statement of comprehensive income for Esrever Ltd for the year ended 30 June 20X1 and a forecast statement of financial position at that date in as much detail as possible. (All calculations should be made to the nearest £1.)

* Question 4

Saddam Ltd is considering the possibility of diversifying its operations and has identified three firms in the same industrial sector as potential takeover targets. The following information in respect of the companies has been extracted from their most recent financial statements.

	Ali Ltd	Baba Ltd	Camel Ltd
ROCE before tax %	22.1	23.7	25.0
Net profit %	12.0	12.5	3.75
Asset turnover ratio	1.45	1.16	3.73
Gross profit %	20.0	25.0	10.0
Sales/non-current assets	4.8	2.2	11.6
Sales/current assets	2.1	5.2	5.5
Current ratio	3.75	1.4	1.5
Acid test ratio	2.25	0.4	0.9
Average number of weeks' receivables outstanding	5.6	6.0	4.8
Average number of weeks' inventory held	12.0	19.2	4.0
Ordinary dividend %	10.0	15.0	30.0
Dividend cover	4.3	5.0	1.0

Required:
(a) Prepare a report for the directors of Saddam Ltd, assessing the performance of the three companies from the information provided and identifying areas which you consider require further investigation before a final decision is made.
(b) Discuss briefly why a firm's statement of financial position is unlikely to show the true market value of the business.

Question 5

You work for Euroc, a limited liability company, which seeks growth through acquisitions. You are a member of a team that is investigating the possible purchase of Choggerell, a limited liability company that manufactures a product complementary to the products currently being sold by Euroc.

Your team leader wants you to prepare a report for the team evaluating the recent performance of Choggerell and the quality of its management, and has given you the following financial information which has been derived from the financial statements of Choggerell for the three years ended 31 March 2006, 2007 and 2008.

Financial year ended 31 March	2006	2007	2008
Revenue (€ million)	2,243	2,355	2,237
Cash and cash equivalents (€ million)	−50	81	−97
Return on equity	13%	22%	19%
Sales revenue to total assets	2.66	2.66	2.01
Cost of sales to sales revenue	85%	82%	79%
Operating expenses to sales revenue	11%	12%	15%
Net income to sales revenue	2.6%	4.3%	4.2%
Current/Working capital ratio (to 1)	1.12	1.44	1.06
Acid test ratio (to 1)	0.80	1.03	0.74
Inventory turnover (months)	0.6	0.7	1.0
Credit to customers (months)	1.3	1.5	1.7
Credit from suppliers (months)	1.5	1.5	2.0
Net assets per share (cents per share)	0.86	0.2	0.97
Dividend per share (cents per share)	10.0	14.0	14.0
Earnings per share (cents per share)	11.5	20.1	18.7

Required:
Use the above information to prepare a report for your team leader which:
(a) reviews the performance of Choggerell as evidenced by the above ratios;
(b) makes recommendations as to how the overall performance of Choggerell could be improved; and
(c) indicates any limitations in your analysis.

(The Association of International Accountants)

Question 6

Liz Collier runs a small delicatessen. Her profits in recent years have remained steady at around £21,000 per annum. This type of business generally earns a uniform rate of net profit on sales of 20%.

Recently, Liz has found that this level of profitability is insufficient to enable her to maintain her desired lifestyle. She is considering three options to improve her profitability.

Option 1   Liz will borrow £10,000 from her bank at an interest rate of 10% per annum, payable at the end of each financial year. The whole capital sum will be repaid to the bank at the end of the second year. The money will be used to hire the services of a marketing agency for two years. It is anticipated that turnover will increase by 40% as a result of the additional advertising.

Option 2 Liz will form a partnership with Joan Mercer, who also runs a local delicatessen. Joan's net profits have remained at £12,000 per annum since she started in business five years ago. The sales of each shop in the combined business are expected to increase by 20% in the first year and then remain steady. The costs of the amalgamation will amount to £6,870, which will be written off in the first year. The partnership agreement will allow each partner a partnership salary of 2% of the revised turnover of their own shop. Remaining profits will be shared in the ratio of Liz 3/5, Joan 2/5.

Option 3 Liz will reduce her present sales by 80% and take up a franchise to sell Nickson's Munchy Sausage. The franchise will cost £80,000. This amount will be borrowed from her bank. The annual interest rate will be 10% flat rate based on the amount borrowed. Sales of Munchy Sausage yield a net profit to sales percentage of 30%. Sales are expected to be £50,000 in the first year, but should increase annually at a rate of 15% for the following three years then remain constant.

Required:
(a) Prepare a financial statement for Liz comparing the results of each option for each of the next two years.
(b) Advise Liz which option may be the best to choose.
(c) Discuss any other factors that Liz should consider under each of the options.

Question 7

Chelsea plc has embarked on a programme of growth through acquisitions and has identified Kensington Ltd and Wimbledon Ltd as companies in the same industrial sector, as potential targets. Using recent financial statements of both Kensington and Wimbledon and further information obtained from a trade association, Chelsea plc has managed to build up the following comparability table:

	Kensington	Wimbledon	Industrial average
Profitability ratios			
ROCE before tax %	22	28	20
Return on equity %	18	22	15
Net profit margin %	11	5	7
Gross profit ratio %	25	12	20
Activity ratios			
Total assets turnover = times	1.5	4.0	2.5
Non-current asset turnover = times	2.3	12.0	5.1
Receivables collection period in weeks	8.0	5.1	6.5
Inventory holding period in weeks	21.0	4.0	13.0
Liquidity ratios			
Current ratio	1.8	1.7	2.8
Acid test	0.5	0.9	1.3
Debt–equity ratio %	80.0	20.0	65.0

Required:
(a) Prepare a performance report for the two companies for consideration by the directors of Chelsea plc indicating which of the two companies you consider to be a better acquisition.
(b) Indicate what further information is needed before a final decision can be made.

Question 8

The Housing Department of Chaldon District Council has invited tenders for re-roofing 80 houses on an estate. Chaldon Direct Services (CDS) is one of the Council's direct services organisations and it has submitted a tender for this contract, as have several contractors from the private sector.

The Council has been able to narrow the choice of contractor to the four tenderers who have submitted the lowest bids, as follows:

	£
Nutfield & Sons	398,600
Chaldon Direct Services	401,850
Tandridge Tilers Ltd	402,300
Redhill Roofing Contractors plc	406,500

The tender evaluation process requires that the three private tenderers be appraised on the basis of financial soundness and quality of work. These tenderers were required to provide their latest final accounts (year ended 31 March 20X4) for this appraisal; details are as follows:

	Nutfield & Sons	Tandridge Tilers Ltd	Redhill Roofing Contractors plc
Profit and loss account for year ended 31 March 20X4			
	£	£	£
Revenue	611,600	1,741,200	3,080,400
Direct costs	(410,000)	(1,190,600)	(1,734,800)
Other operating costs	(165,000)	(211,800)	(811,200)
Interest	—	(85,000)	(96,000)
Net profit before taxation	36,600	253,800	438,400
Statement of financial position as at 31 March 20X4			
	£	£	£
Non-current assets (net book value)	55,400	1,542,400	2,906,800
Inventories and work in progress	26,700	149,000	449,200
Receivables	69,300	130,800	240,600
Bank	(11,000)	10,400	(6,200)
Payables	(92,600)	(140,600)	(279,600)
Dividend declared	—	(91,800)	(70,000)
Loan	—	(800,000)	(1,200,000)
	47,800	800,200	2,040,800
Capital	47,800	—	—
Ordinary shares @ £1 each	—	250,000	1,000,000
Reserves	—	550,200	1,040,800
	47,800	800,200	2,040,800

Nutfield & Sons employ a workforce of six operatives and have been used by the Council for four small maintenance contracts worth between £60,000 and £75,000 which they have completed to an appropriate standard. Tandridge Tilers Ltd have been employed by the Council on a contract for the replacement of flat roofs on a block of flats, but there have been numerous complaints about the standard of the work. Redhill Roofing Contractors plc is a company which has not been employed by the Council in the past and, as much of its work has been carried out elsewhere, its quality of work is not known.

CDS has been suffering from the effects of increasing competition in recent years and achieved a return on capital employed of only 3.5% in the previous financial year. CDS's manager has successfully renegotiated more beneficial service-level agreements with the Council's central support departments with effect from 1 April 20X4. CDS has also reviewed its non-current asset base which has resulted in the disposal of a depot which was surplus to requirements and in the rationalisation of vehicles and plant. The consequence of this is that CDS's average capital employed for 20X4/X5 is likely to be some 15% lower than in 20X3/X4.

A further analysis of the tender bids is provided below:

	Nutfield & Sons £	Chaldon Direct Services £	Tandridge Tilers Ltd £
Labour		234,000	251,400
Materials	140,000	100,000	80,000
Overheads (including profit)	24,600	50,450	18,700

The Council's Client Services Committee can reject tenders on financial and/or quality grounds. However, each tender has to be appraised on these criteria and reasons for acceptance or rejection must be justified in the appraisal process.

Required:
In your capacity as accountant responsible for reporting to the Client Services Committee, draft a report to the Committee evaluating the tender bids and recommending to whom the contract should be awarded.

Question 9

The statements of financial position, cash flows, income and movements of non-current assets of Dragon plc for the year ended 30 September 20X6 are set out below:

(i) *Statement of financial position*

	20X5		20X6	
	£000	£000	£000	£000
Tangible non-current assets		1,200		1,160
Freehold land and buildings, at cost		700		1,700
Plant and equipment, at net book value		1,900		2,860
Current assets:				
Inventory	715		1,020	
Trade receivables	590		826	
Short-term investments	52		—	
Cash at bank and in hand	15		47	
	1,372		1,893	
Current liabilities:				
Trade payables	520		940	
Taxation payable	130		45	
Dividends payable	90		105	
	740		1,090	
Net current assets		632		803
		2,532		3,663
Long-term liability and provisions				
8% debentures, 20X9		500		1,500
Provisions for deferred tax		100		180
		1,932		1,983
Capital and reserves				
Ordinary shares of £1 each		1,400		1,400
Share premium account		250		250
Retained earnings		282		333
		1,932		1,983

(ii) *Statement of income (extract) for the year ended 30 September 20X6*

EBITDA		1,161
Depreciation		660
Operating profit		501
Interest payable: debentures		150
Profit before taxation		351
Income tax		125
Profit attributable to shareholders		226
Dividends: paid	70	
: proposed	105	175
Retained earnings for year		51
Retained earnings brought forward		282
Retained earnings carried forward		333

(iii) *Statement of cash flows*

Net cash flow from operating activities		1,033
Interest paid	(150)	
Income taxes paid	(130)	(280)
Net cash from operating activities:		753
Cash flows from investing activities		
Purchase of property, plant and equipment	(1,620)	
Net cash used in investing activities:		(1,620)
Cash flows from financing activities		
Proceeds from sale of short-term investments	59	
Proceeds from long-term borrowings	1,000	
Dividends paid	(160)	
Net cash from financing activities:		899
Net increase in cash and cash equivalents		32
Cash and cash equivalents at the beginning of the period		15
Cash and cash equivalents at the end of the period		47

(iv) *Tangible non-current assets (or PPE)*

The movements in the year were as follows:

	Freehold land and buildings £000	Plant and machinery £000	Total £000
Cost:			
At 1 October 20X5	2,000	1,600	3,600
Additions	—	1,620	1,620
At 30 September 20X6	**2,000**	**3,220**	**5,220**
Depreciation:			
At 1 October 20X5	800	900	1,700
Charge during the year	40	620	660
At 30 September 20X6	**840**	**1,520**	**2,360**
Net book value:			
Beginning of year	1,200	700	1,900
End of year	**1,160**	**1,700**	**2,860**

You are also provided with the following information:

(i) There was a debenture issue on 1 October 20X5 with interest payable on 30 September each year.

(ii) An interim dividend of £70,000 was paid on 1 July 20X6.

(iii) The short-term investment was sold for £59,000 on 1 October 20X5.

(iv) Business activity increased significantly to meet increased consumer demand.

Required:

(a) Prepare a reconciliation of operating profit to net cash inflow from operating activities.

(b) Discuss the financial developments at Dragon plc during the financial year ended 30 September 20X6 with particular regard to its financial position at the year-end and prospects for the following financial year, supported by appropriate financial ratios.

* Question 10

Amalgamated Engineering plc makes specialised machinery for several industries. In recent years, the company has faced severe competition from overseas businesses, and its sales volume has hardly changed. The company has recently applied for an increase in its bank overdraft limit from £750,000 to £1,500,000. The bank manager has asked you, as the bank's credit analyst, to look at the company's application.

You have the following information:

(i) Statements of financial position as at 31 December 20X5 and 20X6

	20X5		20X6	
	£000	£000	£000	£000
Tangible non-current assets:				
Freehold land and buildings, at cost		1,800		1,800
Plant and equipment, at net book value		3,150		3,300
		4,950		5,100
Current assets:				
Inventory	1,125		1,500	
Trade receivables	825		1,125	
Short-term investments	300		—	
	2,250		2,625	
Current liabilities:				
Bank overdraft	225		675	
Trade payables	300		375	
Taxation payable	375		300	
Dividends payable	225		225	
	1,125		1,575	
Net current assets		1,125		1,050
		6,075		6,150
Long-term liability				
8% debentures, 20X9		1,500		1,500
		4,575		4,650
Capital and reserves:				
Ordinary shares of £1 each		2,250		2,250
Share premium account		750		750
Retained earnings		1,575		1,650
		4,575		4,650

(ii) *Statements of comprehensive income for the years ended 31 December 20X5 and 20X6*

	20X5		20X6	
	£000	£000	£000	£000
Revenue		6,300		6,600
Cost of sales: materials	1,500		1,575	
: labour	2,160		2,280	
: production: overheads	750		825	
		4,410		4,680
		1,890		1,920
Administrative expenses		1,020		1,125
Operating profit		870		795
Investment income		15		—
		885		795
Interest payable: debentures	120		120	
: bank overdraft	15		75	
		135		195
Profit before taxation		750		600
Taxation		375		300
Profit attributable to shareholders		375		300
Dividends		225		225
Retained earnings for year		150		75

(iii) The general price level rose on average by 10% between 20X5 and 20X6. Average wages also rose by 10% during this period.

(iv) The debenture stock is secured by a fixed charge over the freehold land and buildings, which have recently been valued at £3,000,000. The bank overdraft is unsecured.

(v) Additions to plant and equipment in 20X6 amounted to £450,000: depreciation provided in that year was £300,000.

Required:
(a) Prepare a statement of cash flows for the year ended 31 December 20X6.
(b) Calculate appropriate ratios to use as a basis for a report to the bank manager.
(c) Draft the outline of a report for the bank manager, highlighting key areas you feel should be the subject of further investigation. Mention any additional information you need, and where appropriate refer to the limitations of conventional historical cost accounts.
(d) On receiving the draft report the bank manager advised that he also required the following three cash-based ratios:
   (i)   Debt service coverage ratio defined as EBITDA/annual debt repayments and interest.
   (ii) Cash flow from operations to current liabilities.
   (iii) Cash recovery rate defined as ((cash flow from operations proceeds from sale of non-current assets)/average gross assets) × 100.
   The director has asked you to explain why the bank manager has requested this additional information given that he has already been supplied with profit-based ratios.

CHAPTER 29

Analysis of published financial statements

29.1 Introduction

In Chapter 28 we considered the way in which we could 'make the numbers talk' from a set of published financial statements. We explained the importance of taking a 'helicopter perspective' initially and identifying key issues before focusing on specific areas of detail. We showed how powerful ratio analysis could be as an analytical tool provided the ratios were interpreted appropriately. A particularly important issue was the need to differentiate between changes to ratios that were caused by operational and business factors and changes caused by accounting policies and accounting estimates.

When we are interpreting the financial statements of an entity a key issue is the amount of financial information actually available. If we are performing an analysis on behalf of management, or a controlling shareholder, then the amount of financial information available to us is likely to be sufficient to perform any analysis we consider appropriate. On the other hand, where we are performing an analysis from a purely external perspective there will be a limit to the amount of information available to us, because published financial statements generally contain only the information that is required by the appropriate regulatory framework.

Objectives

By the end of this chapter, you should be able to:

- discuss steps taken to improve information for shareholders;
- critically discuss the limitations of published financial data as a source of useful information for interpretation purposes;
- discuss additional entity-wide cash-based performance measures;
- explain the use of ratios in determining whether a company is shariah compliant;
- explain the use of ratios in debt covenants;
- critically discuss various scoring systems for predicting corporate failure;
- critically discuss remuneration performance criteria;
- critically discuss the role of credit rating agencies;
- calculate the value of unquoted investments.

29.2 Improvement of information for shareholders

There have been a number of discussion papers, reports and voluntary code provisions from professional firms and regulators making recommendations on how to provide additional information to allow investors to form a view as to the business's future prospects by (a) making financial information more understandable and easier to analyse and (b) improving the reliability of the historical financial data. This would help ensure the equal treatment of all investors and improve accountability for stewardship.

29.2.1 Making financial information more understandable

There has been a view that users should bring a reasonable level of understanding when reading an annual report. This view could be supported when transactions were relatively simple. It no longer applies when even professional accountants comment that the only people who understand some of the disclosures are the technical staff of the regulator and the professional accounting firms.

Statutory measures

Users need the financial information to be made more accessible. This is being achieved in part by initiatives such as the Strategic Report in the UK with the requirement to publish information on the past year, including a fair review of the company's business, a description of the principal risks and uncertainties facing the company, and a balanced and comprehensive analysis of the performance of the company's business during the financial year.

As regards the future, a description of the company's strategy, a description of the company's business model and the main trends and factors likely to affect the future development, performance and position of the company's business are also required.

Need to understand volatility

There is a need on the part of investors to understand the volatility that can arise as a result of a company's strategy, such as recognising the short- and medium-term impact on earnings of R&D investment. There has been a view that investors are unhappy with an uneven profit trend and that companies have responded by smoothing earnings from year to year to maintain investor confidence.

The ICAEW report produced in 1999 *No Surprises: The Case for Better Risk Reporting* recognised the need for management to disclose their strategies and how they managed risk whilst stating that the intention was not to encourage profit-smoothing but rather a better management of risk and a better understanding by investors of volatility.

29.2.2 Making the information easier to interpret

Traditionally individual investors have referred to financial data which have been paper-based. For further analysis they have been dependent on analysts or access to the various commercial databases such as Datastream for data in electronic format for further analysis.

An increasing number of companies, for example BP, BMW, Colgate, Dell, Lloyds TSB and Vodacom, have been addressing this by providing their annual report in a multi-year downloadable Excel format.

A further advance is being achieved through the eXtensible Business Reporting Language (XBRL) which has been developed to allow information to be described uniformly and tagged. A demonstration website has been developed by Microsoft, NASDAQ and PricewaterhouseCoopers.[1] This is discussed in Chapter 30.

29.2.3 Improving the reliability of financial information

Investors rely on the fact that annual reports are audited and so present a fair view of a company's financial performance and position. However, accounting scandals, such as in Enron, Satyam and the SEC probe in 2012 into the auditing of Chinese companies, have led to a feeling that auditors are not protecting their interests. The profession is aware of this view and of the existence of an expectation gap between what investors expect from an audit and what can reasonably be delivered. This is discussed further in Chapter 31.

Reliability of narrative information in the Annual Report

The following is an indication of the work carried out by an auditor.

- Other information contained in the Annual Report is read and considered as to whether it is consistent with the audited financial statements.
- The other information comprises only the Directors' Report, the unaudited part of the Directors' Remuneration Report, the Chairman's Statement, the Operating and Financial Review and the Corporate Governance Statement.
- The implications for the audit report are considered if there is an awareness of any apparent misstatements or material inconsistencies with the financial statements.
- The responsibilities of the auditor do not extend to any other information.

29.3 Published financial statements – their limitations for interpretation purposes

Assuming that the financial statements have been audited and present a fair view, there remain limitations when attempting to analyse the statements. These can effectively be categorised under the following three headings.

Limitation 1 – Lack of detail

This limitation is due to the amount that corporate entities are required to disclose by the appropriate regulatory framework. Only that information that is required to be disclosed would be subject to objective external scrutiny through audit and that information is strictly limited. For example:

- When analysing the profitability of a corporate entity, whether gross or net profit, the extent to which expenses can be broken down into categories is strictly limited. Most current frameworks require the disclosure of cost of sales and other operating expenses but do not require further analysis. Therefore, when, say, the gross margin shows a variation (either from one period to another for single-entity comparison or between entities) we cannot further investigate the components of gross margin because the published financial statements do not provide the required detail.
- Most frameworks require analysis of expenses into a number of headings but do not prescribe exactly where certain expenses (e.g. advertising) would fit. This means that when we compare the gross margin of one corporate entity with that of another we may not be comparing like with like, because one may have treated advertising as part of cost of sales and another may have treated equivalent costs as other operating expenses and the amount could be significant.

- Lack of detailed information prevents the computation of certain useful ratios in their 'purest' from. For example, one of the ratios we discussed in Chapter 28 was 'payables days' – trade payables as a number of days' credit purchases. If we tried to compute this ratio from the published financial statements we would have a problem – credit purchases are not required to be disclosed in the published financial statements of corporate entities in most regulatory frameworks. It is possible to use cost of sales as a proxy for credit purchases. However, this 'contrived' ratio is not as useful as the ratio would be were credit purchases to be available.

Limitation 2 – The impact of unaudited information

There is a varying amount of information relating to areas such as strategy, risk and KPIs and an ongoing move for improvement. For example, an interesting report issued by the FRC in 1999, *Rising to the challenge: A Review of Narrative Reporting by UK Listed Companies*,[2] found the following:

- For KPIs, the best companies linked KPIs to strategy and provided an explanation of each measure along with some targets, reconciliations, graphical illustrations of year-on-year comparatives and tables to link KPIs to strategy and targets or future intentions. However, many reports still featured an isolated KPI table with no accompanying discussion or link to the remainder of the document.

- For principal risks, best-practice reports provided some context for the risk, indicating whether it was increasing or decreasing, and provided some idea of the impact of a risk crystallising, supported by numbers. However, users would find it difficult to assess risk where there was too little detail or too many risks identified that obscured which were important.

The approach taken in the UK to reporting strategy is discussed further in Chapter 3, Section 3.14.8.

Limitation 3 – Timeliness of information

One of the factors that makes financial information useful is its timeliness. However, the financial information published in the Annual Report is almost always backward-looking and there is an inevitable time lag between the year-end and the date the financial statements are authorised for issue, which may well be up to four months after the year-end.

Possible ways of satisfying the timeliness criterion are to publish continuously, quarterly or half-yearly.

Continuous reporting

Technologically this is achievable, particularly with the adoption of XBRL tagging discussed in Chapter 30. The advantages might be perceived as putting the investor in the same position as management. However, quite apart from the assurance consideration, the reality is that the management has a contextual understanding of the information with an awareness of the probability of possible change. The result could well be that disclosures are deliberately bland.

Quarterly reporting

Here there is a distinct difference in the views of management and investors.

Management might have a view that it is the quality of reporting that is important and increased frequency of reporting diverts management attention away from running the business. In addition, there is a view that it encourages speculative investor activity or short-termism.

Investors might have the opposite view, seeing these reports as essential to enable informed investment decisions. The degree of importance they attach to quarterly information could be influenced by the likelihood of an active investor response to receiving earlier information. Questions that influence their view at a particular point in time include those such as 'Is the company relatively stable?', 'Is the company highly geared when cash flow information might be relevant?', 'Is the company in a fast-changing market when information on product and segment performance might be important?' and 'Is the company subject to highly seasonal movements when an early indication of a change in the trend might be important?'

Half-yearly reporting

The **EU Transparency Directive** revised in 2012 proposes that listed companies should disclose annual and half-yearly financial reports and in the case of issuers of shares, interim management statements rather than quarterly reports.

An **interim statement** must include an explanation of material events and transactions in this period, their impact on the financial position of the issuer, and a description of their financial position and performance.

For **half-yearly reports** the Directive requires annual and half-yearly financial reports to include consolidated financial statements and management reports. EU listed companies will continue to publish management reports with an explanation of material events and transactions that occurred during the first six months of the financial year and their impact on the group's financial position.

29.4 Published financial statements – additional entity-wide cash-based performance measures

When making inter-firm comparisons there is the problem that accrual accounting requires a number of subjective judgements to be made such as the non-cash adjustments for depreciation, amortisation and impairment. Inter-firm comparison schemes overcome this by requiring member companies to restate their results using uniform policies such as restating non-current assets at current values and applying uniform depreciation policies.

External analysts are unable to achieve this and have, therefore, developed other performance measures, often described as non-GAAP, because they are not mandatory or uniformly defined. These measures, discussed in this section, are becoming more frequently met in published annual reports to address specific user needs.

29.4.1 EBITDA

EBITDA is fairly widely used by external analysts. It stands for 'earnings before interest, tax, depreciation and amortisation'.

EBITDA more closely reflects the cash effect of earnings by adding back depreciation and amortisation charges to the operating profit. The figure can be derived by adding back the depreciation and amortisation that is disclosed in the statement of cash flows.

By taking earnings before depreciation and amortisation we eliminate differences due to different ages of plant and equipment when making inter-period comparisons of performance and also differences arising from the use of different depreciation methods when making inter-firm comparisons.

Note that there is no standard definition – for example some companies define it as earnings before interest, depreciation, tax, amortisation, *impairment* and *exceptional items*.

EBITDA shows an approximation to the cash impact of earnings. It differs from the cash flow from operations reported in the statement of cash flows in that it is before adjustment for working capital changes.

Comparing segment performance

EBITDA information is useful where an entity has a number of segments. It allows performance to be compared by calculating the EBITDA for each segment which provides a figure that is independent of the age structure of the non-current assets.

For example, the following is an extract from the Vodafone 2011 Annual Report:

	EBITDA £m	EBITDA margin %
31 March 2011		
Germany	2,952	37.4
Italy	2,643	46.2
Spain	1,562	30.4
UK	1,233	23.4
Other Europe	2,433	
Europe	**10,823**	

Interestingly, the company states that it uses EBITDA as an operating performance measure which is reviewed by the Chief Executive to assess internal performance in conjunction with EBITDA margin, which is an alternative sales margin figure.

29.4.2 Other 'EBITDA-based' ratios commonly produced

These include the following.

EV (Enterprise value)/EBITDA

EV is the value of the whole business calculated as the market capitalisation of equity plus debt, non-controlling interest and preference shares less total cash and cash equivalents.

Assuming for the current year an EV of $199,283m and EBITDA of $29,806m, the EV/EBITDA is 6.69. This is compared to the industry average which is, say, 5.99 which indicates that the company is valued above the industry average. If the company ratio were significantly below the 5.99 it could invite the interest of a takeover. It would be normal to calculate the ratio for a period of say five years to note the trend.

Net debt/EBITDA

This ratio shows the number of years that it would take to 'pay off' the net debt. For example, the following is an extract from the AMEC 2011 Annual Report:

The group is currently in a net cash position. If debt is subsequently required, the long-term net debt is expected to be no more than two times EBITDA. The group may exceed this operating parameter should the business profile require it. However, it is expected that any increases would be temporary given the net operational cash flows of the group.

Debt service coverage ratio

This is defined as EBITDA/annual debt repayments and interest. This ratio is often used in setting debt covenants and by banks assessing a company's ability to repay debt on the terms being sought by the borrower.

EBITDA/interest

This shows the number of times interest is covered. This is also a ratio that banks set as covenant thresholds when agreeing bank credit limits. The following is an extract from the Wienerberger 2011 Annual Report:

	2010	2011	Threshold
Net debt/EBITDA	1.8	1.7	<3.50
Operating EBITDA/interest	4.9	6.8	>3.75

EBITDAR

EBITDAR is a variant of EBITDA that has become popular with analysts in recent times. It stands for 'earnings before interest, tax, depreciation, amortisation and rental expense'.

Adding this rental expense back allegedly makes performance comparisons between entities with different proportions of assets leased under operating leases more valid. It also removes the subjectivity introduced by lease classification as operating or finance.

The following is an extract from the J Sainsbury plc 2012 Annual Report:

Key financial ratios		
Adjusted net debt to EBITDAR[1]	**4.1 times**	4.1 times
Interest cover[2]	**7.5 times**	7.9 times
Fixed charge cover[3]	**3.1 times**	3.1 times
Gearing[4]	**35.2%**	33.4%

1 Net debt plus capitalised lease obligations (5.5% NPV) divided by EBITDAR.

2 Underlying profit before interest and tax divided by underlying net finance costs.

3 EBITDAR divided by net rent and underlying net finance costs.

4 Net debt divided by net assets.

EBITDAR is used as a comparator between companies. For example, Tesco plc in their 2012 Annual Report state that their fixed charge cover remained broadly flat due to increased rent offsetting their reduced interest and increase in operating cash flow. Their target was stated to be a level of cover in the band of 4 to 4.5 times. In its 2011 Annual Report Tesco plc had charted their EBITDAR against Sainsbury's and Morrisons.

EBITDARM

EBITDARM stands for 'earnings before interest, tax, depreciation, amortisation, rental expense and management fees'. The rationale behind this measure is that management fees are extracted from different entities in different proportions. The following is an example from the healthcare sector:

	Care homes for the elderly £	Mental health services £
Fee income	457m	76m
EBITDARM	132m	15m
% margin	28.8%	19.0%

Management charges may not always be totally representative of the services provided. Therefore management fees might sometimes be a form of profit extraction rather than a genuine expense and adding them back once again facilitates inter-entity comparison.

29.5 Ratio thresholds to satisfy shariah compliance

In addition to considering the range of cash-based earnings ratios, investors might also require a company to satisfy certain threshold ratios *before* making an investment. An example is seen with the ratios relevant for shariah compliance.

Shariah law is a regulatory system that is derived from the Islamic religion. Islam commands followers to avoid consumption of alcohol and pork and so adherents do not condone investments in those industries. There is screening to check that (a) business activities are not prohibited and (b) certain of the financial ratios do not exceed specified limits.

This use of ratios is included because of the growing importance of investment in shariah compliant companies. Islamic banking is gaining popularity all over the world with a forecast that investments worth $100 billion would have been made globally in this system by 2010.

There are a number of shariah indices including the Dow Jones Islamic Indexes, the FTSE Global Islamic Index Series, the FTSE SGX Shariah Index Series, the FTSE DIFX Shariah Index Series and the FTSE Bursa Malaysia Index Series. The indices include companies such as Google Inc., TOTAL SA, BP plc, Exxon Mobil Corporation, Petroleo Brasileiro, Novartis AG, Roche Holding, GlaxoSmithKline plc, BHP Billiton Ltd, Siemens AG, Samsung Eectronics, International Business Machines Corporation, Nestlé SA, and Coca-Cola.

Investors interested in establishing whether an entity is shariah compliant are assisted by the service provided by various Islamic indices where the constituent companies have been screened to confirm that they are shariah compliant with reference to the nature of the business and debt ratios.

The indices are compiled after:

- screening companies to confirm that their business activities are not prohibited (or fall within the 5% permitted threshold);
- calculating three financial ratios based on total assets; and
- calculating a dividend adjustment factor which results in more relevant benchmarks, as they reflect the total return to an Islamic portfolio net of dividend purification.

Details are provided below.

Screening

Shariah investment principles do not allow investment in entities which are directly active in, or derive more than 5% of their revenue (cumulatively) from, the following activities ('prohibited activities'):

- Alcohol: distillers, vintners and producers of alcoholic beverages, including producers of beer and malt liquors, owners and operators of bars and pubs.
- Tobacco: cigarettes and other tobacco products manufacturers and retailers.
- Pork-related products: companies involved in the manufacture and retail of pork products.
- Conventional financial services – an extensive range including commercial banks, investment banks, insurance companies, consumer finance such as credit cards, and leasing.
- Defence/weapons: manufacturers of military aerospace and defence equipment, parts or products, including defence electronics and space equipment.
- Gambling/casinos: owners and operators of casinos and gaming facilities, including companies providing lottery and betting services.
- Music: producers and distributors of music, owners and operators of radio broadcasting systems.
- Hotels: owners and operators of hotels.

Key ratios

Shariah investment principles do not allow investment in companies deriving significant income from interest or companies that have excessive leverage. MSCI Barra uses the following three financial ratios to screen for these companies:

● total debt over total assets;

● sum of an entity's cash and interest-bearing securities over total assets;

● sum of an entity's accounts receivables and cash over total assets.

None of the financial ratios may exceed 33.33%.

Dividend adjustment (or 'purification')

If an entity does derive part of its total income from interest income and/or from prohibited activities, shariah investment principles state that this proportion must be deducted from the dividend paid out to shareholders and given to charity.

Dividend purification may be calculated by dividing prohibited income (including interest income) by total income and multiplying by the dividend received. An alternative is to divide total prohibited income (including interest income) by the number of shares issued at the end of the period and multiply by the number of shares held. MSCI Barra applies a 'dividend adjustment factor' to all reinvested dividends.

The 'dividend adjustment factor' is defined as:

$$\frac{\text{Total earnings} - (\text{Income from prohibited activities} + \text{Interest income})}{\text{Total earnings}}$$

In this formula, total earnings are defined as gross income, and interest income is defined as operating and non–operating interest.

29.6 Use of ratios in restrictive loan covenants

Whereas the shariah compliance criteria apply *before* making a financial commitment, lenders might set specific threshold ratios that a company must comply with *after* making a loan in order to limit the lender's risk – these are described as affirmative or negative debt covenants.

When a corporate entity borrows, the borrowing agreement often includes a provision which requires that specified accounting ratios such as gearing (relationship between debt and equity) of the entity be kept below a certain level. The loan agreement would of course have to specify exactly how any ratio is computed for this purpose.

The existence of a debt covenant or covenants has a number of potential implications for an entity and for analysts:

● An entity with a debt covenant that is close to its limit will be unable to raise funds by borrowing, so it will need to raise any required funds by an equity issue. Given the attitude of investors to risk, the return required by equity shareholders in a highly geared entity will be higher than that of an entity in which the gearing is lower. This will affect the overall amount of funding an entity can raise.

● Where a ratio of an entity subject to a debt covenant approaches the limit set out in the covenant, there is an inevitable temptation for the preparers to ensure the ratio is kept within the limit, leading to a potential temptation to misstate the financial statements.

The potential existence of a debt covenant is a factor that should be borne in mind by external analysts. The problem is that the existence of such debt covenants is not normally a required disclosure by relevant regulatory frameworks. Therefore a concerned analyst would need to attempt to obtain this information from the management of the entity. The success or otherwise of this attempt will depend on the bargaining power of the analyst.

29.6.1 Affirmative and negative covenants

Lenders may require borrowers to do certain things by affirmative covenants or refrain from doing certain things by negative covenants.

Affirmative covenants may, for example, include requiring the borrower to:

● provide quarterly and annual financial statements;
● remain within certain ratios whilst ensuring that each agreed ratio is not so restrictive that it impairs normal operations:
  – maintain a current ratio of not less than an agreed ratio – say 1.6 to 1;
  – maintain a ratio of total liabilities to tangible net worth at an agreed rate – say no greater than 2.5 to 1;
  – maintain tangible net worth in excess of an agreed amount – say £1 million;
● maintain adequate insurance.

Negative covenants may, for example, include requiring the borrower *not* to:

● grant any other charges over the company's assets;
● repay loans from related parties without prior approval;
● change the group structure by acquisitions, mergers or divestment without prior agreement.

29.6.2 What happens if a company is in breach of its debt covenants?

Borrowers will normally have prepared forecasts to assure themselves and the lenders that compliance is reasonably feasible. Such forecasts will also normally include the worst-case scenario, e.g. taking account of seasonal fluctuations that may trigger temporary violations with higher borrowing required to cover higher levels of inventory and trade receivables.

If any violation has occurred, the lender has a range of options, such as:

● amending the covenant, e.g. accepting a lower current ratio; or
● granting a waiver period when the terms of the covenant are not applied; or
● renegotiating the credit facility and restructuring the finance, as in the following extract from the 2009 Annual Report of Sunshine Holdings 3 Ltd:

> . . . The Group faces more restrictive financial covenants . . . the directors believe it is likely that the Group will not meet the financial covenants required under the first lien credit agreement.
>
> **Directors' report**
> While the directors fully expect to resolve the covenant issues with a restructuring and/or amendment to the facility agreements, these circumstances represent a material uncertainty regarding the Group's going concern status. . . . the directors have a reasonable expectation that the Group will satisfactorily conclude its covenant issues and will have adequate resources to continue in operational existence for the foreseeable future. Therefore the accounts have been prepared on a going concern basis.

In addition, companies may increase their equity capital, possibly by a rights issue as the current shareholders have a greater incentive to provide additional capital than new investors.

For example, it was reported in 2012 that Lonmin planned a $800m rights issue to avoid possibly breaching its covenants. A rights issue is often made in these circumstances as existing shareholders have a greater incentive than new shareholders to inject further equity capital.

In times of recession a typical reaction is for companies to also take steps to reduce their operating costs, align production with reduced demand, tightly control their working capital and reduce discretionary capital expenditure.

29.6.3 Risk of aggressive earnings management

In 2001, before the collapse of Enron, there was a consensus amongst respondents to the UK Auditing Practices Board Consultation Paper *Aggressive Earnings Management* that aggressive earnings management was a significant threat and actions should be taken to diminish it. It was considered that aggressive earnings management could occur to increase earnings in order to avoid losses, to meet profit forecasts, to ensure compliance with loan covenants and when directors' and managements' remuneration were linked to earnings. It could also occur to reduce earnings to reduce tax liabilities or to allow profits to be smoothed.

In 2004, as a part of the *Information for Better Markets* initiative, the Audit and Assurance Faculty commissioned a survey[3] to check whether views had changed since 2001. This showed that the vulnerability of corporate reporting to manipulation is perceived as being always with us but at a lower level following the greater awareness and scrutiny by non-executive directors and audit committees.

The analysts interviewed in the survey believed the potential for aggressive earnings management varied from sector to sector, e.g. in the older, more established sectors followed by the same analysts for a number of years, they believed that company management would find it hard to disguise anything aggressive even if they wanted to. However, this was not true of newer sectors (e.g. IT) where the business models may be loss-making initially and imperfectly understood. This is illustrated by the developments in the business models for social networking with Facebook, YouTube and Twitter.[4]

Whilst analysts and journalists tend to have low confidence in the reported earnings where there are pressures to manipulate, there is a research report[5] which paints a rather more optimistic picture. This report aimed to assess the level of confidence investors had in different sources of company information, including audited financial information, when making investment decisions. As far as audited financial information was concerned, the levels of confidence in UK audited financial information amongst UK and US investors remained very high, with 87% of UK respondents having either a 'great deal' or a 'fair amount' of confidence in UK audited financial information.

The auditing profession continues to respond to the need to contain aggressive earnings management. This is not easy because it requires a detailed understanding not only of the business but also of the process management follow when making their estimates. ISA 540 Revised, *Auditing Accounting Estimates, including Fair Value Accounting Estimates, and Related Disclosures*, requires auditors to exercise greater rigour and scepticism and to be particularly aware of the cumulative effect of estimates which in themselves fall within a normal range but which, taken together, are misleading.

29.6.4 Audit implications when there is a breach of a debt covenant

Auditors are required to bring a healthy scepticism to their work. This applies particularly at times such as when there is a potential debt covenant breach. There may then well be a temptation to manipulate to avoid reporting a breach. This will depend on the specific covenant, e.g. if the current ratio is likely to fall below the agreed figure, management might be more optimistic when setting inventory obsolescence and accounts receivable provisions and assessing the probability of contingent liabilities crystallising.

29.6.5 Impact on share price

If there is a risk of bank covenants being breached, there can be a significant adverse effect on the share price. For example, it was reported in 2012 that Lonmin's share price dropped sharply by 4.6%, a new 52-week low for the company, following the announcement that it may be in the breach of its covenants with its financial lenders.

However, both the company and the lender might prefer to keep potential breaches private unless there is a risk that enforced disclosure is imminent.

29.7 Investor-specific ratios

The analysis we carried out in Chapter 28 (and the additional performance measures we discussed in Section 29.4 above) was done from the perspective of the performance and position of the entity. In this section we will focus on additional ratios and measures that have as their focus the position of the shareholders of the entity. Some of these measures are 'financial statement measures' and others are 'market-based measures'.

29.7.1 Return on investment

We discussed ROE in Chapter 28 so this section is included as a brief reminder. In Chapter 28 we stated that a primary entity profitability measure is 'Return on investment', i.e. 'Profit'/Capital employed. Where the focus is on the equity shareholders the applicable ratio is ROE where the numerator is the post-tax profit.

If capital employed is funded by sources other than equity, then there is a financial leverage impact on the ROCE when calculating the ROE to reflect the potential benefit to equity shareholders of the company borrowing and investing at a higher rate.

As far as the equity shareholders are concerned, it might appear that the higher the financial leverage the better. However:

- If borrowings are high, it might be difficult to obtain additional loans to take advantage of new opportunities. For example, HSBC raised £12.5 billion in 2009 by a rights issue on the basis that this would give the bank a competitive advantage over its rivals by restoring its position as having the strongest statement of financial position, i.e. high borrowings limit a company's flexibility.

- Interest has to be paid even in bad years with the risk that loan creditors could put the company into administration if interest is not paid.

The relationship is illustrated using data from the financial statements of Vertigo plc for the year ended 31 December 20X9 presented in Section 28.3.1:

	£000
Total assets	4,587
Equity	3,353
Pre-tax profit	116
Tax	25
Sales	3,461

There were 3 million shares in issue. The effect on ROE and EPS is calculated as follows:

Pre-tax margin (3.35%) × Asset turnover (0.755) = Return on assets (2.53%)
    (116/3,461)   (3,461/4,587)

Return on assets (2.53%) × Leverage (1.37) × (1− tax rate) (0.785) = ROE (2.72)
                (4,587/3,353)   (1 − 0.215)

ROE (2.72) × Book value (1.12) = EPS (3.05)
    (3,353/3,000)

29.7.2 Price/earnings (PE) ratio

The PE ratio is computed as:

$$\frac{\text{Market value of a share}}{\text{Earnings per share}}$$

The PE ratio is a market-based measure and a high ratio indicates that investors are relatively confident in the maintainability and quality of the earnings of the entity. Entities in certain sectors (e.g. the retail sector) tend to have higher PE ratios than in other sectors (e.g. the construction sector). Higher PE ratios imply a greater level of market confidence, which usually means that (given the attitude an average investor takes to risk) the entity with a higher PE ratio operates in a sector which is less cyclical.

We will see in Section 29.11 that competitor or industry PE ratios (or its reciprocal, the earnings yield) are used as a base for valuing shares in unquoted companies – comparators being obtained from trade association schemes or sites such as http://biz.yahoo.com/p/industries.html.

Earnings yield

This is the reciprocal of the PE ratio. For example, a PE ratio of 10 becomes an earnings yield of 10% (1/10 × 100).

29.7.3 Earnings per share (EPS)

EPS is computed as:

$$\frac{\text{Profit attributable to the ordinary (equity) shareholders}}{\text{Weighted average number of ordinary shares in issue during the period}}$$

The detailed calculation of basic and diluted EPS was dealt with in Chapter 27.

EPS could be said to be a more reliable indicator of the true trend in profitability than the actual profit numbers because the denominator of the fraction factors in any change in the issued capital during the period. The fact that the weighted average number is used removes the potential inconsistency that arises when dividing a 'period' number like profit by a 'point of time' number like the number of shares.

However, remember that its appropriateness as a performance measure is based on the reliability and subjectivity of the financial statements themselves. This is an important point to remember if directors' remuneration is based on the growth in EPS. Looking at calculation of the EPS of 3.05 (rounded) we can see that it is affected by the profit margin, the rate of asset turnover, the leverage, the tax rate and the number of shares – quite apart from the fact that reducing the discretionary expenditure and simply buying back one-sixth of the shares can lift the EPS by more than 10%.

29.7.4 Dividend cover

Dividend cover is computed as:

$$\frac{\text{Profit for the period}}{\text{Dividends paid}} \quad \text{or} \quad \frac{\text{EPS}}{\text{Dividend per share}}$$

Dividend cover is a measure of the vulnerability of the dividend to a fall in profits. The legality of a dividend payment is normally based on cumulative profits rather than the profits for a single period, but in practice an entity would wish the dividend declared for a particular period to be 'covered' by profits made in that period. Therefore this ratio is seen as a measure of the 'security' of the dividend.

An issue with this ratio is whether a high dividend cover is good or bad. In one sense, a shareholder might be content with a high dividend cover, because this would mean that profits could potentially fall quite significantly without the dividend necessarily falling, and retained earnings are being employed profitably within the company. Alternatively, a shareholder might feel disgruntled that the dividend itself is not higher. Therefore conclusions about whether a change in dividend cover is 'good' or 'bad' need to be made with caution – the trend and inter-firm comparators from the same industry need to be looked at. For example, some companies may target the rate of dividend cover as a key performance indicator as shown in the following extract from the Morrisons 2011 Annual Report:

> Our aim is that dividend cover will be the same as the average for the European food retail sector. Our dividend cover is 2.4 times, in line with the European food retail sector average. This has resulted in dividend growth of 17%.

29.7.5 Dividend yield

Dividend yield is computed as:

$$\frac{\text{Dividend per share}}{\text{Market value of a share}} \text{(expressed as a percentage)}$$

This ratio measures the 'effective' current investment by the shareholder in the entity, because by deciding to keep the share rather than dispose of it the shareholder is forgoing an amount that would be available were the shareholder to make a disposal decision.

This ratio is a 'market-based' ratio, because it is influenced by the share price of the entity. We need to interpret any 'market-based' ratio with caution. In this case a high dividend yield could mean that the shareholder is receiving a very healthy dividend (which would be very positive) or that the share price was very low (which would clearly not be a desirable position either for the entity or for the shareholder).

Indeed, in times of disappointing prices on securities markets dividend yields often tend to be very high because entities are reluctant to cut their dividends for fear the share price will fall even further. A combination of a static dividend and falling share prices leads inevitably to a rise in dividend yields. This would become more apparent if dividend growth were considered in addition to dividend yield.

29.8 Determining value

There are three aspects to consider. One is to assess from an entity viewpoint whether adequate returns (EVA) are being generated, the other is to assess from a shareholder's viewpoint the total shareholder return (TSR), and the third is how either is used in setting directors' remuneration.

29.8.1 Economic Value Added (EVA)

Companies are increasingly becoming aware that investors need to be confident that the company can deliver above-average rates of return, i.e. achieve growth, and that communication is the key. This is why companies are using the annual report to provide shareholders and potential shareholders with a measure of the company's performance that will give them confidence to maintain or make an investment in the company. This is the view expressed in the 2009 Annual Report of Geveke nv Amsterdam:

> A positive EVA indicates that over a specific period economic value has been created. Net operating profit after tax is then greater than the cost of finance (i.e. the company's weighted average cost of capital). Research has shown that a substantial part of the long-term movement in share price is explained by the development of EVA. The concept of EVA can be a very good method of performance measurement and monitoring of decisions.

29.8.2 Formula for calculating economic value added

The formula applied by Geveke is as follows:

> EVA measures economic value achieved over a specific period. It is equal to net operating profit after tax (NOPAT), corrected for the cost of capital employed (the sum of interest bearing liabilities and shareholders' equity). The cost of capital employed is the required yield (R) times capital employed (CE).
> In the form of a formula: $NOPAT - (R \times CE) = EVA$

We will illustrate the formula for Alpha nv, which has the following data (in euros):

	31 March 20X3	31 March 20X4	31 March 20X5
NOPAT	10m	11m	12.5m
Weighted average cost of capital (WACC)	12%	11.5%	11%
Capital employed	70m	77m	96m

The EVA is:

	Percentage change
31 March 20X3: EVA = 10m − (12% of 70m) = 1.6m	—
31 March 20X4: EVA = 11m − (11.5% of 77m) = 2.145m	34%
31 March 20X5: EVA = 12.5m − (11% of 96m) = 1.94m	(10%)

The formula allows weight to be given to the capital employed to generate operating profit. The percentage change is an important management tool in that the annual increase is seen as the created value rather than the absolute level, i.e. the 34% is the key figure rather than the 2.145 million. Further enquiry is necessary to assess how well Alpha nv will employ the increase in capital employed in future periods.

It is useful to calculate rate of change over time. However, as for all inter-company comparisons of ratios, it is necessary to identify how the WACC and capital employed have been defined. This may vary from company to company.

WACC calculation

This figure depends on the capital structure and risk in each country in which a company has a significant business interest. For example, the following is an extract from the 2003 Annual Report of the Orkla Group:

Capital structure and cost of capital
The Group's average cost of capital is calculated as a weighted average of the costs of borrowed capital and equity. The calculations are based on an equity-to-total-assets ratio of 60%. The cost of equity is calculated with the help of the Capital Asset Pricing Model. The cost of borrowed capital is based on a long-term, weighted interest rate for relevant countries in which Orkla operates . . .

The table shows how Orkla's average cost of capital is calculated:

Description	Rates	Relative %	Weighted cost
Weighted average beta	1.0		
× Market risk premium	4.0%		
= Risk premium for equity	4.0%		
+ Risk free long-term interest rate	4.9%		
= Cost of equity	8.9%	60%	5.3%
Imputed borrowing rate before tax	5.9%		
Imputed tax charge	28%		
= Imputed borrowing rate after tax	4.2%	40%	1.7%
WACC after tax			7.0%

In 2012 Orkla's WACC was 10%.

Capital employed definition

The norm is to exclude non-interest-bearing liabilities including current liabilities when determining net total assets. However, there are variations in the treatment of intangible assets, e.g. goodwill may be excluded from the net assets or included at book value or included, as by Koninklijke Wessanen, at market value rather than the historically paid goodwill.

29.8.3 Achieving increases in EVA

EVA can be improved in three ways: by increasing NOPAT, reducing WACC and/or improving the utilisation of capital employed.

● Increasing NOPAT: this is achieved by optimising strategic choices by comparing the cash flows arising from different strategic opportunities, e.g. appraising geographic and product segmental information, cost reduction programmes, appraising acquisitions and divestments.

● Reducing WACC: this is achieved by reviewing the manner in which a company is financed, e.g. determining a favourable gearing ratio and reducing the perceived risk factor by a favourable spread of products and markets.

● Improving the utilisation of capital employed: this is achieved by consideration of activity ratios, e.g. non-curent asset turnover, working capital ratio.

29.8.4 Management attitude to use of EVA

One study[6] identified a number of companies that used value-based measures at head office level, but retained traditional profit measures in their divisions. KPMG, in a 1995 survey of value-based management, described this type of company as 'light users', who report overall results in value-based terms but retain traditional measures within their performance measurement systems.

Turning EVA into a comparative ratio

A new metric has been developed described as EVA Momentum.[7] This relates the change in the EVA £ value to the previous period's sales. The formula is

$$\text{EVA Momentum} = \frac{\text{EVA}^{\text{Period 2}} - \text{EVA}^{\text{Period 1}}}{\text{Revenue}^{\text{Period 1}}}$$

Companies are now being ranked by EVA momentum and it is reported[8] that because it is based on the change in EVA rather than the level, EVA momentum captures profitability performance where it matters most – at the margin. Companies that are losing money but cut their losses dramatically score well on EVA momentum. In contrast, and as you will see, even extremely profitable companies can score poorly on this performance measure if their economic profits are static or declining. As a result, EVA momentum is a great measure for spotting turning points in performance.

29.8.5 Total shareholder return approach

Shareholder value (SV)

It has been a long-standing practice for analysts to arrive at shareholder value of a share by calculating the internal rate of return (IRR %) on an investment from the dividend stream and realisable value of the investment at date of disposal, i.e. taking account of dividends received and capital gains. However, it is not a generic measure in that the calculation is specific to each shareholder. The reason for this is that the dividends received will depend on the length of period the shares are held and the capital gain achieved will depend on the share price at the date of disposal – and, as we know, the share price can move significantly even over a week.

For example, consider the SV for each of the three shareholders, Miss Rapid, Mr Medium and Miss Undecided, who each invested £10,000 on 1 January 20X6 in Spacemobile Ltd which pays a dividend of £500 on these shares on 31 December each year. Miss Rapid sold her shares on 31 December 20X7. Mr Medium sold his on 31 December 20X9, whereas Miss Undecided could not decide what to do with her shares. The SV for each shareholder is as follows:

Shareholder	Date acquired	Investment at cost	Dividends amount (total)	Date of disposal	Sale proceeds	IRR%
Miss Rapid	1.1.20X6	10,000	1,000	31.12.20X7	11,000	10%*
Mr Medium	1.1.20X6	10,000	2,000	31.12.20X9	15,000	15%
Miss Undecided	1.1.20X6	10,000	2,000	Undecided		

* $(500 \times .9091) + (11,500 \times .8265) - 10,000 = 0$

We can see that Miss Rapid achieved a shareholder value of 10% on her shares and Mr Medium, by holding until 31.12.20X9, achieved an increased capital gain raising the SV to 15%. We do not have the information as to how Miss Rapid invested from 1.1.20X8 and so we cannot evaluate her decision – it depends on the subsequent investment and the economic value added by that new company.

29.8.6 Total shareholder return

Miss Undecided has a notional SV at 31.12.20X9 of 15% as calculated for Mr Medium. However, this has not been realised and, if the share price changed the following day, the SV would be different. The notional 15% calculated for Miss Undecided is referred to as the total shareholder return (TSR) – it takes into account market expectation on the assumption that share prices reflect all available information but it is dependent on the assumption made about the length of the period the shares are held.

29.8.7 Performance-based remuneration using EVA and TSR

EVA and managers' performance

In some organisations EVA has been used as a basis for determining bonus payments made to managers. There is some evidence that managers rewarded under such a scheme do perform better than those operating under more traditional schemes. However, research[9] indicated that this occurs when managers understand the concept of EVA and that it is not universally appropriate as other factors need to be taken into account such as the area of the firm in which a manager is employed. The following is an extract from the ThyssenKrupp 2009 Annual Report:

> This management and controlling system is linked to the bonus system in such a way that the amount of the performance-related remuneration is determined by the achieved EVA.

However, there is a risk that this approach can encourage short-termism by focusing on annual targets.

TSR and managers' performance

TSR has been used for performance monitoring, as a criterion for performance-based remuneration and to satisfy statutory requirements.

Performance monitoring
TSR has been used by companies to monitor their performance by comparing their own TSR with that of comparator companies. It is also used to set strategic targets. For example, Unilever set itself a TSR target in the top third of a reference group of 21 international consumer goods companies. Unilever calculates the TSR over a three-year rolling period which it considers 'sensitive enough to reflect changes but long enough to smooth out short-term volatility'.

Statutory requirement
The Directors' Report Regulations 2002 now require a line graph to be prepared showing such a comparison. Marks & Spencer Group's 2012 Annual Report contained the following:

> **Total shareholder return performance graph**
> The graph illustrates the performance of the Company against the FTSE 100 over the past five years. The FTSE 100 has been chosen as it is a recognised broad equity market index of which the Company has been a member throughout the period.

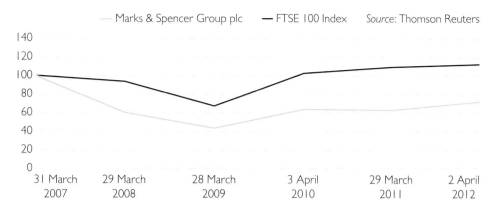

Management and investors assess a company's performance based on the use of ratios described in Chapter 28 and earlier in the present chapter. This follows the pyramid approach of starting with the ROE and drilling down to identify possible causes of change.

The models that attempt to predict corporate failure combine selected ratios to produce a single-figure score. There are a number of such models and we will discuss a selection.

29.9 Predicting corporate failure

In the preceding chapter we extolled the virtues of ratio analysis for the interpretation of financial statements. However, ratio analysis is an excellent indicator only when applied properly. Unfortunately, a number of limitations impede its proper application. How do we know which ratios to select for the analysis of company accounts? Which ratios can be combined to produce an informative end-result? How should individual ratios be ranked to give the user an overall picture of company performance? How reliable are all the ratios – can users place more reliance on some ratios than others? We will consider which ratios have been selected to produce Z-scores and H-scores.

Z-score analysis can be employed to overcome some of the limitations of traditional ratio analysis. It evaluates corporate stability and, more importantly, predicts potential instances of corporate failure. All the forecasts and predictions are based on publicly available financial statements.[10] The aim is to identify potential failures so that 'the appropriate action to reverse the process [of failure] can be taken before it is too late'.[11]

29.9.1 What are Z-scores?

Inman[12] describes what Z-scores are designed for:

> Z-scores attempt to replace various independent and often unreliable and misleading historical ratios and subjective rule-of-thumb tests with scientifically analysed ratios which can reliably predict future events by identifying benchmarks above which 'all's well' and below which there is imminent danger.

Z-scores provide a single-value score to describe the combination of a number of key characteristics of a company. Some of the most important predictive ratios are weighted according to perceived importance and then summed to give the single Z-score. This is then evaluated against the identified benchmark.

The two best known Z-scores are Altman's Z-score and Taffler's Z-score.

Altman's Z-score

The original Z-score equation was devised by Professor Altman in 1968 and developed further in 1977.[13] The original equation is:

$$Z = 0.012X_1 + 0.014X_2 + 0.033X_3 + 0.006X_4 + 0.999X_5$$

where:

X_1 = Working capital/Total assets
(Liquid assets are being measured in relation to the business's size and this may be seen as a better predictor than the current and acid test ratios which measure the interrelationships within working capital. For X_1 the more relative Working Capital, the more liquidity.)

X_2 = Retained earnings/Total assets
(In early years the proportion of retained earnings used to finance the total asset base may be quite low and the length of time the business has been in existence has been seen as a factor in insolvency. In later years the more earnings that are retained the more funds that could be available to pay creditors. X_2 also acts as an indication of a company's dividend policy – a high dividend payout reduces the retained earnings with impact on solvency and creditors' position.)

X_3 = Earnings before interest and tax (EBIT)/Total assets
(Adequate operating profit is fundamental to the survival of a business.)

X_4 = Market capitalisation/Book value of debt
(This is an attempt to include market expectations which may be an early warning as to possible future problems. Solvency is less likely to be threatened if shareholders' interest is relatively high in relation to the total debt.)

X_5 = Sales/Total assets
(This indicates how assets are being used. If efficient, then profits available to meet interest payments are more likely. It is a measure that might have been more appropriate when Altman was researching companies within the manufacturing sector. It is a relationship that varies widely between manufacturing sectors and even more so within knowledge-based companies.)

Altman identified two benchmarks. Companies scoring over 3.0 are unlikely to fail and should be considered safe, while companies scoring under 1.8 are very likely to fail. The value of 3.0 has since been revised down to 2.7.[14] Z-scores between 2.7 and 1.8 fall into the grey area. The 1968 work is claimed to be able to distinguish between successes and failures up to two or three years before the event. The 1977 work claims an improved prediction period of up to five years before the event.

The Zeta model

This was a model developed by Altman and Zeta Services, Inc. in 1977. It is the same as the Z-score for identifying corporate failure one year ahead but it is more accurate in identifying potential failure in the period two to five years ahead. The model is based on the following variables:

X_1 return on assets:	earnings before interest and tax/total assets;
X_2 stability of earnings:	normalised return on assets around a five- to ten-year trend;
X_3 interest cover:	earnings before interest and tax/total interest;
X_4 cumulative profitability:	retained earnings/total assets;
X_5 liquidity:	the current ratio;
X_6 capitalisation:	equity/total market value;
X_7 size:	total tangible assets.

Zeta is available as a subscription service and the coefficients have not been published.

Taffler's Z-score

The exact definition of Taffler's Z-score[11,15] is unpublished, but the following components form the equation:

$$Z = c_0 + c_1 X_1 + c_2 X_2 + c_3 X_3 + c_4 X_4$$

where
X_1 = Profit before tax/Current assets (53%)
X_2 = Current assets/Current liabilities (13%)
X_3 = Current liabilities/Total assets (18%)
X_4 = No credit interval = Length of time which the company can continue to finance its operations using its own assets with no revenue inflow (16%)

In the equation, c_0 to c_4 are the coefficients, and the percentages in brackets represent the ratios' contributions to the power of the model.

The benchmark used to detect success or failure is 0.2.[14] Companies scoring above 0.2 are unlikely to fail, while companies scoring less than 0.2 demonstrate the same symptoms as companies that have failed in the past.

PAS-score: performance analysis score

Taffler adapted the Z-score technique to develop the PAS-score. The PAS-score evaluates company performance relative to other companies in the industry and incorporates changes in the economy.

The PAS-score ranks all company Z-scores in percentile terms, measuring relative performance on a scale of 0 to 100. A PAS-score of X means that $100 - X\%$ of the companies have scored higher Z-scores. So, a PAS-score of 80 means that only 20% of the companies in the comparison have achieved higher Z-scores.

The PAS-score details the relative performance trend of a company over time. Any downward trends should be investigated immediately and the management should take appropriate action.

SMEs and failure prediction

The effectiveness of applying a failure prediction model is not restricted to large companies. This is illustrated by research[16] conducted in New Zealand where such a model was applied to 185 SMEs and found to be useful. As with all models, it is also helpful to refer to other supplementary information that may be available, e.g. other credit reports, credit managers' assessments and trade magazines.

29.9.2 H-scores

An H-score is produced by Company Watch to determine overall financial health. The H-score is an enhancement of the Z-score technique in giving more emphasis to the strength of the statement of financial position. The Company Watch system calculates a score ranging from 0 to 100 with below 25 being in the danger zone. It takes into account profit management, asset management and funding management using seven factors: profit from the statement of income; three factors from the asset side of the statement of financial position, namely current asset cover, inventory and trade receivables management and liquidity; and three factors from the liability side of the statement of financial position, namely equity base, debt dependence and current funding.

The factors are taken from published financial statements, which makes the approach taken by the IASB to bring off-balance-sheet transactions onto the statement of financial position particularly important.

The ability to chart each factor against the sector average and to 25 level criteria over a five-year period means that it is valuable for a range of user needs, from trade creditors considering extending or continuing to allow credit to potential lenders and equity investors and the big four accounting firms in reviewing audit risk. The model also has the ability to process 'what-ifs'.

It appears to be a robust, useful and exciting tool for all user groups. It is not simply a tool for measuring risk. It can also be used by investors to identify companies whose share price might have fallen but which might be financially strong with the possibility of the share price recovering – it can indicate 'buy' situations. It is also used by leading firms of accountants for the purpose of targeting companies in need of turnaround. Further information appears on the company's website at www.companywatch.net which includes additional examples.

29.9.3 A-scores

A-scores concentrate on non-financial signs of failure.[17] This method sets out to quantify different judgemental factors.

Management defects and strategic mistakes

The whole basis of the analysis is that financial difficulties are the direct result of management defects and strategic mistakes which can be evidenced by symptoms. A weighting is then attached to individual defects and mistakes.

For example, in looking at management defects a weighting system might be applied such as:

	Weight
Defects in operational management:	
The chief executive is an autocrat	8
The chief executive is also the chairman	4
The board is unbalanced, e.g. too few with finance experience	2
Defects in financial management:	
There are no budgets for budgetary control	3
Weak finance director	3
There is a poor response to change, e.g. out-of-date plant, old-fashioned products, poor marketing	15

To calculate a company A-score, different scores are allocated to each defect, mistake and symptom according to their importance. Then this score is compared with the benchmark values. If companies achieve an overall score of over 25, or a defect score of over 10, or a mistakes score of over 15, then the company is demonstrating typical signs leading up to failure. Generally, companies not at risk will score below 18, and companies which are at risk will score well over 25.

Symptoms

With an adverse A-score, symptoms of failure will start to arise. These are directly attributable to preceding management mistakes. Typical symptoms are financial signs (e.g. poor ratios, poor Z-scores); creative accounting (management might attempt to 'disguise' signs of failure in the accounts); non-financial signs (e.g. investment decisions delayed; market share drops); and terminal signs (when the financial collapse of the company is imminent).

It is interesting to see the weighting given to the chief executive being an autocrat, which is supported by the experience in failures such as WorldCom in 2002 with the following comment:[18]

'Autocratic style'

WorldCom pursued an aggressive strategy under Ebbers . . . In 1998, Ebbers cemented his reputation when Worldcom purchased MCI for $40bn – the largest acquisition in corporate history at that time . . . But according to one journalist in Mississippi who followed Worldcom from its inception, the seeds of the disaster were sown from the start by Ebbers' aggressive autocratic management style.

However, there are also limitations to participative management which could lead to slow reaction to change in a fast-moving environment.[19]

29.9.4 Failure prediction combining cash flow and accrual data

There is a continuing interest in identifying variables which have the ability to predict the likelihood of corporate failure – particularly if this only requires a small number of variables. One study[20] indicated that a parsimonious model that included only three financial variables, namely a cash flow, a profitability and a financial leverage variable, was accurate in 83% of the cases in predicting corporate failure one year ahead.

29.10 Professional risk assessors

Credit agencies such as Standard & Poor and Moody's Investor Services assist investors, lenders and trade creditors by providing a credit rating service. Companies are given a rating that can range from AAA for companies with a strong capacity to meet their financial commitments down to D for companies that have been unable to make contractual payments or have filed for bankruptcy, with more than 10 ratings in between, e.g. BBB for companies that have adequate capacity but which are vulnerable to internal or external economic changes.

29.10.1 How are ratings set?

The credit agencies take a broad range of internal company and external factors into account. Internal company factors may include:

- an appraisal of the financial reports to determine:
  - trading performance, e.g. return on equity (ROE) and return on assets (ROA); earnings volatility; how well a company has coped with business cycles and severe competition;
  - cash flow adequacy, e.g. EBITDA interest cover; EBIT interest cover; free operating cash flow;
  - capital structure, e.g. gearing ratio; any off-balance-sheet financing;
- a consideration of the notes to the accounts to determine possible adverse implications, e.g. contingent liabilities, whether company is fixed capital or working capital intensive, heavy capital investment commitments;
- meetings and discussions with management;
- monitoring expectation, e.g. against quarterly reports, company press releases, profit warnings;
- monitoring changes in company strategy, e.g. changes to funding structure with company buyback of shares, new divestment or acquisition plans and implications for any debt covenants.

However, experience with companies such as Enron makes it clear that off-balance-sheet transactions can make appraisal difficult even for professional agencies if companies continue to avoid transparency in their reporting.

External factors may include:

- growth prospects, e.g. trends in industry sector; technology possible changes; peer comparison;
- competitors, e.g. the major domestic and foreign competitors; product differentiation; barriers to entry;
- keeping a watching brief on macroeconomic factors, e.g. environmental statutory levies, tax changes, political changes such as restrictions on the supply of oil, foreign currency risks.

29.10.2 Regulation of credit rating agencies

Since the credit crisis there has been severe criticism that credit rating agencies had not been independent when rating financial products. The agencies have been self-regulated but this has been totally inadequate in curtailing conflicts of interest. The conflicts have arisen because they were actively involved in the design of products (collateralised debt obligations) to which they then gave an 'objective' credit rating which did not clearly reflect the true risks associated with investing in them. This conflict of interest was compounded by the fact that (a) agency staff were free to join a company after rating its products, and (b) the companies issuing the products paid their fees.

The following swingeing comments were made by the ACCA:[18]

Regulation of credit agencies
It's a joke that an industry with such influence, particularly during the current volatile economic climate, is self-regulated and only subject to a toothless voluntary code of conduct.

The mere fact that credit rating agencies are paid by the companies they rate puts their independence in jeopardy . . . greater transparency is required . . . We have to strike the right balance when regulating the market between protecting and over-burdening. A range of measures is necessary to bring about transparency in the ratings process . . . Regulation would be part of the solution, but it can't be used in isolation . . . This is a perfect example for when an international set of regulations and other measures are imperative to regain trust in financial markets and avoid further credit crunched victims.

This has led to a call for both Europe and the US to regulate the agencies.

European Commission Agency Regulation[21]

In November 2008, the European Commission adopted a proposal for a Regulation on Credit Rating Agencies, which would require agencies to have procedures in place to ensure that:

- ratings are not affected by conflicts of interest;
- credit rating agencies have a high standard for the quality of the rating methodology and the ratings; and
- credit rating agencies act in a transparent manner.

The intention is that the agencies would remain responsible for the content of the ratings.

29.11 Valuing shares of an unquoted company – quantitative process

The valuation of shares brings together a number of different financial accounting procedures that we have covered in previous chapters. The assumptions may be highly subjective, but there is a standard approach. This involves the following:

- Estimate the maintainable income flow based on earnings defined in accordance with the IIMR guidelines, as described in Chapter 27. Normally the profits of the past five years are used, adjusted for any known or expected future changes.

- Estimate an appropriate dividend yield, as described in Section 29.7.5, if valuing a non-controlling holding.

- Estimate an appropriate PE or earnings yield if valuing a majority holding. In the UK there is now a Valuation Index[22] focused on SMEs which is the result of UK200's Corporate Finance members providing key data on actual transactions involving the purchase or sale of real businesses (in the form of asset or share deals) over the past five years. The average PE ratio at November 2011 stood at 6.0 and the ratio of deal value to EBITDA had increased from 4.6 to 4.9 times. Average deal size in the last two years continued to be just under £3m.

- Make a decision on any adjustment to the required yields. For example, the shares in the unquoted company might not be as marketable as those in the comparative quoted companies and the required yield would therefore be increased to reflect this lack of marketability; or the statement of financial position might not be as strong with lower current/acid test ratios or higher gearing, which would also lead to an increase in the required yield.

- Calculate the economic capital value, as described in Chapter 6, by applying the required yield to the income flow.

- Compare the resulting value with the net realisable value (NRV), as described in Chapter 7, when deciding what action to take based on the economic value.

EXAMPLE ● The Doughnut Ltd is an unlisted company engaged in the baking of doughnuts. The statement of financial position of the Doughnut Ltd as at 31 December 20X9 showed:

	£000	£000
Freehold land		100
Non-current assets at cost	240	
Accumulated depreciation	40	
		200
Current assets	80	
Current liabilities	(60)	
		20
		320
Share capital in £1 shares		300
Retained earnings		20
		320
Estimated net realisable values:		
Freehold land		180
Plant and equipment		120
Current assets		70

The company achieved the following profit after tax (adjusted to reflect maintainable earnings) for the past five years ended 31 December:

	20X5	20X6	20X7	20X8	20X9
Maintainable earnings (£000)	36	40	44	38	42
Dividend payout history: Dividends	10%	10%	12%	12%	12%

Current yields for comparative quoted companies as at 31 December 20X9:

	Earnings yield %	Dividend yield %
Ace Bakers plc	14	8
Busi–Bake plc	10	8
Hard–to–beat plc	13	8

Acquiring a majority holding

You are required to value a holding of 250,000 shares for a shareholder, Mr Quick, who makes a practice of buying shares for sale within three years.

Now, the 250,000 shares represent an 83% holding. This is a majority holding and the steps to value it are as follows:

1 Calculate average maintainable earnings (in £000):

$$\frac{36,000 + 40,000 + 44,000 + 38,000 + 42,000}{5} = £40,000$$

2 Estimate an appropriate earnings yield:

$$\frac{14\% + 10\% + 13\%}{3} = 12.3\%$$

3 Adjust the rate for lack of marketability by, say, 3% and for the lower current ratio (of 1.3:1) by, say, 2%. Both these adjustments are subjective and would be a matter of negotiation between the parties.

Required yield	=	12.3
Lack of marketability weighting	=	3.0
Statement of financial position weakness	=	2.0
Required earnings yield		17.3

The adjustments depend on the actual circumstances. For instance, there might be negotiation over the use of the average of £40,000 with differing views on growth and, if Mr Quick were intending to hold the shares as a long-term investment, there might be less need to increase the required return for lack of marketability.

4 Calculate share value:

$$(£40,000 \times 100/17.3)/300,000 = 77p$$

5 Compare with the net realisable values on the basis that the company was to be liquidated:

		£
Net realisable values = 70,000 + 120,000 + 180,000	=	370,000
Less: Current liabilities		60,000
		310,000
Net asset value per share = £310,000/300,000	=	£1.03

The comparison indicates that, on the information we have been given, Mr Quick is paying less than the net realisable value, but the difference may not be enough to justify acquiring the shares in order to asset strip and liquidate the company to make an immediate capital gain.

Acquiring a minority holding

Let us extend our illustration by assuming that, if Mr Quick acquires control, it is intended to replace the non-current assets at a cost of £20,000 per year out of retained earnings. One of the remaining minority shareholders, Ms Croissant, wishes to dispose of shares and is in discussion with Mr Small who has £10,000 to invest. You are required to calculate for Mr Small how many shares he should aim to acquire from Ms Croissant.

There are two significant changes: the cash available for distribution as dividends will be reduced by £20,000 per year, which is used to replace non-current assets; and Mr Small is acquiring only a minority holding, which means that the appropriate valuation method is the **dividend yield** rather than the **earnings yield**.

The share value will be calculated as follows:

1 Estimate income flow:

	£
Maintainable earnings	40,000
Less: CAPEX	20,000
Cash available for distribution	20,000

Note that we are here calculating not distributable profits, but the available cash flow.

2 Required dividend yield:

	%
Average dividend yield	8.0
Lack of negotiability, say	2.0
Financial risk, say	1.5
	11.5

3 Share value:

$$\frac{£20,000}{300,000} \times \frac{100}{11.5} = 58p$$

At this price it would be possible for Mr Small to acquire (£10,000/58p) = 17,241 shares.

29.12 Valuing shares of an unquoted company – qualitative process

In the section above we illustrated how to value shares using the capitalisation of earnings and capitalisation of dividends methods. However, share valuation is an extremely subjective exercise.

A company's future cash flows may be affected by a number of factors. These may occur as a result of a change of control, action within the company (e.g. management change, revenue investment) or external events (e.g. change in the rate of inflation, change in competitive pressures).

● **Change of control**:
  – Aer Lingus said the offer in 2012 of €1.30 (£1.02) per share by Ryanair was 31% below the €1.87 cash per share based on the company's cash balance of €1bn.

– Ryanair in its offer document said it would grow jobs at Aer Lingus and raise the flag carrier's passenger numbers from 9.5 million a year to 14 million, by cutting Aer Lingus ticket prices and improving the productivity of Aer Lingus staff in order to hold down costs and maintain profit margins.

● **Management change** often heralds a significant change in a company's share price. For example, car and bike parts retailer Halfords' share price jumped after the company appointed a new Chief Executive Officer in October 2012 following the abrupt departure of David Wild in the summer, as it revealed that full-year profits would be at the top end of guidance after a strong second quarter.

● **Revenue investment** refers to discretionary revenue expenditure, such as charges to the income statement for research and development, training and advertising. It also relates to expenditure on costs such as amount of office space provided and travel expense allowed. Where in the recession there had been a reduction in face-to-face meetings and an increase in video and web conferencing, there is ongoing pressure to maintain this process into the future.

● **Changes in the rate of inflation** can affect the required yield. If, for example, it is expected that inflation will fall, this might mean that past percentage yields will be higher than the percentage yield that is likely to be available in the future.

● **Change in competitive pressures** can affect future sales. For example, increased foreign competition could mean that past maintainable earnings are not achievable in the future and the historic average level might need to be reduced.

These are a few of the internal and external factors that can affect the valuation of a share. The factors that are relevant to a particular company may be industry-wide (e.g. change in rate of inflation), sector-wide (e.g. change in competitive pressure) or company-specific (e.g. loss of key managers or employees).

If the company supports the acquisition of the shares, the valuer will be able to gain access to relevant internal information. For example, details of research and development expenditure may be available analysed by type of technology involved, by product line, by project and by location, and distinguishing internal from externally acquired R&D.

If the acquisition is being considered without the company's knowledge or support, the valuer will rely more heavily on information gained from public sources, e.g. statutory and voluntary disclosures in the annual accounts and industry information such as trade journals. Information on areas such as R&D may be provided in the OFR, but probably in an aggregated form, constrained by management concerns about use by potential competitors.[23]

There is an increasing wealth of financial and narrative disclosures to assist investors in making their investment decisions. There are external data such as the various multivariate Z-scores and H-scores and professional credit agency ratings; and there is greater internal disclosure of financial data such as TSR and EVA data indicating how well companies have managed value in comparison with a peer group and of narrative information such as the IFRS Practice Statement *Management Commentary*. It is also easier to access companies' financial data through the Web.

Literature search of qualitative factors which can lead to improved or reduced valuations

There is an interesting research report[24] investigating the nature of SME intangible assets in which the researchers have reported the following:

● **Factors identified in the literature as enhancing achieved price**: transportable business with a transferable customer base; non-cancellable service agreements and beneficial contractual arrangements; unexploited property situations; synergistic and cost-saving benefits; under-exploited brands and products; customer base providing cross-selling opportunities; competitor elimination, increased market share; complementary product or service range; market entry – a quick way of overcoming entry barriers; buy into new technology; access to distribution channels; and non-competition agreements.

● **Factors identified in the literature as diminishing achieved price**: confused accounts; poor housekeeping, doubtful debts, under-utilised equipment, outstanding litigation, etc.; over-dependence upon owner and key individuals; over-dependence on a small number of customers; unrelated side activities; poor or out-of-date company image; long-term contracts about to finish; poor liquidity; poor performance; minority and 'messy' ownership structures; inability to substantiate ownership of assets; and uncertainties surrounding liabilities.

Not all of these satisfy the criteria for recognition in annual financial statements.

Summary

This chapter has introduced a number of additional analytical techniques to complement the pyramid approach to ratio analysis discussed in the previous chapter.

The increasing use of 'non-GAAP' cash-based ratios was discussed to reduce the effect of subjective judgements. The use of ratio thresholds was discussed in determining shariah compliance and in setting debt covenants.

The calculation of EVA and TSR was explained, statuary disclosures in the UK were illustrated and their use in the context of performance-related remuneration was discussed. In addition, this chapter has described the use of ratios in the valuation of unquoted shares.

All users of financial statements (both internal and external users) should be prepared to utilise any or all of the interpretative techniques suggested in this chapter and the preceding one. These techniques help to evaluate the financial health and performance of a company. Users should approach these financial indicators with real curiosity – any unexplained or unanswered questions arising from this analysis should form the basis of a more detailed examination of the company accounts.

REVIEW QUESTIONS

1 It has been suggested that the growth in profits can be achieved by accounting sleight of hand rather than genuine economic growth. Consider how 'accounting sleight of hand' can be used to report increased profits and discuss what measures can be taken to mitigate against the possibility of this happening.

2 Explain how the use of debt can improve returns to equity shareholders in good years and increase their losses in poor years.

3 Telecomsabroad plc has a dividend payout ratio of 95%. Discuss why using the ratio of free cash flow to dividend might influence your assessment of dividend growth.

4 Discuss the difficulties when attempting to identify comparator companies for benchmarking as, for example, when selecting a TSR peer group.

5 The Unilever annual review stated:

> Total Shareholder Return (TSR) is a concept used to compare the performance of different companies' stocks and shares over time. It combines share price appreciation and dividends paid to show the total return to the shareholder. The absolute size of the TSR will vary with stock markets, but the relative position is a reflection of the market perception of overall performance relative to a reference group. The Company calculates the TSR over a three-year rolling period . . . Unilever has set itself a TSR target in the top third of a reference group of 21 . . . companies.

Discuss (a) why a three-year rolling period has been chosen, and (b) the criteria you consider appropriate for selecting the reference group of companies.

6 Discuss Z-score analysis with particular reference to Altman's Z-score and Taffler's Z-score. In particular:

(i)   What are the benefits of Z-score analysis?

(ii) What criticisms can be levelled at Z-score analysis?

7 Identify the two most significant variables in the Z-score, the Zeta model and Taffler's Z-score and discuss why each variable might have been selected.

8 Design variables for your own Z-score model.

9 Explain how and why EVA is calculated.

10 Discuss the advantages and disadvantages of all companies adopting the ratio criteria required to be shariah compliant.

11 Describe the measures taken to reduce the risk that credit rating agencies can mislead investors.

12 The following is an extract from the Bayer AG 2012 Annual Report:

> The value-based indicators aid management's decision-making, especially regarding strategic portfolio optimization and the allocation of resources for acquisitions and capital expenditures. The focus at the operational level is on the key drivers of enterprise value: growth (sales), cost efficiency (EBITDA) and capital efficiency (working capital, capital expenditures), since these directly affect value creation.

Discuss (a) why and how EBITDA is used as a driver for cost efficiency, and (b) how capital efficiency is determined in relation to working capital and capital expenditures.

13 Discuss how the following might be used by a shareholder and by the management:

(i)   The ratio of dividends plus share price movement to the opening share price

(ii) Accounting profit less an additional charge for the use of equity capital.

14 The finance director was investigating a potential acquisition. As part of the exercise she gave your colleague the current value of total assets, the post-tax operating income, the economic life of the assets and the scrap value of the assets with a request to calculate the cash flow return on investment (CFROI) for the company. Your colleague has asked you to explain to him (a) how this is done or where he could find further information about this on the Web, and (b) how the CFROI will be used.

15 Hard Times Ltd has been just about breaking even. It has recently identified a new project which will improve its ROC. Discuss whether entering into the project will always be to the advantage of the shareholders considering WACC.

16 Heavy Debts plc had an agreed debt service coverage ratio, DSCR, of 1.25, where DSCR = monthly net operating income/monthly principal and interest on loan. In 2013 the company's DSCR had fallen to 1.02 which was above breakeven but lower than the agreed rate. The Board believes that it is likely that a covenant default would have a material adverse impact on the value of the underlying businesses. Discuss three possible ways in which the company could deal with this in order to avoid a breach of the covenant.

EXERCISES

* Question 1

Belt plc and Braces plc were in the same industry. The following information appeared in their 20X9 accounts:

	Belt	Braces
	€m	€m
Revenue	200	300
Total operating expenses	180	275
Average total assets during 20X9	150	125

Required:

(a) Calculate the following ratios for each company and show the numerical relationship between them:
  (i)   Their rate of return on the average total assets.
  (ii) The net profit percentages.
  (iii) The ratio of revenue to average total assets.
(b) Comment on the relative performance of the two companies.
(c) State any additional information you would require as:
  (i) A potential shareholder.
  (ii) A potential loan creditor.

* Question 2

Quickserve plc is a food wholesale company. Its financial statements for the years ended 31 December 20X8 and 20X9 are as follows:

Statements of income

	20X9	20X8
	£000	£000
Sales revenue	12,000	15,000
Gross profit	3,000	3,900
Distribution costs	500	600
Administrative expenses	1,500	1,000
Operating profit	1,000	2,300
Interest receivable	80	100
Interest payable	(400)	(350)
Profit before taxation	680	2,050
Income taxation	240	720
Profit after taxation	440	1,330
Dividends in SOCE	800	600

Statements of financial position

	20X9 £000	20X8 £000
Non-current assets:		
Intangible assets	200	—
Tangible assets	4,000	7,000
Investments	600	800
	4,800	7,800
Current assets:		
Inventory	250	300
Trade receivables	1,750	2,500
Cash & bank	1,500	200
	3,500	3,000
Total assets	8,300	10,800
	£000	£000
Equity and reserves:		
Ordinary shares of 10p each	1,000	1,000
Share premium account	1,000	1,000
Revaluation reserve	1,110	1,750
Retained earnings	3,190	3,550
	6,300	7,300
Debentures	1,000	2,000
Current liabilities	1,000	1,500
	8,300	10,800

Required:
(a) Describe the concerns of the following users and how reading an annual report might help satisfy these concerns:
   (i) Employees
   (ii) Bankers
   (iii) Shareholders.
(b) Calculate relevant ratios for Quickserve and suggest how each of the above user groups might react to these.

* **Question 3**

The following are the accounts of Bouncy plc, a company that manufactures playground equipment, for the year ended 30 November 20X6.

Statements of comprehensive income for years ended 30 November

	20X6 £000	20X5 £000
Profit before interest and tax	2,200	1,570
Interest expense	170	150
Profit before tax	2,030	1,420
Taxation	730	520
Profit after tax	1,300	900
Dividends paid in SOCE	250	250

Statements of financial position as at 30 November 20X6

	20X6	20X5
	£000	£000
Non-current assets (written-down value)	6,350	5,600
Current assets		
Inventories	2,100	2,070
Receivables	1,710	1,540
Total assets	10,160	9,210
Creditors: amounts due within one year		
Trade payables	1,040	1,130
Taxation	550	450
Bank overdraft	370	480
Total assets less current liabilities	8,200	7,150
Creditors: amounts due after more than one year		
10% debentures 20X7/20X8	1,500	1,500
	6,700	5,650
Capital and reserves		
Share capital: ordinary shares of 50p fully paid up	3,000	3,000
Share premium	750	750
Retained earnings	2,950	1,900
	6,700	5,650

The directors are considering two schemes to raise £6,000,000 in order to repay the debentures and finance expansion estimated to increase profit before interest and tax by £900,000. It is proposed to make a dividend of 6p per share whether funds are raised by equity or loan. The two schemes are:

1 an issue of 13% debentures redeemable in 30 years;

2 a rights issue at £1.50 per share. The current market price is £1.80 per share (20X5: £1.50; 20X4: £1.20).

Required:

(a) Calculate the return on equity and any three investment ratios of interest to a potential investor.

(b) Calculate three ratios of interest to a potential long-term lender.

(c) Report briefly on the performance and state of the business from the viewpoint of a potential shareholder and lender using the ratios calculated above and explain any weaknesses in these ratios.

(d) Advise management which scheme they should adopt on the basis of your analysis above and explain what other information may need to be considered when making the decision.

Question 4

Sally Gorden seeks your assistance to decide whether she should invest in Ruby plc or Sapphire plc. Both companies are quoted on the London Stock Exchange. Their shares were listed on 20 June 20X4 as Ruby 475p and Sapphire 480p.

The performance of these two companies during the year ended 30 June 20X4 is summarised as follows:

	Ruby plc £000	Sapphire plc £000
Operating profit	588	445
Interest and similar charges	(144)	(60)
	444	385
Taxation	(164)	(145)
Profit after taxation	280	240
Interim dividend paid	(30)	—
Preference dividend paid	(90)	—
Ordinary dividend paid	(60)	(160)

The companies have been financed on 30 June 20X4 as follows:

	Ruby plc £000	Sapphire plc £000
Ordinary shares of 50p each	1,000	1,500
15% preference shares of £1 each	600	—
Share premium account	60	—
Retained earnings	250	450
17% debentures	800	—
12% debentures	—	500
	2,710	2,450

On 1 October 20X3 Ruby plc issued 500,000 ordinary shares of 50p each at a premium of 20%. On 1 April 20X4 Sapphire plc made a 1 for 2 bonus issue. Apart from these, there has been no change in the issued capital of either company during the year.

Required:
(a) Calculate the earnings per share (EPS) of each company.
(b) Determine the price/earnings ratio (PE) of each company.
(c) Based on the PE ratio alone, which company's shares would you recommend to Sally?
(d) On the basis of appropriate accounting ratios (which should be calculated), identify three other matters Sally should take account of before she makes her choice.
(e) Describe the advantages and disadvantages of gearing.

* Question 5

Growth plc made a cash offer for all of the ordinary shares of Beta Ltd on 30 September 20X9 at £2.75 per share. Beta's accounts for the year ended 31 March 20X9 showed:

	£000
Profit for the year after tax	750
Dividends paid	250

Statement of financial position as at 31 March 20X9

	£000
Buildings	1,600
Other tangible non-current assets	1,400
	3,000

Current assets	2,000	
Current liabilities	1,400	
		600
		3,600
£1 ordinary shares		2,500
Retained earnings		1,100
		3,600

Additional information:

(i) The half yearly profits to 30 September 20X9 show an increase of 25% over those of the corresponding period in 20X8. The directors are confident that this pattern will continue, or increase even further.

(ii) The Beta directors hold 90% of the ordinary shares.

(iii) The following valuations are available:

Realisable values

	£000
Buildings	2,500
Other non-current assets	700
Current assets	2,500

Net replacement values

	£000
Buildings	2,600
Other non-current assets	1,800
Current assets	2,200

(iv) Shares in quoted companies in the same sector have a PE ratio of 10. Beta Ltd is an unquoted company.

(v) One of the shareholders is a bank manager who advises the directors to press for a better price.

(vi) The extra risk for unquoted companies is 25% in this sector.

Required:
(a) Calculate valuations for the Beta ordinary shares using four different bases of valuation.
(b) Draft a report highlighting the limitations of each basis and advise the directors whether the offer is reasonable.

Question 6

R. Johnson inherited 810,000 £1 ordinary shares in Johnson Products Ltd on the death of his uncle in 20X5. His uncle had been the founder of the company and managing director until his death. The remainder of the issued shares were held in small lots by employees and friends, with no one holding more than 4%.

R. Johnson is planning to emigrate and is considering disposing of his shareholding. He has had approaches from three parties, who are:

1 A competitor – Sonar Products Ltd. Sonar Products Ltd considers that Johnson Products Ltd would complement its own business and is interested in acquiring all of the 810,000 shares. Sonar Products Ltd currently achieves a post-tax return of 12.5% on capital employed.

2 Senior employees. Twenty employees are interested in making a management buyout with each acquiring 40,500 shares from R. Johnson. They have obtained financial backing, in principle, from the company's bankers.

3 A financial conglomerate – Divest plc. Divest plc is a company that has extensive experience of acquiring control of a company and breaking it up to show a profit on the transaction. It is its policy to seek a pre-tax return of 20% from such an exercise.

The company has prepared draft accounts for the year ended 30 April 20X9. The following information is available.

(a) Past earnings and distributions:

Year ended 30 April	Profit/(Loss) after tax	Gross dividends declared
£	%	
20X5	79,400	6
20X6	(27,600)	—
20X7	56,500	4
20X8	88,300	5
20X9	97,200	6

(b) Statement of financial position of Johnson Products Ltd as at 30 April 20X9:

	£000	£000
Non-current assets		
Land at cost		376
Premises at cost	724	
Aggregate depreciation	216	
		508
Equipment at cost	649	
Aggregate depreciation	353	
		296
Current assets		
Inventories	141	
Receivables	278	
Cash at bank	70	
	489	
Payables due within one year	(335)	
Net current assets		154
Non-current liabilities		(158)
		1,176
Represented by:		
£1 ordinary shares		1,080
Retained earnings		96
		1,176

(c) Information on the nearest comparable listed companies in the same industry:

Company	Profit after tax for 20X9 £000	Retention %	Gross dividend yield %
Eastron plc	280	25	15
Westron plc	168	16	10.5
Northron plc	243	20	13.4

Profit after tax in each of the companies has been growing by approximately 8% per annum for the past five years.

(d) The following is an estimate of the net realisable values of Johnson Products Ltd's assets as at 30 April 20X9:

	£000
Land	480
Premises	630
Equipment	150
Receivables	168
Inventories	98

Required:

(a) As accountant for R. Johnson, advise him of the amount that could be offered for his shareholding with a reasonable chance of being acceptable to the seller, based on the information given in the question, by each of the following:

(i) Sonar Products Ltd;

(ii) the 20 employees;

(iii) Divest plc.

(b) As accountant for Sonar Products Ltd, estimate the maximum amount that could be offered by Sonar Products Ltd for the shares held by R. Johnson.

(c) As accountant for Sonar Products Ltd, state the principal matters you would consider in determining the future maintainable earnings of Johnson Products Ltd and explain their relevance.

(ACCA)

Question 7

Harry is about to start negotiations to purchase a controlling interest in NX, an unquoted limited liability company. The following is the statement of financial position of NX as at 30 June 2006, the end of the company's most recent financial year.

NX
Statement of financial position as at 30 June 2006

ASSETS	$
Non-current assets	3,369,520
Current assets	
Inventories, at cost	476,000
Trade and other receivables	642,970
Cash and cash equivalents	132,800
	1,251,770
Total assets	4,621,290
LIABILITIES AND EQUITY	
Non-current liabilities	
8% loan note	260,000
	260,000
Current liabilities	
Trade and other payables	467,700
Current tax payable	414,700
	882,400
Equity	
Ordinary shares, 40 cent shares	2,000,000
5% preferred shares of $1	200,000
Retained profits	1,278,890
	3,478,890
Total liabilities	1,142,400
Total liabilities and equity	4,621,290

The non-current assets of NX comprise:

	Cost $	Depreciation $	Net $
Property	2,137,500	262,500	1,875,000
Equipment	1,611,855	515,355	1,096,500
Motor vehicles	696,535	298,515	398,020
	4,445,890	1,076,370	3,369,520

NX has grown rapidly since its formation in 2000 by Albert Bell and Candy Dale who are currently directors of the company and who each own half of the company's issued share capital. The company was formed to exploit knowledge developed by Albert Bell. This knowledge is protected by a number of patents and trademarks owned by the company. Candy Dale's expertise was in marketing and she was largely responsible for developing the company's customer base. Figures for turnover and profit after tax taken from the statements of comprehensive income of the company for the past three years are:

	Turnover	Profit after tax
	$	$
Profit for 2004	8,218,500	1,031,000
Profit for 2005	10,273,100	1,288,720
Profit for 2006	11,414,600	991,320

NX's property has recently been valued at $3,000,000 and it is estimated that the equipment and motor vehicles could be sold for a total of $1,568,426. The net realisable values of inventory and receivables are estimated at $400,000 and $580,000 respectively. It is estimated that the costs of selling off the company's assets would be $101,000.

The 8% loan note is repayable at a premium of 30% on 31 December 2006 and is secured on the company's property. It is anticipated that it will be possible to repay the loan note by issuing a new loan note bearing interest at 11% repayable in 2012.

As directors of the company, Albert Bell and Candy Dale receive annual remuneration of $99,000 and £74,000 respectively. Both would cease their relationship with NX because they wish to set up another company together. Harry would appoint a general manager at an annual salary of $120,000 to replace Albert Bell and Candy Dale.

Investors in quoted companies similar to NX are currently earning a dividend yield of 6% and the average PE ratio for the sector is currently 11. NX has been paying a dividend of 7% on its common stock for the past two years.

Ownership of the issued common stock and preferred shares is shared equally between Albert Bell and Candy Dale.

Harry wishes to purchase a controlling interest in NX.

Required
(a) On the basis of the information given, prepare calculations of the values of a preferred share and an ordinary share in NX on each of the following bases:
    (i) net realisable values;
    (ii) future maintainable earnings.
(b) Advise Harry on other factors which he should be considering in calculating the total amount he may have to pay to acquire a controlling interest in NX.

(The Association of International Accountants)

Question 8

The directors of Chekani plc, a large listed company, are engaged in a policy of expansion. Accordingly, they have approached the directors of Meela Ltd, an unlisted company of substantial size, in connection with a proposed purchase of Meela Ltd.

The directors of Meela Ltd have indicated that the shareholders of Meela Ltd would prefer the form of consideration for the purchase of their shares to be in cash and you are informed that this is acceptable to the prospective purchasing company, Chekani plc.

The directors of Meela Ltd have now been asked to state the price at which the shareholders of Meela Ltd would be prepared to sell their shares to Chekani plc. As a member of a firm of independent accountants, you have been engaged as a consultant to advise the directors of Meela Ltd in this regard.

In order that you may be able to do so, the following details, extracted from the most recent financial statements of Meela, have been made available to you.

Meela Ltd accounts for year ended 30 June 20X4

Statement of financial position extracts as at 30 June 20X4:

	£000
Purchased goodwill unamortised	15,000
Freehold property	30,000
Plant and machinery	60,000
Investments	15,000
Net current assets	12,000
10% debentures 20X9	(30,000)
Ordinary shares of £1 each (cumulative)	(40,000)
7% preference shares of £1 each (cumulative)	(12,000)
Share premium account	(20,000)
Retained earnings	(30,000)

Meela Ltd disclosed a contingent liability of £3.0m in the notes to the statement of financial position.

(Amounts in brackets indicate credit balances.)

Statement of comprehensive income extracts for the year ended 30 June 20X4:

	£000
Profit before interest payments and taxation and exceptional items	21,000
Exceptional items	1,500
Interest	(3,000)
Taxation	(6,000)
Dividends paid – Preference	(840)
– Ordinary	(3,000)
Retained profit for the year	9,660

(Amounts in brackets indicate a charge or appropriation to profits.)

The following information is also supplied:

(i) Profit before interest and tax for the year ended 30 June 20X3 was £24.2 million and for the year ended 30 June 20X2 it was £30.3 million.

(ii) Assume tax at 30%.

(iii) Exceptional items in 20X4 relate to the profit on disposal of an investment in a related company. The related company contributed to profit before interest as follows:

To 30 June 20X4	£0
To 30 June 20X3	£200,000
To 30 June 20X2	£300,000

(iv) The preference share capital can be sold independently, and a buyer has already been found. The agreed purchase price is 90p per share.

(v) Chekani plc has agreed to purchase the debentures of Meela Ltd at a price of £110 for each £100 debenture.

(vi) The current rental value of the freehold property is £4.5 million per annum and a buyer is available on the basis of achieving an 8% return on their investment.

(vii) The investments of Meela Ltd have a current market value of £22.5 million.

(viii) Meela Ltd is engaged in operations substantially different from those of Chekani plc. The most recent financial data relating to two listed companies that are engaged in operations similar to those of Meela Ltd are:

	NV per share	Market price per share	P/E	Net dividend per share	Cover	Yield
Ranpar plc	£1	£3.06	11.3	12 pence	2.6	4.9
Menner plc	50p	£1.22	8.2	4 pence	3.8	4.1

Required:

Write a report, of approximately 2,000 words, to the directors of Meela Ltd, covering the following:

(a) Advise them of the alternative methods used for valuing unquoted shares and explain some of the issues involved in the choice of method.

(b) Explain the alternative valuations that could be placed on the ordinary shares of Meela Ltd.

(c) Recommend an appropriate strategy for the board of Meela Ltd to adopt in its negotiations with Chekani plc.

Include, as appendices to your report, supporting schedules showing how the valuations were calculated.

Question 9

Briefly state:

(i) the case for segmental reporting;

(ii) the case against segmental reporting.

Question 10

Discuss the following issues with regard to financial reporting for risk:

(a) How can a company identify and prioritise its key risks?

(b) What actions can a company take to manage the risks identified in (a)?

(c) How can a company measure risk?

References

1 www.nasdaq.com/xbrl
2 www.frc.org.uk/Our-Work/Publications/ASB/Rising-to-the-Challenge/Full-results-of-a-Review-of-Narrative-Reporting-by.aspx
3 J. Collier, *Aggressive Earnings Management: Is It Still a Significant Threat?*, ICAEW, October 2004.
4 M. Falch, A. Henten, R. Tadayoni and I. Windekilde, *Business Models in Social Networking*, Center for Communication, Media and Information Technologies (CMI), Aalborg University, Copenhagen, http://vbn.aau.dk/files/19150157/Falch_3.pdf
5 Alpa A. Virdi, *Investors' Confidence in Audited Financial Information*, Research Report, ICAEW, December 2004.
6 C. Minchington and G.Francis, 'Shareholder value,' *Management Quarterly*, Part 6, January 2000.
7 www.evadimensions.com
8 http://www3.cfo.com/article/2011/11/benchmarking_top-and-bottom-25-eva-momentum-ranking-of-large-companies
9 J. Stern, 'Management: its mission and its measure', *Director*, October 1994, pp. 42–44.
10 C. Pratten, *Company Failure*, Financial Reporting and Auditing Group, ICAEW, 1991, pp. 43–45.
11 R.J. Taffler, 'Forecasting company failure in the UK using discriminant analysis and financial ratio data', *Journal of the Royal Statistical Society*, Series A, vol. 145, part 3, 1982, pp. 342–358.
12 M.L. Inman, 'Altman's Z-formula prediction', *Management Accounting*, November 1982, pp. 37–39.
13 E.I. Altman, 'Financial ratios, discriminant analysis and the prediction of corporate bankruptcy', *Journal of Finance*, vol. 23(4), 1968, pp. 589–609.
14 M.L. Inman, 'Z-scores and the going concern review', *ACCA Students' Newsletter*, August 1991, pp. 8–13.
15 R.J. Taffler, 'Z-scores: an approach to the recession', *Accountancy*, July 1991, pp. 95–97.
16 K. Van Peursem and M. Pratt, 'Failure prediction in New Zealand SMEs: measuring signs of trouble', *International Journal of Business Performance Management (IJBPM)*, vol. 8 (2/3), 2006.
17 J. Argenti, 'Predicting corporate failure', *Accountants Digest*, no. 138, Summer 1983, pp. 18–21.
18 http://news.bbc.co.uk/1/hi/business/4352553.stm
19 www.managementstudyguide.com/limitations-of-participitative-management.htm
20 www.accaglobal.com/databases/pressandpolicy/unitedkingdom/3107831
21 http://ec.europa.eu/internal_market/consultations/docs/securities_agencies/consultation-cra-framework_en.pdf
22 http://www.uk200group.co.uk/Members/SpecialistGroups/SpecialistPanels/CorporateFinance/Sp_Valuations/Sp_Valuations_Home.aspx
23 W.A. Nixon and C.J. McNair, 'A measure of R&D', *Accountancy*, October 1994, p. 138.
24 C. Martin and J. Hartley, *SME Intangible Assets*, Certified Accountants Research Report 93, London, 2006.

CHAPTER 30

An introduction to financial reporting on the Internet

30.1 Introduction

The main objective of this chapter is to explain what XBRL is and how reports in XBRL assist investors and analysts to access and analyse data in published financial statements.

Objectives

By the end of this chapter, you should be able to:

- understand the reason for the development of a business reporting language;
- explain the benefits of tagging in XML and XBRL code data for financial reporting;
- understand why companies should adopt XBRL;
- list the processes a company needs to take to adopt XBRL.

30.2 The reason for the development of a business reporting language

We saw in the previous chapter that various online subscription databases such as Datastream, FAME and OneSource are available, where selected financial reports have been formatted by each of the databases into a standardised format. This allows subscribers to select peer groups and search across a variety of variables. Students having access to such databases at their own institution may carry out a range of assignments and projects such as selecting companies suitable for takeover based on stated criteria such as ROCE, % sales and % earnings growth.

30.2.1 Financial reporting on the Internet in PDF files

At an individual company level we find that most companies have a website to communicate all types of information to interested parties including financial information. Stakeholders or other interested parties can then download this information for their own particular use. Most of the financial information is in the format of PDF files created by a software program called Adobe® Acrobat®. This program is used for the conversion of all their documents, which make up the financial information contained within the annual general reports, into one document, a PDF file, for publication on the Internet. This PDF file can be formatted to include encryption and digital signatures to ensure that the document cannot be changed.

In order for the user to be able to read the PDF files, a special software program called Adobe Reader® needs to be downloaded from the Adobe website www.adobe.com.

30.2.2 Data re-keyed for analysis

Other formats used to display company information are often in Hyper Text Markup Language (HTML). HTML mainly defines the appearance of the information on the computer screen such as placement, colour, font, etc. But even though it is helpful to be able to download the file and read or print the financial information on screen or on paper, when calculations need to be performed the information needs to be retyped unless, as with a few companies, the data is also in Excel format. When we need to consider and evaluate multiple years of a company's financial results or evaluate companies in a sector, this rekeying is an even more time-consuming task and subject to errors.

Other interested parties or stakeholders such as investment analysts, merchant bankers, banks, regulatory bodies and government taxation departments may be able to request information in specific electronic formats, otherwise they also will need to rekey the data.

30.3 Reports and the flow of information pre-XBRL

The information flow from an organisation reporting to stakeholders and regulatory bodies and banks is considerable. The information required is not the same for each of the external parties and so one report is not appropriate.

A typical flow is set out in Figure 30.1 demonstrating how information is collated from Operational Data Stores and coded to the General Ledger (GL) using the chart of accounts

Figure 30.1 Today: a convoluted information supply chain

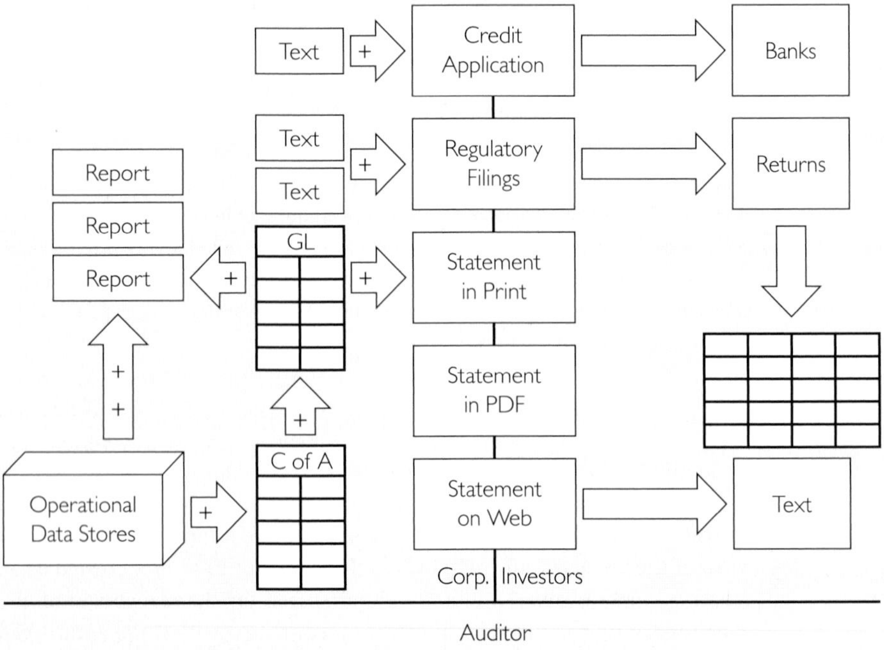

Source: www.xbrl.org.au/training/NSWWorkshop.pdf

(C of A). Once the data has been captured in the GL, statements of comprehensive income, financial position and cash flows can be produced for shareholders and for statutory filing. In addition, separate reports are produced for a variety of other stakeholders such as the tax authorities, stock exchanges, banks and creditors. The reports can be in different formats such as printed statements for internal management and audit use, hard copy annual reports for investors, and summary or full reports on a company's home web page in PDF or HTML format now that this is becoming mandatory or encouraged. This is a very costly process which has led to the development of a special business reporting language called eXtensible **Business Reporting Language** or **XBRL** which is based on XML.

Accountants will become increasingly involved with its development and this chapter provides a brief oversight of a development that is going to make a major impact internationally on the availability of financial data for comparative analysis. Just as the IASB is gradually achieving uniformity of accounting policies, XBRL will gradually achieve uniformity in the presentation of data on the Internet. Note that XBRL is not an accounting standard. It is a language specifically constructed for the exchange of financial information. As with other financial statements, the reader needs to be aware of the accounting standards applicable to the statements under review. XBRL does not in any way attempt to specify accounting rules.

30.4 What are HTML, XML and XBRL?

XBRL is based upon the eXtensible Markup Language or XML. XML itself is an extension of the Hyper Text Markup Language (HTML) which controls the format and display of web pages. We will briefly comment on each.

HTML

HTML is extensively used in website creation for the purposes of display. For example, the following text using HTML would have tags that describe the format and placement of the text:

Assets $50,000
Liabilities $25,000

```
<p><b>Assets    $50,000</b></p>
<p><b>Liabilities    $25,000</b></p>
```

where <p> instructs the item to be printed on the screen (and also where on the screen or in what format) and <b> instructs the item to be displayed in bold print. The </p> denotes the end of the commands and instructs the data to be 'printed' on the computer screen.

XML

XML is a language developed by the World Wide Web Consortium.[1] It goes one step further by allowing for 'tags' to be created which convey identification and meaning of the data within the tags. Thus instead of looking simply at format and presentation, the XML code looks for the text displayed within the code. For example, the user can design the tags used in XML as follows:

Assets $50,000 in this example of XML would be written as

```
<Assets>$50,000</Assets>
```

and similarly for **Liabilities $25,000** the XML code would be

```
<Liabilities>$25,000</Liabilities>
```

The computer program reading the XML code would thus know that the value found of $50,000 within the tags relates to Assets.

XBRL

XBRL has taken XML one step further and designed 'tags' based upon the common financial language used. For example, the terms ASSETS and LIABILITIES are common terms used in financial reports even though the calculations or valuations and the definitions used in different accounting standards may be dependent on those accounting standards applicable to the company.

30.4.1 Advantages of XBRL

Using XBRL means that it is easier for direct system-to-system information sharing between a company and its stakeholders and allows for improved analytical capacity. The numeric data in the financial statements of all companies filing their annual reports will be uniformly defined and presented and available for analysis, e.g. downloaded into Excel and other analytical software. The advantage of using XBRL according to XBRL International[2] is that:

> Computers can treat XBRL data 'intelligently': they can recognise the information in an XBRL document, select it, analyse it, store it, exchange it with other computers and present it automatically in a variety of ways for users. XBRL greatly increases the speed of handling of financial data, reduces the chance of error and permits automatic checking of information.

30.5 Reports and the flow of information post-XBRL

When XBRL is used, (a) information flows from an organisation to stakeholders are much simpler as seen in Figure 30.2, and (b) it is possible for stakeholders to receive information that can be understood by computer software and allow them to analyse the data obtained, as seen in Figure 30.3.

Figure 30.2 With XBRL: multiple outlets from a single specification

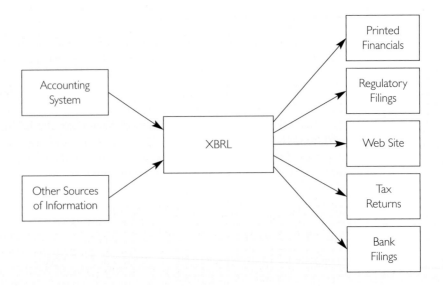

Source: http://xbrl.org.au/training/NSWWorkshop.pdf

Figure 30.3 XBRL: information flow to stakeholders

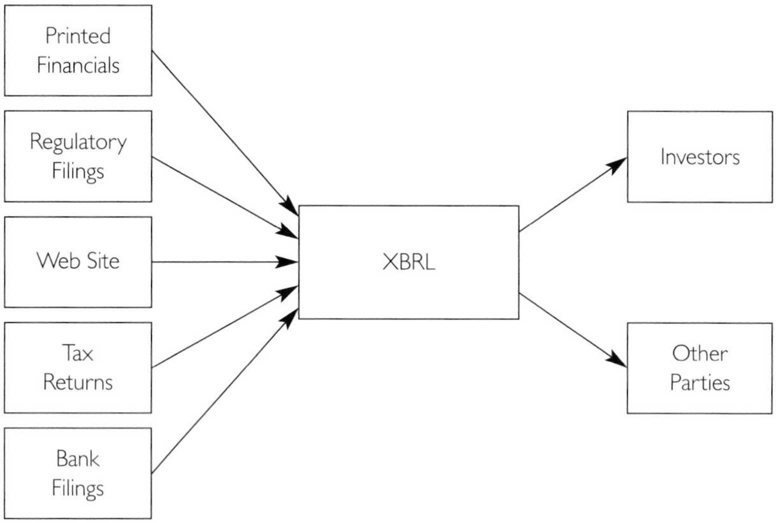

Source: http://xbrl.org.au/training/NSWWorkshop.pdf

30.6 XBRL and the IASB

Tags have been developed as a business reporting language and individual countries are setting their own priorities as to the reports that are being initially developed. As regards financial reporting, the IASB has developed XBRL applicable to IFRSs. We are on course for the content of financial statements to be standardised through IFRSs and for that content to be presented in a standardised uniform digital format.

30.7 Why should companies adopt XBRL?

There are regulatory pressures and commercial benefits concerning the adoption of XBRL.

30.7.1 Regulatory pressures

One of the driving forces has been the pressure from national regulatory bodies for companies to file corporate tax returns, stock exchange and corporate statutory financial statements in XBRL format. In some countries there are specific requirements for financial statements filing.

US developments

The US Securities and Exchange Commission (SEC) required[3] that public and foreign Companies with a float over $5 billion, representing approximately the top 500 companies listed with SEC, that prepare financial statements based on US GAAP must lodge their reports in XBRL from April 2009. Smaller US companies using US GAAP and foreign companies using IFRS must lodge their financial reports from June 2011. All companies lodging their statements in XBRL must also publish this information, on the same day they submit to the SEC, on their corporate websites and this information must be available for 12 months after lodging with SEC. The XBRL-based statements still have the limited liability status as under the voluntary filing programme until 31 October 2014. After this date the XBRL-based statements will have the same legal status as any other financial report. This will have implications for auditors and preparers of the financial reports.

UK developments

UK companies filing accounts at Companies House were notified that from April 2011 online submissions must be prepared using Inline XBRL (iXBRL). iXBRL is a specific form of XBRL that focuses on the human readable format. It was planned for commercial software to be available[4] from spring 2010.

HM Revenue and Customs (HMRC) require similar filing and stated that companies with a turnover of more than £100,000 must lodge online for companies with accounting periods starting from 1 April 2010. For any new business registering for VAT there is no choice: all returns must comply[5] with iXBRL online filing.

Companies House and HMRC requirements mean that all companies submitting online must be familiar with iXBRL and understand the implications for their company.

EU developments and the accounting profession

A policy statement from the Federation of European Accountants (FEE) detailed the impact upon accountants. The impacts considered are the ability to assist with the application of XBRL and the assurance/auditing process of accounting information prepared with XBRL. The accounting profession itself will have to educate their members about all aspects of XBRL.

30.7.2 Commercial benefits

The above is a brief introduction to just some of the XBRL developments that are occurring around the world whereby companies can easily generate tailored reports from a single data set and the data can be readily accessed at a lower cost by regulators, auditors, credit rating agencies, investors and research institutions.

30.8 What is needed to use XBRL for outputting information?

There are four processes, supported by the appropriate software, to be completed to adopt XBRL. The processes are (a) taxonomy design, (b) mapping, (c) creating an instance document, and (d) selecting and applying a stylesheet.

(a) The taxonomy needs to be designed

Taxonomy has two functions. It establishes relationships and defines elements acting like a dictionary. For example, the taxonomy for assets in the statement of financial position would be to show how total assets are derived by aggregating each asset and defining each asset as follows:

	Relationship	Definitions
Non-current assets	a	Not expected to be converted into cash within one year
Current assets		Expected to be turned into cash in less than one year
Inventory	v	Finished goods ready for sale, goods in course of production and raw materials
Trade receivables	w	Amounts owed by customers
Cash	x	Cash and cash equivalents
Subtotal	$v + w + x$	
Total assets	$a + v + w + x$	

The taxonomy also contains linkbases which provide additional information. For example:

- a means to cross-reference with the paragraph in the relevant IFRS;
- an indication of the language used in the financial report, e.g. English, French;
- prompts when a note to the accounts is required for a particular element.

Calculation: contains the validation rules and weights given to monetary items. For example, gross profit is calculated by taking away the cost of sales (COS) from revenue (GP = Revenue − COS). Revenue would be assigned 1 and COS would be minus 1 (noted as − 1) to achieve gross profit, also assigned a weight of 1.

Presentation: is used when reports need to be constructed. Business reports use parent–child type or tree type structures as in the term 'Assets'. Assets is the *parent* of Current and Non-current Assets. Mimicking the business report structures helps users to find the terms they are interested in.

Each country has been developing its own taxonomies. Since the issue by the IASB of the *IFRS Taxonomy Guide* in 2008, future taxonomies could be designed based upon the IFRS guide.

(b) Mapping

The term 'mapping' relates to equating the terminology used in the financial statements to 'names' used in the taxonomy. For example, if the taxonomy refers to 'Inventory' as being products held for sale, but the organisation refers to this as 'Stock in Trade' in the financial statements, then this needs to be 'mapped' to the taxonomy. All the names used in the financial statements, or any other reports, need thus be compared and mapped to (identified with) the taxonomy. This 'mapping' is done the first time the taxonomy is used.

(c) Instance documents

The instance document holds the data which are to be reported. For example, if preparing the statement of financial position at 30 September 2010, entries of individual asset values would be made in this document. This data would then be input to a stylesheet to produce the required report.

	Values	*Date*
Non-current assets	1,250	30.9.2010
Inventory	650	30.9.2010
Trade receivables	310	30.9.2010
Cash	129	30.9.2010

(d) Stylesheets

The format of a required report is specified in a template referred to as a stylesheet where the display is pre-designed. A stylesheet can be used repeatedly as, for example, for an annual report, or new stylesheets can be designed if reports are more variable as in interim reports. The annual report would be displayed in correct format with appropriate headings, currency and scale. For example:

Statement of financial position as at 30 September 2010

	000	*000*
Non-current assets		1,250
Current assets		
Inventory	650	
Trade receivables	310	
Cash	129	
	1,089	
Total assets		2,339

The taxonomy and stylesheets do not need to be changed every time a report is produced. The only changes that are made are those in the instance documents regarding data entries.

Summary of the four processes

A summary is set out in Figure 30.4.

Figure 30.4 Summary of the four processes

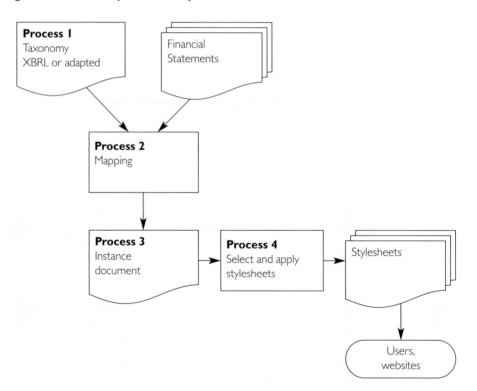

30.9 What is needed when receiving XBRL output information?

Institutional users

Institutions which receive XBRL formatted financial information from companies, such as revenue authorities, stock exchanges, banks and insurance companies, normally require the information to be lodged according to a pre-determined format and their software is specifically designed to be able to extract and display the XBRL data.

Non-institutional users

For other interested parties, specific software is needed to make the XBRL format data readable. In order for the text to be understood by a human in a way that indicates that we are looking at a financial report, it needs to be 'translated', a process known as **rendering**, by computer. 'Rendering' the items contained within XBRL is the current challenge.

Example of rendering

The text below represents the code for XBRL formatted data in an instance document:

Instance document in XBRL

```
<ifrs-gp:AssetsHeldSale contextRef=vCurrent_AsOf" unitRef="U-Euros"
    decimals="0">100000</ifrs-gp:AssetsHeldSale>

<ifrs-gp:ConstructionProgressCurrent contextRef="Current_AsOf"
    unitRBf="U-Euros" decimals="0">100000</ifrs-
    gp:ConstructionProgressCurrent>

<ifrs-gp:Inventories contextRef="Current_AsOf" unitRef="U-Euros"
    decimals="0">100000</ifrs-gp:Inventories>

<ifrs-gp:OtherFinancialAssetsCurrent contextRef="Current_AsOf"
    unitRef="U-Euros" decimals="0">100000</ifrs-
    gp:OtherFinancialAssetsCurrent>

<ifrs-gp:HedgingInstrumentsCurrentAsset contextRef="Current_AsOf"
    unitRef="U-Euros" decimals="0">100000</ifrs-
    gp:HedgingInstrumentsCurrentAsset>

<ifrs-gp:CurrentTaxReceivables contextRef="Current_AsOf" unitRef="U-Euros"
    decimals="0">100000</ifrs-gp:CurrentTaxReceivables>

<ifrs-gp:TradeOtherReceivablesNetCurrent contextRef="Current_AsOf"
    unitRef="U-Euros" decimals="0">100000</ifrs-
    gp:TradeOtherReceivablesNetCurrent>

<ifrs-gp:PrepaymentsCurrent contextRef="Current_AsOf" unitRef="U-Euros"
    decimals="0">100000</ifrs-gp:PrepaymentsCurrent>

<ifrs-gp:CashCashEquivalents contextRef="Current_AsOf" unitRef="U-Euros"
    decimals="0">100000</ifrs-gp:CashCashEquivalents>

<ifrs-gp:OtherAssetsCurrent contextRef="Current_AsOf" unitRef="U-Euros"
    decimals="0">100000</ifrs-gp:OtherAssetsCurrent>

<ifrs-gp:AssetsCurrentTotal contextRef="Current_AsOf" unitRef="U-Euros"
    decimals="0">1000000</ifrs-gp:AssetsCurrentTotal>
```

Looking at the first two lines of code, it is possible to see that the data contain financial information about assets held for sale, that these are 'Current' and that the unit of measurement is in euros and has zero decimals with a value of 100,000. This is possible for a few lines but it would not be feasible to do this for a complex financial statement. Rendering translates the code into readable format as follows:

Rendered XBRL data

CURRENT ASSETS €

Assets held for sale	100,000
Construction in progress, current	100,000
Inventories	100,000
Other financial assets, current	100,000
Hedging instruments, current [asset]	100,000
Current tax receivables	100,000
Trade and other receivables, net, current	100,000
Prepayments, current	100,000
Cash and cash equivalents	100,000
Other assets, current	100,000
Current assets, total	**1,000,000**

The data can now be recognised as belonging to that part of the financial statement where the current assets are listed. This example can be found at http://www.xbrl.org/Example1/.

The rendering process is of particular interest to investors and other third parties who may want to access financial data in XBRL format for evaluation purposes and who may not have software capable of rendering the instance document into human readable format. The ability to render an XBRL document becomes even more important for an investor or analyst seeking to carry out trend or inter-firm comparison analysis. For a more in-depth discussion of the processes involved in rendering visit www.xbrl.org/uk/Rendering/.

30.9.1 How has XBRL assisted the user?

If we take the revenue authorities as an example, they have had their own in-house developed software for carrying out a risk analysis in an attempt to identify those that look as though they should be investigated. Such risk analysis was routine before XBRL but XBRL has allowed the existing analysis software to be refined – this allows obviously compliant companies to be identified and investigation to be targeted where there is possible or probable non-compliance. However, it was still not possible to read the data in human form.

30.9.2 Development of iXBRL

Inline XBRL (known as iXBRL) has been developed so that the XBRL data is capable of being read by the user. It achieves this by embedding the XBRL coding in an HTML document so that it is similar to reading a web page. iXBRL takes a report, say a company's published accounts, in Excel, MS Word or PDF and then 'translates' this to iXBRL. It is then still able to be viewed in human readable format. This would be an advantage for smaller businesses where there may not be accountants with XBRL skills or where the cost would be prohibitive and they also do not need more advanced software. Corefiling's software[6] would be a good example of iXBRL.

This is newly developed software and, if you want to explore this a little further, there are helpful websites – one that offers a software company's view[7] and one that offers another perspective.[8]

How has iXBRL assisted the user?

If we consider the position of the regulators we can see that there is an impact on narrative in reports. For example, there is the requirement of the SEC to include the notes to the business reports in a certain format in the near future. For the larger companies[9] this means that tags have to be developed for many more items than before. The inclusion of the notes to the accounts is not new, but the new requirements from the SEC involve different levels of disclosure within the notes and this will require further development of either a linkbase or a standard approach to the application of stylesheets.

If we continue with the revenue authorities example, the availability of the data in readable format has meant that, once a high-risk case has been identified, it is possible to drill down into the data and highlight relationships that would not have been possible before iXBRL.

XBRL data may be exported to Excel

Facilities are being developed all the time and access to financial data is being constantly improved.

30.9.3 International experience

US experience

In the US, SEC data are being exported to an Excel spreadsheet for analysis. This facility also allows for downloading to Excel spreadsheets and charting operations on screen. However, because companies have different items in their financial reports, it is not possible to make a line-by-line comparison. The user needs to synchronise items and to do this needs to be conversant with the accounting definition of each individual item.

UK experience

In the UK, data that have been submitted to Companies House can be obtained but at a cost.[10] Investors who go to the company's individual website to download the financial information will find that most will be in Adobe Acrobat (PDF) format and not easily copied to Excel for comparative analysis.

XBRL UK reports[11] that both HMRC and Companies House are implementing the recommendations as set out in the Carter report of March 2006. Since the announcement[12] in 2009 this project has progressed and iXBRL has been used to submit returns to both agencies since 2010. The advantage of using iXBRL is that the document produced using this method can be read by humans as the code is 'rendered' in HTML-looking documents. Businesses can continue to use their current software and then as an iXBRL software to render the document in that code.

Singaporean experience

Singapore's Accounting Corporate Regulatory Authority (ACRA),[13] the regulating authority for businesses incorporated in Singapore, has been receiving company reports for most incorporated commercial companies in XBRL format since 2007. Company information can also be purchased from the ACRA website. The information has been extracted from the data lodged with ACRA[14] for a demonstration of the type of analysis available. The demonstration on this website also included evaluation of the company's position in relation to their peers within the industry or the whole industry. This extends the use of business reports from merely financial to the position of the company in the economic environment of their industry sector.

Most investment analysis providers have their analysis and rendering software written in-house to service their investment clients and investment brokers. For investors wanting to do their own investment analysis, there is still a wait for suitable software to obtain XBRL data and then view it on a PC. iXBRL may be able to fill this gap.

Australian experience

In Australia, the Australian Prudential Regulatory Authority (APRA), is the government body that controls and regulates banking and superannuation funds in Australia. It collects regular data using its own Taxonomy D2A (Direct to APRA) based on XBRL. There may be changes to this as the Australian federal government is well on the way to implementing standard business reporting (SBR). The government estimated that the use of SBR, based on XBRL taxonomies, will provide savings per year of $800 million to Australian businesses. The process is facilitated by the Australian Treasury and the government estimates that the application of SBR to the government data has resulted in the elimination of approximately 7,000 data elements.

European experience

In Europe there have been a number of projects in the last few years, some of which have been very extensive. For example, the Dutch project 'Renewal Government Services' is a €250 million project initiated by the Dutch Ministry of Justice and Finance to improve information to be lodged by businesses to government departments and access to published information by third parties. It also provided for €22.4 million for the next four years from 2008 to expand the Dutch taxonomy. It is envisaged that other government areas[15] such as health and education will be the focus of attention for further development of the project. An example of the extended use of XBRL is demonstrated by the government of the Netherlands' use for the yearly budget. The Netherlands also has a taxonomy for use in the banking sector.

IASB and XBRL developments[16]

In January 2013 the IFRS Foundation published for public comment an exposure draft on the *IFRS Taxonomy 2013*. The proposed Taxonomy is consistent with IFRSs, including IASs and the IFRS for SMEs. The IFRS Taxonomy 2013 is a translation of IFRSs as issued at 1 January 2013 into XBRL.

Yet despite a steadily rising number of users and stakeholders, and despite the success of numerous individual initiatives and projects, on a global scale XBRL remains in the early adoption phase. The benefits of XBRL adoption and implementation are being realised, but gradually.[17]

US experience Interactive Data and Financial Statements[18]

In 2009, the SEC issued rules requiring companies to provide financial statement information in the XBRL interactive data format. These rules apply to domestic and foreign companies using U.S. GAAP and will eventually apply to foreign private issuers using International Financial Reporting Standards (IFRS) as issued by the International Accounting Standards Board. The rules require companies' primary financial statements, notes, and financial statement schedules to be provided in XBRL, along with some company identifier information. The rules supplement, but do not replace or change, disclosure using the traditional electronic filing formats in ASCII or HTML. Companies will submit XBRL filings alongside their traditional ASCII- or HTML-formatted filings.

30.9.4 Development of XBRL and iXBRL beyond statutory financial reporting

Sharing data

The development of the SBR projects in Australia, the Netherlands and the US are good examples of the extension and application of XBRL beyond financial reporting and accounting. Development of these projects is an enormous task and requires a lot of planning, design and testing by all parties involved.

The next logical step is for government agencies to share the data submitted rather than businesses having to lodge different reports for different purposes. This will mean in the longer term, however, that governments need to rationalise the formats and volume in which they require businesses to lodge information.

We have discussed the use of XBRL and iXBRL for submitting reports to statutory authorities. There have also been interesting developments in their use for internal accounting.

30.10 Progress of XBRL development for internal accounting

Development in the general ledger area is continuing and will probably be one of the most important developments for companies with consolidation requirements when multiple general ledgers are involved. The general ledger specification has the advantage that organisational data is classified at source and the classification decision with respect to XBRL names will have been made at the Chart of Accounts level.

This is quite a task as the financial statements usually report aggregated data. For example, the total for administration expenses in the Income Statement is usually made up by aggregating a number of different account classifications in the General Ledger. A further consideration is the effect of IFRSs when aggregating expense accounts. For example, the Chart of Account structures for the disclosure of segmentation by product class and by geographical areas are distinctly different. The XBRL code also needs to reflect this.

The XBRL for the General Ledger may also bring great cost savings as data collection at source is automated and the extraction and processing of data into reports can be achieved in a much shorter time. A company such as General Electric has more than 150 general ledgers which are not compatible in use. XBRL has the potential to streamline consolidation processes considerably.

The XBRL Global General Ledger Working Group (XBRL GL WG) within XBRL has released an updated GL module[19] to include the SRCD (Summary Reporting Contextual Data):

> SRCD is a module of the XBRL Global Ledger Framework (XBRL GL) designed to facilitate the link between detailed data represented with XBRL GL and end reporting represented with XBRL for financial reporting (XBRL FR) or other XML schemas.

This module should enable a streamlined preparation of business reports from the general ledger. In February 2010 the GL framework also released the GL module with Japanese labels and this is now awaiting feedback and then a final recommendation.

30.11 Further study

The XBRL International website (www.xbrl.org) has an extensive listing of companies and authorities currently using XBRL. The reader is encouraged to investigate further any of the resources available on the XBRL and other websites such as learn.vubiz.com/ChAccess/XBRL/ where there is an introductory course 'Advances in Business and Financial Reporting'. A number of the links provided will lead to good discussions of the projects and demonstrate how XBRL is applied. Some of the links will also bring the reader to websites in languages other than English (Google translation toolbar may be helpful) and may be of particular interest to readers of this text living in these countries.

Summary

XBRL is still a developing area relating to organisational reporting. In the coming years this will continue and extend beyond the current focus on published financial statements. The general ledger area is developing and this will benefit the organisational information supply chain. Accounting software suppliers are also adopting XBRL in their developments and this will increase accessibility to XBRL. Accounting software companies such as MYOB, aimed at smaller organisations, are also using XBRL in their new developments. Future software development may also make it easier for accountants to use XBRL, especially when a country's taxonomies are in the 'final' approved stage.

Financial statements presented in XBRL format are capable of being downloaded into an analyst's/investor's own spreadsheet (such as Microsoft Excel). The advantage of this is that the analyst/investor does not need to retype the information. The commercial databases which compile specific information for analysts/investors are usually only concerned with public companies listed on the Stock Exchange. XBRL allows any type of financial information to be transferred to a statistical package without having to retype the information. XBRL could thus also benefit not-for-profit organisations and trusts, etc. Professional accounting consultants would also be able to use XBRL in transferring information from a client's accounting package into an analytical tool to prepare information to evaluate business efficiency. This information is often more extensive than the end-of-year financial information.

Large software developers such as SAP announced in February 2009 that 'SAP® BusinessObjects™' is now available for financial publications in XBRL. This conforms to Security and Exchange Commission (SEC) requirements to lodge specific financial information from June 2009. SAP also stated that its software also can be used to lodge financial information using XBRL with HM Revenue and Customs in the UK. The software allows for automatic and easy tagging of the information (see www.xbrlspy. org/sap_announces_xbrl_publishing_support).

Accountants and students wishing to keep up-to-date with these developments are gaining a competitive advantage by creating and developing a 'niche' skill which can only add value to an organisation employing these professionals.

REVIEW QUESTIONS

1 Discuss how an investor might benefit from annual reports being made available in XBRL.

2 Explain how a body such as a tax authority might benefit from XBRL.

3 Explain what you understand by taxonomy and mapping.

4 Explain the use of instance documents.

5 Explain the use of stylesheets.

6 Explain iXBRL and where it is used.

EXERCISES

Question 1

Visit www.us.kpmg.com/microsite/xbrl/kkb.asp to attempt the XBRL tutorial and write a brief note on how you think it will affect the work of a financial accountant.

Question 2

Find the financial reports for a company of your own choice. List the company and describe the format of the Annual Report. See if you can also find information on the *company's own* website about its use of XBRL.

Question 3

The following is an extract from *Digital reporting: a progress report*, an initiative from the Institute of Chartered Accountants in England & Wales commenting in 2004 on possible barriers to the development of increased digital reporting:

Technology is unlikely to be the barrier . . . The barrier, if any, will arise from organisations being unwilling to provide the necessary level of access or information to external users. In addition, issues relating to systems security, particularly control of access to programs and data, would need to be further addressed, as would questions of liability and assurance. The latter two are potentially very big issues indeed.

Whilst there has been major progress by regulators in the US, Australia and the Netherlands, an ICAEW and University of Birmingham (ISARG) Workshop on 25th January 2011 titled 'The future of XBRL in Europe: Impetus, institutions and interrelationships' http://www.icaew.com/~/media/Files/About-ICAEW/What-we-do/thought-leadership/the-future-of-xbrl-in-europe-final-summary-for-release.pdf explored the future of XBRL in Europe and contrasted the US and Pan European drivers:

Pan European development

The U.S. SEC project provides a model of the effectiveness of visionary leadership from the top of a regulatory body to achieve a relatively rapid mandatory implementation. As a model for pan European developments it is limited because of the significantly different institutional environment, goals and processes. It does however raise important questions for consideration. The SEC's stated target market was retail (non-professional) investors in line with its mandate. What could be the focus of the driver for developments in Europe? The SEC was also under pressure to review a significant portion of filings under the Sarbanes Oxley Act that provided a strong internal driver for more efficient processing internally.

Required:
Review the two sources and discuss what equivalent pressures member states are experiencing?

Question 4

Find out more about any of the following topics and write a one-page summary on:

(a) the XBRL general ledger work;

(b) use of XBRL by stock exchanges;

(c) the commitment by the IFRS to the XBRL project;

(d) accounting software companies involved in providing XBRL capabilities;

(e) public utilities that are using XBRL;

(f) government involvement in XBRL.

References

1 www.w3.org/Consortium
2 www.xbrl.org
3 xbrl.sec.gov
4 www.companieshouse.gov.uk/about/pdf/hmrcCommonFiling1.pdf
5 http://search.hmrc.gov.uk/kb5/hmrc/hmrc/results.page?qt=xbrl
6 www.corefiling.com/products/seahorse.html
7 www.tcsl.co.uk/
8 www.xbrlspy.org/to_render_or_not_to_render_xbrl
9 www.claritysystems.com/ap/events/webcasts/Pages/XBRL4Tagging.aspx
10 www.companieshouse.gov.uk/
11 www.xbrl.org/uk/Projects/
12 www.companieshouse.gov.uk/about/pdf/hmrcCommonFiling1.pdf
13 www.acra.gov.sg/
14 http://www.acra.gov.sg/NR/rdonlyres/8F512CAC-84B6-4AE1-8E73-OECC90B45F83/15241/2UsingXBRL_DPPresentation.pdf
15 www.xbrl-ntp.nl/
16 http://www.ifrs.org/XBRL/Pages/XBRL.aspx
17 http://www.ifrs.org/XBRL/Documents/SnapshotIFRSTaxonomyforweb.pdf
18 http://www.sec.gov/spotlight/xbrl/financial-statements.shtml
19 www.xbrl.org/GLFiles/

Bibliography

H. Ashbaugh, K.M. Johnstone and T.D. Warfield, 'Corporate reporting on the Internet', *Accounting Horizons*, vol. 13(3), 1999, pp. 241–257.

R. Debreceny and G. Gray, 'Financial reporting on the Internet and the external audit', *European Accounting Review*, vol. 8(2), 1999, pp. 335–350.

R. Debreceny and G. Gray, 'The production and use of semantically rich accounting reports on the Internet: XML and XBRL', *International Journal of Accounting Information Systems*, vol. 1(3), 2000.

D. Deller, M. Stubenrath and C. Weber, 'A survey of the use of the Internet for investor relations in the USA, UK and Germany', *European Accounting Review*, vol. 8(2), pp. 351–364.

Ernst & Young, *Web Enabled Business Reporting. De invloed van XBRL op het verslaggevingsproces*, Kluwer, 2004.

M. Ettredge, V.J. Richardson and S. Scholz, 'Going concern auditor reports at corporate web sites', *Research in Accounting Regulation*, vol. 14, 2000, pp. 3–21.

M. Ettredge, V.J. Richardson and S. Scholz, *Accounting Information at Corporate Web Sites: Does the Auditor's Opinion Matter?*, University of Kansas, February 1999.

Neil Hannon, 'XBRL grows fast in Europe', *Strategic Finance*, October 2004, pp. 55–56.

Mark Huckelsby and Josef Macdonald, 'The three tenets of XBRL – adoption, adoption, adoption!', *Chartered Accountants Journal of New Zealand*, March 2004, pp. 46–47.

V. Richardson and S. Scholz, 'Corporate reporting and the Internet: vision reality and intervening obstacles', *Pacific Accounting Review*, vol. 11(2), 2000, pp. 153–160.

Mike Rondel, 'XBRL – do I need to know more?', *Chartered Accountants Journal of New Zealand*, vol. 83(5), June 2004, pp. 37–40.

G. Trites, *The Impact of Technology on Financial and Business Reporting*, Toronto: Canadian Institute of Chartered Accountants, 1999.

The following websites were accessed:

www.adobe.com

www.xbrl.org/FRTaxonomies/

www.xbrl.org

www.ubmatrix.com/home/

www.semansys.com

www.edgar.com

PART **7**

Accountability

CHAPTER 31

Corporate governance

31.1 Introduction

The main aim of this chapter is to create an awareness of what constitutes good corporate governance – how to achieve it, the threats to achieving it and the role of accountants and auditors.

Objectives

By the end of this chapter, you should be able to:

● understand the concept of corporate governance;
● have an awareness of how and why governance mechanisms may differ from jurisdiction to jurisdiction;
● have an appreciation of the role which accounting and auditing play in the governance process;
● have a greater sensitivity to areas of potential conflicts of interest.

31.2 A systems perspective

Corporations do not act in a vacuum. They are corporate citizens of society with rights and responsibilities. The way in which they exercise these rights and responsibilities is influenced by the history, institutions and cultural expectations of society. A systems perspective recognises that an entity is not independent but is interdependent with its environment. This has given rise to the need for corporate governance.

Corporate governance is defined by Oman[1] as:

private and public institutions, including laws, regulations and accepted business practices, which together govern the relationship, in a market economy, between corporate managers and entrepreneurs ('corporate insiders') on the one hand, and those who invest resources in corporations on the other.

31.2.1 Good corporate governance – investor perspective

When we pause to contemplate the contribution of corporations to our standard of living, we are reminded how important their contribution is to most aspects of our existence. It is therefore vital that they operate as good citizens in their treatment of the investors who provide their funds and of other stakeholders. This includes actions by management when dealing with investors such as:

- complying with the laws and norms of society;
- striving to achieve the company objectives in a manner which does not involve taking risks which are greater than expected or acceptable to investors;
- balancing short- and long-term performance;
- establishing mechanisms to ensure that managers are acting in the interests of shareholders and are not directly or indirectly using their knowledge or positions to gain inappropriate benefits at the expense of shareholders;
- providing investors with relevant, reliable and timely information that allows them to assess the performance, solvency and financial stability of the business; and
- providing investors with an independent opinion that the financial statements are a fair representation.

This list does not cover all eventualities but is intended to indicate what could be expected from corporate governance – good being determined by the degree that the actions and information flows achieve fair outcomes.

31.2.2 Good corporate governance – other stakeholder perspective

A stakeholder perspective addresses all the other parties whose continued support is necessary to ensure the satisfactory performance of the business. The parties are normally seen as one of the following categories: loan creditors, employees, trade unions representing employees, customers, governments and suppliers.

Good corporate governance might include actions by management such as:

- fair treatment of employees, avoiding discrimination;
- establishing mechanisms for resolving conflicts of interests;
- establishing mechanisms for whistle-blowing so that if inappropriate behaviour is taking place it is highlighted as quickly as possible so as to minimise the cost to the organisation and society;
- paying suppliers, particularly small businesses, promptly within the agreed credit period; and
- providing suppliers with relevant, reliable and timely information that allows them to assess the solvency of the business.

31.2.3 Good corporate governance – stakeholder pressure

As well as there being conflicting interests, there are also differences in the influence that a stakeholder can exert. For example, dominant shareholders, institutional investors and major customers have a greater ability to hold management to account and achieve good corporate governance outcomes. The existence of the ability does not necessarily mean that it is put into effect, since the individual stakeholder's private interest might not be advanced by taking action – it might, for example, divert their management's attention away from their own business.

31.2.4 Good corporate governance – all sectors

The objective is to influence behaviour so that all parties act within the spirit of good governance. The actions and information flows above have been oriented towards business entities but we should expect all organisations to behave in the same way. For example, in the case of a not-for-profit enterprise such as a charity it is important that the money raised be used in a manner consistent with the uses envisaged by the donors, and that an appropriate balance be achieved between administrative costs and the money devoted to assisting the beneficiaries of the charity. The approach to enforcement of good corporate governance by charities varies internationally.

31.3 Different jurisdictions have different governance priorities

The predominant conflicts of interest will vary from country to country depending on each country's history, economic and legal developments, norms and religion.

In the UK and the United States, with their similar considerable reliance on stock exchanges for the financing of public companies, there is a need for an active, efficient capital market. This leads to their focus being on potential conflicts between management and shareholders.

In Germany, where companies have both a board of directors made up of investors as well as an advisory board representing both management and employees, there is a recognition that there is a need to reconcile both management and employee long-term interests and to ensure that both groups are motivated to achieve the organisation's long-term goals.

In south-east Asia, with many of the large corporations having substantial shareholdings owned by members of a single family, the emphasis has been on avoiding conflicts between family and minority shareholders.

In Muslim countries companies should not be involved in activities related to alcohol and gambling; they cannot pay or charge interest and they have religious obligations to make a minimum level of donations. This means there is a need for corporate governance mechanisms to ensure that there is no conflict between commercial activity and religious obligations.

From the above we can see how the governance priorities differ from country to country. They result from the role of the political institutions, the stage of economic development, the diversity of stakeholder perspectives and a country's heritage in so far as it shapes the law, the religion and the social norms.

The large number of multinational companies means that these companies have to be sensitive to the approaches taken in all countries in which they have subsidiary companies and joint ventures. They also have to be aware of the provisions of the US Foreign Corrupt Practices Act 1977 and the UK Bribery Act 2010, particularly as the Bribery Act creates a corporate offence of failing to prevent bribery by persons associated with a corporation.

Just as governance priorities differ, so do the institutions and methods for controlling corporate governance. The institutions include statutory bodies enforcing detailed prescriptive requirements and statutory bodies that encourage voluntary adoption of good practices with disclosure, through to professional accounting bodies that have built the awareness of good corporate governance into their examination syllabi.

31.3.1 Corporate governance culture

In China, Russia and the former communist countries in Eastern Europe, the economies are being changed from state-controlled businesses to privately owned companies. The 'model' of these companies is similar to those in the US and UK. So, the trend is towards the US and UK model of companies' shares being listed on their national stock exchange. This trend to wider share ownership will encourage the development of corporate governance criteria similar to those in the US and the UK. For some countries this is a real cultural shift and it will take time for the concept of good corporate governance to be applied. The following is an extract from an OECD Note of a meeting on Corporate Governance Development in State-owned Enterprises in Russia:[2]

> Finally, as stressed by investors, the OECD, and government officials at this expert's meeting, the emergence of a true corporate governance culture is vital. Such a culture-based approach should involve the understanding of the principles and values behind corporate governance, and replace the 'box-ticking' mechanistic approach in which superficial institutions fulfill certain criteria but do not bring real benefits in terms of effective achievement of corporate goals. This would complement the creation of specific incentives intended to guide the behaviour of economic actors.

31.4 Pressures on good governance behaviour vary over time

History shows that business behaviour is influenced by where we are in the economic cycle, whether it's a time of boom or bust.

31.4.1 Behaviour in boom times

During the booms there has always been a tendency to be over-optimistic and to expect the good times to continue indefinitely. In such periods there is a tendency for everyone to focus on making profits. The safeguards that are in the system to prevent conflicts of interest and to limit undesirable behaviour are seen as slowing down the business and causing genuine opportunities to be missed. Over-optimism leads to a business taking risks that the share-holders had not sanctioned and is, to that extent, excessive.

This is accompanied by a tendency to water down the controls or to simply ignore them. When that happens there will always be some unethical individuals who will exploit some of the opportunities for themselves rather than for the business.

31.4.2 Behaviour in bust times

We see a repetitive reaction from bust to bust. When it occurs some of the malpractices will come to light, there will be a public outcry and governance procedures will be tightened up. Although controls are weakly enforced during boom times, it is a fact of life that vigilance is required at all times. Fraud, misrepresentation, misappropriation and anti-social behaviour will be constantly with us and robust corporate governance systems need to be in place and monitored.

The ideal would be that the controls in place develop a culture that make individuals constrain their own behaviour to that which is ethical, having previously sensitised themselves to recognise the potential conflicts of interest. It is interesting to see the approach taken by the professional accounting bodies which are concentrating on sensitising students and members to ethical issues.

31.5 Types of past unethical behaviour

Some of the unethical behaviour which has been identified in earlier periods and which our governance systems should attempt to prevent are listed below:

- Looting is a term applied to executives who strip corporations of money for their own use, i.e. misappropriation of funds. The misappropriation is often concealed by normal corporate activities such as entering into transactions with associates of the management or dominant shareholders at inflated prices or by falsifying the accounting records and financial statements.

  For example, in the US the SEC filed a complaint[3] against Richard E. McDonald, former CEO and chairman of World Health Alternatives, Inc. ('World Health'):

  > The Commission's complaint alleges that McDonald was the principal architect of a wide-ranging financial fraud at World Health by which McDonald misappropriated approximately $6.4 million for his personal benefit. Also named as defendants are Deanna Seruga of Pittsburgh, the company's former controller and a CPA, . . .
  >
  > A key aspect of the fraud involved the manipulation of World Health's accounting entries . . . repeatedly falsified accounting entries in World Health's financial books and records, understating expenses and liabilities. This made the Company appear more financially sound, and masked McDonald's misappropriation of funds.

- Insider trading, particularly around major events such as a forthcoming company buyout, takeover or development of a new product. Detection is actively pursued by the SEC in the US and penalties are exacted. For example, the SEC charged a former major league baseball player and three others with insider trading ahead of a company buyout and obtaining more than $1.7 million in illegal profits. $2.5 million was paid to settle the SEC's charges.

- Excessive remuneration so that the rewards flow disproportionately to management compared to other stakeholders and often with the major risks being borne by the other stakeholders.

- Excessive risk taking which is hidden from shareholders and stakeholders until after the catastrophe has struck.

- Unsuccessful managers being given 'golden handshakes' to leave and thus being rewarded for poor performance. For example, in Denmark it was reported that 'Banks are facing criticism for giving their CEOs million-kroner "golden handshakes", despite poor performances'.[4]

- Auditors, bankers, lawyers, credit rating agencies, and stock analysts, who might put their fees before the interests of the public for honest reporting.

- Directors who do not stand up to authoritarian managing directors or seriously question their ill-advised plans. For example, it was reported in 2010 that 'A dominant CEO and a weak board of directors was a recipe for disaster at Orion Bank of Naples. Orion failed last November because Chief Executive Jerry Williams and his inexperienced board could not handle the bank's overly aggressive growth strategy, according to a new report by the Federal Reserve's Office of Inspector General'.[5]

- Management setting incentives for employees which encourage action that is not in the firm's interests.

31.6 The effect on capital markets of good corporate governance

Good governance is important to facilitate large-scale commerce. The mechanism of legal structures such as limited liability of companies exists because it allows the capital of many investors to be combined in the pursuit of economic activities which need large quantities of capital to be economically viable. There are also statutory provisions relating to directors' duties and shareholders' rights. This is a good backcloth which is necessary but not sufficient to ensure the effective working of the capital market.

In addition there has to be a high level of trust by shareholders in their relationship with management. Firstly, they need to believe the company will deal with them in an honest and prudent manner and act diligently. This means that shareholders need to be confident that:

● their money will be invested in ventures of an appropriate degree of risk;

● efforts will be made to achieve a competitive return on equity;

● management will not take personal advantage of their greater knowledge of events in the business; and

● the company will provide a flow of information that will contribute to the market fairly valuing shares at the times of purchase and sale.

Failure to achieve appropriate levels of trust will lead to the risk of the loss of potential investors or the provision of lesser amounts of funds at higher costs. Similarly if other stake-holders, such as the bank, do not trust the management, there will be fewer participants and the terms will be less favourable. Another way of addressing this is to say that people have a strong sense of what is or is not fair. Whilst economic necessity may lead to participation, the level of commitment is influenced by the perceived fairness of the transaction.

Also from a macro perspective, the more efficient and effective the individual firms, the better allocation of resources and the higher the average standard of living. If management as a group is not diligent in its activities and fair in its treatment of stakeholders, there will be lower standards of living both economically and socially.

In addition the current focus on corporate social responsibility could be seen as a response to governance failures by some companies. For example, some managers ignored external-ities such as the costs to society of rectifying pollution because management was only judged on the financial results of the firm, and not the net benefit to society.

31.7 Risk management

We have seen with the issue by the IASB of its *Practice Statement* and the UK with its *Strategic Report* that there is a growing pressure internationally for a company to disclose its risk management policy. In any company there is a range of risks that have to be managed. It is not a matter of just avoiding risks but rather of systematically analysing the risks and then deciding how to decide what risks should be borne, which to avoid, and how to minimise the possible adverse consequences of those which it is not economic to shift. A good governance system will ensure that (a) comprehensive risk management occurs as a normal course of events and (b) there is transparent disclosure to shareholders and regulators of the nature, extent and management of these risks.

There is a variety of approaches which could be adopted to the process of identifying the types of risks associated with a company. In this chapter we will discuss briefly strategic, operational and legal/regulatory risks.

31.7.1 Strategic risks

Strategic risk is associated with maintaining the attractiveness and economic viability of the product and service offerings. In other words, current product decisions have to be made with a strong sense of their probable future consequences. To do that the business has to be constantly monitoring trends in the current markets, potential merging of markets,[6] shifting demographics and consumer tastes, technological developments, political developments and regulations so as to capitalise on opportunities and to counter threats. It must be remembered that to do nothing may involve as much or more risk as entering into new ventures. When entering into new projects there needs to be a thorough risk analysis to ensure that there are no false assumptions in the projections, there has been pilot testing, and the question of the exit strategy if the project fails has been seriously considered and costed.

31.7.2 Operational risks

Operational risks include (a) insurable risks, (b) transferable risks and (c) potential hazards.

Insurable risks

These include such risks as physical damage from fire, flood or accident and reputational damage from quality and public liability issues. The question then is 'If this event should happen could we comfortably bear the cost?'. If the answer is no, then we should insure at least for the amount we couldn't afford to bear.

Transferable risks

These include such risks as difficulty recruiting skilled staff to meet orders or dependence on a key supplier.

On staffing, the question may be 'Could work be outsourced?' However, that in itself creates risks such as dependence, quality control, reliability of delivery, lack of involvement in technological developments, and financial risks associated with the subcontractor.

On supply policy, the question may be 'Should the company opt for multiple suppliers?' This would protect against normal hazards such as strikes at the supplier, adverse weather conditions blocking supply, or threats to supply caused by political factors but at a probable increase in cost.

Hazards

In relation to risks like occupational health and safety, the steps involve identification of potential hazards, identifying the best physical process for handling them, and developing standard ways of operating, then training personnel in those standard operating procedures, and regularly checking to ensure those procedures are being followed.

31.7.3 Legal and regulatory risks

This refers to the possibility that the firm will breach its legal or regulatory requirements and thus expose the company to fines and injury to its reputation. This involves being aware of the requirements of each country in which it operates or in which its products and services are used. Further, the staff of the company need to know of the relevant requirements which apply to their activities. They should also have access to advice in order to avoid problems or to address issues that do arise. Once again, standard operating procedures and standard documentation can help reduce the risks. In some companies the protection of intellectual property should be of considerable relevance.

31.8 The role of internal control and internal audit in corporate governance

Adequate internal controls, effective internal audit and full disclosure in financial statements support good governance.

31.8.1 Adequate internal control

In some jurisdictions the company and the external auditors have to explicitly state that the company has adequate internal controls and the accounts present a fair view. In other jurisdictions it is implied that if the company receives a clean audit report that the internal controls are adequate.

In the US when the explicit requirement was introduced many companies spent considerable sums after the introduction of the Sarbanes–Oxley Act 2002 in upgrading their systems, particularly as the CEO and CFO were made personally liable for the effectiveness of the internal controls.

There is an opportunity cost in CEOs focusing on compliance issues rather than on strategic issues and an actual cost in upgrading systems. This led to some arguing that the costs were unjustified.

Whilst the need to consider cost–benefit considerations in relation to all corporate governance measures is a valid concern, it is also important to remember the costs of bad corporate governance. Good governance will not stop all fraud and excessive risk taking but it will stop it from being so widespread. The internal control systems should limit the ability of management to misdirect resources to their personal use or to publish financial statements with material misrepresentation.

31.8.2 Effective internal audit

Sound internal controls combined with an effective internal audit unit should make it more difficult for senior managers to misappropriate resources or misrepresent the financial position. Naturally we know that the more senior the managers the more likely it is that they can override the internal controls or pressure others to do so. It can be argued that such a situation justifies the requirement that the internal audit unit (if one exists) should report to the Audit Committee.

Role of the Audit Committee

The Institute of Internal Auditors Model Audit Committee Charter[7] states that the Audit Committee should:

- Approve
  - the internal audit charter and the risk-based internal audit annual plan.
- Review
  - with management and the chief audit executive the activities, staffing, and organisational structure of the internal audit function.
  - at least once per year, the performance of the Chief Audit Executive and concur with the annual compensation and salary adjustment.
  - the effectiveness of the internal audit function, including compliance with The Institute of Internal Auditors' International Professional Practices Framework for Internal Auditing consisting of the Definition of Internal Auditing, the Code of Ethics and the Standards.
- Ensure
  - there are no unjustified restrictions or limitations; and
  - review and concur in the appointment, replacement, or dismissal of the chief audit executive.

The following is an extract from the Rank Group Audit Committee:

At its meetings in 2010 the committee examined the effectiveness of the Group's approach to:

- assessment of risk – by reviewing evidence of current and emerging risk and the Group's risk management processes;
- internal control – by approving the internal audit plan and reviewing its findings, reviewing the annual and interim financial statements, reviewing the reports of the external auditors and reviewing the effectiveness of the Group's internal audit function;
- action plans to address any failings or weaknesses of internal control; and
- action plans to manage significant risks.

This process has been in place during the year and up to the date of approval of the 2010 annual report and financial statements. It has been reviewed by the board and meets the Internal Control Guidance for directors contained in the Combined Code.

31.8.3 Full disclosure

There are two aspects to full disclosure, namely the financial data and the narrative.

Financial data

There has been a serious problem with the use by companies of off-balance-sheet finance and special-purpose entities (SPEs) which conceal certain of the company's activities.

For example, in the case of Enron, assets whose values were expected to have to be written down or were vulnerable to substantial market fluctuations were sold to special-purpose entities. Under US rules at that time if there was a 3% outside interest then the special-purpose entity's financial affairs did not have to be consolidated. The exclusion of such items led to the group accounts being misleading.

Good governance requires full disclosure in group accounts and it could be argued that the legislators were at fault in creating the possibility for such off-balance-sheet opportunities and the accounting profession for not making representation against their use.

In the US steps have been taken to address three issues: (i) improving disclosure to investors in the securities about the nature of the underlying financial assets; (ii) limiting conflicts of interest between originators of those financial assets and investors in securities issued by corporate SPEs purchasing those assets; and (iii) increasing rating agency scrutiny of securitisation transactions.[8]

Narrative information

The financial data are backward-looking. Comprehensive information would also include items which are likely to be very important in the future even though they are not currently required to be reported. This could in many jurisdictions include matters relating to future sustainability and comprehensive assessments of environmental impacts. Other future-oriented information would have to relate to the company's strategic drivers and opportunities.

Annual reports can also be used as devices to disclose information which is solely oriented to corporate governance. For example, the disclosure of related party transactions is intended to make it more difficult for a major shareholder to exploit the company for their own benefit. Whilst the disclosure does not prevent that, it allows shareholders to view the level of activity and if they find the level of activity a matter of concern they can raise the issue at an Annual General Meeting.

We have discussed the more general issue of the need for the board of directors to identify and report the potential risks which could have a significant impact on the organisation, such as over-reliance on a supplier or customer and exposure to environmental or product liabilities.

Adequate disclosure of risk is now being addressed by the IASB *Practice Statement Management Commentary* and in the UK by the *Strategic Report*.

31.9 External audits in corporate governance

External audits are intended to increase participation in financial investing and to lower the cost of funds. They may be *ad hoc* reports or audit reports giving an opinion on the fair view of annual financial statements.

Ad hoc reports

In the case of lending to companies it is not uncommon for lenders to impose restrictions to protect the interests of the lenders. Such restrictions or covenants include compliance with certain ratios such as liquidity and leverage or gearing ratios. Auditors then report to lenders or trustees for groups of lenders on the level of compliance. In this way auditors facilitate the flows of funds at good rates.

Statutory audit reports

Similarly for shareholders the audit report is intended to create confidence that the financial statements are presenting a fair view of financial performance and position. If that confidence is undermined by examples of auditors failing to detect misrepresentation or material misstatement, the public becomes wary of holding shares, share prices in the market tend to fall and the availability of new funds shrinks. For the audit report to perform its role adequately, a number of things need to occur:

- the auditors are independent;
- the auditors approach the audit with a degree of scepticism;
- the auditors have professional competence;
- the auditors have industry knowledge;
- the profession enforces audit standards; and
- the results of the audit are communicated in a clear manner.

31.9.1 Auditor independence

The external auditors should keep in mind that their main responsibility is to shareholders. However, there is a potential governance conflict in that for all practical purposes they are appointed by the board, their remuneration is agreed with the board and their day-to-day dealings are with the management. Appointments and remuneration have to be approved by the shareholders but this is normally a rubber-stamping exercise.

It is not uncommon for auditors to talk of the management as the customer, which is of course the wrong mindset. To reduce the identification with management and loss of independence arising from a personal interest in the financial performance of the client, a number of controls are often put in place, for example:

- Financial threats to independence:
  - Auditors and close relatives should not have shares or options in the company, particularly if the value of their financial interest could be directly affected by their decisions.

- Auditors must not accept contingency fees or gifts, nor should relatives or close associates receive benefits.
- Undertaking non-audit work the loss of which, if a significant amount, might be perceived as affecting the auditor's independence. This is a contentious issue with some advocating that auditors should not undertake non-audit work, whereas the client might consider it to be cost-effective. All the indications are that current practice will continue with disclosure of the amounts involved.

- Familiarity threats:
  - Appointments, terminations and the remuneration of auditors should be handled by the audit committee.
  - Auditors should not have worked for the company or its associates.
  - Audit partners should be rotated periodically so the audit is looked at with fresh eyes.
  - Audit tests should vary so that employees cannot anticipate what will be audited.
  - It is not desirable that audit staff be transferred to senior positions in a client company. This happens but it does mean that they will continue to have close relations with the auditors and knowledge of their audit procedures. Clients might regard this as a cost benefit.

However, the above are indications and not to be seen as taking a rule-based approach. Good governance is not just a matter of compliance with rules as ways can always be found to comply with rules whilst not complying with their spirit. It is really a question of behaviour – good governance depends on the auditors behaving independently, with professional competence, and identifying with shareholders and other stakeholders whose interests they are supposed to be protecting. Failing to do this leads to what is described as the expectation gap.

31.9.2 Lack of independence – Enron

The following is an extract from the United Nations Conference on Trade and Development G-24 Discussion Paper Series illustrating the dangers when there is a lack of independence:[9]

> Regarding auditing good corporate governance requires high-quality standards for preparation and disclosure, and independence for the external auditor. Enron's external auditor was Arthur Andersen, which also provided the firm with extensive internal auditing and consulting services. In 2000 consultancy fees (at $27 million) accounted for more than 50 per cent of the approximately $52 million earned by Andersen for work on Enron . . . the following assessment by the Powers Committee: The evidence available to us suggests that Andersen did not fulfill its professional responsibilities in connection with its audits of Enron's financial statements, . . . lack of independence linked to its multiple consultancy roles was a crucial factor in Andersen's failure to fulfill its obligations as Enron's external auditor.

31.9.3 Professional scepticism

Professional scepticism is defined[10] as 'an attitude that includes a questioning mind, being alert to conditions which may indicate possible misstatement due to error or fraud, and a critical assessment of audit evidence'. The auditor is explicitly required to plan and perform an audit with professional scepticism recognising that circumstances may exist that cause the financial statements to be materially misstated.

The individual circumstances will vary but there are indicators such as the following that should be considered:

- Internal conditions:
  - Lack of personnel with appropriate accounting and financial reporting skills.
  - Changes in key personnel including departure of key executives.
  - Deficiencies in internal control, especially those not addressed by management.
  - Changes in the IT environment.
- Trading conditions:
  - Operations in regions that are economically unstable, for example countries with significant currency devaluation or highly inflationary economies.
  - Changes in the industry in which the entity operates.
  - Developing or offering new products or services, or moving into new lines of business.
  - Changes in the supply chain.
- Scale of operations:
  - Expanding into new locations.
  - Changes in the entity such as large acquisitions or reorganisations or other unusual events.
  - Entities or business segments likely to be sold.
  - The existence of complex alliances and joint ventures.
- Financial conditions:
  - Going concern and liquidity issues including loss of significant customers.
  - Constraints on the availability of capital and credit.
  - Use of off-balance-sheet finance, special-purpose entities, and other complex financing arrangements.
  - Significant transactions with related parties.

31.9.4 Undue scepticism with reliance on management representations – Structural Dynamics Research Corporation

In the normal course of an audit it is usual to obtain a letter of representation from management, for example providing information regarding a subsequent event occurring after year-end and the existence of off-balance-sheet contingencies. It is confirmation to the auditor that management has made full disclosure of all material activities and transactions in its financial records and statements.

However, the representations do not absolve the auditor from obtaining sufficient and appropriate audit evidence. The following is an extract[11] from an SEC finding relating to two CPAs who were auditing a company which had improperly recorded sales and then written them off in the following accounting period:

> Despite the fact that the language in purchase orders clearly stated the orders were conditional and subject to cancellation, the auditors accepted the controller's explanation and did not take exception to the recognition of revenue on these orders. This undue reliance on management's representations constitutes insufficient professional skepticism by Present (the engagement partner).
>
> Moreover, Present failed to corroborate management's representations regarding conditional purchase orders with sufficient additional evidence that these sales were

properly recorded . . . Overall, Present failed to exercise due professional care in the performance of the audit.

31.9.5 Enforcing audit standards

There are international audit standards. These are set by the International Auditing and Assurance Standards Board (IAASB) which sets high-quality standards dealing with auditing and quality control and which facilitates the convergence of national and international standards.

Whilst the standards are international, the enforcement of the standards is carried out nationally. National practice varies. In the UK, the Financial Reporting Council (FRC) is the independent regulator for corporate reporting and corporate governance. Through its Codes and Standards Committee the FRC has primary responsibility for setting, monitoring and enforcement of auditing standards in the UK.

31.9.6 Governance within audit firms

Within the audit practices there is also the need to apply systems to ensure that there are adequate reviews of the performance of individual auditors and that the individual partners do not take advantage of their positions of trust.

The greatest control mechanism within an audit firm is the culture of the firm. Arthur Wyatt made the following observation:[12]

> The leadership of the various firms needs to understand that the internal culture of firms needs a substantial amount of attention if the reputation of the firms is to be restored. No piece of legislation is likely to solve the behavioural changes that have evolved within the past thirty years.

Impact of consultancy on audit attitudes

Wyatt drawing on his experience in Arthur Andersen and his observation of competitors indicated that in earlier times there was a culture of placing the maintenance of standards ahead of retention of clients; the smaller size of firms meant there was more informal monitoring of compliance with firm rules and ethical standards. Promotion was more likely to flow to those with the greatest technical expertise and compliance with ethical standards, rather than an ability to bring in more fees. The values of conservative accountants predominated over the risk-taking orientation of consultants.

Wyatt's view was that the growth and risk orientations of consulting are incompatible with the values needed to perform auditing in a manner which is independent in attitude.

31.9.7 Detection of fraud

An audit is designed to obtain evidence that the financial statements present a fair view and do not contain material misstatements. It is not a forensic investigation commissioned to detect fraud. Such an investigation would be expensive and in the majority of cases not be cost-effective. It has been argued that auditors should be required to carry out a fraud and detection role to avoid public concerns that arise when hearing about the high-profile corporate failures. However, it would appear that it is not so much a question of making every audit a forensic investigation to detect fraud but rather enforcing the exercise of due professional care in the conduct of all audits. The audit standards reinforce this when they emphasise the importance of scepticism.

31.9.8 The expectation gap

Another area of corporate governance and auditing relates to the expectation gap. The gap is between the stakeholders' expectation of the outcomes that can be expected from the auditors' performance and the outcomes that could reasonably be expected given the audit work that should have been performed.

The stakeholders' expectation is that the auditor guarantees that the financial statements are accurate, that every transaction has been 100% checked and any fraud would have been detected. The auditors' expectation is that the audit work carried out should identify material errors and misstatements based on a judgemental or statistical sampling approach.

Loss of confidence following corporate scandals

There have been a number of high-profile corporate failures and irregularities; for example, in the US, Enron failed, having inflated its earnings and hidden liabilities in SPEs (special-purpose entities). In 2008 the same problem of hiding liabilities appears to have occurred with Lehman Brothers where according to the Examiner's report[13] Lehman used what amounted to financial engineering to temporarily shuffle $50 billion of troubled assets off its books in the months before its collapse in September 2008 to conceal its dependence on borrowed money, and senior Lehman executives as well as the bank's accountants at Ernst & Young were aware of the moves. In Italy, Parmalat created a false paper trail and created assets where none existed; and in the US, the senior management of Tyco looted the company.

This raises questions such as (a) Were the auditors independent? (b) Did they carry out the work with due professional competence? and (c) Did they rely unduly on management representations?

Auditor liability

In each of the above there is good reason for the expectation gap in that the audit had not been conducted in accordance with generally accepted audit standards and there was a lack of due professional care. If the auditors have been negligent then they are liable to be sued in a civil action. In the UK the profession has sought to obtain a statutory limit on their liability and, failing that, some have registered as limited liability partnerships – the path taken by Ernst & Young in 1996 and KPMG in 2002. In Australia some accountants operate under a statutory limit on their liability and in return ensure they have a minimum level of professional indemnity insurance.

31.9.9 Educating users

Many surveys have shown that there has been a considerable difference between auditors and audit report users regarding auditors' responsibilities for discovering fraud and predicting failure. Users of published financial statements need to be made aware that auditors rely on systems reviews and *sample testing* to evaluate the company's annual report. Based on those evaluations they form an opinion on the *likelihood* that the accounts provide a true and fair view or fairly present the accounts. However, they cannot guarantee the accounts are 100% accurate.

A number of major companies have collapsed without warning signs and the public have criticised the auditors. It is difficult when there are such high-profile corporate failures to persuade the public that lack of due professional care is not endemic. In response to these pressures auditors have modified their audit standards to place more emphasis on scepticism.

31.10 Executive remuneration in the UK

It is worth reinforcing the fact that the objective of corporate governance is to focus management on achieving the objectives of the company whilst keeping risks to appropriate levels and positioning the firm for a prosperous future. At the same time, sufficient safeguards must be in place to reduce the risks of resources being inappropriately diverted to any group at the expense of other groups involved.

31.10.1 The problem

The following is an extract[14] from a speech by Vince Cable, Secretary of State in the UK, in 2012:

> The issue is **partly** about 'rewards for failure'. But it is not just that.
>
> There is also a ratchet in executive pay with everyone believing that they should be paid well above average and that they should be benchmarked against US peers when they live and work in the UK. It is of course a logical absurdity for everyone to be paid above the average, let alone in the top quartile. Imagine if this happened with workers' pay awards. There would be galloping wage inflation and loud business objections about our loss of competitiveness.
>
> While it is true that rising executive pay is a global phenomenon, trends in inequality at the very top are very divergent between countries, despite them all operating in the same global economy. There are world class companies in the Nordic countries, Japan, Holland and Germany who take a very different approach to the UK and US.
>
> But let me be clear. There is a legitimate role for high pay for exceptional talent and performance – quite apart from high returns to successful entrepreneurs – and I will defend that.

Since management is the group with the most discretion and power, it is important to ensure they do not obtain excessive remuneration or perks, or be allowed to shirk, or to gamble with company resources by taking excessive risks.

31.10.2 UK government initiatives[15]

The UK government stated that it would:

> . . . introduce in 2012 a new binding vote on a company's pay policy in order to empower shareholders and encourage improved dialogue with the companies they own. This vote will require the support of a majority of shareholders voting to pass. Companies will set out their proposed pay policy as shown in Table A, including potential payments and the performance measures that will be used. They will also have to set out their policy on how exit payments will be calculated. Once approved by shareholders, companies will be required to act within the pay policy and will not be able to make payments outside the scope of that policy. For the first time there will be a real and binding control on pay.
>
> *Table A: Contents of the policy report:*
>
> ● A table setting out the key elements of pay and supporting information, including how each supports the achievement of the company's strategy, the maximum potential value and performance metrics.
>
> ● Information on employment contracts.

- Scenarios for what directors will get paid for performance that is above, on and below target.
- Information on the percentage change in profit, dividends and the overall spend on pay.
- The principles on which exit payments will be made, including how they will be calculated; whether the company will distinguish between types of leaver or the circumstances of exit and how performance will be taken into account.
- Material factors that have been taken into account when setting the pay policy, specifically employee pay and shareholder views.

The Financial Reporting Council (FRC) has announced that it will consult on potential changes to the Corporate Governance Code, including that where a substantial minority of shareholders vote against the policy, a company should publish a statement saying what they will do to address shareholder concerns. This would publicly hold directors to account.

31.10.3 What is fair?

The statistics show[16] that in recent years the remuneration of executives relative to the average employee has been considerably higher than it was 20 years ago, and the remuneration of the top executive compared to the average of the next four executives is also higher than in the past. That seems intuitively unfair – but is it a valid comparison to be referring back to a relationship that existed 20 years ago? Perhaps the question should be whether this higher relative remuneration reflects a greater contribution to performance, whether it reflects that as businesses increase in size the remuneration of the chief executive tends to increase to reflect the higher responsibilities, or whether it has been achieved simply because directors have been effectively able to set their own remuneration.

31.10.4 How to set criteria – in principle

There are a number of issues that will require a judgement to be made:

- What is the right balance between short-term performance and long-term performance?
- What if there are revenues and costs that are beyond the control or influence of management? Should these be excluded from the measure?
- Also, to the extent that performance may be influenced by general economic conditions, should managers be assessed on absolute performance or relative performance?

Relative performance means that if the performance fell from 10% to minus 3% during an economic downturn, and competitors fell to minus 5%, managers would qualify for a bonus recognising that their performance had been relatively better. This may be resented by shareholders who have seen the share price fall.

Often companies resort to outside consultants, but the observation has been made that one doesn't hear of outside consultants recommending a pay cut and they are in part responsible for ratcheting up the levels of remuneration.

31.10.5 Where do accountants feature in setting directors' remuneration?

The equity of the remuneration is not normally seen as an accounting matter, but accountants should ensure transparent disclosure of the performance criteria and of the payments. In some jurisdictions there is legislation setting out in some detail what has to be disclosed.

31.10.6 Performance criteria

Directors are expected to produce increases in the share price and dividends. Traditional measures have been largely based on growth in earnings per share (EPS), which has encouraged companies to seek to increase short-term earnings at the expense of long-term earnings, e.g. by cutting back capital programmes. Even worse, concentrating on growth in earnings per share can result in a reduction in shareholder value, e.g. by companies borrowing and investing in projects that produce a return in excess of the interest charge, but less than the return expected by equity investors.

31.10.7 Institutional investor guidelines

One of the problems is the innovative nature of the remuneration packages that companies might adopt and the fact that there is no uniquely correct scheme. The Association of British Insurers, in its publication *Share Option and Profit Sharing Incentive Schemes* (amended 1998), commented on this very point:

> There is growing acceptance that the benefit arising from the exercise of options should be linked to the underlying financial performance of the company.
>
> Initially, attention focused on performance criteria showing real growth in normalised earnings; however, a number of other criteria have subsequently emerged. The circumstances of each individual company will vary and there is a reluctance, therefore, on the part of institutional investors to indicate a general preference for any particular measurement. On the other hand, a considerable number of companies have stated that they welcome indications of the sort of formulae that are considered to be acceptable. It is felt that remuneration committees should have discretion to select the formula which is felt to be most appropriate to the circumstances of the company in question. Nevertheless . . . it is important that whatever criterion is chosen . . . the formula should be supported by, or give clear evidence of, sustained improvement in the underlying financial performance of the group in question.

The following are examples from the guidelines of criteria which have evolved and which have been adopted:

Absolute Measures or Targets
Normalised earnings per share measured by reference to a percentage margin, for example 2% per annum growth, in excess of inflation over a 3 year period. It is important that the figures for earnings be smoothed where appropriate to avoid distortions arising from one-off extraordinary or exceptional items included within the FRS 3 definition of earnings per share.

Comparative Measures
Outperformance of an index or of the median or weighted average of a pre-defined peer group in the case of basic options: or the achievement of top quartile performance in the case of super-options:

(i) *Normalised earnings per share*
Outperformance of the median or weighted average rate of increase in normalised earnings of a peer group.

(ii) *Net Asset Value per Share*
Net asset value per share measured, for example against a predefined peer group or index.

(iii) *Total Shareholder Return (ie share price performance plus gross dividend per share)*
   Where total shareholder return is used this should be based on exceeding the relevant benchmark within a predefined peer group but, as this formula relies substantially on share price, attainment of the criterion should also be supported by a defined secondary criterion validating sustained and significant improvement in the underlying financial performance.

(iv) *Comparative Share Price*
   Comparative share price relative to a peer group would be an acceptable alternative to total shareholder return, conditional in the same way on a secondary performance criterion validating sustained and significant improvement in underlying financial performance over the same period.

The following is an extract from the United Utilities 2012 Annual Report:

> Our long-term incentive plans are strongly linked to the delivery of long-term shareholder value through the use of operational measures around regulatory outperformance as well as relative total shareholder return (TSR). Shareholding requirements for executives also provide further long-term alignment with shareholders.
>
> **Overview of remuneration policy**
> In determining the total remuneration package and individual elements for executives, the committee looks at both the performance of the individual and the company. It also considers the range of pay in similar companies and continues to be mindful of remuneration issues across the wider workforce.
>
> **Pay benchmarking group**
> The committee uses market data on salary levels and increases to inform, but not specifically to set, the level of base salary. The committee uses this data with caution given the lack of direct comparators and to avoid remuneration being ratcheted up as a result of benchmarking exercises with no corresponding improvement in performance. Pay is benchmarked against companies of a similar size, sector and UK presence taking into account the nature, scope and complexity of operations.

Further details can be found on the company's website.[17]

31.11 Corporate governance, legislation and codes

Investors looking to the safety and adequacy of the return on their investment are influenced by their level of confidence in the ability of the directors to achieve this. Good governance has not been fully defined and various reports have attempted to set out principles and practices which they perceive to be helpful in making directors accountable. These principles and practices are set out in a variety of Acts, e.g. Sarbanes–Oxley in the US and the Companies Act and regulations in the UK, and codes such as the Singapore Code of Corporate Governance 2012 and the UK Corporate Governance Code (formerly the Combined Code).

The various laws and codes that have been published set out principles and recommended best practice relating to the board of directors, directors' remuneration, relations with shareholders, accountability and audit. We now comment briefly on the position in Hong Kong, Malaysia and Singapore where there are common themes coming through from reviews – namely, how to improve good corporate governance and make directors more accountable.

31.11.1 HK Code of Corporate Governance

There is a Hong Kong Code of Corporate Governance which was revised in 2005. Grant Thornton reviewed[18] the operation of the code in 2008 and commented:

> **Improved compliance**
> Our analysis makes it clear that overall compliance is improving. The year 2008 witnessed an increase in the compliance rate of HSCI companies to 62%. This shows that Hong Kong companies are making efforts to comply with the Code and improve their level of transparency. . . . Our review notes that they still lag far behind expectations in many areas, and they should adhere to the Code's principles and best practices with greater determination.

The Stock Exchange of Hong Kong Limited has amended the Code and Listing Rules to promote the development of a higher level of corporate governance among listed issuers and bring Hong Kong in line with international best practices. They come into force in three phases, starting on 1 January 2012. The rules include upgrading matters such as disclosing directors' attendance at board meetings, the establishment of a nomination committee, responsibility for arranging and funding directors' training, the roles and responsibilities of the chairman, the need for a separate shareholder resolution to retain INEDs beyond nine years' service, and provision of directors' insurance.

31.11.2 Malaysian Code on Corporate Governance

The foreword to the Code[19] states that:

> The *Malaysian Code on Corporate Governance* (Code), first issued in March 2000, marked a significant milestone in corporate governance reform in Malaysia. . . . The *Code 2012* (MCCG 2012) focuses on strengthening board structure and composition recognising the role of directors as active and responsible fiduciaries . . . ensuring that the company conducts itself in compliance with laws and ethical values, and maintains an effective governance structure to ensure the appropriate management of risks and level of internal controls.

The revised Code issued in 2012 covers eight Principles with supporting Recommendations.

31.11.3 Singapore Code of Corporate Governance

The Monetary Authority of Singapore issued a revised Code of Corporate Governance[20] on 2 May 2012. It follows the Principles approach with principles relating to the board, remuneration policy, risk management, internal controls, audit and shareholder relations. The Principles are supported by Guidelines. For example, the following is one of the Guidelines relating to remuneration:

> A significant and appropriate proportion of executive directors' and key management personnel's remuneration should be structured so as to link rewards to corporate and individual performance.

Such performance-related remuneration should be aligned with the interests of shareholders and promote the long-term success of the company. It should take account of the risk policies of the company, be symmetric with risk outcomes and be sensitive to the time horizon of risks.

There should be appropriate and meaningful measures for the purpose of assessing executive directors' and key management personnel's performance.

There is a Corporate Governance & Financial Reporting Centre (CGFRC) at the National University of Singapore[21] which aims to promote best practices in corporate governance and financial reporting.

31.11.4 The European Corporate Governance Institute[22]

This is an excellent resource that covers pretty well all the corporate governance codes in the world. It is interesting to refer to the Institute's website to observe the number of new and revised codes since 2010 which reflects the growing importance attached to corporate governance in terms of investor confidence.

For example, in the foreword to the Bahrain Corporate Governance Code issued in 2010 the Government of the Kingdom of Bahrain stated that it:

> . . . is keen to promote good corporate governance principles in Bahrain in order to enhance investor confidence and foster economic development. . . . The Code is based upon nine core Principles of corporate governance that adhere to international best practices . . . We believe that the Code represents the highest standard in current practice, which has been modified to suit Bahrain's unique economic and social climate as a developing country with a strong regulatory infrastructure.

31.11.5 Codes as a partial solution

As the nature of business and expectations of society change, the governance requirements evolve to reflect the new laws and regulations. By anticipating changing requirements, companies can prepare for the future. At the same time they should identify the special areas of potential conflict in their own operations and develop policies to manage those relationships.

Good governance is a question of having the right attitudes. All the corporate governance codes will not achieve much if they focus on form rather than substance. Codes work because people want to achieve good governance. People can always find ways around rules. Further, rules cannot cover all cases, so good governance needs a commitment to the fundamental idea of fairness.

The research on whether good governance leads to lower cost of capital is very mixed, reflecting both the difficulty of identifying the impact of good governance and the fact that some engage with the spirit of the concept and some do not. There are those who question the impact of good corporate governance, and supporting the case of those who doubt that there is a positive impact on performance is an Australian research project[23] looking at companies in the S&P/ASX 200 index which found that companies which the researcher classified as having poor corporate governance outperformed companies classified as having good corporate governance over a range of measures including EBITDA growth and return on assets. There is an ongoing need for further research, particularly as to the effect on smaller listed companies, and it will be interesting to await the outcome.

31.12 Corporate governance – the UK experience

In the UK there have been a number of initiatives in attempting to achieve good corporate governance through (a) legislation, (b) the UK Corporate Governance Code, (c) non-executive directors (NEDs), (d) shareholder activism and (e) audit. We discuss each of these briefly below.

31.12.1 Legislation

Legislation is in place that attempts to ensure that investors receive sufficient information to make informed judgements. For example, there are requirements for the audit of financial statements, majority voting on directors' remuneration policy and disclosure of directors' remuneration. There could be a case for increased statutory involvement in the affairs of a company by, for example, putting a limit on benefits and specifying how share options should be structured. However, the government has gone down the road of disclosure and transparency to encourage and empower shareholder activism.

31.12.2 The UK Corporate Governance Code[24]

The Code is routinely reviewed every two years. The current code was published by the Financial Reporting Council (FRC) in 2012. It sets out standards of good practice in relation to board leadership and effectiveness, remuneration, accountability and relations with share-holders. It is not a rule book but is principles-based and sets out best practice. It relies for its effectiveness on disclosure by requiring companies listed on a stock exchange to explain if they do not comply with its provisions.

The original code made an interesting development by separating its proposals into two parts:

- Part 1 containing Principles of Good Governance (Main and Supplementary) relating to
  - A: directors
  - B: directors' remuneration
  - C: relations with shareholders
  - D: accountability and audit.
- Part 2 containing Codes of Best Practice with procedures to make the Principles operational.

The current updated Code continues to set out broad principles which companies are largely free to choose their own method of implementing. The detailed code provisions are those which companies are required to say whether they have complied with and, where they have not complied, to explain why not. The intention is to combine flexibility over detailed implementation with clarity where there was non-compliance.

The principles and code provisions relating to the board of directors are set out below to illustrate the code's approach. The six principles that relate to directors cover:

A1 the board

A2 chairman and chief executive

A3 board balance and independence

A4 appointments to the board

A5 information and professional development

A6 performance evaluation.

As an illustration of the level of detail, the Principles (A1) and Provisions (A1.3 and A1.4) relating to the board are set out below.

A1 The Board
Main Principle
Every company should be headed by an effective board, which is collectively responsible for the success of the company.

Supporting Principles include:

- The board should
  - set the company's values and standards; and
  - ensure that its obligations to its shareholders and others are understood and met.
- As part of their role as members of a unitary board, non-executive directors should
  - constructively challenge and help develop proposals on strategy;
  - scrutinise the performance of management in meeting agreed goals and objectives and monitor the reporting of performance;
  - satisfy themselves on the integrity of financial information and that financial controls and systems of risk management are robust and defensible.
- As non-executive directors they
  - are responsible for determining appropriate levels of remuneration of executive directors; and
  - have a prime role in appointing, and where necessary removing, executive directors, and in succession planning.

Code Provisions (*relating to NEDs*)

A.1.3 The chairman should hold meetings with the non-executive directors without the executives present. Led by the senior independent director, the non-executive directors should meet without the chairman present at least annually to appraise the chairman's performance (as described in A.6.1) and on such other occasions as are deemed appropriate.

A.1.4 Where directors have concerns which cannot be resolved about the running of the company or a proposed action, they should ensure that their concerns are recorded in the board minutes. On resignation, a non-executive director should provide a written statement to the chairman, for circulation to the board, if they have any such concerns.

Revisions to the code in 2012

The revisions included:

- Boards will be expected to confirm that the report and accounts, taken as a whole, is fair, balanced and understandable and provides the information needed for shareholders to assess the company's performance, business model and strategy.
- A description of the board's policy on diversity, including gender, any measurable objectives that it has set for implementing the policy, and progress on achieving the objectives.
- Evaluation of the board should consider the balance of skills, experience, independence and knowledge of the company on the board, its diversity, including gender, how the board works together as a unit, and other factors relevant to its effectiveness.

31.12.3 Non-executive directors (NEDs)

The main function of non-executive directors is to ensure that the executive directors are pursuing policies consistent with shareholders' interests.[25]

Review of their contribution

Considering the qualities that are required, the Cadbury Report recommended that the board should include non-executive directors of sufficient calibre and number for their views to carry significant weight in the board's decisions. Research[26] indicated that they are concerned to maintain their reputation in the external market in order to maintain their marketability.

NEDs on many boards bring added or essential commercial and financial expertise, for example on a routine basis as members of the audit committee, or on an *ad hoc* basis providing experience when a company is preparing to float or having specific industry knowledge. They are also valued as having a role in questioning investment decisions and entering into unduly risky projects.

Limitations

However, NEDs are not and never can be a universal panacea. It has to be recognised that there may be constraints such as:

● They might have divided loyalties, having been nominated by the chairman, the CEO or other board member.

● This has been addressed by the Code which states 'An explanation should be given if neither an external search consultancy nor open advertising has been used in the appointment of a nonexecutive director. Where an external search consultancy has been used, it should be identified in the report and a statement should be made as to whether it has any other connection with the company'.

● They might have other NED appointments and/or executive appointments which limit the time they can give to the company's affairs.

● This is addressed by some companies such as BUPA[27] that requires non-executive directors to disclose their other significant commitments to the board before appointment, with a broad indication of the time involved; and inform the board of any subsequent changes.

● They might not be able to restrain an overbearing CEO, particularly if the CEO is also the chairman.

● A 2009 survey[28] indicated that a third of non-executive directors feel they are unable to control their chairmen and chief executives, and almost 40% feel they would be unable to sack underperforming board colleagues.

With so many caveats, it would be reasonable to assume that NEDs could not easily divert a dominant CEO or executive directors from a planned course of action. In such cases, their influence on good corporate governance is reduced unless the interest of directors and shareholders already happen to coincide. However, if the issue is serious enough for one or more independent director to resign it is likely that the market will certainly take note.

Independent NEDs and risk – a negative view

Research[29] commented that the view that outside directors brought experience and strategic expertise, together with vigilance in monitoring management decisions, to prevent strategic mistakes and/or opportunistic behaviour by management was not supported by much evidence that governance reduces risks. The researchers found little evidence that governance was effective in reducing the volatility of share prices or the chance of large adverse share price movements. As with the financial sector in the credit crunch, independent directors seem not to be a protection against companies adopting risky strategies.

Independent NEDs and risk – a positive view

However, on a more positive note, the presence of NEDs is perceived to be indicative of good corporate governance, and a research report[30] indicated that good governance has a positive impact on investor confidence. The research examined 654 UK FTSE All-Share companies from 2003 to 2007 using unique governance data from the ABI's Institutional Voting and Information Service (IVIS). An extract from the ABI research is as follows:

> New research from the ABI (Association of British Insurers) shows that companies with the best corporate governance records have produced returns 18% higher than those with poor governance. It was also revealed that a breach of governance best practice (known as a red top in the ABI's guidance) reduces a company's industry-adjusted return on assets (ROA) by an average of 1 percentage point a year. For even the best performing companies (those within the top quartile of ROA performance), that equates to an actual fall of 8.6% in returns per year.
>
> The research also shows that shareholders investing in a poorly governed company suffer from low returns. £100 invested in a company with no corporate governance problems leads to an average return of £120 but if invested in the worst governed companies the return would have been just £102.

There are many highly talented, well-experienced NEDs but their ability to influence good governance should not be overestimated. Their effectiveness might be reduced if they have limited time, limited access to documents, limited respect from full-time executive directors and limited expertise within the remuneration and/or audit committees. When a company is prospering their influence could be extremely beneficial; when there are problems they may not have the authority to ensure good governance.

31.12.4 Shareholder activism

In the UK the need for good corporate governance is affected by how widely shares are held.

In the US and the UK, a large number of financial institutions and individuals hold shares in listed companies, so there is a greater need for corporate governance requirements. In Japan and most European countries (except the UK) shares in listed companies tend to be held by a small number of banks, financial institutions and individuals. Where there are few shareholders in a company, they can question the directors directly, so there is less need for corporate governance requirements.

The following table is an extract from the UK Office for National Statistics[31] showing the holdings in UK shares:

Beneficial ownership of UK shares in 2010

	Pounds (bn) 2010	Percentages 2010
Rest of the world	732.6	41.2
Insurance companies	153.6	8.6
Pensions funds	91.3	5.1
Individuals	204.5	11.5
Unit trusts	118.8	6.7
Investment trusts	37.2	2.1
Other financial institutions	284.5	16.0
Charities	15.1	0.9
Private non-financial companies	40.3	2.3
Public sector	54.4	3.1
Banks	45.0	2.5
Total	1,777.5	100.0

Figures show that at the end of 2010 the UK stock market was valued at £1,777.5 billion. At that date:

● Rest of the world investors owned 41.2% of the value of the UK stock market, up from 30.7% in 1998.

● Other financial institutions held 16.0%, up from 2.7% in 1998.

● Insurance companies held 8.6% and pension funds held 5.1% by value. These are the lowest percentages since the share ownership survey began in 1963.

● UK individuals owned 11.5%, down from 16.7% in 1998.

Individual shareholder influence on corporate governance

With the rest of the world holding 41.2% and individual shareholders holding only 11.5%, it is difficult for the latter group to exercise any significant group influence on management behaviour. In passing legislation, there is an implicit view that individual shareholders have a responsibility to achieve good corporate governance. Statutes can provide for disclosure and be fine-tuned in response to changing needs but they are not intended to replace share-holder activism. When the economy is booming there is a temptation to sit back, collect the dividends and capital gains, bin the annual report and post in-proxy forms.

Shareholder influence has to rely on that exercised by the institutional investors.

Large-block investors' influence on corporate governance

There is mixed evidence about the influence of large-block shareholders. The following is an extract from a Department of Trade and Industry report:[32]

> The report observed from a review of economics, corporate finance and 'law and economics' research literature that there was no unambiguous evidence that presence of large-block and institutional investors among the firm's shareholders performed monitoring and resource functions of 'good' corporate governance. However, management and business strategy research suggests that it does have a significant effect on *critical* organisational decisions, such as executive turnover, value-enhancing business strategy, and limitations on anti-takeover defences.

Feedback from the experts' evaluation of the governance roles of various types of share-holders provided the following pattern:[32]

	Mean	Standard deviation
Pension funds, mutual funds, foundations	4.58	1.50
Private equity funds	4.52	1.76
Individual (non-family) blockholders	4.36	1.70
Family blockholders	4.20	1.63
Corporate pension funds	3.85	1.55
Insurance companies	3.69	1.69
Banks	3.31	1.49
Dispersed individual shareholders	2.18	1.41

The highest scores were assigned to the governance roles of pension funds, mutual funds, foundations and private equity investors:

> Some respondents also suggested that various associations of institutional investors such as NAPF, ABI, etc., play strong governance roles, as do individual blockholders and family owners. At the other end of the spectrum are dispersed individual shareholders whose governance roles received the lowest score. However, it must be kept in mind that none of the individual scores is above 5 indicating that, on average, our experts were rather sceptical about the effectiveness of large blockholders from the 'good' governance perspective.[32]

A further related factor is that US and UK companies have tended to have a low gearing with most of the finance provided by shareholders. However, in other countries the gearing of companies is much higher, which indicates that most finance for companies comes from banks. If the majority of the finance is provided by shareholders, then there is a greater need for corporate governance requirements than if finance is in the form of loans where the lenders are able to stipulate conditions and loan covenants, e.g. the maximum level of gearing and action available to them if interest payments or capital repayments are missed.

However, institutional investors do not represent a majority in any company. Their role is to achieve the best return on the funds under their management consistent with their attitude to environmental and social issues. Their expertise has been largely directed towards the strategic management and performance of the company with, perhaps, an excessive concern with short-term gains. Issues such as directors' remuneration might well be of far less significance than the return on their investment.

The Walker Review of Corporate Governance of the UK Banking Industry[33]

This reviewed corporate governance in the UK banking industry and financial institutions and made recommendations on the effectiveness of risk management at board level, including the incentives in remuneration policy to manage risk effectively; the balance of skills, experience and independence required on the boards; the effectiveness of board practices and the performance of audit, risk, remuneration and nomination committees; and the role of institutional shareholders in engaging effectively with companies and monitoring of boards. The role of the institutional investors is important and a Stewardship Code has been proposed.

The Stewardship Code[34]

The **Stewardship Code** is a set of principles or guidelines issued by the FRC in 2010. Its principal aim is to make institutional investors take an active role to protect the interests of the people who have placed their money with them to invest.

The code consists of seven principles which, if followed, should benefit corporate governance. The principles are:

1 **Institutional investors should publicly disclose their policy on how they will discharge their stewardship responsibilities**. Such a policy should include how investee companies will be monitored with an active dialogue on the board and its policy on voting and the use made of proxy voting.

2 **Institutional investors should have a robust policy on managing conflicts of interest in relation to stewardship and this policy should be publicly disclosed**. Such a policy should include how to manage conflicts of interest when, for example, voting on matters affecting a parent company or client.

3 **Institutional investors should monitor when it is necessary to enter into an active dialogue with their boards**. Such monitoring should include satisfying themselves that the board and sub-committee structures are effective, and that independent directors provide adequate oversight and maintain a clear audit trail of the institution's decisions. The objective is to identify problems at an early stage to minimise any loss of shareholder value.

4 **Institutional investors should establish clear guidelines on when and how they will escalate their activities as a method of protecting and enhancing share-holder value**. Such guidelines should say the circumstances when they will actively intervene. Instances when institutional investors may want to intervene include when they have concerns about the company's strategy and performance, its governance or its approach to the risks arising from social and environmental matters. If there are concerns, then any action could escalate from meetings with management specifically to discuss the concerns through to requisitioning an EGM, possibly to change the board.

5 **Institutional investors should be willing to act collectively with other investors where appropriate**. Such action is proposed in extreme cases when the risks posed threaten the ability of the company to continue.

6 **Institutional investors should have a clear policy on voting and disclosure of voting activity**. Institutional investors should seek to vote all shares held. They should not automatically support the board and if they have been unable to reach a satisfactory outcome through active dialogue then they should register an abstention or vote against the resolution.

7 **Institutional investors should report periodically on their stewardship and voting activities**. Such reports should be made regularly and explain how they have discharged their responsibilities. However, it is recognised that confidentiality in specific situations may well be crucial to achieving a positive outcome.

The FRC proposes to extend these principles to all listed companies.

The Kay Review[15]

The Kay Review of UK Equity Markets and Long-term Decision Making was published in 2012. It recommended that the Stewardship Code should be developed to incorporate a more expansive form of stewardship, focusing on strategic issues as well as questions of corporate governance. This is in keeping with the increasing pressure for companies to report risks and how they are addressing them.

Other recommendations included the following:

● An investors' forum should be established to facilitate collective engagement by investors in UK companies.

● Companies should consult their major long-term investors over major board appointments.

7 'Good corporate governance is a myth – just look at these frauds and irregularities:

- Enron   www.sec.gov/litigation/litreleases/lr18582.htm
- WorldCom   www.sec.gov/litigation/litreleases/lr17588.htm
- Xerox Corporation   www.sec.gov/litigation/complaints/complr17465.htm
- Dell   www.sec.gov/news/press/2010/2010-131.htm
- Lehman   http://lehmanreport.jenner.com/VOLUME%201.pdf'

How realistic is it to expect good governance to combat similar future behaviour?

8 'Stronger corporate governance legislation is emerging globally but true success will only come from self-regulation, increased internal controls and the strong ethical corporate culture that organisations create.' Discuss.

9 In the modern commercial world, auditors provide numerous other services to complement their audit work. These services include the following:

(a) Accountancy and book-keeping assistance, e.g. in the maintenance of ledgers and in the preparation of monthly and annual accounts.

(b) Consultancy services, e.g. advice on the design of information systems and organisational structures, advice on the choice of computer equipment and software packages, and advice on the recruitment of new executives.

(c) Investigation work, e.g. appraisals of companies that might be taken over.

(d) Taxation work, e.g. tax planning advice and preparation of tax returns to HM Revenue and Customs for both the company and the company's senior management.

Discuss:

(i) Whether any of these activities is unacceptable as a separate activity because it might weaken an auditor's independence.

(ii) The advantages and disadvantages to the shareholders of the audit firm providing this range of service.

10 The following is an extract from the *Sunday Times* of 8 March 2009:

> Marc Jobling, the ABI's assistant director of investment affairs, said: 'Pay consultants are a big contributor to the problems around executive pay. We have heard of some who admit that they work for both management and independent directors – which is a clear conflict of interest and not acceptable. We believe that remuneration consultants, whose livelihood appears to depend on pushing an ever-upward spiral in executive pay, should be obliged to develop a code of ethics.'

Discuss the types of issues which should be included in such a code of ethics and how effective they would be in achieving good corporate governance.

11 There has been much criticism of the effectiveness of non-executive directors following failures such as Enron. Some consider that their interests are too close to those of the executive directors and they have neither the time nor the professional support to allow them to be effective monitors of the executive directors. Draft a job specification and personal criteria that you think would allay these criticisms.

12 In 2000, the chairman of the US Securities and Exchange Commission (SEC), Arthur Levitt, proposed that other services provided by audit firms to their audit clients should be severely restricted, probably solely to audit and tax work.[37] Discuss why this has still not happened.

The code consists of seven principles which, if followed, should benefit corporate governance. The principles are:

1 **Institutional investors should publicly disclose their policy on how they will discharge their stewardship responsibilities**. Such a policy should include how investee companies will be monitored with an active dialogue on the board and its policy on voting and the use made of proxy voting.

2 **Institutional investors should have a robust policy on managing conflicts of interest in relation to stewardship and this policy should be publicly disclosed**. Such a policy should include how to manage conflicts of interest when, for example, voting on matters affecting a parent company or client.

3 **Institutional investors should monitor when it is necessary to enter into an active dialogue with their boards**. Such monitoring should include satisfying themselves that the board and sub-committee structures are effective, and that independent directors provide adequate oversight and maintain a clear audit trail of the institution's decisions. The objective is to identify problems at an early stage to minimise any loss of shareholder value.

4 **Institutional investors should establish clear guidelines on when and how they will escalate their activities as a method of protecting and enhancing share- holder value**. Such guidelines should say the circumstances when they will actively intervene. Instances when institutional investors may want to intervene include when they have concerns about the company's strategy and performance, its governance or its approach to the risks arising from social and environmental matters. If there are concerns, then any action could escalate from meetings with management specifically to discuss the concerns through to requisitioning an EGM, possibly to change the board.

5 **Institutional investors should be willing to act collectively with other investors where appropriate**. Such action is proposed in extreme cases when the risks posed threaten the ability of the company to continue.

6 **Institutional investors should have a clear policy on voting and disclosure of voting activity**. Institutional investors should seek to vote all shares held. They should not automatically support the board and if they have been unable to reach a satisfactory outcome through active dialogue then they should register an abstention or vote against the resolution.

7 **Institutional investors should report periodically on their stewardship and voting activities**. Such reports should be made regularly and explain how they have discharged their responsibilities. However, it is recognised that confidentiality in specific situations may well be crucial to achieving a positive outcome.

The FRC proposes to extend these principles to all listed companies.

The Kay Review[5]

The Kay Review of UK Equity Markets and Long-term Decision Making was published in 2012. It recommended that the Stewardship Code should be developed to incorporate a more expansive form of stewardship, focusing on strategic issues as well as questions of corporate governance. This is in keeping with the increasing pressure for companies to report risks and how they are addressing them.

Other recommendations included the following:

● An investors' forum should be established to facilitate collective engagement by investors in UK companies.

● Companies should consult their major long-term investors over major board appointments.

7 'Good corporate governance is a myth – just look at these frauds and irregularities:

- Enron   www.sec.gov/litigation/litreleases/lr18582.htm
- WorldCom   www.sec.gov/litigation/litreleases/lr17588.htm
- Xerox Corporation   www.sec.gov/litigation/complaints/complr17465.htm
- Dell   www.sec.gov/news/press/2010/2010-131.htm
- Lehman   http://lehmanreport.jenner.com/VOLUME%201.pdf'

How realistic is it to expect good governance to combat similar future behaviour?

8 'Stronger corporate governance legislation is emerging globally but true success will only come from self-regulation, increased internal controls and the strong ethical corporate culture that organisations create.' Discuss.

9 In the modern commercial world, auditors provide numerous other services to complement their audit work. These services include the following:

(a) Accountancy and book-keeping assistance, e.g. in the maintenance of ledgers and in the preparation of monthly and annual accounts.

(b) Consultancy services, e.g. advice on the design of information systems and organisational structures, advice on the choice of computer equipment and software packages, and advice on the recruitment of new executives.

(c) Investigation work, e.g. appraisals of companies that might be taken over.

(d) Taxation work, e.g. tax planning advice and preparation of tax returns to HM Revenue and Customs for both the company and the company's senior management.

Discuss:

(i) Whether any of these activities is unacceptable as a separate activity because it might weaken an auditor's independence.

(ii) The advantages and disadvantages to the shareholders of the audit firm providing this range of service.

10 The following is an extract from the *Sunday Times* of 8 March 2009:

Marc Jobling, the ABI's assistant director of investment affairs, said: 'Pay consultants are a big contributor to the problems around executive pay. We have heard of some who admit that they work for both management and independent directors – which is a clear conflict of interest and not acceptable. We believe that remuneration consultants, whose livelihood appears to depend on pushing an ever-upward spiral in executive pay, should be obliged to develop a code of ethics.'

Discuss the types of issues which should be included in such a code of ethics and how effective they would be in achieving good corporate governance.

11 There has been much criticism of the effectiveness of non-executive directors following failures such as Enron. Some consider that their interests are too close to those of the executive directors and they have neither the time nor the professional support to allow them to be effective monitors of the executive directors. Draft a job specification and personal criteria that you think would allay these criticisms.

12 In 2000, the chairman of the US Securities and Exchange Commission (SEC), Arthur Levitt, proposed that other services provided by audit firms to their audit clients should be severely restricted, probably solely to audit and tax work.[37] Discuss why this has still not happened.

The code consists of seven principles which, if followed, should benefit corporate governance. The principles are:

1 **Institutional investors should publicly disclose their policy on how they will discharge their stewardship responsibilities**. Such a policy should include how investee companies will be monitored with an active dialogue on the board and its policy on voting and the use made of proxy voting.

2 **Institutional investors should have a robust policy on managing conflicts of interest in relation to stewardship and this policy should be publicly disclosed**. Such a policy should include how to manage conflicts of interest when, for example, voting on matters affecting a parent company or client.

3 **Institutional investors should monitor when it is necessary to enter into an active dialogue with their boards**. Such monitoring should include satisfying themselves that the board and sub-committee structures are effective, and that independent directors provide adequate oversight and maintain a clear audit trail of the institution's decisions. The objective is to identify problems at an early stage to minimise any loss of shareholder value.

4 **Institutional investors should establish clear guidelines on when and how they will escalate their activities as a method of protecting and enhancing shareholder value**. Such guidelines should say the circumstances when they will actively intervene. Instances when institutional investors may want to intervene include when they have concerns about the company's strategy and performance, its governance or its approach to the risks arising from social and environmental matters. If there are concerns, then any action could escalate from meetings with management specifically to discuss the concerns through to requisitioning an EGM, possibly to change the board.

5 **Institutional investors should be willing to act collectively with other investors where appropriate**. Such action is proposed in extreme cases when the risks posed threaten the ability of the company to continue.

6 **Institutional investors should have a clear policy on voting and disclosure of voting activity**. Institutional investors should seek to vote all shares held. They should not automatically support the board and if they have been unable to reach a satisfactory outcome through active dialogue then they should register an abstention or vote against the resolution.

7 **Institutional investors should report periodically on their stewardship and voting activities**. Such reports should be made regularly and explain how they have discharged their responsibilities. However, it is recognised that confidentiality in specific situations may well be crucial to achieving a positive outcome.

The FRC proposes to extend these principles to all listed companies.

The Kay Review[35]

The Kay Review of UK Equity Markets and Long-term Decision Making was published in 2012. It recommended that the Stewardship Code should be developed to incorporate a more expansive form of stewardship, focusing on strategic issues as well as questions of corporate governance. This is in keeping with the increasing pressure for companies to report risks and how they are addressing them.

Other recommendations included the following:

● An investors' forum should be established to facilitate collective engagement by investors in UK companies.

● Companies should consult their major long-term investors over major board appointments.

- High quality, succinct narrative reporting should be strongly encouraged.

- Companies should structure directors' remuneration to relate incentives to sustainable long-term business performance. Long-term performance incentives should be provided only in the form of company shares to be held at least until after the executive has retired from the business.

- Asset management firms should similarly structure managers' remuneration so as to align the interests of asset managers with the interests and timescales of their clients. Pay should therefore not be related to short-term performance of the investment fund or asset management firm. Rather a long-term performance incentive should be provided in the form of an interest in the fund (either directly or via the firm) to be held at least until the manager is no longer responsible for that fund.

Legal safeguards

Corporate governance has to react to changing circumstances and threats. It evolves and will continue to need to be revised and updated. The law provides minimum safeguards but in the ever-changing complexities of global trade and finance, good governance is dependent on the behaviour of directors and their commitment to principles and values. The UK system is heavily dependent on codes which set out principles and the requirement for directors to explain if they fail to comply. The UK Corporate Governance Code and Stewardship Code will rely for their effectiveness on investor engagement. This recognises that investors cannot delegate all responsibility to their agents, the directors, accept their dividends and be dormant principals.

UK experience and international initiatives

It is interesting to note that what constitutes good corporate governance is evolving with new initiatives being taken globally. For example, the OECD is responding to weaknesses in corporate governance that became apparent in the financial crisis by developing recommendations for improvements in board practices, the remuneration process and how shareholders should actively exercise their rights. It is also reviewing governance in relation to risk management which featured as such a threat in the way financial institutions conducted their business. However, there is some concern that measures that might be essential for the control of the financial sector should not be imposed arbitrarily on non-financial sector organisations.

31.12.5 Audit

Auditors are subject to professional oversight to ensure that they are independent, up-to-date and competent. However, where there is a determined effort to mislead the auditors, for example by creating false paper trails and misstatement at the highest level, then there is the risk that fraud will be missed.

There have been allegations of audit negligence in some high-profile corporate failures, in some of which auditors have been found liable. In part, the financial crisis arising from issues such as the use of special-purpose entities and complex financial instruments has made life more difficult for auditors. This is because pressure groups, such as the investment banks, have influenced the regulators to allow, or not question, practices that have since been found to be highly risky and undisclosed in group accounts.

In general, whilst the audit appears to be a reliable mechanism for ensuring that the financial statements give a true and fair view, there is a need for audit staff to acquire a detailed understanding of the industry being audited and the risks attaching to financial instruments.

Summary

Good governance is achieved when all parties feel that they have been fairly treated. It is achieved when behaviour is prompted by the idea of fairness to all parties. Independent behaviour is expected of the NEDs and auditors and they are expected to have the strength of character to act professionally with proper regard for the interest of the shareholders. The shareholders in turn should be exercising their rights and not be inert. They have a role to play and it is not fair of them to sit on their hands and complain.

Good corporate governance cannot be achieved by rules alone. The principle-based approach such as that of the FRC with the UK Corporate Governance Code recognises that it is behaviour that is the key – it sets out broad principles and a recommended set of provisions/rules which are indicative of good practice, and disclosure is required if there is a reason why they are not appropriate in a specific situation.

Good corporate governance depends on directors behaving in the best interest of shareholders. Corporate governance mechanisms to achieve this include legislation, corporate governance codes, appointment of NEDs, shareholder activism and audit. Such mechanisms are necessary when companies are financed largely by equity capital. It is noticeable that they are being developed in many countries in response to wider share ownership.

Corporate governance best practice is being regularly reviewed and improved internationally.

REVIEW QUESTIONS

1 Explain in your own words what you understand corporate governance to mean.

2 Explain why governance procedures may vary from country to country.

3 What are the implications of governance for audit practices?

4 Auditors should take a more combative position and start with presumptive doubt and a more sceptical frame of mind, even though past experience of the FD and client staff has never revealed any cause for suspicion.

Discuss the extent to which the requirement to adopt a different approach will increase the auditor's responsibility for detecting fraud.

5 The Association of British Insurers held the view that options should be exercised only if the company's earnings per share growth exceeded that of the Retail Price Index. The National Association of Pension Funds preferred the criterion to be a company's outperformance of the FTA All-Share Index.

(a) Discuss the reasons for the differences in approach.

(b) Discuss the implication of each approach to the financial reporting regulators and the auditors.

6 Research[36] suggests that companies whose managers own a significant proportion of the voting share capital tend to violate the UK Corporate Governance Code recommendations on board composition far more frequently than other companies. Discuss the advantages and disadvantages of enforcing greater compliance.

7 'Good corporate governance is a myth – just look at these frauds and irregularities:

- Enron   www.sec.gov/litigation/litreleases/lr18582.htm
- WorldCom   www.sec.gov/litigation/litreleases/lr17588.htm
- Xerox Corporation   www.sec.gov/litigation/complaints/complr17465.htm
- Dell   www.sec.gov/news/press/2010/2010-131.htm
- Lehman   http://lehmanreport.jenner.com/VOLUME%201.pdf'

How realistic is it to expect good governance to combat similar future behaviour?

8 'Stronger corporate governance legislation is emerging globally but true success will only come from self-regulation, increased internal controls and the strong ethical corporate culture that organisations create.' Discuss.

9 In the modern commercial world, auditors provide numerous other services to complement their audit work. These services include the following:

(a) Accountancy and book-keeping assistance, e.g. in the maintenance of ledgers and in the preparation of monthly and annual accounts.

(b) Consultancy services, e.g. advice on the design of information systems and organisational structures, advice on the choice of computer equipment and software packages, and advice on the recruitment of new executives.

(c) Investigation work, e.g. appraisals of companies that might be taken over.

(d) Taxation work, e.g. tax planning advice and preparation of tax returns to HM Revenue and Customs for both the company and the company's senior management.

Discuss:

(i) Whether any of these activities is unacceptable as a separate activity because it might weaken an auditor's independence.

(ii) The advantages and disadvantages to the shareholders of the audit firm providing this range of service.

10 The following is an extract from the *Sunday Times* of 8 March 2009:

Marc Jobling, the ABI's assistant director of investment affairs, said: 'Pay consultants are a big contributor to the problems around executive pay. We have heard of some who admit that they work for both management and independent directors – which is a clear conflict of interest and not acceptable. We believe that remuneration consultants, whose livelihood appears to depend on pushing an ever-upward spiral in executive pay, should be obliged to develop a code of ethics.'

Discuss the types of issues which should be included in such a code of ethics and how effective they would be in achieving good corporate governance.

11 There has been much criticism of the effectiveness of non-executive directors following failures such as Enron. Some consider that their interests are too close to those of the executive directors and they have neither the time nor the professional support to allow them to be effective monitors of the executive directors. Draft a job specification and personal criteria that you think would allay these criticisms.

12 In 2000, the chairman of the US Securities and Exchange Commission (SEC), Arthur Levitt, proposed that other services provided by audit firms to their audit clients should be severely restricted, probably solely to audit and tax work.[37] Discuss why this has still not happened.

13 Discuss how remuneration policies may adversely affect good corporate governance and how these effects may be reduced or prevented.

14 Discuss the major risks which will need to be managed by a pharmaceutical company and the extent to which these should be disclosed.

15 Egypt is a country in which many of the public companies have substantial shareholders in the form of founding families or government shareholders. How do you think that would affect corporate governance?

16 'Management will become accountable only when shareholders receive information on corporate strategy, future-based plans and budgets, and actual results with explanations of variances.' Discuss whether this is necessary, feasible and in the company's interest.

17 The Chartered Institute of Management Accountants (CIMA) has warned that linking directors' pay to EPS or return on assets is open to abuse, since these are not the objective measures they might appear.

   (a) Identify four ways in which the directors might manipulate the EPS and return on assets without breaching existing standards.

   (b) Suggest two alternative bases for setting criteria for bonuses.

18 Review reporting requirements in relation to disclosure of related party transactions and discuss their adequacy in relation to the avoidance of conflicts of interest.

19 Discuss in what situations audit independence could be compromised.

20 Discuss the extent to which a trade union is able to contribute to good corporate governance.

21 In 2012 the Chancellor unveiled a £100m 'employee-owner' scheme that will allow shares worth £2,000 to £50,000 to be exempt from tax if employees give up certain work rights, such as the right to claim unfair dismissal. He said the measure was aimed at the tens of thousands of small and medium-sized firms.

   Discuss the effect of this proposal on corporate governance. Would your view change if the company should be badly managed and trading poorly?

22 Access http://www.oecd.org/tax/exchangeofinformation/42232037.pdf and discuss the type of misuse of charity funds in the UK and one other country.

EXERCISES

Question 1

Manufacturing Co. has been negotiating with Fred Paris regarding the sale of some property that represented an old manufacturing site which is now surplus to requirements. Because part of the site was used for manufacturing, it has to be decontaminated before it can be subdivided as a new housing development. This has complicated negotiations. Fred is a property developer and has a private company (Paris Property Development Pty Ltd) and is also a major (15%) shareholder of FP Development of which he is chairman. The negotiators for Manufacturing Co. note that the documents keep switching between Paris Property Development and FP Development and they use that as feedback as to how well they are negotiating.

Required:
Is there a corporate governance failure? Discuss.

Question 2

Harvey Storm is chief executive of West Wing Savings and Loans. Harvey authorises a loan to Middleman Properties secured on the land it is about to purchase. Middleman Properties has little money of its own. Middleman Properties subdivides the land and builds houses on them. It offers buyers a house and finance package under which West Wing provides the house loans up to 97% of the house price even to couples with poor credit ratings. This allows Middleman Properties to ask for higher prices for the houses.

Middleman Properties appoints Frontman Homes as the selling agent who kindly provides buyers with the free services of a solicitor to handle all the legal aspects including the conveyancing. Most of the profits from the developments are paid to Frontman Homes as commissions. Harvey Storm's wife has a 20% interest in Frontman Homes.

Required:
Are these corporate governance failures? Discuss.

Question 3

Conglomerate plc was a family company which was so successful that the founding Alexander family could not fully finance its expansion. So the company was floated on the Stock Exchange with the Alexander family holding 'A' class shares and the public holding 'B' class shares. 'A' class shares held the right to appoint six of the 11 directors. 'B' class shares could appoint five directors and had the same dividend rights as the 'A' class shares. The company could not be wound up unless a resolution was passed by 75% or more of 'A' class shareholders.

Required:
Is there any risk of a governance failure? Discuss.

Question 4

The board of White plc is discussing the filling of a vacant position arising from the death of Lord White. A list of possible candidates is as follows:

(a) Lord Sperring, who is a well-known company director and who was the managing director of Sperring Manufacturers before he switched to being a professional director.

(b) John Spate, B.Eng., PhD, who is managing director of a successful, innovative high-technology company and will be taking retirement in four months' time.

(c) Gerald Stewart, B.Com, who is the retired managing director of Spry and Montgomery advertising agency which operates in six countries, being England and five other Commonwealth countries.

The managing director leads the discussion and focuses on the likelihood of the three candidates being able to work in harmony with other members of the board. He suggests that John Spate is too radical to be a member of the board of White plc. The other members of the board agree that he has a history of looking at things differently and would tend to distract the board.

The chairman of the board suggests that Lord Sperring is very well connected in the business community and would be able to open many doors for the managing director. It was unanimously agreed that the chairman should approach Lord Sperring to see if he would be willing to join the board.

Required:
Critically discuss the appointment process.

Question 5

(a) Describe the value to the audit client of the audit firm providing consultancy services.

(b) Why is it undesirable for audit firms to provide consultancy services to audit clients?

(c) Why do audit firms want to continue to provide consultancy services to audit clients?

Question 6

How is the relationship between the audit firm and the audit client different for:

(a) the provision of statutory audit when the auditor reports to the shareholders;

(b) the provision of consultancy services by audit firms?

Question 7

Why is there a prohibition of auditors owning shares in client companies? Is this prohibition reasonable? Discuss.

References

1 C. Oman (ed.), *Corporate Governance in Development: The Experiences of Brazil, Chile, India and South Africa*, OECD Development Centre and Center for International Private Enterprise, Paris and Washington, DC, 2003, cited in N. Meisel, *Governance Culture and Development*, Development Centre, OECD, Paris, 2004, p. 16.
2 www.oecd.org/dataoecd/28/62/38699164.pdf
3 www.sec.gov/litigation/litreleases/2009/lr21350.htm
4 http://cphpost.dk/business/ruin-bank-and-earn-ten-million-kroner
5 http://www.heraldtribune.com/article/20100719/COLUMNIST/7191018
6 An example of this is the convergence of computing, telephone, television and entertainment markets as new devices impinge on all fields compared to ten years ago when they were quite distinct fields.
7 https://na.theiia.org/standards-guidance/Public%20Documents/MODEL_AUDIT_COMMITTEE_CHARTER.pdf
8 http://scholarship.law.duke.edu/cgi/viewcontent.cgi?article=3074&context=faculty_scholarship
9 A. Cornford, 'Enron and internationally agreed principles for corporate governance and the financial sector', G-24 Discussion Paper Series, United Nations.
10 ISA 200, *Overall Objectives of the Independent Auditor and the Conduct of an Audit in Accordance with International Standards on Auditing*, paragraph 13(l).
11 www.sec.gov/litigation/admin/3438494.txt
12 A.R. Wyatt (2003), 'Accounting professionalism – they just don't get it!', http//aaahq.orgAM2003/WyattSpeech.pdf
13 http://lehmanreport.jenner.com/
14 http://www.bis.gov.uk/news/speeches/vince-cable-executive-pay-remuneration-2012
15 http://www.bis.gov.uk/assets/BISCore/business-law/docs/D/12-900-directors-pay-guide-to-reforms.pdf
16 L. Bebchuk, M. Cremers and U. Peyer, 'Higher CEO salaries don't always pay off', *The Australian Financial Review*, 12 February 2010, p. 59.
17 http://annualreport2012.unitedutilities.com/Directorsremunerationreport.aspx#longtermincentives
18 *Corporate Governance Review*, Grant Thornton, p. 7, www.gthk.com.hk/web/en/publications/Research/review
19 http://www.sc.com.my/eng/html/cg/cg2012.pdf

20 http://www.mas.gov.sg/en/Regulations-and-Financial-Stability/Regulatory-and-Supervisory-Framework/Corporate-Governance/Corporate-Governance-of-Listed-Companies/~/media/resource/fin_development/corporate_governance/CGCRevisedCodeofCorporateGovernance3May2012.ashx

21 www.cgfrc.nus.edu.sg

22 www.ecgi.org

23 M. Gold, 'Corporate governance reform in Australia: the intersection of investment fiduciaries and issuers', in P. Ali and G. Gregoriou (eds), *International Corporate Governance after Sarbanes–Oxley*, John Wiley and Sons, New York, 2006.

24 http://www.frc.org.uk/Our-Work/Codes-Standards/Corporate-governance/UK-Corporate-Governance-Code.aspx

25 E. Fama, 'Agency problems and the theory of the firms', *Journal of Political Economy*, vol. 88, 1980, pp. 288–307.

26 E. Fama and M. Jensen, 'Separation of ownership and control', *Journal of Law and Economics*, vol. 26, 1983, pp. 301–325.

27 http://www.bupa.com/investor-relations/our-status-and-governance/our-corporate-governance/role-of-the-sid

28 http://www.guardian.co.uk/business/2009/feb/01/ftse-royal-bank-scotland-group

29 A. Abdullah and M. Page, *Corporate Governance and Corporate Performance: UK FTSE 350 Companies*, The Institute of Chartered Accountants of Scotland, Edinburgh, 2009.

30 ABI Research, *Corporate Governance 'Pays' for Shareholders and Company Performance*, ABI, 27 February 2008, Ref: 12/08.

31 http://www.ons.gov.uk/ons/rel/pnfc1/share-ownership---share-register-survey-report/2010/stb-share-ownership-2010.html

32 G. Igor Filatochev, H.G. Jackson and D. Allcock, *Key Drivers to Good Corporate Governance and Appropriateness of UK Policy Responses*, DTI, 2007, www.berr.gov.uk/files/file36671.pdf

33 www.hm-treasury.gov.uk/walker_review_information.htm

34 http://www.frc.org.uk/Our-Work/Codes-Standards/Corporate-governance/UK-Corporate-Governance-Code.aspx

35 http://www.bis.gov.uk/assets/biscore/business-law/docs/k/12-917-kay-review-of-equity-markets-final-report.pdf

36 K. Peasnell, P. Pope and S. Young, *Accountancy*, July 1998, p. 115.

37 'PwC and E&Y in favour of rules to restrict services', *Accountancy*, October 2000, p. 7.

CHAPTER 32

Sustainability – environmental and social reporting

32.1 Introduction

The main purpose of this chapter is to provide an overview of the impact of sustainability on financial reporting. It is intended to provide students with a basic awareness and understanding of the approaches now being undertaken by company management, accounting staff preparing the financial and non-financial data and the professional accountants carrying out audit and assurance assignments.

In Chapter 31 we saw that corporate governance focused on the accountability of the board to the *shareholders* for its strategic control of the assets and its responsibility to act in their best interest. The effectiveness of its control was assessed in financial terms by reference to ratios such as ROCE, ROI, the rate of growth of EPS, earnings and dividend yields.

In the early stages of environmental, social and sustainability reporting the emphasis was on reporting to *other stakeholders*. It is interesting to see that sustainability and corporate governance are beginning to merge as companies see that the two do not have separate audiences. We are at the beginning of a move towards integrated financial reporting.

Reports that started out as PR exercises are now gradually becoming valued by investors and analysts who are requiring a greater degree of detail. It has become important for companies to be transparent about their corporate responsibility and sustainability efforts if they are to remain competitive in a world with a growing number of informed, concerned consumers.

In Part 6 on Interpretation we saw that there is a well-understood process of presenting ratios with the ability to benchmark by inter-period, inter-company and industry comparators. We have not yet achieved this with regard to benchmarking a company's environmental performance. It is still not possible to make comparisons between companies, and attention has concentrated on the comparative year-on-year percentage changes in annual published reports.

Objectives

By the end of this chapter, you should be able to:

- discuss an overview of the development of corporate social reporting;
- discuss the evolution of sustainability reporting including:
  - the Global Reporting Initiative (GRI);
  - the Eco-Management and Audit Scheme (EMAS);
  - the International Organization for Standardization (ISO);
- discuss the accountant's role in a capitalist industrial society;
- discuss the accountant's role in sustainability reporting;
- discuss the evolution of social accounting in the annual report;
- discuss corporate social responsibility reporting;
- comment critically on all of the above areas.

32.2 An overview – stakeholders' growing interest in corporate social responsibility (CSR)

32.2.1 Primary stakeholders

When corporate bodies were first created the primary stakeholders were the shareholders who had invested the capital and it was seen as the directors' responsibility to maximise their return by way of dividends and capital growth. This view was promoted by Milton Friedman[1] writing that:

> few trends would so thoroughly undermine the very foundations of our free society as the acceptance by corporate officials of a social responsibility other than to make as much money for their shareholders as they possibly can.

It follows from this that directors were accountable to the shareholders who in turn should hold them to account. The Friedman approach offered protection for shareholders provided they actually did exercise their ability to hold directors accountable. However, it did not have regard to the interests of any other group affected by a company's decisions, such as employees, suppliers, consumers or the community for the environmental and social impact of a company's operations unless there was a direct financial benefit or risk to the company.

32.2.2 Other stakeholders

Since Friedman's writing in the 1960s companies have been under pressure to be account-able to a growing number of stakeholders. The pressure can be seen to come from various quarters, such as:

- European Union Directives, e.g. the Landfill Directive whose aim was to prevent or reduce negative effects on the environment;
- national legislation affecting financial reports, e.g. in the UK the Companies Act 2006 has a requirement that the business/strategic review in the Annual Report must include information about:
  - environmental matters (including the impact of the company's business on the environment);
  - the company's employees; and
  - social and community issues;
- investor pressure, e.g. see the European Sustainable Investment Forum[2] which is a pan-European network and think-tank whose mission is to develop sustainability through European financial markets; and
- consumers – although consumers are currently largely unaware that negative production externalities are not internalised and that this is why products are cheaper than they should otherwise be; basically, pricing today does not reflect the true environmental cost of production. In the future, an increased ability for consumers to understand the negative environmental impacts associated with production may well influence their purchasing choices. Responsible consumerism will impact on business and will be both a threat and an opportunity.

32.3 An overview – business's growing interest in corporate social responsibility

Companies are now under pressure to act responsibly in their relationships with other stakeholders who have a legitimate interest in the business. Although there was a fear within companies that their financial performance would be damaged if public costs and other stakeholder interests were taken into account, societal pressure has grown since the 1990s.

Management response has polarised between those companies that see environmental expenditure as a means of improving financial performance by gaining a competitive edge and those that act with non-profit motives. Whatever their view, CSR is on the international agenda. For example, the following is a quote from the World Business Council for Sustainable Development:

> CSR is the continuing commitment by business to behave ethically and contribute to economic development while improving the quality of life of the workforce and their families as well as of the local community and society at large.

There are three interesting points to highlight in this quotation. The first is the reference to behaving ethically, the second is the acknowledgement that a company has an economic objective, and the third is the extension to improve the quality of life of other stakeholders which includes environmental and social impacts.

Need to trade profitably

Whilst accepting these three objectives there is an underlying need for a company to trade profitably and make an economic return if it is to be in a position to satisfy the environmental and social benefits. This is reflected in the following extract from the 2012 Annual Report of Imperial Holdings Limited, a company listed on the Johannesburg stock exchange:

> **Sustainability, business integrity and ethics**
> The board has adopted a written code of ethics for the group, to which all operations are required to adhere.
>
> Without satisfactory profits and a strong financial foundation, it would not be possible to fulfill our responsibilities to shareholders, employees, society and those with whom we do business.
>
> However, our corporate actions are not governed solely by economic criteria and take into account social, environmental and political consideration.

32.3.1 The executives' commitment to sustainability

It is interesting to note that a survey, *A New Era of Sustainability: UN Global Compact–Accenture CEO Study 2010*,[3] reported that 93% of CEOs surveyed say that sustainability will be critical to the future success of their companies and will be fully integrated within a decade.

32.3.2 The Board's commitment to sustainability

As far back as 1975 there have been various initiatives in the UK such as the Corporate Report proposing the disclosure of additional information, such as employment and value added reports.

External corporate reporting has been evolving from the simple financial reporting of profits and losses, assets and liabilities to, for example, the *ad hoc* inclusion of information on governance (e.g. disclosure of directors' remuneration), as well as non-financial information such as environmental and social policies.

For the board it is a balance between improving the total shareholder return (TSR) and acting as good corporate citizens. However, adopting environmental and social policies need not mean a reduction in TSR.

Adopting environmental and social policies improves stock market performance

This reflects an understanding as evidenced by research[4] that companies that voluntarily adopted environmental and social policies by 1993 significantly outperform their counterparts over the long term, in terms of both stock market and accounting performance. The evidence indicated that the outperformance is stronger in sectors where the customers are individual consumers, where companies compete on the basis of brands and reputation, and in sectors where companies' products significantly depend upon extracting large amounts of natural resources.

Board composition affects environmental policies

We talk about the board as a unified body. It is, of course, made up of a group of individuals who might well hold different views on committing resources for what they might perceive to be simply a public good. Indeed, with regard to the composition of the board, research[5] indicates that having a higher proportion of outside board directors and having three or more female directors seems to have some positive effect on environmental performance.

Another interesting research finding[6] was that there was a negative relation between board members who had shown past unethical risk behaviour and the environmental performance of the firm. Boards with a higher proportion of risk-prone, unethical members seem to focus less on the environmental concerns of their businesses, which is probably what one would intuitively feel.

If the share capital is provided by a few, the impact of the expenditure becomes far more personal and the board could be under pressure with a reluctance to regard sustainability policies as a source of cost-efficiencies and revenue growth rather seeing them as an avoidable cost.

32.3.3 Reporting environmental performance and impact in the annual report

Narrative references to environmental issues have appeared on an *ad hoc* basis in annual reports. In some jurisdictions there may be, as in the UK, a statutory requirement for a director to act in the way most likely to promote the success of the company for the benefit of its members as a whole, and in doing so to have regard to the interests of the company's employees, the need to foster the company's business relationships with suppliers, customers and others, and the impact of the company's operations on the community and the environment.

Danger of information overload

When considering inclusion of CSR reporting in the annual report, one of the problems has been the volume of data. Companies are overcoming this by issuing summary CSR reports in hard copy and uploading the full CSR report onto their websites. The following is an extract[7] relating to experience in the Netherlands:

In the Netherlands, various companies are aiming for further integration of the CSR information into their annual reports. Companies are increasingly using the Internet in order to reduce the size of their CSR reports. They publish hard copy summary reports, with the full versions available on the Internet.

A survey[8] commissioned by the Global Reporting Initiative (GRI) and The Prince's Accounting for Sustainability Project (A4S) commented that the future steps to be taken should include developing a considered and targeted approach to online investor and analyst communication, focusing on how users interact with online content and the usability of this source of information.

Evolution of stand-alone environmental reports

Companies might find that the environmental data are already so integrated that a single combined report is advisable, or decide that a separate report has the advantage of raising more awareness both in the company and with other stakeholders.

Jurisdictions where there is a legislative requirement

There is legislation in some jurisdictions, such as Denmark, the Netherlands, Norway and Sweden, requiring environmental statements from environmentally sensitive industries either in their financial statements or in a stand-alone report; in other countries, voluntary disclosures are proposed.

The following is an extract relating to a Danish experience[9] where most companies now produce separate Corporate Social Responsibility reports:

> Most Danish companies now publish separate CSR reports, independent of their statutory annual reporting. In recent years, more companies have started integrating their financial and non-financial data into the same report, for instance by adding a section on non-financial data at the end of the report. The companies preparing the best reports, however, are those which grasp the connection between the non-financial data and their business. As a result, these companies have fully integrated non-financial data with financial data in the report. In doing this, the companies clearly demonstrate their full understanding of the value of reporting on non-financial data. They demonstrate that the data are being used as a serious management and communication tool and that they are able to link CSR to business strategy.

Publishing an Environmental Profit and Loss Account

This is a step forward. Developments in financial accounting and reporting remain dynamic and it is fascinating to see the wealth of academic research and business innovation. Many companies are actively engaging with ways in which to report the environmental impact of their operations. One such is the publication[10] by Puma in 2011 of an Environmental Profit and Loss Account which identifies the reasons and the cost of £145m as the environmental impact. It is well worth accessing the corporate site for a more detailed look at its approach. It was not surprising that Puma was also finalist in the 2012 Finance for the Future Awards.

32.4 Companies' voluntary adoption of guidelines and certification

Although there are no mandatory reporting standards, there are a number of schemes such as the Connected Reporting Framework, the Global Reporting Initiative (GRI), the Eco-Management and Audit Scheme (EMAS) and the International Organization for Standardization (ISO).

32.4.1 The Connected Reporting Framework

The Accounting for Sustainability project[11] has developed a Connected Reporting Framework which has been adopted by a range of organisations including Aviva, BT, EDF Energy and HSBC. It explains how all areas of organisational performance can be presented in a connected way, reflecting the organisation's strategy and the way it is managed.

It proposes five key environmental indicators, which all organisations should consider reporting: polluting emissions, energy use, water use, waste and significant use of other finite resources, and the inclusion of industry benchmarks, when available, for key performance indicators, to aid performance appraisal. It is seeking consistency in presentation to aid comparability between years and organisations.

The following is an extract from the 2011 Aviva plc Annual Report:

Accounting for Sustainability
In addition to the online CR Report and summary report in the Annual report and accounts, we also report our performance using Accounting for Sustainability's Connected Reporting Framework, which integrates financial and non-financial data to provide a comprehensive picture of our impacts. We were one of the first companies to help develop the framework and have used this approach for environmental reporting in our Annual report and accounts since 2007. We continue to explore ways to extend this framework and have included customer and community indicators since 2009.

32.4.2 The Global Reporting Initiative (GRI)[12]

The GRI has a mission to develop global sustainability reporting guidelines for voluntary use by organisations reporting on the three linked elements of sustainability, namely the economic, environmental and social dimensions of their activities, products and services.

- The *economic dimension* includes financial and non-financial information on R&D expenditure, investment in the workforce, current staff expenditure and outputs in terms of labour productivity.
- The *environmental dimension* includes any adverse impact on air, water, land, biodiversity and human health by an organisation's production processes, products and services.
- The *social dimension* includes information on health and safety and recognition of rights, e.g. human rights for both employees and outsourced employees.

The Global Reporting Initiative means that parties contemplating a relationship such as assessing investment risk and obtaining goods or services will have available to them a clear picture of the human and ecological impact of the business. Its influence has been growing and there are jurisdictions, such as Sweden, that require a GRI report.

GRI reports have assurance, having been verified by independent, competent and impartial external assurance providers. The assurance providers themselves now have a standard – the AA1000 Assurance Standard.[13] As an example, in the 2011 Aviva Annual Report, Ernst & Young, who were the assurance providers, stated that they were forming a conclusion on matters such as

- inclusivity – whether Aviva had engaged with stakeholders across the business to further develop its approach to corporate responsibility;
- materiality – whether Aviva had provided a balanced representation of material issues concerning Aviva's corporate responsibility performance;
- completeness – whether Aviva had complete information on which to base a judgement of what was material for inclusion in the Report; and
- responsiveness – whether Aviva had responded to stakeholder concerns.

32.4.3 The Eco-Management and Audit Scheme (EMAS)[14]

The Eco-Management and Audit Scheme (EMAS) was adopted by the European Council in 1993, allowing voluntary participation in an environmental management scheme. Its aim is to promote continuous environmental performance improvements of activities by committing organisations to evaluating and improving their own environmental performance.

Just as with GRI reports, verification is seen as an important element and environmental audits, covering all activities at the organisation concerned, must be conducted within an audit cycle of no longer than three years.

In addition to helping internal management, the adoption of such a scheme also assists external auditors when reviewing compliance by the company with legislation.

32.4.4 The International Organization for Standardization (ISO)[15]

The ISO is a non-governmental organisation whose aim is to establish international standards to reduce barriers to international trade. Its standards, including environmental standards, are voluntary and companies may elect to join in order to obtain ISO certification.

One group of standards, the ISO 14000 series, is intended to encourage organisations to systematically assess the environmental impacts of their activities through a common approach to environmental management systems. Within the group, the ISO 14001 standard states the requirements for establishing an EMS and companies must satisfy its requirements in order to qualify for ISO certification.

Benefits from ISO certification

These include:

● *Top-level management become involved.* They are required to define an overall policy and, in addition, they recognise significant financial considerations from certification, e.g. customers might in the future prefer to deal with ISO compliant companies, insurance premiums might be lower and there is the potential to reduce costs by greater production efficiency.
● *Environmental management.* ISO 14001 establishes a framework for a systematic approach to environmental management which can identify inefficiencies that were not apparent beforehand, resulting in operational cost savings and reduced environmental liabilities. Aviva, for example, which we mentioned above, reduced its water consumption by over 25% in 2011.

What criticisms are there of a compliance approach?

Compliance approaches which set out criteria such as a commitment to minimise environmental impact can allow companies to set low objectives for improvement and report these as achievements with little confidence that there has been significant environmental benefit. This is gradually being addressed by industry comparison and by governments also seeking to produce targets and benchmarks.

32.5 The accountant's role in a capitalist industrial society

Shareholder interest initially dominant

In a capitalist, industrial society, production requires the raising and efficient use of capital largely through joint stock companies. These operate within a legal framework which grants them limited liability subject to certain obligations. The obligations include capital maintenance provisions to protect creditors (e.g. restriction on distributable profits) and disclosure provisions to protect shareholders (e.g. the publication of annual reports).

Accountants issue standards to ensure there is reliable and relevant information to the owners to support an orderly capital market. This has influenced the nature of accounting standards, with their concentration on earnings and monetary values.

Other stakeholder interests gradually recognised

However, production and distribution involve complex social relationships between private ownership of property and wage labour[16] and other stakeholders. This raises the question of the role of accountants. Should their primary concern be to serve the interests of the shareholders, or the interests of management, or to focus on equity issues and social welfare?[17]

Pressure for reports to reflect substance

Prior to the formation in the UK of the ASB, the profession identified with management and it was not unusual to allow information to be reported to suit management. If managers were unhappy with a standard, they were able to frustrate or delay its implementation. This meant that the reported results might bear little resemblance to the commercial substance of the underlying transactions.

Creating standards relating to environmental liabilities and assets

Reporting environmental liabilities – IFRSs

Possible environmental liabilities that give rise to a provision include waste disposal, pollution, decommissioning and restoration expenses. There may also be liabilities arising from participation in a specific market, such as vehicle production or the manufacture of electrical and electronic equipment.

We have seen in Chapter 13 that a provision is recognised when an entity has a present obligation as a result of a past event, it is probable that a transfer of economic benefits will be required to settle the obligation, and a reliable estimate can be made of the amount of the obligation (IAS 37).

This information can be commercially important to potential corporate investors as, for example, when deciding on the price to pay to acquire shares on a takeover. For example, acquisitive companies needed to be aware of contingent environmental liabilities,[18] which can be enormous. In the USA the potential cost of clearing up past industrially hazardous sites has been estimated at $675 billion.

Even in relation to individual companies the scale of the contingency can be large, as in the Love Canal case. In this case a housing project was built at Love Canal in upper New York State on a site that until the 1950s had been used by the Hooker Chemicals Corporation for dumping a chemical waste containing dioxin. Occidental, which had acquired Hooker Chemicals, was judged liable for the costs of clean-up of more than $260 million.[19] Existing shareholders and the share price would also be affected by these increased costs.

Reporting environmental assets – IFRSs

There was a question as to whether physical assets acquired to comply with environmental legislation could be classified as an asset for reporting purposes as they were not in isolation creating revenue or reducing costs. This was addressed by IAS 16 *Property, Plant and Equipment* which provides that some elements of tangible non-current assets can be acquired for reasons of safety or are environmental in nature. Although the acquisition of such property, plant and equipment does not in itself qualify them for recognition, they qualify as assets because they enable the institution to obtain additional economic benefits from the rest of its assets which would not have been earned otherwise.

32.6 The nature of the accountant's involvement

32.6.1 Finance directors

FDs have become increasingly involved internally in dealing with issues such as recommending which voluntary code to adopt. Voluntary codes have developed in a largely unstructured way and accountants may be involved in identifying those codes which are appropriate to the business, such as GRI and EMAS.

32.6.2 Accounting staff and systems design

Responding to public interest in the ethical sourcing of raw materials and products, FDs have also become responsible for the design and monitoring of purchasing policies to establish an audit trail. This will become more important as more attention is focused on sourcing. For example, in the 2008 *Environmental Reporting – Trends in FTSE 100 Sustainability Reports*[20] the observation was made that 'the Resource and supply chain are amongst the least discussed environmental issues, despite their growing prominence on the sustainability agenda. The least covered themes across industry sectors are concepts related to resource and supply chain, falling behind themes such as waste and recycling, sustainability, and renewable energy'.

32.6.3 Accounting staff and routine collection of data

In addition, there will be other typical inputs from accountants in each of the three elements, often requiring a greater degree of quantification than at present for the economic and environmental dimensions. For example:

● The economic dimension may require economic indicators such as:
  – profit: segmental gross margin, EBITDA, EBIT, return on average capital employed;
  – intangible assets: ratio of market valuation to book value;
  – investments: human capital, R&D, debt/equity ratio;
  – wages and benefits: totals by country;
  – labour productivity: levels and changes by job category;
  – community development: jobs by type and country showing absolute figures and net change;
  – suppliers: value of goods and services outsourced, performance in meeting credit terms.
● The environmental dimension may require environmental indicators such as:
  – products and services: major issues, e.g. disposal of waste, paper usage, packaging practices, percentage of product reclaimed after use;
  – suppliers: supplier issues identified through stakeholder consultation, e.g. forest stewardship, sustainable logging;
  – travel: objectives and targets, e.g. product distribution, fleet operation, quantitative estimates of miles travelled by transport type.

- Social dimensions may require social indicators such as:
  - quality of management: employee retention rates, ratio of jobs offered to jobs accepted, ranking as an employer in surveys;
  - health and safety: reportable cases, lost days, absentee rate, investment per worker in injury prevention;
  - wages and benefits: ratio of lowest wage to local cost of living, health and pension benefits provided;
  - training and education: ratio of training budget to annual operating cost, programmes to encourage worker participation in decision making;
  - freedom of association: grievance procedures in place, number and types of legal action concerning anti-union practices.

32.6.4 Auditors

Auditors will be increasingly required to provide assurance on the application of standards in the supply chain.[21]

There are mixed feelings towards the need for assurance. Companies that are committed to the voluntary codes (GRI, EMAS, ISO 14001) are more supportive of the need than other companies that are not as familiar with assurance reports. There has, however, been a growing pressure for CSR information to be subject to assurance reports to give stakeholders the same confidence as they have obtained from the audit reports on financial statements. Challenges for UK companies in applying the AA1000 Assurance Standard (2008) include:

- providing more detailed commentary on methodology and recommendations in the statement; and
- focusing more on the materiality, completeness and responsiveness principles rather than just simply checking accuracy of information.[22]

32.6.5 Environmental auditing – international initiatives

Europe

Since 1999 the European Federation of Accountants (FEE) Sustainability Working Party (formerly Environmental) has been active in the project Providing Assurance on Environmental Reports[23] and is actively participating with other organisations and collaborating on projects such as with GRI Sustainability Guidelines.

Canada

It is interesting to see the multidisciplinary approach that is now being taken. For example, the Canadian Environmental Auditing Association (CEAA) is a multidisciplinary organisation whose international membership base now includes environmental managers, ISO 14001 registration auditors, EMS (Eco-Management Systems) consultants, **corporate environmental auditors**, engineers, chemists, government employees, **accountants** and lawyers. The CEAA is now accredited by the Standards Council of Canada as a certifying body for EMS Auditors.[24]

32.6.6 The profession

All of the professional accounting bodies are active in various ways in promoting developments in reporting on environmental and sustainability issues. We briefly comment on a couple of the ICAEW and ACCA activities.

ICAEW – Environmental Issues and Annual Financial Reporting

In 2009 the report *Turning Questions into Answers: Environmental Issues and Annual Financial Reporting*[25] was issued jointly by the ICAEW and the Environment Agency. It identified the main concerns of the users regarding environmental information currently provided in annual reports to be in the areas of:

● Consistency and comparability – in the absence of well-defined disclosure requirements, there is a lack of consistency and comparability.

● Relevance and usefulness – the lack of focus on environmental issues that are of critical importance to specific industry sectors. Disclosure of data does not necessarily reveal the effectiveness of a policy.

● Reliability and assurance – this is regarded as of secondary importance to the above qualities. There are also concerns as to the skills and experience required by assurance providers.

● Materiality – the business review requirement for disclosure of any material environmental issues is unsatisfactory without further guidance.

● Presentation – integration of material financial and non-financial information within annual reports is generally preferred. It will also assist international comparability.

These are all indicators of the need for further work by the accounting profession.

The ICAEW together with NatWest and The Prince's Accounting for Sustainability Project were founder members of the Finance for the Future Awards. These awards look at long-term sustainability from a finance perspective or celebrate accounting for sustainability as the key to creating an innovative business model. They focus in particular on the role that the finance team has to play in reaching these outcomes. One of the award's objectives is to share best practice through development of case studies and educational resources based on the experiences of the nominees and winners.

The ACCA Award schemes

One of the earliest of the award schemes was that of the ACCA. Its 'Awards for Sustainability Reporting' scheme has three award categories for Environmental Reporting, Social Reporting and Sustainability Reporting. Details of the UK and European Sustainability Reporting Award can be found on the ACCA website. Other schemes have been set up using the ACCA criteria,[26] such as the Central European Environmental Reporting 'Green Frog' awards.

These schemes have given environmental reporting a high profile and contributed greatly to the present quality of reports. The schemes now take place in a number of countries and regions. These include Australia, Hong Kong, Malaysia, New Zealand, Singapore, South Africa, Sri Lanka, Europe and North America.

32.7 Summary on environmental reporting

Environmental reporting is in a state of evolution ranging from *ad hoc* comments in the annual report to a more systematic approach in the annual report to stand-alone environmental reports.

Environmental investment is no longer seen as an additional cost but as an essential part of being a good corporate citizen, and environmental reports are seen as necessary in communicating with stakeholders to address their environmental concerns.

Companies are realising that it is their corporate responsibility to achieve sustainable development whereby they meet the needs of the present without compromising the ability of future generations to meet their own needs. Economic growth is important for shareholders and other stakeholders alike in that it provides the conditions in which protection of the environment can best be achieved, and environmental protection, in balance with other human goals, is necessary to achieve growth that is sustainable.

However, there is still a long way to go and the EU's Sixth Action Programme 'Environment 2010: Our Future, Our Choice'[27] recognises that effective steps have not been taken by all member states to implement EC environmental directives and there is weak ownership of environmental objectives by stakeholders. The programme focuses on four major areas for action – climate change, health and the environment, nature and biodiversity, and natural resource management – and emphasises how important it is that all stakeholders should be involved to achieve more environmentally friendly forms of production and consumption as well as integration into all aspects of our life such as transport, energy and agriculture.

32.8 Concept of social accounting

This is a difficult place to start because there are so many definitions of social accounting.[26] The main points are that it includes non-financial as well as financial information and addresses the needs of stakeholders other than the shareholders. Stakeholders can be broken down into three categories:

● internal stakeholders – managers and workers;

● external stakeholders – shareholders, creditors, banks and debtors; and

● related stakeholders – society as represented by national and local government and the increasing role of pressure groups such as Amnesty International and Greenpeace.

32.8.1 Reporting at corporate level

Prior to 1975, social accounting was viewed as being in the domain of the economist and concerned with national income and related issues. In 1975, *The Corporate Report* gave a different definition:

> the reporting of those costs and benefits, which may or may not be quantifiable in money terms, arising from economic activities and subsequently borne or received by the community at large or particular groups not holding a direct relationship with the reporting entity.[28]

This is probably the best working definition of the topic and it establishes the first element of the social accounting concept, namely **reporting at a corporate level** and interpreting corporate in its widest sense as including all organisations of economic significance regardless of the type of organisation or the nature of ownership.

32.8.2 Accountability

The effect of the redefinition by *The Corporate Report* was to introduce the second element of our social accounting concept: accountability. The national income view was only of interest to economists and could not be related to individual company performance – *The Corporate Report* changed that. Social accounting moved into the accountants' domain and it should be the aim of accountants to learn how accountability might be achieved and to define a model against which to judge their own efforts and the efforts of others.

32.8.3 Comprehensive coverage

The annual report is concerned mainly with monetary amounts or clarifying monetary issues. Despite the ASB identifying employees and the public within the user groups,[29] no standards have been issued that deal specifically with reporting to employees or the public.

Instead, the ASB prefers to assume that financial statements that meet the needs of investors will meet most of the needs of other users.[30] For all practical purposes, it disassociates itself from the needs of non-investor users by assuming that there will be more specific information that they may obtain in their dealings with the enterprise.[31]

The information needs of different categories, e.g. employees and the public, need not be identical. The provision of information of particular interest to the public has been referred to as **public interest accounting**,[32] but there is a danger that, whilst valid as an approach, it could act as a constraint on matters that might be of legitimate interest to the employee user group. For example, safety issues at a particular location might be of little interest to the public at large but of immense concern to an employee exposed to work-related radiation or asbestos. The term 'social accounting' as defined by *The Corporate Report* is seen as embracing all interests, even those of a small group.

Equally, the information needs within a category – say, employees – can differ according to the level of the employees. One study identified that different levels of employee ranked the information provided about the employer differently, e.g. lower-level employees rated safety information highest, whereas higher-level employees rated organisation information highest.[33] There were also differences in opinion about the need for additional information, with the majority of lower-level but minority of higher-level employees agreeing that the social report should also contain information on corporate environmental effects.[34]

The need for social accounting to cope with both inter-group and intra-group differences was also identified in a Swedish study.[33]

32.8.4 Independent review

The degree of credibility accorded a particular piece of information is influenced by factors such as whether it is historical or deals with the future; whether appropriate techniques exist for obtaining it; whether its source causes particular concern about deliberate or unintentional bias towards a company view; whether past experience has been that the information was reasonably complete and balanced; and, finally, the extent of independent verification.[35]

Given that social accounting is complex and technically underdeveloped, that it deals with subjective areas or future events, and that it is reported on a selective basis within a report prepared by the management, it is understandable that its credibility will be called into question. Questions will be raised as to why particular items were included or omitted – after all, it is not that unusual for companies to want to hide unfavourable developments.

32.9 Background to social accounting

A brief consideration of the history of social accounting in the UK could be helpful in putting the subject into context. *The Corporate Report* (1975) was the starting point for the whole issue.

It was a discussion paper which represented the first UK conceptual framework. Its approach was to identify users and their information needs. It identified seven groups of user, which included employees and the public, and their information needs. However, although it identified that there were common areas of interest among the seven groups, such as assessing liquidity and evaluating management performance, it concluded that a single set of general-purpose accounts would not satisfy each group – a different conclusion from that stated by the ASB in 1991, as discussed above.[29] The conclusions reached in *The Corporate Report* were influenced by the findings of a survey of the chairmen of the 300 largest UK listed companies. They indicated a trend towards acceptance of multiple responsibilities towards groups affected by corporate decision-making and their interest as stakeholders.[36]

It was proposed in *The Corporate Report* that there should be additional reports to satisfy the needs of the other stakeholders. These included a Statement of corporate objectives, an Employment report, a Statement of future prospects and a Value added statement.

Statement of corporate objectives

Would this be the place for social accounting to start? Would this be the place for vested interests to be represented so that agreed objectives take account of the views of all stakeholders and not merely the management and, indirectly, the shareholders? At present, social accounting appears as a series of add-ons, e.g. a little on charity donations, a little on disabled recruitment policy. Corporate objectives or the mission statement are often seen as something to be handed down; could they assume a different role?

Employment report

The need for an employment report was founded on the belief that there is a trust relationship between employers and employees and an economic relationship between employment prospects and the welfare of the community. The intention was that such a report should contain statistical information relating to such matters as numbers, reasons for change, training time and costs, age and sex distribution, and health and safety.

Statement of future prospects

There has always been resistance to publishing information focusing on the future. The arguments raised against it have included competitive disadvantage and the possibility of misinterpretation because the data relate to the future and are therefore uncertain. The writers of *The Corporate Report* nevertheless considered it appropriate to publish information on future employment and capital investment levels that could have a direct impact on employees and the local community.

Value added statements

A value added report was intended to give a different focus from the profit and loss account with its emphasis on the bottom line earnings figure. It was intended to demonstrate the interdependence of profits and payments to employees, shareholders, the government and the company via inward investment. It reflected the mood picked up from the survey of chairmen that distributable profit could no longer be regarded as the sole or prime indicator of company performance.[36]

The value added statement became a well-known reporting mechanism to measure how effectively an organisation utilised its resources and added value to its raw materials to turn them into saleable goods. Figure 32.1 is an example of a value added statement.

Several advantages have been claimed for these reports, including improving employee attitudes by reflecting a broader view of companies' objectives and responsibilities.[37]

Figure 32.1 Imperial Holdings Ltd value added statement

for the year ended 30 June 2012

	2012 Rm	%	2011 Rm	%
Revenue	80,830		64,667	
Paid to suppliers for materials and services	62,699		49,933	
Total wealth created	**18,131**		14,734	
Wealth distribution				
Salaries, wages and other benefits (note 1)	10,703	59	8,713	59
Providers of capital	1,772	10	1,547	11
– Net financing costs	681	4	554	4
– Dividends, share buybacks and cancellations	1,091	6	993	7
Government (note 2)	1,572	9	1,543	10
Reinvested in the group to maintain and develop operations	4,084	22	2,931	20
– Depreciation, amortisation and recoupments	1,822		1,488	
– Future expansion	2,262		1,443	
	18,131	100	14,734	100
Value-added ratios				
– Number of employees (continuing operations)	47,699		40,898	
– Revenue per employee (000)	1,695		1,581	
– Wealth created per employee (000)	380		360	
Notes				
1. Salaries, wages and other benefits				
Salaries, wages, overtime, commissions, bonuses, allowances	9,959		8,070	
Employer contributions	744		643	
	10,703		8,713	
2. Central and local governments				
SA normal taxation	1,102		1,131	
Secondary tax on companies	90		108	
Foreign taxation	192		151	
Rates and taxes	72		69	
Skills development levy	41		43	
Unemployment Insurance Fund	48		41	
Carbon emissions tax	27			
	1,572		1,543	

Value added 2012 (%)

Employees 59%
Providers of capital 10%
Government 9%
Reinvested in the group 22%

Value added 2011 (%)

Employees 59%
Providers of capital 11%
Government 10%
Reinvested in the group 20%

There have also been criticisms, e.g. they are merely a restatement of information that appears in the annual report; they only report data capable of being reported in monetary terms; and the individual elements of societal benefit are limited to the traditional ones of shareholders, employees and the government, with others such as society and the consumers ignored.

There was also criticism that there was no standard so that expenditures could be aggregated or calculated to disclose a misleading picture, e.g. the inclusion of PAYE tax and welfare payments made to the government in the employee classification so that wages were shown gross, whereas distributions to shareholders were shown net of tax. The effect of both was to overstate the apparent employee share and understate the government and shareholders' share.[38]

In the years immediately following the publication of *The Corporate Report*, companies published value added statements on a voluntary basis but their importance has declined. There was a move away from industrial democracy and the standard-setting regulators did not make the publication of value added statements mandatory.

32.10 Corporate social responsibility reporting

There is recognition that CSR has moved from a PR exercise to being a core business value. This is evidenced by a 2010 survey[39] of CSR trends which reported that 81% of surveyed companies had CSR information on their website and 31% had their reports assured. Companies are also concentrating on those aspects that are of significance to their business. For example, this change in emphasis is illustrated by the following extract from the Ford Motor Company 2009/10 Sustainability Report:

> A key part of our reporting strategy has been the development of a materiality analysis process, which has been a critical tool in helping shape the content of this report. We used the analysis to focus our reporting on those issues determined to be most material to the company.

This has progressed with the approach to CSR becoming increasingly formalised with the setting up of committees reporting to the board and more comprehensive, targeted CSR reports.

There is now a wealth of opportunities for further study of the topic as we now see CSR modules in many university undergraduate and Business School programmes and postgraduate degrees such as the MA in Corporate Social Responsibility at London Metropolitan University.

32.11 Need for comparative data

There is evidence[40] that environmental performance could be given a higher priority when analysts assess a company if there were comparable data by sector on a company's level of corporate responsibility.

We will consider one approach that has taken place to satisfy this need for comparable data using benchmarking.

32.11.1 Benchmarking

There are a number of benchmarking schemes and we will consider one by way of illustration – the London Benchmarking Group,[41] established in 1994. The Group consists of companies which join in order to measure and report their involvement in the community, which is a key part of any corporate social responsibility programme, and which have a tool to assist them effectively to assess and target their community programmes. Organisations such as British Airways, Deloitte & Touche, Lloyds TSB and Pearson are members.

The scheme is concerned with corporate community involvement. It identifies three categories into which different forms of community involvement can be classified, namely charity donations, social or community investment and commercial initiatives, and includes only contributions made over and above those that result from the basic business operations.

It uses an input/output model, putting a monetary value on the 'input' costs which include contributions made in cash, in time or in kind, together with full cost of staff involved; and collecting 'output' data on the community benefit, e.g. number who benefited, leveraged resources and benefit accruing to the business.

32.12 Investors

Investors are gradually beginning to require information on a company's policy and programmes for environmental compliance and performance in order to assess the risk to earnings and financial position. One would expect that the more transparent these are the less volatile the share prices will be, which could be beneficial for both the investor and the company. This will be a fruitful field for research as environmental reporting evolves with more consistent, comparable, relevant and reliable numbers and narrative disclosures.

32.12.1 Socially Responsible Investing (SRI)

This has also given rise to Socially Responsible Investing (SRI) which considers both the investor's financial needs and the investee company's impact on society to an extent that in 2010 over £900 billion in assets were invested in 'ethical' investment funds.

In the UK there is pressure from bodies such as the Association of British Insurers for institutional investors to take SRI principles into account. A number of rating and bench-marking systems are used on behalf of investors and others to grade organisations through the use of ratings and benchmarks based on environmental and other sustainability criteria such as the Dow Jones Sustainability Indices and the FTSE4Good Index.

32.12.2 ABI Socially Responsible Investment Guidelines

In 2007, the ABI issued its updated guidelines on responsible investment disclosure. These are a modification of the Socially Responsible Investment Guidelines launched by the ABI in 2001.

They take account of the EU Accounts Modernisation Directive and the UK Companies Act, as well as recent experience of narrative reporting and the clarification by the UK government of directors' liability for narrative statements. They do not involve substantial change but aim to highlight aspects of responsibility reporting on which shareholders place particular value. This is narrative reporting which:

● sets environmental, social and governance (ESG) risks in the context of the whole range of risks and opportunities facing the company;

● contains a forward-looking perspective; and

● describes the actions of the board in mitigating these risks.

Institutional investors support the revised guidelines, which encourage listed companies to include narrative discussion of the environmental, social and governance (ESG) risks they face. The guidelines also encourage companies to explain what steps they are taking to mitigate and address those risks.

32.12.3 Dow Jones Sustainability Indices

The main impetus for rating and benchmarking systems comes from the growth of interest in SRI. The Dow Jones Sustainability Indices were begun in 1999 and were the first global indices tracking the financial performance of the leading sustainability-driven companies worldwide covering 58 sectors.

Companies are selected for the indices based on a comprehensive assessment of long-term economic, environmental and social criteria that account for general as well as industry-specific sustainability trends. Only firms that lead their industries based on this assessment are included in the indices. There are sub-indices excluding alcohol, gambling, tobacco, armaments and firearms and/or adult entertainment, and global and regional blue-chip indices.

SAM (an investment boutique focused exclusively on Sustainability Investing) annually identifies[42] the top company in each of the 19 supersectors derived from the 58 sectors. The 2012–2013 Supersector Leaders include companies in Australia (2) (Banks and Real Estate); Belgium (1) (Media); Brazil (1) (Financial Services); Finland (1) (Basic Resources); France (2) (Technology and Travel & Leisure); Germany (2) (Automobiles and Industrial Goods); Netherlands (3) (Chemicals, Food & Beverage and Personal & Household); South Korea (3) (Construction, Retail and Telecommunications); Spain (Oil & Gas and Utilities); and Switzerland (2) (Health Care and Insurance). The UK is noticeable for its absence.

32.12.4 FTSE4Good Index Series

The FTSE4Good Index Series provides potential investors with a measure of the performance of companies that meet globally recognised corporate responsibility standards. FTSE4Good is helpful as a basis for socially responsible investment and as a benchmark for tracking the performance of socially responsible investment portfolios.

There is still some way to go, however, with research[43] carried out by Trucost and commissioned by the Environment Agency into quantitative disclosures finding that direct links between management of environmental risks and shareholder value are almost non-existent, with only 11% of FTSE 350 companies making a link between the environment and some aspect of their financial performance and only 5% explicitly linking it to shareholder value.

32.13 The accountant's changing role

Accountants now make positive contributions to sustainability management by their responsible roles in systems and external reporting. They are responsible for the financial systems which provide the raw data for strategic planning, the management of risk, and the measurement and reporting of performance and allocation. For example, they identify environmental costs to measure and report on the efficiency of energy costs and social costs such as the cost of staff turnover and absenteeism.

Accountants have a central role in finance from which they are able to encourage a sustainability culture within an organisation by raising sustainability as a consideration when making decisions. This can be at an operating level, as when they identify environmental or social costs, or at a strategic level when capital investment decisions are being made.

Sustainability information reported to investors and other stakeholders needs to be based on sound systems of accounting and internal control and be externally assured. Professional accountants provide the expertise for the design and operation of systems and external auditors are increasingly providing an assurance capability.

32.13.1 Sustainability and the profession

The professional accounting bodies are building sustainability into their examination syllabi and CPD programmes. For example, the ACCA statement on 'The ACCA and Sustainability' highlights the increasing need for trainees and qualified staff to have an awareness of developments:

> Sustainable development (SD) and corporate social responsibility (CSR) issues are now embedded in ACCA's syllabus. ACCA members need to ensure that they are aware of the changing face of reporting, accounting and assurance and are advising their organisations and clients on the latest developments. The business agenda is changing. Increasing and influential shareholder pressure and enhancing corporate transparency means that a company's reputation becomes its main licence to operate. Companies are trading on their environmental credentials and want to be seen as socially responsible. The threat that the sustainability challenge poses to the future of business and society is such that it is no longer possible to justify the exclusion of SD and CSR issues from the professional syllabus. The professional examinations are, however, only one element of the lifelong learning package that professional bodies are required to provide. ACCA acknowledges the importance of educating members as well as students on the importance of sustainability. CPD programmes will need to incorporate SD and CSR issues – though probably on a sector-relevant basis rather than in a generic form.

32.13.2 Academic programmes

There are numerous undergraduate CSR modules and postgraduate Masters degrees such as at Erasmus University Rotterdam, University of Birmingham, Nottingham University and London Metropolitan University.

There is also active research such as at the Centre for Social and Environmental Accounting Research (CSEAR),[44] the International Centre for Corporate Social Responsibility[45] at Nottingham University Business School, and the Centre for the Study of Global Ethics[46] at the University of Birmingham.

Research interests include environmental and social issues. For example, the Centre for the Study of Global Ethics at the University of Birmingham was a partner in a project aimed at the promotion of corporate social responsibility by way of a methodology for monitoring corporate observance of work-related human rights, core labour and social standards as set out in the Decent Work Agenda and the Social Agenda of the European Union.

The International Centre for Corporate Social Responsibility at Nottingham University has undertaken a number of research projects on CSR and on corporate reporting on gender equality in the workplace.

There is progress being made at varying rates around the world. One of the stimuli has been the environmental, social and sustainability award schemes.

There is a growing interest and experimenting in many companies. As with all initiatives there will be varying views from those opposed to the idea of sustainability reporting, to those who think that the existing initiatives such as GRI are already too complex, to the discussions that will be needed to try to arrive at a uniform model.

Accounting and finance students will find that they will become increasingly involved within companies, not-for-profit organisations, and the profession – working within their accounting speciality and also in multidisciplinary teams. Accounting qualifications will give access to more innovative and rewarding scenarios.

Given the time taken to arrive at a Conceptual Framework for Financial Reporting, it could be quite a while before a consensus is arrived at for a single model – if, indeed, that is the best outcome. In the meantime there will be ongoing academic and professional research and empirical experimenting by companies.

Summary

Sustainability is now recognised as having three elements. These are the economic, environmental and social. It is recognised that advances in environmental and social improvement are dependent on the existence of an economically viable organisation.

As environmental and social reporting evolves, proposals are being made to harmonise the content and disclosure. This can be seen with the publications such as those of the Connected Framework and the GRI working towards an integrated reporting framework.

In addition there are benchmark schemes which allow stakeholders to compare corporate social reports and evaluate an individual company's performance. The management systems that are being developed within companies should result in data that are consistent and reliable and capable of external verification. The benchmarking systems should assist in both identifying best practice and establishing relevant performance indicators.

Corporate social reporting is coming of age. Initially there were fears that it would add to costs and there are present concerns that it is diverting too much of a finance director's attention away from commercial and stragetic planning. However, it is becoming generally recognised that a company's reputation and its attractiveness to potential investors are influenced by a company's behaviour and attitude to corporate governance, social reporting and sustainability.

Companies are reacting positively to the need to be good corporate citizens and it is interesting to see the developments around the world where sustainability, good corporate governance and strategic planning are merging into an integrated system. This will take time but companies are taking up the challenge to be transparent and innovative in their financial reporting. Companies are integrating their non-financial narrative and using the Internet to get their message out to a wider public.

The time has passed since corporate governance, sustainability, environmental and social reporting were seen purely as a PR exercise.

REVIEW QUESTIONS

1 Discuss the relevance of stand-alone environmental reports to an existing and potential investor.

2 Obtain a copy of the environmental report of a company that has taken part in the ACCA Awards for Sustainability Reporting and critically discuss from an investor's and public interest viewpoint.

3 'Charters and guidelines help make reports reliable but inhibit innovation and reduce their relevance.' Discuss.

4 Discuss the implications of the Global Reporting Initiative for the accountancy profession.

5 Discuss *The Corporate Report*'s relevance to modern business; identify changes that would improve current reporting practice and the conditions necessary for such changes to become mandatory.

6 Discuss the value added concept, giving examples, and ways to improve the statement.

7 Outline the arguments for and against a greater role for the audit function in corporate social reporting.

8 Discuss the challenges that accountant and auditor will face with the increasing demand for environmental impact to be reported.

9 'Human assets are incapable of being valued.' Discuss.

10 The following is an extract from the 2011 Tottenham Hotspur Annual Report when considering carrying out an impairment test:

> The Group does not consider that it is possible to determine the value in use of an individual football player in isolation as that player (unless via a sale or insurance recovery) cannot generate cash flows on his own. Furthermore, the Group also considers that all of the players are unable to generate cash flows even when considered together.

Discuss why the players taken separately or together do not have a value in use.

11 The 2011 Tottenham Hotspur plc Annual Report stated

Player costs and transactions

(a) Initial capitalisation
The costs associated with the acquisition of player and key football management staff registrations are capitalised as intangible fixed assets.

(b) Amortisation discounted
These costs are fully amortised on a straight-line basis over their useful economic lives, in equal annual instalments over the period of the respective contracts. Where a contract life is renegotiated, the unamortised costs, together with the new costs relating to the contract extension, are amortised over the term of the new contract.

Discuss possible alternative methods of amortisation.

12 Discuss the impact of the following groups on the accounting profession:

   (a) Environmental groups

   (b) Ethical investors.

13 Nissan, the Japanese car company, decided that 'any environmentalism should pay for itself and for every penny you spend you must save a penny. You can spend as many pennies as you like as long as other environmental actions save an equal number.'[47] Discuss the significance of this for each of the stakeholders.

14 (a) Discuss the significant direct KPIs relating to the air transport industry. (b) Identify which industries you consider to be significant supplier industries.

   (Access to the following is helpful: http://archive.defra.gov.uk/environment/business/reporting/pdf/envkpi-guidelines.pdf)

15 Consumer-oriented models are more likely to be influenced by ethical principles. Discuss.

16 A chemical entity installed new manufacturing equipment at a cost of €1m to comply with environmental regulations concerning the production and storage of chemicals.

   Discuss how this should be dealt with in the Annual Report.

17 Discuss how would it be possible to apply sustainability criteria in determining executive remuneration.

18 A research report[48] found that comparability of extra-financial information between companies is an issue: 61% said they find social information difficult to compare and 41% said they find environmental information difficult to compare, while only 3% said they find it difficult to compare financial information between companies.

   Discuss whether comparability is achievable and, if so, the measures that could be taken to make it possible.

19 Look up an integrated report of a South African company (such as Clicks Group Integrated Annual Report 2011) and discuss what insights you have gained regarding how integral (or not) social and environmental issues are to the achievement of financial objectives in the short and longer terms for the company concerned.

20 The Fourth Company Law Directive requires companies to include, where appropriate, information (key performance indicators – KPIs) relating to environmental and employee matters in their annual report to the extent necessary for an understanding of the company's development, performance or position. Member States, however, may exempt small and medium-sized companies from this disclosure obligation.

   Discuss whether it is appropriate to exempt medium-sized companies and, if so, what other information should they be also exempt from disclosing.

EXERCISES

Question 1

(a) You are required to prepare a value added statement to be included in the corporate report of Hythe plc for the year ended 31 December 20X6, including the comparatives for 20X5, using the information given below:

	20X6	20X5
	£000	£000
Non-current assets (net book value)	3,725	3,594
Trade receivables	870	769
Trade payables	530	448
14% debentures	1,200	1,080
6% preference shares	400	400
Ordinary shares (£1 each)	3,200	3,200
Sales	5,124	4,604
Materials consumed	2,934	2,482
Wages	607	598
Depreciation	155	144
Fuel consumed	290	242
Hire of plant and machinery	41	38
Salaries	203	198
Auditors' remuneration	10	8
Corporation tax provision	402	393
Ordinary share dividend	9p	8p
Number of employees	40	42

(b) Although value added statements were recommended by *The Corporate Report*, as yet there is no accounting standard related to them. Explain what a value added statement is and provide reasons as to why you think it has not yet become mandatory to produce such a statement as a component of current financial statements through either a Financial Reporting Standard or company law.

Question 2

The following items have been extracted from the accounts:

	2005 (€m)	2004 (€m)
Other income	844	980
Cost of materials	25,694	24,467
Financial income	−188	54
Depreciation/amortisation	4,207	3,589
Providers of finance	1,351	1,059
Retained	1,815	1,823
Revenues	46,656	44,335
Government	1,590	1,794
Other expenses	4,925	5,093
Shareholders	424	419
Employees	7,306	7,125

Required:
(a) Prepare a value added statement showing % for each year and % change.
(b) Draft a note for inclusion in the annual report commenting on the statement you have prepared.

Question 3

David Mark is a sole trader who owns and operates supermarkets in each of three villages near Ousby. He has drafted his own accounts for the year ended 31 May 20X4 for each of the branches. They are as follows:

	Arton		Blendale		Clifearn	
	£	£	£	£	£	£
Sales		910,800		673,200		382,800
Cost of sales		633,100		504,900		287,100
Gross profit		277,700		168,300		95,700
Less: Expenses:						
David Mark's salary	10,560		10,560		10,560	
Other salaries and wages	143,220		97,020		78,540	
Rent			19,800			
Rates	8,920		5,780		2,865	
Advertising	2,640		2,640		2,640	
Delivery van expenses	5,280		5,280		5,280	
General expenses	11,220		3,300		1,188	
Telephone	2,640		1,980		1,584	
Wrapping materials	7,920		3,960		2,640	
Depreciation:						
Fixtures	8,220		4,260		2,940	
Vehicle	3,000	203,620	3,000	157,580	3,000	111,237
Net profit/(loss)		74,080		10,720		(15,537)

The figures for the year ended 31 May 20X4 follow the pattern of recent years. Because of this, David Mark is proposing to close the Clifearn supermarket immediately.

David Mark employs 12 full-time and 20 part-time staff. His recruitment policy is based on employing one extra part-time assistant for every £30,000 increase in branch sales. His staff deployment at the moment is as follows:

	Arton	Blendale	Clifearn
Full-time staff (including managers)	6	4	2
Part-time staff	8	6	6

Peter Gaskin, the manager of the Clifearn supermarket, asks David to give him another year to make the supermarket profitable. Peter has calculated that he must cover £125,500 expenses out of his gross profit in the year ended 31 May 20X5 in order to move into profitability. His calculations include extra staff costs and all other extra costs.

Additional information:

1 General advertising for the business as a whole is controlled by David Mark. This costs £3,960 per annum. Each manager spends a further £1,320 advertising his own supermarket locally.

2 The delivery vehicle is used for deliveries from the Arton supermarket only.

3 David Mark has a central telephone switchboard which costs £1,584 rental per annum. Each supermarket is charged for all calls actually made. For the year ended 31 May 20X4 these amounted to:

Arton	£2,112
Blendale	£1,452
Clifearn	£1,056

Required:
(a) A report addressed to David Mark advising him whether to close Clifearn supermarket. Your report should include a detailed financial statement based on the results for the year ended 31 May 20X4 relating to the Clifearn branch.
(b) Calculate the increased turnover and extra staff needed if Peter's suggestion is implemented.
(c) Comment on the social implications for the residents of Clifearn if (i) David Mark closes the supermarket, (ii) Peter Gaskin's recommendation is undertaken.

* Question 4

Gettry Doffit plc is an international company with worldwide turnover of £26 million. The activities of the company include the breaking down and disposal of noxious chemicals at a specialised plant in the remote Scottish countryside. During the preparation of the financial statements for the year ended 31 March 20X5, it was discovered that:

1 Quantities of chemicals for disposals on site at the year-end included:

(A) Axylotl peroxide   40,000 gallons
(B) Pterodactyl chlorate   35 tons

Chemical A is disposed of for a South Korean company, which was invoiced for 170 million won on 30 January 20X5, for payment in 120 days. It is estimated that the costs of disposal will not exceed £75,000. £60,000 of costs have been incurred at the year-end.

Chemical B is disposed of for a British company on a standard contract for 'cost of disposal plus 35%', one month after processing. At the year-end the chemical has been broken down into harmless by-products at a cost of £77,000. The by-products, which belong to Gettry Doffit plc, are worth £2,500.

2 To cover against exchange risks, the company entered into two forward contracts on 30 January 20X5:

No. 03067   Sell 170 million won at 1,950 won = £1:   31 May 20X5
No. 03068   Buy $70,000 at $1.60   = £1:   31 May 20X5

Actual sterling exchange rates were:

	won	$
30 January 20X5	1,900	1.70
31 March 20X5	2,000	1.38
30 April 20X5 (today)	2,100	1.80

The company often purchases a standard chemical used in processing from a North American company, and the dollars will be applied towards this purpose.

3 The company entered into a contract to import a specialised chemical used in the breaking down of magnesium perambulate from a Nigerian company which demanded the raising of an irrevocable letter of credit for £65,000 to cover 130 tons of the chemical. By 31 March 20X5 bills of lading for 60 tons had been received and paid for under the letter of credit. It now appears that the total needed for the requirements of Gettry Doffit plc for the foreseeable future is only 90 tons.

4 On 16 October 20X4 Gettry Doffit plc entered into a joint venture as partners with Dumpet Andrunn plc to process perfidious recalcitrant (PR) at the Gettry Doffit plc site using Dumpet Andrunn plc's technology. Unfortunately, a spillage at the site on 15 April 20X5 has led to claims being filed against the two companies for £12 million. A public inquiry has been set up, to assess the cause of the accident and to determine liability, which the finance director of Gettry Doffit plc fears will be, at the very least, £3 million.

Required:

Discuss how these matters should be reflected in the financial statements of Gettry Doffit plc as on and for the year ended 31 March 20X5.

Question 5

In 2010 there was an explosion, fire, sinking and loss of life on board the mobile offshore drilling unit, the Deepwater Horizon, in the Gulf of Mexico. There has since been a final report issued by The Bureau of Ocean Energy Management, Regulation and Enforcement (BOEMRE)/U.S. Coast Guard Joint Investigation Team (JIT).

Required:

Examine the BP 2011 Sustainability Report[49] and prepare a brief presentation to the group explaining the company's Operating Management System in relation to environmental and social issues and commenting on the extent to which such reports can provide investors with the possible social costs of environmental disasters.

References

1 M. Friedman, *Capitalism and Freedom*, University of Chicago Press, 1962, p. 133.
2 http://www.eurosif.org/
3 http://www.unglobalcompact.org/news/42-06-22-2010
4 R.G. Eccles, I. Ioannou and G. Serafeim, 'The impact of a corporate culture of sustainability on corporate behavior and performance', NBER Working Paper No. 17950, March 2012, http://www.nber.org/papers/w17950
5 C. Post, N. Rahman and E. Rubow, 'Green governance: boards of directors' composition and environmental corporate social responsibility', *Business & Society*, March 2011, vol. 50, pp. 189–223.
6 L.G. Hassel, J.-P. Kallunki and H. Nilsson, 'Implications of past unethical risk behaviour of board members and CEOs on the environmental performance and reporting quality of firms', http://www.sirp.se/getfile.ashx?cid=48377&cc=3&refid=35
7 www.sustainabilityreporting.eu/netherlands/index.htm
8 'The value of extra-financial disclosure: what investors and analysts said', https://www.globalreporting.org/resourcelibrary/The-value-of-extra-financial-disclosure.pdf
9 www.sustainabilityreporting.eu/denmark/index.htm
10 http://about.puma.com/wp-content/themes/aboutPUMA_theme/media/pdf/2011/en/PRESS_KIT_E_P&L.pdf
11 www.sustainabilityatwork.org.uk/strategy/report/0
12 www.globalreporting.org
13 www.accountability.org.uk
14 See http://ec.europa.eu/environment/emas/index_en.htm
15 www.iso.org
16 C. Lehman, *Accounting's Changing Role in Social Conflict*, Markus Weiner Publishing, 1992, p. 64.
17 *Ibid.*, p. 17.
18 KPMG Peat Marwick McLintock, 'Environmental considerations in acquiring,' *Corporate Finance Briefing*, 17 May 1991.
19 M. Jones, 'The cost of cleaning up', *Certified Accountant*, May 1995, p. 47.
20 http://www.spada.co.uk/wp-content/uploads/2008/11/environmental-reporting-spada-white-paper.pdf
21 Information for Better Markets, 'Sustainability: the role of accountants', ICAEW, 2004.
22 www.sustainabilityreporting.eu/uk/index.htm
23 See www.fee.be/issues/other.htm#Sustainability

24 See www.ceaa-acve.ca/aboutus.htm

25 http://www.environment-agency.gov.uk/static/documents/Business/TECPLN8045_env_report_aw.pdf

26 http://www.deloitte.com/view/en_HR/hr/services/enterprise-risk-services/7ac834796ab7b210VgnVCM3000001c56f00aRCRD.htm

27 See http://ec.europa.eu/environment/newprg/

28 R. Gray, D. Owen and K. Maunders, *Corporate Social Reporting*, Prentice Hall, 1987, p. 75.

29 ASB, *Statement of Principles: The Objective of Financial Statements*, 1991, para. 9.

30 *Ibid.*, para. 10.

31 *Ibid.*, para. 11.

32 F. Okcabol and A. Tinker, 'The market for positive theory: deconstructing the theory for excuses', *Advances in Public Interest Accounting*, vol. 3, 1990.

33 H. Sebreuder, 'Employees and the corporate social report: the Dutch case', in S.J. Gray (ed.), *International Accounting and Transnational Decisions*, Butterworth, 1983, p. 287.

34 *Ibid.*, p. 289.

35 AICPA, *The Measurement of Corporate Social Performance*, 1977, p. 243.

36 R. Gray, D. Owen and K. Maunders, *Corporate Social Reporting*, Prentice Hall, 1987, p. 44.

37 S.J. Gray and K.T. Maunders, 'Value added reporting: uses and measurement', ACCA, 1980; B. Underwood and P.J. Taylor, *Accounting Theory and Policy Making*, Heinemann, 1985, p. 298.

38 *Ibid.*, p. 74.

39 http://admin.csrwire.com/system/report_pdfs/1189/original/CSR_TRENDS_2010.pdf

40 Business in the Environment, *Investing in the Future*, May 2001.

41 See www.lbg-online.net/

42 http://www.sustainability-indexes.com/review/supersector-leaders-2012.jsp

43 www.environment-agency.gov.uk/business

44 http://www.st-andrews.ac.uk/~csearweb/aboutcsear/

45 http://www.nottingham.ac.uk

46 www.business.bham.ac.uk

47 M. Brown, 'Greening the bottom line', *Management Today*, July 1995, p. 73.

48 http://www.totalecomanagement.co.uk/2/post/2012/09/what-investors-and-analysts-said-the-value-of-extra-financial-disclosure.html

49 http://www.bp.com/assets/bp_internet/globalbp/STAGING/global_assets/e_s_assets/e_s_assets_2010/downloads_pdfs/bp_sustainability_review_2011.pdf

Bibliography

R.B. Adams and D. Ferreira, 'Women in the boardroom and their impact on governance and performance', *Journal of Financial Economics*, vol. 94, 2009, pp. 291–309.

T. Artiach, D. Lee, D. Nelson and J. Walker, 'The determinants of corporate sustainability performance', *Accounting and Finance*, vol. 50, 2009, pp. 31–51.

J.A. Batten and T.A. Fetherston (eds), *Social Responsibility: Corporate Governance Issues* (Research in International Business and Finance, Volume 17), JAI Press, 2003.

S. Bear, N. Rahman and C. Post, 'The impact of board diversity and gender composition on corporate social responsibility and firm reputation', *Journal of Business Ethics*, vol. 97, 2011, pp. 207–222.

S. Bhagat and B. Bolton, 'Corporate governance and firm performance', *Journal of Corporate Finance*, vol. 14, 2008, pp. 257–273.

K. Bondy, D. Matten and J. Moon, 'Codes of conduct as a tool for sustainable governance in MNCs', in S. Benn and D. Dunphy (eds), *Corporate Governance and Sustainability: Challenges for Theory and Practice*, Routledge, 2006.

S. Brammer and S. Pavelin, 'Voluntary environmental disclosures by large UK companies', *Journal of Business Finance and Accounting*, vol. 33, 2006, pp. 1168–1188.

M.C. Branco and L.L. Rodrigues, 'Issues in corporate social and environmental reporting research: an overview', *Issues in Social and Environmental Accounting*, vol. 1(1), 2007, pp. 72–90.

D. Campbell, 'A longitudinal and cross-sectional analysis of environmental disclosure in UK companies – a research note', *British Accounting Review*, vol. 36(1), 2004, pp. 107–117.

W. Chapple and J. Moon, 'Corporate social responsibility (CSR) in Asia: a seven country study of CSR website reporting', *Business and Society*, vol. 44(4), 2005, pp. 115–136.

P.M. Clarkson, M.B. Overell and L. Chapple, 'Environmental reporting and its relation to corporate environmental performance', *Abacus*, vol. 47, 2011, pp. 27–60.

S.M. Cooper and D.I. Owen, 'Corporate social reporting and stakeholder accountability: the missing link', *Accounting, Organizations and Society*, vol. 32(7–8), October–November 2007, pp. 649–667.

P.K. Cornelius and B. Kogul, *Corporate Governance and Capital Flows in the Global Economy*, Oxford University Press, 2003.

B. Coyle, *Risk Awareness and Corporate Governance*, Financial World Publishing, 2004.

A. Crane, D. Matten and J. Moon, *Corporations and Citizenship*, Cambridge University Press, 2006.

D. Crowther and K.T. Caliyurt, *Stakeholders and Social Responsibility*, Ansted University Press, 2004.

D. Crowther and L. Rayman-Bacchus (eds), *Perspectives on Corporate Social Responsibility*, Ashgate, 2004.

P. De Moor and I. De Beelde, 'Environmental auditing and the role of the accountancy profession: a literature review', *Environmental Management*, vol. 36(2), 2005, pp. 205–219.

J. Derwall, K. Koedijk and J.T. Horst, 'A tale of values-driven and profit-seeking social investors', *Journal of Banking & Finance*, vol. 35, 2011, pp. 2137–2147.

R. Gray, J. Bebbington and M. Houldin, *Accounting for the Environment* (2nd edition), Sage Publications, 2001.

R. Gray, *Social and Environmental Accounting* (Sage Library in Accounting and Finance) (with J. Bebbington and S. Gray), London: Sage, Volumes I–IV, 1664 pp., 2010.

K. Grosser and J. Moon, 'Developments in company reporting on workplace gender equality: a Corporate Social Responsibility perspective', *Accounting Forum*, vol. 32, 2008, pp. 179–198.

N. Guenster, R. Bzauer, J. Derwall and K. Koedijk, 'The economic value of corporate eco-efficiency', *European Financial Management*, vol. 17, 2011, pp. 679–704.

D. Hawkins, *Corporate Social Responsibility: Balancing Tomorrow's Sustainability and Today's Profitability*, Palgrave Macmillan, 2006.

G. Heal, 'Corporate social responsibility: an economic and financial framework', *Geneva Papers*, vol. 30, 2005, pp. 387–409. http://www.genevaassociation.org/PDF/Geneva_papers_on_Risk_and_Insurance/GA2005_GP30(3)_Heal.pdf

L. Holland and Y.B. Foo, 'Differences in environmental reporting practices in the UK and the US: the legal and regulatory context', *British Accounting Review*, vol. 35(1), 2003, pp. 1–18.

A.W. Savitz and K. Weber, *The Triple Bottom Line: How Today's Best-Run Companies Are Achieving Economic, Social and Environmental Success – and How You Can Too*, Jossey-Bass, San Francisco, 2006.

J.L. Walls, P. Berrone and P.H. Phan, 'Corporate governance and environmental performance: is there really a link?', *Strategic Management Journal*, vol. 33(8), 2012, pp. 885-913.

R. Wearing, *Cases in Corporate Governance*, Sage, 2005.

Index